HISTORY

—OF—

LACLEDE, CAMDEN, DALLAS, WEBSTER, WRIGHT, TEXAS, PULASKI, PHELPS AND DENT COUNTIES,

MISSOURI.

Indexed Edition

FROM THE EARLIEST TIME TO THE PRESENT, INCLUDING A DEPARTMENT
DEVOTED TO THE PRESERVATION OF SUNDRY PERSONAL, BUSI-
NESS, PROFESSIONAL AND PRIVATE RECORDS; BESIDES
A VALUABLE FUND OF NOTES, ORIGINAL
OBSERVATIONS, ETC., ETC.

ILLUSTRATED.

Southern Historical Press, Inc.
Greenville, South Carolina

This volume was reproduced from
A personal copy located in the
Publisher's private Library

All rights reserved. No part of this publication may be reproduced,
stored in a retrieval system, transmitted in any form, posted
on to the web in any form or by any means without
the prior written permission of the publisher.

Please direct all correspondence and orders to:

www.southernhistoricalpress.com
or
SOUTHERN HISTORICAL PRESS, Inc.
PO BOX 1267
375 West Broad Street
Greenville, SC   29601
southernhistoricalpress@gmail.com

Originally published: Chicago, IL. 1880
New material Copyright by:
Southern Historical Press, Inc.
ISBN #0-89308-875-7
All rights Reserved.
Printed in the United States of America

PUBLISHER'S PREFACE

The Publisher has choosen to print only half of the original book due to its size. The original book with the new index has 1,318 pages. Due to printing costs and limitation with binding equipment, this creates an enormus difficulty in getting this wonderful book in the hands of the family historian. This is why we have choosen to only print the biographical section of this book with a New Index. We hope the reader understands and enjoys this printing of Goodspeed's History of Laclede, Camden, Dallas, Webster, Wright, Texas, Pulaski, Phelps, and Dent counties.

Southern Historical Press, Inc.

BIOGRAPHICAL APPENDIX.

LACLEDE COUNTY.

F. W. Abbot, agent of the St. Louis & San Francisco Railroad Line at Lebanon, was born in New York City March 4, 1851, and is the son of F. A. and Mary A. (Carrigan) Abbot, natives of New York City and Nottinghampshire, England. F. A. Abbot, the father, is a noted newspaper man, and has been connected with the New York papers and United States press for forty-five years. He furnished news for the English papers before the Atlantic cable was put in. This was done by sealed cans thrown off the Irish coast and picked up by row-boats waiting for that purpose. He is now correspondent for the New Orleans *Picayune*; Galveston *News*, Baltimore *Sun*, and a number of other large daily papers, besides holding a large private correspondence on financial and commercial business. He is one of the most noted correspondents in New York City. His son, F. W. Abbot, attained his growth and received his education in the above mentioned State. In 1871 he went south to New Orleans, and was reporter for the *Picayune*; was also connected with the *Sugar Bowl*, edited by the famous Col. Gilmore, of New Iberia, La. He had charge of the post-office at that place for one quarter as deputy, and was deputy tax collector; also was afterward appointed supervisor of registration, during the Greeley campaign, by Gov. Warmouth, Iberia Parish, and later appointed by Gov. McHenry tax collector of Iberia Parish. Mr. Abbot then drifted back home and went to railroading, first being employed by the Manhattan Elevated Railroad Company, where he remained about two years. He was then induced to come to St. Louis and take a position on the 'Frisco, and was employed in St. Louis for four years. In 1883 he came to Lebanon, Mo., and has since been the general agent of this place. Soon after coming to Lebanon Mr. Abbot was given charge of the Adams Express agency. He was married, in St. Louis, to Miss Helen A., daughter of Prof. Shackford, November 16, 1881, and to this union have been born three children, two now living: Edward H. and Charles S. Mr. Abbot is a member of the I. O. O. F. lodge, and is one of the representative citizens of the county. Since living in Lebanon he has erected a commodious brick residence, and he has also the finest garden, fruits and vegetables to be found in Southwest Missouri. In November, 1888, he was appointed United States commissioner for the Western District of Missouri.

Bailey Adkins, proprietor of the City Mills, was born in Dixon County, Tenn., December 12, 1835, and is the son of Abner and Nancy (Hooper) Adkins, both natives of Tennessee, the father of Dixon County and the mother of Humphreys County. The Adkins family were originally from England, and were early settlers of Virginia. The Hooper family were from Scotland, and immigrated to North Carolina, but afterward moved to Tennessee. The paternal grandfather, Drury Adkins, was a soldier in the War of 1812, was a farmer by occupation, and died in Tennessee. Abner Adkins was also a farmer by occupation, and in 1839 he with his family immigrated with a four-horse wagon to Laclede County, Mo., being about six weeks on the road, and located on the Glaize, the place now owned by Mrs. Hooker. He bought a claim which was not yet improved, and lived on this place but a short time, when they sold out and bought property in Lebanon Township, Goodwin Hollow. Here the father died in 1861. He was captain of militia in Tennessee. There are 360 acres in the homestead, mostly under cultivation. The mother is yet living. They were the parents of five children, four now living: Bailey, Malinda, Abner and William. The one deceased was named Vasa. Bailey Adkins was but five years of age when he came with his parents to Laclede County, Mo. Here he was educated in the rude log school-houses of those early days, and here he assisted on the farm, remaining at home until the death of his father. In 1863 he enlisted in Company H, Eighth Missouri Cavalry, and served until the close of the war, being kept on guard of railroads the principal part of the time. He was mustered out August 12, 1865, came home and resumed farming, which he still continues. In 1887 he took charge of the mill he is now running, and this he has since continued to operate. He owns a fine farm near Lebanon, on which he resides with his mother, brother and sister. He is a member of the G. A. R. and Agricultural Wheel, and is one of the enterprising and successful citizens of the county. He is politically a Democrat.

Dr. Jesse N. Anderson, druggist, of Conway, Mo., was born in Johnson County, Mo., March 30, 1851, and is a son of Jesse C. and Jeanette (Green) Anderson. The father was born in Platte County, Mo., in 1820, and after residing on his father's farm until he attained his majority, he located in St. Charles County, where he engaged in farming, but at the outbreak of the late war he left the plow to engage in that struggle, serving in the Confederate army until 1864, when his health failed, and he was honorably discharged. He then located on a farm in Adams County, Ill., on which he resided until 1867, and then returned to Missouri. After residing in different counties for a number of years he located in Henry County, where he made his home until his death in 1880. His father was a noted minister in the Primitive Baptist Church. His wife was born in St. Charles County, Mo., in 1819, and received a common-school education. She was one of the finest musicians in the county, and was a daughter of Capt. John Green, who was captain of light horse in the War of 1812, and was a very extensive farmer and land-holder of St. Charles County. She became the mother of five children, three of whom are living. Two sons, James W. and Dawson B., served in the Confederate and Union armies, respectively. The latter was a member of the Eleventh Missouri Cavalry, United States Army, and during his hard service contracted sickness which resulted in the loss of his power of speech. After the war he located in Henry County on a farm, where he was highly respected by his neighbors and old army comrades. During the year 1885, while traveling through McDonald County, he was murdered by Irwin Grubb, who was a relative by marriage, but fate speedily overtook the latter, for he was taken from the jail, where he was confined, by the friends and neighbors of Mr. Anderson, and hanged to a tree near the scene of the murder. Dr. Jesse N. Anderson grew to manhood in Newton County, Mo., and during the war was captured by Quantrell, and after being kept prisoner for some time was given his liberty. He was educated at Barry, Ill., and began the study of medicine under Dr. Llewellyn, near Hannibal, Mo. In 1873 he opened a drug store at Palestine, Mo., and soon after entered upon the practice of his profession. He has continued both occupations in various parts of the State up to the present time, and in 1884 located at Conway, where he has since made his home, with the exception of a short time spent in Barton County. He has acquired a large and lucrative practice, and is exceptionally skillful in the treatment of catarrh. During 1884 he was elected to do the practice for five different lodges of Wheelers near Conway. He is a member of the State Pharmaceutical Society, and of the Eclectic Medical Society of the State. In 1873 he married Mary McPherson, a daughter of Dr. T. McPherson, who was one of the leading physicians of Mercer County, Iowa, and Barton County, Mo. He was a regimental surgeon in the Confederate army, and was a prominent Mason and a leading politician. He served as county clerk one term, and died in 1862. Mrs. Anderson was born in Mercer County, Iowa, in 1857, and she and Dr. Anderson are the parents of two children: Ida and Frances. The Doctor is Prelate in the K. P. Lodge of Conway, and is also a member of the A. O. U. W., in which he is examining surgeon. He is a Democrat in politics.

James W. Appling, miller at Lebanon, Mo., and son of James M. and Elizabeth (Barnes) Appling, was born in Wright County, Mo., October 7, 1841. The parents were both natives of Kentucky, and the Appling family were originally from Georgia, but immigrated to Kentucky at an early date. This family is of Scotch-Irish descent. The paternal grandfather, Joel Appling, died in Kentucky, as did also the maternal grandparents. James M. Appling was a farmer by occupation, and in 1835 he, with his family, immigrated to Missouri from Kentucky, coming through with an ox team. This was about the time the Indians were driven from Tennessee, and Mr. Appling experienced some hard times in gathering feed for his cattle. They settled in Wright County, Mo., in the fall of 1835, locating on a squatter's claim, but, however, only lived there a few years, when he sold his claim, and in about 1842 moved to what is now Laclede County. He located about one-half mile north of Old Lebanon, purchased a small farm, unimproved, with the exception of a few acres round a log cabin, and the foundation of this cabin is still standing. Here Mr. Appling lived for many years engaged in tilling the soil, and was subject to all the hardships incident to pioneer life. He has spent his entire life in agricultural pursuits, and is still living at the age of seventy-eight years. The mother died in 1860. They were the parents of nine children, eight now living: Aurelius M., James W., John W., Columbus C., Miles L., Edward H., Sarah A., wife of Miles Elder, and resides in Arizona; Ella M., wife of Thomas Thompson, and is now residing in Kansas. James W. Appling was but a year old when he moved with his parents to Laclede County, Mo., and therefore has been identified with Laclede County all his life. His education was very limited, owing to the fact that school facilities were not of the best, and he assisted his father on the farm until the breaking out of the late Civil War. At the call for troops he shouldered his musket and marched into service August 12, 1861. He enlisted in Company A, Sixth Missouri Cavalry, and was mustered out at St. Louis. He was at the battles of Wet Glaize, Sugar Creek and a great many hard skirmishes. He was in advance of Curtis' army until they struck Pea Ridge, when they stood in reserve for three days. They were in the battle of Prairie Grove in December, 1863, and he was mustered out August 19, 1864. He then returned home and followed farming for three or four years, after which he engaged in milling, and this he has followed ever since. Mr. Appling is a practical miller, having had the experience of many years, and his flour is as good as can be found in Southern Missouri. He was married in 1864, November 28, to Miss Fannie A., daughter of Joseph F. Smith, whose sketch appears elsewhere in these pages. To Mr. and Mrs. Appling were born four children, three now living: Ella B., Jennie M. and Alma M. They have an adopted son, named James L. Mr. Appling is a member of the Masonic fraternity, a member of the I. O. O. F., A. O. U. W. and G. A. R.

James Atchley was born in Bradley County, Tenn., October 6, 1824, and is a son of John and Lizzie Atchley, and grandson of Martin Atchley, who was born, reared and married in Pennsylvania. About 1800 he located in Meigs County, Tenn., on a farm, at which occupation he became quite wealthy, but his death occurred in Bradley County in 1844. He was a soldier in the War of 1812, and was an active member of the Baptist Church. He and wife, who was born in Pennsylvania, became the parents of eleven children, all of whom lived to maturity. Seth, the eldest, now living on the home place in Tennessee, and Mahala (Mrs. Wilson), who resides in Denton County, Ark., are the only ones now living. John Atchley was the sixth child, and was born in Meigs County, Tenn., in 1804, and in 1838 removed with his family to Missouri, locating in Goodwin Hollow, where he died in 1881. He served in the "Old Men's Regiment" during the late war. His wife was born in Kentucky, and died in

1878, having borne a family of eleven children, nine of whom are living at the present time: Noah D., Morgan L., Seth, Miles, Sarah, Elizabeth, Elder, Delilah and James. James Atchley, whose name heads this sketch, was thirteen years of age when his parents came to Laclede County, and here he has since made his home. He served in the Mexican War under Gen. Taylor, and in 1850 took a trip to Pike's Peak, and was engaged in rafting logs on the Missouri and Mississippi Rivers for four years. He was married in 1851 to Miss Nancy Hufft, who was born in Tennessee in 1823, and died in 1865, a devoted member of the Methodist Episcopal Church. The following are their children: Dr. John B., Benjamin and Freeman. Mr. Atchley is a member of the A. F. & A. M., and is the owner of 640 acres of good land, with 320 acres under cultivation.

Levi L. Beckner is a son of Daniel and Mary (Lease) Beckner, and was born in Montgomery County, Va., September 9, 1814. Daniel Beckner was born near Philadelphia, Penn., June 5, 1790, and died in Laclede County, Mo., in 1870; his wife died in Elkhart County, Ind., in 1862 or 1863. They were married in Montgomery County, Va., where they lived until 1827, when they moved to Preble County, Ohio; eight years later they went to Elkhart County, Ind., and in 1839 located in what was then Pulaski County, now Dallas County, Mo., which was their home until the outbreak of the late war, when they returned to Elkhart County, Ind. They were members of the Dunkard Church, in which he was a deacon. He was a Union man during the war, and his sympathies were subsequently with the Republican party. He was assessor of Dallas County, and also served as associate judge in that county one term. Of the family of eleven children, four sons and three daughters are still living, viz.: Levi L.; Daniel, a prominent citizen of Laclede County; Aaron, a farmer of Greene County, Mo.; Eli Harrison, a carpenter of Springfield; May Ann, widow of Moses Hess and living at Elkhart, Ind.; Nioma, who married Louis Wise, a farmer near Marshfield, and Dilicah, now Mrs. Elias Hess, a retired farmer of Marshfield. When eighteen years of age Levi L. Beckner learned the brick-mason's trade, at which he worked in Ohio and Indiana for several years. In 1841 he built the court-house in Bolivar, Mo., which is still used, and at that time the best court-house in Southwestern Missouri, and in 1846 built the court-house at Buffalo, Dallas Co., Mo., which was burned during the war. After removing to Missouri he turned his attention to farming, which he has since continued. February 20, 1842, he married Sarah Ann Miller, who was born in McMinn County, Tenn., May 2, 1822, and is a daughter of John and Elizabeth Miller, natives also of Tennessee. Seven children have been born to Mr. and Mrs. Beckner, of whom five are living, viz.: Amanda, wife of David Hamilton, a farmer of Dallas County; John K. is a farmer and merchant of Webster County, and postmaster of Forkner's Hill Post-office; Abram L. is a farmer and stock raiser of Laclede County; Isabelle Adeline married John J. A. Gibson, of Greene County, Mo., and Isaac N., a commercial traveler for the firm of Wells & Co., of St. Louis. Louisa was the wife of William Wharton, and resided in Greene County at the time of her death.

Mary Ann died when seventeen years of age. The family are consistent members of the Missionary Baptist Church, and the male members are Republicans.

Daniel Beckner, a prominent farmer of Spring Hollow Township, was born in the "Old Dominion," Montgomery Co., Va., August 9, 1821, and is a son of Daniel and Mary Beckner, who were of German descent, and natives of the "Keystone State." The paternal grandfather came from the Fatherland to America some time prior to the Revolutionary War, locating on a farm in Pennsylvania, where he reared a family of five children, of whom Daniel was the youngest son; he was born about 1792. He removed to Virginia when a young man, and in 1827, with his family, which consisted of his wife and nine children, immigrated to Preble County, Ohio, where they resided until 1834 or 1835, when they removed to Elkhart County, Ind. In 1839 they removed to Dallas County, Mo., where the town of Long Lane is now located. There the father died in 1869, having been a member of the county court, and first assessor of the county. His wife was born in 1798, and died in Indiana in 1863. They were both members of the German Baptist Church, and their family consisted of eleven children, all of whom lived to be grown, and seven are living at the present time: Levi, Mary Ann, Daniel, Aaron, Naomi, Delilah and Eli. Those deceased are Isaac, Samuel, James and Catherine. Daniel was in his eighteenth year when he came to Missouri with his father, and he continued to reside on the home place until thirty-seven years of age, but during the war made his home in Indiana. Since that time he has resided on his present farm, having been married to Nancy F. Moore, a native of Kentucky, who came to Missouri when a girl. To them were born two children, Siegel and Jesse, the latter being deceased. The mother was a member of the Missionary Baptist Church, and died in 1863, after which Mr. Beckner married Ellen Schoolfield, a native of Tennessee, by whom he became the father of the following children: Chloe, E. C., Dan, and Levi (deceased). He is a Republican in politics, and served one term as a member of the State Legislature. He is deeply interested in church and school work, and especially in the education and well-being of the rising generations, who are wanted to surpass, if possible, the past.

Thomas Bilderback, one of the oldest and most prominent citizens of Union Township, Laclede Co., Mo., was born in Washington County, Penn., February 3, 1822, and is a son of Daniel and Sarah (Castleman) Bilderback, natives respectively of Virginia and Pennsylvania, the former born March 17, 1797, and the latter February 27, 1794. The parents were married in Pennsylvania in December, 1817, and in December, 1824, they moved to Licking County, Ohio. They lived in Ohio until 1834, when they went to Fountain County, Ind., remaining there until May, 1836, when they settled in St. Clair County, Ill. Early in the year 1837 they settled in Laclede County, Mo., where Daniel Bilderback died October 16, 1863, and his wife in November, 1865. Both were members of the Methodist Episcopal Church, and the first sermon preached in the western part of Laclede County was at the residence of Daniel Bilderback. He devoted his whole life to the pursuit of farming and stock raising, at which he was very successful. In the early history of the county he was associate judge for a number of years. There were ten children born to Daniel and Sarah Bilderback, of whom six are supposed to be living, viz.: Margaret (wife of J. L. Rimmer, a farmer of Wayne County, Iowa, who is also engaged in the hotel business at Confidence), Susan (the widow of Alva Benson, is living in Laclede County), Hester (married S. S. Lowrence, and is now living in Hill County, Tex.), Daniel (went to California in 1852), Henry C. (is a merchant and farmer, in Hill County, Tex.) and Elizabeth (became the wife of P. M. Stewart, and it is not known whether she is living or not). Since his twenty-first year Thomas Bilderback has been engaged in farming, and has been very successful in his chosen occupation. September 27, 1846, he married Sarah J. Rimmer, who was born in South Carolina, and is a daughter of John Rimmer, who came from Tennessee to Missouri about 1845. Mrs. Bilderback died in Laclede County July 4, 1880, a member of the Methodist Episcopal Church for many years, and a loving wife and mother. Of their seven children, five are now living, viz.: Henry L. (who married Sarah L. Cossey, is living near his father), Sarah J. (now Mrs. Alexander S. Luallin, a prominent farmer of Laclede County, was born September 9, 1851), Stephen W. (was born December 29, 1852), Thomas J. (born May 7, 1855), Margaret E. (at home, was born January 19, 1862). Those deceased were Mary E. (born July 28, 1848, died December 21, 1869; she was the wife of A. S. Luallin). The other child died in infancy. During the late war Mr. Bilderback served six months in the State Militia. He has been a member of the Methodist Episcopal Church for many years. He is a Republican in politics, and is an enterprising citizen of Union Township.

Hon. Richard P. Bland, Member of Congress, was born near Hartford, Ohio Co., Ky., August 19, 1835, and is a son of Stouton E. and Margaret (Nall) Bland, who were natives of Kentucky. The family was originally from Virginia, but immigrated to Kentucky in the time of Daniel Boone, and were among the earliest settlers of that country. Stouton E. Bland was a farmer by occupation, and died when comparatively young, being only about thirty-five years of age. The mother lived some years after his death. Of their four children, three are now living: Richard P., Charles C., judge of the Eighteenth Judicial Circuit of Missouri, and Elizabeth, wife of Frederick Tutley, of St. Francois County, Mo. The subject of this sketch attained his growth on the farm in Kentucky, attending the public schools and Griffin's Academy. In 1855 he came to Wayne County, Mo., taught school at Patterson for one term, and in the fall of the same year he went to California, where he studied law. In 1859 he went to Virginia City, Nev., and was admitted to the bar at Carson City United States Court. He then commenced practicing at Virginia City, and here remained until November, 1865, when he came back to Missouri, locating at Rolla, where he practiced law with his brother, C. C. Bland, until 1869, when he came to Laclede County and located at Lebanon. He here practiced his profession until 1872, when he was elected to Congress, and has been re-elected ever since, thus holding his membership for sixteen successive years. In 1877 he purchased the farm where he now lives, and built a large, handsome brick residence, into which he moved one year later. He has resided here ever since, and has a farm of 160 acres of improved land. While in Utah, Mr. Bland was elected county treasurer of Carson County, Utah, which position he held until the office was organized into the State of Nevada, in 1863. While there he was also engaged in the war against the Indians. Since his election to Congress, he has given up his profession. He was married December 19, 1873, to Miss Virginia E. Mitchell, of Rolla, Mo., and by whom he has five children: Fannie, Theodric R., Ewing C., George V. and Margaret. Mr. Bland is a member of the Masonic fraternity, K. T., and is one of the prominent men of the State of Missouri. He has made an excellent Congressman, and has been instrumental in having a great many important bills passed.

Theodore A. Booton (deceased) was a successful farmer and stock raiser of Laclede County, Mo., and was born in the "Sucker State" in 1838, being a son of Laban and Catherine (Shoemaker) Booton, who were farmers, and natives of Virginia and Ohio, respectively, and were of German lineage. Theodore A. Booton was taken by his parents to Knox County, Ill., when a child, and was reared to manhood on a farm, and educated in the schools of Knox County and Peoria. When starting out in life for himself he located on a farm near the home place, where he continued to reside until 1872, when his health became very much impaired, and he and family went to California, where they resided one year. From that time until 1883 they resided in Illinois, and at the latter date sold their property and came to Missouri, taking up their abode near Lebanon, where Mr. Booton was quite extensively engaged in farming and stock raising. He died on the 9th of July, 1886. He served three years in the Seventh Illinois Cavalry Regiment during the late war, and was severely wounded twice. His wife was born in Knox County in 1846, and is a daughter of Asa and Mary (Gaddis) Haynes, who were born in New York and Pennsylvania, respectively. They located in Illinois in 1836, the father being still alive and a resident of Knox County, but the mother died in 1884, having borne a family of eight children, seven of whom are living: Margaret, Elizabeth, Clark, Ann, Nancy, Ellen and Charles. Ellen is the widow of Mr. Booton, by whom she became the mother of six children: Jessie, Clara, Minnie, Theodore, Louella and Leon. Mrs. Booton has a good farm of 290 acres, with 200 under cultivation, and also deals quite extensively in stock. Her husband was a member of the G. A. R., of Lebanon. He died of disease contracted in the army.

J. T. Bradshaw, editor of the *Rustic*, at Lebanon, was born in Clay County, Ill., June 27, 1859, and is a son of Francis A. and Mary (Curry) Bradshaw, natives of Kentucky and England, respectively. The father immigrated to Wayne County, Ill., at an early date, and served an apprenticeship to the carpenter's trade. He then moved to Clay County, Ill., where he followed his trade until the spring of 1869, when he moved to Laclede County, locating at Lebanon, where he has since resided, and where he has since followed his trade. He has built a great number of the houses in Lebanon, and was the contractor for the Laclede Hotel. He is the father of eight children: Belle (wife of J. W. Farris), Edith, James T., Lydia, Edward, Andrew, Mamie and Maude. James T. Bradshaw was reared in Clay County, Ill., until ten years of age, when he came to Lebanon, and was here educated. At the age of twelve years he entered the *Laclede County Leader* office, and served an apprenticeship. During his vacations in the office he attended school. In 1876 he went to Richland, where he had charge of the *Pulaski County Sentinel* during the campaign, but returned to Lebanon in 1878, where he established the Lebanon *Leader*, which publication he controlled until 1880, when he consolidated with the Lebanon *Rustic*, and continued the publication as the *Rustic Leader*, on account of them both being Democrats. In 1881 Mr. Bradshaw went to Joplin, Mo., where he was connected with the *Daily Herald* until early in 1883. He then went to Springfield, Mo., and began working on the *Patriot*, but only remained with that paper a short time. He was then associated with D. C. Kennedy in the publication of the *Daily Leader*, of Springfield, but in 1884 he returned to Lebanon to again take charge of the *Rustic*. In October, 1884, on the death of the editor, Dr. John W. Armstrong, he purchased the paper, and has since continued its publication. This paper is published in the interest of the Democratic party. Mr. Bradshaw was for a short time connected with the St. Louis *Times*, as traveling correspondent. The *Rustic* has a good circulation, and Mr. Bradshaw is an able editor. He was married in April, 1887, to Miss Amie M. Wilson, of Cairo, Ill., and to them has been born one child, Margaret Eugenia. Mr. Bradshaw is a member of the A. O. U. W. and Select Knights. Mrs. Bradshaw is a member of the Presbyterian Church.

Henry L. Brown, postmaster of Conway, Laclede Co., Mo., was born in Webster County, Mo., January 16, 1860, and is a son of George A. and Nancy (Kilburn) Brown, natives of Tennessee, the former born October 26, 1823, and the latter April 7, 1828. The parents were married in their native State December 31, 1844, where they spent the first ten years of their married life, and then moved to Greene County, Mo. About 1858 they located in Webster County, Mo., where they still live. George A. Brown has always been a farmer, and has been very successful in his chosen occupation. He is a Democrat politically, and, with his wife, is a member of the Missionary Baptist Church, in which they take an active part. Eight children were born to the parents of our subject, viz.: Arminta F., who is now the wife of William Cain, a minister of the Missionary Baptist Church, now living in Webster County; Neil S., a carpenter of Conway, Mo.; Allen D., a farmer of Webster County; James J., also a farmer of Webster County; Henry L.; Martha E., who married John H. Smith, a farmer of Webster County; George L., a farmer of the same county, and Millie N. (deceased) was the wife of James L. Rice, of Conway; the latter, who was born in 1866, died May 15, 1888. January 18, 1880, Henry L. Brown married Maria E. Conner, daughter of Solomon Conner, of Dallas County, Mo. Mrs. Brown, who was also a native of Dallas County, Mo., is the mother of two children: Gracie S. and Oscar L. In 1880 Mr. Brown located in Conway, and the following three years was employed as salesman in the establishment of C. Hanson. He then taught school one year in Webster and Laclede Counties, and October 23, 1885, was appointed postmaster of Conway, of which office he is the present incumbent, having served with credit. Mr. Brown is a Knight of Pythias, and in 1887 represented his lodge at St. Louis. He is also a member of the Baptist Church, and Mrs. Brown is a member of the Congregational Church. Mr. Brown is one of the enterprising citizens of Conway, and the family is highly esteemed by all who know them.

John S. Burns, Deputy United States Marshal for the Western District of Missouri, was born in Dallas County September 6, 1844, and is a son of Foster and Elizabeth (Tiller) Burns, and grandson of John Burns. The latter was a native of North Carolina, and located in Tennessee when a young man, where he was married to Margaret Wilson. They located on a farm in Maury County, and in 1836 came to Missouri, locating in Polk County, where he continued farming until he became one of the leading agriculturists of that region, and was an extensive slave-holder. He served in the War of 1812, and was wounded at the battle of New Orleans, and being unable to make his escape was captured by the British soldiers, but was released after a short time. He was a leading politican, and served in the county court, and also represented Polk County in the State Legislature several terms. He was a consistent member of the Cumberland Presbyterian Church, and died September 20, 1863, aged seventy-seven years. His wife was born in Tennessee, and became the mother of a large family of children. She was noted for her piety and hospitality, and died in 1878, at the age of eighty years. Her brother, Gen. Anderson Wilson, was one of the prominent citizens of Tennessee. Foster Burns, the father of the gentleman whose name heads this sketch, was the eldest of the family, and was born in Maury County, Tenn, in 1812, and was reared to manhood and educated in his native State. After attaining a suitable age he engaged in teaching school, which occupation he followed until 1840, and was the author of an arithmetic of considerable merit, but never had it published, and his death occurred just as it was ready for the press. He was married in 1840, and settled on a farm in Polk County, Mo., and in 1844 located in Dallas County, near Buffalo, where he became one of the leading citizens. He was elected sheriff of the county in 1850, but died the same year. He was a member of the Cumberland Presbyterian Church, and his wife, who was born in Kentucky in 1814, was a member of the same. She was a daughter of James Tiller, who was a farmer by occupation, and located in Polk County in 1838. Mr. and Mrs. Burns became the parents of six children, two of whom are living: John S. and Joseph. After the death of Mr. Burns the mother continued to reside on the farm, and succeeded in giving her children a good education. James, the eldest son, received a highschool education, and in 1861 entered the Confederate army, and was on active duty until November, 1864, when he was killed at the battle of Franklin, Tenn. He entered service at the age of nineteen, and after the battle of Iuka was promoted to the rank of captain for gallantry, and was serving on Gen. Cockrell's staff when killed. The youngest son, Joseph, served in the Union army, in the Fifty-first Missouri Infantry. John S. Burns was reared to manhood in Dallas County, and in 1863 enlisted in the Federal army, in the quartermaster's department, and served until the close of the war, being in the Trans-Mississippi Department during the latter part of his service. He returned to his home in Dallas County, and in September, 1866, was married to Miss Nancy Maddux, who was born in Giles County, Tenn., in 1845, and is a daughter of Nathaniel Maddux, an old 1812 soldier. Mr. and Mrs. Burns are the parents of the following family: Foster, Deputy United States Marshal; James, William, Denean, Archibald, Wilburn, Eva, wife of Terrell Bruton, and Florence. In 1878 Mr. Burns was elected sheriff of Dallas County, serving three terms, being re-elected in 1882 and 1884. He made many notable arrests during his term of office, and succeeded in running down and capturing the noted horse thieves, the Crawford brothers, and since being elected to his present office has captured a number of counterfeiters. In March, 1887, he located in Conway, where he has since resided. He is a member of the A. F. & A. M., and is a Royal Arch Mason, Lebanon Commandery, Past Master of the Blue Lodge, and is Master Workman in the A. O. U. W.

Shadrach V. Casey, who is classed among the prominent and enterprising farmers of Gasconade Township, and one of the largest stock farmers of the county, was born December 25, 1837, on the place where he now lives, in Laclede County, Mo. He is the son of Samuel and Lucretia B. (Cayce) Casey. Samuel Casey was born in Roane County, Tenn., March 20, 1799, and as his father died when he was but six months old, Samuel was taken and reared by an uncle, Daniel Biehler, of German descent. Samuel Casey was married in Williamson County, Tenn., and came to Missouri about 1832 or 1833, and purchased the place where our subject lives. He died December 19, 1862. The mother was born in Williamson County, Tenn., January 26, 1817, and was married in that county. She died June 14, 1871. They were the parents of eight children, five of whom grew to maturity, and four now living: Mary J., wife of Mr. Breakfield; Shadrach V., Mrs. Amanda H. Nelson and Mrs. Anna B. Adams. Those deceased were: Thomas B., who was a soldier in the Union army, and came home on furlough; while at home he was taken out by bushwhackers and killed, in 1863; Lucretia E., Samuel H., and one infant, not named. The mother of these children was a member of the Methodist Episcopal Church, and was one of the best of mothers. Her father was a Baptist minister of some prominence, and very wealthy. She was one of thirteen children. Shadrach V. Casey lived on the home place until the fall of 1860, and April 12 of that year he married Miss Mary Ann Nelson, who was born in what was then Pulaski County, now Laclede County, and was the daughter of William and Mahala Nelson. To this union were born a family of four children, all living: William S., Mrs. Mary E. Allen, Mrs. Eliza L. Adams and Thomas H. The mother of these children died August 19, 1868, and Mr. Casey took for his second wife Miss Mary C. Stroup, a native of Wright County, now Laclede County. She was born May 5, 1848, and died November 1, 1883. She was a member of the Christian Church. One child was born to this union, Anna P. After his first marriage Mr. Casey settled on a farm below where he now lives, and there remained but one year. He then returned to the home, and after remaining there one year moved to a place on the prairie nine miles east of Lebanon, and at the end of two years again returned to the home place, where he has since resided. He enlisted in 1862 in the Confederate army, and served about five months as a ranger. He was in one skirmish in Wright County, Mo., and then came home. He was married, the third time, to Miss Mary E. Roberts, who was born in Ohio, and came to Missouri in 1878. She was the daughter of Allen C. and Amanda Roberts, residents of Laclede County. Mr. and Mrs. Casey are the parents of one child, Shadrach Allen. Mr. Casey has a large farm under a good state of cultivation; is a Union Labor man in his politics; has been a member of the school board for many years; is a member of the Masonic fraternity, the Agricultural Wheel, and is a member of the Christian Church. Mrs. Casey is a member of the Methodist Episcopal Church.

C. C. Clendenin, merchant at Lebanon, Mo., and son of Ephraim R. and Pauline (Conway) Clendenin, was born in Randolph Co., Ill., March 25, 1847. The parents were both natives of Randolph County, Ill., the father born in or near Rockwood and the mother born at Old Kaskaskia. The maternal grandfather, Clement C. Conway, was born in Ireland, and immigrated to South Carolina at an early date. From there he moved to Kaskaskia, Ill. He was a hatter by trade, which occupation he followed the principal part of his life. He died on the Ohio River, in 1852, of cholera. The grandfather Clendenin died in Randolph County, Ill. He was engaged in mercantile pursuits for several years in Old Liberty, and was one of the first business men of that place. He resided on a farm the most of his time. The father of our subject lived and died in Randolph County, Ill. In his youth he learned the trade of ship carpenter, which he followed until 1862, when he enlisted in the late war, but the quota being full, he was appointed by Lincoln as enrolling officer for the Southern Illinois District, which position he was filling at the time of his death, which occurred September 20, 1864. The mother is still living, and resides in Walnut, Kas. They were the parents of seven children, four now living: Emma G., wife of James Miln, of Cairo; Colburn C., Charles M. and Adelle. Those deceased were named Sydney, Penelope and Clara. C. C. Clendenin was reared in Liberty (now Rockwood), Ill., where he received a common-school education. He worked on the farm until the death of his father, in 1864, when he served an apprenticeship at the trade of stone cutting, which he followed for twelve years, and worked in the meantime on some of the largest State buildings in Illinois. He assisted in building the Springfield State House, the Southern Illinois Insane Asylum, Normal University of Carbondale, and the penitentiary at Chester. He was contracting for about five years in Illinois. In 1879 he took the contract for all the stone work on St. John's Evangelical Lutheran Church, in Chester, Ill., the finest church building in the county. In 1881 he took the contract for the stone work for the Shiloh Hill College building, in Randolph County, Ill., and the insane asylum on the Randolph County farm. In September, 1881, he came to Lebanon, Mo., and here engaged in the monumental and tombstone business with a partner. This he carried on for two years, then sold out, and was elected constable for Lebanon Township, serving two years. In 1886 he engaged in his present business with L. J. Kaffenberger, and the firm is known as Kaffenberger & Co. Mr. Clendenin was married December 20, 1871, to Miss Maggie L. Gordon, of Jackson County, Ill. To them was born one child, Etta, whose birth occurred October 23, 1872. He is a member of the K. L., National Lodge of Combined Industries, and Sons of Veterans. He is a member of the city council, and president of the town board. Mr. Clendenin is a strong advocate of organized labor, and it was the labor element that elected him to the position of city alderman. He was a delegate to the national convention of the United Labor party that met at Cincinnati, Ohio, May 15, 1888, which nominated Streeter and Cunningham for President and Vice-President.

E. R. Clough, a prominent farmer and stock raiser of Laclede County, Mo., was born in Summit County, Ohio, and is the son of Jeremiah and Susan (Simpson) Clough, natives of Vermont and Pennsylvania, respectively. The Clough family were early settlers of Vermont, and Jeremiah Clough moved from that State to Summit County, Ohio, at quite an early date. Here both parents passed the remainder of their days. Of their seven children, three sons and four daughters, five are now living: Celestia, wife of H. E. Meriner; Jane, wife of T. E. Robinson; Edwin R., Walter W. and Charles. E. R. Clough attained his growth and was educated in Summit County, Ohio. He remained and assisted his father on the farm until 1862, when he enlisted in Company H, One Hundred and Fourth Ohio Infantry, and served until the close of the war. He was at the battle of Knoxville, battle of Atlanta, Franklin, and crossed the mountains to the capture of Fort Fisher. Then his regiment took charge of the surrender of Johnston's army. After his discharge Mr. Clough returned to Ohio, and remained in that State until the latter part of 1865, when he came to St. Louis, thence to Salt Lake City and other cities, prospecting for a location. He visited Old Mexico and Texas, but returned to St. Louis in the latter part of 1866. He was then employed on the now St. Louis & San Francisco Railroad, and remained in the employ of this company until 1869, as railroad conductor on passenger trains. In 1869 he located at Lebanon and engaged in general merchandising, the firm being known as Clough & Lindsay. This partnership was dissolved in 1872, and afterward Mr. Clough engaged in the drug business, which he continued until the spring of 1887, when he moved his stock of drugs to Akron, Ohio. Since that time he has turned his attention to stock raising. He owns over 3,000 acres of land in Laclede County, with several hundred acres under cultivation. He owns one of the finest farms in Laclede County, consisting of 325 acres, all under cultivation, and joining the city of Lebanon. Two hundred acres of this are in meadow land, and on the same he has the fair ground, where he built the race track at his own expense. He has abundance of water on this farm, it being piped 2,500 feet from a magnificent well. Mr. Clough was general superintendent of the Fair the last season, and he is also superintendent of the Lebanon Water Works. He is one of the leading and pushing men of Laclede County, and is a valuable citizen. He owns land in Dakota, Tennessee, Ohio, and has mining interests in Utah. He also has property in Kansas and several other States. He is a member of the Masonic fraternity, Blue Lodge and Chapter, and is a Republican in his political views.

James C. Coffman, farmer and stock raiser of Laclede County, Mo., was born in East Tennessee, on the 11th of January, 1845, his parents being Abner L. and Sarah (Couch) Coffman. He is one of five surviving members of a family of ten children, whose names are as follows: Rachel E. (the wife of A. Lorance), Fernando, Ella (wife of G. B. Gustin) and Houston C. James C. Coffman immigrated to Laclede County, Mo., in 1851, where he has since made his home, and has become one of the prosperous tillers of the soil. In 1863 he espoused the Union cause, enlisting as corporal in the Sixteenth Missouri Cavalry, Company F, and served until the close of hostilities, being mustered out on the 3d of July, 1865. In December, 1870, he was married to Miss M. A. Howard, a daughter of John and Becky (Rouff) Howard, who were natives of Pennsylvania, and immigrated to Laclede County, Mo., in 1866. Mr. Coffman and wife have become the parents of nine children: Rudolph, Ulus, Eugene, Ernest, Effie and Ella. Those deceased are James, John and Mary. Mr. Coffman is a member of the A. F. & A. M., and in his political views is a Republican. He and family attend the Methodist Church.

A. S. Coffman, a worthy farmer of Washington Township, Laclede Co., Mo., was born in McMinn County, Tenn., in 1833, and is a son of John and Elizabeth (Turner) Coffman. After residing in his native State until 1852, he at that date removed to Laclede County, Mo., where he soon after became the owner of some real estate and engaged in husbandry. He has now a fertile and well-cultivated farm consisting of 207 acres, and is considered one of the enterprising and successful farmers of Laclede County. He is a member of the Masonic fraternity, and in 1862 enlisted in Company G, Sixteenth Missouri Volunteer Cavalry, and distinguished himself as first lieutenant, being mustered out of service on the 30th of July, 1865. He participated in a number of severe skirmishes, and was once wounded. In 1854 he was united in marriage to Miss Mary E. Connor, a daughter of Armstrong and Unity (Strickland) Connor, by whom he became the father of fifteen children, thirteen of whom are now living. Mr. Coffman has served as deputy sheriff of Laclede County for six years, and has proved a trusty and competent officer.

Charles Coffman, of Laclede County, Mo., is a son of A. S. and Mary E. (Connor) Coffman, natives respectively of Tennessee and Missouri. The father became a resident of Laclede County, Mo., in 1852, where he owns a good farm and is in comfortable circumstances. He served in the late war as first lieutenant of Company G, Sixteenth Missouri Cavalry. His son Charles was born in Laclede County, Mo., September 12, 1866, and made his home with his father until he attained his twentieth year, when he left the paternal roof, and began doing for himself, homesteading the farm of forty acres on which he is now living. He is one of fifteen children, three of whom are deceased, and September 26, 1886, was married to Miss Ella Edwards, a daughter of Joseph and Catherine (Bohannan) Edwards, who were Kentuckians, and who came to Laclede County, Mo., in 1874, where they have since made their home. Mr. and Mrs. Coffman are the parents of one child, Lawrence E. Mr. Coffman is a stanch Republican in his political views, and is an enterprising and industrious young farmer.

Edward P. Cook, farmer of Gasconade Township, was born in Montgomery County, Mo., March 1, 1823, and is a son of Joel B. and Margaret (Mowser) Cook, who were born in New York and Tennessee, April 17, 1800, and in 1808, respectively. Joel B. Cook is a son of John Cook, who was born in New York, September 7, 1761, and came to Missouri with his family when his son Joel was a young man, locating in Montgomery County, where he was engaged in blacksmithing, gunsmithing, carpentering and mill-wrighting until his death in April, 1845, about four miles below Chamois, in Missouri Bottom, Osage County. Joel B. Cook resided in Osage County, Mo., until 1846, when he located in Pulaski County, and lived until his death, November 25, 1887, being engaged in milling and farming the latter part of his life. His wife died October 29, 1886, having been an earnest and consistent member of the Christian Church. Eleven of their twelve children lived to be grown, and nine are living at the present time: Edward P., John T., Caroline (deceased), Mary, James (deceased), Sarah, George, Nathaniel G., Welton, William J., Lydia A., and Martha (deceased). Edward P. Cook attained his majority in Osage and Montgomery Counties, and in 1849 began selling goods in Waynesville, Pulaski County, but in the spring of the following year took the overland trip to California, where he remained nearly three years, and then returned home via New York City. His return was one accompanied by serious hardship. Associated with his uncle, Lorenz D. Cook, passage was taken on an old steam-wheeler to San Francisco, and thence to the mouth of the San Joaquin River. About a mile up the river near midnight on the night of May 28, 1853, owing to the reported intention of the crew to murder them, Mr. Cook and his uncle undertook to swim ashore, first casting a few sticks of cordwood in the water to assist in their escape. In this effort L. D. Cook was drowned, our subject finally reaching land, and coming upon a temporary habitation where help was accorded him. A two days' effort was made in dragging the river for the body of the unfortunate man, but without success. Subsequently Mr. Cook went to San Francisco, thence to Panama and New York, reaching home in Pulaski County, Mo., about August 1, 1853. He taught school in Pulaski County during the winter following his return, and the next year was married, and commenced farming in Laclede County, on the Osage Fork of the Gasconade River, but since 1857 has been a resident of his present farm. He served in the Missouri State Militia during the latter part of the war. In 1856 he was elected assessor of Laclede County, which position he held by re-election for six years. He was first married to Mary J. Honsinger, who was born in Laclede County January 16, 1829, and died November 19, 1857, having became the mother of the following children: Margaret and William (twins), Joel B. and John E. All died in childhood except Joel, whose death occurred at the age of eighteen years. Sarah M. Maxey became Mr. Cook's second wife. She was born in Tennessee December 5, 1829, and died November 12, 1884, having borne the following children: Mary, Laura, Angeline, Lucy and an infant (deceased). The eldest daughter is the wife of Riley Bench, and Laura is the wife of Oscar Jackson. The latter resides on the home farm with her father. Mr. Cook is also a member of the Christian Church, and belongs to the A. F. & A. M. and the Agricultural Wheel. He is a member of the Union Labor party, and has held a number of offices in his township.

C. H. Corser, farmer and stock raiser, was born in Windsor County, Vt., July 8, 1823, being the son of William and Mary A. (Manuel) Corser. The father was born in Boscoin, N. H., but removed to Vermont when a young man, and there passed the remainder of his life. He was a farmer by occupation, and a soldier in the War of 1812. To his marriage were born eleven children, four now living. C. H. Corser was reared in Vermont, and there received his education. He began learning the iron moulder's trade when nine years of age, at Taftsville, Vt., where he worked for seven years. He then worked at his trade in South Boston, Mass.; Lowell, Mass.; Stockton, Cal.; West Pawlet, Vt., one of the largest factories in the United States; Rutland, Vt., and numerous other places. In 1849 he went to California, and remained in that State for three years, engaged in mining and working at his trade. In 1852 he returned to Lowell, Mass., and May 19, 1853, he was united in marriage to Miss Hattie L. Way, a native of New Hampshire. The fruits of this union are two children: Fred. Augustus and Nettie Louise. In 1872 Mr. Corser and family moved to Laclede County, Mo., purchasing the farm where they now live, which consists of eighty acres, with seventy-five acres under improvement. Mr. Corser's attention is almost wholly taken up with the raising of live stock, especially Holstein and Short-horn cattle. He also has a large orchard, with 300 bearing trees, and is one of the enterprising and intelligent citizens of the county. He is a member of the Agricultural Wheel.

John H. Cotton, farmer, brick and stone mason and plasterer, was born in North Carolina July 16, 1815, being a son of Samuel and Biddie (Purnell) Cotton, who were also natives of North Carolina, in which State the father died. They were the parents of three children: Jacob (deceased), Elizabeth (who is supposed to be dead), and John H. The mother of these children was living when last heard from, forty years ago. At the age of six years John H. Cotton was bound out to a farmer by the name of Wilson Wiseman, with whom he resided until seventeen years of age; then he began the battle of life for himself, and went to Caswell County, N. C. Mr. Wiseman was to have given him educational advantages, but up to seventeen years of age he had received only a few months schooling, consequently he left and began the battle of life for himself. Mr. Cotton learned his trade in Caswell County, N. C., and continued to follow this occupation until 1849, when he came to Laclede County, Mo., with his second wife, whose maiden name was Henslee. He located on the farm now owned by Thomas Turner, but at the end of six months came to his present location, where he has a good farm under cultivation. Mr. Cotton married Mary Ballard (his first wife) August 28, 1838. She was born in Caswell County, N. C., December 23, 1813, and died there February 16, 1842, one week after her second child was born. The following are her children: Martha J., wife of Jacob Kapp, and Addison R. (deceased). November 28, 1843, Mr. Cotton married his second wife, Elizabeth Henslee, who was born in Caswell County, N. C., January 30, 1824. From this marriage there resulted ten children, six of whom are living, namely: Thomas B.; Artelia E., wife of Noah D. Light; Sarah A., wife of Job V. Chalfant; Nannie E., who is a schoolteacher; Elvira, wife of Edward Chalfant, and John M. The mother of these children died on the 20th of July, 1888, having been a member of the Baptist Church since she was nineteen years old, and a model wife and mother. Mr. Cotton is a member of the Christian Church, and belongs to the A. F. & A. M. and the Agricultural Wheel.

B. H. Cowgill, editor of the *Sentinel* at Lebanon, Mo., and son of Elisha Y. and Joannah (Bland) Cowgill, was born in Clark County, Mo., April 21, 1854. The parents were natives of Kentucky, and immigrated to Clark County, Mo., about 1832, being among the first settlers of that county. They remained there until 1864, when they removed to Lewis County of that State, locating at Canton, where both died. They were the parents of four children: B. H., Emma, (wife of Frank C. Devilbliss), Anna (wife of Fred J. Budreau), and George I., who resides in Lewis County, near Canton. The paternal grandfather of these children was a soldier in the War of 1812. H. B. Cowgill attained his growth in Lewis County, Mo., receiving the principal part of his education there at Christian University, and later attended the Christian Brothers College at St. Louis, leaving when in the sophomore class to go to Pike County, Mo., where he was appointed to a position as deputy collector, which position he held for six years. In 1875 he founded the *Pike County Express*, now the Bowling Green *Times*, which he continued to publish until July, 1880, when he sold out to Adjt. Gen. J. C. Jamison. In 1881 Mr. Cowgill removed to Lebanon, Mo., and purchased the *Anti-Monopolist*, changing the name to the *Laclede County Sentinel*, which he still edits.

This paper is conducted independent of party, though during the recent campaign it was identified with the Labor party. It now enjoys a good circulation. Mr. Cowgill has the experience of many years as a newspaper man, and the pages of his paper are newsy and full of interest. He was married in June, 1878, to Miss Alice Sanderson, of Bowling Green, Pike County, and both he and wife are members of the Methodist Episcopal Church. Mr. Cowgill is also a member of Auglaize Lodge No. 192, I. O. O. F., Lebanon Encampment No. 102, I. O. O. F., Wyota Assembly No. 6457, K. of L., and in August, 1888, was elected Judge Advocate of the State Assembly of K. of L. of Missouri.

Simon Dalton was born in Hawkins County, Tenn., March 8, 1825, and in 1849 immigrated to Missouri, locating in Crawford County, from which he came to Laclede County in 1851, and located on the farm on which he is now residing. He is a son of Thomas and Dollie (Light) Dalton, who were natives of Tennessee, and were of English and Dutch lineage, respectively. The former's death occurred during his son Simon's boyhood, and the mother died during the late Civil War. Simon received such education as the schools of his day afforded, and at the early age of fourteen years began the battle of life for himself. His first investment in real estate was eighty acres of land where he now lives, but he afterward entered 120 acres, a portion of which is well improved. Besides his farming interests, he is engaged in raising horses, cattle and hogs, and has a fine young orchard. In 1875 he was married to Pernecia, daughter of James B. Davis, by whom he became the father of four children: James B., married to Adaline Hafly; Lethe, wife of Thomas King; Ruth, and Elizabeth, wife of David Buster. Mrs. Dalton is a member of the Christian Church. Her first husband, Charles K. Phipps, was a soldier in the late war, and died August 18, 1863. Mr. Dalton is a member of the Democratic party, and is one of the leading pioneer settlers of Laclede County.

James Franklin Davis, of Mayfield Township, Laclede Co., Mo., was born in the county in which he now resides, August 22, 1856, and is a son of James Monroe and Charity A. (Casteel) Davis. The former was born in Warren County, Ky., and throughout life was a farmer by occupation, and made a settlement in Laclede County, Mo., as early as 1840, while he was yet a young man. He was married after coming to Missouri, his wife being a native of Middle Tennessee, and their union was blessed in the birth of six sons and three daughters. James Franklin Davis is the eldest of their children, and grew to manhood in Laclede County, and married Florence Brooks, a daughter of Cyrus C. Brooks and Elvira C. (Skelton) Brooks, who were born, reared and married in Alabama, and settled in Missouri about 1868. Mr. and Mrs. Davis are the parents of two sons and one daughter, James Harvey, Thomas Ernest and Ellen, and are worthy and consistent members of the Baptist Church.

S. C. Demuth, grocer at Lebanon, was born in Tuscarawas County, Ohio, May 15, 1832, being the son of Joseph and Mary (Varner) Demuth, natives of Ohio, and grandson of John Demuth, who was a native of Pennsylvania, and who drove a team in the War of 1812.

He was a farmer by occupation, and died in Tuscarawas County, Ohio, at the age of sixty-three years. The father of the subject of this sketch was a mechanic by trade, which he followed the principal part of his life-time. He was elected to the office of county treasurer of his county, and served two successive terms. He was a prominent man and a good citizen. He died in 1867, and the mother many years previous, in 1832. They were the parents of two children, only one now living, S. C. Demuth, who was reared in Ohio and received his education in the schools of that State, completing his education at Granville College. He was placed behind the counter at eleven years of age, and has followed mercantile pursuits ever since, except at intervals, when attending school. In 1856 he went to Northern Illinois, and from there, in 1858, to Clinton County, Ill., where he was engaged in mercantile pursuits until 1876. Previous to this, in 1860, he married Miss Mary James, a native of the State of New York, who immigrated with her parents to Illinois when about eight years of age. To Mr. and Mrs. Demuth were born three children: John V., Frederick and Mary. In 1876 Mr. Demuth moved to Lebanon, Mo., engaging in merchandising, which he has since carried on quite extensively. He has a general line of groceries and a full stock. He has had considerable experience in the mercantile line, and has a thorough knowledge of the business. He is a member of the Masonic fraternity, also a member of the A. O. U. W., and is a Republican in his political principles. He had the misfortune to lose his life's companion in October, 1888. She was in her fifty-fourth year, and was an excellent woman.

James Detherage was born in Warren County, of the "Blue Grass" State, in 1832, and is a son of James and Sallie (Andrews) Detherage, who were born in Tennessee and North Carolina, respectively, and were farmers by occupation. James is one of ten children, and was reared to manhood on his father's farm. In 1854 he was married to Miss Susanna Wood, of Kentucky, by whom he had nine children: Martin, who married Mary Rocter; Winnie, wife of William Rippey; Thomas; Betsey, wife of Henry Wood; Sarah, Mary J., James, Marian and Jesse. Both Mr. and Mrs. Detherage are members of the Baptist Church, in which he is a deacon, and politically he is a Democrat. His first purchase of land was eighty acres in Warren County, Ky., which he afterward sold, and purchased the farm of 160 acres where he is now residing. Besides this land he owns forty acres more, and is one of the best and most thrifty farmers of his locality. He raises good stock of all kinds, and throughout life has been an earnest supporter of the cause of education.

D. R. Diffenderfer, banker at Lebanon, Mo., and son of Michael and Mary (Esterly) Diffenderfer, was born in Lancaster County, Penn., in January, 1821. The Diffenderfer family are of German descent, were originally from Hanover, Germany, and came to America in the celebrated ship "William and Mary" in 1727, which brought over the refugees. Michael Diffenderfer received a grant of land from William Penn, which was called "Michael Diffenderfer's Reserve." He was a farmer, and followed this occupation all his life. He died in Lancaster County, as did also the mother. They were the parents of five children, three now living: David R., Mary (wife of A. G. Sutton), and Frank R. (who is now associate editor of the Lancaster (Penn.) *New Era*). D. R. Diffenderfer received a fair education in the common schools, and at the age of sixteen he went to Pittsburg, Penn., where he learned the drug business. At the end of six years he went to St. Louis, where he again engaged in the drug business, and in 1849 he went to El Paso, Mexico, where he followed the mercantile business until 1861. In 1852 he was appointed by President Millard Fillmore as United States Consul, and continued under President Buchanan's administration. At the time of the firing on Fort Sumter Mr. Diffenderfer was in New York City buying goods, and experienced great trouble in getting through. He was captured in Texas, and imprisoned at Fort Bliss, but only retained a short time. In 1862 he came home, and in 1864 he was united in marriage to Miss Margaret Dunham, a native of New Jersey. To them were born seven children: William, Mary, David, Henry, Jane, John and Grace. After the assassination of President Lincoln Mr. Diffenderfer returned to El Paso, where he was engaged in merchandising until 1871. He then returned to Lancaster, Penn., embarked in the banking business, and this he carried on until after the panic of 1873. In 1876 he came to Lebanon, Mo., and was engaged in railroad contracting until 1886, since which time he has been in the banking business. Mr. Diffenderfer is a Mason, a Knight Templar, and is one of the prominent and leading citizens of Laclede County. His paternal grandfather, David Diffenderfer, served as ensign in the Revolutionary War; was at Valley Forge, and crossed the Delaware River at Trenton with Washington. He was also at the battles of Princeton and Monmouth, and received a wound at the last named place. After recovering from his wounds he re-entered the army, and was captured at the battle of Long Island. He died in Lancaster County, Penn., in his ninety-fourth year.

Richard C. Edmisson, merchant and farmer at Conway, Mo., was born in Dallas County, of that State, September 24, 1854, and is a son of John and Elizabeth (Wollard) Edmisson, both of whom were born in Tennessee. They were married in Dallas County, Mo., in 1848, and resided on their farm in that county until the father was killed for his money, during the late war, by Northern bushwhackers. He was an extensive farmer and stock dealer, and was a leading member of the Baptist Church. They were the parents of eight children, five of whom are now living. After the father's death his widow married again, her second husband being George Davidson, by whom she has two children. He died in 1886, and she now resides on the old home farm with one of her children. Richard C. Edmisson grew to manhood on a farm in Dallas County, receiving a common-school education, and in 1870 went to Texas, where he remained five years, engaged in herding and trading in cattle. He then returned to Dallas County, Mo., and in 1879 was married to Miss Anna Pare, a native of the county, by whom he became the father of one child,

Edna. In 1883 he came to Conway, and embarked in his present business, which has netted him a handsome annual income, and in addition to this work he is quite extensively engaged in stock raising, making the breeding of mules a specialty. He is a Royal Arch Mason, and in his political views is a Democrat.

Amos Edwards, ex-county judge, and farmer of Hooker Township, was born in Brown County, Ohio, June 5, 1842, being the son of Darius and Jane (Geeslin) Edwards, and grandson of Col. George Edwards, who was born in Pennsylvania in 1781, and came to Ohio in 1806. He located on 2,000 acres of land, where he remained until the breaking out of the War of 1812, and then served as colonel of his regiment. He was in a number of the leading battles, and was a brave and gallant officer. He took an active part in all political, national and public matters, and was a very prominent man in his day, being one of the leading men of the State, as well as one of the early settlers. After the War of 1812 he returned to the home place and resumed farming, but after the country had become somewhat settled he engaged in general merchandising, which he followed for many years. He was elected as representative to the Legislature for many terms, and was also a prominent member of the Christian Church. He made many public speeches, and when he got too old to stand up and talk he would sit in a chair. When the Civil War broke out he made one of the leading speeches of his life, directing the people to enlist as soldiers to protect the Union, put down slavery, etc. He died in 1880, at the age of ninety-eight years and eight months. His wife was also a native of Pennsylvania, and died when Amos Edwards was a small boy. She was the mother of ten children, six sons and four daughters, all of whom lived to be grown, but only two of whom are now living, Sandy and Orange; Sandy lives in Kansas, and Orange lives in Ripley, Ohio. Darius Edwards was born in Brown County in 1804, and was reared in that county. He followed farming, etc., all his life, and took an active part in church matters, being a member of the Christian Church. He died in 1879. His wife, Jane Geeslin, was born in 1805, in Brown County, and is now living on the old home place, where their son, Amos, was born. She has good health, is a member of the Christian Church, and is the mother of fifteen children, twelve of whom lived to be grown, and ten are now living: Josiah, Cinderella, George W., Alexander C., Darius (deceased), John B., Mary, Mandania, William H. H., Amos, Martha and Nancy J. (deceased). Sarah Ellen was one of the three that died when a child; the others died in infancy. Amos Edwards grew to maturity in Brown County, where he received his education in the common schools. October 3, 1862, he enlisted in Company E, Seventh Ohio Cavalry, and served three years. In 1865 he was transferred to the invalid corps. At the cessation of hostilities he came to Missouri, Audrain County, where he remained six months. He then moved to Polk County, thence to Laclede, where he has since remained. July 14, 1867, he married Miss Sarah E. Freeze, a native of Tennessee, born May 21, 1845, and the daughter of Martin and Dorcas Freeze, who were old settlers of Laclede County. To

Mr. and Mrs. Edwards were born eight children, six now living: Rosa M., Cora B., Charley D., Lula G., Lillie and Nettie (twins); and those deceased were named Ally D. and Floyd. In 1882 Mr. Edwards was elected county judge for a term of two years on the Greenback ticket. He takes an active part in politics, and affiliates with the Greenback party. He is a member of the Masonic fraternity, and he and wife are members of the Christian Church.

Hon. J. W. Farris, attorney at law and insurance agent at Lebanon, was born in Marion County, Ill., January 20, 1846, and is the son of Hiram K. and Abigail Farris, the father a native of Kentucky and the mother of Indiana. Hiram K. Farris was a resident of Marion County, Ill., for many years, and came there from Indiana in 1840. He was a very prominent man of both Marion and Clay Counties, being elected county clerk of the former county and county judge of the latter. He died in Clay County, Ill., in June, 1865. J. W. Farris remained in Marion County, Ill., until five years of age, and then moved with his parents to Clay County, of the same State. He received his education in the common schools, and October 23, 1861, with the consent of his father, he enlisted in Company K, Forty-eighth Illinois Regiment, and served until 1865, being discharged August 31 of that year. At the time of enlistment he was quite young, and was very anxious to go to the war. His father, thinking of course that he would be rejected when applying, gave his consent, but the lad was so enthusiastic and courageous that he was mustered in. He participated in the battle of Shiloh, where he was slightly wounded in the head with a gunshot; was at the siege of Corinth, siege of Vicksburg, Jackson, Miss., Missionary Ridge, Atlanta, and was with Sherman on his march to the sea. At Scottsborough, Ala., on April 22, 1864, he was promoted to second lieutenant, and April 11, 1865, he was commissioned adjutant of his regiment, which position he held until his discharge. He was mustered out at Little Rock, Ark., and discharged at Springfield, Ill., August 31, 1865. He then returned to his home, and remained there until January, 1867, when he moved to Lebanon, Mo. After moving to Lebanon Mr. Farris engaged in the newspaper business, which he continued for one year. In 1870 he was elected county assessor, and in 1874 he was elected circuit clerk, holding the office for four years. He was appointed probate clerk, and held the office from 1872 until 1880. In 1882 he was elected to the State Senate from the Twenty-second District, and served four years. He was admitted to the bar in 1883, and has since been engaged in the practice of his profession, together with the insurance business. He represents the "American Central Insurance" of St. Louis, "Springfield" (Mass.), "Phenix" of Brooklyn, "North British and Merchants'" of Liverpool, "Fireman's Fund" of San Francisco, "Phœnix" of London, "Connecticut" of Hartford, "Hibernia" of New Orleans, "Southern" of New Orleans, "Liverpool" of London, "Globe," of Liverpool, "Queen" of England and "Fire Association" of Philadelphia. Mr. Farris has been and is a prominent man of the county, and his character is without a stain. He is a Mason and a member of the Blue Lodge, Chapter and Commandery; has also served as Worshipful Master and High Priest of the Chapter. He is at present Eminent Commander of the Commandery, and has been a member of the Grand Lodge since 1876. He is also a member of the G. A. R.

Robert C. Folger was born in Nantucket, Mass., January 6, 1810, his parents being Charles and Judith (Coffin) Folger. The father was also born in Nantucket, his birth occurring in 1780, and he was a son of Charles Folger, grandson of Frederick Folger, and great-grandson of Peter Folger, who was born in England, and came to America on account of religious persecution in his native land. On his way to this country he became acquainted with an Irish girl by the name of Mary Morrel, whom he married in Boston, and soon after settled at Nantucket, where he was engaged in milling and weaving, and reared a family of seven daughters and two sons, his youngest daughter, Abiah, becoming the mother of Dr. Franklin. The father of our subject was a whale-boat builder, a carpenter, and owner in whale ships. He was very successful in early life, but afterward lost $20,000 on sperm oil, in 1842–48, on account of the introduction of coal oil. He died in Nantucket in his eightieth year. His wife was born in 1785, and died in 1848, and became the mother of seven children, two of whom are living, Robert C., and Mrs. Mary Ray, who resides in Rootstown, Ohio. Robert C. learned the carpenter's trade in Nantucket with his father, and followed this occupation for some time after attaining his majority. He located in Illinois in 1845, and was there engaged in tilling the soil until 1884, when he sold out and came to Laclede County, Mo., where he has a farm of 220 acres, nearly all under cultivation. He has traveled quite extensively, having been in all the Northern and Eastern States and Canada, but thinks Laclede County, Mo., the finest place he has ever been in, owing to its many natural advantages and its healthy climate. He was first married to Laura Ann Snow, in Nantucket, who died in 1849, having borne four children, two of whom are living: Nelson, who resides in Fulton County, Mo., and Everett, who resides in Illinois. In 1850 Mr. Folger married his second wife, whose maiden name was Melissa Cross. She was born in Ohio in 1835, but afterward moved to Illinois, where she was married, and is now the mother of these children, who are living: Ginevra (wife of J. Doner), Rosella, Samuel, Winslow (who resides in Iowa) and Clarkson, who is at home. Mr. Folger is a Republican.

Levi C. Fulbright is an old and prominent farmer of Laclede County, Mo., and was born in Haywood County, N. C., February 3, 1811, his parents being William and Rutha (Hollingsworth) Fulbright, who were born in Buncombe and Haywood Counties, N. C., January 8, 1785, and September 28, 1791, and died in Missouri September 22, 1843, and April 30, 1874, respectively. At the age of twelve years the father went to Haywood County, where he grew to manhood and married, and in 1818 moved with his family to Tennessee, coming to Missouri five years later, locating in Springfield, where he resided until his death. He and wife were members of the Christian Church, and became the parents of thirteen children, twelve sons and one daughter, the following of whom are yet living: Levi C., Henry, David N. and E. R. Since 1830 Levi C. Fulbright has been a resident of Laclede County, and since 1845 has resided on his present farm. He at one time owned 677 acres of land, but after the war was compelled to sell a portion of his estate. During the war he served for about six months in the southwest portion of the State in a volunteer company of Confederate infantry, being a participant in the battle of Oak Hill, in which engagement he was beaten over the head with a sword, which has made him deaf for life; he has also almost lost the use of his shoulder and arm. Since the war he has been trying to retrieve his fallen fortunes, but in 1874 his house and all its contents were burned to the ground. He has since rebuilt, and has a cozy and comfortable home. November 29, 1829, he was married to Miss Mary Kyrkendall, who died May 18, 1845, having become the mother of six children, five of whom are living: Susan J. (Hoffman), John L., Matilda Ruth (Story), William H. (deceased), Anna E. (Joiner) and Robert B. Mr. Fulbright afterward married Miss Nancy E. Hillhouse, who was born in Giles County, Tenn., and by whom he became the father of eight children: Roxana (Thompson), Mary L. E. (Jones), Coraline (Pritchett), Ephraim R., Josiah, Daniel, Samuel and Ellen (Jones). Mr. and Mrs. Fulbright are members of the Christian Church, the former being the second person baptized in that church in the county, his first wife having been the first person. His son, Ephraim R. Fulbright, was born in Laclede County, Mo., January 11, 1850, and is a prosperous farmer and stock dealer. He made his parents' house his home until his marriage, and in his boyhood days received a good common-school education. In 1868 he began railroading on the 'Frisco road, and at the end of two years went to Salem, but soon after returned home and engaged in farming and stock trading, which has been his occupation up to the present time, and in which he has been very successful. In 1875 he was wedded to Miss Fannie Oliver, who was born in Camden County, Mo., November 5, 1854, and is a daughter of Giles and Caroline (Evans) Oliver, who were born in Tennessee, and came to Missouri in 1851, and are still residing in Camden County. The following are their children: Henry, Mary M. (Ragan), Fannie, wife of Mr. Fulbright, and William. Mr. Oliver died in 1883, since which time his widow has resided with Mr. Fulbright. To the latter and his wife four children have been born: Guy, Floy, Montia and John W. Mr. Fulbright is a Democrat, and a member of the Agricultural Wheel, and his wife is a member of the Methodist Episcopal Church, South.

Capt. James H. Fulbright. Among those who have secured the confidence and respect of their fellow men, and rank among the progressive and enterprising citizens of the county, may be mentioned Capt. Fulbright, who was the first white male child born in Springfield, Mo., his birth occurring June 12, 1832. His parents, John and Jane (Kyrkendall) Fulbright, were born in North Carolina and Kentucky, respectively, the former's birth occurring in 1795. His father, who also bore the name of John, was of German descent, and was born in Buncombe County, N. C. He (John, Sr.) and five brothers were participants in the Revolutionary War, and in 1810 he came overland to Missouri, settling in Washington County, where he entered a farm and reared part of his children, and lived until his death. His wife, Elizabeth (Coalter) Fulbright, was of German descent, and an excellent German scholar. She was nearly one hundred years old at the time of her death, June 9, 1853. They were members of the Methodist Episcopal Church. They were the parents of five sons, William, David, Martin, Daniel and John, and five daughters, Elizabeth (Williams or Cooper, second husband), Catherine (Evans), Susanah (Daniels), Christener (Goodwin) and Sarah (Smithers). John Fulbright, Jr., was an extensive trader in horses, mules and negroes, and was the first treasurer of Greene County, Mo., having been taught to read and write by his wife. He died in 1862. His wife was born in Kentucky, but was married in Tennessee, whither her parents had moved, her father being one of the very wealthy millers of that State. She died in 1833, having borne seven children, two of whom grew to maturity, one living at the present time. The subject of this sketch, her husband, was reared in Missouri, and served during the latter part of the War of 1812, receiving for his services, before he was twenty-one years old, the grant of a tract of land, a portion of which is now resided on by his son, Capt. Fulbright. He was a member of the Christian Church for over forty years, a Democrat in politics, and died on the 16th of March, 1862. His wife, formerly Miss Kyrkendall, bore a family of seven sons, and died in 1862, after which the father married the widow of Dr. H. Adkins, by whom he became the father of two children, who are now deceased. This lady, second wife of John Fulbright, Jr., died April 3, 1883. Capt. James H. Fulbright resided on the home farm until the breaking out of the late war, when he enlisted in Company I, of the State Guard, and for eleven months served as a private in Parson's infantry. He was then appointed purchasing agent for the division, and at the end of eleven months was transferred to the Confederate army, under Jackson. He also served as receiving agent in Marmaduke's command, and after the surrender of Little Rock was appointed purchasing agent for the division and sent to Texas, where he remained until April, 1864, when he returned, and was with Price on his raid through Missouri. He was made commissary of the Fourth Missouri Regiment, and served until the surrender. June 23, 1865, he landed at St. Louis, where, after about three months, he was joined by his wife, whose maiden name was Mary L. Wilks, and whom he married June 10, 1852, and removed with her to Franklin County from St. Louis, Mo., where he rented land and resided for three years. He then located on the old homestead, in 1868, where he has since made his home. He has always taken a deep interest in politics, and in 1881-83 was elected county judge, which office he filled very creditably. He has also been school director for ten years. He and wife are members of the Christian Church, of which he has been clerk and elder for forty years. He is a member of the A. F. & A. M., the Agricultural Wheel, and is a member of the State Board of Agriculture, being appointed for life by Gov. Marmaduke in August, 1882. His wife was born in

Alabama November 28, 1833, and became a resident of Lawrence County, Mo., when eight years of age, and was here reared to womanhood. The following are her children: Lucy J. (Mrs. Calahan), Elizabeth K. (Kittle), John H. (a very wealthy physician of Ozark, Mo.), Emma L. (Ward), Jemimah P. (Connella), Jesse M. and James H.

Martin V. Fulbright, a successful farmer and stockman, of Laclede County, Mo., was born in Camden County of the same State, and is the son of Daniel and Phoebe (McCloud) Fulbright. Daniel Fulbright was born in North Carolina, and when about twenty-six years of age he came to Missouri direct from North Carolina, and first located in Madison County, near Old Jackson. Here he remained but a few years, and then moved to the Glaize, where he opened up a large farm. He was the owner of one negro, who afterward killed his eldest daughter. Mr Fulbright was first married to Miss Nancy Woolsey, a native of North Carolina, who bore him four children, two now living, John and William, both in Texas. After the death of the mother of these children, Mr. Fulbright married Miss McCloud, a native of Kentucky. When a girl she ran away from home with her little sister, crossed the Mississippi River, and after finding a place for her little sister to live, she went with a family to Laclede County, Mo., where she was married to Mr. Fulbright. This union resulted in the birth of eight children: Mahala, Martin V., James H. (deceased), Merritt C., Daniel L., Leonidas (deceased), Jesse W. and Samuel H. The mother of these children died in February, 1879. The father died December 22, 1856. They were members of the Christian Church, and he took an active part in church and school affairs. He was a Democrat in his political views. Martin V. Fulbright was reared in Laclede County, Mo., and here he has ever since lived. He served in Price's army six months, and was at the battle of Lexington and in several skirmishes. After the war he returned to the home place, where he remained until 1882, when he came to the "Goodwin Hollow," where he has a good tract of land well under cultivation. He was married December 15, 1861, to Miss Nancy Cunningham, who was a native of Tennessee, but who was reared in Kentucky. She came to Missouri in 1859, and located on the Glaize. To Mr. and Mrs. Fulbright were born two children, James D. and Mary F. James D. is married, and lives on a part of the home place. He was married to Miss Mary L. Hickman, a native of Laclede County, Mo., and the daughter of Mastin Hickman, one of the early settlers of this county. To this union have been born three children: Louisa, Mastin V. and Joseph. Mr. Fulbright (subject of this sketch) is a Democrat politically, and he and wife and son are members of the Methodist Episcopal Church.

Thomas M. Gibson, farmer, stock raiser and fruit grower, of Laclede County, Mo., was born in Greenbrier County, W. Va., September 25, 1824, and is a son of John and Mary Gibson, who were born, reared and married in Virginia, and there spent their days. Both the paternal and maternal grandparents were born in the "Emerald Isle," and immigrated to the United States in 1765, locating in Virginia, where they died. Thomas M. Gibson was engaged in farming and stock raising in his native State until 1880, when, thinking to better his condition, he came to Southwest Missouri, and located in Laclede County, Mo., where he has a fine farm, containing 162 acres, six miles southeast of Lebanon, where he has since made his home. October 8. 1846, he was married to Miss Nancy S. Young, a native of Monroe County, W. Va., by whom he became the father of the following children: Elizabeth (wife of J. H. Campbell), Mary J. (wife of A. A. Fleshman), Sarah Y. (wife of William White), Rosaline (wife of T. P. Umphries) and James G. (who married Flora Moffat). In 1862 Mr. Gibson enlisted in the West Virginia volunteer service, and participated in the battles of Lewisburg, Fayetteville and Dry Creek, and served until the close of the war in 1865. Since coming to Missouri Mr. Gibson's labors have met with good success, and his farm, a portion of which is in a high state of cultivation, is principally devoted to raising corn, wheat and oats. In such a section of country as this is—admirably adapted to the raising of grain, hogs, cattle, sheep, horses, etc.—the energetic citizen is bound to succeed. He is a member of the Agricultural Wheel, and he and wife are members of the Cumberland Presbyterian Church. His father was twice married, the first union resulting in the birth of four children: Eliza and Jane (who are deceased), Lydia (wife of James W. Boyd) and Thomas M. The following are the children born to the second union: William, Mary, John, Robert and Julia A.

R. P. Goodall, sheriff of Laclede County, Mo., was born in Orleans County, Vt., December 1, 1838, and is the son of Richard R. and Ruth (Lymon) Goodall, natives of New Hampshire, who immigrated to Vermont at quite an early date. The paternal grandfather was drowned in the Connecticut River while rafting lumber. Richard P. Goodall was a farmer by occupation, is still living, and is a resident of Orleans County, Vt. He is quite a prominent man there, having represented his county two successive terms in the Legislature. He is the father of five children, only two now living: R. P. and Helen. The latter resides at Denver, Col. R. P. Goodall, subject of this sketch, assisted his father on the farm in Vermont until about twenty years of age, and received a good education. At this time he learned the carpenter's trade, which he followed in Vermont. In July, 1861, he was mustered into Company D, Third Vermont Volunteer Infantry, entering the service as a private, and was afterward promoted to the rank of second lieutenant in Company G, at Brandy Station, Va., holding this position until the close of the war. He was engaged in all the battles of the Army of the Potomac: Yorktown, Williamsburg, Fredericksburg, Antietam, battle of the Wilderness, Spottsylvania Courthouse and Salem. He was wounded in the left hand by a gunshot at the Wilderness, but went with his company to Spottsylvania. He was also wounded in the left leg at Salem, and was taken to a hospital, where he remained for about six weeks. He was mustered out at Burlington in 1864, and then returned to Vermont, where he remained until 1867, when he came to Arlington, Mo. He here worked at his trade until 1869, when he came to Lebanon, and there built one of the first frame houses in New Lebanon, for a lady by the name of Hanford.

He continued his trade until 1874, when he was elected sheriff, and re-elected in 1876. Two years later he was defeated by a Greenbacker for the office of collector, and in 1880 he was re-elected sheriff. In 1882 he was elected county collector, and in 1886 he was re-elected to the office of sheriff. He was married November 6, 1879, to Miss Mary Henson, a native of Missouri, and to them has been born one child, R. P., Jr. Mr. Goodall is a member of the Masonic fraternity, Blue Lodge, Chapter and Commandery; also G. A. R., and is a stanch Democrat in his political opinions.

George H. Greenleaf was born in Salisbury, N. H., November 5, 1834, and died at his home in Lebanon, Laclede Co., Mo., December 9, 1886. He was a son of Thomas R. and Mary (Seaton) Greenleaf, who were natives of New Hampshire, and when a small boy moved with his parents to New Philadelphia, Ohio, where he received the greater part of his education. In 1857 or 1858 he came west with his parents to St. Louis, where they located. He then traveled for some time for a wholesale hardware firm of that city, and in 1869 came to Lebanon as a member of the banking firm of P. Vinton & Co., it being the first bank established in Laclede County. He continued a member of the firm until 1873, when they were succeeded by J. S. Sterling & Son. In 1874 Mr. Greenleaf succeeded Sterling & Son, and established the Laclede County Bank, which he continued to manage with great success and to the entire satisfaction of the patrons thereof until his death. He was essentially a self-educated and self-made man, a good and useful citizen, and took an active part in building up the city of Lebanon, and was one of its most honored, prosperous and progressive citizens. He was a member of the A. F. & A. M., the Knights Templar and the A. O. U. W., and was buried with the ceremonies of these societies, the ministers officiating at the funeral services being Revs. J. F. Martin and L. F. Bickford. On the 4th of October, 1870, he was united in marriage, in Old Lebanon, to Miss Lou Harrison, a daughter of John B. and Martha L. (Hyer) Harrison, who were born in South Carolina and Pennsylvania in 1804 and 1812, respectively. John B. Harrison was brought to Missouri when a small boy, and located in what is now Arlington, Phelps County, but in 1847 took up his abode in Laclede County, being among the first settlers of Old Lebanon. His marriage to Miss Hyer took place at Rolla, and for their wedding tour they took a trip to St. Louis on horseback. They became the parents of one daughter, Mrs. Greenleaf, who was born, reared and married in the same house in Old Lebanon. She was educated in the Columbia Christian College, and is the mother of three daughters: May, Anna and Georgia. Mr. Greenleaf was a member of the Congregational Church, of which she remains a consistent member.

M. W. Gustin, editor of the *Graphic*, was born in Branch County, Mich., October 12, 1843, and is the son of Jonathan F. and Lydia E. (Bennett) Gustin, natives of Vermont and New York, respectively. The father immigrated to New York, locating in Genesee Valley, but removed from there to Branch County, Mich., and from there to Elkhart County, Ind., where he remained until 1859, when he removed to Laclede County, Mo., locating in Gasconade Township; there he purchased a farm and entered some land. He now lives in Osage Township, where he is engaged in farming. They are the parents of four children living: S. P., Esther A., wife of R. Gooderich, M. D., and M. W. The last named was reared principally in Indiana. He was brought up on the farm, and followed agricultural pursuits until the breaking out of the war, when in August, 1861, he enlisted in Company A, Sixth Missouri Volunteer Cavalry, and served until August 20, 1864, when he was discharged at St. Louis. He participated in the battles of Monday Hill, Elkhorn and all the campaigns of Southwest Missouri. He was at the siege of Vicksburg, Arkansas Post, second assault at Jackson, and was in the expedition that tore up the New Orleans Railroad. He was in the Red River expedition, where his regiment lost all its quartermaster's and commissary stores, and was in the advance guard, when the assault was made. He served on detached duty most of his time, and after being discharged returned to his home. He was deputy marshal at Rolla for some time, and then engaged in the real estate business in Lebanon, which he carried on for some time. He embarked in the newspaper business in 1869 at Lebanon, removing to Richland, in Pulaski County, and then to Tuscumbia, in Miller County, in the campaign of 1870. After selling out there he re-engaged and was in the newspaper work at Hartville, in Wright County. In 1876 he engaged in farming in Pulaski County, which he carried on until 1878, when he was appointed postmaster at Richland, and held this position until January 26, 1885. In January, 1887, he came to Lebanon and purchased the *Graphic*, which he has since published. He was married in October, 1870, to Miss Sallie E. Manes, of Pulaski County, by whom he has three children: Jessie D., born August 7, 1871; Sempronious B., born November 17, 1873, and Myrtie C., born April 4, 1878. One deceased, Bertha E., was born December 4, 1883. Mr. Gustin is a member of the G. A. R., and has never applied for a pension.

Absalom Gutherie, fruit grower and farmer, and son of John and Sarah (Jinkins) Gutherie, was born in East Tennessee in 1833. The parents were born in Virginia and Tennessee, respectively. The father came to Tennessee about 1800, locating in Claiborne County, and there engaged in farming. He and family came to Dallas County in 1848, and here he continued farming, which occupation he followed in that county until his death in 1854. His wife died in 1852. They had a family of thirteen children, three now living: Absalom, Isaiah and Louisa. The mother was a member of the Baptist Church. Absalom Gutherie came to Missouri when fifteen years of age, and in this State finished his growth. He was educated in the common district schools, and received a very fair knowledge of books. In 1856 he located in Dallas County, and came to his present location in 1869. During the late unpleasantness between the North and South, he served in the Eighth Missouri Volunteer Cavalry, United States Army, for three years, and was one year in the Home Guards. He was in the battles of Prairie Grove, Little Rock and others. He was married to Miss Nancy Davis, daughter of Nathan

L. Davis, who was one of the old settlers of this county. This union resulted in the birth of five children: Wesley; Elizabeth, wife of Jesse Pruett; William; Louisa, wife of Bringle Bringleson; and Elias, at home. Mr. and Mrs. Gutherie are members of the Baptist Church, and he is a member of the G. A. R., Post No. 48, of Lebanon. He is a Republican in politics, and has been school director for the past fifteen years.

Christian Hanson, merchant at Conway, Mo., was born in Denmark December 15, 1841, being a son of Hans Christian and Marian (Martinson) Hanson, who were born in Denmark and were married in 1832. The father was a farmer, and being the eldest son was exempt from military service. He died in 1873. He and wife became the parents of nine children, six of whom are now living, two being residents of America. Christian grew to manhood in Taarup, Denmark, and after attending school the required number of years, supplemented this with an attendance at night school. From 1863 until 1867 he was engaged in traveling throughout the country selling goods, and at the latter date concluded to come to America, and first located in Rolla, Mo., thence to Arlington, where he engaged in the general mercantile business. In 1870 he returned to his native land, but went back to his adopted country the same year, and located in Lebanon. The following year he formed a partnership with Hugh McCain, and in 1872 purchased the interest of his partner and embarked in commercial life on his own responsibility, and has continued up to the present date, meeting with flattering success. He was appointed postmaster of Conway in 1872, and ably filled the office until 1886. He is a very large real estate holder, and cultivates more land than any man in the county. He is also an extensive stock breeder. In 1872 he married Miss Sarah S. Kelley, of Lebanon, a daughter of Rev. Kelley, of the Methodist Episcopal Church, and by her is the father of four children: Emma, Clare, Sarah and Jennie. Mrs. Hanson is a member of the Methodist Episcopal Church, and Mr. Hanson belongs to the Lutheran Church. He is a member of the A. F. & A. M., a Royal Arch Mason, and is a charter member of the K. T. Commandery. He is Past Worthy Master and Present Master in the A. O. U. W. He is M. W. and Deputy Grand Worthy Chief of the I. O. G. T.; also president of the Union Sunday-school Convention. Mrs. Hanson is president of the W. C. T. U.

William J. Heard, farmer, of Franklin Township, Laclede County, Mo., was born in Monroe County, Ind., in 1824, and grew to manhood in Washington County, of the same State, where he enlisted for the Mexican War. He was discharged at Camp Bell Knob, on account of ill health, and then returned to Washington County, Ind., where he remained until 1851, and then went to Harrison County, where he remained about one year. From there he went to Clay County, Ill., and was in that county about six years when he moved to Laclede County, Mo. He located on his present farm between Christmas and New Year's of 1858, and here he has since remained, with the exception of the time spent in the United States service in the late war. He and James Talliaferro organized a company out of their own neighborhood, and he was made first lieutenant and Mr. Talliaferro was made captain. This was in July, 1861. In August of the same year they were attached to Col. Boyd's regiment at Rolla, and then Mr. Heard resigned his lieutenantship and enlisted as a private in the Twenty-fourth Missouri, as a blacksmith; was detailed while at Rolla in March, 1862, and was discharged at St. Louis in March, 1863, because of an injury received in the foot while shoeing a mule in March, 1862. He remained in service until 1863, when his foot was in such a bad condition that he was unfit for duty. He then went to Clay County, Ill., where his family was then living, they having moved there in 1861, and remained there until 1865, when he returned to the home place. He found things here in a bad condition, but his house and barn were not destroyed. During that fall and winter he made 7,000 rails and put them into fence. He had but twenty acres under cultivation after the war, but now has 175 acres well cultivated. He was married July 28, 1844, to Miss S. Jamison, a native of Tennessee, born in 1825, and the daughter of George W. and Ellen (Reno) Jamison, natives of Tennessee. Mr. and Mrs. Heard are the parents of eleven children, eight now living: Mary Ellen, wife of James Power; Martha J., wife of Frank Roupp; Elizabeth, wife of Alex. Simpson; Giles H., William W., Frances C., Charles G. and John H. Those deceased are Sarah A., who died leaving one child and husband, both since deceased; Margaret C., who died when an infant, and Susan A., who also died when an infant. Mr. Heard is a member of the G. A. R., and his wife is a member of the Methodist Episcopal Church, South.

Mastin Hickman, farmer, of Hooker Township, Laclede Co., Mo., was born in Sevier County, Tenn., in 1830, and is the son of Thomas and Sarah (Ward) Hickman, natives of South Carolina and Tennessee, respectively. Thomas was left fatherless at an early age, and afterward came with his mother to Tennessee, and settled on a farm east of Knoxville, where he attained his majority. He then located for himself on a farm, and was a farmer and miller all his life. He was a member of the Masonic fraternity, and died in 1864. He married Miss Ward, who died in 1849; she was the mother of fifteen children, ten boys and five girls, eight of whom are now living: Charlotta, Sarah J., Lavinia, Charles, James H., Mastin, Frederick and Ahaz (twins). Mr. Hickman was married the second time, and had one daughter, Catherine. To his third union no children were born. Mastin Hickman remained on the home place in Tennessee until twenty-six years of age, after which he went to Missouri, locating in Laclede County, near where he now lives, and to his present location in 1865. Here he has since lived. He served in the State Militia, Federal army, for about two years during the war, and rendered effective and valuable service. He was married January 24, 1863, to Miss Mary A. Tennison, born in Crawford County, Mo., September 7, 1842, daughter of Joseph S. and Elvira J. (Cooper) Tennison, natives of Missouri and Tennessee, respectively. Her father is still living, and makes his home with Mastin Hickman. He was born June 9, 1818, in Missouri, and has always lived in this

State with the exception of three months that he spent in Texas. He is a member of the Methodist Episcopal Church, South, and is the only one of his brothers and sisters living. He enjoys good health. His wife came to Missouri when a girl, and by her union to Mr. Tennison became the mother of nine children, seven now living: Newman P., Sarah H., Mary A., Thomas J., Elizabeth L., Frances M. and William M. The mother of these children died December 20, 1873. She was a member of the Methodist Episcopal Church, South, in early life, but later became a member of the Christian Church. To Mr. and Mrs. Hickman were born thirteen children, ten now living: Sarah J. (wife of G. D. Layman), Mary L. (wife of J. D. Fulbright) Joe Ann (wife of Samuel Lomerick), Emett F., James M., Joseph P., George W., Henry C., John F. and Martha D. Those deceased were named Thomas A., Nathaniel and Charlotta C. Mr. and Mrs. Hickman are members of the Methodist Protestant Church, and Mr. Hickman is a member of the Agricultural Wheel.

John B. Hickman, house painter, dealer in wall-paper, prints, etc., was born in Jefferson County, Ohio, September 2, 1843, and is the son of Joseph and Mary A. (Swords) Hickman. The parents were residents of Jefferson County, Ohio, until the death of the father, which occurred in 1849, of cholera. The mother is yet living, and resides in Ohio. Of their six children, four are now living: Sarah A., Margaret A., William and John B. The latter was reared in Steubenville, Ohio, was educated there, and there learned his trade. In August, 1861, he enlisted in Company G, Thirtieth Ohio Infantry, and served until March, 1862, when he was discharged on account of being taken prisoner by bushwhackers. He re-enlisted in May, 1862, in Company F, Eighty-fourth Ohio Infantry, and was discharged in September, 1862, he only enlisting in the three-months service. In June, 1863, he enlisted again in Company H, Eleventh Ohio Cavalry, in the Rocky Mountain service, and was sergeant in both the last enlistments. He was promoted to the rank of first lieutenant, but was cheated out of this position. He was mustered out in July, 1866, and returned home, where he remained until 1868, when he came to Lebanon. He here engaged in his present business, which he has carried on quite successfully ever since. He is a Mason, a member of the A. O. U. W., the G. A. R. and the K. of L., having served as an officer in all the organizations. He was married in 1868 to Miss Jane Hyde, of Ohio, and four children were the result of this union: Joseph W., Hugh E., Georgia and Kinsey R.

George T. Holman, stock farmer, of Auglaize Township, was born in Guilford County, N. C., in 1813, and is a son of James Y. and Mary B. (Hart) Holman, who were born in Virginia and North Carolina, respectively. James Holman was born in 1769, and is a son of John Holman, whose parents were originally from Switzerland, and at a very early day located in Virginia. John Holman was a soldier in the Revolutionary War. James Y. Holman was married in his native State, and was engaged in working at the brick mason's trade and farming. He was first married to a Miss Spencer, a native of Virginia, by whom he had two sons and two daughters, but after her death he removed to Guilford County, N. C., where he was married to Miss Hart, who was born on the 24th of April, 1791, by whom he has one son, George T. In 1816 the mother died, having lived the life of a true Christian, being a consistent member of the Lutheran Church. In 1842 Mr. Holman immigrated with his eldest daughter to Dade County, Mo., where he died on the 3d of August, 1843, having been engaged in teaching school the latter part of his life. From fourteen to eighteen years of age George T. Holman made his home with an uncle in Virginia, and then went to North Carolina, and remained with his father on a farm until his marriage in 1837, when he took charge of the home place until 1842, and then moved to Missouri, locating on a farm in what is now Laclede County. During the late Civil War he served for about three months on frontier duty at Lebanon, but being over age and crippled he could not act in the regular service. He is a Democrat in politics, and served as justice of the peace for several years. He was married to Miss Lucinda Lambeth, who was born in Guilford County, N. C., May 17, 1817, and their union was blessed in the birth of seven children, five of whom are now living: James L., Mary L. (wife of Dr. McCombs), John L. L. (who lives in Idaho Territory, engaged in farming), Andrew J. (who resides near the home farm), William (who farms on the home place); and the following children, who are deceased: George T. W., who died at the age of six years, and Joseph B., whose death occurred when thirty-five years of age. Mrs. Holman, who was an earnest and worthy member of the Methodist Episcopal Church, South, died on the 23d of February, 1881.

Andrew J. Holman, a wealthy farmer of Auglaize Township, and a native of Laclede County, Mo., was born November 19, 1848, and is a son of George T. Holman, whose sketch appears in this volume. Andrew J. grew to manhood on the farm on which his father now resides, and was educated in the district schools of the county, and also attended school in Lebanon for a short time. When reaching manhood he began to improve the farm where he now lives, and in 1872 married and moved onto the place, which consists of 220 acres, with ninety acres under cultivation, the result of his own industry and good management. He has always been a hard worker, both for himself and for his parents, and as a result has a comfortable and pleasant home. Elizabeth Mayfield, his wife, was born May 12, 1855, and is a daughter of W. R. Mayfield, a prominent old settler of the county. Four children have blessed their union: Florence I., Ida M., Jessie M., and Amanda E., who died in infancy. Mrs. Holman died June 2, 1882, having been a zealous member of and worker in the Methodist Episcopal Church, South. In December, 1882, Mr. Holman was wedded to Miss Martha M. Sellers, who was born in Tennessee, and came to Missouri with her parents when ten years of age. She is the mother of one child, Mary E. Mr. and Mrs. Holman are active workers in the Methodist Episcopal Church, South, and he is a member of the A. F. & A. M. and the Agricultural Wheel, and has ever taken a deep interest in all laudable enterprises, contributing liberally to their support.

Benjamin Hooper. Among the many men who have attained prominence in agricultural pursuits in Laclede County, Mo., may be mentioned Mr. Hooper, who was born in Caswell County, N. C., January 20, 1811, and is one of three surviving members of a family of ten children born to the marriage of Woodley Hooper and Priscilla Henderson. The father was born in Virginia, and came to North Carolina, in company with his mother, when a young man, his father having died in Virginia. Woodley was a farmer throughout life, and died in Caswell County in 1852, when about eighty years of age, his wife dying in 1840. The Henderson family became residents of North Carolina about the same time as the Hooper family, and Grandfather Henderson was a very extensive land and slave owner, and spent much of his time in hunting on his extensive farms. He was twice married, and by his first wife became the father of fourteen children, and by his last, five. Benjamin Hooper, whose name heads this sketch, grew to manhood in his native State, and when twenty-one years of age hired out on a farm, receiving for his services $40 per year, but soon after gave up this work and began learning the carpenter's trade, at which he worked for about one year. About this time he and his brother-in-law engaged in the grocery and saloon business, but Mr. Hooper discontinued this at the end of one year, and has since been interested in husbandry. In 1842 he immigrated to Missouri by wagon, with the Turner families, and the first two years resided in Greene County, but since the fall of 1845 has been a resident of Laclede County, and since 1850 has resided on his present farm. During the late war he served one month in the Home Guards, while Price was making his raid through Missouri, but he and family were not molested during the entire war. In 1848 he was married to Miss Alvira P. Gunter, who was born in Alabama in 1826, a daughter of James and Mary R. (King) Gunter, who were born and married in Tennessee, and afterward moved to Alabama. They came to Missouri in 1835, but died in Moniteau County, Mo., in 1872 and 1855, respectively. Three of their ten children are now living: Thomas, Louisa (Dowell) and Alvira (Mrs. Hooper). The latter has been a resident of Missouri since she was nine years old, and to her marriage with Mr. Hooper ten children have been born, only two of whom are living: Sarah J., wife of F. M. McChane, and Benjamin C., who resides on the home farm with his parents. Two other children lived to be grown: Mary P., the wife of G. G. Bloomfield, and Fannie, wife of Benjamin Ballenger. The others died in infancy and childhood. Mr. and Mrs. Hooper have been members of the Christian Church since 1844, and he is a member of the Agricultural Wheel, and in politics is a Democrat. His son, Benjamin C., was born on the home farm in Laclede County in February, 1858, and March 16, 1884, was married to Miss Martha Wallace, who was born in Dade County, Mo., November 30, 1866, and by her became the father of two children: Carl V., and Henry, who is deceased. They are also members of the Christian Church, and he belongs to the Agricultural Wheel. He has a good farm under cultivation, and is well fixed financially.

Isaac Hoskinson, president of the Lebanon Woolen Manufacturing

Co., and son of Isaac, Sr., and Fannie (Thrapp) Hoskinson, was born in Wabash County, Mount Carmel, Ill., February 23, 1829. The parents were natives of Virginia, and Newark, Ohio, respectively. The Hoskinson family were of Scotch origin, and were early settlers of Virginia. Isaac Hoskinson, Sr., immigrated to Lincoln County, Ohio, at quite an early date, and here he married Miss Thrapp. In 1821 he moved to Wabash County, Ill., and here resided until his death, which occurred in the spring of 1830. He was a wheel-wright by trade, and followed the same all his life. The mother died at Mount Carmel in 1864. They were the parents of six children, two now living: Gamaliel, who resides in Boulder, Col., and Isaac, Jr. The latter was brought up in Mount Carmel, where he was educated. He engaged in merchandising at the age of thirteen years, and in 1854 he went to Graysville, Ill., where he was engaged in merchandising until 1856. He then went to Clay County, Ill., and here remained until 1865, when he went to Rolla, Mo. In 1869 he left Rolla and came to Lebanon, where he engaged in merchandising with Hugh McCoin, under the firm title of Hoskinson & McCoin, until 1878. Previous to this, in 1877, the woolen mill was erected, and in this Mr. Hoskinson became a stockholder, and has been its president since its erection. He is also engaged in the real estate business quite extensively, in buying and selling land, both wild and improved. He is interested in about 7,000 acres of land in Laclede County, of which the most is in a wild state. Mr. Hoskinson was elected probate judge of Laclede County in 1872, serving four years; has held several minor offices, and takes a great interest in religious and educational matters. He is a member of the Masonic fraternity, Blue Lodge, Chapter and Commandery. He was married, in 1854, to Miss Jane M. Lutes, a native of York, Penn., and to them was born one child, Myrtle, wife of James T. Moore, representative of Laclede County.

Josephus Hough, one of the old and enterprising citizens of Laclede County, Mo., was born in Highland County, Ohio, in 1817, being the son of Payton and Sophia (Mowery) Hough, both natives of Virginia. Payton Hough was born in 1790; was in the War of 1812, and surrendered under Hull. He came to Ohio when a young man, was married here, and here remained until 1839, when he with his family, wife and four sons located in Gasconade County, Mo., for one year. They then came to Laclede County, and located on the Osage Fork of Gasconade River, where he remained until his death. He took an active part in all public matters; was sheriff in Ohio several terms, and on coming to Missouri held the office of justice of the peace until shortly before his death. In 1872 he was smitten with palsy, and died in April, 1874. He was a member of the Methodist Episcopal Church, South, and in his early life was a Mason. His wife was born in 1793, and died August 20, 1873. To their union were born twenty-one children, four of whom lived to be grown: Josephus, John, Ashford and David. Ashford is now deceased. William Hough, brother of Payton, is still living, and was eighty-three years old March 16, 1889. The grandmother of our subject, and the mother of Payton and William, came to Missouri, where she died in 1843. Josephus Hough was reared in his native State, and was there married in 1839, just before he started west in company with his parents. Her name was Miss Lucinda Kibler, a native of Ohio, and the fruit of this union was one child, Sophia R.; wife of J. Dupugh, who is now living in Oregon County, Mo. The mother died in 1840, at the age of twenty-three. Mr. Hough was again married, October 25, 1845, to Miss Lucretia Wright, a native of Davidson County, Tenn., born in 1825, and the daughter of Benjamin and Elizabeth Wright, natives of South Carolina and Virginia, respectively. They came to Missouri in 1836, and he was a blacksmith by trade. He died about 1851, and the mother about 1852. They were the parents of eight children, four of whom are now living: Mrs. Eliza J. Smith, Benjamin F., William C. and Lucretia, all living in Arkansas but the wife of Josephus. The result of Mr. and Mrs. Hough's marriage was the birth of twelve children, three sons and nine daughters, ten children now living: Mrs. Eliza J. Southard, Mrs. Martha A. Spencer, Mrs. Margrie Brookshir, Mrs. Alvira Smith, Samuel B., Mrs. Catherine Franklin, Cary Frank, Lou, Susie and William H. Those deceased were named Mrs. Melvinia Eads, who died, leaving one child—Lena Belle, who is now with Mr. Hough—and Elizabeth, who died in childhood. Mr. Hough located where he now lives in 1856, and here he has since remained. He enlisted in the old man's regiment during the late war, for ninety days, when they were disbanded. He is a member of the Agricultural Wheel, is with the Union Labor party in his political views, and has been active in all educational matters. Mrs. Hough and family are members of the Methodist Episcopal Church.

Edmund Hulse, one of the many enterprising and successful citizens of Laclede County, Mo., was born September 12, 1848, and is the son of John E. and Mary (Wild) Hulse, natives of England. The Hulses were for several generations back railroad engineers, and the grandfather of Edmund Hulse went to France as an engineer. He was for many years a locomotive engineer, and John E. Hulse was also an engineer for twenty-eight years. He came to this country in 1851, landing in New York, and from there went to Milwaukee, Wis. He afterward returned to England and mounted his same old engine, and in 1866 he came back to America. He remained in Fond du Lac, Wis., for three years, and then came to Laclede County in 1869, locating on a farm, where he remained until 1872, and has been farming ever since. He was the father of seven children, five of whom are now living: Edmund, John, Albert, William, and Adelaide, wife of William Nyberg. Two children died in infancy. Edmund Hulse was eighteen years of age when he came back to Wisconsin, and in 1872 went to Chicago, where he worked as a machinist until in 1880, when he came to Laclede County. He has a good farm in this county, and is doing well. He was first married in 1873 to Miss Margaret Wilder, who was the widow of Hiram L. Wilder, of Chicago. She was born near the last named city, and by her union with Mr. Wilder became the mother of three children. She also had three children by Mr. Hulse, two of whom died. Mary is the only one living. Mr. Hulse took for his second wife Miss Ella E. Wilder, by whom he has five children: Jennie, Edith, Edmund, John and Margaret. Mr. Hulse is a rather prominent man in politics, and affiliates with the Union Labor party. He is a member of the Masonic fraternity at Lebanon; is a member of the A. O. U. W., and he and wife are members of the Methodist Protestant Church.

George R. James, stock farmer, on Osage Fork of Gasconade River, was born in Giles County, Tenn., in 1833, and is the son of George and Dicey James, natives of Georgia and North Carolina, respectively. When George R. was four years old the family immigrated to Missouri by wagon, and located within one mile of where our subject now lives, and here the father died December 27, 1847. He was born April 20, 1799. His wife was born October 19, 1797, and died July 25, 1869. They were married January 13, 1819, and to their union were born seven children, two now living, William R. and George R. William R. lives on Mill Creek, Osage Township, and is engaged in agricultural pursuits. The parents of these children were members of the Methodist Episcopal Church, South. George R. James attained his growth in Laclede County, and assisted his parents on the farm. After the death of his father he took charge of things and lived with his mother until her death. He then took a trip overland to California, where he remained until the fall of 1860, and then returned to the home place by way of New York City, by rail, then to Chicago, thence to Dillon, thence to Rolla, Mo., and from there to the home place by stage. When the war broke out he enlisted in Capt. C. W. Rubey's regiment, and served about two years. At the close of the war he came back to the home place, and after remaining there a short time he came to his present location, where he has resided ever since. He is the owner of a large farm of 1,240 acres, with about 700 under cultivation. He was married October 13, 1861, to Miss Susan Q. Honssinger, a native of Laclede County, Mo., born in 1847, and the daughter of Thomas F. Honssinger, who is one of the oldest settlers of the county. To Mr. and Mrs. James were born nine living children: Mary Ellen, wife of John Bowman; George F., married Emily J. Beard; Quillana E., wife of John R. Wrinkle; William M., Laura D., Lury J., Rosa B., Effie May and Edgar M. Those deceased are Thomas, Isom, Charley W. and an infant. Mr. James is a Democrat in politics, and is a member of the Methodist Episcopal Church, South.

Hon. B. C. Jarrell came to Laclede County, Mo., from his native county of Rockingham, N. C., in 1853, and located near Lebanon, and with his brother, W. G. Jarrell, engaged in the manufacture of plug tobacco until the breaking out of the late Civil War, and in 1862 moved to the place where he now lives. He first made a purchase of forty acres of land, but is now the owner of 200 acres, 120 acres in one tract and eighty acres in the other. His birth occurred February 11, 1826, and he is a son of Jarrett and Eleanor (Lillian) Jarrell, who were of English lineage and natives of North Carolina. The father died in 1836 and the mother in 1830. B. C. Jarrell was educated in

BY THE BROOKSIDE.

Leaksville Academy, N. C., and in the common schools of his native county. After coming west he taught school in Kentucky for some time, and in April, 1849, was married in Madison County, Tenn., to Lucy A. Lassiter, a native of North Carolina, and the daughter of Matthew Lassiter, and their union was blessed in the birth of five children: Salinda I.; William A., who married Catherine James; Mary A., wife of William T. James; Frank Lee and Martha E. Mr. Jarrell is a member of the Masonic fraternity, and in his political views supports the principles of the Democratic party, and has represented his county in the State Legislature. He has also served as surveyor, and he and family are members of the Christian Church, he being a deacon in the same.

Travis Johnson, farmer, stock raiser and fruit grower of Laclede County, Mo., and one of the prosperous men of that county, was born in Roane County, Tenn., January 28, 1825, and is the son of Little B. and Ada (George) Johnson, both born and reared in Knox County, Tenn. The ancestors of the Johnson family came from England, and were early settlers of Tennessee. The paternal grandfather, Edmund Johnson, immigrated to Knox County, of the last mentioned State, as early as 1796, but the Indians were there in great numbers, and he did not stay long. However, he returned to the same place in 1800, and lived there for many years. He died in Roane County, Tenn., over eighty-five years of age. He was a Revolutionary soldier. Little B. Johnson was a farmer, wagon-maker and blacksmith by trade, but the latter part of his life was spent in the Baptist ministry. He organized a great many churches in his time, and died a faithful, upright Christian. He was the father of eleven children, five now living, of whom Travis Johnson is the eldest. The others living are: Patrick, who resides in Lawrence County, Mo.; Lewis C., residing on the old homestead in Tennessee; Rachel, wife of W. R. Herald, and Elizabeth, wife of Samuel Parr, now residing in Tennessee. Two brothers died in Andersonville Prison, Elisha A. and James L. Silas was drowned. Travis Johnson was reared on the farm in Tennessee, and in this State he received his education. In 1845 he was united in marriage to Miss Mary C. Bowman, who bore him six children, four now living: Malissa E., wife of J. H. Brown; Eliza A., wife of James B. Bourman; Parley R., wife of Henry Jones, and Mary C., wife of John L. Stow. In 1859 Mr. Johnson immigrated with his family by team to Laclede County, Mo., locating on Gasconade River, where he purchased 211 acres of land with but few improvements. He has now 100 acres under cultivation on this farm. In 1871 he purchased 218 acres in the same township, and aside from this he has 160 acres of land where he now lives, with about 120 acres under cultivation. Mr. Johnson has turned his attention to stock raising, to which his farms are all well adapted, and he also raises a large amount of fruit. He is one of the leading farmers of Laclede County, and has been a valuable citizen. In the spring of 1883 he moved to Lebanon for the purpose of educating his son, Charles L., a bright young man. After the latter's death Mr. Johnson moved back to the farm, where he now lives. He was a member of the Enrolled Militia during the war, and served in several hard skirmishes. Politically he is a Republican and a strong adherent of that party. He and Mrs. Johnson are members of the Baptist Church.

Col. M. W. Johnson, farmer, was born in Howard County, Mo., on March 15, 1832, and was reared principally in Greene and Camden Counties. His parents, Stebbins and Jerusha B. (Mellen) Johnson, were natives of Connecticut and Massachusetts, respectively. They were married in Steubenville, Ohio, in 1825, and in 1831 removed to Howard County, Mo. Mr. Johnson was a machinist by trade, but upon coming to Missouri he engaged in the milling business, and while on a trip to St. Louis for building material he took the cholera, and died in that city in May, 1833. The mother died at the residence of her son, in Laclede County, in April, 1879, in her seventy-ninth year. They were the parents of four children, two only of whom are now living, Rhoda W. and Marshall W., the latter being the youngest of the family and the subject of this sketch. After the father's death the family moved to Greene County, Mo., and in 1841 to Camden County, and were among the earliest settlers of that county, locating on a farm near the Gunter Spring, which was their home till the children grew to maturity. In 1852 the subject of this sketch entered the employ of Jones, McClurg & Co., who were engaged in a general mercantile business at Linn Creek. Continuing with this firm, he became a member of it in 1858, the style now being changed to McClurg, Murphy & Co., and it prosecuted an extensive business till the outbreak of the Rebellion, in 1861, their business reaching the enormous figure, in that day, for an inland house, of half a million a year. When the war came, Mr. Johnson, being driven from his business and his home by marauding rebels, joined the Osage regiment of Missouri volunteers (Home Guards) an organization called into the service temporarily by Gen. Nathaniel Lyon, then commanding the Department of the Missouri. Upon the disbanding of this organization, in December, 1861, he enlisted in Company G of the Eighth Regiment Missouri State Militia Cavalry, and was appointed quartermaster of the regiment, with rank of first lieutenant, in which capacity he served till March, 1863, when the regiment was reorganized, and he was promoted to the rank and office of lieutenant-colonel of his regiment. This position he held till October, 1863, when, at the request of his former business co-partners, he resigned and took charge again of his business at Linn Creek. In January, 1863, he was united in marriage to Mary E., eldest daughter of ex-Gov. Joseph W. McClurg, and to them were born ten children: Joseph M., Thaddeus S., Frank J., Fannie J., Maggie R., Charles D., Mary B., Louise W., Emma C. and Marshall W., Jr., all now living, save Mary B., who died in early infancy. After closing his old business, which required a number of years, Mr. Johnson was engaged with ex-Gov. McClurg and others in mining, smelting and merchandising at Linn Creek till 1877. In February of that year he moved to his farm, near Lebanon, Mo., where he now resides, engaged in farming, stock growing, etc. His farm contains 280 acres, 200 of which are in cultivation, the residue in timber and pasture. He runs a dairy also, and is getting to some extent in the fruit business. He has an orchard, of his own planting, of 3,000 trees, to which he is adding yearly. He, with his eldest two sons, has also established a cattle ranch, and is opening a farm in Central Dakota. They will have more than 100 acres in crops there this year. Mr. Johnson has never held civil office, save that of county treasurer for eight years, while in Camden, and superintendent of registration for the years immediately following the war. He is a member of the G. A. R., A. O. U. W. and Select Knights.

Luke Joslin, gardener and broom-maker, was born in Washington County, Vt., in July, 1820, and is the son of Luke and Lydia (Graves) Joslin, natives of Vermont, and of English descent, and grandson of Ezra Joslin, who was a farmer by occupation, and who died in Vermont. Luke Joslin, Sr., was also a farmer by occupation, and he too died in Vermont. The mother died in Wisconsin. They were the parents of eight children, three now living: Orrilla, Fannie S. and Luke. The latter was reared and educated in Washington County, Vt., and was there married, in 1843, to Joan A. Ford, a native of Vermont. About 1845 Mr. Joslin removed to Dane County, Wis., purchasing a farm, which he carried on until 1865. In the latter part of 1863 he enlisted in Company H, Eighth Wisconsin Infantry, and served until the close of the war. He served in camp and hospital, and was not called on the field at all. In the summer of 1865 he returned home, and in the fall of the following year he moved to Miller County, Mo., where he resided until 1878, after which he moved to Lebanon, Mo. He here purchased a homestead in the brush, which he has cleared and vastly improved. He carries on his trade, that of broom-making, has a good business, and in connection with this he also carries on gardening, raising all kinds of vegetables. He was elected mayor of Lebanon in 1881, and held the office one term. He is a member of the G. A. R., and he and Mrs. Joslin are members of the Congregational Church. To their marriage were born seven children: Wilburt C., Carrie E., Luke, David D. (deceased), Herbert W., Charles E., Mary E. and Hattie E.

William F. Lambeth is a native of Laclede County, Mo., born in 1846, and is a son of Josiah B. and Sarah A. (Friar) Lambeth, and grandson of Joseph and Lavinia (Fleck) Lambeth, who were prominent residents of the Carolinas. Josiah B. is the youngest of their six children, and was born in Guilford County, N. C., in 1824, and attained his majority in his native State. In 1842 he immigrated to Missouri, locating on the Glaize, and resided in Laclede County until 1861, when he took refuge in Texas, and enlisted in the Confederate army. He was taken prisoner at Vicksburg, but was afterward exchanged, and was given a position in the commissary department. After peace was declared he resided one year in Franklin County, and then took up his abode in St. James, Phelps County, where he sent his children to school, and in the fall of 1867 went to Lawrence County, and purchased land on the head-waters of Spring River. After residing here four years, he next located in Verona, where he died in 1875, and where his widow is still living. He was a member of the A. F. & A. M., and a Democrat in politics. His wife was born in North Carolina in 1819, and after becoming a woman came to Dade County, Mo., with her parents in the fall of 1842, and was married in February of the following year. The following are their children: Joseph, William, Madison, Susan (Latta), Nina (Grammar), Orlena (Ham), and Irving, who resides with his mother. Mrs. Lambeth is now a member of the Christian Church, but earlier in life was a member of the Methodist Episcopal Church, South. William F. Lambeth has always resided in Laclede County, with the exception of one year (1866), when he resided in Franklin County, where he was engaged in farming. In February, 1867, he espoused Miss Malinda Bohannon, who was born in Roane County, Tenn., in 1849, but came to Missouri with her parents when a child, where she grew to womanhood. She was a daughter of John Bohannon and Elizabeth Esther, and became the mother of seven children: John, James, Joseph, William, Andrew, Roenia, who is deceased, and Dee, the youngest. Mr. and Mrs. Lambeth are members of the Christian Church, and he is a stanch Democrat in politics.

J. G. Lingsweiler, one of the most extensive lumber dealers in Southern Missouri, now located at Lebanon, Mo., was born in Buffalo, N. Y., April 13, 1844, and is one of ten children, nine now living, born to John N. and Christiana Lingsweiler, both of whom are natives of Germany. The father of the subject of this sketch was born in 1818, and emigrated from Bavaria, Germany, to America with his parents when about fourteen years of age, or in 1831. His father, John Lingsweiler, was a baker by trade, and died in the State of New York. John N. Lingsweiler, father of J. G., was reared principally in New York State, and received such educational advantages as were available in those early times. He was married in this State, and in 1846 moved to Racine County, Wis., where he purchased a farm, and resided until 1884. He then came to live with his son, J. G., at Lebanon, where he yet lives, and is now in his seventy-first year. The mother is also living, and is in her seventieth year. Their nine children now living are named as follows: John G., Louise, Edward, Mary, William H., Christiana, Carrie L., Frank I. and Julia. J. G. Lingsweiler, the eldest of this family, was but two years of age when he went to Wisconsin with his parents. He was educated partly in that State and partly in Missouri. January 4, 1864, he enlisted in Company H, Twenty-second Wisconsin Regiment, and served until the close of the war. He was with Sherman on his march to the sea, and participated in the battles of Resaca, Burnt Hickory, Lost Mountain, Culp's Farm, Peach Tree Creek, Atlanta (where they had several hard fights), Buzzards' Roost, New Hope Church, Kenesaw Mountain, and several skirmishes on the way to Savannah, and also participated in the grand review at Washington. Mr. Lingsweiler was but nineteen years of age when he enlisted, but, being a strong and vigorous young man, was accepted without difficulty. He fought bravely for his country, and was honorably discharged in July, 1865. In March of the following year he came to Lebanon, where he attended school, then called Lebanon Collegiate School, for two years. He also attended school at Rolla, working for his tuition, and after quitting school he went to Arlington, Mo., where he clerked in a drug store for a short time. He then entered into partnership with a gentleman in the grocery business, and continued at this for about nine months. All this time Mr. Lingsweiler was waiting for the 'Frisco Road to be completed to Lebanon, with a view to going into the lumber business at that place. He started with a small capital, buying as he could, and hauled one car load of lumber from Arlington before the road was completed. He soon built up a large trade, and became quite extensively engaged in the business. He is now one of the most extensive lumber dealers in this section; owns the block where he carries on his business, and has a beautiful brick residence. He is one of the enterprising and prominent business men of Laclede County, and has a host of warm friends. Mr. Lingsweiler is also the owner of several business buildings and dwelling houses. He is a member of the Masonic fraternity, I. O. O. F., in which he passed through the chairs, also a member of the Encampment, K. T. and G. A. R. He has held the office of city alderman and is a member of the school board. He was married in March, 1871, to Miss Emma R. Ostrander, a native of New York, and by whom he has four children: Charlie E., Mabel I., Arthur F. and Myrtle V.

Thomas F. Lockwood, M. D., one of the leading physicians of Conway, Laclede Co., Mo., is a native of Sangamon County, Ill., and was born January 11, 1865. He is a son of Isaac and Sarah (Dunbar) Lockwood, the former of whom was born in Shelby County, Ill., and the latter in Virginia. They are now living in Washington Township, Laclede Co., Mo. The father is fifty-three years of age and the mother fifty-five. They were married in Christian County, Ill., and moved to Shelby County in 1869, whence they came to Laclede County, Mo., in 1878. Previous to his removal to Missouri, Isaac Lockwood worked as a mill-wright, miller and carpenter, and after he removed to Missouri he worked at his adopted trade until a recent date, since which time he has devoted his attention exclusively to farming. He is a member of the Masonic fraternity, and a Democrat in politics. The parents are both members of the Missionary Baptist Church. To their union were born nine children, seven of whom are living: Mary J., wife of Martin M. Sphar, a farmer of Laclede County; Francis M., a farmer of Allen County, Kas.; George H., a farmer of Laclede County; Thomas F., M. D.; William A., at home; Isaac O. and Ira E. (twins), at home. Thomas F. Lockwood received a liberal education in the schools of Laclede County, and began the study of medicine under Dr. A. H. Neal, then of Laclede County. During the sessions of 1885–86 and 1886–87, he attended the Northwestern Medical College, at St. Joseph, Mo., graduating in February, 1887. He then returned to Laclede County and entered upon the practice of his chosen profession, locating in Conway, Laclede County, in June, 1888, where he has a growing patronage. June 20, 1886, Dr. Lockwood married Ellen J. Barr, daughter of Dr. S. B. F. C. Barr, of Laclede County, formerly of Tennessee. One child has been born to Dr. and Mrs. Lockwood, Eda Ethel. Dr. Lockwood also practiced on the Osage River one year, where he was blessed with success, and which practice he still retains. He is one of the rising practitioners of Laclede County, and gives good satisfaction in his work as a physician. He is a most skillful member of the medical fraternity, using the greatest precaution in discharging his professional duty. His aim is to rank among the highest of the profession. The Doctor and wife are members of the Baptist Church. In politics he is a Democrat.

Hon. J. W. McClurg, ex-governor of the State of Missouri, is a native of St. Louis County, Mo., born February 22, 1818, and is the son of Joseph and Mary (Brotherton) McClurg, and grandson of Joseph McClurg, who came to America during the Irish Rebellion of 1798. He came over concealed in the bottom of the vessel, and his family followed shortly afterward. He located in Pittsburg, built the first iron foundry in that city, and here and near Pittsburg passed the remainder of his life. He had a farm near the city, and ran a foundry there for many years. His sons continued the business after he had retired. The father of ex-Gov. McClurg was born in Northern Ireland, and came to America when about twelve years of age. He was also a foundryman, as were his brothers, Alexander and William, and they carried on the business there for a number of years. He died in Ohio while yet engaged in the iron business. The mother died in St. Louis. They were the parents of but two children: James B. (deceased) and J. W. McClurg. The last named was reared in Pennsylvania, whither he had been taken at the age of seven years, but received the principal part of his education in Ohio, where he remained until about nineteen years of age. He then returned to Missouri and made his home with his uncles, James and Marshall Brotherton, both of whom filled the office of sheriff of St. Louis County. J. W. served as deputy sheriff under both of them for about two years. In the spring of 1839 he went to Texas, and remained there for some two years, and was admitted to the practice of law at Columbus, Texas. In 1841 he married, in Washington County, Mo., Miss Mary C. Johnson, a native of Virginia, and this union resulted in the birth of eight children, six now living: Mary E., wife of Col. M. W. Johnson, now at Lebanon; Fannie, wife of C. C. Draper, also at Lebanon; Joseph E., in Dakota engaged in farming; Sarah, wife of Thomas Monroe, resides in Lebanon; Dr. James A., dentist, at Lebanon, and Dr. Marshall J., also a dentist, at Carthage, Mo. After marriage Mr. McClurg turned his attention to merchandising, which he carried on at Hazelwood and Linn Creek, Mo., until the breaking out of the late war, when he was at Linn Creek. In 1861 he enlisted in the Home Guards; was chosen colonel of his regiment, and in 1862 he became colonel of the Eighth Cavalry, Missouri State Militia. He was in this service until after his election to Congress, which was in 1862, from the Fifth District. He then resigned his position in the army to take his seat, and was re-elected in 1864 and 1866. Before the expiration of his last term of office he was elected by the Republican party as governor of the State of Missouri, in 1868, and served one term of two years. He then turned his attention to merchandising, lead mining and steamboating, which he carried on until 1885, at which date he came to Laclede County, and has since been retired from business. He is now in his seventieth year, but still quite well preserved. He has been a very prominent man of the State of Missouri, and has been a strong adherent of the Republican party. He is a member of the G. A. R., and he and Mrs. McClurg were members of the Presbyterian Church. Mrs. McClurg departed this life in December, 1861, at Jefferson City. He remained single. He is now a member of the Methodist Episcopal Church. They were the grandparents of twenty-six children, twenty-four now living. Their son, James A., studied dentistry at St. Louis, and has since been practicing at Lebanon and Marshfield seven or eight years. He was married to Miss Mattie Williams in 1877, and is the father of four children. He is a promising young man, and has built up a good practice. Their son Marshall J. studied dentistry in Philadelphia, Penn., and has now a good practice. He married Miss Effie DeVore, of Carthage.

Dr. James McComb, physician and surgeon at Lebanon, Mo., was born near Jacksonville, Ill., March 12, 1832, and is the son of James and Elizabeth (Lewis) McComb, natives of Knox County, Tenn., and of Scotch descent. The paternal grandfather, William McComb, crossed the ocean to America, and died, after several years, in Tennessee. James McComb, Sr., was reared by an uncle in Tennessee, his parents having died when he was quite young, and attained his growth on a farm. He was married to Miss Lewis in Tennessee, and afterward moved to Morgan County, Mo., where he died in 1837. The mother died several years afterward. They were the parents of ten children, six now living: William, Lewis, Mary, Amy, Dr. James and David. Dr. James McComb was but five years of age when his father died, and he remained with his mother until after her death, which occurred when he was seventeen years of age. He received his early education in the log school-houses, but later attended two years at Warsaw College. He then taught school for two years in order to get money to further his education. In 1856 he attended the State University, in the meantime studying medicine. In 1857 he took his first course of lectures at St. Louis Medical College, and practiced as a first course student until 1865, when he graduated at the Jefferson Medical College at Philadelphia. In 1858 he came to Laclede County, Mo., and located at Lebanon in 1863, where he has since practiced his profession with great success. He is now the oldest practicing physician in the county, and has built up a large and lucrative practice. He was married in 1860 to Miss Mary L. Holman, who was born in North Carolina, and who became the mother of seven children: Charles A., James A., Virgil J. (a druggist), George E. (deputy county clerk), William E., Ernest H. and Floyd J. The latter three are in school. Charles and James graduated in medicine, and are now practicing their profession, the former at Dixon, Mo., and the latter at Bentonville, Ark. The Doctor is a member of the Masonic fraternity, also the A. O. U. W., and he and Mrs. McComb and their children, except the youngest two, are members of the Christian Church.

Judge Anderson McFall, a leading citizen of Union Township, Laclede Co., Mo., was born in Russell County, Ky., January 9, 1838, and is a son of Lindsay and Mary (Bradley) McFall, natives of Kentucky. Lindsay McFall was born in 1808, and has been a farmer all his life; he is now a resident of Russell County, Ky. Mrs. McFall died in 1879, the mother of nine children, six of whom are living, viz.: Sarah E. (wife of I. M. Wells, a farmer of Russell County, Ky.), William (also a farmer of Russell County), James (in Russell County, engaged in farming), Emmerson (in the same county), Susan E. (wife of James Snow, a farmer of Russell County) and Anderson. October 15, 1861, the latter enlisted in Company G, Twelfth Kentucky Volunteer Infantry, and served fifteen months as sergeant, participating in the battle of Mills Springs. He afterward enlisted in Company B, Ninety-fourth Kentucky Militia, of which company he was commissioned captain, and served until the close of the war, when he returned to his home in Russell County, Ky. October 17, 1869, he married Mary C. Oaks, daughter of John W. Oaks. She was born in Russell County December 1, 1854, and died February 15, 1883, the mother of the following children: Julia F., John L. and Sidney C. March 13, 1884, Mr. McFall married Sarah E. Sutton, who was born in Clay County, Ill., January 22, 1861, and is a daughter of Jesse and Nancy J. Sutton, the former of whom died in Clay County, and the mother subsequently married Joshua Robertson and moved to Laclede County, Mo. Mr. McFall has one child by the second marriage, Myrtle Etolia. In 1870 Mr. McFall removed to Laclede County, Mo., and settled in Union Township, which he has since made his home. In 1886 he was elected judge of the Western District of Laclede County by the Democratic party, and for eight years served as justice of the peace of Union Township. He is a member of the Methodist Episcopal Church, and is also a Mason and Knights Templar. He is one of the enterprising citizens of the county, and supports actively all laudable enterprises. Mrs. McFall is a member of the Cumberland Presbyterian Church.

William R. Mayfield, a retired farmer, was born in Casey County, Ky., April 2, 1834, and is the son of James and Mary (Johnson) Mayfield, natives of Tennessee and Kentucky, respectively. The father was a farmer by occupation, was a soldier in the Mexican War, and he and wife were earnest workers in the Christian Church. They moved from Kentucky to Illinois, and later to Missouri, locating in Gasconade Township, Laclede County. Here the mother died, and here the father followed her to the grave in 1853. They were the parents of eight children, all of whom lived to be grown, but only three now living. The eldest, Mrs. Anna Wisdom, is now a widow; James lives in Laclede County, Mo., and William R., subject of this sketch; Mayfield Township was named in his honor. The last named attained his growth in Laclede County, and was left when a boy to do for himself. He began farming for himself, and April 13, 1855, he was united in marriage to Miss Sarah M. Davis, a native of Kentucky, born January 23, 1839, and the daughter of George W. and Elizabeth W. Davis, who were natives of Madison County, Va., and both born in the year 1810. The grandfather, James Davis, was a native of Maryland, and his wife's maiden name was Dent. George W. Davis came from Virginia to Kentucky in 1831, and located in Warren County. He was a grain dealer by occupation. He lived in Kentucky for a number of years, then moved to Tennessee, from there back to Kentucky, and settled in Missouri in the fall of 1839. He located on the Gasconade River, bought land, and here followed agricultural pursuits until his death, which occurred February 6, 1878. He was a member of the Masonic fraternity, and also the I. O. O. F. His wife died November 2, 1883. She was an active worker and a member of the Methodist Episcopal Church, South. They were the parents of eight children. To Mr. and Mrs. Mayfield were born nine children: Sarah E. (deceased), was the wife of A. J. Holman; she died June 2, 1881, leaving three children. [See sketch of A. J. Holman.] Irvin W., W. Melvin, Andrew Q., L. C., Lulu Bell, and three children who died in infancy. August 25, 1880, Mr. Mayfield moved to his farm on Dry Glaize, and in September, 1886, moved to Lebanon. During the war he enlisted in the Forty-sixth Missouri Infantry Volunteers, and served six months, after which he returned home and resumed agricultural pursuits. Mr. Mayfield is a member of the A. F. & A. M. at Lebanon, and he and wife are members of the Methodist Episcopal Church, South, the former having held all the offices of that church.

W. M. Mayfield, farmer and stock raiser, was born in Laclede County, Mo., and is the son of William R. and Sarah E. (Davis) Mayfield. The grandparents on both sides came to Laclede County at quite an early date, and settled in what is now Mayfield Township. W. M. Mayfield grew to manhood in that township, and received a good collegiate education. After finishing his education he engaged in farming, and has followed this occupation ever since. He deals quite extensively in stock, and in this pursuit he has been quite successful. He was married, January 5, 1885, to Miss Lou, daughter of John Esther, of Laclede County, and by whom he had one child, Orin. Mr. Mayfield is a member of the Agricultural Wheel, and he and wife are members of the Methodist Episcopal Church, South.

John Meents, farmer, fruit grower and stock raiser of Lebanon, was born in Hanover, Germany, March 31, 1838, and is the son of Feeke and Reka (Reents) Meents, natives of Germany. The father died in his native country, but the mother is still living, and is a resident of Germany. Their son, John Meents, was reared on a farm in Germany, and was there educated. In 1864 he took passage for New York City, but after reaching that city he went on to Woodford County, Ill., near Peoria, where he remained until 1872, working on a farm, and the last three years engaged in farming for himself. In 1867 he married Miss Tantken Meents, a native of Germany, and to them were born two children: Margaret and Remmer. In 1872 Mr. Meents came to Laclede County, buying the farm where he now lives, which was then all raw land, and improved it until it is now one of the best farms in the county. He has 217 acres of land, all under cultivation. He has a beautiful fruit orchard, with about 2,000 apple, pear and peach trees. He raises a great deal of stock, and is one of the most enterprising farmers of this county. He has accumulated most all he has since coming to America, and has labored hard to improve his place. Mr. Meents has always taken a great interest in educational matters. He and wife are members of the Lutheran Church.

William H. Mizer, a prominent farmer of Laclede County, Mo., was born in Meigs County, Tenn., February 13, 1843, being a son of Michael and Nancy (Hale) Mizer, and grandson of John and Betsey Mizer. John Mizer was born in Germany, and came to America while still unmarried, locating in Tennessee, where he married and reared a family of eight children, Michael being the oldest child. The latter grew to maturity in his native State, and in February, 1843, immigrated to Laclede County, Mo., but eleven years later took up his abode in Gentry County, where he remained about nine years, and died in 1863, at the age of sixty-five years, having been an active worker in the Methodist Episcopal Church. His wife was also born in Meigs County, Tenn., and in November, 1884, died at the home of her son, William, in her sixtieth year. Six of her family of nine children are living, whose names are as follows: George W., William H., Wesley W., Albert B., Lucinda (wife of R. C. Bolles) and Nancy (wife of W. Thrailkill). Those deceased are Elijah H., Minerva and Angeline. Michael Mizer was first married to Betsey Swaford, by whom he had ten children, all deceased. William H. Mizer was educated in the common schools, and was reared to maturity in his native county. In October, 1866, he was married to Miss Mary Clinkinbard, a native of Laclede County, Mo., born October 15, 1849, by whom he has the following children: Elder J., Noah E., William L., Myrtle, Virgil, Luna, Edna, Alice and Etna (who died at the age of three years). On the 1st of January, 1862, Mr. Mizer enlisted in the Fourteenth Regiment Missouri State Militia, and served until the close of the war, being a participant in the battles of Prairie Grove, Pea Ridge, Neosho, and a number of others of minor note. After the war he located in Laclede County, where he has since been engaged in farming, and owns 320 acres of good land, with about 120 acres under cultivation, and is considered one of the successful farmers of Spring Hollow Township. He is a Democrat in politics, and has always taken an active interest in school matters. He is a member of the Christian Church, and his wife belongs to the Baptist Church. The latter's father, James M. Clinkinbard, was born in Tennessee, and came to Laclede County, Mo., in 1844 or 1845, locating near Lebanon on a farm. He died March 20, 1863, in Arkansas, while serving in the Confederate army, but his widow is still living, and is the wife of Martin D. Shipman, one of the old settlers of the county.

L. A. Moore, grocer and proprietor of a meat-market at Lebanon, Mo., was born in Adams County, Wis., January 1, 1854, and is the son of Asa J. and Nancy (Pooler) Moore, the father a native of Maine and the mother of Ohio. The parents were married in Wisconsin, and the father was a farmer by occupation. He enlisted in Company D, Sixteenth Regiment Wisconsin Volunteers, and died of fever while in service near Atlanta, Ga. The widow was left in Wisconsin with five children, the eldest being L. A. He was but eleven years old at this time, and worked hard to assist his mother in supporting the younger children. Finally he was put out with a farmer, and remained with him for some time, receiving a limited education, as he was kept busily at work. In 1872 he came to Lebanon, Mo., where he remained about eighteen months, and then went back to Wisconsin. In 1876 he again returned to Lebanon, and was employed at a low salary as clerk in a grocery store. By economy and industry he accumulated enough money to go into business for himself, and has carried on the grocery and meat-market business since December 3, 1884. Mr. Moore has been quite successful in his business undertakings, and deserves great credit for pluck and energy. He owns a farm near Lebanon, and has a fine orchard of 1,500 apple trees. He was married October 22, 1883, to Miss Mary Glynn, and to them have been born three children: Emanuel, Adelbert and Thomas E. Mr. Moore is a member of the Sons of Veterans.

William Glynn, farmer, and brother of Mrs. Moore, was born in Henry County, Tenn., March 24, 1859, and is the son of Michael and Alice (Reynolds) Glynn, natives of County Galway, Ireland, where they were married, and in 1849 immigrated to America. The father worked on the construction of the M. C. & S. C. Railroad through Tennessee, and afterward moved to Illinois, thence to Iowa, and from there to St. Joseph, Mo., with the intention of buying land, but in 1871 he came on to Laclede County, Mo., where he bought his present farm, consisting of 160 acres. He moved his family on this land in 1873, and is still living there. They have seventy-five acres under cultivation, and all under fence, with good buildings, etc. Mr. Glynn is the father of four children: Mary, wife of the subject of this sketch; William, Thomas and John. The mother died September 22, 1882. William Glynn was but fourteen years of age when he came to this country, and here he received his education. He has worked hard to assist his father in clearing his land, and is a bright young man. He now owns the farm, and is now directing his attention principally to the raising of wheat, at which he has been quite successful. He was married in October, 1888, to Miss Mary Plunkett, a native of Rolla, Mo. Mr. and Mrs. Glynn are members of the Catholic Church.

John Moser, a prominent farmer of Smith Township, Laclede Co., Mo., was born in Campbell County, Tenn., April 15, 1816, being the son of Allen and Susannah Moser, natives of South Carolina and Tennessee, respectively. The father followed farming and blacksmithing for a livelihood, and was a Democrat in his political opinions. He was a soldier in the War of 1812, was a member of the Baptist Church, and died during the late war, over eighty years of age. His father served in the Revolutionary War. Mrs. Susannah Moser died in the year 1850. She was the mother of twelve children, all of whom lived to be grown; but seven are now living. John Moser was the fourth child in order of birth. He was reared on his father's farm in Campbell County, and when twenty-two years of age commenced business for himself. In 1841 he came to Missouri, by wagon, bringing with him his wife, whose maiden name was Mary Murry, and one child. He located in the fall of the same year where he has since lived. He had but $18 after locating on his place, and traded a wagon for his claim, which was 120 acres of bottom land. By hard work and good management he has increased this to 225 acres of good land, with 150 under cultivation. He remained at home during the war; was a Union man, and a Democrat in his political views, although now he is independent. His wife died in 1844, leaving one child, Henry, who died in the Federal army in the fall of 1861. Mr. Moser was married the second time to Miss Lucy Elizabeth Mayfield, daughter of James Mayfield. [See sketch of W. R. Mayfield.] Mrs. Moser died in 1878, and left a family of three children: James, Margaret and John. Margaret died, leaving three children; James is living in Kansas City, and John lives on the old home place. John J. Moser and son farm their land. The latter was born on the home place in 1859, and has always been at home. He was married to Miss Emily J. May, a native of Kentucky, born in 1862, and the daughter of Robert and Ellen May. Ellen May died when her daughter was a small child, and the father is living in Dakota Territory. To John Moser, Jr. and wife, were born five children: Lucy A., Charley W., George A., Harrison and Ida L. Mr. Moser is a member of the Agricultural Wheel, and he and wife are members of the Methodist Episcopal Church, South.

A. Nelson. The Ozark Plateau Land Company is represented by A. Nelson as general manager. This company own about 140,000 acres of land, located in Laclede, Webster, Camden and Dallas Counties, which is sold off in any quantity, on long time and easy payments. Mr. Nelson was born in Oneida County, N. Y., and is the son of John A. and Clarissa (Hamlin) Nelson, and grandson of Elijah Nelson, who was born in England and who immigrated to the State of New York at quite an early date. He located in Westchester County, N. Y., where he purchased a large tract of land, cleared it, and here passed the residue of his days, dying in 1848. He first came there in the latter part of the seventeenth century, and was in his ninety-second year at the time of his death. He purchased a silver watch, manufactured at Peakhill, England, which he brought over with him. It bears the date of 1727, and is now in the possession of A. Nelson. He was also one of the first subscribers to the first bibles that were sold only by subscription, and this volume is also in our subject's possession. John A. Nelson and wife were born in Westchester County, N. Y., on the Hudson River, and in this State they were reared. The father was a farmer by occupation and a prominent citizen. He served six months in the War of 1812, and died in Wayne County, N. Y., in July, 1865. The mother died in 1835. They were the parents of five children, only two now living: Fannie E., who resides in Buffalo, N. Y., and Absalom, subject of this sketch. He was reared on the farm, and received a meager education in Oneida County, N. Y., being obliged to grub stumps in his boyhood days instead of attending school. After his marriage to Miss Nancy A. Jackson, a native of Oneida County, N. Y., and of English descent, he moved to Buffalo, N. Y., still retaining his farm, however, in Oneida County. He here engaged in the lake and canal transportation business, which was quite an extensive calling, and which he carried on for about twenty-five years. Twenty-three years of this time he was a resident of Buffalo City. He was a citizen of Wayne

County, N. Y., for three years, where he had a large farming interest, and also kept up his business in Buffalo. In 1883 he moved to Lebanon, and in connection with his company purchased 177,000 acres of land, which company he still represents, as stated above. This concern is represented by a well-posted gentleman, in behalf of Mr. Nelson, who has a thorough knowledge of this county and its lands, having gone all over them before purchasing. Mr. Nelson is quite extensively engaged in farming, and is a man universally respected. He is chairman of the Republican city committee, and took an active part in the campaign of 1888. Mr. and Mrs. Nelson are the parents of five children: Homer A., Arthur T., Harry A., Alfred J. and Laura A., and both are members of the Methodist Episcopal Church. Mr. Nelson is a member of the Masonic order, and also a member of the K. of H. He has spent a great deal of his time and money in building up the county, in the way of stock, fruit and grain, etc., which he has exhibited at the St. Louis Exposition, to show what Laclede County could do. He has made fine exhibits at Springfield on stock, etc., and has always taken the premium. He is certainly one of the leading and enterprising citizens of this portion of Missouri, and deserves great credit for his enterprise.

A. H. Nicks, deputy collector of Laclede County, Mo., was born in Hickman County, Tenn., December 2, 1817, and is the son of John and Anna (Richards) Nicks, natives of Guilford County, N. C., and Pennsylvania, respectively. The paternal grandfather, John Nicks, was of English descent, and was a farmer by occupation. He immigrated from England to North Carolina at a very early date, and there passed the remainder of his life. The father of the subject of this sketch was also a farmer. In 1858 he came to Missouri, locating in Howell County, where he died in 1859. The mother died in Tennessee. To their marriage were born ten children, three now living: Betsey A., Alfred H. and Mary. A. H. Nicks remained on the farm in Tennessee until seventeen years of age, when, in 1836, he was employed as clerk in the mercantile business. He followed mercantile pursuits until 1857, when he moved to Howell County, Mo., where he was engaged in farming for some time. The same year of his arrival he was elected sheriff of Howell County, but his opponents thought it not fair. They issued a few warrants, and had a trial, but the judge decided in favor of Mr. Nicks, and he held the office for one term. He was married in 1844 to Miss Flora N. Porter, a native of Williamsport, Tenn. To them were born four children: William M., Mary B., Brown S. and Robert A. In 1862 Mr. Nicks enlisted in the war under Col. McFarland, in Company B, and was first lieutenant all through the service under Col. Price. He was engaged in the battles of South Fork and Farmington, Miss. At the close of his service, in 1864, his financial condition was not of the best, as he had but $1 left. He moved to Pulaski County, engaged in farming and the study of law, and was admitted to the bar in 1876, after which he practiced for some time. In 1869 he removed to Laclede County, locating in Gasconade Township, where he purchased a farm, and there he has since made his home. He was commissioned city collector September

18, 1888, and is one of the prominent men of the county. He owns between 600 and 700 acres of land on the Gasconade River, which is very valuable, and has 200 acres under cultivation. He has made all his property by hard work and economy, and is now ready to enjoy the fruit of his labor. He is a member of the Masonic faternity; a member of the Grange, of which he was president for some time, and a member of the Agricultural Wheel, of which he is a member of the trade committee. Mrs. Nicks is of the prominent Porter family.

Jasper N. Norman, farmer and merchant, was born in Camden County, now Laclede County, in 1841, his parents being Moses and Lucinda (Nichols) Norman. Moses Norman was born in Tennessee in 1793, and came to Missouri from Mississippi in about 1837 or 1838. He located in what is now Camden County in about 1840, and entered the place where his son Jasper N. is now living. Here he died in 1873. He was a United States mail contractor while in Mississippi. He was a Democrat in his political views before the war, but since that event he has voted with the Republican party. His wife, Mrs. Lucinda (Nichols) Norman, was born in Illinois in 1828, and on becoming a young woman she came to Missouri with her people. Here she married Mr. Norman, and is still living at the home place. She bore Mr. Norman eight children, seven now living: Jasper N., Newton, Caledonia, Sarah J., Taylor, Caroline, Mattie, and Solomon, who died when a child. Jasper N. Norman attained his majority in this county, where he has always lived. At the opening of the war Mr. Norman enlisted in the Osage Regiment, Company A, United States Army, and served about one year. He was wounded accidentally, and was afterward discharged and came home. He was married, in 1865, to Mary S. Wright, who bore him six children, two now living: Ida and Nellie; Ida is the wife of Robert B. Regan. The remainder of the children died when young, with the exception of Lucy, who died at the age of sixteen years. Mrs. Norman died in 1872, and Mr. Norman was married the second time, to Miss Minnie Doss, in 1885. She was born in Northern Missouri, and by her marriage to Mr. Norman became the mother of three children: Grace, Archie and Harrison. Mr. Norman is a member of the I. O. O. F., and is a Republican in politics.

H. H. Oberbeck, a worthy and wealthy farmer of Laclede County, Mo., is a native of Prussia, born August 15, 1841, being a son of William and Caroline (Frazer) Oberbeck, who were also born in Germany. They spent the greater portion of their lives in their native land, but the father made a visit to America. He was a cabinetmaker by trade, and became the father of nine children, eight of whom are living: Carr, Caroline, Lottie, Henry, August, Herman H., Frederick and Minnie. Herman H. Oberbeck, whose name heads this sketch, learned the cabinet-maker's trade in his native land, and followed that occupation for many years, and in the spring of 1867 sailed for America, taking passage at Bremen and landing at New York City. He first located in St. Louis, where he worked at his trade for about seven years, and then engaged in the wholesale and retail liquor business, afterward investing in a stock of groceries also.

In 1877 he came to Laclede County and purchased 407 acres of land, with 100 under cultivation. He is quite extensively engaged in raising cattle and hogs, and is one of the progressive farmers of the county. In 1865 he wedded Miss Minnie Steinberger, a native of Germany, who died in 1886, having borne a family of seven children: Minnie, Annie, Henry, August, Mary, Lena and Ida. In June, 1888, he was married to Mollie Weirauch. He is a member of the Agricultural Wheel.

I. M. O'Dell, farmer, stock raiser, and native of Laclede County, Mo., was born November 15, 1849. His father, Samuel O'Dell, who was of Scotch-Irish descent, and a native of Tennessee, born in the year 1800, was twice married. He immigrated with his first wife (Cynthia Walker) to Illinois in 1830, and after residing in Macoupin County for six years his wife died, leaving seven children, whose names are as follows: Elizabeth, wife of A. A. Lowrance; Enoch, who moved to Grayson County, Tex., in 1857, and at the breaking out of the war espoused and served in the Confederate cause; Jonathan, Jeremiah and John, who served in the Federal army, and were killed in the battle of Franklin, Tenn.; James and Eliza. Being discouraged by sickness Mr. O'Dell immigrated to Laclede County, Mo., in 1836, settling on the Osage Fork of the Gasconade River, ten miles south of Lebanon, at which place he continued to reside until his death in 1881. He was married the second time in 1838, to Mary S. Devazier, who was of German descent, also a native of Tennessee, and who preceded him to Laclede County only a few months. She was the mother of nine children: W. C. and A. F., who served in the cause of the Union, the latter being killed in the battle of Pleasant Hill, La.; S. H., who died in infancy; B. A., who resides in Callahan County, Tex.; I. M. was chosen by his father to be executor of his estate; S. S., Maggie, Jennie and Kate, all of Laclede County, Mo. Mary (Devazier) O'Dell died December 17, 1888. Mr. O'Dell located on the farm on which he now resides in 1882, and is considered one of the first farmers of his section of the country. He was married February 9, 1873, to Miss Lizzie Workman, a daughter of Green and Martha Workman, who were Tennesseeans by birth. In 1858 she, in company with her sister, Mrs. Sylvia Younger, came to Laclede County, where she met and married Mr. O'Dell, by whom she became the mother of one child, Grace, who died October 18, 1876. Mr. O'Dell is a Democrat, and belongs to the A. F. & A. M. Throughout life he has never been more than thirty miles from his birthplace.

W. H. Owen, merchant, and president of the Bank of Lebanon, is a native of Kent, England, born February 3, 1840. At the age of fourteen, or in 1854, with an uncle, he took passage at Liverpool, and landed at Boston, Mass. After arriving in America he attended school during the winters, and worked during the summers. This he continued until eighteen years of age, when he entered a store at Adrian, Mich., as clerk. He remained here for about four years, and then went to Waterford, Mich., where he engaged in general merchandising until 1865. In the spring of 1866 he went to St.

Louis, and was employed as traveling salesman for a wholesale dry goods house, with whom he remained until 1877. He then came to Lebanon, located, and here engaged in the general mercantile business. Previous to this, in 1873, he married Miss Hannah Ward, of St. Louis. Two children, William H. and James W., were the result of this union. Aside from his mercantile business, Mr. Owen is also engaged quite extensively in farming, and is a prominent grain buyer. He employs a great many men in his store and in his other enterprises. He has 600 acres of land, with most of it under cultivation. On the organization of the Bank of Lebanon he was made its president, and on the organization of the Laclede County Agricultural Society, in 1885, he was made its president. He is politically a stanch Republican. He is one of the leading and influential citizens of Laclede County, and is a valuable citizen.

John J. Paine, stock farmer, was born in Vigo County, Ind., in 1825, and is the son of A. and Sarah (Searing) Paine, natives of Massachusetts and New York, respectively. The grandfather Paine lived at Lowell, Mass., and owned a large manufacturing establishment, and the father of our subject became dissatisfied because he could not be overseer of the factory, and came to Indiana, where he engaged in farming. He also followed the cooper's trade during the winters. He was well educated, took an active part in political affairs, and died in 1837 or 1838. The mother was married the second time to Mr. Rickman, and died in 1885 in Indiana. She was the mother of ten children by her first marriage, three now living: George A., Marvin M. and John J. There were no children born to the second marriage. J. J. Paine remained at home until sixteen years of age, when he went to learn the tanner's trade, and served five years for his board, clothes and six months' schooling. When in his twenty-second year he went to Hendricks County, Ind., where he engaged in the tanner's trade, but continued here but two years, when he moved to Clay County, and here followed his trade, also farming a small tract for five or six years. He moved to Missouri in 1853, locating first five miles southeast of Lebanon, and in the spring of 1855 he bought the Dunkin tan-yard, on the place now owned by Judge Rupard, which yard he ran for four or five years. In 1860 he sold out, and bought the farm that he now owns. He left this farm in 1863, went to Franklin County, Mo., and in the fall of the same year went to Indiana, where he raised one crop. In the fall of 1865 he returned to the home place, where he has since resided, and removed to his present location in 1878. He was married in September, 1846, to Miss Sarah J. Bronaugh, a native of Kentucky, who bore him eight children, four now living: Robert A., John T., Sarah N. (wife of Charles L. Johnson), and Clara Bell (wife of James Rupard). Those deceased were named Mary, Lucia, George and Martha. The mother of the above children died March 21, 1876. She was a member of the Methodist Episcopal Church, South. Mr. Paine then married Mrs. Mary E. Mayfield, who was born February 6, 1839, in Warren County, Ky., and who was the widow of John E. Mayfield. She was the daughter of James and Sarah Hendricks, natives of Kentucky. They came to Missouri when she was a small girl, and here she married Mr. Mayfield, by whom she had four children: Lucy E. (wife of Alfred Carter) and Sarah N. (wife of George Walker. Two are deceased, James H. and William R. Mr. Paine is a member of the Agricultural Wheel, is a Democrat in politics, and has held the office of justice of the peace for several terms. Mrs. Paine is a member of the Methodist Episcopal Church, South, as was also the first Mrs. Paine.

Rufus Phillips, one of the leading citizens of Union Township, Laclede Co., Mo., was born in Cheshire County, N. H., March 7, 1822, and is a son of Reuben and Rebecca (Foster) Phillips. The ancestors of our subject were among the first families who came from England to this country, in 1620 or 1622, and it was a member of this family who was the first mayor of Boston. Reuben Phillips was born in Worcester County, Mass., March 24, 1788, and was the son of Gideon Phillips, who was born in Phillipston, Worcester Co., Mass., November 7, 1763. The latter served five years in the American army; was commissioned lieutenant; participated in the battles of Brandywine, Bunker Hill, Monmouth and others, surrendering at Yorktown, having been slightly wounded several times. Joshua Phillips, father of Gideon, was also a native of Phillipston, Mass., which place took its name from this family. Rufus Phillips, a son of Gideon Phillips, was killed on Lake Champlain during the War of 1812. Richard Phillips, brother of Gideon, was in the American navy during the Revolution, and was taken prisoner and carried to Dover, England, where he was kept for about three years. Pain Phillips, Gideon's twin brother, was also a Revolutionary soldier for five years. Reuben Phillips, father of our subject, was a member of the Legislature several sessions, and died in Keene, Cheshire Co., N. H., in September, 1861. Rebecca (Foster) Phillips was born in Massachusetts May 16, 1798, and died in New Hampshire June 18, 1842. She was a daughter of Enoch and Rebecca Foster, the former of whom served as lieutenant in the United States army during the Revolution, participating in many battles. Reuben and Rebecca Phillips were members of the Congregational Church. To their union were born six sons and four daughters, all of whom grew to maturity: Joseph S. enlisted in the Federal army in the late Civil War, and received a wound at Helena which caused his death; Washington is now living at Nelson, N. H., engaged in farming; he was also in the Federal army; Simeon W. (deceased) served in the Confederate army during the late war; Reuben M. was a resident of New Hampshire, but was lost in the wreck of Burnsides during the war; A. J. was a resident of Laclede County, Mo., and lost his life while in the Confederate service, at Linn Creek; Rufus, subject of this sketch; Eliza A. Pond (deceased); Lestina A. Beal (deceased); Mary S., widow of William Towns, resides in New Hampshire, and Caroline E. Wilbur died in Michigan. In 1843, at the age of twenty-one years, Rufus Phillips graduated at the Hancock Academy, Hillsborough County, N. H., and the following three years he engaged in school teaching. He then went to Philadelphia, where he enlisted in the First United States Dragoons, Company H, Taylor's division, and served eighteen months, when he was mustered out at Fort Gibson, and subsequently went to Laclede County, Mo., where he again turned his attention to teaching school for several years. He afterward embarked in farming and stock raising, and was appointed commissioner to locate swamp lands in Laclede, Wright, Barton, Webster and other counties, and assisted in laying out the town of Lamar, Barton County. He built the first steam mill in Laclede County, at Phillipsburgh, served as the first surveyor of Laclede County, and was its second representative. In 1861 he organized Company F of the Missouri State Guard, of which he was made captain; he was wounded and taken prisoner at Springfield, held fourteen months in Illinois and exchanged at Vicksburg, after which he remained in the Confederate service until the close of the war. March 4, 1851, Rufus Phillips married Rebecca J. Anderson, who was born in Laclede County, Mo., March 20, 1828, and was a daughter of Jacob Anderson, who was born in North Carolina, and was one of the earliest settlers of Laclede County. Mrs. Phillips died September 8, 1877, the mother of six sons and three daughters, five of whom are living, viz.: Heseltine A., wife of William C. Howell, of Miller County, Mo.; Reuben T., a minister of Tyler City, Smith Co., Tex.; Andrew D., a farmer of Laclede County, Mo.; Rufus S., a school-teacher of Laclede County; Maggie E., at home. Those deceased were Isaac N., Parker Duff, and Celestine, a twin of Heseltine. July 3, 1878, Mr. Phillips married Phoebe Harris, a native of Webster County, Mo., born November 27, 1846, and a daughter of John D. Harris. Of the five children born to this union four are living, viz.: John G., Lucy Arminta, William E. and Charles J. The parents are members of the Methodist Episcopal Church. Mr. Phillips is a Royal Arch Mason, and a Democrat.

William Phillips was born in McMinn County, Tenn., in 1836, and is a son of Robert and Nancy Phillips, who were born in Tennessee, and were of Dutch and Irish descent. They moved to Laclede County, Mo., in 1849, and entered 160 acres of land on Brush Creek, afterward purchasing 100 acres of land on Osage Fork of the Gasconade River. Here they were engaged in farming until 1857, when they went to Jefferson County, Ill., and after farming for some time the father engaged in the mercantile business, and died in 1873. Eleven children were born to their union, William Phillips being their eighth child. He was reared and educated in Tennessee and Missouri, and in January, 1861, was married to Nancy J. Hemphill, of North Carolina, a daughter of Alfred and Maria Hemphill, who were natives of North Carolina, where the father died. The mother is now residing in Missouri. To Mr. and Mrs. Phillips six children have been born, only two of whom are living: Nancy, wife of Philip Owens, and James Monroe, who resides with his parents. The family attend the Baptist Church, and Mr. Phillips is a member of the Agricultural Wheel, and in his political views is a Democrat. His first purchase of land was eighty acres where he now lives.

John M. Quinn, a successful agriculturist of Laclede County, was born in County Tyrone. Parish of Cookstown, Ireland, February 22, 1817, being the son of Edward and Catherine (McCloskey) Quinn, natives of the same parish. The former was a school-teacher by profession, and passed an examination by the board of excise, and but for his death would have received a government appointment. John was reared and educated with his mother's family (they being manufacturers and exporters of linen cloth), and was apprenticed to them to learn the manufacture of linen cloth, subsequently making alternate trips to Glasgow and Edinburgh, Scotland, in their interest, between 1836 and 1844. In the spring of the latter year he took passage at Liverpool for America, landing at New York twenty-eight days afterward, but after a short time in that city followed up his determination to come west by going via the Hudson River to Albany, and thence on rail to Buffalo, the rails of the road at that time being wooden, covered with hoop iron—a decided contrast to the appointments of to-day. In October he started for Chicago, taking a lake boat, but the first night out a hurricane so disabled the craft that it was necessary to put in port for safety. The trip was later successfully accomplished. About this time political feeling was at fever heat, and no little excitement attended the contest between Clay and Harrison. Chicago was then a mere hamlet, and before long Mr. Quinn went to Joliet, Will Co., Ill., taught school one year, and then returned to Jersey City, N. J., where he remained a short time. In February, 1845, he set out for Little Rock by way of New Orleans, resuming teaching in the former city in the Old Academy, but owing to sickness he returned to Jersey City, later entering the employ of a New York publishing house. In 1849 he married Miss Bridget Reynolds, by whom he had five children: Frank, John, James, Mary E. and Anna Teresa. From 1849 until 1856 Mr. Quinn was occupied in merchandising in New Brunswick, N. J., then accepting a position as shipping clerk in the New York Custom-house under Schell, then collector of customs, which position he left in 1861, and from that time until 1866 gave his attention to stock-raising in Wilmington, Ill. In August of this last mentioned year he started for Southwest Missouri overland, and after traveling in an emigrant wagon over 400 miles arrived at Lebanon September 1. For three months he lived in a camp, being obliged to haul the timber for his house a distance of sixty miles. Mr. Quinn, though now in his seventy-first year, is remarkably well preserved for a man who has passed through the many hardships he has. In July, 1887, he had the misfortune to lose his life companion. He was initiated into the Odd Fellows Lodge No. 6, I. O. O. F., in New Brunswick, N. J., in 1853, and is now one of the prominent citizens of Laclede County. His attention is directed to stock and fruit raising, and at this he has been quite successful.

John M. Ragland, attorney at law of Conway, Mo., is a native of Washington County, Ill., born August 23, 1852, being a son of John and Martha (Spence) Ragland, both of whom were born and reared in Kentucky. They were married in 1827, and a year later moved to Washington County, Ill., where the father assisted in the early settlement of that county. He was an extensive farmer and stock raiser, and about 1858 moved to Laclede County, Mo., and located on a farm of 320 acres on Brush Creek, where he spent the remainder of his days. He was an active member of the A. F. & A. M., and during the latter part of his life was a devoted member of and worker in the Primitive Baptist Church. Mrs. Ragland's father was a Protestant Irishman, and was a leading minister in the Presbyterian Church. Out of a family of twelve children born to Mr. and Mrs. Ragland, eight are now living. Three sons served in the Union army during the late war: Silas, who lost his life during service; William C., who now resides in Washington County, Ill., and is a minister of the Primitive Baptist Church, and James H. Mrs. Ragland died in October, 1855, and the widower was afterward married twice; his third wife is still living. He died on the 1st of February, 1881. John M. Ragland grew to manhood in Laclede County, and received his education in the common schools and at Hartville, Mo. In 1873 he began the study of law in the office of W. S. Pope, and two years later entered upon the practice of his profession, being admitted to the bar in Marshfield in 1886. He opened an office at Conway, and besides the practice of his profession is engaged in the real estate business. He owns a fine farm of 200 acres, and gives considerable attention to stock raising. He was married in September, 1874, to Miss Maria Devlin, of Laclede County, a daughter of Charles D. Devlin. She was born in Laclede County April 19, 1857, and is the mother of six children: Arthur H., Simeon W., Gertrude M., J. M. Hubert, Clarence E. and Nora E. In October, 1888, Mr. Ragland engaged in the drug business in Conway. He is a member of the K. of P., keeper of the R. and S., and he and wife are members of the Christian Church, he being an elder in the same. The Ragland family are of Scotch descent, and so far as known are the descendants of two brothers, who came from Scotland to the United States previous to the Revolutionary War, in which conflict the great-grandfather of our subject was an active participant. They have been a family of farmers and attorneys, and some of them have become distinguished members of the bar.

William Richey, a wide-a-wake, thorough-going tiller of the soil, of Hooker Township, Laclede Co., Mo., was born in Union County, Ohio, in 1833, and is the son of James and Sarah (Newhouse) Richey, natives of Pennsylvania and Ohio, respectively. The father was born in 1798. The grandfather, William Richey, was a native of Scotland, and came to America with his parents. They located in Beaver County, Penn. William Richey was a soldier in the Revolutionary War, and immigrated to Marietta, Ohio, in the year 1813. He was a farmer by occupation, and continued at this near Marietta until 1815, when he moved to Union County, Ohio. He was eighty-eight years of age at the time of his death. James Richey was also a farmer, and at an early day moved to Delaware County, Ohio, where he married and passed the remainder of his days. He died in 1885. He was a Whig in politics, and a member of the Presbyterian Church. The mother was born in Pickaway County, Ohio, in 1801, and grew to womanhood in Delaware County, where she married and lived until her death in 1881. She was a member of the Methodist Episcopal Church, and the mother of seven children, all now living: Newton,

Martha, Nancy, William, Mary, Eura and James. William grew to manhood on the Sciota River, Ohio, and followed farming in Delaware County until he came to Laclede County, Mo., in 1882. He was a soldier in the late war, enlisting in Company C, One Hundred and Twenty-first Ohio Volunteer Infantry, and served eight months. He was at the battle of Perryville, Ky., and others. He was married August 20, 1861, to Miss Martha Newhouse, a native of Delaware County, Ohio, born April 14, 1844. This union resulted in the birth of eight children: Eliza (died in childhood), Robert, Alexander, Sarah, Ralph, Ada, Samuel and Mary. Mr. Richey is a Republican in his political views, is a member of the I. O. O. F., and a member of the United Brethren Church.

Capt. Charles W. Rubey was born in Cooper County, Mo., in December, 1836, and is the son of Urbin E. and Kittie (Cockerell) Rubey, both natives of Virginia. The parents immigrated to Cooper County, Mo., at quite an early date, and remained there for a number of years. The mother died in 1842, and the father received his final summons in Macon City, Mo., in 1864. He was a stock dealer most of his time, and also carried on a large farm. He was the father of eight children by his first wife, four now living: Thomas T., Charles W., Sarah J. (wife of L. W. H. Wright) and Nancy C. (wife of Sanford Wilson, of California). By his second marriage Mr. Rubey became the father of four children, two now living: William L., and Alice E., wife of Edwin Winters. Capt. Charles W. Rubey was quite small when his parents left Cooper County, and he was reared principally in St. Louis, where he was educated. Later he engaged in the grocery business, which he carried on until 1860, when he came to Lebanon. Previous to this, in 1858, he married Miss Mary J. Nesbit, who bore him two children, one now living, Thomas L. Mrs. Rubey died in 1863, and Mr. Rubey was married in 1865 to Miss Lizzie L. Duval. At the commencement of the war Mr. Rubey acted as messenger for the United States army, and in 1862 he went in as captain of the State Militia. He was afterward promoted to the rank of lieutenant-colonel of the same. In November, 1863, he organized a company and went into the Sixteenth Missouri Cavalry, he being its captain, which position he held until the close of service. During the last year of service he was on Gen. John B. Sanford's staff, at district headquarters, Springfield, Mo. He participated in all the engagements of Price's raid through Missouri, in 1864, and was wounded at the battle of Newtonia, in the shoulder, by a gunshot. He was also injured at Big Blue by his horse falling upon him. He was mustered out of service June 30, 1865, and came back to Lebanon, where he has since been engaged in farming, stock dealing and merchandising. In 1878 he was elected clerk of the circuit court, and recorder, which office he held for eight years. He is largely interested in real estate, wild lands and town property, and owns, with his associates, the land where the town is now laid off. Capt. Rubey is one of the enterprising and intelligent citizens of Laclede County. He is a member of the Masonic lodge, G. A. R. and Loyal Legion of the United States.

Lewis R. Rupard, ex-county judge, and a successful agriculturist of Smith Township, Laclede Co., Mo., was born in Williamson County, Tenn., September 23, 1822, being the son of Erasmus and Nancy (Noll) Rupard, and grandson of Peter Rupard, who was a native of the Carolinas, and of Dutch descent. He was an extensive farmer, and was the father of three sons and five daughters, all of whom grew to maturity, married and reared families of their own. They are all now deceased with the exception of two. Erasmus Rupard was the eldest of the family. When about sixteen years of age he came to Williamson County, Tenn., with his parents, and there he finished his growth, married in 1819, and remained in this county until 1828, when he immigrated to St. Charles County, Mo., and rented land. In 1844 he moved to Polk County, Mo., and two years later to Hickory County, where he remained until his death, which occurred in May, 1883. He was married the second time in 1846, and became the father of four children, all deceased but one, Benjamin F. The mother of this child died in 1883. The mother of Lewis R. Rupard died in 1830, leaving a family of eight children, seven of whom grew to maturity. Those now living are Parlee, wife of A. J. Coshow; Lewis R.; Elizabeth, wife of H. J. Zumwalt, in Curry County, Oreg., and William, in Dallas County, Tex. Those deceased were named John D., who died in Texas and left a family; Erasmus, died in Texas and left a family; Peter, who died at the age of six months, and Nancy, who died in June, 1845, in Polk County, Mo. The father, after the death of his first wife, became a member of the Methodist Episcopal Church, and later a member of the Baptist Church, in which he took an active part, and held several minor offices while in Hickory County. Lewis R. Rupard was reared in St. Charles County, Mo., and went to Polk County in August, 1844. Later he went from there to Texas County, Mo., where he was one year engaged in logging and the lumber business, and was then hired as a foreman for a time. He was clerk in a mercantile establishment, and superintendent of lumber yards belonging to Truesdell & Burnett, for nearly five years. April 6, 1848, he married Miss Elizabeth J. Craddock, a native of Virginia, born November 10, 1825, and the daughter of Asa L. and Nancy Craddock, both natives of Virginia. Her parents came west about 1835 or 1836, and finally located in Laclede County, Mo., where the father died in 1853. The mother died in 1857 in Texas County. They had eleven children, these now living: Asa, James, Elizabeth and Nancy. Those deceased were named Eliza, Lucinda, John, Matilda, Clayborne, Mary and Stark. In 1850 L. R. Rupard moved to Laclede County, and since then has engaged very extensively in stock raising and farming. He is the owner of 750 acres of land in the Gasconade River Valley, 300 under a good state of cultivation. By his marriage to Miss Craddock he became the father of ten children, eight of whom lived to be grown, and six are now living: Erasmus and Nancy Ann (twins), William, John, James and Joseph. Those deceased were named Mary, Matilda, Lucinda and Grant. The last two were twins. Nancy Ann is the wife of William Monday, in Camden County. Mr. and Mrs. Rupard have a grandson, Robert Elmer Beck, living with them.

BIOGRAPHICAL APPENDIX. 749

He was born in 1882, and his mother, Mary (Rupard) Beck, died nineteen days after he was born, leaving two other children, William S. and Edina. Erasmus married a Miss Craddock, and they have five children, three now living: Ella, May and Elijah. Nancy Ann married William Monday, and had five children, two living, Mary and Robert. William married Miss Dyca Harrell, and has two children, Pearl and Beulah. John R. married Miss Harrell; he is residing in Texas. Joseph married Miss Mollie Kinchloe, and to them were born five children: Bettie, Nancy A., Robert, Ethel and Joseph. Matilda died at the age of eighteen years. James Rupard married Miss Clara Paine, who bore him three children: Elsie, Edward and Wallace. Mr. Rupard, subject of this sketch, is a member of the I. O. O. F., Agricultural Wheel, and in 1866 he was elected county judge, serving two years, and was re-elected in 1876. In 1882 he was elected to the same position for four years. In 1888 he was nominated by the Democrats to represent that county in the Lower House. He has been justice of the peace for a number of years, and has always taken great interest in educational matters, having served in the capacity of president and superintendent of public schools since 1852. He took an active interest in the support of the Federal Government in the late War of the Rebellion, and has always been consistent politically, casting his first presidential vote in 1844 for James K. Polk. He has affiliated with the Democratic party up to the present time; was one of that number of fifty who had the courage to vote for the Democratic nominee (George B. McClellan) in 1864, when radicalism was rampant in Southwest Missouri, and the country overrun by what was then known as Kansas Jayhawkers.

Francis M. Russell, one of the most prominent citizens of Union Township, Laclede Co., Mo., was born near his present place of residence, on the Osage Fork, in what was then Pulaski County, Mo., August 18, 1839. He is the son of Jeremiah and Celia (Wade) Russell, natives of Warren County, Ky. The father was born in 1803, and died in Laclede County, Mo., February 23, 1880. He was a successful farmer and merchant, selling goods at Jericho for ten years, and was postmaster at that place. The mother was born in 1809, and died in Laclede County, Mo., May 10, 1876. They were married in Kentucky, and afterward moved to Illinois, where they resided ten years, or until March, 1837, when they moved to the neighborhood in which our subject now lives. He was a Democrat in politics, and a member of the Primitive Baptist Church. To their marriage were born eleven children, five now living: George W., W. R., Francis M., Theresa, wife of G. W. Steen, and Mary, wife of Capt. E. McMahan. Francis M. Russell received his education in the country schools, and finished at the academy at Lebanon. He then assisted his father in the mercantile business until the opening of the late war, when he enlisted in Capt. Campbell's company of Missouri State Guards, but was afterward in Woods' battalion, Confederate service, Capt. Wickersham's company, which was organized for Capt. Wickersham by Mr. Russell, who came through the Federal lines to organize the company. He was not with the command any length of time, he being a scout, and rendering valuable work for the Confederacy. He was in the battle of Wilson's Creek, Lexington, Price's raid, and was twice taken prisoner, first by Col. Woods, near Mr. Russell's home, and taken to Lebanon, where he was retained about three months in 1863. The second time he was taken prisoner by Capt. Robert Butts, and was six days in prison at Springfield, when he escaped. His scouting was done from White River in Arkansas to north of where he now lives. His experience during the war was varied as well as dangerous. When the war cloud of battle had cleared away Mr. Russell went to Louisiana, and April 7, 1867, married Miss Nannie Daniel, a native of Shelby County, Tenn., born October 22, 1847, and the daughter of M. E. Daniel. Soon after their marriage Mr. and Mrs. Russell moved to Texas, but afterward moved back to Louisiana. In 1871 they moved to Laclede County, Mo., where they have since resided, his occupation being that of a farmer and stock dealer. He has been south and west with mules since coming back to Missouri; has perhaps handled more mules than any one man in Southwest Missouri, and during the time has bought over $500,000 worth of mules alone. As a trader he has been very successful. In 1880 and 1881 he was engaged in merchandising at Conway, but was burned out, and did not again resume the business. Mr. Russell is now the owner of 500 acres of excellent land in Laclede County, Mo., it being considered the best stock farm in the county. His farm is about three and a half miles southeast of Conway, on the Hartville and Buffalo road. He is a Mason, a K. T., is a member of the A. O. U. W., a member of the Wheel, and is a Democrat in politics. To his marriage were born six children: Mary Ella, Florence Leona, Ida Lee, Emma Josephine, Jeremiah Edwin and Clara.

William H. Schmalhorst, one of the leading citizens of Union Township, Laclede County, residing one mile east of Conway, was born in the Kingdom of Prussia in 1825, and is a son of Henry Christopher and Ann Maria Schmalhorst, both natives of Prussia, who came to the United States about 1839, by way of New Orleans, and located in Perry County, Mo., where they engaged in farming, but lived only a few years after their arrival in this country. Of their six children four were living at the time of the parents' death. William H. was employed most of the time working out at farming in his early life. January 17, 1847, he married Isabella Whybark, who was born in Perry County, Mo., in 1830, and is a daughter of Samuel P. Whybark, a farmer of that county, who is now eighty-seven years of age. In 1854 our subject and wife located on their present farm in Laclede County, where he bought a claim of forty acres, with improvements, for $500, to which he has since added the balance of a section of some of the best land in that section of Missouri. Mr. and Mrs. Schmalhorst are the parents of eleven children, all of whom are living, viz.: Nancy N., wife of J. C. Leonard, a farmer of Barton County, Mo.; Mary E., who married J. J. Miller, a farmer of Webster County, Mo.; Cordelia I., now Mrs. John A. Durbie, a farmer near Marble Falls, on the Rio Grande River, Texas; Frances Patterson, wife of James T. Patterson, a farmer of Webster County, Mo.; Margaret, married

Frank P. Knight, a farmer of Laclede County; Samuel H., who is living near Conway, Mo., a farmer and stock raiser; Levi, also a farmer of Laclede County; Victoria C., at home; Moses D., who will graduate at Drura College, Springfield, Mo., in the spring of 1890; William L. and David E. Mr. and Mrs. Schmalhorst and all but two of the children are members of the Presbyterian Church, and Mr. Schmalhorst has been an elder in the church for twelve years or more. He is a Republican in politics, and during the late war served as orderly-sergeant in the State Militia. He was justice of the peace of his township a short time, but has never aspired to political office. He is one of the most prominent citizens of Laclede County, and is ever ready to support all educational and religious enterprises for the good of the community. He built a grist-mill on his farm in 1867, which he successfully operated until 1887, when he sold out. The family have the respect and high esteem of all who know them.

Joab Scott, retired, was born in Bedford County, Tenn., February 28, 1818, being the son of Jesse and Jennie (Dial) Scott, and grandson of Jordan Scott, who was formerly from South Carolina, but moved to Alabama, where he passed the remainder of his life. The maternal grandfather, Jeremiah Dial, served seven years in the Revolutionary War, and was but sixteen years of age when he entered the service. In 1790 he immigrated to Bedford County, Tenn., and there resided until his death. He was a farmer and school-teacher by occupation, and was a well-educated man. Jesse Scott, father of our subject, was reared in Tennessee, was a farmer by occupation, and was a soldier in the War of 1812. In 1842 he immigrated to Wright County, Mo., and entered a tract of land, which he labored hard to improve. He died there in 1873. The mother died in 1828. Young Scott was educated in Tennessee, and assisted on the farm until 1839, when his parents moved to Missouri with an ox team, and after a six weeks' trip landed in what is now Laclede County, but what was then Pulaski. They located on Brush Creek when there were but three other families living on the creek, and when the county was not sectionized. He remained on his farm until 1873, when he moved to Lebanon, where he has since resided. In 1849 Mr. Scott was elected sheriff, and served four years, being the second sheriff elected after the organization of the county. He was appointed by the county court as swamp land commissioner in 1885, and served until 1860. In 1872 he was elected county collector, and served four years. He was appointed the first assessor of Laclede County, and served one year. He was also appointed county court justice, and served one year, to fill an unexpired term. Mr. Scott is one of the pioneers of Laclede County, and is prominently identified with the interests of the same. He has labored hard during his life, but can now sit down and during his declining years enjoy the fruit of his energy. Mr. Scott is a member of the Masonic fraternity, and he and wife are members of the Christian Church.

Judge John Wesley Smith, one of the leading citizens of Union Township, Laclede Co., Mo., was born in Lincoln County, Tenn., in 1812, August 2, and is a son of John W. and Lucinda (Gibson) Smith, natives, respectively, of Rutherford County, Tenn., and Davidson County, N. C. The parents were married in Tennessee, and lived in Lincoln County until 1837, when they moved with their family to Greene County, Mo. The father, who was born in 1790, was a farmer all his life; he died in Greene County in 1878, having survived his wife eight years. The latter was born in 1791, and was the mother of eight children, three of whom are now living: Rev. R. D., who is a minister of the Christian Church, now preaching at Evansville, Ind.; Margaret Ann, the wife of Judge R. D. Dillard, a farmer of Greene County, and John Wesley. At the age of twenty-one years the latter married Matilda Clayton, a native of Lincoln County, Tenn., who was born in 1815, and was a daughter of Stephen Clayton. Mrs. Smith died in Lincoln County in 1836, the mother of one child, also deceased. In 1838 Mr. Smith married Margaret Clark, a native of North Carolina, born in 1817, and a daughter of Spencer Clark. She died in Pope County, Mo., in 1852, leaving five children, all living, viz.: Sarah Jane (wife of W. S. McMenus a farmer of Scott County, Kas.), Nancy E. (wife of Alexander Wilhoit, a farmer of Laclede County, Mo.), Rebecca F. (who married Joseph McMenus, also a farmer of Laclede County), John W. (at home), and Margaret Ann (now the wife of R. H. Tucker, a farmer of Laclede County). In 1853 Mr. Smith married Fidelia M. Wait, a daughter of Russell Wait; she was born at Hatfield, Mass., February 24, 1827. To this union have been born four sons, viz.: Finis E. (a farmer near Phillipsburg), Martin S. (also a farmer of Laclede County), Marcus B. (who died in infancy) and Albert R. (who was born April 3, 1855); the latter married Mary E. Cook, by whom he had one child, Albert R., Jr., and was one of the most enterprising farmers and best citizens of Laclede County at the time of his death, which occurred March 25, 1888. Soon after his marriage our subject engaged in farming, which he continued several years. He moved to Polk County, Mo., in 1851, where he lived until 1853, when he removed to Laclede County, where he has since lived. In 1852 he engaged in merchandising, in which business he continued until 1869. Soon after the close of the war he was appointed judge of the county court, which office he held with credit to himself for seven years. He has also served fourteen years as notary public since coming to Missouri, and has been commissioned justice of the peace seven times. He has now retired from the active duties of public office. In 1832 he was elected an elder of the church, which title he has ever since retained with honor. He is a member of the Masonic fraternity, and in politics is a stanch Prohibitionist, having cast the only Prohibition vote in Phillipsburg precinct. Mrs. Smith is a highly educated woman, and has spent forty-two years of her life teaching. She was a pupil in the North Amherst Academy, and also in the Gothic Seminary at Northampton, Mass., a school of high reputation, and now holds a certificate signed by Drs. Pearson and Brooks, with Dr. Roswell C. Hawks, president of the Mount Holyoke Female Seminary, South Hadley, Mass. From these institutions of learning she has received valuable documents.

Joseph F. Smith, retired, was born in Portsmouth, N. H., September 15, 1816, and is a son of Francis and Martha (Mitchell) Smith, the former a native of New Market, N. H., and the latter a native of Kittery, Me. They moved to Portland, Me., where the father died, but the mother died in Jersey City, N. J. The father was a shoemaker by trade, and followed this occupation during his youth. He was for many years a cutter in one of the largest establishments in Portland. He was a soldier in the War of 1812, and the father of six children, two now living: Samuel, who resides in Kansas, and Joseph F., who was reared in the city of Portland, Me., where he was educated. He served an apprenticeship to the carpenter's and joiner's trade, and was engaged in Boston, Mass., for one summer. He then went South, and helped build up Brunswick, Ga. He assisted in building the first house that was erected in this noted city, going to the woods to hew the timber. He afterward returned to Portland, where he remained a short time, and in 1860 he landed in Lebanon, Mo., coming up on the 'Frisco Railroad, as far as it was completed, which was some distance from Rolla. There he hired wagons to move his property to Lebanon. Previous to this, however, in 1842, he married Miss Martha J. Stearnes, a native of Westfield, Mass., and lived in Chicago one year. He moved from there to St. Louis, where he resided about fifteen years, being engaged in the manufacturing business with Clark, Renfrou & Co., Eagle Foundry. Before leaving he was a partner in the St. Louis Agricultural Works. At this time the population of St. Louis did not exceed 80,000. After coming to Lebanon, Mo., Mr. Smith erected the first steam mill in that city, and this he operated until 1872. During the war he was taken prisoner, was put in the guard house, but was brought out in order to grind their grist, though watched over with a guard and gun. Afterward he had to sleep in the woods for safety. The country was as yet sparsely settled, and Mr. Smith witnessed many hardships during the war, but he stood up to his principles manfully, and pulled through all right, although his life was often threatened. He is now retired from active business life, and is enjoying the fruits of his industry. He has been a member of the I. O. O. F. for over forty years, becoming a member of the St. Louis Lodge No. 5 while living in St. Louis. He is also a member of the Encampment, and is Past Chief Patriarch, having been elected to the Grand Encampment. This is an organization in which Mr. Smith has always taken a great interest, and has been a good and useful member. To Mr. Smith's marriage were born six children, four now living: Fannie, wife of James Appling; Isabel, wife of T. H. Jones; Charles A., and Jennie, wife of Dr. C. F. Wright, of Springfield. Mr. and Mrs. Smith are members of the Congregational Church. While living in St. Louis Mr. Smith was engaged in building circular saw-mills. He put up saw-mills in different portions of the Union, and traveled thousands of miles in order to do so.

C. A. Smith, proprietor of Laclede Roller Mills, and son of Joseph F. and Martha J. Smith, was born in St. Louis June 5, 1848. He was reared in St. Louis until about twelve years of age, when in 1860 he came with his parents to Lebanon, Mo., and here he has since resided. He attended school after coming here until of age, and during the late war was employed as chief clerk in the provost marshal's office. At the age of twenty-one he took charge of the flour and saw-mill which his father had built and owned in Old Lebanon, and operated until 1869. He has since continued the business alone, with the exception of four years, from 1872 to 1876, during which time he had a partner, Mr. J. W. Appling, his brother-in-law. In 1872 he moved the machinery from the old town, having erected a new mill building in the new town of Lebanon, and in 1881 put in the roller process. He now has the best equipped mills in this section. He also runs a saw-mill in connection with his flouring mills. He has recently built a band saw-mill at Arlington, Mo., at an expense of $6,000, which he is now operating. Mr. Smith's band saw-mill was the first in the State of Missouri to be erected outside of St. Louis. He was married in 1876 to Miss Mattie S. Hubbard, of Springfield, Mo., and by whom he has four children living: Charles T., Homer F., Virgil A. and Pauline Smith. One is deceased, named Arthur Paul (who died June 17, 1886, aged twenty months and ten days). Mr. and Mrs. Smith are members of the Congregational Church. He is one of the enterprising and intelligent business men of Laclede County.

George Smith. Prominent among the enterprising and successful farmers of Laclede County, and among those deserving special recognition for their long residence in this county, stands the name of the above mentioned gentleman, who was born in Wilson County, Tenn., July 8, 1825, and is the son of William H. and Lucy W. (Piercy) Smith, natives of Maryland and Virginia, respectively. William H. was born in 1800, and came to Georgia with his parents when a child. They soon after moved to Tennessee. He was the eldest of three children, and attained his growth in Tennessee, where he was married in 1820. In 1838 he and family moved to Missouri, and lived in different counties for some time, but finally settled in Laclede County, Mo., within a mile and a half of where his son George now lives. Here he died in 1877. He led a quiet life, and was a good citizen. His wife, Mrs. Lucy (Piercy) Smith, was born in 1805, and was the daughter of Baswell and Sophia (Woodard) Piercy, natives of Virginia, who came to Tennessee when Mrs. Smith was a small child. They moved to Missouri about the same time the Smith family moved to this State. Mr. Piercy died in 1853, and Mrs. Piercy in 1855. They had four children: Jack, Frank, Martha and Lucy, all deceased but the last named, the mother of our subject, who is still living with her children: George, William B. and Mary (Woodard). One child, Jack, is deceased. Mrs. Lucy Smith is a member of the Methodist Episcopal Church, South, and has enjoyed good health until within the last five years. George Smith, subject of this sketch, received a rather limited education in the old subscription schools of early times, and at the age of twenty-eight started out for himself. He located on the place where he now lives, and here remained until 1885, when he returned to his former place, and there he has since resided. He was married to Miss Anna Craddock, daughter of Edmond and Elizabeth Craddock, both natives of Virginia. Her father died in 1855, and the mother in 1886. Of their fourteen children, Anna was the sixth child in order of birth. She is now living, and is the mother of eight children, one now living, James H., who is the youngest of this family. Four of these children died in infancy; Ellen, died when eight years old; William, choked to death at the age of two years; George, died at the age of eleven months. James H. was born in 1862, and is now living with his parents. He was educated in the common schools and at Lebanon, and is a promising young man. Mr. Smith has been an invalid for over twenty years, and all the business is done by his son, James H. He is a Democrat in politics, and his wife is a member of the Methodist Episcopal Church, South.

William B. Smith, a prominent stock dealer of Auglaize Township, Laclede Co., Mo., was born in Wilson County, Tenn., in January, 1831, and is a son of William H. and Lucy (Piercy) Smith, and grandson of George Smith, who came to Tennessee, where he was married and where his wife died, when William H. was a small boy. George Smith after his marriage moved to Rutherford County, Tenn., and remained in this county until 1845, when he came to Pulaski County, Mo., and later settled in Madison County, where he passed his last days. In early life he had followed the saddlery business. His family consisted of three children, all of whom grew to maturity: William H., Robert and Martenia, all now deceased. William H. was born in Virginia, and came to Tennessee when a child. Here he grew up, married, and afterward settled in Wilson County, Tenn., where he farmed until 1839. He then came to Missouri, locating in Ripley County, now Dent County, but afterward moved to Madison County, where he remained one year. He then moved to Pulaski County, now Laclede County, and finally died in Laclede County in 1880. He had improved a large farm in this county. His wife, Lucy (Piercy) Smith, was born in Virginia, and came to Tennessee when a child. She was married in this State, and became the mother of five children, three now living: George Smith, living on Gasconade River, William B. and Mary Titterington. Mrs. Smith was born in 1802, and is still living at Richland with her daughter, Mrs. Mary Titterington. Mrs. Smith is a member of the Methodist Episcopal Church, South, and takes an active part in all religious work. William B. Smith was but eight or nine years of age when he came to Missouri with his parents, and here he grew to manhood. He received a good common-school education, and December 20, 1855, he married Miss Eglentine Fitzgerald, a native of McMinn County, Tenn., born in 1837, and the daughter of Joseph and Nancy (Thomas) Fitzgerald. Her father was born in Jackson County, Tenn., in 1804, and remained in his native county until seventeen years of age, when he went to Alabama, and from there to East Tennessee. Here he remained until 1852, when he came to Missouri and located on the farm where William B. Smith now lives. He went to Texas during the war, and died there in 1866. His wife was born in Warren County, Ky., in 1808, and was the daughter of James and Mary (Morris) Thomas, who were of English and Welsh descent. Grandfather Morris was killed by the Indians, and some member of the Morris family was a signer of the Declaration of Independence. The parents of Nancy Thomas came to Tennessee, where they passed their last days. Their family consisted of these children: Sarah, Mary, James, Esther, John, Eglentine, Joseph and Edward. Those deceased were named Margaret and Rachel. The mother of these children is yet living, and is one of the oldest members of the Christian Church, having joined the church when twenty-two years of age. After marriage, in 1856, Mr. Smith located in Smith Township, where he remained until 1871, when he came to the present location, where he has a good farm of 480 acres, with 150 under cultivation. To his marriage were born thirteen children, but the eldest, James, died when two years of age; Lulu, wife of John Winfrey; Joseph, George, Edwin, Willie (at home), Mollie, Robert, Imogene, Hugh, Merton, Eglentine and Ethel. Mr. Smith does not take a very active part in politics, but votes the Democratic ticket. He is a member of the Masonic fraternity, and is one of the county's most successful farmers and stock raisers.

W. Spohn, farmer, was born near Dayton, Ohio, June 16, 1833, and is a son of Elias and Mary (Kellar) Spohn, natives of Maryland. They immigrated to Montgomery County, Ohio, and settled near Dayton in 1816, being among the earliest settlers of that region. They purchased a farm, and here the father lived until his death, which occurred when he was nearly ninety years of age. He served in the War of 1812, was at the battle of Baltimore, and was present at the death of Gen. Ross. Of the nine children born to his marriage W. Spohn is the youngest. He was educated near Dayton, and when seventeen years of age he was apprenticed to the cabinet-making trade, and served his time. He worked at his trade until coming to Missouri, since which time he has been engaged in agricultural pursuits. Previous to coming to Missouri he lived one year in Greene County, Ohio, and sixteen years in Logan County, of the same State. In 1870 he came to Laclede County, Mo., purchased a farm, and here he has since resided, near Lebanon, engaged in stock raising in connection with his farming interests. He owns ninety acres of land, nearly all under cultivation, and has one of the best small farms in Laclede County. He was married in 1855 to Miss Victoria Sharp, a native of Logan County, Ohio, and they became the parents of six children, five now living: Clara, Myrtie, Chase, Justin and Ernest.

Dr. John Q. Titterington, physician, farmer and stock dealer, of Laclede County, Mo., is a native of Cumberland County, Ky., where he was born February 12, 1826. His parents, Adam and Sarah (Smith) Titterington, were originally from Belfast, Ireland, and Virginia, respectively. The father, who was born in 1783, was educated in his native city, and when eighteen years of age came to the United States, and located in Kentucky, where he was married to Miss Smith, who had moved there with her parents at an early day. He was engaged in farming and school-teaching for a number of years, and was a graduate in medicine, but never practiced that profession. On coming to America he took an active interest in politics, and was a

Jacksonian Democrat. He was a member of the Christian Church, and died August 17, 1856, at the age of seventy-six years, his wife dying in 1837. She was born in 1794. Their union was blessed in the birth of twelve children, all of whom grew to maturity, and five are now living: James (the eldest of the family, was a graduate of the Louisville (Ky.) Medical College, and was one of the oldest practitioners of Laclede County, but is now a resident of Pulaski County), John Q., Daniel (a house carpenter, of Dallas, Tex.), Alfred W. (a practicing physician, of Richland, Mo.) and Elizabeth (widow of Mr. Merrit). The father was married twice, and by his second wife became the father of two children: Caroline (Mrs Hamilton, of Clarksville, Tenn.), and a son, who is deceased. Their mother died in 1864. Dr. John Q. Titterington grew to maturity in Christian and Caldwell Counties, Ky., and received his education at Princeton, Ky., and in 1850 began the study of medicine under Dr. Young, two years later entering the St. Louis Medical College, and the following year began practicing his profession in Laclede County, Mo., and the next year located in Marionville, Lawrence County. After residing in this place for seven years he entered the Confederate army as second surgeon, and served four years, after which he located in Greene County, Ill. Here he resided only ten months, when he again settled in Missouri, taking up his residence in Franklin County, and in 1869 came to Laclede County, where he has since made his home. He has a very extensive practice, and is one of the acknowledged leaders of the medical profession in Laclede County. June 1, 1854, he was married to Elizabeth Wilks, who was born in Alabama March 9, 1836. She came to Missouri with her parents when a child, and located in Lawrence County, on Buck Prairie, where descendants of the family are still living. Two of their five children are living: Jesse M. (who is a graduate of the Nashville Medical College, and is now one of the leading physicians of Marionville, Mo.), and Mary (Mrs. Smith, of St. Louis). Those deceased are James H. (who died in infancy), Sarah A. (whose death occurred at the age of about two years) and Robert D. (who died when twenty-two years of age). He was a graduate of the Christian Biblical College, of St Louis, and the St. Louis Medical College before he was twenty-one years of age; was one of the most promising young men of the county, and gave promise of becoming one of the leading physicians of the State. He had built up a good practice, and was respected and esteemed by all who knew him. He died on the 27th of October, 1888.

Hillory M. Turner, farmer, of Auglaize Township, was born in Caswell County, N. C., in 1821, and is a son of Thomas and Celia (Wear) Turner, whose sketch appears in another portion of this work. Hillory M. attained his majority in North Carolina, and was educated in the common schools of Caswell County. In 1858 he began tilling the farm on which he now lives, but during the late Civil War made his home in Texas, residing in that State until 1866, when he returned to the home place. On the 17th of September, 1857, he was united in marriage to Miss Mary M. Hawkins, who was born in Pulaski County,

Mo., and by her became the father of the following family of children: William, Alice, John, May, Edward, Blanche, Virgil and Zoe. Those deceased are Robert and an infant not named. Mr. Turner is a Democrat in politics, and has always taken a deep interest in all matters pertaining to the public weal. He is a member of the A. F. & A. M., the Agricultural Wheel, and he and wife are members of the Methodist Episcopal Church, South.

Andrew J. Turner, ex-judge of the county and a prominent farmer of Auglaize Township, was born in Caswell County, N. C., in 1835, and is a son of Thomas and Celia (Wear) Turner. The father was born in Halifax County, Va., November 15, 1790, and was the youngest child of Martin and Elizabeth Turner. Martin was born in England and came to the United States when a child, his parents both dying on the ocean while *en route* to America. He attained his majority in Virginia, and after becoming grown was married to a Miss Lipscomb, who was born in King Williams County, Va., about 1810. After their marriage they went to North Carolina by wagon, and reared their family of ten children in Caswell County. Thomas Turner was in his twentieth year when his parents moved to North Carolina, and while a resident of that State he enlisted in the War of 1812, serving until the close. He was one of the leading men of his county, and in 1842 came with his family, overland, to Missouri, making Springfield their home for two years. He then located in what is now Laclede County, where he improved a large farm and resided until the breaking out of the late war, when he went South and resided in Texas four years, then returning to the farm in Missouri, where he died in 1875. His wife was born in Caswell County, N. C., in 1800, and died February 1, 1862, while a resident of Texas. Four of their eight children are now living: Hillory M., William and Meriwether (deceased), John C. (deceased), Robert D., Mildred S. (deceased), Andrew J. and Thomas B. The father was first married to Elizabeth Fisher, by whom he had one son, Rufus A., who is residing in Texas. Mr. Turner was a member of the A. F. & A. M. Andrew J. Turner grew to manhood in Laclede County, and attended the common schools and the high-school of Lebanon. He has resided on his present farm since 1858, with the exception of six years during the late war, when he moved his family to Texas, and there enlisted, in February, 1862, in Company G, Winston's Battalion, being afterward transferred to the Missouri Department, in which he served during the remainder of the war. He was at the battles of Lexington, the first siege of Corinth, Prairie Grove and Little Rock. After the cessation of hostilities he returned with his family to Missouri (1867), and in 1874 was elected judge of the county court for a term of two years. November 18, 1858, he married Miss Laura L. Payton, who was born in Maury County, Tenn., March 13, 1840, and is a daughter of Henry and Elizabeth Payton, who came to Laclede County, Mo., in 1855, and engaged in farming. The father died in 1857, but the mother is still living, and makes her home with Mr. Turner. Mrs. Payton was born in Maury County, Tenn., September 29, 1807, and after the death of Mr. Payton was married to John Ragland, a native of Virginia, who died in 1876. Of the five children born to her first union three grew to maturity, but all are now deceased, with the exception of Mrs. Turner. To Mr. and Mrs. Turner nine children have been born: Ella, wife of Samuel R. Fulbright; Thomas A., Robert B., Bettie F., Maude A., Henry P., Elmo M., Edna E. and Myrtle O. Mrs. Turner is a member of the Christian Church, and he is a member of the A. F. & A. M., of the Blue Lodge and the Agricultural Wheel. He is a stanch Democrat in politics.

Thomas B. Turner was born in Caswell County, N. C., July 3, 1837, and is a son of Thomas and Celia (Wear) Turner, a short biography of whom is given with the sketch of Andrew J. Turner. Thomas B. is the youngest son of the above parents, and was brought by them to Missouri at an early day, and attended one term of school (his first) at Springfield. After locating in Laclede County his educational advantages were very limited, owing to the newness of the country, and what schooling he received was in the primitive log school-house of pioneer times. He remained with his parents until the breaking out of the late Civil War, when he enlisted and served for a short time in Pleasant's Battalion, and then came home on furlough, but was captured by the Federals and taken to Rolla, thence to St. Louis, and was afterward taken to Alton, Ill. At this place his health became very much impaired, and in compliance with the prison surgeon's advice, he took the oath of allegiance, and returned home. Here he remained until the summer of 1862, when he obtained a passport and went to his parents in Texas, and the following year went with a command under Townson to the Gulf of Mexico, where he remained until the early winter of 1864, and then went to the Red River country. He then joined Company I, Fourth Missouri Cavalry Volunteers, Marmaduke's brigade, Burbridge's regiment, and served until Price made his raid through Missouri. He was captured in Kansas, taken to Fort Scott, thence to Warrensburg on foot, and from there by rail to St. Louis, where he was retained two or three months. He was next taken to Johnson's Island and thence to Akin's Landing, then to Richmond and afterward to Mobile, but before reaching the latter place, the city had surrendered. Mr. Turner was then paroled and made his way back to his command, but was taken sick at Atlanta, Ga., and was obliged to remain in that city six weeks. News then came that Lee had surrendered, but Mr. Turner was delayed again at Vaiden, Miss., on account of sickness, and did not reach home for three or four months. He made his way to his friends in Texas, and in the fall of 1867 returned with them to Laclede County, where he has since been extensively engaged in farming and stock raising. His wife, who was formerly Miss Josephine T. Jordan, was born in Dahlonega, Lumpkin Co., Ga., June 22, 1847, and was educated in the Fountain Hill Academy, of Tennessee, which institution she attended four years. She was then engaged in teaching school from fifteen to twenty-four years of age, the most of the time in Johnson and Camden Counties, Mo. Her marriage with Mr. Turner was blessed in the birth of four children: Claude J., Walter L., Jeane L. and Ora T. Mr. Turner is a member of the A. F. & A. M., the A.

O. U. W., and he and wife are members of the Christian Church. Mrs. Turner's parents, John and Sarah (Scruggs) Jordan, were born in Virginia and Tennessee, respectively, and the father was a saddler and a farmer and stock dealer by occupation. In 1848 he made a trip south, and is supposed to have been killed by a band of free negroes, who at that time infested the country. His widow was married in Tennessee in 1856, and came to Missouri in the fall of 1860, and is at present residing in Greene County, Mo. She became the mother of one daughter, Mrs. Turner. Mrs. Turner is a granddaughter of Rev. John Scruggs, of Monroe County, Tenn., a history of whose family is given in the History of East Tennessee.

Judge W. I. Wallace, circuit judge of the Fourteenth Judicial Circuit, and one of the prominent men of Laclede County, Mo., is the son of Zebina and Lucinda (French) Wallace, who were of Scotch-Irish descent. The Wallaces trace their genealogical ancestry back to the earliest colonists immigrating to Massachusetts. The paternal grandfather, Seth Wallace, was born in Massachusetts, but immigrated to the State of New York, where he passed his last days. He was a farmer by occupation, as were most of the family; was a soldier in the Revolutionary War, and was noted for his bravery. Zebina Wallace resided in Vermont until 1859, when he moved to Dane County, Wis., purchasing a farm near Madison, and here resided until his death, which occurred in 1881. He was a tanner by trade, which he learned in his youth, but his last days were spent on the farm. The mother died in 1883. They were the parents of nine sons, seven yet living: William, Christopher, Dewitt C., Jonathan C., Francis E., Washington I. and Joseph W. One remarkable feature of this family is that on the father's side the grandfather and father died at the age of eighty-five years, and on the mother's side the grandparents died at the age of eighty-five and eighty-four, respectively. Judge W. I. Wallace was born December 25, 1840, on the Green Mountains, in Franklin County, Mass. Here he was reared until fifteen years of age, when he went with his parents to Wisconsin, and in that State received his education. Being desirous of fitting himself for a professional life, he chose the law course, and took particular interest in his choice. He attended the University of Wisconsin, where he graduated in the year 1864. He also attended the Ann Arbor College, where he graduated in the law course in the spring of 1866. He came directly to Lebanon, Mo., where he entered into partnership with A. D. Groesbeck, a leading attorney and a very estimable gentleman. The firm continued as Groesbeck & Wallace until Mr. Groesbeck's death, which occurred in 1870. Since that date Mr. Wallace has continued the practice alone. His unusual ability won for him a large practice and considerable prominence. In 1868 he was elected prosecuting attorney, anp served until 1870. In 1876 he was sent as a member to the State Senate, where he served faithfully for four years. In 1884 he was elected to his present position of circuit judge (he having seven counties in his circuit), and was re-elected in 1886. He has held several other offices of public trust, and has filled all in an honorable and satisfactory manner. In 1863 he enlisted in Company D, Fortieth Wisconsin Infantry, and served until the regiment was mustered out. He was offered an officer's position, but refused to accept. He participated in many of the severe skirmishes, and was a brave and gallant soldier. He was married in 1876 to Miss Louisa Groesbeck. They have one child, Clara. Judge Wallace and wife are members of the Congregational Church, and he is also a member of the Masonic fraternity, and has passed all its degrees.

George S. Warner, of Union Township, Laclede County, was born in Shelby, Orleans Co., N. Y., December 11, 1853, and is the son of Joseph B. and Lodema (Rusk) Warner, natives of Connecticut, now living in Orleans County, N. Y., at the advanced ages of eighty-nine and eighty-eight years, respectively. The parents removed to Orleans County after their marriage, where they have since lived and devoted their attention to the pursuit of agriculture. Both have been members of the Methodist Episcopal Church for many years. They have had eight children, four sons and four daughters, viz.: William J., a farmer of Laclede County, Mo.; Mary D., widow of William F. Parker, of Kalamazoo, Mich.;, Octavo, at home; Sarah, wife of Ogden Bailey, of Orleans County, N. Y.; James, a farmer of Orleans County; George S.; Francis, a farmer near Cleveland, Ohio; Antoinette, wife of Ira Howland, a farmer near Centerville, N. Y. When in his twentieth year George S. Warner was employed by the United States Express Company as a messenger between Davenport and Keokuk; he was afterward in the employ of the American Express Company from Burlington to Council Bluffs, and later worked for the Union Pacific Express Company from Cheyenne to Ogden. In 1878 he located in Laclede County, Mo., on a farm, which he had bought two years before, and which he has since successfully conducted. He now owns 236 acres of land, and has one of the finest farms in the county. March 4, 1884, Mr. Warner married Martha O'Neal, who was born in Virginia in 1864, and is a daughter of Thomas A. O'Neal. One child has blessed this union, whose name is Frances Lodema. Mr. and Mrs. Warner are members of the Methodist Episcopal Church. Mr. Warner is also a member of the Masonic fraternity, and in politics his sympathies are with the Democratic party. He is one of the enterprising young men of Laclede County, and is deservedly popular.

Conrad Weissgerber was born in Hessen Darmstadt, Germany, June 19, 1821, being the son of Adam and Catharine Weissgerber, both natives of Germany. He was a burgomaster and prominent man, both in church and State. He was a soldier under the English Government for sixteen years, and fought in Spain. He died at the age of seventy-two. His mother died in 1841. They had seven children, all of whom grew to maturity, two of whom are living in Germany. Conrad Weissgerber came to this country in the spring of 1847, at the age of twenty-four years. He landed at New Orleans, and worked at cabinet-making for about eight years. He then went to Warren County, Mo., where he stayed for two years, and then went to Davenport, Iowa, where he met with great losses, through a cyclone striking the town. He then went to Chicago, where he was married on the 26th of July, 1856, to Miss Theresa Doffeller, a native also of Germany, by whom he became the father of four children, of whom only one is living, his son George, who is in Baton Rouge, La., engaged in farming. Mr. Weissgerber now moved to Baton Rouge, La., where he, together with his brother Christian, opened a confectionery business, but the war breaking out soon after, they went back to Chicago, where Mrs. Weissgerber died in 1864. In 1865 Mr. Weissgerber took for his second wife Miss Emma Kunze, a native of Germany, who came to this country at the age of fifteen. This marriage resulted in the birth of four children, of whom three are living: Lena, Otto and Theresa. In 1866 he came to Laclede County, where he followed farming in Hooker Township. He is the owner of a large tract of land, and is one of the representative farmers of the county. He is a member of the Lutheran Church, and is an honest, upright citizen. He moved to Lebanon in 1888, where he now resides.

R. J. Wickersham, postmaster at Lebanon, Mo., was born in Woodford County, Ky., June 6, 1834, being the son of Isaac and Nancy (Wiggs) Wickersham, the father a native of Virginia and the mother of Kentucky. Isaac Wickersham moved to Springfield, Ill., at quite an early date, and here he engaged in merchandising with R. F. Herndon's father, who is now one of the most extensive merchants of that city. From there Mr. Wickersham moved to St. Louis, where he embarked in the livery business and dealt in stock quite extensively. He moved to Lebanon, Mo., in 1859, and in 1861 he moved to Arkansas. He died in Carthage, Mo. His son, R. J. Wickersham, was reared in Kentucky until eight years of age, when he accompanied his parents to Springfield, Ill., and here he was educated. He then went with his parents to St. Louis, where he assisted his father in buying and taking care of stock. He came to Lebanon in 1859, and at the breaking out of the war he raised a company and started out with it as its captain. He took his company south, and in Arkansas it was disbanded, and he entered the Confederate service. Mr. Wickersham again raised a company on the border of Arkansas, and joined Col. Robert Wood's Battalion, Confederate States Army, in which he was major. After Price's raid through Missouri Mr. Wickersham was promoted to the rank of lieutenant-colonel, and was paroled at Shreveport, La. On their transportation on Red River on the steamer "Kentucky," when about ten miles below Shreveport, the vessel sank, and some 1,500 lives were lost. Mr. Wickersham lost two valuable horses and all his possessions. He participated in the battles of Springfield, Mo., Pea Ridge, Jenkins' Ferry and others. He was paroled at Shreveport, La., in 1865, and afterward returned to Cotton Plant, Ark., where he made his home until 1868, when he came to Lebanon, Mo., in 1869. Since that time he has been engaged in buying stock for a St. Louis firm, and has probably bought more stock than any man in the Southwest. In 1885 he was appointed postmaster, which office he has held since. He was mayor of the city one term, but resigned before the term expired. He was married August 6, 1855, to Miss Mary Weigle, of St. Louis, and by whom he has nine children: Nannie, wife of Josiah Ivey; Ella, wife of William Watt, resides near Lincoln, Neb.; Lou., wife of Arthur L. Palmer; Mattie, wife of Eugene Hooker; Bettie L., Sallie, Mary, Abra and Vic.

James H. Wickersham, county clerk, was born in Versailles, Woodford Co., Ky., and is the son of Isaac and Nancy (Wiggs) Wickersham, both natives of Kentucky. The parents moved to Springfield, Ill., at an early period, and here the father engaged in merchandising, which he followed for seven years. On leaving, R. F. Herndon succeeded him, and this gentleman is now one of the largest merchants of Springfield. Mr. Wickersham moved to St. Louis, where he remained for ten years, being engaged in the stock business and in merchandising. He was a stone mason by trade, which occupation he followed in his youth. Both parents are now deceased. Of the ten children born to their union four are living: Sarah, Richard, James and John The subject of this sketch was reared principally in St. Louis, and there received the greater part of his education, finishing at Lebanon Academy, whither he had moved in 1857. In 1861, in a company commanded by R. J. Wickersham (a brother), he enlisted and went out as lieutenant. After the siege of Vicksburg he was promoted to the rank of captain, in which position he remained until the close of the war. He was engaged in all the principal battles of the campaign: Springfield, Elk Horn, Corinth, Baker's Creek, siege of Vicksburg, Rome (Ga.), Altoona, Peach Tree Creek, Atlanta (Ga.), Franklin (Tenn.) and Blakely (Ala.). He was captured at Vicksburg and paroled. After six weeks in camp he was captured at Blakely, Ala., sent to Ship Island, thence to New Orleans, thence to Jackson, Miss., and paroled. After the war he located at Cotton Plant, Ark., where he was engaged in merchandising until 1870, when he returned to Lebanon. In 1872 he went to St. Louis, where he engaged in the real estate business and where he remained until 1874. He then returned to Lebanon, and traveled for the Lebanon Woolen Manufacturing Company until 1876, when he was employed by Wallace Bros., wholesale and retail merchants, as book-keeper, and there remained until elected to the office of county clerk in 1886, his term expiring in 1890. Mr. Wickersham is a public-spirited and enthusiastic citizen. He is a Democrat in his political views.

George Wood, a farmer residing in Osage Township, Laclede Co., Mo., was born in Warren County, Ky., January 25, 1824, being a son of George and Winnie (Lawny) Wood, natives of Virginia and North Carolina, respectively. They were among the early pioneers of Kentucky, and became the parents of nine children, the father dying in 1855, and the mother in 1882. The father was a shoemaker by trade. George Wood, their son, received a common-school education in his native county, and while still residing there was married in 1855 to Miss Mary M. Downey, a native of Kentucky, and a daughter of Abram and Patsey Downey. Mr. Downey was the father of seven children, a farmer by occupation, and has been dead for many years. Soon after his marriage Mr. Wood came to Laclede County, Mo., and purchased 240 acres of land, forty acres of which were cleared. He now owns 360 acres of land, 200 acres of which are cleared and in cultivation, and for the past thirty years he has been extensively engaged in rearing cattle, horses, hogs and sheep. He and wife became the parents of eleven children, two of whom are deceased. Those living are Martha E. (wife of William Owens), Carter (married to Lydia Edwards), Thomas, Jane, David W., Eli, Charley, Alice, Mary and Frank. Winnie A. and Abram died while young. Mr. and Mrs. Wood are members of the United Baptist Church, and he is a Democrat politically, and has served many years as a member of the school board. He is one of the thorough farmers of Missouri, and is recognized as one of the leading citizens of his county.

Isom Wood, stock farmer of Osage Township, was born in Tennessee in 1832, and is the son of James and Sarah (Davis) Wood, both natives of South Carolina. They came to Tennessee with their parents when children, and grew to maturity in that State. They were married there, and when Isom Wood was a small boy they moved to Indiana, settling in Gibson County, where they remained until 1854. They then came to Stoddard County, Mo., where they purchased land, etc. He was a soldier in the War of 1812, and led a very active life as a farmer. He died in 1864 at the age of sixty-nine years. The mother died in May, 1863, at the age of sixty-four. To their union were born twelve children, all of whom lived to be grown, and four are now living. Isom Wood was the seventh child in order of birth, and remained at home until twenty five years of age, when he married, in March, 1857, Miss Fannie M. Bollinger, who was born and reared in Stoddard County, Mo., and who is the daughter of Frederick and Margaret Bollinger, natives of North Carolina. Her parents came to Missouri when she was a child, and located in Stoddard County, where Mrs. Wood grew to womanhood. By this union Mr. and Mrs. Wood became the parents of eight children, three of whom are deceased: Albert L., Henry, Richard, Margaret (wife of George Simpson) and Julia A. (at home). Albert and Henry are married, and live in Laclede County, Mo. Mr. Wood and wife are members of the Baptist Church, and he is a member of the Masonic fraternity. He is a Democrat in politics, and is at present postmaster at Drynob Post-office, he being appointed in 1881. After his marriage Mr. Wood settled on the home place, where he remained until after the death of his parents, when he sold his interest and moved to Texas in 1867. He returned to Arkansas the following year, and after a residence of about one year in that State moved to Stoddard County, Mo., and then to Laclede County two years later. Here he has since resided. He served in the State Militia six months under Jeff. Thompson, and during the latter part of the war he served in the Enrolled Militia for three months, when Gen. Price was making his raid in Southern Missouri. He was wounded at Belmont, Mo., while on duty.

H. T. Wright, circuit clerk and hardware merchant, of Lebanon, was born in Portland, Me., January 30, 1848, and is the son of Henry B. and Harriet (Hayes) Wright, both natives of Maine, and of English origin. The Wright family were among the colonists who settled in

Massachusetts in 1620, and one Christopher Wright, of whom mention is made in the late English histories, was one of the Guy Fawkes plotters. The paternal grandfather, Christopher Wright, was born in Marshfield, Mass., and immigrated to Portland, Me., where he was among the earliest settlers. During his early life he was engaged in merchandising, and his latter days were spent as director in some large institution. The maternal grandfather, Reuben Hayes, was born in North Yarmouth, Me., and spent his entire life there. He was a tiller of the soil. Henry B. Wright, father of our subject, was born in Portland, Me., and here passed his days. He died in December, 1853. He was for eighteen years president and secretary of the Ocean Insurance Company, of Portland, Me. H. T. Wright, our subject, was the only child born to his parents. He secured a good practical education in the schools of Yarmouth, and at the age of sixteen he went to sea, where three years afterward he was made second in command, and made voyages to Europe, South America, Australia and Callao, Peru, on the western coast. He followed the sea for six years. In the winter of 1870 he came west and located at Lebanon, Mo., where he followed farming until 1874, being then elected county clerk, which office he held until 1876. In 1883 he engaged in the hardware business, which he has since conducted. In 1886 he was elected to the office of clerk of the circuit court, a position he still holds. He is a member of the school board, being president of the same at this date. He is secretary of the Laclede and Lebanon Loan and Building Associations; is a member of the Masonic fraternity, of which he is Past Master, Past High Priest and Past Eminent Commander. He was married in 1873 to Miss Martha L. Munger, a native of Oswego, N. Y., who bore him six children: Harriet B., Grace E., George R., James H., Henry F. and Louisa T. Mrs. Wright is a member of the Congregational Church.

Robert N. Young, a prominent merchant, postmaster and express agent of Phillipsburgh, Laclede Co., Mo., was born in Ripley County, Mo., May 12, 1847, and is a son of Jeremiah and Margaret Ann (Neil) Young, also natives of Ripley County, Mo. The parents removed to Carroll County, Ark., when Robert N. was a child, and afterward went to Franklin County, whence they removed again to Baxter County, where they lived until their deaths. The father was accidentally killed, during the late war, by his own party, and died in 1863, at the age of forty-five years. Mrs. Young died in 1862. Both were members of the Methodist Episcopal Church. When a young man, Jeremiah Young learned the carpenter's trade, becoming very successful, and at the time of his death he owned considerable property. Of their family of eight children four are now living, viz.: Campbell W., a blacksmith by trade, is a resident of Arkansas; Mary C. is the wife of R. O. Hardy, and is a school-teacher of Conway, Mo.; Maggie is the wife of James Hughes, foreman of the woolen mills at Lebanon, Mo. Robert N., the second child in the family and the oldest now living, received his education in Arkansas, and after his father's death he went to Springfield and enlisted in Company B, Second Missouri Light Artillery, Federal service, and served until

December 20, 1865. He was then discharged, the war having closed, and arrived in Phillipsburgh, Mo., the following Christmas Day, and Laclede County has ever since been his home. After the war he learned the blacksmith's trade, at which he worked for twelve years in different parts of the county. He then located in Phillipsburgh and engaged in the mercantile business, starting in with a limited stock of groceries. He now carries a general line of goods, and is doing a good business. He owns the old homestead, in Baxter County, Ark., consisting of 320 acres, a good portion of which is under cultivation, and also a farm in Union Township. December 29, 1866, Mr. Young married Sarah T. Popejoy, who was born in Dallas County, Mo., in 1848, and is a daughter of Alexander Popejoy. Two sons have been born to them, Charles J. and Timothy N. In 1871 Mr. Young was appointed postmaster of Phillipsburgh, which office he has ever since held, with credit to himself and the satisfaction of the community. He is also ticket agent and express agent of the railroad, and is one of the live and energetic citizens of Phillipsburgh. He is a Mason and a member of the G. A. R., and politically is a Democrat.

PULASKI COUNTY.

W. Spencer Adams, a farmer and stock raiser of Liberty Township, was born in Clark County, Ky., in 1827. His father, Elcanah Adams, was born in Culpeper County, Va., in 1806, and was married in Kentucky in 1825 to Margerie Tredway, who was born in Clark County, Ky., in 1804, and was a daughter of Joel Tredway, whose wife was a sister of Judge William and Col. John Thornton, two prominent citizens of Northwestern Missouri. After their marriage the parents of our subject removed to Ray County, Mo., where the mother died in 1881. The father was a soldier in the Mormon War in Missouri, and died in Kansas in 1865. The latter was a son of J. Spencer Adams, of Virginia, an early settler of Kentucky, a soldier in the War of 1812, and a large slave-holder. He lived to be over one hundred years old, and was of English descent. W. Spencer Adams was the eldest of seven children, of whom five are now living. He was reared in Ray County, Mo., and received his education in the common schools. In 1851 he married Martha A. Phillips, daughter of Jesse and Polly Phillips, natives of Kentucky and early settlers of Ray County, Mo., where Mrs. Adams was born. Six children have been born to Mr. and Mrs. Adams, all of whom are living, viz.: Rufus, Thomas Luther, of Laclede County, Mo.; Nancy Jane, wife of Franklin Miller; Margerie Catherine, Mollie L., wife of Joseph Miller, and Stacy, who married Albert Harrison, of Laclede County. Having lost his property during the war Mr. Adams moved to Pulaski County, then a comparatively new country, and as a reward of honest industry and enterprise he has been successful in the pursuit of agriculture, now owning a good farm of 160 acres on the Gasconade River. During the war he served two or three years in the Missouri State Militia, and, though formerly a Whig, has been a Democrat since the war. In 1849 he crossed the plains to California, but was unable to mine, and returned the following year by way of the Isthmus of Panama. Mrs. Adams is a member of the Baptist Church.

Andrew R. Bailey, postmaster of Bailey, and a successful farmer of Pulaski County, Mo., was born in Mahoning County, Ohio, in 1842, and is the eighth of ten children born to the union of David and Elizabeth (Early) Bailey, who were of Scotch and Irish descent, born in Connecticut and Pennsylvania in 1800 and 1804, and died in Ohio in 1862 and 1872, respectively. The father was a farmer, and became a resident of Ohio in 1805, and he and wife were worthy and consistent members of the Presbyterian Church. Andrew R. Bailey received his early education in Coitsville, Ohio, and remained with his parents until the breaking out of the war, when he enlisted in Company C, Fifty-seventh Regiment Pennsylvania Volunteers, and after participating in the siege of Yorktown, the battles of Williamsburg and Fair Oaks, being wounded in the latter engagement, he received his discharge in December, 1862, and returned home, where he was married in 1864 to Miss Artie M. Brownlee, who was born in Coitsville, Ohio, in 1847. Her parents, Thomas and Martha Brownlee, were of Scotch descent. To Mr. and Mrs. Bailey were born five children: Preston T., Mattie, Carrie L., Lester M. and Jennie E. In 1865 Mr. Bailey removed with his family to Mercer County, Penn., and in 1876 immigrated to Missouri, locating in Pulaski County, where he owns a fine farm of 417 acres. He has 125 acres under cultivation, and is in a prosperous condition financially. He votes the Republican ticket, and in 1864, while residing in Ohio, was elected to the office of assessor, holding the position one term, and after moving to Pennsylvania was elected to the same office, which he held three consecutive terms. In 1880 he was appointed census enumerator for Roubideaux and Piney Townships, in Pulaski County, and in 1879 was made postmaster of Bailey Post-office, which received its name from him. He and wife and three children are members of the United Presbyterian Church.

Bland N. Ballard, farmer and stockman, of Cullen Township, Pulaski Co., Mo., is a native of Sangamon County, Ill., born in 1834. His father, Bland N. Ballard, was a native of the "Palmetto State," born in 1800, and when a young man went to Overton County, Tenn., where he met and married Miss Margaret Smelser, who was a native of that county, born in 1801. In 1833 he moved to Sangamon County, Ill., and four years later came to Pulaski County, Mo., where he spent the remainder of his days, dying in 1861. He was an influential citizen of Pulaski County for many years, and held the following offices: sheriff and collector, circuit and county clerk, a member of the State Legislature and probate county judge. To him and wife, who died in 1873, six children were born, Bland N. being their third child. He resided with his father until the latter's death, and then his mother made her home with him. His marriage to Miss Sarah White was celebrated in October, 1867. She was born in Springfield, Mo., in 1841, and became the mother of five children: Maggie, Olive, Charles, Cora and Sallie. Her death occurred in March, 1878, and in January, 1879, Mr. Ballard wedded Elizabeth Bradford, a daughter of Neely Bradford, by whom he became the father of four children: Lucy, Samuel, Neely and Winnie. Mrs. Ballard was born in Phelps County, Mo., in 1842. Mr. Ballard's first investment in land was seventy-six acres, which he bought in 1866, but he has since increased his acreage until he now owns 102 in the home tract and 198 acres in another. In 1888 he erected a handsome and commodious two-story frame residence, at a cost of $800. In 1861 he enlisted in Company A, under Col. Stein, and served four years, being a participant in a number of engagements. He was captured near Fort Smith, and taken to St. Louis, where he was kept a prisoner for about nine months, when he was paroled, and returned home. He has always been a Democrat in politics, has been a member of the Methodist Episcopal Church, South, for about fifteen years, and is a Master Mason.

Wellington Barlow, a farmer and nurseryman of Liberty Township, was born in Washington County, Va., in 1822, and was the sixth in the family of ten children born to Jacob and Dorcas (Gross) Barlow. Jacob Barlow, who was a soldier in the War of 1812, died about 1830. A part of the family subsequently removed to Kentucky, where the mother died about 1850. She was a member of the Baptist Church, and was a daughter of John Gross, an Englishman. Wellington received his education in the common subscription schools, to which he was obliged to walk several miles. January 1, 1845, he married Nancy, daughter of Nathaniel Stamper, a native of North Carolina, but one of the pioneers of Kentucky, where Mrs. Barlow was born. Mr. Stamper afterward removed to Missouri, where he lived until his death, which occurred about 1883. Of the twelve children born to Mr. and Mrs. Barlow, six are now living: Pennis, Joseph W., Sarah (wife of John Nelson), R. Lincoln, Catherine and Sherman. In 1848 Mr. Barlow removed to near Burlington, Iowa, where he lived until 1866, then coming to Pulaski County, Mo., on the Gasconade, where he has since improved and still owns a good farm of 160 acres, on which, in 1868, he established a nursery. In this business he has been very successful. He raises some small stock, but pays particular attention to the growth of apple and peach trees. Mr. Barlow is a Democrat in politics, and cast his first presidential vote for Polk in 1844. He has been a member of the Baptist Church since about 1840. Mrs. Barlow died in the fall of 1877, having also been a member of the Baptist Church for many years.

Hon. Solomon Bartlett, farmer, and proprietor of a saw and grist mill on the Gasconade River, in Cullen Township, was born in Miller County, Mo., in 1831, being a son of John M. and Elizabeth (Russell) Bartlett, who were born in Kentucky in 1798 and 1800, and died in Missouri in 1871 and 1848, respectively. The father was of French descent, and was married about 1818, coming to Miller County, Mo., in 1820, but afterward became a resident of Moniteau County. Seven of their twelve children are living: Solomon, Nancy (widow of

B. P. Sailling), Louisa, John G., Reuben H., Hiram F. and Sarah. Solomon resided on his father's farm until seventeen years of age, when he left home and took the overland route to California, making the trip in ninety days. He spent three years in that State working in the mines, and in 1853 returned home via the Isthmus of Panama and New York City, and located in Moniteau County, where he was engaged in merchandising for three years, and then sold out, and the following two years was engaged in farming. In 1854 he married Miss Martha Matthews, who was born in Boone County, Mo., in 1833, and died in 1874, having borne two children: Crocia Ann, wife of A. B. Brownfield, and George W. In 1877 Mr. Bartlett married Miss Martha Bond, who was born in Miller County, Mo., in 1846, and died in 1881. In 1857 he became a citizen of Pulaski County, Mo., and purchased sixteen acres of land, and began operating a saw and grist mill which was on the land. He erected his present mill in 1866, which is provided with two buhrs, the saw-mill being run by water power. In politics he is a Democrat, and in 1864 was elected to the State Legislature, and served one term. The same year he enlisted in Company A, Forty-eighth Regiment Missouri Volunteer Infantry, United States Army, as second lieutenant, and was promoted to first lieutenant, and in June, 1865, was discharged at St. Louis. After the war he was elected as supervisor of registration, and served two years.

Larkin Rufus Bates, farmer and stock dealer, of Cullen Township, was born in Phelps County, Mo., in 1838, and is a son of Larkin and Elizabeth (Thrailkill) Bates, who were born in Kentucky in 1801 and 1800, and died in Missouri in 1850 and 1858, respectively. They were married about 1820, and soon after immigrated to Missouri, locating in Phelps County, where they resided until 1841, when they came to Pulaski County, and settled on the farm now owned by their son, Larkin R. Bates. They were among the pioneer settlers, and the father built a saw-mill on his farm, the site of which is now owned by Solomon Bartlett. Larkin Rufus Bates is the sixth of their eight children, and is the only one now living. He resided with his parents until their respective deaths, and in February, 1858, was married to Miss Alice Ann Matthews, a daughter of William Matthews. She was born in Miller County, Mo., in 1841, and died in 1863. Three years later Mr. Bates wedded Miss Matilda Howard, a daughter of Silas Howard. She was born in Pulaski County in 1843, and became the mother of two children, Thomas and Effie. The mother of these children died in 1874, and three years later Mr. Bates took for his third wife Miss Mollie Howard, a sister of his second wife. She was born in Hickory County, Mo., in 1859, and is the mother of four children: Alfred, Viola, Matie and Charles. Mr. Bates owns the old homestead, where he has lived since he was three years old. It consists of 400 acres, with 175 acres under cultivation, and is one of the best bottom land farms (if not the best) in the county. He deals quite extensively in stock, and is among the most successful and enterprising citizens in Pulaski County. He is a Democrat in politics, and cast his first presidential vote for George B. McClellan. In July,

1861, he enlisted in Company A, Forty-eighth Regiment Missouri Volunteer Infantry, United States Army, and served eleven months, being discharged at Benton Barracks in 1865, having been corporal of his company. In 1862 he was elected sheriff and collector of the county, and served four years. He is a Master Mason.

William Addison Bates, farmer and stock dealer, of Cullen Township, and native of Pulaski County, Mo., was born in February, 1845, being a son of Albert and Christian (Turpin) Bates. The former was born in the "Blue Grass" State, and when quite young came with his father, James Bates, to Pulaski County, Mo., being among the first settlers of the county. Albert Bates and his wife were married in 1838, and soon after located on Big Piney, where he died in 1845, in the prime of life. His wife was also born in Kentucky, and after his death married Abraham Skaggs, who was killed during the war. She died in 1853, leaving four children, who were born to her first marriage: James L.; Mary J., now Mrs. Franklin; Avirella, widow of John Robinson, and William A. The latter was an infant when his father died, and was only eight years of age when his mother died. He made his home with his Aunt Sallie Carmack until eighteen years of age, when the war broke out about this time, and Mr. Bates cast his destinies with the Confederacy, enlisting in June, 1861, in Company A, McBride's division, Price's command, and after serving six months, and participating in the fight at Springfield, returned home. In July, 1864, he again joined the army, enlisting in Company A, Forty-eighth Regiment Missouri Volunteer Infantry, United States Army, under Col. Blodgett, and received his discharge at St. Louis, Mo., June 20, 1865. In the fall of the latter year he engaged in the saloon business at Waynesville, but sold out two years later and purchased a general mercantile stock, in which business he was engaged until 1886, having G. W. Colley for his partner ten years and R. L. Christeson one year. In June, 1886, Mr. Bates moved to the farm where he now lives. He owns 388 acres of fine bottom land, and is one of Pulaski County's best farmers and most highly esteemed citizens. In 1867 he united his fortunes with those of Miss Sytha Lorena Mitchell, a daughter of Samuel Mitchell. Mrs. Bates was born in Pulaski County in 1849, and has borne six children, whose names are as follows: Cora Lee (wife of Dr. L. Tice, of Waynesville), Bertie G., Fred R., Walter A., Stella, and an infant son, Claude M. Bates. Mr. Bates is a Democrat politically, and in 1870 was elected treasurer of Pulaski County, being re-elected in 1876.

William L. Bradford, ex-collector of Pulaski County, Mo., resides about two miles southwest of Waynesville, and was born in 1839 in Pulaski County (now Phelps), and is one of five children born to the marriage of Isaac Neeley Bradford and Martha Duncan, both of whom were natives of Kentucky, the former born in 1804. In 1822 he came to what is now Phelps County, Mo., with his father, Adam Bradford, and located on the farm now owned by R. B. Duncan. They were among the first whites to settle in that region, and there Adam Bradford died in 1850. Isaac N. married and settled in Spring Creek Township, where he passed the remainder of his life, his death occurring in 1882. After his wife's death, in 1839, he married Frances Mary Vance, who bore him six children and yet survives him. William L. Bradford was reared to manhood on his father's farm, and received a common-school education. At the age of twenty-two years he became the architect of his own fortunes, and August 4, 1861, enlisted in the Missouri State Guards for six months. After his time had expired he re-enlisted in the First Missouri Cavalry, Gates' regiment, and was sergeant of Company F. He was at Pea Ridge, Iuka, Corinth, Grand Gulf, Baker's Creek, Big Black and the siege of Vicksburg, being captured at the latter battle, but was soon paroled and rejoined his command. He was then at Kenesaw Mountain, where he was wounded in the right leg by a bomb, and was disabled for thirty days. After recovering he again entered the field, and was in the battles of Atlanta, Jonesboro, Dalton, Altoona Mountain, Franklin and Fort Blakely, being captured at the latter engagement. After being paroled at Jackson, Miss., he returned home, and in the year 1867 became a citizen of Pulaski County, Mo., and in January of the same year was united in marriage to Missanaiah Sophia Tilley, a daughter of Wilson and Elizabeth (Tippett) Tilley, of Pulaski County. Mrs. Bradford is a native of the county, and was born in 1849. After their marriage they lived upon rented land for six years, and in 1873 bought 175 acres of land where they now make their home. At present Mr. Bradford is the owner of 420 acres of land in the home farm and 120 acres in Liberty Township. He has been a life-long Democrat in politics, and his first presidential vote was cast for Douglas in 1860. In 1882 he was elected sheriff of Pulaski County, and two years later became collector, being re-elected in 1886, and filled the duties of this office faithfully and well. He is a Master Mason, and he and wife have been members of the Methodist Episcopal Church, South, for eight years, and for six years he has been recording steward for Waynesville Circuit.

James A. Bradford, a prosperous farmer of Piney Township, is a Phelps County Missourian, born in 1848, and is a son of Isaac and Frances M. (Vance) Bradford. The father was born in Kentucky in 1805, and in 1825 immigrated to what is now Phelps County, Mo., where he was engaged in farming. He was married the same year to Martha Duncan, but she died November 30, 1839, and November 19 of the following year he wedded Miss Vance. The latter lady bore him six children, four of whom are living. James A. Bradford, their fourth child, made his home with his parents until 1872, when he was married to Miss Bettie C. Lenox, who was a daughter of Hamilton and Maria Lenox, and was born in Phelps County, Mo., in 1850, and bore one child, Ada L. Mr. Bradford married his second wife in 1879. Her maiden name was Martha W. Root, and she was born in Phelps County, Mo., in 1855. They are the parents of four living children: Sally M., Marion E., Lucy E. and Clara E. Mary L. is deceased. Mrs. Bradford is a daughter of Martin and Lucy L. Root, who were born in Kentucky and Ohio, respectively. In 1881 Mr. Bradford settled on his present farm of 217 acres, seventy acres of which are under cultivation. He is a Democrat in politics, and in

1874 was elected justice of the peace of Cold Spring Township, Phelps Co., Mo., but declined to serve. He is also a member of the County Wheel. His mother is a daughter of Samuel and Lucy (Rutt) Vance, who were born in 1876 and 1873, and died in 1841 and 1843, respectively, and is yet living, and resides with her children. The paternal grandparents, Adam and Frances (Neely) Bradford, came to Missouri in 1825, and died in 1849 and 1876, respectively. The latter's father and grandfather were killed by the Indians in Tennessee. The great-grandfather, Andrew Vance, was a native of Virginia, and was a soldier in the Revolutionary War.

Alexander Bryan, a retired farmer of Pulaski County, is a native of Ballard County, Ky., and was born in March, 1823. He was the fourth in the family of six children, four sons and two daughters, born to Moses A. and Eliza (Weaver) Bryan. The mother, who was born in Kentucky, died in her native State when our subject was five years old, and about one year later the father took his family to Maury County, Tenn. Moses A. afterward married Elizabeth Carival, and in 1858 located on the Gasconade River, in Pulaski County, when the county was almost a wilderness and white settlers were few. He was an enterprising farmer, and lived in Pulaski County until his death, which occurred in 1873. He was a member of the Baptist Church for many years. Alexander Bryan was fifteen years of age when he came to Pulaski County, and in early life devoted much attention to hunting. He is a farmer by occupation, and owns 155 acres on the Gasconade River, where he has a good home; he also owns a two-thirds interest in a flour and saw-mill in Richland, and after the war was engaged in the hotel business at Waynesville for many years. In 1861 he enlisted in the Confederate army, and served about nine months under Gen. McBride, six months as bass drummer. He afterward was enrolled in Company A, Forty-eighth Missouri Volunteer Infantry, United States Army, where he served eleven months, and then went to his old home in Tennessee, and was subsequently sent on garrison duty to Camp Douglas, Chicago, where he remained until June, 1865. When but seventeen years of age Mr. Bryan was united in marriage with Sarah Jones, who died about 1848; five years later he married Caroline York, who only lived three years after marriage, and died leaving one son, Samuel, who died about 1882. Mr. Bryan afterward married Mary, daughter of William and Elizabeth Carmack, and of the six children born to their union only three daughters are now living. Politically Mr. Bryan is a Democrat.

George C. Cain, one of the wealthiest farmers of Pulaski County, Mo., was born in 1823 in what is now Pulaski County, and is the only surviving member of a family of four children born to the marriage of Jonathan and Narcisia (Henson) Cain, who were born in Tennessee in 1797 and 1805, and died in 1834 and 1882, respectively. They became residents of Crawford County, Mo., in 1820, and were there married and spent the remainder of their lives. They were among the very early settlers and farmers of that region, there being more Indians than whites in the section at that time. After the father's death his widow married a Mr. Riddle, by whom she had four children, only one of whom (Elias) is still living. The maternal grandparents, George and Silence (Whipple) Henson, were Tennesseeans, and came to Missouri in 1819, spending the remainder of their days in Pulaski County, where George followed the occupation of blacksmithing. George C. Cain, whose name heads this sketch, has always resided in what is now Pulaski County, and received such education as the early schools of Missouri afforded. In 1840 he began life for himself as a farmer, and until 1844 was also engaged in rafting lumber to St. Louis. At the latter date he was married to Miss Elizabeth Jackson, who was born in Tennessee in 1821, and died in 1868, having borne a family of ten children, seven of whom are still living: Mary (Mrs. Underwood), George W., Frances (Mrs. Christeson), Jesse, Linda (Mrs. Christeson) Thomas and Louisiana (Mrs. Drake). In 1872 Mr. Cain married Miss Rebecca Underwood, a native of Tennessee, born in 1837, and a daughter of Samuel and Martha Underwood (the former was a sailor), by whom he has three living children: Isaac, Lizzie and William. His first wife was a daughter of John and Polly (Hughes) Jackson, who moved from Tennessee to Missouri in 1841, and there engaged in farming. Only three of their eleven children are now living. Mr. Cain made his first purchase of land in 1852, but has since made purchases from time to time until he has become the owner of 2,400 acres of good land. He has given seven of his children two good farms each, and still has 1,000 acres of his own. His property has been accumulated by raising corn and feeding it to stock, which illustrates what can be done in Arkansas by energy and judicious management. In 1865 he enlisted in the State Militia, in Company B, and received his discharge at Waynesville the same year. He is a Republican in politics, casting his first presidential vote for James K. Polk in 1844.

George R. Cannefax. Among the important industries of Pulaski County, Mo., worthy of special mention is the flouring mill operated by Mr. Cannefax. He is a native of the county, born June 24, 1837, and up to the age of thirteen years resided on his father's farm in Missouri. He was then seized with the "gold fever," and determined to seek his fortune in the mines of California. He took the overland route, driving a team of horses, and reached Placerville, Cal., just six months after starting from Independence, Mo. From Placerville he went to Cold Springs, where he began work prospecting, and discovered a rich placer claim, which he afterward sold. He next went to Volcano, Cal., where he discovered another rich claim, from which he took from fourteen to twenty-seven ounces of ore per day. He worked this claim eight months, and was then taken sick, and was unable to do any work for about four months. Up to the age of twenty-eight years he resided in the following cities in the West: Placerville, Cal., in 1859; Virginia City, Nev., in 1860; Austin, Nev., in 1863; Virginia City, in 1864, where he played in McGuire's Opera House; San Francisco, in 1865, from which place he started home on August 3 of the same year, reaching Springfield, Mo., on September 3. He met with many stirring adventures during his career in the West, and was quite successful in his mining ventures.

After his return home he kept a saloon in Mount Vernon, Mo., for eighteen months, and then engaged in the milling business, which he has since followed. March 20, 1866, he was married to Miss Josephine Haley, who was born in McMinnville, Tenn., in 1850, and by her became the father of eight children: Mattie, wife of B. F. Hunter; Hattie, Caroline, Naomi, Ruthie, Loren, Clyde and Walter. He came from Lawrence County, Mo., to Dixon in 1877, and has had charge of the Dixon Flouring Mills since November 22 of that year. He has a comfortable and pleasant home, and owns Lots Nos. 6, 7, 8 and 9, in Block 24, of Dixon. He is a Democrat, a Mason and a member of the A. O. U. W. His wife's parents, George and Abigail (Ray) Haley, were natives of Tennessee, and were farmers by occupation. In 1861 the father enlisted in the United States army, and was forage master during the most of the war. Four of their five children are living: Josephine (Mrs. Cannefax), Azaline (Mrs. Freeman), Ruth (Mrs. Rollins) and Bettie (Mrs. Cherry). The parents of Mr. Cannefax, Joseph and Sarah (Callahan) Cannefax, were born in Kentucky and Virginia, in 1798 and 1802, respectively. They moved from Kentucky to Springfield, Mo., in 1840, and there the father spent the remainder of his days, dying in 1846. He was a millwright and miller by trade, and a thorough mechanic of wood and iron. Only three of his twelve children are living: George R., Robert and I. Binda (Mrs. Crow). Mr. Cannefax had three brothers in the Mexican War: John, William and Chesley. The first and last mentioned died while in the service. The grandparents, Radford and Louisa Cannefax, were among the earliest settlers and farmers of Greene County, Mo. Radford Cannefax was born in Kentucky about 1842. The maternal grandmother, Margaret Callahan, was born in Tennessee, and died about 1849.

Elijah Jordan Christeson, one of Pulaski County's oldest citizens, was born in Adair County, Ky., November 24, 1819, and is a son of Elisha and Agnes (Drake) Christeson, and grandson of Robert Christeson, who was born in Maryland, and immigrated to Adair County, Ky., about 1793–94. Here he spent the remainder of his days, dying about 1825, at the age of sixty-six years. His son, Elisha, was also born in Maryland, December 15, 1790, and grew to manhood and married in Adair County, Ky. In 1829 he immigrated to what is now Pulaski County, Mo., and settled on the farm now owned by his daughter Eljelina. Here he reared a family of twelve children, and lived to the ripe old age of ninety-four years. He was one of the very earliest settlers of the county, his nearest neighbor residing four miles distant, and owing to the primitive state of the country he was obliged to go twenty-four miles to mill. His wife, whom he married in 1815, was born in the State of Virginia in 1800, and died in 1873. Five of their children are living, whose names are as follows: Elijah J.; Permelia, widow of Levi Henshaw; Malinda, wife of John W. Nelson; Walker W. and Eljelina. Elijah J. was ten years old when he came with his parents to Pulaski County, Mo., and made his home with them until twenty-five years of age, receiving his education in the primitive log school-house of early days. In 1844 he married Sarah C. Colley, who was born in Caldwell County, Ky., in 1825, and a daughter of Cyrus Colley, and by her became the father of eleven children: James, Thomas J., Cyrus E., Elizabeth (wife of James Dixon), George E., John, Cynthia J., Sarah A. (wife of Charles French), Frank and William H. The eldest, Martha, married James Hudgens February 2, 1862, and died June 1, 1863. In 1845 or 1846 Mr. Christeson entered 160 acres of land about five miles from Waynesville, where he located and has since made his home. He has added acre by acre to his farm until he now owns 280 acres of fine land, well adapted to raising all the cereals. He is the oldest settler of the county, having lived here for fifty-six years, and in politics has been a life-long Democrat. He has held a number of offices in the county, among which are constable, sheriff, collector, judge and public administrator, and has filled the duties of several of the offices for a number of terms. Since 1861 he has been blind (caused by neuralgia), which is a severe trial to him, but he has a remarkably good memory, and can remember with distinctness events that happened many years ago. He has always led an honest, upright and unselfish life, and is universally respected and esteemed. His wife is a member of the Free Will Baptist Church; he is not a member of any church, but believes in the Bible as a true moral guide, and in the Christian faith as set forth by the Protestant doctrines.

Commodore P. Christesson, farmer, of Union Township, Pulaski Co., Mo., and a native of the same, was born January 20, 1853, and is a son of Elijah and Lucretia (Carpenter) Christesson, the former being born in Kentucky in 1790, and died in 1875. He moved from his native State to Missouri in 1829, settling in Pulaski County, and after a short residence in Texas returned to Missouri, and spent the remainder of his days in tilling the soil. He was married five times, and became the father of eleven children, his last wife, the mother of Commodore P., bearing him six children. Only three of the number are living: Commodore P., Lafayette and James Pleasant. The maternal grandfather, Solomon Carpenter, was born in Tennessee in 1796, and died in 1871. He was a farmer by occupation, and was a soldier in the War of 1812, being a participant in the battle of New Orleans, January 8, 1815, in which engagement he was wounded in the head. Commodore P. Christesson was reared and educated in his native county, and at the age of twenty-one years engaged in farming on his own responsibility. By industry and good management he has become the owner of 390 acres of land in three different tracts, and has 150 acres under good cultivation. His union with Miss Malinda Cain, who was born in Pulaski County February 11, 1857, has been blessed in the birth of six children, five of whom are living: Elijah C., Lillie P., William C., Commodore F. and Mary E. He is a member of the A. O. U. W., and in 1876 cast his first presidential vote for R. B. Hayes. Mrs. Christesson's father, George Cain, who was born in Pulaski County, a farmer by occupation, was twice married, his first wife being Elizabeth Jackson, by whom he became the father of nine children, seven of whom are living: Mary N. (Underwood), George W., Sarah F. (Christesson), Jesse R., Malinda S.

(Christesson), Thomas G. and Louisiana C. (Drake). His second union was blessed in the birth of four children, three living: Isaac, Lizzie O. and William.

Robert L. Christeson, general merchant, of Waynesville, Mo., and a native of Pulaski County, was born on the 29th of January, 1862, being a son of Robert L. Christeson, who was born in Adair County, Ky., in 1823. In 1829 he came to Pulaski County, Mo., with his father, Elisha Christeson, and located about six miles south of the county seat, on Roubideaux Creek. He died in 1862, and his wife, whose maiden name was Charlotte Tilley, died two years later. They were the parents of only one child, Robert L., whose name heads this sketch. After the death of his parents he was taken to rear by his grandmother, Mrs. Elizabeth Tilley, with whom he resided until he was fourteen years of age, and at that time began making his home with his guardian, W. L. Bradford, remaining with him until twenty years old. He attended the common schools in early life, and in 1878 entered Morrisville Institute, in Polk County, Mo., which he attended three years, graduating in 1881. The following year he worked on a farm, and in September, 1883, in company with W. A. Bates, began merchandising in Waynesville, but sold his interest to Mr. Bates nine months later, and in September of the same year purchased the entire stock, and took as a partner W. P. Skaggs, the firm being known as Skaggs & Christeson. September 19, 1887, they were burned out, with a loss of $5,000, but Mr. Christeson soon engaged in the same business on his own responsibility, and has since continued, meeting with good success. He has a large and select stock of goods, and as a consequence his enterprise is patronized largely by the town and county. October 2, 1887, he married Miss Jennie Coffman, a daughter of John and Mary Coffman. She was born in Kentucky in April, 1864, and died July 8, 1888, having borne one child, Lida. Mr. Christeson is a Master Mason, and is a member of the Methodist Episcopal Church, South, as was his wife.

Daniel A. Claiborn, farmer and merchant at Hancock, Mo., was born in Smith County, Tenn., in 1839, and is a son of Onsley and Frances (Robertson) Claiborn, who were born in Virginia and Tennessee, in 1802 and 1814, respectively. Both are yet living, and reside in Camden County, Mo., whither they had come from Tennessee in 1849. The father is a farmer, and in 1850 was elected judge of the Camden County courts, serving two terms. Six of his eight children are now living: John L., William F., Susan J. (Stone), N. T. (Mitchell), Elvira E. (Barr) and Daniel A. The paternal grandparents are Daniel and Anna Claiborn. The maternal grandparents, David and Mary (Hunter) Robertson, came from Tennessee to Missouri in 1839, where they engaged in farming. David Robertson was a soldier in the War of 1812, and was at the battle of New Orleans. Daniel A. Claiborn resided in Camden County, Mo., until the breaking out of the late Civil War, receiving a common-school education, and in 1862 enlisted in Company D, Twenty-ninth Missouri Infantry, United States Army, and participated in the battle of Chickasaw Bayou, in which he was wounded in the arm by a minie-ball, which necessitated amputating the limb. He was taken to the hospital at St. Louis, and returned home the following March. In 1863 he was married to Miss Jane E. Huffman, who was born in Camden (now Laclede) County, Mo., in 1845. She is a daughter of M. J. and Elizabeth (Daniels) Huffman, being one of their ten children, whose names are as follows: Jane E. (Claiborn), Mary (Arnold), Caroline, Robert, Susan (Biggs), Missouri (Blakely), Martha (Bean), John, and Jacob and Jesse (twins). Two hundred acres of Mr. Claiborn's fine 800-acre farm are under cultivation, and he has a nice residence and good bearing orchard. He also owns a general mercantile store in Hancock, which has been established since 1887. He is a Democrat in politics, and he and wife are the parents of the following family: Onsley, H. A., Eddie, Drura, Fannie, Belle, Inauda, Carrie and Arthur. Mr. Claiborn served two terms (or from 1882 to 1886) in the county court of this county.

John J. Clark, treasurer of Pulaski County, Mo., and dealer in general merchandise at Waynesville, was born in Camden County, Mo., in 1842, and is a son of Benjamin Clark, who was born in the "Old North Carolina State" in 1819. About 1833 the latter went to Middle Tennessee with his father, Zachariah Clark, and two years later immigrated to Missouri, locating in Pulaski County, twelve miles west of the county seat. Here Zachariah purchased land, and began making him a home in the dense forest. He died in Camden County, Mo., at his son Benjamin's home. About 1841 the latter settled in Erie, Camden County, and about three years later bought a farm in the southeast part of the county. In 1858 he returned to Pulaski County, and purchased a farm near Richland, where he resided until December 7, 1888, when he died. He served as assessor of Camden County for about twelve years, and in 1856 was elected sheriff and collector of the county, serving one term. His wife was born in Tennessee, and died in 1869, having become the mother of nine children. John J. is the eldest of the family, and was reared on a farm, making his home with his parents until 1868. He received a good common-school education, and at the age of twenty engaged in pedagoguing, which occupation he continued four terms. July 15, 1861, he enlisted in Company F, First Regiment Missouri Volunteer Infantry, Confederate States Army, and served six months. He was in the battles of Wilson's Creek, Lexington and Horse Creek, and then returned home, but January 26, 1863, enlisted as a teamster in the Government employ, hauling supplies from Rolla to Lebanon, Mo. August 24, 1864, he joined Company C, Forty-eighth Regiment Missouri Infantry, United States Army, and was mustered out on the 29th of June, 1865. After the war he engaged in farming and teaching school, and was also engaged in selling goods for several years. October 18, 1868, he wedded Miss Matilda L. Riddle, a daughter of Isaac and Martha (Rapp) Riddle, of Pulaski County, Mo. Mrs. Clark was born in the county in 1848. In 1878 Mr. Clark was elected county and circuit clerk of Pulaski County, and in 1882 was elected circuit clerk and *ex-officio* recorder, which position he held four years. In July, 1887, he commenced merchandising in Waynesville, his partner being J. M. Long, but in September the building and contents were consumed by fire, at a loss of $600. Mr. Clark re-engaged in the business in October of the same year, and has a remunerative and increasing trade. In November, 1888, he was elected treasurer of the county, and is now filling the duties of that office. He is a Democrat in politics, and his wife is a member of the Christian Church.

Hon. George W. Colley, ex-merchant, farmer and stock-dealer, of Waynesville, Mo., was born in Caldwell County, Ky., June 9, 1829. His father, Cyrus Colley, was of Irish descent, and was born in York County, S. C., in 1800, and when he was a small boy was taken by his parents to Caldwell County, Ky., where he grew to manhood and was married to Miss Elizabeth Howard. He was a carpenter by trade, but during the latter part of his life followed the occupation of farming. In 1832 he immigrated to the State of Missouri and located six miles west of Waynesville, where he became the owner of 300 acres of land in "Colley Hollow," which was named in his honor, he being the first white man to settle there. He became a prominent citizen of Pulaski County, holding the office of county judge a number of terms, and was also appointed commissioner by the county court to sell the lots of Waynesville, having assisted in laying out the town. He was one of the first settlers of what is now Pulaski County, and his nearest neighbor, who was Isaac N. Davis, lived three miles distant. His next nearest neighbor was William Gillespie, who resided at a distance of five miles. His nearest milling point was twenty-five miles distant. His wife, who is yet living and resides with her daughter, Mrs. Sarah Christeson, was born in Caldwell County, Ky., in 1805, and became the mother of ten children, eight of whom are living. George W. Colley is their eldest son and third child, and was about four years of age when he was brought to Pulaski County, Mo. He grew to manhood on the old homestead, and received a fair common-school education, and at the age of twenty years began clerking in a general store at Waynesville, which belonged to his uncle, Silas Howard. After following the same occupation in Springfield for some time, he, in the fall of 1850, returned to Pulaski County and took charge of a store about one-fourth of a mile from his home, and in the spring of the following year established a store at Waynesville, his partners being his uncle, Silas Howard, and J. A. Rayle. At the end of one year Mr. Colley purchased his partners' interest, and William Stewart became a member of the firm. Mr. Colley continued this business the greater portion of the time up to 1883, with different partners, and at that date sold out, and has since devoted his time to farming and stock dealing. He is the owner of the old homestead, and is one of the largest land-holders of the county, his acreage amounting to 1,000. In 1858 he was united in marriage to Miss Elwiza N. Mitchell, a daughter of Samuel and Elizabeth (Nash) Mitchell. She was born in Pulaski County in 1839, and is the mother of five children: Frank L., mail agent on the Missouri Pacific Railway; James M. and Charles H., who keep a livery and feed stable; Ida V., wife of H. E. Rollins, who is circuit court clerk of Pulaski County, and Alfie. Mr. Colley has been a life-long Democrat in politics, and has served his party as deputy sheriff two years, assessor and county treasurer, but resigned the latter office the same year he was elected (1856.) In September, 1864, he enlisted in Company A, Forty-eighth Missouri Infantry, as sergeant, and served until he received his discharge at St. Louis, June 29, 1865. In 1865 he was appointed sheriff and collector of Pulaski County, and the following year was re-elected to the same office. Two years later he was elected to the State Legislature and served one term, and at the end of that time became county treasurer, serving in this capacity until 1876. In 1885 he was appointed deputy collector of internal revenue of the First District of Missouri, but resigned the position at the end of two years. He is a member of the Masonic order, Lodge No. 375 of Waynesville (being a Master Mason), and his family are members of the Methodist Episcopal Church, South.

Daniel B. Colley, a prominent farmer and stock raiser of Cullen Township, is a son of Judge Cyrus and Elizabeth (Howard) Colley, and was born in Pulaski County, at the mouth of Colley Hollow, in 1833. Cyrus Colley was born in York County, S. C., in 1800. He received a limited schooling, and his mother having died when he was quite young, he was bound out to learn the blacksmith's trade, but owing to ill treatment he soon sought other employment. In 1825 he married Elizabeth Howard, daughter of William Howard, of Kentucky. She was born in Caldwell County, Ky., in 1805, where they lived after marriage until 1831, when they removed to Southern Illinois, and one year later located in what is now Pulaski County, Mo. They finally settled in what is now known as Colley Hollow, which is one of the richest valleys in the county. There Mr. Colley improved a good farm, on which he spent the remainder of his life. He was one of the pioneers of Pulaski County, and in an early day served one term as county judge, holding the same office just prior to the war, during which time the railroad company endeavored to obtain support for the proposed railroad, to which Mr. Colley was actively opposed, and it is probably due to his perseverance and determined opposition that Pulaski County is without the burdensome railroad debt hanging over so many counties in Missouri. He was a man of great industry and endurance, and had the interests of the county at heart. He was an active worker in the Democratic party, and one of the most enterprising farmers of his time. He died November 4, 1876. In a family of six sons and four daughters, Daniel B. Colley was the fifth. His education was that obtained in the common schools. In 1860 he married Rachel Gillespie, whose father, William Gillespie, was a pioneer of Pulaski County. She was born in Pulaski County, and died in December, 1866, leaving one child, Clara, now the wife of Rev. L. H. Davis. September 10, 1871, Mr. Colley married Mrs. Margaret E. Hobbs, widow of Joseph Hobbs. She was born in Pulaski County in 1840, and has three children by her first husband, viz.: Le Roy J., William W., and Josie J., who married James M. Colley. The parents of Mrs. Colley were Wilson and Elizabeth Tilley, natives of North Carolina and Tennessee, respectively, who settled in what is now Pulaski County about 1829. Mr. Tilley was killed September 10, 1864, by a band of militia, who burned his house and robbed him of his money. His wife is still living, and of their twelve children four daughters and one son are still living, and rank among the highly esteemed families of their respective communities. The parents were members of the Methodist Church. Three children were born to Mr. Colley by his second marriage, only one of whom survives, Daniel Burkley. After the war Mr. Colley settled on his present farm, which adjoins the old homestead, and where he now has a well-improved farm of 140 acres, about sixty acres under cultivation. He engaged in farming until 1866, when, having been elected circuit and county court clerk, he removed to Waynesville. He held the office continuously for eight years, and at the expiration of the last term returned to his farm, where he now lives. In political faith he is a Democrat.

William J. Cook, farmer, merchant and postmaster at Cookville, Mo., is a native of Osage County, Mo., and was born in 1842. His parents, J. B. and Margaret (Mouser) Cook, were born in New York and Pennsylvania, in 1800 and 1806, respectively. The former was a farmer by occupation, and at the age of eighteen years immigrated from his home to Osage County, Mo., and in 1845 came to Pulaski County, where he died on the 25th of November, 1877. William J. Cook is the tenth of their twelve children, and until he attained the age of twenty-two years his time was employed in attending the common schools and assisting his parents on the farm. In 1863 he was married to Miss R. M. Barnard, a daughter of Mrs. Susan Barnard. She was born in Indiana in 1841, and died on the 26th of April, 1887, having borne a family of six children. In January, 1888, Mr. Cook married Miss Jessie, a daughter of George and Salisba Goldsberry. She was born in Iowa in 1865. In 1883 Mr. Cook located on his present farm, which consists of 320 acres. It is situated on the Roubideaux River, and 100 acres are in a good state of cultivation. In 1872 Cookville Post-office was established, and Mr. Cook was appointed its postmaster. In connection with the post-office he keeps a stock of general merchandise, which brings him quite a nice little sum annually. He is a Democrat in politics, and is a member of the Masonic fraternity.

Hiram D. Craft, farmer, of Pulaski County, Mo., was born in Hancock County, Ind., in 1844, and is a son of William and Emily (Williams) Craft, who were of English and Scotch descent, respectively, born in 1812 and 1813. The father became a resident of Illinois at an early day, and was a farmer by occupation. In 1866 he became a resident of Kansas, and died in that State in 1872. His wife is still living, an active old lady, aged seventy-six years, and makes her home with her son Abraham. Eight of her twelve children are living, Hiram D. being the sixth of the family. He remained with his parents until eighteen years of age, and then enlisted in the Union army, Company E, Seventy-ninth Illinois Infantry, and served over two years, participating in the battles of Stone River, Missionary Ridge, Chickamauga and Kenesaw Mountain, being wounded in the latter battle, which occasioned the loss of the sight of one eye. In 1866 he was married to Mary Margaret Paul, a daughter of John and Mary Paul. She was born in Kentucky in 1847, and became the mother of eight children, whose names are as follows: Edwin, William, Charley, Albert, Emery, Neva, Thomas and Minnie. Since his marriage Mr. Craft has resided in Pulaski County, where he has a good farm of 190 acres, with sixty under cultivation, located on the Roubideaux River. He takes a deep interest in the cause of education, and makes his home in town during the winter seasons in order to give his children the benefit of the town schools. He is a strong Republican, and he and wife are members of the Baptist Church.

Charles H. Davis, prosecuting attorney of Pulaski County, is one of the most prominent and successful young legal practitioners of the county. His birth occurred in Hickory County, Mo., in 1860, and in the family of two sons and two daughters born to Hon. Daniel E. and Mary P. (Foster) Davis he was the second. The parents were natives of Pulaski and Hickory Counties, respectively, and married in Hickory County, where they lived until Charles H. was two or three years of age, when they moved to Pulaski County, which was their home until 1881; in the latter year they located in Springfield, where the father, who is a carpenter and joiner by trade, is now proprietor of the Robinson Avenue Planing Mills. He represented Pulaski County two terms in the General Assembly ten or twelve years ago, and during the late war was captain of a company in the Forty-eighth Missouri Infantry, Federal Army. He is a member of the A. F. & A. M. and A. O. U. W., and he and wife belong to the Methodist Church. Isaac N. Davis, paternal grandfather of our subject, was an early settler of Southern Missouri, a farmer by occupation, and died in Pulaski County several years before the war. Charles H. Davis was reared on a farm, and received a good common-school education at Richland. When nineteen years of age he began doing for himself in the insurance business, and at the same time studied law with J. A. Bradshaw, with whom he remained until about one year after he was admitted to the bar, which was in September, 1880. He has since been successfully engaged in the practice of his chosen profession in Pulaski and adjoining counties, and is one of the promising young lawyers of Missouri. He is a fluent speaker, and his career has every promise of being a brilliant one. In 1882, when but twenty-two years of age, he was elected prosecuting attorney, to which office he has been twice re-elected. He is a Democrat in politics, and is a member of the A. F. & A. M., of which lodge he has served as secretary and treasurer. May 25, 1882, he married Ida, daughter of Alexander and Mary Bryan, of Richland. Mr. and Mrs. Davis have a fine home in Richland, and are members of the Methodist Church. Mr. Davis is also an insurance and loan agent, and for six years acted as real estate agent for the 'Frisco Railroad Company.

Henry Decker, farmer, of Pulaski County, Mo., was born in Kentucky in 1829, and is a son of David and Mary (Townsend) Decker, who were born in Kentucky in 1804 and 1807, respectively. They moved from Kentucky to Illinois in 1852, thence to Arkansas, thence to Illinois, and in 1853 located in Pulaski County, Mo., where the father died the same year. His widow is still living. They became the parents of eighteen children, twelve of whom are living: Henry,

Caroline (Back), Mahala (Hancock), Tabitha (Bailey), Basheba (Tucker), Welcome, Marion, Martha (Carmack), Merritt, Sarah (Becktow), Anderson and Nancy (Clent). The paternal grandparents, Henry and Patsey Decker, were born in North Carolina, the former's death occurring in 1845. They moved to Kentucky at an early day, and there Mr. Decker engaged in farming and blacksmithing. Henry Decker, whose name heads this sketch, spent his early years in Kentucky and never had a day's schooling in his life. At the age of twenty-one he began working at the gunsmith's trade for himself, and in 1852 was married to Miss Martha Decker, who was born in Kentucky in 1829, and a daughter of Landick and Patsey Decker, of North Carolina, the father a farmer and teacher by occupation. Henry Decker and wife became the parents of one son, Landick. This wife died, and he afterward married again, and by this wife became the father of eight children: William Thomas, Polly J. (Denton), Marion, Richard, Katie (Porter), Jemima (Dickson), Jackson and Ambrose. In 1861 Mr. Decker enlisted in Company A of the State Guards, under Col. Johnson, and was at the battles of Springfield, Pea Ridge and Prairie Grove. He received his discharge at Van Buren, Ark., in 1862, having served during the war as captain of a division train. His family resided in Illinois during this period. He is a Democrat, and his first presidential vote was cast for Franklin Pierce in 1852.

James M. Farrar is one of the prominent citizens of Richland, where he has been engaged in the drug business since 1879, and since 1885 has published and edited the *Cyclone*. He was born in Franklin County, Mo., October 7, 1858, and is the fifth of seven children born to Hon. Reuben H. and Virginia (Jones) Farrar. Reuben H. Farrar came to Missouri when small with his father, Richard Farrar, a native of Virginia, and an early settler of Franklin County, Mo., where he lived until his death a few years ago. Reuben H. Farrar served as assessor and collector of Franklin County, and in 1864 and 1865 represented that county in the Legislature; he removed to Lebanon in 1867, where he held the office of justice of the peace continuously from 1872 until his death, which occurred in 1886. He was a Republican in politics, and during the late war commanded a company of infantry of Missouri troops. Mrs. Farrar died when James M. was small, and the latter, at the age of ten years, entered the printing office at Lebanon, where he was employed for three years; he then spent four years in his brother's drug store in the study of chemistry, and subsequently went to St. Clair, Franklin County, where he engaged in the drug business until 1879; in the latter year he located at Richland, and again engaged in the drug business. December 24, 1879, Mr. Farrar married Miss Phena Morrow, of Springfield, Mo., who was born near Ottawa, Canada, and when quite young went with her parents to Minnesota, where they both died, and she was adopted by Dr. C. L. King, who afterward moved to Springfield. Mr. and Mrs. Farrar are the parents of three children. Mr. Farrar is a Republican in politics, in which he takes an active interest. He served as city treasurer of Richland three years, and since has been alderman five years. He is a member of the A. F. & A. M., and has held various offices in the lodge, and is also a member of the A. O. U. W., and Select Knights A. O. U. W., being major of the Ninth Missouri Regiment of the last named order. Mr. Farrar is a large stockholder in the new bank to be located in Richland, and has been a prominent figure in many of the enterprises of that city.

James K. Foote, postmaster at De Bruin, Mo., was born in Orange County, Ind., in 1848, and is a son of William and Adaline (Pinnick) Foote, who were born in Indiana in 1823 and 1826, and died in Indiana and Missouri in 1877 and 1888, respectively. They were the parents of fourteen children, nine of whom are living: James K., Mary E. (wife of George T. McNeff), Nancy A. (wife of James M. Lane), Cammaliza, Malinda F. (wife of G. W. Mickler), William H., Minnie A. (wife of Alfred H. Williams), Evaline M. and Asher L. William Foote's father was a Virginian, and after residing in Tennessee and Kentucky for some time moved to Indiana, where he died in 1862, at the age of seventy-five years. James K. Foote spent his boyhood days on a farm, and resided with his parents until twenty-one years of age. His marriage with Miss Laura J. Briner was celebrated in 1875. She was born in Orange County, Ind., in 1857, and is the mother of the following children: Nora A., Mabel M., Edson E. and Artiemecie. In 1872 Mr. Foote flat-boated to New Orleans, La., and in 1873 took up his abode in Texas, and at the end of two years and seven months returned to Indiana, and in the fall of 1875 went to Cherokee County, Kas. Here he resided until 1878, when he again returned to Indiana, and in the fall of 1879 came to Pulaski County, Mo., and in 1881 purchased forty acres of land about six miles west of the county seat, it being a portion of the old Cyrus Colley farm. In 1883 he was appointed postmaster of De Bruin. In his political views he is a stanch Republican. In religious belief he and wife are Seventh-Day Adventists.

Samuel F. Giddens was born in Knox County, Tenn., May 27, 1806. When fifteen years old he was thrown upon his own resources by the death of his father, Roger Giddens, and soon began an apprenticeship at the trade of carpenter in Knoxville, becoming in time an adept at his avocation. He resided for awhile in Monroe County, and at the age of twenty-one was married to Elizabeth J. Brown, born in South Carolina in 1810. In 1830 he immigrated to Illinois, but finding the country sparsely settled and unprofitable to his trade, he returned to Tennessee, and was there when Gen. Scott removed the Indians west, being one of the many who dug for the supposed hidden treasures of the "red man of the forest." In 1838 he resumed his trade as carpenter and millwright in Williamson County, Ill., doing considerable building in that locality, and in 1848 he moved to Walker County, Ga. This undertaking did not prove satisfactory, and in 1852 he located in Texas County, Mo. (then Pulaski, but now Phelps), where he built the principal part of the town of Relfe for Mr. Coppage (still living and ninety years of age). This place is now owned by the latter's son-in-law. It was named by Mr. Giddens. In 1855, in company with others, he started for Kansas, but upon reaching Webster County heard of John Brown's depredations in that State, and consequently stopped here until things were more quiet. During this time he resumed his chosen calling, and built the first house in Marshfield. In 1856 he settled in Johnson County, Ark., and followed farming and boat building until 1861, when, the war breaking out, and he claiming himself a Jefferson Democrat, he incurred the displeasure of the South, and was forced to hide, his wife following him, for safety. Four of his boys enlisted in the service. The suffering and tortures this respected and honored citizen was obliged to undergo cannot be imagined. He finally reached Pulaski County, Mo., and subsequently enlisted in the army as wagon boss, at which he was occupied at the time of his death, at the age of fifty-six, December 20, 1862. He belonged to the Missionary Baptist Church. His wife died in Texas County January 31, 1887. They were the parents of fifteen children, five boys and ten girls. Three sons, John B., Samuel B. and A. R., are ministers of the gospel. W. V. is a merchant, and William G. is the eldest and a farmer. The latter received a meager education in the subscription schools of his young days, and remained at home with his parents until twenty-one, when his marriage occurred to Miss Mary Ann Isbel, daughter of James and Nancy Isbel, born in Monroe County, Tenn. In 1850 Mr. Giddens moved to Illinois, in 1853 to Texas County, Mo., in 1854 started for Kansas, but stopped in Webster County, and in 1857 his wife died, having borne three children: Nancy E., wife of F. A. Dodson; John K., and Mary C., married Frank Tucker November 14, 1877, and died August 10, 1879. In 1858 he married Nancy C. Clark, daughter of Levi and Nancy Clark. She was born in Walker County, Ga., in 1831, and became the mother of nine children, six living: Deliah A., wife of George Rogers; George W., James F., Margaret; Amanda, wife of Andrew Musgraves, and Eliza A., wife of Price Williams. Mrs. Giddens died in Pulaski County January 1, 1873. Mr. Giddens married for his third wife, March 15, 1878, Mrs. Mary Tucker, *nee* Ready. They have one child, R. T. January 20, 1889, he immigrated to Miller County, Mo., where he has purchased land. He owns 380 acres, 200 of which are in cultivation. Himself and wife are members of the Missionary Baptist Church. Politically he is a Democrat. John K. Giddens is the oldest son of William G. Giddens, and was born in Webster County, Mo., in 1854, remaining with his parents until he reached his majority, and only receiving one year and a half's schooling. In 1876 he was married to Miss Susan Welch, who was born in Maries County, Mo., in 1858, and is the daughter of James and Maria Welch. She died in 1883, having borne two children, one of whom, Lidia May, born July 15, 1880, died July 4, 1881; Hattie P. was born September 9, 1883, and is still living. His second wife was Miss Thursia E. Lane, who was born in Hamilton County, Ill., in 1858. She is a daughter of Jacob C. and Nancy Lane, and is the mother of one child, Susie A. Mr. Giddens owns about 480 acres of land, and has about 150 acres under cultivation. Like his father, he is a Democrat in his political views.

Hugh Godfrey, liveryman of Richland, Mo., was born in the "Old

North State" about 1830, and is a son of Thomas and Elizabeth (Moss) Godfrey, who were also North Carolinians, and moved to Indiana about 1840. Here they resided eight years, and after a short residence in their native State took up their permanent abode in Washington County, Ind., where the mother died. The father afterward married again, and moved to some other State, and was never afterward heard from. He was a farmer by occupation. Hugh Godfrey is the second of six children, and in early life received but a meager education. He was married in North Carolina, January 5, 1857, to Susan, daughter of Caleb Sawyer, by whom he became the father of nine sons, one of whom is deceased. Richard and Alexis are farmers in Miller County, as is James; Joseph, Thomas, Frank, Caleb, George and Isaac live in Pulaski County; Caleb is a railroad man. In 1859 Mr. Godfrey removed to Washington County, Ind., and from there removed to Carroll County, Mo., and from 1869 to 1882 was a resident of Miller County. Since that time he has resided in Richland, and for three years carried the mail to Brumley, but since that time has been engaged in the livery business, and is in good circumstances, being the owner of several lots in Richland, and a good livery barn, seven horses, four buggies and two hacks. He is a Democrat politically, and he and wife are members of the Christian Church.

L. D. Groom, a dealer in general hardware, farm implements, wagons, etc., at Richland, was born in Camden County, Mo., in 1853, and is a son of James F. and Amanda (Cockrill) Groom. James F. Groom was born in Kentucky in 1811, and during life devoted his attention to farming and carpentering; he was a Republican in politics, and served several years as justice of the peace. His death occurred in 1866. Mrs. Amanda Groom was also a native of Kentucky, and was born in 1821; she died in 1882. The paternal grandfather of our subject was Enoch Groom, a native of Virginia, who was of Irish descent, and was a carpenter by trade. Dr. Anderson Cockrill, the maternal grandfather of L. D. Groom, was born in Virginia, and moved to Kentucky, from which State he removed to Missouri in 1837, and fifteen or twenty years later went to California, where he remained until his death, which occurred about 1862; he was a prominent medical practitioner, and also a minister of the Baptist Church. L. D. Groom was reared to the pursuit of farming, and received a common-school education. After attaining his majority he spent a short time at the academy as a student, where he was subsequently engaged two years as a teacher. In 1877 Mr. Groom married Maggie, daughter of A. J. and Mary E. Combs, formerly of Kentucky, and early settlers of Camden County, where Mr. Combs died in 1884; he was a farmer and stock trader. Mrs. Combs is still living. Mrs. Groom is a native of Camden County, and is the mother of three children. After his marriage Mr. Groom turned his attention to farming until 1881, when he removed to Richland and engaged in the grocery business until 1883, under the firm name of Combs & Groom; in the latter year he established his present business, and carries a stock of general hardware, etc., worth about $5,000. He has been mayor of Richland since 1887, and is one of the enterprising men of the town. He is a member of Richland Lodge No. 382, A. F. & A. M., and is also a member of Linn Creek Lodge No. 307, I. O. O. F. Mrs. Groom is a member of the Christian Church.

Samuel R. Hale, a farmer of Piney Township, Pulaski Co., Mo., was born in Tennessee in 1847, and is a son of W. G. and Susanna (Brookshire) Hale, who were born in Tennessee in 1824 and 1823, respectively. The father is of Irish descent, a farmer by occupation, and is now a resident of Kentucky. From 1851 to 1868 he resided in Missouri, but since the latter date has been a resident of the "Blue Grass" State. Samuel R. Hale is the eldest of six children, and was but four years old when he was brought to Missouri. He has lived in Pulaski County since 1852, and up to the time of attaining his majority remained with his parents and attended school. In 1869 he was married to Mrs. Mary Ann (Deer) Bradford, widow of I. N. Bradford. She died May 11, 1879, having borne four children, two of whom are living. In January, 1879, Mr. Hale married his second wife, Prudence Huckins, who was born in Ripley County, Ind., in 1860. She is a daughter of F. S. and Emily J. Huckins, and has borne four children, two living. Since his marriage Mr. Hale has resided the most of the time in Pulaski County, where he owns a good farm of 186 acres, 115 of which are under cultivation. He is a Democrat in politics, and in 1868 was elected justice of the peace, and served two terms. He also served two years as deputy sheriff of the county, and from 1884 to 1886 served again as justice of the peace, being re-elected in the latter year for two years. He is a member of the A. O. U. W. and the Free Will Baptist Church.

Rev. Alexander Hendrix is a resident of Piney Township, Pulaski Co., Mo., and was born in North Carolina March 27, 1831, being a son of Jesse and Abi (Worthington) Hendrix, who were North Carolinians, born August 23, 1809, and September 8, 1809, respectively. The father was of English descent, a farmer by occupation, and always resided in his native State, but died in Georgia in 1855, while there on business. His widow is still living, and since 1871 has resided in Rush County, Ind., with her sixth son, Henry L. She is a member of the Baptist Church, and became the mother of eleven children, all of whom grew to maturity, and eight are now living. Rev. Alexander Hendrix is the eldest of the family, and made his home with his parents until twenty years of age, attending the district schools during the winter months. In 1851 he was married to Miss Mary E. Haneycutt, who was born in Stanley County, N. C., in 1830, and is a daughter of Edmond and Malitia (Morgan) Haneycutt, both of whom were of Dutch descent. Seven children were born to Mr. and Mrs. Hendrix, five of whom are living. Mr. Hendrix resided in his native State for three years after his marriage, and in 1854 immigrated to Indiana, and in 1869 came to Missouri, locating in Pulaski County, where he has since lived. He joined the Union Baptist Church in 1850, and was ordained in Indiana a minister of the Pleasant Grove Baptist Church. He has organized a number of churches, and since coming to Missouri has joined the Friendship Baptist Church, and was chosen its pastor. In 1870 he was elected missionary of the Gasconade River

Baptist Association, and was afterward chosen missionary of the Dixon Baptist Association. He is now pastor of three churches. Since being ordained he has been instrumental in saving many souls. He has preached about 2,436 sermons, baptized 635 different persons, and has received into the church about 1,320 persons. He has a good farm of 223 acres, 100 of which are under cultivation, and is president of the County Wheel organization. He is a Republican.

W. S. Hicks, farmer and merchant, of Roubideaux Township, was born in Tennessee in 1827, and is a son of James and Mary (Marlow) Hicks, who were born in North Carolina and Virginia, December 15, 1779, and April 15, 1790, respectively. The father was a farmer and school-teacher, and in 1813 moved to Dickson County, Tenn., where he died January 31, 1860, followed by his wife June 27, 1867. To them were born fourteen children, twelve of whom lived to maturity, and only four of whom are now living. W. S. Hicks is the eighth of the family, and remained with his parents until twenty-five years of age. In 1854 he was married to Miss Margare J. Moore, who was born in Pulaski County, Mo., in 1837, and is a daughter of William and Elizabeth Ann Moore, and by her became the father of one child, James W., who was born in Pulaski County, Mo., January 8, 1856, and resides with his parents. He is a representative young man, and was elected assessor of his native county in 1886, and made an efficient officer. In 1855 Mr. Hicks settled on the farm where he now lives, and besides this property is the proprietor of a good general mercantile store, which was established in 1874, which brings him in a comfortable income. He is a Democrat in politics, and is an influential and enterprising citizen. He is the owner of 300 acres of land, 140 of which are under cultivation, but at one time was the owner of 1,760 acres. His land is well improved, being furnished with good buildings, and is situated on the Roubideaux River. He is a member of the Masonic fraternity, and he and wife are members of the Missionary Baptist Church.

William Wilson Hobbs, collector and ex-sheriff of Pulaski County, Mo., of which county he is a native, was born August 25, 1862, being a son of Joseph J. and grandson of Vincent Hobbs. The former was born in Cape Girardeau County, Mo., in 1839, and died in 1864. He was a farmer by occupation, and when a young man came to Pulaski County, Mo., with his father, and settled in Hobbs Hollow, which was named in his father's honor, he being the first white settler of the region. He was married to Margaret E. Tilley, who bore him three children, and after his death his widow married D. B. Colley, by whom she became the mother of one child. William W. Hobbs is the second child, and lived with his mother until he grew to manhood, being reared on a farm. March 18, 1885, he was wedded to Miss Cora E. Mitchell, a daughter of James M. and Sarah N. (Musgrave) Mitchell. Mrs. Hobbs was born in Cedar County, Mo., January 1, 1859, and she and Mr. Hobbs are the parents of two children: Lena and Roy. In 1881 he became a salesman in the general mercantile store of W. A. Bates, of Waynesville, and in the summer of 1884 acted as deputy sheriff of the county, being elected to the office in the fall of that year and re-elected two years later. In 1888 he was elected county collector, to begin the duties of the office in March, 1889. He is a Master Mason, a Democrat in politics, and he and wife are members of the Methodist Episcopal Church, South.

John H. Imboden, general merchant, of Dixon, Mo., is a son of George and Eliza (Hughes) Imboden, and grandson of John Imboden and wife, formerly a Miss Goloday. The latter couple were born in Pennsylvania in 1780 and 1798, and died in 1865 and 1876, respectively. They moved from their native State to Virginia, thence to Missouri in 1830, the grandfather serving in the War of 1812. His son, George, was born in Virginia March 9, 1822, and after moving to Missouri was married to Miss Hughes, who was born in Washington County of that State. She was a daughter of William Hughes and wife, nee Kirkpatrick, who were born in Kentucky in 1792, and died in 1876 and 1827, respectively, and she inherited German blood from her father (her grandfather having come from Germany), and Scotch-Irish blood from her mother. Her union with Mr. Imboden was blessed in the birth of nine children, eight of whom are living: James W., John H., T. V., George W. (deceased), J. S., B. F., C. A., Eliza A. (Love) and Albertson. John H. Imboden spent his early days in Maries County, Mo. During 1871 he attended McKendree College, Lebanon, Ill., and in 1872 entered the Caledonia Collegiate Institute, Caledonia, Mo., and the following year became a student in the State University of Missouri. The following year he began teaching school and clerking in a store in Dixon, Mo., and the same year was married to Miss V. A. Basham, who was born December 3, 1853, and by her is the father of two children, Minnie and Mabel. February 22, 1875, he came to Pulaski County, and was engaged in clerking and teaching school until 1879, when he established his present business, a Mr. Murphy being his partner. Since July of that year the firm has been Imboden & Spalding. They have been located in their present building since 1880, and are having a large and lucrative trade. He has been a Mason since attaining his twenty-first year, and has always voted the Democratic ticket. He was the first mayor of Dixon, being elected in 1878, and since 1885 has been postmaster of the town. His wife is a daughter of Edmund and Mahala (Jones) Basham, natives of Tennessee, Mr. Basham being a farmer, blacksmith and merchant by occupation. The following are their children: Elizabeth (Johnson), John, Nancy (Christman), Perry, V. A. (Imboden), Amanda (Bridges), S. F. (Price), Florence (Herd), Martelia (Johnson) and James.

James L. Johnson, prosecuting attorney of Pulaski County, Mo., and native of the same, was born in 1854, and is a son of David and Rebecca (Bates) Johnson. The former was born in the State of Kentucky about 1823, and when a boy was brought to Pulaski County, Mo., by his father, John Johnson, who settled about two miles north of the county seat. In 1850 he took the gold fever, and went to California by the overland route, and after remaining in that State for two years returned to Pulaski County, and the following year was married. His death occurred in 1863. His wife was born in Tennessee about 1825, and died in 1862. They were the parents of four children,

James L. being the only one now living. He was quite small when his parents died, and he was taken to rear by Solomon Bartlett, with whom he remained seven years. His days were spent in working in a saw and grist mill, and attending the common schools during the winter seasons. He was very desirous of obtaining an education, and during 1872–73 attended school at Richland, and in 1874–75 attended the School of Mines at Rolla. He became a disciple of Blackstone in the latter year, his preceptor being Hon. William Rollins, of Waynesville. In March, 1877, he was admitted to the bar, and immediately entered upon the practice of his profession, being also appointed by Gov. Phelps prosecuting attorney of Pulaski County, in April of the same year, to fill the unexpired term of Hon. William Rollins, who had died. He served in this capacity two years, and during 1880 and 1881 was engaged in tilling the soil. At the latter date he entered the teacher's profession, but after a short time resumed his practice in Waynesville. In November, 1888, he was elected to his present position. May 6, 1877, he married Mary Bostic, who was born in North Carolina in 1858, and to them have been born five children: Oscar, Effie, Ernst, Josephine and Vera. Mr. Johnson is a Democrat, and he and his wife are members of the Christian Church. Mrs. Johnson is a daughter of B. D. Bostic, who came from Richmond County, N. C., in 1868.

Anderson Keith, merchant and farmer, and a native of Miller County, Mo., was born on the 10th of July, 1848, and is a son of John and Catherine (Whittle) Keith, who were born in Indiana and Kentucky, respectively, the former's birth occurring in 1820. He was taken to Kentucky when small, and was reared on a farm, receiving a common-school education. He removed to Miller County, Mo., at an early day, and during the late war served in the Home Guards, the State Militia and the regular army until the close of the war. He has been very successful, and is said to be one of the neatest farmers of the county. The following are his children who are living: Anderson, Paradine, James, Martha Jonathan, Francis, William R. and Simon P. Those deceased are Elizabeth, Polly A. and Henry. The mother of these children died in 1872, after which Mr. Keith married Susan Dean, of Miller County, by whom he has five children: George, Sallie, Melvin, Cordelia and Mary. Anderson Keith was reared on a farm in Miller County, Mo., and received a common-school education. He remained with his parents until twenty years of age, and then began life for himself, and was married to Martha E. Smith, a daughter of Thomas L. and Mary J. (Gaston) Smith, who were natives of Illinois, where their daughter was born. She was taken to Pulaski County when quite small, then to Miller County, where the father died. The mother is still living. Mrs. Keith became the mother of four children, three living: William T., Albert N. and Arthur L. Mary C. is dead. In 1876 Mr. Keith came from Miller County to Pulaski County, and purchased his present farm of 100 acres, sixty acres being under cultivation. He farmed exclusively for four years, but since that time has given a portion of his time to the mercantile business. Through his influence a post-office was established at

Hawkeye in 1881, and he was appointed its postmaster, and has since been filling the duties of that office. He and wife are members of the Christian Church, and he is a Republican in politics.

William C. Kelso was born in Rockbridge County, Va., May 24, 1825, and is a son of Joseph and Martha (Allen) Kelso, who were born in the same county, the former in January, 1774, and the latter September 25, 1780. He was a miller and farmer by occupation, and died on his farm in Virginia in 1867. His two brothers, James and Hugh, were soldiers in the Revolutionary War. Four of his eleven children are now living: Hugh, Ewing, Martha and William. The following died on or near the old homestead at Kelso Gap, Va.: Polly, Jane, Elizabeth and Sallie. John A. and Speece died in Missouri, and Walker in Florida. Hugh and Elizabeth (Culton) Kelso, the paternal grandparents, were natives of Ireland and Virginia, respectively, the former coming to the United States when a young man, and spent the remainder of his days in Virginia. John and Jane (Montague) Allen, the maternal grandparents, were of Scotch parentage, and natives of Virginia, where they lived and died. William C. Kelso, whose name heads this sketch, remained in his native State until eighteen years of age, and while there was educated for the Presbyterian ministry, but instead chose farming as his calling through life. He assisted his father, when not in school, until coming west, and after coming to Missouri located in Lewis County, where he entered land and lived two years. He then went to Illinois, where he resided for three years, and again came to Lewis County, and for thirty-one years was engaged in farming and dealing in real estate near Monticello. In 1851 he was wedded to Miss Cordelia L. Turner, of Kentucky, by whom he became the father of four children: Martha, Stotira, Mary and Joseph. The mother of these children died on the 9th day of July, 1864, and Mr. Kelso was then married to Miss Mary B. Carlley on the 1st of May, 1866. She was born August 30, 1849, and is a daughter of Herbert and Leah (Shully) Carlley, who were born in Pennsylvania, and of German descent. Mrs. Kelso was born in Adams County, of that State, and was eight years of age when brought to Missouri. Mr. Kelso is an old-time Democrat, and at one time represented Lewis County in the State Grange, but has never held any office. He located in Vernon County, Mo., in 1881, and the latter part of 1883 came to Pulaski County. He has a good farm of 250 acres, 100 being under cultivation, and in connection with his farming gives considerable attention to stock raising. He and wife, who is a member of the Baptist Church, are the parents of three children: William C., Alexander S. and Lottie.

Edward Lingsweiler, dealer in lumber, brick, lime, and all kinds of building material at Richland, is a native of Racine County, Wis., and was born in 1847. He is a son of John I. and Christina (Shero) Lingsweiler, natives of Germany, the former born January 1, 1818, and the latter about 1820. They immigrated to the United States in 1831 with their parents, and were married in Buffalo, N. Y. About 1844 they removed to Racine County, Wis., where they lived until 1884, and in the latter year located at Lebanon, Mo., where they still live. Mr. Lingsweiler is a well-to-do farmer. Edward Lingsweiler received his education in the common schools of Racine County, Wis., and was reared on a farm. In 1878 he went to Lebanon, Mo., and the following two years clerked for his brother, John G., in the lumber business. The brother then removed to Richland, and established a lumber business under the firm name of Lingsweiler Bros., which continued until January, 1883, when John G. retired, and our subject has since conducted the business alone with remarkable success. In November, 1884, Mr. Lingsweiler married Zippora Farrar, daughter of Reuben and Virginia Farrar, and a native of St. Clair, Mo. Mr. and Mrs. Lingsweiler have three children. They are members in good standing of the Methodist Episcopal Church, where Mr. Lingsweiler is a steward and trustee. He has a fine residence in Richland, and good business property. He is a Republican in politics, and a member of the A. O. U. W. and Select Knights of Richland.

Joseph Martin Long, sheriff of Pulaski County, Mo., was born in Greenup County, Ky., March 19, 1855, and is a son of George W. and Mary Ann (Gray) Long, and grandson of Martin Long, who was born in Botetourt County, of the "Old Dominion," and by occupation was a sailor in early life and a cooper in later years. He moved to Kentucky at an early date, his son, George W., being born in Greenup County, of that State, in 1824. The latter was married in his native county, and in the fall of 1855 moved to Hancock County, Ky., and sixteen months later to Spencer County, Ind., residing there until 1867, when he took up his abode in Pulaski County, Mo., locating three miles south of the county seat. Here he died in 1877. He was of French and German descent. His wife was also born in Greenup County, Ky., in 1834, and is the daughter of Joseph Gray. She is yet living, and since 1885 has been the wife of J. O. R. Reeves, and is residing in Wright County, Mo. To her marriage with Mr. Long three children were born: William P., Francis M. and Joseph M. The latter was about twelve years of age when he first became a resident of Pulaski County. His early days were spent in following the plow and attending the common schools, and on the 23d of August, 1874, he espoused Miss Matilda, a daughter of John J. and Catherine Laughlin. She was born in 1859, and died in 1877, having become the mother of one child, Luther. Mr. Long afterward wedded Miss Margaret J. Logan, a daughter of Anthony and Margaret Logan. Her birth occurred in Pulaski County, Mo., in 1858, and their union has resulted in the birth of three children: Sarah Ann, Henry Martin and Lydia Adelia. Until 1885 Mr. Long was engaged in husbandry, at which date he moved to Waynesville, and began keeping a grocery, but sold out at the end of two years, and engaged in blacksmithing. After a short period he discontinued this business, and resumed the sale of groceries, forming, in 1887, a partnership with J. J. Clark in the general mercantile business, which partnership continued until they were burned out. After this Mr. Long became a salesman for Mr. Clark. In 1888 he was elected on the Democratic ticket, whose principles he has always espoused, as sheriff of Pulaski County, and is the present incumbent of that office. During 1886-87 he served as deputy sheriff of the county, and gave good satisfaction. In the fall of 1883 he moved to Jack County, Tex., where he resided eleven months, and then returned to Missouri. He and wife worship in the Baptist Church.

Hon. Joe McGregor, attorney at law, of Waynesville, Ohio, was born in Osage County, Mo., June 14, 1857, and is a son of Dr. Allan L. and Anna M. (Mosby) McGregor, and grandson of James McGregor, who was born in Scotland, and came to the United States in 1812 or 1813, locating in Wheeling, W. Va. He died in Keokuk, Iowa, in 1881. His son Allan was born in Wheeling in 1827, and became a citizen of Osage County, Mo., in 1851, where he entered the teacher's profession, taking up the study of medicine at the same time, afterward attending Pope's Medical College at St. Louis, Mo., from which institution he graduated. He practiced his profession in Osage County until 1862, when he moved to Maries County, and in 1871 became a citizen of Pulaski County. Here he was actively engaged in practicing medicine until the summer of 1888, when he was stricken with paralysis, and has since been unable to attend to his work. In politics he is stanch Democrat, and in 1880 was elected on that ticket to represent Pulaski County in the State Legislature, serving one term. He is one of the foremost citizens of the county in which he resides, and is highly honored and esteemed by his fellow men. His wife was born in Kentucky in 1834, and died in 1858, and after her death he espoused Miss Susan McKnight, who died in 1881. Two sons were born to each marriage: Allan and Joe to the first, and James and Pryor to the last. Joe McGregor attended the common schools in boyhood, and at the early age of fifteen years engaged in "teaching the young idea," receiving a first-class certificate from Judge V. B. Hill, who was school examiner of Pulaski County at that time, and followed that occupation for about seven years in Phelps, Maries and Pulaski Counties. In 1880 he became connected with the *Pulaski County Tribune*, published at Waynesville, his partner being D. Rainey. He was connected with the paper for three years, and then sold his interest, and the same year was admitted to the bar, having been an earnest student of Blackstone for some time. In 1884-85 he took the senior law course in the State University at Columbia, Mo., and in March, 1885, graduated with the degree of LL. B. Since that time he has practiced his profession in Waynesville, being also engaged in abstracting and the general real estate business, and has in his possession the only complete set of abstract books in the county. He is a stanch Democrat and an active worker for his party, and has frequently been a delegate to State and judicial conventions. He is a member of the Masonic fraternity, and September 25, 1886, was married to Miss Fanny Price, who was born in Maries County, Mo., in 1869, and by her is the father of one child, Ralph.

Samuel J. Manes, an attorney at law of Richland, was born in Miller County, Mo., in 1840, and is a son of Jacob W. and Emeline (Hice) Manes, natives of Tennessee and North Carolina, respectively.

The parents were early settlers of Miller County, where they were married about 1834, and there they spent the remainder of their lives, with the exception of four years spent in Arkansas. The father, who was a farmer by occupation, served eighteen years as justice of the peace in Miller and Ozark Counties, and died in the latter county in 1852. The mother is still living, and has been a member of the Baptist Church for sixty-four years, of which church her husband was also a member. The paternal grandfather, Seth Manes, was of Welsh descent, and was a Revolutionary soldier. He died in Hawkins County, Tenn. At the early age of thirteen years Samuel J. Manes engaged in farming, and a few years later he learned the blacksmith's trade, which he followed with remarkable success until 1885. He then abandoned his trade and took up the study of law, and was admitted to the practice of the legal profession in October, 1886, since which time he has earned for himself a place in the ranks of the successful attorneys of Pulaski County. He has an extensive practice, which is steadily increasing. He was elected justice of the peace in 1886, of which office he is the present incumbent. He was a soldier in the late war in the United States army, in Company A, Sixty-fifth Illinois Infantry Regiment, and was mustered out at the close of the war in Greensborough, N. C. Mr. Manes was first married, in 1857, to Abigail Lane, who died in 1858, and the following year he married Margaret Reed, who was the mother of six children: J. T., J. O., W. J., S. J., A. E. and M. J. Manes. His third wife was Mary E. Burhans, whom he married in 1872, and who was the mother of two children, Ida M. and Bertha E. In 1888 Mr. Manes married Lucinda Long, who still survives, and is a member of the Baptist Church. She is the mother of one child, S. J. Manes, and is a noble wife. Mr. Manes owns 160 acres of land two and one-half miles from Richland, as well as some good property in the town. He is clerk of the Baptist Church, a Republican in politics, and an enterprising citizen.

George S. Marks was born in Juniata County, Penn., April 23, 1836, and is a son of Jacob and Anna (Snyder) Marks and grandson of Jacob Marks. The latter was born in Hanover, Germany, and came to the United States previous to his marriage, with his two brothers, John and Peter, who had been millers for the king of their province in their native land, and had to flee the country owing to an edict passed by him. Jacob settled in Perry County, Penn., where he engaged in farming, and was afterward married to a Miss Kleener, she also being of German birth. They both died in Juniata County, having become the parents of the following children: John, Jacob, Luke, Katie (Campbell), Polly (Hildebrand), Hannah (Bell) and two other daughters, who married Costetters. The son, Jacob Marks, was born in Perry County, Penn., February 14, 1800, and by self-application acquired a good education and an excellent knowledge of surveying, filling the office of surveyor of Juniata County for a number of years. He was also engaged in teaching school for twenty-three years, sixteen of the years being spent in teaching two schools. During the Mexican War he volunteered his services, but was never sent to the front, and was also a volunteer in the late war. He resided in his native county until his death in May, 1872. His wife was born in Union County, Penn., October 25, 1798, and received a good education, her father, John Snyder, being a wealthy farmer. She was married on October 22, 1819, to Mr. Marks, to whom she bore twelve children, nine now living: Phoebe A., Andrew N., Daniel H., Louisa J., Peter A., Margaret E., George S., Isaiah W. and Lydia H. Those deceased are John L., Jacob S. and Susannah. The mother of these children died January 2, 1851. John Snyder, her father, was born in Philadelphia County, Penn., in 1772. He was a farmer and manufacturer by occupation, and was a brother of Simon Snyder, who was governor of the State of Pennsylvania for six years, Snyder County being named in honor of the family. John Snyder was married to Susannah Grabiel, who was born in Northumberland County, Penn., in 1776. She was an infant at the time of the Sunberry massacre, December 25, 1776, and was in her mother's arms when the latter was foully murdered by the Indians. She was rescued by her father, who succeeded in making his escape, and who afterward established Fort Grabiel as a protection against the Indians. During the Revolutionary War he served with distinction as major. George S. Marks resided in his native State until he was twenty-one years of age, receiving no early educational advantages, but has since acquired a fair English education. He worked on a farm and at railroading while in his native State, and in June, 1856, immigrated to Calhoun County, Ill., where he attended school for a short time, and afterward clerked for Lewis Swarens and Jacob Crater for about eighteen months. He then farmed in Pike County, Ill., for about three years, and January 9, 1859, was married to Mary A. Long, a daughter of Thomas S. and Fannie (Deemen) Long. The father was born in Bucks County, Penn., October 3, 1807, and lived to maturity near Easton. He was a farmer, and in 1835 immigrated to Pike County, Ill., where he died November 23, 1884, aged seventy-seven years. His wife was born in the same county as himself, her birth occurring November 7, 1810. She is still living. Their daughter, Mary A., was born in Pike County, Ill., November 27, 1839, and by Mr. Marks became the mother of eight children, seven of whom are living: Alice J., Fannie B., William S., Thomas Grant, Addie May, Charles E. and Orpha B. Eva Maud is deceased. Mr. Marks resided in Illinois until 1868, when he moved to Vernon County, Mo., and at the end of sixteen years came to Pulaski County, where he has a fine farm of 550 acres, with 150 in a good state of cultivation. He also laid out Marks' addition to the town of Crocker, and owns sixty lots. In 1862 he enlisted in Company I, Ninety-ninth Illinois Volunteer Infantry, and served as orderly-sergeant and first lieutenant, being in the service over two years and a half. He was in the battles of Hartville, Vicksburg, Fort Gibson, Raymond, Champion's Hill, Black River Bridge, Jackson and a number of others. He was discharged at Springfield, Ill., December 16, 1864. He is now a member of the G. A. R., and a member of the Pilgrim Knights, Oriental Masonry, Masonic Lodge for twenty-four years, and for thirty years has been a member of the

American Bible Society. His wife is a member of the Cumberland Presbyterian Church.

James M. Mays, farmer and stock raiser, of Liberty Township, was born in Hawkins County, East Tenn., in 1828, being a son of William and Crotia (Miner) Mays, who were born, reared and married in Halifax County, Va. They afterward removed to Hawkins County, Tenn., and there spent the remainder of their lives, the father dying at the close of the war and the mother six years later. The father was a farmer and stock raiser, and was a soldier in the War of 1812. His father, Beverly Mays, was a Virginian, and resided in his native State for many years, but during the latter portion of his life removed to Tennessee, where he spent the remainder of his days, and is now resting in the family burying ground in that State. James M. Mays is the eighth of thirteen children, three of whom are living in Pulaski County, two in Tennessee, one in Kentucky, two in California and one in Oregon. Two sons served in the Federal army during the late war, and two in the Confederate army. One of the latter, the youngest of the family, Charles T. H., was killed at Altoona Pass, Ga., near the close of the war. James M. was educated in the common schools of East Tennessee, and at the age of twenty began life for himself, coming to Pulaski County, Mo., in October, 1847, and was engaged in clerking for his brother-in-law in Waynesville until 1850. In the latter year he, in company with eighty persons, started on the overland trip to California, driving ox-teams, and after a seven-months' journey reached their destination. He mined successfully for three years, and then went to the valleys, where he invested his means in cattle, and was engaged in stock raising until 1857, when he returned to Waynesville via the Isthmus of Panama and Cuba. He soon after made a visit to his parents in East Tennessee; then he and a brother-in-law, J. A. Rayl, engaged in the mercantile business in Waynesville. About a year later Mr. Mays established a store in Camden County, which he continued to conduct until the breaking out of the war, and since that time has been engaged in farming. In 1860 he was married to Elizabeth, daughter of Judge William and Mary Gillespie, who were natives of North Carolina, and were among the earliest settlers of Pulaski County, locating on the farm, which was then densely covered with woods, now owned by Mr. Mays. The mother died about 1853, and the father several years later. Mr. Gillespie was a man of prominence and influence, and was one of the judges of the Pulaski County Court. Mr. Mays became the father of four children, but only three of them are now living. He resided on a farm until about 1883, and then came to Richland to educate his children. He owns 340 acres of land, the greater portion of which is rich bottom land, and all this he has obtained by his own exertions and the aid of his worthy and intelligent wife. He was formerly a Whig in politics, but now supports the principles of the Democratic party. His wife is a member of the Christian Church, and one daughter is a member of the Methodist Church.

C. Miller, attorney at law, Dixon, Mo., is a native of Fayette County, born in Vandalia, in the State of Illinois, December 25, 1833.

He is the son of John C. Miller and Nancy Dudley Miller. His father was born in Grainger County, Tenn., in the year 1799, and died on his farm on Spring Creek, which was first Pulaski, then Maries, and now Phelps County, Mo., his death occurring June 10, 1867. His mother, Nancy Dudley Miller, was born in the city of Portsmouth, Va., and died June 10, 1872, at Rolla, Mo. Her genealogy dates back to the earliest English settlements in America, whose ancestry were of the Dudley family, of England. The father resided upon and operated a fine farm, taught school, was elected judge of the county court and justice of the peace for many years. He was a participant in the War of 1812, and received a serious wound in the battle at Pensacola, Fla., which made him an invalid throughout life, and finally caused his death. He was the father of ten children, eight of whom are living, and all reside in Phelps County, Mo., with the exception of C. Miller, whose name heads this sketch. The latter spent his early life in Phelps County, and there received a good education in the common schools and at home. He began life for himself at an early age, first engaging in the mercantile business in Maries County, Mo., and in 1859 and 1861 established two stores in Pulaski County. At the latter date he opened a store in Rolla, and in 1862–63 served as sheriff of Phelps County. About this time he assisted in organizing the Thirty-sixth Regiment Missouri Infantry Volunteers, and was in command of Company B of this regiment for some time. At the age of eighteen, while yet residing with his father, he began the study of law, and continued reading for many years, accumulating a large library of law books, which, however, was unfortunately burned in 1869. He was admitted to the Pulaski County bar in 1874, and has since devoted his attention to the practice of his profession in the Eighteenth and Ninth Judicial Circuits. He is the oldest notary public in the county, now holding his sixth commission. He has a fine farm of 400 acres, 150 of which are under good cultivation. All is under fence, and makes one of the best farms in the county. In 1855 he was married to Miss Charlotte B. Love, who died the same year. Afterward he married his second wife, Miss Annie Fleming, who was born in Nashville, Tenn. They have two daughters living, Flossa Dudley and Gertrude May, and one son and one daughter deceased. Mr. Miller is a Republican, and cast his first presidential vote for Abraham Lincoln in 1860.

Richard Miller, farmer and stock raiser, of Piney Township, Pulaski Co., Mo., was born in Baden, Germany, in 1832, and is a son of Joseph and Josephine (Whachter) Miller, who were born in 1797 and 1807 and died in 1857 and 1860, respectively. The father was a blacksmith and farmer, and he and wife were the parents of four children. Richard immigrated to Canada in 1852, and at the end of two years removed to Davis County, Ill., and a year later located in Douglas County, Kas. About four years later he went to New Orleans, La., where he spent two years as a cook on a steamer. His next move was to Franklin County, Mo., and after a residence of seven years in that county he came to Pulaski County, where he has since made his home. In 1862 he was married to Miss Julia Kelly, who was born in Franklin County, Mo., in 1844. She is a daughter of Peter and Bridget Kelly, and is of Irish descent, and the mother of four children. Mr. Miller has an excellent farm of 336 acres, and has 200 acres in a good state of cultivation, and ships one car load of cattle and hogs per year. He is a Republican in politics. Both he and his wife are members of the Catholic Church.

John Morgan (deceased), farmer, of Pulaski County, Mo., was born in Tennessee in 1817, and was the third of eight children born to the marriage of Reuben Morgan and Elizabeth Dowel, who were natives of North Carolina. The father was of Irish descent, a farmer by occupation, and died in what is now Phelps County, Mo., when about fifty years of age. His wife was born about 1797, and after his death made her home with her son John, and died in 1862. John was educated in the district schools near his home, and resided with his parents until his father's death. August 26, 1845, he was united in marriage to Miss Mary A. Tilley, who was born January 4, 1828, in the State of Tennessee, and by her became the father of ten children, six of whom are living: Rebecca, wife of Curtis York; George, Loura R., Lottie W., John B., and Mattie, wife of Ransom Rollins. Mr. Morgan located with his parents on the farm now occupied by his widow at the age of sixteen years, and became an enterprising and influential citizen of the county. He died in 1877, December 30, and left a farm of 240 acres, 160 under cultivation, to his wife. It is located on the Roubideaux River, and is valuable land. Mr. Morgan was a Democrat in politics, a member of the Masonic fraternity, and an earnest believer in the Christian faith. His widow is a member of the Methodist Episcopal Church, South. Mrs. Morgan's parents, Wilson and Elizabeth Tilley, were of Scotch and Irish descent, respectively.

Hon. John O. Morrison is a native of Barren County, Ky., and was born in 1836. He was the fourth in the family of three sons and eight daughters born to Joseph F. and Martha (Faulkner) Morrison, both natives of Culpeper County, Va., and born respectively in 1800 and 1806, whence, when young, they removed with their parents to Kentucky, where they were married and spent the remainder of their lives. The father was a farmer by occupation, and died in April, 1860; his widow died October 2, 1862. The maternal grandfather of our subject, James Faulkner, was born in Virginia, and died in Pettis County, Mo., several years before the war. John O. Morrison was reared on a farm within thirty miles of Mammoth Cave, Ky., and received his education in the common schools. He remained with his father's family, assisting in the support of the younger members, until 1867, when he went to Barry County, Mo., and there spent one year as a clerk. He then engaged in merchandising at Linn Creek, under the firm name of Crouch & Morrison, which was successfully conducted until 1872; in the latter year Mr. Morrison formed a partnership with a Mr. Moulder, and entered the mercantile business at Richland. In 1886 Mr. Moulder sold his interest to Capt. Benjamin D. Dodson, with whom Mr. Morrison continued in business until February, 1888, when the firm was dissolved by mutual consent, and both members retired. Mr. Morrison was prominent in organizing the Pulaski County Bank at Richland, of which he is president and one of the principal stockholders. He owns a fine farm of 400 acres in Camden County, about ten miles north of Richland, besides considerable town property, and is one of the prominent and wealthy citizens of Pulaski, which place he has taken an active interest in building up. He was a member of the city council for several years, and November 6, 1888, was elected by the Democratic party, by a large majority, to represent Pulaski County in the Legislature. He is a member of the A. F. & A. M., having taken the Royal Arch and Commandery degrees; he is also a member of the A. O. U. W. October 12, 1869, Mr. Morrison married Alice Ferguson, a native of Hannibal, Mo., who died February 10, 1870. In July, 1873, Mr. Morrison married Joe Ann, daughter of Benjamin D. and Joe Ann Dodson. Mrs. Morrison was born in Glaize City, Camden County, in February, 1854, and is the mother of one child. Capt. Benjamin D. Dodson was born in East Tennessee, but when quite young went with his parents to Alabama, subsequently removing to Camden County, Mo., where he was reared and lived many years, but is now a resident of Richland. The maternal grandmother of Mrs. Morrison, Mary K. (Haden) Sprout, was born in Virginia in 1810, and at the age of about five years went with her parents, Joseph and Nancy Haden, to Kentucky, where the father died, and about 1839 the family removed to Springfield, Mo., then but a village; there the mother died, leaving four children. Mary K. was married in 1831, in Kentucky, to John Sprout, who died in 1835, and in 1840, in Springfield, Mo., she was united in marriage with John DeBruin, who died about 1857; she has since lived a widow, and now has her home with Mr. Morrison. She is one of the pioneers of Southern Missouri, and for forty-nine years has been a consistent member of the Christian Church. Mr. and Mrs. Morrison are also members of the Christian Church.

W. S. Musgrave, senior member of the general mercantile firm of Musgrave & Rollins, who have been the successors of Morrison & Dodson since February, 1888, was born in 1847, and is a son of Bennett H. and Sarah (Nelson) Musgrave, natives of Jackson County, Tenn., the former's birth occurring in 1803. Both were formerly married in Tennessee, and after coming to Pulaski County, Mo., lost their respective companions, and were afterward married. The mother died in 1871, and the father in 1864, on the Pacific Ocean, while *en route* to California, and was buried at sea. He was a farmer throughout life, and accumulated a considerable portion of this world's goods. In 1850 he crossed the plains to California, where he was engaged in mining and farming for three years. At the latter date he returned home, and from 1856 to 1861 lived in Colley Hollow, on the St. Louis and Springfield road, where he kept a tavern known as the California House, which still bears that name. W. S. Musgrave, whose name heads this sketch, is the younger of two brothers; the elder, George, who was with his father at the time of his death, died in California about 1885. W. S. was educated in the common schools, and at the age of sixteen years began doing for himself. During the late war he drove

Government teams, and in March, 1865, joined a company of Missouri Rangers for one year, but was mustered out in July of that year. After the war he farmed until 1880, and then came to Richland and became the owner of a hotel known as the Richland House, now known as the "Home." A year later he discontinued this business and began clerking in the dry goods establishment of G. W. Morgan & Co., and at the same time ran a furniture store, continuing the latter business until 1888, when he sold out and engaged in his present occupation, the stock being valued at $6,000. January 30, 1868, he was married to Aggie, a daughter of Allen and Perlina Stevens, who were formerly of Adair County, Ky., but became early settlers of Pulaski County. Mrs. Musgrave, who was a worthy and consistent member of the Methodist Church, died on the 18th of July, 1888, leaving her husband and two sons and one daughter to mourn her loss. Mr. Musgrave is a Democrat, and cast his first presidential vote for S. J. Tilden, in 1876, and has held the office of alderman. He is a member of the A. O. U. W., Lodge No. 212; Select Knights, Lodge No. 115, and is Worthy Master in the A. F. & A. M., Lodge No. 382.

William H. Murphy, attorney at law, of Crocker, Mo., was born in Franklin County, Mo., October 26, 1844, and is a son of Isaiah T. and Rebecca J. (Clark) Murphy. The father is also a native of Franklin County, born November 18, 1815, and owing to the wild condition of the country in his boyhood days, he was compelled to be very diligent in order to obtain an education. From 1866 to 1868 he resided in Miller County, and at the latter date came to Hancock, in Pulaski County, where he supplied beef to the contractors until the completion of the road. He and his sons, T. A. and W. H., opened a store in Hancock in 1869, continuing until 1875, when he sold out to his sons and removed to Miller County, and after farming there until 1882 moved to Dixon, and is now farming near that place. His wife was born in Virginia, and with her parents moved to Illinois, thence to Missouri, where she met and married Mr. Murphy, by whom she became the mother of nine children, five of whom are living: Thomas A., William H., Perron F., Frank W. and Robert C. Those deceased are Lilburn, Anvil M., Mary and Emma. The paternal grandfather, Isaac Murphy, was born in Kentucky, and immigrated to Missouri before its admission into the Union as a State, settling on the land on which the town of Washington is now located. He was the first circuit and county clerk of the county, and there resided until his death. William H. Murphy was reared in his native county, and at the age of eighteen years enlisted in Company E, Thirty-first Missouri Volunteer Infantry, and served until the 18th of December, 1864, when he was wounded at Macon, Ga., while with Sherman on his march to the sea. He was at Chickasaw Bayou, being wounded and taken prisoner on the 30th of December, and sent to Vicksburg, and at the end of one month was taken to Jackson, where he was confined two and one-half months, after which he was paroled and sent to New Orleans. He was next sent to New York City, thence to Benton Barracks at St. Louis, Mo. He subsequently joined his command near Chattanooga, Tenn., and participated in the battles of Lookout Mountain, Missionary Ridge, Resaca, Kenesaw Mountain, Atlanta, and numerous others. He was discharged at Central Park Hospital, New York City, and returned to Franklin County, Mo., where he accepted a position on a steamer running from St. Louis to Omaha, being assistant engineer for two years. After residing with his father one year he went to Hancock, where he located the town. In December, 1869, he was married to Miss Sallie Kanada, who is a daughter of Charles and Lucy Kanada, and was born and reared in Franklin County. They have four children: Arthur P., Kate C., Mary and William H., Jr. Mr. Murphy began the study of law in 1865, and in 1876 was admitted to the Pulaski County bar, and has since practiced his profession in Maries, Phelps, Pulaski and Miller Counties. He is also engaged in the lumber business in Crocker, and owns 800 acres of land, 200 acres of which are under cultivation. In 1874 he was elected president of the Pulaski County Court to fill an unexpired term, and in his political views is a stanch Republican. He is a member of the I. O. O. F., and is a Select Knight in the A. O. U. W. He has been postmaster of Dixon and Hancock. He and wife are members of the Methodist Episcopal Church.

James B. Overbey was born in Mecklenburgh County, Va., February 14, 1833, being a son of Cain and Sallie (White) Overbey, both of whom were born and reared in the same county as our subject. A few years after their marriage they moved to Granville County, N. C., where they were engaged in farming, but at the end of one year returned to Virginia, and there spent the remainder of their days. Both the paternal and maternal grandparents were natives of Virginia, the former family being of English descent. Grandfather Overbey died near Clarksville, Ky., aged about eighty years. James B. Overbey remained in Virginia until eighteen years of age, and then went to Cleveland County, N. C., where he made his home for fifteen years, where he was engaged in buying land and farming. In 1853 he was married to Miss Jane Glasscock, who was born and reared in that county, and by her became the father of six children: Alfred W., Mary J., Lucy B., James R., Marcus L. and Zulia F. He moved to Lafayette County, Ill., his wife dying the first year of their residence there, and in 1868 he wedded Lydia Deardeuff, a daughter of Stephen and Margaret Deardeuff. She was born in Ohio March 17, 1853, but was reared principally in Illinois. She received good school advantages, and her marriage with Mr. Overbey was blessed in the birth of seven children, six of whom are living: William T., Tura A., John L., Franky E., Dora M. and Elmar A. Docia B. is deceased. In 1871 Mr. Overbey immigrated to Missouri, and settled on the farm of 200 acres where he now lives. He served in the Confederate army during the late war, in Company A, Thirty-fourth North Carolina Volunteer Infantry, and received his discharge at the end of three and a half years, having participated in the battles of Cedar Mountain, the seven days fight at Richmond, Malvern Hill, Bull Run, Chancellorsville, Gaines Mill, Sharpsburg, Harper's Ferry and Gettysburg, being captured in the retreat from the latter battle. He was kept a prisoner at Washington, D. C., and Point

Lookout for sixteen months, and was then taken to Savannah, Ga., where he was exchanged and returned home. Since coming to Pulaski County, Mo., he has given his attention to farming, and is doing well financially. He and wife are members of the Christian Church, and he is a member of the Agricultural Wheel, and in politics is a Democrat.

William Pemberton may be mentioned as one of the prosperous farmers of Pulaski County, Mo. He was born near Paris, in Middle Tennessee, October 3, 1832, and is a son of Thomas and Dica (Winfrey) Pemberton, and grandson of William Pemberton, who was of German descent, a Virginian by birth, and immigrated to Kentucky at an early day, going from there to Illinois, where he died. His wife, whose maiden name was Nancy Skaggs, was also born in Virginia. The maternal grandparents, James and Winnie Winfrey, were also born in Virginia. Thomas and Dica Pemberton were born and married in Kentucky. They afterward moved to Missouri, and settled in what was then Miller County in 1834. Five years later he went to Illinois, and during a residence of five years in that State was engaged in farming. After returning to Missouri he resided two years in Miller County, and then moved to Camden County, where he died January 12, 1860. After his death his widow resided with her son William, and died at his home March 9, 1886. The following are their children: William, Alexander, Nancy, Eliza and Melvina. Winnie, Lewis and Ruthie are deceased. William Pemberton was brought to Missouri when about two years of age, and was reared to a farm life in Miller and Camden Counties. He received a fair education in the subscription schools of his day, and made his home with his parents until grown. At the age of twenty-two years he began farming for himself with his grandfather, and February, 23, 1854, was married to Lucinda Wade, a daughter of John and Rhoda (Barnett) Wade. She was born in Kentucky, and at the age of twelve years came to Missouri, and was married in Miller County to Mr. Pemberton, by whom she became the mother of ten children, five of whom are living: Thomas. Nancy J., Preston, Sarah M. and William R. In 1859 Mr. Pemberton located on his present farm of 220 acres, the country at that time being very sparsely settled, there being no schools or churches, and but one house between his home and Crocker. During the late war he did effective service in the State Militia, and with this exception has always lived the peaceful life of the farmer. He has always supported the Republican party, and his wife is a member of the Methodist Episcopal Church.

Loss Peterson, farmer, of Union Township, Pulaski Co., Mo., was born in Sweden in 1832, and is a son of Peter Peterson, who married a Miss Ingera. They were also born in that country, the father being a farmer and a carpenter by occupation. They were the parents of four children, two of whom are living: Loss and Paer G. The paternal grandfather was Peter Peterson, who was born in Sweden, and there spent his days. Loss Peterson went to Denmark in 1854, where he was engaged in farming until 1867, when he immigrated to the United States and located at Urbana, Ohio, making his home in that town for ten years, being engaged in tilling the soil. He then concluded to try his luck a little farther westward, and accordingly located in Missouri, where he purchased the farm of 188 acres where he now lives. He has eighty acres under cultivation, and is already considered one of the thrifty farmers of the county. In 1859 he was wedded to Miss Esther Grangoard, who was born in Schleswick Holstien, Germany, March 14, 1834, and by her is the father of three children: Ingera, Peter and Anna Margareta. Mr. Peterson is a Democrat politically, and his first presidential vote was cast for Samuel J. Tilden in 1876. He is a member of the Agricultural Wheel, and he and family worship in the Lutheran Church. His wife is a daughter of Hans C. and Anna Margareta (Nicholson) Grangoard. The father is a shoemaker, and he and wife are the parents of nine children, two of whom, one son and one daughter, are residing in America.

George W. Pippin was born in Hickory County, Mo., January 28, 1856, and is a son of William and Nancy J. (Tilley) Pippin, who were born in Tennessee and Pulaski County, Mo., respectively. The father was taken to Alabama when young, and was reared on a plantation in that State, coming to Pulaski County, Mo., about forty years ago, and settling on the farm on which his son, George W., now lives. He served during the late war, and he and wife became the parents of eleven children, the following being those living: Virginia, George W., William J., Thomas J., Aniah, Alice, Charley, Joseph, Bland and Lizzie. Robert is deceased. Mrs. Pippin died in March, 1881, and Mr. Pippin in May, 1879. The grandfather, Hill Pippin, was a native of Tennessee, and died in Missouri. Grandfather Tilley was also a Tennesseean, and became a resident of Pulaski County, Mo., before Waynesville was established. Grandmother Tilley is still living, and is in her eighty-first year. George W. Pippin, whose name heads this sketch, was reared in Hickory County until eleven years of age, receiving a good common-school education. He began life for himself at the age of twenty-one, being engaged in farming on the home place, and September 17, 1882, was married to Miss Docia Rollins, who was born and reared in Pulaski County. Her parents, James M. and Sarah J. (Martin) Rollins, were born, reared and married in Scott County, Va., and immigrated to Missouri in 1858, settling on a farm in Pulaski County. Mr. and Mrs. Pippin are the parents of three children: Alvah, Thomas C. and Olive G. They reside upon a farm of 100 acres, all under cultivation, and are doing well financially. He is a Democrat and a member of the Methodist Episcopal Church, and his wife is a member of the Missionary Baptist Church. Her paternal grandparents were born in Virginia, and her maternal grandparents in Tennessee and North Carolina, respectively.

John Price, proprietor of a grist and saw-mill in Liberty Township, and also a farmer and stock dealer of the same, was born in Washington County, Tenn., in 1850, and is a son of Hiram and Lucinda Jane (Craddock) Price, who were probably Tennesseeans, and came to Ozark County, Mo., about 1854, where they resided a number of years, and from 1860 to 1865 lived in Adair County. From that time until 1878 they again resided in Ozark County, and after a residence of about five years in Texas took up their abode in Laclede County, Mo., where they now make their home. The father is a successful farmer and stock dealer, and for some years sold goods on his farm. He has been married twice. His first wife died about 1852, and he afterward married Miss Nancy J. Smith, by whom he had three children, two of whom are living. Both he and wife have been members of the Baptist Church for many years. John Price is the younger of two children, his sister, Mary Ann, being the wife of J. W. Hawkins, of Ozark County, Mo. John's early days were spent in Ozark and Adair Counties, but his educational advantages were quite limited. After the war he attended school for about twelve months, and received more practical benefit from this schooling than from all his previous attendance. He was married in Webster County, Mo., when but eighteen years of age, to Sarah E. Williams, who was born in Tennessee, and died in 1874, having borne three children. Mr. Price's second marriage was consummated March 9, 1880, to Malinda J., daughter of Daniel Smith, formerly of Kentucky. She was born in Pulaski County, and became the mother of two children. Mr. Price resided in Ozark County a few years after his first marriage, and after living about one year in Texas came to Pulaski County, and was engaged in stock trading in Richland until 1886, when he located on his present farm. He has 120 acres of land in two farms, all of which he has earned by his own effort, and has a fine residence, which he has erected since his purchase. He is a Democrat in politics, and has served as constable and deputy sheriff; he is a member of the A. O. U. W., Lodge No. 115, and the Select Knights, Lodge No. 212. He is a liberal contributor to all public enterprises, and spares no pains to give his children good educations. Mrs. Price is a member of the Baptist Church.

Rev. Henry Roam, minister of the Christian Church at Swedeborg, Mo., and also a farmer and stock raiser of Liberty Township, was ordained in 1884 by Elder John Glover, and since that time has expounded the doctrine of the Christian Church in Pulaski, Camden and Laclede Counties. He is the pastor of the Pleasant Grove congregation, but owing to ill-health has been compelled to abandon many other congregations. He united with the church in 1861, and has since been a faithful member and active worker for the grand cause of Christianity. He had been an elder for some years prior to his ordination, and had occupied pulpits at different times in the absence of the regular pastor. He was born in Overton County, Tenn., in 1835, was reared on a farm, and in early life had meager educational advantages. In April, 1853, he was married to Rhoda, a daughter of Thomas Jefferson and Lydia Strain, by whom he became the father of eleven children, six sons and three daughters living. He came to Pulaski County in 1857, and in 1867 settled on his present farm near Swedeborg. He owns 400 acres of land in different farms, and has about 150 acres under cultivation, and has proved himself to be one of the industrious and honorable citizens of the county. He started in life a poor boy, but by the breaking out of the war had accumulated considerable means, all of which were destroyed during that conflict. He was then obliged to commence anew, with broken health, and by close application to business, good management and economy has secured a good home for his declining years. In July, 1864, he joined Company A, Missouri Infantry, United States Army, at Waynesville, Mo., and went with the regiment to Rolla, where he was taken sick. He remained with the regiment, however, until it was ordered to Tennessee, and while at Spring Hill was sent to the hospital at Nashville, in which he was kept eight or ten days. Later he was removed from there to Louisville, Ky. Up to this time he could not write his name, but while in the hospital he was seized with a desire to write a letter to his family, and requested one of the officers in charge to set him a copy, which he soon mastered, and in a short time was able to write his name, and soon wrote a letter home. He remained at Louisville until May, 1865, when he was sent to his regiment at Chicago, and in June to St. Louis, where he received his discharge. He then returned home, and has since been engaged in preaching the gospel, farming and stock raising. He has spared no pains to educate his children, and has done all in his power to promote the welfare of the community in which he has resided. He has been a life-long Democrat, and cast his first presidential vote for Buchanan in 1856. His wife and six children are also members of the Christian Church. His parents, Rev. Isaac and Elizabeth (Ward) Roam, were born, reared and married in North Carolina, and about 1832 moved to Overton County, Tenn., where the father died in 1862, at the age of seventy-one years. The mother is still living, and has resided in Pulaski County since 1872. Both were members of the Christian Church for many years, and reared a family of nine children, seven of whom are living. The father was a minister of the Christian Church for many years, and was also a miller and farmer. He was thrown on his own resources at an early age, and would work wherever he could find employment. He grew to manhood without obtaining any schooling, but in after years became an exceptionally well-informed man. He was a soldier in the War of 1812. His father was a wealthy German, who came to the United States and settled in North Carolina, and when Isaac was about eight years of age he was making preparation to start on a visit to his native land; but before starting, and while making preparation, his dead body was found in a creek in North Carolina. The mother lived until Isaac was a man.

 James M. Rollins, a farmer and stock raiser of Liberty Township, is a son of Harrison and Elizabeth (Hobbs) Rollins, and was born in Russell County, W. Va., in 1830. The parents were natives of Virginia, the father born about 1790, and the mother in 1799, and they spent their entire lives in their native State. Harrison Rollins, who was a farmer, was of French descent; he died in 1856, and his wife about twelve years later. James M. Rollins was the second in a family of eleven children, six of whom grew to maturity. He received his education in the common schools, and in 1851 he married Sarah J., daughter of Rev. Elisha and Emily Martin, natives, respectively, of Virginia and North Carolina, who afterward settled in Virginia, where Mrs. Rollins was born and reared. The parents subsequently removed to Tennessee, which was their home until their death; the father was a Baptist minister for many years. Of the nine children born to Mr. and Mrs. Rollins, six sons and two daughters are now living, all in Pulaski County. After his marriage Mr. Rollins lived about two and a half years in Tennessee, when he returned to Virginia, where he lived until 1859; he then went to Pulaski County, and for two years rented a farm, on which he improved 100 acres. In 1861 he settled on his present farm, which was then nearly all forest; he owns in all 540 acres, and has 200 acres cleared and well improved. In August, 1862, he enlisted in Company M, Third Iowa Cavalry, and operated principally in Missouri and Arkansas; he was present at the battle of Little Rock, where his regiment was the first to raise the Union flag on the State House, and also at the battle of Saline. He was captured in Arkansas, May 4, 1864, taken to Camp Ford, Tex., and afterward to Camp Gross, and was discharged at New Orleans, after an imprisonment of seven months and ten days. He joined his command at Louisville, Ky., went to Tennessee, and after a visit home on furlough again joined his command at Atlanta, Ga.; at the close of the war he received an honorable discharge at Nashville, Tenn., and returned home. In 1868 he was elected sheriff and collector of Pulaski County, and was re-elected in 1870; he served as justice of the peace a short time after the war, and has been postmaster of Bellefonte since about 1875. In 1873 he established a store on his farm, which he successfully conducted until 1877. He is a Democrat in politics, and is a member of the Baptist Church, of which church Mrs. Rollins is also a member.

John A. Schlicht, miller, of Pulaski County, Mo., is a son of Paul and Anna M. (Lortz) Schlicht, who were born in Hafstetten, Bezirk, Regensburg, Upper Bavaria, and Wohunfurch, in Middle Bavaria, in 1821 and 1818, respectively. The father always followed the occupation of milling, and in his youth received a good education in the schools of Munich, being the master of four languages on leaving school. He served in the War of 1848, and on that account was exiled and went to Switzerland, where he remained two years. He then resumed milling in his native town, and in 1870 immigrated to America, where he died in 1884. He was the father of two children: John A. and Frank, the latter being a miller of Wright County, Mo. The male members of the family for seven generations back have been millers. John A. Schlicht resided in the old country until twenty years of age, and there received an excellent education, being a fine scholar in English and French. He also studied mechanical engineering, and at the age of fourteen entered a machine shop, where he worked two years. The two following years he spent on the ocean, as cadet on a Government vessel, and then returned home and engaged in milling, continuing this occupation until coming to the United States in 1866. He landed at Castle Garden, New York City, without a pair of shoes, but soon after found employment at Danbury,

Conn., working at the milling business for G. Grofuth & Son. He next went to Rochester, N. Y., thence to Lebanon, Mo., where he was manager of J. F. Smith's Mills for six years. In 1876 he purchased the Gasconade Mill, which was then a small water mill, and since then has added the full roller process, the capacity of which is sixty barrels per day, and has both steam and water power. In 1868 he was married to Miss Margaretta, a daughter of Peter Hohman, who is residing in the old country. Mrs. Schlicht immigrated to the United States in 1865, and settled at Rochester, N. Y., where she married Mr. Schlicht. She has two children: Charles and Theressa. Besides his mill, which has a permanent water supply from a large spring near by, Mr. Schlicht owns 200 acres of good land, and gives considerable attention to raising stock. He is a strong Democrat, and is a member of the I. O. O. F.

Oliver W. Shockley, farmer, was born in Gasconade County, Mo., June 22, 1841, being a son of Owen and Elizabeth (Briggs) Shockley. Owen was born in Tennessee, near Nashville, December 3, 1801, and was there reared to manhood on a farm, receiving a common-school education. November 30, 1874, he was married to Miss Briggs, who was born in Tennessee November 10, 1809, and for several years after his marriage resided in Davidson County. He then came to Gasconade County, Mo., but at the end of about three years returned to Tennessee, where he lived one year. From that time until his death, which occurred April 22, 1855, he resided in Gasconade County. He was a farmer throughout life, and a minister of the Methodist Episcopal Church for thirty years. Three of his nine children are living: Sarah, Oliver W. and Mahala. Those deceased are Andrew J., Samuel J., James M. H., Matilda, Malinda and Nellie. Mrs. Shockley died in Gasconade County on the 12th of August, 1869. The grandfather, Richard Shockley, was born in Virginia, and both he and wife died in Tennessee. The maternal grandparents were also Virginians, and settled in Tennessee at an early day, the grandfather dying in Arkansas and the grandmother in Tennessee. They were of German descent. Oliver W. Shockley received a common-school education in his boyhood days, was reared on a farm, and after the death of his father assisted in supporting the family, remaining with his mother until twenty-six years of age, when he was married, May 12, 1869, to Elizabeth J. Lewis, a daughter of John and Lotta (Perkins) Lewis. After residing in Gasconade County for three years after their marriage, they moved to Pulaski County, where he has since been engaged in farming, and now owns 500 acres of land, with 200 acres under cultivation, being also quite extensively engaged in stock raising. In 1861 he enlisted in the Federal army, and served four years in Company M, Fifth Iowa Cavalry, being a participant in numerous bloody battles. He was wounded at Duck River, and was discharged at Camp Dennison, Ohio. He is now the father of five living children: Robert F., Cora, Elizabeth, Isaac and Emmet. Those deceased are Charlotte, John O., Oliver and Ollie. Mr. Shockley is a member of the Masonic fraternity, and is a Republican politically. Mrs. Shockley's father was born in Tennessee, was a farmer by occupation, and previous to his marriage came to Gasconade County, Mo., where he resided until his death. His wife was born in Osage County, Mo., and became the mother of nine children, four of whom are living: Elizabeth, Mary I., Emma A. and Louisa V Those deceased are Tabitha, Samuel W., Sarah C., Hiram and Rebecca T. Mr. Lewis died in Gasconade County in 1865, and his wife in 1879. Both the paternal and maternal grandparents were born in Tennessee.

Charles H. Shubert, attorney at law, of Richland, and the successor of J. A. Bradshaw, was born at Linn Creek in 1858, and is the eldest of six children born to Garret B. and Bridget (Foy) Shubert. Garret B. Shubert was born in Philadelphia, Penn., in 1829, and when fourteen years of age went to sea; he made two trips around the world, and served in various capacities on board ship for fifteen years. Upon leaving ocean sailing he landed on the Pacific coast in California, about 1849, and spent the last few years in steamboating on the Mississippi River. Soon after his marriage in St. Louis, in 1857, he removed to Linn Creek, which has since been his home, with the exception of several years during the war. April 10, 1863, he was commissioned lieutenant of the Eighth Cavalry, Missouri State Militia, and served as lieutenant and adjutant until April 13, 1865, when he resigned, his operations having principally been in Missouri and Arkansas. At the close of the Civil War he was sent as quartermaster of the Fourteenth Missouri Cavalry to fight the Indians, returning to his home at Linn Creek in the fall of 1865. He subsequently spent four or five years flat-boating on the Osage River. In 1871 he was elected probate judge of Camden County, which office he held until 1875, being elected to the same office in 1878, and serving until 1886. From 1878 to 1882 he was presiding judge of the county court, and since 1884 has been county collector. He is a stanch Republican in politics, and an active worker for his party. His father, George Shubert, was of German descent, and a native of Pennsylvania; he was a skillful mechanic, and died at Portsmouth, Ohio, when Garret B. was but twelve years of age. Charles H. Shubert received a good education in the public schools of Linn Creek, and when sixteen years of age he entered the county and circuit court offices, where he studied law, being admitted to the Camden County bar when twenty years of age. He was successfully engaged in the practice of the legal profession at Linn Creek until his removal to Richland, in February, 1888. He is a fluent speaker, and one of the promising attorneys of Richland. He served as prosecuting attorney of Camden County, and has held other minor positions. He is a Republican politically; is a member of the A. F. & A. M. and A. O. U. W. and Select Knights. In 1879 he married Eliza R., daughter of Dr. Joel C. and Ellen V. Crouch. Mr. and Mrs. Crouch removed to Camden County from Kentucky about 1850, where the former died in 1873 and the latter in 1878. Mr. Crouch was a well-known physician of Camden County for many years. Mrs. Shubert died in June, 1883, leaving one son, Leslie.

William A. Skaggs, farmer and stock raiser, of Liberty Township, is a native of Wayne County, Tenn., where he was born in 1821 being a son of Mastin and Lucly (Abbott) Skaggs, who were born, reared and married in Virginia, and about 1818 came to Wayne County, Tenn. About 1828 they removed to Weakley County, of that State, and a year later came to what is now Camden County, Mo., where they lived until 1841, and then took up their abode near Waynesville, where the father died in 1863 and the mother in 1844. They were worthy tillers of the soil, and were among the early pioneers of Missouri, coming to the State when the country was almost a wilderness, inhabited by Indians and wild animals, and throughout their career improved several good farms. The grandfather was Jacob Skaggs, a German, who died in Tennessee. William A. Skaggs is the second of eight children, and was reared to manhood on different farms in Missouri. At the age of twenty-three years he began farming for himself, and the following year was married to Susanna, a daughter of Jesse Dean, who was formerly of Tennessee, where Mrs. Skaggs was born, but came to Pulaski County, Mo., about 1836, where he spent the remainder of his days. His wife, who died in 1866, became the mother of three sons: Mastin, Jesse (deceased) and Jacob. Since 1849 Mr. Skaggs has lived in Liberty Township, where he owns a fine farm of 411 acres, all the result of his own labors and good management. He was engaged in merchandising in Swedeborg about one year, but the greater portion of his life has been spent in farming. He has been a Democrat all his life, and his first presidential vote was cast for Polk in 1844. He has served as justice of the peace six years, and for many years has been a member of the Baptist Church. His present wife, whom he married in 1868, and whose maiden name was Margaret Hibbs, is also a member of the Baptist Church, her people coming to this county in 1841. Mr. Skaggs served four years in the late war in the Confederate army, under Gen. Price, in Company I, Sixth Missouri Cavalry, operating in Missouri, Arkansas and Tennessee, and was a participant in the battles of Des Arc, Prairie Grove, Pea Ridge, Deep River, and many minor engagements. He was with Price on his famous raid through Missouri, and November 1, 1864, was captured and taken to St. Louis, thence to Alton, and afterward to Rock Island, Ill. Here he was released May 20, 1865. He was captured in Kansas, with Gen. Marmaduke and eighty-three of his men.

Albert Smith, one of Cullen Township's best farmers, was born in Isle of Wight County, Va., in 1821, being a son of Daniel and Rebecca (Justice) Smith, who were natives of the "Old Dominion," and the parents of twelve children, Albert being the only one now living. He was reared on his father's farm, and gave the proceeds of his labor to his father until he was twenty-one years of age, when he began doing for himself, and became overseer on a large plantation in his native State. In 1858 he went to Louisiana, where he followed the same occupation, and in the spring of 1861 came North with the last regular boat that plied the Mississippi River. He landed at St. Louis, Mo., on the 22d of May, and soon after went to Peoria, Ill., but soon returned to St. Louis, and in September enlisted in the telegraph department for three years. Three months later the regiment was disbanded, and he took charge of a train of wagons, and about twelve months later began driving ambulances in St. Louis for Jefferson Barracks. He afterward joined the telegraph repair department, and served until the close of the war. After the close of hostilities he went to Collinsville, Ill., where he was married in June, 1865, to Mrs. Lottie (Robinson) Gibson, who was born in Lincoln County, Mo., in 1816. In June, 1866, Mr. Smith became a citizen of Pulaski County, Mo., and by industry and good management has become the owner of 307 acres of fertile land. He is a Democrat in politics, and a member of the Methodist Episcopal Church, South. Mrs. Smith departed this life July 25, 1884. His father, Daniel Smith, was a soldier in the War of 1812, and participated in the "whisky insurrection."

James R. Smith, farmer, of Tavern Township, Pulaski Co., Mo., was born on the 27th of January, 1857, in Cole County, Mo., and is a son of Thomas M. and Cena (Messersmith) Smith. He resided in his native county until eight years of age, when he was brought to Pulaski County, being reared to manhood on a farm near Crocker. He received a good public school education, and subsequently attended school in Richland two terms. He remained with and assisted his father on the farm until he reached manhood, and at the age of twenty-three years began the battle of life for himself. After coming to Crocker he was engaged in teaching school for two years, and in September, 1878, was married to Miss Zula Overbey, a daughter of James B. and Jane Overbey. She was born in North Carolina, and was quite small when brought to Missouri. She grew to mature years, and married Mr. Smith in Pulaski County, and has become the mother of five children: Minnie M., Rosa N., Edna E., James T. and Ida J. One child died in infancy. Mr. Smith settled on his present farm previous to his marriage, and is now considered one of the prosperous agriculturists of the county. In his political views he supports the principles of the Democratic party.

Dr. G. W. Stevenson, a prosperous physician, residing about twelve miles south of Waynesville, Mo., was born in Kentucky in 1818, and is the second of six children born to the marriage of Zadock Stevenson and Alsie Appleton. The former was born in France in 1752, and during the colonists' struggle for liberty came to America with Marquis de La Fayette, and was an active participant in the Revolutionary War. He also served in the War of 1812 and the Black Hawk War, and died in 1859, at the age of one hundred and seven years. He was a minister of the Methodist Episcopal Church, and was the father of thirteen children, seven of whom were born to a former marriage. His wife, Alsie, was born about 1790, and died in Mississippi about 1860. At the age of seven years Dr. G. W. Stevenson was sent to France by his parents to receive his education, and at the age of thirteen returned home, and after a time entered the medical colleges of Cincinnati, Ohio, Indianapolis, Ind., and completed his medical education in Kentucky, at the age of thirty. He practiced his profession ten years in Indiana, three years in Illinois, and then came to Missouri, where he is yet actively engaged in practicing. In 1861 he enlisted in the Confederate army, serving as orderly-sergeant under Gen. Price until he received his discharge in August, 1865. He received five wounds, but none of them were very serious. He has always been a Democrat in politics, and while residing in Illinois served as judge of his county for eighteen months. He was elected sheriff of Lawrence County, Ark., in 1850, and has been urged many times by his friends to run for office. In 1854 he was united in marriage to Miss Lucy M. Garrison, who died in March, 1871, having become the mother of three children. In 1874 he married his second wife, the widow of Pleasant Solomon. She was born in Tennessee in 1836. Dr. Stevenson's children are as follows: Emily, widow of John Ousley; Mary (deceased) and George. The Doctor is a Mason, and he and wife are members of the Missionary Baptist Church.

Prof. John W. Stewart, principal of the Richland Institute, and attorney at law, is the second born in the family of five children of William P. and Mary (Gordon) Stewart, and was born in Maury County, Tenn., on the 28th of December, 1848. William P. Stewart was born in North Carolina in 1824, and is of Scotch origin. He married in Tennessee, and in 1859 removed to Lebanon, Mo., where he still lives; he was formerly engaged in the boot and shoe business, but is now a farmer. The paternal grandfather of our subject, Charles Stewart, was also a native of North Carolina, and was an early settler of Maury County, Tenn., where he died. The maternal grandfather was John Gordon, who was born in North Carolina, and died in Maury County, Tenn., of which county he was a pioneer. John W. Stewart received the principal part of his education at Lebanon Academy, then the best school in Laclede County, and in 1868, at the age of twenty years, he taught his first school in Dallas County, and afterward taught near Lebanon. He was assistant teacher in the Lebanon public schools for years, one year principal of the Ozark school, and one year principal of the Lebanon graded schools. In 1875 he graduated from the law department of the University of Michigan, at Ann Arbor, after attending one year, having previously read one year in a law office, and devoting considerable attention to the study of law while he was engaged in teaching. In August, 1875, he was admitted to the Laclede County bar before Judge W. F. Geiger. In 1877 he became editor and publisher of the Richland *Sentinel*, which he ably conducted until 1880, when he removed to Steelville, in Crawford County, and during the campaign of that year he published the *Crawford County Sentinel*. In December of the same year he sold out and returned to Richland, and the following year became principal of the Richland Institute, to which he has since devoted almost his entire attention. He is one of the most active educational workers in the county, and as such is well and favorably known. During the summer vacation for several years past Mr. Stewart has conducted a normal school at Richland, with remarkable success, and it has been of almost inestimable value to the educational interests of the county, greatly advancing the standard of the teachers in the county. In 1878 Mr. Stewart married Mary, daughter of Oliver and Caroline Gillespie, natives of Pulaski County, their parents being early settlers. Mrs. Gillespie still resides in the county. Of the five children born to Mr. and Mrs. Stewart four are now living. The parents are members of the Christian Church. Mr. Stewart is a member of the I. O. O. F. and A. O. U. W.

Alexander P. Sutton, a farmer of Roubideaux Township, is a Virginian, born in Washington County in 1837, and is a son of William and Rachel (McCrary) Sutton, both of whom were born in Virginia, the former's birth occurring in 1809. He is a farmer by occupation, and is now residing in Kentucky with his son James. Mrs. Sutton died in her native State in 1837, having borne four children. After her death the father married Tilda Rose, in 1840, by whom he became the father of seven children. In 1860 Alexander P. Sutton was married to Nancy M., a daughter of T. R. and Catherine Harmon. She was born in Whitley County, Ky., in 1838, and died in March, 1882, having borne a family of eleven children. Two years later Mr. Sutton married his present wife, whose maiden name was Barbara C. Steward, and by her became the father of five children. August 13, 1862, he enlisted in Company F, Seventh Kentucky Regiment, and served about three years. His eyesight was injured in the service. His early educational advantages were very limited, but, knowing the value of a good knowledge, he takes a deep interest in all matters pertaining to the cause of education. Since 1870 he has been a resident of Missouri, and is the owner of a good farm of 160 acres in Pulaski County, besides eighty acres in another tract on the Roubideaux River, having in all sixty acres under cultivation. Mr. Sutton is a Republican in politics, and he and wife are members of the Missionary Baptist Church.

Jacob Teeple was born in Pulaski County, Mo., in November, 1839, and is a son of Jacob and Nancy (Bilyeu) Teeple, who were born in Tennessee, the former in 1802, and died in 1862 and 1865, respectively. They were married in Illinois, and in 1832 moved to Missouri, where the father engaged in farming and stock raising. He held the office of justice of the peace for a great many years, and was also judge of the Pulaski County Court. He served in the Black Hawk War, and was a participant in the engagement at Rock Island, Ill. The maternal grandparents, Peter and Diana (Blackwell) Bilyeu, were Tennesseeans, and at an early day moved to Illinois, where they engaged in farming. Jacob Teeple, whose name heads this sketch, is the only surviving member of a family of nine children, eight besides himself, whose names are Peter, G. W., John R., Isaac, Margaret, Diannah, Nancy (Strain) and Hannah (Denton); he was reared in his native county, receiving his education in the common schools. In July, 1861, he enlisted in Company C, Frazier's regiment, Price's army, and at the battle of Springfield was captured and taken, in company with twenty-eight others, his father being of the number, first to Rolla, and then to St. Louis. Here he was retained two months, and was then taken to Alton, Ill., thence to Johnson's Island, where he was exchanged. He then rejoined his regiment at Little Rock, Ark., and served in the Trans-Mississippi Department until the close of the war. He was in a number of hotly contested battles, and in June, 1865, was paroled with Gen. Kirby Smith and returned to Missouri. He soon after went to Illinois, where he resided until 1869, having married in the meantime (1867) Miss Mary A. Plain, who was born on the 8th of December, 1848, and then returned to Missouri, where he has by hard work and judicious management become the owner of a fine farm of 324 acres, 175 of which are under cultivation. A family of nine children was born to himself and wife, only four of whom are living: Charles Elbert, John Elmer, James A. and Hannah Lavonia. Those deceased are Robert Lee, Minnie F., Lillie May, Emma Ellen and an infant unnamed. The family attend the Christian Church, and Mr. Teeple is a Democrat, his first presidential vote being cast in 1860 for John C. Breckenridge. He is a charter member of the Grange. Mrs. Teeple's parents, John and Mary A. (Workman) Plain, were born in Kentucky and Tennessee, respectively, the former's birth occurring in 1821. They moved from Kentucky to Illinois, thence to Missouri in 1865, and after several changes located permanently in Illinois in 1871, where they are yet residing. Seven of their eleven children are living: Mary A. (Teeple), Malinda (Wilson), Isabel (Lemon), Nancy (Ross), Ella (Wilson), Alice (Malhoit) and Laura May (Malhoit).

Hon. James Titterington, an extensive fruit grower and stock raiser, and a retired physician of Richland, was born in 1825, in Cumberland County, Ky., and when about three years of age removed with his parents to Christian County, Ky., where he was reared, and remained until 1850. He then went to Missouri, spent one year in Miller County, and subsequently located in Laclede County. In March, 1875, he settled in Richland, which has since been his home. He received a good common-school education, and began the study of medicine with Dr. James F. Drane, in Christian County, Ky. He took one course at the Transylvania Medical College, Lexington, Ky., and began his practice with his preceptor. He met with remarkable success in the practice of his chosen profession, which he continued about thirty-seven years, and, with one exception, he is the oldest practitioner in this section of Missouri, his practice extending through Pulaski, Miller, Laclede and the surrounding counties. He was financially successful, and at the outbreak of the late war owned 1,200 acres of land and a large quantity of stock. He has given each of his children good farms, and still owns about 300 acres. Soon after the war he bought a flour and saw-mill in Laclede County, which, in 1877, he removed to Richland, and successfully operated for six years. For the past ten years Mr. Titterington has been extensively engaged in fruit growing, and has on his place 1,300 apple trees and about 150 peach trees. In 1854 he served as assessor of Laclede County, and in 1873–74 represented that county in the Legislature. He was appointed postmaster of Hazel Green in 1860, which office he held fourteen years, and after serving as postmaster of Richland one year he resigned. He is a member of Richland Lodge of the A. F. & A. M., and of the Farmers & Mechanics Mutual Aid Association. In 1852 Mr. Titterington married, in Laclede County, Mary B., daughter of Judge William H. and Lucy Smith, formerly of Tennessee, who removed to Laclede County about 1845, where the father died in 1878. The mother is still living, at the age of eighty-five years. Mrs.

Titterington was born in Missouri, and is the mother of six children, three of whom are living, viz.: Lucy M., wife of Dr. W. L. Ragan; Sallie, widow of William M. Dodson, and Dr. James L., a graduate of Missouri Medical College, and a practicing physician of Laclede County. The parents of our subject were Adam and Sallie (Smith) Titterington, the former of whom was born in England about 1784, and came to this country when quite young. He followed school teaching all his life, and was well known as such in Kentucky. He also devoted some attention to farming before his death, which occurred in 1857. He was twice married, and his first wife, whose maiden name was Sarah Smith, was born about 1794, and was a daughter of Moses Smith, an Englishman, who served in the Revolution, and died in Cumberland County, Ky. Of the six sons and four daughters born to Mr. and Mrs. Titterington, five of the sons became prominent physicians, and Dr. Richard M. served as surgeon in Gen. Morgan's brigade during the late war. Mrs. Sarah Titterington died in Christian County, Ky., in 1837.

Dr. Alfred W. Titterington, a practicing physician and surgeon of Richland, is a native of Christian County, Ky., and was born in 1837. His father was Adam Titterington, who was born in Yorkshire, England, about 1784, and when thirteen years of age immigrated to the United States, where he was engaged in teaching forty-five years, and was one of the leading educators of Kentucky; he was twice married, his first wife, whose name was Sarah Smith, being the mother of ten children, of whom our subject, Alfred W., was the tenth. Adam Titterington was also a well-to-do farmer, and died in 1857. Mrs. Sarah Titterington was born in Virginia in 1794, and died in Christian County, Ky., in 1837. She was a daughter of Moses Smith, whose birthplace was England. He served during the Revolutionary War, and died in Cumberland County, Ky., at the advanced age of ninety years. Alfred W. Titterington received his education in the common schools of his native State, and when a young man spent two years flat-boating on the Cumberland River, after which he returned home, and the following three years was engaged in the study of medicine with his brother, Richard M., in Crittenden County, Ky. He was there actively engaged in the practice of his chosen profession until 1858, when he removed to Laclede County, Mo., where he was a successful practitioner for thirty years. He located in Richland in 1880, where he also has an extended practice. The Doctor owns 151 acres of land on the river, twenty acres near Richland and forty acres in another tract. In August, 1862, he enlisted in Company G, Eighth Missouri Infantry, Confederate Army, and served three years, spending one year as hospital steward at Little Rock. In 1879 he married Clara, daughter of Samuel Wilson, a farmer and stock raiser of Laclede County, Mo., who died during the war. Mrs. Titterington was born in Laclede County, Mo., and is the mother of two children. She is a member of the Christian Church. Mr. Titterington is a member of Richland Lodge No. 382, A. F. & A. M., and is also a member of the A. O. U. W.

Simeon Traw, a farmer and stock raiser, and one of the pioneers of Pulaski County, was born in Washington County, Va., in 1818, and is the eldest of the seven sons and two daughters born to David and Christina (Fudge) Traw, who were natives, respectively, of Pennsylvania and Virginia. The parents were married in Washington County, Va., and when our subject was but four years of age the family removed to Adair County, Ky., where the father died about 1842; he was a farmer by occupation. The mother died in Camden County, Mo., since the war, and both were members of the Christian Church. They were of German descent, and of their family of nine children all grew to maturity, and seven are still living, who have families of their own, and rank among the enterprising citizens of their respective neighborhoods. Simeon Traw received but a limited common-school education in his native State, and in 1837, at the age of nineteen years, he married Susan, daughter of Josiah and Minerva Smith, natives of Virginia, who afterward removed to Cumberland County, Ky., where Mrs. Traw was born. Eight children have been born to Mr. and Mrs. Traw, but three of whom are now living, viz.: John, Josiah and James B. Mr. Traw located in Pulaski County in 1841, when the white settlers were few and the Indians, bear, elk and wild turkeys plentiful. After living about two years on the Gasconade River he removed to Camden County, where he lived on the Wet Glaize until 1881; in the latter year he settled in Richland. He owns about 600 acres of land in two tracts in Pulaski County, being the result of long years of industry and enterprise. The family is one of the most prominent and well known in the county. Mr. and Mrs. Traw are consistent members of the Christian Church, and for many years have been identified as among its most active workers. Mr. Traw is a Democrat in political faith, and cast his first presidential vote for Van Buren in 1840.

Joseph H. Turpin was born in Pulaski County, Mo., January 13, 1846, and is a son of Thomas and Nancy J. (Barnett) Turpin. The father was born in Kentucky, and after residing in Indiana for a short period came to Pulaski County, Mo., when eight years old. He was born in 1806, and his parents were said to be the first white settlers in the county. The country was then a wilderness, inhabited by Indians, who were of a friendly disposition, and there were no schools, churches or houses for many miles. Thomas acquired a good education by studying at home, and throughout life followed the occupation of farming, dying in 1871. His wife was born in Kentucky, and by Mr. Turpin became the mother of six children, two of whom are now living: Joseph H. and Eliza A. (Yakely). Martha, Mary, Thomas and John are deceased. Mrs. Turpin died in 1871. Both the paternal and maternal grandparents were Kentuckians, and died in Missouri. Joseph H. Turpin, whose name heads this sketch, was born, reared and educated in Pulaski County, and remained with his parents until their respective deaths. During the late war he served in Company A, Forty-eighth Missouri Volunteer Infantry, and was at first stationed at Rolla on post duty. He was ordered to Nashville during Hood's campaign, and was afterward at Columbia, Tenn., on post duty. He was subsequently on garrison duty at Chicago, and then returned to St. Louis, Mo., where he received his discharge at Benton Barracks, in 1865. He then resumed the peaceful pursuit of farming, and September 13, 1875, was married to Tennie (Anderson) Jewell, who was born in Tennessee, and was brought to Missouri when small. Four children were born to their union: Thomas H., Amanda J., John E. and James R. (deceased). Mr. Turpin tilled the home farm until 1876, when he purchased some land on Gasconade River, moved upon it, and has been a resident of Pulaski County for a long time, owning 350 acres of land, with about 200 acres under cultivation. He is a Republican politically, a member of the Agricultural Wheel, and his wife is a member of the Christian Church.

C. D. Wale is a native of the State of Kentucky, and was born in 1848. He is the eighth in the family of eleven children born to H. O. and Sallie (Brewington) Wale, the former of whom was born in Virginia in 1808, and the latter in Kentucky in 1812. H. O. Wale was a farmer, and was a son of Martin Wale, who settled in Kentucky in an early day; the latter took an active part in the War of 1812, and participated in the battle of Tippecanoe under Gen. Harrison. C. D. Wale attended the common schools in early life, and later spent a year and a half in college. In 1862 he joined Gen. Morgan's troops in the late war, was with him on his famous raid, and later stopped at his home a short time on the way north, and subsequently joined Gen. Lyon's command, with whom he served until near the close of the war. He was captured at Salina, Tenn., in May, 1865, and taken to Nashville, where he took the oath of allegiance, and returning home turned his attention to farming. In 1875 he went to Chariton County, Mo., where he was engaged in agricultural pursuits until 1881, when he located at Richland, and the following five years engaged in the drug business. This he afterward abandoned in favor of the milling business, in which he is now occupied, having an interest in and serving as proprietor of the Richland Roller and Saw Mill. In 1875 Mr. Wale married Emma Swain, daughter of George T. and Matilda Swain. Mrs. Wale was a native of Kentucky, and died October 3, 1885, leaving five children. In October, 1887, Mr. Wale married Miss Lottie McFarland, who is still living, and is a member of the Methodist Episcopal Church. Mr. Wale is a member of the I. O. O. F.

Capt. Henry E. Warren is one of the oldest and most enterprising merchants of Richland. He is the eldest of three children born to Charley and Susan (Armstrong) Warren, both natives of Tennessee, who came to Pulaski County, Mo., in 1866; the mother died in 1877, but the father, who is a farmer by occupation, is still living. His father, who was Rev. Charley Warren, a Methodist minister for many years, was of English descent, and was one of the early settlers of Tennessee, but died in Virginia, which was his native State. The parents of our subject were also members of the Methodist Church. Henry E. Warren received a good common-school education, and spent two years at Holston College, Tenn. In 1863 he enlisted in the United States Army, Company A, Ninth Tennessee Cavalry, and after serving about four months as a private was made sergeant-major of his regiment, and one year later was promoted to the position of first lieutenant of Company H. Six months afterward he was commissioned captain of Company E, which position he held until the close of the war, being mustered out at Knoxville, Tenn., in September, 1865. He participated in many prominent engagements of the war in Tennessee and Virginia. He came to Missouri with his parents in 1866, served as deputy county clerk a short time, and subsequently clerked in a store at Arlington two years. He then went to Richland, and in 1869 established a general merchandise business, and is the only merchant who has since been continuously engaged in business at that place. He carries a stock of dry goods, clothing, hardware, harness, saddles, etc., worth about $6,000, and the annual sales amount to about $30,000. He represented Pulaski County in the State Legislature in 1886, having been elected on the Democratic ticket, and served with credit to himself and the county. In March, 1869, Mr. Warren married Lottie, daughter of Judge Samuel and Eliza Gibson, natives of Missouri and Tennessee, respectively. Mrs. Warren was born in Camden County, where her father died; her mother is still living. Judge Samuel Gibson was probate judge of Camden County several years, and was also judge of the Camden County Court, a man of considerable ability and influence, and a member of the Methodist Episcopal Church. He married Eliza Ballard, daughter of B. N. Ballard, one of the pioneers of Pulaski County, where he spent the remainder of his life, and was prominent in public affairs. Mrs. Warren died in the autumn of 1888, leaving a family of eight children. She was a consistent and devoted member of the Methodist Episcopal Church for many years, and was mourned by many sincere friends. Capt. Warren is one of the most enterprising business men of Richland, and is a man of more than ordinary ability.

Rev. John J. Watts, school-teacher, farmer and minister, is a native of Warren, Lincoln (now Knox) Co., Me., born on the 27th of September, 1839. He is a son of William Watts, grandson of Samuel Watts, and great grandson of John Watts, and great-great-grandson of William Watts. The latter was born in Casco, Scotland, March 4, 1720, and married Margaret McLellan, of Casco, Scotland, in 1740, very soon after their marriage coming to America, and settling in Boston, Mass. They had three children, and died there. Their oldest child, John Watts, was born in Boston November 8, 1742, married Elizabeth McNeal, of Boston, July 15, 1761, moved to St. George, Me., in 1764, and in 1774 removed to Warren, Me. They had nine children, and he died August 10, 1817. His widow died November 4, 1819, aged eighty years. Their seventh child was Samuel Watts, who was born in Warren, Me., October 15, 1777, married first Elizabeth Lermond, December 3, 1797, and second Nancy Jones in 1812. He had eight children by each wife, and died May 1, 1862. Elizabeth, his first wife, died March 27, 1812. His second child was William Watts, who was born in Warren, Me., April 6, 1800, married Deborah Jones January 29, 1833, had four children, and died March 2, 1871. His wife died December 24, 1860. Their fourth child was John Jones Watts, subject of this sketch, who was educated in his native town of Warren, and at the age of twenty years went to work in a ship yard, but at the breaking out of the war enlisted in Company B, Twenty-fourth Regiment Maine Volunteer Infantry. October 4, 1862, he received a commission of second lieutenant, which office he held during service. Owing to the expiration of his term of service (nine months' call) he was honorably discharged at Augusta, Me., August 25, 1863, having served under Gen. N. P. Banks in the siege of Port Hudson, La. In the fall of 1863 he started for California. He worked in a saw-mill on Humboldt Bay for two years, and then returned home, but again went to California in 1868. At the end of one year he was called home by the sickness of his father, and remained until September 8, 1871, when he immigrated to Missouri, and settled in Phelps County. Ten years later he located in Piney Township, Pulaski County, where he owns a good farm of 160 acres, eighty acres of which are under cultivation. In 1858 he experienced religion, and joined the Baptist Church in Warren, Me., and March 10, 1874, joined Beaver Creek Baptist Church, of Phelps County, Mo., and in 1877 was licensed by that church to preach, being ordained two years later. He has long been an instructor of the young, and is now teaching his eighteenth term of school. He first joined the Masonic fraternity in 1862 in his native town, but is now a member of the Spring Creek Lodge No. 347, of Phelps County, Mo. September 1, 1872, he was married to Miss Mary Jane Woolsey, who was born in Phelps County, Mo., January 10, 1858, and is a daughter of William and Matilda (Hudgens) Woolsey. She is a member of the Baptist Church, and is the mother of three children, one of whom died at the age of four years.

D. P. Webster, M. D., a prosperous physician of Pulaski County, Mo., was born in the "Buckeye State" in 1848, and is a son of John T. and Mary A. (Pulliam) Webster, who were born in Virginia in 1822, and Kentucky in 1824, respectively. The former died in 1881, but the latter is still living. The father was one of the worthy tillers of the soil, and at an early day moved from his native State to Ohio, thence to Illinois in 1856. He was the father of six sons, whose names are as follows: Nathan W., Norman, George W., Moody J., Dr. D. P. and J. G. George Webster, the paternal grandfather, was born in Virginia, and died in 1846. He was a private in the War of 1812, a boot and shoe maker by trade, and at an early day moved from Virginia to Ohio. His wife, whose maiden name was Nancy Erton, was born in Washington, D. C. The maternal grandparents, Nathan and Ann (Galloway) Pulliam, were born in Kentucky in 1789 and 1791, and died in 1858 and 1860, respectively. Nathan was a minister in the Christian Church, and moved from Kentucky to Ohio. Dr. D. P. Webster became a resident of Illinois when eight years of age, and spent his early life in that State, receiving his education in the Pittsfield High-school. After attaining a suitable age he began reading medicine under C. H. Doss, of Pittsfield, Ill., and from 1877 to 1880 was a student in the American Medical College at St. Louis, Mo. He graduated in the latter year, and entered upon the practice of his profession at Hulls, Ill., where he remained two years. After a residence of two years in Greene County he located in Kansas, where he made his home until 1886, when he came to Dixon, Mo., and here has since made his home and established a good and lucrative practice. In 1878 Miss Annie Giles, who was born in Illinois in 1857, and is a daughter of Samuel and Mary (Crawford) Giles, became his wife, and is the mother of two children, Ethel, and Zoe, who died in infancy. Dr. Webster is a Republican in his political views, and cast his first presidential vote for Abraham Lincoln in 1864. He is also a member of the Christian Church and the I. O. O. F. Mrs. Webster's father and mother were born in Tennessee and Pennsylvania, in 1830 and 1836, respectively. The latter died in 1884.

John W. Wheeler, a successful and prosperous miller, of Union Township, Pulaski Co., Mo., was born in Osage County, of that State, in 1855, and is a son of William E. and Minerva (Sherrill) Wheeler, and grandson of John and Eliza B. (Wise) Wheeler. The latter were born in Virginia and Kentucky, in 1791 and 1799, and died in 1848 and 1845, respectively. They were married in Kentucky, and in 1825 moved to Manchester, Mo. William E. Wheeler is one of their five children, four living, whose names are as follows: Charlotte M. (Miller), Frances A. (Keith), William E., Lydia B. (Mason) and Luther H. (deceased). William E. was born in Mason County, Ky., March 16, 1825, and received a good education in a high-school of St. Louis, and at the age of eighteen began clerking in a store in that city, spending the years 1848 and 1852 in traveling over Southwest Missouri, selling a patent medicine for Dr. I. H. Hale, of Manchester, Mo. In January, 1848, he espoused Miss Sherrill, who was born in Tennessee in 1829, and is a daughter of Samuel Sherrill, who married a Miss Gatewood, also natives of Tennessee. The father was a farmer and cabinet workman, and was a soldier in the Black Hawk War. Catherine (Murphy) is their only living child in a family of seven children. Mrs. Wheeler died July 19, 1877, having borne a family of twelve children, eight of whom are living: John W., Nathan, George W., Ray, Ellen, Mollie (Stokes), Fanny (Hutsell) and Cora. Mr. Wheeler settled in Osage County in 1852, and after a short residence in Miller County came to Pulaski County, Mo., in 1868. He purchased his present farm of 139 acres in 1873, and soon after built his present large flouring mill. He is a Mason, a Democrat and a member of the Methodist Episcopal Church, South. He served for some time in the State Militia during the late war. His son, John W., whose name heads this sketch, received a common-school education, and in 1872 came to Pulaski County, where he was engaged in milling until 1875, when he engaged in farming. From 1878 to 1879 he clerked in a store in Hancock, Mo., and in 1881 re-engaged in milling, which occupation has received his attention ever since. He owns a good farm of eighty acres, with thirty acres under cultivation, all of which he has earned by his own industry and good management. He and wife, whose maiden name was Harriet Lipscomb, and whom he married in 1875, are the parents of five children: Minerva, Ollie, William, Luna and Mary. He is a Democrat, and his first presidential vote was cast for S. J. Tilden in 1876. Mrs.

Wheeler is a daughter of Wade and Mary (Baker) Lipscomb, natives of Tennessee, who came to Missouri at a very early day. The father was a miller and distiller, and the following are the names of his children: Sarah (Keaton), Susannah (Clark), Amanda (Layman), Julia (Hutsell), John F. and Harriet (Mrs. Wheeler).

Edward G. Williams, county and probate clerk of Pulaski County, Mo., is a native of Bedford County, Va., born in 1843, and is a son of Edward D. and Martha E. (Jones) Williams, and grandson of Samuel Williams, who was a Virginian by birth, and died about 1848. Edward D. Williams and his wife were born in Cumberland County, Va., in 1806, and removed to Phelps County, Mo., in 1867, where the father died in 1887. While residing in his native State he was hotel proprietor at Christiansburg and Jacksonville, but the latter portion of his life was spent in farming. His wife is yet living, and resides in Roanoke, Va. The following are her children who are living: Samuel G., an attorney of Roanoke, Va.; Martha E., widow of A. L. Staff, of Rolla, Mo.; Albert W., traveling for a wholesale clothing house of Baltimore, Md.; Henrietta B., wife of Samuel B. Thurman, of Lynchburg, Va.; Marie S., wife of William E. Webber, of Phelps County, Mo.; Edward G., and James M., a salesman in a grocery store at Springfield, Mo. Edward G. Williams began his business career by clerking in a store in Lynchburg, Va., but at the end of two years entered the army. In February, 1861, he enlisted in Company E, Eleventh Virginia Infantry, Confederate States Army, and was in the battles of Bull Run, Antietam, the seven days fight below Richmond, Plymouth, Drury's Bluff, Dranesville, Williamsburg, Seven Pines, Fredericksburg, Second Manassas, Sharpsburg, Boonsboro and Gettysburgh, receiving a severe wound in the leg at the engagement at Drury's Bluff. The leg was amputated the same day, and he was in the hospital at Richmond, Va., for seven weeks, and was then sent home. He was orderly-sergeant of his company for about one year. In 1866 he left his native State and came westward, locating in Rolla, Mo., and in February, 1869, became a citizen of Waynesville, having been appointed to the office of deputy clerk of the circuit, county and probate court. In 1874 he was elected circuit and county clerk of Pulaski County, serving four years, and from 1878 to 1882 clerked in a store in Hancock. At the latter date he was elected county clerk, and was appointed probate clerk, being re-elected county clerk in 1886, and re-appointed probate clerk. He is now faithfully filling the duties of these offices. February 15, 1885, he was united in marriage to Mrs. Emeline Bostic, who was born in Randolph County, N. C., in 1845. He is a Democrat, and cast his first presidential vote for Horace Greeley in 1872.

M. W. Wright was born in Baltimore, Md., in 1822. His father, William J. Wright, was a native of England, and came to the United States about 1818, settling in Baltimore, where the family lived until the outbreak of the war, then returning to England, leaving our subject in this country. The latter received his early education in the private schools of Baltimore, and spent two years at the Normal School in Wilmington, Del. When fifteen years of age he left home and went to New Orleans, where he was employed for four or five years with Hewitt, Norton & Co., commission merchants. In 1849 Mr. Wright embarked for California, going by way of the Isthmus of Panama, and spent three years in the gold mines with fair success. He returned to New Orleans in 1852, and from there went to Louisville, Ky., where he worked in the Louisville, New Albany & Chicago Railroad shops until 1856, part of the time having charge of an engine. In 1856 he went to St. Charles County, Mo., and turned his attention to farming, which occupation he followed until 1875, when he removed to Pulaski County. In 1859, in St. Charles County, he married Charlotte Chambers, who died in 1865, leaving two children. In 1870 Mr. Wright married Mrs. Mary Scofield, daughter of Moores and Nancy Burbanks, natives, respectively, of New England and Ohio, the former of whom died in 1835 and the latter in 1868. Mr. and Mrs. Burbanks, who were married in 1810, settled in St. Charles County in 1808, and were among the earliest white settlers of that county. Mr. Burbanks and Mr. Alexander Chambers (father of Charlotte Chambers) were comrades in the War of 1812, and served under Col. Nathan Boone. Mr. Chambers settled in St. Charles County in 1802. Mr. Wright owns 140 acres of land in Pulaski County and a home in Richland. In 1878 he was elected justice of the peace, which office he held until 1886, and from 1880 to 1882 he was associate judge of the Western District of the county court. Politically he is a Democrat.

William T. Wright, presiding judge of the county court of Pulaski County, Mo., and editor and publisher of the *Pulaski County Democrat*, of Waynesville, was born in Mercer County, Mo., in 1849, and is a son of David T. and Catherine E. (McEffee) Wright. William T. is the third born, and attended the common schools until the age of twelve years, when he entered the printing office of his father. In 1869 he became a member of the Pioneer Printing Company at Chillicothe, Mo., and was one of the publishers of the *Christian Pioneer* and the Chillicothe *Constitution*. In 1873 he was elected collector of Chillicothe Township, and the following year went to Milan, in Sullivan County, Mo., where he engaged in the grocery business. He continued in this business for nearly two years, and in February, 1876, he established the Brookfield *Chronicle*, at Brookfield, Mo., and in the spring of 1877 came to Lebanon, where he was employed on the *Rustic and Journal*. In the fall of 1879 he came to Waynesville and bought the Pulaski *Tribune*, and continued its publication until the summer of 1880. From 1880 until the spring of 1888 he was engaged in farming, at which time he became editor and proprietor of the *Pulaski County Democrat*. In November, 1887, he was married to Mary J. Strong, only daughter of Henderson Strong. Mrs. Wright was born in Pulaski County in 1858, and is the mother of one child, Frank. Mr. Wright is a stanch Democrat, and in 1884 was elected associate judge of the county court, and two years later was elected presiding judge of the same. He was also clerk of the city of Richland for several years, and is a Select Knight, a member of the A. O. U. W. and A. F. & A. M. lodges at Richland.

Jacob N. Wrinkle, a farmer and stock raiser of Liberty Township, is a native of Knox County, Tenn., and was born in 1836. He was the third in the family of eight sons and two daughters born to John and Sophia A. Wrinkle, who were also natives of Knox County, Tenn., the former born in 1806 and the latter in 1811. John Wrinkle was a farmer by occupation, and his father, George Wrinkle, whose birthplace was Knox County, Tenn., was killed in a storm in that county by a falling tree. The latter, with his brother Jacob, and the maternal grandfather of our subject, were soldiers in the War of 1812. John Wrinkle died in February, 1879. His wife is still living. They were both members of the Baptist Church. Jacob N. Wrinkle attended the common schools and Woodlawn Academy, where he prepared to enter the State University, but trouble with his eyes prevented further study. January 5, 1857, he married Emma C., daughter of Leroy A. and Ann Eliza Kidd, natives of Virginia, who moved to North Carolina, and later to Knoxville, Tenn., where the mother died and the father still lives. Mrs. Wrinkle is a native of Virginia, and is the mother of thirteen children, ten of whom are living. In 1860 Mr. Wrinkle moved to Pulaski County, and has since lived most of the time in Liberty Township, having settled on his present farm in 1882. He is one of the largest land owners in the county, owning about 1,000 acres, and very little of which is under cultivation. He lost considerable property during the war, and in 1864 removed to Boonville, where he rented a farm for one year, and then returned to Pulaski County. In March, 1872, he removed to Lebanon, where he lived one year, and was part of the time employed as a clerk in the warehouse of Wallace Bros. In 1879 Mr. Wrinkle took a trip through the western country, and has twice, once in 1866 and again in 1880, returned to his old home in Tennessee. Since 1862 he has auctioneered for the public in Laclede, Camden and Pulaski Counties, where he is well known as a salesman, in which line he has been remarkably successful. In politics he is in sympathy with the Democratic party. He is a member of the Agricultural Wheel.

H. H. Wrinkle, one of the leading merchants of Richland, carries a stock of general merchandise, including dry goods, hardware, etc., to the value of about $8,000, his annual sales averaging about $30,000. Mr. Wrinkle first engaged in merchandising October 1, 1879, the firm being known as Wallace Bros. & Co. It was afterward known as Evington & Co., and since August, 1885, Mr. Wrinkle has conducted the business alone and with remarkable success. He was born in Knox County, East Tenn., February 4, 1852, and is the youngest but one of eight children born to John and Sophia Wrinkle. The father was born in Tennessee in August, 1806, where he spent his entire life and died in 1881; he was a well-to-do farmer, and a member of the Baptist Church for many years. He was a son of John Wrinkle, a native of Germany, who came to the United States with his parents and settled in Virginia at an early day, whence the family removed to Knox County, Tenn., their home for three generations. The mother of our subject was also a native of Tennessee, and was born about 1813; she is still living in Knox County. H. H. Wrinkle was reared on a farm and attended the common schools until about seventeen years of age, after which he spent two years at the University of Nashville. He taught school near his home two years, and in 1878 went to Lebanon, Mo., where for one year he was employed as clerk for Wallace Bros., with whom he was afterward in partnership, as above stated. In 1879 Mr. Wrinkle married Fannie E., daughter of James Anderson Gass, of Tennessee. Mrs. Wrinkle, who is a member of the Methodist Church, South, died February 11, 1886, leaving three children. In April, 1888, Mr. Wrinkle married Lizzie Knerr, a native of York County, Penn. Her parents were John and Julia Knerr, who were born in Berks County and York County, Penn., in 1824 and 1806, respectively, and afterward removed to York County, Penn., where the father died in 1881 and the mother in 1884. Mr. Wrinkle is a member of the Methodist Church, and his wife of the Presbyterian. Politically he is a Republican.

William J. Yowell, farmer and stock raiser, was born in Phelps County, Mo., in 1855, and is a son of Easton and Nancy J. (Bradford) Yowell, who were born in Kentucky and Missouri in 1822 and 1832, respectively. The father was of Scotch descent, and a farmer by occupation, and when young immigrated with his parents to Phelps County, Mo., where he married and died, the latter event taking place in 1859. His widow still survives him, and is living with her second husband, J. H. Wilson. William J. Yowell is the third of five children, and resided with his mother and step-father until he attained his majority. He attended the district schools until he was sixteen years of age, and then completed his education in the high-school of Spring Creek, graduating at the age of nineteen years. Miss Ida Walters, a daughter of Joseph and Mary E. (Morris) Walters, became his wife in 1877. She was born in Platte County, Mo., in 1862, and is the mother of two children. After his marriage Mr. Yowell located in Platte County, where he resided six years, and then came to Pulaski County and purchased the farm of 126 acres where he now lives. He has 110 acres under cultivation, and his farm ranks among the best in the county. He is quite extensively engaged in stock raising, and ships from three to five car loads of cattle and hogs annually. He is a Democrat in politics, and a member of the Missionary Baptist Church. His wife belongs to the Christian Church.

WEBSTER COUNTY.

Micajah Aldridge, miller, and son of Richard and Lucy (Pleasant) Aldridge, was born in Caswell County, N. C., May 10, 1832. The parents were natives of North Carolina, and died in Webster County, Mo., the father in 1853 and the mother in 1867. The family came to Missouri as early as 1839, and settled in Webster County. Micajah Aldridge is the fourth of eight children, seven of whom are now living.

He assisted his father on the farm until grown, and in 1852 commenced tilling the soil on his own responsibility. He was married in June, 1854, to Miss Elizabeth Moore, who was born in North Carolina January 20, 1831, and who bore him seven children: Martha A., born March 28, 1855; Candice S., born July 15, 1865; Allie B., born October 20, 1869, and Sterling Roy, born October 26, 1875, living, and three deceased: an infant, born March 8, 1859; Williamson, born April 25, 1860, died June 11, 1860; and an infant daughter, born March 6, 1863, died July 29, 1863. Mr. Aldridge continued farming until 1885, when he sold his farm, one of the best in Webster County. He was for many years one of the most extensive tobacco growers in that county, and was quite successful in this enterprise. In the fall of 1880 Mr. Aldridge removed to Marshfield, where he carried on the lumber business until about 1885, and also engaged in the livery business, which he still continues. He is engaged in buying grain, and also runs a flouring mill. He has been very successful in all his business ventures, and is one of the leading business men of Marshfield. In politics he is Democratic, of the uncompromising type, and cast his first presidential vote for James Buchanan. He was a Mason for several years, and Mrs. Aldridge is a member of the Methodist Episcopal Church, South. His paternal grandfather served through the Revolutionary War, and died in Caswell County, N. C.

Thomas Anderson, farmer and stock raiser of Union Township, was born in Putnam County, Tenn., December 9, 1844, and is the son of Edward and Lucinda (Mahaney) Anderson, natives of Virginia. They died in Putnam County, Tenn., the father when Thomas Anderson was but fourteen years of age, and his wife one year later. They were married in the last named county, and both were members of the Methodist Episcopal Church. He was a successful tiller of the soil the principal part of his life. There were born to their union two sons and five daughters, four now living: V. W.; Adaline, wife of Alfred Jones, who is now deceased; Margaret J., wife of R. B. Waller, and Thomas. The latter, after the death of his parents, came with his brother to Missouri, and located in Laclede County. In 1862 he enlisted in Company G, Sixteenth Cavalry, Federal army, and in 1863 he re-enlisted in Second Missouri Light Artillery. He was mustered out November 18, 1865, and was four months on the plains after peace was declared, fighting the Sioux Indians. He was in many severe battles and skirmishes in Missouri and Arkansas during the war, but his hardest fighting was done on the plains, where he was first sergeant in the Second Missouri. He was never wounded nor taken prisoner. In 1866 he married Miss Malinda Jane McFarland, a native of Kentucky, born in 1845, and to this union ten children were born, all living: Francis M., Henry R., Margaret J., I. N., Thomas J., Allen A., John L., Eula B., Minnie E. and V. Ernest. In 1867 Mr. Anderson came to Webster County, where he turned his attention to farming and stock raising. He is the owner of 480 acres of as good land as is to be found in the county, with over 200 acres under cultivation. He is a member of the Masonic fraternity, the A. O. U. W., the Wheel, the G. A. R., and is a Democrat in politics.

Scott Atkins, presiding judge of the Webster County Court, and a resident of Washington Township, was born in Lee County, Va., near a place called Rose Hill, August 12, 1833, being the son of Morris and Lucinda (Peek) Atkins, natives of Summers County, Va., near New and Kanawha Rivers. The father was born January 1, 1801; the mother was born October 3, 1803. After his marriage Mr. Atkins moved, in 1829, to Grainger County, Tenn., where they resided until the spring of 1846, and then immigrated to Gasconade County, Mo.; here he died July 28, of the same year. He was a member of the Baptist Church; was a gunsmith by trade, and a manufacturer of edged tools. He was a Democrat in politics. The mother was a member of the Primitive Baptist Church. After the death of her husband she moved back to Claiborne County, Tenn., near where they had formerly lived, and here died in July, 1857. Their son, Scott Atkins, at the age of twenty-two years, married, in 1885, and after marriage engaged in agricultural pursuits, which he has continued ever since. He also learned the carpenter's trade, at which he has continued to work until within the last two years. In 1856 he moved to what is now Leavenworth County, Kas., with the intention of making the place a permanent home. The border troubles being at their worst, it was no fitting place to live, and after staying about one year he moved to Polk County, Mo., where he resided until 1860, when he moved to Webster County, Mo. This has since been his home. He is the owner of a well-located and well-improved farm. He served in the State Militia at various times and places until 1864, when he enlisted in Company B, Forty-eighth Missouri Infantry, Federal service, and was mustered out in 1865, at Chicago, Ill., at Camp Douglas. He was at the battle of Nashville, Tenn., on December 15 and 16, and was in many places guarding the railroads, and was in a railroad wreck near Spring Hill, south of Nashville, in February, 1865, where an entire train was precipitated down an embankment, except locomotive and tender. After the war he returned to Webster County, Mo. In November, 1882, he was elected presiding judge of Webster County, and re-elected in 1886, which position he now holds. The Judge is a member of the G. A. R., is a Republican in his political views, and is one of the prominent men of the county. Mrs. Atkins is a member of the Methodist Episcopal Church. The subject of this sketch has three sisters and one brother, living in what is now Union County, Tenn., formerly a part of Grainger and Claiborne Counties. The brother, Samuel Atkins, is a prominent physician and merchant, who is now located on the bank of Clinch River. The sisters are Mesdames Walker, Capps and Haynes. The eldest brother was killed by being thrown from a horse while quite young.

Floyd E. Barnes, miller, was born in Kendall County, Ill., March 23, 1851, and is the son of Judge E. W. and Rosina (Morgan) Barnes. The father was born in Ohio in 1823, and is now a resident of Carthage, Mo. The family came to Missouri in 1865, settling in Lebanon for a short time, and then came to Marshfield. The father held the office of probate and county judge for two terms, commencing with the year 1876, and was also president of Webster County

Bank. In 1881 he moved to Carthage, Mo. While living in this county he was one of its prominent citizens, and was universally respected. Mrs. Rosina (Morgan) Barnes was born in New York in 1829, and died at Marshfield in 1875. Floyd E. Barnes was the elder of two children born to his parents, was reared on a farm, and received his education in the common country school. At the age of twenty-one he began for himself; was deputy postmaster, and ran a book and stationery department in connection. Prior to this he was employed in his father's mill, and in 1872 he began the hardware business in partnership with Freeman Evans, under the firm title of Barnes & Evans, the partnership continuing until 1887. In February, 1888, Mr. Barnes engaged in the milling business, buying one-half interest in the Barnes & Bolinger Mill, and has been quite successful in this pursuit. He was married in 1871 to Miss Emma Hampton, a native of Dade County, Mo., born in 1864, and the daughter of Dr. Noah H. Hampton, who was born in Tennessee, and who came to Missouri in early life. Of the seven children born to Mr. and Mrs. Barnes three are now living: Cora, born in 1872; Minnie, born in 1877, and Warren, born in 1882. Mr. Barnes is a Republican in his political views, and cast his first presidential vote for U. S. Grant in 1872. He is a member of the A. O. U. W., and is one of the best men of the county. Mrs. Barnes is a member of the Congregational Church.

John Bass was born on the 25th of November, 1828, in Marion County, Tenn., and is a son of Andrew Bass, who was born in North Carolina, but was reared and married in Tennessee, in which State his wife, whose maiden name was Ellen Smith, was born. They located near Springfield, Mo., in 1830, where Mr. Bass homesteaded and entered land, and on which he resided until his death, which occurred about 1863. He was quite a hunter, and killed many deer and a few bears. Eight sons and five daughters grew to mature years, and all became the heads of families, and five sons and five daughters are living at the present time. John Bass was reared in Greene County, and was there married in 1850 to Miss Samentha Owens, who was born and reared in Greene County, and immediately engaged in tilling the soil on his own responsibility. He became the owner of his present property in 1868, which consists of 125 acres, but at one time his land amounted to 400 acres, the most of which he gave to his children. He has about 100 acres of cleared land, and a substantial residence and other buildings. His wife died in 1856, leaving two children: Sarah C., wife of W. A. Stratton, of Greene County, and Jasper A. J., who is married and resides in Webster County. In 1857 Mr. Bass married his present wife, Miss Angeline Hartley, who was born in Tennessee and reared in Webster County, being a daughter of Jesse Hartley. Their union has been blessed in the birth of four children: Jesse W., who is married and is a resident of the county; John W., also married; Margaret F., wife of David Bodenhamer, and Benton, a young man of eighteen years. Mr. and Mrs. Bass are worthy and consistent members of the Missionary Baptist Church.

Adam M. Blunt is one of the old settlers of Webster County, Mo., and was born in Mecklenburgh County, N. C., August 4, 1819, his father, James Blunt, being also a North Carolinian. Dorcas Moore, who was of Irish descent, and was also born in North Carolina, became the latter's wife, and died in her native county when her son Adam was a small boy. James Blunt died in 1830. Adam Blunt remained in North Carolina until 1835, when he went to Texas and enlisted in Col. Steele's independent regiment, serving nine months. After residing in Tennessee until 1839, he came to Missouri, and was married in Lincoln County, March 1, 1843, to Nancy G. Williams, who was born in North Carolina June 16, 1828, a daughter of John and Fannie Williams, of North Carolina. After residing in Missouri for about two years they moved to Arkansas, but shortly after returned to Missouri, and up to 1854 resided in Lincoln County. From that time until the present he has remained in Webster County, with the exception of one year (1877) when he lived in Texas. He has sixty acres of his 105-acre farm under cultivation, and has a comfortable residence and good barns and orchards. In 1861 he enlisted in the Twenty-fourth Missouri Infantry, United States Army, and served until he received his discharge in October, 1864, being promoted to first sergeant, and participated in a number of engagements, the following being the most important: Pea Ridge, Ark., and Tupelo, Miss. He received his discharge at St. Louis, and after returning home was elected lieutenant of a company of State Militia. He is a Republican in politics, and a member of the G. A. R., and the following are the children born to his union with Miss Williams: James L., Alfred M., Lavina (wife of George Spradling), Daniel L., George, Huldah J. (wife of William Potter) and Sarah E. (wife of W. D. Edwards). Those deceased are John C. (who was killed February 2, 1862, while serving in the United States army), Mary F. (who was married, and died September 20, 1878), Martha E. (married, and died April 19, 1879), Joseph A. (who died July 12, 1871, aged sixteen years) and an infant. Mr. Blunt and wife are members of the Christian Church. Their son, Alfred M. Blunt, was born in Lincoln County, Mo., July 30, 1849, but was reared to manhood in Webster County, and remained with his father until twenty years of age, enlisting in 1863 in the Sixteenth Missouri Cavalry, and, after participating in the battles of Big Blue, Independence, Boonville and the fights with Price in Missouri, he received his discharge on the 29th of June, 1864, and returned to his home, where he was married September 3, 1868, to Miss Ruthie E., a daughter of Thomas W. Potter, who was formerly from Illinois. She was born and reared in Greene County, Mo., and in 1874 she and Mr. Blunt located on their present farm of eighty acres, forty of which are under cultivation. They have made many improvements since locating, and have a comfortable home and out-buildings, and a good bearing orchard of 125 trees, besides a young orchard of 500 trees. He is a Republican in politics, and has served part of two terms as constable of his township. His wife died on the 4th of October, 1885, leaving the following family: Sarah E. (wife of Jasper Miller), Mary E., Celia, James and Thomas. Two infants are deceased. August 7, 1887, he wedded Edith Atkinson, a daughter of John Atkinson (deceased). She was born in Arkansas and reared in Missouri. Mr. Blunt is a member of the Agricultural Wheel.

Joseph D. Bodenhamer, another successful agriculturist of Grant Township, is a native of Webster County, Mo., born March 5, 1854, being the son of William Frederick and Mary E. (Rudd) Bodenhamer. The father was born in Tennessee in 1822, and came to this county with his parents about 1836. He was a Republican in politics, a soldier in the late war, and was captain of Company B, Twenty-fourth Missouri. He represented Webster County, Mo., in the Legislature, and was one of the leading men and early settlers of this part of the State. He took a leading part in the affairs of the county, and was a man universally respected. He died in Webster County in 1887. The mother was born in North Carolina in 1833, and died in August, 1887. They were the parents of four children, three now living, of whom Joseph D. is the eldest. He was reared to manhood on the farm, and now owns the old homestead. He attended the county schools in his boyhood; has all his life followed agricultural pursuits. He is the owner of 240 acres of land in Grant Township. January 18, 1882, he was united in marriage to Miss Matilda A. Goodwin, who was born in Illinois in 1867, and who is a daughter of Thomas Goodwin. One child is the result of this union, named Ella Maude, whose birth occurred in June, 1884. Mr. Bodenhamer has been a resident of Grant Township all his life; is a Republican in politics, and is a highly respected man.

The Bodenhamer family is one of the oldest in Webster County. Jacob Bodenhamer, father of P. G., a well-known citizen, settled in the present limits of this county, in April, 1837, in Township 30, Range 19. He raised a family of sixteen children, the three youngest being born in that neighborhood, where he lived until 1844, then removing to Pierson Creek, Greene County. C. W. and W. F., his eldest sons, still remain here. The family originally came from Giles County, Tenn., and upon locating here found but four other families: Spencer Clark, Mrs. Sally Hoover, George Kepley and A. E. Goss, Sr. Reference to this is made elsewhere in this volume.

Samuel T. Brannock, farmer and stock raiser of Grant Township, is a native of Orange County, N. C., born May 8, 1828. His parents, A. N. and Susan (Foster) Brannock, were both natives of Orange County, N. C., the former born in 1800, and died in his native State at about the age of eighty, where the mother also died at about the age of eighty. The paternal grandfather, William Brannock, was a native of Maryland, and died in North Carolina. The maternal grandfather, George Foster, was a native Virginian, and was one of Gen. Washington's body guards during the Revolutionary War. His death occurred in North Carolina when more than eighty years of age. Samuel T. Brannock, subject of this sketch, is the elder of two children born to his parents. He was reared on the farm, and like the average country boy received his educational training in the common schools of his county. In 1852 he removed to Haywood County, West Tenn., where he lived for two years, and then came to what was then Greene, now Webster County, Mo. He now resides in Grant Township, about seven miles west of the county seat, where he owns

100 acres of well-improved land. Mr. Brannock enlisted in the Missouri State Guards, in September, 1861, for six months, and in May, 1862, he enlisted in Company F, Third Missouri Cavalry, of the Confederate army, and served until the close of the war. He was paroled at Shreveport, La. December 24, 1850, Mr. Brannock married Miss Fannie Boswell, who was born in Caswell County, N. C., July 19, 1823, and died in Webster County, Mo., December 18, 1886, leaving these children: William W., Julia A.. Alexander N. and Mary A. In politics Mr. Brannock is a conservative Democrat, and prior to the late war was one of the assayers of Webster County. In 1876 he served by appointment in the same office for one year. He is one of the popular men of Webster County, of which he has been a resident for thirty-four years.

Christopher W. Brooks, a leading and prosperous merchant of Marshfield, was born in Caswell County, N. C., February 5, 1844, and is the eldest of six children born to the marriage of Robert H. and Letha (Boswell) Brooks, both natives of North Carolina. Christopher Brooks, grandfather of our subject, was a native of North Carolina, and died in his native State when Christopher W. Brooks was about nine years of age. Robert H. Brooks was reared and married in Caswell County, of his native State, to Miss Letha Boswell, of the same locality. After his marriage he farmed there a few years, and in the fall of 1854 moved to Missouri, settling where his son William now resides. He was mustering officer while in North Carolina, and held a major's commission. Mr. Brooks died January 19, 1862, and his wife, July 25, 1888. Young Brooks removed with his parents from North Carolina to Western Tennessee, and after a residence in that State of three years he came to what was then Greene County, now Webster County, Mo., and here his parents died. He was reared to manhood engaged in agricultural pursuits, and received a good practical education in the common schools. He continued farming until 1876, when he removed to Marshfield and engaged in the mercantile business, to which, in 1879, he added a stock of agricultural implements. In 1866 he was married to Miss Joe Stella Dameron, a native of North Carolina, born in 1845, and who came with her parents to Missouri about 1851. Mr. and Mrs. Brooks became the parents of six children: McNey, Robert H., Stella, Nellie Edna and Shirley. Mr. Brooks is a Democrat in politics, and was county assessor for three years. He is a member of the Masonic fraternity, Mount Olive Lodge No. 439, and also the I. O. O. F., to which he has belonged for several years. He has been a resident of Webster County for thirty-four years, and is a highly respected citizen. He and wife are members of the Methodist Episcopal Church, South.

George A. Brown, one of the oldest settlers and most prominent citizens of Union Township, Webster County, was born in Giles County, Tenn., October 26, 1823, and is a son of Dickson and Naomi (McBride) Brown, both natives of North Carolina. Dickson Brown was born January 31, 1802; he received a liberal education in Giles County, Tenn., and when a young man taught school in connection with farming. While teaching school in Lauderdale County, Ala., in 1822, he met Miss Naomi McBride, who was visiting there, and they were married August 22, of that year. They lived in Giles County, Tenn., until about 1827, when they moved to Hardin County, Tenn., where they lived a time, then went to Maury County, Tenn., and later removed to Wayne County; they subsequently lived in Lawrence County, Tenn., and in 1854 moved to Dade County, Mo. In 1865 they settled in Webster County, Mo., where he died March 9, 1868. He turned his attention exclusively to farming after removing to Missouri, and though at one time elected justice of the peace refused to serve, being no office seeker. Mrs. Brown was born in North Carolina April 2, 1801, and died March 17, 1878. Both were members of the Missionary Baptist Church, in which church he was a deacon. Of their ten children seven are now living, viz.: George A.; Eliza Jane, wife of J. B. Dixon, a carpenter of Webster County, Mo.; L. K., a farmer and minister in Hardin County, Tenn.; E. G., a farmer of Webster County, Mo.; Naomi R., who married Thomas Spear, a carpenter of Dade County, Mo.; J. W., a farmer of Webster County, Mo., and E. M., a resident of Colorado. Those deceased are Mary A., Dixon L. and Julia Ann. When twenty-one years of age George A. Brown began for himself as a farmer, which occupation he has successfully followed all his life. He is now the owner of one of the best located and improved farms in the county. He left Tennessee in 1853, and went to Greene County, Mo., where he remained one year, and then removed to his present farm. During the war he served as sergeant and lieutenant in Col. J. F. McMahan's regiment, State service. December 31, 1844, Mr. Brown married Nancy Kilburn, who was born in Maury County, Tenn., April 7, 1829, and is a daughter of Allen Kilburn, of Scotch descent. This union has been blessed with eight children, viz.: Arminta F., wife of William Cain, a farmer of Webster County, and a minister of the Missionary Baptist Church; Neal S., of Conway, Mo.; A. D., at home; James G., also at home; Henry L., postmaster of Conway; Martha E., wife of John Smith, a farmer of Webster County; George L., at home, and Millie N., who was born March 31, 1866, became the wife of J. L. Rice, of Conway, and died May 15, 1888, at the age of twenty-two years. Mr. and Mrs. Brown have been connected with the Missionary Baptist Church since their marriage, and their children are all members of the same church. The family have the respect and esteem of all who know them, and have done much toward the upbuilding of the community. Mr. Brown is a Democrat in matters political.

Samuel H. Caldwell, retired farmer and merchant of Henderson, Mo., was born in Lee County, Va., November 30, 1833. His father, Samuel Caldwell, was a Kentuckian, but was reared, educated and married in Virginia, the latter event being to Miss Eliza Cissel, of Virginia. In 1840 they came to Greene County, Mo., where they reared their family and spent the greater part of their remaining days, the father's death occurring in Henderson about 1875. Samuel H. Caldwell remained with his father until eighteen years of age, and

March 17, 1853, was married in Webster County to Miss Sidney C. Caldwell, a daughter of Col. Andrew Caldwell, who died at Chester, Ill., having served in the War of 1812. Mr. Caldwell first located in Cole County, Ill., but in 1856 came to Henderson, and the following year opened a tan-yard, which business he had learned in boyhood, and followed this occupation until 1864. He owned all the land where the town of Henderson now is, and assisted in laying out the town, the first store being built about 1868 by A. T. Graves, Dr. Allen and Mr. Caldwell. The latter has served as county assessor and justice of the peace, and during the late war served in the State Militia, being called out on two or three occasions. His wife is a member of the Methodist Episcopal Church, and their union has been blessed in the birth of the following children: W. S., a farmer of Webster County; Frederick J., a dentist, and Ollie J., who resides with her parents.

James P. Callaway is a son of Parham and Nancy (Kirk) Callaway, both of whom were born in North Carolina, the parents having been reared and married in that State. They became residents of Webster County, Mo., December 1, 1852, and here the father died May 1, 1864, having served as a soldier for a short time before his death. James P. Callaway was born October 4, 1849, in Stanley County, N. C., but received his education and rearing in Webster County, Mo. January 15, 1878, he espoused Miss Martha M. Bruton, daughter of Dr. D. P. Bruton (deceased) and Mary (Miller) Bruton. She was born and reared in Webster County, Mo., being now the mother of four children: Roxie R., Atlee B., Parham P. and Lawrence A. In the fall of 1880 Mr. Callaway was nominated and elected sheriff of Webster County, and at the expiration of his term as sheriff was elected county collector, serving by re-election until 1887, and filled the duties of both these offices very efficiently and to the satisfaction of all concerned. He located on his farm about 1887, and is now the owner of 520 acres of land. He has a commodious residence, good barns for his grain and stock and a nice young orchard. He and wife are members of the Christian Church.

Alexander M. Cantrell, a well-to-do farmer and stockman of Webster County, Mo., was born in McMinn County, Tenn., December 4, 1836, being a son of Gabriel and Nancy (Smith) Cantrell, both of whom were Tennesseeans by birth. The father was a teacher by profession, and served several years as sheriff of McMinn County, and died there in 1849. In 1853 his widow and family moved to Missouri, locating in Dade County, and two years later in Webster County, settling on what is known as Cantrell's Creek. Alexander M. remained with his mother until about twenty-five years of age, and in November, 1861, he enlisted at Rolla in Col. Phelps' regiment for six months, and at the end of that time went to Illinois, where he was engaged in farming for three years. In July, 1862, he was married, in Webster County, to Miss Harriet Manry, who was a daughter of Edward Manry, of Alabama. He became a resident of Webster County in 1860, and is now deceased. Mrs. Cantrell was born in Tennessee. In October, 1867, they moved back to Missouri, and purchased their present farm of 360 acres, which was then in a very wild state. About half of his farm consists of bottom land, and 200 acres are cleared and under cultivation, and furnished with excellent buildings. He also has another tract of 119 acres well improved. He is a member of the Agricultural Wheel, and has always supported the principles of the Republican party. His children's names are as follows: Elmina, wife of Alexander Hall; Hezekiah, who is married and resides in Webster County; John D., Mary, Dora, Martha, Clementina, Edward, Charles, Elva and A. Logan. Mr. and Mrs. Cantrell are members of the Protestant Methodist Church.

Felix G. Cantrell is a brother of Alexander M. Cantrell, whose sketch appears above, and was born in McMinn County, Tenn., on the 6th of January, 1841, and came to Webster County, Mo., with his mother in 1855. Here he resided until the fall of 1861, when he went to Illinois, and was engaged in farming in Madison County until the fall of 1866, when he returned to Missouri and purchased the old home place, which consists of 440 acres all in one body, nearly one-half of which is bottom land, with 140 acres under cultivation. He has a substantial frame residence, commodious barns and other out-buildings, and his orchard supplies him with sufficient fruit for home use. He was married in Webster County, Mo., on the 9th of December, 1866, to Malinda Jane Pitchford, who was born in Kentucky and reared in Webster County, and by her is the father of the following children: Joseph Sherman, Ulysses S. Grant, William Gabriel, David Sheridan and Martha Arabelle. The mother of these children died April 11, 1885, and Mr. Cantrell's marriage to Mrs. Trephena Gilleland took place in Wright County. She is a daughter of Robert Pool, of Wright County, and was the mother of two children by her first marriage, Parthena and Robert Gilleland. By this last marriage there is one child, Abraham Cantrell. Mr. Cantrell is a member of the Baptist Church.

Joseph P. Cantrell, whose name is synonymous with the farming and stock raising interests of Webster County, was born in Tennessee, October 16, 1847, and is the son of Gabriel and Nancy Cantrell, whose maiden name was Miss Smith. The parents were both natives of Tennessee, and the father died in this State about 1849 or 1850. The mother died in Webster County, Mo., at about eighty years of age. The family came to Missouri in 1853, and lived here for two years in Dade County, but about 1855 they removed to Webster County, and settled on Cantrell's Creek, in High Prairie Township, being among the early settlers in that part of the county. Joseph P. Cantrell is one of a pair of twins, and the youngest in a family of fourteen children, nine of whom are living. He remained on the farm until twenty years of age, and then began life for himself, without education, and can neither read nor write. Notwithstanding all this he is at present one of the successful farmers and stock traders of the county, and has bought and shipped a large amount of stock from this county to St. Louis. He owns a farm in High Prairie Township, which consists of 470 acres, and for ten years he has been engaged in the stock business. He was married in 1868 to Miss Caroline Cantrell, who was born in Webster county, Mo., and whose parents were early settlers of this county. Mr. and Mrs. Cantrell have nine children: John G., William, Nancy, Malissa, Joseph, Ada, Emma, Messie and Mattie. Mr. Cantrell has been a resident of Webster County for thirty-five years or more, and is an honest, industrious citizen. He is a Mason, member of the Niangua lodge, and is a Republican in his political views.

Edmund P. Cardwell, a prominent farmer and stockman of Webster County, Mo., was born in Roane County, Tenn., on the 8th of July, 1822, and is a son of John and Faney (Ganes) Cardwell, who were born, reared and married in Virginia. They moved to Tennessee about 1814, and in 1833 located in what is now Pulaski County, but two years later purchased land where the town of Marshfield now is, but sold out the following year, and from that time until his death resided near Dallas. Edmund P. Cardwell received the education and rearing of the average farmer's boy, and in July, 1844, was united in marriage to Miss Eda Bruton, a daughter of David Bruton, both of whom were born in Tennessee. He has owned several different farms in Webster County, and since 1868 has resided on his present farm. In 1869 he engaged in the mercantile business in Bloomington, and continued that occupation with good success for about seventeen years. April 13, 1879, his wife died, having borne two children: America F., who is now deceased, and Thomas G., whose sketch appears below. In September, 1879, he married his second wife, Anice Elizabeth Bruton, a daughter of Enoch Bruton. She was born in Wright County, Mo., and is the mother of two children: Caledonia W. and Jessie May. The father is a member of the Missionary Baptist Church. Thomas G. Cardwell was born in Greene County, Mo., March 16, 1848, and remained with and assisted his father on the farm until he attained his majority. In 1868 he was married to Miss Martha Phillips, who was born and reared in Webster County, and by her is the father of eight children: Albert L., Robert E., Jesse N., William E., Thomas A., Mattie R., Eugenia B. and Susan D. They have a good farm of 125 acres, on which they have resided since 1873, and have 100 acres of land under cultivation, with a neat residence and good barns. The family worship in the Baptist Church, and are considered among the prominent citizens of the county.

Alexander G. Cardwell was born in Webster County, Mo., on the 14th of December, 1837, and is a son of Dr. Thomas P. and Katie (Steward) Cardwell, who were born in Virginia and Tennessee, respectively. After their marriage they resided in Tennessee for a number of years, and about 1830 moved to Missouri, locating in what is now Webster County, where the father made a farm, reared his family, and resided until his death in September, 1882. He was a practicing physician for many years, and served several terms as justice of the peace. His five sons and five daughters lived to mature years, and four sons and three daughters are living at the present time. Alexander G. Cardwell was reared near his present place of abode, and during the late Civil War served in the Home Guards and State Militia. In 1858 he was united in marriage to Miss Sarah Mobley, and soon after located in Douglas County, where he resided about three years, sin⁀ ⁀ which time he has been a resident of Webster County. In 1865 he settled on 183 acres of raw land on Finley Creek, and by industry and good management has succeeded in putting 100 acres of his farm under good cultivation, and has erected a good residence and barns. He also owns another farm of 160 acres, with about sixty under cultivation. His wife died in the spring of 1883, having borne four children: William Thomas, Perry W., Linda B. and Samuel Tilden; and in the fall of 1885 he was married to Miss Elizabeth Denny, who was born and reared in Webster County, and died on the 6th of June, 1888. Mr. Cardwell is a member of the Free-will Baptist Church.

Lewis S. Cass, farmer, stock raiser and trader of East Dallas Township, was born in Madison County, N. Y., November 3, 1837, being a son of Hon. Dudley Cass, who was born and reared in New Hampshire. The latter went to New York when a young man, and there met and married, in Madison County, Miss Martha Robbins, who was also a native of New Hampshire. In 1843 Mr. Cass moved with his family to Wisconsin, settling in Kenosha County, where he made a farm and reared his family, then came to Missouri, and lived with his son in Springfield until 1870. His death occurred in 1884, at the age of seventy-three years. He served as colonel in a company of militia at one time, and was a member of the Wisconsin Legislature one term. His widow survives him, and resides in Springfield with her daughter, Theresa A. Cass, a maiden lady. Her two sons are Lewis S. and Kimble, the latter being a resident of the old homestead in Wisconsin. Lewis S. Cass was reared to manhood in Wisconsin, and received a good education in the common schools and an academy in Kenosha County, in which institution he took a three-years' course. He afterward engaged in teaching in Wisconsin and Northern Illinois for three years, and afterward located on a farm in Lake County, of the latter State, but at the end of two years removed to Benton County, Iowa, where he spent two years in farming and stock raising. In the spring of 1866 he moved to Missouri, and located in Springfield, where he taught in the public schools for two years. From 1869 to 1885 he was engaged in merchandising in that city, and while there built two good business blocks and a good brick residence. After selling these he purchased his present farm of 444 acres on Dry Creek, a goodly portion of which is bottom land, and 250 acres are under cultivation. He has a commodious two-story frame residence, two large frame barns and one log barn, very large. In 1862 he was married, in Kenosha County, Wis., to Miss Charlotte Collier, who was born, reared and educated in New York, and by her is the father of six children: Mary, Burdella, Dudley, Emma, Fannie and Lydia. Mrs. Cass is a member of the Baptist Church, and Mr. Cass belongs to the K. of H., and while a resident of Springfield served as city alderman of his ward.

Daniel E. Cates, a prominent merchant of Webster County, Mo., was born in Bedford County, Tenn., October 2, 1835, and is a son of John S. and Elizabeth (Hime) Cates. The father was a son of Thomas Cates, and was born in Tennessee, on the way from North Carolina to Tennessee, his birth occurring on the 12th of January, 1808, and his death June 1, 1880. His wife was born in Bedford County, Va., December 25, 1809. She is yet hale and hearty, and is living in Bedford County, Tenn. Both parents were members of the Cumberland Presbyterian Church for many years, and the father was a Mason (joined 1847) and a member of the I. O. O. F. (1846). He was a stone mason and a farmer by occupation, and was very skillful at both callings. The Cates family are of English descent, and the grandfather, Thomas, was born in North Carolina, and died in Bedford County, Tenn., when the subject of this sketch was a young boy. There were eleven children born to the marriage of John S. Cates and Elizabeth Hime, the following of whom are living: Mary E., widow of Pascal Brown; John R.; Martha J., widow of J. M. Rives; Daniel E., Joseph H.; Finetti F., wife of J. M. Thomas; Locadia R., wife of J. B. Dwyer; Justinna E., wife of D. H. Dwyer, and Caldonia C., wife of John F. Dwyer. Those deceased are James P. and Giles P. Daniel E. Cates was in his twenty-fourth year when he married Miss Sarah L. Evans, a daughter of A. H. and Ellen C. (Holt) Evans, who were born in Tennessee April 6, 1818, and August 27, 1814, and died in their native State July 1, 1880, and June 26, 1868, respectively. Mrs. Cates was born in Bedford County, Tenn., November 3, 1840, and is the mother of three children: Zarilda F., born January 23, 1860, the wife of J. W. Whitehurst, a merchant of Republic, Mo.; J. H., who was born March 9, 1868, and is engaged in the mercantile business with his father, and Giles G., who was born January 12, 1876, and resides at home. After his marriage Mr. Cates first turned his attention to farming, which he continued to follow until coming to Missouri, in the fall of 1883, since which time he has been engaged in the mercantile business in Niangua, where he has acquired a large and lucrative trade. He was engaged in merchandising during the war, and although he had his goods taken from him twice, he has accumulated considerable of this world's property. He is a Republican in politics, and he and wife are members of the Cumberland Presbyterian Church.

Col. George L. Childress, a prominent citizen of Webster County, Mo., is a son of Hon. R. L. and Hannah (Lacy) Childress, who were born, reared and married in Knox County, Tenn. They became residents of Cherokee County, Ala., about 1833, and in 1851 came to Greene County, Mo. (now Webster County), and here the father served in the constitutional convention in 1864. In 1866 and 1868 he was elected to represent Webster County in the State Legislature, and prior to the war was county school commissioner, and also held other offices. His death occurred on the 30th of January, 1885, his wife having died in 1862. George L. Childress was reared to a farm life, and in his youth received only fair educational advantages. At the breaking out of the war in 1861 he enlisted first in the Home Guards, then for six months in the Phelps Regiment Missouri Infantry, and at the expiration of that time joined the Eighth Missouri Volunteer Cavalry, and for his bravery and efficient service was promoted first to the rank of captain, then to major, and lastly to lieutenant-colonel, holding the latter position until he received his discharge at the close of the war, being mustered out at St. Louis August 4, 1865.

He participated in the battles of Prairie Grove, Little Rock, Pumpkin Road, and was in numerous sharp skirmishes. After the war he settled on the old home place, and in 1876 was wedded to Miss Harriet A. Aldredge, who died in March, 1886, having borne a family of six children, whose names are as follows: Mary B., Frances E., Lillie E., Robert B., Creed A. and Linna M. Mr. Childress' present wife, whose maiden name was Louisa Newton, was born in Mercer County, Mo. Besides farming Mr. Childress deals very extensively in railroad ties, piling, posts and lumber, which he ships west, which enterprise has proved quite remunerative. He has always supported the principles of the Republican party, of which he has ever been a prominent member, and was appointed adjutant-general under Gov. McClurg for two years, but resigned at the end of one year. He is a member of the G. A. R.

Anderson H. Chitty, proprietor of the Chitty Hotel at Marshfield, Mo., and son of Dixon and Mahala (Lawson) Chitty, was born in Marion County, E. Tenn., August 16, 1840, and is the fifth of eight children born to his father's first marriage. The father was born in Ray County, E. Tenn., August 14, 1808, and died September 15, 1882, at Marshville, Mo. He was a farmer and stock trader by occupation, and during the late war lost $100,000, all he possessed. The mother was born in Marion County, E. Tenn., in 1815, and died in her native county in 1855. Their son, Anderson H. Chitty, remained on his father's farm until 1863, when he enlisted in Company C, Thirty-second Tennessee, Confederate Army, and served until the war closed. After the war he continued farming in Tennessee until 1869, when he came to Marshfield. Previous to this, October 16, 1867, he was united in marriage to Miss Mary Wallace, a native of Jackson County, Ala., born September 17, 1847, and daughter of William and Elizabeth (Parker) Wallace. Her father was born in Raleigh, N. C., February 29, 1813, and died September 30, 1864, in Jackson County, Ala. The mother was born January 14, 1832, and died February 9, 1883, in Jackson County, Ala. Mrs. Chitty is the third of ten children born to her parents, nine now living. After coming to Marshfield, in 1869, Mr. Chitty followed farming until 1874, when he engaged in the hotel business, and June 16, 1880, bought his present hotel. He has also been engaged in stock trading, and took stock south for seven winters, and this he has continued more or less ever since. He has one of the best hotels in Southwest Missouri, and is a wide-awake business man. To Mr. and Mrs. Chitty have been born two children, Willie D., born May 31, 1871, and Gayford Wallace, born June 21, 1888. Mr. Chitty is a Democrat politically, and cast his first presidential vote for Horace Greeley. He is a member of Webster Lodge No. 163, I. O. O. F., and he and wife are members of the Christian Church.

Samuel C. Crawford, one of the leading merchants of Webster County, Mo., was born in Washington County, Ark., November 4, 1860, being the son of Samuel C. and Elizabeth (Harron) Crawford, natives of Tennessee and Washington County, Ark., respectively. The father was born May 20, 1818, and the mother October 29, 1825.

He is a farmer, has followed this occupation all his life, is a Democrat in politics, was justice of the peace for three years, and he and wife are members of the Methodist Protestant Church. He served in the Confederate service during the war, and was a brave and gallant soldier. He and wife are now living, and are residents of Washington County, Ark. They were the parents of thirteen children, ten of whom lived to be grown, and nine now living. Of this family Samuel C. is the youngest. He remained with his parents until 1882, when he began for himself by farming and dealing in stock in Washington County, Ark. The same year he came to Missouri, locating in Webster County, and October 4, 1884, engaged in merchandising. He carries a stock of goods valued at from $2,000 to $2,500, with annual sales that equal from $8,000 to $12,000. In connection with his mercantile business he also buys and handles a great deal of railroad ties and lumber. November 25, 1877, he married Miss Tobitha M. Alexander, a native of Morgan County, Mo., born in 1857, and the daughter of H. H. Alexander. Two children have blessed this union: Martha Elizabeth and Samuel L. Mr. Crawford is a Democrat in his political views, and is a member of the Masonic fraternity.

William M. Crump, resident of Niangua, Webster Co., Mo., and a native of that county, born July 15, 1856, is the son of Adam and Mary (Puett) Crump, natives of North Carolina. The father died in Webster County, Mo., December 17, 1862, at the age of thirty-five, and the mother died in the same county April 24, 1884. They were married in North Carolina and came to Missouri in 1849, being among the first settlers of the county. He was a farmer all his life with the exception of a year and a half, 1854 and 1855, when he was in the mines of California, and where he was quite successful. He served a short time in the Federal army, was a Democrat in politics, and both he and wife were members of the Methodist Episcopal Church, South. To their marriage were born four children, three now living: John P., farmer in Webster County, Mo.; William M., and Nancy C., wife of Davis Tuttle, of North Carolina. Mary E. died when three years of age. William M. Crump remained with his mother until after her death, and followed the occupation of a farmer and stock raiser, which he still continues. He is the owner of a well-improved and well-located farm, and is one of the successful and enterprising young farmers of the county. In January, 1878, he chose for his companion in life Miss Winifred A. Dameron, daughter of John S. Dameron, who is a native of North Carolina and an old settler of Webster County, Mo. Mrs. Crump was born in the last named county in 1861, and by her union to Mr. Crump became the mother of four children: Mary A., Ella M., Georgie L. and Inez R. Mr. Crump is a Democrat in politics, and he and wife are members of the Methodist Episcopal Church, South, of which he has been class leader.

William G. Davis, of Webster County, Mo., is a son of Charles and Ruth (Gearhart) Davis, who were born, reared and married in Tennessee, and about 1841 located in Missouri, settling near where their son, William G., now resides. The father died in September, 1878, having served several terms as justice and assessor of his township. William G. was born in Jackson County, Tenn., August 24, 1832, and until attaining his majority made his home with his parents. In 1861 he enlisted in the Home Guards for three months, and at the expiration of that time enlisted in Company E, Forty-ninth Illinois Volunteer Infantry, United States Army, and served until he received his discharge at the close of the war. He was at Fort Donelson, Pittsburgh Landing, Little Rock, and participated in several fights and skirmishes of less note. He was wounded in the arm by a gunshot at Pleasant Hill, La., and was in the hospital for about two months, and after receiving his discharge, January 9, 1865, he returned to Webster County and engaged in tilling the soil, and by industry and good management has become the owner of 210 acres of land, eighty-five of which are under cultivation, furnished with good buildings and an orchard of 100 select trees. November 5, 1868, he was wedded to Miss Nancy Caroline Powell, who was born in Giles County, Tenn., and is a daughter of Elias Powell, now deceased, and by her became the father of the following children: Charles B., Amanda J. and James Edmond. Mr. and Mrs. Davis are members of the Christian Church, in which he is an elder, and he belongs to the Agricultural Wheel, and in his political views is a stanch supporter of the principles of the Republican party.

Judge John H. Davison, merchant and farmer of Jackson Township, was born in Polk County, Mo., October 30, 1843, but was reared in Dallas County, and made his home with his father until nineteen years of age, when he spent six years in his native county, engaged in farm labor. While a resident of that county he was married, on the 19th of December, 1861, to Miss Susan V. Ragsdale, who was born in Kentucky, but was reared in Polk County, of which county her father, Joel Ragsdale, was a pioneer. In 1861 Mr. Davison enlisted in the Home Guards, and in 1864 joined the Enrolled Missouri Militia, Fifteenth Cavalry, and served until the close of the war, being mustered out at Springfield. He was in the battle of Lexington, Mo., and during his six months' service, in 1861, was captured, but after being retained a short time was paroled and returned home. In the spring of 1865 he and family moved to Dallas County, where he partly made two farms, and is the owner of one of them at the present time. He was engaged in the mercantile business in Thorpe, Mo., in 1883–84, but sold out and engaged in the same business in Charity. Since July, 1885, he has resided in Webster County, and has built him a store, residence and blacksmith shop, and carries on the general mercantile business very successfully. He also started a grist and sawmill in 1886, which brings him in a nice little income annually. While residing in Dallas County he served one term as county judge, being elected on the Greenback ticket in the fall of 1882. In 1888 he was elected public administrator of Webster County. He is a Master Mason, and he and wife are the parents of the following children: Margaret R., wife of G. B. Richardson; Joel Thomas, who is a partner in the store and mill with his father; George W., who resides on the farm in Dallas County; Lewis H.; Sarah J., wife of W. E. Salsman; Oliver C. and Charles A. Two children are deceased: Catherine, who died at the age of six years, and an infant. Mrs. Davison is a member of the Christian Church. Judge Davison's parents, Bracket and Delilah (Hardison) Davison, were born in Tennessee and North Carolina, respectively, and after their marriage resided in Tennessee a few years, and in 1838 located in Polk County, Mo., taking up their abode in Dallas County in 1851. The father was a soldier in the War of 1812 under Gen. Jackson, and was at the battle of New Orleans. He died in Dallas County September 29, 1863.

Judge John Denney, a prosperous farmer of Webster County, Mo., was born in Wayne County, of the "Blue Grass State," on the 21st of February, 1825, his father being Benjamin Denney, of Virginia. The latter was reared in his native State, and when a young man went to Kentucky, where he became acquainted with and married Miss Mary Mounce, who was born and reared in that State. Her father, John Mounce, was one of the early pioneers of that State, and many interesting anecdotes are told of his encounters with the red man and his fights with wild animals. Mr. Denney resided in Kentucky for a number of years after his marriage, and in the fall of 1836 immigrated to Webster County, Mo., which was then a part of Pulaski County, and entered and cleared the farm on which the Judge is now living. Here he died in 1842, having lived a useful life. Judge John Denney is self-educated, his learning having been mostly acquired since reaching years of maturity, and since his father's death he has resided on the home farm, and has a comfortable and commodious residence and pleasant surroundings. He served in the Enrolled Militia during the late war, and was called out several times. In the fall of 1878 he was elected judge of Webster County, and has held this office for ten consecutive years, the duties of which he has filled with honor to himself and to the satisfaction of his constituents. His wife is a member of the Freewill Baptist Church, and their children's names are as follows: Crafford, who is married and resides in the county; Thomas L., who was married, and died in 1881; Mary T., who died in September, 1882, aged twenty-three years; Ellet G., married and living in Webster County; William T., who died at the age of eighteen, in January, 1882; Louisa H., the wife of William Philpot, of Douglas County; Riley and Sophronia.

Samuel B. Dugger, merchant, real estate dealer and station agent at Northview, Mo., was born at Carlinville, Macoupin Co., Ill., in 1834. While a boy he learned the printer's trade, and when only eighteen years of age he, associated with his brother, Jefferson L., published the Macoupin *Statesman*, of which paper our martyr President, Abraham Lincoln (then practicing law at Springfield, Ill.), was a frequent contributor. At the age of twenty-one Mr. Dugger started and published the Menard *Express*, the first newspaper ever published at Petersburgh, Ill., which he sold out, soon after, to the friends of Congressman Thomas L. Harris, and moved to Atlanta, Ill., where he commenced the publication of the *Logan County Forum*, which he continued to publish about three years, when he, in connection with the same brother above mentioned, commenced the publication of the *Kansas Daily Register*, at Leavenworth, Kas., in the days of the "Free

State" and "Border Ruffian" war for ascendancy. From Kansas he returned to Illinois, where he continued in the newspaper business until the breaking out of the late War of the Rebellion, when he was appointed United States Internal Revenue Assessor and Collector for Macoupin County, Illinois, in which capacity he continued to serve until after the inauguration of President Grant, when he resigned and re-engaged in the mercantile business at Carlinville, Ill. During the war he also served as deputy provost marshal, and superintended the enrollment and draft. During the year 1870 he assisted in the organization of the National Building Company, an association of experts and capitalists engaged in the construction of gas and water works for cities throughout the South and West, with headquarters at St. Louis. Being chosen secretary of that company, he moved to St. Louis, and had the active management of the business of the company until 1875, when he again resumed the mercantile business, in St. Louis, and continued therein until 1880. During that year his attention was attracted to the great advantages offered by Southwest Missouri, and on visiting Webster County he was so favorably impressed that he bought a body of land immediately surrounding Northview Station, from the St. Louis & San Francisco Railway Company, to which place he removed his family, opened a general store, and was appointed railway station agent, postmaster, etc. In his business and social relations, since the time of his settlement here, he has established an enviable reputation throughout the country as an intelligent and enterprising citizen, and a fair-minded and honorable business man. In 1855 Mr. Dugger became a member of the Masonic fraternity in Illinois; served four years as Master of Mount Nebo Lodge No. 76, and three years as High Priest of Burke Chapter of Royal Arch Masons, at Carlinville, Ill. He took the Council degrees of Royal and Select Master, as well as the order of High Priesthood, at Chicago, and became a member of Belvidere Commandery of Knights Templar at Alton, Ill. Since coming to Northview he has transferred his membership to Springfield, Mo. During his residence in Illinois he held several positions and served in numerous capacities in the Grand Lodge of that State. As Grand Standard Bearer, he assisted in laying the corner-stone of the Douglas Monument at Chicago, and also assisted in depositing the remains of President Lincoln in his tomb at Springfield. Mr. Dugger has been married twice, his first marriage being to Miss Kate M. Odell, of Illinois, who died in 1872, having borne the following children, who are now living: Jarrot P., now a prominent business man in Chicago; Helen M., wife of Frank P. Kimbrough, of St. Louis; Mary C., wife of William A. Colby, also of St. Louis. and Samuel O., who resides near Marshfield, Mo. In 1875 Mr. Dugger was married, in St. Louis, to Miss Eliza M. Riegel, who was born in Seneca County, N. Y., and educated at Syracuse. She is a lady of more than ordinary mental culture, and was a successful teacher in the public schools of Syracuse, N. Y., and St. Louis, Mo., previous to her marriage. They are the parents of one son, Albert Arthur, now living with them. Mr. Dugger is a progressive and public-spirited man; believes in building and maintaining schools and churches (being an active member of the Methodist Episcopal Church himself), and in encouraging every good work that will contribute to the happiness and prosperity of the people, and improve the moral and social condition of the community in which he lives, as well as of the country at large.

Freeman Evans, treasurer of Webster County, and dealer in general hardware at Marshfield, was born in Sumner County, Tenn., January 19, 1841, and is a son of James and Ann (Barr) Evans. The family immigrated to Missouri in 1849, settling in St. Clair County, where the parents of Mr. Evans died in 1852. Freeman Evans is the third of seven children born to his parents, three now living. His boyhood was spent on the farm, and a limited education was obtained in the common schools. In 1857 he left the farm and began learning the tinner's trade at Greenfield, but in 1858 went to Springfield, where he continued his trade until 1861, when he enlisted in Capt. Phelps' regiment of the State Guards. A short time afterward he joined the Sixth Missouri Cavalry, under Col. Wright, and three months later was discharged on account of physical disability. In August, 1862, he again entered the service, joining the Eighth Missouri Cavalry, and continued in service until the close of the war. He was honorably discharged in August, 1865, and returned to Springfield, Mo., where he resumed his trade. In 1867 he came to Marshfield, engaged in the stove and tin business, and two years later added a stock of general hardware. He is the second oldest business man in Marshfield, and is doing a prosperous business, although he was burned out three times. He is a Republican in politics, and was elected county treasurer of Webster County in 1876, serving in that position two years. In 1883 he was appointed by Gov. Crittenden to serve for a short time, and in the fall of that year he was again elected to the same position, his term expiring in January, 1889. He was married in 1866 to Miss E. V. Thomas, a native of Greene County, Mo., and to them were born four children: Harvey E., Maggie, Maud E. and Bessie. Mr. Evans is a Mason, a member of Webster Lodge No. 98, is also a member of the Methodist Episcopal Church, and is one of the leading citizens of the county.

L. Farnsworth, a progressive farmer and stock raiser of Webster County, Mo., was born in Monroe County, Ohio, February 11, 1840, and since the fall of 1887 has been a resident of his present farm, which consists of 120 acres of land, with about 100 acres under cultivation. His farm is supplied with very good buildings, an excellent young orchard, and since his residence here Mr. Farnsworth has fenced the place and greatly improved it in other respects. His parents, John and Polly (Lamon) Farnsworth, were born in Tennessee and Ohio, and were married in the latter State, where the mother died in 1844. Our subject remained in his native State until seventeen years of age, then went to Iowa and worked as a farm hand until the spring of 1861, when he went to Illinois, and was engaged in tilling the soil in Pike County till August of the following year, when he enlisted in Company C, Ninety-ninth Illinois Infantry, and served until he received his discharge at the close of the war. He was at Baton Rouge, Magnolia Hill, Champion's Hill, Black River, the siege and surrender of Vicksburg, and Jackson, Miss. During all this time he was never off duty, never received a wound, and was never in the hospital or taken prisoner. After peace was declared he returned to Pike County, Ill., and was there married, on the 13th of September, 1866, to Amanda J. Benson, of that county, a daughter of Thomas Benson, now deceased, but her death occurred in Carroll County, Mo., January 2, 1887, having borne a family of seven children: Anna Laura, born November 16, 1868; Arthur Roscoe, born February 18, 1870; Lottie May, born April 2, 1872; Oscar, born August 17, 1874; William, born September 3, 1876; Edgar, born July 31, 1878; Elmer, born March 5, 1881. Mr. Farnsworth is a member of the G. A. R., Ben Grigsby Lodge, No. 305, of Carroll County, Mo., and is a member of the Union Labor party.

Dr. Thomas S. Florance, a successful practitioner of Marshfield and vicinity, was born in Dallas Township, Webster Co., Mo., November 8, 1853, being the son of James and Sarah S. (Bouldin) Florance. The father was born in Caswell County, N. C., November 4, 1818, and the mother was born in the same county June 11, 1817. They now reside in Webster County, in Dallas Township. As early as 1841 the father came to Webster County, Mo., remaining one year, and then returned to North Carolina, but in 1844 he came back to Webster County, and settled in Dallas Township on the farm where he now lives. Tolliver Florance, grandfather of Dr. Florance, was a native of North Carolina, born in 1787, and died in his native State in 1872. The subject of this sketch is the fourth of six children born to his parents. He was reared on the farm in Dallas Township, and secured a fair education in the common schools. In 1874 he came to Marshfield, began the study of medicine in the office of Dr. C. S. Wallis, and subsequently attended the Missouri Medical College at St. Louis, from which he graduated in 1877. He then began the practice of his profession in Dallas Township, Webster County, and there continued a successful practice until November, 1888, when he removed to Marshfield, and is practicing there at the present. He was married, in 1875, to Miss Mary E. Johnson, a native of North Carolina, born October 13, 1863, and the fruits of this union are four children: Inez, born June 23, 1876; Ollie G., born August 23, 1878; Robert, born February 18, 1881, and Walter J., born January 15, 1886. Politically a Democrat, his first presidential vote was cast for Grover Cleveland in 1888. He is a member of the Masonic fraternity, Mt. Olive Lodge, No. 439, and he and wife are members of the Methodist Episcopal Church, South.

John Freeman is a successful merchant of Seymour, Mo., and was born on the 4th of January, 1833, in Roane County, Tenn., both of his parents, B. D. and Elizabeth (Fortson) Freeman, being born in the same State, where they were also reared and married. After residing in Anderson County, Tenn., for some time they moved to Missouri in 1848, and located in what is Webster County at the present time, where they made a farm, reared their family, and where the father died in 1883. Since fifteen years of age John Freeman has been a resident of Missouri, with the exception of about fifteen years spent in gold mining on the Pacific slope. He made the journey overland to California in 1852, reaching that State at the end of three months, and during his residence in the West was engaged in the mercantile and livery business as well as mining, and also fed stock a portion of the time. In 1865 he returned home via Nicaragua, New York City and St. Louis, and settled in Webster County, where he engaged in farming and dealing in cattle, which occupation he continued until 1882, when he entered into the mercantile business at Waldo, where he sold goods for two years, and then moved to Seymour and embarked in his present business, which is bringing him in a nice annual income. He carries a large and select stock of general merchandise, and does an annual business of $20,000. In December, 1865, he was married to a widow lady, Mrs. Elizabeth C. (Amick), a daughter of Lorenzo and Cynthia Amick, and the widow of Abraham McMahan, by whom she had one child, Elijah. Mrs. Freeman was born in Webster County, and she and Mr. Freeman are the parents of the following children: Lorenzo D., Mary M., John T., Robert J. and Laura M. Mr. Freeman is a Master Mason in the Masonic fraternity, and he and wife are members of the Cumberland Presbyterian Church.

John Fuson, of the mercantile firm of Fuson & Co., of Seymour, Mo., was born in Wilson County, Tenn., on the 7th of March, 1823, and is a son of Jonathan Fuson, a native of Virginia. The latter was married in his native State to Margaret Malon, who was born in Tennessee, and afterward moved to the latter State and made a farm in Wilson County, but in the fall of 1829 moved to Wayne County, Tenn., where he reared his family and resided until his death, which occurred about 1856. Their son John's early days were spent on a farm, and he was married there on the 12th of November, 1844, to Mary E. Grimes, a daughter of William Grimes. She was born in Tennessee, and died in 1858, having borne a family of four children, all of whom are residents of Missouri: W. T., J. A., R. B., and Mary J., wife of J. A. Tate, of Wright County. Mr. Fuson married his second wife, whose maiden name was Sophronia Galleyly, in 1858, in Tennessee. She is a daughter of Morris Galleyly, of that State, and is the mother of three sons and two daughters: John M., who is married and resides in Texas; Dr. F. B., who is married and is a resident of Mansfield; James W., whose sketch immediately follows this; Emma C., wife of Prof. W. R. Jackson, of Webster County, and Fanny, wife of P. S. Wilks, of Seymour. In 1860 Mr. Fuson moved to Illinois, and continued to reside in Union County, of that State, until 1869, when he moved to Missouri and located in Webster County, and has since been engaged in merchandising at Seymour, in which business he has been quite successful. He and wife are members of the Missionary Baptist Church, in which he has been a deacon for about forty years. James W. Fuson was born in Union County, Ill., on the 31st of December, 1861, and in 1869 located with his parents in Wright County, Mo. He received a common-school education, and when about eighteen years of age entered a drug store in Hartville as clerk, which occupation he followed for two years. He then spent about two years as a traveling salesman, but in 1884 located at Seymour, and engaged in the hardware business in company with P. S. Wilks, the style of the firm being Fuson & Wilks. Mr. Fuson afterward purchased Mr. Wilks' interest, and the firm is now known as J. W. Fuson & Co. Mr. Fuson erected his present business house in the fall of 1886, and carries a large and choice line of heavy and shelf hardware, also farming implements, harness, saddles, etc. He was married here on the 12th of June, 1887, to Miss Tempa S. McMahan, a daughter of W. T. McMahan, whose sketch appears in this work. She was born, reared and educated in Webster County, and is the mother of one daughter, Opal W. Mrs. Fuson is a member of the Cumberland Presbyterian Church, and Mr. Fuson is a Master Mason, and is Senior Warden of his lodge. He is also city treasurer, and is considered one of the enterprising and successful young business men of the county.

Valentine Garner. Prominent among the worthy tillers of the soil and stock men of Webster County, Mo., who deserve honorable mention, is Mr. Garner, who was born in Randolph County, N. C., December 10, 1813. His parents, John and Susan (Halla) Garner, were born in the same State, and in 1816 settled in Tennessee, and after residing in Wilson County, of that State, for a number of years, moved to Illinois, where both parents and three grown children died of cholera in the fall of 1834. Valentine Garner accompanied his parents to Illinois in 1831, and is next to the youngest of their ten children, he and his brother William being the only surviving members of the family. He came to Missouri in 1834, and December 31, of the same year, was married to Sarah Edington, who was born and reared in Tennessee. Her father, James Edington, was one of the early pioneers of the county. Mr. and Mrs. Garner spent the winter of their marriage in Illinois, and the following May returned to Webster County, Mo., where they have since resided. He purchased raw land (346 acres), on which he erected a house in 1840, and now has 200 acres of his farm cleared and well improved. His marriage has been blessed in the birth of the following children: Nancy, wife of George Linn, of California; John, also residing in California; William, who resides in Webster County; Martha, wife of Benjamin Shields, of Webster County; Dialtha, wife of P. D. Grigsby, of California; Frances, wife of John Shook, of Webster County; Mary, wife of W. P. Letchworth; Anna, wife of Jones Mackey; James and George, both of whom are married and reside in Webster County, and Julia, who is the wife of Robert Chaffin. The following children are deceased: Jane, Susan, Amanda and Sarah. Mr. and Mrs. Garner are members of the Christian Church, and he is an elder in the same.

Joiner Gentry may be ranked among the prosperous farmers and stock men of Webster County, Mo., and was born in Jackson County, Ala., October 13, 1832, and is the son of Bartlett and Priscilla (Monday) Gentry, the father's birth occurring February 15, 1803, in North Carolina. About 1831 he went to Alabama, thence ten years later to Missouri, locating where the town of Seymour now is. He made this place his home until 1861, when he went to Texas County, Mo., where he is still residing at the age of eighty-six years. Joiner Gentry was reared in Webster County, and during the late war served in the Home Guards and in the quartermaster's department, and returned home after the cessation of hostilities and engaged in farming, which occupation he has continued in Webster County up to the present time, with the exception of three years spent in Douglas County. His farm of 204 acres was in a very wild state at the time of his purchase, but he has made valuable improvements, and now has about 150 acres under cultivation, sixty acres in grass, and has a commodious frame residence and out-buildings. He became a member of the Masonic order in 1860, and is now a Master Mason. December 27, 1860, he was married to Miss Martha Smith, who was born in Indiana, but was reared in Missouri, and by her is the father of the following family: Willie Sherman, Amos B., Charles O., Mary J., Robert C. and Martha Ann. Mr. and Mrs. Gentry are members of the Christian Church. She is a daughter of Amos and Jane Smith, who were born in Kentucky in 1798 and 1804, respectively, and are in all probability the oldest residents of Webster County. They were married in 1824, and have one son sixty-four years of age.

Rev. Jacob Good was born in Rockingham County, of the "Old Dominion," on the 4th of October, 1825, his father being Jacob Good, of Virginia. The latter grew to manhood and was married in his native State to Miss Eve Wideck, who was also of Virginia. In 1858 he determined to seek his fortune in the West, and accordingly moved to Greene County, Mo., where he died in 1865, his wife having died in 1836. Jacob Good, whose name heads this sketch, immigrated to Tennessee in 1839, and located in Robinson County, but in 1853 came to Missouri and settled in Greene County. August 29, 1844, he was married, in Tennessee, to Emeline E. Ruffin, a native of Tennessee, and after locating in Missouri engaged in tilling the soil, teaching school and preaching the Gospel, having been ordained a minister of the Missionary Baptist Church in 1853. In 1863 he located in Marshfield, where he was engaged in the mercantile business for about four years, after which he spent a few years on a farm, and in 1883 moved to Seymour, where he began selling lumber, afterward adding furniture and undertaking goods. He is doing a thriving business, and besides this property owns a one-third interest in the flouring mills of Seymour. In connection with his ministerial work he has been moderator of the Webster County Association for the past twenty-one years, and in his connection with the church has been instrumental in saving many souls. He is a Master Mason in the Masonic fraternity, and he and wife are the parents of the following named children: Thomas A., who is married and resides in Colorado; Joel B., married and a resident of Henry County, Mo.; John W., married and residing in Seymour, Webster County; Rutha A., wife of H. L. Walker, a resident of Seymour; Jacob W., married and also residing in Seymour, and Albert B. One daughter, Mary C., died at the age of six years.

Thomas Goodwin, one of the leading farmers and stock traders of Grant Township, Webster Co., Mo., and a son of Adam and Elizabeth

(Ezel) Goodwin, was born in White County, Ill., August 24, 1844. Adam Goodwin was born in Carmi, Ill., or where Carmi now stands, in the latter part of the last century, and died in that city in 1859. His father, Elijah Goodwin, was one of the first settlers of White County, Ill., and died near Carmi in 1854, at the age of eighty-nine years. He built the scaffold at Carmi on which Leadbetter, the murderer, was hung. Mrs. Elizabeth (Ezel) Goodwin was born in Alabama, and died at Carmi when her son, Thomas Goodwin, was but two years of age. The latter was the first child by his father's second marriage. He grew to manhood on the farm, and received a common education in the country schools. In August, 1861, he enlisted in Company D, Fifty-sixth Illinois Regiment, and was at the battles of Pittsburg Landing, Corinth, Chattanooga, and was sent from Chattanooga to the Trans-Mississippi Department, under Steele, at Little Rock. He was honorably discharged July 25, 1865, at Pine Bluff, Ark. After the war he returned to Carmi, where he tilled the soil until 1870, when he came to Webster County, Mo., and here resided for six years. He then removed to Kansas, remained there for four years, and in 1881 settled in Webster County, where he now lives, in Grant Township. He is the owner of 370 acres of land, all the result of his own industry. In 1866 he took for his wife Miss Emaline Douthit, who was born in Carmi, Ill., in 1847, and who bore him six children: Matilda, Thomas, Hays, Rosa K., Emaline and Hattie. Mr. Goodwin is a Republican in politics, and cast his first presidential vote for Grant. In 1878 he was appointed county judge in Pratt County, Kas., by Gov. St. John, and was elected to the same position three terms, but resigned the office in 1881. He is a member of the G. A. R., Marshfield Post 225, and he and wife are members of the Methodist Episcopal Church.

D. L. Graham, harness dealer, was born in Van Buren County, Ark., November 17, 1826, and is the son of Joel and Catherine (Winkler) Graham. The father was born in North Carolina in 1776, and died in Van Buren County, Ark., in 1852. The mother was born in Missouri in 1788, and died in Van Buren County, Ark., in 1848. The father was a harness maker by trade, and in connection was also engaged in farming. D. L. Graham is of Scotch-German descent, and is the third of eight children, only two now living, himself and a brother, Aquilla Graham, now a resident of Texas. Mr. Graham learned the harness maker's trade from his father, and this he followed for some time. In 1855 he married Miss E. J. Roberts, who was born in Smith County, Tenn., May 3, 1836, and is the daughter of Z. B. Roberts, who died in California in September, 1888. In 1857 Mr. Graham moved to Marshfield, Mo., and here he has since resided. In 1866 he began the harness maker's business on his own account in this town, and has since continued without interruption. He has been quite successful, and is the oldest business man in Marshfield, having been a resident of that city for thirty-one years. His first store stood where the county jail now is, and his first residence was a cabin, 16x16 feet. This was burned in December, 1860, and was the first house destroyed by fire in the city. Mr. Graham is a Democrat in politics, is a member of the Masonic lodge, and he and wife are members of the Methodist Episcopal Church, South.

Joshua H. Graves, dealer in hardware, agricultural implements and groceries, and son of Ira and Mary (Wilson) Graves, was born in Franklin County, Mass., January 12, 1835. His father was born in 1781, and died in Michigan in 1868, while on a visit in that State. He was a soldier in the War of 1812. The mother was born in the latter part of the last century, and died in Pennsylvania at more than eighty-five years of age. She began going to school in 1800. The paternal grandfather, Ira Graves, was born on the New England coast, and died in New Hampshire at an advanced age. Joshua H. Graves was the third of nine children born to his parents, four of whom are living. At the early age of seven years he was put to work in a cutlery factory in Massachusetts, and there remained for about three years. At the age of ten years he was bound out to a farmer for five years, but he only served about one-half of that time, when he returned to the factory mentioned above. Here he remained until fifteen years of age, and then with his parents moved to Pennsylvania, where he worked on a farm until May 16, 1861. He then enlisted in Company C, of the Pennsylvania Reserve Volunteer Corps, and in August of the same year he was transferred to the (Twelfth Regiment Pennsylvania) United States troops. He was wounded at the battle of Fredericksburg, Va., was at the battle of Antietam, and in all was in twenty-two engagements. He was honorably discharged, as sergeant, February 15, 1864, and came to Marshfield in 1868, where he has since resided. He assisted in building the court-house of Webster County. Mr. Graves then engaged in the furniture business, which he continued until 1883, and has since been occupied in his present business. He was married in May, 1867, to Miss Hannah S. Hogle, a native of St. Lawrence County, N. Y., born in 1844, and the daughter of John Hogle. Two children, Myrtle, born in 1871, and Clara, born in 1882, were the result of Mr. and Mrs. Graves' marriage. Mr. Graves is a Republican in politics, and cast his first presidential vote for J. C. Fremont. He is a member of the I. O. O. F., and is an excellent citizen. Mrs. Graves is a member of the Methodist Episcopal Church.

John D. and James Green, farmers and assessors of Webster County, Mo., were born in Marion County, Tenn., December 7, 1845, and September 13, 1847, respectively. Their parents, Samuel and Elizabeth (Wilburn) Green, were also Tennesseeans, and for a number of years after their marriage resided in their native State, coming to Missouri about 1851, and settling on a farm in the southwest portion of Webster County, where they reared their family of four sons and six daughters: William, who resides in Arkansas; Dr. S. P., a physician of Boone County, Ark.; John D., James; Sarah, wife of T. Barnhart; Malinda, wife of Elijah Morrison; Velveyrettie, Delasia, Martha J. and Ortelia. John and James Green grew to maturity in Webster County, and in their boyhood days received but limited educations in the common schools. After reaching maturer years, they saw the need of good educations, and began attending higher institutions of learning, and acquired a thorough knowledge of the common and higher English branches. They were then engaged in teaching school in Webster County and elsewhere for some time, and in 1875 went to

Montana Territory, where they remained until the fall of 1877, and then returned home and embarked in merchandising at Rogersville, but about a year later their store building and contents were consumed by fire, and they abandoned the mercantile business and engaged in farming. They own 160 acres of valuable land in one tract, and have about fifty acres cleared and under cultivation, besides owning fourteen acres adjoining Rogersville, where they reside with their sisters. They have a pleasant and comfortable residence, and their property shows the result of industry, taste and prosperity. The Green brothers are Republicans in politics, and are stanch supporters of the principles of that party.

C. H. Greer, sheriff of Webster County, is a native of Claiborne County, Tenn., born April 4, 1847, the son of Hon. W. W. and Sarah (Teel) Greer. The father was born in North Carolina about 1801, and died in Claiborne County, Tenn., in 1886. He was a farmer and politician; was sheriff of Claiborne County for eighteen years, and represented the same county in the Lower House of the Tennessee Legislature for six years; was also a member of the Tennessee Senate for one term, and was an uncompromising Democrat all his life. The mother was born in Tennessee, and died in her native State when her son, C. H. Greer, was but six years of age. The latter remained with his father on the farm and received a common-school education. He then engaged in farming in Tennessee, and continued this until 1869, when he came to Missouri, settling in Webster County, and here carried on agricultural pursuits for one year. In 1870 he entered the employ of the Marshfield Milling Company as engineer, and continued to fill that position for sixteen years, or until 1886, when he was elected sheriff of Webster County by a majority of thirty-five votes. Two years later he was defeated for the same position by a majority of fifty-six votes, and the State Democratic ticket was defeated by 160, attesting, beyond a doubt, the popularity of Mr. Greer. He is one of the best sheriffs the county has ever had, and is honorable to a fault. He was married in 1867 to Miss Mary A. Burchfield, who was born in Claiborne County, Tenn., in 1859, and who became the mother of four children: John W. and William M. (twins), Robert H. and Ida L. Mr. Greer is a Mason, member of Webster Lodge No. 98, of which he was Master for two years, and represented the same in the Grand Lodge. He is also a member of the Odd Fellows lodge, and he and wife are members of the Methodist Episcopal Church, South. He is one of the representative citizens of the county.

Newton F. Grier, farmer, stock raiser, and native of Webster County, Mo., was born on the 18th of July, 1840. His father, Samuel Grier, was born in North Carolina, and was there married to Elizabeth Pleasant, who was also born in Caswell County, N. C. They moved to Missouri as early as 1834, and purchased land in what is now Webster County, where they reared their family and resided until their respective deaths, the father's demise occurring in August, 1871. Of ten children born to them nine lived to maturity and became heads of families, and four brothers and four sisters are living at the present writing. Newton F. Grier's boyhood days were spent in attending the common schools and assisting his father on the farm, and in 1861 he enlisted in the Confederate army, in Col. Snavel's regiment, but was wounded by a gunshot in the thigh at the battle of Pea Ridge, being permanently disabled, and was obliged to return home. He was married in Webster County, in March, 1867, to Sarah E. Smith, whose father, William Smith, was an early emigrant from Tennessee to Missouri, and about two years after his marriage located on his present farm of 260 acres. He has 150 acres of land in a good state of cultivation, and has a commodious and comfortable residence. His wife died in December, 1879, having borne a family of three sons and one daughter: Tasso, Samuel, Dorsey and Ollie. In September, 1880, Mr. Grier married Mary E., the daughter of John Morton, and by her has two children, Everett and Roxie. The family worship at the Baptist Church.

Gus Gumpertz, a leading merchant and business man of Marshfield, is a native of Cologne, Germany, born July 16, 1842, being the son of Simon and Sibiela Gumpertz, natives of Germany. The father was born in Deutz in 1794, and died in New York City in 1860, and the mother was born in Sigburg, on the Rhine, in 1803, and is now residing in St. Louis, Mo. Their son, Gus Gumpertz, was the fifth of a family of eight children by his father's second marriage. He obtained a good common education in the schools of his native country, and in 1855 immigrated with his parents to the United States. They settled in New York City, and here Mr. Gumpertz learned the cigar maker's trade, which he conducted on his own account in 1857. They remained in New York until 1860, and in 1861 Gus Gumpertz enlisted in Company E, Eighth New York Volunteers, and served for about one year. In 1862 he went to California, and for two years was engaged as a clerk in a dry goods store. In 1865 he returned to the East, and went to Carrolton, Ill., where he engaged in general merchandising, which he continued for nine years. In 1871 he came to Marshfield, where he has since been occupied in the same occupation, and has met with well-deserved success, having done an average business per annum of not less than $60,000. By the cyclone of 1880 he lost $10,000. He is a practical business man and up with the times. He was married in 1870 to Miss Hattie Cole, of St. Louis, formerly of White Hall, Ill., and who was born in 1850. They have one son, Simon, born in 1875. Mr. Gumpertz is a conservative Democrat. His brother, David, who died in New York City in 1887, was a soldier in the late war, serving four years.

Peter F. Hailey is one of the prosperous farmers and stock raisers of Webster County, Mo., and is a native of Bedford County, Tenn., born January 1, 1826, being a son of Tavner and Joyce (Thompson) Hailey, who were born, reared and married in Henry County, Va., and subsequently moved to Maury County, Tenn., and afterward to Bedford County. About 1839 they located in what is now Webster County, Mo., and here the father died about 1866, having served in the War of 1812. Since attaining his thirteenth year Peter F. Hailey has resided in Webster County. He made the paternal roof his home until twenty-six years of age, then was married in 1851 to Martha Ann

Wammack, a native of Tennessee, and shortly after located on a farm in the neighborhood of where he now lives, where he has a good 100 acre farm, nearly all of which is under cultivation, and a substantial two-story residence, and good barns and orchard. He served about one year in the Missouri State Militia during the late war, and was in the fight at Lone Jack. He received his discharge in May, 1863, and then returned home and re-engaged in the peaceful pursuit of farming. He and wife are members of the Missionary Baptist Church. They are the parents of the following children: James T., a physician of Douglas County, Mo.; William; Mary T., wife of George W. Hicks; Martha J., wife of James McBerry; A. Lincoln and Joyce.

Coffee Carroll Haggard is a successful farmer residing near Northview Post-office, Mo. He was born in Roane County, Tenn., June 16, 1819, and is a son of Samuel and Elizabeth (Montgomery) Haggard, who were also Tennesseeans. The former served in the War of 1812, and throughout life made his home in his native State, where he reared his family. Coffee C. Haggard remained with his father until grown, and was married in his native State, January 6, 1839, to Lucinda Emory, a native of Roane County, but in 1849 took up his residence in what is now Webster County, where he is still residing. The farm he purchased was very slightly improved, but is now under cultivation and otherwise well improved. It consists of 160 acres, with eighty under cultivation, and he has forty acres at Northview, on which is a nice residence, where he makes his home. August 8, 1862, he enlisted in the Eighth Missouri Cavalry, and served until the close of the war, and was a participant in the fights at Little Rock, Cotton Plant and numerous skirmishes, and filled the following offices, in the order in which they are named: Duty sergeant and commissary sergeant. He was mustered out at Little Rock, and discharged at St. Louis, in August, 1865. He and wife are the parents of two children: William Carroll, who is married and resides near his father, and Amanda, who is the wife of Henry Bumgarner. On the 24th of September, 1888, Mrs. Haggard died, having been a faithful wife for over forty-nine years, and a kind, watchful mother. Mr. Haggard is one of the oldest and most highly esteemed citizens of Webster County, and is favorably known throughout this part of the State. Not to know Uncle Coffee Haggard would be equivalent to not knowing the country. Wherever he is known his word is as good as his bond; no one would think of asking him for security, even if he should give his note, of which very few, if any, are in existence. Being one of the early pioneers, his residence here ante-dates the county itself, the territory now comprising Webster being then embraced in Greene County. To his less favored neighbors he is ever charitable and neighborly, none going away from his door empty handed when knowingly in want.

Oscar T. Hamlin, attorney at law, was born in Pickens County, S. C., August 5, 1866, and is the son of Rev. J. R. and Mary A. (King) Hamlin, natives of North Carolina, the father born about 1826 and the mother about 1828. They removed from their native State to South Carolina about 1856, and from there to Bourbon, Crawford

Co., Mo., in 1869, where they now reside. The father is a Baptist minister, and has followed his ministerial duties for thirty years. Oscar T. Hamlin is the youngest living of nine children born to his parents. He first attended the public schools, and then spent two years at the Salem Graded School, in Dent County. Later he spent two years at the Southwest Baptist College, at Bolivar, Polk Co., Mo., and in December, 1885, he began the study of law. In March, 1887, he entered the law office of his brother, at Bolivar, Mo., and October 18, 1887, was admitted to the bar at that place. He came to Marshfield, Mo., in January, 1888, and here has since continued the practice of his profession, meeting with good success. He is a Democrat in his political opinions, and cast his first presidential vote for Grover Cleveland. He is a member of the Baptist Church, and is an honorable, upright citizen.

Abram Harges was born in Marion County, Tenn., in September, 1819, and is a son of Abner Harges, who was married in Tennessee to Nancy Smith, and there reared his family and spent the remainder of his days. Abram Harges remained in his native country till October 31, 1837, at which time he joined the United States service to serve in the Florida War. After having served faithfully he was honorably discharged at Baton Rouge, La., May 10, 1838, and then returned to his native country, Tennessee, and remained till 1839, when he came to Missouri. He then made three trips back to Tennessee. He married in Marion County, Tenn., September 12, 1848, Miss Louisa Mitchell, a daughter of John Mitchell, who was formerly from North Carolina, and one of the pioneers of Tennessee. After his marriage he located permanently, in 1850, in Webster County, Mo. His occupation has always been farming. He enlisted for ninety days in the Home Guards in 1861 in the behalf of the Government. The following are the children born to his marriage: John, William, Canzada (wife of William Wilson), Thomas Jefferson, Julia Ann, Catherine (wife of James Smith), Mary Mahuldia (wife of Michael Dykes) and Abraham, Jr. Mr. and Mrs. Harges are members of the Free Will Baptist Church, he being a deacon in the same.

John H. Hartley, educator and farmer, was born in Webster County, Mo., on the 4th of April, 1864, and received a good education in the public schools and at the Southwest Baptist College. After completing his studies he engaged in the profession of teaching in Webster County, and has followed that occupation for four years. Almarinda Wommack became his wife on the 4th of December, 1886, and their union has been blessed in the birth of one child, Sophia A., an infant. Mr. and Mrs. Hartley are members of the Baptist Church, and she is a daughter of Wilson Wommack, and was born, reared and educated in Greene County. Mr. Hartley is a son of R. B. and Elizabeth (Jackson) Hartley, who were born in North Carolina and Tennessee, respectively, the former of whom came to Missouri with his father, Jesse Hartley, at a very early day. He grew to manhood, and was married in Webster County, and is still a resident of the county, engaged in farming. He served in the State Militia during the greater part of the late war.

William Z. Haymes was born in McMinn County, Tenn., January 13, 1833, and is a son of Judge William Haymes, who was born and reared in Virginia, and was married in Tennessee to Rebecca Zeigler, also a native of Virginia. In 1839 they moved to Missouri and settled in what is now Webster County, and took up a claim, where he reared his family. He is still living, and is now seventy-nine years old. He served as one of the county judges during the late war, and has always been noted for the liberality with which he contributes to enterprises for the public weal. William Z. Haymes, his son, has resided in Webster County ever since he was a small boy, and made his home with his parents until he attained his majority, and the following year was married to Miss Rebecca E. Jones, of North Carolina, their union taking place March 8, 1854. She was reared and educated in Webster County, whither she had come with her father, William Jones, and the year after her marriage she and Mr. Haymes located on their present farm, which consists of 250 acres, with 150 under cultivation, well improved with good buildings and a good bearing orchard of apple and peach trees. Although a Republican in politics, he has been postmaster of Conklin since 1880, and for a number of years he has been a member of the Masonic fraternity, in which he is a Master Mason. He and wife are members of the Methodist Episcopal Church, and are the parents of the following children: Sarah T. (wife of J. W. Watkins), Estella, Virginia T. (wife of Judge George A. Day), Mary R. (wife of S. K. Barnes), Adelaide (wife of Joseph Thomas), Martha E., Walter O., Jacob E. and Maggie J. William S. died in 1867, at the age of three years. Mr. Haymes served about six months in the State Militia, and in 1862 was elected first lieutenant of Company F, Seventy-fourth Enrolled Missouri Militia, but was discharged at the end of six months for disability, and returned home.

Dr. Messer Highfill, physician and surgeon at Marshfield, is a native of Webster County, Mo., born in Jackson Township, Webster Co., Mo., May 6, 1858, and is the eldest in a family of seven children, six now living. His father, J. E. Highfill, was born in West Tennessee August 15, 1836, and is now residing in Jackson Township, this county, having immigrated to this county from his native State when about fourteen years of age. The mother of Dr. Highfill, Nellie (Norton) Highfill, was also born in West Tennessee, March 16, 1835, and died in Webster County, Mo., August 30, 1887. Dr. Highfill was reared on the farm, and first, after finishing at the common schools, completed his education by attending one term at the Waldo Graded School, and also one term at the Ebeneazer Graded School, in Greene County. He first began teaching school in 1877, and continued teaching more or less until 1885. He began the study of medicine in 1877, in the office of Dr. N. H. Hampton, now a resident of Springfield, Mo. Mr. Highfill attended lectures at the Missouri Medical College at St. Louis, and graduated from that institution March 4, 1887. March 29, of the same year, he located in Marshfield, commencing the practice of his profession, and here still continues. He has a good practice, and is a successful physician. In 1885 he was united in marriage to Miss Jennie Hoover, a native of Webster County, born January 10, 1865, and the daughter of George and Sarah Hoover. One child, Willie E., born July 16, 1888, is the result of this union. Dr. Highfill is a Democrat in his political views, and cast his first presidential vote for Gen. Hancock. Mrs. Highfill is a member of the Methodist Episcopal Church, South.

Thomas Russell Hightower, one of the leading citizens of Union Township, Webster Co., Mo., was born in Caswell County, N. C., May 1, 1839, and is a son of Dovorex and Cicily (Gooch) Hightower, natives, respectively, of Knox County, Tenn., and North Carolina. The parents were married in North Carolina in 1816, where they lived until the fall of 1850, when they removed to Greene County, Mo., and three years later located in Webster County. When a young man the father learned the stone-mason's trade, at which he worked in connection with farming all his life, and was very successful until the outbreak of the Civil War, during which he lost heavily. He was a Democrat politically, and in his death, which occurred September 17, 1872, Webster County lost one of its most enterprising residents. Mrs. Hightower died in October, 1858, a member of the Primitive Baptist Church. There were eight sons and eight daughters born to the parents of our subject, of whom four sons are now living, viz.: Joshua, a farmer of Niangua Township, Webster County; Eppa, a farmer of Wright County, Mo.; Abner, a farmer of High Prairie Township, Webster County, and Thomas Russell. The latter received his education in the common schools, and his home was with his parents during their life-time, providing and caring for his father during the last years of his life. He started in life for himself with limited means, but industry and good management have added 280 acres to the eighty acres left him, and he now owns a farm of as good land as there is in Webster County. March 4, 1860, he married Martha Walker, daughter of Robert Walker; she was born in Cedar County, Mo., June 5, 1843. To this union were born six children, only two of whom are living, viz.: Matilda A., wife of George Tory, and John R., at home. Mrs. Martha Hightower died October 25, 1882, having been a worthy and consistent member of the Methodist Episcopal Church, South. November 19, 1883, Mr. Hightower married Martha Hyde, daughter of John and Malinda Hyde; she was born in Webster County, Mo., November 19, 1850, and is the mother of two children: Albert Cleveland, who died at the age of twenty-one months, and Irvin Earl. Mr. Hightower is a Democrat in politics, a member of the Masonic fraternity, and a member of the Methodist Episcopal Church, South. He is one of the enterprising men of the county, and is highly respected by all who know him. Mrs. Hightower is a member of the Baptist Church.

George Hoover, a farmer and stockman of Jackson Township, was born in Davidson County, N. C., September 11, 1832, and in 1835 came to Missouri with his mother, Sarah (Goss) Hoover, his father, Felix Hoover, having died in Tennessee on the way. Both were North Carolinians. George and his mother located in Greene County, and about 1840 moved to what is now Webster County, taking up their abode near the farm on which George now resides. In these two counties our subject grew to manhood, but was married in the latter county to Miss Sarah F. Pipkin, their marriage being celebrated on the 3d of July, 1860. She was born and reared in Greene County, Mo., and is a daughter of Lewis Pipkin, who was formerly from Tennessee, and was one of the early settlers of Greene County. Since his marriage Mr. Hoover has resided on his present farm, and is the owner of about 350 acres of fertile land, about 200 acres of which are cleared, and furnished with a large, two-story frame residence, a good frame barn and other out-buildings, and an orchard of 200 trees. He and wife are members of the Methodist Episcopal Church, South, and he is a Master Mason in the Masonic order. Their children's names are as follows: Louis F., who is married and resides near his parents; Jane, wife of Dr. Highfill, of Mansfield, whose sketch appears in this work; Christina, Mary, Samuel C., George W., Maud Elizabeth and Johnny (who is seven years of age). Four children died in infancy; Margaret Alice died at the age of two years; Robert Franklin died in 1885, aged twenty-three years, and Sarah F. also died that year, at the age of nineteen years.

Silas A. Hoover, who keeps a livery and feed stable at Seymour, Mo., was born in Webster County, near Seymour, February 1, 1859, and is a son of Jesse and Amanda A. (Cross) Hoover, who were natives of the "Old North State," and were there reared and married. They moved to Missouri in 1854, settling on a farm, where they reared their family, and here Silas A. Hoover grew to manhood. February 28, 1878, he was married, in Douglas County, to Miss Martha Ellen, a daughter of William Carrick, who was formerly from North Carolina. She was born in North Carolina, and there resided until fifteen years of age, when she came to Missouri with her parents, and settled in Douglas County. After their marriage they farmed for seven years, and then moved to Seymour and engaged in the livery business, in which he has been quite successful. His business was established in 1885, and he is now the owner of two good stables, and commands a lucrative patronage. He is a member of the I. O. O. F., and he and wife are consistent members of the Baptist Church, and the parents of the following named children: Ida S., Daniel A., Amanda E., Mary E. and William S.

John W. Hubbard, farmer and sheriff of Webster County, Mo., was born near Danville, Mo., August 1, 1859, and is a son of Bird Hubbard, who was a Virginian, and was brought to Missouri in his childhood by his father, William Hubbard, and settled in Montgomery County, of which they were among the pioneers. Bird Hubbard was married in that county to Miss Sultana Grooms, and was engaged in manufacturing tobacco until the breaking out of the war, when he enlisted in a Missouri cavalry regiment, United States army, and served until the close of the war, when he returned to his family and engaged in farming. About 1875 he went to Texas, and located in Eastland County, near Eastland City, where he still resides. His son, John W. Hubbard, resided in his native county until 1880, when he became a resident of Webster County, and two years later moved to Texas, where he spent about one and a half years, since which time he has been residing on his present farm in Webster County, Mo. He is a member of the Republican party, and was elected sheriff of Webster County on that ticket, receiving a handsome majority. On the 8th of June, 1879, he was married to Miss Laura E. Harmon, a daughter of William H. Harmon, of Marshfield, Mo., by whom he is the father of the following family of children: Nellie S., Della Lee, Ella O. and John A.

Dr. William H. James was born in Blount County, Tenn., April 17, 1827, and is the eldest of nine children born to John and Elizabeth H. (Kelly) James, and of Scotch-Irish descent. The paternal grandfather, John James, Sr., was a native Virginian. John and Elizabeth (Kelly) James were both natives of Blount County, Tenn., the former born in 1805, and died in Webster County, Mo., in 1872, and the latter born in 1808, and died in Johnson County, Mo. The father was a farmer by occupation, and in 1837 he and his family immigrated to Missouri, settling in Johnson County, where Dr. William H. James attained his growth. He obtained a good practical education, and in 1844 began the study of medicine in the office of Dr. William Huff, a native of old Kentucky. Later he began the practice of his profession in Johnson County, in 1847, and continued there about two years, when he went to California. He remained on the Pacific slope for twenty years, and during that time was engaged in merchandising, mining and in the practice of his profession. He returned to Missouri in 1869, and settled in Webster County. In 1877 he came to Marshfield, where, in addition to the practice of his profession, he has carried on the drug business, which he still continues, doing a good trade and business. He was married in California, in 1856, to Miss Lucy A. Wade, who was born in Virginia in 1837, and seven children were the result of this union, six of whom are living: John T., a druggist, living in Hamilton, Tex.; Dr. W. C., a graduate of Vanderbilt University at Nashville, Tenn., and of Bellevue Hospital Medical College, in New York City (is now located at Springfield, Mo.); Jefferson B., a jeweler at Marshfield; Virginia Lee, Edward and Mary. Dr. James is a Democrat in his political opinions, and cast his first presidential vote for Franklin Pierce. He is one of the leading citizens of Webster County, and is an intellectual, clever gentleman. Mrs. James is a member of the Methodist Episcopal Church, South.

Hon. Robert W. Jameson is a son of Samuel and Rebecca (Rease) Jameson, who were born in New Jersey and Delaware, respectively, and were married in Tennessee. Some six years after the latter event they immigrated to Christian County, Ky., and at the end of seven years took up their abode in Knox County, where they made their home for thirteen years. Monroe County, Tenn., then became their home, and there the father died in 1836. Robert W. Jameson was born in Knox County, Ky., June 8, 1811, and made his home with his parents until he attained his majority, receiving the greater part of his education in Tennessee. In 1837 he was married, in McMinn County, to Miss Esther L. Thomas, a native of Alabama, and after his marriage continued to reside in Tennessee, engaged in farming until 1843, when in the spring of that year he started over-

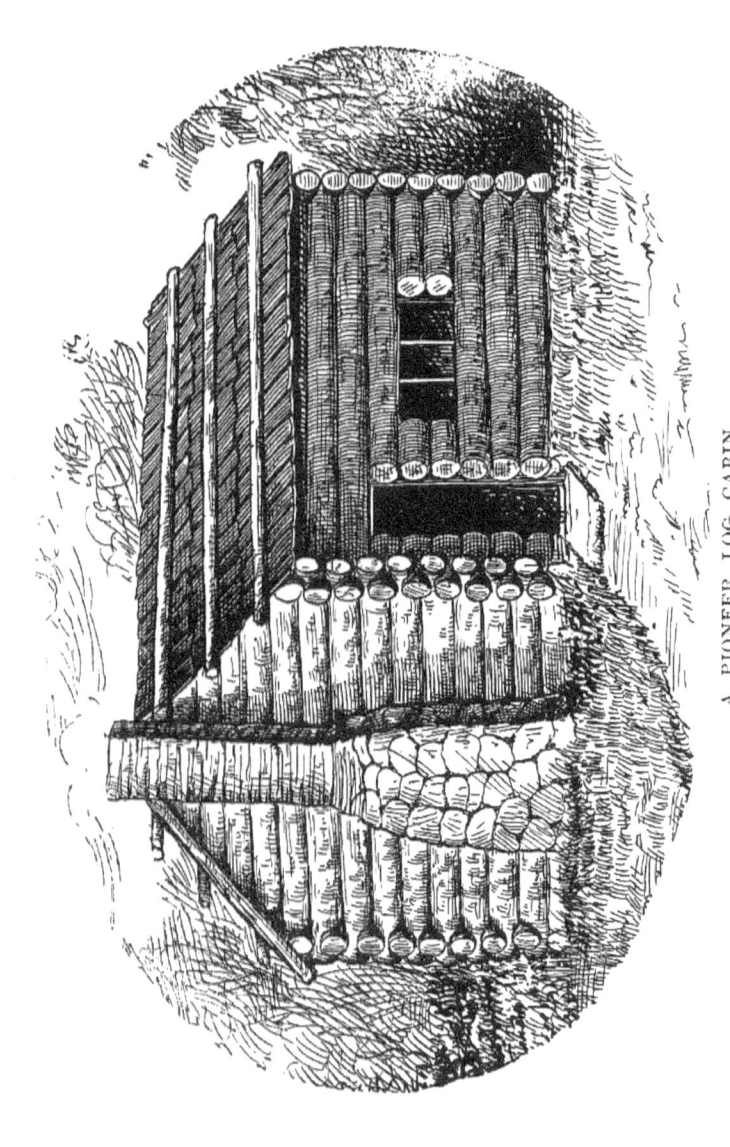

A PIONEER LOG CABIN.

land with ox teams to Missouri, but was delayed by sickness, and did not reach this State until August following He has now 500 acres of valuable land, with 200 acres under cultivation, and is considered one of the thrifty farmers of Webster County. He was raised a Whig in politics, and held to that party until the Rebellion, and since that time has supported the principles of the Democratic party. He served as justice of the peace eight years, and one term as judge, when Webster was a part of Greene County, and after it was made a separate county served as its judge one term. He was elected a delegate to the convention called to pass ordinances of secession, and helped to defeat that measure. In 1864 he was elected to represent Webster County in the State Legislature, and served through two sessions of that body, being re-elected in 1876, and served one term with honor to himself and to the satisfaction of his constituents. Since that time he has been retired from politics. His wife died June 23, 1860, having borne eleven children, seven of whom are living: Thomas T., Sarah M. (wife of Dr. J. M. Hunt), Z. T., Martha E. (wife of J. B. Owens), Nancy F., Abigail J. and Robert W. Mr. Jameson is a Master Mason.

Hiram Jennings is a native of Missouri, born in Webster County on the 18th of January, 1853, and is a son of John and Elizabeth (Sartin) Jennings, who were born in North Carolina and Kentucky, respectively. About 1840 they moved to Greene County, Mo., but shortly after located on their present farm in Benton Township. Hiram Jennings grew to manhood in Webster County, and remained with his father until he attained his majority, when he was married in this county, on the 17th of January, 1875, to Miss Artelia Watts, a native of the county, and a daughter of James Watts. After his marriage he resided on his father's farm for a few years, being engaged in trading in stock, and in 1880 moved to his present farm, and engaged in mercantile pursuits in a small way, but has gradually increased his business until he now has a large and lucrative trade. He also has an excellent farm of 210 acres, and has about seventy-five acres under cultivation. His children's names are as follows: Ellis L., Laura B. and John E. Mr. Jennings has been postmaster of Sarvis Point since 1882, and has proved to be an efficient officer.

William E. Jones, a successful farmer and stock raiser of East Dallas Township, was born in the "Old North State" September 19, 1828, and is a son of Aquilla Jones, who, like his son William E., was born and reared in Davidson County, N. C. He was married there to Miss Susanna Tacher, and in 1870 moved to Missouri, settling in Marshfield, where he resided until his death, April 25, 1873. His widow survives him at the age of eighty-three years, and resides with her son, William E. The latter was reared in North Carolina, and February 12, 1857, was there married to Miss Mary A. Zink, who was also a native of Davidson County. Her father, Jacob Zink, was a prominent North Carolinian. In 1873 William E. Jones removed with his family to Missouri, and settled in Webster County, where he purchased the farm of 160 acres where he now resides. The farm was only slightly cleared at that time, but he has added many improvements, and has about 100 acres under cultivation. He has a good two-story residence and an orchard of 250 bearing apple trees, and 1,050 young trees of the Ben Davis variety, and he intends putting out 1,000 more trees of the same variety. Besides his home farm he has 160 acres of land, with seventy acres under cultivation, situated about a half mile from his home, on Dry Creek, a portion of which is bottom land. Mr. and Mrs. Jones have been blessed with a family of six children: Jacob, Sarah (wife of W. L. Alsup), Charles W., Mollie L., Robert A. and Anna. The family worship in the Baptist Church, and Mr. Jones is a strong supporter of Democratic principles.

Eli W. Jones, another old settler and enterprising citizen of Washington Township, Webster Co., Mo., was born in Marshall County, Tenn., November 26, 1836, and is the son of James and Ailee Jones, both natives of North Carolina. James Jones was born October 12, 1794, and died in Dallas County, Mo., May 14, 1863. He married Miss Bills about 1815, and afterward they moved to Marshall County, Tenn., but later found their way to Missouri, where they located in what is now Washington Township, Dallas County. Here the mother also died. James Jones was a Democrat in politics; was a member of the Baptist Church, as was also his wife, he being a minister in the same, but never taking money for preaching. In connection with his ministerial duties he also followed farming. To James and Ailee Jones were born eleven children, seven now living: Lemuel, Susan C., Edwin C., Garsham B. (deceased), Polly Ann, Solomon B. (deceased), Sarah M., James M. (deceased), Elizabeth P., Eli W. and Keziah M. (deceased). Lemuel represented Dallas County in the Legislature several years before and during the war, and after that eventful time represented Webster County three terms. After going to Texas he represented McLennan County in the Legislature. He was captain of a Confederate company during the war, as was also Edwin C., who was also a prominent man, and represented Hot Springs County in the Legislature. Eli W. Jones, when twenty years of age, or on September 6, 1856, married Miss Ann Eliza Campbell, daughter of George W. Campbell, and a native of Dallas County, Mo., born May 10, 1840. By this union eleven children were born: Edwin W. (farmer of Dallas County, Mo.), Medretta (wife of Augustus Latimer), Mary Frances (wife of Herbert McFadin), James F., Martha F. (wife of Frank Hollis), Joseph Lee, Ida A., Charley, Robert E. and Nella F. One child, who died at the age of thirteen, was named Lemuel A. After his marriage Mr. Jones remained on the old homestead until 1880, when he moved to his present place of residence, and has followed farming all his life. He has never been an office seeker, would not under any consideration be a candidate, although all his brothers have held different public offices. He is a member of the Masonic fraternity, a Democrat in politics, and one of the best citizens of the county.

Isaac C. Jones was born in what is now Webster County, Mo., February 16, 1851, and grew to manhood on the farm on which he is now residing. He was married here on the 28th of April, 1872, to

Miss Alice Clayton, a native of Laclede County, Mo., and a daughter of John W. Clayton, by whom he has five children: William Campbell, V. May, Charles L., Bingham H. and Sadie. June C. died August 7, 1881, aged five years. Mr. Jones is the only child of Judge J. B. and Evaline (Jamason) Jones, who were born in North Carolina and Kentucky, respectively, the former's birth occurring June 21, 1818. Evaline Jones was born May 30, 1822, in Kentucky. J. B. was taken to Tennessee when a lad of five years, and was there reared to manhood and married, the latter event taking place in McMinn County August 10, 1842. They farmed in that State for about four years after their marriage, then came to Missouri, and settled in what is now Webster County in 1846. Six years later they located on the farm on which Isaac is residing, and were obliged to labor very hard for a number of years to clear the land and get it under cultivation. He served one year in the State Militia during the late war, and was county judge four years. His death occurred on the 11th of October, 1888. Mrs. Evaline Jones is a member of the Methodist Episcopal Church, South.

Judge Joseph Keller, a well-to-do farmer and successful stock raiser of East Dallas Township, is a Tennesseean, born in Bedford County November 15, 1840. His parents, Rev. F. A. and Catherine (Green) Keller, were born, reared and married in Bedford County, Tenn., and were engaged in farming in that county until 1855, when they started to move to Missouri, but the father died at the residence of a brother, in Perry County, Ill., November 25, of that year. He was a minister of the Baptist Church, and after his death his family remained in Illinois until February of the following year, when they pushed on to Missouri, and settled in Webster County, and purchased a farm, on which they resided until the breaking out of the war. Judge Keller is the eldest of a family of five children, and made his home with and assisted his mother until the breaking out of the war, and March 12, 1862, enlisted in the Fourteenth Missouri Cavalry of State Militia, and served until receiving his discharge for disability, in January, 1863. He participated in several skirmishes, and was wounded by a gunshot while on detail duty. January 17, 1859, he married Miss Martha Burks, who was born in Coffee County, Tenn., a daughter of J. W. Burks, one of the pioneers of Webster County. Soon after he began making a farm in Benton Township, where he resided until 1877, when he located on his present farm of 280 acres, about 115 of which are under cultivation. He has 180 acres under fence, and a pleasant and comfortable dwelling house. Since the war Mr. Keller has been a stanch Republican in politics, and in 1880 was elected justice of Benton Township, and six years later was elected one of the judges of the county court, and was re-elected in 1888. He and wife have a family of seven children: James F. (who is married, and resides in the county), W. R. (who is married, and is a teacher of Webster County), John L. (at home), Mary J., Sarah C., Sophia E. and Charles Winfield. The Judge, wife and oldest daughter are members of the Missionary Baptist Church, and the Judge is church clerk. He is also a Master Mason in the Masonic order.

Allen Kilburn is one of the earliest settlers of Union Township, Webster Co., Mo. He is a native of Jackson County, Ga., and was born February 1, 1808, the third in a family of eleven children born to Daniel and Nancy (Watkins) Kilburn, the former born in South Carolina and the latter in Virgina. The parents were married in Georgia, where they lived until our subject was about eight years of age, when they moved to Williamson County, Tenn.; four years later they went to Lawrence County, Tenn., where the mother died in 1857. Mr. Kilburn subsequently moved to Hardin County, Tenn., where he died in 1866, at the age of eighty-five years. Both were members of the Baptist Church. Daniel Kilburn was a farmer all his life, and served in the War of 1812. But one child besides our subject survives, who is Martha, the wife of William A. Davis, a farmer near Booneville, Miss. When young, Allen Kilburn started in life for himself as a farmer with limited means, but industry and good management have won for him success, and he now owns a well-improved farm in Webster County, after having given his children a start in life. When nineteen years of age he married Millie Watkins, who was born in Williamson County, Tenn., July 8, 1811, and was a daughter of Pleasant Watkins. Sixteen children were born to this union, six of whom are still living, three sons and three daughters, viz.: William P. (a farmer of Webster County, Mo.), James J. (a farmer and miller of Webster County), Joel N. (a farmer of Chautauqua County, Kas.), Nancy Lee (wife of George A. Brown, a prominent farmer of Webster County, Mo.), Mary Jane (who married J. D. Whittenburg, a farmer and stock dealer of Webster County), and Eliza Dickard (who married William Dickard, deceased) is now living in Taney County, Mo. After their marriage our subject and wife lived in Maury County, Tenn., for two years, and then moved to Lawrence County, Tenn., where, with the exception of one year spent in Calloway County, Ky., they lived until 1854; in the latter year they removed to the present location in Webster County, Mo., then known as Wright County. Mrs. Kilburn died January 6, 1888, having been a member of the Christian Church thirty-five years. While in Tennessee Mr. Kilburn served seven years as justice of the peace, and after removing to Missouri he held the same office in Union Township, Webster County, eighteen years. He has been a member of the Christian Church since 1849, and has served as deacon. He is a Republican in politics, and is one of the most enterprising of Webster County's residents. He takes an active interest in the educational and religious enterprises of the community, and is highly respected by many friends and acquaintances.

Frederick King, attorney at law, real estate, loan and abstract agent, and publisher of the *Standard*, was born in Sharon, Litchfield Co., Conn., in 1843. He was reared on a farm, remaining there until 1861, when July 13 he enlisted as private in Company I, Fifth Regiment Connecticut Volunteers, and served until July 22, 1864. He was in Banks' command, in the Shenandoah Valley, and in the Army of the Potomac until September, 1864, taking part in the engagements at Chancellorsville, Gettysburg and many minor battles. Subsequently he was in the First Brigade, First Division, Twentieth Corps, Army of the Cumberland, from October, 1864, serving in Tennessee, North Alabama, and with Sherman on the Atlanta campaign, participating in all the great moves and battles of that campaign. Following this Mr. King resided in Washington, D. C., for four years, from April, 1865, to March, 1869, after which he came west to Greene County, Mo., in March, 1869, and located near Republic, in that county, purchasing a farm. He began the study of the legal profession, and was subsequently admitted to the practice of law. In March, 1885, he moved to Marshfield, and has since resided in this place. He was Eminent Commander (and charter member) of St. Johns Commandery No. 20, Knights Templar, at Springfield, for two terms. In 1888 Mr. King was elected delegate from the Thirteenth District to the Republican National Convention at Chicago, voting for Gen. Harrison. His connection with the affairs of Webster County has proved fortunate for the people of this community. As a member of the real estate, loan and abstract firm of King & Moore he has built up a good business. Professionally his standing is widely recognized, while no little influence is exerted in the publication of the *Standard*.

Dr. Herndon H. Lea, one of the first physicians of Webster County, Mo., was born in Cocke County, Tenn., October 1, 1816, and is one of the representative citizens of the county. His parents, Eppey H. and Mary Lea, were natives of North Carolina and Jefferson County, Tenn., respectively. The father was born January 8, 1791, and died in Knoxville, while on a business visit, October 5, 1883, although at the time of his death his home was in Anderson County, Tenn. The mother was born in 1792, and died in Jefferson County, Tenn., in 1838. They were married on a farm in the last named county in 1811, and afterward moved to Cocke County, Tenn., then to Jefferson County, and still later to Anderson County of the same State. Mr. Lea was a soldier in the War of 1812, was a farmer, and both he and wife are members of the Methodist Church. To their union were born eleven children, ten of whom lived to be grown, and six of whom are now living: Dr. H. H.; Martha, wife of Spencer Hand, of Roane County, Tenn.; Elizabeth, widow of Joseph Binns; Nancy, widow of Charleton Fairless; Gideon B. R., and Frances, wife of William Taylor. After the death of the mother of these children Eppey H. Lea married Miss Eaton, who bore him one son, William. Dr. Herndon H. Lea studied medicine at home and under Dr. Tate, of Clinton, Anderson Co., Tenn. In 1845 he left home for a two weeks' business trip down Clinch River, but came to Missouri, locating at Hartville, Wright Co., Mo., where he resided until 1863, when he went to Clyde Station, in Illinois, and remained there until 1869, when he moved to the farm where he now lives, and where he owns 180 acres of some of the best land in Webster County. He continued to practice medicine until he was elected clerk of the Wright County Circuit Court, which position he held until 1855. In January of the year previous he sold goods at Hartville, and was engaged in buying and selling all kinds of stock. Since coming to Missouri he has been engaged in farming and stock raising. While in Anderson County, Tenn., he was colonel of the militia for four years. In the last election, without his knowledge, he was elected justice of the peace. On May 5, 1846, he married Miss Martha Love, daughter of Col. Thomas B. Love, and a native of Haywood County, N. C. She died in 1848, at the age of twenty-six years, and is the mother of one daughter, who is now the wife of Leonard A. Morphis, an artist, residing near Dr. H. H. Lea. January 9, 1853, Dr. Lea married Miss Nancy H. Officer, a native of McMinn County, Tenn., born November 11, 1828, and the daughter of Jefferson B. Officer. No children were born to the first union. Mrs. Lea is a member of the Methodist Episcopal Church; the Doctor is a member of the Masonic fraternity, is a Democrat in politics, and is one of the most enterprising citizens of this section of the State of Missouri. In 1850 he was assistant United States marshal, and took the census of Wright County. From 1854 to 1861 he and John M. Gorman built, by themselves, the school-house at Hartville, and he has been a liberal contributor to the building of many churches.

Welcome Letchworth was born in Claiborne County, Tenn., January 20, 1813, and since 1832 has been a resident of Missouri, his parents, Aaron and Elizabeth Letchworth, having come to the State at that date. The father was born in Virginia, but was reared and married in Tennessee, and resided in that State until his death. He was a soldier in the War of 1812. Welcome Letchworth went to Hamilton County at the age of seventeen years, and was there married and remained until 1832, when he resided from that time until 1850 in Mississippi County, Mo., and since the latter date has been a resident of Webster County. His first purchase was forty acres of land, but he is now the owner of 200 acres in the home place, and eighty acres in another tract, with over 140 acres under cultivation. Game was very abundant when he first located here, and hunting has always had considerable fascination for him, and many are the deer, bear, wolves and other wild animals that have fallen victims to his skill as a marksman. While residing in Mississippi County he was engaged in trapping, also, but never followed that occupation after coming to Webster County. At the breaking out of the Rebellion he enlisted in the first company of Home Guards that was organized in the county, and although he participated in a number of skirmishes was in no general engagements. Elizabeth Gower, whom he married on the 17th of August, 1832, died on the 17th of February, 1886, having been a faithful help-mate for nearly fifty-two and a half years. They have one child living, Isabella Catherine, wife of T. M. Stone. Thompson, a son, died at the age of twenty-two years, and John M. died in the hospital in St. Louis in the fall of 1861, aged twenty years. Other children died in infancy. Mrs. Lydia C. Plank, widow of Henry Plank, who died in 1875, and daughter of Joseph Williams (deceased), became the wife of Mr. Letchworth in 1889.

Four children were born to her first marriage: Della, wife of Joseph Kilburn; Sarah, wife of Sigel Owen; Laura and Amanda. Mr. Letchworth and wife are members of the Missionary Baptist Church, and he has been a deacon in the same for a number of years.

Hon. Matthew Long, one of the prominent and successful farmers of Webster County, Mo., was born in Columbus, Ohio, August 3, 1824, being the son of William and Rebecca M. Long. The father was born in 1781, and died in Columbus, Ohio, in 1851. He built the third house on the present site of Columbus, Ohio, in 1813. Mr. Long's father was one of the leading men of Columbus for many years, and filled many positions of honor and trust. He helped to make Franklin County what it is. The mother of the subject of this sketch was born in 1791, and died at Columbus, Ohio, in 1861. Hon. Matthew Long received his educational training in the public schools of Columbus, and at Central College, of that county. At the age of eleven years he entered the treasurer's office of Franklin County, and for six years was deputy county treasurer and collector under his father, spending his winters in the office and his summers in school. For seven and a half years he was a clerk in the book store of Whiting & Huntington, in Columbus, afterward for two years in the same business and at the same place, under the firm name of Randall, Aston & Long. Always having a desire to be a farmer, and his health failing him, he sold his interest in the store and purchased a farm in Licking County, and for ten years followed agricultural pursuits on the farm. In 1863 he removed to Iowa County, Iowa, where he continued farming for ten years. Five years of that time he was president of the Iowa County Agricultural Society. He is a Republican in his political views, and represented Iowa and Poweshiek Counties in the State Senate for a term of four years, to the entire satisfaction of his constituents. In 1873 he removed to Des Moines, Iowa, where for twelve years he was secretary of the State Insurance Company, and under his management it was very successful, having in that time increased its assets over $600,000. In 1884 Mr. Long resigned his position with the State Insurance Company to accept the secretaryship of the Southern California Insurance Company, at Los Angeles, Cal., where he was equally successful. Finding he had overtaxed his strength, after filling this position for over a year he resigned, but was again unanimously elected to the same position, with a large increase of salary and a two months' vacation. Mr. Long feeling the great need of a change again offered his resignation, which was accepted, and he was then immediately presented by the company with $500 in gold, which was in addition to his regular salary. In 1886 he came to Webster County, settling on his farm of 320 acres, and is now engaged in farming, making Short Horn cattle and Berkshire hogs a specialty. He is also a practical farmer, and is president of the Webster County Farmers' Club. He was married, in 1846, to Miss Mary Tuttle, a sister of Dr. Tuttle, president of Wabash College, at Crawfordsville, Ind. Mrs. Long was born in New Jersey, November 6, 1821. Four children were born to the union of Mr. and Mrs. Long: William L., Jacob T., Margaret E. and Ellen. Mr. Long is a member of the Masonic fraternity, Royal Arch and K. T. He is a Presbyterian, but as there is no church of his faith in Marshfield, he is now connected with the Methodist Episcopal Church, and is one of the representative men of this portion of Missouri.

William L. Long, cashier of the Merchants' & Farmers' Bank of Marshfield, Mo., was born in Columbus, Ohio, June 16, 1846, and is the son of Matthew and Hannah M. (Tuttle) Long. Matthew Long was also a native of Columbus, Ohio, his father having built the third log cabin where that city now stands. Matthew Long moved to Licking County, Ohio, where he remained until 1863, at which date he moved to Iowa County, Iowa, and was there engaged in farming for about ten years. His son, William L. Long, completed a course of study in the public schools, and then spent three years at Wabash College, Crawfordsville, Ind., where he lived with his uncle, Joseph F. Tuttle, who is a Presbyterian minister, and who has been president of the above mentioned institution for nearly thirty years. After leaving the college Mr. Long taught school during the winters and farmed during the summers for several years. In the fall of 1871 he went back to Ohio, and was there married to Miss Lottie P. Condit, daughter of Philip Condit, a merchant at Jersey, Licking Co., Ohio. About a year after marriage Mr. Long and a friend of his, Dr. O. W. Archibald, now superintendent of the Insane Hospital at Jamestown, Dak., traveled over Southern and Southwestern Iowa, and both located at Glenwood, Mills County, of that State, about 1872. Mr. Long spent one year in the post-office at that place, and was then elected principal of the public schools. This position he held for eight years, and after being re-elected for the ninth year resigned and accepted a position in the office of the State Insurance Company of Des Moines, Iowa. This company his father had served about ten years as secretary, and his brother as head of the note department. After serving with the book-keeper for several months Mr. Long was appointed examiner of applications, in which position he served the rest of the three years of his stay in the insurance office. About this time his father and brother took a trip through Southwest Missouri, for the latter's health. The father purchased 320 acres of land lying immediately north of Marshfield, and here the brother remained. About a year later Mr. Long moved to Marshfield, having been elected principal of the school at that place, which position he held for three years. After this he spent one year on his father's farm, and was then elected cashier of the Merchants' & Farmers' Bank at Marshfield, which opened its doors for business the 13th of August, 1888. To Mr. and Mrs. Long were born two children: Elizabeth C., a native of Glenwood, Iowa, born November 3, 1874, and Matthew P., who was also born at Glenwood, Iowa, September 4, 1876.

Russel McCormmach is one of the well-to-do farmers of Webster County, Mo., and was born in Jackson County, Tenn., on the 9th of September, 1830. His father, Johnson McCormmach, was born in Virginia on the 6th of July, 1806, and when a young man went to Tennessee with his parents, where he was married to Miss Mercilla Brown, of that State, on the 10th of May, 1827. In January, 1856, they moved to Webster County, Mo., where a farm was made, on which they resided until 1865, when they took up their abode in Pike County, Mo. There the father died November 8, 1870. Russel McCormmach was reared in Tennessee, and was there married in April, 1854, to Mary King, of that State. He came to Missouri with his parents, and after a short residence in Webster County located in Taney County, near Forsyth, where he cleared a small farm, and resided for about three years. In 1859 he settled upon his present tract of land in Webster County, which comprises 240 acres, and is one of the best farms between Marshfield and Seymour. He has 100 acres of land under cultivation, on which are excellent buildings and plenty of good water. He and wife, who died April 28, 1871, became the parents of six children: Alfred J., William T., John C., James Russell, Sarah Ann (wife of Thomas Hale) and Mary M. (wife of William Moore). Mr. McCormmach's present wife was Miss Lydia Julian, who was born in Knox County, Tenn., on the 12th of December, 1842, by whom he has the following children: Ollie L., wife of Nathaniel L. George; Leroy, Huldah J., Joseph P., Harriet M. and Martha L. His wife has three children by her first husband, Solomon Scott. Their names are, respectively, Larken R., Mary L. (wife of Samuel Mitchler) and Stephen R. A. Mrs. McCormmach is a member of the Methodist Episcopal Church, and he is a stanch Democrat in his political views. In July, 1862, he enlisted in the Eighth Missouri Volunteer Cavalry, and served as a private until the close of the war, being a participant in the battles of Little Rock, Pilot Knob, Prairie Grove, Pumpkin Bend fight and a number of skirmishes.

Col. John F. McMahan. Prominent among the many enterprising and successful citizens of Southwest Missouri stands the name of Col. McMahan, who was born in Bedford County, Tenn., November 24, 1826, the son of James and Temperance (Mason) McMahan, and grandson of John McMahan, who came to the United States from Ireland after the Revolutionary War, and located in East Tennessee. James McMahan was born in Sevier County, Tenn., January 4, 1800, left his home at the age of twelve years, and was in the War of 1812. He was of Scotch-Irish descent. His wife was born in North Carolina January 7, 1804, and both are now deceased, the father dying May 13, 1853, and the mother in Webster County, Mo., in 1872. They lived in Bedford County, Tenn., until 1838, then after a short residence in Coffee County, of the same State, they moved to Missouri, and located near where Seymour now is. Here they passed their last days. The father was overseer until coming to Missouri, and after that he was engaged in farming until his death. They had born to their union nine sons and three daughters, five sons and one daughter now living: Col. John F., Joseph, William T., Dubson, Robert, and Huldah, wife of Jefferson P. Chaffin. Those deceased were named as follows: James; Samuel, who died at Springfield; Abram, who was killed near Seymour during the war; Elijah, died in Texas in 1885; Elizabeth, died in 1838 in Tennessee, and Temperance, died in 1847 in Missouri. In 1846 Col. John F. McMahan volunteered in the Mexican War, and in 1847 was placed in Company G, Third Regiment Missouri Mounted Infantry, commanded by Col. Ralls. He served until the fall of 1848, and was in many battles with the Indians. He then attended school for some time, and later crossed the plains to California. In 1851 he returned home, engaged in farming and dealing in stock, and January 3, 1856, he married Miss Margaret E. Young, a native of Henry County, Tenn., born December 26, 1833, and the daughter of James Young. This union has been blessed by six sons and one daughter: James T., the eldest, died when in his twenty-first year; Mason Y. is at home; John F., now at home; Samuel R., engaged in merchandising; Robert C., at home; Charles W., at home, and Mattie E., at home. In 1857 Col. McMahan commenced farming where he now lives, where he first purchased 160 acres of land, and to this has added 850 acres in Webster County and 480 acres in Laclede County. He has over 600 acres under cultivation. In the early part of 1862 he organized a company, and was commissioned captain of Company D, Seventy-fourth Enrolled Missouri Militia, August 6, 1862. December 20, the same year, he was commissioned major of the Seventy-fourth Regiment, and October 1, 1863, he was promoted to the rank of lieutenant-colonel of the Seventy-second Missouri Enrolled Militia Infantry. June 17, 1864, he was commissioned colonel in the Sixteenth Missouri Cavalry, Federal army, and was discharged from service July 6, 1865. During the time of service he was at the battles of Boonville, Mo., Independence, Mo., and Big Blue. His regiment was in Newtonia, but the Colonel was absent on account of sickness. During every engagement the Colonel could be found in the thickest of the fight, but was fortunate in not being wounded. Previous to his war record, in 1854, the Colonel was elected to represent Wright County when barely old enough to take a seat in the House of Representatives, and was instrumental in organizing Webster County. Just twenty years later he was elected to represent Webster County in the Legislature, and in 1880 he was elected to represent the Twenty-third Missouri District in the State Senate. In 1872 he was elected associate judge, and in 1878 was elected president of the county court. He voted the Whig ticket until the war, and since that time has affiliated with the Democratic party, has always been active in political affairs, and has been in several conventions. He is a member of the Masonic fraternity, is a member of the Farmers' and Mechanics' Mutual Aid Society, and Mrs. McMahan is a member of the Methodist Episcopal Church, South.

William T. McMahan was born in Bedford County, Tenn., February 5, 1832, and is a son of James and Sarah T. (Mason) McMahan, natives respectively of Virginia and Tennessee; they moved to Missouri about 1841, and settled on a farm near where the town of Seymour now is, where the father made his home until May, 1853. William T. was reared in Webster County. In September, 1858, he was married to Miss Susan Freeman, a daughter of Littleton Freeman, formerly of Tennessee, but now a resident of Wright County, Mo. Mrs. Susan McMahan was born November 10, 1838. In the spring of 1860 they purchased eighty acres of their present farm, which they have since increased from time to time, until they now own 408 acres, with 340 under cultivation. They have large and comfortable buildings on their farm and a good bearing orchard of 400 trees. This with other improvements and conveniences makes for them one of the finest homes in the county. At the breaking out of the Rebellion, William T. enlisted first in the Home Guards, then in the State Militia, and in the fall of 1864 in the regular United States service, in the Forty-eighth Missouri Infantry, and served until the final close, when he returned home. Their children are as follows: James was born September 21, 1859, and was married to Eva A. Trimble, of Webster County; Arabella, born June 16, 1861, wife of John B. Foster, of Marshfield, Mo.; Clella J., born November 26, 1862, wife of W. H. Oliver, of Webster County; Mattie E., born November 24, 1864, wife of Perrie T. Hyde, of Webster County; Tempa S., born November 2, 1866, wife of J. W. Fuson, of Seymour; Hulda F., born November 6, 1868; Samuel D., born May 5, 1872; William T. Jr., born July 4, 1875; Lillie and Rosa were born March 13, 1878; Lillie died August 22, 1878, and Rosie died March 6, 1880. Mr. McMahan is an energetic and wide-a-wake farmer, and deals largely in mules. He is a Master Mason, and Mrs. McMahan is a member of the Cumberland Presbyterian Church.

Robert McMahan, an enterprising citizen of Union Township, Webster Co., Mo., was born in Webster County, then known as Wright County, on the 23d of December, 1848. His parents, James and Temperance (Mason) McMahan, were natives of Middle Tennessee, in which State they were married and lived until 1839, when they removed to Webster County, Mo., and located near where the town of Seymour is now situated, afterward moving to near Waldo. The father, who was a successful farmer, died in 1853, and the mother in 1872. Of their family of eleven children, six are now living, viz.: John F., a prominent farmer of Webster County; Joseph, a stock trader of St. James, Mo.; William, a farmer and stock dealer near Seymour, Mo.; Hulda, wife of Perry Chaffin, of Webster County; Dobson is a farmer of Belle County, Tex., and Robert. The latter received a common-school education in his native county, and when twenty-one years of age engaged in farming and stock raising, which he has ever since continued with marked success. He now owns a well-improved farm in a desirable location in Union Township, the greater portion of which is under cultivation. July 21, 1878, he married Annie Foster, daughter of Jesse Foster, who came with his family from East Tennessee, and located in Webster County, where Mrs. McMahan was born June 21, 1851. Jesse Foster is deceased, but his widow is still living near Waldo, on the old homestead, with her youngest son. Five children were born to Mr. and Mrs. McMahan, viz.: Hulda Temperance, born May 25, 1879, died August 24, 1879; John R., born May 26, 1881; Bertha May, born January 27, 1883; Thomas W., born June 5, 1885, and Effie Myrtle, born November 23, 1887. Mrs. McMahan is a member of the Methodist Episcopal Church, South. In politics our subject is in sympathy with the Democratic party.

James McMahan was born in Wright County, Mo., on the 21st of September, 1859, and is a son of William T. McMahan, whose sketch appears in this work. He grew to manhood in his native county, and from early boyhood was reared on a farm, becoming skilled in the duties of farm labor, and received a good practical education in the common schools of Webster County. He made the paternal roof his home until after he attained his majority, when he was married in this county on the 30th of August, 1881, to Eva A. Trimble, a daughter of Rev. A. D. and M. E. Trimble, who were formerly from Tennessee. Mrs. McMahan was born, reared and educated in that State, being a graduate of Mary Sharp College, of Winchester, Tenn. Previous to her marriage she spent a number of years as a teacher of instrumental music, and after that event located with her husband on their farm of 160 acres in Webster County, Mo.; 130 acres are under cultivation and furnished with good buildings and a young orchard, which promises to supply them with plenty of fruit. They have one daughter, Rosa Lee, a miss of six years. Mrs. McMahan is a member of the Missionary Baptist Church. Her father was a minister of that denomination, but is now deceased. Her mother re-married, and is now residing in Springfield, Mo.

Prof. John H. Magill. Among the educators of Missouri worthy of honorable mention is Prof. Magill, who is now superintendent of public instruction of Webster County. His birth occurred on the 12th of April, 1857, in Crawford County, Ill., and until fifteen years of age he made that county his home, and there received his education, attending the Olney High-school, in which institution he made very rapid progress in his studies. When only eighteen years of age he taught a country school, and after his term was completed entered the Normal School at Danville, Ind., taking a teacher's course. He then took a scientific course in the college at Carmi, Ill., and during a four and a half years' attendance at this institution was engaged in teaching book-keeping and penmanship. In 1882 he became a resident of Webster County, Mo., and had charge of the Mountain Dale Seminary for three years, and then became principal of the Henderson Academy, which he has successfully conducted up to the present time. He makes a specialty of thoroughly preparing teachers for their work, and has won an enviable reputation as an instructor in Webster County, his school enrolling from 150 to 175 pupils throughout the year, which is a high average for a private school in Southern Missouri. In April, 1887, he was elected superintendent of the Webster County schools, and has filled the duties of this position with honor to himself and to the entire satisfaction of all concerned. In the summer of 1887 he held a teacher's institute for two weeks, for the especial purpose of preparing teachers for their work, and owing to his encouragement and advice newer and better methods are being adopted for instructing the young. He was married in Greensburg, Ind., in 1882, to Miss Anna G. Stagg, who was born, reared and educated in the "Hoosier" State. They have two children, Della and Ralph. One son, Logan, died when three years old. Prof. and Mrs. Magill are members of the Methodist Episcopal Church, South, and he is a

Master Mason. He is a son of John and Emeline (Martin) Magill, who were also natives of Illinois. The father was a farmer and stock trader, and made several trips south to New Orleans. He died in his native State, his wife surviving him at this date (1889).

Archibald Marlin, one of the old and representative citizens of Washington Township, Webster Co., Mo., who has been a resident of Greene, Polk, Dallas and Webster Counties, was born in Marion County, Mo., April 4, 1823, being the son of Thomas and Polly (Rice) Marlin, natives of Kentucky and Tennessee, respectively. The father was born in 1782, and died in Webster County, Mo., in 1861. The mother died in Marion County, Mo., when Archibald Marlin was about seven years of age. The parents remained in Tennessee until 1820, and then came to Marion County, Mo., where they resided until 1833, when they moved to Pope County (then Greene County). Their nearest neighbor was ten miles distant, and everything was then wild and unsettled. Thomas Marlin was a farmer all his life; was a Democrat until 1860, when he voted for Lincoln. He was a soldier in the War of 1812, and while living in Pope County, Mo., was in the Legislature one term; was also county judge, justice of the peace, etc., and was a well-known and prominent citizen. Seven children were born to his marriage, six of whom are now living: James, Spencer, Archibald, Malinda, William and Mary. Archibald, when twenty-three years of age, was married to Amanda Hogan, daughter of Andrew Hogan, and a native of Tennessee, born May 3, 1824. By this union five children were born: Madison, Wallace, Helen, wife of John Rice, of Dallas County, Mo.; Delmer and Mary. When first married Mr. Marlin began farming and dealing in stock, which he has continued until the present time, and although he started with limited means, by industry and economy he is now the owner of a good farm. In 1844 and 1845 he was engaged in mining lead on James Fork of White River. At different times Mr. Marlin has held the offices of justice of the peace, constable, etc. He is a member of the Agricultural Wheel, and is a Republican in politics. He has lived where he is now located for fifty-four years, and is highly respected by all who know him. Mrs. Marlin is a member of the Baptist Church.

William A. Martin. Among the men of Webster County, Mo., who have attained prominence as tillers of the soil and stock men, may be mentioned Mr. Martin, who was born in Marion County, Tenn., March 19, 1841, but was reared to manhood in Webster County, Mo., whither he came with his parents, James D. and Catherine (Thompson) Martin, in 1852. The father was born in Virginia, and after attaining manhood went to Tennessee, where he was married, and after a few years' residence in that State, moved to St. Louis County, Mo. In August, 1861, he joined Company B, Twenty-fourth Missouri Infantry, and served until his death, in May, 1864, at Pleasant Hill, La. William A. Martin enlisted at the same time, in the same company as his father, and was at the battle of Pleasant Hill, and in a great many skirmishes, and was severely wounded in the right shoulder by a gunshot at the former engagement, being in the hospital at New

Orleans and Memphis for about five months. He received his discharge at St. Louis, January 11, 1865, homesteading the same year the farm of 200 acres where he now lives. He has about 150 acres under cultivation and well improved, and his farm is situated about eight miles from Marshfield. He has always supported the measures of the Republican party, and in the fall of 1884 was nominated and elected sheriff of Webster County, and ably filled the duties of that office for two years. Since then he has resided on his farm. February 19, 1865, he was married to Miss Mary L. Turner, who died in Webster County on the 16th of April, 1868, and he took for his second wife Miss Sarah L. Morton, a native of North Carolina, and daughter of George Morton, who died during the war. Two children were born to his first marriage, Laura M. and Charles F. The following are the children of his last marriage: Mary S., and James P. and Matilda C. (twins). Mrs. Martin is a member of the Methodist Episcopal Church, and he belongs to the A. O. U. W. and G. A. R.

Christian Mikkelsen. Prominent among the leading citizens of Webster County, Mo., stands the name of the above mentioned gentleman, who was born in Denmark September 23, 1835, and is the son of Hans and Christine Mikkelsen, natives of Denmark, where they both died, he when the subject of this sketch was about one year old, and she in 1862 or 1863. They were members of the Lutheran Church, and he was a trader and farmer by occupation. To their marriage were born two sons and four daughters, Christian Mikkelsen being the youngest of this family. He remained with his mother until eighteen years of age, when he went to Copenhagen, and entered the king's stable as a driver, remaining there for seven years. He then went home for a short time, and in 1860 came to the United States, locating in Gasconade County, Mo., and afterward in Maries County, of the same State. In August, of the following year, he married Miss Ann M. Petersen, who was born in Denmark in 1839, and who came to the United States one year after Mr. Mikkelsen. The same year after his marriage Mr. Mikkelsen enlisted in Company D, of the Sixth Missouri Cavalry, Federal army, and was in the service nearly one year, when he was discharged on account of disability. He then came to Webster County, Mo., and for several years was engaged in working on the 'Frisco Railroad, running a boarding-house and keeping teams. In 1869 he bought the farm where he now resides, and engaged in agricultural pursuits. Although when coming to the United States his means were limited, he has since been very successful, and has one of the best farms in the county. March 10, 1878, Mrs. Mikkelsen died. To their marriage were born seven children, four now living: Christian P., Hans, Jacob P. and Charles Louis. Those deceased were named Christiana and Anna (twins), who died when ten months old. In 1879 Mr. Mikkelsen married Miss Mary Virginia Owens, a native of Tennessee, born in 1839; she died one year after her marriage. In 1880 he married Mette Marie Gammelgaard, a native of Denmark, born in 1844. Mr. Mikkelsen is a Republican in politics, and he and family are members of the St. Paul's Lutheran Church.

John F. Miller, farmer and stock raiser of Webster County, Mo., was born in Stark County, of the "Buckeye State," August 18, 1849, and is a son of John Miller, who was born in Northumberland County, Penn., and removed to Ohio when a young man, settling in Stark County, where he was engaged in merchandising for about fifteen years. He served as postmaster of his town at the same time, and was married in Stark County to Elizabeth Keplinger, a native of Ohio, and there reared his family. His later years were spent in tilling the soil, and his death occurred on the 16th of May, 1883. John F. Miller was reared to manhood on a farm, and received his education in the common schools, and took a two-years' course in the Mount Union College, at Mount Union, Ohio, completing the course in 1867. He then engaged in pedagoguing, which occupation he continued in Wayne County for two years, and December 8, 1870, was married in Columbiana County to Miss Jane Hahn, who was born, reared and educated in that county, completing her schooling in Mount Union College. She was also a teacher by profession, and was a daughter of Adam Hahn, who was born in Columbiana County in 1812. After their marriage Mr. and Mrs. Miller located on a farm in Stark County, but in 1883 sold out and came westward, looking for a suitable location in Kansas, Nebraska, Illinois and several other Western States. Mr. Miller then returned to Ohio, and in the spring of 1885 removed to Missouri with his family, and in August of that year purchased and located on the farm on which he now resides. He has a tract of land consisting of 400 acres, and has 200 acres cleared and under cultivation, and well improved, with a large two-story residence, good barns, and a fine orchard of twelve acres. He is quite extensively engaged in dealing in and breeding thoroughbred Short-Horn cattle, and has a very fine herd at the present time. He has always supported the measures of the Democratic party, and has held the office of township trustee for three consecutive terms, and has also been a member of the county committee of Webster County. He was also congressional committeeman from his district in 1888, and is a Master Mason in the Masonic fraternity, a member of Lodge 499, of Columbiana County, Ohio. He and wife are the parents of the following family: Frank, Dean, John, Marion, Harvey, Melvin and Bessie.

Capt. Friley Washington Moore, another prominent citizen of the county, was born in Jamesville, Martin Co., N. C., February 22, 1820, being the only living representative to the marriage relation of William B. and Sarah J. (Cooper) Moore, and is of Irish-English extraction. His father was born at Jamesville, N. C., about 1798, and died in his native town about 1834. He was a carpenter and book-keeper by occupation. The mother of Mr. Moore was also a native of Martin County, N. C., and died at Jamesville in the thirty-sixth year of her age. The paternal grandfather of Mr. Moore was Mathias Moore, a native of the "Emerald Isle," and who came to the United States at a very early date. He settled in North Carolina, was an inn-keeper for some time, and died in 1824, at a good old age. Humphrey Cooper, the maternal grandfather of our subject, was a native of England, and died in North Carolina. Capt. Friley W. Moore obtained a common-school education, and at an early age began clerking in a store at Jamesville. In January, 1841, he went to Williamston, N. C., where he clerked in the store of Rev. C. B. Hassell, at a salary of $125 per annum, with board and washing, and with the understanding that his wages were to be increased at the rate of $50 per year if mutually satisfied. He continued here for four years, and in 1844 bought out his employer. His marriage occurred February 17, 1846, to Miss Martha Ann Clomon, of Rainbow Banks, N. C. She died in Marshfield, Mo., June 22, 1876, and was a most estimable woman, and for many years was a member of the Methodist Episcopal Church, South. In 1848 Mr. Moore sold his store to his old employer, and then engaged in the saw-mill and lumber business, selling his manufactures in New York City, Philadelphia and Boston. After three years he sold his business to a Virginia company, and in 1856 was elected president of the Roanoke Steam-boat Navigation Company, becoming commander of the steamer "John Styles." In 1861 he sold the steamer to the State of North Carolina for use in the Confederate service, and her name was changed to the "Albemarle" of the Confederate States, Mr. Moore being commissioned her captain by Gov. Ellis, of North Carolina. Capt. Moore resigned his position in June, 1862. The "Albemarle" was captured by the Federals a short time after his resignation, and the same year she sank in Pamlico River. The same year Capt. Moore was appointed salt commissioner and collector of internal revenue for the Second District of North Carolina under William K. Lane, serving in this position until the close of the war. He then again entered mercantile pursuits, and in 1867 came to St. Louis, where he carried on business for one year. In February, 1868, he came to Marshfield, and here he has since resided. When first coming here he engaged in the tanning business, which occupied his attention for two years, after which, for one year, he was engaged in the real estate business. He then resumed merchandising, which he now continues, and at which he has been unusually successful. In politics the Captain is an uncompromising Democrat, and is a leading politician of that party. He was made an Odd Fellow in 1847, at Philanx Lodge No. 10, in North Carolina, and is now a member of Webster Lodge No. 163. Capt. Moore has one son by his marriage, William J.

Hon. Joseph T. Moore. Prominent among the leading men of Marshfield, and among those deserving special recognition for their long residence in Webster County, stands the name of the above mentioned gentleman, who was born in Giles County, Tenn., January 11, 1839. His parents, Jonathan F. and Mary (Camper) Moore, were both natives of Tennessee, and both born in the year 1818. The father died in Webster County, Mo., in 1844, and the mother in the same county in 1876. They were the parents of two children, their daughter dying in 1863. Joseph T. Moore is the only one of the family now living. In the fall of 1839 he came with his parents to what was then Pulaski County, and settled on the James Fork of White River. This county was afterward changed to Wright County, and then to Webster County. Mr. Moore was mainly self educated, and in April,

1861, he enlisted in the Home Guards, and served with them until the Wilson's Creek battle, August 10, 1861. He then went to Raleigh and enlisted in Col. John S. Phelps' regiment, and here continued until he was discharged by reason of expiration of term of service. He then enlisted in the Eighth Missouri Cavalry, and upon the organization of Company B he was elected second lieutenant. He was discharged in the winter of 1863, on account of physical disability. He was at the battles of Pea Ridge and Prairie Grove, and rendered effective and useful service. Having regained his health, he entered the militia service of the State of Missouri, and was elected captain of Company A, and continued in that position until peace was declared. He then began farming in High Prairie Township, where he now lives, and where he owns 204 acres of land. He taught one term of school in the fall of 1869. Previous to this, in 1863, he married Miss Sarah White, who died in 1870. To this union were born three children. Mr. Moore was married the second time, in 1872, to Miss Martha Jane Morton, who was born in North Carolina in 1850, and they have seven children. Mr. Moore has resided in this part of the State for forty-nine years, and is a representative citizen of the county. He has been a life-long Republican in politics, casting his first presidential vote for Lincoln in 1864. In 1878 he was elected justice of the peace, and re-elected in 1882. In 1886 he was elected representative of this county by 122 majority, being the first Republican (straight) elected to the Legislature from this county in sixteen years. In 1888 he was elected to the same office by 158 majority. He is one of the leading Republicans of the county, and is a member of the G. A. R., Post No. 225.

James Thomas Morris, of the mercantile firm of Morris & Bouldin, was born in Greene County, Mo., June 20, 1853, being a son of Robert and Martha (Thornton) Morris, who were born, reared and married in Tennessee. They moved to Missouri about 1840, locating in Greene County, but the father's death occurred at Pilot Knob in 1863, he having served eighteen months in the Eighth Missouri Volunteer Cavalry. James T. Morris remained with his mother in Greene County, Mo., until he attained his majority, receiving the advantages of the common schools. After starting out in life for himself he was engaged in farming in Greene County for about three years, then sold out and removed to Barry County in 1879, and was occupied in merchandising at Eagle Rock for about eighteen months. He disposed of his stock about this time, and in March, 1880, moved to Henderson and embarked in business under the firm name of Wharton & Morris, but after some time Mr. Wharton retired, the firm now being known as Morris & Bouldin. Mr. Morris built their present business house in 1884, and owing to his many sterling business qualities he has established a good trade. In 1887 he was appointed notary public, and in his political views is a Republican. In March, 1875, he was married to Mary L. Wharton, who was born in Greene County, and by her is the father of two children: James C. and Clarence R. He and wife are members of the Methodist Episcopal Church, South, and she is a daughter of Emsley Wharton, who was a native of North Carolina.

John W. Nelson, an enterprising farmer of Ozark Township, Webster Co., Mo., was born in Huntingdon, Penn., May 18, 1849, and is the son of John and Elizabeth (Heffner) Nelson. The father was born in Pennsylvania in 1820, and is now living in Bedford County, that State. In 1862 he enlisted in the Eighteenth Pennsylvania Cavalry, and was first lieutenant of Company K. February 4, 1863, he was severely wounded, near Fairfax, Va., by Mosley's guerrillas. The mother was born in Huntingdon County, Penn., in 1829, and died in her native county in 1851. John W. Nelson was the second of three children, two of whom are now living. His father being a miller, the early life of Mr. Nelson was spent in his father's mill, but in 1864 he began working on the farm at $7 per month, and in 1868 he rented a farm and began working for himself. This occupation he continued for nine years, and then purchased a portion of the farm he had rented, and here cultivated the soil until the fall of 1885, when he came to Webster County, Mo., settling where he now lives, and here he has since remained. He is an industrious farmer, and was married October 6, 1870, to Miss Hannah R. Mann, who was born in Bedford County, Penn., November 13, 1850, and who is the daughter of George and Hester (Zimmers) Mann, natives of Pennsylvania. Mr. and Mrs. Nelson are the parents of an interesting family of children: Myrtle, born in 1871; Mary E., born in 1874; Maggie M., born in 1876; Elsie E., born in 1879, and William Roy, born in 1882. Mr. Nelson is a Democrat in politics, and he and wife are members of the Methodist Episcopal Church.

John L. Pryor is a prosperous farmer and stock man of Hazelwood Township, Webster Co., Mo., and was born in Marion County, Tenn., on the 16th of December, 1836, being a son of William and Nancy (Griffith) Pryor, who were also Tennesseeans, and who moved to Greene County, Mo., in the fall of 1840, and to Douglas County in 1858. Here the father resided until the fall of 1881, when he went to the Indian Territory, where he had two sons living, and there died January 5, 1888, at the age of seventy-five years. His wife died in 1857. John L. Pryor grew to manhood on a farm in Christian County, Mo., and remained with his father until he reached manhood, and on the 26th of July, 1860, was married in Douglas County, Mo., to Miss Catherine Kerr, a daughter of James H. Kerr, formerly a Tennesseean. Mrs. Pryor was born in that State, and by Mr. Pryor is the mother of five children: Nancy Olive (wife of William S. Haley), Mary E, Amanda, Dona Jane and Araminta S. They lost four sons in infancy, and one daughter, Lydia J., at the age of fourteen years, in 1884. In the fall of 1862 Mr. Pryor enlisted in the Enrolled Militia, Sixth Provisional Cavalry, and served until March, 1864, when he went to Illinois and enlisted in the One Hundred and Fiftieth Illinois Volunteer Infantry, serving as corporal until February, 1866, when he received his discharge, being mustered out at Atlanta. He returned to Missouri in the fall of 1866, and located near where he now lives, and since the fall of 1883 has been residing on his present farm of 120 acres, seventy-five of which are under cultivation, and furnished with fair buildings. Mr. and Mrs. Pryor are members of the Christian Church.

William M. Puett, one of the leading citizens of Webster County, Mo., is a native of Caldwell County, N. C., where he was born on the 27th of May, 1855. His parents, Joseph N. and Irene (Loudermilk) Puett, were born in Caldwell County, N. C., the former's birth occurring in 1832, and the latter's birth occurring in 1840. Joseph N. Puett died July 4, 1858, at the age of twenty-six years. His widow is still residing in Caldwell County, and is the wife of George W. Crump, a farmer. Joseph N. Puett was a farmer by occupation, a Democrat in politics, and a member of the Lutheran Church. The mother is a member of the Methodist Episcopal Church, South, and by Mr. Puett became the mother of four children, three of whom are living at the present time: Mary (wife of Charles A. Bradford), William M., Caroline S. (wife of Thomas Lofton), and Joseph N. (who died February 13, 1882, at the age of twenty-two years). To her last marriage four children were born, two of whom are living. At the age of twenty-two years William M. Puett came to Missouri, and first engaged in farming on rented land, but afterward purchased the farm on which he is now residing, which is a fertile and well-improved tract of land. November 27, 1881, he was united in marriage to Ellen Copening, a daughter of Jacob Copening. She was born in Webster County, Mo., May 17, 1864, and is the mother of six children, two of whom are living: John J. and Virgie Irene. Mr. Puett is one of the enterprising young citizens of the county, and bids fair to become one of its wealthy inhabitants. He and wife are members of the Methodist Episcopal Church, South, and he is a member of the Masonic fraternity, and supports the principles of the Democratic party.

Samuel Y. Puryear, farmer and stock raiser of Webster County, Mo., was born in Bedford County, Tenn., January 7, 1833, and is a son of Robert H. Puryear, who was born and reared in Virginia. The latter served in the War of 1812, and when a young man went to Tennessee, where he met and married Miss Mary Blythe, whose birth occurred in North Carolina. They resided in Tennessee until 1857, when they moved to Missouri, and located on the farm on which their son Samuel Y. now resides, and here the father's death occurred on the 6th of September, 1860. His twelve children grew to mature years, but one son afterward died in Mexico, during the war with that country, and another died in Tennessee. Samuel Y. Puryear came to Missouri from his native State on horseback, in the year 1855, and selected the location on which his father afterward settled. In the fall of 1861 he enlisted in the Confederate service, Third Missouri Cavalry, and served until the close of the war, participating in the battles of Cape Girardeau, Jenkins' Ferry, Pilot Knob, and was with Price on his raid through Arkansas and Missouri. He was discharged at St. Louis, Mo., in 1865, and went to Illinois, where he resided four years, and then returned to Missouri, and took charge of the home farm, which he has since managed. He owns a tract of land consisting of 400 acres, all in one body, near Seymour, and has about 150 acres under cultivation, on which are erected a neat dwelling house and good barns. His orchard consists of about 100 bearing trees. Mr. Puryear is unmarried, and a sister, who is also unmarried, resides with and keeps house for him.

Henry Rabenau, merchant, and dealer and shipper of railroad timber, lumber and wood, at Fordland, Mo., was born in Hesse Darmstadt, Germany, April 27, 1827, and at the age of twenty-two years immigrated to the United States, locating first at Allegheny City, Penn., where he was engaged in merchandising for about twelve years. During this period he also dealt in real estate to some extent, in which business he was quite successful. In 1864 he purchased 1,600 acres of land in Webster County, but located at Rolla, and took a Government contract for furnishing beef for the Union army. In the fall of 1865 he located on his land in Webster County, and was engaged in farming until 1881, when he rented his land and moved to Fordland, and engaged in his present business, building his present business house in March, 1884. He carries a well-selected general mercantile stock, and handles about 800 car loads of timber per year. He is the present proprietor of the Fordland *Journal*, edited by G. P. Garland, and in all his business transactions his labors have met with well-deserved success. He was married in Pennsylvania, February 5, 1851, to Mary Anna Baker, who was born in Germany, and died in April, 1885. The following are their children: Henry A., William J., Caroline Louisa (wife of J. H. Williams), Charles J. and Louis G. In January, 1888, Mr. Rabenau was married in Webster County to Miss Mary Angeline Renner, who was born in Tennessee, and is a daughter of John Renner. They are members of the Christian Church, and he is a Master Mason in the Masonic fraternity.

John J. Redmond, a leading citizen of Webster County, Mo., and son of Matthew and Ann (Burne) Redmond, was born in Liverpool, England, June 24, 1833. The parents left England in 1848, immigrated to Canada, located near London, and here died at the age of eighty-eight. Mr. Redmond was a man of education, and was a member of the I. O. O. F. John J. Redmond was the youngest of a family of nine children, six now living. He came with his parents to America when sixteen years of age, and commenced clerking in London, Canada, in a general grocery, where he remained for five years. He then came to the United States, locating in Ramsey County, Minn., where he farmed, taught school and was justice of the peace, for four years. He then came to St. Louis, and entered the employ of the Southern Pacific Railroad (now 'Frisco), and remained in their employ until 1870. He then came to Niangua, where he was engaged in merchandising, milling, and was ticket agent and Adams Express agent, postmaster and notary public, until 1883. During the late war he was captain of a company of militia, but previous to this, December 25, 1856, he married Miss Emily Nicholson, daughter of Sampson Nicholson, and a native of London, Canada. To this union were born three children: John N., Emily and Sarah. Mr. Redmond is a member of the Masonic order, and the Commandery at Lebanon, and is a Democrat in his political views.

Nicholas Rhodes was born in Knox County, Tenn., March 19, 1823, being a son of John Rhodes, of North Carolina. The latter went to

Tennessee with his father when a lad of twelve years, grew to manhood in that State, and there married Mary Cox, a native of Knox County, Tenn. He was a soldier in the War of 1812, under Gen. Jackson, and also served in the Florida War. He died in Knox County, Tenn., in 1870, at the age of seventy-seven years. Both grandfathers (Rhodes and Cox) were soldiers in the Revolutionary War. Nicholas Rhodes resided in Knox County until twenty-five years of age, and then began the battle of life for himself. He was married on the 9th of September, 1849, in Greene County, Mo., whither he had come in 1848, to Margaret Caldwell, of Greene County, Mo. She came to this county with her parents in 1839. Robert Caldwell, her father, served in the War of 1812, and also in the late Civil War, and died in 1866, at the age of seventy-seven years. Sarah Caldwell, wife of Robert Caldwell, died in 1880, at the age of eighty-eight years. Mr. Rhodes now has a good farm of 160 acres, on the Pomme de Terre River, on which he has resided since March, 1856. By industry he has succeeded in clearing his farm, and now has eighty acres of land under cultivation, and a neat one-story residence. He and wife have a family of three sons and one daughter, whose names are as follows: Robert E., John F., Sarah H. (wife of J. M. Morton) and William T., a young man twenty-three years of age. During the late Civil War Mr. Rhodes served for some time in the Home Guards, and afterward in the Enrolled Militia, and at the end of nine months received his discharge on account of disability.

Rev. Robert E. Rhodes is a native of the State and county in which he now resides, and was born April 28, 1850, being a son of Nicholas Rhodes, who was born and reared in East Tennessee. The latter came to Missouri about 1848, and located in Webster County, where he was united in marriage to Margaret Caldwell, who was also born in East Tennessee. They cleared and put under cultivation a large farm, and here reared their family. The father served in the Federal army during the late war, being in the Home Guards and Enrolled Militia. Robert E. Rhodes remained with his father until twenty-three years of age, and was married on the 8th of August, 1872, to Dollie H. Grier, a sister of N. F. Grier, whose sketch appears in this work. After his marriage he located on a farm in Grant Township, and in 1877 came to his present location. He owns a part of the Grier homestead, and his acreage amounts to 210 acres, with about 135 acres under cultivation, on which are a good residence, barn and other out-buildings. He and wife are members of the Missionary Baptist Church, and he has been a licensed preacher of that denomination since September, 1888. He is a missionary for the Greene County Sunday-school Association, and, while he has charge of no church, preaches nearly every Sunday. Mr. Rhodes devoted his attention to farming and stock trading exclusively from 1870 to 1887. Until this latter year he was an infidel in belief, but, in his efforts to obtain proof to substantiate his claims, a critical study of the Bible led him to see his condemnation as a sinner, and the doom awaiting him. As he himself says: "Then I called upon God for mercy, and to save me. He did, and I have been telling others the story ever since."

William S. Riggs, farmer and stock raiser and dealer, was born in Maury County, Tenn., February 26, 1829, and is a son of A. J. and Peternella (Wray) Riggs, who were North Carolinians, and were married in their native State. After moving to Tennessee they settled in Maury County, where they spent the remainder of their days, the father dying in 1852. William S. Riggs remained with his parents until twenty-one years of age, when he began doing for himself, and in 1854 went to Texas, and afterward returned to his home in Tennessee via Missouri. In 1855 he took up his abode in Greene County, Mo., and was there married in March, 1856, to Miss Emily J. McCracken, who was born in Tennessee, but was reared in Greene County. They engaged in farming near Springfield, and in 1867 moved to that city and engaged in keeping a hotel, following this occupation for twenty years. In 1885 he purchased the farm where he now resides, but has only lived upon it since 1887. His farm consists of 350 acres, nearly all of which is bottom land, and 250 acres are under cultivation and well improved with good buildings. He has a nice bearing orchard of six acres, and has one-half acre in vineyard. Mr. Riggs ships considerable stock, but usually finds a ready market at home. His children's names are as follows: Mary, wife of H. Thackery, residing in Springfield; Robert, who is married and resides on the home farm; William S. and John A. The last two named are twins.

Daniel Wesley Robertson, the leading lumber dealer in Marshfield, Mo., is a native of Henry County, Tenn., where he was born May 14, 1844, being the son of James R. and Eleanor (Neese) Robertson, natives of North Carolina. The father of Mr. Robertson was born April 5, 1813, and died April 22, 1850. The mother died in October, 1865. They were married in their native State, and afterward removed to Henry County, Tenn., where they remained until 1842. They then settled in Greene County, where the father died, but the mother died in Webster County, Mo. Mr. Robertson, like the average country boy, assisted his mother on the farm, and received his education in the common schools. In 1862 he enlisted in Company D, Sixteenth Missouri Cavalry, and served nearly three years. He was wounded at Boonville, Mo., and was mustered out of service in July, 1865. After coming home he engaged in running a carding machine for about three years, and then for two years was interested in the furniture business. After this for eight years he was occupied in tilling the soil, and since 1880 he has been carrying on his present business, having a full line of lumber, sash, doors, paints, glass, etc. He is doing a good business, and is the owner of the old Barnes estate of this city. He was married, July 7, 1864, to Miss Mattie A. Shackelford, who was born in Greene County, Mo., August 8, 1845. To that union were born these children: Ida Ellen, born August 22, 1866, and died October 23, 1866; William Martin, born October 9, 1867, and died December 7, 1887; John Wesley, born March 11, 1869; Charles Calvin, born July 27, 1871; James Garland, born January 21, 1873; Daniel Alphonso, born June 3, 1874; Joseph Henry, born March 28,

1876; Ann Nettie, born July 29, 1877; Robert Josiah, born July 23, 1879; Eva Blanche, born December 14, 1882, and Christopher Wallace, born October 28, 1886. Mr. Robertson is Democratic in his political views. He is a member of the Masonic fraternity, the G. A. R., and he and Mrs. Robertson are members of the Methodist Episcopal Church, South. He has four brothers and one sister, whose names are as follows, all now living: M. N., A. J., John S., James M. and Elizabeth Ann (Buck). John S. Robertson and Elizabeth Ann Buck live in Montana Territory, the others in Webster County, Mo.

James Lawrence Rush, a leading criminal lawyer of Missouri, was born in Westmoreland County, Penn., November 9, 1832, being the eldest of eight children born to the union of John H. and Margaret (Riley) Rush. The father was born in 1806, and died at Bedford, Penn., in 1870, and the mother was born in 1807, and died in 1882. James L. Rush received a common-school education, and at the age of seventeen years he went to Baltimore, Md., and learned the carriage-maker's trade, which he continued until twenty-one years of age. He then worked at his trade for one year at Washington, Penn., when he went to Bedford and entered the law office of Judge William McClay Hall, being admitted to the bar in 1857. In 1858 he came to Marshfield, Mo., and here carried on the practice of law until the breaking out of the late Civil War, when he joined the Webster County Home Guards, and served as such for three months. After the battle of Wilson's Creek he acted as a Union scout during the retreat on Rolla. Later he entered the Sixth Provisional Regiment as adjutant, detached from the Enrolled State Militia, and at the organization of the Sixteenth Regiment he was made major, and took part in the campaign against Price in 1864. During the last four months of the war he was on detached service at Springfield, Mo., with Gen. Sanborn, as acting judge advocate. Since the war Mr. Rush has been engaged in the law practice at Marshfield. He is a Democrat in politics, and in 1860 he was elected county surveyor. He was also elected county attorney seven years later, and was the Democratic elector from the Thirteenth Missouri District in 1888. July 1, 1860, he was united in marriage to Miss Frances E. Nichols, and she and one of eight children were killed in the cyclone of 1880. Mr. Rush is a Mason, also a member of the G. A. R., and is one of the prominent men of Marshfield.

Edwin W. Salmon. It is the truth to say that "man is the architect of his own fortune." Circumstances may make or mar his prospects to a certain extent, but a determined will will bend even the force of circumstances to its bidding. So-called genius has little to do with the success of men in general, but the possession of keen perception, sound judgment and determination, essential elements in any successful calling, is sure to accomplish the aims hoped for. Among the representative and truly substantial and worthy citizens of Marshfield, no one occupies a more prominent position than Edwin W. Salmon, whose association with its financial interests, and familiarity and connection with the commercial affairs of the community, have added materially to his popularity and recognition as a business man. Born at Versailles, Morgan Co., Mo., March 14, 1856, he is the son of William W. and Ann G. (Tutt) Salmon, a family well and favorably known in the vicinity of Clinton, Mo., where the father now resides. The former was born in Greenville County, S. C., in 1833, his wife's birth occurring in Rappahannock County, Va., in 1835. Edwin's paternal grandfather, Ezekiel Salmon, a native of South Carolina, became an early resident of Missouri (1839), and died in Morgan County in 1851. William Salmon upon starting in life for himself first engaged in merchandising, and subsequently turned his attention to farming and stock raising, his business, which he started at Versailles in 1852, being interrupted and broken up by the war. In 1863 he removed to St. Louis, resuming his mercantile interests there until 1870, in the latter part of which year he located in Henry County, of which Clinton, his present residence, is the county seat. Edwin W. Salmon, the eldest of a family of eleven children (eight of whom survive), received an excellent common-school education, improving the opportunities with which he was favored, and in February, 1873, he entered the bank of Salmon & Salmon, at Clinton, there obtaining an admirable business training, which well qualified him to establish the Bank of Marshfield, in June, 1885. The success of this now well-known financial institution has been steady and solid, and it has proved an important factor in the material advancement and reputation of Marshfield. Mr. Salmon, as its head, has manifested an ability and force of character which at once mark him a man above the ordinary. His strict integrity, earnest and sound financial judgment, and his uprightness and honor in all matters of business and private life, have gained for him the confidence of all, and he is worthy of the esteem and respect shown him and his family. Public spirited, enterprising and reliable, he has ever lent his influence to the growth and development of his adopted home, and has liberally supported all just measures tending to its benefit. October 10, 1883, Miss Lucie A. Milburn, of Baltimore, Md., daughter of Alexander Milburn, became his wife. Mrs. Salmon's birth occurred in 1861. One child has blessed their union, Milburn Tutt, born November 9, 1884. Mrs. Salmon is a member of the Episcopal Church.

George W. Silvey. In giving a history of the enterprising and successful business men of Webster County, Mo., a brief sketch of Mr. Silvey is in order. He is a prosperous farmer and stock raiser of the community, and was born in Roane County, Tenn., February 25, 1826, having been a resident of Missouri since 1837, when he immigrated here with his parents, Charles and Lucretia (Howard) Silvey, from Mississippi, whither they had moved from their native State in 1834. He was reared on a farm on Finley Creek, and at the age of twenty-three years was married, on the 11th of October, 1849, to Minerva J., a daughter of Charles Denny, one of the pioneer settlers from Kentucky. Mrs. Silvey was born in Kentucky, and after her marriage she and Mr. Silvey settled on their present farm of 324 acres, which was then raw land, heavily covered with timber. He has now 125 acres cleared and under cultivation, on which are erected a good dwelling-house and fair out-buildings. Their family of children are as follows: Charles, who was married, and is now deceased; Smiley, who is married, and resides in the county; Letitia Ann (deceased), wife of Cornelius Lofton; William, who is married and resides in the county; Catherine, wife of Frank Wright, of Douglas County; George, who was married, and is deceased; Jackson is married, and lives in Taney County, Mo.; Zerilda, wife of E. G. Denny; Susan, wife of John Wright; James, Elizabeth and Thomas. The family attend the Free Will Baptist Church, of which Mr. and Mrs. Silvey are members, and during the late war Mr. Silvey served in the Home Guards and State Militia for some time.

Nathan T. Smith was born in Roane County, Tenn., July 13, 1831, and is a son of William and Mary (Turner) Smith, also Tennesseeans. The family located in Webster County, Mo., about 1843, where the father became a successful husbandman, and served a number of years as justice of the peace. His death occurred in March, 1871. His wife survives him, and is in her eighty-third year. Nathan T. Smith came to Missouri with his parents when a lad twelve years old, and grew to mature years in Webster County. He remained with his father until he attained his majority, and in 1861 enlisted in the Missouri State troops, under Gov. Jackson's call, but at the end of six months joined the regular Confederate service, being with Col. Green's cavalry regiment, and served until receiving his discharge in the fall of 1863. He enlisted as a private, but was promoted to orderly sergeant, which position he held the most of the time during his service. He was at Elkhorn and Helena, and after receiving his discharge went to Texas, where he resided until the spring of 1866. While in that State he was married, July 30, 1865, to Elizabeth J. Roberts, a native of Roane County, Tennessee. She was reared and educated in her native State, and when a young lady eighteen years of age, came with her father, John J. Roberts, to Missouri. The latter served as justice of the peace in Tennessee, and died in Texas in September, 1883. Since 1866 Mr. Smith has been residing on his present farm, which consists of over 300 acres, with 150 under cultivation. He has a comfortable residence, and a good young orchard of over 100 trees just beginning to bear. Mrs. Smith was previously married to Hardin McPherson, who was a soldier in the Confederate army, and was killed at the battle of Wilson's Creek, August 10, 1861. One daughter was born to their marriage, Alice Mattie, wife of James Galbrith. To Mr. and Mrs. Smith have been born the following family: Mary Lucy (wife of James M. Toughstone), Jessie Lorena, John W., Bessie Adella and Oscar Lee. Two sons and one daughter died in childhood. The family attend the Christian Church, and Mr. Smith is a member of the Masonic fraternity, and is Master of Mount Olive Lodge, No. 439. He also belongs to the A. F. & A. M.

William L. Smith, editor and proprietor of the Marshfield *Chronicle*, is a native of Webster County, Mo., born May 19, 1857, being the son of C. C. and Sarah (Nichols) Smith. The father was born in Tennessee in 1829, and the mother in North Carolina in 1833. The family came to Webster County in 1844, settling twelve miles south of the county seat, and in 1869 moved to Marshfield. William L. Smith is the eldest of five children. He remained on his father's farm until about thirteen years of age, and since then has resided in Marshfield. He received a common-school education, and October 9, 1872, he entered the office of the Marshfield *Democrat*, where he began learning the printer's trade, and has since continued that calling. Since January, 1877, he has been publishing the *Chronicle*, which is newsy and full of interesting matter. Mr. Smith is a member of the Masonic fraternity, also a member of the I. O. O. F., and is Democratic in his political views.

Prof. William W. Thomas, superintendent of the Marshfield Public Schools, and one of the leading educators of this part of Missouri, is a native of Hastings, Mich., born April 22, 1861, being the eldest of three children born to the union of Edgar M. and Marietta (Fifield) Thomas. Edgar M. Thomas was born near Detroit, Mich., in 1834, and died in his native State in 1875. He was a farmer by occupation, and for some time was a resident of Grand Rapids, where he was engaged in the manufacture of pumps, but later he carried on the general insurance business. The mother, Mrs. Marietta (Fifield) Thomas, was born in New York State in 1844, and is now a resident of Webster County, Mo. Prof. William W. Thomas began life for himself at thirteen years of age. He first attended the public schools of Michigan, and after coming to Missouri he attended Henderson Academy. In 1888 he graduated at the Delaware (Ohio) Commercial College. In 1880 he began teaching school in Christian County, Mo., and in 1885 and 1886 he was associate principal of Henderson Academy. He came to Marshfield in the fall of 1887, took charge of the Marshfield schools and is doing good work. He is a self-made man in every sense, and is a successful and practical teacher. He was married December 25, 1886, to Miss Mary E. Langston, daughter of J. W. and Mary (Cargill) Langston, and a native of Greene County, Mo., born in 1864. One child, Edgar, who was born November 12, 1887, is the result of this union. Prof. Thomas is an earnest Republican in his political views, is a member of the I. O. O. F., and he and Mrs. Thomas are members of the Methodist Episcopal Church, South.

Rev. George W. Thompson was born on the top of Cumberland Mountain, in Marion County, Tenn., on the 19th of February, 1831, and is a brother of Andrew J. Thompson, whose sketch immediately follows. He was there reared to manhood, and in 1851 located in St. Louis, Mo., coming the following year to what is now Webster County, and locating near his present place of residence. He did his share in helping to improve the county, and assisted in laying out the town of Marshfield in August, 1855. January 6, 1859, he espoused Miss Mary L. Shook, who had come from her native State of Tennessee to Missouri when a miss of six years, and settled with her father, William B. Shook, in Webster County. Six days after their marriage they settled on their present farm, which was then raw land, and which consisted at first of forty acres. He has since purchased adjoining lands, and is now the owner of 280 acres, about 100 of which are cleared and under cultivation. His property is well improved with good, substantial buildings, and Mr. Thompson may well be proud of the success which has attended his efforts, for he began life a poor boy, but has acquired a nice property. He served about two months in the Home Guards during the war, and also served as justice of the peace at one time during this period. He is a member of the Agricultural Wheel, and since 1875 has been a local preacher in the Methodist Protestant Church, his wife being also a member of this denomination. The following are their children: George W., Jr., Francis Marion, William Jackson and Eva Ellar. Seven children died in infancy and early childhood.

Andrew J. Thompson, farmer and stock raiser, of Webster County, Mo., was born in Marion County, Tenn., May 16, 1833, and is a son of Moses Thompson, who was born in Virginia, and went to Alabama when a young man, where he met and married Miss Mary Thompson, who was born and partially reared in North Carolina. After residing about fifteen years in Alabama they moved to Marion County, Tenn., where they reared their family, and died about 1863. Andrew J. is the youngest of their ten children, all of whom lived to become the heads of families. He and one brother, David, enlisted in the Confederate army, the former being with a Texas company, and died near Little Rock, Ark. Andrew J. enlisted in May, 1862, and served as a private until the close of the war, being the greater portion of the time on detail duty in various capacities. He was in the hospital for a short time, and received his discharge at Marshall, Tex., in the spring of 1865. He was married in Hill County, Tex., August 16, 1860, to Miss Hannah Norman, a widow lady, and daughter of John McBride, who was originally a Kentuckian. She was born in Lauderdale County, Ala., but was reared principally in Kentucky, and after her marriage to Mr. Thompson moved to Arkansas, from which State he enlisted in the Confederate army. After the war they located in White County, Ark., where they were engaged in farming up to 1877, but sold out in November of that year, and came to their present farm of eighty acres. The land is well located, and is furnished with plenty of pure limestone water, and improved with good buildings. Mr. Thompson is president of the County Agricultural Wheel, a Master Mason, and his wife is a member of the Missionary Baptist Church. They have no children of their own, but have reared two orphan children.

William H. Triplett was born in Monroe County, Tenn., June 15, 1836, and is a son of James M. and Tircy (Freeman) Triplett, who were born in the Carolinas. In 1849 they located in Pope County, Ill., where they farmed and reared their family, and where the father's death occurred in the spring of 1886. William H. Triplett grew to manhood in Illinois, and was married in Pope County, September 25, 1856, to Miss Mary Jane Hazel, born March 25, 1838, a daughter of Alfred M. Hazel, both of whom were born in Illinois. After his marriage he farmed in Pope and Johnson Counties up to 1870, when, in the fall of that year, he located in Franklin County, Ark., and farmed three years. In the spring of 1874 he moved to Kansas, Cherokee County, but in the fall of 1875 came to Webster

County, Mo., where he purchased the farm of 240 acres where he now resides, on which he has made some valuable improvements. He has given land to his children, and now only has eighty acres, nearly all of which is under cultivation. He has about thirty-three acres in orchard, and has a comfortable home and good out-buildings. He is a Republican in politics, and while a resident of Illinois served four years as constable. He is a Master Mason, and he and wife are members of the Missionary Baptist Church, and are the parents of the following family: James A., born February 1, 1858, is married and resides near his father; William T., born April 7, 1860, is also married and resides near his father; Martha J., born June 6, 1862, wife of W. H. Newcomer; Della, born May 8, 1865, wife of J. D. Melton; Mary L., born January 16, 1868; Grant, born October 27, 1870; Charles F., born May 3, 1874, died September 7, 1878; Reuben W., born May 28, 1877, and Elsa Ann, born September 13, 1882. In 1881 Mr. Triplett engaged in the grist-milling business, and owned a one-half interest and carried on the mill for six years, but in 1887 exchanged his interest for another farm of eighty acres, fifty acres in cultivation, all in good condition, with eleven acres in young orchard.

Samuel C. Trimble. In every calling in life, whether of a professional, commercial or agricultural nature, there are always some men who attain the highest round in the ladder of success, and such a man is Mr. Trimble, who is a prosperous merchant of Seymour, Mo., and was born in what is now Webster County, Mo., on the 9th of April, 1850. His parents, Judge John C. and Rhoda (Proctor) Trimble, were born, reared and married in Kentucky, and about 1837 moved to Missouri, locating in what is now Webster County, where they cleared a farm and reared their family. He was elected the first judge of Webster County, and served sixteen consecutive years, and in January, 1883, engaged in the mercantile business in Seymour, the firm name being J. C. & S. C. Trimble. This business he carried on until his death, August 26, 1887. Samuel C. Trimble was reared to a farm life until sixteen years of age, and after working at the milling business for eight years in Webster County, began merchandising at Waldo, where he remained four years. The two following years were spent in the same business at Hardwell, and after the railroad was built at Seymour he located at this point, where he has since been a successful merchant, and carries a large and select stock of general merchandise. He also sells lumber for railroad purposes, and in every enterprise in which he has been engaged his efforts have been attended with the best of success. He was married in Wright County, Mo., on the 19th of December, 1872, to Miss Laura B. Freeman, a daughter of Littleton Freeman. She was born and reared in Wright County, and is the mother of three children: Anna Lee, Fannie May and Samuel E. Mr. and Mrs. Trimble are members of the Christian and Baptist Churches, respectively, and he is a Master Mason, and is Junior Warden of his lodge.

William Tunnell, of Ozark Township, Webster Co., Mo., is a North Carolinian, born November 6, 1821, being a son of Burgess and Penelope (Bumpus) Tunnell, who were of Virginia and North Carolina stock, respectively. They were married in the latter State, and about 1829 moved to Virginia, where the father died shortly after. His widow afterward married again, and moved to Henry County, Mo. William Tunnell grew to manhood in Virginia, and shortly after attaining his majority was married to Elizabeth Kinser, and moved to Missouri, arriving here November 3, 1843, and homesteaded and bought land in Webster County. In 1863 he moved to Marshfield and enlisted in the Home Guards, serving about one year, when he was called on guard duty to Springfield during the battle of Wilson's Creek, and was promoted to the rank of orderly. He had learned the blacksmith's trade in his youth, and for about six months, in 1862, was in the Government employ at Springfield. After moving to Marshfield he conducted a blacksmith shop for a number of years, but about two years after the war engaged in the hotel business, and continued that occupation for about five years. From that time until November, 1882, he was engaged in farming, and at the latter date was appointed to take charge of the county poor farm, and has about twenty-one persons under his care. He expects soon to resign his position, as his age is beginning to tell upon him. July 18, 1881, his wife was taken from him. To their union were born the following children: F. M., Joseph L., Nancy J.; Sarah C., wife of Daniel Hathaway; George W. and William J. F. M. Tunnell served in the Federal army during the Rebellion. Mr. Tunnell married his second wife, Mrs. Mary Beamy, in May, 1885. She was born in Indiana, but was reared in Iowa. Her maiden name was Casteel, and she settled in Webster County about 1853. They are members of the Missionary Baptist Church, and Mr. Tunnell belongs to the I. O. O. F.

Samuel W. Walton, merchant and lumber dealer and shipper, and postmaster of Diggins, Mo., is a native of the State, born in Cooper County November 25, 1846, and is a son of William P. Walton, who was born in Virginia, and who, about 1838, located in Cooper County, Mo., where he met and married Louisa J. Turley. The latter was also born in Missouri, and is a daughter of Samuel Turley, who was one of the early Kentucky settlers of Missouri. Mr. Walton was engaged in farming in Cooper County for a number of years, and about 1868 moved to Henry County, where he died about 1873. His wife survives him, and resides in Eureka, Kas., with one of her sons. Samuel W. Walton was reared and educated in his native county, and after becoming grown engaged in the mercantile business in La Mine, Mo., where he sold goods and was postmaster for five years. In March, 1882, he moved to Webster County and settled on his present place of residence, which was before the Kansas City, Springfield & Memphis Railroad was established. He erected him a store-house, and was appointed postmaster of Stella, but at the end of one year resigned, and the office was discontinued. The post-office of Diggins was established in June, 1886, and he was appointed and still serves as postmaster. He built his present business house in 1887, and is carrying on a thriving general mercantile business. He also sells and ships lumber, and handles on an average 1,000 car loads per year. January 1, 1866, he wedded Miss Laura Tyler, who was born and reared in Cooper County, and died May 4, 1880, being a daughter of William Tyler, who was one of the early settlers of Missouri from Virginia. She became the mother of six children: Daisy D., wife of James R. Kibler; Charles B., who is married, and in business with his father; Hattie T., William P., Mollie E. and Jesse B. On Christmas Day, 1883, Mr. Walton married Miss Clara E. Layton, a native of Webster County, and a daughter of T. G. Layton. They have two children, James E. and Freeman. Mr. Walton is a member of the Baptist Church.

Oliver Wells, postmaster at Marshfield, Mo., and dealer in books, stationery, etc., is a native of Lincoln County, N. C., where he was born February 19, 1845, being the son of James and Mary J. Wells, and grandson of James Wells. The latter was a native of Wales, who came to the United States and settled in South Carolina, serving as a soldier in the Revolutionary War, and taking part in the battles of King's Mountain, Ramseaur's Mill and other minor engagements in that section of the country. He died and was buried near Yorkville, S. C., in his ninety-first year. The maternal grandfather of Mr. Wells was a Methodist preacher, a Virginian by birth. James Wells, father of our subject, was born in South Carolina in 1799, and died in North Carolina in 1858. He was a contractor and builder by occupation. Mary Munday, Oliver's mother, was born near Spottsylvania Court House, Va., in 1803, and died in North Carolina in 1885. Of this union twelve children were born, Oliver being the youngest; eight are now living. Oliver Wells obtained a common-school education, and enlisted in the Confederate army, when but a boy of sixteen, on the 15th day of June, 1861, in Company K, First Regiment North Carolina Volunteers, D. H. Hill, colonel commanding. This regiment reorganized, and was afterward known as the Eleventh North Carolina State Troops, and Mr. Wells was made a member of Company I, in which he remained until the close of the war. He was twice wounded, first at Gettysburg in the memorable Picket charge, again at Bristoe Station, on the Orange & Alexander Railroad, and was taken prisoner three times. He took a part in all the hard-fought battles of Lee's army, holding several positions of honor and trust. After the surrender he learned the brick-layer's trade. In 1868 he went to East Tennessee, and in 1869 to Kansas, and on the 20th of April, 1870, he arrived at Marshfield, Mo., working at his trade in Marshfield and Springfield until 1885, when he was appointed postmaster by President Cleveland. He has filled that position to the satisfaction of all, and is one of the country's best citizens. In 1879 he married Miss Martha W. McCulloch, a native of Missouri, born in the year 1856. They have four children, viz.: Mary Edith, Daniel Lee, Clara Jane and Thomas. In 1880 Mr. Wells took the census of Ozark Township, the township in which Marshfield is located, and has filled the office of constable in that township for two terms. He is a member of three secret societies, and is an agreeable and accommodating gentleman.

P. P. Wells deserves honorable mention as one of the prosperous stock men and farmers of Webster County, Mo. His birth occurred December 4, 1846, in Orange County, N. C., and he is a son of W.

W. and Rachel (Compton) Wells, who were also born and reared in Orange County, their marriage taking place in that county. They made their native State their home until 1851, when they located on a farm in what is now Webster County, Mo., where they reared their family and still reside. Their son, P. P. Wells, received a good common-school education, and remained with and assisted his father on the farm until he attained his twenty-first birthday, when he began the battle of life for himself, and was married February 26, 1867, to Miss Mary E. Pumphrey, of Ozark County, and soon after located on a farm in Dallas County, where he was engaged in tilling the soil for several years. After spending two years in Ozark Township they returned to Dallas Township, where Mr. Wells began handling and trading in stock, which business he has made quite a success. He ships several car loads of stock annually, which net him a nice income per year. Nearly all of his farm, which amounts to eighty-six acres, is under cultivation, and furnished with fair buildings. Besides this property he owns a good residence and fifteen acres of land adjoining Henderson. His is a Master Mason, a Democrat in politics, and he and wife have reared the following family: Rachel F. (the eldest, was the wife of J. D. Foster, and died in June, 1888), W. C., J. F., Rosa E. and Maggie M. Mrs. Wells is a daughter of William G. Pumphrey, one of the pioneers of Ozark County.

R. Jason White, merchant of Seymour, Mo., is a son of Moses and Amanda J. (Freeman) White, both of whom were born in Tennessee. They were married in Wright County, Mo., and have since been engaged in farming in that county. R. Jason White, whose name heads this sketch, grew to manhood in Wright County, and at the age of twenty years began clerking in a drug store in Hartville, and in 1881 came from that town to Mansfield, and followed the same occupation in that place for some time. In February, 1884, he came to Seymour, and for four years was a clerk in the general mercantile establishment of S. C. Trimble, and at the end of that time engaged in the general grocery business, which is proving quite a success. He was married in Webster County, on the 11th of October, 1885, to Frona Goss, a daughter of Jacob Goss, of Webster County. She was born, reared and educated in the county, and is the mother of two children, Charles H. and Verba. She is a member of the Missionary Baptist Church. Mr. White served as a member of the town board in 1887, and was town treasurer in 1886.

Jonathan D. Whittenburg, farmer and stock raiser of Ozark Township, and one of the leading men of Webster County, is a native of Northern Georgia, and was born November 26, 1836, being the son of James and Sarah C. Whittenburg. The father was born in Tennessee in 1809, and now resides in Ozark Township, this county. In early life he removed from Tennessee to Georgia, and in 1857 the family immigrated to Missouri, settling on the Ozark, in Webster County. The mother, whose maiden name was Davis, was born in Tennessee in 1804, and died in Webster County, Mo., in 1878. Jonathan D. Whittenburg was reared on his father's farm, and was a pupil in the country schools. He began farming for himself at the age of twenty-four years, and is now the owner of 200 acres of good land, all well improved. He is the inventor of "Whittenburg's Safety Flood Fence," which was patented September 22, 1885, and which is one of the best fences of the kind ever placed on the market. Mr. Whittenburg was married in 1860 to Miss Mary J. Kilburn, who was born in Lawrence County, Tenn., in 1839, and who is the daughter of Allen and Millie (Watkins) Kilburn. Mr. and Mrs. Whittenburg are the parents of four children: Thomas, born in 1861; Martha, born in 1866; Margaret, born in 1867, and Dickey, born in 1875. Mr. Whittenburg is a Democrat in politics, and he and Mrs. Whittenburg are leading and much esteemed members of the Christian Church.

David A. Williams, M. D., a leading physician of Webster County, Mo., was born in Henry County, Tenn., September 18, 1854, and is a son of Richard M. and Lucy (Walker) Williams, who were also born in Tennessee, the former's death occurring at Eureka Springs, Ark., whither he had gone for his health, June 19, 1885, and the latter's in Henry County, Tenn., when David A. was quite young. After his wife's death Mr. Williams married Mary C. Callaway, who is still living in Webster County. They resided in Tennessee until 1870, when they came to Missouri, and purchased the farm on which Mrs. Williams is now living. He was a successful farmer, and in his political views was a Democrat. He belonged to the Christian Church and the Masonic fraternity. During the Mexican War he served under Gen. Taylor, and participated in all the principal battles fought under that leader. Seven children were born to his marriage with Miss Walker, six of whom are living: J. T., George W., Richard C., David A., Annie (wife of John Butts) and Willie; Charles is deceased. Four children were born to his last marriage: Charles T., James R., Zanoda F. and Marion E. Dr. David A. Williams was educated in the seminary at Lebanon, Mo., and in 1879 began studying medicine under his brother, George W., and during 1881 and 1882 he attended the Missouri Medical College, receiving a diploma in 1883, since which time he has practiced his profession with good success in Niangua, Mo. January 1, 1883, he was married to Miss Mollie E. Thompson, a daughter of John A. Thompson, by whom he has two children: Gertrude, who died when an infant, and Hallie E., who is now three years old. Dr. and Mrs. Williams are members of the Christian Church, and he is a Mason and Democrat.

Malcolm Wilson. Prominent among the leading and successful farmers of Ozark Township, and among the Democratic politicians of considerable note, stands the name of the above mentioned gentleman, who was born in North Carolina March 21, 1833. His parents, Nathan and Drusilla (Tew) Wilson, were both natives of Sampson County, N. C. The father died in Tennessee at seventy-six years of age, and the mother died in her native State when fifty-four years of age. Their son, Malcolm Wilson, was the ninth in a family of fourteen children, six of whom are now living. Agricultural pursuits formed his chief employment during boyhood, and his educational training was received in the country schools. In 1855 he was united in marriage to Miss Martha Spense, who died in August, 1864, leaving two children, John A. and William H. The same year of his marriage he moved to Benton County, Tenn., and engaged in farming, which he continued until 1864, when he began the carpenter's business, and carried that on in Tennessee and other States until 1876, when he moved to Missouri, settling on his present farm, about two miles north of Marshfield, where he has 165 acres of good land, and where he is considered one of the best farmers in Webster County. In 1869 Mr. Wilson married Mrs. Volumia I. Smith, whose maiden name was Poindexter. She was born in Tennessee December 31, 1832, and was the daughter of F. A. Poindexter. Mr. Wilson has always been an ardent supporter of the principles of the Democratic party, and cast his first presidential vote for James Buchanan. In the fall of 1888 he ran as the independent Democratic candidate for representative. Mr. Wilson has made his own way in life, and has been quite successful. He lost $1,000 by the failure of the bank at Marshfield, in 1884, and has taken a leading part in the litigation caused by the failure of that institution.

CAMDEN COUNTY.

R. H. C. Appleton, a dealer in general merchandise and a farmer of Adair Township, Camden County, was born in that county January 22, 1854, and is a son of John and Levina (Elmore) Appleton, both natives of Tennessee. John Appleton, who was a blacksmith and farmer, was born in 1823; he moved from Tennessee to Jefferson City, Mo., and afterward located at Linn Creek, Mo. He was twice married, and was the father of sixteen children, eleven of whom are still living. The paternal grandfather of our subject was John Appleton, a native of South Carolina, who afterward went to Tennessee, and was a farmer, millwright and carpenter; he served in the War of 1812, participating in the battle of New Orleans, and his wife was Polly (Pepper) Appleton, of Virginia. John Appleton, Sr., died in 1843. Mrs. Levina Appleton died in 1863. She was a daughter of Ebenezer Elmore, of Tennessee. R. H. C. Appleton has devoted the greater part of his attention to the pursuit of farming, but in 1879, as a member of the firm of A. J. Campbell & Co., he engaged in the mercantile business at Osage Iron Works Post-office, which he continued until 1881; in the latter year he purchased and moved to a farm of 150 acres in Adair Township, which he still owns, and has about 100 acres under cultivation. He also owns other landed property, in all amounting to about 622 acres. In March, 1887, he purchased a new stock of general merchandise, and in partnership with Henry Dougherty opened a store at Osage Iron Works, which they still conduct with success. In 1881 Mr. Appleton married Miss Rosa E. Carroll, who was born in Camden County, Mo., in December, 1855, and is a daughter of George and Cordelia A. Carroll, natives of Kentucky. Of the children born to Mr. and Mrs. Appleton only one survives, Myrtle Eve. In politics Mr. Appleton is a Democrat.

Dr. John W. Armstrong (deceased). The Armstrong family first became represented in the United States a short time previous to the Revolutionary War, and were of Anglo-Saxon origin. The great-grandfather, James Armstrong, located in Fauquier County, Va., and there his son, Mason Armstrong, was born. The latter came to Kentucky with two of his brothers, Roland and James, about 1810, and here they married and settled down to tilling the soil, but Mason remained single until after the War of 1812, in which struggle he took an active part under Gen. Harrison, and then returned home and married Mary Crook, who was born in Madison County, Ky., and was a daughter of John Crook and a sister of Maj. Crook. Mason Armstrong was a minister of the Methodist Episcopal Church, and died in 1856, at the age of seventy-two years. His son, James M. Armstrong, was born in Kentucky, and graduated from the Transylvania Medical College, of Lexington, Ky., in the spring of 1844, and in 1855 came with his family to Missouri and located in Elston Station, Cole County, where he resided until the breaking out of the late Civil War, when he enlisted as a surgeon in the service and served until the close. He then returned to his home, and located with his family at Sarcoxie, where he died in March, 1884. His wife, whom he married October 27, 1837, and whose maiden name was Mary J. Searcy, was also born in Kentucky, and is an active worker in the Methodist Episcopal Church, South. Dr. John W. Armstrong is the eldest of their ten children, and was born in Kentucky on the 26th of September, 1838, and there resided until 1856, when he came to Missouri with his parents and located on a farm. He attended school at Liberty and Danville, Ky., and was a close student all his life, and wrote a biography of the Armstrong family, which is considered quite valuable. He became eminent in his professional career, and was a man of decided mental endowments, being the editor and publisher of the *Rustic Stoutland*, which paper he also founded. He removed his machinery to Linn Creek, thence to Lebanon, but the paper still retains its original name. The first paper was issued on the 14th of June, 1873. He was a man of very active habits, and owing to his excellent judgment was a man of influence wherever he resided, and was alike esteemed for his social and business qualities. In the fall of 1860 he came to Camden County to practice medicine, but in 1862 enlisted in the Confederate army, in the Trans-Mississippi Department, Company K, Sixteenth Missouri Infantry, as a private, and made an honorable and faithful soldier. July 4, 1863, he was wounded at Helena, Ark., which finally resulted in his death October 28, 1884, at the age of forty-six years, one month and two days. August 27, 1865, he espoused Miss Lucy E. Dodson, at Bonham, Texas, but she was born in Camden County, Mo., on the 30th of January, 1844. [The sketch of her father, Dr. Dodson, appears in this work.] To their union the following children were born: James W., Joseph S., Mary Ella (Sellers), Benjamin A., John R., Charles H. and Elizabeth D. Mrs. Armstrong lives on the home place with her family, and is an active member of the Methodist Episcopal Church, and owns over 600 acres of valuable land, about 200 acres of which are well under cultivation.

George Arnhold, a prosperous miller and farmer of Camden County, Mo., was born near Frankfort, Prussia, on the 14th of February, 1835, and is a son of Henry and Elizabeth (Moore) Arnhold, who were also natives of Prussia, the father being a miller by trade, which occupation he followed the greater part of his life; he was the owner of a mill near Frankfort-on-the-Main. He and wife both died in their native land, having become the parents of eight children, five of whom are living: Christopher, who resides in Cole County, Mo.; John, who manages the old home mill in Germany; Sophia and Dora, who are also in Germany, and George, who is the youngest of the family. He learned the miller's trade with his father, and after attaining the requisite age to enter the German army, concluded to come to America, and took passage at Bremen, and after a forty-four days' voyage landed at New York City. Here he remained about five months working at his trade, and then went to Rochester, N Y., thence to Detroit, and afterward to Chicago, then to St. Louis, and finally to Jefferson City, Mo., in 1855. He was in the latter city when the war broke out, and he enlisted in the Home Guards, serving two years and participating in several hard skirmishes. He located on his present farm of 200 acres in 1878, and since that time has made many improvements, and has about half of his farm under cultivation. His grist-mill is located on the Big Niangua, six miles west of Linn Creek, and is one of the most extensive in Camden County. In connection with this he operates a saw-mill, farms, and is extensively engaged in raising stock, having met with good success in all these undertakings. He was married in 1859 to Miss Dora Schortt, a native of Germany, by whom he has seven children: August, William, Ameil, Henry, Louisa, Sophia and Clara. Mr. and Mrs. Arnhold are members of the Lutheran Church, and he belongs to the I. O. O. F. lodge.

E. F. Avery, another enterprising and industrious farmer of Osage Township, was born in Londonderry, Rockingham Co., N. H., August 18, 1830, and is the son of Foster and Rebecca (Robinson) Avery, natives of Massachusetts and New Hampshire, respectively. The great-grandfather Avery was a native of Scotland, and on the Robinson side the ancestry can be traced back to the "Mayflower." Foster Avery was but nine years of age when he went with his parents to New Hampshire, and in that State he passed his last days. He was a farmer by occupation. He was the father of eight children, four sons and four daughters. Jeremiah M., Ephraim F., Sarah, wife of Louis Stiles, of Massachusetts, and Eda A., wife of Nathaniel Ballou, who now resides in Iowa, are the ones now living. E. F. Avery was reared and educated in New Hampshire, and afterward went to Lowell, Mass., where he worked in a cotton mill until twenty-one years of age. In 1851 he went to Wisconsin, locating in Waupaca County, where he remained for some time, and then moved to Eau Claire County. He continued to live there until 1871, engaged in farming, and then came to Laclede County, Mo. In 1872 he was employed on the St. Louis & San Francisco Railroad, where he remained until 1876, at which date he was employed on the Missouri Pacific Railroad as freight conductor. In 1878 he retired from the railroad business and moved on his farm in Laclede County, where he lived until 1886, when he moved to his present property in Camden County. This consists of 294 acres, with a good portion under cultivation, and is considered one of the finest farms in the county. Mr. Avery was married in 1851 to Miss Olive H. Cole, a native of Vermont. To them were born five children, four now living: Emma, wife of J. R. Pierce, is now residing in Wisconsin; Edna C., wife of John B. French, of St. Louis; Roy, married to Miss Effie T. Churchill, and Charles E. While living in Wisconsin Mr. Avery was chairman of the board of supervisors one term.

Dr. Jacob M. Bollinger, a successful practicing physician of Camden County, Mo., was born in Hickory County, Mo., February 12, 1850, being a son of Wright M. and Sarah A. (McSwain) Bollinger, and grandson of Jacob and Sarah (Moreland) Bollinger. The grandfather was of German nationality, and moved from Tennessee to Illinois, from there to Camden County, Mo., in 1833, and finally located in Polk County, where he died. He was a farmer by occupation; was a private in the War of 1812, and was at the battle of Mobile, Ala. The maternal grandparents (Salina Hall grandmother's maiden name) moved from Kentucky to Polk County, Mo., about 1837. He was a farmer and stone-cutter by occupation. Wright Bollinger was born in East Tennessee in 1812, and died July 10, 1882. His wife was born in Kentucky in 1822, and is still living. He moved with his parents from Tennessee to Illinois, from there to Camden County, Mo., in 1833, and then to Hickory County, Mo., in 1837. He was in the Home Guards in the late war. Of the five children born to his marriage, all are living in Hickory County, Mo., with the exception of Dr. Bollinger. These children are named as follows: Jacob M., Joseph C., Salina D. Mashburn, Sarah F. Bollinger and Jerusha B. Richardson. Dr. Bollinger spent his youthful days in Hickory County, Mo., and at the age of nineteen years began farming. He was married August 30, 1868, to Miss Margaret R. Dixon, who was born June 30, 1854, in Greene County, Mo., and who was the daughter of Hiram and Nancy R. (Pitts) Dixon, both natives of Kentucky. Mr. and Mrs. Dixon moved from Kentucky to Hickory County, Mo., with their parents, were married in the last named State, and there passed the most of their lives. He was a farmer, and served in the late war. They were the parents of ten children, five now living: William M., Sarah J. Moore, George W., John T. and Mrs. Margaret R. Bollinger. The maternal grandmother of Mrs. Bollinger, Rhoda (Ricks) Pitts, was born in Kentucky, and moved from that State to Hickory County, Mo. Dr. Bollinger became the father of seven children by his marriage, five now living: George F., Nancy A., Hiram M., Lee and Rosa May. Those deceased are Wright M. and an infant unnamed. Dr. Bollinger began reading medicine under able instruction at fourteen years of age, in 1874, and practiced in Polk and Hickory Counties from 1879 to 1882.

He attended Joplin College of Physicians and Surgeons in 1882 and 1883, graduating in the last named year. He then engaged in the practice of his profession at Elixir Springs, Dallas County, Mo., also practiced in Elkton, Hickory Co. in 1884, and came to Mack's Creek in March, 1885, where he has since been occupied in the active duties of his profession. He has bought property and permanently located at Mack's Creek. He is the owner of 130 acres in one tract, forty acres in another, and a good frame house in the town, with land adjoining. He is a member of the Masonic fraternity, and is a Republican in politics, casting his first presidential vote for U. S. Grant in 1872.

Valentine Bowers, merchant and postmaster at Decaturville, Mo., was born in Carter County, Tenn., in 1855, and is a son of Rev. Abraham N. and Mary (Ellis) Bowers, and grandson of Valentine Bowers, who was also a minister, and who lived to be about eighty-six years of age. Rev. Abraham N. Bowers and wife were born in Carter County, Tenn., and after they had a family of four children moved to Gentry County, Mo., going two years later to Morgan County, Mo., where the father resided until 1881, when his son Valentine took him to Eureka Springs, Ark., where he died on the 21st of August, 1881, at the age of fifty-five years. He was actively engaged in ministerial work throughout his career in Missouri, and by his consistent Christian life, and earnest endeavor, did much to further the cause of Christianity. His widow is still living on the home farm in Morgan County, in her fifty-eighth year, and always labored earnestly to aid her husband in his ministerial duties. The following are her children who are living: Daniel, Valentine, Reece, James, John, Jacob, Isaac, Polly and Barbara. Those deceased were Archey, Lyda, Abigail, and two infants who died unnamed. Valentine Bowers attained his maturity in Morgan County, Mo., and obtained a good common and high-school education, and prepared himself for teaching by also attending normal school. He then followed the occupation of pedagoguing for eight years in Morgan and Camden Counties, and in March, 1883, engaged in the mercantile business at Decaturville, where he has since successfully held forth. He was appointed postmaster of the town in 1883, and since his residence here has held the office of school director. Miss Mattie Oszmus became his wife on the 28th of October, 1881. She was born in Pettis County, Mo., and is a daughter of Andrew and Jane Oszmus, who were natives of Germany and Indiana, respectively. The father came to America when nineteen years of age, landing at New Orleans, and afterward located in Indiana, where he was married. He then moved to Pettis County, Mo., and at the close of the war to Camden County, where he is still living, engaged in farming, near Linn Creek. The following are his children: Maggie, Willie, Mattie and Mary (deceased). Mr. and Mrs. Bowers are the parents of one child, named Gracie. They belong to the Baptist Church, and he is a member of the A. F. & A. M., and in his political views is a Democrat.

Joseph W. Burhans, merchant, farmer and stock dealer, and the presiding judge of Camden County, Mo., was born in the State of

New York October 10, 1842, his father and mother, James and Eliza (Brown) Burhans, being natives of New York and Connecticut, and of English and German descent, respectively. In 1845, after their marriage, they moved to Rock County, Wis., where they engaged in farming. The father enlisted to serve in the War of 1812. He died July 1, 1865, in Rock County, Wis., at the age of sixty-nine years and six months, his wife's death occurring in Stoutland, Mo., in 1883, at the age of sixty-six years. Her grandfather was a soldier in the Revolutionary War, and she was the second wife of Mr. Burhans, and an active worker in the Baptist Church. The following are the names of their children: James W. Burhans, Richland, Mo. (half brother); Joseph W., Lavinia C. (Hudson), Mary E. (Manes), Stephen S., Frank D., Nancy E. and Adora. The last two children are deceased. Joseph W. Burhans grew to manhood in Wisconsin, and after obtaining sufficient education engaged in pedagoguing, which occupation he followed in Mason, Tazewell and Cass Counties, Ill., for about ten years, after which he came to Missouri (in July, 1872), locating in Stoutland, where he is now engaged in general merchandising, and is doing a business of over $20,000 per annum. He owns several large farms, including a tract of 2,000 acres in Kansas. In 1886 he was elected judge of Camden County on the Republican ticket, and is always one of the first men in the county to patronize worthy public enterprises and to aid church and educational institutions. He is one of the wealthiest men in the county, and deserves much credit for the success which has attended his efforts, for all his property, with the exception of about $800, has been acquired by his own exertions. On the 2d of August, 1871, he was united in marriage to Miss Lizzie Waite, who was born and reared in Vermont. She moved to Illinois in 1867, and is a daughter of Jacob U. and Elizabeth (Ramsdall) Waite, who were also born in Vermont, and died in 1879 and 1872, respectively. They were the parents of the following children: Lizzie, Mary E., Daniel, Emma, George, Lottie (deceased), Pliny J. and Eva.

L. P. Chalfant is a son of David H. and grandson of David Chalfant, of Chester County, Penn., the latter being of Quaker origin, who was drafted to serve in the Revolutionary War. The Quakers being opposed to fighting, a dispute arose between his parents and the man he was bound out to as to who would pay the penalty of the draft, when he ran away and joined Washington's army at Valley Forge, and was severely wounded at the battle of Brandywine, from the effects of which he died at the age of seventy-eight years. He was born in Chester County, Penn., but moved to and reared his family in Fayette County, and there followed the occupations of farming and blacksmithing. His son, David H. Chalfant, was his third child, and spent his life in Fayette County, dying in 1875. He and wife, whose maiden name was Eliza Patterson, became the parents of seven daughters and two sons, only two of the family being now alive: L. P., and Martha, wife of H. C. Gearing, residents of Pittsburg, Penn. Mrs. Chalfant, who was a consistent member of the Methodist Episcopal Church, died in 1852; was a daughter of Col. Robert Patterson, a native of Pennsylvania, who obtained his title in the War of 1812, being a colonel under Gen. W. H. Harrison. His family consisted of five children, four daughters and one son, whom he reared in Fayette County, Penn. He represented that county a number of years in the State Legislature. L. P. Chalfant, whose name heads this sketch, was born in Fayette County, Penn., in 1822, and remained under the home roof until about twenty years of age, when he went to Pittsburg, and began working at his trade, that of blacksmithing, which he had previously learned, but after a short time hired out as a deck hand on the steamboat "Mayflower," and afterward became fireman on the "Expert" under his uncle. He went up the Arkansas River to Little Rock, where he gave up his position on the boat, and resumed work at his trade in a foundry, continuing there about thirteen months, then rejoined the "Expert" as assistant engineer, and returned to Pittsburg in the spring of 1844. He afterward worked on the steamer "Majestic," running between Pittsburg, Penn., and Cincinnati, Ohio, during the summer, and in the fall he went back to the Arkansas River again on the steamer "Archer." In the following spring he returned to Pittsburg; boated on the Ohio River during the summer, when he went with the steamer "Archer" to St. Louis, where the boat ran for awhile on the Upper Mississippi. Late in the fall he went up the Missouri River, where he spent the winter of 1845-46, and arrived at St. Louis in the spring. From 1846 to 1855 he was engaged as engineer on various boats, and running on all the principal rivers emptying into the Mississippi, making his home at St. Louis until 1855, when he came to Linn Creek, and worked for McClurg, Murphy & Co. until 1862, and two years later returned to steamboating on the Mississippi River, being connected with the boat "Minnehaha." At a later period he returned to Linn Creek on the "Zouave," and a short time afterward purchased his present farm, and on which he has since lived. He helped to build the steamer "Emma" for Draper, McClurg & Co., which boat he managed for about ten years, and also made trips on other boats for this company. In the fall of 1847 he made trips up the Osage River on the "St. Louis Oak," and is one of the oldest Missouri River engineers now living. When the war broke out he enlisted in the Forty-seventh Enrolled Missouri Militia, of which he was captain and adjutant, and was also captain of the Ninth Provisional Enrolled Missouri Militia, and during his two years' service was in no regular engagement. He served as Deputy United States Marshal under Mr. Sitton in 1861, and under Mr. Wallace in 1862. In March, 1848, he was married to Maria Russell, in St. Louis, who was born in Philadelphia, Penn., and was brought to St. Louis, Mo., when about four years of age, where she was reared to maturity. Her father, Isaiah Russell, was an old steamboat pilot and mate between St. Louis and New Orleans, and was pilot on the gun-boat "Essex," his son James being on the "Arkansas" when they had a fight below Vicksburg. The former was victorious, and the father saw his son crawl up the bank, as his boat struck the shore, and make his escape. Mr. Chalfant and wife became the parents of seven sons and four daughters, all of the latter dying in childhood save Joan Hester, who lived to be fourteen years of age. The sons' names are as follows: Joab V., James L., Henry W., William D., Edward C., Francis A. and George R. Mr. Chalfant is a Republican in politics, originally a Whig, and was a delegate to the State convention, in 1870, at Jefferson City, and at St. Louis, Mo., in 1872. He is a member of the A. F. & A. M., and is temperate in his habits.

H. W. Chalfant, circuit clerk of Camden County, and one of the prominent men of the county, was born in the city of St. Louis April 28, 1855, being the son of Louis P. and Maria (Russell) Chalfant, both natives of Pennsylvania, the father born in Montgomery County and the mother in Philadelphia. Louis P. Chalfant when nineteen years of age went on the river to learn engineering and boating, which business he followed for a number of years, principally on the Mississippi and Missouri Rivers. He continued boating until about sixty years of age, and located in Camden County, Mo., in July, 1855, at Linn Creek, where he followed boating on the Osage River. He served three years in the State troops during the late war, and after cessation of hostilities he purchased a farm on the Wet Auglaize River, which he still owns and where he is now living. The mother of our subject came to St. Louis with her parents when there were but few families living there, and purchased a farm on which a part of the city is now standing. Her father was a pilot on the Mississippi River, and was in the United States navy employ at the time of his death, running a Government vessel. He was aboard the gun-boat "Essex" when she had her battle with the "Arkansas," at the time she ran the blockade. H. W. Chalfant was but an infant when he came to Linn Creek with his parents, and here he grew to maturity, receiving such education as the schools of those days afforded. He was reared to farm life, and followed this occupation until elected to the office of sheriff in 1884, which position he held one term. In 1886 he was elected to the circuit clerk and recorder's office, which position he now holds. He is also engaged in farming, and is one of the substantial and enterprising citizens of the county. He was justice of the peace two terms before elected sheriff. He was married December 27, 1877, to Miss Sarah A. Smith, a native of Camden County, who bore him four children: Ida M., Sarah M., Fred G. and Florence G. Mr. and Mrs. Chalfant are members of the Christian Church.

A. S. Churchill, late editor of the *People's Tribune*, at Linn Creek, was born in Laclede County, Mo., October 15, 1866, and is the son of C. B. and Elizabeth (Ellis) Churchill, the father a native of Kentucky and the mother of Missouri. He is one of six children, five now living: Effie, wife of Roy Avery; Armistead S.; Lena B., wife of Dr. D. H. Kouns; Harry and John, at home. The one deceased was named Edith, and her death occurred in 1873. A. S. Churchill, subject of this sketch, remained and assisted on the farm until 1884, and received a liberal education. In 1884 he came to Linn Creek and clerked in the store of his father for a short time, when he took charge of the drug store and ran it for one year. During the summer of 1886 he was engaged in farming, and in August of the same year he returned to the store, remained one year, and then taught one term of school. In January, 1888, he, in partnership with E. F. Shubert, founded the *People's Tribune*, and continued but a short time when Mr. Churchill bought out his partner and continued the publication alone until January 1, 1889, when he leased his paper to E. F. Shubert and W. T. S. Agee. Mr. Churchill is now employed as clerk in the store of F. Hooker, and is a promising young man.

S. E. Darnell, general merchant and postmaster at Climax Springs, Mo., was born in Ohio in 1844, and is a son of Samuel and Nancy (Logan) Darnell, natives of Pennsylvania and Ohio, respectively, the former's birth occurring in 1820. He moved from his native State to Ohio when a boy, and in 1869 located in Camden County, Mo., where he was engaged in carpentering and millwrighting. His parents, Samuel and Hannah (Tibbs) Darnell, were Virginians, and became early residents of Ohio, where they spent the remainder of their days, the father being engaged in carpentering and boat building. The maternal grandparents, Moses and Jane (Brookhaw) Logan, were born in Ireland and Ohio, respectively. The former crossed the ocean and settled in Ohio, where he was engaged in farming until his death. S. E. Darnell, whose name heads this sketch, is one of seven children, six now living, whose names are as follows: John, Anna (Lane), Richard, Caroline (Carter), Lewis Darnell and S. E. The latter spent his early life in his native State, and at the age of twenty-four embarked on the sea of life for himself, and in 1882 moved to Camden County, Mo., and a year later to Climax Springs, where he established his present general mercantile business, which stock is valued at about $2,000. For the first six months he was in partnership with George Blevins, but has since been sole proprietor, and has managed the business alone. He is a Democrat in politics, and since 1888 has been postmaster of the town. In 1874 he wedded Miss Anna Griesel, who was born in Germany in 1856, and is a daughter of George and Catherine (Leidheiser) Griesel, who were also Germans, and came to America in 1861, settling in Camden County. Their children are as follows: Anna (Darnell), Adam, William, George, Louisa, Matilda, Sophia, Antulp and Della. Mr. and Mrs. Darnell are the parents of the following children: Ardella, Emma, James, Cora and Everett. Mr. Darnell is a Mason.

S. J. Davis, blacksmith at Linn Creek, was born in St. Francois County, Mo., October 28, 1832, and is the son of Severe and Sarah (Parrick) Davis, natives of Kentucky and North Carolina, respectively. The father immigrated with his family to St. Francois County, Mo., at an early day, and there died. He was a successful farmer. In about 1844 the widow and family immigrated to Camden County, and located on the Little Niangua River. There were plenty of Indian camps, and the place was very wild. The mother was afterward married to Benjamin Shumate, and they moved to Laclede County, Mo., where she died. Of the six children born to her first marriage S. J. Davis is the only one now living. He was about twelve years of age when he came to this county, and here he was reared on the farm. At the age of seventeen he was apprenticed to learn the blacksmith trade, which he learned at Buffalo, remaining about six years. In 1849 he came to Camden County, and located at Mack's Creek, where he carried on the business for himself. In 1861 he came to Linn Creek, where he has since conducted the business alone. He is also an undertaker, and manufactures coffins and furniture. In 1861 he enlisted in the State Militia, and for about three years was company blacksmith. He was married in 1847 to Miss Mary Sharp, by whom he has one child, deceased. His second marriage was in 1854, to Miss Margaret Johnson, who bore him two children, one living, Cornelia. His third marriage was to Miss Catherine Johnson, by whom he had four children, one living, John W. His present wife is Miss Elizabeth Skinner, by whom he has four children: Sarah, Belle, Mattie and Tea. Mr. and Mrs. Davis are members of the Methodist Episcopal Church; he is a member of the Masonic fraternity, the I. O. O. F. and Agricultural Wheel. He has held the office of justice of the peace for some four years.

Henry Debery, farmer, was born in Carroll County, Ohio, December 5, 1847, being a son of Thomas and Emma (Johnson) Debery, who were born in Maryland and New Jersey, respectively. They both became residents of Ohio when very young, and were reared and married in Carroll County. When about eighteen years of age the father was crippled by falling from an apple tree, and he afterward learned the shoemaker's trade, following this occupation until he came to Missouri in 1861. He then resided on the farm in Glaize Township until his death, in 1875, at the age of sixty-six years. He was a member of the Presbyterian Church while residing in Ohio, but after coming to Missouri united with the Methodist Episcopal Church, in which he was an active member. He was also an active politician, and a strong Union man during the war, and furnished the Government with valuable information regarding the people and country. His wife is still living, and resides on the home farm in Camden County. Their eight children are named as follows: Henry, Alexander, John, George; Mary, wife of D. R. Miller; Albert, Isaac and Thomas C. Henry Debery attained his majority in Camden County, and received a fair education in the common schools. At the early age of sixteen years he enlisted in the Second Missouri Light Artillery, at Lebanon, Battery K, serving mostly at St. Louis and along the Mississippi River. In 1865 his company was transferred to the plains and Montana to fight the Indians, and he participated in the battle fought on Powder River in Montana, which lasted about fifteen days. During this siege the troops suffered severely from hunger, and were finally obliged to eat their own horses and mules to keep from starving to death. From this point they returned to St. Louis and were disbanded. Mr. Debery farmed the home place for two years, but since his marriage, which occurred in 1867, he has been engaged in farming for himself, and has been a resident of his present farm since 1878. He has held the office of county assessor since 1886, having also held a number of minor offices. His wife, whose maiden name was Samantha Shaha, was born in Ohio, and when a child was brought to Missouri by her parents, Jackson and Elizabeth Shaha, who were also natives of the

"Buckeye State." Mrs. Debery is the eldest of their eight children, and is the mother of the following children: Ella; Effie, wife of Joseph Evans; Charles, Vallie, Emma, Lilburn, Virgil, Atha and Montez. Mr. Debery is a stanch Republican in politics, a member of the G. A. R. Post of Montreal, the A. O. U. W., and he and wife are members of the Methodist Episcopal Church.

Dr. William M. Dodson is one of the oldest settlers of Auglaize Township, Camden Co., Mo., and was born in Tennessee January 11, 1811, being a son of James and Lucy (Davis) Dodson, who were born in Virginia and Tennessee, respectively, the former's birth occurring about 1772, and his death on the 23d of December, 1832. When he was about eleven years old he removed to Tennessee with his parents, and located in what is now Sevier County. Here he grew to manhood on a farm, and after his marriage, in 1804, he became a disciple of Æsculapius, and eventually became an eminent physician. From East Tennessee he moved to Middle Tennessee, and located on a branch of Duck River, where he erected a very fine grist-mill, and resided here about eight years. He next took up his abode in Jackson County, Ala., thence, about seven years later, to Jefferson County, Tenn., and from there to Hawkins County, and finally to Boone County, Mo. He died in Camden County, while on his way with his family to Springfield, but left his wife and children in fairly good circumstances, he having been the owner of a number of slaves and considerable real estate. The mother was born in 1787, and died November 18, 1847, both she and her husband having been consistent members of the Baptist Church. Five of their ten children are living at the present time: William M., Dr. James N. B., Lucy (Estes), Zilpha (Brockman), and Benjamin D., a farmer and merchant of Richland. James N. B. was the first clerk of Camden County [see history], and is now living, retired from active business life, in Nevada, Mo. Dr. William M. Dodson was almost a man grown when he came to Missouri, and his education was acquired in the common schools of Alabama and Hawkins County, Tenn. He began the study of medicine after coming to Missouri, being under the instruction of his father, and after the latter's death continued his medical studies under his brother James, taking a course of lectures at Lexington, Ky., in the winter of 1836–37. He commenced practicing in the summer of the latter year, at Glaize City, Mo., continuing there until 1847, when he moved to his present location, where he has practiced the healing art, off and on, up to the present time. He was the only physician in the county for many years, and as he was very successful, his practice extended over a circuit of forty-five miles. February 21, 1843, he was married to Mrs. Mildred E. Bagerly, a native of North Carolina, born in 1817. She and her first husband came to Missouri in 1840, and here the latter died in 1842, after which his widow came to Camden County, to take the boat for Kentucky, but here met and married Dr. Dodson, by whom she is the mother of two children: Lucy E., the widow of Dr. J. W. Armstrong, and Penelope, wife of Josiah Traw. Dr. and Mrs. Dodson are active workers in the Methodist Episcopal Church, South, of which he has been a member since 1845, and is now a deacon, and he has always kept his home well supplied with church and medical journals, and has kept thoroughly up with the times. He is a Democrat in politics, and although he has often been urged to run for office, he has invariably refused. During the late war he was appointed chaplain of a company in the Confederate States army, but resigned on account of ill health, and joined his family in Texas, whither he had moved them in 1861. They returned to Missouri in July, 1866, where they have since made their home.

James N. B. Dodson was born in Camden County, Mo., in 1852, being a son of Benjamin D. and Joannah (Sprout) Dodson, who were born in Alabama and Kentucky, respectively, and were among the early settlers of Camden County. [For history of grandparents see sketch of Dr. William M. Dodson.] James N. B. Dodson, our subject, was reared on a farm near where he now lives, but received only limited early educational advantages, as the schools of his day were few and far between, and were of an inferior kind. He afterward took a one year's course at the Richland Institute, and at the age of nineteen years embarked in business for himself, and for about eight months was engaged in selling goods at Marshfield, but his health became badly impaired, owing to confinement to the house, and he then came home and remained with his parents until they moved to a place near Richland, in 1874. In 1887 he came to his present place of abode, where he has a good farm well under cultivation, and is considered by all as one of the progressive farmers of the county. In 1880 he was elected to represent Camden County in the State Legislature, and served with distinction for two years. He has also been a delegate to the State convention several different times, and has ever been a strong supporter of Democratic principles. He contributes freely to churches, schools and all worthy public enterprises, and is a member of the A. F. & A. M. In February, 1883, he was married to Miss Lola M. Stroud, in Benton County, Ark. She was born in Laclede County, but was reared in Benton County, being a daughter of A. B. and Mary I. Stroud, who were born in Tennessee, and came to Arkansas previous to their marriage. The father was a Union man, and came to Laclede County, Mo., during the war, but he and wife are now residing in Jasper County, Mo. Mrs. Dodson is the fourth of their seven children, and she and Mr. Dodson are the parents of two children, Lola M. and Joan Z., and are members of the Christian Church.

Benjamin W. Earnest, a progressive farmer of Camden County, Mo., was born in Morgan County, of the same State, in 1854, and is a son of Amos and Mary (Wilson) Earnest, who were born in Tennessee in 1812 and 1818, and died in Morgan County, Mo., whither they had moved in 1839, in 1870 and 1869, respectively. The father was a farmer and blacksmith, and after leaving his native State resided for a time in Indiana. Their children are as follows: Addie (Cooper), Isaac, Jerusha J. (Allender), B. W. and John M. Benjamin W. Earnest resided in Morgan County until seventeen years of age, then engaging in farming for himself. He has been a resident of Camden County since 1882, and owns a tract of land consisting of

450 acres, with about eighty acres under cultivation. He is a Republican in politics, and cast his first presidential vote for Rutherford B. Hayes in 1876. He and family attend the Methodist Episcopal Church, South. His wife, whose maiden name was Mollie Roe, and whom he married in 1881, was born in Cooper County, Mo., in 1862, and is the mother of two children: Maggie and Henry. Her parents, Samuel and Zerilda (Lee) Roe, were born in Maryland and Missouri, respectively. The father was taken to Cooper County, Mo., when about five years of age (1821), and there he was engaged in farming and blacksmithing. He was justice of the peace of the county for fifteen years, and has been postmaster of Proctor, Mo., for the past six years. The following are their children: Lizzie (Greene), Samuel, Kelly, William, Mollie (Earnest) and James.

James C. Earp. Among the farmers of Camden County, Mo., whose efforts have been attended with a goodly degree of success may be mentioned Mr. Earp, who was born in Miller County September 21, 1843. His parents, John C. and Mary (Record) Earp, were born in Tennessee and Illinois, respectively, the former immigrating with his father, Josiah Earp, to Miller County, Mo., at an early day. After residing in this county for a number of years he came to Camden County in 1856, and here died on the 16th of January, 1870. His widow and five of his six children are still living. Grandfather Earp was born in Ireland, and when quite young came to the United States, locating first in Tennessee, but died in Hickory County, Mo. He was a lieutenant in the War of 1812. James C. Earp's brothers' and sisters' names are as follows: Josiah (who was killed in the late war), John C., William L., Mary A. (wife of Monroe Stevens), Narcissus J., wife of W. J. Miller. The subject of this sketch was reared on farms in Hickory and Camden Counties, and resided on the old homestead until December, 1881, when he located on his present farm. His home farm consists of 600 acres, with 125 acres under cultivation, besides which he owns two other tracts, each consisting of 146 acres, which are well adapted to raising stock. In 1870 he was married to Miss Sarah Kelly, by whom he has seven children: Olive M., Annie S., Thompson J., Carrie M., John M., Fannie J. and Virgil. Mr. and Mrs. Earp are members of the Christian Church.

Andrew Estes, a farmer of Adair Township, Camden County, was born in that county in 1843, and is a son of John G. and Lucy (Dodson) Estes. John G. Estes was born in Alabama in 1809. He was a farmer by occupation, and when young moved to Missouri, where he met and married Lucy Dodson, a native of North Carolina, who was born in 1816. Of the ten children born to them five are now living, viz.: Mary G. Smith, Susan Russell, Zilpha Foster, Penelope Gibson and Andrew Estes. Elizabeth Chitwood and Lucy Simpson (deceased) were married and reared families before their deaths. The paternal grandparents of our subject were Andrew and Mary (Gibson) Estes, natives of South Carolina, who removed from their native State to Tennessee, and in 1832 to Boone County, Mo., subsequently settling in Camden County. The maternal grandparents of Andrew Estes were James and Lucy (Davis) Dodson, who immigrated to Missouri from Tennessee. James Dodson was a physician, and Mrs. Dodson was a relative of Jefferson Davis. John G. Estes, father of our subject, died in 1862; his widow is still living in Camden County. Andrew Estes spent his early life in attending the common schools of his native county, and at the age of nineteen began life for himself as a farmer of the same county. July 4, 1861, he enlisted in the Confederate army, Company A, Sixteenth Missouri Cavalry, under command of Col. Johnson and Capt. Charles Hawthorne. He participated in the battles of Springfield, Lexington, Pea Ridge and Prairie Grove, and was taken prisoner near Fayetteville, Ark., in 1863; he was confined at the latter place three weeks, and was then taken to Springfield, Mo., where he remained until March, 1863, when he enlisted in the United States army, Company D, Eleventh Missouri Cavalry, Col. William D. Woods, Capt. Holstein, and served until discharged in August, 1865. In 1867 Mr. Estes married Mary Foster, who was born in Camden County, Mo., in 1847, and is a daughter of Williamson and Nancy (Brown) Foster, natives of Kentucky, whose four living children are James, Thomas, Leonard and Mary. Jonas Brown, maternal grandfather of Mrs. Estes, served in the War of 1812; his wife was Mary (Hart) Brown. Mr. and Mrs. Estes are the parents of nine children, viz.: Elizabeth, Nancy P., Martha E., Jenora, John W. Lucy A., Ethel and Eltha (twins) and Andrew A. Mr. Estes bought his present home in 1873; he owns 120 acres of good bottom land, of which forty acres are under cultivation. In politics he is a Democrat.

Joshua Farmer, of Camden County, Mo., was born in Montgomery County, Va., April 13, 1837, and is a son of John and Christina (Bishop) Farmer, who were born in Virginia, and there made their home for many years, but immigrated with the paternal grandfather, Joseph, to Missouri, in 1838, locating in Cole County, but died in Miller County. They experienced many dangers and privations in their trip westward, and had considerable difficulty in crossing the mountains, which were at that time infested by numerous gangs of cut-throats and robbers, but were piloted safely through by a man by the name of John Gausley, who did not know the meaning of fear. John Farmer, the father of Joshua Farmer, came to Missouri at the same time, and entered a tract of land in Cole County, ten miles south of Jefferson City, and here resided until 1851, when he moved to Fremont County, Iowa, and at the end of four years to Andrew County, Mo., but finally located on the Osage River, near Linn Creek, where he purchased a farm and remained until the war broke out, at which time he moved North. At the close of hostilities he returned to Missouri, and died at Linn Creek. His wife died in 1873. Two of their nine children are living: Joshua and Joseph M. The former was an infant when brought to Missouri, and until seventeen years of age resided in Cole County. In 1861 he enlisted in Company B, Second Battalion, but at the end of six months the company was disbanded, and Mr. Farmer enlisted in the Ninth Missouri Cavalry, and from July 13, 1863, to July 13, 1865, served with this company, and fought bushwhackers in Northern Missouri. In 1869 he purchased his present farm on the Osage River, consisting of 300 acres, and is now considered one of the prosperous farmers and stock men of the county. In 1860 he wedded Miss Zeruviah A. Roberts, who died in 1871, having borne four children, who are all deceased: Mary Francis, Joseph William and two infants. In 1871 he married his second wife, Miss Fannie L. Edwards, who died August 23, 1874, leaving one child, Margaret J. Mr. Farmer's third wife, Indiana A. Farmer, whom he married in 1874, has borne seven children, five living. The names of those deceased were James Edward and William E. Mr. and Mrs. Farmer are members of the Christian Church, and he belongs to the I. O. O. F.

Dr. T. J. Feaster, a successful druggist at Climax Springs, Camden Co., Mo., was born in Benton County, Mo., October 12, 1861, and is one of five surviving members of a family of six children born to the marriage of E. S. Feaster and Deborah (Cobb) Feaster, who were born in Tennessee and South Carolina, in 1827 and 1825, respectively. They moved from their native States to Benton County, Mo., about fifty years ago (about 1839), and here are now residing, having followed the occupation of farming throughout life. In 1861 the father enlisted in the Confederate army, and served under Gen. Price throughout the war, participating in all the battles in which that general was engaged. He was wounded at Wilson's Creek, and was confined in the hospital for three months, and surrendered at Shreveport. His father was born in Tennessee, and his wife's parents were natives of North Carolina. His children are as follows: Mary (Bailey), George, W. A., Elizabeth (Brown), deceased; Dr. T. J. and Emma (Nowell). Dr. T. J. Feaster made his home in Benton County until nineteen years of age, then entering the Morrisville Collegiate Institute, which institution he attended during 1880–81. He was then engaged in "teaching the young idea" for about five terms, and also read medicine under Dr. T. J. Sheldon, of Quincy, Hickory Co., Mo., and in 1887 attended the medical department of the University of Kansas City, Mo., graduating in February, 1888, after which he began practicing his profession at Climax Springs; he has gained the confidence and esteem of the public, and has acquired an extensive practice. He is a member of the Masonic fraternity, and is a Democrat, casting his first vote for Grover Cleveland in 1884.

J. W. Francisco is a prosperous farmer and general merchant of Spring Valley, Mo., and was born in Saline County, Mo., in 1849, his parents being J. G. and Sarah (Wood) Francisco, both natives of Kentucky. The former's birth occurred in 1812, and his death in Missouri, in October, 1888, his wife dying in 1880. They became residents of Saline County, Mo., in 1837, and there followed the occupation of farming, and reared their family of four children: Sophia L. (Ross), Anna J. (Martin), Mollie E. (Martin) and J. W. The latter was reared in his native county, and at the age of twenty years engaged in farming for himself, and was married in 1867 to Miss Fanny Martin, who was born in Clark County, Ky., in 1846. Her parents, Samuel T. and Eliza (Jones) Martin, were also born there, and moved to Missouri about 1850, where they reared their eleven children:

G. Thomas, Samuel D., Charles, Frank, Fanny (Francisco), Bettie (Yantis), Mary (Francisco), Kate (Garvin), Helen (Moberly), Anna (Parks) and Hester. Mr. and Mrs. Francisco are the parents of the following children: George T., Woodie E., Anna J., John S., Mary E. and Murray C. Mr. Francisco owns 160 acres of valuable land, with forty acres under cultivation, and his mercantile stock is valued at $1,500. He and family attend the Presbyterian Church, and he is a Democrat. His paternal grandparents, John and Julia (Lewis) Francisco, were born in Virginia in 1760 and 1780, and died in Missouri in 1844 and 1859, respectively. They moved from Virginia to Kentucky, thence to Missouri in 1837, and were there engaged in farming. The grandfather was a soldier in the Revolutionary War at the age of sixteen, and was at the battle of Cowpens. He was colonel of a regiment in the War of 1812, and received one severe wound during his service. The maternal grandparents, Thomas and Sarah Wood, were also Virginians, and at an early day moved to Danville, Ky., where they owned hotel, and he was judge of Mercer County Court.

H. George, county clerk, was born in Russell County, Ky., October 20, 1841, and is the son of H. and Jane (Wilson) George, both natives of Kentucky. In the spring of 1842 the parents immigrated to Miller County, Mo., and located four miles west of Brumley. The father entered a large tract of land, which he improved, and which is now known as the William Pope farm. He remained on this a number of years, and then removed to Camden County in the fall of 1854, purchasing a farm in Jackson Township, known as the James Wilson farm, which is one of the oldest settled farms in the county. It was improved when he purchased it, and on this farm he spent his last days, his death occurring in March, 1855. The mother is yet living in this county, having married William A. Bradshaw. They were the parents of nine children, eight now living. H. George was but an infant when he came with his parents to the State of Missouri, and in this State he attained his growth, receiving a liberal education, and followed the occupation of farming and teaching until 1878. He was then elected county court justice, and was also appointed public administrator. In 1880 he was elected sheriff and collector of revenue, which position he held for four years, being re-elected in 1882. In 1886 he was elected county clerk of Camden County, which office he now fills. He owns two good farms, of 250 acres in each tract. He has an unusually fine vineyard on one of his farms. In the spring of 1861 he married Miss Luticia Ulmon, of Miller County, and to them have been born five children: Josiah M., Elizabeth J. (wife of W. R. Waters), Samuel H., Milton L. and Frederick A. In August, 1861, Mr. George entered the Federal service, in the Osage Regiment, Home Guards, Company G, commanded by Capt. William A. Bradshaw. He is a member of the Masonic fraternity, and a member of the A. O. U. W., and is an enterprising and intelligent citizen and prominent man.

Mrs. Eliza J. Gerhardt, *nee* Wallace, is a resident of Russell Township, Camden Co., Mo. She was born in Benton County, Mo., in 1839, and is a daughter of Jacob and Catherine (Rice) Wallace, the former of whom was born in Madison County, Mo., in 1809, and the latter in North Carolina in 1814. In 1838, when the country was new, the parents removed from Madison to Benton County, Mo., where they still live. Jacob Wallace, who is now seventy-nine years of age, is an active, well-preserved man for his years, and still delights to hunt as in his former days. Mr. and Mrs. Wallace are the parents of eight children, viz.: Eliza J. Gerhardt, Ellen Smith, George W., James, William, Mary Sally, John Wesley and Alzada Franklin, the two latter deceased. All four of the sons served in the Union army during the late Civil War, in which service John Wesley lost his life. Our subject spent her early life in her native county, and in 1856 married August Gerhardt, a native of Germany, who was born in 1834, and came to the United States when seventeen years of age. He first located in Cole County, Mo., but subsequently went to Benton County, where he worked at his trade of wagon-maker. In 1862 he enlisted in Company F, Eighth Missouri Cavalry, and served until the close of the war, receiving his discharge in 1865. Eleven children were born to Mr. and Mrs. Gerhardt, eight of whom are living, viz.: Johanna E. Derrick, Frederick J., Katherine E. Smith, Harmon W., Adolph N., Ulyssimus S. A., Laura and Pinky A. In 1874 Mr. Gerhardt engaged in a general merchandising business in Duroc, Mo., in partnership with Mr. Campbell, whose interest he afterward bought out, and in 1883 he moved to Coelleda, where he purchased the present home and built the store. He owned 160 acres of land, and built all the houses in the little town of Coelleda. Mr. Gerhardt served four years as justice of the peace in Benton County, and was a Republican in politics. He was a member of the Lutheran Church, while Mrs. Gerhardt is a member of the Missionary Baptist Church.

George Griesel, farmer and miller at Climax Springs, Mo., was born in Germany in 1826, and is a son of Adam and Anna E. (Sharp) Griesel, who were also Germans, born in 1774 and 1789, and died in 1840 and 1867, respectively. The father was a farmer, and served as justice of the peace and city appraiser, and was captain of a company of Home Guards in his native land. He was in the war from the time he was sixteen until he was thirty-two years of age, with Napoleon Bonaparte, and was at the battle of Waterloo, under command of Gen. Blucher. Five of his six children came to America, but only two are now living, George and Jacob, of Sacramento, Cal. The grandparents, Jacob and Anna E. Sharp, were also Germans. George Griesel received a good education in his native land, and in his boyhood days learned the millwright's trade. When twenty years old he was mustered into the army, and was discharged at the age of thirty, having participated in the war between Germany and Denmark in 1850–53. In 1854 he was married in his native land to Catherine E. Leidheiser, who was born in 1834, and is a daughter of John A. and Ann E. (Tibmar) Leidheiser, who were tillers of the soil, and the parents of eleven children, three of whom crossed the ocean to America, and four are yet living: John A., Conrad, Martha E. and

Catherine (Mrs. Griesel). Mr. and Mrs. Griesel are the parents of the following family: Ann E. (Darnell), Sophia C., Lou, John A., William A., George K., Mary M., Antulf and Della May. Since 1859 Mr. Griesel has been a resident of Camden County, Mo., and was first engaged in operating the mill for Mr. Arnholdt, but when it was burned during the war he rented land and engaged in farming, and since 1867 has resided on his present farm, and has been occupied in milling. He is a Republican in politics, and cast his first presidential vote for Abraham Lincoln in 1860. He and wife belong to the Lutheran Church.

James Harvey Hall, one of the successful agriculturists of Osage Township, Camden County, is a native of Laclede County, Mo., born October 12, 1861, being a son of James and Mary (Porter) Hall, the father a native of Virginia, and the mother of Kentucky. The father, with his brother William, immigrated to Laclede County, Mo., quite early, and located twenty miles south of Lebanon. They entered land which was wild and unbroken, and remained there until the breaking out of the late Civil War, when the father enlisted, and while in service took a fever and died, as did also his brother. The mother came to Laclede County with her parents when about eight years of age, and, when grown, was married in that county to Mr. Hall, by whom she had two sons: William Edgar, who died February 3, 1888, and James Harvey. The mother was again married, to John Frieze, who is also deceased. By the last marriage she had four children: Louis, George, Ina B. and Arty. The widow now resides near Lebanon. James H. Hall was reared and educated in Laclede County, Mo., and in 1881 he took a trip to Texas, where he worked on a cattle ranch. In 1885 he moved to where he now lives, and is the owner of 200 acres of good land, with about seventy-five under cultivation. He was married May 5, 1886, to Miss Edna Selby, who was born in Camden County February 16, 1869. They have one child, Thomas E., born October 7, 1887. Mrs. Hall's parents were Legrand and Rebecca E. (Neal) Selby, natives of Ohio, but now deceased. She is their only living child, and was reared by her paternal grandparents, Thomas and Huldah Selby. Mr. Hall is a wide-a-wake, stirring young man, is a successful farmer, and deals quite extensively in stock, especially hogs.

F. Hooker, merchant at Linn Creek, and son of John A., and Sallie A. (Cherry) Hooker, was born in Laclede County, Mo., March 13, 1854. His parents immigrated to Laclede County, Mo., at a very early day, settling near the Osage Fork, and were among the first settlers of that county. Here the father died. He was in the nursery business at the time of his death. He was a soldier in the Confederate army during the late war; was with Price, and was captured and cast into prison, where he was kept for some time. He was also wounded during his service, by a gunshot in the ankle. He was the father of two children—a son and daughter: Fernando, and Helena A., wife of Mr. Odenweller. F. Hooker, subject of this sketch, was reared by his father to the nursery business, and also in the mercantile business. At the age of fourteen he drifted out to do for himself. He was employed with D. W. Faulkner, a merchant of Lebanon, as clerk, and remained with him for about six years. In 1878 he came to Linn Creek, where he engaged in the mercantile business in partnership with E. W. Craig, which continued until the fall of 1880, when W. P. Hooker bought out Mr. Craig, and the business was continued under the firm name of F. & P. Hooker. After continuing a short time at this, both sold out, and F. Hooker engaged in the business for himself, and carried it on alone for about two years. He again sold out and went to Tuscumbia, Miller County, and carried on the mercantile business there until August, 1888, when he returned to Linn Creek. Here he has since remained, and has been engaged in the mercantile business. He carries a full line of general merchandise, and is a good business man. He was married in 1884 to Miss Belle Freeman, by whom he has two children: John A. and Lena M. He kept the post-office at Linn Creek for about two years.

Ephraim Hopkins, a successful tiller of the soil, was born in Marion County, Tenn., September 1, 1829, and is the son of John and Rebecca (Phillips) Hopkins, natives of North Carolina. The parents immigrated to Tennessee at a very early date, and at a time when the Indians were still there. The father was a farmer by occupation, and passed the latter part of his life in Tennessee. The grandparents on both the Hopkins and Phillips sides were soldiers in the War of 1812, and Grandfather Hopkins died while in service. To John and Rebecca (Phillips) Hopkins were born eleven children, four now living: Elisha C., Ephraim, James F. and Elizabeth (widow of William Hicks). The subject of our sketch was reared and educated in Tennessee, and made his home in Nashville for about twelve years, and was there engaged in teaming. About 1853 he, accompanied by his brother, Elisha C., came to Camden County in search of a location, and here Ephraim settled in about 1857. He entered a portion of the land, and bought a part. He owned 881 acres, and has about 150 acres under cultivation. He has deeded this land to his children: John, Alpha, Charley and George W. He has made nearly all the improvements, and has a good farm. He was constable for two years during the war. In 1855 he married Miss Angelina Thomas, a native of Kentucky, who bore him nine children, six now living: John, Rebecca (widow of Dr. Lyon), Christopher C. (deceased), Margaret, James (deceased), Alpha, Charles, George W. and Sarah Ann (deceased). The mother of these children died in March, 1882, and Mr. Hopkins took for his second wife Miss Sarah Herald, a native of Tennessee, who came to Tennessee with her parents in about 1866. In July, 1861, Mr. Hopkins enlisted in Company B, under Gov. McClurg, and served until disbanded, in December, 1861, when he was taken sick, and remained in the hospital at Jefferson City until February, 1862. He was on scouting duty most of the time while in service, and now receives a pension, as his eyesight was affected. He is a member of the G. A. R., and an enterprising citizen.

G. S. Howard, farmer, was born in Cole County, Mo., in 1837, and is a son of William and Urana (Roberts) Howard, who were born in Tennessee, but were reared and married in Cole County, Mo. The father was a farmer, and served in the late war in McClurg's company, and died in 1874. His children are as follows: Charlotte (Hasty), Elvira (Bench), Elizabeth (Starks) and G. S. The latter was reared on farms in Cole and Benton Counties, and when eighteen years of age began working for himself as a farm hand. In 1860 he married Miss Lucy Wisdom, who was born in Camden County, Mo., and a daughter of Pollard and Charity (Mashburn) Wisdom, natives of North Carolina, and by her became the father of the following children: William J., Mary F. (Hicks) and Virginia A. The mother of these children died in 1874, and three years later Mr. Howard wedded Mrs. Marilla J. (Roney) Huffman, a daughter of Thomas G. and Elizabeth Roney, of Tennessee, by whom he is the father of four living children: Effie C., Edna E., Ernest B. and Fred. This wife died on the 29th of February, 1888. In 1862 Mr. Howard enlisted in Company G, of the Missouri State Guard, and was discharged in 1865. When first married his entire property consisted of one horse, but he rented land for about ten years, and in 1870 purchased the farm he had been renting, and in 1883 bought the farm where he is now living, giving for it $2,100 in cash. He is now the owner of 320 acres of land, mostly good bottom land, on the Little Niangua River, about 175 acres of which are under cultivation. He is a Democrat, and cast his first presidential vote for Breckinridge in 1860.

B. F. Kendrick ranks among the successful farmers of Camden County, Mo., and was born in Washington County, Ark., July 30, 1848, being a son of John and Eliza A. (Hines) Kendrick, who emigrated from Alabama to Tennessee, thence to Illinois, and from there to Arkansas at quite an early day. They located in Washington County, where the father's death occurred, but the mother died in Camden County, Mo. B. F. Kendrick is the youngest of their eight children, and until sixteen years of age was a resident of Arkansas. He was a member of the Enrolled Militia at Fayetteville, Ark., during the late war, and was in several hard skirmishes, and after the death of his father was left to fight the battle of life alone, and until 1874 resided in the following counties in Missouri: Moniteau, Pettis, Cooper, and at the latter date came to Camden County and resided for a number of years at Climax Springs. Since that time he has resided on the farm of 130 acres where he now lives. It is nearly all under cultivation, well improved, and is admirably adapted to stock purposes, in which Mr. Kendrick is considerably interested. In 1870 he was married to Lucinda Beard, by whom he has a family of seven children: William, Eliza A., George, Laura J., Mary, John and Lizzie. The mother of these children died April 30, 1884, and on the 20th of September of that year he wedded Catherine Nicholson, by whom he has two children, Benjamin and Dora. Mr. Kendrick is a member of the Masonic fraternity, and is one of the successful farmers and honored citizens of the county.

Pleasant King, judge of the probate court, Camden County, was born in Osage County, Mo., December 20, 1850, being the son of Hugh L. and Delilah (Groves) King, and grandson of John S. King, who immigrated with his family to Osage County, Mo., at a very early date, and located on the Missouri River, where he established what was known as "King's Landing." He was there engaged in the mercantile business, which he continued until the breaking out of the war. He died a few years later. He was a prominent man and a good citizen. Hugh L. and Delilah (Groves) King were natives of Georgia and Missouri, respectively. The father was a farmer by occupation, and this he followed the principal part of his life, although when young he had followed merchandising with his father at "King's Landing." He remained in Osage County, Mo., until his death, which occurred in 1867. He served in the Home Guards and militia organizations during the late war, and held a number of official positions, and was a prominent man in Osage County. The mother is yet living, and resides in Camden County. They were the parents of six children, three living: Judge Pleasant, Laura, wife of John Bunch, and Oliver L. The three deceased were Luella, Sophronia and an infant. Judge Pleasant King was principally reared in Osage County, Mo., where he was educated. He was brought up on a farm, but entered the profession of teaching at nineteen years of age, and continued in that work until admitted to the bar. He remained in that county until 1882, when he removed to Richland, Pulaski Co., Mo., where he was engaged in the practice of law and newspaper business. He was admitted to the bar in Osage County, Mo., in October, 1882. He established the *Cyclone* at Richland, Mo., which publication he continued until 1885, when he sold out. In 1886 he came to Linn Creek, and the same year was elected probate judge, which office he still holds. He is also engaged in the practice of law and real estate business, and represents the Phœnix (of Hartford) and the German (of Freeport, Ill.) insurance companies. He was married January 16, 1873, to Miss Anna Agee, of Osage County, Mo., who bore him five children: Ray, Ilma, Edith, Edgar and Nilla, three of whom are now living, namely: Ray, Edith and Nilla. Judge King is a member of the A. F. & A. M. and I. O. O. F. lodges.

George W. Miller, postmaster and merchant at Linn Creek, and son of Samuel D. and Aultana J. (Stevens) Miller, was born in Camden County, Mo., August 17, 1852. His father was a native of Overton County, Tenn., and his mother of Wake County, N. C. Samuel D. Miller immigrated to St. Louis, Mo., from Kentucky with his mother about the year 1833, where they remained only a few years. In about 1837 they removed to Camden County, where they were among the first settlers. He located on Shawnee Bend, where he resided some time, and then entered and bought large tracts of land. He lived at the time of his death in Jasper Township, near the mouth of the Glaize. He was a farmer by occupation, and died in 1876. The mother died Febuary 12, 1886. They were the parents of ten children, seven now living: Sarah, wife of Edmund Spearman; Mary, wife of John C. Earp; Ann E., George W. and John R. (twins), William J., and Theresa C., wife of Thomas E. Ezard. G. W. Miller attained his growth and received his education in Camden County, Mo. He was reared on the farm, which occupation he followed until 1882, when he engaged in the mercantile business at Cape Galena,

Morgan County, with Jesse W. Caffey, remaining with him for two years. In 1884 he engaged with Owen A. Nelson in merchandising, and the firm was known as Miller & Nelson for about one year, when the former bought out Mr. Nelson and carried on the business alone until December, 1887, when David Moulder purchased a half interest, and the firm has since continued as Miller & Moulder. They carry a general line of merchandise, and are wide-a-wake, enterprising business men. Mr. Miller was appointed postmaster in January, 1888. He was appointed county treasurer to fill a vacancy, and held the position for seven months. In April, 1884, he married Miss Florence M., daughter of Frank M. King, by whom he had two children, both deceased. Mr. Miller now owns an interest in the old home farm, and 200 acres of unimproved land. He also owns property in Linn Creek, and is one of the leading and intelligent citizens of Camden County. He is a member of the Masonic fraternity, and is a Democrat in his political views.

David Moulder, merchant, and one of the pioneers of Camden County, Mo., was born in Grainger County, Tenn., May 25, 1840, and is the son of Valentine and Ann (Yaden) Moulder, both natives of Grainger County, Tenn., and of Italian and German descent. The paternal grandfather was an early settler of Tennessee. Valentine Moulder was a farmer by occupation, and immigrated with his family to Camden County, Mo., in 1842. He came through in wagons, and located in Osage Township, about seven miles northwest of Linn Creek. He entered about 200 acres of land, with about five acres cleared, on which was a little log cabin, which is still standing. He set to work to improve his place, and soon had a number of acres under cultivation. On this farm he remained until his death, which occurred in 1862. The mother died in 1852. They were the parents of nine children, three now living: David, Mary E. (wife of T. P. Groom) and Bertha R. (wife of C. M. Piercy). The father represented Camden County in the Legislature two terms, 1852 and 1856; held the office of county judge for about four years, and was a very prominent man in this county. He had a host of friends. His son, David Moulder, was two years of age when he came to Camden County, Mo., with his parents, and thus it may be seen that he has been identified with the interests of Camden County almost all his life. He received his education in the old subscription schools, and was obliged to walk three and one-half miles to attend the same, the school-house being of log, with a hole for a door and a crack for a window. He assisted on the farm, and when the late war broke out he enlisted in the Missouri Militia and served three years. He was engaged in several hard skirmishes, and had one hair-breadth escape, a ball passing through his hat brim. At the close of the war he engaged in merchandising at Linn Creek, which vocation he has since continued, and is the oldest merchant at Linn Creek. He sold goods ten years at Richland, Pulaski County. Mr. Moulder carries a general line of merchandise, and now owns Gov. McClurg's old mansion, which was built under the Governor's supervision thirty-five years ago. He also owns the farm, consisting of 300 acres. Mr. Moulder was elected county treasurer in 1874, re-elected in 1876, and resigned in 1877 on account of his removal to Richland. He was married in 1865 to Miss Sallie Selby, by whom he has ten children living: Ellen, Jessie L., Cora M., Thomas V., Charles, George C., John D., Elect E., Emma M. and Sallie. Mr. Moulder is a member of the Masonic fraternity, and is a stanch Democrat politically.

Hon. Thomas H. B. Moulder, farmer, was born in Camden County, Mo., August 12, 1844, being a son of George W. and Ann (Yaden) Moulder, who were born in Tennessee, and immigrated to Missouri about 1831, and six years later to Camden County, locating on the fork of the Big and Little Nianguas. The father was judge of the county courts for some years, and was a prosperous farmer and stock man. Hon. Thomas H. B. Moulder has always resided on a farm in his native county, and by good management and industry has become the owner of a tract of land consisting of 400 acres, with about 150 acres under cultivation, and on which are some very valuable improvements. His farm is mostly bottom land, and is well adapted to raising stock, which occupation receives much of Mr. Moulder's attention. The post-office of Cave Pump is located at his residence, and he fills the duties of postmaster, and in 1882 served one term as a member of the State Legislature. In 1878 he was elected to the office of county assessor, and was re-elected in 1880, filling the duties of all of these offices in a very efficient manner and to the entire satisfaction of his constituents. Nancy E. Foster, a native of Camden County, became his wife in 1866, and the mother of his nine children, eight of whom are living: Frederick J., Hattie L., Juliett, Sidney, Ann E., George A., Bettie and John P. In 1862 Mr. Moulder enlisted in Company D, Twenty-ninth Missouri Volunteer Infantry, and served nearly three years. He was at Vicksburg, Arkansas Post, and was captured at Greenville, Miss., by the rebels, and was kept a prisoner at Pine Bluff, Ark., and Little Rock. After being paroled and exchanged he rejoined his regiment at Corinth, Miss., and participated in several skirmishes near Tuscumbia, Ala., and Iuka, Miss., and at the battle of Lookout Mountain was wounded by a gunshot in the left foot, which necessitated his being taken to the hospital, where he remained nine months. He was then transferred to the Veteran Reserve Corps, with which he remained for about nine months, being stationed at Camp Douglas, Chicago, and received his discharge in July, 1865. He is now a member of the G. A. R., and draws a pension for his wound; he has been a member of the Masonic fraternity for many years.

Owen A. Nelson, county treasurer of Camden County, Mo., was born in Posey County, Ind., August 29, 1854, and is the son of Alexander G. and Sarah A. (Highman) Nelson, the former a native of Posey County, Ind., and the latter of Iowa. The father was a blacksmith by trade, but never followed it for a livelihood, for farming was his principal occupation. He left Indiana at the beginning of the late war, and went to White County, Ill., where he remained until 1868, when he moved with his family to Camden County, Mo., and located near Linn Creek, where he died in 1881. The mother is still living.

They were the parents of four children, all sons: Owen A., John W., George W. and Grant. Owen A. Nelson was but a small lad when his parents moved to White County, Ill. He assisted his father on the farm until 1868, when he came to Missouri, locating in Camden County, where he has since made his home. He was elected treasurer of Camden County in 1886, and re-elected in 1888. He is a prominent citizen of the county. He was married in 1876 to Miss Mary A. Russell, by whom he had two children: William G. and George E. Mrs. Nelson died in 1881, and he married for his second wife, February 1, 1883, Miss Amanda J. Scofield, a native of Iowa, who bore him one child, Hugh R. Mrs. Nelson is a member of the Baptist Church, and he is a member of the Masonic fraternity and the I. O. O. F. His grandfather Nelson was an early settler of Posey County, Ind.

Maj. Thomas O'Halloran was born in the "Emerald Isle" in 1827, and there resided until 1848, when he immigrated to the United States with his brothers, Maurice and James, and his sister, Eliza. After landing in New York City they remained there three or four months, and then went to Chicago, where the sister died in the fall of 1848. The brothers then came to Missouri, Maurice and James locating in St. Charles County, on a farm, where the former died a short time after. James is now living in Pulaski County. Maj. Thomas O'Halloran remained in St. Louis until about 1856, where he was engaged in pork packing, and then came to Camden County, and began working in the pork packing house of Murphy, McClurg & Co.; then he came to his present farm, which he had purchased the previous year, and on which he has resided ever since, with the exception of a short time during the late war. He enlisted as a private in the Forty-seventh Enrolled Militia, and August 12, 1862, was commissioned captain of a company he organized, and September 18, 1862, rose to the rank of major, and afterward to lieutenant-colonel of the Forty-seventh Regiment. He resigned in 1864, after doing honorable and active service. In the fall of 1863, while at home on furlough to put up his winter's meat, a party of six men rode up and inquired of his family the way to Mineral Point, Linn Creek and Tuscumbia. Soon after they left the house the Major thought something was not right, and mounted his horse and started after them. When he reached them they asked him which of the three roads led to Linn Creek. He told them not to matter about the roads, but to consider themselves under arrest as prisoners; to which one of them, who afterward proved to be Maj. Rucker, of the Confederate army, replied that he thought it rather cool for one man to take six men; but Maj. O'Halloran marched them down the road, single file, for about a mile and a half, where he secured help to disarm them, and found on their persons over 300 letters for Southern sympathizers in Northern Missouri and St. Louis. For this act of bravery the Major received a vote of thanks from the State Senate, and won the respect and admiration of all his friends. He came to the home place when the war was over, and has since been actively engaged in improving his farm of 440 acres, and has 150 acres in a fine state of cultivation. December 28, 1858, he was married in Linn Creek, by Lewis Coy, to Miss Frances

M. Murphy, by whom he became the father of eight children, two being deceased: William D., who died at the age of six years, and Thomas W., whose death occurred when twenty-three years old. Those living are Edwin C., James, Mary E. (wife of Berry Hendricks), Fannie B., John M. and Katie F. Mr. O'Halloran is a Republican in politics.

James J. O'Halloran, a successful farmer and stock man of Camden County, Mo., was born July 28, 1861, and is a son of Maj. Thomas O'Halloran, whose sketch precedes this. He was reared on his father's farm, and received his education in a subscription school, which was conducted at their residence, and also attended the high-school of Richland. When about eighteen years of age he began farming for himself, and November 27, 1887, was wedded to Miss Jessie Moulder, a daughter of David Moulder, a sketch of whom is herein given. Mrs. O'Halloran was born at Linn Creek in 1870, and is the mother of one child, Bessie. Mr. O'Halloran has a large tract of land, with about 115 acres under cultivation, all of which is the result of his own energy and good management; he also has a fine residence and substantial out-buildings. In connection with farming he is engaged in stock raising to some extent, and like his father supports the principles of the Republican party.

William Osborn, general merchant at Mack's Creek, Camden County, Mo., was born in Scott County, W. Va., in 1831, his parents, Stephen and Lavisa (Bledsoe) Osborn, being natives of Virginia, born in 1802 and 1806, and died in 1865 and 1852, respectively. The parents moved from their native State to Kentucky; thence to Camden County, Mo., in 1841, where they engaged in farming. Five of their twelve children are now living: Ambrose, Nelson, Franklin, Malinda and William. After residing with his parents until twenty-one years of age, William Osborn started out in life for himself as a farmer, and was married in 1852 to Miss Elizabeth Nicholson, who was born in Georgia in 1831, and a daughter of Isaac and Zena (Dawson) Nicholson, who were planters of Georgia, and the parents of nine children. Previous to the war Mr. Osborn had shot over 1,000 deer, principally for their hides, and many other animals also fell victims to his skill as a marksman. In April, 1861, he enlisted in the Osage Regiment of Missouri Home Guards, and was discharged therefrom in December, 1861, after which he enlisted, in 1862, in the State Rangers, and was discharged in 1863. He re-enlisted August 16, 1863, in Company D, Eighth Missouri Cavalry, and was discharged May 20, 1865, at Springfield, Mo., having participated in the battles of Jefferson City, Boonville, Big Blue, Mine Creek, Independence, Newtonia and others. After the war he followed farming until 1868, at which time he began merchandising at Lead Mine, Dallas Co., Mo., and went from there to Urbana, Mo., where he resided during 1878 and 1879. At the latter date he came to Mack's Creek, and established himself in his present business, which has proved quite remunerative. He belongs to the Christian Church, the Masonic fraternity and the G. A. R., and in his political views is a Republican, having cast his first vote for Winfield Scott in 1852. The following are his children who are living: Isaac, Franklin, William, Lucy A. (Harold),

Malinda (Bryant), Mary J. (Hack) and Matilda (Ricker). The paternal grandfather, James, was a Virginian, and at an early day moved to Kentucky. The maternal grandfather was Ambrose Bledsoe.

William J. Payne, postmaster and tobacco manufacturer at Zebra, Mo., was born in Bedford County, Va., in October, 1835, and is the son of William and Nancy E. (Ashwell) Payne, both natives of Virginia, where they passed their last days. The father was a tiller of the soil and an honest, industrious citizen. His son, William J. Payne, was reared and educated in Bedford County, Va., and was reared to farm life. At the age of twenty-two he began to learn the tobacconist's trade, and worked in a tobacco manufactory for some time. August 18, 1861, he enlisted in Company I, Fifty-eighth Virginia Volunteer Infantry, and served nearly four years. He was commissioned as a lieutenant of his company, and came out in the same position. He was at the battles of McDowell, Cross Keys, Winchester, Richmond, Front Royal, battle of Wilderness, Fredericksburg, Spottsylvania and several other hard engagements. He was wounded on June 27, 1863, by a grape-shot, and was again wounded in 1864 by a gunshot. At the time of his first wound he was permitted a leave of absence, and went to the rear. He served most of his time as adjutant and drill-master. At the close of the war he went back home, and remained there until 1868, when he left, came west, and in 1878 he engaged in hauling ties and railroading. In 1879 he married Miss Elizabeth Frazier, a native of Meigs County, Ohio, who bore him one child, William H. In 1881 Mr. Payne moved to where he now resides, in Camden County, and is the owner of 167 acres of land, thirty acres under cultivation. He has made all the improvements, having first settled in the brush when he could not see a man at a distance of fifty yards. He is a member of the Agricultural Wheel, and is an enterprising and much respected citizen.

Hiram L. Pease, dealer in general merchandise, and stock dealer at Climax Springs, Mo., was born in Fremont, Ohio, January 25, 1860, and is a son of John R. and Mary (Meade) Pease, who were born in Connecticut and New Hampshire in 1805 and 1828, and died in Ohio in 1860 and 1873, respectively. They moved to the "Buckeye State" at an early day, and were there married and spent the remainder of their lives. The father was a farmer and tinner, and was mayor of Fremont for some time. He was twice married, and by his first wife became the father of one child, and five by his second wife: John R., Edwin E., Helen (Merriam), Francis, one deceased, and Hiram L. The maternal grandparents died in New York and Ohio, at the ages of eighty-five and seventy-three, respectively. Hiram L. Pease received his education in the schools of Fremont, and also attended Blake's Preparatory School, at Gambier, Ohio. When he attained his majority he began life for himself, and was engaged in surveying real estate for six months, and in 1883 went to Montana, where he followed the same occupation for some time, and then returned to his native State. March 7, 1884, he came to Camden County, Mo., where he has since been engaged in stock dealing, and in partnership with B. F. Swindler established his present mercantile business at

Climax Springs, the firm being known as Pease & Swindler. December 1, 1888, he purchased Mr. Swindler's interest, and has since successfully conducted the business alone. He carries a stock valued at about $2,000, and besides this property owns eighty acres of land and live stock valued at $1,000. He is a Republican in politics, and cast his first presidential vote for Benjamin Harrison in 1888. He also belongs to the I. O. O. F.

L. I. Roach (deceased) was born on the farm where his widow now resides, near Linn Creek, December 30, 1837, and was one of a family of six children, whose parents removed from Tennessee and settled in the then new and almost unexplored State of Missouri in the year 1831. At the time of Mr. Roach's birth Missouri was a Territory and a wilderness, Camden County containing only about 100 inhabitants. It comprised a portion of Pulaski County, and was afterward organized as Kinderhook County. During the year 1841 he was deprived by death of both parents, and the family was left penniless, the means of his father having been exhausted (at his direction) in the payment of debts. In conformity with a then existing statute, "Little Jack," as he was then called, was apprenticed to one Hiram Bagley, a tailor, whom he left in 1847 because of harsh treatment. He was re-apprenticed to one James A. Crain, a farmer, with whom he remained until the latter died, in 1851. He was then employed by various farmers until 1854, and during that time he attended school four months and a half, this scanty draught of the fountain of knowledge representing the full extent of his educational advantages. He then turned his attention to navigation, beginning his career in the humble capacity of night watchman on one of the Osage steamers. At the commencement of the Rebellion he possessed pilot papers authorizing him to run from St. Louis to the head-waters of the Osage River, but rapid as had been his advancement in his chosen occupation, he responded to his country's call, and left the deck for the battle-field, enlisting in the Osage Regiment of the Missouri Home Guards, with which he remained until its disbandment in December, 1861. He then enlisted in the Eighth Missouri Cavalry, and served three years and three months. His regiment was in active service, and Sergeant Roach was in nearly all the principal engagements that occurred on Missouri soil. He rendered valuable service as a scout and bearer of dispatches, and afterward retained a lively recollection of several narrow escapes and thrilling adventures. When peace was declared Mr. Roach returned to the river, and followed the vocation of pilot until December, 1866, when on the tenth of that month he was united in marriage to Miss Frances M. Crain, only daughter of his late master. To their union were born six children, Rebecca J., Susan E., James L., Sidney C., Martha A. (deceased) and William M. In 1868 Mr. Roach was elected sheriff and collector, which position he held two years. In 1870 he was elected clerk of the county and circuit courts, and in 1874 he was re-elected to this office, and also to the position of probate judge. For the ensuing four years he discharged the duties of four county offices, and gave such general satisfaction that in 1878 he was urged by the most influential men of both parties to become a candidate for re-election to all the offices which he had so acceptably filled. The work was too onerous, however, for even his methodical habits, but he was retained in two clerkships by a handsome majority. In 1883 he was elected for the fourth time to the position of county clerk. He was admitted to the bar as a prosecuting attorney in February, 1883, and soon became an ornament to the profession. Among other business ventures he was engaged in the mercantile business at Gunter, Mo. He owned a large tract of land adjoining Linn Creek, and had, but a few years previous to his death, completed his handsome and well-constructed residence, in which the widow and family now reside. Mr. Roach was a self-made man in every respect, and none had more friends than he. He was liberal and always ready to help any public enterprise for the benefit of his county. He died January 29, 1886.

G. B. Shubert, collector of internal revenue for Camden County, Mo., is a native of Philadelphia, Penn., born March 11, 1829, and is the son of George and Eliza (Beckhorn) Shubert, both natives of Philadelphia, Penn. His great-great-grandfather was in winter quarters at Valley Forge with Washington, and his wife walked and carried her husband's clothing a distance of ninety miles. The Shuberts are of an old Philadelphia family. The paternal grandfather was a shoemaker by trade, as was also the maternal grandfather, both of whom died in the "City of Brotherly Love." George Shubert was a carpenter and ship joiner, which trade he learned in Philadelphia, and which he carried on in that city until 1833, when he immigrated with his family to Portsmouth, Ohio, where he still continued his trade. He was delegate to the convention that nominated William H. Harrison to the presidency of the United States, and died before he got to vote. He lies buried in Portsmouth. The mother then went back to Philadelphia, where she died in 1880. They were the parents of five children, three now living: Garrett B., Henry, and Georgiana, wife of Harvey Gillett, of Hastings, Minn. Garrett B. Shubert was quite small when he went to Ohio with his parents, and he remained there until the death of his father, when he went with his mother back to Philadelphia, where he remained until fourteen years of age. He then followed the sea for about eight years, sailing principally to South America and Europe. He made one voyage around Cape Horn, in 1849, to California, where he remained a little over one year, being engaged in mining on Yuba and Feather Rivers. He returned to Boston, Mass., in 1851, made several voyages to Europe, and in 1855 gave up the sea and went on the Mississippi River. He began as a deck hand, and was promoted to several higher positions before he gave it up, which he did after being on the river about two years. On May 7, 1857, he landed at Linn Creek, and accepted a position with Gov. McClurg as mate of his steamships and captain of his flat-boats. He was constantly employed by the year until the war broke out, when in June, 1861, he enlisted in the Home Guards, and afterward, while trying to organize a company, was captured by the rebels and carried to Fort Smith, where he was kept under provost guard. He was retained about three months, and then made his escape and came home, where the second day after his arrival he enlisted in the Missouri State Militia

Cavalry, and was made quartermaster-sergeant. About a year later he was made quartermaster, which position he held until February, 1865, when he was transferred to the Fourteenth Missouri Veteran Cavalry, holding the same position. He was discharged November 1, 1865. He participated in a great many hard skirmishes, but never received a wound. At the close of the war he came back to Linn Creek, and has since been engaged in farming, etc. Previous to the war, in 1857, he married Miss Bridget Foy, a native of New York, but who was reared in Louisiana. To this marriage were born six children: Charles, Henry; Eliza, wife of J. W. McIntire; Edward F., editor of the *People's Tribune*; Mary F., wife of Sherman Agee, and George. In 1871 Mr. Shubert was elected probate judge to fill an unexpired term. In 1878 he was elected probate judge and president of the county court, holding the position four years. In 1882 he was re-elected probate judge, which position he held until 1887. In 1884 he was elected county collector, and re-elected in 1886-88, this making his third term for county collector. He has been deputy clerk for both courts, and also deputy sheriff for a number of years. Judge Shubert is one of the most prominent citizens of Camden County, and has made a host of friends. He is a member of the G. A. R., and is the owner of 240 acres of land, with about fifty acres under cultivation and well improved.

William F. Simpson, county surveyor of Camden County, and a farmer of Adair Township, was born in Tennessee in 1845, and is a son of William C. and Lucretia T. (Garner) Simpson, both natives of Tennessee, the former of whom was born in 1810. The parents moved from Tennessee to Camden County, Mo., in 1847. William C. Simpson was a farmer, and served as county surveyor for about twenty-seven years; he was also assessor several terms and commissioner of public schools. Of the eight children in this family but four are now living, viz.: Sophia Ann Pritchett, Nancy E. Freeman, John D. and William F. William C. Simpson, who died in 1882, was a son of James Simpson and Levina Simpson; the former, a farmer, was born in Virginia, and died in 1860. Mrs. Lucretia T. Simpson died in 1860. She was a daughter of Louis Garner, who moved from his native State, Tennessee, to Camden County, Mo., about 1857. William F. Simpson spent the greater part of his early life in Camden County, Mo. In 1863 he enlisted in Company K, Second Missouri Light Artillery, United States Army, under command of Col. Nelson Cole and Capt. Confare, with whom he served in the capacity of duty sergeant and second lieutenant, operating in Nebraska and Montana, until 1865, receiving his discharge at St. Louis. November 15, 1866, he married Lucy Estes, who was born in Camden County in 1840, and was a daughter of John G. and Lucy (Dodson) Estes. Mrs. Simpson died in 1881, and June 9, 1886, Mr. Simpson married Mary J. Russell, who was born in Camden County in 1856, and is a daughter of Andrew A. Russell. They have one child, William Andrew. Mr. Simpson was justice of the peace in Auglaize Township for six years, and upon the death of his father, in 1882, he was appointed county surveyor, which position he still holds. In politics he is a Republican.

He is a Mason, a member of the I. O. O. F. and G. A. R., and also belongs to the Christian Church.

Josiah Stanley, attorney at law and carpenter, of Climax Springs, Mo., is a native of Wayne County, Md., where he was born in 1841, being a son of Richard H. and Naomi (Beeson) Stanley, who were born in North Carolina in 1808 and 1814, and died in Howard County, Ind., in 1858 and 1882, respectively. They first moved from their native State to Wayne County, but afterward located in Howard County in 1851, where the father followed his trade of carpentering, and where they reared their family, which consisted of seven children, five now living: Nancy A. (Kemp), Josiah, Lydia (Poole), Richard Henry and Melissa (Smith). William died during the late war from the effects of a wound received at the battle of Murfreesboro, Tenn., and Mary (Mrs. Gardner) died in 1878, having borne one child. Josiah Stanley spent his early life in Howard County, Ind., and at the early age of sixteen began the battle of life for himself as a carpenter. April 17, 1861, he enlisted in Company D, Sixth Indiana, three months troops, under Capt. Thomas J. Harrison, United States army, but after receiving his discharge, in August of that year he joined Company D, Thirty-ninth Regiment Indiana Cavalry, of which company he was afterward made sergeant. He was promoted to second lieutenant in April, 1862, and in May, 1864, became captain of his company, and was discharged on the 31st of December, 1864, at Savannah, Ga., having taken an active part in the battles of Shiloh, Corinth, Perryville, Murfreesboro, Liberty Gap, Hoover's Gap, Rousseau's raid in Alabama, Gen. McCook's raid in Georgia, Chattanooga, Chickamauga, and was with Gen Sherman on his march to the sea. He was wounded near Waynesboro, Ga., November 24, 1864, by a gunshot in the right knee, which wound still troubles him, and confines him to his room for months at a time. He was taken prisoner at Murfreesboro. In 1865 he married Miss Sarah A. Brownfield, who was born in Indiana in 1844, a daughter of Samuel and Sarah (Boyd) Brownfield, both of whom were of Irish descent, and whose children's names are as follows: William, Ellen and Sarah A. (Mrs. Stanley). Eight of their nine children grew to maturity. Mr. Stanley has served as notary public for a number of years, and also as justice of the peace. He is a Republican, his first vote being cast for Grant in 1868, and is a member of the Masonic fraternity, the I. O. O. F. and G. A. R. He and wife became the parents of one son, Albert Sherman, who died at the age of twelve years. They have reared two orphan children: William M. Brownfield and Stanley Gardner.

J. W. Vincent, editor of the *Reveille*, at Linn Creek, was born in Jackson, Miss., May 14, 1859, and is the son of Joshua S. and Susan (Williams) Vincent, the former a native of New York and the latter of the Emerald Isle. The father has had quite a notable career. He was a printer by trade, entering his apprenticeship at the age of fourteen years, and was at work on the New York *Tribune*, under Horace Greeley, at the time of the Mexican War. He abandoned his business and enlisted in Company I, First Regiment, sailed around Cape Horn, and in 1848 landed in California, where he served two years and a half, being discharged at San Diego. He was wounded twice in a skirmish with the Indians; was a sergeant, and after being discharged remained about seven years in California, being engaged in mining. He bought the Clear Lake property, near San Francisco, which is now quite extensive property. There he ran a public inn or resort, which he carried on for three years. This property was purchased under a Mexican Government grant, and he was in litigation over this for some years, as there was an opposition grant, which was a forgery, being afterwards proven as such. An assassin was hired to put him out of the way, and a load of buckshot was fired into his neck one morning while he was sitting in his hotel, seriously wounding him. However, he recovered, sold out in 1856, and returned to New York State, where he worked on several of the leading papers in the cities of that State, also being foreman of the Milwaukee *Sentinel* for some time. He was sent south as a correspondent of this paper, finally locating in Mississippi, and at the time of the breaking out of the war was at work on the Jackson *Mississippian*, and set up the Mississippi ordinance of secession when first issued. In 1861 he left and went to Wisconsin, and from there to Jackson County, Ill., where he founded the *New Era* at Carbondale, which he ran for about three years. In 1868 he came to Linn Creek and founded the *Reveille*, which publication he continued until 1880, when his son, J. W., purchased the office, and has since continued its publication. The father was married in Milwaukee, Wis., and has but two children: Joshua W. and Henry M. The father is a resident of Linn Creek. J. W. Vincent was about nine years of age when he came to Linn Creek with his parents. Here he completed his growth, received a common-school education, and learned the printer's trade of his father. In 1880 he purchased the paper of his father, as before stated, and this sheet is edited in the interests of the Republican party, and is a spicy journal. Mr. Vincent was married first, in 1880, to Miss Mary E. Shoop, who bore him one child, Mary Ida, and died in 1883. In September, 1884, Mr. Vincent chose for his second wife Miss Elizabeth M. Foster, by whom he had three children, one now living, Mabel. Mr. Vincent is a Past Master Mason, and was Master of the late Grange lodge.

John Vogel is one of the prosperous farmers residing on the Little Niangua River, in Camden County, Mo. He was born in Germany in 1842, and in 1853 came to America with his parents, Frederick and Elizabeth (Miller) Vogel, who were born in that country in 1810 and 1807, respectively. They settled in Cole County, Mo., where the father followed his trade of tailoring, and reared his family, which consisted of eleven children. Seven are living at the present time, and four of his sons were soldiers in the Union army. At the age of eighteen years John Vogel began life for himself, and entered the Union army, enlisting in 1861, in Company K, Fifth Missouri Cavalry, and received his discharge in July, 1865. He is now a member of the G. A. R., and is a stanch Republican in politics, casting his first presidential vote for Abraham Lincoln in 1864. He came to Camden County in 1870, and purchased his present fertile valley farm, consisting of 220 acres, 100 of which are under cultivation, and here has since resided with his family. December 26, 1868, he wedded Miss Louisa Arnholdt, who was born in Cole County in 1847, and by her is the father of the following named children: Bertha, Ida, William, Henry, Charles, Peter and George, all of whom attend the Lutheran Church, of which the father and mother are members. Mrs. Vogel's parents, Christopher and Purlina (Frisb) Arnholdt, were born in Germany, and came to America in 1842, locating in Cole County, Mo. They moved to Camden County in 1856, purchasing a good farm on the Little Niangua River. He was engaged in farming and milling until his mill was burned by bushwhackers in 1864, and after the war he located in Jefferson City, Mo., and has since been engaged in the mercantile business, being now a resident of Brazito, Mo.

A. J. Watson, one of the prosperous farmers of Camden County, is a native of Cooper County, Mo., born June 6, 1857, and is the son of Cornelius and Elvira (Johnson) Watson. The father immigrated to Missouri from Kentucky at an early day, and located in Camden County, where he remained a short time. He then moved to Cooper County, Mo., where he died in 1865. The mother is yet living. They had four children: Harriet E. (wife of William Ray), Andrew J., Henry F. and Eliza (wife of Alexander McDowell). The father participated in the late war. He was captured by the Union forces, and cast into prison, where he died. He was reprieved, but was not able to come home. He was a farmer, which occupation he had followed the principal part of the time. A. J. Watson was reared, until nine years of age, in Cooper County, when he moved with his mother to Camden County in 1866, and located in Osage Township. He remained with his mother until twenty-one years of age, and in November, 1877, he married Miss Mary E. Hibdon, a native of Morgan County, Mo., by whom he has four children: Sarah A., Dolly E., Rosa B. and Maude D. After marriage Mr. and Mrs. Watson moved to their present farm, and bought 700 acres of land, with about 150 under cultivation. He has made all the improvements, which are first-class, and as good as can be found in Camden County, with a good residence and barn. He deals in stock of all kinds, and his farm is well adapted for this purpose. Aside from his farming interest, Mr. Watson is also engaged in the drug business at Linn Creek, having purchased the drug store of H. H. Wines in January, 1889. He is a member of the Masonic fraternity, and Mrs. Watson is a member of the Baptist Church.

John White was born in Camden County, Mo., in 1857, and is an enterprising citizen of his native county. His father, Thomas White, was a farmer by occupation, and was born in Indiana in 1834; he drove a Government team during the late war, and he married a Miss Medley. Of their children four are living, viz.: John, Riley H., Caroline (now Mrs. McCamish) and Luroney Carlisle. His second marriage, to Mrs. Sarah Fisher, resulted in the birth of two children: Robert and James T. Mrs. W. had three children by a former husband: Joseph, Fanny and Samuel Fisher. The paternal grandfather of our subject was Moses White, who was born in New Jersey, from which State he moved to Illinois, thence to Indiana, and in 1840 to

Camden County, Mo. He was a farmer, and died in 1868. John White was reared to the pursuit of farming in Camden County, and was deprived of the privileges of an education even in the common schools, for which deficiency he made up to a large extent by studying alone. He worked at farming until 1882, and, having saved $100, he invested that amount in a stock of groceries, which he opened at Olive City, Camden County; after one month he moved to Osage Iron Works, where he engaged in more general merchandising, in partnership with J. T. Washburn, and the firm has been remarkably successful. They carry a complete stock of general merchandise, own their store building and residence, as well as 278 acres of land in Camden County and 320 acres in Morgan County. February 5, 1888, Mr. White married Miss Jennie Leighty, who was born in Johnson County, Mo., in 1869, and is a daughter of Peter and Ellen Leighty, natives of Pennsylvania. Mr. and Mrs. White's only child, Ellsworth Oron, who was born October 26, 1888, died January 26, 1889. Mr. White has been postmaster of the Osage Iron Works for the past five years, and has filled the office with credit to himself and to the satisfaction of the community. He is a Democrat in politics, and a member of the Masonic fraternity, as well as the Methodist Episcopal Church, South.

Josiah L. Winfrey, a prominent stock farmer of this community, was born within six miles of where he now lives, on what is known as Conn's Creek (named after his grandfather), on the 12th of February, 1838, his parents being James M. and Eleanor M. (Conn) Winfrey, who were Tennesseeans, and his grandfather being also James M. Winfrey, and a native of Tennessee. The latter moved to Kentucky with his family in the early part of the 30's, and located on the Wet Auglaize, near the mouth of Brumley Creek, where he lived until 1863, in which year he died. He was twice married, but had no family by his second wife. His first union was blessed in the birth of seven children, two of whom are now living, Thomas and William C., both of whom are living in Miller County, Mo., the former being a Predestinarian Baptist minister. James M. Winfrey, the father of our subject, was only a lad when brought to Missouri, but remained with his parents until grown, then married and located on Conn's Creek, but being of a rather roving disposition, remained here but a short time, and until about 1848 or 1849 resided on and improved good farms in Dallas, Polk, Camden and Miller Counties. He then located on the farm where his widow now resides, and there died March 13, 1863, having been a member of the Osage Regiment of Missouri Home Guards, United States Army. His wife was born in 1829, being a daughter of Josiah Conn, who was a Tennesseean. He moved from his native State to Alabama, where he taught school, but at an early day removed to Missouri, locating on the prairie which afterward took the name of Conn's Creek. He taught school after coming to Missouri, and also preached the Gospel and farmed. Four of his eight children are now living: Eleathea, Eleanor M., Peggie and Josiah J. To James M. and Eleanor Winfrey were born the following family: Josiah L., William C., Benjamin E., Sarah E., Eleathea, Zilpha, James M., Thomas L., Pennington, John C., Marshal

C. and Francis T. Benjamin, Eleathea and Pennington are deceased. Josiah L. Winfrey was reared in his native county, and served during the Rebellion in Company C, Osage Regiment Missouri Home Guards, as sergeant for about six months, and was then taken to Jefferson City to guard that city. He afterward served as orderly-sergeant in Company C, Forty-eighth Missouri State Militia, and during the war purchased the farm where he now lives, on which he has resided since peace was declared. He was elected county assessor in the fall of 1872, which position he held four years, taking the census of 1876, and has held the office of justice of the peace a number of years, being the present incumbent of that office. At one time he was engaged in selling goods at Montreal, Mo., and in 1859 took the "gold fever," and made a trip to Pike's Peak, but did not remain there long. January 10, 1861, he was married to Rebecca M. Amos, who was born in Alabama, and came to Missouri with her parents in 1857. Her death occurred August 21, 1882, she having become the mother of eight children, seven of whom are living: Mary E., Valonia J., Rebecca M., Eliza E., Melissa S., Sarah A., Josiah L. and Zilpha J. Josiah L., the only son, died at the age of eleven months. Mr. Winfrey was married the second time July 23, 1885, to Melvina C. Carlton, whose maiden name was George. She was a daughter of Ira H. George, and was born in Russell County, Ky., coming to Missouri in 1850, when she was nine years old. By her first husband, Milton, who died in 1859, she became the mother of two children: Eveline E. and William R. Her second husband, Franklin S. Carlton, died September 22, 1882, and left four children, all deceased but one, Merinda I. John H., Sarah A. and an infant are deceased. Mr. and Mrs. Winfrey have one of the handsomest homes in the county. They are members of the church, Mr. Winfrey being also a member of the A. F. & A. M. and the G. A. R., being Past Commander of Montreal Lodge No. 342. In his political views he is a stanch Republican.

DALLAS COUNTY.

Francis M. Adams, a substantial and prominent citizen of Washington Township, Dallas Co., Mo., was born in Montgomery County, Tenn., January 24, 1832, and is the son of Philip and Rebecca (Nanny) Adams, natives of Virginia. The father died in Dallas County, Mo., in 1859, at the age of fifty-six years. The mother is still living, in her eightieth year, is a resident of the last named county, and is a member of the Christian Church. The father is a Democrat in politics, was constable while living in Tennessee, and during the mustering of the militia was major. He started life without means, but was a successful farmer, and was in comfortable circumstances at the time of his death. During the Mexican War he enlisted, but was never called into the service. He was the father of seven children, four now living: Francis M., Martin V., Jasper N. and Julia D. At the age of eighteen Francis M. Adams engaged in the mercantile business at Conyersville, Tenn., and was in business there eleven years, or until 1859, when he came to Missouri, and located in Dallas County, intending to go into the mercantile business, but on account of the war abandoned this idea. In June, 1862, he enlisted in Company A, Woods' Battalion, Confederate service, and was on duty until his surrender at Shreveport, La., in June, 1865. He was orderly sergeant most of the time, when not holding the office of lieutenant. He was in many battles—Pea Ridge, Camden, Alexander and Price's raid. He received a flesh wound at Indianapolis. Mr. Adams was a heavy loser by the war, and after that eventful period he went back and located in Henry County, Tenn., where he farmed and dealt in stock for eleven years. He then came back to Dallas County, Mo., where he has since resided. Previous to the war, December 20, 1855, he married Miss Emily A. Simmons, daughter of Levi and Eliza Simmons, and a native of Henry County, Tenn., born November 14, 1837; she died in Dallas County, Mo., May 22, 1859. She was a member of the Primitive Baptist Church, and an excellent woman. To this union was born one daughter, Elzerene, wife of B. F. Norris, now of Henry County, Tenn. December 20, 1860, Mr. Adams married Miss Rebecca J. Haymes, daughter of William and Rebecca Haymes, natives of East Tennessee, Hawkins County. She was born in what is now Webster County, Mo., April 22, 1844, and by her marriage became the mother of six children, three of whom are now living: Emily D., wife of Christopher H. Whittenburg, farmer in Dallas County; William A. and Alta J. Those deceased are: Frances R., who was the wife of G. B. Franklin, and who died December 2, 1886, when twenty-two years of age; Mary O., an infant, and Philip A., who also died when an infant. Mr. Adams is a farmer by occupation, is a Democrat in politics, a member of the Masonic fraternity, and his wife is a member of the Methodist Episcopal Church, South.

John M. Alford, merchant and farmer, and one of the principal stock dealers of Dallas County, Mo., was born in Knox County, Tenn., February 9, 1822, and is a son of John and Jane (McElhattan) Alford, also Tennesseeans, who immigrated to Carroll County, Ark., in 1852, and there spent their declining years. The father was a farmer, and also carried on milling in his early days, and of his large family of children there are living at the present time: Malinda, Robert, John M., Orlando D., Thomas, Margaret, Rebecca and Mary. John M. was reared on a farm in his native State, and was married in Meigs County, Tenn., March 4, 1840, to Lucinda Cardell, by whom he became the father of two children, Robert and William. In 1855 he came with his family to Dallas County, Mo., and reached Four Mile Prairie November 5, 1855, where he purchased a claim that was partly improved, with about ten acres cleared, and on which was a little log house. In 1856 he entered several forty-acre tracts, 160 acres being prairie land and the rest in timber, and here has lived up to the present date. He now owns 1,600 or 1,700 acres of valuable land, the most of which is under cultivation, and is an extensive dealer in the better class of stock. He has a good residence and other buildings on his farm, and a look over his home farm shows the thrift and energy that has put his place in its present admirable condition. Since 1862 he has been engaged in the mercantile business at Wood Hill Post-office, and in his public as well as social career would prove a valuable addition to any community. He married his present wife, whose maiden name was Hannah Hallomon, April 13, 1847, and nine of their ten children are now living: Pleasant, Jeremiah, Sarah, Matthew, Charles, Thomas, Owen, Susan, Mary and John.

John P. Andrews, a physician and farmer of Urbana, Dallas County, is a son of Mark and Virginia W. (Thompson) Andrews, and was born in Buffalo, Mo., in 1847. Mark Andrews was born in Virginia in 1812, and was a physician by profession, practicing medicine for several years in Dinwiddie County, Va., before his removal to Dallas County, Mo., where he also engaged in the practice of his profession until his death, which occurred in 1866. He had twelve children, of whom nine are now living, viz.: Martha Darby (only child by a previous marriage), Virginia Fletcher, Emily Darby, Lucy Reser, Harriet Coon, Joseph Andrews, Susan Darby, Mark Andrews and John P. Andrews. The paternal grandfather of our subject died of small-pox in the army, during the War of 1812. John P. Andrews spent his early life in Dallas County, Mo. He subsequently attended college at Mount Pleasant, Iowa, and later read medicine with Drs. Slavens & Vaughn, of Urbana, having previously been engaged in school-teaching. In 1873-74 he taught in the Urbana High-school, and the following year the Morrisville School. In 1876-77 he had charge of the Dadeville School, and in 1877-78 was principal of the Rondo Institute, Polk County. In 1881 he entered the St. Louis Medical College, which he attended three consecutive terms, graduating in 1884. He then returned to Dallas County, and immediately began the practice of his chosen profession at Urbana, in partnership with Dr. Vaughn, his former preceptor. In 1874 Dr. Andrews married Miss Rintha Hightshoe, who was born in Indiana in 1849, and is a daughter of David and Elizabeth (Burne) Hightshoe, natives of Ohio and West Virginia, respectively. Of the seven children born to Dr. and Mrs. Andrews, five are now living, viz.: Henrietta V., Zula R., Alice, Rolla and Bessie. The Doctor is a member of the Methodist Episcopal Church, and in politics his sympathies are with the Republican party.

Dr. Morgan L. Atchly, an eminent physician and surgeon of Dallas County, Mo., was born November 16, 1837, in Meigs County, Tenn. He is one of eight surviving members of a family of ten children born to the marriage of John Atchly and Elizabeth Eubanks, who were natives of the "Old Dominion," and early immigrants to Tennessee. About 1838 they took up their abode in Goodwin Hollow, Laclede Co., Mo., where they entered land amounting to about 340 acres, the most of which was heavily covered with timber. In time it became one of the finest farms in the county, and is now owned by their two sons, Seth and James. The father died about 1882, and his wife in 1878. The following are their children who are living: Noah D., James, Seth, Miles, Dr. Morgan L., Sarah, Delilah and Elizabeth. Dr. Morgan L. Atchly grew to manhood on a farm in Missouri, and received such education as the schools of that day afforded. He began the study of medicine in 1860, and in 1864 was appointed assistant surgeon, and was stationed at Hartville and Lebanon, serving in this capacity for about two years. He attended his first course of lectures at Cincinnati, Ohio, in 1863, and after the close of the war he completed his medical studies and graduated from the Eclectic Medical College of St. Louis, Mo., in 1872. He first practiced his profession at Lebanon a short time, then located in Phelps County, and in 1867 came to Louisburg, where he has since been an active and very successful practitioner. He derives a very lucrative income from his profession, and in connection with the "healing art" gives much of his attention to farming, being the owner of about 246 acres of land, with about 170 acres under cultivation and well improved. On coming to Dallas County, his possessions consisted of a good education, a pair of pill bags and six "bits," but his energy was boundless, and as a result he is now one of the successful physicians and wealthy farmers of the county. He is a member of the Dallas County Medical Association. In 1868 he was united in marriage to Miss Sophronia Marsh, by whom he had one child, Maude, the wife of C. C. Carter. His wife died in 1870, and the following year he wedded Virginia T. Lindsey, who has borne him four children: John A., Jessie E., Inez and Virgil M. The Doctor is a member of the I. O. O. F., and he and wife are consistent members of the Baptist Church.

J. A. J. Baker is a worthy and successful tiller of the soil, of Dallas County, Mo., in which county he was born on the 8th of April, 1847. He is a son of Abraham and Mary B. (Breshears) Baker, who emigrated from Tennessee to Dallas County, Mo., at an early day, the father's death occurring here. His widow afterward married Noah Bray, whose sketch appears in this work. J. A. J. Baker was reared and educated in and has always been a resident of Dallas County. By industry and judicious management he has become the owner of a fertile farm of 240 acres, and has about eighty acres under good cultivation, and furnished with commodious and substantial buildings. He is one of the enterprising farmers of the county, and is always interested in enterprises which tend to benefit the county in which he resides. In 1870 he was united in the bonds of matrimony to Miss Sarah E., a daughter of J. M. Alford, and by her is the father of six children: James S., Mary A., Hannah E., Lucy, Maude and Susie. Mr. and Mrs. Baker are members of the Baptist Church. During the late war he served about six months in Company C, Forty-sixth Missouri Volunteer Infantry.

John T. Bass, farmer, was born in Wilson County, Tenn., May 2, 1844, his parents being Dolphin and Rutha (Bennett) Bass. The father was born in Tennessee, and in 1852 immigrated with his family to Dallas County, Mo., locating near Louisburg, where he entered a tract of land, consisting of 280 acres, and soon had a large portion of it under good improvement. Here he died in 1857, but his widow is still living, and resides in Texas. Six of their eight children are now living: John T., Harriet, Lucy, Solomon (deceased), Henry, Nancy, Louis (deceased) and William. The father was twice married, and had by his first wife six children, but only two are now living: James and Elijah. J. T. Bass was reared on a farm, and educated in the common schools of Dallas County, and in 1862 enlisted in the Enrolled Militia, Company D, Fifteenth Missouri, and after two years' service enlisted in the United States service, serving in the same company. He was in several hard skirmishes, and after receiving his discharge, in 1865, came home, and has since been engaged in farming and stock raising, making a specialty of raising mules and cattle. He owns 440 acres of land, besides some town property, and gives considerable attention to raising fruit. In February, 1865, he was married to Emeline Gammon, a daughter of George P. Gammon, and by her is the father of four children: Wellington, who is in the mercantile business at Louisburg; Walter, Ottie and one deceased. Mr. and Mrs. Bass are members of the Baptist Church, and he is also a member of the Masonic fraternity.

John M. Beck, a prosperous farmer and stock dealer of Dallas County, Mo., was born in Gasconade County, Mo., March 10, 1851, and is a son of John C. and Phoebe (Rennington) Beck, who were born in New York and Kentucky, respectively, and were married in Illinois. In 1846 they came to Missouri, settling in Gasconade County, but in 1857 took up their residence in Dallas County, locating on a partially improved farm of 160 acres on Four Mile Prairie, where they made valuable improvements and lived until their deaths, February 8, 1882, and December 19, 1888, respectively. The following are their children who are living: Rodolphus, John M., Joseph R., Jasper N., and Sarah E., wife of J. L. Cook. John M. Beck was educated in the common schools, and is now the owner of a fine farm of 240 acres, 120 of which are under cultivation and well improved. He raises and deals in mules and cattle, and ships to St. Louis, which business has proved highly remunerative. He is a member of the Masonic fraternity, the Agricultural Wheel, and is considered one of the sagacious and enterprising farmers of the county. He was married in 1881 to Miss Sarah E. Wisdom, a daughter of Parson C. Wisdom.

Christian H. Behrens is one of the leading merchants of Dallas County, Mo., and was born on the 12th of January, 1856, in Lee County, Iowa, his parents, Henry and Hannah (Burgdorf) Behrens, being natives of Hanover and Brunswick, Germany, respectively. Henry Behrens came to America in 1845, and located in St. Louis, Mo., and about 1847 went to Lee County, Iowa, where he purchased a farm and resided until his death, which occurred in 1872. His widow and eight of his eleven children are living, the latter's names being as follows: Christian H., Henry J., William J., August C., Hannah, Charles C., Martha and Frederick E. Christian H. Behrens resided with his parents on the farm until twenty-three years of age, and received his education in the schools of his native county, obtaining his academic education in Primrose Academy, and also attended several German schools of a high order. After leaving the farm he entered the employ of the large mercantile house of Chonca & Brown, of Fresno, Cal., but about the end of 1882 he came to Buffalo, and on the 11th of December, 1882, engaged in the mercantile business, which he is still successfully carrying on, the firm being now known as C. H. Behrens & Bro. Mr. Behrens started with quite a small stock of goods, but by industry and good management his store has reached its present admirable proportions, and nets him and his brother a handsome annual income. In the spring of 1887 their present building was completed, which is a commodious and handsome three-story brick, the largest mercantile house in the county, and a credit to any city, and is well stocked with all kinds of dry goods, groceries, boots, shoes and clothing, and agricultural implements. Although they have resided in Buffalo but a few years, they are already well known throughout the county as enterprising, honorable and reliable business men, and have accordingly secured a large and lucrative trade. On the 28th of November, 1878, C. H. Behrens was united in marriage to Miss Etta Able, who died in 1880, having borne one child, Aaron, and on the 25th of October, 1881, he wedded his present wife, Miss Matilda Able, by whom he became the father of three children, who are all deceased. He and wife are members of the Presbyterian Church, and he is ever ready to give material aid to undertakings of worth, and to further the interests of the churches and schools and enterprises of any kind beneficial to the town and county. Politically Mr. Behrens is a strong Democrat, although being reared in the great Republican State, Iowa. He is well versed in the German and American languages, and is an expert accountant.

Nathaniel L. Bennett. Among the prominent citizens and farmers of Dallas County, Mo., may be mentioned Mr. Bennett, who was born in Maury County, Tenn., November 27, 1835, being a son of Moses G. and Sarah (Woolard) Bennett, natives, respectively, of North Carolina and Maury County, Tenn., the former's birth occurring April 9, 1813, and the latter's March 2, 1817. Both are yet living, and reside in Dallas County, Mo., with their children. Moses G. Bennett is a Democrat in politics, and is a very successful farmer, and accumulated a great deal of property by industry and close application to business. He has been quite extensively engaged in stock dealing, and always finds a ready market for a great deal of his stock near home. Five of his ten children are now living: Nathaniel L., Harriet (wife of J. D. Newport), James C., Martha J. (wife of J. W. Jones), and John M. Besides his own children he has given a good home to five orphan children; the following are the names of his children who are deceased: Mary, Lockey A., Margaret D., Jackson and an infant. Nathaniel L. Bennett remained on the home farm until twenty years of age, and then engaged in farming and stock raising on his own responsibility, and is now the owner of 300 acres of as good land as there is in Dallas County. He has given considerable attention to raising blooded horses, many of which have won good records on the race-track, and also makes a specialty of training horses for driving and the saddle. His cattle are of the Short-Horn and Galloway breeds, and he was the first man to introduce good hogs in the lower part of Dallas County, they being of the Poland-China and Berkshire breeds. He has also handled Cotswold sheep. His farm is abundantly watered, and is admirably adapted for stock purposes. After serving in the State Militia for about six months during the late war, and participating in the battle of Lexington, he, in 1863, joined Company I, Sixteenth Provisional Cavalry, United States Army, and served until the close of the war, being in the following engagements: Jefferson City, West Point, Boonville and a number of others. March 6, 1856, he was married to Elizabeth Henson, a daughter of Benjamin Henson. She was born in Dallas County February 14, 1842, and became the mother of ten children, all but two now living: Moses W., who died when an infant; Mary F., wife of N. C. Stafford; Harriet D., Sallie R., who died August 21, 1888; Lucinda J., Albert D., Ben D., Jack T., Edmond and George M. Mrs. Bennett is a member of the Missionary Baptist Church, and Mr. Bennett is a member of the A. O. U. W. and the Union Labor lodge.

John C. Bennett deserves honorable mention as one of the prosperous farmers of Dallas County, Mo. His birth occurred in Clark County, Ill., December 26, 1842, and he is a son of Philip and Ann (Marrs) Bennett, who were Kentuckians. After becoming grown the father went to Clark County, Ill., where he entered land and made him a home, and was one of the pioneer settlers. He was married in Illinois, his wife having been reared principally in Indiana, and by her he became the father of eight children: William M., John C., Marion F., Lafayette, Pauline J., Philip A., Emerson and Margaret A. The parents immigrated to Dallas County, Mo., in 1855, and located in Washington Township, where they made their home for four years; then sold out and moved one mile south of Buffalo, where the father resided until his death in 1886, at the age of seventy-five years, three months and five days. The mother survives him, and is in her seventy-sixth year. Since about thirteen years of age John C. Bennett has been a resident of Dallas County. He obtained a common-school education, and at the breaking out of the war served three months in the Dallas County Home Guards, in Capt. Eldredge's company, of Col. Edwards' regiment, and in 1862 enlisted in the Missouri State Militia Cavalry, in Capt. Worley's company, of Col. Richardson's regiment, the regiment being consolidated in 1863 with the Fourth Regiment, Col. Hall commanding, he being a member of Company L. In the fall of 1864 he re-enlisted in Company H, Thirteenth Missouri, United States Cavalry, commanded by Col. Catherwood, and received his discharge in May, 1866, at Fort Leavenworth, Kas., the latter part of the time being spent in quelling the Indians in Kansas and Colorado. He was in the battles of Pea Ridge, Neosho, Newtonia, Cane Hill and Prairie Grove, and also participated in many sharp skirmishes; was with the command on Price's raid, and was present when Maj.-Gens. Marmaduke and Cabell and a regiment of Confederate infantry were captured. After nearly five years' service he returned to his home and spent the summer and fall in school, and during the winter crossed the plains to the mountains and back, and in the spring of 1867 was married, and located on the tract of land where he now lives. He has about 200 acres under cultivation, and about 480 acres in the tract, and gives much of his attention to stock raising and dealing in stock. March 31, 1867, he wedded Miss Rachel Wright, by whom he has eight children: Emma (wife of John F. Fowler), Ella, Sheridan, Sherman, Emmett, John, Odessa and Ressa. The family attend and are members of the Christian Church, and Mr. Bennett has served five years as county assessor, and is a member of the G. A. R. He is a Republican in politics, and his motto is, do unto others as you would have others to do unto you—to say but little and do a great deal.

Marion Francis Bennett was born in Clark County, Ill., September 10, 1844, and is a son of Philip and Ann (Marrs) Bennett, natives of Nelson and Monroe Counties, Ky., respectively. The former's birth occurred on the 31st of December, 1810, and his death in Dallas County, Mo., April 5, 1886. His wife was born September 22, 1813, and their marriage was consummated in Illinois, and they continued to make that State their home until 1855, when they took up their abode in Dallas County, Mo. Their union was blessed in the birth of eight children who lived to be grown, seven of whom are now living: William M., John C., Marion Francis, Lafayette, Philip A., Paulina J., wife of William Joyner, and Margaret, wife of Monroe Cofer. Those deceased are Emerson, who was twenty-six years of age at the time of his death, and two infants. Marion Francis Bennett resided with his parents until the breaking out of the war, when he enlisted in the State Militia, and served until 1863, when he became a member of Company I. Sixteenth Missouri Cavalry, and was in the service the remainder of the war, then turning his attention to the peaceful pursuits of farming and stock raising, which occupations have proved tolerably successful under his skillful management. He is a stanch Republican in politics, and served as postmaster of Spring Grove for five years. February 3, 1867, he espoused Miss Mary O'Bannon, a daughter of John O'Bannon, one of the first settlers of Dallas County. She was born in Dallas County, Mo., May 17, 1848, and has borne a family of ten children: William S., George W., Edith, John O., Lizzie, Ann, Philip, Maude, James L. and Arthur.

Levi Brunner, a prominent citizen of Dallas County, Mo., was born in York County, Penn., September 6, 1834, and is a son of Peter and Sallie Brunner, who were born in Pennsylvania. The former died in his native State in 1882, at the age of seventy-seven years. After the death of his wife, whose demise occurred when Levi was a small child, Mr. Brunner wedded Elizabeth Misenbelder, who died in 1886. He followed the occupation of farming throughout life, and was a worthy member of the German Reformed Church. In early life he was a Whig in politics, but later in life became a Republican. To his first union four children were born, Levi being the only one now living, and his last union resulted in the birth of seven children, five of whom are living. Levi resided with his parents until twenty-four years of age, and then went to Tippecanoe County, Ind., but only resided there a short time, when he went to Lincoln County, Ill., where he made his home three years. From that time until 1868 he resided in Webster County, Mo., since which time he has made his home in Dallas County. In 1869 he purchased 120 acres of land, to which he has added until he now owns a good farm, with 100 acres under cultivation. When starting out in life for himself it was without means, but by industry and judicious management he has acquired his present property. December 25, 1862, he espoused Miss Catherine Fry, daughter of Daniel Fry. She was born in York County, Penn., in 1829, and died in Dallas County, Mo., in April, 1886, having become the mother of five children: William H., Jacob, John T. and Sarah E. Emanuel died in Illinois when an infant. Mr. Brunner is a member of the German Reformed Church, and throughout life has been a member of the Democratic party. While residing in his native State he learned the carpenter's trade, but has given most of his attention to farming.

Emanuel Bower, a farmer of Lincoln Township, Dallas County, is a native of the State of Pennsylvania, and was born December 11, 1817. His parents were Michael and Susanna Bower, who first moved from Pennsylvania to Ohio, thence to Indiana in 1835, and two years later located in Dallas County, Mo. Michael Bower, who was a blacksmith and farmer, was born in 1796 and died in 1876; his wife was born in 1796 and died in 1869. They were the parents of sixteen children, but five of whom are now living, viz.: Michael, Margaret, now Mrs. Yeager, of Dallas County; Emanuel, Luvina, who became a Mrs. Stout, and is now living in California, and William, a resident of Dakota; he married Miss Louisa Beasly about 1851. Emanuel Bower spent the greater part of his early life in Ohio, and was eighteen years of age when he went to Missouri, and three years later began an independent life and devoted his attention to the pursuit of agriculture. In 1842 he married Miss Pulina J. Yeager, who was born in Tennessee in 1826, and is a daughter of Elijah and Hannah Yeager, who moved from Tennessee to Illinois, and thence to Missouri in 1834. Elijah Yeager was a farmer and minister. To the union of Mr. and Mrs. Bower were born nine children, six now living, viz.: Hannah Carter, Susan Smith, Mary Reser, William Bower, Jennie Whelock and Vernon Bower. As a result of industry and good management Mr. Bower became the owner of 900 acres of land; he has given each of his children a farm, and now cultivates 160 acres. He is a Republican in politics, and with his wife is a member of the Methodist Episcopal Church.

Noah Bray, a wealthy retired farmer, and one of the early residents of Dallas County, Mo., was born in Gallia County, Ohio, January 29, 1819, and was there reared and educated. In 1840 he concluded to seek his fortune in the West, and came down the Ohio and Mississippi Rivers on a steamboat to Boonville, Mo., and from there walked to Dallas County, a distance of 110 miles, in three days. He had a brother who had previously located here, and he made his home with him and immediately engaged in farming. He raised one crop, then married Elizabeth Darby, of Polk County, and purchased the farm on which he now lives, which consisted of 160 acres, on which he erected a little log house, and continued to live in this manner until he could make better improvements, which he soon did. The country was in a very primitive state at this time, and they raised their own cotton and flax and made their own clothes. Mr. Bray has resided in Dallas County for nearly half a century, and has seen the country grow from a wilderness into highly cultivated farms, and handsome residences take the place of the little log cabins of early days. He organized a company of militia during the war, was elected its captain, and while visiting at home was captured by the "Johnnies," but succeeded in eluding their vigilance and made his escape. On December 24, 1840, his marriage occurred, and his union has been blessed in the birth of six children, three of whom are living: Elizabeth J., wife of William Alford; Mary M., wife of M. D. L. Jones, and Frances A., wife of W. A. Southard. Mrs. Bray died January 21, 1851, and September 18, 1851, Mr. Bray married Mary Baker, who has borne him five children: William R., Noah J., General F., Naomi, wife of M. Alford, and Margaret, wife of J. L. Austin. Mr. Bray owns 500 acres of land, with about 250 acres under cultivation, and has also been extensively engaged in stock dealing. He held the office of justice of the peace six years, public administrator six years, deputy sheriff of the county two years, and was also county commissioner two years. He and wife are members of the Baptist Church, and he is a member of the Masonic fraternity. His parents, William and Elizabeth (Denny) Bray, were born, reared and married in Surry County, N. C., and immigrated to Ohio in 1811, being among the early settlers of Gallia County. They entered 167 acres of unimproved land, and there spent the remainder of their days. The father was a soldier in the War of 1812, and he and wife became the parents of twelve children, nine sons and three daughters, but only three of the family are now living: William, Noah and Reuben.

Thomas M. Brown, attorney at law, Buffalo, Mo. Prominent among the many wide-a-wake and enterprising citizens of Dallas County stands the name of the gentleman whose brief biography follows. Schooled and reared in the cradle of necessity, Mr. Brown has shown by his very successful life here, during the past eight or nine years, the sterling worth of his manhood, and has drawn around him many friends, the result of his close application to public and private matters, and a masterful completion of his work. He is a native of Illinois, was born in La Salle, Ill., February 4, 1854, and is the son of John M. and Mary (Mulholland) Brown, natives of the Emerald Isle, who sought for themselves in their early life a home on the American Continent. John M. Brown was a merchant by occupation, and followed this occupation in Illinois for some time. He then removed from there to Missouri, and subsequently (projecting a journey to Pike's Peak) he located in Johnson County, Kas., where he passed the remainder of his life. Mrs. Brown afterward returned to the Missouri home, where she subsequently became the wife of John M. Guthridge, and bore him six children. Our subject grew to manhood on the farm of his foster-father, and obtained a fair common-school education. Upon attaining his majority, he sought the Lone Star State, where he spent nearly a year. He had been reared to hard manual labor, and used it as his stock in trade, but the State of Texas did not furnish him, as he thought, remuneration sufficient for his labors, and he returned to old Missouri. He here completed a good schooling, and afterward taught school. His early inclinations were for the study of law, and to this end the young man bent his energies. As soon as he could afford it, he entered a law office, his preceptor being the Hon. Daniel P. Stratton, of Stockton, Mo., from whose office he was admitted to the bar in 1880. Mr. Brown immediately cast about for a location, and for awhile he was at Hartville, in Wright County, Mo., where he made many strong and true friends, but did not stay there long, and located here. He came here in the spring of 1880, and in the fall of that year he was nominated and elected to the office of prosecuting attorney of Dallas County, a position he filled most acceptably during his term. To his credit it may be said that upon his retirement the citizens of Dallas County testified to their appreciation of his services by re-electing him to that office, and continuing him as their prosecuting attorney for another term. Upon his retirement from public life, Mr. Brown gave close attention to his practice, and has placed himself in the front rank of his profession. He is a versatile speaker, a deep reasoner, a logician of the old school on financial matters, and in this respect, which is certainly a cardinal principle in his character, we question very much whether he has any superiors, and few equals, in this judicial district. He has "hewed to the line," and made a success of his efforts. He owns over 1,000 acres of farm land, a very considerable city property here, a half interest in the Dallas County Bank and perquisites. He has a lucrative practice, and is to-day blessed with a realization of his early hopes when coming here, nominally a penniless attorney. Mr. Brown was happily married in Cedar County, Mo., January 20, 1881, to Miss Josie M. Beck, daughter of Isaac F. and Martha (Fielder) Beck, worthy citizens of Cedar County, Mo. Mrs. Brown is a lady of estimable attainments, and has, with her husband, the universal respect of all acquaintances. They are members of the Christian Church, and Mrs. Brown is a worthy and active member of the Ladies' Aid Society. Mr. Brown is a Master Mason, and a member of Reddick Lodge No. 361. He is a genial gentleman, affable and courteous to every one he meets; has a sound head, well set on a strong and healthy body. He enjoys his successful life here, however, very unostentatiously. We present his portrait.

J. P. Brownlow, banker of Buffalo, Mo., and one of the prominent and enterprising residents of Dallas County, was born in Giles County, Tenn., August 17, 1841, and is a son of James and Isabel (McCreary) Brownlow, who were also natives of that State and county, the former being killed during the late war by the soldiers, and the latter dying in Dallas County, Mo., in 1882. J. P. Brownlow received a limited early education, owing to the scarcity of good schools at that period, but acquired a fair knowledge of the "three R's." In 1861 he enlisted in the Confederate army, in Company K,

Third Tennessee Regiment, under Col. Brown, who afterward became governor of Tennessee, and participated in the battle of Fort Donelson, where he was wounded by a grape-shot in the right arm, and was afterward discharged and joined the Ninth Tennessee Cavalry, and was elected a lieutenant in Gen. Forrest's command. At the battle near Franklin he was wounded by a gunshot in the left shoulder, but was not disabled from duty. He was also in the battles of Nashville, Resaca and in a great many hard skirmishes, and was mustered out and discharged in April, 1865, at Gainesville, Ala., after which he returned home, and was engaged in farming until 1873, when he came to Dallas County, and located in Benton Township, about five miles from Buffalo, where he tilled the soil and was interested in stock trading and raising until 1882. He then came to Buffalo, where he has since made his home. All his business enterprises have been attended with good results, and in both social and business life he ranks among the first men of the county, and is a liberal giver to all worthy enterprises, having been one of the liberal contributors to the beautiful Baptist Church which has lately been erected in the town. He was married on December 4, 1859, to H. J. Ussery, a native of Tennessee, by whom he has seven children: Arabella F., Sallie P., John E., Joseph F., Cecil A., Cora and Katie. Mr. and Mrs. Brownlow and their four oldest children are worthy and consistent members of the Baptist Church, and are highly esteemed residents of the county.

Cornelius Brundridge is a representative of one of the oldest families in Dallas County, they having first become residents in 1838. He was born in Washington County, Mo., September 30, 1829, and is a son of David and Susan (Williamson) Brundridge, who were born in Kentucky and Ohio, respectively, and died in Dallas County, Mo., in 1875, their deaths occurring June 18 and June 11. The former was about sixty-three years of age, and the latter sixty-five. Their marriage took place in Washington County, whither they had moved with their parents at an early day, and they continued to reside there until the latter part of 1838, when they became residents of Dallas County. They were members of the Methodist Church for many years, and took great interest in the cause of Christianity. The father was a member of the State Militia during the late war, and until the breaking out of the Rebellion was a Democrat politically, after which he became a Republican. He was a strong Union man, and throughout a long and useful career was engaged in farming. Eight of his children are still living: Cornelius, William A., Sophronia (wife of Wilson Cooksey), John, Nancy (wife of Thomas Hardison), Abraham, Delila (wife of John Cooksey) and James D. Cornelius Brundridge resided with his parents until twenty-four years of age, and then engaged in tilling the soil for himself, which he has continued, in connection with stock raising, up to the present time, and has accumulated a goodly property. When the war broke out he first served six months in the State Militia, and then enlisted in Company I, of the Eighth Cavalry, United States Army, and after serving faithfully for three years was honorably discharged, having been a participant in the following engagements: Little Rock, Grand Prairie and others. April 10, 1853, he was married to Serena Lofton, a daughter of John Lofton. She was born in Maury County, Tenn., January 4, 1830, and is the mother of seven living children: Susan (wife of John Lofton), Sarah (wife of Beverly Gammons), Martha J. (wife of John Saunders), G. F., Annie, Ella, John W. and Bell. Those deceased are Margaret and Amanda. Mrs. Brundridge is a member of the Methodist Episcopal Church. He belongs to the G. A. R., and is a Republican in politics.

Judge William H. Buckner, associate judge from the Southern District of Dallas County, also postmaster and merchant at Thorpe, was born in Cocke County, Tenn., January 24, 1842, and is the son of Thomas and Elizabeth (Carter) Buckner, natives of Cocke County, Tenn., and Virginia, respectively. The father was born March 23, 1819, and is now living on the farm of his son, Judge William H. The mother was born April 14, 1822, and is also living. They were married in Cocke County, Tenn., and lived there until the fall of 1869, when they came to Dallas County, Mo., where they have since resided. He for years was a minister in the Missionary Baptist Church, but of late years, on account of ill health and old age, has stopped preaching. He served over two years in the Third North Carolina Mounted Infantry, Federal service, and was in different battles. The Buckner family is of English and Irish descent, but the Carter family is of French and Irish. To Mr. and Mrs. Buckner were born four children: William H., John W. (deceased), Elizabeth (deceased) and Nancy E., wife of Reuben I. Carter, a farmer of Dallas County, Mo. William H. received his education in Cocke County, Tenn., and in March, 1862, he enlisted in Company C, Eighth Tennessee Infantry, Federal Army, as orderly sergeant, and later as commissary sergeant, being honorably discharged at Knoxville, Tenn., August 18, 1865. He was in the siege of Knoxville, Dandridge and Blue Springs, Va.; then with Sherman to the sea; was at Buzzard's Roost and Resaca, Cartersville, Ga., and numerous other engagements, serving with honor and credit. After the war he began farming for himself, which he continued during the summer, and worked at the carpenter trade during the winter time. This he continued until June 6, 1884, when he formed a partnership with J. H. Davidson, and opened up a store at Thorpe. Here, after merchandising for a year, Mr. Buckner bought out his partner, and continued the business alone until 1886, when he formed a partnership with S. C. Robertson, and in March, 1888, the latter gave up his partnership interest, and J. W. W. Thompson took his place, where he has remained since. In 1882 our subject was elected justice of the peace, and in 1888 was elected judge from the Southern District of Dallas County. He has been school director and district clerk for twelve years. December 24, 1865, he married Miss Mary Eliza Holt, a native of Cocke County, Tenn., and the daughter of Josiah and Millie Holt. She was born in 1844, and died in her native county August 7, 1868. Two children were born to this union: Joseph A., a farmer in Henry County, Mo., and another son, who died in infancy. January 20, 1869, Judge Buckner married Miss Martha J. White, who was born in Cocke County, Tenn., October 30,

1843, and who is the daughter of Daniel and Elizabeth White. To Judge and Mrs. Buckner were born ten children: Sarah E., born October 23, 1869, and died October 1, 1888, wife of N. S. Binkley, of Dallas County, Mo.; David W., James D., born October 13, 1873, and died April 4, 1874; Eliza J., John H., Margaret A., Levi A., Lavina, born in February, 1881, and died August 10, 1881; Charles C. and Ira P. In 1885 Judge Buckner was appointed postmaster at Thorpe. He is a Republican in politics, and an enterprising citizen.

Andrew Johnson Butts, M. D., one of the leading practitioners of Dallas County, Mo., and a resident of Jackson Township, was born January 8, 1863, and is the son of John W. and Mary (Crawford) Butts, natives of Franklin, Ky., and North Carolina, respectively. John W. Butts moved with his parents to Missouri when a young man, and located in Dallas County, where he remained until the breaking out of the Civil War. He then enlisted in the Confederate army, serving until the battle of Helena, Ark., where he was taken prisoner, retained as such nine months at Alton, Ill., and fourteen months at Fort Delaware. He was in different battles, and was wounded at Pea Ridge, Ark. After the war he went to Texas, and settled in Lamar County, but afterward moved back to Dallas County, Mo. Here he remained one year, and in 1881 returned to Texas, locating in Denton County, and there died February 23, 1883, at the age of forty-two or forty-three. The mother is now living in Laclede County, Mo., and is the wife of William Benton. While in Texas the father served for some time as deputy sheriff, but his principal occupation was farming and stock raising, in which he was very successful. He was a Democrat in politics. To their marriage were born five children, three now living: A. J., Nettie and Hasie. The two last named are living with their grandfather, H. G. Butts. The two deceased were Walter and an infant. Andrew J. Butts was reared by his grandfather, and received a very liberal education at the home schools. In 1884 and 1885 he attended lectures at the Missouri Medical College, and again in 1887 and 1888, graduating on the 6th of March of the last named year. Soon after he came to his present location, where he has a large practice, which is constantly increasing. January 24, 1885, he married Miss Ellen McMillan, a native of Hardeman County, Tenn., and the daughter of James McMillan, an old settler of Dallas County, Mo. This union has been blessed by two children, Mallie and Willie. Dr. Butts is a Democrat in politics and a good citizen.

Charles L. Curtice, dealer in marble and granite monuments, tombstones, etc., at Buffalo, Mo., is a native of the "Empire State," having been born on the 10th of November, 1842, in Washington County, N. Y. His father was a well-known Free-will Baptist minister, while his mother was a Wing, of the Wings of Troy, N. Y. Charles L. Curtice was reared and educated in his native State, and at the age of seventeen began teaching school in Wisconsin, to which State his widowed mother removed in the previous year, his father dying while the son was only twelve years old. When the Civil War broke out he enlisted, on the 27th of April, 1861, in Company F, Twentieth Illinois

Volunteer Infantry. On the 27th of November, 1861, he was discharged, but re-enlisted on the same day in Company C, Sixth Illinois Cavalry. He was on the famous Grierson raid, and participated in the siege of Port Hudson, the last fight at Nashville, and a large number of lesser engagements. He was captured twice by the enemy, once by the guerrillas, but, although he was run by blood-hounds, he escaped, and after eleven weeks returned to his regiment at Memphis, Tenn. He was discharged November 27, 1865, at Camp Butler, Ill., making his term of service four years and seven months. For two years after his discharge he taught school in Franklin County, Ill. In 1868 he came to Dallas County, Mo., and for about eighteen years he taught in the schools of Dallas and adjoining counties. He also homesteaded and improved a farm during the intervals of teaching. He was married while on veteran furlough, on the 27th of April, 1864, to Miss Nancy E. Tinsley, of Franklin County, Ill., by whom he has had six children: Alice, married and living in Gunnison, Colo.; Willie, who died in November, 1884, at the age of fifteen years; Mamie, Walter, Cecil and Neva. His wife is a lineal descendant, on her father's side, of one of the oldest German families, her grandmother being a Molkey, a near relation of the Baron Von Moltke. Mr. Curtice is a member of the A. O. U. W. and the G. A. R., and he and his wife are members of the Christian Church.

William H. Darby, a carpenter and farmer of Urbana, Dallas County, was born in what was then Polk and is now Hickory County, Mo., in 1842. His parents were Daniel and Phoebe (Evans) Darby, the former of whom was born in Ohio in 1799, and the latter in 1801. After their marriage they moved from Ohio to Illinois, and later settled in Polk County, Mo. Of their thirteen children six are still living, viz.: Ezra, Ruami, Ephraim, William H., George W. and Isabelle, all living near Urbana, Mo. Daniel Darby was a wagon-maker and farmer, and served as justice of the peace many years; he died in 1862, and his widow in 1880. The paternal grandfather of our subject was Jedediah Darby. William H. Darby spent his early life in his native county. In 1863 he enlisted in Company F, Seventh Missouri State Militia Cavalry, under command of Col. John F. Phillips and Capt. B. H. Wilson, and took part in the battles of Jefferson City, Boonville and Big Blue, Mo., and Westport and Mine Creek, Kas., receiving an honorable discharge in 1865. In the same year he married Emily Andrews, who was born in Buffalo, Mo., in 1843, and is a daughter of Mark and Virginia (Thompson) Andrews, both natives of Virginia. Mark Andrews was a physician and farmer, and moved from Virginia to Buffalo, Mo., in 1840, and thence to near Urbana, Hickory Co., Mo., in 1850. In the Andrews family were ten children, seven of whom are still living, viz.: Martha Darby, Virginia Fletcher, Emily Darby, Lucy Reser, John Andrews, Joseph Andrews, Harriet Coon, Susan Darby and Mark Andrews. Mr. Darby owns 160 acres of land, of which eighty-five acres are under cultivation. He served as justice of the peace in Hickory County four years, and in 1880 bought and removed to his present home in Dallas County. He is a Democrat in politics, and cast his first presidential vote for Abraham

Lincoln in 1864. Mr. and Mrs. Darby are members of the Methodist Episcopal Church, South.

Joseph Davis is a farmer and miller of Urbana, Dallas Co., Mo., where he was born in 1842. His parents were Shepherd and Nancy (Cox) Davis, the former born in New Jersey in 1819, and the latter in North Carolina in 1822. They first moved from New Jersey to Illinois, whence they went to Dallas County, Mo., in 1839, returning to Illinois in 1843. In their family of three children our subject is the only survivor. Shepherd Davis, who was a farmer by occupation, died in 1849. The paternal grandparents of our subject were Ezekiel and Rachel Davis, natives of New Jersey, who subsequently moved to Illinois; the former was a farmer and cooper. Mrs. Nancy Davis was a daughter of John and Sarah (Owens) Cox, who went to Illinois from North Carolina, and in 1839 removed to Dallas County, Mo. John Cox was also a farmer. Joseph Davis was reared to farming in his native county, and in 1863 he enlisted in Company I, Eighth Missouri Cavalry, Union Army; he participated in the battles of Little Rock, Brown's Station, Pumpkin Bend and Augusta, and received an honorable discharge in August, 1865, when he returned to his home in Dallas County. Mr. Davis owns 540 acres of land, and a three-fourths interest in a flouring and saw mill at Urbana, as well as three lots in the town of Urbana. In 1872 he married Miss Rosetta White, who was born in Grant County, Wis., in 1849, and is a daughter of Nathan White, a native of the State of Tennessee, and a farmer by occupation. Mr. and Mrs. Davis have four children, viz.: Olive Lula, Cora Nancy, Oscar Lee and Ruiah Rowena. Mr. Davis is a member of the Masonic fraternity, and his political sympathies are with the Republican party.

George Delaplain, sheriff of Dallas County, was born in Licking County, Ohio, September 15, 1835, and is a son of John and Orpha (Overturf) Delaplain, the former being an early settler of Ohio. He immigrated to Polk County, Mo.; in 1849, but in 1852 came to Dallas County and located in Benton Township, where he lived until his death in 1871. His wife died in 1859, having borne a family of nine children, five of whom are yet living. George Delaplain resided in his native State until fourteen years of age, and continued to make his home with his parents until 1855, when he was married and began doing for himself. In August, 1862, he enlisted in the Eighth Missouri Cavalry, Company I, serving three years, and was in a number of skirmishes, but was in no regular engagement, as he was on scouting duty the most of the time. He also served as blacksmith of his company, and after receiving his discharge on the 2d of August, 1865, went to Illinois, whither his family had moved for protection. He remained there about one year, then moved back to Dallas County, where he has since been engaged in farming, and is the owner of ninety acres of land in Benton Township, the most of which is under cultivation. He was elected to the office of county sheriff in 1882, and was re-elected in 1886 and in 1888, and in his official capacity, as well as socially, he stands high in the estimation of the people. He was first married to Isabel Patterson, of Ohio, by whom he became the father of five children, four of whom are living: Elvira, Orpha, Eva and Adam. His second marriage was to Miss Mary J. Cowden, who bore him one child, Charles, and his next marriage was to Miss Adaline Johnson. His present wife was Mary Battoms, who was born in Tennessee. He is a member of the A. O. U. W. and G. A. R., and he and wife belong to the Baptist Church.

Silas Dillion, an enterprising farmer of Lincoln Township, Dallas County, was born in Virginia in 1819, and is a son of William and Mary (Plyburn) Dillion, both natives of Virginia, who were born respectively in 1793 and 1787, and spent their lives in their native State. They had a family of ten children, seven of whom still survive, viz.: Louis Dillion, Jacob Dillion, Lydia Sink, Silas Dillion, Jesse Dillion, Reed Dillion, Tyra Dillion. Those deceased are Becky Bonson, Polly Dillion and Moses Dillion. William Dillion, who was a farmer, died in 1846; his widow lived until 1876. The paternal grandparents of our subject were Jesse and Elizabeth (Blankenship) Dillion, of Virginia, where the former was a large planter and slaveholder. Silas Dillion was reared in his native State, where he spent his early manhood. In 1840 he went to Kentucky, and engaged in teaming until 1843, when he returned to Virginia, but the following year again went to Kentucky. In 1847 he married Elizabeth J. Vaughan, who was born in Kentucky in 1830, and was a daughter of Jeremiah and Frances (Barker) Vaughan, also natives of Kentucky, the former a farmer and merchant. Mrs. Dillion died in 1869, leaving seven children, viz.: Mary Frances Brown, Jeremiah, Anna E. Wattenboyer, William, Robert, Jennie E. Bonner and Crawford. In 1871 Mr. Dillion married Sarah E. Sample, a native of Tennessee, and a daughter of John and Elizabeth Sample, of that State. By his second marriage Mr. Dillion has five children, viz.: Dona Belle Crudginton, Jacob, John L., Mella S. and Rebecca J. In 1862 Mr. Dillion enlisted in Company E, Missouri State Militia, under command of Col. McClurg and Capt. Allen, and served until the close of the war, participating in the battles of Sentinel Prairie and Vaughn Station. He removed from Kentucky to Missouri in 1856, and first settled in Polk County, where he remained one year, and then went to Hickory County, removing to Dallas County in 1865, which has since been his home. He owns 278 acres of land, 100 acres of which are under cultivation, and devotes his attention entirely to farming. In religion he is a Free Will Baptist, and politically he is non-partisan.

Jacob Drake, dealer in saddles, harness, bridles, collars, whips, etc., at Buffalo, Mo., is a native of Jackson County, Ind., and was born in December, 1841, and when four years of age was taken by his parents, Jacob and Sarah (Sheline) Drake, to Vinton County, Ohio, where they resided until 1856. Coming west they located in Dallas County, Mo., where the father entered 160 acres of land, heavily covered with timber and totally unimproved. Here he erected a little log cabin, in which he lived until he could make better improvements, which was done in a few years. In 1869 he removed to Kentucky, where he spent the remainder of his days, his death occurring in 1875. He was born in Massachusetts in 1809, his wife having been born in the "Keystone State." Five of their eleven children are living at the present time. Jacob Drake, the subject of this sketch, resided in Ohio until about sixteen years of age, since which time he has lived in Dallas County, Mo. When the war broke out he enlisted first in Company F of the Home Guards, but shortly after joined Phelps' six months regiment, and after serving over seven months he joined Company A, Eighth Missouri Cavalry, serving as corporal until the close, doing duty principally as a scout, and participating in a number of sharp skirmishes. He was mustered out and discharged in August, 1865, after nearly four years' service, and was engaged in farming until the spring of 1881, when he was elected county collector, and served four years. He was also engaged in the real estate business until June, 1888, since which time he has been occupied in his present calling, the firm being known as Drake & Lovan, and besides this property he owns several houses and lots in Buffalo. He is a member of the G. A. R. and A. O. U. W., and he and wife, whose maiden name was Delilah B. Robbins, and whom he married in 1866, are members of the Methodist Episcopal Church. They have an adopted child, named James P. Drake, but his father's name is F. M. Routh. The child was born March 9, 1886; his mother, A. J. Routh, died when he was nine days old.

John S. Edmisson (deceased). In giving a history of the prominent and progressive citizens of Dallas County, the biographical department of this work would be incomplete without mentioning the Edmisson family, who have been represented in Missouri since 1837, at which date John S. Edmisson and his parents, Emanuel and Nancy (Johnson) Edmisson, located in Washington Township, Dallas County, where they entered land and were among the first settlers. He was born October 20, 1820, in Hardin County, Tenn., but received a fair education in the schools of Dallas County. July 8, 1847, he was married to Miss Elizabeth Wollard, and removed to Washington Township, where he was robbed and killed by the militia on the night of the 25th of September, 1863. He was a very successful farmer and stock dealer, and all his property was acquired by his own energy and judicious management, as he started in life a poor boy and received no assistance from his parents. He held a number of offices in the county, and had been clerk of the Baptist Church, of which he was a member, for a number of years. Five of his seven children are now living: George T.; Louisa R., wife of James L. Randle; Richard C.; Nancy M., wife of John H. Williamson, and Robert N. His wife is still living, aged sixty-one years, and after his death she was married to Dr. George Davison, of Murray County, Tenn., by whom she became the mother of two children: Joshua S., and Mary J., wife of John A. Brown. The Doctor died January 4, 1887, and was a member of the Christian Church, and also came to Missouri when seventeen years of age. His wife's parents were Nathaniel and Margaret (Hardison) Wollard, natives of Murray County, Tenn., where also their daughter Elizabeth was born, November 29, 1827. They came to Dallas County about 1837, and settled on a farm in Washington Township, where the father was killed by the militia September 1, 1863, his house having been robbed and burned by them. He was a minister of the Baptist Church, and was a peaceable and law-abiding citizen. Emanuel Edmisson died at the home of his son, John S., in Jackson Township, in July, 1857.

George T. Edmisson, a son of John S. and Elizabeth (Wollard) Edmisson, is a prominent attorney and notary public of Buffalo, Mo., and was born in Dallas County September 11, 1849, and was reared on farms in Jackson and Washington Townships, being educated principally in the latter. In August, 1877, receiving appointment to fill a vacancy as county clerk, he gave up farm life, and began filling the duties of his office. He was elected to the office in 1878, which position he filled until January 1, 1883, and during this time his spare moments were spent in studying Blackstone, and he was admitted to the bar in 1887, being appointed notary public the same year. He is building up an excellent and lucrative practice, and promises to stand at the head of his profession at no distant day. He enlisted in the Fifty-sixth Missouri Infantry, United States Volunteers, April 1, 1865, and served until peace was declared, although he was only sixteen years of age. He is a member of the Masonic fraternity, Blue Lodge, Chapter and Commandery, and his wife, whom he married October 29, 1868, is a member of the Baptist Church. Her maiden name was Amanda M. Stafford, and they are the parents of the following children: Lizzie, Felix C., George I., Robert E. and Albert P. Four children are deceased. Mr. Edmisson's connection with the professional and social affairs of Buffalo has proved fortunate for the residents of this community. Active, painstaking and thorough in everything attempted, he has aided very materially in advancing the interests of the place, and his career as a representative, progressive citizen has won for him extensive and honorable acquaintance.

Curtis C. Edmisson is a leading citizen of Washington Township, Dallas Co., Mo., and is a son of Emanuel and Nancy (Johnson) Edmisson, who were natives of North Carolina and Kentucky, respectively. The father died in Dallas County, Mo., in 1854, at the age of sixty-two years, the mother also dying there in 1840, when a comparatively young woman. They were married in Johnson County, Ky., whither the father had emigrated when a young man, and after residing in that State for a few years went to Tennessee, and afterward to Missouri, being among the very early settlers of Dallas County. In 1849 the family went to Randolph County, Ark., but returned to Missouri in 1853, locating in Hickory County, where the mother's death occurred. After her death Emanuel married Widow Nancy McVey, who is now living in Dallas County at an extreme old age. The father was a Democrat and a farmer throughout life, and he and wife became the parents of fourteen children, twelve of whom lived to be grown, Curtis C. being the eleventh of the family. He and a brother and three sisters are the only ones living at the present time. Their names are as follows: Martha (widow of George H. Hill), Ellen (widow of Thomas Hill), Nancy (wife of John Allcorn), Curtis C., and S. R., who is a mechanic of Dallas County. In 1857 Curtis C. left home, and crossed the plains to California, making the trip in six months. The year before he had started to make the trip, but after he and his friends had passed Fort Kearney, they had a fight with the Indians, in which one of the men was wounded, and Mr. Edmisson remained to care for him until his death. By that time the train had advanced such a distance that he was unable to join it, and he returned home and started the next year, and during a fourteen years' residence in the West was engaged in mining in Oregon, Nevada, Washington Territory, Idaho Territory, Montana Territory, Utah Territory, Wyoming Territory and British Columbia. He also followed teaming and farming, and in all these occupations was quite successful, having surmounted difficulties to which many men would have succumbed. He can tell many thrilling experiences of his Western life, and for some time, while residing in Montana, filled the office of justice of the peace. Since returning to Missouri he has been engaged in farming and stock dealing, and is a wealthy and enterprising citizen of the county, being the owner of a well-improved and well-located farm. On the fourteenth of December, 1871, he was married to Rhoda R. C. Randles, a daughter of Robert O. Randles, by whom he is the father of the following children: John R., Nancy Olive, Lillie Melvina, Curtis O., William R., James F., Ella R., and the following, who are deceased: Ida M. and Cora L. Mrs. Edmisson was born in Dallas County, Mo., April 4, 1854, and is a member of the Baptist Church. Mr. Edmisson is a Mason, and a member of the Agricultural Wheel.

Benjamin S. Fraker was born in Knox County, Tenn., May 14, 1818. His paternal grandparents, Michael Fraker, and wife, came to this country from Germany in 1700, first settling in Virginia and then in Tennessee, where they died in 1700. They reared a large family of children, who became successful farmers. One of the sons, Michael Fraker, Jr., moved to Kentucky in an early day, and was instrumental in the building of a town called Frakertown. The maternal grandparents of Benjamin, Christian Sandes and wife, Mary, also settled in Tennessee in 1700. The former was a blacksmith by trade, a calling in which he made a good living. Christian Fraker, father of the subject of this sketch, was born August 19, 1782, and died in 1828, in full fellowship with the Methodist Church, of which he had lived a devoted member. He was a successful farmer, and accumulated considerable property. His wife, Mary Sandes, daughter of Benjamin Sandes, was born November 29, 1785, and died in 1854. After her husband's death she came with five children to Missouri, in the fall of 1842. The following constituted the family: Margaret, born September 20, 1804, died in 1833; Michael, born March 22, 1806 (also deceased); George W., born December 9, 1807, died in 1886; Mary, born February 23, 1810, died in 1829; Robert, born January 7, 1812, died in 1832; Sarah, born March 23, 1814, died in 1880; Elizabeth, born May, 8, 1816; Benjamin S., our subject; Catherine, born April 17, 1820, died the same year; Susan, born April 22, 1822, died in 1849; Martha J., born February 4, 1824, died in 1843; and Nancy E., born February 24, 1826. Benjamin and Nancy are the only ones now living, the latter keeping house for her brother. She has been a member of the Methodist Episcopal Church, South, for many years. Benjamin S. Fraker was the youngest son, and with his sister Nancy resided with and cared for his mother until her death. In 1842 he came to Missouri, to him a land unattractive by reason of the presence of a multitude of snakes and wild animals, though good hunting (of which he was fond) abounded. In 1843 he took up his abode in Dallas County, which has since been his home. During the war he lost heavily, but has since managed to retrieve his fallen fortunes, and is now in good circumstances, and is considered one of the enterprising and prosperous citizens of the county. His farm consists of 240 acres of excellent land, and is well adapted to stock raising, an enterprise in which Mr. Fraker has taken considerable interest. He has always been a stanch Democrat, and for the past thirty years has been a steward in the Methodist Episcopal Church.

Judge John Franklin. Among the many prominent and esteemed citizens of Dallas County, and among those deserving special recognition for their long residence in the same, stands the name of the above mentioned gentleman, who was born in Moniteau County, Mo., August 20, 1834, and is the son of John and Susan (Foster) Franklin, natives of North Carolina. John Franklin was married in North Carolina, and afterward immigrated to East Tennessee, going from there to Central Illinois, where he remained for some time, but afterward moved to Moniteau County, Mo. Later they moved to Dallas County, of the same State, and here both died, the father in 1862, at the age of eighty-six, and the mother in 1851, at the age of fifty-five years. They were both members of the Baptist Church for many years, and he was a Republican in politics after the organization of that party. To their marriage were born eleven sons and one daughter, and of this large family only two are living: Nancy and John. Nancy is the wife of Green Stafford, who was a Union soldier, and died during the war. She is now living in Jasper Township, Dallas County. Judge John Franklin remained with his parents until their deaths, taking care and providing for them in their old age. In August, 1861, he enlisted in Company B, Twenty-fourth Missouri Infantry, Federal Army, and served sixteen months and a half, when he received a gunshot wound in the right side, which disabled him from further service. Previous to the war, December 23, 1852, he married Miss Lavina Flannagan, who was born in Illinois July 16, 1832, and who is the daughter of Thomas and Nancy (Holly) Flannagan. This union resulted in the birth of six sons and one daughter: Andrew J., William T., Albert J., George R., Joseph H., Almus M. and Mary. Judge Franklin has been a farmer and stock raiser all his life, and as such has been successful. He has 240 acres of land, with the greater portion under cultivation and well improved. In 1872 he went to Wilson County, Kas., and lost considerable money on this venture, but has since made good the loss. He is a member of the Masonic lodge, and is J. W. of Reddick Lodge No. 361, also a member of Lodge No. 430, I. O. O. F., at Buffalo, and is a member of the Wheel. He was constable of Jasper Township for eight years, and in 1882 was elected county judge, and re-elected in 1884. He is a Republican in politics, and he and wife are members of the Free Will Baptist Church.

D. M. Gammon is a merchant of Louisburg, Mo., and was born in Roane County, Tenn., August 1, 1841, his parents being George and Malinda (Galbreath) Gammon, who were born in Virginia, but were reared and married in Tennessee, whither they had moved at an early day. They remained in that State until 1860, and then came to Dallas County, Mo., and located on what is known as Four Mile Prairie, where they purchased a large tract of land and resided until their respective deaths. D. M. Gammon is one of eight surviving members of their family of eleven children, and received his education and rearing in his native State. When about twenty years of age he came to Missouri with his parents, but continued on his western course, and resided in Kansas for about eight months. In March, 1862, he rejoined his parents, and enlisted in Company B, Fourteenth Missouri State Militia, which was consolidated in February, 1863, with Company A, Fourth Missouri State Militia, and served until April, 1865, being a participant in the battle of Prairie Grove and several hard skirmishes. At Air Rock, Mo., he was wounded by a gunshot in the right knee, and was taken to the hospital, where he remained about fourteen months. After receiving his discharge he returned home, and was engaged in husbandry until 1875, when he began merchandising at Louisburg. He has been deputy postmaster of the town for several years, and is a member of the I. O. O. F. In 1865 he espoused Miss Margaret Knox, by whom he has six children: Charles O., Leonard T., William, Eva, Margaret and Stella. Mr. Gammon is a member of the Cumberland Presbyterian Church.

Francis M. Gann, who is also classed among the prominent and enterprising citizens of Dallas County, was born in Hamilton County, Tenn., March 12, 1848, and is the son of Cornelius and Lydia (Morland) Gann, natives of Tennessee and North Carolina, respectively. The father was born August 3, 1819, and died in Dallas County, Mo., December 3, 1875. The mother was born in 1817, and is still living on the old homestead in Washington Township, Dallas Co., Mo. They were married in Tennessee, where they lived until 1853, when they came to Webster County, Mo., and there resided until 1857. They then came to Dallas County, and located in the neighborhood of where their son, Francis M., now lives. He was a successful farmer, the result of industry and good management; was a Republican in politics, and both he and wife were members of the Baptist Church for many years, he being deacon of the same. In 1861 he enlisted and served six months in the State Militia, or Home Guards, then enlisted in Company B, Twenty-fourth Missouri Infantry, Federal Army, and served until honorably discharged at St. Louis, Mo., in the latter part of 1864. He was in the battles of Pea Ridge, Tupelo, Miss., Pleasant Hill, La., and many other skirmishes. To his marriage were born ten children, our subject being the fourth: Sarah E., Martha J., Delilah, Francis M., Thomas (deceased), Nancy, Sallie, James M., John and Henry D. Thomas was born March 12, 1850, and died November 1, 1888. Of this family Francis M. is the eldest son. He remained at home and assisted in taking care of the balance of the family until seventeen years of age, or until August, 1864, when he enlisted in Company F, Sixteenth Missouri Cavalry, Federal Army, and served until June 23, 1865, he being the youngest soldier in his regiment. September 10, of the last named year, he married Miss Clara J. Alley, a native of Kentucky, born November 23, 1847, and the daughter of Wiley and Charlotta (Shelton) Alley. This union was blessed by the birth of ten children, viz.: James W., who died when seven years of age; Rebecca Ann, wife of T. F. Legan, a farmer of Dallas County, Mo.; John W., at home; Martha J., at home; Starling C., also at home; George R., died in his third year; Marion, Joseph, Franklin N., Lucy E. and Thomas J. When first married Mr. Gann began life as a farmer, and this he has since continued. He is the owner of a well-located and well-improved farm, and he and wife are members of the Missionary Baptist Church, Mr. Gann at present being clerk of the same. He is a Republican in politics, and is a member of the G. A. R.

Joseph S. Goheen, editor of the *Dallas County Democrat*, was born in Greene County, Ill., May 24, 1855, and at the early age of fourteen years began learning the printer's trade, serving an apprenticeship in the office of the *Register*, at White Hall, Ill. He afterward went to Texarkana, Ark., where he worked as a journeyman for a number of years, and then became foreman in the job printing department of the Springfield *Herald*, with which paper he was connected for some time. In the fall of 1888 he came to Buffalo, Mo., and took charge of the *Dallas County Democrat*, and became proprietor of the establishment in January, 1889, and owing to his many years' experience in the newspaper business and knowledge of political affairs, the *Democrat* has become one of the most flourishing papers of the county. It is published in the interests of the Democratic party, and is newsy, entertaining and instructive. In 1878 he was married to Miss Nettie Light, a native of Macoupin County, Ill., and by her is the father of three children: Jo-Nettie, Charles and Harry.

B. W. A. Henson, one of the leading stock traders and dealers of Dallas County, Mo., and the son of Benjamin and Fanny (Wollard) Henson, was born in Dallas County, Mo., near his present place of residence, April 17, 1848. The parents were natives of Tennessee, and both died when the subject of this sketch was a young lad. Benjamin Henson, a farmer by occupation, was one of the first settlers in Dallas County. To his marriage were born four children: Elizabeth, wife of N. C. Bennett, a prominent citizen of this county; William T., also a Dallas County farmer; Catherine, wife of Timothy Cloud, of Hot Springs County, Ark., and B. W. A. The last named, after the death of his parents, lived with his grandparents, his uncle, Robert Randels, and with N. L. Bennett. He has farmed the most of his life, and in connection has dealt and traded in stock. May 26, 1867, he married Miss Minerva A. Davis, who was born in Dallas County, Mo., December 8, 1850, and who is the daughter of Woodford J. Davis. Six living children were born to this union: William T., Benjamin F., Augusta E., Charles F., Cora D. and Mamie E. Those deceased were named: Thomas E., who died October 25, 1868, at the age of five months, and John I., born July 13, 1878, and died December 13, 1881. In 1880 Mr. Henson began selling goods where he now lives, which he continued four years, and was appointed postmaster at Greasy, which position he has since filled. He is the owner of some of the best land in Dallas County, 700 acres in all, with 320 in the home place. Though starting life with limited means, Mr. Henson has, by industry and good management, been unusually successful, and is now in very comfortable circumstances. He is a Democrat in politics, and he and wife are members of the Missionary Baptist Church. He has, for some time past, been extensively engaged in stock business, and it is said that he handles more stock than any other man in Dallas County. He is a warm supporter of the educational interests of the community, and, indeed, supports all worthy movements tending to the welfare of his native county.

George W. Herd, one of the leading merchants of Dallas County, doing business at Charity, was born in Tennessee September 26, 1828, being the son of John and Rebecca (Martin) Herd, natives of Kentucky and North Carolina, respectively. The father was a farmer all his life, and died in Tennessee when the subject of this sketch was a very small child. After his death the mother moved to Macoupin County, Ill., here married James Derrick, and soon after moved to Missouri, locating in Greene County (this county was soon after changed to Webster County), when George W. Herd was but seven years of age. The mother was a member of the Methodist Episcopal Church, and died in 1875, at the age of seventy-two. By her first marriage she became the mother of two sons: James C. (deceased) and George W. The former died in Greene County, Mo., January 20, 1888, at the age of sixty-one. He was a farmer. By the last marriage were born two children: Joshua, and Cynthia J., wife of Alex. Blay. George W. Herd was nineteen years of age when he started for himself as a farmer, and this business he has continued up to the present, in connection with rearing and dealing in stock. In January, 1880, he opened up a general store at his present location, where he has remained ever since. August 26, 1848, he married Miss Sarah M. Drumheller, a native of Sumner County, Tenn., born December 22, 1831, and the daughter of Nicholas L. and Eliza (Hollis) Drumheller. This union has been blessed by the birth of nine children: Rosa J. (wife of William T. Henson, a farmer of Dallas County), Eliza C. (wife of Solomon B. Jones, a farmer of Texas), James T., (farmer, of Dallas County), Phœbe V. (wife of L. F. Jones, merchant, of Buffalo), Sarah C. (wife of J. W. W. Thompson, farmer, of Webster County), Lougenia M. (wife of A. J. Graves, a Methodist minister now on the Buffalo Circuit), Parthena (wife of S. B. Robertson, a blacksmith) and Alma, at home. There was one who died—Mary R. Mr. and Mrs. Herd are members of the Missionary Baptist Church, and he is a Democrat in his political views.

Warrenton Hunt, liveryman and farmer, of Buffalo, Mo., was born in Washington County, Tenn., November 22, 1835, and is a son of Dr. Peter and Easter (Morrison) Hunt, who were also natives of that

State and county. They immigrated to Dallas County, Mo., in the spring of 1840, and located on what is known as the Straitor farm, near the Rock Spring Camp-ground. Here they resided until after the war, then went to Arkansas for the father's health, but his death occurred in Polk County in 1874. He was a practicing physician, which profession he carried on in connection with farming, and bore an excellent reputation among his medical brethren. His wife died in 1843. He was married four times, and reared a large family of children. Warrenton Hunt was about five years of age when he was brought to Dallas County, and was here reared to manhood on a farm. Owing to the scarcity of schools in his boyhood days, he received no schooling, but managed to acquire enough education by self application to fit him for the ordinary business affairs of life. He remained with his father until the Rebellion broke out, then enlisted in the Home Guards, but after a short time was furloughed, and returned home and engaged in threshing wheat. He followed this occupation for two years, and as the men were all serving in the war, he was assisted in this work by the women. He then joined Company H, Eighth Regiment Enrolled Missouri Militia, and served until the close of the war as commissary sergeant, and participated in several hard skirmishes, but in no regular fight. In 1865 he returned home, and purchased 183 acres of land, all under fence and well improved, where he continued to reside and deal in stock until November, 1885, when he moved to Buffalo, and engaged in his present business, in which he has been quite successful. September 12, 1869, he was married to Miss Martha Olinger, by whom he has six sons and one daughter: William T., James R., Ella (wife of G. B. Austin), Adolphus F., Marcus F., Jasper I. and Varda V. Mr. Hunt is a member of the A. O. U. W., and he and wife belong to the Missionary Baptist Church.

C. F. Johnson may be mentioned as one of the successful farmers and stock dealers of the county. He was born in Karlstead, Sweden, November 4, 1844, his parents being John J. and Margret A. (Swenson), Johnson, both of whom lived and died in their native land. Three of their eight children are now living. C. F. Johnson was reared and educated in his native land, and before coming to America learned and worked at the stone-mason's trade. In May, 1865, he embarked for the United States, taking passage at Gottenburg, Sweden, and landed at Castle Garden, New York City, after a fourteen days' voyage. After residing in that city for about four months, he went to Chicago, thence to St. Louis, and worked in the latter city at the stone-mason's trade for about four years, and for about three years worked on the San Francisco Railroad construction. He was then employed on the construction of the Laclede & Fort Scott Railway, and worked on it until it stopped work at Buffalo, in which city he located in 1873, purchasing the farm of 305 acres on which he is now residing. In all he owns 700 acres of valuable land, fairly well improved, all of which he has acquired by industry and economy, and can now enjoy the fruits of his labor. He has given a great deal of attention to dealing in hogs and cattle, which he ships to St. Louis, and the county fair ground is located on Mr. Johnson's farm, and consists of twenty acres. March 8, 1874, he was wedded to Rebecca P., a daughter of Thomas P. and Polly A. (Rice) Welch, and by her is the father of seven children: Alfred L., William O., Walter T., Minnie D., Charles F., Margret A. and Fannie J. Mr. Johnson is a member of the Masonic fraternity, and his wife belongs to the Christian Church.

John Washington Jones, a successful agriculturist and fruit grower of Jackson Township, Dallas Co., Mo., was born near his present place of residence February 24, 1852, and is the son of Bills and Altha (Randles) Jones, natives of Tennessee. The father was born in 1821, and died in Dallas County, Mo., January 10, 1876. The mother died on January 9, 1874, when forty-six years of age. They were married in Missouri, and lived and spent the principal part of their lives in Dallas County. The father was a farmer and stock raiser, at which he was quite successful. He was a member of the Masonic fraternity, was a Democrat in politics, and was sheriff of Dallas County in 1860. To his marriage were born twelve children, eight now living: Mary, wife of J. W. Henderson; Sarah, wife of J. C. Bennett; Solomon B., John Washington, Lemuel T., Robert L., James E. and Green S. One deceased was named Nancy, and three died in infancy. John W. Jones, the subject of our sketch, was married March 6, 1870, to Miss Martha Bennett, a native of Dallas County, Mo., born May 25, 1853, and to this union were born seven children, viz.: Moses B., James F., Nathaniel L. (deceased), Sarah A., Jackson B., Solomon L. and Christopher Alonzo. Mr. Jones is a Democrat in politics, and ever since his marriage he has been successfully engaged in farming and stock raising. He is the owner of a well-improved and well-located farm, and is also engaged quite extensively in the fruit business, raising apples mostly. He and wife are members of the Missionary Baptist Church.

Dr. Samuel J. Latimer, a leading physician of Dallas County, Mo., was born in Washington County, Mo., April 22, 1833, being the son of Samuel and Nancy (Bottom) Latimer, both natives of Green County, Ky. The father was born December 19, 1795, and died in Webster County, Mo., July 19, 1873. He had followed agricultural pursuits, and was first married to Miss Elizabeth Garrett, who died in Missouri. He afterward married Mrs. Day, who was the widow of John Day, and whose maiden name was Bottom. She was born July 18, 1797, and died in Webster County, Mo., December 15, 1885. After his second marriage Mr. Latimer and wife lived in Macoupin County, Ill., a short time, and then moved to Washington County, Mo., where they resided until November, 1837. At that date they moved to Webster (then Polk) County, Mo., settling on Niangua Creek, and while living on one farm he was a resident of three different counties. He was a Democrat in politics, and he and wife were members of the Methodist Episcopal Church, South. He held numerous minor offices in Washington County, Mo., and was one of the much esteemed citizens of the county. His father, Jacob Latimer, was a native of Virginia, who went to Kentucky with Daniel Boone, and helped fight the Indians at Crab Orchard. To Samuel Latimer and his second wife were born a large family of children, five of whom are now living, Dr. Samuel J. being the eldest. The others were named as follows: Margaret Ann and Martha Ann (twins), William H. and Jacob L. (twins), Lydia M. (deceased). By his first marriage Mr. Latimer became the father of one son, Dr. G. W., and two daughters, the last two only living, Adaline and Nancy G. By her first marriage Mrs. Latimer became the mother of five sons and one daughter; three are living: Edward, Allen and Hiley. Dr. Samuel J. Latimer received his education chiefly at home, and at the age of nineteen began teaching school in Dallas County. This he continued at irregular intervals for several years. From 1852 to 1856 he was engaged in teaching school, attending school as a student, or filling the place of salesman in general merchandise at St. Luke, Newburg and Breezeville, Mo. September 13, 1855, he chose for his life companion Miss Mary F. Mehaffey, who was born in Pulaski County, Mo., August 18, 1835, and who is the daughter of Dr. A. D. Mehaffey. The fruits of this union were eight children: Nancy A., born October 2, 1856, and died June 26, 1870; Wesley B., born in Dallas County, Mo., September 12, 1858; Samuel A., born May 6, 1861; Mary M. M., born January 1, 1864; Sarah E., born December 4, 1866; Nathan W., born November 25, 1869; Ida J., born August 29, 1872, and Cora B., born September 21, 1875. In the spring of 1857 Dr. Latimer purchased a farm in Dallas County, Mo., where he has since continued to reside. He is an ordained minister in the Methodist Episcopal Church, South, and has been licensed to preach since 1858. He studied medicine under Drs. A. D. Mehaffey and G. W. Latimer, his father-in-law and elder half-brother, who were both respectable practicing physicians of Dallas and Webster Counties, Mo. Dr. Samuel J. Latimer has been actively engaged in the practice of medicine since January, 1862. His wife and five of his children are members of the Methodist Episcopal Church, South. He is a member of the Masonic fraternity; also of the National Grange and Good Templars organizations. He is a Democrat in politics, and believes firmly in the doctrine of "the greatest good to the greatest number."

C. C. Lightner, of the firm of Lightner Bros., proprietors of a general store in Urbana, Dallas County, was born in Lewis County, Mo., August 6, 1852, and is a son of J. M. and Elizabeth (Snapp) Lightner, natives, respectively, of East Tennessee and Vermilion County, Ill., and born in 1828 and 1834. The parents located in Hickory County, Mo., in 1859. J. M. Lightner was a blacksmith and farmer. In 1861 he enlisted in the Missouri State Militia under Capt. Lindsey, and served three years. He died August 23, 1885, the father of three children, two of whom are living, our subject and George W. The paternal grandparents of our subject were Christopher and Nancy (Glass) Lightner. The former, a blacksmith by trade, was born in Pennsylvania, and was of German descent. He died in 1861. C. C. Lightner spent his early life in Dallas County, Mo., and attended the common schools; he afterward attended Johnson's Commercial College of St. Louis, where he graduated in 1878. When eighteen years of age he began life for himself, and chose farming and stock raising as an occupation, which he abandoned in 1878, and with his father and brother established his present business, under the firm name of J. M. Lightner & Sons. In 1884 the firm became Lightner Bros., under which style it is successfully conducted. October 4, 1873, Mr. Lightner married Miss Ellen Bower, a native of Dallas County. She was born in 1855, and is a daughter of E. and Pelina (Yeager) Bower, the latter of whom died in 1881. Three children have been born to Mr. and Mrs. Lightner, viz.: Georgia C., Jessie L. and Rosa Cornelia. Mr. Lightner is a Democrat politically, and has served as postmaster of Urbana for more than six years.

Ezekiel Lindsey, an early and prominent settler of Dallas County, Mo., has been a resident of the same since 1836, whither he came with his parents, Sterling and Mary (Azbell) Lindsey, from his native State of Tennessee. He was born in Lawrence County September 7, 1819, and there received a fair English education, and made his home with his father until the latter's death. He spent two years in the Cherokee Nation, and in 1850 went to California, taking the overland trip, and after mining two years in that State returned home, and in the fall of that year purchased a drove of mules, which he took to Texas, being absent until 1854. He then returned home and married, but took his wife to Texas with him, and there made his home until 1868, serving during the late war on the frontier. In the fall of that year he returned to Dallas County, Mo., and has since resided on his present farm of 220 acres, the greater part of which is under cultivation. He deals some in stock, is engaged in fruit growing, and up to 1880 was in the mercantile business, but has since been occupied in farming. He was first married to Mrs. Elizabeth A. Tinnell, a daughter of Col. Miles Vernon, by whom he had nine children, seven now living: Larissa (wife of Greenstreet Mitchell), Vivia and Alice (twins, wives of D. M. Rush and Thomas Booth, respectively), Luella (wife of A. Bottom), Nellie, Melvin and Lester. The mother of these children died December 8, 1883, and in July, 1885, Mr. Lindsey wedded Mrs. Martha A. (Bridges) Hucaby, a daughter of Joseph and Susanna (Hogg) Bridges, who settled in Polk County, Mo., in 1845. Mr. and Mrs. Lindsey are members of the Missionary Baptist Church, and he is a Royal Arch Mason, and is one of the prosperous farmers of the county. His parents were born in the Eastern States, and were early immigrants to Tennessee. The father was born in 1797, and after residing in Tennessee for a number of years moved with his family to Dallas County, Mo., and located near Louisburg, on the prairie, where he took a "squatter's claim," and after the land was put on the market by the Government, entered eighty acres. He erected a very primitive log cabin, in which he lived for a number of years, and then made better improvements. All their clothing was home-made, and at that day a suit of jeans was considered a very handsome outfit. Neighbors were very scarce, but the woods and prairies were covered with wild game of nearly all kinds, and Mr. Lindsey has many a time stood on the prairie and seen a drove of 100 deer. He was a skillful marksman, and his cabin was always plentifully supplied with choice wild meats. He and wife became the parents of twelve children, but only six are living at the present time: Ezekiel, Sterling W., Mary (wife of Henry Sawyer), Elizabeth (wife of William Hale), Emily J. (wife of J. Drum) and Hannah B. (wife of T. J. Hayes). Those deceased were Eliza, Drucilla, William C., John J. and Daniel A.

S. W. Lindsey, one of the largest stock dealers in Dallas County, Mo., and also a prominent farmer of the county, was born in Lawrence County, Tenn., March 18, 1833, his parents being Sterling and Mary (Azbell) Lindsey, a short history of whom is given in the sketch of Ezekiel Lindsey. They were the first family to settle in that part of the county, and suffered many privations incident to pioneer life. They had to go sixty miles to Waynesville to get their seed-corn, and their clothing was all home-spun. The father was a tanner by trade, and would often kill deer and make moccasins out of their hides. He was also a cooper, and made nearly all their household utensils. He entered two forty-acre tracts where Louisburg now stands, and the deeds for these were among the first recorded. Here he made his home until his death March 4, 1846, his wife dying September 12, 1867. Sterling W. Lindsey, whose name heads this sketch, has been a resident of Dallas County since about three years of age, but owing to the scarcity and very primitive condition of the schools of that day, he never went to school but about three months, and that was to a private teacher. He worked hard to help improve the home farm in his boyhood days, but in 1853 left the paternal roof to seek his fortune in the gold mines of California. He took the overland route, and made the journey in three months and twenty days, the objective point being Sacramento. He took a drove of cattle with him, and while there turned his attention to stock dealing, which occupation met with fair success. While on his way he killed buffalo, deer and panthers, and can tell many anecdotes of thrilling interest connected with some of his hunting expeditions, as well as some of his experiences with the more civilized inhabitants of that region. In 1855 he returned to the old homestead in Missouri, and resumed farming, and has also been largely engaged in stock dealing. He has a large farm well adapted to stock raising, and has driven large droves of cattle through to Illinois and sold them at Jacksonville and other points. His land amounts to about 500 acres, nearly all of which is under cultivation, and well supplied with water. In 1861 he enlisted in the Home Guards, and served for six months, and the following year enlisted in the Enrolled Militia, and was stationed at Buffalo the most of the time. In 1864 he joined Capt. Brown's company, and was transferred afterward to Capt. Sullivan's company, in which he served until the close of the war. His first wife, Mary Drum, whom he married in 1857, bore him two children, Carroll J. and Daniel J., and died in April, 1864; and in August, 1865, he wedded Martha Paine, by whom he has ten children: Ella, wife of Charles E. Burton; Minnie, Anthony, Emmet, Jeanette, Bertha, Blanche, Berniece X., Roscoe and Grant. Mrs. Lindsey is a member of the Missionary Baptist Church, and he is a member of the G. A. R. He has in his possession a paper, the *New England Weekly Journal*, published at Boston, on Queen Street, April 8, 1728, and also has a powder-horn dating

1763, made by William Betts, his name being engraved on the horn. He has a small round table made of sixty-three different kinds of wood, made by a man by the name of Gardner, and also a walking-stick of hickory that grew up by the side of Davy Crockett's house in Tennessee.

M. G. Lovan. The manufacturing interests of Dallas County, Mo., are ably represented by M. G. Lovan, who is a manufacturer and dealer in harness, saddles, hardware, etc., and is also treasurer of the county. He was born in Hopkins County, Ky., August 22, 1842, and is a son of William M. and Maria (Carnahan) Lovan, who were also Kentuckians, the paternal grandfather being one of the early pioneers of that State. The father of our subject was reared on a farm in his native State, and after his marriage learned the saddler's trade, which occupation he followed most of his remaining days. From 1844 until 1847 he resided in Greene County, Mo., and at the latter date removed to Dallas County, locating in Buffalo, where he worked at his trade for several years, but died in Polk County, Mo., in 1875. His wife died in Dallas County, having borne a family of seven children, five of whom are living: James R., Marshall G., Mary E. (wife of John O'Bannon), Henry G. and Gertrude (widow of Peter Wilson). Marshall G., whose name heads this sketch, was brought to Missouri when two years of age, and was educated in Buffalo, where he also learned the harness and saddler's trade of his father, which calling he has since followed. In 1862 he enlisted in the Missouri State Militia, which was afterward a part of the Eighth Regiment, and after serving three years was discharged in April, 1865. In 1878 he was elected county treasurer, and served by re-election three successive terms, and was again elected in 1886 and re-elected in 1888. He has been a prominent citizen of Dallas County for a great many years, and was married in 1864 to Miss Mary E. Bledsoe, by whom he has five living children: Alfonso B., Leonidas, Ida, Marshall E. and Edmund A. Mr. and Mrs. Lovan are members of the Baptist Church, and he is a stanch Republican in his political views.

T. C. Lovell, merchant, came to Buffalo, Mo., in 1873. He was born in East Tennessee, and when quite small both his parents died, and he was reared by strangers. The most of his early life was spent in Hickory County, Mo., on a farm, but when the Rebellion broke out he was residing near where Peirce City, Mo., is now located. He enlisted at Neosho in the six months' service, and at the expiration of that time he enlisted in the three years' service, joining Company G, Eighth Regiment Volunteer Infantry, in 1862, serving three years under Capt. Curry and taking an active part in the battles of Neosho, Lone Jack, Prairie Grove, Banks' raid up Red River, Jenkins' Ferry and others, and was paroled at Alexandria, La., in June, 1865. At this time his worldly possessions consisted of a few dollars, and his wearing apparel was in rather poor condition, but he decided to come to St. Louis, Mo., with a comrade, which he did, and afterward located in Linn Creek, which place he reached with only 25 cents between him and starvation, and this he gave to his friend to buy tobacco. Here he met Gov. McClurg, who took an interest in his welfare and found him employment. He went to work making rails, but not being used to such labor his hands soon gave out, and he was obliged to give this up for a time. At this time he did not know a single letter of the alphabet nor one figure from another, but Gov. McClurg kindly gave him employment for five or six years, and he also attended school a portion of the time, and thus secured a fair business education. He worked on the farm one year, and the balance of the time was employed in the store and warehouse. In 1873 he came to Buffalo with $700, and engaged in the mercantile business in partnership with Frank C. Wilson, but at the end of a few years Mr. Lovell formed a partnership with S. B. Roll, but since the election of the latter to the office of probate judge Mr. Lovell has been in business alone. He carries an excellent stock of dry goods and groceries, and occupies a large, two-story brick building, receiving from the sale of his goods a snug annual income. He is in every respect a self-made man, and deserves great credit for the success he has achieved and the difficulties he has overcome. Starting in life with no friends, home or education, he now has all, and has won the confidence and respect of all who know him by his genial nature and strict integrity. After his parents' deaths he was bound out to a man who promised to send him to school, but failed to live up to his promise. Accordingly Mr. Lovell ran away and hired out for $10 per month, but was taken sick, and after a nine months' siege the war broke out. In 1878 he was married to Miss Alice J. Ramsay, of Buffalo, Mo., who is a member of the Presbyterian Church, and a daughter of A. A. Ramsay.

Daniel W. McCoy, miller and merchant at McCoy's Mills, was born in Armstrong County, Penn., April 22, 1854, and is the son of Andrew and Susan (Binkard), McCoy, natives of Pennsylvania. The father is living in Warren County, Penn., and is engaged in agricultural pursuits, but the mother died when the subject of this sketch was three years of age. Their family consisted of four children, Daniel W. being the third in order of birth. At the death of his mother, he was taken by Washington Campbell (no relation), and remained with him until sixteen years of age. He then started for himself; first went to the oil regions of Pennsylvania, where he remained for three or four years, and then went to Iowa, remaining in that State until 1886, when he came to his present place of residence. For several years he was on the Ohio and Mississippi Rivers as engineer. In 1879 he turned his attention to milling, and in 1886 fitted up the mill property he is now operating, where he has a splendid custom. He has recently opened up a general store in connection with the mill. In 1881 he selected his companion in life in the person of Miss Ladornia Cook, of Pennsylvania. They have two children: Maud and Myrtie. Mr. McCoy is a Republican in politics, and Mrs. McCoy is a member of the Methodist Episcopal Church.

Solomon M. McGee, one of the prominent and enterprising citizens of Jackson Township, Dallas Co., Mo., was born in Hardeman County, Tenn., May 8, 1836, his parents being William and Louisa (Martin) McGee, natives of North Carolina and Kentucky, respectively. The father was born April 2, 1802, and died in Dallas County, Mo., in 1872, March 1. The mother was born in 1815. They were married in Tennessee, and lived in Hardeman County of that State until they came to Missouri, and located in Taney County, in November, 1851, coming in March, 1854, to Dallas County. They then located where the subject of this sketch now resides, and here the mother is still living. She is a member of the Methodist Episcopal Church, as was also Mr. McGee, who was a Republican in politics. He was a farmer and stock raiser, and although he left his people in North Carolina and started out with little or no means, he was very successful in all his business enterprises. They were the parents of ten children, Solomon M. being the second child, and eight of whom are now living: John O., Solomon M., Delila B. (wife of Jacob Drake), Mary Ann (wife of P. T. White), Margaret (wife of Jerome H. Powell), James W., Frances (wife of I. J. Wingo), Louisa T. (wife of John Popejoy). Those deceased were named Jane and William H. Solomon M. McGee remained at home until twenty-one years of age, when he began for himself as a farmer and stock raiser, which occupation he has since continued. September 2, 1858, he married Miss Margaret E. Robbins, a native of Sangamon County, Ill., born December 15, 1841, and the daughter of William and Catherine Robbins. To Mr. and Mrs. McGee have been born a large family of children: Gilson F., William K., Dialtha C. (wife of Nathaniel Dornan), Amanda F., Rosie E., Jacob, John T., Solomon A., Martin L., Charles E., Sarah Louisa. Gilson F. is a farmer in Christian County, Mo., and the remainder of the children are at or near home. July 29, 1862, Mr. McGee enlisted in the Eighth Missouri Cavalry, Company A, Federal Army, and served until July 20, 1865, when he was honorably discharged at St. Louis. He was in the battle of Prairie Grove and in many skirmishes. Mr. McGee is not a member of any church, but takes an active part in church support. He is a member of the Masonic fraternity, a member of the Agricultural Wheel, and is a Republican in politics; is also a member of the G. A. R.

J. K. P. Maddux is one of the representative farmers of Dallas County, Mo., and was born in the State March 9, 1845, and is a son of Alfred B. and Caroline (Brown) Maddux, the former a native of Tennessee and the latter of South Carolina. They located in Dallas County, Mo., in 1849, but are now residing in Jackson County, Mo. J. K. P. Maddux is one of their eleven children, and since four years of age has been a resident of the county. In 1862 he enlisted in the State Militia, and was at the battles of Neosho, Prairie Grove, and on the Price raid, and during his three years' service in the field was ever a faithful and trusty soldier. After his marriage he located on the farm on which his father first settled on coming to the county, but in 1881 removed to his present valuable farm, consisting of 335 acres, which is well improved with excellent buildings and a small orchard. He is an extensive stock man, and in all his enterprises for the accumulation of this world's goods he has met with good success. He was married in 1865 to Miss Martha A. Southard, by whom he has seven children: Tamza C., wife of B. Edmondson; Mary E., Rebecca, John,

Burton, Clarence and Ernie. Mrs. Maddux is a member of the Methodist Episcopal Church.

John J. Montgomery, a well-known farmer of Lincoln Township, Dallas County, was born in Pulaski County, Mo., in 1826, and is a son of William and Nancy (Ballew) Montgomery, natives of North Carolina. William Montgomery was born in 1792, and was a farmer and blacksmith; he moved from North Carolina to Tennessee, from there to Crawford County, Mo., and later to what was then Pulaski and is now Dallas County. He served as justice of the peace in Pulaski County for several years, and was one of the first county judges of Dallas County; he died in 1853, and his wife, who was born in 1800, died in 1854. They had twelve children, five of whom are still living, viz.: John J., Margaret A. Morrow (formerly Margaret Davis), Charity C. Poynter, Thomas J. B. and Nancy E. Leckie. The paternal grandfather of our subject was John Montgomery, of North Carolina, a farmer by occupation. The maternal grandfather was Jesse Ballew, also a native of North Carolina, who located in Missouri about 1820. John J. Montgomery spent his early life in Pulaski and Dallas Counties. In 1850 he went to California with his father, where they farmed and kept a hay-yard until 1855, when he returned to Dallas County, Mo., having been very successful financially. In 1861 our subject enlisted in the Missouri State Militia, under command of Capt. Williams, where he served one year, and then enlisted in Company D, Eighteenth Missouri Volunteers, Confederate Army, under command of Col. Hunter; he participated in the battles of Prairie Grove, Helena, Mansfield, Pleasant Hill, Saline River, and served until the close of the war. In 1856 Mr. Montgomery married Julia W. Clark, who was born in Indiana in December, 1836, and is a daughter of George and Nancy (King) Clark, natives, respectively, of Vermont and Kentucky. Three children have blessed this union, viz.: John William, Gilford W. and Allie Virginia. After the war Mr. Montgomery moved to Texas, where he remained three years, and then returned to Missouri, where he has since lived. He owns about 600 acres of land, 100 acres of which are under cultivation, and which he devotes entirely to farming. He is a member of the Masonic fraternity and of the Methodist Episcopal Church, South. Politically he is a Democrat.

T. J. B. Montgomery. This gentleman ranks among the prominent agriculturists and stock raisers of Dallas County, Mo., and was born in the township in which he now resides January 29, 1840, his parents being William and Nancy (Ballew) Montgomery. They were born in the "Old North Carolina State," and in the year 1817 moved to Tennessee, and in the year 1818 immigrated to Pulaski County, Mo., in which county they got a tax receipt (dated in 1824) for the year 1823, which is now in the possession of T. J. B. Montgomery. They located in Dallas County, on the Little Niangua River, but shortly after moved to Four Mile Prairie, and, as soon as the land was put on the market by the Government, he entered a large tract, and erected a little log cabin, which was a very primitive construction. He was one of the first settlers of the county, which was in a very wild and unsettled state at this time, and could stand in his cabin door and shoot down a deer with his rifle almost any day. They raised flax, which they hackled, spun and wove into clothing, their every-day clothes being made of the tow and their Sunday suits of the fine flax. During the "gold fever" of 1849, Mr. Montgomery and his son went to California, and while there, striving to accumulate a competence for his family, he died, and was buried in Colusa County. His wife died in Dallas County, having borne a large family of children, only five of whom are now living: John J., Margaret (widow of David Morrow), Charity C. (wife of T. J. Poynter), Thomas J. B. and Emeline (widow of Dr. Leckie). The early days of Thomas J. B. Montgomery were spent at hard labor on his father's farm, which he assisted in clearing. For a short time he attended school in the little log cabin, the teacher being hired by his father and their neighbors, but he derived little benefit therefrom, as the most of the time his services were required at home. With the exception of one winter spent in Texas, he has resided on a farm in Dallas County all his life, and is now the owner of 373 acres of valuable land, 150 acres of which are well improved and under cultivation. He makes a specialty of raising stock, and is also interested in growing fruit, his farm being well supplied with excellent orchards. He has shown his brotherly spirit by joining the Masonic fraternity and the Agricultural Wheel, and in 1861 enlisted in the Home Guards, being afterward transferred to the Enrolled Militia, serving throughout the Rebellion. In 1862 he wedded Miss Augustine M. J. Edwards, a native of Dallas County, Mo., by whom he is the father of eight children: Evy M. (wife of E. E. Eason), William C., Cora E., Irena F., Thomas B., Daisy D., Bunnie and one deceased. Mrs. Montgomery is a member of the Methodist Episcopal Church, South.

Hon. W. L. Morrow, of Buffalo, Mo., is one of two surviving members of a family of six children, the other member being Lafayette J. Morrow, and was born September 24, 1817, in Warren County, Tenn., whither his parents, Robert and Julia (Simpson) Morrow, had emigrated from their respective States of North Carolina and Virginia about 1811. The father was a soldier in the War of 1812, and was a participant in the battle of New Orleans, and about 1827 immigrated with his family to Washington County, Ill., where they remained until 1835, locating then in Alabama. In 1843 they became residents of Greene County, Mo., the father's death occurring in Ozark in 1849. The mother died in Illinois in 1830, and the father afterward married, and by his second wife became the father of five children: Thomas B., Robert A., Monroe I., Mary and Josephine. Hon. W. L. Morrow, whose name heads this sketch, remained with his father during his various changes of residence, and in 1844 came to Dallas County and embarked in the mercantile business, buying goods at St. Louis and hauling them through in wagons until the railroad was built. His early days were attended by many hardships and privations, but by his indomitable will and energy he surmounted these difficulties and became one of the prosperous business men of the county. He conducted his mercantile establishment in Buffalo until January, 1888, when he sold out to his son, William L., Jr., and has since been retired from the duties and cares of active business life. His real estate in the county amounts to about 1,500 acres, all of which is well improved and very valuable property, and on one of his farms, on Section 22, Township 37, Range 19, a valuable lead mine was discovered by a Mr. Hatfield, and was explored about 1883. A shaft was sunk to a depth of sixty feet, and mineral was found in abundance, about 80,000 pounds being removed from it. When properly developed it gives promise of becoming very valuable. In 1844 Mr. Morrow was united in marriage to Miss Sarah Brown, a native of Georgia, by whom he has six children: William L., Jr., Robert, George, Julia, Harriet and Tabitha. Mr. Morrow was postmaster for several years in Buffalo, and also filled the position of county treasurer for a number of years. He was a member of the convention called by the Legislature to take steps in regard to the Rebellion, and in 1880 was elected to represent Dallas County in the State Legislature, serving one term. He and wife are worthy members of the Methodist Episcopal Church.

T. B. Morrow, of the firm of Behrens & Morrow, lumber merchants, of Buffalo, Mo., was born in Benton (now Calhoun) County, Ala., January 2, 1842, and is a son of Robert and Elizabeth (Joiner) Morrow. When about two years of age he was taken to Greene County, Mo., by his father, and here the latter died about 1849, and he was reared to a mercantile life by the Hon. William L. Morrow, whose sketch appears in this work. At the breaking out of the war he enlisted in the State Militia, and afterward in the Fifteenth Missouri Volunteer Cavalry, and served until the close of the war, being mustered out in 1865. He was in Price's raid, but was in very few battles, being quartered most of the time at Springfield, assisting in the quartermaster's department. After the war he returned to Buffalo, where he remained in the mercantile business until 1872, when he was appointed to the office of county clerk, and in 1874 was elected to the office, the duties of which he filled until 1877, when he resigned and again engaged in merchandising. This occupation he continued to follow until January, 1886, when he sold out and engaged in the lumber business with H. J. Behrens. They have conducted this business very successfully, and handle an immense amount of lumber annually, the firm being considered one of the most prosperous and enterprising in the county. He was married in 1866 to Miss Mary A. Gammon, by whom he has four children: Lizzie, Etta, Queeny and one deceased. Mr. and Mrs. Morrow are members of the Methodist Episcopal Church, and he is a member of the Masonic fraternity.

Hon. George W. O'Bannon. In every calling in life, whether of a professional, commercial or agricultural nature, there are always some men who attain the highest round in the ladder of success, and win the confidence, respect and esteem of all who know them, and such a man is Mr. O'Bannon, whose name heads this sketch. He was born in Dallas County, Mo., on the 15th of April, 1841, and is a son of John and Nancy (Proctor) O'Bannon, who were natives of Kentucky, to which State the paternal grandparents came from North Carolina at a very early day. John O'Bannon was reared and married in Kentucky, and in 1840 immigrated with his family to Dallas County, Mo., coming through to this State in a "prairie schooner," drawn by a yoke of oxen. He entered several hundred acres of prairie land in Jackson Township, where he made a crop the first year, and on which he, himself, erected a little shanty, in which he lived for a number of years. He eventually became a very wealthy land-owner, and by industry and good management his farm became one of the best improved in the county. Here he died in 1877, having lived a long and well-spent life. His widow and five children survive him, the names of the latter being Phoebe, George W., John, Mary and James P. George W. O'Bánnon assisted his father on the farm until sixteen years of age, and was then engaged in attending and teaching school at Buffalo until the breaking out of the war, when he enlisted in Company I, Sixteenth Missouri Cavalry, and served until July, 1865, and participated in all the skirmishes along the Big Blue River, Boonville, Jefferson City, and was slightly wounded three times, being shot through the hand, arm and shoulder. He went out as lieutenant, and held that commission until he received his discharge. He then returned home, and has since been engaged in the mercantile business, being one of the oldest business men of Buffalo. His house was erected in 1882, and is a two-story brick and basement, and he carries a large and select stock of general merchandise, and has also large farming interests in Dallas County. In 1871 he was elected to represent Dallas County in the Twenty-sixth General Assembly, and served one term. He has also been county treasurer for several years, and is a member of the Masonic fraternity. He was united in marriage, in 1868, to Miss Rebecca Maddux, a native of Dallas County, by whom he is the father of six children: Floyd, Claude, Daisy, Myrtle, Ralph and Arthur. Mr. and Mrs. O'Bannon are members of the Methodist Episcopal Church.

John O'Bannon, dealer in furniture and undertaking goods at Buffalo, Mo., is a native of Dallas County, and was born on the 10th of February, 1845, his parents being John and Nancy (Proctor) O'Bannon, a short history of whom is given in the sketch of Hon. George W. O'Bannon. The gentleman whose name heads this sketch was reared in Dallas County, and until seventeen years of age was engaged in tilling the soil on his father's farm, but when the late Civil War broke out he left the plow to enlist in Company I, Sixteenth Missouri Cavalry, and was a faithful soldier until peace was declared. He participated in a number of hard skirmishes, and while on duty, commanding a squad of men, was thrown from his horse and had his left leg broken. He was taken to the Lebanon Hospital, where he remained two months, when he was able to rejoin his command, and was given the office of first duty-sergeant, which position he held until the spring of 1865, when he received his discharge. The first year after his return home he was engaged in teaching school, being then engaged in agricultural pursuits until 1868, when, in the fall of that year, he was elected to the office of county sheriff and collector of Dallas County, being re-elected to both offices in 1870. Two years later these offices were divided, and Mr. O'Bannon was re-elected collector, and after holding the position one year resigned on account of failing health, and engaged in the mercantile business, which he carried on for about three years. He then sold drugs until 1885, when he engaged in his present business, in which he is commanding a large and lucrative trade. He owns a valuable farm near Buffalo, and gives much of his attention to raising stock, especially mules. On the 16th of September, 1866, he was united in the bonds of matrimony to Miss Mary E. Lovan, by whom he has the following named children: William, Effie, Minnie and Roscoe. Mr. and Mrs. O'Bannon are consistent members of the Christian Church, and he is also a member of the Masonic fraternity and the A. O. U. W. of Buffalo, Mo.

J. P. O'Bannon, the popular and efficient circuit clerk and recorder of Dallas County, Mo., is a native of the county, born July 3, 1858, and is a son of John and Nancy (Proctor) O'Bannon, who were Kentuckians by birth. They immigrated to Dallas County, Mo., in 1840, and located eight miles south of Buffalo, in Jackson Township, where they entered several hundred acres of Government land, on which they reared their family. The country in that region is still called O'Bannon Prairie in honor of the family, and here the father died in 1878. His widow is still living, and resides with her children. J. P. O'Bannon, whose name heads this sketch, is deserving of more than ordinary mention for the interest he has manifested in all movements tending to the material progress and welfare of the locality in which he has always made his home. Commencing in life for himself under circumstances which, it might seem, were not the most fortunate, he has improved to the utmost the opportunities with which he has come in contact, and by an upright, honorable course has gained the esteem and respect of a wide circle of friends—his life-long residence in the county contributing largely to his extensive acquaintance. In youth he received a common-school education in this county, and remained at work on the farm until the fall of 1882, when he was elected to the office of circuit clerk and recorder, and was re-elected in 1886 on the Republican ticket, a fact highly complimentary to his efficiency and esteem. In 1876 Louisa E. Robbins, of Dallas County, Mo., an estimable lady, became his wife, and their union has resulted in the birth of four children: Howard, Lillie, Roswell G. (deceased) and Gertrude. He and wife are members of the Christian Church. In his political views he has always been a stanch Republican, which party has been greatly benefitted by the interest he has taken in the development of the principles upon which it is founded; he is a member of the State Republican Central Committee of his district, chairman of the Twentieth District Senatorial Committee of Missouri, and is also chairman of the County Republican Committee. He owns considerable real estate in Dallas County, and is always ready to give material aid to advance its interests. His position as a substantial, representative citizen of the community is well established. He is a member of Buffalo Lodge No. 430, I. O. O. F., and a Mason.

A. J. Patterson, of Dallas County, Mo., ranks among the prosperous farmers and stock raisers of the county, and was born in Licking County, Ohio, January 31, 1843, and is a son of Thomas and Isabel (Hawkins) Patterson, who were natives of Guernsey County, Ohio, and died in Polk County, Mo., and Ohio, respectively. The father came to this State in 1849, and died in December, 1851, having followed the occupation of farming throughout life. He was twice married, and

by his first wife became the father of seven children, only one of whom is now living, A. J. Patterson. The following are the children born to his second union: Francis M., Campbell, and Lucretia, wife of John Stokeley. A. J. Patterson was quite a small lad when his parents died, and from that time until the war broke out he made his home with an uncle in Dallas County, and in April, 1861, enlisted in the Home Guards, serving three months. He then went to Illinois and enlisted in Company B, One Hundred and Sixteenth Volunteer Infantry, and took an active part in the following battles: Arkansas Post, Vicksburg, Jackson, Missionary Ridge, siege of Atlanta, siege of Jonesboro, Fort McAllister, Kenesaw Mountain, and was with Sherman on his march to the sea, and served in nineteen hard battles. He was mustered out at Washington City, and was discharged at Springfield, Ill., June 28, 1865, having served his country faithfully for three long years. He remained in Macon County, Ill., until 1869, when he went to Elk County, Kas., where he remained until 1877, then came to Dallas County and purchased the farm where he now resides, consisting of 240 acres, with about 140 acres under cultivation. He has made all the present improvements on his farm, and has one of the most valuable places in the county, and as it is well adapted to raising stock, being well supplied with water and grass, he gives the greater part of his attention to raising cattle and other animals. He is a stanch supporter of Republican principles, and is a member of the G. A. R. and the Agricultural Wheel. He was married in 1862 to Miss Louisa Calhoun, a native of Virginia, by whom he has two children, Nellie and Thomas. This wife died in 1874, and he took for his second wife Miss Lora Nicholson, of Ohio. They are members of the Methodist Episcopal Church.

J. T. Pendleton, county clerk of Dallas County, Mo., was born in Cumberland County, of the "Blue Grass State," December 16, 1847, his parents being George L. and Martha A. (Cole) Pendleton, who were born in Kentucky and Virginia, respectively. They were married in Kentucky, and immigrated to Warrick County, Ind., in 1862, and three years later removed to Effingham County, Ill.; thence to Hickory County, Mo., in 1866, where the father died in the month of February, 1887; his wife's death occurred in Effingham County, Ill. Eight of their family of ten children are living at the present time, whose names are as follows: Tabitha P., John T., George T., Russel G., Mary S., Armedia, Susan and Sarah A. John T. Pendleton, whose name heads this sketch, was reared on a Kentucky farm, and made his home with his parents during their residence in Indiana, Illinois, and also came with his father to Hickory County, Mo., in 1866. Here he attended the common schools, and the school at Buffalo in 1869, and was also engaged in teaching at intervals, but in 1875 removed to Dallas County, locating at Urbana, where he engaged in the mercantile business, which occupation he followed at that point until 1882, when he located in Louisburg, remaining one year engaged in the mercantile business. In December, 1882, he was elected county clerk, and removed to Buffalo, where he has since made his home, being re-elected to the same office in 1886, and is at present ably filling the duties of this position. He is a member of the Masonic fraternity and the I. O. O. F., and has been a member of the County Republican Committee, also a member of the Senatorial Committee, and filled the office of postmaster at Urbana for seven years. He was first married to Cynthia A. Lindsey, who died in 1873, leaving one child, Neva, and in 1875 he was married to Alice Wright, of Hickory County, by whom he has four children: Luther E., Bertram E., Clara G. and one deceased. Mrs. Pendleton is a member of the Methodist Episcopal Church.

Hon. William P. Porter, attorney at law, of Dallas County, Mo., and a representative citizen of the county, is a native of Perry County, Tenn., and was born April 20, 1851, being a son of William C. and Matilda (Ledbetter) Porter, who were born, respectively, in South Carolina and Tennessee. The former was a farmer by occupation, and in 1860 immigrated to New Madrid County, Mo., where he purchased a farm, and remained until 1868, when he removed to St. Francois County, and there resided until his death, in 1884. His wife died in 1878, their union having been blessed in the birth of eight children, five of whom are living: Martha, Mary, Henry, Sarah and William P. The latter has resided in Missouri most of the time since he was nine years of age, and received a good education in the schools of Farmington, and when twenty-seven years of age began the study of law under F. M. Carter, being admitted to the bar at Farmington in 1880. Since that time he has been in the active practice of his profession, and has become one of the foremost members of the legal fraternity in Dallas County. In the fall of 1888 he was elected on the Republican ticket to represent this county in the House of Representatives, and has also held the offices of assistant prosecuting attorney and justice of the peace, and was filling the duties of the latter office when he was admitted to the bar. He was married in 1871 to Laura Bradshaw, a native of Illinois, by whom he is the father of eight children: Nettie F., William W., Robert H., Lula B., Maude, Ellis B., Mabel and Mollie. Mr. and Mrs. Porter are members of the Methodist Episcopal Church, and he belongs to the A. O. U. W. When the war closed Mr. Porter's father had been stripped of all his personal property by the rebels, and he was left a poor man, and the subject of this sketch had a poor show in life. When about eighteen years of age his father turned him loose to do for himself. He at once engaged himself to a stone-mason to labor for money to pay his expenses, etc., at school. In this way he acquired all the means with which he educated himself. In 1874 he moved to Meridian, Tex., and commenced the publication of the *Bosque County Standard*, an independent paper in politics. Not liking Texas, he returned within a few months after locating there, to Missouri.

Hon. M. L. Reynolds. No worthy history of Dallas County could fail to make honorable mention of the Reynolds family, prominently identified with its earliest settlement. Mark Reynolds, grandfather of the gentleman whose name heads this sketch, a native of South Carolina, was reared principally in Georgia, and as a soldier in the War of 1812 participated, among others, in the battle of New Orleans, also serving in the Florida War. Subsequently he resided near Nashville, Tenn., rearing a family of five sons and five daughters, with all of whom, except the oldest son, John (who became a resident of Illinois), he moved to Pulaski (afterward Polk) County, Mo., in 1831; and afterward he settled on the place now occupied by his grandson, M. L. Reynolds, at the Buffalo Nurseries, in Dallas County. [Mention is made of this elsewhere in the present volume.] For thirty years he was a member of the Baptist Church. He was the first assessor of the county, and served for eighteen years. His children have mostly married. Elizabeth married John Wells, who was famous as being one of the best millwrights of his day, and building Brice's, Bennett's, Edwards', Hamilton's and Haynes' mills, on Niangua, and many of the Sac River mills; Dianna married Charles Self, who died soon after; Nancy married Peter Self, father of William J. Self; Charlotte married Eaton Tatum; Ailie remained single until her death; William Reynolds married Darcus Wisdom, sister of Rev. Colum Wisdom, of whom Elizabeth Reeser, wife of Solomon Reeser, this county, is their only child; Cyrus, his youngest son, married Theodosia Wisdom, also a sister of Rev. Colum Wisdom; Mark Reynolds married Margaret Cox; they had born to them six sons and five daughters, of whom John J. Reynolds, near Buffalo, James K. and Mark B., near Urbana, Mo., are the only surviving sons, and Sarah Brush, widow of the late B. L. Brush, of Howard, Kas., Nancy L., wife of James B. Garrison, and Margret, J., wife of John Thomas, all of Urbana, Mo., are the surviving daughters. Robert D. Reynolds is mentioned farther on. These children are well known by the early settlers of this country as being prominent among its pioneers. It was largely by the assistance of their strong arms and determined will that the giants of the forest stubbornly succumbed, and the then wild and desolate prairies were converted into broad, fertile fields and comfortable homes. Many were the obstacles that had to be surmounted, and many the hardships endured. At the period when they first came no mills were in existence save a wooden mortar and pestle, in which the grain was beaten. Springfield contained the nearest and only store and a blacksmith shop. There were no roads, nothing but trails made by Indians and buffalo. R. D. Reynolds, father of M. L., was quite young when brought here. He assisted his father in opening up his farm, and during the summer season managed a large team of cattle, turning the prairie sod. In 1843 he was married to Eliza Adams, daughter of William Adams, who had a few years before moved from Tennessee, and one among the early settlers of this country. After living one year with his father-in-law he settled a claim adjoining his father's, where he remained one or two years, and then moved to Fort Smith, Ark. One year later he returned to his former home, but upon the breaking out of the Mexican War he enlisted in Col. Gilpen's battalion of Mounted Dragoons, and was elected and served as orderly sergeant of Capt. Jones' company, serving as escort and keeping the line of communication open from the States through the Indian Territory and New Mexico, wintering at Santa Fe. After peace was restored he returned to his former home, and in 1850 bought his father's farm, and moved upon it, where he resided until his death. He was a Whig until the party went down, when he voted with the Democratic party. In 1860 he voted for Stephen A. Douglas, of Illinois, and when the war clouds began to hover over the nation, he was one of the first to gather around the flag of his country. In January, 1861, he assisted in raising the first flag for the Union in Dallas, afterward serving conspicuously in organizing Home Guards and militia companies for the preservation of the Union. He was first lieutenant of one of the Home Guards companies, and after the retreat of the troops from Springfield to Rolla, Mo., he re-enlisted in the Twenty-fourth Regiment of Missouri Volunteer Infantry, in which he served until November, when he was taken with measles, suffered a relapse, and was discharged on account of disability. After the close of the war he resumed the nursery business, which he had begun in 1857. In 1864 he voted for Abraham Lincoln; in 1868, for Ulysses Grant, and again in 1872, and in 1876 for Peter Cooper; in 1880 his last ballot was for James B. Weaver. In the year 1873 he made a profession of religion, and joined the Missionary Baptist Church, of which he lived a consistent member until his death, in 1858. He joined the Masonic fraternity, and was a devoted and consistent member. He was patriotic, public spirited and charitable, and lived to be a useful citizen, and died on the 17th day of October, 1883, regretted by all. His widow, who survives him, lives at Nichols Junction, Mo., with her youngest daughter, Mrs. Tippin. They had born to them eight children, four sons and four daughters; four are dead, two sons and two daughters. Those who are living are Sarah A., wife of T. J. Normon, who now lives at Rome, Iowa; Margaret J., wife of G. T. Tippin, who lives at Nichols Junction; George W. Reynolds, unmarried, lives with his brother, M. L. Reynolds, near Buffalo, Mo., and M. L. Reynolds, the eldest of the surviving children. He was born January 9, 1846, in Dallas County, Mo.; the educational facilities of the country during his rearing being very limited, and his parents being poor, he received only such an education as the common schools, which were of a poor grade, would afford. At the early age of fourteen his father put him forward in the business transactions of life as salesman and collecting agent for his nurseries. At the early age of fifteen he enlisted in the first companies of Home Guards, and after they were disbanded enlisted in the Seventh Missouri Cavalry, where he served about five months, re-enlisting in Battery K, Second Missouri Light Artillery, where he served until the close of the war, eleven months of the time serving as clerk in the commissary department. After the war closed in the States, he went with an expedition, against the Indians, into the Yellowstone country, and after returning home in December, 1865, he went to school for a short time at Buffalo, Mo., following which he engaged in the mercantile business. In December, 1866, he was married to Susanna Vanderford, daughter of R. M. Vanderford, of Polk County, Mo. Sixteen months after their marriage, to them was born a son, but their happiness, like all things earthly, came to an end, for in one short month both mother and child were consigned to the grave. After this he took an interest with his father in the Buffalo Nurseries, which the latter had founded in the year 1857. In January, 1870, he married Sarah A. Cowden, daughter of W. O. P. Cowden, of Polk County, Mo. They have had born to them, and now living, five children: Eliza J., aged eighteen years, and the wife of E. L. Yarbrough;

William D., aged sixteen; Mark W., aged fourteen; Eugene H., aged twelve years; Lillie May, aged eight years. Mr. and Mrs. Reynolds and their two eldest children are members of the Missionary Baptist Church. In the year 1879 he was elected as a member of the Thirtieth General Assembly of the Legislature of the State of Missouri, and assisted in the revision of the statutes of the State. He was a member of the national nominating convention assembled at Chicago, Ill., June 9, 1880, which nominated Gen. James B. Weaver for President. His politics were Republican until the year 1876, since which time he has voted the Greenback and Union Labor tickets, his vote and influence always being cast with what he considered the best interests of the whole people. In 1883 he purchased his father's interest in the Buffalo Nurseries, since which time he has conducted the business alone, having about 120 acres of land engaged in the growing of fruit, shade and ornamental trees. In the year 1886 he also bought of Mr. Holemon the Springfield Nurseries, situated at Nichols Junction, three miles west of Springfield, Mo., and has now about sixty-five acres there engaged in propagating trees. The two nurseries require about thirty hands in propagation of trees, and about thirty traveling salesmen, making some sixty men constantly employed by him. He has always been an earnest and constant promoter of horticulture and agriculture, and especially the former. He has always been an earnest supporter of and liberal contributor to schools and churches, as well as all public enterprises. To say the least, he has never allowed himself to be second in aiding and encouraging public movements.

Wesley S. Rice ranks among the successful farmers of Dallas County, Mo., and was born in Hawkins County, East Tenn., March 23, 1834, his parents being James S. and Frances (Harper) Rice, the father a native of Tennessee and the mother of North Carolina. They lived and died in Claiborne County, Tenn., having reared a family of seven children, five of whom are now living: Harper H., Calvin H., Wesley S., Mahala L. and Roadman H. Wesley S. Rice was reared on a farm in his native State, and was there also educated, subsequently engaging in teaching a portion of the time before the war. In 1856 he and his brother, Roadman H., immigrated with a family by the name of Dodson to Missouri, coming in wagons, and only had $20 between them. They settled in Dallas County, and during the summer were engaged in farm labor, and in the winter attended school. This they continued until 1858, when Wesley S. crossed the plains and spent one summer at Pike's Peak, where he was engaged in gold mining. He returned to Missouri in the fall of that year, and resumed farming, and saved enough money to purchase eighty acres of land in 1859. He purchased his present farm in 1862, and by industry and good management has made some valuable improvements on each, and is now considered one of the wealthy farmers of the county. He joined the Home Guards in 1861, and in January, 1862, enlisted in the Missouri State Militia, Company A, as a Mountain Ranger, but the ranks kept filling so fast that it was made the Fourteenth Regiment. He held the office of orderly-sergeant of his company, and was at the battles of Pea Ridge, Neosho, and several minor engagements. In 1864 he re-enlisted in the veteran service, Company H, Thirteenth Regiment, Missouri Cavalry Volunteers, and served on the plains against the Indians, being wounded and taken to Benton Barracks Hospital, where he laid for two or three months. He was mustered out and discharged on the 27th of April, 1866, and returned to the peaceful pursuit of farming, which occupation has since received his attention. He now owns 540 acres of land, with about 150 under cultivation, and is also engaged in stock buying and raising. He has two fine orchards on his farm, which furnish them with various fruits. He was married in 1866 to Julia A., a daughter of Spencer and Rosanah J. (Benthall) Dobson, natives of Tennessee, and early settlers of Dallas County, Mo. Mr. and Mrs. Rice are the parents of ten children: Luvernia F. (wife of J. H. White), Rosa B. (deceased), Roadman B., Rosa T., wife of I. C. Killion; Christian B., Virginia A., Wesley W., Levi H., Oliver O. and Estella M. Mrs. Rice is a member of the Primitive Baptist Church. Mr. Rice is one of the progressive men of the county, having always favored advancement. His motto is "Onward and Upward" in internal improvements, science, religion and education. Knowing by personal experience the great need of an education, he is endeavoring to give to his children the benefits of at least the common schools.

W. G. Robertson, prosecuting attorney of Dallas County, was born in Jefferson County, Mo., December 10, 1850, and is a son of James A. and Mary J. (Cundiff) Robertson, who were born in Missouri and North Carolina, respectively. The paternal grandfather, William Robertson, was one of the early settlers of Missouri. James A. Robertson is still residing in Hickory County, Mo., and throughout life has followed the occupation of farming. He served in the late war, in the Eighth Missouri State Militia, and participated in several hard-fought battles. W. G. Robertson is one of his nine children, was reared and educated in Hickory County, and when about twenty-six years of age began the study of law, having been previously engaged in farming. He pursued his studies under F. M. Wilson, of Hermitage, now the county clerk of Hickory County, and was admitted to the bar of Dallas County in October, 1880, and in September, 1882, moved to Buffalo, where he has since been actively engaged in practicing his profession, and has won an enviable reputation among the legal fraternity of the county. He was elected prosecuting attorney of the county in 1886, and discharged the duties of his office in so acceptable a manner that he was re-elected to the same position in 1888. He owns a small farm one mile west of Buffalo, all of which is under cultivation, but he gives his entire attention to his profession. He is a member of the I. O. O. F. lodge at Buffalo. From October, 1878, to July, 1882, he served as postmaster at Hermitage, Mo. October 17, 1869, he espoused Miss Margaret Alexander, by whom he has three children: Ida B., Laura A. and Eva W. On the 29th of August, 1879, he wedded his present wife, Miss Sarah E. Darman, who has borne him four children: Lula E., Harry W., Minnie and Gracie. Mr. and Mrs. Robertson are members of the Methodist Episcopal Church.

David M. Rush, county collector, was born in Barren County, Ky., November 27, 1849, the grandson of John Rush, a Virginian, born in 1776, who was in the battle of New Orleans in the War of 1812; for that service he received a 40 and a 120-acre land warrant. David's father, Daniel W. Rush, born in Allen County, Ky., in 1824, married Rhoda J. Chapman in 1848, immigrating to Polk County, Mo., in 1852. Four of their six children survive: David M., Mary E. (wife of John Tompkins), Rhoda A. (now Mrs. R. B. Lee) and William R. John J. died in 1868, aged twelve, and Maletha, in 1883, aged twenty-two. David M. remained on his father's farm until 1870 (his mother having died in 1861), and in 1871 left the public schools to enter a select school at Urbana, Mo. A portion of his three years' course was devoted to the higher mathematics. After teaching from 1874 to 1881 he engaged in the patent right business for several years, during which time he secured two patents of his own invention, one for a washing machine, and the other for an adding machine, both a success, and of acknowledged ingenuity in mechanical construction. In 1878 Mr. Rush married Vivia Lindsey, of Louisburg, Mo. Their four children are Dolores, Lascelles, Loise and Norma L. In 1886 he was elected as a Republican county collector of Wright County, and served with such satisfaction that he was renominated in 1888 without opposition, and was, of course, elected, running several votes ahead of his ticket. He has been a Mason since 1875. His wife is a member of the Missionary Baptist Church.

E. L. Schofield, editor and proprietor of the Buffalo *Reflex*, was born in Allamakee County, Iowa, on the 27th of December, 1859, his parents, James and Cornelia (Seely) Schofield, being natives of the "Empire State," and early immigrants to Illinois and Iowa. When about seven years of age E. L. Schofield came with his parents to Buffalo, Mo., and was here reared to manhood and educated. His early days were spent at farm labor, but he also learned the machinist's trade, but never followed it for a livelihood. In September, 1888, he purchased the *Reflex*, which paper he has since successfully published, it being devoted entirely to the interests of the Republican party, and it is one of the spicy and ably edited papers of the county, and promises to further the interests of the Republican party to a great extent. In connection with his paper Mr. Schofield is also engaged in studying law, and will soon become a member of the legal fraternity of Dallas County. He was married in 1884 to Miss May Clark, of Bolivar, Mo., by whom he has one child, James C. He is a member of the I. O. O. F., and is a half-brother of Gen. Schofield, of Civil War fame.

William J. Self may properly be mentioned as one of the leading farmers of Dallas County, of which he is a native. His parents, Peter and Nancy (Reynolds) Self, were born, reared and married in Tennessee, and about 1835 immigrated to Dallas County, Mo., coming in covered wagons, and located on the land now owned by J. J. Reynolds. Here he erected a very primitive log cabin, and as soon as the Government put the land on the market he took a claim, and began clearing his land. Indians and wild game of all kinds were plentiful in the region at that period, but they were little troubled by either.

They did their marketing at St. Louis, but all their clothing was homemade. In 1859 the parents moved to Arkansas, where they both died, the former's death occurring in 1863. Five of their eight children are living at the present time, whose names are as follows: Polly (wife of James Hatfield), William J., Charlotte (wife of Col. John D. Allen), Eliza (wife of Jacob Mendenhall) and Ruth (wife of L. D. Little). William J. Self, whose name heads this biography, was born on the 26th of January, 1838, and has always resided on a farm in Dallas County, in which he was the third child born. His early educational advantages were very meager, and he never entered a school-room until after ten years of age, and that was a little log cabin with a dirt floor and no windows. He has always been noted for his energy and thrift, and is now the owner of a valuable farm of 240 acres, all under fence, and with 125 acres under cultivation. He has a handsome and commodious residence, substantial out-buildings, and is an extensive dealer in stock. He enlisted in the Home Guards for three months in 1861, and after serving about two years with the Rangers he enlisted in Company D, Fifteenth Missouri Volunteer Cavalry, and was mustered out in July, 1865. After the war closed he returned home, and bought the land where he now lives, which was then heavily covered with timber. He has been married four times, his first marriage being to Miss Sarah Cox, in 1857, who died six weeks later, and in 1859 he espoused Elizabeth Cowden, by whom he had three sons: James H., Francis M. and William R. This wife died in July, 1863, and in August, 1865, he wedded Mary McGinnis, who also bore him three children: Mary E., Mark L. and Nancy J. The mother of these children died in 1873, and a year later Mr. Self was married to Sarah Shaw, by whom he has four children: Albert J., Minnie P., Lulu E. and Edward W. Mr. and Mrs. Self are members of the Baptist Church, and are much esteemed as citizens and neighbors.

Z. L. Slavens, a physician and farmer of Urbana, Dallas County, is a native of Springfield, Mo., and was born February 13, 1834, being the second child born in Springfield. His parents were James H. and Amanda L. (Roundtree) Slavens, natives, respectively, of Kentucky and North Carolina. James H. Slavens, was born in 1809, and when a boy went from his native State to Illinois, and from there to Montgomery County, Mo., in 1815, locating where Springfield now stands, in Southwestern Missouri, in 1831, and he was the first minister of the Methodist Episcopal Church in that part of Missouri. The following year, 1832, he married Miss Amanda L. Roundtree, who was born in 1816, and was a daughter of Joseph Roundtree and Nancy (Nichols) Roundtree, who moved from North Carolina in 1818, and thence to Springfield, Mo., in 1829, taking as a claim the land upon which Springfield is now built. To James H. and Amanda L. Slavens were born seven children, of whom four are now living, viz.: Dr. Z. L., Nancy A. Price, Lucius B. and Luther J. James H. Slavens was sent as a missionary to the Peoria and Shawnee Indians in Kansas, among whom he labored one year, when he returned to his home in Greene County, Mo., where he engaged in farming and teaching. In 1843 he took up the study of medicine, to the practice of which he devoted considerable attention until his death, which occurred in 1888. He served as surgeon in Gov. Phelps' Enrolled Militia during the late war. The paternal grandfather of our subject, Stewart Slavens, who was a farmer by occupation, was born in Virginia in 1786, and died in 1866. Mrs. Amanda L. Slavens died March 16, 1886. Dr. Z. L. Slavens spent his early life principally in his native place. He attended the high-school at Ebenezer, Mo., two years, and later John A. Stephens' Select School, of Springfield, Mo., one year. He began the study of medicine in 1856, under Dr. E. T. Robertson, of Springfield, and in 1857 and 1858 he attended lectures at the Missouri Medical College, St. Louis. He began the practice of his chosen profession in Laclede County, Mo., in 1858, and from there went to Buffalo, Dallas County, in 1859, where he practiced until the war broke out, when he took his family to Indiana. In 1862 he entered the army as surgeon of the One Hundred and Fifteenth Indiana Infantry, under command of Col. John Mahan, and served one year, receiving an honorable discharge. He returned to Indiana and practiced medicine until 1865, when he again went to Buffalo, Mo., where, with the exception of a short time spent in Webster County, he remained until 1875, at that time removing to Urbana. In February, 1860, Dr. Slavens married Irene Z. Stanley, who was born in Indiana in February, 1839. Her parents were Horace and Sarah (Willoughby) Stanley, natives of Tennessee. They located in Buffalo, Mo., in April, 1839, and built one of the first houses on Buffalo Head Prairie. Horace Stanley died in 1863. Sarah Stanley died in 1877. They have three children living, viz.: Mrs. Minerva Morrow, Mrs. I. V. Cummins and Mrs. Slavens. Dr. and Mrs. Slavens have four children, viz.: Mrs. Alice L. Lightner, Lieut. T. H. Slavens, Mrs. M. I. Reser, of Urbana, and Robert B. Slavens, still at home. Lieut. T. H. Slavens graduated with honor from the West Point Military Academy in 1887, and was commissioned a lieutenant and assigned to duty in the Fourth Cavalry, United States Army, now stationed at Fort Lowell, Arizona Territory. Dr. Slavens is a member of the Masonic fraternity, is a Methodist, and in politics a Republican.

L. J. Slavens, a general merchant of Urbana, Dallas Co., Mo., was born in Buffalo, Mo., November 14, 1849, and is a son of Dr. James H. Slavens and Louisa A. (Rountree) Slavens. James H. Slavens was born July 30, 1809, and in 1818 went from Kentucky, his native State, to Illinois, and thence, in 1820, to Montgomery County, Mo. In 1832 he married Louisa A. Rountree, who was born in North Carolina August 31, 1816. Seven children blessed this union, three of whom are deceased, viz.: Dr. Joseph W. R. Slavens, Thomas F. Slavens and Louisa Almarinda Slavens; four are still living, viz.: Dr. Z. L. Slavens, Mrs. N. A. Price, L. B. Slavens and L. J. Slavens. Dr. James H. Slavens, father of our subject, was a minister, and did honorable service as a missionary to the Indians one year. He moved to Buffalo, Mo., in 1844, where he practiced medicine and preached, and from there moved to Ebenezer, Mo., in 1850, where he spent two years, and subsequently removed to Webster County, Mo., returning to Buffalo in 1859. In 1861 he went to Indiana, and afterward located in Springfield, Mo. In 1865 he bought a farm near Buffalo, and in 1875 settled in Urbana, where he lived until his death, which occurred June 23, 1888. During the war he served as surgeon in Col. John S. Phelps' regiment, United States Army. He was a successful medical practitioner, to which he devoted the greater part of his attention, commanding a large patronage wherever he went. He was a son of Stewart Slavens, of English descent. The mother of our subject died March 16, 1886; her parents were Joseph and Nancy (Nichols) Rountree, natives of North Carolina. Joseph Rountree located where Springfield now stands, before the town was founded, where he lived until his death, which occurred December 27, 1875, at the advanced age of ninety-three years. He was a farmer, and served as county judge. L. J. Slavens spent his early life in Webster and Dallas Counties, Mo., receiving a common-school education. At the age of eighteen he engaged in school-teaching, which he pursued for about twelve years. May 5, 1878, he married Josephine Lindsey, who was born in Hickory County, Mo., December 11, 1855, and is a daughter of Lycurgus and Lucy (Toby) Lindsey. Lycurgus Lindsey, a native of Kentucky, is now a farmer of Hickory County, Mo.; he served as lieutenant of Company B, Eighth Missouri State Militia Volunteers, under Capt. Cosgrove. Mrs. Slavens was the third in a family of seven, two of whom, Mrs. Cynthia A. Pendleton and Mrs. Mary E. Creed, are deceased. The remaining four now living are Mrs. Matilda Coon, Mrs. Emma Thurston, Mrs. Laura White and Eugene Lindsey. Mr. Slavens engaged in his present business, at Urbana, in 1881. He was appointed notary public in 1876, which office he still holds. They have three children: Joseph Rountree, Mary Louisa and Inez Lucy. Mr. Slavens is a member of the Methodist Episcopal Church. Politically he is a Republican.

W. Smithpeter. The milling interests of Dallas County, Mo., are ably represented by Mr. Smithpeter, who is the proprietor of the Buffalo Roller Mills, and is a dealer in flour and meal and native lumber. He was born in Laclede County, Mo., on the 2d of July, 1849, his parents, Alfred and Mary C. (Dugger) Smithpeter, having immigrated from their native State of Tennessee to that county in 1840. Here the father purchased 700 acres of timber land, and succeeded in improving a great portion of it previous to his death, which occurred in 1861, he being killed by bushwhackers. His widow and six of his ten children are still living, the latter's names being Angeline (wife of G. Dethurum), Albert, Wilburn, Ellen (wife of M. H. Case), Marietta and Florence. Wilburn Smithpeter, whose name heads this sketch, was reared and educated in Laclede County, Mo., and remained with his parents until twenty-one years of age. In 1870 he came to Buffalo and engaged in the drug business, which business he followed until 1883, when he purchased the mill he is now operating. In 1887 he put in the roller process, and now manufactures as fine flour as can be had in any city, and supplies the demand for many miles around. His mill is a three-story frame building, run by steam, and has a capacity of fifty barrels per twenty-four hours. He also owns a valuable and well-improved farm of sixty acres, and is engaged in the lumber business, having a saw-mill attached to his gristmill. Mr. Smithpeter is one of the progressive citizens of the

BIOGRAPHICAL APPENDIX. 969

county, and has done all in his power to encourage worthy enterprises. He is a member of the Masons, the I. O. O. F. and the A. O. U. W., being a Select Knight in the latter. In 1873 he was married to Lydia A. Shemberger, a native of Indiana, by whom he has two children: Charles W. and Herbert V. He and wife are worthy and consistent members of the Christian Church.

James M. Stafford is one of the oldest settlers of Dallas County, Mo., and was born in Hardeman County, Tenn., February 5, 1827, and is a son of Bird and Lucy (Parker) Stafford, both of whom were born in North Carolina, and died in Dallas County, Mo., whither they had come from Hardeman County, Tenn., in 1840. March 3 he landed on the place where he died. The father was a soldier in the War of 1812, and, although previously a Democrat, during the late war was a strong Union man. He was a successful blacksmith and farmer, and in 1863 was married to Miss Eliza Wingo, but died three years later. To his first union eleven children were born, James M. and L. L. being the only ones who are now living. The former served during the Mexican War, and was in a number of fierce battles with the Indians on the plains. After the war he returned home and began working at the carpenter's trade, but afterward engaged in farming and blacksmithing. He was without means on starting in life for himself, but his labors have been attended with good success, and he became the owner of 600 acres of land, but has given all but 360 acres to his sons. He served for a short time during the late war, a part of the time acting as orderly sergeant. May 30, 1850, he was married to Avaline Maddux, a daughter of Nathaniel and Rebecca Maddux, natives of Polk County, Tenn., and early settlers of Dallas County. Mrs. Stafford was born September 21, 1832, and died in Dallas County, Mo., August 4, 1871, having borne a family of twelve children, ten of whom are living: Amanda M. (wife of George T. Edmisson), Lucy E. (wife of E. D. Fortner), Newton C., Laura E. (wife of J. M. Bennett), Rebecca J. (wife of Thomas Routh), Martha A. (wife of J. L. Hardison), John P., Harriet T. (wife of William Norton) and Margaret S. (wife of George S. Wingo). Nathaniel Bird, William A. and Sarah E. are deceased. December 25, 1873, Mr. Stafford wedded Mary B. Harmon, a daughter of James Harmon. She was born in Missouri, and died in Dallas County November 25, 1882, having borne five children: Lydia L., Felix C., Hettie B., Floyd and Mary Ellen. Mr. Stafford is an elder in the Cumberland Presbyterian Church, and is a Democrat in politics, and a member of the Masonic fraternity.

J. S. Thurston, a dealer in harness and saddlery, of Urbana, Dallas County, was born in Benton County, Mo., in 1857, and is a son of William S. and Matilda V. (Phillips) Thurston. William S. Thurston was born in Kentucky in 1832, and the following year was taken by his parents, William S. and Polly Ann (Stanley) Thurston, to Benton, now Pettis, County, Mo. He went to Iowa in 1880, and in 1881 enlisted in the Missouri State Militia, and served one year. He returned to Benton County, Mo., in 1866, and in 1871 located in Dallas County. He is a farmer and stock raiser, and the father of thirteen children, of whom the following are still living: J. S., Maggie

A., Sally, Robert, John C. and Nancy A. The paternal grandfather of our subject was born in Kentucky in 1793, and died in 1839; he did honorable service in the War of 1812, for which his widow received a pension. Mrs. Matilda Thurston was born in Wisconsin in 1836, and was a daughter of Hiram Phillips, a farmer and stock dealer of that State: she died in 1882. J. S. Thurston spent his early life in Iowa and Missouri, removing from Iowa to Missouri in 1864 or 1865, and settling in Dallas County in 1868. November 26, 1878, he married Miss Emma Lindsey, a native of Hickory County, Mo., who was born in 1858, and is a daughter of Lycurgus and Lucy (Toby) Lindsey, the former born in Kentucky in 1829, and the latter in Indiana in 1837. Lycurgus Thurston is a farmer, and in 1861 he enlisted in and served as captain of the Home Guards at Preston, Mo. Mr. and Mrs. Lindsey are the parents of seven children, of whom five are living, viz.: Josephine, Emma, Matilda, Laura and Eugene. Amos Lindsey, father of Lycurgus, was born in Kentucky in 1787, and died in 1877; he married Polly Madison, an own cousin of President James Adams. Mr. and Mrs. Thurston are the parents of three children, viz.: William Lycurgus, Shepherd Oscar and Thomas Fulton. Mr. Thurston owns fifty acres of land, as well as a house, two lots and two acres of land in Urbana. Politically he is a Republican. He has served as deputy sheriff of Dallas County two years.

Thaddeus S. Tinsley, Sr., of Dallas County, Mo., is a descendant of an old Virginia family, who immigrated to Tennessee at quite an early day. His parents, John and Alice (Mulkey) Tinsley, were born, married and spent their lives in Jackson County, Tenn. They were farmers by occupation, and became the parents of fifteen children, eleven of whom are yet living: William, Philip, Emily, Ruth, Amos, Milton, Elizabeth, Thaddeus S., Martha, Lucretia and Lucinda. Thaddeus S. Tinsley is of English origin, and was born on the 31st of March, 1832, in Jackson County, Tenn., and received his education and rearing in his native county. He was married in 1854 to Miss Julia A. Fowler, of French descent, by whom he has ten children: John H., married to Mary Hendrickson February 1, 1883; Lydia, wife of R. A. McCowan; Alice, wife of J. L. Hendrickson; Lee, Vanus E., T. S., May, Zela, Clay and Idylle. In 1873 Mr. Tinsley immigrated with his family to Dallas County, Mo., where he eventually became the owner of 700 acres of land, but has sold some, and given to his children, until he now only owns 315 acres, with about 225 acres under cultivation. He has given the most of his attention to stock raising, as his farm is well adapted for this purpose, and in this occupation has been more than ordinarily successful. He and wife and eight of the children are members of the Church of Christ, and their two sons, Lee and T. S., are ministers of that church.

A. R. Vanderford was born in Ross County, Ohio, on the 30th of March, 1818, and since the fall of 1838 has been a resident of Dallas County, Mo. The father, Eli Vanderford, was born in Maryland, and at a very early day immigrated to Ohio, where he was married to Susannah Ratcliff, a native of North Carolina. They moved to Missouri at the above mentioned date, coming through in covered wagons, and reached Dallas County one month after starting out. They purchased the farm now owned by the Coffer family, on which they erected a little log cabin, and lived in this for a number of years, until they were able to make better improvements. At the land sale in January, 1839, he purchased 160 acres of land for himself, and 160 acres for his son, A. R. Vanderford, whose name heads this sketch. He then entered several tracts of land near by, and at one time was an extensive real estate owner, but divided his property among his children. He and wife were among the first settlers of the county, and here spent their remaining days. Their son, A. R. Vanderford, was about twenty years of age when he came to Dallas County, and after his father purchased him his farm he bent all his energies to clearing it and getting it in a tillable condition. He has lived on this farm ever since he came to the county, and now owns 300 acres of land, with about 200 acres under fence and in cultivation, and with good improvements. In 1840 he was married to Malinda Gordon, a daughter of Noah and Nancy (Bartlett) Gordon, who came to Missouri in 1835, and located in Polk County. Here the mother died, but the father's death occured in Pulaski County. Mr. and Mrs. Vanderford are the parents of nine children, five now living: Monroe, John C., Jasper N., Marion F. and James B.; those deceased are Julia A., Nancy P., Almira and an infant. Mr. Vanderford cast his first vote for Gen. Harrison, and he and wife are members of the Christian Church. Jasper N. Vanderford, their son, is the presiding judge of the Dallas County Court, and was born in the county on the 2d of August, 1849. His early days were spent in attending school and assisting his father on the farm, and he now has a valuable farm of 120 acres, on which are some valuable improvements. His present office, to which he was elected in 1886, expires in 1890. He has always taken a deep interest in religious matters, as well as other enterprises for the public weal, and might well be considered a valuable acquisition to any community. December 8, 1869, he wedded Miss Jane Van Horn, by whom he has the following children: William M., Laura B., Ida M., Joseph A., Charles N., Annie, Dora E., Minnie J. and Pearl. Mr. and Mrs. Vanderford are worthy members of the Christian Church.

Z. L. West, an enterprising farmer and lead miner of Miller Township, Dallas County, was born in Gasconade County, Mo., August 11, 1825, and is a son of William and Elizabeth West, the former a native of Kentucky, who moved to St. Louis, Mo., in 1809, and to Gasconade County in 1811, where he was one of the earliest settlers. He erected the second house built on the Gasconade River, and had many a dispute and fight with the native Indians. He was a farmer by occupation, and the father of eight children, four girls and four boys, of whom our subject is the only one residing in Missouri. William West died in 1854. Z. L. West spent his early life in Gasconade and Maries Counties, Mo., and when but sixteen years of age began an independent life as a farmer. In 1849 he married Miss Mary M. Harris, a native of North Carolina, and a daughter of Micajah and Barsheba Harris. Mr. and Mrs. West are the parents of nine children, of whom five are living, viz.: William M., Mary E., Courtney, Zachariah, Sarah M. Duff and Wesley. The family moved to

Dallas County, Mo., in 1848, where Mr. West purchased a claim, and as a result of industry and good management has built up his present home. He owns 244 acres of land, upon which he has good improvements and a good, comfortable house. In 1884 he enlisted in Company I, Sixteenth Missouri Mounted Infantry, took part in the battles of Jefferson City, Big Blue and Mine Creek, and received his discharge at the close of the war at Springfield, Mo. Mr. West is a member of the G. A. R., and is a Republican in politics.

Frank C. Wilson, the popular druggist of Buffalo, Mo., was born December 25, 1847, in Camden County, Mo., his parents being James and Sarah (Britton) Wilson, and his grandfather James Wilson. The latter immigrated to Camden County, Mo., at a very early day, before the Osage Indians had left the country, the State then being a Territory. His nearest neighbor lived at a distance of twenty-seven miles, and his nearest market was St. Louis, whither he would repair when in need of supplies, driving a yoke of oxen. His first residence was a little log cabin, with clapboard doors and roof, and was located about ten miles from the Osage River, on the Auglaize stream. He was a noted hunter, and his cabin was always supplied with choice wild meats, which animals fell a victim to his skill as a marksman. He was an extensive farmer and stock dealer, and made a specialty of raising fine horses, being a great admirer and an excellent judge of these animals. About 1858 he took up his residence in Caldwell County, Mo., and died near Breckenridge. His eldest son, Sampson, was sheriff of a territory now comprising (but then called Kinderhook County) several counties, of which Jefferson City was the county seat. James Wilson, the father of Frank C. Wilson, was born in Camden County, Mo., and was a farmer and trader by occupation, and was captain of Company I, Osage Regiment of Missouri Home Guards. Hon. J. W. McClurg was colonel. He and Capt. McVey carried the first message for Gen. Sigel from Lebanon to Rolla. In the spring of 1861 Mr. Wilson was commissioned recruiting officer for the Union army at Springfield by Gen. Lyon. He died at Jefferson City October 13, 1861. His wife was born in South Carolina, and died at Cassville, Mo., having become the mother of eight children, six of whom are living: William L., Frank C., Mary J., Martha M., Allen H. and Charles M. Frank C. Wilson is the eldest of the family now living, and was reared and educated in Camden County. At the age of eighteen years he engaged in teaching school, but shortly after embarked in mercantile life, and continued in the business until 1873, when he established the Lebanon *Journal*, which he continued to publish until 1880, and then came to Buffalo and engaged in milling, stock trading and the mercantile business. He has now a complete stock of drugs and all the fixtures usually carried by a druggist. He is one of the prominent business men of the town, and is a member of the I. O. O. F. and the A. O. U. W., and has served as postmaster of Buffalo for three years. In 1872 he was married to Jennie H. Booth, by whom he has two children, Minnie A. and Annie B. Mr. and Mrs. Wilson and their eldest daughter are members of the Presbyterian Church.

Hon. Nathaniel J. Wollard. Prominent among the leading and

enterprising citizens of Dallas County, Mo., stands the name of the above mentioned gentleman, who was born in Dallas County, Mo., October 16, 1844, and is the son of Nathaniel and Margaret (Abel) Wollard, natives of North Carolina and Virginia, respectively. The father was born August 6, 1792, and died in Dallas County, Mo., September 1, 1863. He was a Primitive Baptist minister, and in connection with his ministerial duties carried on farming, at which he was very successful. At the time of his death he was the second largest tax payer of Dallas County. He was a soldier in the War of 1812; was in the battles of Horseshoe, New Orleans, Tippecanoe and others. He was in active ministerial duty for over forty years, and preached in the greater part of Southwestern Missouri. When twenty-one years of age, poor and almost penniless, he walked 800 miles to Tennessee, and located in Maury County, where he resided until 1837, when he came to Missouri and located near where his son, Nathaniel J., is now living. He was married first to Margaret Hardison, in Tennessee, about 1816. She died in Dallas County, Mo., and Mr. Wollard married the mother of our subject in 1841. She was born January 12, 1808, and is now living with her son, Nathaniel J. Wollard. She was the daughter of John David Abel and the widow of Calvin Newport. She came with Mr. Newport from Roane County, Tenn., in 1836, and located in Wright County, where she married Mr. Wollard. To this union were born four children: Louisa P., Nathaniel J., Silas B. and James M. (deceased). Nathaniel J. remained at home until 1863, when he enlisted in Company B of Woods' Battalion, Confederate States Army, and served two years, or until the close of the war. He was in many battles—Dardanelle, Pine Bluff, Pilot Knob, Jefferson City, Big and Little Blue, Neosho and others. October 22, 1865, he married Miss Alice Randles, a native of Dallas County, Mo., born December 6, 1846, and the daughter of James Franklin Randles. The fruits of this union were these children: Mary L. M., died in infancy; James F., John S., Moses W., Sarah E. M., Robert P., Estella D., Quincy Lee, died at the age of six years; Martha, died in infancy; Permelia E., and Omega F., who died in infancy. After the war Mr. Wollard engaged in farming and stock raising, at which he has been unusually successful. In 1881 he engaged in mercantile business at Buffalo, the firm title being Randels & Wollard, and at the end of one year the title was changed to Wollard & Co. He was in business about five years, when he sold out. In 1872 he was elected justice of the peace, and served six years, when he was elected county judge from the Southern District. In 1882 he was elected by the Greenback party to represent the county in the Legislature, and in 1884 he was re-elected by the Greenback and Democratic parties. In 1886 he was nominated for State senator by the Union Labor party, but declined. In 1881 he was instrumental in establishing the Dallas County Fair Association, being elected vice-president of the same the following year, and afterward president. Mrs. Wollard has been a member of the Missionary Baptist Church from early girlhood, and recently Mr. Wollard has joined the same church. He is a member of the Masonic fraternity, is a member of the I. O. O. F., the Agricultural Wheel, in which lodge he takes a great interest, is president of the County Wheel, and a delegate to the State Wheel. He was elected in 1888 to represent the State of Missouri at the National Wheel at Meridian, Miss. Mr. Wollard is one of the representative citizens of Dallas County, and at all times takes an active interest in Sunday-schools, he being vice-president of the Washington Township Sunday-school Union. When first elected to that position there were but two Sunday-schools; now there are eleven, and over 900 scholars. At the present time Mr. Wollard is engaged in building a fine church house on his premises, which will be a credit to any locality, and as he leaves out fail in his enterprises it doubtless will be completed.

PHELPS COUNTY.

Dr. Samuel F. Arthur was born August 20, 1850, in Dent County, Mo., and is the son of John and Elizabeth (Hyer) Arthur. John Arthur was born in the State of Kentucky, was of Scotch descent, receiving a common-school education, and immigrated to Missouri about 1838; he settled at Meramec Iron Works, working in the smelting furnace, and was engaged in the same business in Crawford County for five or six years, and after that went to Dent County, entered land, and there he now resides. During the late war he was quartermaster in the Confederate army. Elizabeth Hyer was born in Pennsylvania, of German parentage. She came to Missouri when young, was married to Mr. Arthur in Crawford County, and bore him twelve children, five now living: Samuel F., Mary, Mattie, Alice and Katie. Those deceased were named John, James, Lewis, Ellen, Lizzie, May and Julia. The paternal grandparents were both natives of Kentucky, and spent their entire lives there. Grandfather Hyer was a native of Germany, and immigrated to Pennsylvania, then to Ohio, and afterward to Missouri, where he died. Dr. Samuel F. Arthur was reared in Dent County, Mo., and received a good ordinary education. At the age of twenty he began the study of medicine, reading under his uncle, Dr. John Hyer, of Lake Springs, Dent County, for two years, graduating March 11, 1874. He then came to Edgar Springs, where he has since been practicing. He has been quite successful, and has an extensive practice. He was married, March 29, 1875, to Miss Josie M. Lenox, daughter of Francis M. and Elizabeth Lenox. Mr. Lenox was from Calloway County, Ky., and followed mercantile pursuits after coming to Missouri. He represented Phelps County and also Dent County in the Legislature. His father, David Lenox, was one of the pioneer settlers of Phelps County, and a minister in the Baptist Church years afterward. Dr. Arthur was defeated by fourteen votes for the office of representative of Phelps County. He was coroner for one term. He is a Democrat in politics, is a member of the I. O. O. F., K. of P., and the Masonic fraternity, and is a member of the Rolla District Medical Society, being elected vice-president in 1883.

John Baker, farmer, was born in Osage County, Mo., December 5, 1839, and is the son of Matthew S. and Hettie (Tabor) Baker, and grandson of James Baker, who was a native of the "Blue Grass State," and a soldier in the War of 1812. His wife, Rebecca (Small) Baker, was also a native of Kentucky, and was of Irish descent. James Tabor, the maternal grandfather of the subject of this sketch, was born in North Carolina, and immigrated to Tennessee at an early date, making the journey on pack-horses. His wife, Delila Tabor, was also from North Carolina, and also died in Tennessee. Matthew S. Baker was born in Wayne County, Ky., July 12, 1814, and remained in that State until six years of age, when he immigrated with his parents to Marion County, Tenn., remaining there for a number of years. He was educated principally by his own exertions, and later taught school. He immigrated to Missouri in 1835, settling in what is now Osage County, where he remained until 1855, engaged in farming. He then moved to Phelps County, remained there until 1860, and then moved to Camden County, where he was killed July 12, 1863. During his life he never held any office higher than justice of the peace. His wife, Hettie Tabor, was born in Rutherford County, Tenn., May 28, 1814, and bore him twelve children, seven now living: John N., Matthew S., Delila A., Elizabeth, Hettie M., Nancy R. and Oliver T. Those deceased are Thomas H., Malinda J., James H. and two small children. Mrs. Baker died in Phelps County, Mo., December, 1885, at the age of seventy-four years. John Baker, the subject of this sketch, was reared on his father's farms in Osage and Phelps Counties, Mo., and as the country was sparsely settled, and schools and churches hardly known, his education as a consequence suffered. At the age of twenty-one he enlisted in Company A, First Missouri State Troops, but was afterward in Robert's Company A, and served eight months, during which time he engaged in the Cole Camp fight. He was discharged at Springfield, Mo., after which he went to Rolla, where he remained until Price's raid. He then made two trips across the plains with Government supplies as far west as Denver and New Mexico. He then came home and cared for his mother, and December 20, 1866, he married Mrs. Sarah J. (Coldiron) McCommon, daughter of William and Mary (Howard) Coldiron, both of whom were born in Kentucky. Mrs. Baker was born January 8, 1842, in Laurel County, Ky., and came to Missouri when twelve years of age. By her union to Mr. Baker were born five children, four now living: Sarah A., Mary H., James M., John W. and an infant deceased. Mrs. Baker was the mother of a child by her former marriage. This child, William M., is deceased. Mr. Baker is the owner of 500 acres of land, 300 under cultivation. He is a member of the Masonic fraternity, also the Odd Fellows lodge, and is politically a Democrat.

Peter Baumgartner, proprietor of St. James Livery Stable, and dealer in wines, liquors and cigars, has been a resident of St. James, Mo., since January, 1878. He was born in Germany in 1852, and at the age of two years was brought to the United States by his parents, until four years of age residing in Pennsylvania. Since that time he has been a resident of Maries County, Mo. The father, Anton Baumgartner, was a farmer and carpenter, and died in Maries County in 1887. His wife, Mary, is still living, aged about seventy years. Their son, Peter, is the second of four children, and was educated in the common schools of Maries County. In March, 1872, he was married to Missouri Isabella Jones, who was born and reared in Missouri, and died in 1878, leaving three children, only one of whom is living. In March, 1879, Mr. Baumgartner married his second wife, whose maiden name was Jennie Ann Brown. She was born in Gasconade County, and is the mother of four children. In 1886–87 Mr. Baumgartner served as mayor of St. James. He has a good business block and livery barn in the town, keeps from fifteen to twenty horses, and has an excellent lot of vehicles, all of which he has earned by hard labor and good management since he attained his twenty-second birthday. He is a Democrat, and cast his first presidential vote for Tilden in 1876, and is a member of the I. O. O. F., Big Spring Lodge No. 237. He is also a member of the Triple Alliance, and belongs to the Catholic Church. His business amounts to about $5,000 annually.

Edmund Ward Bishop, one of Rolla's oldest citizens and most highly esteemed men, is a native of Dutchess County, N. Y., born in 1820, and is the son of Morris and Merab (Botsford) Bishop. Morris Bishop, a native of Connecticut, born about 1774, was a teacher of music and penmanship, and a soldier in the War of 1812. He died in 1825. His wife was born near Jordan, N. Y., on the Erie Canal. Edmund W. Bishop was but five years of age when his father died, and he was taken by an uncle, with whom he remained two years. The uncle then died, and young Bishop went to work on a farm for Jeduthan Roe. He was to receive board, clothes and three months' schooling for his services. At the end of eight years he had received but fifty-three days' schooling, and was old enough to see the necessity of a thorough knowledge of books, consequently he demanded the fulfillment of his contract, and was refused. Being of a determined nature he left for Coudersport, Potter Co., Penn., where his mother and brother lived, reaching there just in time to see his mother die. This was in 1836. The distance was over 300 miles, and young Edmund made the journey, the greater portion of the way, on foot. He worked three years as a carpenter, and during fall and winter months attended school at Coudersport Academy. At the end of three years he taught school for three months, for $10 per month, boarding round with parents of pupils. The following two years he attended school at the academy, working nights and mornings to pay his board, at the end of which time he taught the village school three months for $45 per month. After completing his school term he attended one term at Batavia High-school. The following summer he hired as ax-man for an engineer corps, making a preliminary survey of the Philadelphia & Erie Railroad. His next work was to superintend the rafting and selling of lumber for Ives & Dykes, taking their rafts down the Allegheny and Ohio Rivers to Cincinnati. In six months he became clerk and supply agent, and after two years' faithful service the company failed, and Mr. Bishop lost all his wages. In 1848 he received a contract on the Canisteo division of the New York & Erie

Railroad, which he completed under discouraging circumstances, owing to limited condition of money matters, but realized fairly on his contract. For the following sixteen years Mr. Bishop continued as railroad constructor, contractor, and assisted in building the Buffalo & Niagara, Hamilton & Toronto, Catawissa and the Williamsport & Elmira Railroads. In 1855 he went to St. Louis, and became employed on the St. Louis & San Francisco Railroad, working on this road for four years. He then disposed of his interest in the contract, and became a citizen of Rolla, where he immediately took steps looking to the improvement and prosperity of the town. He speculated largely in real estate, donated land for the county seat, superintended the building of the court-house and jail, after which he engaged in agricultural pursuits near Rolla. He assisted in the organization of the Rolla Flouring Mills, superintending the erection of the same. He was also one of the originators of the National Bank of Rolla, and is one of its directors. He is a stockholder in the Rolla Woolen Mills, and has been a member of the school board and city council. He was president of the Agricultural and Horticultural Society during its existence, and was appointed and afterward elected a member of the State Board of Agriculture. He was also instrumental in the establishment of the School of Mines, donating 160 acres of land and his time for the purpose. In 1861 and 1862 Mr. Bishop was major of the Enrolled Militia stationed at Rolla, being appointed by Gov. Gamble. Gov. McClurg appointed him a member of the Mining Bureau, and in 1876 Gov. Hardin appointed him president of the Centennial Commission of Phelps County, also appointing Mrs. Bishop of the ladies' department on the same commission. October 21, 1858, he married Miss Jane Sellard, daughter of James and Judith Sellard, of Bradford County, Penn. This union resulted in the birth of four children: Jennie, wife of John P. Harrison, deputy circuit clerk of Phelps County; Julia, wife of Joseph Pool; Flora, wife of W. W. Wyshon, and Edmund W., Jr. In politics Mr. Bishop was a Democrat before the war, and since that time has been a Republican. He was a delegate to the national convention at Philadelphia in 1868, and has been a delegate to every State convention in Missouri since the organization of the Republican party. In 1876 he was nominated for the Legislature, running ahead of his ticket, but the county being largely Democratic he was of course defeated. He is a prominent temperance worker, is a member of no church, but is a firm believer in Christianity. Starting in life for himself at the age of sixteen, without means, and possessed of but very little education, Mr. Bishop has amassed a comfortable fortune, and is one of the substantial citizens of the county. He owns large tracts of land and fine property in Rolla, which he has accumulated by his marked business capacity, skillful financiering and economy. He has lost thousands of dollars by going security for his friends. Since the war he has paid $20,000 in taxes.

Hon. Charles C. Bland, judge of the Eighteenth Judicial Circuit of Missouri, is a native of Ohio County, Ky., and the son of S. Edward and Margaret (Nalle) Bland. S. Edward Bland was of English descent, born in Kentucky, and was a miller and farmer by occupation.

The mother was of Scotch descent, and was also a native of Kentucky. To their union were born four children: Richard P., Congressman of the Eleventh Congressional District of Missouri, and author of the famous Bland Silver Bill; Elizabeth, wife of Fred Tetley, at Bonne Terre, Mo.; Ella, who died in childhood, and Judge Charles C. The latter was born February 9, 1837, and was left an orphan when very small. At the age of fourteen he came to Missouri, and attended the Arcadia College for three years. In 1857 he entered the teacher's profession, and followed this at Pilot Knob and Caledonia for some time. In 1859 he went to Mississippi, taught one term of school, and in the spring of 1860 he went to Dent County, Mo. Previous to this, in 1858, he commenced the study of law, and in the spring of 1860 was admitted to practice at Salem. In August, 1862, he enlisted in Company D, Thirty-second Missouri Infantry Volunteers, United States Army, and was elected captain of his company. He was in the siege of Vicksburg, Jackson, Lookout Mountain, Atlanta campaign, Jonesboro and numerous other battles and skirmishes. He was discharged at Chattanooga, November 18, 1864, and after the war he located at Rolla, where he resumed his practice. He was a member of the school board of Rolla for several terms, was mayor of that city two terms, and in 1880 was elected judge of the Eighteenth Judicial Circuit of Missouri, which comprises Phelps, Crawford, Dent, Texas and Pulaski Counties. He was elected by a majority of 1,500, and in 1886 he was re-elected, having no opposition in either nomination or election. He has been frequently called outside of his district to preside at important trials—notably to Springfield, on the famous Cora E. Lee case, charged with the murder of Mrs. Sarah Graham in the year 1888. In May, 1872, he married Miss Hattie B. Keene, who is a native of Ohio. Seven children have been born to this union: Thomas C., Richard E., Harry O., Charles P., Ione, Joseph and George R. In 1881 Judge Bland was appointed by Gov. Crittenden as a member of the Board of Curators of the Missouri State University, to fill a vacancy, and in January, 1887, was re-appointed by Gov. Marmaduke for six years, and is a member at the present time. He is the owner of about 500 acres of land in Phelps County, and a beautiful home in the outskirts of Rolla. He is a Democrat in his political views, and cast his first vote for Bell and Everett in 1860. Judge Bland is one of the leading and popular men of Phelps County, and no one is better respected. He is a member of the Masonic fraternity, being a member of the Blue Lodge and Royal Arch Chapter of Rolla. Judge Bland lost his wife in April, 1888.

Emil G. Boisselier (deceased) was for many years an extensive hardware merchant and brass manufacturer of St. Louis, Mo., the firm being known as Kupferle & Boisselier. They established their business previous to the late Civil War, and continued in the business until about 1874, at which date Mr. Boisselier died, and his widow then succeeded him in the business, continuing until 1886. Mr. Boisselier was born in Bremen, Germany, in 1835, where he received a good business and classical education. His father died when he was quite young, and he learned the trade of brass moulder and finisher, and when about fifteen or sixteen years of age came to

America, and located in St. Louis, Mo., where he worked at his trade for some years, with good success, before he established his own business. He deserves much credit for the many difficulties he encountered and overcame in his business career in that city, for he was thrice burned out, losing nearly all his stock each time, but returning to his trade he earned money with which to commence anew. He met with remarkable success in his endeavors, and so popular and influential did the firm become that it has continued under the old name up to the present time. During the late war they filled large contracts in furnishing supplies for the Government, and on the death of Mr. Boisselier the city lost one of its honored citizens, as well as one of its most enterprising and successful business men. He was married in St. Louis, in 1861, to Miss Elizabeth, a daughter of Ditmer and Mary Freudenstein, by whom he became the father of six children: Thomas H., Wilhelmina (who died in 1864, at the age of two years and three months), Emil G., Charles W., Harry H. and Katie G., all of whom received good educations in St. Louis, and are now residing with their mother on their valuable farm of 320 acres in Phelps County, on which they located in 1887. They have a beautiful and commodious two-story frame residence, and have made valuable improvements on their house and farm since locating here, and although reared in the city, bid fair to become successful and wealthy farmers. Mrs. Boisselier was born in Germany, and when four years of age was brought to the United States by her parents, and was reared and educated in Ripley County, Ind., where the father died in 1879 and the mother still lives. They were members of the Lutheran Church. Mr. Boisselier was a Republican in politics, but was not an active politician. His sons are also Republicans.

Hon. James R. Bowman. Prominent among the ex-judges of Phelps County, Mo., is found the name of Mr. Bowman, who is a retired farmer and stock dealer, and one of the county's wealthy and enterprising citizens. He is the eighth of twelve children, six of whom are living, and was born in Overton County, Tenn., in December, 1826, being reared among the mountains of that State. He only received the advantages of the common schools while residing with his parents, and after the death of his mother, about 1836, the family became scattered, and he found a home with a neighbor, with whom he lived until he became grown, being obliged to work very hard, and receiving but little schooling. October 14, 1845, he was married to Livona C. Yeagor, who was also born and reared in White County, and a daughter of James and Sarah Yeagor, who were born in Tennessee and Ohio, respectively. To Mr. Bowman and wife eleven children were born, only six of whom are living at the present time. They resided in their native State until 1851, when they came to Wright County, Mo., and eight years later located in Laclede County. During the war and until 1866 they resided in Jacksonville, Ill., and at the latter date came to Phelps County, where he has since resided. He was engaged in selling goods in St. James for five years, but since that time has been occupied in farming and stock raising, his real estate consisting of 1,500 acres in Phelps County, 1,000 acres in Wright County, and about that amount in Texas County. The place on which he resides is beautifully located, and is one of the most valuable farms in Missouri. He has a beautiful residence, and all his property has been acquired by his own industry and judicious management. He was postmaster of Hartsville, Mo., for four years, and was also assessor of a portion of Wright County for two years. In 1860 he was elected associate judge of the county court of Laclede County, which office he held until the provisional government of Missouri deposed him. He was then appointed associate judge of Phelps County by Gov. Brown, being twice re-elected, and then served four years as probate judge, and at the same time was *ex-officio* chairman of the county court. In 1878 he was elected to the State Legislature, and served one term. He was reared a Whig in politics, but is now a supporter of Democratic principles. He is a Knights Templar in the Masonic fraternity, of which order he has been a member since 1864, and is a member of the Commandery at Lebanon and the Chapter at Rolla. He served about six months in the State Guards of Missouri during the late war, and operated in Arkansas and Missouri. He and family attend the Christian Church, his wife having been a member of that denomination since her youth. His parents, James and Rachel (McKorkle) Bowman, were born in Virginia and East Tennessee, respectively, and after their marriage resided for some time in Overton County, and then removed to White County, where they spent the remainder of their lives. The father was an industrious and moderately successful farmer, and died during the war. The grandfather, John Bowman, was of English descent, a farmer by occupation, a native of Virginia, and a soldier in the Revolutionary War. He died in Roanoke County, Tenn., in 1841, aged about ninety years. Grandfather Robert McKorkle died in Warren County, Tenn.

Mrs. Elizabeth Branson, residing a short distance east of Rolla, Mo., was born in South Carolina in 1810, and is a daughter of Robert and Nancy (Neice) Campbell, who were born in South and North Carolina, about 1780 and 1779, respectively. Mrs. Branson is the third of their nine children, and while residing in Gasconade County, Mo., was married to James Harvey Hawkins, by whom she became the mother of three children: William Jefferson, Joseph Marion and Jacob Monroe. Mr. Hawkins was a farmer by occupation, and died in Gasconade County, Mo., in 1844. Two years later his widow married David Branson, who was also a farmer by occupation, born in 1810, and died in 1881 on the farm where his widow is now residing. She resides with her youngest son, Jacob Monroe, and is a member of the Christian Church.

Dr. Daniel D. Burns was born in Phelps County, Mo., February 24, 1855, and is a son of Dr. Edward S. and Elizabeth (Mings) Burns. Dr. Edward S. Burns was born near Peoria, Ill., had limited chances for an education when a boy, but afterward acquired a good academic and medical education. He remained in Illinois until twenty-one years of age, and then came to Phelps County, where he married Miss Elizabeth Mings, returning afterward to Illinois. After remaining here a short time he moved to Nebraska, and practiced medicine in that State until 1861, when he enlisted in the Union service as assistant surgeon, and was in service for three years, when he was discharged on account of disability. He returned to Missouri in 1866, settling in Phelps County, on Mill Creek, where he died in 1883. Elizabeth Mings was born in Kentucky, but was reared in Missouri, where she married Dr. Burns, and bore him eight children, seven now living: Quintus D., Daniel D., William C., Mary F., Nettie E., Eva M. and Edward F. The one deceased was named Elizabeth C. Mrs. Burns is now living on the old homestead in Phelps County. The paternal grandparents were natives of Scotland, and the maternal grandfather was of German parentage, but was born in this country, and was a soldier in the Mexican War. Dr. Daniel D. Burns attained his growth principally on the farm, and received a common-school education. At the age of eighteen he commenced reading medicine under his father, and began practicing in 1884. He has an extensive practice, and is very successful. January 8, 1880, he married Miss Permelia F. Anthony, daughter of John M. Anthony; both father and daughter were born and reared in Phelps County. To Dr. and Mrs. Burns were born three children: Melvin H., Grover C. and Elsie. Dr. Burns was an elector at large for the Union Labor party in 1888, and is politically a Union Labor man. He is a member of the A. O. U. W. (Select Knights), K. of P. and K. of L. Mrs. Burns is a member of the Baptist Church.

Nathan L. Burwell, proprietor of the hotel at Newburg, Mo., was born July 15, 1854, in Covington, Ky., and is the son of John and Sarah Mountjoy (Best) Burwell. The paternal grandparents were natives of New Jersey, and immigrated to Zanesville, Ohio, where they spent the remainder of their days. They were of Scotch parentage. John Burwell was born at Zanesville, Ohio, was a civil engineer by occupation, and was engaged on the Slack Water Navigation Works on the Muskingum River, continuing at this business until thirty-five years of age. He went to Covington, Ky., about 1845, but later moved to Ohio, where he died in 1870. He was superintendent of the Bloom Forge Iron Works for Gaylord & Co., of Portsmouth, at that time. His wife was born in Kentucky, attained her growth in that State, and was there married to Mr. Burwell, by whom she had eleven children, four now living: Mary, widow of Hobert Weatherby; John B., Stephen B. and Nathan L. Mrs. Burwell died in Ironton, Ohio, in 1859. Her parents were natives of Kentucky, where they lived and died. Nathan L. Burwell received a liberal English education in the schools of Portsmouth, and remained with his father until his death. At the age of sixteen he began life for himself by engaging in the iron business. He came to Missouri in 1881, engaging as bookkeeper at Nova Scotia Iron Works, Dent County, where he remained for a year and a half. He then occupied the same position at Ozark Iron Works, in Phelps County, remaining until the works closed in the latter part of 1883. Mr. Burwell then opened the 'Frisco Eating House at Newburg, where all trains stop for meals, and there he has since remained. He was married in 1873 to Miss Ella Lloyd, a native of Sampsonville, Ohio, and the daughter of William Lloyd. Mr. Burwell now runs a thriving business, feeding on an average seventy-five people per day. He is a strong Republican in politics, and an excellent citizen.

Joseph Campbell, another prominent and enterprising citizen of Rolla, is a native of the County Armagh, Ireland, and was born August 17, 1829. His father's people were known as the Maghery Campbells, and were of Scotch descent, having immigrated and settled in the north of Ireland at an early day. His mother's people were known as the Hatters' Campbells, having followed the trade of hatters as a profession. The subject of this sketch, Joseph Campbell, was the eldest son of a family of ten children, six sons and four daughters. He received his education in the common schools of his native place, and worked on his father's farm until the age of eighteen years, when he concluded to seek his fortune in America, where by force of energy and industry he won for himself his present enviable position. On reaching this country he worked for a time on a farm, and while on a visit to New York City he met a relative, with whom he went to Ohio, and engaged with him in the capacity of clerk and superintendent, the former having a contract on a railroad near Cleveland, Ohio. On the completion of this work he moved to Virginia, which was then the scene of unusual activity in railroad building, remaining near Fairmont, W. Va., nearly three years. He came to Missouri in 1855, and secured a contract on the Iron Mountain Railroad, which was then in its inception. This was his first venture on his own account, and proving remunerative, he continued in the business of railroad building, receiving a contract on the Southwest Branch of the Pacific Railroad (now the 'Frisco Railroad) near Stanton, which being completed, he took another contract further west on the same road, in Pulaski County. About this time, 1860, the banking firm of John J. Anderson & Co., of St. Louis, failed, and he lost the accumulations of many hard years' earnings by this failure. The Civil War then occurred, which stopped operations in the building of the road. Mr. Campbell remained idle a year, and embarked in the mercantile business at Rolla, the firm name being Campbell & Co., Mr. Pat Long being the company. This venture proved very profitable. Mr. Long died in 1865, and Mr. Campbell continued to conduct the business until 1868, when it was merged into the house of Campbell, Love & Co., himself becoming a partner in the new firm. They continued together until 1871, when Mr. S. M. Smith purchased the stock of Campbell, Love & Co. Mr. Campbell, in connection with Mr. R. A. Love and W. M. Smith, engaged in the management and operation of the Rolla Mills, Mr. Love retiring in 1879, and Mr. Smith later, but Mr. Campbell remained in the mill, and has continued to serve in the capacity of president to the present time. Mr. Campbell is also a director and acting president of the National Bank of Rolla, and his connection with that institution has materially contributed to the high standing which the bank enjoys. Mr. Campbell was married June 16, 1868, to Miss Elizabeth Garvey, a native of St. Louis, and the daughter of James and Catherine (Judge) Garvey. Eight children were born to Mr. and Mrs. Campbell, six now living: Mary, Joseph, Kate, Eugene, Bessie and John. Mr. Campbell is a man of marked business capacity, and one of the most solid, substantial citizens of Rolla. He was a member of the school board of Rolla for ten years, and for many years a member of the city council. He is a member of the Masonic order, having taken the degree of Royal Arch, and is a conservative Democrat in his political opinions. In 1883 he was appointed by Gov. Crittenden a member of the Board of Curators of the State University to fill the unexpired term of A. M. Millard, who resigned. Mr. Campbell was reappointed by Gov. Marmaduke in January, 1885, for six years longer, or a full term.

John D. Carpenter, M. D., one of the successful practitioners of Rolla, and the son of Benedict K. and Sarah Ann (Rodenbo) Carpenter, was born in Pontiac, Mich., in 1853. Benjamin K. Carpenter was born in Orange County, N. Y., in 1810; is of American descent, and a farmer by occupation. When married he lived at Pontiac, Mich., where he now resides. In early life he followed merchandising in New York, but in 1835 moved to Pontiac, Mich., settling in the wild woods, and built the first frame house and barn in that community. He has lived the greater portion of his life on the same farm. Sarah Ann (Rodenbo) Carpenter was born in Steuben County, N. Y., is of German descent, is still living, and is sixty-four years of age. They are the parents of four children: William E., farmer at Pontiac, Mich., and a member of the Legislature; John D., Carrie and Charles H., at Pontiac. Dr. John D. Carpenter received his collegiate education at Agricultural College, at Lansing, Mich., and in 1872 he entered the teacher's profession, following this five years. In 1877 he commenced the study of medicine, his preceptor being Dr. Carleton Graves, of New York, and in 1878 entered the University Medical College of New York City, graduating in 1881. The same year he located at Rolla, Mo., where he entered upon his practice. From 1884 to February, 1887, the Doctor was absent from Rolla; was in Springfield, Mo., a portion of the time. In July, 1884, Dr. Carpenter married Miss Jennie Van Campen, who was born in Romeo, Mich. They have two children, Gertrude and Grace. In 1883 and 1884 Dr. Carpenter took a post graduate course in the School of Medicine and Surgery at St. Louis, and is one of the most thoroughly posted medical men in Phelps County. He is a skillful surgeon, and a man much esteemed and respected by the public and at large. He is a Democrat in his political views, is a member of the Rolla District Medical Society, of the I. O. O. F., and also a member of the A. O. U. W.

Charles Cartall is a general merchant and dealer in lumber and building material of all kinds at St. James, Mo., in which city he has been engaged in his present business since 1880. He keeps a large and well-selected stock, and is enjoying a correspondingly large patronage. He was born in Brunswick, Germany, in 1838, and is a son of George and Johannah Cartall, who spent their entire lives in Germany, and died at about the age of eighty years, the father being a florist throughout life. Charles is next to the youngest of five children, and attended the public schools from the age of six to fourteen years of age, and then served a six years' apprenticeship in a store. Having always had a desire to travel, and believing that the new world offered better opportunities for a young man to advance, he concluded to go to the United States, and landed in New York in August, 1857, where he remained a short time, working at anything he could find to do, and afterward worked his way to Buffalo, thence to Canada, spending two years in the latter country, after which he came to St. Louis, Mo. He next accepted a situation at Alton, Ill., remaining there one year, after which he clerked in Lane's Prairie, Mo., and that vicinity for two years, and then went to Knob View, where he clerked for T. J. Kinsey until the latter's death, about the close of the war. Mr. Cartall then purchased the stock of goods, and was engaged in business in Knob View until 1880, his enterprise being attended with remarkable success. He had about $800 of his hard earnings to commence with, and is now, although having met with several heavy losses, one of the well-to-do citizens of Phelps County. Besides his business block he owns forty acres near St. James, with his handsome residence, and two other farms in the county, of 160 and eighty acres, respectively, all of which has been obtained by his good management and energy. He is a Republican, and cast his first presidential vote for Lincoln in 1864; is also a member of the Commandery and a Royal Arch Mason, and belongs to the A. O. U. W. In October, 1866, he was married to Miss Minnie, a daughter of William Wagner, formerly of Germany. Two sons and three daughters are living of seven children born to them. Mr. Cartall and wife are members of the Lutheran Church.

David E. Cowan, circuit clerk and *ex-officio* recorder of Phelps County, Mo., was elected to his present position in November, 1886, by a majority of 207 votes. Mr. Cowan is a native of Phelps County, and was born December 7, 1858; he was educated in the district schools, and attended nearly two years at School of Mines at Rolla, subsequently remaining and assisting on his father's farm until 1878, when he entered the teacher's profession, following this for two terms near Edgar Springs, his birth-place. The year 1879 he spent on the frontier of Texas, and from 1880 to 1886 he engaged in tilling the soil and dealing in stock. He is the son of Dr. Robert B. and Susannah B. (Lenox) Cowan, grandson of William B. Cowan, and great-grandson of William Cowan, who was a native of Scotland, and an attorney by profession. He was at one time an opponent in a lawsuit with Patrick Henry. William B. Cowan was a native of Virginia, as was also his son, Dr. Robert B. Cowan, whose birth occurred in Nodaway County in 1825. He was a graduate of Mary's and William's College, and was a very intelligent gentleman. In an early day he came West, locating in St. Louis, and afterward settled in Washington County, in Bellview Valley. Here he died in 1864, at the home of his daughter, Mrs. Mary A. Bates, in Pulaski County. Dr. Cowan received his education in the common schools, and his medical education at McDowell's Institute, in St. Louis, graduating as an M. D. at about the age of twenty-three. He settled in Phelps County, Mo., when a young man, and about 1854 he married Miss Susannah B. Lenox. She was born in Phelps County, Mo., in 1833, and is the daughter of Elder David and Elizabeth (Brown) Lenox, who were natives of Kentucky, coming to Missouri at an early date. Elder David Lenox was an Old School Baptist minister of this section of Missouri, and was a man of marked influence in church and society.

He died during the war, in Arkansas. Dr. Robert B. Cowan died January 10, 1879. He was actively engaged in the practice of his profession from the time of graduating until up to within a short time of his death, being one of the leading physicians and surgeons of Phelps County for many years. He was quite successful, being the owner of 800 acres of land, 600 acres being in one tract. His wife is yet living, and is the mother of eight children, seven of whom are living: Elizabeth C., wife of W. W. Lenox, M. D., of Lake Springs, Dent Co., Mo.; David E.; Robert B., M. D., of Phelps County, Mo., and a graduate of the Missouri Medical College, at St. Louis; William H., farmer; John W., Travis J. and Francis M. David E. is a Democrat in politics, is a member of the Masonic order, and also a member of the I. O. O. F.

Dr. Robert B. Cowan, son of Robert B. and Susan B. (Lenox) Cowan, was born in Phelps County, Mo. Robert B. Cowan, Sr., was born in Virginia, near Pilot Knob, received a good education, and practiced medicine for many years after coming to Missouri. He settled in Phelps County, and here died in 1869. Susan B. Lenox was born in Phelps County, Mo. (then Pulaski County), and was there married to Mr. Cowan, bearing him eight children: Elizabeth C., wife of Dr. W. W. Lenox; David E., Robert B., William H., John W., Travis J., Francis M. and Margaret. Mrs. Cowan is now living near Edgar Springs, and is fifty-two years of age. Grandfather Cowan was a native of Virginia, as was also his wife; there they lived and died. Grandfather Lenox and wife were born in Kentucky, immigrated to Missouri about 1821, and settled in Crawford County, where Mr. Lenox built the first mill in that county. Dr. Robert B. Cowan was reared at Edgar Springs, this county, and received his education at the Springs. He remained on his father's farm until twenty years of age, when he began the study of medicine under Dr. S. F. Arthur, where he remained for a short time. After that he studied under Dr. Lenox, of Lake Springs, for six months. He then graduated from the Missouri Medical College in March, 1881, after which he located in Spring Creek for a short time. He then came to Relfe, but after remaining for four years engaged in the practice of his profession, he moved to Edgar Springs, where he remained only a short time, and then moved back to Relfe. Dr. Cowan was married September 9, 1885, to Mrs. Sallie J. Bradford, daughter of L. L. and Amanda Coppedge. They have no children. Dr. Cowan is a member of the Rolla District Medical Association, is a member of the Masonic fraternity, the I. O. O. F., and is a Democrat in politics. He gives his entire attention to the practice of his profession.

Prof. George W. Davis, principal of the St. James High-school, is among the popular and successful educators of Phelps County, Mo., and has bent all his energies to perfect himself in his chosen calling; and it may be truthfully said that his labors have met with flattering success. He was born in Lake County, Ill., in 1853, and is a son of Alson W. and Hannah Davis, both of whom were born in Steuben County, N. Y., in 1828. Alson W. Davis removed to Lake County, Ill., when Chicago was a mere trading post, and was reared and married in that county. In 1859 he returned to Steuben County,

N. Y., and while there enlisted in the First New York Artillery for three years, or during the war, and after about two years' service with the Army of the Potomac was discharged on account of ill-health, but after about six months' rest improved so in health that he again joined the army, enlisting in Company G, Twenty-second New York Cavalry. He was taken prisoner at Weldon Railroad, near Richmond, Va., in 1864, and was kept in captivity in Andersonville, Libby, Florence and Charleston prisons, and died a paroled prisoner at Annapolis, Md., April 4, 1865, and is buried in the National Cemetery. He was a cabinet-maker by trade, and was a son of Lemuel C. Davis, who was of Welsh descent, and a farmer of Connecticut, and died in Lake County, Ill. Judge Noah C. Davis, of the New York Supreme Court, who was appointed by President Grant, is his nephew. Our subject's mother was a daughter of Samuel Davis, a brother of Lemuel C. The former was also a native of Connecticut, and was a soldier in the Revolutionary War. He died in Steuben County, N. Y. In 1867 Prof. George W. Davis and his mother came to Phelps County, Mo., and here the mother is still living, the wife of Charles Baker, whom she married in 1867. Prof. Davis is an only child, and was reared on a farm, receiving a common-school education, until fourteen years of age. After coming to Missouri he was sick for a long period, which left him a cripple for life. From 1885 to 1888 he attended the Cape Girardeau Normal School, graduating from the "C" and "B" courses, and began his career as a pedagogue in 1874, and with the exception of one year, when he was in school, has taught up to the present time. He is entering on his second year's work at St. James, and bids fair to become among the foremost educators of the day. He is a member of the I. O. O. F., Big Spring Lodge No. 237, and in his political views supports the principles of the Republican party, his first presidential vote being cast for Hayes. His step-father, Mr. Baker, was born in Hampshire, England, in 1825, and as his parents were quite poor he was compelled to begin the battle of life for himself at a very early age, receiving but very little schooling. When about ten years of age he hired out as a shepherd boy, which occupation he continued for some five years, receiving about 4 shillings a week for his services, and the following four years worked at gardening. He was then employed in a dock-yard for about two years, at which time he had accumulated enough money to enable him to come to the United States (1850), and spent some years in various parts of the Western States and Territories trading with the Indians. He was engaged in carpentering in Illinois about ten years, and then came to Missouri in 1867, where he has since lived, actively engaged in agricultural pursuits.

Henry Dean, a successful agriculturist of Rolla Township, was born in Nashville, Tenn., February 11, 1832, and is the son of Moses and Mary (Binkley) Dean. Moses Dean was born in Wilkes County, N. C., in 1800, and was of French descent. He went to Davidson County, Tenn., before marriage, and there resided until 1844, when he moved to Crawford County, Mo., locating five miles southeast of Rolla, where he owned 220 acres of land. He died in 1858. Mary (Binkley) Dean was born in Pennsylvania in 1803, and was of German descent. She died in 1865. She was the mother of twelve children, Henry Dean being the tenth. He was twelve years of age when his parents moved to Phelps County, Mo.; was reared and grew to manhood on the farm, and remained with his parents until he had reached his majority. April 1, 1852, he married Miss Elizabeth Matlock, daughter of John Matlock, and a native of East Tennessee, born in 1832. They have three living children: Charles M., sheriff of Phelps County, Mo.; Mary M., wife of Harrison Williams, and Stephen D., a farmer. After marriage Mr. Dean settled near the old home place, and here Mrs. Dean died April 7, 1862. October 7, following, Mr. Dean married Miss Nancy Smith, a native of North Carolina, born in 1840. To this union was born one child, Bettie. Mr. Dean is one of the old settlers of Phelps County, having been a resident of the same since his twelfth year. For the past twelve years he has been a citizen of Rolla or lived in its vicinity. He is the owner of 1,000 acres of land in Phelps County, is a life-long Democrat, is a member of the I. O. O. F., the Masonic order, and he and wife are members of the Christian Church. During the war Mr. Dean was in service one year in Parson's Brigade, being assistant commissary of the same. In 1874 he was elected collector of Phelps County by a majority of sixty-eight, and in 1876 he was re-elected by a majority of 380.

Charles M. Dean, sheriff of Phelps County, Mo., is a native of this county, born in 1853, and the son of Henry and Elizabeth (Matlock) Dean. [For further particulars of parents see sketch of Henry Dean.] Charles M. Dean is the eldest of four living children, and attained his growth on the farm, where he remained, assisting his father, until twenty years of age. In 1871 he married Miss Catherine Billings, who was born in Chillicothe, Ohio, in 1853. To this union was born an interesting family of seven children: Albert, Bettie, Ella, Lewis, Josie D., Wesley and Grace. Mr. Dean followed agricultural pursuits until 1886, when he was elected sheriff of Phelps County by a majority of 156. In the year 1888 he was re-elected by a majority of 657, on the Democratic ticket. Mr. Dean is a member of the I. O. O. F., also the K. of P., and he and wife are worthy and consistent members of the Christian Church.

Stephen D. Dean is a successful and enterprising farmer of Phelps County, Mo., and was born in that county in 1859, being a son of Henry and Elizabeth (Matlock) Dean, who were born in Tennessee in 1832 and 1831, respectively. The father was a farmer, and when ten years of age came to Missouri, where he afterward married. Here the mother died in 1862, having borne a family of five children, Stephen D. being the youngest. Mr. Dean married his second wife, Nancy Smith, of North Carolina, in 1862, and by her is the father of two children. Stephen D. Dean remained at home until twenty-one years of age, and was then united in marriage to Miss Jane Montgomery, a daughter of Thomas and Mary Montgomery. She was born in Maries County, Mo., in 1861, and is the mother of five children: Daisy M., Edna Jane, Mary Etta, and Harry and Clifford, who are deceased. Mr. Dean owns a good farm of 183 acres, 100 of which are under cultivation, on which he has resided since his marriage in 1880. He is a successful farmer, and in his political views supports the principles of the Democratic party. His wife is a member of the Christian Church.

Daniel Donahoe, dealer in general merchandise at Rolla, was born in Queens County, Ireland, on the 1st day of November, 1842. He immigrated to the United States with his parents in 1853, and located in Franklin County, Mo. His father, William Donahoe, was a contractor on the Missouri Pacific Railroad at the time that road was under construction between St. Louis and Kirkwood. He afterward followed agricultural pursuits in Franklin County, where he died on the 18th of January, 1878, at the age of sixty-five years. His mother, Sarah (Walsh) Donahoe, was also a native of Queens County, Ireland. She died at her home in Franklin County on the 9th of December, 1885, at the age of seventy-two years. Daniel Donahoe was the eldest of six children, four of whom are dead, and the other, William, is now an engineer on the St. Louis & San Francisco Railroad. Judge Donahoe, as he is now popularly known, commenced railroading on the Missouri Pacific Railroad at the breaking out of the war, in 1861. He continued on this road only one year, when he was transferred to what was then known as the Southwest Branch of the Missouri Pacific Railroad, but is now known as the St. Louis & San Francisco Railroad. He continued to run on this road for eight years, and was conductor on the first time table freight train that was run over the road. In 1869 Mr. Donahoe gave up railroading and located in Lebanon, Mo., where he engaged in merchandising. On the 5th of July, 1870, he married Miss Mary Ann Murray, daughter of Patrick and Mary Murray. This lady was born in St. Louis on the 11th of November, 1851, and was nineteen years of age at the time of her marriage. She is agreeable and courteous in personal character and conversation, generous and frank in disposition, and in fine has always been a blessing and a comfort to her husband, her children, and all around her. Six children were the result of this union: Katie Marie, Mary Anna, William Patrick, Daniel Francis, Sarah Blanche and Cornelius Murray. The same year of his marriage Mr. Donahoe became a resident of Rolla, where the following year he resumed merchandising, at which business he has since continued. In politics he is a Democrat; was a member of the city council of Rolla for six years, having been elected to this position three times in succession. In December, 1882, he was appointed by Gov. Crittenden judge of the county court, to fill a vacancy caused by the death of R. H. Flannigan. He performed his duty so well that in 1884 he was elected by a rousing majority, and in 1886 was re-elected to the same position. It is conceded by all that Judge Donahoe is a skillful financier and a strictly honest man. It was during his term of office that the $25,000 debt of Phelps County was liquidated without increasing the rate of taxation, a result that could only be accomplished by economy and good management in the members of the court. As a public servant Judge Donahoe justly deserves the confidence which has been placed in him by the people of Phelps County. Himself and family are members of the Catholic Church.

William T. Evans, a worthy and enterprising citizen of Edgar Springs, was born in Jackson County, Ala., July 13, 1839, and is the son of John P. and Sarah A. (Gay) Evans. Grandfather Evans was a native of Tennessee, was a soldier in the Revolutionary War, and spent the latter part of his days in Alabama. Grandfather Gay was an early settler of Alabama. John R. Evans was born on a farm in Alabama, received a good education, and during the late war was in the State Militia at Rolla, serving for about three months, but never in active battle. He immigrated to Phelps County, Mo., in 1860, rented land on Spring Creek, which he afterward bought, and there he has since resided. When Mr. Evans first located in the county neighbors were few and the country was wild and unsettled. He is still living on the farm purchased in 1864, and is now in his sixty-fifth year. Mrs. Sarah (Gay) Evans was born, reared and married in the same county in Alabama, and received a good common-school education. To her union with Mr. Evans were born thirteen children, nine now living: William T., John W., Catherine, George A., Caledonia, Missouri A., Melvina, Jennie and Martha L. Mrs. Evans is also now living. William T. Evans went to Texas when five years of age, and remained in that State for six years, after which he immigrated to Phelps County, Mo., with his parents, in 1860. He received a common education, and assisted his father on the farm until nineteen years of age, when he began life for himself by hiring out on a farm. He then worked on the 'Frisco Railroad for one year, after which he returned home, rented land and farmed for one season. September 10, 1871, he married Miss Mary A. Lanning, daughter of William and Nancy (Ledgerwood) Lanning. Mr. Lanning was born and reared in Tennessee, was a farmer, and immigrated to Missouri when about grown. Mrs. Lanning was born in Indiana, and came to Missouri when young, marrying Mr. Lanning in Phelps County. Mrs. Evans was born August 14, 1850, and remained at home until grown, when she married Mr. Evans. This union resulted in the birth of seven children, six now living: Nancy A., Mary E., Sarah E., John A., Lucy E., Martha J., and William E., who is now deceased. After marriage Mr. Evans lived on Spring Creek for about six years, then sold out and moved to Shannon County, Mo., where he remained six years. In 1884 he returned to Phelps County, Mo., settled where he now lives, and is the owner of 214 acres of land, with about ninety under cultivation. Mr. Evans is a Democrat politically, is a member of the Masonic fraternity, and he and wife are members of the United Baptist Church.

Frederick C. Flint, broker and speculator of Rolla, and one of the prominent citizens of Phelps County, Mo., is a native of Steuben County, N. Y., and the son of Edward and Jane (Clute) Flint. The father was born in New York State, was of English descent, and was a farmer and blacksmith by occupation. In 1833 he moved to Crawford County, Ohio, and the following year to Lucas County, in 1835 to Jackson County, Mich., and in 1837 to Lake County, Ind. He died in 1860. His wife, Jane (Clute) Flint, was born in New York State, and died in 1865, at the age of seventy-two. They were the parents of ten children, Frederick C. being the fourth. He made his home with his parents and assisted on the farm until twenty-four years of age, when in 1841 he married Miss Caroline Morris, a native of New York, born in 1822. They have three children: Asa, Wilbur and Leonard. Wilbur is a grocery merchant in Rolla, and was born in Lake County, Ind., in 1852. At the age of thirteen he commenced working on the Pittsburg & Fort Wayne Railroad, where he remained seven years in the capacity of brakeman and conductor. He then worked three years in a saw-mill at Grand Rapids, Mich., four years for P. D. Armour in Chicago, one year on the dock in Chicago, and the past four years he has spent engaged in merchandising in Rolla. In 1887 he married Miss Mary Gift, a native of Pennsylvania, born in 1859, and to them has been born one child, Carrie. Frederick C. Flint followed farming in Lake County, Ind., until 1865, when he sold out and moved to Valparaiso, where he engaged in merchandising. In 1874 he sold out and became a resident of Rolla, Mo., speculating in notes, etc. In 1867 he lost his wife, and he afterward married Miss Lizzie McDonald, a native of New York, born in 1857. Mr. Flint is a good business man and a well-to-do citizen. He is a stanch Republican, and he and wife are members of the Methodist Episcopal Church.

William Fort, collector of Phelps County, Mo., and now a resident of Rolla, is a native of Chillicothe, Ross Co., Ohio, and was born in 1846, being the son of William Fort and Sarah Weast, and grandson of Thomas Fort, who with two brothers emigrated from England to America. They were shipwrecked, and Thomas was the only one who reached America. He located near Dover, N. J., and was the father of three sons: William, Charles and Thomas. William Fort, Sr., was born in Dover, N. J., in 1814, and was a mechanic by trade in early and middle life, but his last days were spent engaged in agricultural pursuits. He went to Staunton, Va., was married there, and in 1835 moved to Ross County, Ohio. In 1853 he moved to Crawford County, Mo., where he passed the remainder of his days. He died May 12, 1881. The mother was of Pennsylvania Dutch descent, born in Harrisburg, Penn., in 1816; is yet living, and resides in Rolla, Mo., with her daughter, Nancy, wife of A. S. Long. She is the mother of four sons and seven daughters, ten of whom are now living: Henry, in Cuba, engaged in the manufacture of wagons, plows, etc.; Mary, wife of F. S. Atteberry, in Crawford County, on the old homestead of William Fort, Sr.; Nancy, wife of A. S. Long, a merchant in Rolla; Sarah, wife of Rev. I. J. K. Lumbeck, pastor of the Methodist Episcopal Church at Rolla; William; Libbie, wife of John Bannon, hardware merchant in St. Louis; James, mechanic in Los Angeles, Cal.; Charles, mechanic in 'Frisco Shops at Springfield, Mo.; Rhoda, wife of C. F. Patton, farmer in Franklin County, Mo., and Henrietta, wife of L. D. Viemann, merchant at Oak Hill, Crawford Co., Mo. William Fort was but seven years of age when his parents moved to Missouri. He was reared on a farm, and in connection followed blacksmithing until nineteen years of age, when he commenced clerking in a store in Rolla, and remained in this capacity for eighteen years. In 1884 he was elected collector of Phelps County, Mo., in a Democratic county of about 400 votes, and in 1886 he was re-elected to the same position. He was the only Republican in the county elected, thus forcibly illustrating his popularity. In 1872 he was united in marriage to Miss Mary Niven, who was born in Logan County, Ohio, at Bellefontaine, in 1853. Three children are the fruits of this union: Nellie, Edward L. and Lillie. Mrs. Fort died July 3, 1883, and December 31, 1885, he married Miss Dell McDougal, who was born in New York State. One child, Albert, is the result of this union. Mr. Fort is a member of the I. O. O. F., and also a member of the K. of H.

James M. Freeman, merchant at Relfe, was born October 20, 1837, in Hamilton County, Tenn., and is the son of Britton and Elizabeth (McMullen) Freeman. Britton Freeman was born in Roane County, Tenn., in April, 1816, grew to manhood on a farm, and received his education in the common schools. He assisted largely in removing the Indians from Georgia and Tennessee to the Indian Territory. His two brothers, James and Thomas, served in the Mexican War, the former a captain and the latter a colonel. Mr. Freeman immigrated to Missouri in 1848, settling in Wright County, where he engaged in farming. Here he died in 1863. During his life in Tennessee he was both colonel and major of the State Militia. He lost his wife in 1842, and three years later married Miss Harriet A. Dyke, of Tennessee. By his first marriage, to Miss Elizabeth McMullen, a native of Roane County, Tenn., he became the father of three children, all living: James M., George W., and Clemantine, wife of George W. Hickey, of Arkansas. The second marriage resulted in the birth of six children, three now living: William, John, and Ellen, wife of F. E. McDonald. Those deceased are Edward (who was killed by the Indians in 1863), Dodson and Marion. James M. Freeman lived in Tennessee until eleven years of age, then immigrated to Missouri, and settled in Wright County, where he remained until twenty-six years of age, receiving a common-school education. He worked for his father until twenty years of age, then traded in stock for eight or ten years, and in 1863 came to Missouri, settling in this county, near St. James, where he dealt in stock until 1866. He then moved to the place where he is now living, farmed for a year, and then engaged in the mercantile business, which he has since followed in connection with his farming interests. He was married in January, 1865, to Miss Martha E. Coppedge, a native of Phelps County, Mo., and the daughter of Lindsey L. and Amanda (Dodd) Coppedge. Mr. Coppedge was a native of Kentucky, and settled where Newburg, Mo., now stands, in 1823, while the Indians were still in the county. To Mr. and Mrs. Freeman were born three children, two now living: Mary E. (wife of John H. Rillmon) and Loring L. The one deceased was named Edward L. During the war Mr. Freeman served six months in the State Militia, in Company G, Seventh Missouri Regiment; was in the battle of Pea Ridge, and was discharged at Van Buren, Ark. He has been postmaster at Relfe, and has been notary public for three years. He is the owner of 680 acres of land in this county, 200 acres under cultivation. He is a member of the Masonic order, and is a stanch Democrat in his political views.

Hon. Cyrus H. Frost, president of the National Bank of Rolla, was born February 11, 1816. His parents, Simeon and Mary (Woods) Frost, were natives of Jessamine County, Ky., born in 1789 and 1790, respectively. They were married in their native county and State, and in 1821 immigrated to Washington County, Mo. The father was a farmer by occupation, and also carried on the blacksmith trade. About 1835 he removed to Steelville Valley, Crawford County, Mo., the county seat being located on a portion of his farm. The mother died in 1839, and the father ten years later. Of their eight children all lived to be grown and married. They are named as follows: Hamilton J., James M., Cyrus H., Edmund F., Christopher E., George H., Martha J. and Mary A. Cyrus H. was reared in Jessamine County, Ky., until five years of age, and then his parents moved to Missouri, where he completed his growth on a farm, giving the proceeds of his labor to his parents until twenty-one years of age. In 1837 he was appointed as assessor of Crawford County, and in 1838 he was appointed sheriff, being elected to that position, and was re-elected to the same position in 1840. He then engaged in merchandising for a short time at Steelville, when he sold out, went to Texas County, Mo., and was there elected sheriff, serving three years. About 1843 he commenced the study of law, and was admitted to the bar in Steelville. In August, 1845, he married Miss Hannah Leek, who was born in East Tennessee in 1820, and who bore him six children, only one now living, Sarah J., wife of Hon. A. A. Flett, of Salem, Mo. In 1848 Mr. Frost was elected to the State Legislature from Texas County, and served until 1855, when he resigned to accept the office of clerk of Texas County. He served in this capacity until 1862, when, owing to the unsettled condition of affairs by the late war, he became a citizen of Rolla. In the fall of 1862 he was elected State senator for Rolla District, and served four years. After his term of office had expired he established a claim and real estate office in Rolla, also practiced law, and in 1870 he was elected to the Legislature from Phelps County as a Liberal Republican, and served one term. He then returned to his former work, in which he remained engaged until 1884, when he was so unfortunate as to lose his eyesight by cataract. In 1870 Mr. Frost was one of the leading spirits of the organization of the Bank of Rolla, was a charter stockholder, was elected a director and also its president. The following year the bank was reorganized into the National Bank of Rolla, and Mr. Frost was again elected president, a position he has held from the time mentioned until the present, being elected each succeeding year. Mr. Frost also assisted in the erection of Rolla Flour Mills and Grant Hotel. He is one of the old and highly esteemed citizens of Phelps County, and is a man who has always been one of the prominent factors in all public enterprises, and his acts of charity and benevolence are numerous and commendable. He is now in the evening of life, but it is an honor and credit to Rolla and Phelps County that such a man has lived within its borders. For many years he held public offices of trust and honor, and never can it be said that he betrayed a trust or deceived a friend. He is a Republican in politics, is a member of the Masonic fraternity, Royal Arch, and he and Mrs. Frost are members of the Presbyterian Church.

John S. Frost, M. D., residing five miles north of Rolla, was born in Acton, Me., in 1834, and is a son of George W. and Sarah E. (Farnham) Frost, who were also born in Maine. The father received a good education in an academy in Portsmouth, N. H., and afterward engaged in the practice of law and merchandising. His wife was born in 1807, and died in Granby, Canada, in 1888, having borne a family of five children, of whom John S. was the fourth. At the age of eighteen years he, having made that science a study, began lecturing on phrenology, and at the age of twenty years took a partial course in medicine in New York City. He received an academic education in Granby, Lower Canada, and is well versed in Greek and Latin. He taught school one year near Baltimore, Md. He moved to Missouri in 1857, locating at Vienna, Maries County, in 1858, and in 1863 moved to his present home, near Rolla, Phelps Co., Mo. He was married to Miss Esther Spencer in 1865, who was born in Cincinnati, Ohio, in 1831, and by her is the father of two living children: Esther Jane and Henry Cleino. Since 1863 he has resided on his present farm of 300 acres in Phelps County, Mo., and during all this time has been an active medical practitioner. He was ordained a minister of the Baptist Church in 1865, and has expounded the doctrine of that church at various times up to the present date. He is a Democrat in politics, and in 1860 was elected coroner of Maries County, Mo., but refused to act. He is a member of the I. O. O. F., and his wife is a member of the Rebecca Lodge, and also belongs to the Baptist Church. He has been appointed notary public by three different governors of Missouri, and is particularly noted for aiding all eleemosynary and educational enterprises in his locality. John S. Frost is a descendant of among the oldest families of the United States. His foreparents immigrated to what is now the State of Maine in March, 1656, from Tiverton, England.

Pleasant M. Gaddy, a worthy and successful farmer of Phelps County, Mo., was born in East Tennessee August 13, 1831, and is a son of Harmon A. and Rebecca (Ray) Gaddy, who were born in North Carolina and Tennessee in 1812 and 1815, respectively. The father moved to Tennessee when a boy, thence to Missouri in 1838, and in 1849 located in what is now Phelps County, where he was engaged in farming until his death in 1871. The following are his children who are living out of a family of thirteen: F. M., Eliza (Mrs. Stawhun), Jeremiah, Harmon A., Emily (Mrs. Collier), Louisa (Mrs. Aldrich), Harriet J. (Mrs. Mitchell), Rutha M. (Mrs. Dotson) and Martin F. The paternal grandparents, Jeremiah and Celia (Adams) Gaddy, it is supposed, came either from North or South Carolina, the grandmother being a descendant of the Adams family of historic note. The maternal grandparents, Abner and Ruth (Sparkman) Ray, were Tennesseeans, and farmers by occupation, and the grandfather was a private in the War of 1812, and was a participant in the battle of Horse Shoe Bend. At the age of seven years Pleasant M. Gaddy was brought from Tennessee to Missouri, where, at the age of twenty years, he began life for himself as a farm hand, and is now the owner of a fine property, his real estate consisting of 400 acres, with 175 under cultivation, and he is also the owner of some property in Rolla. He served as sheriff of Phelps County, Mo., in 1876 and 1880, and was appointed county collector in 1884. In 1850 he married Miss Lucinda Bell, who was born in Franklin County, Mo., in 1831, and by her is the father of seven children: Louisa (Mrs. Samler), Sarah (Mrs. Sloan), George W., Samuel, Hila (Mrs. Miller), Harmon and John. Mr. Gaddy has been a Mason for many years, and also belongs to the A. O. U. W., and in his political views is a Democrat. Mrs. Gaddy is a daughter of Daniel and Elizabeth (Ridenough) Bell, who were early settlers of Missouri, and the parents of thirteen children. The father was twice married, and had four children by his first wife.

William R. Hale, farmer of Phelps County, Mo., was born in St. Louis County, Mo., on the 13th of August, 1849, being a son of M. C. and Sarah J. (Robertson) Hale, both of whom were born in Tennessee in 1820, and are now living in Phelps County, where they located in 1830. The father has held the office of justice of the peace for many years, and has also served as assessor of Phelps County. Six of his nine children are now living: Samuel G., William R., Alexander B., John A., Caroline (wife of John A. Perry) and Lucy (wife of John Roster). The grandparents, Zachariah and Elizabeth (Hale) Hale, were born in Maryland and Tennessee in 1786 and 1791, and died in 1841 and 1854, respectively. Zachariah moved first to Tennessee, thence to Missouri in 1830, where he spent the remainder of his life. He was a soldier in the War of 1812. The great-grandfather Robertson served in the Revolutionary War under Gen. Greene, and was with him on his retreat through North Carolina and South Carolina, and took part in the battles of Cowpens and Yorktown, being present when Cornwallis surrendered. William R. Hale was five years old when brought to Phelps County, Mo., and here he was reared to manhood, marrying, in 1873, Miss Susan A. Yowell, who is one of five surviving members of a family of ten children born to the marriage of Lindsey L. Yowell and Sarah A. Wilson. Mrs. Hale's brothers and sisters are as follows: Napoleon B., Amanda J. (Mrs. Paulsell), Lindsey L. and Charles E. Mr. Hale owns 200 acres of good farming land, with 110 acres under cultivation. He is a Mason, a Democrat, and he and wife are the parents of seven children: Minnie L., Ida M., Nicholas L., John A., William R., M. C. and Lindsey L.

Thomas M. Hanrahan, son of Thomas and Ellen (Quinlan) Hanrahan, was born in Phelps County, Mo., March 28, 1857. The father, Thomas Hanrahan, was born in Ireland, and immigrated to the United States when about thirty years of age, having married his first wife in his native country, where she died. He landed in New York, worked on the principal railroad in Pennsylvania, and remained there a number of years, after which he traveled quite extensively throughout the United States, being engaged in railroad contract work. He came to Missouri about 1860, settling at Rolla, and was there during the war, working for some time for the Government, but never taking an active part in the war. Before the extension of the railroad to Springfield he freighted between Rolla and that place, and when the railroad was begun he returned to agricultural pursuits. He continued to work on the 'Frisco Railroad until about fourteen years ago, then worked at the Meramec Iron Works for some time, and is now engaged in farming. He is eighty years of age. His wife, Ellen (Quinlan) Hanrahan, was born in County Clare, Ireland, and there remained until about thirty years of age. Unlike her husband, she received a common-school education, and after reaching the United States was married to Mr. Hanrahan in New York. Four children were born to their union, three now living: Jeremiah, Thomas and Bridget. The one deceased was named James. Mrs Hanrahan is still living, and is nearly eighty years of age, but is strong and vigorous. Their son, Thomas M. Hanrahan, was reared principally in this section of Missouri, and when small attended the Catholic schools of Rolla, after which he went to Webster County and attended school there a short time. His next schooling was in Dent County, and after twenty-two years of age he began earning his own means, although remaining at home until he was twenty-five years of age, engaged in teaching, and paying for his own schooling. February 7, 1883, he married Miss Rebecca J. Dunham, who was born and reared in Texas County, Mo., and who is the daughter of Richard H. and A. (Morris) Dunham, natives of Tennessee. By her marriage to Mr. Hanrahan she became the mother of two children, both living: Jeremiah and Mary. After marriage Mr. Hanrahan moved to Rolla, where he attended the School of Mines, remaining there for about seven months. He then moved to Relfe, taught five months, then farmed for a year, also taking charge of the public school at Edgar Springs for two years. He was then elected school commissioner, moved to Rolla, where he again entered the School of Mines, and while there accepted a position and taught eight months in the Rolla schools as first assistant. Since that time he has had charge of the Edgar Springs School. He was elected school commissioner by a majority of 100 votes over three candidates. Mr. Hanrahan was reared a Catholic, and in his political views is a Democrat.

Hon. James B. Harrison, a successful legal practitioner of Rolla, is a native of Laclede County, Mo., and was born in 1854, being the son of Benjamin B. and Penelope (Dodson) Harrison. Benjamin B. Harrison was born in Phelps County, Mo., in 1818, and is the son of James Harrison, who was a native of South Carolina, and who immigrated to Missouri in the fall of 1817, settling in what is now Phelps County, where the village of Arlington is now located. He here engaged in merchandising, also in farming, and was postmaster of the burg. James Harrison was one of the first white settlers in Phelps County, and he had a brother by the name of Thomas who located in Callaway County the same year. James Harrison died about 1845. Benjamin B. Harrison was one of the first white children born in what is now Phelps County. He was married in Lebanon, Mo.; was the first merchant in the town, and donated the land for the county seat. He followed merchandising up to the time of the late war, and after that he devoted his time to farming. He died in 1886. His wife, and the mother of the subject of this sketch, was born in the State of Missouri, and died about 1854. She was the mother of three children, two now living: Lycurgus L. and James B. The last named was educated in the schools in Lebanon and at Missouri School of Mines in Rolla. At the age of twenty years he began teaching school, and continued this for three terms. During his teaching he studied law, and in 1876 entered the law department of the State University at Columbia, where he graduated in 1877. He entered upon his practice at Lebanon, but soon went to Waynesville, Mo., and in 1880 from there to Rolla, where he has since resided, engaged in the practice of his profession. He is a Democrat in politics, and in 1882 was elected as probate judge of Phelps County, serving four years. During the year 1886 he was elected prosecuting attorney, and served two years. He married a daughter of Judge V. B. Hill, of Pulaski County, Mo., by the name of Miss Ada Hill, who is a native of Pulaski County, Mo., born in 1856. They are the parents of four children: Benjamin H., Georgia, Lucile and James.

Edward M. Harrison, druggist at Rolla, was born in Phelps County, Mo., March 5, 1867, and is the son of Thomas C. and Maria M. (Moore) Harrison, and grandson of John P. Harrison, who was born in Virginia, as was also his wife. He immigrated to Missouri, but before the admission of the State into the Union, settled near Arlington, and his house was the only one in that country. The maternal grandparents of our subject were also early settlers in this section of Missouri. Thomas C. Harrison was born in Phelps County, Mo., February 21, 1822, near Arlington, where by his own efforts he received a fair education. He remained at home and assisted on the farm until nineteen years of age, when he married and began life for himself. He engaged in merchandising at Arlington, which he continued until his death from sun-stroke July 28, 1880. During his life in this county he represented the people at Jefferson City; was also a prominent member of the Masonic order. Maria M. Moore was born at Hartville, Wright County, Mo., in 1840; was educated in that county, and married J. W. P. Poole. After his death she married Mr. Harrison, and became the mother of five children, three now living: Lizzie L., Daisy and Edward. The two deceased were named Mamie and Mattie. She was the mother of a child by her first marriage, who was named Joseph W. Poole, and who is now living in Rolla. Mrs. Harrison died August 13, 1874. Edward M. Harrison attained his growth near Arlington, and attended the district schools. He came to Rolla when sixteen years of age, and April 4, 1881, entered the public schools, attending two years, and received a first-class certificate of $96\frac{1}{5}$ per cent. He then entered the School of Mines, attended two terms and took a select course. He then clerked for two years in a drug store at Newburg, after which he attended the Missouri Medical College at St. Louis for one year. He then returned to Newburg, where he clerked in a drug store for six months. He then came to Rolla, worked in the county collector's office as deputy during the winter of 1887–88, and on March 14, 1888, was united in marriage to Miss Linda Minium, daughter of John and Harriet Minium, natives of Pennsylvania, who came to Missouri and settled near Rolla in 1869. Mrs. Harrison was born August 16, 1867, in Meadville, Penn. April 23, 1888, Mr. Harrison opened the drug store he now has, and is doing a profitable business, his prescriptions running 5,000 a year. He carries a full line of drugs, chemicals, clocks, paints, oils, etc. Mr. Harrison is a member of the A. O. U. W. and Select Knights, and his wife is a member of the Methodist

Episcopal Church. They are both musicians, and Mrs. Harrison is a graduate of Western Conservatory of Music.

Perry D. Hawkins, junior member of the firm of Marshall & Co., at Newburg, Mo., was born in Phelps County, Mo., January 11, 1854, being the son of Robert P. and Rhoda (Bryant) Hawkins. Robert P. Hawkins, who was born in Georgia, was the third son of Solomon Hawkins and Sophronia Isabel (Duncan) Hawkins. Solomon Hawkins was born October 23, 1798, in Greenville District, South Carolina; was reared upon a farm, securing a limited education, and married, December 18, 1821, Sophronia Isabel Duncan. In 1826 he removed from South Carolina to the State of Georgia, remaining there four years, and then came to Missouri in the winter of 1831, and opened a farm on the Gasconade River, near the mouth of Little Piney. In the year 1836 he moved to and opened a farm on Cave Spring Creek, where he lived the remainder of his days. He was noted for sobriety and industry, and filled several offices in the county in which he lived with honor to himself and credit to the county. He lived in four counties without moving from the old homestead—Crawford, Maries, Pulaski and Phelps. He died January 30, 1867. His wife, Sophronia J. Hawkins, is still living with her daughter, Eliza L. Woody, of Miller County, Mo., and is quite smart for her age, which is eighty-five years. They reared a family of five girls and seven boys: William J., James P., Robert P., Alfred, Perry Eaton (the only son now surviving), Melissa Susanna, Mary M., Eliza Louisa (the two last named the only surviving daughters), John B., Amanda M., Permelia Elizabeth and an infant son. Robert P., the third son, was born in Georgia, coming to Missouri with his father when a small boy, in the year 1831. He settled near Arlington, and was there engaged in farming, and during the late war was in the State Militia. He was also justice of the peace in his township. He was married March 27, 1850, to Rhoda Bryant. By this marriage there were four children born, three of whom are living: Perry David, John P. and Rhoda J. (who married Daniel Fulbright). Rhoda Bryant, his wife, died January 28, 1858. Robert P. Hawkins' second marriage was July 15, 1860, to Margaret E. Young. By this marriage he had four sons, only one of them now living, Ivy Wilbert. Mrs. Margaret (Young) Hawkins died in November, 1870. Mr. R. P. Hawkins died December 3, 1871. Perry D. Hawkins was reared principally on the farm near Arlington, attending school at Arlington and Richmond, and the School of Mines at Rolla, Mo. He remained on the homestead until twenty-six years of age, being engaged in farming, and went from there to Arlington, and clerked in the store of A. M. Murphy for one year, after which he bought out the stock and continued at this one and a half years. In May, 1884, he came to Newburg, where he has since been engaged in general merchandising. Mr. Hawkins was married October 4, 1883, to Miss Lizzie Marshall. She is a daughter of Rev. George Marshall, who was born in Ireland in 1831, and came to this country when a boy, receiving his education at Union College, New York, and Princeton Theological Seminary, New Jersey, from which he graduated, and was licensed to preach at Albany, N. Y. He was ordained and installed pastor of the

Presbyterian Rock Church, at Fair Hill, Cecil Co., Md., May 13, 1856, and continued in charge of this church until his death, February 27, 1861. His wife, Isabel Campbell, was also a native of Ireland. To their union were born four children; two of them died when young, Willie and Georgina. His wife, Isabel (Campbell) Marshall, died in 1864, and the remaining two children, Lizzie and Carrie, came to Missouri with their uncle and aunt, who took charge of them after their parents' deaths. Carrie married Charles Wood, and Lizzie, P. D. Hawkins. Mrs. Hawkins was born in Fair Hill, Cecil Co., Md., came to Missouri when quite young, and was reared principally in that State. She attended the public schools in Phelps County, also in Mount Vernon, Ill., and St. Louis, Mo. She is a member of the Presbyterian Church. Mr. Hawkins is a member of the A. O. U. W., of the Masonic fraternity, and is the owner of a farm besides his mercantile business. He is politically a Democrat.

Dr. Samuel H. Headlee. Among the men of Phelps County, Mo., who have attained prominence in the healing art, and who are worthy of special mention, is Dr. Headlee, who was born in Maury County, Tenn., in 1826, and is the eldest of eleven children born to the marriage of Judge Elisha Headlee and Rachel Steele, who were born in North Carolina in 1801 and 1803, respectively. Elisha immigrated with his parents to Tennessee after becoming grown, and there married and lived until 1836, when they located in Greene County, Mo., when the country was in a very wild and unsettled state. They improved a good farm, and here the father died in 1876, having lived a long and useful life. He served as justice of the peace, public administrator and county judge, and was at one time candidate for the Legislature on the Democratic ticket, but owing to that party's minority was defeated. His father was probably born in New Jersey, of Welsh descent, and was a soldier in the Revolutionary War. He died in Greene County, Mo., in the 30's, his wife having previously died in Tennessee. The maternal grandfather of Dr. Headlee, Samuel Steele, removed from his native State of North Carolina to Tennessee at an early period, and in 1836 came to Greene County, Mo., where he died at a ripe old age, his wife also having died in Tennessee. Dr. Headlee resided in Greene County from the age of ten years up to manhood, and received a common and high-school education. His clothing until he reached manhood, even to the buttons, was made at home. About 1848 or 1849 he began the study of medicine, continuing three years, and then entered the Missouri Medical College at St. Louis, from which institution he graduated in 1857, after having practiced in the meantime to some extent. He first entered upon his practice in Wright County, and in 1863 located in Lebanon, and the following year came to St. James, which was then situated almost in the wilderness, and has since been actively engaged in practice. He served a short time as surgeon in the Confederate army during the late war, and was one of the curators of the University of Missouri for some years, but resigned the position in 1878, being that year elected to represent his senatorial district, which then consisted of Phelps, Crawford, Dent, Pulaski, Maries, Miller and Camden Counties, in the State Senate, and served one term of four years. He has also been a member of the town council and school board. He is a Democrat in politics, and is a member of the Masonic and I. O. O. F. fraternities, having held all the offices in both lodges.

Horatio S. Herbert, postmaster of Rolla, and a member of the firm of Herbert & McCrae, editors and proprietors of the Rolla *Herald*, was born in Erie, Penn., in 1837, and is the son of Rev. James and Harriet (Weston) Herbert. The parents removed to Lawrenceburg, Ind., from there in 1847 to Indianapolis, in 1855 to Schuyler County, Ill., and in 1870 to Sullivan County, Mo., where they now reside. Horatio S. Herbert was educated in the common schools, and in the graded schools of Indianapolis. At an early age he entered a printing office, and in 1855 entered the high-school, where he remained two years. He then went to Milan, Mo.; was in a printing office here for some time, but in 1859 went to Lebanon, Mo., where he became editor of the Laclede *Journal*. At the end of one year he bought the paper and material, and was editor and proprietor until 1861. This year Mr. Herbert cast his fortune with the Confederacy, and became a member of the State Guard of Missouri, afterward joining Gen. Price's army; and going to Arkansas, was in the fight at Pea Ridge. His command was ordered to Corinth, was in the fight at Iuka Springs, siege of Vicksburg, and after he was exchanged he joined the command of Gen. J. E. Johnston at Atlanta. He was wounded at Altoona, but rejoined his regiment three months later; was in the fight at Mobile, and in 1865, at the surrender of Fort Blakely, was sent to Black Island, where he was released in June, 1865. After the war Mr. Herbert went to Central Mississippi, where he clerked in a store and in a printing office until 1868, when he went to Rolla, Mo. Previous to this, in 1860, he married Miss Tennie A. Hooker, daughter of Benjamin and Martha Hooker, of Lebanon, Mo. To this union were born two children: Hattie, wife of A. M. Millard, and Bessie. After coming to Rolla Mr. Herbert was employed on the *Herald*, but in 1869 purchased the office and paper. In 1879 Charles McCrae became a partner, and they have since been proprietors of the same. The *Herald* has a large patronage, and wields an important influence. Mr. Herbert is prominent in politics, being one of the influential Democrats of Phelps County, and in 1885 was appointed by President Cleveland as postmaster of Rolla, to compensate partially for the good he had done the party.

Menzo House, farmer and stock raiser of Phelps County, Mo., was born in Herkimer County, N. Y., in 1834, and is a son of Abraham P. and Elizabeth (Shaut) House, who were also born in Herkimer County, where they married and lived until 1834, since which time they have resided in Steuben County, N. Y., the father being eighty-six years of age and the mother eighty-four. They have been worthy members of the Wesleyan Methodist Church for many years, and the father is a prosperous farmer. His brother, Coonrod P., was a soldier in the War of 1812, and his father, Peter, aided the colonists in their struggle for liberty during the Revolutionary War. The maternal grandfather, Jacob Shaut, was of German origin, and spent his entire life in Herkimer and Steuben Counties, N. Y. Menzo House is the sixth of eleven children, eight of whom lived to be grown, and in his boyhood days acquired a common-school education. He was married in February, 1856, to Harriet Helen, a daughter of Hiram and Mary Weeks, of Herkimer County, N. Y. Here, it is supposed, the father died, but the mother's demise occurred in Steuben County in 1870. Mr. and Mrs. House became the parents of six sons and four daughter, four sons and two daughters of whom are living. They made Steuben County their home until 1867, when they came to Phelps County, Mo., and settled on their present farm, which now consists of 200 acres, with 150 acres under cultivation, on which is erected a handsome and commodious residence. During the late war Mr. House served three years in the Federal army as a volunteer in Company K, One Hundred and Seventh New York Infantry, about fourteen months of the time being spent with the Army of the Potomac, and participated in the battles of Resaca, Peach Tree Creek, Dallas, New Hope Church and Atlanta. He was captured at Rutledge, Ga., November 19, 1864, and was taken to Florence, S. C., where he was retained until March 3, 1865, at which time he returned home on furlough, and soon after rejoined his regiment. While serving with the Army of the Potomac he was in the battles of Antietam, Chancellorsville, Gettysburgh, Falling Water and many others of less note. Mr. House has been a Republican all his life, and has served as justice of the peace a number of terms. He and wife are members of the Methodist Episcopal Church. For a number of years he has been agent for the W. A. Wood binders and mowers.

Hon. John Gregory Hutcheson. Prominent among the old and much respected citizens of Phelps County stands the name of John G. Hutcheson, a retired merchant and business man of Rolla. He was born in Monroe County, Tenn., in 1820, and is the son of James and Mary Hutcheson, the father being a native of Virginia, born in 1781. He was married in his native State, and soon moved to Monroe County, Tenn., but in 1834 immigrated to the State of Missouri, locating in what is now Maries County, where he settled, and where he passed the remainder of his life. He died about 1844. He was one of the first white men to settle in Central Missouri, and came by ox team, making the trip in about six weeks. His wife, Mary (Gregory) Hutcheson, was also a native of the State of Virginia. She died in 1850. She was the mother of eleven children, seven sons and four daughters, five of whom are now living: James M. (in Lawrence County, Mo.), William (in Maries County), Martha (widow of Z. Blackwell, in the Indian Nation), Mary E. (wife of P. Johnson) and John G. The last named was fourteen years of age when his parents landed in Missouri. He remained on the farm until about twenty-four years of age, and January 30, 1845, was married to Miss Juliana Avery, a native of Alabama, and the daughter of John and Elizabeth Avery, who were natives of Alabama, and who immigrated to Missouri in 1832, settling in what is now Maries County, they being the first settlers. To Judge and Mrs. Hutcheson were born six children, four of whom lived to be grown: Marion C. (deceased), Mary (deceased, and wife of John Gill), Sarah E. (wife of William Carr, in Leavenworth, Kas.), and Imogene (wife of Paul N. Davey, in Carthage, Mo.). Judge Hutcheson located in Phelps County, Mo., five miles north of the county seat, after marriage, and bought 380 acres of land. He followed farming until the late war, when he rented his farm, and moved to Rolla, where he conducted a livery and feed stable. After the war he and W. Smith sold goods one year. In 1866 he with five men erected the Rolla Mills, and he was a partner two years, meeting with good success. He invested $4,000, and sold out for $8,000. In 1868 he purchased a drug store, and was in that business for four years. For the last fifteen years Judge Hutcheson has been leading a quiet life, donating a portion of his time to looking after the interest of his farm of 200 acres, one mile northeast of Rolla. In politics Mr. Hutcheson is a life-long Democrat, casting his first presidential vote for James K. Polk in 1844. In 1870 he was elected probate judge, served four years, and has also served as county court justice twelve years. The Judge is one of the old residents of Phelps County, and among her most highly esteemed citizens. He is a member of the Masonic order, and his wife is a member of the Missionary Baptist Church.

Dr. William T. Hutcheson, druggist, of Newburg, Mo., was born in Crawford County, Mo., September 28, 1849. This county was afterward changed to Phelps, and then to Maries County; thus the Doctor has lived on one farm and in three counties. His parents, Robert E. and Virginia (Keatley) Hutcheson, are natives of Knox County, Tenn., and St. Louis County, Mo., respectively. The father moved to Missouri when nine years of age, settling where he now lives, and in that time the name of the county has changed four times. He has followed farming all his life, was fairly educated, and was married to Miss Virginia Keatley, who bore him eight children, six now living: James M., William T., Eliza J., Mary E., Sarah A. and Robertus A. Those deceased were named Theodore F. and John C. Mr. Hutcheson, during his life in Crawford County, was made county judge, and held the same office fourteen years in Maries County, where he was also engaged in milling and farming. Mrs. Hutcheson was the daughter of Thomas Keatley, who was an early settler from Virginia, a soldier in the Black Hawk War, and of English parentage. The paternal grandparents of the subject of this sketch were natives of Ireland, and came to the United States at an early date. Dr. William T. Hutcheson was reared principally on a farm in Phelps County. He received a good English education, and during the late war traveled over the country. After that he began the study of medicine, and was in a drug store at Rolla for Dr. M. C. Hutcheson for two years. He then practiced with Dr. Glenn for two years as a student, after which he attended one course of lectures at the St. Louis Medical College. He then located at Relfe, Phelps County, practiced one year, then went to Rolla, where he was in the drug business two years, engaging in general merchandise afterward for one year. Later he moved to Maries County, purchased land, and here followed agricultural pursuits in connection with the practice of his profession. Again, in 1877, he attended lectures at St. Louis, and graduated from the medical college at that place, after which he went to Arlington, Phelps Co., Mo., and here followed his profession until 1886. Previous to this, in 1884, Dr. Hutcheson ventured into the drug business, and as this requires all his time he has retired from professional life. He was married in 1875 to Miss Sarah A. Livesay, a native of Dent County, Mo., and the fruits of this union were four children, three now living: Lulu D., William R. and M. Grace. The one that died was named J. Emmet. Mrs. Hutcheson died August 29, 1886. The Doctor has been postmaster at Newburg for four years, is a member of the Masonic order, and although a young man is one of the oldest Masons in this section of the county. Besides his drug business the Doctor is the owner of 600 acres of land in this county. He is a stanch Democrat in his political views.

Thomas M. Jones, attorney at law, and real estate and insurance agent, of the firm of Frost & Jones, was born in Pulaski County, Mo., in 1861, being the eldest of five surviving children born to the marriage of Thomas A. Jones and Cynthia Leake, natives, respectively, of Indiana and Virginia. The father was born in Indianapolis in 1838, and when about nine years of age came with his father, John G. Jones, to where Washington, Mo., is now located, where he was reared to manhood. He was married in and has been a resident of Pulaski County for over twenty years, and is a prominent Baptist minister. His father, John G., was a cabinet-maker by trade, and died in 1862 in Pulaski County. His father, the great-grandfather of our subject, Thomas A. Jones, came from Wales at a very early day, his wife being a native of Scotland. William Leake, the maternal grandfather, was born, reared and married in Virginia, and about 1833 came to Missouri, locating in Pulaski County, where he died in 1873, aged ninety years. He was a soldier in the War of 1812, and was a well-to-do farmer. His father, William Leake, was a Revolutionary soldier, and died in Virginia. Thomas M. Jones, whose name heads this sketch, resided on his father's farm until fifteen years of age, and from that time until twenty-two years of age was in school, during which period he studied civil engineering in the Missouri School of Mines and Metallurgy. In 1883 he became a member of the present firm, and gives promise of becoming one of the prosperous citizens of the county. He has been engaged in pedagoguing, his first term being taught when he was sixteen years of age. Soon after becoming the partner of Mr. Frost he took up the study of law, and in 1887 was admitted to the Phelps County bar. He has been city treasurer for three years, and is also secretary of the executive committee of the Missouri School of Mines and Metallurgy. In 1888 he was elected public administrator for Phelps County. He is a member of the Masonic fraternity, the I. O. O. F., and in politics is a Democrat. On June 24, 1886, he was married to Miss Lucy B., daughter of William and Lucy A. Morse, formerly of Massachusetts, and by her is the father of two children. She was educated in the public schools of the county and at the Missouri School of Mines and Metallurgy. Her father located in Rolla during the war, and there died in 1870, having been one of the prominent merchants of the town. He also held the office of probate and associate county judge, and was at one time mayor of Rolla.

Col. William C. Kelly, prosecuting attorney of Phelps County, Mo., was born November 18, 1836, in Maury County, Tenn., the son of Hardy and Elizabeth (Shelton) Kelly, and grandson of Elijah Kelly, who was of Irish birth. Hardy Kelly was born in South Carolina in 1796, and was a Methodist minister by profession. When a young man he went to Maury County, Tenn., with his father, and was married in that State. In 1840 he moved to Carroll County, Ark. now Boone County, and in 1856 he moved to Springfield, Mo. In 1861 he became a resident of Rolla, where he died in 1866. He was engaged in ministerial work for about thirty years, being a local preacher. Elizabeth (Shelton) Kelly was born in Maury County, Tenn., in 1800, and was the daughter of Stephen Shelton, who was a physician by profession, and of considerable note in Tennessee; was the author of "Shelton's Domestic Medicines." Mrs. Kelly died in 1876. To Hardy Kelly and wife were born eleven children, seven of whom are now living, Col. William Kelly being the third in order of birth. He was educated in the common schools, but has added materially to this by observation and general reading. He attained his growth on his father's farm, and at the age of eighteen became a disciple of Blackstone, Hon. James P. Spring, of Fort Smith, Ark., being his preceptor. In 1855 he was admitted to the bar at Springfield, Mo., and commenced practicing in Greene County, where he continued two years. In 1856 he married Miss Margaret D. Ross, a native of Tennessee, and six children were the results of this union: Alice, wife of F. P. Rutherford, of Houston, Mo.; Jefferson D., Christopher L., Lulu, John and James B. In 1857 Mr. Kelly went to Marshfield, Mo., where he remained until 1861, when he joined the State Guards, and was elected major of the First Missouri Regiment, in McBride's brigade, which joined the army under Gen. Price. He was in the fight at Wilson's Creek, Dry Wood and Lexington. About six months after he was appointed by Gen. Price to recruit a regiment in Missouri and Arkansas. He raised eight companies, and was elected lieutenant-colonel, but Gen. Hindman reorganized the army, discharging all the officers who had been elected, and filled their places by appointment. But an officer with the ability of Col. Kelly could not remain idle, and he was appointed by Gen. Price to conscript troops for the Confederate service for the north sub-district of Arkansas, which position he filled up to the raid of 1864. He was then placed on the staff of Gen. Marmaduke, and a part of the time was in command of about 100 men, being a scout of that general. After the war Judge Price, of Springfield, Mo., and Col. Kelly, formed a law partnership at Batesville, Ark., which lasted two years, when Judge Price moved to Springfield and Col. Kelly to Rolla, where he has remained in the practice of law up to the present time. In 1872 he was elected by the Democratic party as prosecuting attorney of Phelps County, and has since filled that position. He is a man of high legal ability, being one of the leading members of the Phelps County bar, and has filled the office of prosecuting attorney in an efficient and able manner. He has carefully guarded the public welfare, sparing neither time nor hard work to do his duty, and his whole duty, showing impartiality in performing the obligations of his office. He is a fluent speaker, and challenges the high esteem of all his many friends. Mrs. Kelly died in 1881, and March 22, 1883, Col. W. C. Kelly married

Mrs. Mary J. Ellis, who died in June, 1884. In December, 1886, he married Miss Lucretia Fore, a native of Kentucky. The Colonel is a member of the Masonic fraternity, Royal Arch Chapter, was High Priest for four years, and is also an ancient member of the I. O. O. F.

William A. Kitchen, another successful agriculturist of Phelps County, and a resident of Edgar Springs, was born April 11, 1831, in Crawford County, Mo., afterward Phelps County. His parents, George P. and Elizabeth (Adams) Kitchen, were both natives of Kentucky, and the father was by occupation a farmer. He received a thorough education at Louisville College, and immigrated to Missouri about 1828, settling near Newburg, or where that town now stands. Indians still remained in the country, but were friendly; very few white people were in the county, and game of nearly every description abounded in plenty. In connection with farming, Mr. Kitchen also taught school during the winter months. He died in this county in 1844. He was the father of eight children, five now living: Elias D., William A., Conrad, Margaret J. and Mary A. Those deceased were named Andrew J., Sarah E. and George N. The paternal grandfather, Anthony Kitchen, was probably a native of Virginia, and immigrated to Kentucky at an early day. In 1828 he came to Phelps County, Mo., where he died in 1868. He was a colonel in the War of 1812, and while in Kentucky was a member of the State Militia. He was a tailor by trade. His wife, Margaret Kitchen, also died in this county. Grandfather Adams was born in Kentucky, and was of German descent. William A. Kitchen was reared principally in Phelps County, receiving his education in the district schools, and during his boyhood days remembers seeing the Indians. He remained at home until twenty years of age, and then hired out for about five years. He then purchased the land where he now lives, which consists of 330 acres, only about seven being under cultivation when bought by Mr. Kitchen, but now having 115 acres cultivated. November 30, 1854, Mr. Kitchen married Miss Rebecca Newport, a native of Illinois, and the daughter of Richard and Sarah (Matthews) Newport. To Mr. and Mrs. Kitchen were born eight children, five of whom are now living: Sarah E., George D., William J., James E. and Margaret E. The ones deceased were named as follows: Cynthia A., Charles L. and Richard M. Mrs. Kitchen died in January, 1883, and February 13, 1887, Mr. Kitchen married Mrs. Margaret L. (Turner) LeSueur, who has borne him one child, Edna C. During the war Mr. Kitchen was in the State Militia for six months, Company D, being confined to this State. He was discharged at Springfield. Since in early life he has been engaged in farming, giving this his entire attention. He is a Democrat in his political principles.

John B. Lamb, a well-to-do farmer of Phelps County, Mo., and a native of the same, was born in September, 1851, and since nineteen years of age has been the architect of his own fortunes. He has always followed the occupation of farming, and by industry and economy has become the owner of 265 acres of good land, ninety acres being in a high state of cultivation. Miss Sarah Louisa Scott, who was born in Washington County, Mo., in 1846, became his wife in 1870, and by her he became the father of seven children, six of whom are living:

America L., Lemuel W., Amanda C., Louisa E., John E., Nora E. and William Thomas (deceased). Mr. Lamb is a Democrat in politics. His wife, who died March 9, 1887, was a daughter of William C. and Jane (Hensley) Scott, who were farmers and natives of Missouri. Mr. Lamb is a son of Thomas and Elizabeth (Plank) Lamb, who were born in 1827 in Missouri and Tennessee, respectively, and in 1843 located on the place where they are now residing. The following are their children: John B., Nancy J. (Talbott), and William Riley. The grandparents, John and Catherine (Adams) Lamb, were born in 1798 and 1800, respectively. The former's birth occurred in Virginia, and he died in 1873. His wife is still living, and resides in California. The maternal grandparents, Benedict and Rachel (Gallahorn) Plank, were born in Tennessee, and died in 1858 and 1833, respectively. Both families were wealthy farmers.

John Lenox. The success which has attended the career of Mr. Lenox as an agriculturist is a striking illustration of what can be done in Missouri by a young man who possesses pluck, energy and a determination to succeed. He was born in Kentucky in March, 1831, and is a son of John and Susannah (Hutson) Lenox, the former of whom was born in Kentucky in 1796, and died in 1849. In 1814 he came to Missouri with Daniel Boone, with whom he hunted and trapped for several years. He then returned to Kentucky, and after his marriage resided in that State for several years, and again came to Missouri, settling in Crawford County with his family. He and an elder brother, William, assisted in laying out the town of Jefferson on his first visit to the State, and when he returned he engaged in farming, entering 160 acres of Government land. The following are his children who are living: Thomas, John, Taylor, Hamilton, Elizabeth (Mrs. Dutton), Susannah (Mrs. Adams) and Margaret A. (Mrs. Bassett). The paternal grandfather, Charles Lenox, was born in Scotland, and was a soldier in the Revolutionary War. The maternal grandparents were Kentuckians. John Lenox, whose name heads this sketch, was brought to Missouri when four years of age, and spent his early life in Crawford, afterward Pulaski, and now Phelps County. Miss Sarah A. D. Kidwell, who was born in Callaway County, Mo., in October, 1831, became his wife in 1854. She is a daughter of William and Hester (Armitage) Kidwell, both of whom were born in Kentucky. The father was a book-keeper in some iron works, and served as sheriff of Calloway County for several terms. Mrs. Lenox is the only surviving one of their five children. The father died in 1834, and the mother in 1865. In 1861 Mr. Lenox enlisted in Capt. Frank's company, Col. Johnson's regiment, Confederate States Army, and during his six months' service operated in Southern Missouri and Arkansas. He is a Democrat in politics, and cast his first presidential vote for Franklin Pierce in 1852. The following are his children: Mary J. (Mrs. Faulkner), Henry E., Samuel H., Willie Ann, Francis E., Sarah L. and Harriet E.

D. T. Lenox, farmer, stock dealer and raiser, and a native of Phelps County, Mo., was born in 1847, being a son of David and Elizabeth (Brown) Lenox, who were natives of Kentucky, the former's birth occurring in 1797. He was ordained a minister of the Baptist Church in the early part of his career, and throughout life was an influential and highly respected citizen. He died in 1863, at the age of sixty-six years, and his wife, who was born in 1801, died in 1868. They were the parents of twelve children, D. T. Lenox being the ninth of the family. He remained with his parents until their respective deaths, and in 1867 was married to Miss Sarah Burkitt, a daughter of Wheeler and Catherine Burkitt, by whom he became the father of six children: Bessie, Hamilton, Catherine, Kenard and Isaac (twins) and Madge. Mr. Lenox resides on the old home farm, which was entered by his father about 1825, and which now consists of 700 acres of good land, with 400 acres in a fine state of cultivation and well improved. He ships from two to three car loads of cattle annually, and two car loads of hogs, all of which are raised on his farm. His buildings are all in good condition, and he has a fine cattle barn, 60x80 feet. He keeps from sixteen to twenty mules to work his farm, and is a man of good business qualifications, as his success shows. His farm is principally bottom land, located on Dry Fork Creek. In 1879 he was elected by the Democratic party of Phelps County as collector, and served one term. He is a member of the I. O. O. F. and the Masonic fraternity.

Grandason B. LeSueur is another prominent resident of Phelps County, Mo. He was born in Henry County, Va., March 7, 1805, was reared on a farm, and received a common-school education. He remained with his parents until twenty-seven years of age, and then, October 4, 1831, married Miss Ingram, who bore him nine children, three now living: William M., Elizabeth, wife of Gabriel Prillaman, of Virginia, and James A. Those deceased were named Martel P., Catherine O., Martha A., Stephen W., George G. and Rebecca E. Mr. LeSueur immigrated to Phelps County, Mo., in October, 1869, and settled where he now lives. Mrs. LeSueur was born February 21, 1809, and died August 28, 1873, at the age of sixty-four years. Mr. LeSueur has been a farmer all his life, and at one time ran a tannery in Virginia. Martel LeSueur, father of the subject of this sketch, was of French parentage, and most likely born in France. He was a soldier under the direct command of Col. William Washington in the Revolutionary War, and served the entire time. He was engaged at the Cowpens and at Bunker Hill. He was a farmer by occupation, and June 10, 1781, was married to Miss Elizabeth Bacon. He died August 6, 1843, at the age of eighty-six, and his wife died September 6, 1844, at the age of seventy-nine years. Elizabeth Bacon, the mother, was born in England, coming to the United States when small, and here married Mr. LeSueur in Virginia. Grandason B. LeSueur is eighty-four years of age, is strong and vigorous, can read without glasses, and is now living with his son. He has been a member of the Primitive Baptist Church sixty-four years past; was baptized by Stephen Hubbard, in Union Church, Patrick County, Va., and is a strong Democrat in his political views. William M. LeSueur attained his growth in Franklin County, Va., received a good practical education, and when nineteen years of age learned the tanner's trade, which he followed in Virginia for twenty years. January 19, 1856, he married Miss Paulina J. Turner, a native of Henry County, Va., born October

19, 1832, and the daughter of Thomas K. and Caroline (Pyrtle) Turner. Her parents were also born in Virginia, and the father was a gunsmith by trade. Her paternal grandparents were both born in Virginia, and that family is one of the oldest in this country, as is also the Pyrtle family. William M. LeSueur enlisted in the Confederate service, Company B, Thirty-sixth Virginia Infantry, McCauslin brigade, Whorton's division, and served one year. He was at Mount Jackson and Middleton battles; was captured at Waynesborough, Va., March 2, 1865, and imprisoned at Fort Delaware for about four months. After being discharged at Norfolk, Mr. LeSueur tanned for the Government, and also for soldiers' families. He had three brothers also in the Confederate service. Mr. LeSueur has no children of his own, but has reared two boys, Henry B. and James W. White, who were left orphans. He has also reared his brother's four children: Ellen V., Ida C., Exeony E. and Thomas G.

John Simpson Livesay, treasurer of Phelps County, and hardware merchant in Rolla, a member of the firm of Livesay & Love, is a native of Franklin County, Ill., born December 16, 1852, being the son of John W. and Martha (McDonald) Livesay. John W. Livesay was a native of Maury County, Tenn, born in 1827, of Welsh descent. He went with his parents to Illinois when young, locating in Macoupin County, and afterward in Franklin County, where John W. taught school for three years. In December, 1853, he moved to Salem, Mo., and engaged in mercantile pursuits there for nine years. In 1862 he moved to St. James, in Phelps County, and in 1865 became a citizen of Rolla, where he already had a store. Besides this he had one in Salem. Mr. Livesay continued merchandising until 1878, when, owing to ill health, he was obliged to abandon it. He located on his farm one and a half miles west of Rolla, where he lived a quiet and retired life. He died August 14, 1886; was treasurer of Dent County for several terms, and was postmaster at Salem for several years. He was a man of large business capacity, and made a large amount of money. His wife was a native of Raleigh, N. C., born in 1829 and died May 7, 1887. They were the parents of ten children, five living: James D., Lewis A., John S.; Mary J., wife of Frank Beers, and Amanda M. John S. was but an infant when he was brought to Missouri; was reared as a salesman in his father's store, commencing when he was sixteen years of age. He was educated at St. James, at Rolla, and at the State School of Mines. April 11, 1882, he married Miss Eliza E. Love, a native of Phelps County, Mo., born September 2, 1855, and the daughter of Robert A. and Amanda Love. Mr. Livesay worked for his father until 1878 or 1879, and then hired to Robert A. Love, becoming a partner in 1881. This partnership continued until 1886, when Mr. Livesay was elected county treasurer of Phelps County by a majority of 269. In 1888 he was re-elected to the same office by a large majority. In November, 1886, he and Thomas E. Love purchased a hardware store in Rolla, and have since continued that business. They carry a first-class stock of hardware, stoves and tinware, and are live, energetic men. Mr. Livesay is a Democrat in his political views, and is true to his party. In June, 1883, he was elected a member of the city council, and served four years, being the youngest member ever elected to that position. He is a member of the I. O. O. F., Lodge No. 135, of Rolla, and of the Masonic Lodge No. 213, at this place, and Mrs. Livesay is a member of the Missionary Baptist Church.

A. S. Long, dealer in general merchandise, Rolla, Mo., and one of the oldest and most extensive merchants in the place, is a native of St. Louis County, Mo., where he was born in 1835, being the son of Joseph and Jane (Martin) Long. The father was a native of Virginia, and when a young man went to St. Louis County, Mo., where he was married. He was not permitted to live the allotted time of man, but was cut down in the prime of life. He died in 1836, at the early age of about twenty-one years. He left a wife and two sons. His widow was born in St. Louis County, Mo., in 1816, and died in 1883. In 1838 she married H. R. Edgar, who is yet living, and is ninety years old. He lives in Maries County, Mo., Mrs. Edgar being the mother of five children by her second marriage. Albert S. Long was the eldest of the two children born to the first marriage. He was an infant when his father died, and in 1836 he moved with his mother to Maries County, Mo., where she located and passed the remainder of her days. A. S. obtained his growth on the farm, and gave the proceeds of his labor to his step-father until he was nineteen years old. He then left home and went to the Meramec Iron Works, working on a farm for two years at very small wages. After two years he entered the store of William James as clerk, to learn the business of selling merchandise. April 23, 1857, he was married to Nancy Fort, daughter of Sarah and William Fort, a native of Ross County, Ohio, born September 10, 1840. The result of this marriage was five boys and one girl, four boys and one girl deceased. Edwin is still living. In 1862 Mr. Long went to Rolla, where he worked for Faulkner & Graves for four years. In 1866 he engaged in business on his own account, with D. W. Malcolm and A. Demuth as his partners, but sold out to them in 1869, and embarked in the manufacture of wagons with Mr. Ginish. In 1870 Mr. Long established a general merchandise store on his own responsibility, commencing on a small scale, but year after year he added to his business, until to-day he is one of the leading merchants of Phelps County. In 1882 he erected a two-story brick, 90x40 feet, with two stores side by side, both of which he occupies. He carries a first-class stock of goods, clothing, hardware, etc., the stock being valued at $20,000. Although commencing life with limited means, Mr. Long has made a success of all his enterprises, and is today one of the solid, substantial business men of Rolla. In politics he is a stanch Republican, casting his first presidential vote for Bell and Everett, in 1860. He is director and stockholder in the First National Bank of Rolla, and has held this position for the past twelve years. He is a Master Mason, and he and Mrs. Long have been members of the Methodist Episcopal Church for twenty years, in which he has been steward for fifteen years.

Robert A. Love, dealer in general merchandise at Rolla, and senior member of the firm of Robert A. Love & Son, was born in Floyd County, Ind., in 1832, and is the son of Isaac and Pheba (Conley) Love. Isaac Love was born in Tennessee in 1782, and was of

Scotch-German descent. He was married in his native State, and afterward started for Missouri, but stopped in Floyd County, Ind., where he remained until 1832, when he came to Phelps County, Mo., and located eight miles north of the county seat. He was a farmer by occupation, but the latter part of his life he sold goods. He died in 1865. The mother was born in Knox County, East Tenn., in 1792, and died in 1868. She was the mother of twelve children, eleven of whom lived to be grown, and our subject being the youngest. He was but six weeks old when his parents moved to Missouri, and was reared to manhood in Phelps County. February 2, 1853, he married Miss Amanda Miller, daughter of John and Nancy Miller, and a native of Tennessee. She was born in 1828. Ten children have been born to this union: Eliza E., wife of John S. Livesay, treasurer of Phelps County, Mo., and hardware merchant of Rolla; George L., member of the firm of R. A. Love & Son; Thomas E., hardware merchant in Rolla, and a member of the firm of Livesay, Love & Co.; Nellie C., wife of Noel A. Kinney, express agent at Rolla; Charles F., salesman in his father's store; Triza Carrie, died March 18, 1876, at the age of eighteen; James W., born December 2, 1861, died July 5, 1865; Lea M., born April 10, 1863, died September 7, 1866; Eddie A., born October 11, 1872, died March 5, 1873, and one child, born September 2, 1857, died at birth. Mr. Love resided near the old home place until 1860, when he moved to Rolla, and during the war was captain of Company A, Sixty-third Regiment Home Militia. In 1864 he was elected sheriff of Phelps County, and two years later was re-elected, filling that position for four years. In 1867 he became a partner in the mercantile firm of Campbell, Love & Co., and in 1867-68 they erected the Rolla Flour Mills, at a cost of $40,000. After the mill was erected Mr. Love sold his interest in the store, and the mill firm was the same. He remained in the mill for eleven years, and in 1870 established a store, the firm being Love, Smith & Co. About 1872 he sold his interest, and the following year bought new property, established a store, and in 1876 his son, George L., became a partner, and from that date until the present the firm has been R. A. Love & Son. Mr. Love retained an interest in the mill until 1879, and is the next oldest merchant in Rolla. He is a Republican in politics, casting his first presidential vote for Bell and Everett. He was a member of the school board of Rolla two terms, and a member of the city council a number of years, and he has been a member of the Missionary Baptist Church for seventeen years, and his wife for thirty years, he having been deacon ever since joining the church. He is a Master Mason, and an excellent citizen. In every sense of the word Mr. Love is a self-made man, receiving little or no schooling, and never attending school more than two months at any one time in his life; he commenced for himself very poor, the first money he received ($9) being in payment of six weeks of labor at rafting down the Gasconade River. He is now well-to-do and of acknowledged prominence.

Charles M. McCrae, member of the firm of Herbert & McCrae, editors and publishers of the Rolla *Herald*, is a native of the Isle of Cape Breton, born in 1853. His parents, Frank and Isabella (Campbell) McCrae, were born in Scotland, and went to Nova Scotia when single, and were there married. In 1856 they moved to Canada West, and in 1870 moved to Fort Scott, Kas. Frank McCrae was a sea captain, and had charge of a merchant ship up to the time he moved to the United States. His ship plied between Halifax and British India. He was accidentally killed in 1878, by being struck on the head while assisting in moving a large rock. His wife, Isabella (Campbell) McCrae, died from the effects of a fall on the ice in 1888. She was twice married, her first husband being John McKenzie, by whom she had four children. She was also the mother of four children by her second husband, Charles M. being the youngest. He was seventeen years of age when his parents moved to the United States, and never attended school after he was eleven years of age. When twelve years of age he entered the printing office and worked on the Woodstock (Canada) *Sentinel*, then under the management of John McWhinnie & Son; served an apprenticeship of four years, and his case mate was W. S. Barnes, the famous fast type-setter, now of Philadelphia. Mr. McCrae then worked two weeks on the Detroit *Free Press*, and in 1870 went to Fort Scott, Kas., where he became employed on the Fort Scott *Monitor*, remaining seven months, and then went to St. Louis, and was in a job office. In the fall of 1871 he came to Rolla, Mo., and began working on the Rolla *Express*, and soon took the foremanship of the Rolla *Herald*, under Van Deren & Herbert. In 1879 he became one-half owner of that paper, and since then the firm has been Herbert & McCrae. The *Herald* has the largest circulation of any paper in Phelps County, and is very ably edited. Its politics are purely Democratic, and it is a newsy local paper. September 27, 1882, Mr. McCrae married Miss Edwarda Rogers, who was born in Lynchburg, Va., in 1862. They have two children: Charles Edward and Rowe Francis. Mr. McCrae is a member of the A. O. U. W., Select Knights, K. of H., and Mrs. McCrae is a member of the Baptist Church.

Otto P. Margedant, merchant at Edgar Springs, Mo., and son of Mattias and Frederica (Richter) Margedant, was born in St. Louis, Mo., July 28, 1836. The father, Mattias Margedant, was born in Dusselldorf, Germany, in 1816, and was a printer by trade, which occupation he followed before coming to America, working in jobbing offices. He immigrated to the United States when a young man, came to St. Louis after a year's residence in New Orleans, and was here engaged in the printer's business, which he followed until his death in that city in 1850. The mother, Frederica Richter, was born in Canstadt, Germany; came to the United States when quite a young woman, but after her marriage to Mr. Margedant in Germany. They had one child born to their union, Otto P. After her husband's death Mrs. Margedant married a Mr. Huffsmith, and is now living in St. Louis, Mo. Otto P. Margedant was reared principally in St. Louis, received a good education, and when young learned the trade of mathematical and philosophical instrument maker, but never followed it. During the time of his residence in St. Louis he was employed by McDowell & Bro., general merchants, and also taught school in Illinois. He began life for himself in 1866 by going to Texas County, Mo., where he taught school for eight years. He also engaged in merchandising at Licking for about ten months. At the opening of the late war he enlisted in Company C, Eighth Missouri Infantry, Confederate States Army, enlisting as a private, afterward orderly-sergeant, and then promoted to the rank of second lieutenant, serving altogether three years and six months. Among the battles in which he participated are the following: Wilson's Creek, Fremont's Body Guard, Prairie Grove, Pleasant Hill, La., Jenkins' Ferry, Ark., evacuation of Little Rock. He was wounded at Prairie Grove. After the war he returned to Texas County, Mo., where he remained until 1876, when he came to Edgar Springs, this county. He was engaged in lead mining on Little Piney for one year, and then taught school for one year. After that he engaged in the drug business for some time, sold out and engaged in his present business, which is the largest of its kind in Edgar Springs. In 1858 Mr. Margedant married Miss Jennie Dooley, of Texas County, Mo., and daughter of Thomas Dooley. Mrs. Margedant was born in Cole County, Mo., and by her marriage to Mr. Margedant became the mother of ten children: Sarah J., Emma F., Henrietta, Agnes, Lillian, Edwin L., Albert, Walter, Oscar and Florence. Mr. Margedant is a Democrat in politics, is a member of the Masonic fraternity, the K. of L., and he and Mrs. Margedant are both members of the Methodist Episcopal Church, South. He has been postmaster of this office for nine years.

Charles N. Martin, farmer and stock raiser of Dawson Township, Phelps Co., Mo., was born in St. Louis County, Mo., in 1838, and when an infant was taken by his parents to what is now Maries County (then Crawford), and was there reared to manhood, receiving such education as the schools of that day afforded. After attaining his majority he began the battle of life for himself, with no capital whatever but his hands and a goodly supply of pluck and energy, and these have been the means of placing him in the independent position he now occupies. He first spent two seasons in St. Louis County, where he was engaged in overseeing, and during the late war he was extensively engaged in dealing in cattle, but also served as lieutenant-captain in the Missouri Militia for some time. While on his way to St. Louis with a drove of cattle he was captured by a scouting band of Shelby's command, and was with them during the battle of Osage, but soon after succeeded in effecting his escape, and made his way home. On the 7th of January, 1866, he was married to Miss Valeria, a daughter of James and Mary E. Simpson, who were born in Virginia and Missouri, and died in the latter State August 15, 1888, and 1850, respectively. The father was reared in Indiana, and about 1840 located in Crawford County, Mo., and in 1861 took up his residence in Phelps County. After his wife's death he went to California, where he remained about ten years, and then returned to Missouri and married again. Mrs. Martin is his only living child. She was born in Crawford County, Mo., and by Mr. Martin is the mother of nine children, six of whom are living. They have all received good educations, and his eldest son spent some years in the Indiana Normal School, at Valparaiso. He is now one of Phelps County's best teachers, and is an excellent penman. He is now studying medicine. Mr. Martin has 480 acres of land, the home farm comprising 280 acres. He has been a Democrat all his life, and his first vote was cast for Douglas in 1860. He is also a member of the A. O. U. W., and his wife is a member of the Baptist Church, and his eldest son and daughter of the Christian Church. His parents, Madison and Anastasia (Perry) Martin, were born in St. Louis County, Mo., in 1812, and were there reared and married. In 1838, about three years after their marriage, they settled in what is now Maries County, on Spanish Prairie, where they still live. The grandfather, David Martin, was born in North Carolina, and while yet a boy came with his father, Adam Martin, to St. Louis, and settled near Bridgetown, when the city was a small French hamlet. There David lived until 1838, and then came to Maries County, where he died in 1867. He was a soldier in the War of 1812. Adam Martin was the first man to bring a four-wheeled wagon to St. Louis, and was one of the pioneers of that county. He was of English descent, and many of his descendants still live in St. Louis County. Jackson Perry, grandfather of the gentleman whose name heads this sketch, was a French Canadian, and came to St. Louis when young, where he spent the remainder of his life, dying in 1859 at an advanced age. He reared a large family of children, who located in different portions of the West, but many of his descendants still reside in St. Louis County.

Hon. Robert Meriwether, judge of the probate court of Phelps County, Mo., and a resident of Rolla, is a native of Lewis County, Mo., where he was born in 1853. Judge Meriwether received his rudimentary education in his native county, and his collegiate education at Louisiana, Mo., attending the college at that place for three years. In 1870 he became a disciple of Blackstone, and in 1872 was admitted to the bar to practice in Louisiana. Six years later he became a resident of Phelps County, Mo. At the age of eighteen he engaged in the teacher's profession, and followed this occupation for five years, teaching one year in Phelps County. In 1875 he married Miss Alice J. Bondurant, a native of Lewis County, Mo., born in 1855, and the daughter of Joseph A. Bondurant. Two children are the fruits of this union, Carl and Roy B. Judge Meriwether resided at St. James until 1884, when he came to Rolla and here continued his practice. In 1886 he was elected probate judge of Phelps County, by a majority of 600, by the Democratic party. The Judge is a young man of fine legal ability, and is one of the coming attorneys of Phelps County. He is highly respected and a very excellent citizen. He is a member of the A. O. U. W. and Farmers & Mechanics Mutual Aid Association of St. Louis, and Mrs. Meriwether is a member of the Methodist Episcopal Church, South.

Lea H. Miller, farmer, of Phelps County, Mo., was born in Knoxville, Tenn., in 1826, and is a son of John C. and Nancy (Dudley) Miller, who were born in Tennessee and North Carolina in 1798 and 1810, and died in 1867 and 1870, respectively. They were married in the father's native State, and in 1827 moved to Indiana, thence to Illinois in 1830, and took up their abode in Crawford County, Mo. (now Phelps County) in 1835. They came to this State overland, with ox teams, and bought out a settler, Mr. Newberry, and entered the land, 120 acres. John C. Miller served as justice of the peace for several years, and was also judge of Pulaski County, Mo., for four years. At the early age of fourteen years he enlisted in the War of 1812, and served three years, being crippled by a four-horse cannon wagon, which wound finally caused his death. He was a participant in the battle of Horse Shoe Bend. The following are the names of his children: Lea H., Chesteen, William W., George R., Mrs. R. A. Love, Mrs. Matthew Wynn, Mrs. John Welch and Mrs. E. P. Ferrill. The grandfather, George Miller, was born in Ireland, and was a harness maker and saddler. His wife, whose maiden name was Aggie Conley, was born in East Tennessee, and was of German descent. The maternal grandfather was a farmer. Lea H. Miller, whose name heads this sketch, was reared in his native county, and began life for himself at the age of twenty-three years. He was married in 1852 to Miss Nancy Jane Love, who was born in Knoxville, Tenn., in 1830, she being one of the children born to the marriage of Pleasant M. Love and Dialtha Armstrong, natives of Tennessee, in which State the father served as justice of the peace. He was a farmer, and at an early day moved to Missouri. Lea Miller's wife died in 1859, having borne two children: Letitia, wife of John Welch, and T. W., of Springfield, Mo. In 1865 Mr. Miller married Mrs. Mary (Holloman) Hawkins, a daughter of Edmund B. and Mary (Barrett) Holloman, who were born in North Carolina in 1773 and 1783, and died in 1843 and 1858, respectively. They moved to Tennessee in 1807, thence to Missouri in 1812, at the time of the great earthquake and sinking of that portion of the State. The father was a farmer, and at the age of sixteen years was drafted into the army to serve in the War of 1812. Mrs. Miller had one child by her first husband, Mrs. Mary E. Welch, of Rolla, Mo. She and Mr. Miller have one son, Lea E., who still makes his home with his parents. The family attend the Methodist Episcopal Church, South, and Mr. Miller is a Republican, and cast his first presidential vote for John C. Fremont.

Levi Mitchell, a prominent farmer of Spring Creek Township, and the son of William and Elizabeth (Stonecypher) Mitchell, was born in Morgan County, Tenn., March 22, 1842. William Mitchell was born in North Carolina, and there married in an early day, subsequently moving to Cape Girardeau County, Mo., where he bought a farm and settled on the Mississippi River. He afterward went back to Tennessee, but finally settled in Dent County, his death occurring in Phelps County, Mo., in 1880, at the age of eighty-four years. His wife was also born in North Carolina, in which State she was married, and by her union with Mr. Mitchell became the mother of twelve children, eight now living: Polly, Jane, Mahala, Andrew, Peter, William, Levi and Julius. The children deceased were named as follows: Sallie, Abigal, James and Jesse. Mrs. Mitchell also passed her last days in this county. Levi Mitchell, subject of this sketch, remained in Tennessee until sixteen years of age, after which he came to Missouri with his parents and settled in Dent County, where he finished his growth. He worked on the farm, receiving limited chances for an education, and at the breaking out of the late war enlisted in Company B, Missouri Volunteer Infantry. His war record is an interesting one. His brother William and himself were in the battle of Wilson's Creek, where the former was wounded and left. The latter then took part in the engagements at Drywood and Lexington; was taken sick, but rejoined the army at Springfield, meeting with his brother again. He was then discharged, returned home, and in the summer of 1862 the brothers enlisted in Colman's cavalry, and went to Batesville, there being dismounted. They were left at that place on account of sickness, and were discharged October 12, 1862, after which a journey, slow and painful, was commenced toward Missouri. At Mammoth Spring, the head of Spring River, bushwhackers were found who piloted the weary travelers home. A week after arriving Levi Mitchell was taken as a prisoner to Rolla, Phelps County, tried for his life, was discharged and came home. He was again taken—to Salem, but again discharged, since which time farming has been his occupation. Mr. Mitchell was married November 15, 1866, to Miss Susan E. Rheinerson, who was born and reared on the farm where they now live. Seven children were born to this union, six now living: Margaret E., Martha F., Cynthia A., Augusta I., Josie A. and Alfred L. The one deceased was named Nancy J. Since his marriage Mr. Mitchell has been engaged in farming, and is now the owner of 340 acres, 150 under cultivation. He is a member of the Agricultural Wheel, the Grange, and is a stanch Democrat in his political views.

Robert T. Parker, civil engineer and surveyor, Phelps County, Mo., was born in New Castle, County Limerick, Ireland, in 1826, and is a son of Robert and Elizabeth (O'Brien) Parker, who spent their entire lives in their native land. The father was a farmer and landlord, and a wealthy citizen. Robert T. is the tenth of their twelve children, and was educated in a private school, receiving excellent mathematical and classical training, and between the ages of twenty and twenty-two years was engaged in studying civil engineering, and in 1848 came to the United States. He spent some time in the South in the interests of the Mobile & Ohio Railroad as civil engineer, and in 1851 came to Missouri, and for nine consecutive years was connected with the Missouri Pacific Railroad. Since that time he has been in the employ of the St. Louis, Iron Mountain & Southern Railroad; the St. Louis & San Francisco Railroad; the Missouri & Western Railroad, and the Louisiana & Missouri River Railroad, which has occupied the greater part of his time up to the present date. He is one of the most thorough and practical civil engineers in Missouri, and has also done considerable work in Kansas and Arkansas for the 'Frisco Railway Company. In 1887 he was appointed by Gov. Marmaduke surveyor of Phelps County, and in November, 1888, was elected to the same office. He has always been a Democrat in politics, and an earnest worker for his party. He owns a farm of 120 acres near St. James, on which are 3,500 apple trees and 800 peach trees. Besides this property he has a residence in the town, all of which has been earned by his energy and judicious management. He is a member of the Masonic fraternity, Lodge No. 230, and also belongs to the Royal Arch Chapter of that order. He was married in Franklin County, in 1858, to Miss Sarah Smith, who was born in Missouri, and died in 1861, having borne one child that died one year later. In March, 1881, he was wedded to Miss Emma Vining, who was born in Indiana, and came to Missouri with her parents soon after the war.

They have one child. Mr. Parker belongs to the Protestant Episcopal Church, and his wife belongs to the Methodist.

Hon. Luman F. Parker, attorney at law, of Rolla, is a native of Lexington, Greene Co., N. Y., where he was born in 1847, being the son of Luman F. and Elizabeth (Wylie) Parker. Luman F. Parker, Sr., is a native of the State of New York, born in 1813, and his wife was born in the same year, also in that State. He was a machinist by trade, and when married was living in Shenango County, N. Y. He afterward located in Greene County, and in 1847 moved to New Britain, Conn., and thence to Meriden, Conn., where he now resides. He was for many years engaged in the manufacture of locks. The mother is also living. Of their five children Luman F. was the third, and was but six months old when his parents moved to Connecticut. He received a good academic education in New Britain, Conn., and in 1868 entered the teacher's profession, first coming to St. Charles County, Mo., where he taught one year, and then going to Franklin County, Mo., where he taught three years. In the fall of 1872 he came to Rolla, and was employed as principal of the public schools, it being the first term taught in the building now owned by the State School of Mines. During his teaching he commenced the study of law, and in 1873 was admitted to the bar in Rolla by Judge Elijah Perry. The year previous to this he was married to Miss Sallie B. Maupin, who was born in Franklin County, Mo., in 1851. They have three children: Luman F., Jackuelin O. and Grace M. Immediately after being admitted to the bar Mr. Parker entered upon the practice of his profession, and for four years was in partnership with Hon. E. A. Seay, of Salem. Hon. Luman F. Parker is one of the leading legal practitioners of Central Missouri, his practice extending over the Ninth and Eighteenth Judicial Circuits, or over nine counties. He is a man of great eloquence, and a man of force and power before a jury. He is one of the best civil lawyers in the State. In politics he is a stanch Republican; was a delegate to the national convention at Chicago in 1888, and for the past ten years has been a delegate to every State convention. He is the leading man of the Republican party in Phelps County, being a thorough organizer and political worker, and believing strictly in his party and its principles. Mr. Parker is a member of the Masonic order, Royal Arch, and has been Master of Lodge No. 213 at Rolla for the greater portion of the time in the past ten years. He is an ancient member of the I. O. O. F. lodge, and is attorney for the National Bank of Rolla.

James Ramsey, a successful tiller of the soil, was born August 26, 1848, in Maries County, Mo., being the son of Robert L. and Mary (Avery) Ramsey. Robert L. Ramsey was one of the pioneer settlers of Maries County; was a blacksmith by trade, and an excellent one at that, following the same for a number of years. He then engaged in the mercantile business in that county, and while a resident of that county, when it embraced Phelps, Maries and Pulaski, was assessor. He died in Maries County in 1885, at the age of nearly seventy-six years. His wife, Mary (Avery) Ramsey, was a native of Pennsylvania, and of German descent. She immigrated to Missouri, was here married to Mr. Ramsey, and bore him quite a family, four now living: James, Lewis N., Robert S. and Dinah. Mrs. Ramsey still survives, and is a resident of Maries County, Mo. James Ramsey, subject of this sketch, was reared principally on a farm in Maries County. He received a fair education, and remained at home until grown, after which he clerked for James Christmon in Dixon for three years. He then returned to Maries County, farmed for six years, and then came to Phelps County, where he now lives. He was married March 17, 1870, to Miss Malinda Christmon, daughter of James Christmon, and a native of Maries County, Mo. This union was blessed by the birth of twelve children, nine now living: Noah, Mary, Monroe, Ada, Robert L., Margaret, James, Cora and Charley. Three deceased were named Oliver, Beady and Bonie. When settling in this county, in 1881, Mr. Ramsey bought 300 acres of land, 100 being under cultivation, and now has 200 acres under cultivation, all fine bottom land. Mr. Ramsey has now turned his attention to stock raising, and is feeding 150 head of cattle. He also raises other stock. He is a Democrat in his political views.

Alexander J. Rauch. In all avocations in life, whether of a professional, commercial or agricultural nature, there are some men who, by their many sterling qualities, have attained prominence. Such a man is Mr. Rauch, who is one of the leading citizens and successful business men of Phelps County. He is one of five surviving members of a family of ten children, and was born in St. Clair County, Ill., in 1861, receiving his primary education in the district schools of his native county, and at the age of thirteen began attending the high-school of St. Louis, remaining in the latter three years. The two following years were spent in teaching school in St. Clair County, since which time he has been engaged in the milling business, first at Freeburg, Ill., afterward in Belleville, of that State, where he was assistant superintendent, and lastly at St. James, Mo., where he has been since 1883. He has been very successful throughout his business career, and through his good management and business ability has become the owner of 640 acres of land, 200 of which are under cultivation. At this time he is engaged in operating the flouring mills at this point, the only manufacturing establishment of the place. The company is known as the W. H. Bowles Milling Co., of which Mr. Rauch is secretary and superintendent. He has always labored in the interests of the Republican party, and his first presidential vote was cast for James G. Blaine, in 1884. He is a member in good standing of the A. O. U. W. His wife, whose maiden name was Miss Belle Dunlap, and whom he married in 1883, is a member of the Catholic Church. Mrs. Rauch was born in St. Clair County, Ill., and is the mother of two children. Her parents, Thomas and Nancy Dunlap, were also born in St. Clair County, and there the father died. The mother is living in Marshall, Mo., and is the widow of W. F. Bamber. Mr. Rauch is a son of John and Frederica (Telcher) Rauch, who were born in Germany in 1819 and 1825, respectively. The former came to the United States in 1830, and the latter in 1842. They were married in St. Clair County, Ill., about 1846, and are still living. The father is a well-to-do farmer, and from 1868 to 1870 was engaged in manufacturing agricultural implements in Carlinville, Ill. His father, John William Rauch, came to the United States in 1830, and died in St. Clair County.

Charles Roster, life insurance and real estate agent, also general merchant, at St. James, Mo., was born in Hesse Darmstadt, Germany, in 1848, and is a son of Henry and Margaret (Goff) Roster, who were born in Waldeck, Hesse Cassel, in 1822 and 1820, respectively, and in 1851 came to the United States, and after residing in Ross County, Ohio, until 1867, came to Phelps County, Mo. They have since resided near St. James, and have two good farms, comprising 720 acres in all, with 300 acres under cultivation. The father has also followed the occupation of iron-making, off and on, throughout life, but since his residence in Phelps County has given the most of his attention to farming. Charles Roster is the eldest of their seven children, five of whom are living, and was only four years of age when brought to the United States. All his schooling was received in Ohio before he was fourteen years of age, but by self-application since becoming grown he has acquired a good education. About 1874 he began farming for himself, which occupation he gave up to engage in the saloon business two years later, and in 1878 engaged in clerking, continuing three years, in the dry goods house of Sutton & Young. In 1881 he again embarked in business on his own responsibility, but in 1883 his brother, Christopher, became his partner, the firm being known as Roster & Bro. until October, 1887, when Charles retired. Some time prior to this, however, he had been selling the Osborne Harvester and Mower, and is now engaged in that business, and is also a successful life insurance and real estate agent, and is about to embark in the mercantile business again at St. James. He has served on the town board three terms of several years each, and has been a member of the school board many years. He has ever been an active worker for the Republican party, and his first presidential vote was cast for Hayes, in 1886. He is also a member of the A. O. U. W., and in March, 1880, was married to Miss Elizabeth Auckman, who was born in Austria, and at an early day came with her father, Andrew Auckman, to the United States. The latter served the full term in the army of his native country, and is now a farmer, residing in Crawford County. Mr. Roster is the father of three children, and is sparing no pains to give them good educations.

James B. Sally, clerk of the county court of Phelps County, Mo., was elected to his office in November, 1886, by a Democratic majority of 611 votes, this being the largest majority ever received in the county with or without opposition. Mr. Sally was born in Phelps County May 27, 1857, and was educated in the public schools and the School of Metallurgy at Rolla. After residing until twenty years of age on his father's farm, he engaged in teaching school as a means of gaining a livelihood, and taught one term at Elm Spring. In 1878 he was appointed deputy county clerk, and served until 1886, with the exception of one year, 1882, when he acted in the capacity of deputy collector. In 1883 he was married to Sarah, a daughter of ex-Judge John R. Bowman, whose sketch appears in another part of this work. She was born in Phelps County, was educated in the common schools, and by Mr. Sally became the mother of two children. Mr. Sally cast his first presidential vote for Hancock in 1880. He has taken all the degrees in the Masonic fraternity, being at the present time a Knights Templar, and is also a member of the I. O. O. F., Cuba Encampment. Mrs. Sally is a member in good standing in the Christian Church. Mr. Sally is a son of John A., and grandson of George Sally, who was born in Franklin, Ky., in 1806, and is of French descent. When he was a very small boy his parents died, and he was taken to rear by an uncle, with whom he remained until he was ten years of age, and then started out in life for himself. Two years later he landed in Phelps County, Mo., with a party of emigrants, and here he grew to manhood and afterward made his home. He was married to a Miss Lenox, who bore him four children, John A. being the second child, and for fifty-five years resided on one farm, which consisted of 600 acres, and is at present in possession of his heirs. He died on the 12th of March, 1888. His wife died many years ago. His son, John A., was born in Phelps County, Mo., in the 30's, and was reared on the farm on which he now resides. His marriage with Miss Margaret Coppedge was celebrated in Phelps County in 1853. She was born in the county in 1833, and is a daughter of Henson and Nancy (Kitchen) Coppedge, who were born in Kentucky, and came to Phelps County about 1820, being among the first white settlers of this part of the State. Mr. Coppedge was a prosperous merchant for many years, and died in the county in November, 1888, in his eighty-eighth year. He was a member of the Old School Baptist Church.

Hiram M. Shaw, proprietor of the Grant House, of Rolla, Mo., was born in Washington County, N. Y., in 1827, and is the son of Hiram and Lois (Miller) Shaw, and grandson of Thomas Shaw, who was born at Middleburg, Mass., May 1, 1753. Hiram Shaw, Sr., was born in Lee, Mass., November 1, 1794, and was a contractor and builder by occupation. When a young man he went to Hampton, N. Y., where he married, February 10, 1820, Miss Lois Miller, who was born January 25, 1798, in Hampton, N. Y. She was a sister of Rev. William Miller, who predicted that the world would come to an end in 1843, and all his followers were known the world over as "Millerites." Mrs. Shaw, however, was not a follower. Hiram Shaw was a soldier in the War of 1812. He died in 1852, and his wife died January 14, 1886. They were the parents of five children, only three now living: Lois E., wife of Levi W. Manchester, who resides on the old homestead of Hiram Shaw; Hiram M., and George T., who is in San Francisco, Cal., engaged as a lumber merchant. Hiram M. Shaw was educated in the common schools of his native county, and remained with his parents until twenty years of age, when he commenced learning the carpenter's and builder's trade, remaining three years before he was responsible for his work. He worked as a journeyman for a short time, after which he commenced on his own responsibility, erecting farm houses in his native county. In 1855 he followed Horace Greeley's advice, and started westward, landing at Dubuque, Iowa, where he took a clerkship in the Julian House for two years. In the year 1860 he went still farther west, and at last found himself at Pike's Peak, Col., but in January, 1862, he returned to Dubuque,

Iowa, and in the fall of the same year he came to St. Louis, Mo., where he entered the Government service at Jefferson Barracks. He here superintended the building of the hospitals, and after the war was employed to superintend the erection of warehouses and magazines for the navy. After remaining in the employ of the Government for four years, in 1867 he became a resident of Rolla, and here followed agricultural pursuits for one year. February 1, 1869, he leased a small frame house and commenced keeping hotel. He remained in this house until 1876, when a stock company was formed to erect a new brick hotel, with Mr. Shaw the principal stockholder. They erected a three-story brick, 35x70 feet, and in 1883 an addition of 38x75 feet was added. The house was named Grant House, and is one of the best equipped hotels in South Central Missouri. It contains thirty sleeping rooms and an opera hall. The entire building cost about $25,000, Mr. Shaw being the one who planned the design. In 1857 he married Miss Josephine A. Hunter, a native of Fort Edwards, N. Y., and to this union were born three children: Lois J., Kate E. (deceased) and Josephine A. Mrs. Shaw died in July, 1866, and January 29, 1874, Mr. Shaw married Miss Mary A. Clark, who was born in Fair Haven, Vt., and who bore him three children: Olive Helen, Hiram Miller and Oliver Clark. Mr. Shaw is a man who thoroughly understands the hotel business, and has been instrumental in making the Grant House what it now is. He keeps the best hotel in South Central Missouri, and his house is widely known as being a first-class hotel in the fullest sense of the term. He is an affable and pleasant gentleman, and his wife and daughter Lois are most estimable ladies, looking carefully after the interests and comfort of the guests of the hotel. Mr. Shaw is a Republican in politics; was a member of the school board six years, and was president of the board for the same length of time.

Hon. F. W. Shinman, farmer and stock dealer, of Phelps County, Mo., was born in Erie County, N. Y., in 1842, being a son of Adam and Henrietta Shinman, who were born in Germany in 1805 and 1818, respectively. After having borne five children the mother died, but the date of her death is not known. Her sister afterward married Mr. Shinman, and their union was blessed in the birth of four children. Mr. Shinman died in Erie County, N. Y., in 1872. At the age of sixteen years F. W. Shinman left home and began learning the cooper's trade in Niagara County, N. Y., and in 1865 was married to Miss Rose Barns, of Oakland County, Mich. She was born in Bristol County, that State, in 1845, and became the mother of six children: F. W., Jr., Etta, Albert, Lena, Walter and Louis. Soon after his marriage Mr. Shinman engaged in the cooper business at Auburn, Mich., but afterward located at Mulford, being also joint owner and manager of a saw-mill at East Saginaw. In 1876 he moved to Rolla, Mo., where he engaged in manufacturing barrels for the Rolla Flouring Mills, continuing two years, and then purchased a half interest in a saloon, and also embarked in buying stock and grain. In 1882 the saloon caught fire and was burned to the ground, but Mr. Shinman soon after built a brick building at his own expense, but sold out the following year, and purchased the farm of 240 acres on which he is now residing, and on which he has lived since 1888. He was recently elected on the Democratic ticket to represent Phelps County in the State Legislature, and since childhood has been a member of the Lutheran Church. He is a Mason, and his wife is a member of the Methodist Episcopal Church, South.

John L. Short, M. D., surgeon in charge of the Rolla Eye, Ear, Nose and Throat Infirmary, of Rolla, was born at Iberia, Miller Co., Mo., in 1853, being the son of Evan L., and Nancy A. (Jones) Short, grandson of Ruben Short, and great-grandson of John Short, who was born in Virginia in 1756, and died in Linn County, Iowa, in 1836. His wife, Mary Hansford, was born in 1758, and died in 1821. She spoke and read the German language. John Short was of Welsh descent; was a Baptist minister, but in the year 1825 he and his son, Wesley Short, Alexander Campbell and B. W. Stone renounced the Baptist doctrine, and took up the Christian faith. John Short immigrated to Kentucky in pioneer times, and lived on bear meat one year. He was a soldier in the Revolutionary War. Ruben Short was born October 15, 1794, in West Virginia, and he and his father, John Short, moved to Kentucky, and from Kentucky to Linn County, Iowa, in 1817. In 1830 Ruben Short moved to Greene County, Iowa, and in three years moved to Sangamon County, Ill., where he purchased 200 acres of land. In 1837 he sold out for $5 per acre, and moved to Miller County, Mo. He died in Arkansas in 1867. Evan L. Short went to Illinois with his parents, and in the winter of 1835 went to Linn County, Iowa, where he taught his first term of school. In 1837 he went to Miller County, Mo., and hauled goods from St. Louis, Mo., one trip taking him thirteen days. He made a trip south to Mississippi and Louisiana with a drove of horses, and sold out and boarded a steamer at Vicksburg and returned home. After returning north he entered a select school for a term of six months; in fact all his education was received by private instructions. In 1838–39 he taught a public school two terms in Cole County, Mo., near Jefferson City, and in 1840 taught a school in Miller County. During his teaching he commenced reading medicine. In 1841 he married Miss Nancy Ann Jones, who was born in 1824, and who was the daughter of William B. and Didama (Burks) Jones. In 1844 Evan L. Short moved to Benton County, and the following year to Morgan County, and two years later returned to Miller County, where he has since resided. Evan L. Short practiced medicine for over twenty years, but the past few years he retired to quiet life. He is the father of eleven children, six sons and five daughters, Dr. John L. Short being the sixth child in order of birth. He received a good literary education in the common schools, was reared on the farm until twenty-one years of age, and was never out of the sight of his mother two days at a time during that time. He commenced the study of medicine under his father at an early age, and in 1874 commenced practicing in Dyer County, Tenn. He was there three years, and then returned home and located at Crocker, Pulaski Co., Mo., where he practiced until 1884. In 1878 he married Miss Martha Jane Tramble, who was born in Van Burensburg, Ill., in 1863. They have two children: Rosa E. and Nancy A. In 1884 Dr. Short removed to Kansas City, and attended the medical department of the University of Kansas City, where he graduated as an M. D. He practiced his profession in Kansas City until 1887. In 1887 he came to Rolla, Mo., where he commenced his practice. In September, 1888, he founded the Eye and Ear Infirmary of Rolla, securing the assistance of the leading physicians and best business men of Rolla. For the short time it has been organized the institution has grown rapidly, and the Doctor is meeting with marked success, having patients from several States, and a large patronage at home, and all are fully satisfied with the treatment. Dr. Short is a very skillful physician and surgeon, and has gained a wide-spread reputation as an eye and ear specialist, which is due to the remarkable cures that follow his treatment. He is a member of the Rolla District Medical Society, is a member of the I. O. O. F., the A. O. U. W., is a Republican in politics, and he and wife are members of the Christian Church.

Joseph A. Smith, retired merchant of Rolla, is a native of Grainger County, Tenn., and was born in 1832. He remained on his father's farm until sixteen years of age, when he commenced as a salesman in a general store, which business he followed until hostilities broke out between the North and South. His sympathies being with the Southern people caused him to enlist in the Confederate army, in April, 1862, in Company I, Fifty-ninth Regiment Tennessee Infantry Volunteers. He was in the siege of Vicksburg, New Hope Church, and all through the battles in the Shenandoah Valley, being in many severe skirmishes. He was captured at Vicksburg, and after being exchanged was in the cavalry service. He was in service until peace was declared, after which he returned home, and in 1866 immigrated to Phelps County, Mo., where he and T. C. Harrison established a general store at Arlington. In about three years Mr. Smith sold his interest to Mr. Harrison and came to Rolla, where he resumed merchandising. December 31, 1868, Mr. Smith married Miss Mary E. Godwin, of Grainger County, Tenn., where she was born in 1843. The fruits of this union are seven children: Ella, Tenna, Carrie, Joseph H., James M., Annie and Kate. After coming to Rolla Mr. Smith followed merchandising until the spring of 1888. For the last four years the firm was Smith Bros., he and his brother, James L., being the partnership. Mrs. Smith is a member of the Missionary Baptist Church. Mr. Smith is a Democrat in politics, and was tax collector of Grainger County one term. He is the son of Samuel and Elizabeth (Dyer) Smith, and grandson of Thomas Smith, who was a native of Virginia. [For further particulars of parents see sketch of James L. Smith.]

James L. Smith, collector of Phelps County, Mo., was born in Grainger County, Tenn., in 1834, and his parents, Samuel and Elizabeth (Dyer) Smith, were both natives of the last named county, born in 1809 and 1808, respectively. Samuel Smith was a farmer, merchant, distiller and blacksmith by occupation. He was quite a successful business man, being worth $40,000 before the war, but lost it all during that struggle. In 1868 he immigrated to Phelps County, Mo., where he died in 1881. His wife died in 1851. They were the parents of nine children, James L. being the third child. He assisted on the farm until sixteen years of age, and then went to Loudon, where he hired as a salesman in a general store. Here he remained four years, and then clerked on a steamer in the Tennessee River a few months. In 1855 and 1856 he was in Texas, and in 1858 went to California, where he remained until 1860. The year following he enlisted in Company I, Fourth Battalion Tennessee Cavalry, and was in service four years. He was in the fight at Champion's Hill, siege of Vicksburg, Winchester, Charleston, and many severe skirmishes, but never received a wound. He surrendered at Knoxville after peace was declared. In 1865 he left his native State, immigrated to Phelps County, Mo., and here hired to Joseph Campbell in the mercantile business, where he remained four years. In 1867 he married Miss Anastasia Rayl, a native of Cooper County, Mo., born in 1842, and they have seven children: William H., Edmund W., Joseph S., Charles B., Wesley M., Allen and Frank (twins). In 1872 Mr. Smith was elected sheriff, was re-elected in 1874, and from 1876 to 1880 he was engaged in farming and merchandising. In the last named year he was elected treasurer of Phelps County, and two years later was re-elected. From 1884 to 1888 he followed farming and sold goods. In November, 1888, he was elected as county collector of Phelps County. Mr. Smith is the owner of 320 acres of land, located eight miles north of the county seat. He has been a life-long Democrat in his political principles; is a Royal Arch Mason, a member of the A. O. U. W., and Mrs. Smith is a member of the Missionary Baptist Church.

Ernst Soest, farmer, and agent at Rolla for the Anheuser-Busch Brewing Company, of St. Louis, is a native of the Kingdom of Prussia, Germany, born in 1844, and is the son of Ernst and Emily von Soest. Ernst von Soest, Sr., was a farmer by occupation, and the subject of this sketch was reared to agricultural life on a North German estate. In 1863 he was one year in the regular army, and in 1867 came to the United States and direct to Rolla, Mo., where he purchased a farm of 310 acres, one and one-half miles east of the county seat, where he has since resided. In 1872 he established an ice house on the farm, and has since supplied the city of Rolla with ice, putting up 250 tons per annum. In 1885 he became agent for Anheuser-Busch, of St. Louis, to handle their beer, and his territory includes Pulaski, Phelps, Texas, Dent, Shannon, Maries and Crawford Counties. Mr. Soest has 250 acres under cultivation, and has one of the finest farms in Phelps County. He has the farm well improved, with fine buildings, pastures, fish ponds, etc., and has a beautiful place. Mr. Soest is a good business man, and one of Rolla's most solid citizens. In 1875 he married Miss Anna Schelling, who is a native of Germany, born in 1854, she having come to this country in 1872. They have three children: Adelia, Walter and Herbert. Mr. Soest is a Republican in politics, is a member of the Knights of Honor, also the Knights of Pythias, and he and wife are members of the German Lutheran Protestant Church.

J. L. Stewart, freight conductor on the St. Louis & San Francisco Railroad, between Newburg and St. Louis, is a native of Adams County, Ohio, where he was born in 1849, being a son of J. M. and

Martha J. (Ellis) Stewart, who were also natives of the "Buckeye State." The father is still living, but the mother died when her son, J. L., was about ten months old. The latter grew to manhood on his father's farm, and received his education in the common schools and the National Normal School at Lebanon, Ohio, which institution he attended two and one-half years, graduating in 1865. He was then engaged in teaching the "young idea" for about five years, and served as superintendent of the Western Union public schools in the county of his birth. About 1872 he came to St. Louis, Mo., and worked as book-keeper for Alex. Repine for about two years. He then went to Vinita, Ind. Ter., and took charge of the St. Louis & San Francisco Railway Company's yards, and with the exception of three years, from 1883 to 1886, has been in the employ of that company ever since in various capacities, but principally as yard master. By his industry and good management he has become the owner of a fine farm of 220 acres, and is considered by all to be an enterprising and successful business man. He is a member of the I. O. O. F., the Knights of Honor, and is a Knights Templar in the Masonic fraternity, and belonging to St. Louis Commandery No. 1. He has always been a Democrat in politics, and October 10, 1880, was married at Rolla to Miss Susan Cansler, who was born in Tennessee, and came with her parents, Nathaniel and Martha Cansler, to Rolla. Here they both died. The father was a carpenter. Mr. and Mrs. Stewart have two little children. Mrs. Stewart is a member of the Methodist Church.

William Stimson has been a general merchant of St. James, Mo., since 1884, and was born about ninety miles from London, England, in 1848. His parents, William and Jane (Gregory) Stimson, were also of English birth, and when our subject was about two years of age immigrated to the United States, locating in Cleveland, Ohio, where they made their home until about 1859, at which time they took up their abode in Phelps County, Mo., settling about twelve miles south of St. James, where the family still owns a good farm. The father was killed about 1874 by a runaway horse. He was a brick mason by trade, and while residing in his native land was a member of the I. O. O. F. The mother is still living, and resides at St. James, aged about seventy-three years, and is a worthy and consistent member of the Episcopal Church. William Stimson is the third of their four children, and received his education in the public schools of Cleveland, Ohio. After coming to Missouri he clerked in St. James for a number of years, and then engaged in merchandising at Stimson's Iron Bank, on their farm, where he continued until 1884, since which time he has resided in St. James. He carries a stock valued at about $2,000. He has served as postmaster of St. James about four years, and is a stanch Republican in politics, and is an active worker for that party. He is a member of the A. F. & A. M. and the A. O. U. W. October 25, 1887, he was married to Miss Lizzie M., a daughter of Richard and Elizabeth Chandler, of Cleveland, Ohio. The father was formerly a sailor. Mrs. Stimson is a member of the Baptist Church.

William Ten Eyck, farmer of Phelps County, Mo., but retired merchant of St. James, was born in Wyoming County, N. Y., in 1827, and is a son of William and Chloe (Warren) Ten Eyck, who were born in Summerville, N. J., and on the Mohawk River, N. Y., respectively. They resided near New York City until shortly before their deaths, when they went to their son William's in Pennsylvania, and there the mother died in 1863, at the age of seventy years. The father died at St. James, Mo., in 1871, aged eighty-seven years. He was a shoemaker and tanner by trade, and was a son of Rev. Coonrod Ten Eyck, who was born in New Jersey, and was of Low Dutch origin. He was a descendant of one of three brothers who came to America at a very early day and settled in New Jersey. Coonrod served in the Revolutionary War, and throughout life was a Presbyterian minister, and died in Wyoming County, N. Y., where he had lived many years. The grandfather of our subject, Mr. Warren, was a prominent and wealthy citizen of York State. William Ten Eyck, whose name heads this sketch, is the ninth of fourteen children, and was educated in the public schools of New York. In 1848 he went to Curwensville, Penn., where he was successfully engaged in the mercantile business for twenty years. While there he was married in 1855 to Miss Jane Thompson, who was born in Pennsylvania, and by her became the father of five children, four of whom are living. Mr. Ten Eyck resided in Pennsylvania until 1869, then came to St. James, and was engaged in merchandising with his usual success for about twelve years. Since that time he has been engaged in farming and stock raising, and besides his 400-acre farm has twenty acres of well-improved town property. He has always been industrious and enterprising, and has spared no pains to educate his children, and has always been ready to support laudable enterprises. He has been a Republican all his life, and his first presidential vote was cast for Gen. Taylor in 1848. He and wife are worthy members of the Presbyterian Church. Their son, John W. Ten Eyck, is agent and operator for the St. Louis & San Francisco Railway at St. James, which position he has held since December 27, 1884. He was born in Curwensville, Penn., in 1859, and came with his parents to Phelps County, Mo., in 1869. He was educated at St. James, and spent much of his time working in his father's mercantile establishment, being now a member of the firm. He is an active worker for the Republican party, and his first presidential vote was cast for Garfield in 1880. He is a bright and enterprising young man, and is a member of the A. O. U. W. Mrs. Ten Eyck's parents, John and Sarah Thompson, were of Irish and German descent, respectively, and were natives of Pennsylvania. The father was judge of the county court of Clearfield County for a number of years, and also held the office of justice of the peace. He was a blacksmith by trade.

Lewis Henry Thompson, proprietor of the livery and feed stable of Rolla, was born in Dutchess County, N. Y., in 1842, and is the son of Platt and Harriet (White) Thompson. The father was born in Connecticut in 1813, was a farmer by occupation, was married in Dutchess County, N. Y., and in 1856 he moved to Kalamazoo County, Mich. He died in 1883. The mother was born in 1817 in New York, and is yet living. Of the two children born to their union Lewis Henry Thompson was the elder. George F. is engaged in farming four miles from Rolla. Lewis H. was educated in the common schools of New York State and Michigan. At the age of fifteen he commenced book-keeping in Kalamazoo, Mich., and there continued ten years. He was quartermaster clerk in the army in 1864 and 1865, and also spent one year at Jefferson Barracks. He then spent a year on the plains on an expedition against the Indians. During the year 1866 he kept books at Little Rock, Ark., and in 1867 he became a citizen of Rolla, where he established a livery and feed stable, continuing ever since in the business. He first started on a very small scale, had only one horse, and the first man he hired it to never returned it, and he was compelled to start anew. His first experience did not prevent him from buying other horses and starting out again. From that time until the present he has gradually been increasing his business, until at the present date he has the best livery and feed stable in South Central Missouri. In 1877 he erected his present barn, which is 57x80 feet, and stables seventy-five horses. At present Mr. Thompson has twenty horses, twenty vehicles, a hearse, and everything pertaining to a first-class stable. This is the only stable in Rolla. Mr. Thompson is a perfect gentleman, and is respected by all. He has never married, and his mother keeps house for him. He is a Republican in politics, and was a member of the city council of Rolla one term. Mrs. Thompson is a member of the Presbyterian Church.

William Vetter, dealer in wines and fancy liquors at St. James, Mo., is a native of Prussia, born in 1838, and is a son of Clarl and Frederica Vetter, who were born and always resided in Prussia. William attended school until fourteen years of age, and then learned the trade of baker, working at that five years. He was a soldier in the Prussian War, and participated in the war with Austria. In 1867 he came to the United States, and worked in Columbus, Ohio, until 1871, at which time he came to Missouri, and spent some time working in the iron mines near St. James. While engaged in this employment he was buried in the mines, but was finally rescued, but received injuries which nearly caused his death and which have left him a cripple for life, he being unable to stand for six months. He afterward found employment in the Meramec Iron Works, in Phelps County, near St. James, but was compelled to work for a long time in a sitting posture before he was able to stand and do his work, and even at the present time it is impossible for him to perform manual labor. In 1876 he established his present business, which he has conducted with success, and in addition to this work he has been quite extensively engaged in dealing in live stock, and is a thorough-going, enterprising, and consequently successful, business man. He started in life with no capital, but by good management and industry has become the owner of 325 acres of land near St. James and eighty acres in Crawford County. In 1877 he was married to Miss Margaret Sigler, who is of German birth, and by her is the father of five children, three boys and two girls. Mr. Vetter is a Republican in his political views. He owns good property in the town of St. James.

John Weber, an old and highly esteemed citizen, residing on Corn Creek, in Spring Creek Township, three miles northwest of Edgar Springs, was born in the city of Philadelphia, Penn., on the 24th of

January, 1819, his parents being John M. and Elizabeth (McQueen) Weber. The father was born near the river Rhine, in Holland, November 10, 1794, and at the age of twelve years came to the United States with his mother and one brother, and settled in Philadelphia, where he grew to manhood and was married. He learned and worked at the baker's trade in Philadelphia, but about 1823 moved to Rutherford County, Tenn., and engaged in farming. He knew nothing of this business, but was taught by his wife, who was born in Prince George County, Va., October 18, 1793. They lived in Tennessee until 1830, then moving to Saline County, Ill., where the father died in 1867 and the mother in 1869. John Weber, whose name heads this sketch, is the second of eight sons and three daughters, and remained with his parents until nineteen years of age. September 17, 1840, he married Eliza J. Powell, who was born in Gallatin County, Ill., January 22, 1824. In 1844 he became a citizen of Phelps County, Mo., and located adjoining the present site of Rolla, and here he erected the first house in that section. In 1876 he moved to the farm where he now lives, his acreage consisting of 580 acres. His wife died in September, 1859, having borne a family of ten children: John O., who died in 1860; Elizabeth (deceased), died in 1882, the wife of William Yowell; William E.; James H., who died in 1884; Annie J., wife of A. J. Weber, her cousin; Mary E., died in 1859; Archibald N.; Margaret E., who died in 1887, the wife of James Ray; Americus C., and Joseph M. (deceased), died in 1860. In March, 1860, Mr. Weber married Mrs. Sarah Crites, who was born in Tennessee, and died in 1862, having borne one child, Sarah E., who is deceased. On the 22d of February, 1863, he married Mrs. Lucinda F. Yowell, *nee* Sally. She was born in Phelps County, Mo., in 1836, and she and Mr. Weber are the parents of eight children: George E.; Mattie A., wife of James Dunham; Laura, wife of Louis Aurebach; Minnie L. (deceased), died in 1873; Andrew J., Charles A., Albert F. and Nellie I. Mr. Weber is one of the oldest citizens of Phelps County, and commands the respect and esteem of all who know him. He has been a life-long Democrat in politics, and has shown his brotherly spirit by joining the Masonic order and the I. O. O. F.

DENT COUNTY.

Dr. W. L. Arnot, merchant and farmer of Dent County, Mo., was born in Jefferson County, Tenn., in 1830, and is a son of Holbert and Elizabeth (Kirkpatrick) Arnot, both of whom were born in the "Old Dominion." The former was born about 1790, and died about 1845, in Jefferson County, Tenn., being of Scotch-Irish descent, and a farmer by occupation. Mrs. Arnot was born about 1795, and died about 1842. Eight of their ten children grew to maturity, Dr. W. L. Arnot being the fifth of the family. After his parents' death he went to North Carolina, where he made his home with a sister for three years, and then returned to Tennessee and worked at the cabinet trade for a short time, but owing to ill health was obliged to give up this trade. He then entered Tuscalum College, and at the end of one year was transferred to Hiwassee College, which institution he attended three years. The following three years were spent in reading medicine under Dr. Drake, of St. Clair, Tenn., and after passing examination under the medical board of that place he was given a diploma. He then moved to Cole County, Mo., and the first year taught school and practiced his profession, but shortly after gave all his attention to the latter occupation, and became one of the leading physicians of the county. In 1864 he was arrested on a charge of being disloyal to the Government, and was taken to St. Louis for trial, and was sentenced to the military prison at Alton, Ill., for five years at hard labor. He was there from May till November, and was then sent to Polk Island, Ill., to take charge of the hospital as physician, and there remained until February of the next year, when he succeeded in making his escape (one of the most remarkable as well as notable incidents of the war), and went to Macoupin County, Ill., where he enlisted in the Union army, and was mustered in at Jacksonville. He served in Company G, Twenty-eighth Regiment Illinois Veteran Volunteers, and at the close of the war was sent to the Rio Grande River with the Thirteenth Army Corps, being mustered out of the service at Brownsville, Texas, May 9, 1866. He then returned to Dent County, Mo., and resumed the practice of his profession and teaching school, following the latter occupation two terms in the town of Salem. He also sold drugs and practiced his profession in Dent County until 1871, when he sold out and purchased his present farm. From that date until 1876 he practiced medicine in Arkansas, but at the latter date he and family moved to the farm, and he has since given the most of his attention to farming, stock raising and merchandising. His farm consists of 480 acres, with 130 under cultivation, and is well improved, with a two-story frame dwelling, and besides this he has two 120-acre farms and forty acres in another. September 23, 1877, he was married to Lucy J. Brigman, who was born in Dent County, Mo., in 1846, and is a daughter of Edmond and Nancy Brigman. They have three children. Dr. Arnot is a Republican, and is a member of the Second Advent Church.

John Arthur, tiller of the soil and stock raiser of Watkin Township, was born in Washington (now Marion) County, Ky., March 20, 1814, and is one of the old and enterprising citizens of the township. He is the son of Barnabas and Nancy (Vaughn) Arthur, the former probably a native of Virginia, and the latter a native of Washington County, Ky. The mother died a few years after her marriage, and the father married again and removed to Boone's Lick, in North Missouri, where he spent one year, returned to Kentucky, and at the end of one year removed to Franklin County, Mo., and again returned to Kentucky, but later removed to Crawford County, Mo., where they both, father and step-mother, passed their last days. Mr. Arthur was one of the pioneers of South Missouri, settling there when it was a wilderness, and when it was probably a Territory. He reared four sons and a daughter, John Arthur being the only one living of the first family. He was reared principally where Meramec Iron Works were when that country was one vast wilderness, teeming with bear, wolves, panthers, elk, deer, etc., and it was common for fifteen years to see from 1,000 to 1,500 Shawnee Indians. He was reared with very little schooling, and when not working, generally spent a great deal of his spare time in hunting with the Indians, and learning the Shawnee language, in which he learned to converse readily. Before he was twelve years of age he had killed bear. When old enough, he began working in the old Meramec Iron Works, where he was employed until twenty-four years of age. In 1839 he married Miss Elizabeth, daughter of Samuel and Elizabeth Hyer, whose sketch appears in another part of this work. Mrs. Arthur was born in Cumberland County, Penn., and by her union to Mr. Arthur became the mother of twelve children, five now living: Mattie, wife of Dr. Frank Craven, of Licking; Dr. Samuel, of Phelps County; Alice, wife of Alfred Craven of Licking; Anna Mary, wife of J. H. McFarland, and Kate, wife of Joseph Hodges. The eldest, a daughter, named Julia, died in 1883, leaving her husband, James T. Whitelaw, a lawyer, now of Dodge City, Kas., and three children. When first married Mr. Arthur settled on his present farm, on Hyer's Branch of Dry Fork, and was one of the first settlers of that creek. Here he has since lived, and is one of the prominent and enterprising farmers and extensive land-owners of the county, owning about 1,400 acres, with about 300 under cultivation. He began life in the woods, coming to his home with a yoke of cattle and a cart, the latter containing all his household effects. He has hauled wheat to St. Louis for 50 cents a bushel, with an ox team, taking twenty days to make the trip, when he would lay in a supply of groceries for one year. The nearest post-office at that time was Meramec Iron Works. By industry, economy and good management he has accumulated a good property, and now, when getting old, can enjoy the result of his labor. He has long been known as an honest, industrious and upright citizen, and at present is largely engaged in stock raising, and is making considerable effort to improve the grade of stock in the county. He has taken an active part in upbuilding the county, and has spared no pains to educate his children. The eldest was educated at the Convent of Visitation, St. Louis. The son is a graduate of Missouri Medical College, and is now a successful practicing physician of Phelps County, Edgar's Prairie. The remainder of the children were educated principally at home, by private tutors. Mr. Arthur is a Democrat in his political views, his first presidential vote being for Martin Van Buren in 1836. He has been a member of the Masonic fraternity for forty years, Royal Arch degree, and Mrs. Arthur has been a member of the old Primitive Baptist Church since May, 1888.

Samuel Asbridge is a native of North Carolina, born in 1812, and is a son of Joseph and Sarah (Pounds) Asbridge, who were born in Maryland and North Carolina, in 1750 and 1752, and died in Kentucky in 1835 and 1826, respectively. The father was a farmer, and his father was also an agriculturist, of English birth, and a soldier in the Revolutionary War. Samuel Asbridge is the seventh of eight children (six of whom grew to maturity), and made the paternal roof his home until after the death of his mother. He received very meager school advantages, and at an early day began earning his own living. In 1833 he was united in marriage to Jane Bonner, who was a daughter of William and Anna Bonner, and was born in Tennessee in 1814, and died in 1871, having borne seven children, only one, a daughter, now living. After his marriage Mr. Asbridge resided in the State of Kentucky two years, and from that time until 1852 resided in Tennessee, and at the latter date took up his abode in Dent County, Mo., where he has continued to reside up to the present time, having spent the time in farming with the exception of two years, when he was engaged in the livery business in Salem. He owned at one time 640 acres, but now owns only 257½ acres, with 100 acres under cultivation. In 1885 he deeded one and a half acres on which to erect a church, which is denominated the Union Church, and is the largest country place of worship in the county. February 14, 1874, he was married to Mrs. Elizabeth Price, widow of William Price, and daughter of John and Rachel Hagler. She is of German descent, was born in Union County, Ill., in 1844, and became the mother of three children, two of whom are living: Sidney L., who was born June 1, 1873, and is the wife of H. Pewett, and Rachel Melvina, who was born in August, 1875. In 1865 he enlisted in the Eighty-fourth Regiment Missouri Infantry, Federal service, and since the late Civil War has been a Republican in politics. He and wife are members of the Christian Church.

Rev. John M. Ashlock, assistant manager and wood receiver of Sligo Furnace, was born in Washington County, Mo., in 1842, and is the son of Benjamin and Mary (Robinson) Ashlock, the father born in Obion County, Tenn., about 1823, and the mother in St. Francois County, Mo. They were married in Washington County, and there the father died in 1846. The mother afterward married William Polk. She was a member of the Baptist Church, and died in October, 1883. Mr. Ashlock was a mason by occupation, and the son of Col. James Ashlock, who was of German origin, and who was reared in Obion County, Tenn. He was a mason and furnace builder, and a colonel in the War of 1812, under Jackson. His father, William Ashlock, was a native of Germany, and came as a soldier to the American colonies with Gen. Braddock, being with him in his defeat in the French and Indian War. He served with Gen. Washington all through the Revolutionary War, serving as national guard, and was present at the Declaration of Independence. He was a firm friend and associate of Gen. Washington. John Robinson, the maternal grandfather of subject, was a native of Ireland, and came to the United States when young. He settled in St. Francois County, Mo., at quite an early date, followed farming, and finally died in Washington County, where he had moved. Rev. John M. Ashlock was the eldest of three children, and received a limited education in the common schools, being obliged to go six miles, that being the nearest school. At the age of about eighteen or twenty he began for himself as a farm hand, but soon after was employed by an iron company at Irondale, and has been connected with the iron works more or less ever since. In 1861 he married Miss Henrietta Brooks, who was born in Kentucky, and who died in 1880, leaving three children. In 1881 Mr. Ashlock took for his second wife Miss.

Lizzie, daughter of Henry and Mary Benson, of Kentucky and Iowa, respectively. Mrs. Ashlock was born in Phelps County, Mo., where her father died. Her mother is still living. Mr. Ashlock's last union resulted in the birth of two children. Mr. Ashlock has always been a great reader of good literature, and although his education was rather limited, he has, by his own efforts, become a well-informed man. In 1864 he joined Company B, Fifth Missouri Volunteer Infantry, as a regular color bearer with the rank of corporal. He operated in Missouri and Tennessee, and was mustered out at St. Louis in August, 1865. Soon after the war he united with the Missionary Baptist Church, and began to apply himself to the study of the Scriptures, with which he soon became familiar, and then chose a higher calling, being ordained as a minister in 1868. He then devoted his entire time for many years to his ministerial duties in Washington, Maries and Crawford Counties. He was located at Osage for nearly two years, and was pastor of several churches from there to Midland, and was pastor of the church at Sligo the first six years there. Since his residence at Sligo he has married 101 couples, and a great many before coming there. Politically a Republican, his first presidential vote was cast for Hancock in 1880. He is an ardent advocate of the prohibition of the liquor traffic. Mrs. Ashlock has been a member of the Baptist Church since 1880.

Capt. Robert Mortimer Askin, hardware and furniture dealer, of Salem, Mo., was born April 10, 1838, in the city of Dublin, Ireland, being the son of John and Sarah S. (Shea) Askin, and grandson of John Askin, who was a native of England and a plumber by trade. He died in Ireland. John Askin, Jr., was born in Ireland in 1808, but was of English descent. He was also a plumber by trade, and died in his native country in 1873. His wife, Sarah S., was born in Ireland in 1807, and died in 1880. She was the mother of seven children, three now living, but only two came to America: William A. and Robert M. The last named and his brother came to Canada with their uncle, William Shea, on a visit in 1852. William Shea located in Upper Canada, and at the end of twelve months Robert M. and William A. did not wish to return to Ireland. They lived in Canada four years, and while there worked at the tinner's trade. In 1856 Robert M. came to the United States, and located in Jefferson County, N. Y., at Belleville, and here Robert M. worked at his trade until 1859, when he returned to Canada. In 1860 he returned to the States, and stopped in Missouri, locating in St. Louis in August, 1862. He enlisted in Company E, Thirty-second Missouri Regiment Infantry Volunteers, for three years or during the war, at Steelville, Mo. He was in the fights at Vicksburg, Lookout Mountain, Missionary Ridge, and was all through the Atlanta campaign, with Sherman to the sea, through the Carolinas by way of Richmond, and was at Washington, D. C., during the grand parade. He then went back to Louisville, Ky., where he was discharged July 18, 1865. His regiment was in fifty-two battles and skirmishes, and he never received a scratch or wound; was not absent but once, from December 9, 1863, to February 8, 1864, on recruiting service. He was not sick during entire service. He entered the service as a private, and October 20, 1862, he was commissioned second lieutenant. April 4, 1864, he received the commission of captain of his company. After the war he located at Steelville, Crawford County, and established a hardware and tin store. In 1870 he moved to Cuba, and there engaged in his old trade, but nine years later he came to Salem, where he has since been engaged in the hardware and furniture business. February 22, 1866, he married Miss Clara Alice Jamison, daughter of Homer Jamison, and a native of Washington County, Mo., born in 1849, died January 22, 1873, leaving two children, William Clarence and John Herbert. April 12, 1876, he married Frances Amelia Watros, a native of New York, born in 1850. They have four children: Arthur W., Adney E., Myrvin L. and Matie Amelia. Mr. Askin is one of Salem's best business men, and is the only furniture dealer in the town. He carries a first-class stock of goods, and is a man well respected by all who know him. He is a stanch Republican in his political views; is a member of the Masonic fraternity, the A. O. U. W. and the G. A. R. He was a member of the school board for a time, and he and wife are members of the Episcopal Church.

Asa H. Bain is considered one of the successful farmers of Dent County, Mo., and although born in Maury County, Tenn., was reared and educated in Dent County, Mo. He was born on the 1st of August, 1841, and is the seventh of ten children born to the marriage of Frederick Bain and Susannah Andrews, and is a grandson of William Bain. The latter was of Scotch descent, and lived and died in North Carolina, the latter event taking place at the age of one hundred and two years. Frederick Bain was born in the "Old North State" March 26, 1809, and died in the State of Arkansas in 1859, having been a Southern trader in horses and mules. His wife was also born (1808) in North Carolina, and died at the home of her son Asa, in September, 1875. She was of Scotch-Irish descent, and was married in 1828, and became the mother of ten children, nine of whom are living. On the 7th of October, 1875, Asa H. Bain was married to Miss Mary M. Craig, who was born in Dent County, Mo., April 19, 1853. She is a daughter of James E. and Edith Craig, and is the mother of four children: James F., H. Asbury, Susannah C. and Mary S. In July, 1861, Mr. Bain enlisted in Company D, Tenth Missouri Infantry, under E. Kirby Smith, Parson's brigade, Price's division, Confederate States Army, and served until June, 1865, being a participant in the battles of Springfield, Prairie Grove and Helena. In the last engagement he received two wounds. After the close of the war he returned to his farm of 165 acres in Missouri, and has since been actively engaged in tilling the soil. His land is well improved, and is furnished with a good orchard and buildings. He served two years as constable of Current Township, and was president of the County Wheel one term. His wife is a member of the Baptist Church, and he has always been a Democrat in his political views.

William Barksdale, a prosperous farmer of Dent County, Mo., was born in Tennessee in 1836, and is a son of Stephen I. and Sarah (Waler) Barksdale, who were born in Tennessee in 1812 and 1811, and died in Shannon and Dent Counties, Mo., in 1879 and 1883, respectively. The father was of English descent, and a farmer by occupation, and became a resident of Dent County, Mo., about 1840. Six of their eight children grew to maturity. Three were living at the time of William's marriage; two besides himself: Henry, who died at Neosho, Mo., in 1861, while in the State service, and Wallar, who died in the Confederate service at Pine Bluffs, Ark., in 1862. William Barksdale was the eldest of the children, and is the only son. Up to the time of his marriage, in 1859, his time was employed in assisting his father on the farm, and in attending the district schools during the winter seasons. His wife, whose maiden name was Mary E. Daugherty, was born in Tennessee on the 28th of February, 1841, and was a daughter of Saciah and Sally Daugherty. She became the mother of seven children, six living, and died on the 18th of January, 1875. In January, 1886, Mr. Barksdale married his second wife, Mrs. Dinwiddie. Since 1859 Mr. Barksdale has resided on the farm he now occupies, but during the Civil War he was compelled to change his place of abode, and located in Fulton County, Ark., where he remained two years, and then moved to Shannon County, Mo., and in 1881 returned to his present farm. He is the owner of 640 acres of land, 480 acres comprising the home farm, and has 150 acres well tilled and under good cultivation. He is one of Dent County's most prosperous and successful farmers, and is much esteemed as a neighbor and friend. He is a Democrat in politics, and is a member of the County Wheel organization.

John F. Bass, a prosperous farmer, residing about eleven miles south of Salem, Mo., was born in the "Old Dominion" in 1832, and is a son of Robert and Jane (Nasry) Bass, who were also born in Virginia, in 1788 and 1800, respectively. The father was of Irish lineage, and in 1851 immigrated with his family to Tennessee, where he continued to make his home until 1856, when he took up his abode in Dent County, Mo., and there resided until his death in 1862. His wife's death occurred in 1870, also in Dent County. Four of their nine children are living, John F. Bass being the fourth member of the family. He made his home with his parents, and received his education in Virginia. In 1879 he was united in marriage to Miss May Shelton, who was born in Tennessee in 1853, and is the mother of five children: Lee, Jackson, Benjamin, Sarah and Minnie. Soon after his marriage he located on the farm of 301 acres where he now lives; 120 acres are under cultivation, and well improved, with good buildings, fences and orchard. Mr. Bass has always been a Democrat in politics, and in 1861 enlisted in Company E, First Regiment Missouri Infantry, and served until the close of the war, being a participant in the battles of Oak Hill, Lexington, Dry Wood, Hartville and numerous skirmishes. At the latter engagement he received a wound in the hand, which left it badly crippled. He is one of the pioneers of Dent County, and one of its substantial and honorable citizens. Mrs. Bass is a daughter of Berrymond and Sarah Shelton, both of whom are living.

John Thomas Benton, of Salem, wholesale agent for Anheuser-Busch, of St. Louis, Mo., is a native of Crawford County, Mo., where he was born in 1847, being the son of Henry W. and Nancy T. (King) Benton. Henry W. Benton was born in Jefferson County, Mo., in

1804, and is a farmer by occupation. He was left fatherless at the age of three years, and was reared by his sister in his native county. Previous to his marriage he moved to Crawford County, Mo., where he now resides and where he has since lived. He is the oldest resident of Crawford County now living. He is the father of seven children: Rhoda Ann, wife of Calvin Brand, in Crawford County, Mo.; James S., on the old home place; Catherine E., wife of James M. Avery; John T., Henry E., Julia Ann, wife of Val Blanton, and Elijah P. Mrs. Nancy Benton, mother of these children, was born in the State of Kentucky in 1813, and came to Crawford County, Mo., with her parents, Joseph and Rhoda King, when thirteen years of age. Her parents are both deceased. Mrs. Benton is living, and she and her husband have lived together over fifty years. John Thomas Benton remained with his parents on the farm until twenty-two years of age, and June 7, 1867, he married Miss Nancy Evaline Jones, daughter of James and Evaline (Province) Jones, and a native of Izard County, Ark., born in 1845. To this union were born two children: James E., barber in Salem, and Julia Ellen. In 1869 Mr. Benton moved to Scotia, Crawford Co., Mo., and worked at the furnace. In 1873 he removed to Midland Furnace, where he remained until 1882, when he became a resident of Salem, Mo., where he now resides. For the past year he has been agent for Anheuser-Busch's Brewery of St. Louis. Mr. Benton lost his first wife in 1872, and in the year 1885 he married Miss Maggie E. Garner, who was born in Dent County, Mo. They have one child, Birdie. Mr. Benton is one of the finest men, physically, in the State of Missouri, standing six feet, four and a half inches in his stockings, and weighs 320 pounds, there not being a pound of surplus flesh on him. He is a Democrat in politics, and cast his first presidential vote for Greeley in 1872.

Franklin C. and Hardy Blackwell, proprietors of livery and feed stable at Salem, were born in 1856 and 1864, respectively, being sons of James H. and Nancy M. (Barnes) Blackwell, grandsons of William and Mary (Halbert) Blackwell, who were natives of Virginia, coming to Missouri at a very early date, and settling in Crawford County. William died in 1856, at the age of sixty-three, and his wife is yet living, and is now in her eighty-ninth year, her birth occurring in 1801. James H. Blackwell was born in 1822, and died in 1866 in Dent County, eight miles north of Salem, where his widow now lives on the old homestead of 393 acres. She was born in Tennessee, later moving to Alabama, and came to Dent County, Mo., with her parents, Thomas and Elizabeth Barnes, who located four miles north of the county seat. Mrs. Blackwell is the mother of nine children: Sarah, wife of Harvey McDonald; Eliza J., wife of James L. Chambers; Frances, wife of Thomas Frank; James T., Rachel, wife of Samuel Roney; Franklin C., John P., Nancy, wife of George Plank, and Hardy. Franklin C. was reared on his father's farm, and in 1884 was elected constable of Spring Creek Township, and was also appointed deputy sheriff of Dent County. In 1886 he was elected sheriff of Dent County, and served the people faithfully for two years. In September, 1888, Blackwell Bros. bought the livery and feed stable of Powell Bros., and are doing a good business. They have nine horses, three buggies, three hacks and one wagon. They are young men of good business capacity, and gentlemen in every sense of the word. They keep a first-class stable. In October, 1877, Franklin C. was united in marriage to Miss Sarah Ann Norris, who was born in Dent County, Mo., in 1860. They have one child, Emmet H. In 1886 Hardy Blackwell married Miss Jane Peck, a native of Dent County, Mo., born in 1866, and the daughter of Thomas Peck. They have one child, Arley Fulton. In politics the Blackwell brothers are Democrats, and Franklin C. and wife are members of the Christian Church.

Robert Jackson Bowman, a successful tiller of the soil in Spring Creek Township, whose residence is situated four miles east of Salem, was born October 18, 1831, in Washington County, Tenn., and is the son of Isaac and Agnes (Young) Bowman, both natives of Washington County, Tenn. Isaac Bowman was born in 1812, and was a farmer by occupation. About 1844 he moved to Barren County, Ky., where he now resides. He was a soldier in the Confederate army during the late war; was captured at Vicksburg, Miss., and retained some time. His wife died in 1887. They were the parents of twelve children, Robert J. being the ninth. He was about thirteen years of age when his parents moved to Kentucky, and was reared on a farm, where he remained until over twenty years of age. In 1854 he married Miss Nancy Jane Peden, daughter of Benjamin and Mary Peden, and a native of Kentucky, born in 1832. Eight children were born to Mr. and Mrs. Bowman: James L., farmer; Benjamin, merchant; Joseph, Matthew, John, William, Juda, wife of Jube Carthy, and Mary, wife of Eli Mosher. In 1870 Mr. Bowman left Kentucky, and immigrated to Dent County, Mo., where he bought 300 acres of land four miles east of the county seat, where he located and where he has since resided. He is a Democrat in politics, and his wife is a member of the Missionary Baptist Church.

Thomas Jefferson Bowman. Prominent among the many enterprising farmers and stock raisers of Watkins Township stands the name of the above mentioned gentleman, who was born in Greene County, Tenn., in 1833, the son of Benjamin and Millie (Skyles) Bowman, also natives of Greene County, Tenn., where they remained until about 1852 or 1853, when they moved to what is now Dent County, and here the father died two years later, at the age of sixty-five years. He was a farmer, and one of the early settlers of the county. The mother died in 1871; she was the daughter of William Skyles, who was also an early settler of Greene County, Tenn., and died in that State while *en route* for Missouri. He was with Gen. Jackson in one of the Indian wars, and was at the battle of Horseshoe Bend. Sparling Bowman, grandfather of the subject of this sketch, was born in Maryland, and was one of the first white settlers of Greene County, Tenn., where he died. He was a soldier in the Revolutionary War, was also in the Indian wars, and was sheriff of Greene County many years, and one of its best citizens. Thomas Jefferson Bowman was the third of six children born to his parents; he received a limited education in the common schools of Tennessee, and moved with his parents to Dent County, Mo., where in 1858 he married Miss Elizabeth, daughter of Robert and Prudence Thompson, natives of Virginia and South Carolina, respectively. Mrs. Bowman was born in Tennessee, and came to Dent County about 1851 or 1852. Her father died in Arkansas about 1862, and her mother in Phelps County shortly after coming to Missouri. To Mr. and Mrs. Bowman were born two children, Benjamin F. and Thomas J. Since his marriage Mr. Bowman has lived on and adjoining the old farm on which his father first settled. He is the owner of 400 acres of land. In 1863 he served about four months in the Federal army, in Company B, Forty-eighth Missouri Infantry, on guard at Rolla. He has been a Democrat in his political views all his life, and cast his first presidential vote for James Buchanan in 1856, and for every Democratic candidate since. Mrs. Bowman is a member of the Methodist Episcopal Church, in good standing.

Millard F. Browne, local manager of Plank Iron Bank, for Dent Iron Company, and postmaster of Eden Post-office, also general merchant at the bank, whose annual sales equal about $10,000, established the store July 6, 1882, under the title of Sankey & Browne, and since about 1885 Mr. Browne has been sole owner and proprietor. He has also been manager of the iron bank since November, 1887. He was born in Washington County, Mo., October 11, 1855, being the son of Rev. Solomon and Mary Ann (Love) Browne, natives of Virginia, born in 1799, and Missouri, born in 1819, respectively. They were married in Reynolds County, Mo., in 1842, and settled in Washington County, where he lived until 1873, when he moved to Salem. He died there February 18, 1888, at the age of eighty-nine. He was a Cumberland Presbyterian minister for nearly forty years, and delivered his last sermon a few months before he died. He was married three times, the subject's mother being his last wife, and was the father of twenty-one children, five by the first wife, seven by the second and nine by the last. He lived in Missouri for nearly sixty years; was a very prominent divine, and became well known throughout Southeast Missouri. His father was a Scotchman, a Revolutionary soldier, and died in Kentucky. Mrs. Mary Ann (Love) Browne died in Salem in September, 1877, and was first a member of the Baptist Church, but afterward joined the Cumberland Presbyterian Church. Her father, Judge William C. Love, was an early settler in Reynolds County, and is now living in Iron County, nearly one hundred years old. He was a farmer by occupation, was in the Mexican War, and was presiding judge of Reynolds County Court for many years. Millard F. Browne was the sixth of nine children, and received his education in the common country schools, and his parents afterward moved to Salem, where he attended the schools there for two years, giving Prof. Linch his note at 10 per cent., which he paid with money earned afterward. He taught two terms of school, one during vacation and one after finishing school. He then began as weighmaster for Dent Iron Company, in Phelps County, and about twelve months after he was made manager of the Clinton Bank, in Phelps County, where he remained until he came to Plank Bank, and where he assumed the duties as above stated. He was married April 30, 1882, to Miss Maggie Ann McGinnis, the daughter of Hugh and Mary McGinnis, natives of Ireland, who came to the United States when young. The father died in Crawford County, but the mother is still living. To Mr. and Mrs. Browne were born three children. Mr. Browne is a member of the A. O. U. W., a member of the Masonic fraternity, the I. O. O. F., and has been postmaster of Eden for the past fifteen months. He is a Democrat in his political views, and his first presidential vote was for S. J. Tilden, in 1876.

John Larkin Callahan, farmer and stock raiser of Watkins Township, and one of the pioneers of Dent County, Mo., was born in North Carolina in 1814, being the son of Robert and Mary (Welch) Callahan, both natives of North Carolina, where they lived until their son John L. was three years of age. They then moved to Illinois, and when John L. was about nine years of age they moved back to Middle Tennessee. In 1836 they came to what is now Dent County, where the father died in 1856 or 1857, at the age of sixty-eight. The mother died in 1884, at the age of eighty-eight years. The father was a soldier in the War of 1812, and was with Jackson at New Orleans. He was justice of the peace for many years, and was a class leader in the Methodist Episcopal Church. He was one of five sons, three of whom were Methodist Episcopal preachers. His father, James Callahan, was a lieutenant in the Revolutionary War with Gen. Marion. He died in North Carolina. John Larkin Callahan was the eldest of five sons and four daughters. He never attended school but three months, but learned considerable in the Sunday-schools at home, and mostly by his own effort. In 1834 he was married, in Weakley County, Tenn., to Miss Mary, daughter of John and Elizabeth Welch, who were formerly from North Carolina, but who moved to Illinois, where Mrs. Callahan was born. She died April 26, 1879, and was the mother of thirteen children, three sons and two daughters now living: John Robert, Larkin A., Thomas A., Sarah (widow of Michael McCluster) and Eliza J. (wife of W. G. Edmondson). In 1879 Mr. Callahan took for his second wife Mrs. Martha Welch, *nee* Hayes, who was born in Overton County, Tenn., and came to Dent County with her brother when small. After his first marriage Mr. Callahan came to Dent County, Mo., being among the first settlers. In this county he has since lived, and is one of its prominent citizens and successful farmers. Since 1850 he has lived on his present farm, and at one time owned about 1,200 acres, but now has 640 acres, after giving his children farms. He filled the office of justice of the peace for many years, and is an honest, upright citizen. He has been a lifelong Democrat in his political views, casting his first presidential vote for Martin Van Buren in 1836, and for every Democratic candidate since. He has been Master of the Grange since its organization, and is a member of the Wheel. He has been a member of the Methodist Episcopal Church for twenty years, and his first wife was also a member of that church. His present wife belongs to the Baptist Church. Mr. Callahan has accumulated the most of his property by his own efforts. His brother, W. C. Callahan, one of the pioneer and most efficient Baptist ministers of Dent County, died in 1887, after many years of earnest and successful ministerial work. Another brother, Capt. James Callahan, commanded a company for one year in the Federal army, and died at Salem while on duty. Another brother was a Federal soldier on duty at Rolla, where he was taken sick and discharged.

Elbert C. Comstock, owner and proprietor of Lecoma Flour Mills, was born in Chautauqua County, N. Y., in 1852, and is a son of Asa and Eliza (Christman) Comstock, natives of Pennsylvania and New York, born in 1801 and 1806, respectively. They were married in New York, and in 1857 immigrated to Houston County, Minn., where they remained until 1867, and then moved to Dent County, Mo., where the father died in 1883, but the mother previous to this, in September, 1875. He was a farmer, a miller, running a saw-mill in New York for many years, and was an honest, upright citizen. His ancestors, three brothers, came over in the "Mayflower," and one settled in Connecticut, one in Rhode Island, and the other in the West. Elbert C. Comstock was the youngest of five sons and seven daughters, three sons and seven daughters now living. He was educated in the common schools, and remained on the farm until after his father's death. In March, 1874, he married Miss Kittie, daughter of Frank M. and Phalinda   , natives of Chautauqua County, N. Y. They moved from there to Tennessee during the war, and in 1872 removed to Wisconsin, where the father still lives. Mrs. Comstock was born in New York, and came with her parents to Dent County. After his marriage Mr. Comstock followed farming, and was also engaged in the mill business in 1882 with J. M. Lenox, both having an interest in the same until 1885, since which time Mr. Comstock has been sole owner. The mill has a capacity of fifty barrels per day, steam power, and was the first mill in Watkins Township. Mr. Comstock is the owner of the old home place of 380 acres, with 160 acres where the mill is, and 200 acres under cultivation. He is a Republican in politics, and his first presidential vote was for Gen. Grant in 1872. He is a member of the A. O. U. W., of Lecoma Lodge 279, transferred from Salem Lodge, and is one of the substantial citizens of the county. His father settled in the woods and improved a good farm. Mrs. Comstock is a member of the Presbyterian Church, but was formerly a Methodist.

Thomas H. Condray, superintendent of Hawkins Iron Bank for Midland Blast Furnace Company since the bank opened in 1880, and who had previously been the company's blacksmith at Salem, was born in Claiborne County, Tenn., four miles from Cumberland Gap, in 1833. William H. and Elizabeth (Welch) Condray, his parents, were natives of Tennessee, where they still live, the father eighty-three and the mother eighty-one years of age. William H. Condray is of French extraction, and his wife of Irish. He was a farmer by occupation. The grandfather of our subject, William Condray, was a native of North Carolina, a Revolutionary soldier, and died in Claiborne County, Tenn., at the age of one hundred and two. The maternal grandfather, Joseph Welch, was a native of Virginia, of Irish descent, and served in the War of 1812, with Jackson. He was a wheelwright by trade, and died in Claiborne County, Tenn. Thomas H. Condray was the second of three children, one son and two daughters, born to his parents. He received but little schooling, and his education was received mainly at home by the light of the pine-knot fire. When young he learned the blacksmith trade, which he followed for many years in connection with farming. He was married in 1856 to Miss Sarah A., daughter of Lewis Chumbley, of Claiborne County, Tenn., and eleven children, ten now living, were born to this union. Two sons are engineers at the Hawkins Iron Bank, and one son is foreman in one department in the bank. Mr. Condray lived in Claiborne County, Tenn., until 1870, when he came to Crawford County, Mo., and lived there three years engaged in farming and blacksmithing. He then went from there to Benton Creek Iron Bank, and in 1876 to Salem, where he was blacksmith for the company by whom he is now employed. He has a farm of eighty-five acres in Norman Township, and the Condray Post-office at Hawkins Bank was established in 1885, and named for Mr. Condray. He is a Republican in politics, his first presidential vote being for Fillmore in 1856, and he and wife have been members of the Baptist Church for thirty years. He has served the company by whom he is employed faithfully and industriously since he has been under their employ.

Christopher C. Cox is a Tennesseean, born March 5, 1843, being a son of Nicholas and Eliza (Birlew) Cox; the former's birth-place is unknown, but he was of Scotch-Dutch descent, a farmer by occupation, and died in Laclede County, Mo., while on his way to Texas. His wife was born in South Carolina in 1822, and died June 15, 1887, in Maries County, Mo., having borne a family of eleven children; seven grew to maturity, and Christopher C. is the fifth of the family. When he was two years of age his parents immigrated to Missouri, and he continued to reside with his mother until 1863, when he enlisted in Company L, First Regiment Light Artillery. In July, 1865, he came to Maries County, Mo., and February 8, 1887, was married to Josephine Callahan, widow of Thomas Callahan. She was born in Smithville, Lawrence Co., Ark., in 1847, and by her first husband became the mother of one child. Mr. and Mrs. Cox are members of the Methodist Episcopal Church, South, and he is a Democrat, and belongs to the I. O. O. F. After coming to Dent County, Mo., in 1873, he worked in a tobacco factory in Salem for about four years, and three years later located on the farm of 200 acres where he now resides. His wife has 240 acres of land. Mrs. Cox's parents, Green and Elizabeth Woods, were of Scotch-Irish and English descent, respectively, and the former was a presiding elder in the Methodist Episcopal Church, South. They were born on the same day in the year, the father's birth occurring in Washington County, Mo., in 1814, and the latter's in Franklin County, Ga., in 1814.

Harry Cross, one of the prominent agriculturists and stock raisers of Watkins Township, was born in Suffolk County, England, in 1856, and is the son of Harry and Susannah Cross, and grandson of Pearl Cross, who was born on the farm in Suffolk County, England, on which his son and grandson were born, and which has been in the family for over one hundred years. Harry Cross, Sr., was born in 1819, and his wife in 1829. He was well educated and was in comfortable circumstances. He and wife were members of the Episcopal Church, and excellent citizens. Of their family of nine children, all died of consumption with the exception of Harry, Jr. He was educated at home until twelve years of age, and then received a good high-school education in German, French, Latin, English, etc. He was reared on a farm, and for three years managed a large estate. Just prior to coming to America, which was in 1882, he married Miss Kate, daughter of Henry and Anna Bellerby, all natives of York City, England, where the parents still live. He came immediately to Dent County, Mo., and settled on his present farm of 300 acres, about 150 acres improved, and nearly all the result of his own efforts. He is making a specialty of raising thorough-bred Suffolk horses, fine mules and Southdown sheep. He has a fine imported stallion, which his father raised in England, and sent him in 1887. Mr. Cross is one of the most practical and thorough-going farmers and stock breeders of the county. His farm is situated about seventeen miles northwest of Salem, and about twelve miles south of Rolla. His horse was awarded the first premium at St. James Fair, in 1888, for first draft horse, and first premium for best horse for all work. Mr. Cross has probably the only thorough-bred Suffolk horse in Missouri, and is doing more to improve the horses of Dent County than any one man. He is a Republican in politics, and his first presidential vote was for Harrison, in 1888. He is a member of the Agricultural Wheel, Lecoma Lodge, and he and wife are members of the Episcopal Church.

John Cummins, another farmer and stock raiser of Spring Creek Township, was born in Washington County, Mo., in 1831, and is the son of Samuel and Elizabeth (Cole) Cummins, both natives of Lawrence, Ky., where they were reared, married, and in an early day removed to Washington County, Mo. (This was soon after the War of 1812). There they spent the remainder of their lives. The father died about 1875, at the age of eighty-four, after a life of probably over sixty years on one farm. At the age of nineteen he enlisted in the War of 1812. His parents were from Ireland. The mother died about 1870. John Cummins is the youngest but three of eleven children born to his parents. He was educated in the common subscription schools of Washington County, and in 1851 was united in marriage to Miss Angeline, daughter of Joseph and Mary Millsap, natives of Tennessee and Illinois, respectively. Her parents were married in Illinois, where Mrs. Cummins was born in 1834, and where she remained until about four years old. They then moved to Franklin County, Mo., and then to Washington County, where the father died about 1844. The mother died in St. Francois County in 1880. After the death of Mr. Millsap she had married again. To Mr. and Mrs. Cummins were born six children, three now living: Mary J., wife of Enoch Spriggs; Julia A., wife of James Gayhart, and Eliza, wife of John Copeland. In 1854 Mr. Cummins came to Dent County, settling in the woods on his present farm, in a hunter's cabin, and there remained two years. After some years he used this cabin for a smokehouse, and now has moved it to his barn, and uses it for a corn-crib. He has 320 acres of land, with about ninety under cultivation, all the result of his own hard labor. In 1859 Mr. Cummins went to Pike's Peak, where he spent some months in the mines, and met with fair success. He expected to return the following year, but did not on account of the approaching war. During the war he was three years in the Federal army, enlisting August 11, 1862, in Company D, Thirty-second Missouri Volunteer Infantry, and operated in Missouri, Arkansas, Mississippi, etc. He was in the battles of Haines' Bluff, Arkansas Post, and the last two years of the war he was at Camp Burnside, Ind., guarding prisoners, where he was mustered out at the close of the war. He is now one of the prominent farmers and stock raisers of the county, and spares no pains for the improvement of his stock. He is a Democrat in his political opinions, and his first presidential vote was for Pierce in 1852. Mr. Cummins is a member of the Agricultural Wheel, and Mrs. Cummins and the eldest daughter are members of the Presbyterian Church. The other two daughters are members of the Christian Church.

John M. Daugherty. Among the many enterprising farmers and stock raisers of Spring Creek Township, none have done more to improve the stock or to develop the agricultural interests of the county than Mr. Daugherty. He was born in Overton County, Tenn., in 1832, and is the son of Surkiah and Sarah (McDonnell) Daugherty, both natives of Tennessee. The parents came to Dent County, Mo., in 1854, settling on Meramec, and in 1861 the father joined Gen. Price's army, under Col. E. T. Twingo; was wounded at Wilson's Creek, and died from the effects three days later. He was captain of a company. He was of Irish descent, and was a well-to-do farmer and stock raiser. The mother died in Arkansas in 1865, and both were members of the Christian Church. John M. Daugherty was the eldest of nine children, five sons and four daughters. He received a good common-school education, and came with his parents to Dent County in 1854. He was married, in 1860, to Miss Mary V. Barksdale, daughter of Stephen I. K. and Sarah Barksdale, both natives of Tennessee, where Mrs. Daugherty was born. They came to Dent County about 1839, and were among the early settlers of the county, where the mother died about 1874. The father died in Shannon County, in 1878. He was a soldier for six months in the Confederate army. To Mr. and Mrs. Daugherty were born three children, one son and two daughters: Jefferson B., Ellen and Etta. In 1861 Mr. Daugherty joined Company G, Fourth Missouri Volunteer Cavalry, for six months, and after about four months he was discharged on account of disability. He was captured in August, 1864, in Shannon County, was imprisoned at Rolla a number of weeks, and was then paroled on honor not to return to the Confederate army. In 1862 he returned to Shannon County, where he lived until 1880, and then came to his present farm, near Salem. This farm consists of 245 acres, all well improved. He owned the old home place on Meramec, which consisted of several hundred acres, which he gave to his children. In 1873 he and his father-in-law built a flour and saw-mill on Jack's Fork of Current River, Shannon County, and operated the same for years with success. In 1867 he was appointed circuit and county clerk and recorder of Shannon County by the governor, and in 1868 he was elected circuit clerk and recorder, which office he held for twelve or fourteen years, or until he resigned, being elected three times. He is a Democrat in politics, his first presidential vote being for Buchanan in 1856. He has been quite largely engaged in dealing in stock since his majority, and is one of the enterprising farmers of Dent County.

James Douthart Dilworth, farmer of Spring Creek Township, who resides one mile west of Salem, was born in Anderson District, S. C., June 30, 1827, and is a son of Billy Green and Rebecca (Adkinson) Dilworth, natives of the same district of South Carolina, born in 1790 and 1805, and died in 1840 and 1865, respectively. Billy Green Dilworth was of Irish descent, and a farmer by occupation. His wife was of English descent. Nine children were born to their union, James D. Dilworth being the fifth in order of birth. He was reared and grew to manhood on a farm, and when thirteen years old his father died. He remained with his mother and sisters, looking after their comfort, until he was thirty years of age. In 1852 he, his mother and sisters came to Dent County, Mo., and located five miles north of Salem, where he entered 200 acres of land for 25 cents per acre. In September, 1857, he married Miss Martha E. Dill, who was born in Wayne County, Tenn., in 1837, and who bore him one child, Mary McCullock, wife of James W. Reddick. In August, 1861, Mr. Dilworth enlisted under Capt. McSpadden in the Missouri State Militia, and in 1864 enlisted in the general service of the Confederate States army. He was in quite a number of severe skirmishes, and was in service until the surrender, being in Texas at that time. He was neither captured nor wounded. Mrs. Dilworth died May 23, 1865, and in August, 1867, he married Mrs. Sarah Jane Walker, *nee* Ray, daughter of James H. Ray. Five children were the result of this union: Rebecca E., teacher in the public schools of Salem; Julia Ann, Emma Lake, Abbie and Billie Green. In 1874 Mr. Dilworth located where he now lives, and is the owner of 920 acres of land, and is one of Spring Creek's best farmers. He is a Democrat in politics, is a Mason, and he and wife and three children are members of the Baptist Church.

Elbridge L. Dye, member of the planing and saw-mill, and also a member of the lumber firm, of Dye Bros., of Salem, was born in Taylor County, W. Va., in 1847, and is the son of Alexander E. and Elizabeth (Bradfield) Dye, and grandson of Vincent and Frances (Montgomery) Dye, who were natives of Vermont. Alexander Dye was born in Wheeling, W. Va., in 1816, and was a contractor and builder by trade. When a young man he went to Monroe County, Ohio, with his parents, and in this county was married to Miss Bradfield. They remained in this county a short time, and then moved to Tyler County, W. Va., and in 1852 moved to Clay County, Ill. In 1869 he became a citizen of Buffalo, Dallas Co., Mo., and erected the court-house of Dallas County the same year. In 1870 he came to Salem, Dent County, built the court-house for that county, and in 1871 he came to Rolla, where he erected the school building for the School of Mines. In 1873 he built the jail of Dent County. His wife died in 1871. She was born in Virginia in 1822, and after her death Mr. Dye married Mrs. Mary C. Jamison, *nee* Hudspeth, who yet survives, and is now Mrs. William McMurtray. Alexander Dye died in 1876. He was the father of six children by his first wife and two by his second. Elbridge L. Dye was one of the children born to the first marriage. He was educated in the common schools, came to Missouri with his parents, and at about the age of fifteen commenced working at the carpenter's trade with his father.

He remained with his parents until twenty-one years of age, and in 1868 went to Marshfield, where he erected several good buildings in the town. In 1869 he worked on the court-house in Buffalo, and in the fall of 1870 he bought a half interest in a planing-mill and lumber yard with Lewis Martin. In 1877 he married Miss Ary B. Sprague, who was born in Bartholomew County, Ind., in 1858. They have four children: Leslie E., Frank W., Mary A. and Isaac R. In 1880 Isaac Dye, brother of the subject of this sketch, purchased an interest in the firm, and the same year the firm added a saw-mill. In 1882 Mr. Martin sold his interest to Dye Bros., and from that date until the present the firm has been known as Dye Bros. Planing-Mills. Elbridge L. built the public school building in Salem, the Salem Hotel and the Baptist Church. The firm has erected the Dent Block, Christian Church and many buildings of less note. Mr. Dye has made the plans for every church in Salem, and is a skillful workman. The Dye Bros. are successful business men, and look to the welfare and prosperity of Salem, assisting in all laudable and public enterprises. He is a Democrat in politics, is a member of the A. O. U. W., was a member of the city council for eight years, and was president for seven years. He is a member of the school board, and his wife belongs to the Cumberland Presbyterian Church.

Minor Elayer, member of the Clark Mercantile Company, of Salem, was born in Franklin County, N. Y., in 1849, being the son of Joseph and Mehitabel (Brown) Elayer, grandson of Joseph and Margaret (Dumont) Elayer, and the great-grandson of Joseph Elayer, who was a native of France. Joseph Elayer, Sr. (grandfather of subject) was born in Canada in 1797, and moved to the United States about 1858, and located in Franklin County, N. Y. He died in Salem, Mo., at the home of his son Joseph. His wife died in New York about 1853, and was the mother of fifteen children. Joseph Elayer, father of subject, was the eldest child born to his parents. He was reared on a farm, and at the age of twenty-one came with his parents to the United States, locating in Franklin County, N. Y. In 1854 he married Miss Mehitabel Brown, who was born in Lower Canada in 1821, and the fruits of this union were four children: Minor, Milo, blacksmith at Salem; Marquis, farmer, and Harvey, a member of the Clark mercantile firm, of Salem. Mr. Elayer became a citizen of Salem, Mo., in 1866, and bought 200 acres adjoining the town, where he located, and where he has since resided. At one time he was the owner of 1,160 acres of land, and was one of Dent County's most substantial citizens. He has divided his property with his children, and now lives with them. He is a Republican in politics, and he and wife are members of the Methodist Episcopal Church. His son, Minor Elayer, came to Salem, Mo., with his parents in 1866, and was on the farm until twenty-five years of age. At the age of twenty-one he began teaching, and followed this profession for five years, three or four months each year. December 13, 1871, he married Miss Maria Williams, a native of Monongalia County, W. Va., born in 1849, and came with her parents, W. P. and Eliza Williams, to Dent County, Mo., in 1857. To Mr. and Mrs. Elayer were born three children: Edward W., Ruth and Jessie Martha. In 1876 Mr. Elayer began clerking for A. H. & H. B.

Clark, and remained with them until September, 1888, when the present firm was formed, with Mr. Elayer as a member. They have the largest stock of goods in Salem, and have by far the largest trade, their sales amounting to $100,000 per year. Mr. Elayer is a Republican in politics, is a member of the A. O. U. W., and he and wife are members of the Methodist Episcopal Church.

Calvin Floyd, farmer, stock raiser and engineer, of Watkins Township, was born in Meigs County, Tenn., in 1849, being the son of Nimrod and Mahala (Keller) Floyd. The father was of English extraction, was a farmer by occupation, and died when his son, Calvin Floyd, was quite small. The mother was born in North Carolina, and after the death of her husband she and the children, eight sons and two daughters, came to Dent County, Mo., and settled on Dry Fork, Texas Township, where they improved a good farm. The mother is still living; is residing on Pigeon Creek, where she has a farm of sixty-seven acres. She is a member of the Missionary Baptist Church; has lived a widow for nearly thirty-two years, and has reared a large family in a new and wild country. Her eight sons and two daughters are all living in Dent County, and are among the well-to-do and respected citizens of the same. Calvin Floyd received a limited education, and at the age of twenty-one began for himself as a farmer. In 1871 he married Miss Eliza J., daughter of C. P. Pinckney and Jane Thorp, formerly of North Carolina and Tennessee, respectively. They came to Dent County, Mo., at an early date, and here passed the balance of their lives. The mother died when Mrs. Floyd was quite young, and the father in June, 1888. He was one of the wealthy farmers of the county, was an industrious citizen, and a good man. He reared six children. He was left an orphan at an early age, and was consequently thrown upon his own resources, but in spite of many drawbacks, he kept steadily at work, and soon accumulated a good fortune. To Mr. and Mrs. Floyd was born one child, a daughter, named Alphia. Soon after his marriage Mr. Floyd settled on his present farm, which consists of 529 acres, with 180 under cultivation. He is a good farmer, and since 1882 he has been running a steam thresher. He is extensively engaged in feeding cattle and hogs, having in his present lot forty hogs and fifty-three cattle. He does his own shipping, and is one of the practical farmers and stock raisers of the county. He is a Democrat in politics, and his first presidential vote was for McClellan in 1864. Mrs. Floyd is a member of the Baptist Church.

John B. Fox, farmer and stock raiser of Watkins Township, was born in Haywood County, West Tenn., in 1838, and was brought by his parents to what is now Dent County, where the father died about 1844. About three years later the family removed to what is now Texas County, near Licking, where the son was reared to manhood, with very limited educational advantages. He was one of four sons and three daughters, who were reared by his widowed mother. She was born in South Carolina, has been a member of the Methodist Church for a great many years, and is now eighty-five years of age. Her father, Lewis Campbell, first moved to Tennessee, and later to Texas County, Mo., where he died. He was of Irish descent. William Fox, father of subject, was probably born in Tennessee, and his father, Enoch Fox, was of Dutch descent, and he and two brothers were in the War of 1812. John B. Fox was married in 1861 to Miss Julia A., daughter of William and Rachel Ratleff, natives of Pike County, Ky., born in 1811 and 1819, respectively. They came to Texas County, Mo., in 1858, and during the war went to Nebraska, where he remained one year. He then went to Bourbon, County, Kas., where the father died in 1868, and the mother in 1874. Mrs. Fox was born in Pike County, Ky., and to her union with the subject of this sketch were born eleven children, four sons and three daughters now living. He lived for about three years during the war in Phelps County, Mo., then returned to Texas County, and in 1867 to Dent County, where, since 1868, he has resided on his present farm. He has 560 acres now in the woods, and 280 acres improved. He served about six months, in 1862, in the Confederate Army, Company A, First Missouri Cavalry, in Missouri and Arkansas, and was in several skirmishes. He was captured in Shannon County, January 1, 1863, and imprisoned at Rolla one month, when he was paroled under bond, and returned home. He is a Democrat in politics, casting his first presidential vote for Breckenridge in 1860. He is a member of the I. O. O. F., Spring Creek, No. 416, also a member of the Grange, and a member of the Agricultural Wheel, both of Victor Mills Lodge. Mrs. Fox is a member of the Christian Church.

Milton Godbey, M. D., of Salem, Mo., was born in Pulaski County, Ky., April 3, 1845, and is the son of Rev. Josiah and Sena (Kelly) Godbey, and grandson of William Godbey, who was a native of Caroline County, Va., born in 1781. Josiah Godbey was born June 30, 1817, in Pulaski County, Ky., and remained at home until twenty years of age, when he married Miss Sena Kelly, daughter of Samuel and Nancy Kelly. This was in 1837. Ten children were born to their union: William C., John E., Martha J., Sarah H., Milton, Samuel M., Josiah, Maggie, Thomas and Sena A. In 1833 Josiah Godbey was converted, and commenced studying for the ministry, though by his own efforts. In 1841 he entered the ministry of the Methodist Episcopal Church, by joining the Kentucky Conference as an itinerant, being ordained two years later in Louisville, Ky., by Bishop Morris. He continued to preach the Gospel in Kentucky, meeting with good success, for eleven years. In September, 1852, he moved to Cooper County, Mo., and for over thirty-five years has been engaged in his ministeral duties in Missouri. Dr. Milton Godbey went to Cooper County, Mo., with his parents when a boy of eight years, and received his literary education in the common schools of that county, but later attended the public high-school in St. Louis. In 1866 he commenced the study of medicine, his preceptor being Dr. A. H. Conkwright, of Sedalia. In 1867 he entered the Ohio Medical College at Cincinnati, and in 1868 commenced practicing at Jonestown, Mo., in Bates County. In March, 1870, he graduated as an M. D. at the Ohio Medical College, and afterward practiced in Bates County, until 1875, when he came to Salem, Mo. Here he has since resided, actively engaged in the practice of his profession, to which he has devoted his whole time and attention. He has a large practice, and is one of the leading physicians of the county. On January 31, 1872, he married Miss Robertha P. Simpson, who was born at Harrisonville, Cass Co., Mo., February 20, 1854. They have three children deceased: Annie, Jervase and Frank; three are living: Milton E., Pearl and Elizabeth S. In politics the Doctor is a Democrat, casting his first vote for Seymour in 1868; is a member of the Rolla District Medical Society, and has been its president several terms. He is a member of the United States Pension Examining Board of Dent County, and has been president of the same since its organization, eleven months ago. He is a member of the A. O. U. W., and he and wife are members of the Methodist Episcopal Church, South.

Peter Guthoerl, another enterprising farmer of Spring Creek Township, was born in the Kingdom of Prussia, Germany, in 1843. His parents, Jacob and Catherine (Krame) Guthoerl, were natives of Prussia, born in 1807 and 1809, respectively. John Jacob Guthoerl was a farmer by occupation, and died in 1845. In 1854 his widow and two children came to America, and located in Athens County, Ohio. In 1856 she married Jacob Bruhlman, who was a native of Switzerland, and in 1866 they moved to Crawford County, Mo., where he died in March, 1874. Mrs. Bruhlman is yet living, and resides with her son Peter. Her other child, John Jacob Guthoerl, was wounded at the battle of Peach Tree Creek, July 22, 1864, and died the 28th of the same month, at the age of twenty-six. Peter Guthoerl came to the United States with his mother when eleven years of age, and attained his growth on a farm. September 5, 1861, he enlisted in Company E, Eighteenth Ohio Volunteer Infantry, as private, and was in the fights at Murfreesboro, Chickamauga, Mission Ridge, Nashville and many severe skirmishes. He was in service until November, 1865, being discharged at Camp Chase, Ohio, but was mustered out at Augusta, Ga. April 17, 1865, he was made sergeant of Company A, Eighteenth Regiment Ohio Infantry, and in May, 1865, he was appointed and commissioned, by John Brough, of Ohio, as second lieutenant of Company I, Eighteenth Regiment. These promotions were for bravery, patriotism and fidelity to the Union cause. After the war he returned to Athens County, Ohio, and in 1869 came to Crawford County, Mo., and in 1870 bought 220 acres of land in Dent County, Spring Creek Township, where he now resides. Since then, or from 1870 to 1874, he made several trips to Texas and the Indian Territory. December 24, 1876, he married Miss Missouri Jane Earney, a daughter of Judge Martin and Lydia (Deal) Earney, of Crawford County, Mo., who were among the first settlers in Crawford County. Judge Earney died in October, 1881, at the age of seventy years, but his widow is yet living. She was not outside the county for fifty years, until the winter of 1888–89, when she made her son-in-law, Peter Guthoerl, a visit. She is seventy-nine years of age. Mrs. Guthoerl was born January 10, 1853, in Crawford County, Mo., and to this union were born five children: Lydia C., Laura, Ingersoll, Firnim and William A. Mr. Guthoerl now owns 415 acres of good land, and is a well-to-do citizen. He is a stanch Republican in his political views, casting his first presidential vote for Lincoln in 1864. He is agnostic in his belief.

George A. Head, farmer, stock dealer, and a prominent citizen of Norman Township, was born in Warren County, Penn., in 1843, and is the son of George W. and Zannetta M. (Smiley) Head, natives of Tompkins County, N. Y., born in 1812 and 1820, respectively. They were married there in about 1836, and afterward removed to Warren County, Penn., where the mother died in 1845, and the father in about 1856. Both were members of the Methodist Church, the father being a millwright by trade. William Head, grandfather of subject, was born in New Jersey, and was of English parentage. When a small boy his father's house was attacked by Indians, who murdered and scalped the entire family with the exception of William, whom they thought they had killed. As he grew to manhood he naturally had a strong hatred for the red race, and soon became one of the greatest Indian fighters of the East. He at last followed them into Michigan, where it was supposed he was roasted by the reds. William Smiley, the maternal grandfather of subject, was born in New Jersey, was of Scotch descent, and was a soldier in the War of 1812. He died in Dent County, in 1875, after having lived here a few years. George W. Head was married three times, his first wife, subject's mother, bearing him four children. George A. Head was the third child in order of birth. He was educated in the common schools, and remained at home until the death of his father, when he began for himself, as a hand in the lumber woods, until the opening of the war. He then joined Company D, One Hundred and Eleventh Pennsylvania Infantry, in the Potomac army, and remained with the same until the fall of 1863. He then joined the Army of the Cumberland, and was mustered out at Washington City. He was in the fights at Chancellorsville, second Bull Run, Cedar Mountain, Gettysburg, Lookout Mountain, and all through the Atlanta campaign to the sea. He was at the grand review at Washington, D. C. He was never captured nor wounded, and was never in the hospital but a few days. He served over four years, and was never absent but fifteen days, when he went home on a furlough. He was married in 1866 to Miss Margaret S., daughter of William and Eliza Porter, natives of New York and Ireland, respectively. Her parents came to Dent County, Mo., in 1870, and here the father died in 1882, at the age of sixty-six, but the mother is still living. Mrs. Head was born in Chautauqua County, N. Y., and by her marriage became the mother of four children, three now living. In 1866 Mr. and Mrs. Head moved to Dent County, where, some time later, they settled on their present farm, which consists of 243 acres, at the head of Norman Valley, with about 160 acres under cultivation. Mr. Head deals largely in stock; has some fine Durham cattle, Berkshire and Chester White hogs and Merino sheep. He is a stanch Republican in politics, casting his first presidential vote for Lincoln in 1864. He is a member of the A. O. U. W., Salem Post of the G. A. R., and is also a member of the Grange order. Mr. Head is a live and thoroughgoing farmer, and has done much to raise the standard of agriculture and intelligence in his neighborhood, having been reared in a country of good schools, where farming was made a science. Mrs. Head is a cultured and refined lady, and although almost an invalid for some years, her influence in the family is wielded in the direction wherein only a mother's is felt and remembered.

David Headrick. Among the prominent features of Watkins Township stands the farming and stock dealing interests, which have developed within the last few years in an extraordinary manner, and no one has aided in developing this interest more than the gentleman whose name heads this sketch. He was born in North Carolina in 1825, and is the son of Francis and Elizabeth (Smith) Headrick, and grandson of Francis Headrick, who was a native of Pennsylvania, and served as fife major for six years and nine months in the Revolutionary War. He died in North Carolina, at the almost unheard-of age, one hundred and five years. The maternal grandfather of our subject, David Smith, was a native of North Carolina, where he spent all his life. Francis and Elizabeth (Smith) Headrick were born in Davidson County, N. C., where they passed their entire lives. The father died in 1857, and the mother ten years previous. The father was of Pennsylvania Dutch descent, was a Democrat in politics, a well-to-do farmer, and a member of the Baptist Church. David Headrick was the younger of two children, a son and daughter, born to his parents. The daughter, Margaret, married Mr. Leonard Beck, who now resides in North Carolina. David Headrick was the only one of his father's family to leave the native State. His education was rather limited, and at the age of twenty-one he began business for himself, in the gold mines in the winter and on the farm in summer. In March, 1847, he married Miss Mary B., daughter of Philip and Mary Frank, who were natives of Pennsylvania, but who immigrated to North Carolina at an early date. The father died in that State, but the mother came to Dent County, where she also died. Mrs. Headrick was born in Davidson County, N. C., and to her marriage were born nine children, three sons and three daughters now living. In 1857 Mr. Headrick and family moved to Dent County, Mo., settling in a shanty on his present farm when the same was covered with dense woods. He has now 320 acres of land, with about 160 cleared, all the result of his own efforts. He is a successful farmer and stock raiser. He has been postmaster at Celina since Grant's first term. During the war he served about three months in the Confederate army, with Capt. Coleman, in Arkansas, in 1863, as forage master. Politically he has been a Democrat all his life, and his first presidential vote was for Gen. Cass in 1848. He has voted for every Democratic candidate since. Mrs. Headrick has been a member of the German Reformed Church from early girlhood, and they are classed among the best citizens of Dent County.

Frank Headrick, farmer and stock raiser of Watkins Township, and son of Christopher C. and Margaret (Billings) Headrick, was born in Davidson County, N. C., in 1830. His parents were born in Davidson County, N. C., in 1799 and 1801, respectively, and came to Haywood County, Tenn., in 1834. The next year he moved to Dent County, Mo., on Dry Fork, then near Victor Mills, on the farm now owned by his son Silas, and there he and his faithful companion passed their last days. He died in 1868, and the mother in 1873. The country was a wilderness when they first settled in Dent County, and the nearest post-office was Meramec Iron Works. Both were members of the Missionary Baptist Church. Frank Headrick was the third of four sons and one daughter, and came with his parents to Missouri when about eight years of age. He received a limited education in the schools of the woods, and attended one term of school in Tennessee, his parents having stopped one season in that State on their way to Missouri. In 1853 he crossed the plains to California, and assisted in driving a drove of 700 cattle, being nearly six months in making the trip. He spent nearly seven years in the gold mines of California, and during that time experienced all the hardships incident to mining life. He then returned to Missouri, by way of the Isthmus, and arrived home March 3, 1860. He served during the entire war in the Confederate army, Company C, of a battalion of sharp-shooters, in Arkansas and Louisiana, skirmishing over nearly all of Arkansas. He was in the fight at Helena, Ark., Pleasant Hill, La., Jenkins' Ferry, Ark., and others. He surrendered at Shreveport in June, 1865, after over four years of hard service, without being captured or wounded. He then returned to Dent County, and in 1869 was united in marriage to Miss Mary E. Burkitt, a native of Phelps County, Mo., and the daughter of Thomas W. and Catherine Burkitt. Thomas W. Burkitt came to Phelps County at quite an early date, and when quite young worked at the Meramec Iron Works, where he learned the blacksmith trade. He died when Mrs. Headrick was a little girl. Mrs. Burkitt is still living, and is a sister of Dr. John Hyer, whose sketch appears elsewhere in this work. To Mr. Headrick and wife were born five children, three now living. Mr. Headrick lived on the old home farm until 1880, and then purchased the old Anderson Johns farm on Dry Fork, which consists of 420 acres, 100 under cultivation and well improved. He is a Democrat in politics, and his first presidential vote was for Pierce in 1852. He is a Master Mason of Salem Lodge No. 225.

Major Silas Headrick, proprietor of Salem Hotel, of Salem, Mo., and son of Cristopher C. and Margaret (Billings) Headrick, was born in Davidson County, N. C., in 1831. His parents were natives of Davidson County, N. C., born in 1799 and 1801, respectively. Christopher C. Headrick moved to Haywood County, Tenn., in 1834, and the following year moved to Dent County, Mo., and located in Watkins Township, the farm now being owned by his son Silas. He died here in 1868. His wife died in 1873. They were the parents of four children, three now living: James, Franklin and Silas. The last named was but four years of age when his parents came to Dent County, Mo., they being among the first white settlers of the county, which was full of Indians and wild animals. Silas assisted his father on the farm until thirty-eight years of age, and in 1861 he enlisted in Capt. Frank's regiment, Missouri State Militia, and in the spring of 1862 he enlisted in the regular service under Col. Coleman. After his regiment was disorganized he joined Col. Pindall's battalion of sharp-shooters, and was in service until in 1865, when he surrendered at Shreveport, La. He was in the battles of Wilson's Creek, Lexington, Pleasant Hill, La., and Jenkins' Ferry, Ark. He was captured at West Plains and retained one month, and was the first prisoner exchanged during the war. He enlisted as a private, was promoted to the rank of first lieutenant, and later to major of his regiment. After the war he returned to Dent County, where in 1866 he married Mrs. Nancy Plank, nee Plank, daughter of Benedict Plank, and a native of Tennessee, born in 1837. To Mr. and Mrs. Headrick were born seven children: Frederick, May, wife of Alex. Putman; James, Jeremiah, Riley, Annie and Myrtle. Mrs. Headrick had one child by her former marriage, who was named America, and who became the wife of Isaac Dunham. Mr. Headrick followed agricultural pursuits until 1874, when he was elected collector of Dent County, and was re-elected in 1876. For the past five years he has been merchandising in various places in the county, and in the fall of 1888 he sold his stock of goods at Victor Mills, and leased the Salem Hotel at Salem, taking possession December 3, 1888. He keeps a first-class house in every respect, and looks well after the comfort of his guests. He is a Democrat in politics, a member of A. O. U. W., Select Knights of same, and his wife is a member of the Baptist Church.

Ex-Judge Cicero P. Hedrick, manager and stockholder of Victor Roller Mills, was born in Davidson County, N. C., in 1850, being the son of Alfred and Elizabeth (Goss) Hedrick, and grandson of Adam Hedrick, who was born on the same farm in Davidson County, N. C., as his son and grandson, and there spent his entire life. He was killed at a muster drill by a drunken man when his son Alfred was a boy two years old. He was the son of Capt. Peter Hedrick, who came to America at an early date, and served as a captain in the Revolutionary War; he had also one son in that war. His barn was burned by Tories during the latter part of the war. He died on the farm on which his great-grandson, ex-Judge Cicero P. Hedrick, was born. Joseph Goss, maternal grandfather of our subject, was born in North Carolina, where he spent all his life as a slave-holder. He was of German descent. Alfred and Elizabeth (Goss) Hedrick were also natives of Davidson County, N. C., born in 1824 and 1832, respectively. They lived in their native State until 1874, when they came to Dent County, Mo., and here the mother died in 1881. The father is still living, and is a farmer by occupation. During the late war he served about one year in a North Carolina regiment of infantry, in the Confederate army. He is a Democrat in politics, and a member of the German Reformed Church, of which his wife was also a member for many years. They were the parents of six sons and three daughters, three sons and two daughters now living. Of this family ex-Judge Hedrick was the second child. He attended school two winters previous to the war and only two months afterward, most of his knowledge of books being acquired by his own efforts. He began for himself at the age of twenty-two as a farm hand, and continued as such for nine years. He came with his parents to Dent County, Mo., and in 1878 was united in marriage to Miss Tennessee, daughter of James C. and Emily Connell, formerly of Tennessee, but early settlers of Dent County, where Mrs. Hedrick was born. Her mother is still living, but the father died in Cape Girardeau County, Mo., about 1872. He served through the Federal army as a captain. Judge C. P. Hedrick followed farming in Dent County, Mo., until 1884, when he learned the carpenter's trade, and followed the same until July, 1888, when he assumed charge of the Victor Mills, which he assisted in building. He is a

Democrat in his political views, and his first presidential vote was for O'Conor in 1872. He is a member of Edgar Springs Lodge No. 416, I. O. O. F., and he and wife are members of the Methodist Episcopal Church, South. He served four years as justice of the peace, from 1882 to 1886, and in the last named year he was elected associate judge of county court from the Second District, and served one term. He has been notary public three years, and has held numerous minor offices nearly ever since his majority. He has a fine farm of 200 acres, eighty acres under cultivation, all well improved. His father has been postmaster at Taladego Post-office since 1882.

James Hickman, of Salem, Mo., was born in Monroe County, Ohio, in 1828, being the eighth of eleven children. He remained at home, working on the farm and attending school, until he attained his majority, and in 1851 was united in marriage to Miss Elizabeth Kinney, who was born in Ohio in 1833. Her parents, Timothy and Rachel Kinney, moved from Ohio to Carroll County, Mo., in 1865, and in 1870 moved to Dent. The father is still living. Mr. and Mrs. Hickman became the parents of seven children, five of whom are living. One son, Siles P., resides at home, two sons and one daughter reside in Dent County, and the oldest daughter in Howell County. One of their daughters died in Ohio, in 1865, and one son in Missouri. On the 31st of December, 1861, Mr. Hickman enlisted in Company G, Seventy-seventh Regiment of Ohio Volunteer Infantry, and participated in the battles of Shiloh and Corinth. April 25, 1864, while in the State of Arkansas, he was taken prisoner and kept at Camp Fort Tex., until February 25, 1865, when he was exchanged, and returned home on a furlough of sixty days, and on account of poor health was allowed to remain. He received his discharge March 8, 1866. His eyesight was badly injured during the war, and with the exception of a short period he has been totally blind ever since. Until 1872 he resided in Monroe County, Ohio, since which time he has been a citizen of Dent County, Mo. He owns a good farm of 280 acres, with 100 under cultivation, on which are a commodious, two-story frame residence, large barn and other necessary buildings, and has five acres in orchard, consisting of young and bearing trees. He has 320 acres of timber land, located a short distance from the home place, and his wife has 160 acres of land on Current River, in Dent County. This river runs through the farm, and furnishes good water power, on which she has caused a grist-mill to be built, and has placed it in charge of her oldest son, Timothy, who is a millwright and miller. Mr. and Mrs. Hickman were members of the Protestant Methodist Church when in Ohio, but have never united with any church in Missouri. Mr. Hickman is a Republican in politics, and is a son of William and Mary (Green) Hickman, the former being a native of Pennsylvania. He died in Monroe County, Ohio, in 1858, at the age of sixty-eight years, whither he had moved at an early day. His wife was of English lineage, and died in Ohio, in 1856, at the age of sixty years.

Timothy Hickman, farmer and millwright, was born in Monroe County, Ohio, in 1852. His parents' history appears in another part of this work. Timothy was educated in the common schools of Ohio, and resided with his parents until his marriage, in 1880, to Miss Susan

E. Roberts, who was born in Dent County, Mo., in 1857, being a daughter of Hugh and Sarah Roberts. The first year after his marriage Mr. Hickman resided on his father's farm, which he tilled. In 1881 he bought a farm in Current Township, on Current River, which he still owns. In 1883 he took charge of a grist-mill, located on an adjoining farm belonging to his mother, and controls and manages the mill as though it were his own. The mill was erected in 1883. It has two sets of buhrs, runs by water, and is patronized by the public twenty-two miles distant, thus showing Mr. Hickman's popularity as a good miller. In connection with these duties, he also successfully manages a farm of 170 acres, and has eighty acres under cultivation. He is a Republican in politics, and in 1882 was elected to the office of justice of the peace, and served with credit for two years. He is postmaster at Montauk Post-office, a member of the Agricultural Wheel, and he and wife are members of the Cumberland Presbyterian Church.

Charles William Hobson, farmer and stock dealer and raiser, of Norman Township, was born in Randolph County, Ind., October 27, 1837, his parents being Arthur and Catherine (Moffatt) Hobson, natives of Chatham County, N. C., born in the early part of the nineteenth century. They were married in their native State in about 1831 or 1832, and removed, probably, to Randolph County, Ind., and from there in 1838 to what is now Dent County, Mo. They settled near the head of Dry Fork, and here the father improved several farms. Later he moved to Henry County, Mo., but about two years later returned to Dent County, where the mother died about 1864. In 1866 the father went to visit a son in Iowa, and shortly afterward started to return to Missouri, and from that time no trace of him has ever been found. He was one of the first settlers of Dent County, and one of its honorable and industrious citizens. He was of a roving disposition, and was a wagon-maker and blacksmith by trade. He was a natural mechanic, and could make anything from wood or iron. The mother was of Scotch-Irish descent, and her father, Charles Moffatt, was probably born in the old country, and died in North Carolina. Charles William Hobson was the sixth of six sons and six daughters, seven now living, four in Dent County. He received a limited common school education, and March 29, 1857, he married Miss Cynthia A., daughter of James D. and Levisia (Coppedge) Watkins, natives of Virginia and Kentucky, and born in 1800 and 1807 respectively. Mr. and Mrs. Watkins came to Dent County when young, were married there, and settled on Dry Fork about 1830, where they improved a good farm. They were among the first settlers of that creek, and Watkins Township was named for Mr. Watkins. He died in June, 1863, and the mother in November, 1883. Mr. Watkins was justice of the peace for a number of years. To Mr. and Mrs. Hobson were born nine children, five sons and two daughters now living. Since the war Mr. Hobson has lived in Norman Township, with the exception of a short time. He has improved five good farms, and has lived on his present farm for three years. This consists of 272 acres, 100 under cultivation. In 1872 and 1873 he followed merchandising on his farm near Plank Bank. He is a Democrat in his political views, casting his first presidential vote for J. C.

Breckinridge in 1860. He is a member of the Grange, the Wheel, and he and wife and two sons are members of the Missionary Baptist Church. His eldest brother, Joab, served as a private in the Mexican War, and was also in a Missouri regiment during the late Civil War. He is now farming in Newton County. Another brother, Aaron S., was for three years in the United States Cavalry. He is now in Iowa, farming.

Hiram Hodges. Among the prominent and most successful farmers and stock raisers of Watkins Township stands the name of Mr. Hodges, who was born in Ripley County, Ind., in 1820, being the son of Samuel and Elizabeth (Razor) Hodges, natives of Abbeville District, S. C., and grandson of Richard and Sarah F. Hodges, who emigrated from South Carolina to Kentucky, where they expected to find plenty of cheap land for their children, but were disappointed, and about two years later moved to Ripley County, Ind., where the grandparents passed the remainder of their days. Samuel and Elizabeth (Razor) Hodges were reared and married in South Carolina, and about 1810 or 1812 they moved with Mr. Hodge's parents to Kentucky, and from there to Indiana. The father enlisted for the War of 1812, but peace was declared before he entered the service. He was justice of the peace in Indiana for many years, and about 1846 came to Missouri, settling in Dent County, where he died about 1873, at the age of eighty-four years and six months. His wife died in 1873, at the age of eighty-four years, six months and eleven days. They were members of the Baptist Church. Her father, Peter Razor, was a Revolutionary soldier, and a native of Germany. Hiram Hodges is the sixth of eleven children, six sons and five daughters. He received a liberal education in the common schools of Indiana, and March 11, 1841, he married Miss Rhoda Ann, daughter of James B. and Eva Leeds. Mr. Leeds was born in New Jersey, where he lived until thirteen years of age, and then came with his parents to Ohio, where he was married about 1816. Later he removed to Ripley County, Ind., where he spent the rest of his life, engaged in tilling the soil. His wife was born in Virginia, and went to Ohio with her parents. By his marriage Mr. Hodges became the father of thirteen children, five sons and four daughters now living: Samuel, Benjamin M., Hiram L., Elizabeth, wife of W. H. Craig, of Shannon County; Ellen R., James J., Sarah J., wife of William R. Love; Helen M., wife of Jefferson Daugherty, and George W., an attorney. The same year of his marriage Mr. H. came to what is now Dent County, in Gladden Valley, where he improved a good farm, and a few years after he removed down the valley to what is now Shannon County. Here he lived in different parts of the county for a number of years, and in 1856 he returned to Dent County, settling on Pigeon Creek, where he improved another good farm, and remained there until 1871. He then came to Salem, was for ten years engaged in merchandising at that place, and then returned to the farm, where he lived until 1884. He then moved to his present farm on Dry Fork, which consists of 332 acres of good farming land. Besides this he still owns his old farm of 400 acres, well improved, with about 260 acres under cultivation. He followed merchandising with success in

Shannon County, hauling his goods from St. Louis with ox-teams, and soon after purchased a saw-mill in Parker Hollow, and operated the same for many years, meeting with good success. He has been sawmilling ever since, and now owns one near the head of Meramec. In 1870 he built a flour mill at Salem, which he and G. R. Kenamore operated with success for a short time, when Mr. Hodges sold out, but one year later purchased the entire mill, and afterward took W. R. Love as a partner. They then operated the mill until 1881, when they sold out. Mr. Hodges has given his children good educations, and has liberally contributed to all worthy enterprises. Mr. Hodges was formerly a Whig, casting his first presidential vote for Harrison in 1840, but since the war he has affiliated with the Democratic party. He and wife have been faithful members of the Baptist Church for many years, and are excellent citizens. Mr. Hodges and eldest son now own a flour custom mill eight miles south of Salem, and Mr. Hodges has also a business block in Salem. He is a stockholder in the Bank of Salem.

William T. Holman, another successful farmer and stock raiser of Watkins Township, was born in Overton, now Clay County, Tenn., in 1844, and is the son of William and Nancy (Barksdale) Holman, and grandson of William Holman, a native of North Carolina and an early settler of Tennessee, where he died. The parents of our subject were natives of Tennessee, where they remained until 1845, when they moved to what is now Dent County, Mo., where they improved a good farm. In 1860 they removed to Washington County, where the father died in 1886. The mother had died many years previous, and after her death the father had married Miss Zilla Woods, whose father was one of the first settlers of Washington County. Mr. Holman was a successful farmer and stock raiser, and one of the pioneers of Dent County. He raised a company of soldiers, of which he was made captain, and started to assist in one of the Indian wars, but his services were not needed. He was a member of the Christian Church. William T. Holman, subject of this sketch, was the third of six children, and was educated in the common schools, and a few months at Arcadia. He remained with his father in Washington County until 1870, when he returned to Dent County and assumed charge of the old farm then owned by his father. He was married in 1871 to Miss Levicia A., daughter of Abner and Jane Harrison, natives of North Carolina and Tennessee. Her parents came to Dent County in 1852, and there they have since lived. Mr. Harrison is one of the wealthiest farmers and stock raisers in the county. He was born in 1818. Mr. Holman, after his marriage, lived on the old farm until 1886, when he removed to his present farm, a tract of land containing 1,085 acres, the most of it the result of his own efforts in farming and stock raising. To his marriage were born six children, three now living. He is a Democrat in politics, casting his first presidential vote for Seymour in 1868. For ten or eleven years he has been successfully engaged in breeding Short-horn cattle, beginning with a two-year-old heifer, which he paid $110 for, and now has probably the finest herd in the county. He was among the first to introduce the stock in the county, and he has also been engaged in breeding Poland-China hogs, of which he has a fine lot.

Dr. John Hyer, retired physician and surgeon at Lake Spring, was born in Lancaster County, Penn., in 1810, the son of Samuel and Elizabeth (Mitchell) Hyer, and grandson of Louis Frederick Hyer, who was born in Wolfenddettle, Germany, and came to America at an early day. He was a forgeman, as were all his sons, and died in Lancaster, Penn. His wife, Mary E. (Weaver) Hyer, was born in Pennsylvania, and was of German descent. She died in Cumberland County, Penn. The maternal grandfather, John Mitchell, was born in England, and was a wealthy Philadelphia merchant. He and wife died in that city when the subject's mother was an infant. She was born in 1785, in Philadelphia, and was then adopted and reared by the Llewellyn family, who came to America with William Penn. The descendants are now living on the old home farm near Philadelphia. The father, Samuel Hyer, was born in Lancaster County, Penn., in 1779, and was married near Philadelphia. He first settled in Lancaster County, Penn., in 1817, then in Cumberland County, of the same State, then in Wheeling, W. Va., thence to Bainbridge, Ohio, and in 1837 to Missouri, where for a year or two he was at the Meramec Iron Works. He then moved to Lake Spring, when there were but few settlers, and there passed the remainder of his life. The mother died in 1855, at the age of seventy, and the father in 1862, at the age of eighty-three. Both were members of the Methodist Church from early youth. Mr. Hyer was a forgeman, which occupation he followed many years after he left Pennsylvania. He was formerly a wealthy merchant, but became a bankrupt by indorsement for friends. He was a man of great activity, energy and good business ability. Dr. John Hyer was the second of eight children born to his parents, and the eldest son. He was reared in the common schools of Pennsylvania, and clerked in his father's store until about twenty-one years of age, when he began the study of medicine with his brother-in-law, Dr. William W. Stigleman, whose wife now lives with Dr. Hyer. He then taught school to pay his expenses while studying three years. In 1838 he came to this portion of Missouri, settling at Lake Spring, where he began his practice, and continued at this with remarkable success until after the war. He is one of the very first practitioners in South Central Missouri, as well as one of the most successful ones. He still prescribes for some of the old settlers. In 1842 he married Miss Mary Ann, daughter of William and Eliza Ruth, and a native of Pennsylvania, born near Philadelphia, where the parents spent all their lives. Mr. Ruth was a blacksmith by trade. Mrs. Hyer came to Missouri in 1840, with the Doctor's sister, Mrs. Ann Stigleman. To the Doctor and wife were born three children: Elizabeth P., wife of Judge Robert W. Fyan (she was killed at Marshfield, by the cyclone of 1880, the house blowing in); Martha L., wife of Dr. Edward B. Bowles, of Maries County, and Mary Ella, wife of Alexander C. Donnan. The daughters all received good educations, and the eldest daughter finished at the Convent of the Visitation, St. Louis. The second daughter finished at Troy, Ohio, and the youngest in the high-schools in St. Louis. Mrs. Hyer died in 1855, at the age of thirty-three years. She was a devout member of the Methodist Episcopal Church, all the daughters being members of the same. Dr. Hyer is among the substantial men of Dent County, owning 2,000 acres of land in Dent and Phelps Counties. He is well known through South Central Missouri, and is an honorable, upright citizen. In 1842 he represented Crawford County in the Legislature, when that county extended over a large part of South Central Missouri, and again, in 1848, he represented that county in the Lower House of the same body. During that session he petitioned the Legislature and organized Dent County. In 1860 he represented his senatorial district, then consisting of Crawford, Maries, Phelps, Dent, Shannon, Ozark and Pulaski Counties, in the Legislature, and was elected to the Confederate Congress, but did not serve. He was a member of the Constitutional Convention, in 1874, which revised or formed a new State Constitution. His father established a postal route from Jefferson City and Houston, and the Doctor was the first postmaster at Lake Spring Post-office, which position he held until the war. After that eventful period he was postmaster again until 1887. In his political views he has been a Democrat all his life, and his first presidential vote was for Gen. Jackson, in 1832. He is a Royal Arch Mason, and a worthy member of the Baptist Church.

Joseph H. Jadwin, farmer and merchant of Texas Township, was born in Texas County, Mo., in 1852, being a son of Valentine and Nancy (McDonald) Jadwin, who were born in Tennessee in 1830 and 1831, respectively. The former was of Dutch lineage, a farmer by occupation, and about 1833 emigrated with his parents from Tennessee to Missouri, locating in Texas County, but his death occurred in Dent County in June, 1887. His widow is still living, and resides on her farm about ten miles south of Salem. Joseph H. Jadwin is the eldest of eight children, and made his home with his parents until his marriage. He attended the country schools until nineteen years of age, and then attended the high-school of Salem for about two years. He taught his first term of school when nineteen years of age, and continued that occupation in Dent, Texas, Howell and Shannon Counties for thirteen years. On the 14th of October, 1879, he was married to Miss Emeline Jack, who was born in Dent County, Mo., in 1863, being a daughter of James and Susan Jack, both of whom were of Dutch origin, and natives of Tennessee. The former died in 1882, but the latter is still living. Mr. and Mrs. Jadwin are the parents of one child. The first two years of their marriage they resided on a farm on Dry Fork, and then moved to Gladdin Valley, where he was engaged in farming and general merchandising for six years, doing a good paying business. He has a well-improved farm of 160 acres, on which are erected a good residence and commodious and substantial out-buildings. He is a Democrat politically.

John Thomas Johns. Classed among the prominent and successful farmers and stock raisers of Watkins Township stands the name of the above-mentioned gentleman, who was born in Texas Township, Dent Co., Mo., August 25, 1840. His parents were Elijah and Elizabeth (Craddock) Johns, natives of Kentucky, born near the years 1815 and 1818, respectively. They were married in Kentucky about 1837, and came to Dent County, Mo., about 1839. The grandfather, Elisha Johns, was a native of Virginia, and of Scotch-Irish descent.

The maternal grandfather of our subject, John Craddock, was also a native of Virginia, and married Sarah Bartlett. Both died in Kentucky. When Elijah Johns, father of subject, first came to Dent County, he settled in Texas Township, and later in Watkins Township, where his son John T. now lives. He died in 1860. He was a successful and industrious farmer, and moved to Dent County when there were very few settlers. The mother is still living. John Thomas Johns was the eldest of eleven sons and one daughter, five sons and one daughter now living, and all but one brother in Dent County. He received his education in the common schools of Dent County, and in 1862 he enlisted in Company B, Tenth Missouri Cavalry, Federal Army, and operated in Arkansas, Tennessee, Mississippi, Louisiana, Alabama and Georgia. He was in the battles of Pea Ridge, Tupelo, and various other expeditions and skirmishes. He was with Gen. Wilson on his raid through Georgia and Alabama, and was discharged at Nashville, Tenn., as a corporal, in October, 1865, after over three years' service. He enlisted twice, the last time as a veteran. In March, 1866, he married Miss Mary, daughter of Judge James M. and Nancy Jones, who were early settlers of Dent County, where they died, the father in 1877 and the mother in 1873. To Mr. Johns' marriage were born eight children, four sons and four daughters. After his marriage Mr. Johns lived for some time on Little Piney, in Phelps County, but since then he has lived on the old home place, and is the owner of 500 acres of good land, all the result of his own efforts, and with about 100 acres under cultivation. In 1884 he was appointed justice of the peace, and served about one year. Politically he is a Republican, casting his first presidential vote for Abraham Lincoln in 1864. He is a member of the Agricultural Wheel; he and wife are members of the Baptist Church. Mr. Johns, like many others, could not write his name until during his first service while in the war. He then learned to write, and has since become considerable of a reader, and is considered a well-informed man on any subject. He has taken great pains to educate his children, and his eldest son finished his education at Salem, and is now one of Dent County's best teachers. Mrs. Johns' parents came to Missouri in 1843, and her father was a soldier in the Federal army; was a justice of the peace for some years, and served one term, at least, as county judge. He and wife were members of the Baptist Church.

Dr. A. J. Jones, retired physician, but now a prosperous merchant of Franklin Township, Dent Co., Mo., was born in Williamson County, Tenn., April 8, 1838, being a son of William and Julia (Crosner) Jones, both of whom were born in the same county as their son, A. J. The father was of Irish descent, a farmer by occupation, and was born about 1808, and died in his native county December 8, 1837. The mother was born on the 7th of February, 1813, and is now residing in Obion County, Tenn. In December, 1839, two years after her husband's death, she married Jackson Coleman, who died in Tennessee in 1886. Five children were born to her first union (all sons) and nine by her second. The maternal grandfather of A. J. Jones, Henry Crosner, was born in Williamson County, Tenn., in 1775, and died in 1865, having been a soldier all through the Revolutionary War. A. J.

Jones made his home with his mother until sixteen years of age, and received a good education in the country schools of his native State. He then went to Kentucky, where he had a brother teaching school, and stayed with and went to school to him for two years. He then attended the high-school of Lebanon, Tenn., one term, shortly after beginning the study of medicine under Dr. A. V. Hawkins, and at the end of eighteen months entered the Medical University of Nashville, which institution he attended from January, 1859, to March, 1860. In the latter year he located in Fulton County, Ky., where he entered upon the practice of his profession, and the following year was married to Fanny Dodge, who was born in Christian County, Ky., May 18, 1833, being a daughter of Jarred and Sally Dodge, who were of German descent. The mother died December 11, 1888, at the home of Mrs. Jones, with whom she had made her home for many years. She was about eighty-one years of age. After Mr. Jones had practiced his profession in Fulton County for about two years, he moved to Union City, Tenn., locating in Rolla, Phelps Co., Mo., about three years later. Four years later he came to Dent County, locating on a farm, and also practiced his profession until 1882, since which time he has gradually given up his profession on account of ill health. In February, 1883, he opened a general mercantile store, in connection with a general line of drugs, and is doing a lucrative business. He is a Democrat in politics, and has been frequently solicited to accept various offices, but has invariably declined the honor. He and wife are members of the Methodist Episcopal Church, South.

Jonathan D. Jones, farmer and stock raiser, is a native of Obion County, Tenn., born in 1842, and is a son of J. W. and Martha A. (Doak) Jones. The former was born in North Carolina, near Raleigh, in 1838, and died in Dent County, Mo., November 27, 1888, having been a resident of the county since 1855. He was a farmer, and of Irish descent, and at an early day immigrated to Tennessee, where he was married, his wife having been born in Wilson County, of that State, about 1820, and is now residing with her sons in Dent County. Jonathan D. Jones is the second of her ten children, seven of whom grew to maturity. He made his home with his parents until about twenty-one years of age, receiving his education in the district schools, and in 1861 volunteered in the Southern army, but after serving six months came home, and February 15, 1865, enlisted in Company E, Eleventh Regiment Veteran Volunteer Infantry, of the Federal army, serving until January, 1866, seven months after the close of the war. He then returned to Crawford County, Mo., where he had been married to Miss E. J. Brickey in 1863. She was born in Crawford County, Mo., in 1846, and is the mother of eight children, five now living. Her parents, Cornelius and Keziah A. Brickey, were of German descent. Since 1866 Mr. Jones has been a resident of Dent County, and in 1868 he located on the farm of 300 acres where he now lives; 140 acres of land are under cultivation, and besides this property he has a forty-acre tract of timber land. He has a good bearing orchard, and is in a prosperous condition financially. He is a Democrat politically. Mrs. Jones is a member of the Christian Church.

George R. Kenamore, Deputy United States Collector of Internal Revenue of the First District, Fifth Division of Missouri, was born in Maury County, Tenn., in 1846, being a son of Grant Allen and Emily Frances (London) Kenamore, and grandson of William and Polly (Johnson) Kenamore. William Kenamore was a native of North Carolina, born in 1792, and at an early age immigrated to Middle Tennessee. He was a soldier in the War of 1812, with Gen. Jackson, and died in 1862, near Springfield, Mo., having become a citizen of that place in 1854. His wife, Polly Johnson, was born in 1784, and died in 1870. Her father, Abner Johnson, was a soldier in the Revolutionary War, and was wounded at Guilford Court House. He was born in 1759, in North Carolina, and died in 1850. Grant A. Kenamore was born in Maury County, Tenn., February 14, 1824; was reared and married in his native county, where he remained until 1854, and then immigrated to Greene County, Mo. About 1856, he became a resident of Salem, Dent Co., Mo., and located one-half mile from the county seat, but the following year moved into the town. At the commencement of the war his sympathies were with the Southern people, but for the Union, and when the dismemberment came he remained true to the old flag, casting his destinies with the North. In April, 1863, he enlisted in Company G, Ninth Regiment Missouri State Militia, and later, in 1864, raised a company in Dent County, and in September of that year was elected captain of Company D, Forty-eighth Missouri Infantry Volunteers, commanded by Col. Wells H. Blodgett. This regiment was on active field duty until February, 1865, at which time it was ordered to Chicago, Ill., and here Mr. Kenamore remained until the expiration of his term. He then returned to Salem, and in May, 1865, was appointed by Gov. Thomas C. Fletcher captain of a Dent County company of State Militia for home protection. He stood by his people faithfully and well. Capt. Kenamore was a man who had the entire confidence of the people, and he rendered effective service for them when a trusty and worthy man was needed. After the war he engaged in merchandising for several years in Salem, being a partner with W. R. Love a few years. He also traded in stock, speculated in real estate, and did a quite extensive business in various lines of commercial activity. He was successful in all his business transactions; was county surveyor of Dent County for about six years, and was probate judge when the war began. He died July 7, 1885. His wife, Emily F., was a native of Maury County, Tenn., and died in 1874. After her death Capt. Kenamore married Mrs. Lizzie Durham, *nee* McSpadden, who yet survives. Capt. Kenamore was the father of two children: William B., who died in November, 1884, at the age of thirty-six, and George R., who was educated in the common schools, and at the early age of sixteen enlisted in Company D, Forty-eighth Missouri Infantry, and was in service six months. After the war he engaged in merchandising, and has been occupied in this the greater part of the time since. In November, 1887, he was made Deputy United States Internal Revenue Collector, by Freeman Barnum. December 23, 1873, he married Mrs. Emma Henthorn, *nee* Craiger, a native of Indiana, born in 1850, and the daughter of James P. Craiger, of Carlisle, Ind.

They have two children: Rufus Clare and Charles. Mr. Kenamore is a life-long Democrat in his political views, casting his first presidential vote for Seymour in 1868; was county treasurer of Shannon County, Mo., for four years, and has frequently been a delegate to the various conventions. He is a Master Mason and a member of the A. O. U. W. His wife is a member of the Christian Church.

Rudolph Kessler, proprietor of the Mammoth Livery and Feed Stable at Salem, was born in the Kingdom of Prussia, Germany, August 19, 1844, and is the son of Rudolph and Mary Elizabeth (Miller) Kessler. Rudolph Kessler, Sr., was born in the Kingdom of Prussia, Germany, in 1818, and was a miller and distiller in his native country. He came to America in 1857, locating in Pilot Knob, Mo., and soon went to Madison County, where he purchased a farm and tilled the soil the remainder of his days. He died in 1883. His wife was also a native of the Kingdom of Prussia, Germany, born in 1825, and is yet living on the old home place. She is the mother of six children: Rudolph, Emily D., wife of Jacob Kessler; Charles, in Mine La Motte, Mo.; Joannah, Lena and John. The last three are at home. Rudolph was thirteen years of age when he came to America with his parents, and remained with them until they moved to the farm, when he commenced working at Pilot Knob. At the opening of the war he was employed in the Government stables at Pilot Knob. In 1863 he enlisted in Company M, Eighth Missouri Mounted Infantry, and served about six months, when he was discharged. He then enlisted in Company F, Fiftieth Regiment Mounted Infantry, and served about four months. He was in the battle of Pilot Knob. He was wagon-master while in the Eighth Regiment, and was quartermaster-sergeant in the Fiftieth Regiment. After the war he lived in Wayne County for a year, and from 1866 to 1872 he was at home in Madison County. In the last named year he came to Salem, and bought an interest in the livery and feed stable with Richard Pohlman, the firm being Pohlman & Kessler for over two years. Mr. Kessler then bought Mr. Pohlman's interest, and from that time until the present he has been sole owner. He keeps an average of twelve horses, seven buggies, five spring wagons, one lumber wagon and a hack to all trains. In 1881 he erected his present stable, which is 30x80 feet, with a thirty-foot shed on one side and a 130-foot shed on the rear, twenty-two feet wide. Mr. Kessler keeps a first-class stable—the best and most complete stable in Salem or in Dent County. By his long experience in the business he knows the needs of the traveling public, and keeps his stable and traveling apparatus in first-class order. He is courteous, obliging, and a true gentleman. In 1872 he married Miss Rosa Weaver, daughter of John C. Weaver. She was born in Warren County, Ohio, in 1850, and by her marriage became the mother of four children: Rudolph, John, Lizzie and Rosa. Mr. Kessler is a Republican in politics, and was a member of the city council two years. He is a member of the A. O. U. W. and Select Knights. He and wife are members of the German Lutheran Church.

Isaiah Larkin, a prosperous farmer of Dent County, Mo., was born in Jefferson County, of that State, in 1843, and is a son of George W. and Elizabeth J. (Stobaugh) Larkin, who were born in Kentucky in

1813 and 1815, and died in Dent and Jefferson Counties. Mo., in 1871 and 1853, respectively. They were married in their native State, and soon after immigrated to Missouri, locating in Jefferson County, of which they were pioneer settlers. Isaiah is one of four surviving members of their family of nine children, and remained on the home farm until he attained his majority, receiving no schooling, and consequently acquired but little education. In 1865 he was married to Ruthie Turley, who was born in Jefferson County, Mo., in 1843, and by her became the father of eleven children, ten of whom are living: Maley, George, William, Rosa, Isaiah, Dolly A., Effie, Dovie, Magnolia and Albert. For fourteen years after his marriage Mr. Larkin resided in Jefferson County, Mo., since which time he has lived on his farm of 160 acres where he now lives. He has about seventy-five acres under cultivation, well improved and with a good bearing orchard. He is an enterprising citizen, and has given his children, who are all single and reside at home, good educational advantages. He is a Democrat, and his wife and oldest daughter are members of the Baptist Church. Mrs. Larkin's parents, Zadock and Margaret Turley, were of Irish and Dutch descent, and were born in Kentucky and Virginia, respectively.

Dr. Wilson M. Lenox, a practicing physician and surgeon of Lake Spring, was born in what is now Phelps County, Mo., in 1843. He is a son of Hamilton and Permelia M. (Harrison) Lenox, and grandson of William Lenox, a Virginian by birth, but who went to Kentucky at a very early day, and was an intimate friend of Daniel Boone, whom he aided against the Indians, both in Kentucky and Missouri. He was also a soldier in the Black Hawk War, when his son Hamilton was but a boy. The family moved from Kentucky to Missouri, and spent a number of years in Callaway and other counties of Northern Missouri. They then came to Phelps County, at still quite an early period, and here died. He was of a migratory disposition, and spent much of his time with the Indians in the wild Southwest, where he figured prominently in civilizing the same. His father was of Scotch descent; was a soldier in the Revolutionary War, and was wounded at the battle of Cowpens. The ancestors of our subject on the father's side trace their lineage back to three brothers who were natives of Scotland; two of them came to America and from them sprang the Lenox families in America. Dr. Lenox's maternal grandfather, James Harrison, was a native of Virginia, and went to South Carolina when a young man, was married there, and at a very early period, about 1820, came to Missouri and settled where the town of Arlington is now located. He owned a very large and valuable tract of land, on which he spent the remainder of his days. He was one of the most influential and prominent citizens of Southern Missouri in his day. He served as a judge, was notary public, county and circuit clerk, etc.; in fact, he transacted nearly all the business affairs of the people for years in South Central Missouri, acting as a general tribunal. His sons became representative citizens of Missouri. The Doctor's great-grandfather, Benjamin Harrison, was a native of Virginia, of English descent, and a Revolutionary soldier. He is originally of the same family as President Benjamin Harrison. Dr. Lenox is the sixth of twelve children, and was educated at Jacksonville, Ill., and Lebanon Academy. At about the age of seventeen he began the study of medicine with his uncle, Dr. James P. Harrison, of Arlington, who was a graduate of McDowell Medical College, St. Louis. He studied with him until the opening of the late war between the North and South, and then enlisted in the Confederate army, and was afterward made medical purveyor of Parson's division of the Confederate army for the remainder of the war, operating in Missouri and Arkansas. He was at the battle of Wilson's Creek, Pea Ridge, Cane Hill, Camden, etc. After the war he went to Northeastern Texas, where he practiced with success for nearly two years. He returned to Missouri in 1867, located at Rolla until 1872, and one year later settled at Lake Spring, where he has since practiced with his usual success. He is one of the most prominent physicians of Dent County. At different times he has attended different medical institutions at New Orleans, Camden, Ark., St. Louis, etc., and graduated from the St. Louis College of Physicians and Surgeons in 1883. He was a delegate to the National Democratic Convention at Chicago, in 1884, which nominated Grover Cleveland. He was also a delegate to the State Convention in 1870, and has frequently been a delegate to congressional conventions, etc. He is a member of the State Medical Association, and also of the Minor Medical Association. He cast his first presidential vote for Horace Greeley in 1872, and it is hardly necessary to add, after reading the sketch so far, that he is a Democrat in his political views. He is a Royal Arch Mason of Rolla Chapter, and like his ancestors on both sides, is a prominent and representative citizen. His first marriage occurred in February, 1876, to Miss Martha Frances Bradford, a native of Phelps County, Mo., and the daughter of John D. and Margaret A. (Lenox) Bradford, who were early settlers of Phelps County. Mrs. Lenox died in October, 1882, and September 29, 1884, the Doctor married Miss Elizabeth C. Cowen, daughter of Dr. Robert B. and Susannah B. (Lenox) Cowen, granddaughter of William B. Cowen, and great-granddaughter of William Cowen, who was from Scotland, and was a lawyer in Virginia. The grandfather of Mrs. Lenox was also a native of Virginia; was known as Col. Cowen, and was probably a soldier in one of the early wars. He was a wealthy Virginian, and died in Pulaski County, Mo. The father of Mrs. Lenox was born in Bedford County, Va., and came with his father when a boy to St. Louis, and afterward to Phelps County, where he spent the rest of his life. He died in 1869; was a practicing physician at Edgar Springs for fifteen years, and was a graduate of McDowell Medical College, St. Louis, Mo. His wife, and the mother of Mrs. Lenox, is still living, and is residing near Edgar Springs. Mrs. Lenox was educated at various schools in Dent and Phelps Counties, and at the Ursuline Convent of St. Louis. She is a refined and educated lady. Both wives were second cousins of Dr. Lenox.

Abner H. Leonard, farmer and stock raiser of Spring Creek Township, was born in Iredell County, N. C., in 1827, and is the son of Robert and Cynthia (Johnson) Leonard. Robert Leonard was born in North Carolina in 1781, and the mother was born in the same State, but was about ten or twelve years younger than her husband.

She was an orphan, and was Mr. Leonard's second wife. Mr. Leonard removed to Gilmore County, West Tenn., about 1833, and came to what is now Dent County, and settled on Spring Creek, near Salem, and was one of the first white settlers of the county. He improved a good farm, where he died January 5, 1857. He was fond of hunting, and spent much time in this pursuit when game was plenty. The nearest post-office was Steelville, and they did the principal part of their marketing at St. Louis, where they went with their ox teams, carrying with them hides, furs, beeswax, wheat, etc., which they exchanged for groceries, etc., enough to last the family a year. They were generally fourteen or fifteen days in making the trip. The next day after Mr. Leonard arrived in Dent County he started through the woods to borrow or buy some corn. There were no settlements near him, and to prevent getting lost he blazed the trees as he went along, so that he could follow them in getting back. Joseph S. Leonard, the great-grandfather of Abner H. Leonard, was a native of Ireland, but came to America prior to the Revolutionary War. His son William, who was the grandfather of Abner H., was living at Wilmington, N. C., during the Revolutionary War, and when Robert was but seven days of age the British captured the city, but the father being sick the family was not molested. He was a rope-maker by occupation. The mother of our subject died in 1844. Mr. Leonard was the father of eighteen children, nine by each wife. Abner H. Leonard was the fourth child born to the last marriage. He was reared in the wilds of Dent County, where there were no schools until he was nearly grown. He never attended school but a few months, and the principal part of his education was obtained by the light of the fireplace in the evenings at home. The woods at that time were full of bear, elk, wolves, panthers, wildcats, etc., and young Leonard spent a great deal of his time in hunting; was an unusually good shot, and many deer fell at the report of his gun. In 1850 he married Miss Mary Ann, daughter of John and Anna Stagner, who were natives of North Carolina, and who afterward moved to Kentucky, where Mrs. Leonard was born. About 1840 Mr. Stagner moved to Salem, and afterward spent a few years in Southwestern Missouri, but later returned to Dent County, where both died, on Dry Fork, the mother about 1856 and the father about 1866. He was the first justice of the peace, and married the first couple in Spring Creek Township. Both were members of the Methodist Episcopal Church. To Mr. Leonard and wife were born seven children, four now living: John W., William R., James F., and Eliza Ellen, wife of John A. Jones, living on her father's farm. The same year of his marriage Mr. Leonard settled on his present farm, which consists of 280 acres, with seventy-five under cultivation. He served about three years in the Federal Army, Company D, Thirty-second Missouri Volunteer Infantry, and operated in Arkansas, Mississippi, Louisiana, Alabama, Georgia, North Carolina, South Carolina and Tennessee, under Sherman, and was in the first engagement at Chickasaw Bayou, Arkansas Post, Lookout Mountain, Missionary Ridge, and was in all the Georgia and Atlanta campaign to the sea. He was at the grand review at Washington, D. C. He was discharged at Louisville, Ky., July 18, 1865, and was never wounded nor captured during service. Politically he was formerly a Whig, his first presidential vote being for Gen. Tayler in 1848, but he is now a Republican. Mr. Leonard has spared no pains in educating his children, and is justly proud of his efforts in that direction. He and wife have been members of the Methodist Episcopal Church since soon after the war, and three of the children are members of the same church. Mrs. Leonard has been almost blind for ten years.

Robert A. Leonard, a successful tiller of the soil and a prominent stock dealer of Norman Township, is the son of Joseph and Elizabeth (Walls) Leonard, and the grandson of Robert Leonard, who was one of the pioneers of Dent County, and whose history appears elsewhere in this volume. Joseph Leonard was a native of North Carolina, and came with his parents to what is now Dent County in 1833, where he married, and afterward settled near Salem, where he died in 1878, at the age of sixty-five. He was a carpenter, and built some of the first houses in Salem. He was justice of the peace for many years, and was a member of the Methodist Episcopal Church. The mother was born in Tennessee, and came with her parents to Dent County when young. Her father afterward moved to Laclede County, where he died. She is still living, is about seventy-six years of age, and has been a member of the Methodist Church for many years. She is the mother of ten children, five sons and five daughters, Robert A. being the fourth. He was born in Spring Creek Township, Dent Co., Mo., in 1844, and received a good practical education in the common schools. At the age of eighteen he enlisted in Company E, Eleventh Missouri Cavalry, United States Army, and operated mostly in Arkansas and Mississippi. He was in the battle of Brown's Prairie, Ark.; was in many skirmishes, and served until the close of the war. He was mustered out at New Orleans, July 25, 1865. He then returned home, and November 4, 1868, he married Miss Mary McCaupin, a native of Tennessee, who came with her parents to Dent County when a child. Six children were born to Mr. and Mrs. Leonard, who lived in Texas Township until 1882, when they moved to their present farm on Dry Fork. Here they have 320 acres of land, with about 150 under cultivation, and Mr. Leonard has done a great deal in improving the stock of the county. He is a stanch Republican politically, casting his first presidential vote for Gen. U. S. Grant in 1868; is a member of the G. A. R., Agricultural Wheel, A. O. U. W., and he and wife have been members of the Methodist Episcopal Church for a great many years. Mr. Leonard has spared no pains in educating his children and in the general upbuilding of the county.

Josiah Lewis, farmer of Franklin Township, Dent Co., Mo., was born in Maries County, Mo., in 1830, and is a son of John and Thankful (Short) Lewis, who were born in Tennessee and Kentucky, in 1780 and 1798, respectively. The father was of English descent, a farmer by occupation, and while yet single moved from his native State to Missouri, where he spent the remainder of his days, and later died. Ten of their twelve children grew to maturity, Josiah being the sixth of the family. He made the paternal house his home until his father's death, and in 1861 was married to Miss Mary Jane Bugg, who was born in Kentucky in 1840, and died in 1864, having borne one child that died in infancy. In 1862 he enlisted in Company B, Cavalry Brigade, Confederate States Army, serving until the close of the war, and being a participant in the battle of Iron Mountain. He has resided on his present farm of 200 acres since the close of the war, and has about fifty acres under cultivation. He is one of the worthy citizens of the county, and, owing to his many admirable traits, has many warm personal friends. He has always supported the principles of the Democratic party, and is one of the pioneer citizens of Dent County.

Judge William Robert Love, president of the bank at Salem, and dealer in general merchandise at that place, is a native of Lincoln County, Tenn., born in 1823, and the son of Robert King and Margaret Catherine Love. Robert K. Love was born in Wilkes County, N. C., in 1790, and is the son of John Love, who was a native of Scotland. Robert Love immigrated to Tennessee when a young man, and was living in Lincoln County when married. In 1830 he moved to Washington County, Mo. (now Reynolds County), and here passed the remainder of his life engaged in farming. He died in 1843. His wife was born in Lincoln County, Tenn., in 1801, and died in 1838. She was the mother of six children, five of whom are still living: William R., John A., Dallason S., Elizabeth J. and Sarah A. William R. Love was reared and grew to manhood on a farm, and remained with his parents as long as they lived. In 1844 he married Miss Sarah P. Larimore, a native of Tennessee, born in 1825, and the daughter of James Larimore. Six children were the result of this union: Elizabeth, wife of B. M. Hodges; Dallason, who is in the store with his father; Andrew H., Mary, wife of Lucius Judson, attorney at law; William B. and Horace J. Mr. Love lived in Iron County until 1860, when he came to Dent County, and located two miles south of Salem. In the fall of 1862 he commenced merchandising in Salem, and about 1863 John W. Livesay became a partner. They did an immense business for upward of twelve years, having stores at Salem, Rolla and St. James at the same time, and during the year 1867 Mr. Love was a resident of Rolla. He was also in partnership with W. A. Young a few years in Salem. In November, 1883, the Bank of Salem was organized, and Mr. Love was elected president, which position he has held since its organization, he being the principal stockholder and prime mover in its organization. About 1875 he erected a large, three-story brick hotel, at a cost of $10,000, including the room in which he has his general store. Mr. Love is the owner of a large estate, and is perhaps the wealthiest citizen in the county. He is a man who has always led an active life, and has made a marked success financially. He commenced in life a poor boy, but by close application to business and economy he has accumulated a good property. In 1863 Mr. Love was appointed county treasurer of Dent County, was elected and served in all thirteen years. Later he was county judge for three years, being presiding judge. Mr. Love is a member of the Masonic fraternity, has been a life-long Democrat in his political views, and Mrs. Love is a member of the Baptist Church.

James D. McGee, farmer of Franklin Township, Dent Co., Mo.,

was born in Tennessee in 1825, being a son of John and Margaret (Dixon) McGee, who were born in Tennessee, the former about 1797 and the latter in 1799. John McGee was of Irish descent, and throughout life followed the occupation of farming. In 1845 he emigrated from his native State to what is now Dent (then Crawford) County, Mo., and there spent the remainder of his days, dying about 1865. His wife was of Scotch descent, and also died in Dent County, in 1886, having borne a family of seven children, only three of whom are now living. James D. McGee is the fourth member of the family, and made his parents' house his home until forty-five years of age. His boyhood days were spent in attending the district schools and working on the farm, and in 1869 he espoused Miss Sarah Pettigrew, who was born in Alabama about 1844, and was a daughter of Edward and Nancy Pettigrew. She was a member of the Cumberland Presbyterian Church, and died in 1876, having borne a family of three children. In 1877 Mr. McGee married his second wife, Miss Catherine Hutchison, who was born in Tennessee about 1846, and died in 1883, leaving two children. She was also a member of the Cumberland Presbyterian Church. Mr. McGee has a fine farm of 460 acres, eighty acres of which are well improved and in a good state of cultivation. He is one of the pioneers of Dent County, and in his political views is a Democrat.

Rev. Thomas MacGlashan, member of the firm of MacGlashan & Mitchell, manufacturers of wagons and buggies and owners of a general repair shop at Salem, Mo., was born in Scotland in 1832, being the son of Alexander and Betsey (MacDonald) MacGlashan, both natives of Scotland. Alexander's ancestors were strong supporters of Prince Charles Edward Stuart, and when he lost his cause all his followers above a certain rank were to be court-martialed. Alexander MacGlashan's ancestors were included in the ranks, and to avoid detection one brother changed his name to MacGlashan, hence the name. Some fled to America, and afterward became famous in the Revolutionary war under the name of MacDonald. Alexander MacGlashan was a millwright and sawyer by trade. He passed his entire life in his native country, and died in 1834 from the effects of an injury received in a mill. His wife, Betsey MacDonald, was born in 1812, and her ancestors were of the MacDonalds of Keppoch. She is still living in her native country. After the death of her husband she married James MacDonald, who is also deceased. Rev. Thomas MacGlashan is the only child by the first marriage, and he was but two years of age when his father died. When large enough he commenced working with his step-father, who was a wheel-wright and house builder by trade. He attended school until he was sixteen years of age, and afterward became tutor to the Duke of Athole for two years. After that he became overseer in one of the Duke's saw-mills, where he remained seven years, and for the following two years and a half he was overseer of the mills for one Mr. McInroy, of Lude. About 1859 he became land steward for Gen. Sir John McDonald, having command of all his large landed estate. Gen. Sir John died, and his son, Gen. Alastair MacDonald, succeeded his father. He is at present commander of the forces in Scotland. Mr. MacGlashan could not agree with Gen. Alastair, and accordingly, in 1868, he immigrated to America and located in Milwaukee. The following year he immigrated to Licking, Mo., and here opened up a wagon and builder's shop, which was consumed by fire, with the tools, etc., six weeks later. In 1866 he married Miss Christina Cameron, a native of Scotland, who was born in 1842. They had one son, Thomas Angus Ewan. In 1872 Mr. MacGlashan came to Salem, and did not even have three cents to pay postage on a letter. He commenced house building as soon as possible, and in a short time engaged with John Eaton, blacksmith, to manufacture wagons for him. From that time until the present he has been more or less engaged in the manufacture of the same. In 1881 the firm was formed. They have manufactured 275 wagons, making about fifty per annum, and also manufacture buggies. Their work is all first-class, all being warranted to give satisfaction. Mr. MacGlashan is a Republican in politics; was justice of the peace of Salem for two years, and taught three terms of school in Crawford County, Mo.,—1870, 1874 and 1875. Mr. MacGlashan is one of the solid, substantial business men of Salem, and has made all his property by economy and good management. He is a member of the A. O. U. W. When a young man he professed religion, and prepared to enter the Presbyterian ministry, but owing to sickness he was compelled to abandon it. After coming to the United States he became a member of the Baptist Church, and in 1870 was licensed to preach; had charge of the Baptist Church at Salem one year. Off and on for the past sixteen years he has been Sunday-school superintendent. His wife is a member of the Baptist Church.

Dr. J. N. McMurtrey, a prominent practitioner of Salem, and druggist of the same place, was born in Madison County, Mo., in 1842, being the son of Alexander and Rebecca (Powell) McMurtrey, and grandson of Alexander McMurtrey, who was a minister by profession. In his early life he practiced the Presbyterian doctrine, but in later years the Christian faith. About 1811 he immigrated to Southeast Missouri, locating in what is now Madison County, and was in that State before it was admitted into the Union. He was one of the very first white settlers in that section of the State, and a prominent man, being one of the pioneer preachers. Alexander McMurtrey, Jr., was married in Madison County, Mo., and in 1847 moved to Independence, Mo., where he died in 1850, while yet in the prime of life. He was of Scotch-Irish descent. Mrs. Rebecca (Powell) McMurtrey was born in North Carolina in 1802, and died in Salem, Mo., in 1882. After the death of Mr. McMurtrey, she married Samuel Aldridge, who is also deceased. She was the mother of thirteen children, all by the first marriage, and seven now living. Of this family Dr. J. N. McMurtrey is the youngest boy. He received his literary education at Bluff Springs, Tenn., and at Miami University, Oxford, Ohio. At the age of twenty-one he began teaching, and followed this in Marshall County Ill., one term. In 1866 he commenced the study of medicine in St. Louis, and in 1868 graduated as an M. D. in the Eclectic Medical College at Cincinnati, Ohio. October 21, of the following year, he married Miss Eliza J. Kindig, who was born in Woodford County, Ill., in 1847. To them were born six children: Jessie, Walter, Tessie,

Clifford, Deane and Percy. After graduating Dr. McMurtrey came to Salem, Mo., where he entered upon the practice of his profession, and this he has actively followed ever since, with the exception of 1870, when he was in Henderson County, Ill. One year later he established a drug store at Salem; has a first-class stock of drugs, as large if not the largest in Dent County. Dr. McMurtrey has a large and lucrative practice, and is one of the leading physicians and surgeons of Dent County. He is a stanch Democrat in his political views, casting his first vote for Horace Greeley. He was postmaster at Salem from July to the fall of 1887, and is a member of the I. O. O. F. and A. O. U. W. He and wife and eldest daughter are members of the Missionary Baptist Church.

Moses M. McSpadden, farmer and stock raiser of Short Bend Township, and the son of Capt. John and Elizabeth (Apperson) McSpadden, and grandson of Moses McSpadden, was born in Washington County, Va., in 1823. His grandfather was probably born in North Carolina, and died in Virginia about 1827. He was of Scotch-Irish origin, and a well-to do farmer. The parents of our subject were both natives of Virginia, where they lived until 1828, when they moved to Missouri by land, crossing the river at St. Louis, which was at that time a small town. They lived in St. Charles County for about three years, and then removed to Franklin County, where he built a powder-mill on Spring Creek. He died about the time it was completed, which was in 1834. He was a millwright and miller, and an enterprising citizen. He was captain of the militia in early days, and was a surveyor of either St. Charles or Franklin County. He was a member of the Presbyterian Church. His wife died a few months prior to his death. She was the daughter of Dr. John Apperson, a native of Virginia, who came to Missouri at an early date. He died in Franklin County, Mo., in 1835, and was a well-known and prominent physician and surgeon for many years. He was of Scotch descent. He reared a large family; one of his sons, John, was a soldier in the War of 1812; another son, Randolph W., now of California, is father-in-law to Senator George Hearst, of California. Moses M. McSpadden, subject of this sketch, is the eldest of four children, one son and three daughters, and is the only one now living. He was left on orphan at the age of ten or eleven, and was mostly reared by a cousin, Moses Berry, of Franklin County. He received a limited country-school education, and when about fifteen years of age he went to Washington County, attended school and worked on a farm. He lived some years with Randolph W. Apperson, who was his guardian. He came to Dent County, Mo., in 1849, and established a store on the Meramec, in Meramec Township, where he remained for about three years. In 1852 he was married, in the house where he now lives, to Miss Juliann Millsaps, daughter of James and Elizabeth Millsaps. Her father died many years ago in St. Francois County, and her mother, who was born in 1808, died near Salem in 1880. Mrs. McSpadden was born in Washington County, Mo. Her grandfather, Thomas Higginbotham, who was a native of Georgia, left home when young on account of a step-mother, and was married in Tennessee to Miss Elizabeth Ross. He then moved to Missouri, when it was still a Territory, and settled in Washington County, where his wife died many years ago. He then, in about 1836, settled on a farm, where the subject of this sketch now lives, and there died in 1851, at the age of eighty-seven. He was known as Capt. Higginbotham, having served as captain in the War of 1812. His father, Joseph Higginbotham, was a native of Ireland, and commanded a company in the Revolutionary War. To Mr. McSpadden and wife were born five children, one son and four daughters now living (one died in infancy): Elizabeth, wife of Moses H. McSpadden; Alcey Jane, wife of Dr. Andrew H. Love; Emeline A. and Joseph M. Soon after marriage Mr. McSpadden settled in Salem, where he followed merchandising a few years, and then settled in the woods near Salem, where he improved a good farm. He lived there until 1887, and then came to his present farm, which consists of over 360 acres. In all he has 1,300 acres, and a business block in Salem. In 1853 Mr. McSpadden was elected county and circuit court clerk for six years, and re-elected in 1859, but was removed during the war. Again, in 1874, he was elected circuit clerk, and served four years with credit and satisfaction. He declined to be re-elected. He has been a Democrat in politics all his life, and his first presidential vote was cast for Franklin Pierce in 1852. He was formerly a member of the Masonic fraternity, now demitted, and has been a member of the Presbyterian Church for many years. At the breaking out of the Mexican War in Texas he joined Company I, of Col. Albert Sidney Johnston's regiment (Third Texas Infantry), for six years, but after three months was discharged on account of ill health. Some time after he volunteered his services, but was rejected. He served as sergeant. The lumber in Mr. McSpadden's house was sawed by a whip-saw on the farm, and is one of the oldest houses in Dent County, the stone chimney bearing the date of 1838. Mr. McSpadden was the first man to be elected county and circuit clerk and recorder of Dent County, and is one of the old and much respected citizens of the county.

William C. Martin, retired farmer and stock raiser, and one of the much esteemed citizens of Spring Creek Township, was born in Roane County, Tenn., in 1826, his parents being George and Matilda (Childers) Martin, who probably spent all their lives in Tennessee. The father died about 1832 or 1833, and the mother followed him to the grave after her son, William C., came to Missouri. He was one of six children, and the only one who ever came to Missouri. He received a very meager education, and remained with his mother until twenty-three years of age. In 1849 he moved to Dent County, where he was married, in 1852, to Miss Rachel M. Barnes, a native of Alabama, born in 1830, and the daughter of Thomas and Elizabeth Barnes, who moved from one of the Carolinas to Alabama. In about 1844 the family removed from Alabama to Arkansas, and the next year from that State to Dent County, where her father died in 1880. The mother is still living, and is eighty-four years of age. Her father and mother came from Ireland at an early day. Her father left home before she was born, and she never saw him. Mrs. Martin's father was of Scotch origin. To Mr. and Mrs. Martin were born four sons and one daughter, all living: Eliza Jane, now Mrs. John Thomas

Watson; William T., John Westley, Francis Marion and George Washington, all of whom have had the best educational advantages. The youngest is a graduate of Dixon (Ill.) College. Since the war Mr. Martin has lived on his late farm, four miles north of Salem, and was the owner of 300 acres of land. He has just recently sold to his son-in-law. He dealt largely in stock, and is one of the county's most substantial citizens. He was formerly a Whig in politics, but of late years has been a Democrat, and his first presidential vote was cast for Zachary Taylor in 1848. He and wife have been members of the Baptist Church for many years, and are members in good standing.

W. T. Martin, railroad and express agent of Salem, was born in Dent County, Mo., in 1855, being the son of William C. and Rachel Minerva (Barnes) Martin. William C. Martin was born in Roane County, Tenn., in 1826, and when a young man immigrated to Dent County, Mo. He was married here in 1852, and located four miles north of Salem, where he has since resided. He is the owner of 320 acres of land, and is a successful farmer. His wife, Rachel M. (Barnes) Martin, was born in Lauderdale County, Ala., in 1830, and is the daughter of Thomas and Elizabeth Barnes, who were natives of Alabama, and who came to Dent County, Mo., in 1844, and located seven miles northeast of the county seat. Thomas Barnes died about 1880, at the age of eighty, and his wife is yet living, and is eighty-four years of age. To Mr. and Mrs. Martin were born five children: Eliza J., wife of John T. Watson; William Thomas, John W., Francis M. and George W. William T. was educated at Salem Academy, and at the age of eighteen he began teaching, which profession he followed for three terms in Dent County, Mo. He was reared and grew to manhood on the farm, making his home with his parents until twenty-one years of age. In 1877 he married Miss Amanda J. Goade, who was born in Crawford County, Mo., January 6, 1859, and who bore him six children: Charles E., Ernest E., Minnie M., Pearl, Mattie and Lee. In 1879 Mr. Martin and family came to Salem, where he teamed for two years for William James, hauling iron ore. In 1881 he commenced working for the St. Louis, Salem & Little Rock Railroad, now 'Frisco Railroad, as assistant agent and assistant clerk for E. B. Sankey, superintendent of the same branch. For twenty months he was baggage and express agent for the Salem branch, and in February, 1887, he was given his present position. He is a member of the A. O. U. W., and is a Democrat in politics, casting his first presidential vote for Tilden in 1876.

Jordan Miner was born in Reynolds County, Mo., in 1829, and is the next to the youngest of a family of eight children, five of whom are living. He made the paternal roof his home until twenty-six years of age, and received what education he has in the old subscription schools. About 1855 he went to California, and after working in the gold mines of that State for about four years, returned to Dent County, Mo., and purchased the farm of 218 acres on which he is now residing. He has ninety acres under cultivation, and is considered one of the enterprising and successful farmers of the county. January 16, 1859, he was married to Miss Margaret E. Parker, who was born in Franklin County, Mo., in 1840, and is a daughter of David A. and Sarah Parker, who were of Irish and Dutch descent, respectively. Mr. and Mrs. Miner became the parents of eight children, only four of whom are now living. H. H. Miner, their oldest child, remained with them until twenty-two years of age. During that time he advanced his education as far as it was possible in the common schools. After two years of wild adventure in the West, he returned, and began his studies in the Home College at Salem, which he had to leave several times to teach school to secure means to defray his expenses. He began the study of the legal profession, was admitted to the bar April 2, 1888, and ran for circuit attorney in the same year, being defeated by a small majority. His office is with the Salem *Monitor*. Mr. Jordan Miner is a member of the County Wheel, and he and wife are members of the United Christian Church. His parents, Laban E. and Elizabeth (Moran) Miner, were born in Kentucky, about 1791, and died in Reynolds County, Mo., in 1863 and 1866, respectively. They were reared and married in their native State, and in 1818 immigrated to Missouri, being among the pioneer citizens of Reynolds County. The father was of English and the mother of Irish descent.

Samuel Morrison, hardware merchant and dealer in farming implements at Salem, Mo., was born in Coshocton County, Ohio, in 1839, being the son of William and Sarah (Kimberly) Morrison. William Morrison was born in Holmes County, Ohio, in 1807, and was of Scotch-Irish descent. He was a farmer by occupation, and died in Coshocton County, Ohio, in 1852. His wife, Sarah Kimberly, was born in Holmes County, Ohio, in 1809, and died in 1864. They were the parents of five children, two of whom are living. Samuel Morrison was the eldest of this family. He remained on the farm until eighteen years of age, when he went to Minnesota, and remained two years. From 1859 to 1860 he was part of the time in Iowa and part of the time in Illinois. In December of the last named year he went to Vigo County, Ind., and was there at the breaking out of the war. April 17, 1861, he enlisted in Company H, Thirteenth Indiana Infantry Volunteers, and served for three years. He was in the fight at Rich Mountain; was with McClellan on the Peninsula, Winchester, Morris Island, Jacksonville, Fla., Cold Harbor, siege of Petersburgh, Fort Fisher, Goldsborough, Raleigh, and was discharged at Indianapolis September 19, 1865. He was mustered out as captain of his company the last eight months, but previous to that he was first lieutenant. During his service he was neither wounded nor captured. After the war he resided for two years in his native county, and then went to Missouri, and, locating in Salem, engaged as salesman in a store. In 1869 he was appointed deputy sheriff of Dent County, and served four years. While filling that office he became a partner of Rufus Kenworthy in a hardware and tin shop, the firm title being Morrison & Kenworthy for thirteen years. In 1883 Mr. Kenworthy sold his interest to Mr. Morrison, and since that time Mr. Morrison has conducted the business on his own responsibility. He was married in 1872 to Miss Eliza R. Linsey, who was born in Cincinnati, Ohio, in 1852. An interesting family of five children were the fruits of this union: William S., Grace L., Clarence M., Guy W. and Carl T. Mr.

Morrison is a Republican in politics, is a member of the I. O. O. F., charter member, also a member of the G. A. R., and was one of the charter members. He and wife are members of the Presbyterian Church, and he is a member of the A. O. U. W., and a charter member of the Select Knights. Samuel's grandfather, William Morrison, was a native of Virginia, and about the year 1801 he went to what is now Holmes County, Ohio. He was a soldier in the Revolutionary War, also in the War of 1812; was first lieutenant of Adam Johnson's company; was mustered into service August 25, 1812, and mustered out September 25 of the same year. In the War of 1812 he wore a yellow hunting shirt, trimmed with white fringe, and carried a trusty rifle, tomahawk and scalping knife. His company was called "The Mansfield Frontier." Samuel Morrison had two brothers, Marcus and John Morrison, in the army. Marcus was in Company G, Eightieth Indiana, and died of typhoid fever at Danville, Ky., in September, 1863. John was a member of Company D, One Hundred and Forty-second Regiment, Ohio, and died of chronic diarrhœa in the hospital at City Point, Va., in August, 1864.

Ex-Judge Franklin M. Moser. Foremost among the enterprising and successful farmers and stock raisers of Spring Creek Township stands the name of Judge Moser, who was born in Independence County, Ark., in 1838, and is the son of Eli and Maria (Bowen) Moser, natives of North Carolina and Arkansas, respectively. When a young man Mr. Moser went to Arkansas, where he married Miss Bowen. He was married twice, and had seven children by his first marriage and six by the last. He was a well-to-do farmer, and an enterprising citizen. The mother died in 1848, and the father in 1860. Both were members of the Methodist Church. John Moser, grandfather of subject, was a native of Germany, and he and wife came to the United States soon after the war, settling in North Carolina, but spent the last part of their days in Arkansas. Ex-Judge Franklin M. Moser was educated in the common country schools of Arkansas, and was obliged to walk two or three miles in order to attend the same. At the age of twenty-one he began for himself by farming, and at the breaking out of the late unpleasantness between the North and South, he enlisted in Company I, Eleventh Arkansas Volunteer Infantry, Confederate Army, and was in service until the close of the war. He was at the battles of Corinth, Iuka, siege of Vicksburg and Baker's Creek. After the fall of Vicksburg he served in the transportation department; was in the battle of Jenkins' Ferry and many skirmishes. He surrendered at Shreveport, La., in May, 1865. He was wounded in the thigh at Corinth, was captured, and held prisoner for about six months on parole, and afterward was exchanged, and rejoined his regiment at Vicksburg, where he was again captured and paroled. He then started for home, but in about two months was exchanged, and rejoined his command near Camden, Ark. After the war he returned home. Previous to the war, in 1858, he married Miss Sarah A., daughter of Daniel and Margaret (Suminett) Moser. She was born in Tennessee, as were also her parents, and afterward moved to Arkansas, where her father died in 1857, and the mother in 1874. To Mr. Moser and wife were born seven children, four sons and three daughters, all living in Dent County. Mr. Moser lived in Arkansas until 1869, and then moved to Dent County, Mo., on Dry Fork Creek, ten miles north of Salem, where he resided until 1883, and then moved on his present farm, three miles northeast of Salem. He has an excellent farm of 230 acres, 110 under cultivation, with good buildings and orchard, and nearly all his property is the result of his own labor. He improved a farm on Dry Fork and one in Arkansas. He is a natural mechanic, and has worked at the trade of blacksmith, carpenter and mason. In 1880 he was elected associate judge from the Second District; was re-elected in 1882, and again in 1884, serving six years, and increasing his majority each time. He is a Democrat politically, and his first presidential vote was for J. C. Breckinridge in 1860. He is a member of the Masonic fraternity, Salem Lodge No. 225, and has held offices as high as Senior Warden. He and wife are members of the Methodist Episcopal Church, South; two of the children are members of the same church, and one of the children is a member of the Baptist Church.

Judge James Madison Orchard, postmaster of Salem, was born in Washington County, Mo., and is the son of John and Rosanna (Ashbrook) Orchard. John Orchard was a native of Kentucky, born in 1801, and was of Scotch-Irish descent. When eighteen years of age he immigrated to Missouri, when that State was a Territory, and located in Washington County. Here he was married, and in 1847 he came to Dent County, Mo., locating on the Meramec, and in 1850 settled on a farm six miles southeast of the county seat. He at first owned 180 acres, but has added to this 320 acres. He was sheriff of Washington County, Mo., one term. He died in 1865. His wife, Rosanna (Ashbrook) Orchard, was born in Washington County, Mo., in 1805, and died in 1873. To them were born eight children, only three now living: Alexander H., George W. and James M. The last named was educated in the common schools of his native county, was reared on a farm, and in 1849 commenced teaching a four months' school, but when half through with the term resigned, and started to California to obtain his share of the hidden wealth in the "Eureka State." He went overland, it taking him six months to make the long and perilous journey, and remained in that State until 1853, working in the mines, after which he returned East and became a citizen of Salem, Mo. He then engaged in merchandising, his father and his brother, William A., being partners. In 1854 Mr. Orchard was appointed postmaster, the name of the office being Dent Court-house, now Salem, and held the position until about 1858, he being the first postmaster at that place. In November, 1856, Judge Orchard was married to Miss Martha E. Ware, nee Mitchell, daughter of Spencer Mitchell, who was one of the pioneer settlers of Texas County, Mo. Mrs. Orchard was born in Tennessee in 1829, and by her marriage became the mother of seven children: John M., assistant professor of mathematics at Naval Academy at Annapolis, Md., and graduate of the same, ranked as lieutenant of the United States Navy; Albert E., who died in January, 1888, at the age of twenty-six; Charles H., manager of Clark Mercantile Co., of Salem, Mo.; Mary L., wife of Dr. C. A. Dunnavant, at

Kirkwood, Mo.; Julia R., wife of J. W. Simms, at West Plains, Mo.; William D., at Pueblo, Col., and Ruah. Judge Orchard continued in partnership with his father and brother until 1858, when the firm sold to John W. Livesay, and in 1860 Judge Orchard became a partner in a general store, but one year later they boxed their goods and shipped them to St. Louis. Subsequently Judge Orchard sold his interest to Mr. Wheeling. In 1862 he began shoemaking, which occupation he followed until the fall of 1865, and after the war he commenced practicing law, having been admitted to the bar in 1855. In November, 1887, Judge Orchard was appointed by Postmaster-General W. F. Vilas to the position of postmaster at Salem, and this office he is now holding. He is one of the old citizens of Dent County, and is one of the influential and most esteemed members. For one year he was probate judge of Dent County, and was county commissioner for a short period. He is a life-long Democrat in his politics, casting his first presidential vote for Franklin Pierce in 1852. He is a Royal Arch Mason, and he and wife are members of the Missionary Baptist Church, of which he has been a member for forty-one years and a deacon for twelve years. Mrs. Orchard, by a previous marriage, became the mother of one child, Spencer H. Ware, who is circuit clerk of Shannon County, Mo.

Charles H. Orchard, secretary, treasurer and general manager of the Clark Mercantile Company, at Salem, of which he is also a member, was born in Salem, Mo., in 1860, and is the son of J. M. and Martha E. (Mitchell) Orchard. Charles H. Orchard was educated in the Salem public schools, and at the age of sixteen began clerking in a store at that place. At the age of nineteen he began as bookkeeper and assistant manager at West Plains, in the branch store of H. B. Clark & Bro. at that place, where he remained for two years. Then for two years he was salesman at Salem for the same firm. For about two years he was manager of their branch store at Cuba, and then returned to West Plains, where he became a partner of Hill & Co., successors to H. B. Clark & Bro. He remained there for a short time, or until he began for the present firm, which was organized September 1, 1888, as successors to A. H. & H. B. Clark. They are carrying a general stock of merchandise, with a capital stock of $15,000. Mr. Orchard was married in 1887 to Miss Alice M., daughter of Capt. F. L. and E. E. Withaup, and who was born near Richland, Mo. Her parents are now living in Salem, Mo., and her father was captain in the United States army during the late war. Mrs. Orchard is a member of the Episcopal Church, and by her marriage became the mother of one child. Mr. Orchard is a Democrat in his political principles, and his first presidential vote was for Grover Cleveland in 1884. He is a member of the A. O. U. W., West Plains Lodge, and is a member of the Baptist Church.

Hon. John E. Organ, editor and publisher of the Salem *Monitor*, at Salem, Mo., was born in Champaign County, Ohio, April 7, 1838, and is the son of James and Amanda L. (Parry) Organ. James Organ is a native of the "Keystone State," born in 1802, and was married in Ohio. He immigrated to White County, Ind., in 1848, and in 1858 moved to Dent County, Mo., where he now resides.

His wife, Amanda L. (Parry) Organ, was born in Augusta County, Va., in 1810, and died in 1881. She was the mother of seven children, John E. being the second. He was educated in the common schools of Indiana and Ohio, studying mathematics under a private instructor. He came with his parents to Dent County in 1858, and during that year, and in 1859, followed the teacher's profession. In the last named year he was elected surveyor of Phelps County, and served until the breaking out of the Civil War, when, in 1861, he enlisted in a detached cavalry company, Confederate States army, in the State Guard, and was second lieutenant of the same. At the end of six months he recruited a company, or nearly so, and in March, 1862, was captured and held prisoner six months, being exchanged at Vicksburg, where he enlisted in Company E, Eighth Regiment Missouri Infantry, and was made first sergeant of the company. He served until June, 1865, when he surrendered at Shreveport, La., under Kirby Smith. He was in the fights at Prairie Grove, Little Rock, Pleasant Hill, Jenkins' Ferry and others. After the war he returned to teaching, and followed this for several terms. August 20, 1867, he married Miss Martha L. Burkitt, a native of Phelps County, Mo., born June 14, 1843. This union resulted in the birth of four children: Minnie, James B., Perry and Daisy E. In 1873 Mr. Organ bought the Salem *Monitor*, and has since been its publisher. In 1874 he was elected to the State Legislature by the Democratic party; in 1878 was again elected, and still again in 1884. In 1880 he was an elector for the Eleventh Congressional District, on the National ticket, for Hancock and English. In 1886 his name was presented to the Democratic Convention, Twenty-second Senatorial District, for nomination to the State Senate, against five competitors, but he was defeated after a protracted campaign of nearly four months, two dead-locked conventions, and more than 800 ballots, only lacking one vote of a nomination on several, and but for the treachery of one delegate he would have been successful. Mr. Organ is a very extensive land-holder, owning about 40,000 acres, and has also considerable interest in iron mines, and large property in Salem. Mr. Organ is a man well posted politically, better, perhaps, than any other man in Dent County; he is an able writer, a practical newspaper man, and one of the most influential men of Dent County. He is a member of the A. O. U. W.

Jesse B. Pemberton, farmer and merchant of Stone Hill, Mo., is a native of Wilson County, Tenn., born in 1821. His father, Richard Pemberton, was born in Virginia about 1793, and resided in his native State until his removal to Tennessee, where he met and married Miss Nancy Glasby, who was born in that State about 1808. Subsequently they moved to Saline County, Ill., where they spent the remainder of their days, dying in 1881 and 1874, respectively. Ten of their twelve children grew to maturity, Jesse B. being the third child. He resided under the paternal roof until he attained his majority, and was then married to Miss Mary Womack, a native of North Carolina, born in 1817. She was a daughter of William and Abigail Womack, and became the mother of six children, five of whom are living: Levi T., Eliza J. (wife of George Harrison), J. Brown, John W. and Martha

A. (wife of Thomas McGee). The mother of these children died in 1875, and the following year Mr. Pemberton espoused Miss Ruthie S. Young, a daughter of Green D. and Mary Young, born in Illinois in 1833. He has a good farm of 203 acres, on which he has resided since 1866, and has seventy acres under cultivation. The farm is well supplied with good running water, and is provided with good buildings and a good bearing orchard. In 1875 Stone Hill post-office was established, and he was appointed postmaster, which position he has held up to the present time. In 1884 he opened a general store on a small scale, but his efforts in this line have met with such good success that he now does an annual business of $4,000. He is a strong Prohibitionist, and has held the office of justice of the peace of Dent County ten years, and is a Royal Arch Mason.

Levi T. Pemberton, farmer and stock raiser of Linn Township, was born in Wilson County, Tenn., November 30, 1846, and is a son of Jesse B. Pemberton, whose sketch appears in this work. He is the second of six children, and made his parents' house his home until twenty-five years of age, when he began the battle of life for himself, and on February 20, 1873, was united in marriage to Miss Mary Holman, who was born in Dent County, Mo., October 27, 1847. Her parents, William and Nancy Holman, who were natives of Overton County, Tenn., came to Missouri about 1845, and were among the first settlers of the Meramec Valley, in Linn Township. Soon after his marriage Mr. Pemberton located on a farm in Meramec Township, but at the end of nine years moved to the farm of 284 acres on which he now resides. It is one of the best in the Meramec Valley, and 100 acres are under good cultivation. He has always been a highly respected citizen, and in his political views is a Democrat, and is also a member of the order of Good Templars. He and wife are members of the Methodist Episcopal Church.

John T. Pettigrew, of Dent County, Mo., was born in Monroe County, E. Tenn., in 1832, being a son of Ebenezer and Lucinda (Smith) Pettigrew, both of whom were born in Georgia about 1795. The father was of Irish descent, and died in Monroe County, Tenn., in 1839, leaving a wife and seven children to mourn his loss. About six years after his death his widow gave up housekeeping, and in 1852 immigrated with five children to Washington County, Mo., where she was joined by her two other children in 1854 and 1878, respectively. The eldest son died in 1888, and the mother in Dent County, Mo., in 1875. Owing to the early death of his father, John T. Pettigrew received but little schooling, and since twelve years of age has fought the battle of life for himself. He has always made farming his chief calling in life, and December 25, 1855, was married to Miss Mary Brown, who was born in Washington County, Mo., in 1839, and died in Dent County in 1856, eleven months after her marriage. In June, 1859, Mr. Pettigrew, married his second wife, whose maiden name was Isabelle McGee. She was born in Tennessee in 1831, and is a daughter of John and Margaret McGee. She died on the 14th of August, 1884, having borne a family of five children, three of whom are living: John Y., Albert B. and Ida L., all of whom reside with their father. When Mr. Pettigrew's first wife died he went to his father's birth-place in Georgia, but returned home in 1859, and was married to his second wife, locating soon afterward on the farm of 235 acres on which he now resides. He gave his eldest son forty acres, and has 195 acres left, 100 of which are under cultivation. He was one of the pioneers of Dent County, and resides six miles south of the county seat. In 1861 he enlisted in the rebel army, in Company G, First Regiment, Seventh Division, of the Missouri State Guard, and participated in the battles of Oak Hill and Dry Wood. After serving four months he was taken prisoner near Lexington, Mo., and by taking a pledge to remain neutral during the war was discharged and came home. He is a Democrat in politics, and although not a member of any church, is a believer in the Christian faith.

George W. Powell, manager of the Midland Blast Furnace Company's store, at Hawkins, since August 27, 1881, and son of Joseph E. and Cynthia A. (Elliott) Powell, was born in Crawford County, Mo., in 1852. The parents were born in North Carolina and Tennessee, respectively, were married in Tennessee, moved to Central Illinois, where they remained until about 1844, and then came to Crawford County, Mo. Here the father died in 1872, at the age of sixty-five, and the mother died in 1880, at the age of sixty-four or sixty-five. The father was a successful tiller of the soil, and improved a good farm in Steelville Valley. He and wife were members of the Methodist Episcopal Church, South, for many years. Of their twelve children, nine sons and three daughters, George W. Powell was the tenth. He attained his growth on the farm, and received his education in the common schools and in Steelville Academy. At the age of nineteen he began teaching, and followed this occupation for nine or ten years in Crawford, Washington, Phelps, Texas and Gasconade Counties, meeting with good success. The last two years he was principal of Cuba School, and during vacation he clerked, etc., until he came to his present position. He and his brother, Benjamin F., recently established a store at Cook Station, which is now in charge of the latter. Mr. Powell has a farm of 200 acres in Norman Township, nearly all the result of his own industry and hard work. He was married May 9, 1882, to Miss Mary A., daughter of David and Lucinda Bressie. The father died in Tennessee, while in the Union army, but the mother is still living in Dent County. To Mr. and Mrs. Powell were born three children. Mr. Powell is a Democrat in politics, his first presidential vote being for Greeley in 1872, and his wife is a member of the Baptist Church. Mr. Powell had two brothers in the Confederate army: Henry E., who was captured at Big Blue, and died in the St. Louis Hospital, and German H., who died in Little Rock, Ark., while in service. He was a chaplain, and died soon after the battle of Prairie Grove, in which he participated. Mr. Powell is postmaster at Condray post-office.

John Reynolds Ray, watch-maker, jeweler and dealer in general merchandise at Salem, was born in Henderson County, Tenn., in 1843, and is the son of James H. and Elizabeth (Wallace) Ray, and grandson of Robert Ray. James H. Ray was born in Orange County, N. C., in 1812, and was of Irish descent. When young he went to Henderson County, West Tenn., with his father, and was here married. In

1846 he immigrated to Dent County, Mo., and located one-half mile north of Salem, where he resided until 1852, when he settled four miles west of the county seat. He died in 1883. The mother is yet living. She was born in Orange County, N. C., in 1818, and is now residing on the old home place. They were the parents of twelve children, nine of whom are now living. John R. Ray was the fifth child in the order of birth, and was only three years of age when he came with his parents to Dent County, Mo. He was reared in this county, and February 25, 1864, he enlisted in Company E, One Hundred and Twenty-second Regiment Illinois Infantry, and was discharged November 4, 1865, at Vicksburg, Miss. In the fight at Tupelo, Miss., he was wounded in the right hand. He was also in the battles of Nashville and Fort Blakely. He received his primary education in the common schools of Dent County, and after the war attended the public schools in Salem. In 1866 he entered the teacher's profession, and followed this ten terms, all in Dent County, his lowest wages being $30 per month and the highest $40 per month, his terms being all four months each. He met with good success, never teaching in a district but what he was offered the same school a second time, four schools two terms each. November 11, 1868, he married Miss Jane Dill, a native of Wayne County, Tenn., born in 1842, and the daughter of Alfred Dill. To this union were born two children: Lolo and Bennie. Mr. Ray followed farming until February, 1874, and then worked at the carpenter's trade until 1877. He then commenced working at the watch-maker's and jeweler's business, and in 1885 added groceries. In 1887 he added dry goods, and at present carries a good stock of each, being one of the leading business men of Salem. He is a Democrat in politics; was a member of the city council two years, and was city clerk one year. He is a member of the Masonic fraternity, and he and wife and children are members of the Methodist Episcopal Church, South, he having been a member for ten years, and for nine years has been a member of the official board.

Ransom Reddick, of Dent County, Mo., was born in Weakley County, Tenn., in 1830, and is the son of David and Mary B. (Martin) Reddick, who were born in South and North Carolina in 1789 and 1794, and died in Dent County, Mo., in 1851 and 1884, respectively. The father was of Dutch descent, and came to Missouri in December, 1837, where he spent the remainder of his days. Mrs. Reddick made her home with her son Ransom after his marriage, and from early womanhood was a member of the Baptist Church. All of her ten children grew to maturity, and Ransom is her ninth child. He has resided in Missouri since his seventh year, and made his home with his parents until his father's death, and two years later was married to Miss Susan W. Inman, who was born in Williamson County, Tenn., in 1835, and is a daughter of Ezekiel and Lillie Inman, who came to Missouri in 1839. To Mr. and Mrs. Reddick two children were born, James W. being the only one living. He is married, resides with his parents, and tills the home farm. In July, 1862, Mr. Reddick enlisted in Company E, Missouri Infantry, and served as a private for about two years, when he returned home, and was engaged in farming and mining in Phelps County one year. He then gave the whole of his attention to farming and stock raising until 1871, when he came to Salem, and was engaged in hauling iron ore for two years. From that time until 1879 he farmed in Phelps County, and at the latter date returned to Salem, and kept a boarding house in connection with his teaming. Since 1880 he has resided on his present farm, which now consists of 179 acres, with 110 acres under cultivation. His land is well improved, with good buildings, and he has just erected a barn 30x50 feet. His wife is a member of the Christian Church, and he is a Democrat, and cast his first presidential vote for Buchanan.

Duncan Robertson, farmer and stock raiser of Current Township, Dent Co., Mo., is a Scotchman, born in 1858, and is the son of Peter Robertson, who was also born in Scotland, in 1827, and died in Missouri January 3, 1886, whither he had come in 1868. He was a farmer and stock raiser, and was married in his native country to Miss Margaret McLachlan, whose birth occurred in 1830. She is yet living, and resides in Texas County, Mo., with her son Peter. Duncan Robertson is the fifth of ten children, and lived with his parents until twenty-two years of age, receiving about four years of schooling in his native land, and about the same in the United States. After starting out in life for himself he began working on the grade of the Memphis Railroad, being made overseer of a gang of men, and by economy and industry accumulated sufficient means to enable him to purchase the farm of 124 acres where he now resides. He has sixty acres well improved, with good buildings and a thrifty young orchard. He is an industrious and enterprising citizen, and is an accommodating neighbor. He has always been a Democrat in politics, and March 7, 1886, was married to Miss Nancy Stubbs, who was born in Tennessee in 1868, by whom he has one child. Mrs. Robertson is a daughter of Andrew J. and Malinda Stubbs.

Eben Blachley Sankey, division superintendent of Salem Branch of the 'Frisco Line, with residence at Salem, and superintendent of the Missouri Iron Company's mines, in Dent County, is a native of New Castle, Penn., where he was born in 1837, being the son of Ezekiel and Sarah (Jones) Sankey, and grandson of Maj. Ezekiel Sankey, who was born in Mifflin County, Penn., in 1772, and moved to Lawrence County, of the same State, in 1798, being one of the first settlers of Western Reserve Harbor. He was sheriff of Mercer County; was a man of sterling integrity and great influence. He died in 1813. Maj. Ezekiel Sankey, Jr., was born near New Castle, Penn., in 1806, and at the age of sixteen hired out to work on a farm at $6 per month, taking his pay in store trade as he needed it, and working thus for three years. At the age of nineteen he began serving an apprenticeship at the shoemaker's trade, which occupation he followed some five years. He ran the first canal-boat, the "Alpha," between New Castle and Beaver, in 1834. One year later he erected the first warehouse in New Castle, and the same year was elected major of a volunteer battalion of Mercer County, and served several years. He was engaged as contractor on public works of several States, among which were the New York & Erie Railroad, the Pennsylvania Railroad, Baltimore & Ohio Railroad, Sandy & Beaver Canal in Ohio, and subsequently figured prominently in projecting the Pittsburg & Erie Railroad. In 1861 he entered the employ of the United States Government in repairing railroads that had been destroyed by rebels. He was engaged in merchandising for a few years in New Castle, and was at one time proprietor of the old "Mansion House." In 1863 and 1864 he was proprietor of the Leslie House. Maj. Sankey was a man of decidedly progressive ideas, and always took an earnest and active interest in all matters pertaining to the improvement and upbuilding of his surroundings. He was a man of more than ordinary talent, had great originality and inventive powers, of unusually clear discernment and remarkable shrewdness, which elements, combined with irrepressible will and energy, revealed the secret of his success. To these characteristics must be added his genial, social nature and his open-hearted benevolence. He was married in 1832 to Miss Sarah S. Jones, and they reared ten children. Mrs. Sankey died September 11, 1861, and Maj. Sankey died November 20, 1888. Eben B. Sankey was educated in the public schools in New Castle, Penn., and as early as 1854 engaged in railroad work, first as chainman and afterward as rodman and assistant engineer, until 1857. Railroad building for a period being nearly suspended, he followed various other pursuits, until 1862, when he was employed as assistant engineer in the construction of the New Castle & Beaver Valley Railroad from New Castle to Homewood, continuing with the company as engineer and road master until 1865, when, the oil excitement being at its height, he resigned and went to Petroleum Center, Venango Co., Penn., where he opened and carried on for about two years a land surveying office. In 1868-69 he superintended the building of the Etna Iron Furnaces, at New Castle, Penn., and in 1869-70 the Vigo Furnace, in Terre Haute, Ind. In 1870-71 he built the Hubbard Branch of the Ashtabula & Youngstown Railroad. On September 29, 1868, he married Miss Julia E. Woodward, of Taunton, Mass., who by her marriage became the mother of four children: Bessie P., Paul H., Ruth V. and Eben Wallace. In February, 1872, Mr. Sankey moved from New Castle, Penn., to Missouri, for the purpose of taking charge, as chief engineer, of the construction of the St. Louis, Salem & Little Rock Railroad, completing the same in July, 1873. After this he was general freight agent of the same up to February, 1879, at which time he became superintendent and general freight agent. He continued in this service until December 1, 1886, when the road was purchased by the St. Louis & San Francisco Railway Company, and afterward operated by it as the "Salem Branch," he being appointed division superintendent of same, which position he now (1889) occupies. From 1873 to the present time he has been superintendent of the Missouri Iron Company's ore mines, opening up the Simmons Mountain, Jamison, Preston & Clark mines, of Dent County, and the Smith & Clinton mines, of Phelps County. For the past eight years Mr. Sankey has been president of Dent Iron Company. He moved to Salem in 1874, and is one of the influential citizens of the county. He is a Republican in politics; is chairman of the Republican County Committee, a member of the school board and city alderman. He was a delegate to the Republican National Convention which met at Chicago, Ill., in

1884, from the Eleventh Congressional District, and was one of five from Missouri who voted for James G. Blaine on the first ballot, continuing to do so until nominated. He is a Mason, and a member of the Presbyterian Church. Mr. Sankey is first cousin to Ira D. Sankey, the noted singer of Moody and Sankey fame. Mrs. Sankey is a devoted Episcopalian.

Joseph Y. Shults was born in Henry County, Mo., in 1842, and is a son of Jacob and Mary (Young) Shults, who were born in Kentucky and Missouri in 1802 and 1808, and died in 1867 and 1848, respectively, the former's death occurring in the State of Arkansas. He was of Dutch descent, a farmer by occupation, and came to Missouri when about seventeen years of age. Joseph Y. Shults, when four years of age, was left without a mother to care for him. He continued to make his home with his father until about sixteen years of age, when he began the battle of life for himself, working on a farm, and received $8 per month for his services. He continued to follow agricultural pursuits until 1863, when he enlisted in Company A, Eleventh Regiment Missouri Cavalry, United States Army, and served until June 5, 1865, when he received his discharge. He then returned to Dent County, Mo., and August 7, 1867, was united in marriage to Miss America Nelson, who was born in Dent County, Mo., February 2, 1848, by whom he became the father of eleven children, all living: Reuben O., Emma E., Henry J., Joseph M., Elisha M., Lewis A., Mary L., Walter C., Effie M., Spurgeon R. and Haden L. Mr. Shults has resided on his present farm of 253 acres ever since his marriage, and has about 100 acres of his farm under cultivation, on which are a good orchard, a residence and out-buildings. He is an enterprising citizen of the county, and what education he has was acquired in Dent County in the primitive log school-house of early times. He is a member of the County Wheel, and in his political views is a Republican, and cast his first presidential vote for Lincoln. He and wife are members of the Missionary Baptist Church.

John L. Skeeters is a farmer of Dent County, Mo., and was born in East Tennessee in 1820, being a son of William and Mary (Legg) Skeeters, who were born in Kentucky and Tennessee in 1791 and 1800, and died in Texas and Alabama in 1883 and 1845, respectively. The father was a farmer, and carpenter by trade, and came to Missouri from Alabama in 1871, but from 1880 until his death resided in the "Lone Star State." John L. Skeeters was the second of their twelve children, and resided with his parents until he attained his majority, receiving his education in the country schools, and then came to Missouri, but a year later returned to Alabama. In 1849 he was married to Miss Susan McCoren, who was born in that State in 1831, and is a daughter of Isaac and Rebecca McCoren. To them were born ten children, six of whom are living: William I., Elizabeth (wife of Joe Nelson), Samuel W., Martha C. (wife of Henry Duckworth), Vickie (wife of William Tune) and Dora. In 1852 Mr. Skeeters removed from Alabama to Missouri, and entered forty acres of land in Dent County, which he has since increased to 750 acres, with 175 acres under cultivation, well improved with good buildings and orchard. He is a Democrat in politics, and about 1854 was elected justice of the peace, in which capacity he served twelve years, and was afterward elected again, and served four years, filling the duties of that office in a very creditable manner. He and wife are worthy members of the Baptist Church.

Erasmus B. and William F. Smith, blacksmiths and wagon manufacturers of Salem, Mo. E. B. Smith was born in Washington County, Mo., May 19, 1847, and is a son of Benjamin F. and Emily (Wells) Smith, the former a native of Pennsylvania and the latter of Kentucky, born in 1813 and 1817, respectively. They were married in Kentucky in 1833, and removed from there to Washington County, Mo., in 1840, where the father was killed by falling in machinery in the saw-mill in 1860. He was a blacksmith, a farmer also, and ran a saw-mill, and was postmaster at Rock Springs at the time of his death. He owned a good farm, and was an industrious, honest man. He was a member and an active supporter of the Christian Church, as was also his wife. Erasmus B. was one of fourteen children, ten of whom lived to be grown. He was reared in Washington County, educated in the common schools, and was but thirteen years of age when his father died. He was then the eldest son at home, and the main support of the family devolved upon him, which deprived him of further schooling until about grown, when he spent a few months in school at his own expense. At the age of about eighteen he began for himself working on a farm, and in 1868 he went to New York, where he took passage for California, being twenty-four days in making the trip. He there learned his trade, and returned home in 1869, where the next year he married Miss Margaret Ann Griffith, daughter of Thomas and Sarah Griffith, both natives of Wales, but who came to the United States when young, living in Cincinnati, Ohio, for awhile, and then moved to Washington County, Mo., where they are both now living. Mrs. Smith was born in Cincinnati, and by her union to Mr. Smith became the mother of two children, both sons. The same year of his marriage Mr. Smith returned by rail to California, where he worked at his trade until 1875, when he went to Nevada. From there he went to Washington County, Mo., in 1876, and ran a shop at Palmer until 1878, when he moved to Dent County, and farmed until 1884, when he sold his farm and moved to Salem. He here established his present business, in company with John Gunnett, and in 1885 Mr. Gunnett sold to Mr. Smith's nephew, William F. Smith, who is his present partner, and they have since had a successful business, with a capital of about $1,500. In the year 1887 they sold thirty-eight wagons, all their own work. Mr. Smith has a good home in Salem, all the result of his hard work and good management. He also has one-third interest in the house of Smith, Tennyson & Ramsey, at Salem, with a stock of about $3,000. Politically a Democrat, his first presidential vote was for Seymour in 1868. He is a member of the Masonic fraternity, Lodge No. 225, took degrees in 1869, and he and wife are consistent members of the Christian Church. William F. Smith is the son of William S. Smith, who is the eldest brother of Erasmus B. Smith. William S. Smith was born in Kentucky in 1834, and came with his parents to Washington County when a boy. There he married, and with the exception of a few years before the war, when he was engaged in saw-milling in Dent County, has lived there all his life. He is a farmer, a blacksmith, and has been justice of the peace for many years. William F. Smith was born in Washington County, January 21, 1860; was reared on a farm and educated in the common schools. He learned his trade at the age of seventeen, which he has since followed principally. He is a Democrat in politics, and his first presidential vote was cast for Grover Cleveland in 1884. He is a member of the Masonic fraternity and the I. O. O. F. lodge. His mother, Emily (Simpson) Smith, is the daughter of Joseph Simpson, a native of Kentucky. William F. is one of four sons and five daughters born to his parents. His father is a member of the Christian Church, and his mother of the Methodist Episcopal Church.

William Sparks, a wealthy agriculturist and stock raiser of Dent County, Mo., has resided on his present fine farm of 440 acres since his marriage, which took place in 1875. He has 120 acres under cultivation, and is now completing a large, two-story frame residence at a cost of $1,500. He has a thrifty orchard of 700 trees, and is considered one of the successful farmers of the county. He was born in Wilkes County, N. C., in 1846, and when twenty-nine years of age was married to Miss Sarah J. Shirley, who was born in Dent County, Mo., January 15, 1849, a daughter of Jacob and Lucinda Shirley, both of whom died when Mrs. Sparks was quite young. She is the mother of six children, and is a member of the Methodist Episcopal Church. Mr. Sparks has always been a Democrat in politics, and is a son of Reuben and Blineld (Gray) Sparks, who were born in Wilkes County, N. C., about 1812 and 1829, respectively. The father was of German descent, a farmer by occupation, and in 1868 immigrated with his family to Dent County, Mo., where he died in 1881. He and wife became the parents of ten children, eight of whom are living. Six reside in Dent County, one in Douglas County, and one in Kansas.

Capt. William T. Stepp, an enterprising farmer and stock raiser of Spring Creek Township, was born in Clark County, Ill., in 1841, and is the son of Samuel and Parthena (Smith) Stepp, who were born near Lexington, Ky. They were married in Clark County, Ill., and here they both died, the father when William T. was two years of age, and the mother when he was seven years old. The mother was married three times, her first husband being Mr. Sheapley, and her last husband a Mr. Porter. Mr. Stepp was a farmer by occupation, and the only child born to his union was William T. Stepp, who, after the death of his parents, lived with his half-brother until twelve years of age. He then began as a cabin boy, cook, etc., on the Mississippi, and there continued for two years. He then learned the plasterer's trade at Terre Haute, Ind., which he followed there until the breaking out of the war. He then enlisted in Company H, Thirteenth Indiana Volunteer Infantry, Union Army, serving one year as a private, one year as a corporal, and about one year as duty sergeant. In December, 1864, he was made captain of Company E, of the same regiment, which he commanded until September, 1865. He was discharged at Goldsborough, N. C., after over four and a half years of service. He was in the fight at Rich Mountain, Winchester, Malvern Hill, Petersburg and vicinity, was at Charleston, Morris Island, etc., his regiment being in twenty-two regular engagements. He was also at Cold Harbor, and Forts Darling and Fisher. He was wounded in the left arm at Cold Harbor, June 1, 1864, and this has left him a cripple for life, but he was only off duty about sixty days, when he was commissioned captain. He made his home at Terre Haute, Ind., until 1867, when he came to Dent County, and taught school that winter. The next year he and Perry Barricklow, an army comrade, founded the Salem *Monitor*, which our subject was connected with for about eighteen months. In the meantime, in 1868, he was elected collector and sheriff of Dent County, and re-elected in 1870, holding the office four years with credit. In 1869 he married Miss Mary J. James, daughter of Stephen C. and Keziah James, formerly of Tennessee, but early settlers of Wayne County, Mo. They came to Dent County about 1846 or 1847, where Mrs. Stepp was born, and here the father died in November, 1869, and the mother in January, 1870. To Mr. Stepp and wife were born four children, one son and three daughters. In 1873 Mr. Stepp was made business manager of a stock company which founded the *Western Success* at Salem, which he controlled until after the campaign of 1876, and in 1877-78 he was deputy collector of internal revenue for the Second (now the First) District of Missouri. In 1879 Mr. Stepp was appointed gauger for the same district, holding the position until change of administration in 1885. Since then he has devoted his time and attention to farming. Mr. Stepp has lived on his present farm, which consists of 327 acres, 110 under cultivation, since 1878, and has made a success of farming. He is politically a Republican, and his first presidential vote was for Abraham Lincoln in 1864. He is a member of the I. O. O. F., Salem Lodge No. 118, is a member of the G. A. R., and also a member of the Agricultural Wheel.

W. Andrew Sturgeon, a prominent agriculturist of Watkins Township, and a successful stock dealer, was born in Lauderdale County, Ala., in 1849, his parents, John N. and Ersly J. (Howard) Sturgeon, both being natives of Lauderdale County, Ala., born about 1827 and 1828, respectively. They remained in their native county until about 1852, then removed to Arkansas, and a year later to Dent County, Mo. He here settled in the woods, improved a farm, and here the father died in 1880. The mother is still living on the old farm, and is a member of the Baptist Church. W. Andrew Sturgeon is the eldest of seven children, three sons and two daughters now living, and received his education at Lake Spring Seminary. He began for himself at the age of eighteen by renting land of his father, and in March, 1873, he married Miss Lizzie, daughter of Bluford and Julia Arthur, natives of Kentucky and Pennsylvania, respectively. Both the father and mother came to Missouri at a very early day. After marriage Mr. Arthur, (father of subject's wife,) settled in Dent County, where he died before the war. The mother is still living in Dent County. To Mr. Sturgeon and wife were born four children, all living. Mr. Sturgeon has been a resident of Watkins Township from early boyhood, and for fifteen years in the neighborhood of his present farm. He has about 600 acres of land, 200 under cultivation, and is one of the stirring, wide-a-wake farmers of the township. He has been engaged in farming and stock raising all his life, and has been very successful at the same. He is a member of the Agricultural Wheel, and is a Democrat in his political views, casting his first presidential vote for S. J. Tilden in 1876.

Edward Swiney. In every calling in life, whether of a commercial, agricultural or professional nature, there are always some men who attain the highest round in the ladder of success, and Mr. Swiney may be mentioned as one of those men, for he has not only attained considerable of this world's goods, but he has won the confidence, esteem and respect of all with whom he has come in contact. He was born in Washington County, Mo., December 25, 1829, and is one of six surviving members of a family of nine children born to the marriage of John Swiney and Elizabeth Highley. They were born in Kentucky and Virginia in 1803 and 1805, respectively. The father was a forgeman by trade, and helped to make the first iron ever made in Missouri, at what is known as Massas Iron Works. He was of Irish descent, and died in the city of Chihauhau in 1848, while serving in the Mexican War. His widow resides in Iron County, Mo., with her daughter, Mrs. Susan Thomas. Edward Swiney, the immediate subject of this sketch, resided with his parents until eighteen years of age, when he enlisted in the Mexican War, in Company D, Third Regiment Missouri Mounted Volunteers, being mustered into service on May 8, 1847, receiving his discharge October 19, 1848. While in the service he was thrown from a horse and injured his left arm, which has been practically useless ever since. In 1851 he was united in marriage to Miss Susan Thompson, who was born in Washington County, Mo., in March, 1828, by whom he is the father of eight children: Elizabeth and Ellen (deceased), Julia A., John M., James H., Isaiah N., Edward L. and Thomas D. At the time of Mr. Swiney's marriage he located on a farm in Washington County, where he resided until 1857, when he moved to Dent County, where he owns 280 acres of land, with sixty-five under cultivation. He also owns 660 acres in Shannon County. In 1873 he was elected justice of the peace of Sinking Township by the Democratic party, receiving all but one vote, and filled this position four terms of two years each. In 1882 he was elected county judge of his district, being re-elected in 1884. His wife is a member of the Methodist Episcopal Church, South, and is a daughter of Morgan and Nancy Thompson.

Dr. D. P. Thurber, physician and surgeon for Sligo Furnace Co. since March, 1887, and general practitioner, was born in Moundsville, W. Va., in 1849, being the son of N. U. and Mary A. (Pickard) Thurber, natives of New York and Ohio, respectively. They were married in the last named State, and in about 1844 or 1845 they removed to West Virginia, where they remained until about 1869 or 1870, when they came to Wayne County, Mo., and here the father died in 1880. In early life he followed merchandising at Moundsville, and in about 1847 or 1848 he invented a grain fanning-mill, which was a profitable and successful invention. After this for several years he was engaged in their manufacture in South Carolina and Tennessee. After his removal to Missouri he carried on farming and stock raising. About

1862 he joined the Twelfth Virginia as regimental quartermaster, in the United States army, afterward brigade quartermaster, remaining as such until the close of the war, in the Army of the Potomac. His father was an Englishman, and settled in Long Island in early days. Our subject's mother died in Ohio in 1884, where she moved after the death of her husband. She was a member of the Methodist Episcopal Church and he of the Baptist. He was married twice. Dr. D. P. Thurber was one of three children, two sons and one daughter, born to his father's second marriage. He was educated in Moundsville Academy, and at the age of nineteen began the study of medicine in Moundsville, W. Va., graduating from Missouri Medical College, at St. Louis, in 1870, after a two years' course. He began near Moundsville, W. Va., where he practiced for some time, and since then has practiced in Ohio, Missouri and Texas, meeting with great success. In 1879 he was married at New Alexandria, Ohio, to Miss Anna Chilton, a native of Pennsylvania, and the daughter of William and Louisa Chilton. Mr. Chilton died when his daughter was quite small. To the Doctor and wife were born six children. Dr. Thurber came to Sligo Furnace in 1887. He has been considerable of a traveler in his day, and he and a brother were in the fruit business in New York City for a short time. During the war, and when but fourteen years of age, he enlisted in Company A, Fourteenth Virginia Cavalry, and served until the termination of hostilities. He is a Democrat in politics, casting his first presidential vote for Lincoln in 1864, and is a member of the A. O. U. W.

John Emery Watson. Prominent among the enterprising farmers and stock raisers of Short Bend Township stands the name of the above mentioned gentleman, who was born in Prince George County, Md., in 1825. His parents were William C. and Mary (Gibbons) Watson, both probably natives of Prince George County, Md. The father was born in 1794, was married there, and there the mother died when her son, John Emery, was but a small boy. The family afterward removed to Fauquier County, Va., and in about 1835 or 1837 they moved to Dent County, Mo., on Meramec, where they improved a good farm. Mr. Watson died soon after the war. He was a soldier in the War of 1812, and was a member of the Methodist Church. His father, Leonard B. Watson, was probably born in Maryland, was of English origin, and was a soldier in the War of 1812. He came to Missouri with his son, and died in Crawford County, where William C. lived for the first two years as a renter. John Emery Watson is the third of five children, and is the only one now living. He received a limited education, which he improved later in life by observation, study and reading. At the age of seventeen he began for himself by farming, and in 1847 and 1848 he married Miss Mary Ann, daughter of William and Mary Ann (Halbert) Blackwell, natives of Virginia and South Carolina, respectively. To Mr. Watson and wife were born twenty children, fifteen sons and five daughters, seven sons and two daughters now living: John Thomas, James A., Mary A., wife of William Harkey, of Texas; Lorenzo Dow. G. T. Beauregard, Rhoda R., Prince Albert, Orin P. and Samuel J. Tilden. With the exception of about four years spent in Salem to educate his children, Mr.

Watson has lived in Short Bend Township, and on his present farm since before the war. He has over 700 acres in all, and has property in Salem, also owning a park stocked with deer. There are three caves on his farm, and in one is a fine spring and small lake. One of the caves has been explored one-fourth of a mile, and has also fine prospects for iron of superior quality, also some lead and some silver and copper ore. Mr. Watson has given his large family of children a good education, and some of them are numbered among the best teachers of Dent County. In 1865 he served four months in the Union army, in the troops stationed at Salem, and enlisted for one year, but at that time the war closed and he was discharged. He was formerly a Whig in politics, but is now a Democrat, casting his first presidential vote for Gen. Taylor. Mr. Watson is a member of the Masonic fraternity, a member of the Agricultural Wheel, and Mrs. Watson and two daughters are members of the Methodist Church. One son is a member of the Baptist Church. While in Salem Mr. Watson was interested in wagon-making; was also engaged in the butchering business, and for a short time was occupied in merchandising. Mrs. Watson was born in Crawford County, and her father was born in Virginia, and when about three years old came with his father, Jesse Blackwell, to St. Francois County, where he married Miss Mary Halbert. In about 1832 or 1833 he removed to Crawford County, Mo., and a few years afterward removed to Dent County, in Norman Valley, where he died shortly before the war. He was a soldier in the Black Hawk War; was very wealthy, and before the war built a large brick house. His wife is still living, and is ninety-four or ninety-five years of age. Her father, Rev. James Halbert, was a South Carolina Primitive Baptist minister, and was for many years in Southeast Missouri. He was an early settler of St. Francois County, and died near Steelville.

John Calvin Welch, collector of Dent County, and one of the prominent citizens of Spring Creek Township, is a native of Dent County, Mo., and was born November 8, 1840. He is a son of Thomas and Eliza (Reddick) Welch, and grandson of John Welch, who was a native of North Carolina, and at an early date immigrated to Tennessee. He resided in Weakley County, Tenn., a number of years, and then came to Dent County, Mo., locating six miles west of the county seat, where he died about 1857, at the age of ninety years. He was a soldier in the War of 1812, with Gen. Jackson. Thomas Welch was born in Tennessee in 1812, was married in Weakley County, of that State, and then came to Dent County, Mo., the same year as his father. He settled on Dry Fork, six miles from Salem, where he now resides. He was the owner of 600 acres of land, but being of a benevolent disposition, has given it all to his children. He is yet living, and is one of the pioneer settlers of Dent County. When first settling there his nearest neighbor was forty miles south, and he would frequently go twenty miles to a house raising, and twenty-five and thirty miles to mill. His wife, Eliza (Reddick) Welch, died in 1852, and after her death Mr. Welch married Mrs. Caroline Jadwin, *nee* Howell, daughter of Christopher Howell. Thomas Welch is the father of twelve children, seven by the first marriage and five by the second, all of whom lived to be grown: Melissa, wife of Joseph M. Howell; Joseph M. (deceased); John C., Thomas J., Eliza, wife of Jasper Plank; Jane, wife of J. S. Cooley; Phœbe E., wife of W. C. Inman; Current R., General A., James G., Josephine, wife of Samuel Skeeters, and Albert S. John C. Welch attained his growth on a farm, and made his home with his parents until the breaking out of the late war, when he cast his destinies with the South. In 1861 he enlisted in Freeman's company, Missouri State Militia, for six months, but at the end of six months he was captured and taken to Alton, where he was retained until September, 1862. He was then exchanged, and enlisted in Company F, Ninth Missouri Infantry, as orderly-sergeant. After the fight at Pleasant Hill he was promoted to the rank of second lieutenant,. and surrendered at Shreveport, La., in June, 1865. In December of the following year he married Miss Martha E. Wofford, daughter of Smith Wofford, and a native of Middle Tennessee, born in 1846. To this marriage were born seven children: James C., Thomas F., William G., Joseph M., Iona, Bertha, Walter H. After the war Mr. Welch resumed farming, and continued at this until 1886, when he was elected collector of Dent County, by a majority of 262, on the Democratic ticket. He is a member of the I. O. O. F., and his wife is a member of the Missionary Baptist Church.

William W. Williams, who is closely connected with the farming and stock raising interests of Norman Township, was born in Wales in 1817, and is the son of David and Sarah Williams, natives of Wales, where they spent all their lives. The mother died during the Civil War, and the father died about ten years before. Of their seven children, five sons and two daughters, William W. is the youngest. He was reared on a farm in his native country, and received a very limited education. About 1840 he came to the United States, and lived in Pennsylvania until 1866, when he came to Dent County, Mo., and settled on his present farm, which now consists of 500 acres, with 150 under cultivation, all the result of his own labor. He was engaged in coal mining in Pennsylvania, and farming and stock raising in Missouri. His farm is located nine miles north of Salem, and is a fine place. He served a short time in Company A, Forty-eighth Pennsylvania Volunteer Infantry, and was on guard duty in Pennsylvania. He was married in 1849 to Miss Jane Thomas, who was born in Pennsylvania, and died in June, 1851. She bore him one child, who is also deceased. Mr. Williams is a Republican in politics, his first presidential vote being for Taylor in 1848. His three brothers and one sister came to the United States, and the sister died in Salem. She was the wife of William Williams. Mr. Williams is the owner of 200 acres near Meramec River, and a house and lot in Salem, all the result of his own hard work, and has cleared nearly all his land by his own individual labor. He has always been very industrious, and, although seventy-one years of age, does considerable hard work. In early life he made several sea voyages, and has had a varied experience.

Col. Edmund T. Wingo, attorney at law and justice of the peace, of Salem, was born in Amelia County, Va., December 23, 1818, and is the son of John and Mary (Hutchings) Wingo. John Wingo was born in Amelia County, Va., in 1788, and was of English descent.

He was the son of John Wingo, Sr., who was a native of England. John Wingo, Jr., was a farmer by occupation, and in 1829 his wife and six children went to Missouri with her brother, Charles Hutchings, who located in Washington County, Mo. John Wingo remained behind to dispose of some property and settle up business; was taken sick, and died in 1830. The same year his widow moved to Madison County, Mo., and bought a farm, where she died about 1832. After her death the children remained with their uncle until 1837, when Edmund T. went to Montgomery County, Tenn., to live with his uncle, John Hutchings, and attend school. The following year he returned to his birth place, in Virginia, and continued going to school, living with his uncle, William Green, who had married a Hutchings. In 1844 he graduated from William and Mary's College at Williamsburg, Va., and received a diploma to practice law, practicing for fifteen months in Amelia. He then moved to Liberty, Bedford Co., Va., and in January, 1846, was married to Miss Mary J. Fizer, a native of Bedford County, Va., born in 1822. One child was born to this marriage, Jacob W., who is now deputy postmaster of Salem, Mo. In May, 1847, Mrs. Wingo died, and Mr. Wingo went to Botetourt County, Va., where he taught a four months' term of school. In September, 1850, he married Miss Sarah Stull, a native of Botetourt County, Va., born in 1808. In the fall of 1850 he returned to Washington County, Mo., with his wife and nine negroes. At the end of six months he sold all his negroes except one, and returned to Virginia, where he remained until 1857, when he again came back to Missouri, but this time located in Salem, where he resumed the practice of law, in which business he has since been engaged. In 1860 he organized a cavalry company in Dent County, and in 1861 he organized the First Regiment, Seventh Division Missouri State Guard, and he was elected colonel of the same. In 1862 he was commissioned brigadier-general of the Seventh Division Missouri State Guard, and at the battle of Lexington he was shot in the right shoulder while dismounting from his horse. He was with his regiment until it was disorganized, which occurred in 1862. Col. Wingo is a man now in the evening of life, and is as highly esteemed and as universally respected as any man in the county. He is a man of fine legal ability, good judgment, and is scrupulously honest. He has a pleasant disposition, is courteous and accommodating, and is a man who is fond of a joke and is witty in giving them. He has been a life-long Democrat, casting his first presidential vote for Gen. Cass in 1848. He has been in official life the greater portion of his days; was lieutenant of militia in Virginia, a notary public; was a Douglas elector in 1860; was elected to the State Legislature in 1882, and is now justice of the peace. Col. Wingo's second wife died April 14, 1886, and in October of the same year he married Miss Lucinda E. Wheeling, who was born in Washington County, Mo., in 1842, and who is a member of the Baptist Church. Col. Wingo is a pleasing and forcible speaker, and he has been one of the most influential men of Dent County; was a candidate for the nomination of circuit judge, and carried Dent County, Mo., by a large majority, but was defeated in foreign counties. The number of votes he has always commanded in Dent County illustrates to a nicety his high standing among his own people. He is a member of the Masonic fraternity, and is a strong believer in the Christian faith, and is very charitable and liberal in giving to laudable enterprises.

TEXAS COUNTY.

Judge John N. Angel, of Texas County, Mo., was born in De Kalb County, Tenn., December 13, 1832, and is a son of Martin B. and Lucy (Stover) Angel, natives of Virginia and Tennessee, respectively, both of whom died in Illinois, he in Jackson County in 1857, when about sixty years of age, and she in Union County in 1884, aged eighty years. They had moved from the mother's birth-place in 1853, and spent the rest of their days in Illinois, where the father was engaged in tilling the soil and teaching school. He was a Whig, and while residing in Tennessee filled the office of justice of the peace, and was also a member of the Masonic fraternity. Mrs. Angel was a member of the United Baptist Church, and she and Mr. Angel became the parents of four sons and three daughters, two sons and two daughters of whom are now living. Judge John N. Angel was quite young when he started in life for himself, but being plucky and persevering he began learning the blacksmith's trade, and afterward turned his attention to farming, and has been connected with every mail line except that which leads to Rolla, being engaged in the latter business in Southern Missouri for the past eighteen years. During the latter part of the Rebellion he was in the Government service as teamster. Since 1851 he has been a resident of Texas County, Mo., and in 1852 was appointed to the office of constable, being elected to the office the following year, and in addition to this has served as justice of the peace seven years. In 1866 he was appointed assessor of the county, which position he held four years, and in 1886 was elected justice of the peace, being elected, two years later, judge of the Western District, which position he is still filling. June 15, 1853, he married Miss Frances J. Wood, a daughter of Hon. John C. Wood. She was born in Wilson County, Tenn., January 4, 1835, and died in Texas County, Mo., January 23, 1880, having become the mother of the following children: James W., who was born July 9, 1855, and is now a resident of Texas County; Isabella A., born May 13, 1857, and now the wife of S. H. Fry; Susan B., born September 18, 1862, and Hershel A., born March 17, 1869. Those deceased are John C. Willis, born September 19, 1866, and died at the age of two years; Sarah Rebecca, born August 26, 1859, and died March 27, 1862, and Horace, born August 8, 1872, and died September 15, 1872. Mr. Angel began life a very poor boy, and on coming to Texas County, Mo., his entire capital consisted of 45 cents, but by industry and judicious management he is now one of the prosperous citizens of the county.

J. M. Angell, manager of the Cabool Roller Mills, was born in

Coffee County, Tenn., and reared in Pottawatomie County, Kas., where in early manhood he took up milling. At ten years of age he became an apprentice to that trade in a mill in Smith County, Tenn., and in 1869, or at the age of fourteen, he, in company with an elder brother, G. W. Angell, who is now a leading miller and citizen of Pottawatomie County, Kas., left their Tennessee home and sought for themselves a home in the Sunflower State. On their way J. M. took the small-pox, and after arriving in Kansas went through a siege of that dread disease at St. Mary's. After recovering he completed a good schooling, and then carried on milling in St. Mary's, Kas., for about eight years. He then left that city with his brother, went to Wamego, Kas., where they erected a fifty-barrel mill, which they carried on about eleven months, and then met with reverses in their business by a complete destruction of their mill by fire. J. M. then went to Clay Center, Kas., where he carried on a 150-barrel mill for two years, and then left this lucrative position to "go on the road," as traveling man and expert for leading milling and manufacturing houses. In this capacity he has worked for several years. During the time he has remodeled and built anew many of the important mills throughout Washington Territory, Wyoming Territory, Nebraska, Kansas and Missouri. His latest works have been at Mountain Grove and Cabool. He is a member of the Masonic fraternity, and is an Odd Fellow.

John Banch, merchant and miller, and son of Frank and Mary Banch, was born in Germany, in the Province of Schweried, Mecklenburg, April 19, 1834. His father was a merchant tailor by trade, and in connection carried on farming. John Banch was the fifth in order of birth of four sons and three daughters. He was reared in his native country, completing a fair education, and in 1856 came to America. He landed in New York City, spent a year in New Jersey, then a year in Wisconsin, and then spent some time in traveling in the South and West. He was in Missouri at the breaking out of the war, and in 1861 he enlisted in the three months' service, in the Second Missouri, and at the end of that time went to Illinois, subsequently enlisting in the One Hundred and Forty-fourth Illinois, Company K, and served until the termination of hostilities. He was married in Milwaukee, Wis., in 1865, to Miss Catherine Steffen, a native of Germany, from Prussia, born June 20, 1848, and the daughter of John Peter and Agnes (Bell) Steffen, who came to the United States in 1851, and located near Milwaukee, Wis. After the war Mr. Banch and family moved to Missouri, and here they have since resided. To their marriage were born two sons, John H. and William Frederick, both engaged in business in Cabool. Mr. Banch is a member of the Lutheran Church, and his wife of the Roman Catholic. He has served his locality with credit in the school board of his district and other municipal offices. He is a member of the G. A. R. He built a large store and mill here and a store at Dykes Post-office, and aside from this he has farming interests here and at Dykes.

John E. Barnes, M. D., of Licking, Mo., was born in Philadelphia, Penn., September 25, 1829, being the son of John and Elizabeth (Repsher) Barnes, natives, respectively, of Massachusetts and Pennsylvania, he of English descent and she of German on her mother's side. The parents were married by the rector of the Swede Church in Philadelphia, the oldest church in that city. The father died there when the subject of our sketch was a babe, and the mother was married twice afterward. She died in Philadelphia, at about the age of seventy-five. John E. Barnes is the only child of the first marriage. When about nine years of age he began to make his own way in the world, and in his teens worked for about four years in a large mercantile house in Philadelphia. He spent his earnings in educating himself, taking a course in the University of Pennsylvania up to the junior year. Having acquired a thorough medical education, he located at Raymond, Miss., where he married Miss Mary A. L. Warner in 1853. She was born in Florida. After practicing for some time at Jackson, Miss., Dr. Barnes returned to Philadelphia. About this time, train after train of sick and wounded soldiers were coming into the city, no hospital accommodations being sufficient for them. The citizens met in the Doctor's parlor and formed the Citizens' Volunteer Hospital Association, of which he was chosen president, but not accepting, was chosen vice-president. He served for a time as assistant surgeon of the above mentioned association, and in 1868 moved to Missouri, locating in Dade County, where he remained two years, and later came to this county, where he still lives, engaged in the practice of medicine to a limited extent. He is a local elder in the Methodist Episcopal Church, South, and his wife is a member of the Baptist Church, and both are much respected citizens. The Doctor is the owner of 560 acres of land, and for eighteen years has been a resident of Texas County. He is a Democrat in his political views, and has been probate judge of this county one term. He has been a member of the Odd Fellows lodge for about thirty-six years and a Mason for about twenty-five years; has held the positions of District Deputy Grand Master and Grand Chaplain of the Grand Lodge of Missouri.

Perry Barricklow. The milling interests of Texas County, Mo., have an energetic representative in the person of Mr. Barricklow, who was born in Dearborn County, Ind., October 8, 1837, and is a son of Farrington and Patsy (Buchanan) Barricklow, grandson of Daniel, and great-grandson of Van Dyke Barricklow, who was a native of New Jersey, and a soldier in the Revolutionary War, being wounded at King's Mountain. His son Daniel was also born in New Jersey, and Farrington was born in Fayette County, Penn., in 1804. He was reared on a farm, and in his early days was a medical student. He removed with his parents to Dearborn County, Ind., in 1816, and in 1832 was married to Miss Buchanan, who was a daughter of James Buchanan, of Bedford County, Va., of Scotch-Irish parentage. In 1856 Farrington Barricklow and his brother Henry removed to Kansas, and laid out the town of Palmyra, now Baldwin City. In 1861 Perry Barricklow enlisted in Company H, Thirteenth Indiana Volunteer Infantry, under J. C. Sullivan, and served until July, 1864. He returned to Kansas, and was engaged in teaching school for a short time. He came to Missouri in 1866, and established the Cassville *Republican*, the first paper published in Barry County, and the following year went to Dent County, and established the *Monitor*, the official paper of the county, and which is still being published by Hon. J. E. Organ. He next went to Rolla, and managed the *Express* for five years, and in 1877 came to Houston as editor of the Houston *Democrat*, but shortly after purchased a mill on Big Creek, which he still manages. He was married in 1869 to Miss Ama C. Matthews, daughter of Ransom B. Matthews, of Salem, Mo.

William O. Bartholomew, miller, and who is also engaged in the loan business, is a native of Scotland, and was born at Inverkeithing, Fifeshire, June 14, 1860, being the son of Robert and Mina O. (Sutherland) Bartholomew. The father was a physician and surgeon in the old Edinburgh School of Medicine, and a F. R. C. S. E. He had a large practice, and spent about forty years in professional work at Inverkeithing. His son, William O., received a liberal training in the schools of his home, and at the age of fourteen he became an apprenticed clerk in a wholesale warehousing and grocery trade, completing a through apprenticeship at it. He held afterward, with this firm (Traill & Fletcher), a traveling position for three years. Leaving this business and his native land in 1881, he journeyed to British Guiana, where he was engaged in the raising and manufacture of sugar, which he prosecuted actively for fourteen months, abandoning it reluctantly in consequence of ill health, and returned to his native heath, whence, after spending a few months with his old firm (Traill & Fletcher), he again departed, this time for America, and landed in New York. He then started out immediately for Kansas City, Mo., and spent some time in traveling from that point through Kansas, Texas and the Indian Territory, finally selecting as a location Texas County, Mo., in the early part of 1883. Here he engaged in hog breeding, which he followed for about a year, and then embarked in the saw-mill business, with which he has been identified ever since, in the meantime adding loan business, representing Eastern capital. He was married, in Texas County, to Miss Norma Kendall, daughter of Nathaniel Kendall, of White Hall, Ill. Mr. Bartholomew is a member of the Ancient Order of the Scottish Clans, and in affiliation with Clan McGregor, of Springfield, Mo. He is a notary public of Cabool, through the commission of Gov. Morehouse.

James P. Bates is a son of P. Quinton and Mary (Waymon) Bates, natives, respectively, of Kentucky and Pennsylvania. Both parents removed to Phelps County, Mo., with their parents when young, and were there reared to maturity and married, coming shortly after to Texas County, but only resided here a short time, when they returned to Phelps County, where the mother died in the full bloom of womanhood. In 1849 Mr. Bates went to the Black Hills to dig gold, and there died. He was a Democrat, and a successful and enterprising business man. James P. Bates is the oldest of three surviving members of a family of five children, and was born in Texas County, Mo., February 28, 1837, and was reared to the saw-mill business, receiving his education in the old subscription schools of early days. When about fifteen years of age he began the battle of life for himself, and was first engaged in driving oxen for $10 per month, and was then occupied in rafting, making twenty-five trips down the rivers to St. Louis. Since 1863 he has been engaged in operating a saw-mill, and in connection with this manages his large farm of 640 acres, the most of which is exceptionally good land. He has always been a Democrat in politics, and is a member of the Masonic fraternity, and is considered one of the successful business men of the county, having made all his property by his own exertions. In 1860 he was married to Elizabeth Harper, nee Reardon, a native of Ireland, born June 28, 1839. She was reared in London, England, but came to America when about sixteen years of age, and is now the mother of one child, Mary F.

James W. Beard, an enterprising agriculturist of Texas County, Mo., was born in Williamson County, Tenn., December 11, 1830, being the son of Bird and Sarah (Kenneday) Beard, both natives of North Carolina. When young they went with their parents to Tennessee; were married in that State, and there the father followed agricultural pursuits. He was a Whig in politics, and lived to be about fifty-seven years of age. The mother was a member of the Christian Church, and died at the age of over seventy years. They were the parents of six children, five sons and one daughter, the fourth child being James W., the subject of this sketch. He grew to manhood on the farm, and received his education in the old subscription schools. At the age of seventeen he commenced for himself, by working out for wages, and in 1852 he came to Texas County, Mo., where the following year he brought his mother and sister, in a one-horse wagon, drawn by a blind mule. When they reached their place of destination $1.50 was all the available funds in their possession. During the war Mr. Beard served six months in the State Militia, Confederate army. Previous to this, in 1857, he married Miss Telitia J. Sisk, who bore him nine children, six sons and three daughters. His wife died in 1874, and the following year he married Miss Mary E. Giddeons, and by her became the father of five children, two sons and three daughters. Both wives were professing Christians. In 1881 Mr. Beard moved to his present property, and some time after built a store, which he ran for two years. He owns eighty-five acres of land, and for thirty-six years has been a resident of this county. He is a Democrat in his political views.

Jesse Franklin Beeler, a prominent farmer and stock raiser of Burdine Township, was born in Sullivan County, Tenn., December 22, 1805, and is one of the old and much esteemed citizens of the county. He is the son of Daniel and Margaret (Sharrartz) Beeler, and the grandson of Jacob Beeler, who served all through the Revolutionary War, and drew a pension until his death, for services rendered. He was an American by birth, but of Swedish descent. Margaret Sharrartz was the daughter of Conrad Sharrartz, a European, who came to America with his parents when he was but five years of age. On both sides of Jesse F. Beeler's ancestry may be found people of excellent standing and business ability. Both the grandparents are buried in the Beeler cemetery, Sullivan County, East Tenn., near the Virginia line. When the subject of this sketch was but four years of age his parents moved to Claiborne County, Tenn., where he grew to manhood. He assisted his father on the farm, and after his twenty-third year he followed boat building and farming, and made trips to points south of his home, in Alabama and other States, trading with Indians and others with different stock or articles of merchandise. He subsequently farmed and traded in horses, doing business through the South a great deal, and dealing often with the Indian traders. He was also identified with the distillery business. In 1850 or 1851 he came to Missouri, and located first in Jefferson County, where he followed farming, principally, until 1868, when he came to Texas County, and located upon his present farm, two miles east of Cabool. He married his first wife, Mary Dyer, in Grainger County, Tenn., whom he buried there in the Beeler grave-yard. She left him five daughters: Cynthia Jane, deceased wife of Green Harrington; Mary Orlena, deceased wife of Reeves Beevers; Matilda Caroline, wife of Judge John Hagenbush; Martha Elizabeth, wife of James Wiley, merchant of Moselle, Mo., and Melissa Ann, wife of James Jones, of St. Louis, Mo. Mr. Beeler married his second wife, Elizabeth Sellers, in Grainger County, Tenn., and buried her on the way to Missouri, at Eastport. She left him a son and daughter: Margaret Ellen, wife of Robert Lemmens, and James K. P., a substantial farmer of Texas County. Mr. Beeler is a member of the Missionary Baptist Church; is a member of the Agricultural Wheel, and while yet a comparatively young man filled the position of a commissioned officer in the State Militia. In Tennessee he served as justice of the peace for about fifteen years, and about the same length of time in East Tennessee. Mr. Beeler at this writing is eighty-four years of age, and says he is thankful to God for the many favors and blessings conferred by that omniscient Creator.

Henry H. Bell, farmer and stock raiser of Texas County, and one of its acknowledged energetic, industrious citizens, was born in Jackson County, Mo., May 15, 1838, his parents being Samuel and Margaret (Vaughan) Bell, who located in Jackson County, Mo., from Kentucky, in 1832. There the father, a farmer by occupation, died in 1854, at the age of fifty-nine years. He was a stanch Democrat during life, and with his wife was connected with the Methodist Church. They had a family of ten children, of whom six sons and one daughter survive, four sons and their sister living in California. Henry H. Bell spent his boyhood days on his father's farm in his native county, receiving but a limited education. His disinclination for work in early years created within him a disposition for a roving life, and in 1854, at the age of sixteen, he crossed the plains to California with a drove of cattle and ox-teams. August 18, 1855, he left San Francisco for the Isthmus of Panama, at which point he took ship for the island of Cuba, and there changed for New Orleans. After numerous dangers and perils he reached the old home in Jackson County, but during his absence changes had occurred, death having claimed his father and two sisters. Through his influence and persuasion, the mother, three brothers and his sister finally decided to remove to California, the trip being made overland (after many dangers, seen and unseen), in 1857, and there the mother still resides, near Healdsburg, where the children have grown up, reared families, and become well-to-do. Henry, not contented among friends, again left home, and passed not a little time in the mountains, crossing the snow-capped Sierra Nevadas in mid-summer, and experiencing more than once the sensation of being snow-bound in early spring. An account of his adventures in detail, interesting and romantic as they are, cannot be given within the limits of the present work. They would constitute a volume in themselves. At the age of twenty-six years Mr. Bell became convinced that there was truth in the old adage, "A rolling stone gathers no moss," and immediately set to work with an energy and determination quite in contrast with his former characteristics. May 15, 1866, he embarked from San Francisco for New York, and returning to Missouri was married in Lexington, December 25, 1866, to Miss Ann E. Geer. Following this he moved upon a farm in Jackson County, but in 1878 settled in Lexington, La Fayette County, coming later to Texas County, in 1884. His purchase of 460 acres of fine land includes 230 acres in cultivation, all of which has been redeemed from what was a heavy growth of timber and brush. The past winter he fed 100 cattle for market, in reaching which a stampede was experienced. Mr. Bell's decided apathy to laziness in any form, and his sincere earnestness and industry in every enterprise, gave him the cognomen of "The Working Bell" in Jackson County, a reputation fully sustained in La Fayette and Texas. He thinks honesty and hard work the best policy, if not very remunerative. He and wife have five children living: Maggie L., Cora T., Edwin E., Henry J. and Samuel G. Mr. Bell is a man of positive convictions, a stanch advocate of temperance, genial and social in disposition, and a favorite of all. He is small in stature, enjoys good health, and can always appreciate a good joke.

John R. Blankenship, merchant, and one of the oldest business men of Houston, Mo., was born in Polk County, Tenn., March 24, 1842, his parents being Spencer and Mariah (Scoggins) Blankenship, natives of Virginia and North Carolina, respectively. They both died in Texas County, Mo. He was born in 1809, and was seventy-six years of age at the time of his death. She was born in 1810, and died in 1886. They were married in North Carolina, whither the father had moved when a young man, and afterward moved to Polk County, Tenn., where they remained until 1860, when they came to Missouri and located in Texas County. He was quite successful in his business transactions, but lost all during the late war. He was a Democrat previous to the war, and after that a Republican in politics. Both he and wife were members of the Missionary Baptist Church. To their union were born ten children, eight now living. One son, Stephen, died in the Federal army. John R. Blankenship remained on his father's farm until the breaking out of the war, when he enlisted in Company F, of the Fifth Missouri State Militia, and later in Company I, of the Twelfth Missouri Cavalry, Federal Army, and rendered effective service until disabled from measles, when he was discharged. After leaving the army he attended school at Clarksburg and Jefferson City. In 1866 he engaged in the mercantile business on Howard Creek, and one year later he came to Houston, where he engaged in his former business, and has continued at this ever since. When starting for himself his means were limited, but by close attention to business he has been very successful. In 1869 he quit the dry goods business for drugs and groceries, etc. He is a member of the Masonic fraternity, a Republican in politics, and has been president of the school board for the last six years. He filled the office of treasurer for four years, being elected in 1868, and was elected to the same position in 1878, serving two years.

James Bradford. Among the earliest settlers of this part of Missouri was the above mentioned gentleman, whose birth occurred in Washington (now Marion) County, Ky., in 1807. His father was a native of Maryland, and when young went to Virginia, then to Tennessee, where he married Miss Nancy Cole, and became the father of four children. His wife having died he moved to Kentucky, and there married Miss Frances Nealy, who bore him twelve children, of whom James Bradford was the second in order of birth. In 1827 all the family moved to Missouri, and settled at Coppedge's Mill, in Phelps County, their nearest neighbor being fifteen miles away. Here James, his father and brothers spent much time in hunting bear, panther, elk, etc. It was his good fortune to meet Miss Anna Turpin, to whom he was married. She was the daughter of Josiah Turpin, who settled in what is now Pulaski County about 1816. She was born in 1811. Having lived in Phelps County until 1838, James Bradford and family moved to Texas County, Mo., where for a livelihood Mr. Bradford followed farming and saw-milling. He was a man of energy and good business talent. He began a poor man, but accumulated a good fortune, which was lost during the war. For two years he was judge of the county court of Texas County. Prior to the war Mr. Bradford was a Democrat, but after that a Republican, and both he and wife were members of the Methodist Episcopal Church. In 1864 he lost his wife, and later he married Mrs. Sarah I. Crow, nee Welborn. By his first wife he had twelve children, and by his second four children. He died in 1877. Josiah Bradford is the third child of the first set. He was born on April 1, 1834, at the mouth of Spring Creek, Phelps County, Mo. He was reared a farmer's boy, and received but littled education, not attending more than twelve months altogether. By observation and close application to his books he has made up for this deficiency to a great extent. May 15, 1856, he married Miss Elizabeth Halbert, a native of Texas County, Mo., and by her became the father of seven children: America, Columbus, Josiah G., Hugh, Florence A., Arthur and Huber. Mr. Bradford and all his family are members of the Methodist Episcopal Church, and Columbus is a minister in the same. August 9, 1862, Mr. Bradford enlisted in Company C, Thirty-second Missouri Volunteer Infantry, United States Army, and served nearly three years. He was in the battles of Chickasaw Bayou, siege of Vicksburg, Lookout Mountain, Missionary Ridge, capture of Atlanta, march to the sea, and was never wounded or taken prisoner. He was discharged at St. Louis, and has followed farming principally since. In 1865 he was appointed by the county court surveyor of this county. From 1868 to 1873 he filled the office of sheriff and collector; was a strong Democrat until 1864, since which time he has affiliated with the Republican party. He is a member of the G. A. R. He owns 320 acres of land, and as a business man has been quite successful, having worked out his own possessions.

Hon. Thomas N. Bradford, of the mercantile firm of J. S. Campbell & Co., of Licking, Mo., was born April 22, 1841, in Texas County, Mo., and is the son of James and Anna (Turpin) Bradford. [See sketch of parents under Josiah Bradford.] He is the sixth child born to his parents, and was reared on a farm, where he received a very limited education in the subscription schools of that day. In July, 1861, he enlisted in the Missouri State service, and remained about seven months. In 1864 he crossed the plains to California, where he teamed for some time. He then returned to the East, where he followed milling and merchandising for some time, or until 1872, when he was elected sheriff of Texas County. Two years later he was elected sheriff and collector, holding the office one term. In 1882 he was chosen to represent his county in the State Legislature, and since that time he has been engaged in merchandising and farming. December 25, 1867, he married Miss Dora Wilson, a native of Phelps County, by whom he has eight children, three sons and five daughters. Mrs. Bradford died June 11, 1886, and on August 27, 1887, he married Mrs. T. B. Wells, nee Janes, who is an active worker in the Presbyterian Church. Besides his interest in the store, Mr. Bradford is the owner of 300 acres of good land, notwithstanding the fact that he began life a poor boy. He is a strong Democrat in politics; is a Mason, being Master of Latimer Lodge No. 395.

Rev. Martin Collins Brown, or "Parson Brown," as he is familiarly known, pastor of the Cumberland Presbyterian Church of Cabool, was born in Bedford County, Tenn., January 14, 1831, and is the son of Jesse and Mary (Hicks) Brown, and grandson of Hezekiah Brown, one of the pioneers of Flat Creek, Bedford Co., Tenn. His nativity is uncertain. Jesse Brown was a native of Tennessee, and was a farmer by occupation. He went to Illinois in 1840, and located near Shawneetown, where he died one year later, at the age of forty-one years. His wife, Mrs. Mary (Hicks) Brown, was a native of South Carolina, and the daughter of James Hicks, who was a native of Ireland and who settled in South Carolina in pioneer days. Rev. Martin Collins Brown was the seventh child and only son in a family of ten children. He attained his growth on his father's farm, and in 1850 was united in marriage to Miss Cordelia Brown, of Illinois. He then farmed and taught school for about seven years, and in 1854 he professed religion, and with his wife joined the Cumberland Presbyterian Church. About eighteen months after this he united with the presbytery of that church, and began preaching, and at the same time carried on his teaching. Up to 1867 he traveled as a missionary through Southern Illinois, and in the spring of that year he went to Franklin County, Kas., where he remained, engaged in his ministerial work, until 1871, when he returned to Franklin County, Ill. In the spring of 1876 he moved to Texas County, locating on a farm on Elk Creek, and remained there until this year. He has 180 acres of valuable land; is a breeder of hogs and cattle, and is doing well. He is the father of these children: Jesse M., of Elk Creek; Emily, wife of Morgan Stotts, a farmer of Bates County, Mo.; Wiley Luther, a farmer of Elk Creek; Julia, deceased wife of George Marsh, of Washington Territory, and who left a daughter; Agnes, wife of Gideon Harmon, of

Piney Township, Texas Co., Mo.; George B., a farmer; Charity M., James M., Josie Minnie and Maggie T. Of this family all are well educated, and bright lights in their social relations. The three eldest sons have taught school. Parson Brown is a public-spirited gentleman, and contributes liberally to all objects having for their aim the general advancement of his locality. He has assisted greatly in the building of a new Cumberland Presbyterian Church at Cabool, and has rendered considerable aid to other church work.

George W. Brown, a leading citizen of Texas County, Mo., was born in Guilford County, N. C., in April, 1834, his parents being William R. and Elizabeth (Bevel) Brown, who were born in Guilford County, N. C., December 26, 1808, and June 2, 1811, respectively, and were there reared and married, the date of the latter event being July 27, 1831. In the fall of 1834 they went to Wilson County, Tenn., where the father died July 8, 1846, when comparatively a young man. He was of Scotch descent, and his father was a soldier in the Revolutionary War. In the fall of 1857 George W. Brown emigrated with his mother from Tennessee to Texas County, Mo., and here the mother, who had married a Mr. Michael Shaver, in April, 1859, after her husband's death, spent the remainder of her days, dying January 14, 1880, having been a worthy member of the Baptist Church for many years. Five children blessed their union: Mary C., wife of George Putnam; Eliza A., wife of W. T. Allman (she died in Benton County, Ark.); Francis (died in Wilson County, Tenn.), George W. and William J. George W. was the eldest son, and after his father's death took care of and provided for the remaining members of the family, being engaged in farming. In the early part of 1863 he enlisted in Company E, Third Missouri Cavalry, United States Army, but was afterward transferred to Company A, of the Eleventh Missouri Cavalry, serving until the close of the war, and participating in many battles, among which were Jenkins' Ferry, Prairie de Hand, Little Missouri River, Little Rock, the Biometer battle east of Little Rock, and many others. October 16, 1865, he was married to Mary A. Long, of Wilson County, Tenn., who was born September 10, 1839, and by her became the father of seven children, the following of whom are living: Thomas J., Albert M., Charles H., Martha and Josiah. James W., who was born April 16, 1857, died September 12, 1859, and John H., born May 7, 1869, died January 11, 1882. Mr. Brown has been a member of the Baptist Church for thirty-four years; is a member of the Masonic fraternity, and votes the Republican ticket.

Elder John W. Brown, who is prominently identified with the farming and stock raising interests of Burdine Township, Section 22, was born in Mississippi County, Mo., April 26, 1840, his parents being George Wesley and Lucinda (Scott) Brown. Elder John W. Brown was left motherless when a few months old, and his father died in August, 1883. He was reared in St. Francois County, Mo., and was obliged to make his own way in the world. He first contracted chopping cord-wood, and added farming to this. After the late Civil War he came to Texas County, purchasing a fine tract of land, consisting of 240 acres, where he located and where he has since lived. He was married in St. Francois County, Mo., to Miss Hettie Jones, a native of Missouri, born in Bollinger County, and the daughter of Thomas and Delilah (Pullum) Jones, natives of North Carolina. To Mr. and Mrs. Brown were born six sons, all living: William Isaac, a farmer of Texas County, who married Miss Sarah Keen, and has a family; John Wesley, a farmer of Wright County, who married Miss Evalina Dye; Thomas Benton, a student at Mountain Grove High-school, a school-teacher; James Harvey, Albert L. and Christopher C. yet remain on the farm with their parents. They buried their two daughters, Martha Delilah and Mary Melvina. Mr. and Mrs. Brown have extended their Christian charities to other children than their own, and have adopted two little orphans girls, Rhoda Elizabeth Klymer and Mary Catherine Drennon. Mr. Brown has served on the school board of his district, and has worked as a local minister for the past twenty years, in the Baptist Church, of which he, his wife and children are all members.

William J. Brown was born in Wilson County, Tenn., December 2, 1842, and is a son of William R. and Elizabeth (Bevel) Brown, a short history of whom is given in the sketch of George W. Brown. William J. Brown resided with his mother until he joined the State Militia, but afterward went with his mother to Cole County, Mo., where he lived for some time, and after a short stop in Pettis County, returned to Texas County in the fall of 1870, where he has since made his home. About 1866 he was married to Sarah G. Thons, a daughter of R. G. Thons. She was born in Guilford County, N. C., April 14, 1845, and died in Texas County, Mo., December 17, 1876, having been a consistent member of the United Baptist Church for a number of years. Their children are as follows: George W., Jr., Lily Bell, F. R., Thomas Jerry and Mary Caroline. In 1877 he married Nancy Cox, who was born in Tennessee, and died in Texas County, Mo., April 5, 1883. She was also a member of the United Baptist Church, and was the mother of three children, two of whom are living, Jimmie and Cora Bell. Mr. Brown has been a farmer and stock raiser all his life, and as such has been very successful, and is now a member of the Agricultural Wheel. He is a member of the United Baptist Church, and is a liberal supporter of religious and educational institutions, and in his political views is a Democrat.

Alfred H. Brown, liveryman, and one of the wide-awake, thorough-going business men of Texas County, was born in Cattaraugus County, N. Y., January 28, 1853, and is the son of Charles and Angeline (Hardin) Brown. The father died about 1861, and the mother afterward married Frank Cummings, with whom she moved to Missouri. They settled in Audrain County in 1868, where Alfred H. Brown was educated, and where he grew to manhood. He was reared to agricultural pursuits, and this occupation he adopted and followed until 1882, when he moved to Texas County, settling at Cabool, where he has since been engaged in the livery business. He has all the requisites necessary for a first-class barn, and being a practical business man, and a genial, pleasant gentleman, would make a success of any undertaking, and especially of this. He was married in Texas County, November 25, 1885, to Miss E. A. Rust, who was born in that county May 28, 1868, and who is the daughter of J. R.

Rust, a native of Missouri. To Mr. and Mrs. Brown's marriage relations were born two children, both sons, Frank Earl and Charles Joseph. Mr. Brown is a member of the I. O. O. F., and a member of the city council.

John Cameron is one of the worthy farmers of Texas County, Mo., and is a son of Malcom and Rose (Craig) Cameron, both of whom were born in County Antrim, Ireland, and were there also reared and married, their five children being also born there. The father was a weaver by occupation, and in 1847 sailed for America, landing at Montreal, Canada; two of his children died while on the voyage, and were buried at sea. The father and eldest son took ship fever, from which they died soon after landing, the widow and remaining children being cared for by the wife of Rev. Willoughby until they could secure homes elsewhere. While with this lady John Cameron was sent to school, and secured a fair education. He was born in April 1838, and at the age of ten years became errand boy in a printing office, for which he received his board and clothes. At the age of thirteen years he began learning the plumber's trade, at which he served an apprenticeship of five years, and worked at his trade in Canada until 1865, when he went to New York, and worked in that city and in Brooklyn until 1877, when he took up his abode in Texas County, Mo., where he is the owner of 360 acres of land, which he earned by working at his trade. On his arrival here he had never ridden a horse or driven a team, and the first year he was compelled to hire his plowing done, but the second year took hold himself, and has become one of the best farmers in the neighborhood. In 1870 he was united in marriage to Miss Agnes C. Bell, who was also born in County Antrim, Ireland, and by whom he is the father of seven children: Rose Ella, John, David M., Jennie B., William W., James R., and Aggie, who is deceased. Mr. Cameron is a Republican in politics, and he and wife belong to the Methodist Episcopal Church.

John S. Cameron, principal of the Licking schools, and one of the prominent educators of Texas County, Mo., was born in the Grampian Hills of Scotland, July 1, 1848. He was reared and educated in the old country, where he took an academic course, and his boyhood days were passed on his father's farm. In 1869 he and his parents immigrated to America, and located near Licking, where the father died at the age of seventy, but the mother is still living, and is seventy-six years of age. In their family were eleven children, seven of whom are living. John S. Cameron, soon after coming to this country, began teaching, which profession he has continued since, nine terms in succession being taught in one district. In 1883 he was chosen county school commissioner of Texas County, which position he held for four years. He is now teaching his twenty-first term in the public schools, having been principal of Licking schools three years. In connection with his profession he is interested in farming, and is the owner of 236 acres of good land. In 1877 he wedded Miss Emma H. Barnes, a native of Texas County, and by her became the father of three children: Rosabella, Ewan J. and Eva E. Mr. Cameron is one of the oldest and most successful educators in Texas County. He is a Democrat in politics, is a member of the Masonic fraternity, and both he and Mrs Cameron are members of the Baptist Church.

William F. Cavaness, farmer, is a son of Edward and Lovie J. (Craven) Cavaness, who were born in Virginia and North Carolina, respectively. The father was taken to North Carolina when four years of age, and was there reared to manhood and married. His wife died about 1840, and he afterward married Mary A. Johnson, with whom he came to Texas County, Mo., in 1856, and here spent the remainder of his days. dying in 1865. His widow still survives him. Their family consisted of eight children, and six children were born to his first marriage. William F. Cavaness is the third child born to the first union, and was born in Randolph County, N. C., August 4, 1833, and received no schooling in his early days. He worked on his father's farm until twenty-one years of age, and then began working for himself, hiring out by the month for a year, since which time he has been engaged in farming for himself, and now owns about 783 acres of land, with about 100 acres under cultivation, all of which has been acquired by his own exertions. In 1853 he was married to Miss Martha J. Ward, a native of North Carolina, and two years later moved to Texas County, Mo. His wife died in 1857, and in 1859 he espoused Sarah Brown, a native of Randolph County, N. C. Thomas M. and Mary E. are the children born to his first union, and Alexander W., William E., Andrew D., Martha M., Alfred O. and Lorenzo are the children of his second union. Mr. Cavaness is a Republican politically, and a Mason, and he and wife are members of the Baptist Church. In 1863 he enlisted in the Sixth Provisional Regiment, United States Army, and served seven months, holding the office of fifth duty-sergeant.

L. A. Cochrane, dealer in hardware, was born in Jefferson County, Ill., March 1, 1849, being the son of John and Margaret (Roberson) Cochrane, and grandson of John Cochrane, Sr., who was a native of South Carolina, and whose father was a native of Scotland, and a soldier in the Revolutionary War. Margaret (Roberson) Cochrane was a native of Georgia, and the daughter of Joshua Roberson. L. A. Cochrane was one of a family of two sons and two daughters. He was reared in Illinois, and obtained a good education in the public schools of Jefferson County, Ill., supplementing it with academic training at Spring Garden Academy, of Jefferson County. He then taught school for three years, read medicine, and entered the Rush Medical College, of Chicago, Ill. He practiced first in Clay and Franklin Counties, and at Eureka Springs, but abandoned this profession at that place to embark in manufacturing there, and afterward at Winona Springs, Ark. In May, 1875, he came to Cabool, and has been identified with the manufacturing interests of the county since. In 1887 he opened a branch store at Winona, Mo. He was married in New Burnside, Ill., to Miss Mary E. Goode, a native of Kentucky, and to them have been born two sons: Victor Hugo and Leroy. Mrs. Cochrane is a member of the Presbyterian Church. Mr. Cochrane is an Odd Fellow, Treasurer of Cabool Lodge No. 433; has served on the school board of Cabool, and has built and improved property here.

David T. Collier, of Licking, was born in Stewart County, Tenn., September 1, 1838, being the son of Jesse and Mahala F. (Ellis) Collier, born, respectively, in Virginia and Stewart County, Tenn. The father moved to Tennessee when young, was married there, and about 1840 moved to Illinois, and the following year to Missouri, where they spent the rest of their lives with the exception of a year passed in Texas. Mr. Collier was a plain, well-to-do farmer, and the mother was a member of the Methodist Church. Politically the father was a Democrat, and during the war served in the Confederate army a short time. They both lived to be about sixty-three years of age. In their family were thirteen children, ten sons and three daughters. David T. Collier was the eighth child, and was educated in the common schools. His minority was spent working on the farm, but at the age of twenty-two he began the study of medicine under Dr. S. W. Wood, of Lebanon, Mo. In 1863 he graduated from the Cincinnati College of Medicine and Surgery, and afterward came to this part of the State. In 1865 he located in Licking, where he has been more or less actively engaged in the practice of his profession. For about seventeen years he carried on merchandising in Licking. In 1862 he married Miss Mahala Tilley, a native of Pulaski County, Mo., and to them were born ten children, eight now living: Byron, Ida, Mamie, Claud, Effie, Everett, Lillian and Burt. Dr. Collier has practiced his profession for twenty-six years, and is a successful physician. He is associated with Rolla District Medical Association and Texas County Medical Society. He is a man who takes an active interest in all the worthy enterprises of his community. In connection with the practice of his profession Dr. Collier is interested in farming, and has 500 acres of land. He is a Democrat in politics, a Royal Arch Mason, and Mrs. Collier is a member of the Methodist Episcopal Church.

William Burrell Connelly, farmer and stock raiser, was born in Southern Alabama, February 1, 1834, being the son of William and Elvira (McClendon) Connelly. The father was a native of Limerick, Ireland, and came to America when a lad. He had left his home for that of a sea-faring life, which he abandoned as a soldier in the War of 1812. He then located in Alabama, and for several years taught school and followed farming. In 1835 or 1836 he went to Tennessee, and spent six years in that State, engaged in agricultural pursuits, in Henry and Madison Counties. He came to Missouri in 1842, locating in New Madrid County, of that State, but afterward moved to St. Francois County, where he died in 1871, after a residence there of about eleven years. He died in full communion with the faith of the Methodist Church. His worthy wife followed him in 1885, and is buried beside him; she was also a member of the Methodist Church. Of their family of four sons and four daughters, one son and two daughters survive. The daughters are Sarah and Lavinia, respectively, and Mrs. John Merritt and Mrs. William Pratt. William Burrell Connelly grew to manhood in Missouri, and spent four months in Missouri State Service and six months in the United States Federal service during the late war, the latter part of which he was second lieutenant of Company F, Forty-seventh Regiment Missouri Volunteer Infantry. He then followed merchandising and farming in St. Francois County until 1870, when he came to Wright County, and in 1873 came here and located upon his present farm. He married, in

Ste. Genevieve County, Miss Sarah Ann Barnes, daughter of Jehu and Elizabeth Dodson (Parks) Barnes, natives of North Carolina, who made an early settlement in Ste. Genevieve County. Mr. and Mrs. Connelly have eight children, three sons and five daughters: Elvira, Mrs. Bell; Sarah Ann, James Franklin, William Lincoln, Cora Blanche, Jehu Barnes, Lillie Jane, Estella Mabel, and have buried their eldest child, Mary Elizabeth, the wife of G. M. Roberts. Mr. Connelly has served with credit for several terms on the school board of his district, and is a stanch Republican in his political views.

Dr. Benjamin Franklin Craven, a prominent and successful practitioner of Licking, Mo., was born in Randolph County, N. C., August 2, 1845, being the son of Rev. John W. and Henrietta (Johnson) Craven. The father was a native of North Carolina, born October 2, 1821, and was licensed to preach in the Methodist Episcopal Church, South, in 1849, although his principal occupation through life was farming and merchandising. The mother was born October 26, 1820, in Virginia. After marriage they lived in North Carolina until 1857, when they came to Texas County, and settled within three miles of Licking, where they spent the remainder of their lives. He died December 30, 1884, and she August 31, 1887. Their family consisted of eight children, six sons and two daughters, only three sons now living, of whom two are M. D.'s. The oldest living one of these children is Dr. Benjamin F. Craven, who came with his parents to Texas County when twelve years of age. He received a good literary education in the common schools in youth, and assisted his father on the farm. When about twenty-one years of age he began the study of medicine with Dr. D. T. Collier, of Licking, and in 1867 entered the Missouri Medical College at St. Louis, where he graduated in 1869. He then located at Lake Spring, in Dent County, and practiced a year with Dr. John Hyer, after which he practiced by himself. In 1872, and while in the last named county, he married Miss Mattie L. Arthur, a native of Dent County. Two children were born to this union, one of whom is now living, John Arthur. The same year of his marriage Dr. Craven removed to Licking, where he has had a good practice since. For about fifteen years he has made a specialty of the eye, being quite successful in treatment. In the spring of 1888 he took a post graduate course at Missouri Medical College, paying especial attention to the eye. He is a member of Rolla District Medical Association, Texas County Medical Society, and is a member of the A. O. U. W. He lives on his farm adjacent to the town, and has the advantage of both country and city. As a physician Dr. Craven has met with success, and has devoted himself exclusively to his profession. He is a Democrat in politics, and is a man who takes an interest in all worthy enterprises. He and wife are members of the Methodist Episcopal Church, South.

James A. Craven, merchant at Licking, Mo., was born March 28, 1848, in Randolph County, N. C., and is the son of John W. and Henrietta R. (Johnson) Craven. He was reared to agricultural pursuits, and received a very limited education in the old-time schools. At the age of nineteen he began clerking for Dr. D. T. Collier for $13 per month, and two years later he became a partner of his father in the store at Licking. In all he was in partnership with his father for about twelve years, and with the exception of about six months he has been engaged in merchandising in this town since, keeping a general store. The firm has changed names several times, his last partner being Joel Sherrill. In 1888 Mr. Craven became sole proprietor, and now runs one of the most extensive stores in Licking. He was married September 8, 1879, to Miss Mary E. Sherrill, daughter of Joel Sherrill. Ten children were born to this marriage, eight now living: Rosa D., Joel W., Elbert E., Wesley H., James M., Eunice, Helen and Alfred F. July 23, 1888, Mrs. Craven died. Both he and wife were members of the Methodist Episcopal Church, South. He is a Mason, being Chaplain of Latimer Lodge No. 395, and is a Democrat in politics. In connection with merchandising he also runs a farm, and is the owner of 262 acres. As a business man he has been quite successful, having made most all he has by his own efforts. He has never aspired to any official position, but for eight years he has been notary public.

Alfred Randolph Craven, M. D., one of the successful practitioners of Texas County, is a native of Randolph County, N. C., born January 3, 1854, and is the son of John W. and Henrietta R. (Johnson) Craven. He was reared to farm life, and educated in the old subscription schools. At the age of twenty he entered a store as salesman, where he continued for ten years. When about twenty-five years of age he commenced reading medicine, and in 1887 and 1888 he took a course of lectures at Missouri Medical College. In the spring of 1888 he took a post graduate course, and in 1888 he opened an office five miles north of Licking. In 1879 he married Miss Alice Arthur, a native of Dent County, and the fruits of this union are four children: Mildred B., Mattie E., Ashbury F. and an infant. In connection with his profession Dr. Craven carries on farming, and is the owner of 100 acres of land, besides property in Licking. He is a pleasant, agreeable gentleman, and has a good practice for so short a residence in the vicinity. He is a Democrat in his political views, and both he and Mrs. Craven are members of the Methodist Episcopal Church, South. He has been a resident of Texas County for thirty-two years, and has the confidence and esteem of all who know him.

William W. Cronin, of the firm of Cronin Bros., dealers in general hardware and agricultural implements, was born in Colchester, Conn., February 14, 1855, being the son of Daniel and Catherine (O'Niel) Cronin, both natives of Fermoyle Parish, County Kerry, Ireland, and come of old Irish stock in that locality. They were married in their native county, and in 1852 left the land of their birth and immigrated to America. They settled at Colchester, and here the father passed an active and useful life. He died the 4th of November, 1888, at the ripe old age of eighty-six. His son, William W. Cronin, attained his growth in Connecticut, and completed a thorough knowledge of plumbing and tin-smithing, and carried on journeyman work until 1882, when he and his brother D. W. opened the first hardware store in Texas County, at Houston, and they still carry on that branch. In 1883 they opened another store at Cabool, which they have since continued with great success. At White Hall, Greene Co., Ill., Mr.

Cronin married Miss Mary Kendall, daughter of Nat Kendall, a farmer of that place, and a native of Maine. To Mr. and Mrs. Cronin were born two children, a son and daughter: Annie and Jeremiah. Mr. Cronin is a member of the Roman Catholic faith, served as president of the school board for three years, was one of the original incorporators of Cabool, and served as village trustee. He is a member of the A. O. U. W., and is a K. of L.

David T. M. Crow, farmer, of Sherrill Township, was born in Morgan County, Ala., January 6, 1833, and is the son of Dickerson and Malinda (Matkin) Crow, born in South Carolina and Kentucky in 1809 and 1808, respectively. When young both moved to Morgan County, Ala., where they married and lived until 1837, when they came to St. Francois County, Mo., and three years later to Texas County, settling five miles north of Licking, on Spring Creek, where the mother still lives. Although starting with little means, Mr. Crow soon became a well-to-do farmer, and was a prominent citizen of the county. During the war he represented Texas County in the Legislature; had been a Democrat before that time, but after peace was declared he affiliated with the Republican party. Both he and wife were members of the Methodist Episcopal Church. He died July 7, 1870. In their family were ten children, nine sons and one daughter, of whom our subject is the third in order of birth. He assisted his father on the farm, and attended the common schools, being obliged to walk as far as five miles to attend the same. At the age of twenty-one he commenced for himself by farming, which has been his business ever since. November 1, 1859, he married Miss Martha J. Burnes, a native of North Carolina, born February 20, 1832, and to this union were born four children: James F., Jennie (deceased), Lucy (deceased) and Jacob D. In August, 1861, Mr. Crow enlisted in Company B, Bowen's battalion, in which he served about a year, and was then transferred to the Tenth Missouri Cavalry, United States Army, where he served three years. He was in a number of minor engagements. After the war he returned home and engaged in tilling the soil. In 1857 Mr. Crow entered 320 acres of land, where he now lives, and since then he has added eighty acres more. He is a hard-working, industrious man, and has about 100 acres under cultivation. He has been a resident of this county for forty-eight years, and is one of its best citizens. He was a Democrat before the war, but since that eventful struggle he has affiliated with the Republican party. He and wife are members of the Methodist Episcopal Church.

Zachariah T. Denison, farmer and stock dealer of Sherrill Township, was born in Hart County, Ky., February 1, 1847, and is the son of Zachariah and Margaret (Isbel) Denison, who came to this county in 1848, settling on the farm where the subject of this sketch is now living, and there followed farming. Previous to this the Denison family had emigrated from Virginia to Kentucky. Mr. Denison was a Democrat in politics, and died at the age of fifty-one. Mrs. Denison was a member of the Methodist Episcopal Church, and died at the age of forty-two. Both passed their last days in Texas County. Their family consisted of ten children, six sons and four daughters, Zachariah T. being the second in order of birth. Like the majority of country boys, he assisted his father on the farm and attended the common schools, where he received but a limited education, owing to the breaking out of the Civil War. He remained under the parental roof until about nineteen years of age, when he began farming for himself. October 6, 1868, he married Miss Sarah C. Johnson, a native of Texas County, Mo., and the daughter of Frank Johnson. This union resulted in the birth of eight children: Henry C., Francis L., Samantha L., Delilah A., Lucy C., Frances L., Amanda E. and Maggie T. Soon after marriage Mr. Denison located on the farm where he now lives, and is now the owner of 360 acres of land, of which about 125 are under cultivation. In connection with his farming interest he has been engaged in buying and shipping stock. As a business man he has met with excellent success, and is considered one of the solid, substantial men of the county. He is a man who takes an active interest in schools, churches and other laudable enterprises, and has been a resident of Texas County for forty years. Mr. Denison is a Democrat politically, and he and wife are members of the Baptist Church.

James H. Denison, a prosperous young stock man, farmer, and native of Sherrill Township, Texas Co., Mo., was born on the 15th of January, 1854, receiving his education in the old subscription schools of early times, and being compelled to walk a distance of three miles to receive such instruction as could be obtained at that day. At the age of nineteen years he began the battle of life for himself, with no capital but a horse, saddle and bridle, but by industry and good management he has become the owner of 160 acres of valuable land, about seventy-five acres of which are under cultivation and well improved. On the 23d of October, 1873, he was married to Miss America E. Haggard, who was born in Texas County, Mo., August 21, 1857, and by her is the father of five children, whose names are as follows: Moletna F., Mary E., McCuin Z., James W. and Ceba C. Mr. and Mrs. Denison are members of the Christian Church, and he is a Democrat in politics. They have resided on their present farm since 1878, and are considered among the first citizens of the county.

James R. Duke, proprietor of the Clipper Stables at Houston, Mo., was born near Richmond, Va., on the 11th of September, 1849, his parents being Richard and Elizabeth Ann (Pulland) Duke, whose deaths occurred in Texas County, Mo., in 1860, the mother's being about six months after the father's. They moved from their native State of Virginia to Ohio, thence to Illinois, residing in Pike and Jasper Counties, and in 1858 came to Texas County, Mo., where they afterward made their home. The father learned the stone-mason's trade when a young man, and worked at this occupation in connection with farming and trading, and in his political views was a Democrat throughout life. Mrs. Duke was a member of the Methodist Episcopal Church. Three of their six sons are living at the present time: Minon E., a prominent farmer of Texas County, residing near Houston; James R., and William M., a farmer of Maries County, Mo. James R. Duke was educated in Houston, and after the death of his parents made his home for some time with Nat Rogers, and then began making his home with James P. Bates, of Texas County, Mo., with whom he resided for a number of years. When starting out in life for himself he worked at anything he could get to do to make an honorable living, but was principally engaged in hauling logs. He afterward engaged in farming, and began dealing in stock, which occupations have proved remunerative, and he has taken a great deal of stock to St. Louis. He now owns a valuable farm adjoining Houston, on which is a substantial residence and good out-buildings. Nannie A. Sutton, who was born in Texas County, Mo., and is a daughter of Valentine Sutton, became his wife October 14, 1876, and their union has been blessed in the birth of the following children: Arthur William, born August 24, 1877; James R., who died at the age of eighteen months, having been born May 24, 1879; Jennie J., born September 26, 1881; Charles H., born December 30, 1884, and Bessie. Mrs. Duke is a member of the Methodist Episcopal Church, and Mr. Duke belongs to the I. O. O. F., and in his political views is a Democrat.

Daniel G. Elliott. The manufacturing interests of Texas County, Mo., are ably represented by Mr. Elliott, who is the proprietor of the Elliott Foundry, which house was established in 1875. Its original dimensions were 20x40 feet, and was run by horse-power, but it is now a building 40x120 feet, and is fitted up with some of the very best machinery to be had, his engine being twelve horse-power and of the best make. His iron-work is all done during the summer months and his wood-work during the winter season, some of the products of his establishment being all kinds of farm machinery, such as plows, cane-mills, etc. On starting his foundry he was the owner of twenty acres of land, but he now owns 206 acres and is one of the prosperous men of the county. He was born in Coshocton County, Ohio, September 21, 1834, his parents being Thomas and Lucy (Sanders) Elliott. The father was born in Ireland, and was brought to the United States by his parents when five years of age. They located in Ohio, but in 1856 went to Sangamon County, Ill., where Thomas died in 1879, at the age of sixty-five years. His wife died in Ohio about 1842. Four of their sons are yet living: Simon, who is a moulder by trade, resides in Kansas; Nathan is a farmer of Johnson County, Mo., but in his younger days was also a moulder; Thomas is a blacksmith and moulder of Sangamon County, Ill., and Daniel G., our subject. At the age of twelve years the latter entered his father's wagon and general machine shop, in which he worked until sixteen years of age, at which time he had become such a skillful workman that he commanded journeyman's wages. In 1853 he went to Ohio, and engaged in business at his father's old stand, where he remained until 1862, then enlisted in Company H, of the Ninety-seventh Infantry, and served as orderly-sergeant until May 15, 1865, when he was mustered out at Columbus, Ohio, having participated in many battles, among which were Stone Hill and Missionary Ridge. After the latter battle he was on detached duty the rest of the war, and then returned to Ohio, and resumed business at the old stand until the spring of 1867, when he located on a farm in Texas County, Mo., but soon after gave this up and worked at carpentering and other mechanical work until 1875, since which time he has been engaged in his present business. April 26, 1855, he was married to Catherine Henderson, who was born in Ohio in 1835, and by her is the father of three children: Sanders S., Mary Lucy, wife of James Tate, and William T. Mr. and Mrs. Elliott are members of the Methodist Episcopal Church, and he is a member of the G. A. R., and a Republican in politics.

Hon. John R. Farris, merchant and farmer, is a native of Missouri, born on Big Piney Creek, Texas County, April 24, 1842, and is a son of James and Caroline (King) Farris, natives of Scott County, Mo., and North Carolina, respectively, and grandson of John Farris, who was born in Tennessee. The Farris family were of Scotch-Irish descent, and trace their ancestors back to before the Revolutionary War. These ancestors made settlements in Virginia and Tennessee, and the great-grandfather of the subject of this sketch served with distinction in the War of the Revolution. Hon. John R. Farris, after reaching man's estate, followed the occupation of his father, that of a farmer and stock raiser. June 21, 1861, he enlisted in Company G, McBride's First Regiment Infantry, State service, and served six months. He then entered Freeman's brigade, Confederate service, cavalry, serving all through the war; was commissioned the last two years of the war as captain and aid-de-camp of Gen. Freeman. After the war Mr. Farris returned to Missouri and carried on farming, to which, in 1883, he added merchandising. He was married in Crawford County, Mo., to Miss Missouri Snelson, daughter of John Snelson, a native of Missouri, originally from Ohio. To Mr. and Mrs. Farris were born five sons and three daughters: Rosa, wife of A. M. Turner; Albert (deceased), Della, Lee, Walter R., Ferdinando, Maggie and Johnnie. Mr. Farris, wife and daughter Della are members of the Cumberland Presbyterian Church; the wife and daughter are active workers in the same, and Mr. Farris is an elder. In 1884 he was elected to represent Texas County in the Thirty-third General Assembly, and served on the committee of insurance. He is a Blue Lodge Mason. He pays considerable attention to the fine stock breeding of jacks, horses, cattle and hogs. His fine farm of 120 acres adjoins Cabool.

Albert T. Fengler, dealer in groceries and bakery supplies, was born in Breslau, Silisia, Prussia, Germany, March 8, 1843, being the son of Ernest and Emelia Fengler, who came to America in 1848, and settled at Dubuque, Iowa, where their son, Albert T., grew to manhood, and afterward enlisted in the Federal army, Company F, One Hundred and Thirty-fourth Volunteer Infantry, 1862-63; served about eight months, when he received an honorable discharge. He then went into the Government's employ as clerk in the quartermaster's department, and served in that capacity until cessation of hostilities. Leaving this business, he was engaged for some time upon various interests in the Government's employ, and traveled quite extensively through the South, but principally in Mississippi and Louisiana. He then returned to Dubuque, but came to Cabool in 1882, where he has since been engaged in merchandising. He built his present store, 60x20, in 1884, and is a stockholder in the Blankenship Springs Improvement Company. He is a charter member of the G. A. R., Pardee Post No. 352, at Cabool. He was reared in the Lutheran faith. He was one of five sons, Richard, Emil, George,

Albert and Trangott, and three daughters born to his parents; one son, Emil, died on the battle-field of Chickamauga as a soldier of the Chicago & Galena Union Railway Regiment Illinois Volunteers. The father, Ernest Fengler, died a worthy Union soldier in the hospital at Evansville, Ind.

Richard T. Foard was born in Halifax County, Va., April 20, 1839, and is the son of William F. Foard and Jane W. (Tuck) Foard, natives, respectively, of Person County, N. C., and Halifax County, Va. The father was born April 12, 1812, and is still living in Guilford County, N. C. His wife was born October 10, 1814, and died in 1867, after which Mr. Foard married a Mrs. Hall, who is still living. He was married three times, his first wife being Nancy Tuck. Although a heavy loser by the war, he is now a well-to-do farmer. He is a member of the Methodist Episcopal Church, South, and politically he is a Democrat. The grandfather Tuck was orderly-sergeant in the War of 1812. Richard T. Foard is the second of eleven children, and until twenty years of age resided on the home farm. He then went to Guilford County, N. C., where he spent some time in running a grist-mill for his father and farming, and a short time previous to the breaking out of the Rebellion was made first lieutenant of Company B, of the State Militia, and was held in reserve until 1863, when he entered active service. In 1867 he came to Missouri, and has since been engaged in farming and stock raising in Texas County, where he has over 700 acres of fine land. In 1872 he was elected justice of the peace, and in 1876 was elected sheriff of the county, being re-elected in 1878 and 1880, serving until 1882. He was married to Mary Kirkman in 1861. She was born in North Carolina in 1839, and died in Texas County, Mo., September 6, 1872, having been a consistent member of the Methodist Episcopal Church, South, for a number of years. On January 21, 1877, Mary Emely White, a daughter of Hon. J. C. White, became his wife. Her birth occurred in Texas County, Mo., April 5, 1852, and her union with Mr. Foard has been blessed in the birth of four children, three of whom are living: Novella J., Mary J., Bulah F., and William B., who died at the age of five years and five months. Mr. Foard is a Democrat, a Mason and a member of the I. O. O. F., and he and wife belong to the Methodist Episcopal Church, South.

James C. Fox. Prominent among the farming and stock raising representatives of Texas County, Mo., stands the name of James C. Fox, who was born in Haywood County, Tenn., March 9, 1833, and is one of twelve children, four now living, born to William and Susan (Campbell) Fox. The parents were, respectively, of Tennessee and Alabama, and after marriage they lived for some time in Haywood County, Tenn. About 1840 they came to Texas County, Mo., in an ox-wagon, drawn by three yoke of oxen, and there made their home. He was a small farmer, but was a great lover of the chase, and died in the prime of manhood. He was a Whig in politics, and a member of the Methodist Church, South. The mother is also a member of that church, and is still living, being eighty-five years of age. Their son, James C. Fox, was reared on the farm, and had very limited educational advantages. He was but a lad when his father died, and he was obliged to hire out. His father had bought a farm on credit, and it being taken he had to help support his mother and the younger children. In 1856 he married Miss Martha E. Martin, a native of Tennessee, and to them were born nine children, six now living: Nancy C., William B., Susan E., James M., Mary M. and Thomas O. Both Mr. and Mrs. Fox are members of the Missionary Baptist Church. After marriage they settled in Sherrill Township, and with the exception of about two years have lived there ever since 1840. He owns 200 acres of land, with about 100 under cultivation, and although he started a poor boy, he now is ready to enjoy the fruits of his labor. He is a Democrat in his political views.

John Geers is a prosperous stock man and farmer of Texas County, Mo., and is the third of five children born to the marriage of William L. Geers and Desdemona Higgins, natives, respectively, of Kentucky and Illinois. They were married in the latter State, and settled in Madison County, where they were engaged in farming, and where the father died in 1849. His widow is still living, and is considerably advanced in years. John Geers was born in Madison County, Ill., March 20, 1841, and was reared on a farm, receiving a common-school education. In August, 1862, he enlisted in Company C, One Hundred and Seventeenth Volunteer Infantry, United States Army, and was a faithful supporter of the "Stars and Stripes" for three years. The battles in which he took part are as follows: Pleasant Hill, Nashville, Fort Spanish, Fort Blakely and several others. He was never wounded nor taken prisoner, and after his return to Illinois was married, February 27, 1866, to Sarah A. Radcliff, also a native of Madison County, and moved soon after to Chariton County, Mo., where he engaged in farming. While his wife was on a visit to her old home she was taken ill, and died in 1871, leaving three children: Nicholas G., Okalona and Joan. Since 1874 Mr. Geers has been a resident of Texas County, and was here married, November 4, 1877, to Mary E. Williams, a native of North Carolina, born July 11, 1862, and by her is the father of five children: William L., Mary C., Charles F., John E. and Lucy D. Mr. and Mrs. Geers are members of the Missionary Baptist Church, and he is a member of the Masonic fraternity, and a Republican in his political views. He has been twice nominated for county sheriff, and although the county has a Democratic majority of 800, he came within sixty-one votes of election in the last race. He owns 524 acres of land, with about 140 acres under cultivation, and has been quite successful in his business enterprises.

Thomas N. Gibson is a son of William F. and Rachel (Brookshire) Gibson, and was born in Rutherford County, Tenn., October 27, 1834. His father was born in the "Palmetto State," June 7, 1810, and immigrated in wagons with his parents to Tennessee when twelve years of age, settling in Rutherford County, where he resided until 1835, when he located in Linn County, Mo., where he is still living, at the age of seventy-nine years, and has been justice of that county for twelve years. To him and wife, who was born in Rutherford County, Tenn., twelve children have been born, eight of whom are living: George W., Mary C., Amanda, Sarah, James W., Daniel R., David A., and Thomas. Those deceased are Martha A., Elizabeth, John and an infant. Mrs. Gibson died July 27, 1856, after which Mr. Gibbons wedded Rebecca Schrock, by whom he has three children: Robert L., Andrew J. and Lucy. The grandfather, Thomas N. Gibson, was born in Ireland, and immigrated to the United States when a young man, settling in South Carolina during the Revolutionary War. Ruth A. Fowler, his wife, was born in London, England. Grandfather Brookshire was also of Irish birth, but his wife was of Dutch extraction. Thomas N. Gibson, whose name heads this sketch, was reared in Linn County, Mo., and received the education which was accorded the average farmer's boy of his day. At the age of twenty-three years he wedded Mary A. Purden, who was born in Boone County, Mo., and five children have blessed their union: Huldah, Jeanette, Lloyd, Dora and Byron. August 25, 1876, the mother of these children died, and Mr. Gibson then espoused Mrs. Sarah V. (Cline) Haney, a daughter of Isaac and Theresa Cline, both parents and daughter being natives of Clark County, Va. To Mr. and Mrs. Gibson, who were married in 1877, two children have been born: John T. and Pearl. Mr. Gibson resided in Linn County, Mo., until 1867, and from that time until 1886 resided in Sullivan County, coming to Texas County at the latter date. He served as justice of Linn County, and is the present postmaster of Big Creek, and in his political views is a stanch Democrat. He is a worthy member of the Methodist Episcopal Church, South, and is one of the county's well-to-do farmers.

Joel S. Halbert, one of the prominent farmers of Texas County, Mo., is the son of Eli G. and Frances (Sherrill) Halbert, both natives of Tennessee, born in 1805 and 1812, respectively. In early life they both came to St. Francois County, where they married in 1828. About 1843 they came to Texas County, Mo., and made Sherrill Township their home the remainder of their lives. Mr. Halbert was one of the leading farmers of his day, and in connection for some time ran a store in Licking. He held the position of county judge, being presiding judge at the time of his death, which occurred in 1872. He was a Democrat in politics. The mother was a member of the Missionary Baptist Church, and died in 1875. They were the parents of thirteen children, six of whom are living, one son and five daughters. Joel S. Halbert was born December 27, 1840, in St. Francois County, and was the sixth child in order of birth. He attained his growth on the farm, and received the greater part of his education in the old subscription schools, receiving a fair education for that day. In June, 1861, he enlisted in Capt. John Nichols' company, Missouri Infantry, State service, where he served six months. He then joined the regular Confederate army, and served three years. In the State service he participated in the battles of Wilson's Creek, Dry Wood and Lexington, Mo. In the regular service he participated in the battles of Helena, Ark., Mansfield, La., and Jenkins' Ferry, Ark., and was neither wounded nor taken prisoner. He held no office save corporal. After returning home he was married, December 31, 1867, to Miss Martha J. Thornton, a native of this county, who was born March 13, 1849. To this union were born ten children: Eureka P., Eli C., Estella P., Ephraim G., Frances A., Mary E., Eva M.,

Bertha C., Bessie M. and Carrie. Mr. Halbert has carried on farming all his life, and is the owner of 302 acres, with about 125 acres under cultivation. As a business man he has been very successful, although commencing with limited means, and he is now the owner of a good property, notwithstanding that he came from the war penniless and that he has been burned out once since. Mr. Halbert is a Democrat in politics, is a member of the Masonic fraternity, and he and wife are members of the Missionary Baptist Church.

Henry Harmon was born in Greene County, Tenn., August 25, 1828, his parents being Philip and Catherine (Fry) Harmon, born in Jefferson County, Tenn., and Virginia, respectively. They were married in Tennessee, and there resided until 1857, when they came to Texas County, Mo., where the father worked at the blacksmith's and wagon-maker's trades until his death, in 1865, at the age of sixty-six years. He was a successful business man, but owing to going security for others, lost considerable money. He was a Democrat, and he and wife were earnest members of the Methodist Episcopal Church. The latter's death occurred in 1861, at the age of about fifty-two years. Six of their ten children are now living. Henry Harmon is their third child, and made his home with his parents until twenty-two years of age, and then began his career as a farmer, in which calling he has been quite successful. September 19, 1850, he was married to Sarah Carter, who was born in Tennessee, and died in Greene County of that State when twenty-two years old, having borne two children, George W., and Anderson, a farmer of the county. Her oldest son was a practicing physician of Texas County. Mr. Harmon took for his second wife Eliza Matilda, a daughter of Jesse Elmore. She was born in Bradley County, Tenn., February 9, 1829, and died in Texas County, Mo., when fifty-three years of age. To them was born one daughter, Martha E., wife of John Beck, a farmer of the county. After the death of his wife Mr. Harmon wedded Eliza Rippee, in 1870. She was born in Dickson County, Tenn., in 1831, and her union with Mr. Harmon resulted in the birth of four children, only one of whom is living, Ada. Those deceased are Robert L., Mary E. and Cordelia. Mr. and Mrs. Harmon are members of the Methodist Episcopal Church, and he is a Mason and a member of the I. O. O. F. He is a Democrat politically, and does all in his power to support the principles of his party.

Henry J. Herrick, attorney, farmer and prominent citizen of Texas County, Mo., now residing in the suburbs of Houston, was born in Huron County, Ohio, near the city of Norwalk, August 9, 1832, and is the son of Lot and Lola (Sutliff) Herrick, natives of Utica, N. Y., and New Haven, Conn., respectively. The Herrick family came from England before the Revolutionary War. Mr. and Mrs. Herrick were married in Norwalk, Ohio, where the father had gone when a young man. They remained there until 1833, when they removed to De Kalb County, Ind., and lived there the remainder of their lives. Both were members of the Methodist Episcopal Church, and both died in 1879. He was a Whig in politics, and afterward a Democrat. He held official positions in De Kalb County for many years, and was very proficient in mathematics, although he could neither read nor write until after his marriage, when his wife was his teacher. To his marriage were born seven children, four now living: Catherine (wife of William S. Goodell, deceased), Electa J. (wife of Charles Ryan), Henry J. and George W. (who is an attorney and farmer, of Farmer City, Ill). Henry J. Herrick received his education at Ann Arbor, and graduated in the law department in 1861. He then practiced his profession one year in De Kalb County, Ind., and in 1863 moved to Princeton, Mercer Co., Mo., where he remained until October, 1864, when he enlisted in Company D, Fifty-fifth Regiment; was afterward commissioned assistant adjutant-general of Missouri, ranking as captain, and was on detached duty in the Federal army. He was for a time provost-marshal at Chillicothe, Mo. In 1866 he located at Trenton, Mo., and entered the law firm of Shanklin & Austin. Two years later, as Shanklin, Austin & Herrick, they organized the Shanklin & Austin Bank. Mr. Herrick remained with the bank for five years, and was then elected prosecuting attorney, which position he held for six years. He remained in Grundy County until 1879, when he began to travel, and was in many States and localities. In 1881 he came to Houston, and one year later was connected with Edward A. Seay in the law practice. Mr. Herrick is a prominent criminal lawyer, and has been unusually successful. August 23, 1863, he married Miss Sarah Fusselman, a native of De Kalb County, Ind., born in 1837, and the daughter of Henry Fusselman. To this union was born one child, Henry L., who died when eight years of age. Mr. and Mrs. Herrick are members of the Christian Church, and Mr. Herrick is a member of the Masonic lodge; was Master of the lodge at Trenton one year, and represented that lodge at the Grand Lodge. He has taken all the degrees in York Masonry, is a Knight Templar, and belongs to Godfrey D. E. Commandery, No. 24, at Trenton, Mo. He is a Democrat in his political views.

Virgil M. Hines, attorney, of Houston, Mo., was born in Warren County, Ky., October 23, 1851, and is the son of Vincent K. and Ann M. (Stone) Hines, both natives of Warren County, Ky., and both now living at Windsor, Henry Co., Mo. Vincent K. Hines was born August 7, 1815, and his wife in 1819. They were married in Warren County, Ky., January 15, 1840, and resided there until 1867, when they moved to Johnson County, Mo., where they resided until December, 1875. They then moved to Windsor, Henry County, where they now reside. Both are members of the Methodist Episcopal Church, South, and he is a Democrat in politics. He followed farming until 1875, when he engaged in merchandising at Windsor, and continued at this until 1888, when he retired from business. He has been successful in all his business transactions. The Hines family came from Virginia to Kentucky, and were among the very earliest settlers of that State. William Hines, grandfather of our subject, it is thought, was a soldier in the War of 1812. He died in Kentucky. The Stone family were also early settlers of Kentucky. To Mr. and Mrs. Vincent Hines were born six sons and four daughters, nine children now living: James H., John W., died in 1871, when twenty-four years of age; W. M., V. M., Frank B., V. G., Mary, wife of W. Y. Cross; Jane, wife of T. C.

Craig; Julia, widow of E. H. Wall, and Ida, wife of Eli Dawson. Virgil M. Hines remained on his father's farm until twenty-one years of age, when he began farming for himself. In 1871 he attended school at Springfield, and afterward at Central College, Fayette, Mo., in the fall of 1872. He studied law under N. Blackstock, at Knobnoster, and entered the law department of the State University of Missouri in the fall of 1874, and graduated in the spring of 1876. In 1877 he came to Houston, Mo., where he has since practiced very successfully. In 1884 he was elected prosecuting attorney of Texas County, Mo., and re-elected in 1886. On September 13, 1879, he was married to Miss Florence Owsley, a native of Johnson County, Mo., born in 1855, and the daughter of John N. Owsley. One child has been the result of this union, Leslie. Mr. Hines is a member of the Methodist Episcopal Church, South, and is a Democrat in politics.

Robert F. Hoeck, blacksmith at Sargent, was born in Leavenworth, Kas., September 15, 1862, and is the son of Gustav Hoeck, a native of Germany, from Bealefelt, who came to America when a young man. He worked at the carpenter's and builder's trade at Fort Leavenworth, Kas., and while at that place chose for his companion in life Miss Arnestine Heymann, also a native of Bealefelt, Germany. Mr. G. Hoeck, in December, 1888, celebrated his thirty-third year in the Government's service, quartermaster's employ, as a carpenter and builder. To his marriage were born two sons and a daughter, Robert F. being the second child. He learned the trade of blacksmith at Leavenworth, Kas., and followed it there for five years. After this he spent two years in traveling all over the Union, and finally, January 4, 1886, he moved to Texas County, where he has since made his home. He was married at Sargent to Miss Mary Sieg, who was born in Germany. One daughter, Bertha, was born to this union. Mr. Hoeck is a member of the A. O. U. W. society, and he and wife are both members of the Presbyterian Church. Mr. Hoeck is the owner of considerable property in Cabool and vicinity, and is one of the county's best citizens.

Spencer M. Hubbard, clerk of Texas County Court, was born in Texas County, Mo., February 5, 1857, and is the son of John H. and Louisa C. (Mitchell) Hubbard, natives of Randolph County, Mo., and White County, Tenn., respectively. The father was born April 8, 1821. He attended medical college at St. Louis, but graduated at New York City. He then practiced medicine in Pocahontas, Ark., for some time, and then came to Texas County, Mo., in about 1848, where he resided until his death, with the exception of the last two years of the war, when he resided in Gasconade County, Mo. He was one of the first physicians in Texas County, and, it may truthfully be said, one of the best. He was a member of the Masonic fraternity, and a Democrat in politics. He died March 6, 1867. The mother was born September 22, 1834, and is the daughter of Spencer and Susan Mitchell, now of Salem, and two of the oldest people in Southern Missouri. They were among the first settlers of that State. Mrs. Hubbard is still a resident of Texas County. In 1872 she married John C. Lea, who died in 1884. She is a member of the Christian Church. By her marriage to Dr. Hubbard, which occurred in 1852, were born six sons and one daughter, viz.: James M., a physician in Wright County, Mo.; John H., Martha Ann, wife of R. B. Lynch, of Plato, Mo.; S. M., Charles B., a farmer of Texas County, Mo.; Frank P., also a farmer in Texas County, but who has also studied medicine, and Robert P., who is now attending the School of Physicians and Surgeons at St. Louis, Mo. Spencer M. Hubbard, subject of this sketch, received his education at Salem, Mo., under Prof. Lynch. After this he farmed, taught school, and studied medicine under his brother, James M. In 1880–81 he attended medical lectures at St. Louis, and in the latter year he located at Elk Creek, Texas County, where he engaged in the practice of his profession. Soon after he went to Mountain Grove and formed a partnership with his brother. In 1884 he came to Cabool, where he again began the practice of medicine, which he continued until elected county clerk, in 1886. June 7, 1877, he married the daughter of Robert W. and Clara (Bundy) Hardin, who were also among the earliest settlers of Texas County, Mo. Mrs. Hubbard was born in Wright County, Mo., February 5, 1859, and by her marriage became the mother of four children: Eunice, James H. and Tom. Minnie died when one year, one month and fifteen days of age. Mrs. Hubbard is a member of the Methodist Episcopal Church, South, and is an excellent lady. Dr. Hubbard is a member of the Masonic fraternity, I. O. O. F., and is a decided Democrat in politics.

Alexander Jadwin, one of the old and prominent citizens of Texas County, Mo., was born in De Kalb County, Tenn., November 30, 1815, and is a son of Joseph and Mary (Van Hooser) Jadwin, natives of Virginia, who died in Texas County, Mo., in 1858, at the age of eighty-three, and in 1854, aged sixty-six years, respectively. Both became residents of Tennessee when quite young, and married in Warren County, and resided there and in De Kalb County until 1843, when they came to Missouri and located in Texas County, where they spent the remainder of their days. The father was a farmer, and a son of Joseph Jadwin, who was born in Scotland, and served seven years in the Revolutionary War under Gen. Morgan, participating in many battles, and was wounded in the thigh at the battle of Cowpens. Seven children were born to the marriage of Joseph and Mary (Van Hooser) Jadwin, only two of whom are now living: Martin C., a farmer residing in Dent County, Mo., and Alexander, whose name heads this sketch. The latter, having learned the blacksmith's trade, began doing for himself at the age of seventeen years, and worked at his trade in Smithville, Tenn., until 1851, when he came to Missouri, locating at Houston, where he was engaged in blacksmithing three years, and then entered the land on which he is now living, and has since been engaged in farming and stock raising. In 1856–57–58–59 he was sheriff and collector of Texas County, and afterward served two years as county judge and four years as probate judge. January 5, 1843, he wedded Elizabeth North, a native of Bradley County, Tenn., born March 23, 1817. She was a consistent member of the United Baptist Church for many years, and died November 18, 1873, having borne the following children; Manson M., who served in Company B, Col. Burbridge's regiment, Confederate States Army, and was killed at

Saline; Mary Angeline (deceased); William C., who is now collector of Texas County; Nannie (deceased), was the wife of S. G. Cannady; Mattie A., Laura E., Sarah E., Joseph E. and Matilda P. Mr. Jadwin is a Mason and a Democrat, and is one of the enterprising and successful farmers of the county.

William C. Jadwin, collector of Texas County, Mo., was born in De Kalb County, Tenn., April 2, 1848, and is the son of Alexander and Elizabeth (North) Jadwin, both of whom are natives of Tennessee. The father is now living in Texas County, Mo., whither he moved in 1851, and where he has resided ever since. He was born in 1818; has followed farming all his life, and has made a success of the same. He learned the blacksmith trade when a young man, which he followed in connection with farming until recent years. He is a Democrat in politics. In 1857 he was elected sheriff and collector of Texas County, and served four years. In 1878 he was elected probate judge of Texas County, and served four years. His wife was a member of the Missionary Baptist Church, and died in Texas County, Mo., in 1872. They were the parents of eight children, six now living: W. C., Martha, Laura, wife of L. A. Fourt; Sarah, wife of J. M. Brown; Joseph E. and Matilda. Those deceased were named Manson M., who was killed at Jenkins' Ferry during the war, and Nancy, who was the wife of S. G. Cannady. William C. Jadwin was educated in Texas County; was reared on a farm, and followed this occupation until elected to his present position. In 1877 he was elected school commissioner, and held the office six years. February 20, 1876, he married Miss Nancy Hardin, daughter of R. W. Hardin, of Texas County. By this union was born one child, Walter E. Mr. Jadwin is a member of the Masonic fraternity, the I. O. O. F., and is a Democrat in his political views.

Frank L. Johnson is one of the leading citizens of Texas County, Mo., but his birth occurred in Blount County, Tenn., July 22, 1821. His parents, William and Sarah (Johnson) Johnson, were distant relatives, and both are now dead. The father's death occurred when Frank L. was a young lad, and after his death his widow married Amaziah Ballinger, and moved to Texas County, Mo. Frank L. Johnson, early left an orphan, was taken to be reared by his grandfather. He was educated in Tennessee, but when a boy of thirteen years his grandfather died, and he had to begin the battle of life for himself, working as a farm hand until coming to Missouri, in 1849, and is now the owner of 520 acres of land, the result of a life-time of hard labor. He also gives considerable attention to raising stock, which he ships to Arkansas, and all his business ventures have been attended with good results. In 1841 he was married to Margaret Johnson, a daughter of William Johnson, who, like himself, was born in Blount County, Tenn., but her death occurred in Texas County, Mo., previous to the war. The following are their children who are now living: Decatur, Columbus F., Sarah E., Mary, Paulina J. and Hettie A. Those deceased are Julia, Nancy, Elvira E. and William T. In 1860 Mr. Johnson wedded Mary Roberts, who was born in North Carolina March 10, 1839, and is a daughter of James Roberts. Eight children have blessed this union: Lewis L., Charles M., Clinton A., Jeremiah, Foster L. and Amanda. Malinda and Margaret are dead. In connection with farming and stock raising Mr. Johnson has been engaged in blacksmithing, and at one time served as blacksmith of a company in the Missouri State Militia. He is a Mason, a member of the G. A. R., and a Democrat in politics, but is not a strict party man.

Hon. James W. Jones. Among the prominent citizens and prosperous farmers of Texas County, Mo., who started in life for themselves with a very small portion of this world's goods, but who have attained a secure and high position on the ladder of success, may be mentioned Mr. Jones, who is the youngest of ten children, and was born in Clinton County, Ky., April 20, 1823. He acquired a good education in his youthful days, and at the age of twenty years left home, and came to Chariton County, Mo., where he was first engaged in breaking hemp at $12 per month, and at the breaking out of the Mexican War enlisted in Company K, Second Missouri Cavalry, under Col. Sterling Price, and was out twelve months, participating in the battles of Cannatta, Lamputher and Toas. At the last named battle he received a wound in the left thigh that came very near being fatal. In 1850 he went to California, driving an ox team as far as Salt Lake, and made the rest of the way on horseback. He was engaged in mining in that State until 1853, then went to Australia, where he mined for about a year, then returned to his home, and engaged in farming in Chariton County. During the late war he served for a short time in the Missouri State Guard, and April 3, 1855, was married to Mary Porch, a native of Tennessee, born May 28, 1821, her father being Israel, the first settler of Porch's Prairie, in Chariton County. To Mr. and Mrs. Jones a family of three children were born: Jonathan, John and an infant (deceased). Both sons are married, and residing near their parents. Mr. Jones is the owner of 1,000 acres of land, with about 300 acres under cultivation, and owing to his many sterling business qualities his labors have been attended with good success. While in Chariton County he held the office of justice of the peace, and in 1877-78 he represented Texas County in the State Legislature. He is a Democrat and Mason, and a son of Jonathan and Mary (Humphries) Jones, who were born, respectively, in North Carolina and Georgia. At at early day the father moved with his brother, on pack-horses, from North Carolina to Kentucky, and settled in Clinton County, whither the mother came when a young woman. They were married and spent their lives in that county, and were engaged in agricultural pursuits, and in his political views the father was a Democrat. They were members of the Presbyterian and Baptist Churches, and died at the ages of sixty-five and seventy-three, respectively.

Michael C. Jones. Prominent among the successful and enterprising citizens of Texas County, and among those deserving special recognition for their long residence in the county, stands the name of Mr. Jones, who was born in Edmondson County, Ky., June 17, 1827, being the son of Felix W. and Onor (Jones) Jones, natives of Edmondson County, Ky. Felix W. Jones died in Illinois in 1875, when about seventy years of age. His wife died in Kentucky when the subject of this sketch was a small child. She was a distant relative of her husband, and was a member of the Baptist Church. After her death

Felix W. Jones married Miss Catherine Cockerill, who is still living, and is a resident of Bates County, Mo. She was born in Barren County, Ky. Mr. Jones followed farming all his life, and lived in Edmondson County, Ky., until 1848, when he moved to Franklin County, Ill. He afterward moved to Marion County, Ark., where he resided a few years, and then moved back to Franklin County, Ill. He was a Whig in politics, and afterward a Republican. He was a member of the Baptist Church. Michael C. Jones was the eldest of five children born to his parents, all now living: Michael C., Olive, wife of Benjamin Anthony (deceased); Chylon, Iradel, and Marcellus, who is now a resident of Choctaw Nation, Indian Territory. Michael C. Jones was quite young when he left his home and went to Hardin County, Ky. He followed farming in that county for two years, and then lived in Edmondson County, Ky. In 1849 he went to Franklin County, Ill., where he resided until the spring of 1852, and then went to Texas, remaining there a short time, and then went to Arkansas. Here he found a company going to California, and went with them across the plains, and assisted in driving 800 head of cattle. After reaching that State he followed mining for three years, and then returned by way of Nicaraugua and New Orleans. He remained in Franklin County, Ill., a short time, and then made another trip to Texas, but soon moved to Williamson County, Ill., where he lived until in 1871, and then moved to where he now resides. He is the owner of 160 acres of as good land as is to be found in the county. December 29, 1856, he married Miss Nancy Henry Clayton, a native of Warren County, Ky., born in 1835, and the daughter of Foster Clayton. To Mr. and Mrs. Jones have been born one daughter, Eliza Hubbard, wife of Frank Payne Hubbard. Mr. Jones is a Democrat in politics, and is a member of the Masonic fraternity. To Mr. Hubbard and wife have been born two children: Grace May and Henry H.

Enoch Keen, farmer and stock raiser, one mile east of Sargent, in Burdine Township, was born in Bedford County, Tenn., October 27, 1825, and is the son of Matthias and Rachel (Brown) Keen, natives of Tennessee. Matthias Keen served as a soldier in the Creek Indian War. The Keens were of English descent, and the Browns of Scotch extraction. Enoch Keen was one of six sons and four daughters born to his parents. He was reared on a farm in Bedford County, Tenn., and while yet a young man his parents moved to Missouri, and settled in Franklin County, where Enoch married Miss Nancy Napier, a native of Illinois, and the daughter of Patrick and Allie (White) Napier, both natives of Kentucky. In 1870 Mr. Keen and family came to Texas County, settling on their present farm, and here they have since remained. To their union were born nine children, six sons and three daughters: Allie Jane, wife of J. R. Stogdill, of Texas County; Mary, wife of J. J. Mitchell [see sketch]; Sarah, wife of W. I. Brown, now residing near Sargent; Lewis Wesley, John P., William M., James E., Thomas P. and George W. Of these children Mrs. Allie Jane Stogdill has two sons and two daughters; Mrs. Mary Mitchell has one son; Mrs. Sarah Brown has four sons and one daughter; Lewis Wesley resides in Shannon County, Mo., and has three sons and one daughter; John P. is at home, unmarried; William M. is unmarried; James E. is married, and has a son and daughter; Thomas P. resides in Carter County, Mo., is unmarried, and George W. is unmarried. Mr. Keen owns a large farm, of 700 acres altogether, in Texas County. He devotes considerable attention to the breeding of a good grade of cattle. He is a Democrat in politics, and has served on the school board of his district.

Col. John S. Kirwan was born in Lempster, Sullivan Co., N. H., June 22, 1840. His parents, Hugh and Bridget (Hanigan) Kirwan, were born in the counties of Galway and Rosscomon, Ireland, respectively, and were the parents of ten children, five boys and five girls. John, the youngest of the family, is the subject of this sketch. In May, 1840, Mr. Hugh Kirwan and his family immigrated to America, locating in Sullivan County, N. H., and engaged in farming. In 1851 he died, at the age of sixty-five years, and his widow and the remainder of his children at home, Timothy, Ann, Cecelia, Delia and John, moved to the city of Manchester, N. H., where John attended school, and at times worked in the factories. In 1855 he entered the dry goods house of H. Doherty & Co., 339 and 341 Washington Street, Boston, Mass., as salesman, and remained there until 1856, when he returned to Manchester, N. H., and acted as salesman for Wright & Gill and W. A. Putney & Co. In 1858, at the age of eighteen years, he ran away from home, and enlisted in the Regular Army (First, now the Fourth, Cavalry), at Boston, Mass. He was sent from Boston to the school of instruction for cavalry at Carlisle Barracks, Penn., and later joined his regiment at Fort Riley, Kas., on the last day of May, and on the following day, June 1, 1859, the command started for the Upper Arkansas River, for the purpose of observing the movements of the Indians, and to protect the mail and Pike's Peakers (it being the time of the Pike's Peak craze). In September, 1859, the Comanche and Kiowa Indians declared war, killing Mr. Peacock, who was keeping a ranch on Walnut Creek. Kirwan's company, "K," was kept pretty busy the fall and winter of 1859-60, fighting Indians and building Fort Learned, on Pawnee Fork, Kas. The spring and summer of 1860 found him with Maj. Segwick (afterward Maj.-Gen. Segwick, commanding the Sixth Army Corps, who was killed at the battle of Spottsylvania, Va.). In August, 1860, he was engaged with Indians at Blackwater, about forty miles north of the Arkansas River, where the Indians were defeated. First Lieut. J. E. B. Steward (afterward the famous rebel general) was in command. Immediately after this battle the Indians sued for peace. Maj. Segwick was ordered to build a fort, then called Fort Wise (now Lyons), at a place called Bent's Fort, on the Upper Arkansas River. The company of which he was a member remained at Fort Wise until the fall of 1861, when it was ordered to Fort Leavenworth, Kas., and from there to West Point, Ky., being assigned to the command of Maj.-Gen. Buell, by whom it was ordered to reinforce Gen. Grant in front of Fort Donelson. It arrived there just after the surrender, and was ordered to Nashville, Tenn. On arriving, Companies G and K were assigned as escort to Gen. Buell, and participated in the battles of Shiloh, Miss., and in front of Corinth, and from there to Huntsville, Ala., and Bridgeport, Tenn., and in the great duel race between Gens. Buell and Bragg to the Ohio River, participating in the battles of Perryville, or Chaplin Hill, and Crab Orchard, Ky. Immediately after Crab Orchard, Gen. Buell was relieved by Rosecrans, and the name of the army changed from the Army of the Ohio to the Army of the Cumberland, and the Fourth Regular Cavalry was assigned as escort to Gen. Rosecrans, and was recruited up to its maximum strength. On the 1st of December, 1862, young Kirwan was made a corporal in his company, and on the day after the battle of Stone River he was promoted to the rank of sergeant. On the 10th day of April, 1863, he was captured by the enemy, while leading a charge of eighteen men on the Louisburg Pike, about five miles south of Franklin, Tenn. Six of his men were killed, and he and the remainer of the squad were captured and sent to Libby Prison, Richmond, Va., where he remained two months, and being exchanged, again joined his company on the 19th day of June, just in time to participate in the advance on Shelbyville, Tullahoma and Decherd, Tenn. At Decherd he was detailed by the War Department to report to Andrew Johnson, military governor of Tennessee, for the purpose of drilling and organizing the different regiments of Tennessee cavalry then being organized for the Union. On the 1st of October, 1863, Mr. Kirwan was commissioned lieutenant of Company C, Twelfth Tennessee Cavalry, and on the 20th of the same month promoted to captain of the same company, and at short intervals promoted to the rank of major, lieutenant-colonel and colonel of his regiment. In December, 1863, he was ordered to take command of the post at Charlotte, Dickson County, Tenn., and to clean out the bushwhackers in that vicinity, which he did, killing and wounding quite a number, and capturing 157, which he sent to Nashville to be tried by military commission. In 1864 he was busily engaged against the rebel generals, Forrest, Wheeler and Williams, and fought them at Elk Creek, Florence, Triune and Pulaski, in Alabama and Tennessee. In the fall of 1864 Col. Kirwan was ordered to relieve Col. Clift of the command of the brigade composed of the Fifth, Tenth and Twelfth Tennessee Cavalry, United States Volunteers, then stationed in front of Gen. Hood at Florence, Ala., and was placed as Third Brigade of Gen. Ed. Hatch's Division. Col. Kirwan fought Hood's army on its march on Nashville, at Campbellsville, Spring Hill and at Franklin, Tenn., where he lost many officers and men, among whom was Maj. Morgan Boland, a brave officer, who was mortally wounded while leading his regiment in a charge. Col. Kirwan was with the cavalry corps on Gen. Thomas' right wing at the battle of Nashville, December 15 and 16, and assisted in breaking the enemy's left wing and capturing eighteen pieces of artillery and 3,000 prisoners. He was also engaged in the pursuit of Gen. Hood to the Tennessee River, and fought his last battle on Christmas Day, 1864, at Robinson's Hill, Tenn. At Sugar River, Ala., Col. Kirwan was placed in command of 500 picked men to cut off Hood's rear guard and wagon train before it crossed the Tennessee River, which he did (or what was left of it). He was then ordered, with the rest of the cavalry, to Gravelly Springs, Ala., and from there to Eastport, Miss., where he remained until the 1st of May, 1865, when he was ordered with his regiment to St. Louis, Mo. He received a new outfit of horses and equipments, and was ordered to report to Gen. Dodge at Leavenworth, Kas., and then ordered by Gen. Dodge to establish a temporary military post at the 100th meridian, on the north fork of the Solomon River, Kas., where the city of Kirwin, Kas., now stands. Col. Kirwan remained there with his regiment, fighting the Indians and furnishing a guard for the corps of engineers that were surveying the land for the Government, until November, 1865, when the regiment was ordered to Leavenworth to be mustered out of service. Immediately after being mustered out of the service, Col. Kirwan located in the Solomon Valley, in Ottawa County, Kas., and opened the first store in the now city of Minneapolis. In 1866 Col. Kirwan was elected a delegate from Ottawa County to the State Republican Convention at Topeka, Kas., and was there elected one of the vice-presidents of that convention. In 1867 he moved to St. Louis, Mo., and became a member of the Metropolitan police force of that city, first as sergeant and then as captain of police. In 1870 he resigned from the police, and took the stump, with the rest of the liberal Republicans, in favor of the enfranchisement of those whom he lately fought. In 1871 (October 1) Col. Kirwan entered the St. Louis post-office, and worked there for sixteen years and two months, resigning from there on December 1, 1887. On January 1, 1880, he bought part of the farm he now owns (five miles east of Houston, on the Salem road, and one and one-half miles west of Raymondville), and has since been adding to it. He is now the owner of 330 acres, which are well stocked. Col. Kirwan is, and always has been, a Republican in politics. He cast his first vote for Abraham Lincoln in 1864. Col. Kirwan's discharge and papers from the army show that he was in twenty-five battles during the war and with Indians, and had some narrow escapes and thrilling adventures during seven years' service. His mother and two sisters, Ann and Cecelia, moved to Missouri in 1859, and settled in Osage County, where his mother died in 1860, aged sixty years. The elder sister, Ann, married a Mr. King there, and in 1861 moved to Texas County, near Raymondville, where her husband died, and she again married, in 1870, Mr. William H. Wilson. The second sister, Cecelia, married Mr. John McKenna, in St. Louis, Mo., in 1866. She is also a resident of Texas County, near Raymondville. His sister Delia married Mr. George MacKenzie, and lives in Minneapolis, Kas. Col. Kirwan has been married twice; to his first wife, Jennie Greener, daughter of Nicholas and Ellen Greener, at Nashville, Tenn., in November, 1863. She died of cholera in St. Louis, October 20, 1867. He married again, Jennie Bierman, daughter of John M. and Rosenna Bierman, at St. Louis, Mo., February 7, 1869. He has one child living by his first wife, Ellen Cecelia Kirwan, now the wife of Mr. Benjamin Osborn Holt, and is also a resident of Texas County. Col. Kirwan and his near relatives are all members of the Catholic Church. Both his wives were converts to that religion.

 Christopher Kofahl, a successful tiller of the soil of Sherrill Township, Texas Co., Mo., was born in Hanover, Germany, August 2, 1825, and is the son of Hans Christopher and Magdalene (Richs)

Kofahl, both of whom were born, reared, married and died in Hanover, Germany. The father was a well-to-do farmer. In their family were nine children, five sons and four daughters, only two of whom came to America, our subject and sister. His early life was spent on his father's farm and in school, where he received a limited education. At the age of fifteen he commenced learning the carpenter's trade, and worked four years as an apprentice. In 1847 he left home for America, and landed at New Orleans. He worked at Vicksburg, Miss., for a time, and then went to Greenburg, where he spent the summer of 1848. That winter he returned to Vicksburg, and in 1849 removed to St. Louis, but later removed to Cincinnati, where he worked in a factory for some time, and then returned to Vicksburg. Some months were spent at Yazoo City, Miss., then back to Cincinnati, and then again returned to Yazoo, where, May 13, 1852, he married Miss Mary E. Housman, a native of Hanover, Germany. She came to this country in 1851, and in 1858 they came to Texas County, and settled on the farm where they now live. There were only eighteen acres cleared at that time, but since then he has increased it to about 140 acres. He knew nothing about farming except what little he had learned in childhood, and had to start almost from the beginning. He, however, has made a complete success of it, and now owns 500 acres. During the war he served about eight months in the Confederate army, being sergeant. He is a Democrat in politics, and a member of the Methodist Episcopal Church, South, as was also his wife, who died December 30, 1888. They were the parents of eleven children, nine now living: John C., Henry, William, Magdalene C., Ellen, Louis C., Robert E. L., James C. and Benjamin F. In connection with his farming interest Mr. Kofahl has also handled machinery for the McCormick Harvesting Machine Co. for about ten years. He has been a resident of Texas County, Mo., for the past thirty years, and is a much respected citizen.

John W. Kyle. Among the prominent men of Texas County, Mo., who embarked on the sea of life with little or no capital, but who are now considered among the wealthy citizens of the county, may be mentioned Mr. Kyle, who was born in Westmoreland County, Penn., July 24, 1837, his parents being Samuel and Diana (Kelley) Kyle, who were natives of Pennsylvania, and there lived and died, the father's death occurring at the age of fifty-two years, during the cholera epidemic, and the mother's in 1872, when seventy-three years of age. They were members of the Missionary Baptist Church, and the father was a Whig in politics, and a shoemaker by trade, and followed this occupation until a few years before his death, when he turned his attention to farming. John W. Kyle is the third of their six children, and after his father's death made his home with his mother until nearly eighteen years of age, when he was apprenticed to a blacksmith, and served three years for $100. At the end of this time he entered the employ of the man for whom he had been working, receiving for his services $3 per day. He then worked for some time in Pittsburg, Penn., but in July, 1861, he enlisted in Company F, of the Twelfth Pennsylvania Reserve Corps, serving with credit nineteen months, participating in all the battles in which the Army of the Potomac took part. At the second battle of Bull Run he received a very severe wound in the head from a bursting shell, which confined him to the hospital for over two months, after which he was honorably discharged. Shortly after he went to Rockford, Ill., and then came to Rolla, Mo., and worked in the Government shops for nearly three years. In 1866 he came to Texas County, Mo., and in 1877 put up a shop in Houston, where he worked at his trade for fourteen years, since which time he has been engaged in farming and stock trading, his efforts in this line meeting with good success. July 3, 1864, his union with Miss D. L. Barber was consummated. She was born in North Carolina, a daughter of T. Y. Barber, and she and Mr. Kyle became the parents of ten children: Lilie May, Mary J., James W., Charles A., John H., Elizabeth M., Caroline L., Ethel C., Cecily and Florence K. Mrs. Kyle is a member of the Christian Church, and Mr. Kyle is a Mason, and a Republican in politics.

[Since the above was written Mr. Kyle has been the victim of a sad and fatal accident, one which has thrown gloom upon the community, and occasioned a loss sincerely felt. On February 14 Mr. Kyle left his home, some two miles south of Houston, to attend to some business in town. While returning he fell from his horse, striking upon his head, and causing almost instant death. The wound which he received during the war had caused at times dizziness or unconsciousness, and it is supposed the fall occurred during one of these spells. He was buried by the Houston Masonic Lodge, of which he had been an honored member.]

Hon. Charles Harvey Latimer (deceased) was born in Cape Girardeau, Missouri Territory, February 29, 1820, his parents being natives of Kentucky. They made a settlement in Washington County, Mo., a short time before it was admitted as a State, and here Charles H. Latimer grew to manhood. He adopted agricultural pursuits as an occupation, and in 1840 came to Texas County, where he was for many years extensively engaged in the lumber interests of that State. He then abandoned this business and returned to tilling the soil, which he continued for some time. The latter part of his life was spent as a minister in the Methodist Church, South. He died in 1875, at Jefferson City, Mo., while serving as a member of the General Assembly of the State. He had joined many of the good citizens of Jefferson City in their efforts to quell the mutiny of convicts of the State Penitentiary, and while individually engaged in this constabulary work he contracted pneumonia, which carried him off to join the silent majority inside of two days. He was a man of strong force of character, magnetic in attractions as a public speaker, and esteemed by all for his sterling worth and honesty of character. He left a family of two children: Mrs. Mires, wife of Hon. J. W. Mires [see sketch], and Joseph W., a merchant of Cabool, children of his marriage to Miss Sarah Black, a native of Washington County, Mo. Her parents were natives of Tennessee, and pioneers of Washington County, Mo. Mr. Latimer was a genial gentleman, affable to all, and stood high in the esteem of all who knew him. He was a prominent member of the Masonic fraternity, and was the founder of Texas Lodge, No. 177, at Houston. His remains were brought home by his son-in-law, and buried with full Masonic honors at Elk Creek, and in full connection with the faith of the Methodist Church, South.

Guilford A. Leavitt. In every community and among all classes there are always some men who become leaders in whatever they do, whether of a professional, agricultural or commercial nature; and these same men are the ones who, perhaps unconsciously, take an active and prominent interest in promoting any movements which may be thought capable of tending to the welfare of the city or vicinity where they reside. Such a man is Mr. Leavitt, who was born in Conneaut, Ashtabula Co., Ohio, June 8, 1844, the son of James and Jerusha (Bliss) Leavitt, natives of Ashtabula County, Ohio, and Massachusetts, respectively. The father is now a resident of Houston, Mo., and is engaged in merchandising. In his younger days he followed farming, which he continued until about 1876, when he came to Missouri and located at Houston. He served in the Seventh Michigan Infantry one year, was lieutenant, and was in the battles of Balls Bluff and Winchester. He is a member of the I. O. O. F. and the G. A. R. lodges. He has been a Republican since the Whig party became defunct. His son, Guilford A. Leavitt, received his education in the common schools of Michigan, and in 1867 he graduated from the Law School at Ann Arbor. In 1868 he came to Houston, Mo., where he has since been engaged in the practice of his profession—general country practice. In the fall of 1864 he enlisted in Company C, Twenty-ninth Michigan Infantry, and served until the fall of 1865. He was with the Army of the Cumberland, was in the battles of Decatur and Murfreesboro and many skirmishes. He was promoted to the rank of lieutenant. Before the time he began the study of law he followed farming, but since then he has practiced his profession with very satisfactory results. He at one time had an extensive criminal practice, but of late years has confined himself to office practice. In March, 1871, he married Miss Julia W. White, daughter of Dr. Thomas G. White. To this marriage were born these children: Albert W., Serene F., Amelia and James B. Mr. Leavitt is a member of the Masonic fraternity, and has represented Houston Lodge in the Grand Lodge. He is also a member of the G. A. R., and is a decided Republican in his political principles. In 1888 he attended the State convention that nominated Kimball. Mr. Leavitt is the owner of the noted Glenwood Stock Ranch, consisting of 280 acres of land, adjoining the comparative lines of Houston. He purchased this place of Dr. White in 1884, with the intention of making stock farming his chief occupation. Since then he has built one of the finest barns in the State of Missouri. This is fitted up with all the latest improvements, with machinery for cutting and grinding feed, and he expects soon to add a system for preserving his feed in a green state. He also expects to make other additions, fish ponds, etc. Mr. Leavitt deserves great credit for being the first and only man to bring good stock to Texas County, and is now the only man in the county extensively engaged in this enterprise. He has a herd of Short-horn cattle; also some very fine horses, which are of the same stock as "Jay Eye See" and "Maud S."

Tyre M. Lingo. Among the men of Texas County, Mo., who

have attained the highest round in the ladder of success, owing to his earnest endeavor and persistent effort, may be mentioned Mr. Lingo, who is a successful attorney at law, farmer and stock man, and a son of James and Jane (Thompson) Lingo, who were born in Virginia in 1777, and Campbell County, Ky., in 1787, respectively. James Lingo was reared chiefly in his native State, but after attaining manhood went to Kentucky, where he met and married Miss Thompson, and when Daniel Boone moved from that State westward, they came in the same company, and located in St. Louis County, Mo., and in 1824 took up their abode in Madison County, Ill., where the father died in 1834, his wife dying in Jefferson County of that State in 1844. He was a Whig in politics, and the only official position he ever held was that of magistrate. He and wife were members of the Presbyterian Church, and became the parents of nine children. The paternal grandfather was an Englishman by birth, and on coming to America espoused the cause of the colonists in the Revolutionary War, being killed in battle. Tyre M. Lingo, whose name heads this sketch, is the fourth child born to his parents, his birth occurring in St. Louis County, Mo., August 20, 1821. Owing to the primitive condition of the schools in his boyhood days, his early educational advantages were limited, but by devoted application to his books, and without the aid of any one, he has become one of the best informed men of the county. At the age of seventeen he began hiring out by the month, driving an ox team to Missouri, but was married in Illinois, September 12, 1847, to Miss Martha C. Anderson, who was born in Illinois February 24, 1832, and by her became the father of twelve children: Liza J., Miram, Mary E., Laura, Benajah A., William E., George M., Alice, Berry A., Lewis E., James R. and Charles F. In 1852 he took up his abode in Osage County, Mo., where he fed cattle for Silas Brickey, and during this time trouble arose between Brickey and one of his renters, and as there was only one lawyer in reach, Mr. Lingo was called upon to defend his employer. Although he had never looked into a law book he gained the case, which success secured for him some notoriety, as his opponent was an able lawyer, and on his second case he was pitted against two lawyers, and also came off victorious. From that time on his services were often required in legal difficulties, and when the Missouri Pacific Railroad was being built he was employed as attorney for the road, being also appointed overseer of the same. He then ran a wagon-shop for six months, and practiced law for about one and a half years in Osage County, and in 1857 moved to Texas County, where he has since made his home, and where he was admitted to the bar in 1859, by P. H. Edwards. He served for a short time in the United States army during the late war, and then returned home and re-engaged in farming, and has also been occupied in practicing his profession. He at one time owned 1,800 acres of land, but has given to his children until he now only owns 400 acres, with about 160 acres under cultivation. He is a man of fine constitution, and gives promise of spending many more years of usefulness in Texas County.

Col. William Lavender Lyles, late editor and proprietor of the *Mountain Howitzer*, of Salem, and now of the Houston *Herald*, was born in Newberry District, S. C., in 1829, being the son of Robert and Jane (Lavender) Lyles, both natives of Newberry District, S. C., born in 1776 and 1786, and died in 1847 and 1857, respectively. Robert Lyles was the son of Ephraim Lyles, who was a Revolutionary soldier. Robert Lyles was twice married, and Col. William L. Lyles was the eldest child by the second marriage. He remained at home as long as his father lived, and in 1849 he and his mother and sister moved to Pickens County, Ala., and the following year to Chickasaw County, Miss. Here he purchased land, and followed farming until the breaking out of the late war. In the fall of 1861 he raised Company B, Twenty-fourth Mississippi Regiment, was elected captain of the same, and served until the close of hostilities. He was at Shiloh, Perryville, Corinth, Resaca, Murfreesboro, Kenesaw Mountain, Atlanta, and at Jonesboro, where he was shot in the neck, which disabled him for years, not being able to eat food for seven days. He was at the hospital at Griffin, Ga., but was not paroled until the surrender. At Dalton, Ga., he was promoted to the rank of lieutenant-colonel. After the war he engaged in merchandising at West Point, and in 1867 he went to Oxford, Miss., where he remained until 1873, and then moved to Salem. He here followed merchandising a short time, and in 1878 was elected to the position of circuit clerk and *ex-officio* recorder of Dent County, serving four years. The subsequent four years he was in the real estate business, and in 1886 he established the *Mountain Howitzer*, editing its columns until recently. On the 24th of January, 1889, Col. Lyles sold this paper to Mr. John C. Pugh, and purchased the Houston *Herald* of Mr. Beauregard Ross, of Houston, Mo., and took charge of the same February 10, 1889. His motto is: "My gun is the Press; my ammunition, Truth, Justice, Morality and Democracy, deliberately aimed." His journal is a newsy, bright sheet, and has a good circulation. Col. Lyles is a true Christian gentleman, and an esteemed citizen. During the years 1870 and 1872 he was a member of the State Legislature in Mississippi. In 1853, previous to the war, he married Miss Elizabeth P. Kilgore, who was born in Greenville District, S. C., in 1834. They have three children: Pleasant L., Edgar K. and Cecil E. Col. Lyles is a member of the Masonic fraternity, is a Democrat in his political views, casting his first presidential vote for Pierce in 1852, and he and wife are members of the Baptist Church, of which he is a deacon.

Stephen D. Lyles, M. D., one of the leading practitioners of Texas County, was born in Monroe County, Ill., October 25, 1858, and is the son of Alfred Newton and Mary (Walker) Lyles, natives of North Carolina. The father died in Illinois in 1863, and the mother in Missouri in 1870. He was a Methodist Episcopal minister, was also engaged in farming, and at one time was a circuit rider. After the death of her husband Mrs. Mary Lyles moved with her family to Greene County, Mo., where she died. After the death of his father Stephen D. Lyles was obliged to make his own living. He came to Licking, lived with Lot Smalley four years and attended school there. He then lived with Dr. George M. Orr and studied medicine under him. In 1880 and 1881 he attended lectures at Keokuk, Iowa, and immediately afterward came to Houston, where he began practicing.

September 10, 1884, he married Miss Frances M. Mitchell, daughter of P. D. Mitchell, of Texas County. This union resulted in the birth of two children, Mary and Josephine. In April, 1887, Dr. Lyles opened a drug store at Houston, and has been quite successful in this business. He is examining surgeon of Texas County and has been connected with the post-office at Licking for several years. He is a member of the Masonic fraternity, and is a Republican in politics.

Rev. Dabney B. Lynch, one of the pioneers of Texas County, and one of that county's most prominent citizens, was born in Madison County, Ky., February 14, 1810, and is the son of David Lynch, a native of Virginia and a Revolutionary soldier, who moved to Kentucky at an early date, and in 1819 came to Missouri, settling in St. Charles County. Rev. Dabney B. Lynch came to Texas County, Mo., in 1826, where he has lived since with the exception of three years, and has probably resided in Texas County longer than any other white man. He has been a farmer all his life and a Missionary Baptist minister since 1856. September 23, 1847, he married Miss Serena McKinney, who died June 16, 1883. There was born to this union a large family of children, five of whom are now living, viz.: John H., Susan C., James S., Ervin T. and Martin W. The Lynch family are of German descent and first located in Virginia, the city of Lynchburg taking its name from this family.

John T. Lynch, one of the leading citizens of Houston, Texas County, Mo., was born in that county May 10, 1841, and is the son of David and Polly Ann Margaret (Fourt) Lynch. The father was born in Virginia, March 15, 1803, and died in Texas County, Mo., May 15, 1865. The mother was born December 13, 1813, and died in Texas County, Mo., February 24, 1852. They were married in Warren County, Mo., November 19, 1837. The Lynches were of Irish descent, and settled in what is now Lynchburg, Va., which was named from the family, previous to the Revolutionary War. David Lynch was a son of Henry Lynch, of Virginia, whose father was an old Revolutionary soldier. David Lynch's grandfather was also Henry Lynch. David Lynch came to Texas County, Mo., in 1823; operated mills on Piney River and engaged in the lumber and timber business, rafting the timber and lumber to St. Louis. He afterward turned his attention to farming, which he continued many years. He was a successful business man and was one of the county's best citizens. At the organization of Texas County he was appointed one of the judges of the county court; and the court met at his residence for a number of years afterward. At one time he was in the State Legislature from Texas County. He was a Whig in politics, and both he and wife were members of the Methodist Church. To their marriage were born seven children, five now living: Prof. William H., a noted educator of Southern Missouri, now at Mountain Grove Academy; John T., Ransom B., a physician; David A., also a physician, and Hayden W., a farmer. John T. Lynch received his education at Lathrop Academy, in Boone County, Mo., in 1857, 1858 and 1859, and from that time until the breaking out of the war, he was with his parents. In 1863 he enlisted in Company K, Sixth Provisional Enrolled Missouri Militia, and soon after was in Company K, Sixteenth Cavalry, Missouri Volunteers, where he served as regimental commissary-sergeant until June 30, 1865. After the war he located in Houston and for the next five years was in the sheriff and collector's office as deputy. For a number of years after that he followed milling and farming, but of late years has been in the abstract and real estate business. January 16, 1866, he was married to Miss Cordelia Ann Mires, a native of Bedford County, Tenn., born October 30, 1846, and the daughter of George W. and Elizabeth Ann Mires. She died in Texas County, Mo., November 3, 1866. To this union was born one daughter, Cordelia Ann Lynch, now the wife of Hon. John D. Young, of Houston [see sketch]. April 22, 1871, Mr. Lynch married Miss Sarah H. Rodgers, a native of Cooper County, Mo., born December 25, 1839, and daughter of Nathaniel K. and Elizabeth Rodgers, now both dead. Mr. Rodgers was a carpenter and moved to Texas County in 1853. He died there in January, 1862, when sixty-five years of age. Mrs. Rodgers died in August, 1888, when eighty-five years of age. By the last marriage Mr. Lynch became the father of three children: Minnie E., Thomas H. and Mary F. Mr. Lynch is a member of the G. A. R., and has been the adjutant of his post since its organization, August 2, 1887. He is a Republican in politics and cast his first vote for Uncle Abe in his second election in November, 1864. Mr. Lynch was one of the two who took the United States census in the year 1870, and one of the five who took the United States census in 1880.

Robert C. McBride, farmer and ex-sheriff, of Texas County, Mo., is a son of James H. and Mildred A. (Barnes) McBride, who were born in Harrodsburg, Ky,, and Cooper County, Mo., in 1814 and 1824, respectively. The father was of Scotch-Irish descent, and when a young man came to Missouri and engaged in merchandising at Paris but soon after began the study of law and was admitted to the bar, establishing himself after his marriage in Springfield, and afterward represented Greene County in the State Legislature. He went to California in 1850 and at the end of three years returned home and resided in Springfield until 1859, when he became a resident of Texas County. The same year he was elected circuit judge, and served until the late war broke out, when he was appointed brigadier-general of the State troops by Gov. Jackson, and commanded a brigade at Wilson's Creek and Lexington, but just before the battle of Pea Ridge he resigned and was commissioned brigadier-general in the Confederate army. After about a year's service he resigned on account of failing health and returned home where he died in March, 1864, of consumption. He was an able lawyer and a judge that stood high in his circuit, a Royal Arch Mason and a Democrat. His wife was a member of the Christian Church, and died in June, 1873, having borne a family of nine children, two sons being in the Confederate army, the elder being killed at Batesville, Ark. Robert G. McBride is the fifth child and was born in Springfield, on the 16th of May, 1849. He received very meager educational advantages, and after the death of his father and his eldest brother, the burden of caring for the family fell mainly on him. He first engaged in hiring out as a farm hand, and as soon as he could engaged in farming for himself, and now owns

200 acres of land with about sixty under cultivation, all of which he has made since his marriage. September 29, 1870, he was married to Mary J. Rider, a native of Tennessee, by whom he has seven children: Edward H., Obal C., Jennie B., Callie L., Ewing E., Florence M. and Robert C. Mrs. McBride is a member of the Christian Church, and Mr. McBride is a Democrat and in 1880 was elected sheriff of Texas County, which office he held six years, with two years intermission. He is a member of the Masonic and I. O. O. F. fraternities.

James McCaskill, merchant of Summerville, Mo., was born in Maury County, Tenn., February 13, 1854, his parents, William and Mary (Blassingame) McCaskill, being born, reared and married in Giles County, Tenn. In 1855 they immigrated to Shannon County, Mo., where they entered land and settled down to farming and stock dealing, which occupations were attended with good results. During the late war he served the entire time, with the exception of six months, under "Old Pap" Price, and was with him on his raid through Arkansas and Missouri. He was captured on Pike Creek, Shannon County, but made his escape and returned to his command. After the war he resided in Shannon County until 1876, when he came to Texas County where he died on the 17th of April, 1881. He and wife were the parents of the following children: Eliza, James, George, John, Elizabeth, William, Zimri, Levi, Alice and Dona. Mrs. McCaskill is now living with a daughter on the old homestead. The paternal grandparents were natives of the "Old North State," and immigrated to Tennessee at an early day, making the journey in wagons. The grandfather served during the War of 1812 under Gen. Jackson, and became one of the prominent residents of Tennessee. James McCaskill was reared principally in Shannon County, Mo., but received very limited early educational advantages, owing to the scarcity of schools in those days. He resided on the home farm until twenty-four years of age, and was then married to Alcy Summer, a daughter of Jesse and Ditha Summer, who were early settlers of the county, the town of Summerville being named in honor of the family. On the 1st of May, 1881, Mrs. McCaskill died, and three years later Mr. McCaskill wedded Miss Orpha, a daughter of William and Eliza Weakley, who were from Bloomington, Ill., and by her is the father of two children: Cecil and Myrtle. Mr. McCaskill has been a merchant of Summerville for a number of years, and in 1886 bought the milling plant of the town, which was conducted on a small scale until 1888, since which time the roller process has been added at a cost of $3,000, and the mill is now doing an extensive and profitable business. He is also engaged largely in farming and stock dealing, and is one of the progressive citizens of the county. He is the postmaster of Summerville, and in his political views is a Democrat.

David McKinney, an old and honored resident of Texas County, Mo., was born in Campbell County, Tenn., August 19, 1814, being a son of James and Sarah (Gouge) McKinney, who were born in Tennessee and died in Missouri in 1872, aged eighty-five years, and 1874 aged eighty years, respectively. They were married in Campbell County, Tenn., and at an early day removed to Cole County, Mo., taking up their residence in Texas County about 1845, where the father was engaged in farming. He was a Democrat and his wife was a member of the Baptist Church. At the age of twenty-two years David McKinney began farming for himself, and resided in Cole County for two years after his parents left, then also came to Texas County where he owns a valuable and productive farm. He was engaged in school teaching while in Cole County, and at one time was elected assessor of the county. Since coming to Texas County he has served three terms as county judge, one of these terms being presiding and probate judge, and has also filled the positions of public administrator and justice of the peace, being elected to these offices on the Democratic ticket, which party he has always supported. In 1836 he married Nancy Wade, who was born in Cole County, Mo., in 1818, and died in Texas County in 1862, being a daughter of William Wade. To them were born the following children: Margaret, Missouri, Monroe, Martha J., James William, Sarah, C. G., Alonzo, Ellen, Mary, Pinkney, and J. D. November 15, 1863, Mr. McKinney married Isabella, a daughter of J. S. Winningham. She was born in Overton County, Tenn., February 24, 1836, and by Mr. McKinney became the mother of the following children: Andrew J., Robert B., Nancy, Chelly, Ida and Jacob L. Mr. McKinney has fifty-eight grandchildren and ten great grandchildren. He and wife are members of the Missionary Baptist Church, and he is a member of the Masonic fraternity.

Peter T. Mason, farmer and county judge-elect, is a son of Dexter and Laura (Parker) Mason, who were born in Vermont and New York, in 1811 and 1810, respectively. When young they both became residents of Massachusetts, where they were united in the bonds of matrimony, and soon after moved to New York, then to Ohio where they spent about four years, and then returned to New York. In 1858 they became residents of Texas County, Mo., and when the Rebellion broke out the father and his three eldest sons enlisted in the Union service, while the mother and younger children returned to New York. The father and two of his sons returned home to New York, but the other son died in the hospital at St. Louis. In 1866 the family again returned to Texas County, Mo., and in 1875 and 1876 Dexter Mason represented Texas County in the State Legislature, the latter year being appointed by Gov. Hardin an honorary member of the Board of Managers, from Missouri, at the Centennial Exposition. He was a Democrat in politics, a farmer by occupation, and died at the age of seventy-three years, his wife's death occurring at the age of seventy-five. Their family consisted of four sons and two daughters, Peter T. Mason being their youngest child. He was born in Cattaraugus County, N. Y., October 22, 1847, and owing to the unsettled condition of the country during the late war, his early education was somewhat neglected. At the early age of thirteen years he began hiring out by the month, and on the 15th of November, 1866, was married to Miss Barbara Collie, who was born in Scotland on the 22d of August, 1847, but came to America when nine years of age. Her union with Mr. Mason resulted in the birth of eight children: William D., Herbert C., James R., Frank, Edwin, Elizabeth L., Roy M. and

Grace. Mrs. Mason died February 29, 1888. Soon after his marriage Mr. Mason came to Texas County, where he now has a good farm of 215 acres, 130 acres of which are under cultivation. He is a Democrat, a Mason, and November 6, 1888, was elected to the office of county judge, the duties of which he is filling very creditably.

Alfred Merrell (deceased) was born in North Carolina May 26, 1818, and was there reared to manhood and married, his union being to Miss Margaret Canoy, who was also born in North Carolina, September 20, 1820. They resided in their native State until 1837, then emigrated westward, and settled in Pulaski County, Mo., where they made their home for twenty years, then coming to Texas County, where he died on the 28th of January, 1865. He learned the cooper's trade in early life, but throughout his later career gave the most of his attention to farming. Previous to the war he had voted the Democratic ticket, but he afterward supported the principles of the Republican party. His wife was a member of the Methodist Episcopal Church, and she and Mr. Merrell became the parents of seven sons, only three of whom are living at the present time. The youngest, John, was born in Phelps County, February 20, 1849, and received no educational advantages whatever in his youth, never having learned to read or write. He made his home with his mother until August 17, 1873, when he was married to America C. Collins, a native of Texas County, born August 16, 1853, by whom he has eight children: Eleanor, Mary, Alfred, Louisa F., John, Philip, Margaret M. and George M. Since 1881 he has resided on his present farm of 165 acres, where he has acquired an excellent reputation as a farmer and stock raiser. He is a Democrat; his wife belongs to the Missionary Baptist Church.

Dan Merrell is a son of Alfred Merrell, whose sketch appears above, and was born in what is now Phelps County, Mo., June 30, 1846. His early days were spent in laboring hard on his father's farm, and his education was badly neglected. After reaching manhood he learned to read and write, and at the age of nineteen years he engaged in agricultural pursuits, which has been his life occupation. In 1869 he was married to Ruth E. Tate, a native of Texas County, who bore him two children, Missouri C. and Margaret B., and died in 1880. Two years later he married Mary C. Wallace, who has also borne him two children, Hattie E. and Amanda M. Ever since his first marriage Mr. Merrell has resided on the old home farm, and is now the owner of 165 acres of valuable land, about ninety acres of which are under cultivation, and in connection with his agricultural labors he has been engaged in running a threshing machine for the past seventeen years. He is a Republican in politics, and a member of the Methodist Episcopal Church.

Hon. J. W. Mires, physician and surgeon, Cabool. Prominent among the many good citizens of this community, and among those deserving recognition for their long residence in Texas County, stands the name of the above mentioned gentleman, whose brief biography follows. Dr. Mires has passed the last twenty-nine years of his life among the people of Texas County, and has been in active practice as a physician and surgeon; for eighteen years has been identified with its mercantile and farming interests as a principal factor, has held a seat in its councils, represented its interests ably and well in State matters at Jefferson City, twice as its representative, has been prominently before its people as one of its educational men, and in many other ways has added to its interests by his sterling worth and public spirit. He was born in Wilson County, Tenn., September 17, 1843, being the son of George W. and Elizabeth A. (Telford) Mires, grandson of Peter and Diana (Carter) Mires, and the great-grandson of Charles Mires, who was born in Germany. Peter Mires and wife were natives of Wilson County, Tenn., and George W. Mires and wife were also natives of Tennessee, and he was a farmer by occupation. Of the history of the Mires branch of the family in America, it is known that Charles Mires came from Germany to America with his parents prior to the Revolutionary War, and made a settlement in the Carolinas. They were mainly farmers, although we find them in the professions, trades and as artisans. Elizabeth A. (Telford) Mires was the daughter of Hugh A. and Mary W. (Brown) Telford, natives of Tennessee and South Carolina, respectively, worthy people, who after making a settlement in Southeast Missouri, where their daughter was born, returned to their Tennessee home in Wilson County. In the spring of 1860 George W. Mires made a settlement in Texas County, Mo., and here followed the teachings of the political doctrines of his native State. When the Civil War broke out he joined the Confederate army, and lost his life in 1864. He left two sons and a daughter. Dr. J. W. Mires was attending school at the opening of the war, and was but eighteen years of age. He remained engaged in his studies until 1862, when he left school for the battle-field, enlisting in Company I, Thirty-second Missouri Volunteer Infantry, Federal Army, and rendered honorable and active service until at the battle of Resaca, Ga., when he received a gunshot wound in his right groin, which incapacitated him for further field duty. In January, 1865, he was honorably discharged. The following six years of his life were spent in patient and industrious toil for the purpose of furthering his designs for a medical education. He completed a thorough course of study in the St. Louis Medical College at St. Louis, Mo., and graduated from that institution in 1872. Dr. Mires has served very creditably as a deputy county official in 1867-68 [see history], and after graduating located at Houston, the county seat of Texas County, and here he became an active worker in the general development of his locality, particularly to the advancements of its educational interests, and became one of the important factors in the establishment of the Houston Academy. He served as its trustee and upon the building committee. He then left Houston, and locating at Elk Creek again performed similar duty to the educational interest of that place, and likewise at Cabool. In each of these places he became to their educational institutions an important aid, contributing liberally upon each and every occasion, and serving faithfully and well officially. He has always identified himself with the Democratic party, and has on many occasions served his party well in their caucus deliberations, both upon county and State matters. In 1875 he filled the unexpired term in the Legislature of his honored father-in-law, the Hon. Charles H. Latimer [see sketch], and in 1880 he was elected to represent Texas County. In his legislative associations he formed many strong attachments for his seniors in the Assembly, and by his honorable bearing added an important luster to the "Lone Star" County. He served with credit upon the committees of Militia, Retrenchment and Reform, and upon Claims, serving as chairman in the latter. Socially Dr. Mires is of a genial disposition, and has drawn around him a host of friends. He is a Master Mason of several years standing, serving in the Blue Lodge as Past Master six times. He has been master of Barnes Lodge, Cabool, since its organization, and served as District Deputy Grand Master of the State in 1886. He has an interesting family of two sons, Benjamin and Edison, children of his union to Miss Elizabeth P., daughter of Hon. Charles H. Latimer. Dr. Mires buried his first wife, Miss Margaret Missouri Rutland, in 1870, and in 1874 he buried Walter, their only child.

Judge Philander Davis Mitchell, farmer, and judge of Texas County, Mo., was born in White County, Tenn., June 1, 1827, being a son of Spencer and Mary M. (Lewis) Mitchell, who were born in Virginia and Tennessee, April 8, 1804, and November 9, 1808, respectively. Spencer Mitchell moved to Tennessee with his parents when a boy, where he grew to manhood, married, and throughout life followed the occupation of farming. He became a resident of Texas County, Mo., in 1834, the town of Licking then consisting of two houses, and held a number of offices in the county, such as justice of the peace, sheriff and collector. He is a Democrat, a Mason, and his wife is a member of the Methodist Episcopal Church, South, he being a Presbyterian in belief. Judge Philander Davis Mitchell is the eldest of their ten children, and received a fair education in the old subscription schools of early times. At the age of twenty-one years he began farming for himself, and March 24, 1853, was married to Miss Mary L. Halbert, who is a native of Texas County, born November 30, 1832. Their five children's names are as follows: Travis B., Spencer E., Frances M., Mary E. and Philander H. Since their marriage they have resided on their present farm, which consists of 600 acres, with about 125 acres under cultivation, and besides this property he has given his children good farms. All his property has been acquired by his own good management and industry, and he deserves much credit for the success which has attended his efforts. He was justice of the peace for four years before the war, and during that struggle served for about six months in the Missouri State Guard, and toward the close of the war served about the same length of time in the regular Confederate army. He is a Democrat politically, and since 1886 has served as judge of Texas County. Both he and wife are members of the Methodist Episcopal Church, South, and he has been Worthy Master of the Masonic lodge two terms.

Sherrill Lewis Mitchell, M. D., was born in Texas County, Mo., June 22, 1862, being the son of Sherrill L. and Sarah (Bradford) Mitchell, natives of Tennessee and Missouri, respectively. When a child, the father moved to Texas County, where he married and still lives, being a farmer by occupation. He has been county judge for about six years; was magistrate many years, and during the late unpleasantness between the North and South he served three years in the Union army. Both parents were members of the Methodist Church. In their family were eleven children, nine of whom are living, five sons and four daughters. Dr. Sherrill L. Mitchell was the fourth in order of birth. He received his education in the common schools and at Salem Academy, and remained on the farm until about twenty-one years of age, when he studied medicine under Dr. George Orr, of Licking. In 1883 he entered the Missouri Medical College, and graduated from that institution in 1885. He afterward located at Licking, where he has enjoyed a good practice since. In 1887 he took a post graduate course at the Polyclinic School, St. Louis. He is a member of the Rolla District Medical Association and Texas County Medical Society, being president of the latter. January 25, 1885, he married Miss Anna Freeland, daughter of M. D. Freeland, and became the father of two children, Nellie and Ernest. December 30, 1888, his wife died. She was an excellent woman, and a member of the Christian Church. In connection with his practice, Dr. Mitchell is senior member of the drug firm of Mitchell & Hill. He has been a resident of this county all his life, and is a wide-awake, stirring young man. He is a Republican in politics, and is a member of the Methodist Episcopal Church.

Thomas Lorenzo Moore was born in Quantico, Wicomico County, Maryland, on the 24th day of October, 1855. Leaving there in the spring of 1877, he entered the printing business at Charleston Mo., and remained only one year, when he embarked in the mercantile business at Blodgett, Scott Co., Mo. Three years later, or in the fall of 1882, he sold out, and was appointed committee clerk in the State Senate during the General Assembly, and held the position until removing to Stoddard County, as manager and book-keeper of the Gregory Lumber Company. In 1884 he came to Cabool, and started the *Record*, which he now owns, and conducts in a manner reflecting credit upon himself, and proving of substantial benefit to the people of the community. In the summer of 1886 he was elected city alderman, and also city clerk. In 1888 he was elected as representative to the General Lodge of the I. O. O. F., of the State of Missouri, from the district comprising Wright, Howell, Shannon and Texas Counties. The same year he was also elected justice of the peace for Burdine Township, Texas County. He is a Democrat politically, the principles of which party are warmly sustained through the medium of his publication.

John H. Moran, another prominent farmer of Sherrill Township, and an enterprising citizen of the county, was born in St. Louis County, May 10, 1842. His father, Derby Moran, was a citizen of that county, an Irishman by birth, and a man of Catholic education, having been educated for the priesthood in the old country. His mother, Bridget Morisey, was a sister to the noted John Morisey, the pugilist, of New York. They had three boys and one girl. The father, mother and daughter died in St. Louis; the three brothers, Moses W., John H. and Thomas M., came to Licking, Texas County, in 1857, and entered into business, going south in 1861, where Moses, the oldest, died in 1864. After the war and a tramp through the States, John H. Moran came back to Texas County, where he had some land, and engaged in blacksmithing, in Licking, in 1866. He was successful enough to accumulate good farm property and buy several hundred acres of land. In 1878 he married Miss Annie Halbert, daughter of Judge E. Halbert, of Texas County. They have two children, Hampton, named for Gov. Wade Hampton, and Vesta, named for Senator George Vest. Mr. Moran and family lived in Licking until the cyclone of 1880 swept that town away, when they moved to their farm, "Valley View," four miles north of Licking. Mr. Moran is a genial, social fellow, well posted, and though not connected with any church, assists everybody and everything tending to the good of society and the country. His wife belongs to the Methodist Episcopal Church, South. Mr. Moran thinks he has some things to be proud of in the history of events of Texas County. He received the title of colonel from Sim West, and that of judge from Gen. Jo. Bradford. He believes himself to have been the first person in the county to get married in church; also the first in the county to obtain a patent for an invention. He was, besides, one of the first presidents of a Democratic club in the county. He is for Cleveland and D. R. Francis in 1892.

E. P. Murrill, who is also closely associated with the farming and stock dealing interests of Texas County, was born in Jefferson County, Mo., July 29, 1844, being the son of Elias (born November 4, 1810) and Jane A. (Perkins) Murrill (born October 28, 1861), natives of Kentucky, and grandson of Hardin Murrill, who was also a native of Kentucky, and who settled in Ste. Genevieve County, Mo., as did also the family of John Perkins, father of Jane A. (Perkins) Murrill. Both were, it is supposed, Revolutionary soldiers. The Perkins were large people, long-lived, and were Baptists in their religious views. The Murrills were of medium stature, and were members of the Baptist Church. Among them may be found merchants, artisans, farmers and professional people. E. P. Murrill grew to man's estate in Missouri, and during the latter part of the war was in the Union service for nearly seven months. He farmed in Jefferson County until 1873, and then spent eleven years in Franklin County, Mo., or until 1884, when he moved to Texas County of the same State, and there invested in land. He was married in Jefferson County, Mo., May 18, 1869, to Miss Lucy Maness, a native of Missouri, born December 5, 1847, and the daughter of Elijah Maness, born September 7, 1811, and Mary Ann (Murell) Maness, natives of Tennessee and Missouri, respectively. Mr. and Mrs. Murrill have reared three sons and two daughters: Constantine Briggs, born February 17, 1870; George Riley, born August 27, 1871; Mary Ann, born September 2, 1873; Daisy May, born November 9, 1876, and Ross Perkins, born November 8, 1878. Mr. Murrill has served on the school board of this district for many years, and he and wife are members of the Methodist Episcopal Church, South.

Rev. Wesley Nall, pastor of the Methodist Episcopal Church, Houston charge, and a resident of Elk Creek, Cass Township, was born in Chatham County, N. C., July 26, 1822. He is a son of John and Dorcas (Ansley) Nall, and grandson of John Nall, Sr., who was the son of a Revolutionary soldier, and presumably of English descent. The Nalls were people of large stature; were very tenacious of their religious faith, and were early settlers of the "Palmetto State." Rev. Wesley Nall was the eldest of a family of seven sons and three daughters. He remained and assisted his father on the farm in North Carolina until in his seventeenth year, when, in October, 1838, he removed with his parents, who were identified with Marshall and Dickson Counties, Tenn., five years; then to Missouri in 1843. Here the father made a home for himself and family upon Elk Creek for nineteen years. He died in Johnson County, Kas., in 1865, in his sixty-seventh year, at the home of his second son, Thomas. His wife followed him in 1875, in her seventy-fifth year. Rev. Wesley Nall was reared to the faith of the Methodist Episcopal Church, and August 29, 1842, he embraced the religion of Christ. August 7, 1847, he was licensed to exhort, and, in October, 1851, to preach, having followed his ministerial duties for over forty-one years. He married, July 26, 1847, Miss Nancy Self, a native of St. Louis County, Mo., and the daughter of Fountain and Sarah (Sullins) Self, natives of Kentucky and Missouri, respectively. To Mr. and Mrs. Nall were born these children, three sons and two daughters living: Samuel, of San Francisco, Cal., and a carpenter and builder by occupation; G. C., who is also a carpenter of the same place; Sarah, wife of Austin Grisham, of Elk Creek; A. B., of Kansas City, Mo., and Naomi Jane, wife of Richard Forsythe, of Willow Springs, Mo.; another son, John F., died in Kansas, January 25, 1882, aged twenty-six years, and left a son and daughter. Mr. and Mrs. Nall also lost three other children in infancy. Mr. Nall is a Blue Lodge Mason, and has served in the school board of his district. He has 200 acres of land in one tract, 100 under cultivation, and his post-office is Elk Creek, Mo.

William Scott Nichol, a leading merchant, tobacco manufacturer, saw-miller and farmer, was born in Hickman County, Ky., April 16, 1840, the son of David and Martha (Mitchell) Nichol, both of whom were born in Virginia, he in 1798 and she in 1808. When young both immigrated to Tennessee, where they married, and afterward removed to Kentucky. In that State the father died in 1850. He was a practical tanner, and carried on a large tan-yard business, but in connection ran a large farm. He was a Whig in politics, and both were members of the Methodist Episcopal Church. In their family were eight children, six sons and two daughters. In 1856 the mother and children came to Texas County, Mo., and located one-half mile from Licking, though there was only a log store to mark the place. The mother died here in her eighty-second year. William S. Nichol was the youngest but two of this family. In youth he aided in tilling the soil, and attended the common schools, in which he received a limited education, on account of the war breaking in on his studies. In September, 1861, he enlisted in Col. Coleman's regiment, Confederate service, and remained about a year, when he was then made hospital steward. In 1864 he was taken prisoner, and held at Rolla. Judge C. C. Bland finding him there, secured his parole and took him into his store, and some time afterward Mr. Nichol had the pleasure of recompensing him by casting the tie vote for Mr. Bland as judge. After the termination of hostilities Mr. Nichol began the manufacture of tobacco, which he has followed ever since, turning out a product now of about 10,000 pounds per year. In connection he runs a large farm, owning some 400 acres. In 1880 he opened a store in Licking, and has one of the largest stocks of goods in town. He is also interested in a saw-mill. September 9, 1869, he married Miss Mary Weller, a native of Washington, Ohio. They have no children of their own, but have reared an orphan boy, Frank Mautz, who is now associated with Mr. Nichol in his business enterprises. Mr. Nichol is a very successful business man, having made all he has by his own efforts. He is a Democrat politically, and he and wife are members of the Methodist Episcopal Church.

Thomas F. Nicholas, circuit clerk and recorder of Texas County, Mo., is a native of Texas County, Mo., born February 28, 1852, and is the son of Walker and Isaminda (Elliott) Nicholas, natives of Missouri and Indiana, respectively, and both deceased, he in the State of Louisiana, March 17, 1885, when fifty-five years of age, and she in Texas County, Mo., March 21, 1852, at the age of eighteen or nineteen, when the subject of this sketch was an infant only twenty-one days old. The father when a boy came from Washington County, Mo., to Texas County, of the same State, and was married February 14, 1851, and remained in that county until after the death of his wife. He then, when Thomas F. was one year old, left him in Missouri, and March 1, 1853, went to California, and was engaged in mining for nine years, or until about the breaking out of the late war. Returning to Missouri he enlisted in the Confederate army, and served as forager or wagon-master until cessation of hostilities. He then went to Central America, engaging in the timber business and trading, but afterward returned to Louisiana, about the year 1869 or 1870, where he turned his attention to farming. He then married Miss Mary Barrow, who is now living in Louisiana. To Mr. Nicholas and his first wife was born one child, Thomas F., the subject of this sketch. While his father was in California Thomas F. was left in care of Miss Mary Hamilton, an unmarried lady, who is now living with our subject. The latter received his education at the schools in Texas County, worked on the farm, also cut cord-wood and worked in saw-mills, and in 1875-76-77 he taught school in Texas County. In 1878 he was elected circuit clerk and recorder on the Democratic ticket. Since then he has been re-elected twice to the same position by the Democratic party, and the last time had no opposition. April 9, 1876, he married Miss Drucilla Farris, a native of Missouri, and the daughter of James Farris, one of the first settlers of Texas County, Mo. To Mr. and Mrs. Nicholas have been born three children: Mary, Orlena and Daisy. Mrs. Nicholas is a member of the Baptist Church, and Mr. Nicholas is a decided Democrat in his political views. He is a member of the Masonic lodge, and has represented the same twice in the Grand Lodge of the State. He is also a member of the I. O. O. F. His success has been attained by a life-time of hard labor and attention to his official duties.

John O'Hearn, Cabool. Among the many prominent and public-spirited citizens of Texas County, and among the notable ones of Cabool, stands the name of Mr. O'Hearn, who was born in the Emerald Isle, Parish of Kildorray, County Cork, June 24, 1847, and carries with him in his citizenship here full characteristics of the progressive people of his fatherland. His parents, Michael and Ellen (Sullivan) O'Hearn, were worthy people of Ireland, and came of a long line of ancestry there. They died when John was a mere lad, and he was left to the guardianship of an uncle by marriage, Michael Welch, who reared and educated him until thirteen years of age, when he went out to work. At the age of eighteen he took passage for America, paying the same by his own earnings, and sought for himself a home in the New World. He remained for several years in the State of Michigan, and during that time he not only gained a thorough knowledge of American customs and wages, but also, in his frugality, some means. After spending about seventeen years in honorable occupation in that State, he immigrated to Kansas, when, after an experience of about two years in that State, he decided to cast his fortunes in Missouri, and located, for some two years, in Rich Hill, Mo. He then moved to Texas County in 1882, just at the juncture when Cabool needed pushing and enterprising characters, invested here, and here he has made a notable mark in commercial circles, for be it said to his credit that he stands the equal of any of Texas County's business men for keen business acumen and progressive character. Increasing his business, he has enlarged upon many of the industrial interests of this locality, and but few interests here, whether of merchandising, farming, school or church, but have been benefitted by his generous contribution and liberal patronage. He is a leader in his work, and stands high in the citizenship of his locality. He has built and improved the property largely, is the owner of some fine buildings here, and is the owner of a good farm, etc. He was happily married in Jackson, Mich., to Miss Bridget Nestor, a lady of estimable attainments, and the daughter of John and Annie (McNeil) Nestor, natives of the Emerald Isle, from County Clare. Mr. and Mrs. O'Hearn are members of the Roman Catholic Church, although both are liberal in their contributions to other church and society work. Mr. and Mrs. O'Hearn enjoy the respect and esteem of all who know them. Mr. O'Hearn has always identified himself with the political faith of Democracy, and has rendered his party important aid here on many occasions. We bespeak for him a worthy recognition on the part of the Texas County Democracy, at no distant day. He is an affable gentleman, and has drawn around him a host of friends.

George Paulding, farmer, was born in Allegheny County, Penn., January 7, 1821, and is a son of John W. and Alice (Cassilly) Paulding, the former being born at Fishkill, N. Y. His boyhood days were spent on a farm, but he afterward learned the hatter's trade, which occupation he followed until 1842, having immigrated to St. Louis, Mo., in 1828, in which city he resided until 1852, when he went to Portland, Ore., where all news of him was lost until 1887, when a notice of his death appeared in a newspaper. His wife was of Irish descent, and died when her only child, George, was a small boy. Mr. Paulding afterward married Ann Dillon, of St. Louis, who was also of Irish lineage, and by whom he became the father of four children: John H., Hiram, Walter and Joseph. The grandfather, John Paulding, was born in New York, and was a soldier in the Revolutionary

War, and was one of the three men, Isaac Van Wert and David Williams being the other two, to capture the British spy. Maj. Andre, for which service he was awarded a medal. He was of German descent, and a farmer, by occupation. George Paulding, the gentleman whose name heads this sketch, was seven years old when he came to St. Louis, but a year later went to Belleville, Ill., where he attended school until he was thirteen years of age, then returned to St. Louis and remained four years, working at the hatter's trade. In 1838 he settled in Texas County, Mo., and since that time has followed farming for a living. He was one of the first settlers of the region, the country at that time being in a very wild and unsettled state, deer, bear, elk and other wild animals roaming the woods at will. There were no churches or schools, and religious services were conducted at the homes of the settlers. In February, 1842, Mr. Paulding wedded Miss Julia A. Turpin, who was born and reared in Arkansas, the following being the children born to their union: John M., William W., Alfred D., Adaline and Isabella. James F., Benjamin, George and Mary are deceased. The mother of these children died in December, 1866, after which Mr. Paulding wedded Mrs. Margaret A. (Cabble) Roberts, a native of Tennessee. Three of their five children are living: Henry, Lizzie, Agnes (living), and Ellen and Joseph (deceased). Mr. Paulding is a wealthy farmer and prominent citizen of the county, and has faithfully filled the offices of assessor, surveyor and presiding and probate judge of Texas County, being elected to these offices on the Democratic ticket. He is a charter member of the I. O. O. F., and he and wife are members of the Christian Church.

Charles E. Peter, representing the Western Land & Cattle Company, of Kansas City and London, England, was born near Edinburgh, Scotland, April 21, 1863, and is the son of Henry T. and Elizabeth (Peter) Peter, natives of Scotland, and cousins. The father died in his native country in March, 1886, when seventy-nine years of age, but the mother is still living, and is fifty-seven years of age. Both were members of the Scotch Episcopal Church. The father was a manufacturer of linen cloth on an extensive scale, his being one of the oldest establishments of the kind in Scotland. There were born to their marriage four children, three now living, and Charles E. being the youngest. He received his education at Dollar Academy and Edinburgh, and soon afterward served a five years' apprenticeship as engineer, in the foundry at home. Later he went to Dundee, then to London, where he worked for the "P. & O." Steamship Company, in the capacity of engineer, for six months. He then went home soon after, and in February, 1885, he came to the United States, locating in Texas County, where he took charge of the property belonging to the Western Land & Cattle Company. Mr. Peter is a Democrat in politics, is a citizen of the United States, and intends to make this country his home. In connection with managing the property of the Western Land & Cattle Company Mr. Peter is also engaged in farming on an extensive scale.

George Franklin Pettigrew, postmaster at Cabool, was born in East Tennessee, Bradley County, October 21, 1846, to the marriage of Edwin and Rebecca (Robinson) Pettigrew, natives of Georgia and

Tennessee, respectively. The Pettigrew family were of Scotch-Irish stock, and trace their ancestors back to early settlers in Virginia. Rebecca (Robinson) Pettigrew was the daughter of Basil Robinson, a native of Tennessee. In 1853 Edwin Pettigrew left his Tennessee home in Bradley County, came to Missouri, made a home in Washington County, and there George F. Pettigrew grew to manhood. He completed a good education in the public schools in that county, and in early life followed the teacher's profession for several terms. He then left the school-room in 1870, and engaged in farming and merchandising in Crawford County, Mo., which he carried on until 1881, when he came to Cabool, Texas County. He served in the Federal army, State Militia, for twelve months while in his eighteenth year, and afterward was postmaster at Wilson's Mills for about a year. Upon removing to Sligo he was appointed postmaster, by Gen. Grant, at that place, and after coming to Cabool received his appointment as postmaster here under President Arthur, and has held the position ever since. After coming here he formed a partnership with J. R. Farris, and is engaged in general merchandising. He was married in Crawford County, Mo., to Miss Ann A. Snelson, a native of Missouri, and the daughter of John C. Snelson, also a native of Missouri. To this union were born three sons and a daughter: Albert, Marshall E., George R. and Mabel A. Mr. and Mrs. Pettigrew are members of the Cumberland Presbyterian Church, and he is an elder in the same, a position he has creditably and honorably filled for the past ten years. He is a trustee in the New Church Building Association of the Cumberland Presbyterian Church. He has been city treasurer of Cabool since its organization, was agent for the Adams Express Company for two years, and is a member of the school board, being at present the honored president. He is a Blue Lodge Mason.

Gabriel M. Pike, farmer and stock man, was born in Grainger County, Tenn., in January, 1825, and is a son of Benjamin and Mary (Hooker) Pike, who were born, reared and married in the "Old North State," moving to Tennessee soon after the celebration of the latter event, where they spent the remainder of their lives. The father was a Democrat, and he and wife were members of the Methodist Church. Gabriel M. Pike was the fifth of their seven children, and although he has a fair English education his early educational advantages were very limited. He worked with his father as a collier until 1843, then drove a team for his passage to Missouri, but after working two years in Pulaski County he found himself but little better off than when he came to the State, and he engaged in rafting on the river for ten years, working on the Piney, Gasconade, Missouri and Mississippi Rivers to St. Louis, making in all some forty trips, and traveled homeward on foot most of the time. He then purchased a tract of land on Piney River and engaged in farming, but during the war served six months in the State Militia, and then kept a grocery in Rolla for about seven months, returning to his farm in 1865. June 25, 1876, he was married to Miss Mary Truesdell, who was born in Texas County December 19, 1845, and by her is the father of four children: Alva E., Benjamin M., Nancy T. E. and Robert. By good management and industry Mr. Pike has become the owner of about 500 acres of land, 150 of which are under cultivation, and besides this has other property, which makes him one of the heaviest tax payers in the county. He deserves much credit for the success which has attended his efforts, as he came to the county without any capital whatever, and has been, in every respect, the architect of his own fortune. He is a Democrat politically, and is a member of the Masonic fraternity.

Jabez D. Randall, farmer, is a son of Ornan and Esther (Stafford) Randall, who were born in Rhode Island and Vermont, respectively, but were married in New York. The father served in a regiment of artillery during the War of 1812, and from the jar occasioned by firing the guns he became quite deaf. From New York they moved to Bradford County, Penn., and in 1855 immigrated to Texas County, Mo., where they were engaged in farming, and where the mother died at the age of fifty-seven years. The father returned to Pennsylvania, and there died at about the age of eighty years. Their family consisted of twelve children, five sons being soldiers in the Federal army during the late war, and one in the Confederate. Jabez D. Randall, one of the sons, was born in Bradford County, Penn., March 5, 1846, and was there reared on a farm and received a common-school education. In May, 1863, he enlisted in Company B, Fifth Cavalry, of Missouri State Militia, and served until the close of the war, being a participant in the battle of Boonville. After peace was proclaimed he returned to his parents' home in Missouri, and here has been engaged in husbandry up to the present time, being now the owner of 249 acres of land, eighty of which are under cultivation. He is a Republican in politics, was committee-man from his district, and has been constable of Sherrill Township for two years. January 1, 1867, he espoused Miss Mary A. Bradford, a daughter of James Bradford. She was born in Texas County on October 6, 1847, and her union with Mr. Randall has been blessed in the birth of five children: James L., Esther A., Oscar A., Leslie C. and Iva F. (deceased). Mr. Randall and wife belong to the Methodist Episcopal Church, and are worthy citizens of the county.

William Ray, manager of the Diamond Flour Mills, of Licking, was born in Phelps County, Mo., April 15, 1848, and is the son of David and Elizabeth (Crow) Ray, natives of Kentucky, though they lived for some years in Tennessee. They came to Missouri in 1847, and after living a short time in Greene County moved to Phelps County, where the mother died in 1851, leaving six children, two sons and four daughters. After her death the father married again, and became the father of nine children by his last union. He was a well-to-do farmer, was a Democrat in politics, and lived to be sixty-five years of age. The mother was a member of the Baptist Church. William Ray was the youngest but one of the children born to the first marriage. He was educated in the old subscription schools, but the war coming on cut short his school life. At the age of twenty he began for himself by tilling the soil, but has had a general experience in business. He ran a livery stable for some time, then a grocery store in Rolla, and in 1874 he came to Texas County, where he established a grocery store in Licking. He ran a mail line from Rolla to West Plains, and afterward engaged in the hardware business at

Licking, then dry goods, and in 1887 he took charge of the above mill. He owns 360 acres of good land. November 4, 1874, he married Miss Emma Halburt, a native of this county. Five children were born to this union: Lizzie F., Sanford D., Theale V., Alra and an infant. Mr. Ray as a business man has been quite successful, and is one of the representative men of the county. He is a Democrat in politics, is a member of the Masonic fraternity, and he and wife are members of the Baptist Church.

David Asher Robertson, merchant, and a native of Kentucky, was born in Crittenden County August 6, 1858, the son of William and Narcissa (Asher) Robertson, natives of Kentucky, and grandson of Stephen Robertson. The Robertson family were large people, of strong physique, and were disciples of the Presbyterian faith. Narcissa (Asher) Robertson was the daughter of William R. and Esther (Love) Asher, natives of South Carolina, and granddaughter of William Asher, Sr., who was in the War for Independence, and served with credit and honor. He was a farmer by occupation, and lived to a good old age. He died in Kentucky, whither he had removed. The Ashers were members of the Cumberland Presbyterian Church, as are the Ashers of the present day. David Asher Robertson was reared in Kentucky, and obtained a fair education in the public schools of Crittenden County. The father died in 1871, and it devolved upon David A. to carry on the farm. In February, 1880, he came to Missouri, locating in Butler County, and there remained for three years, when he moved to Texas County, and settled at Cabool. In 1886 he embarked in merchandising upon a nominal capital, and has increased it to a large and lucrative business. He was married in Kentucky to Miss C. Shaw Black, a native of Kentucky, and the daughter of John T. and M. Jane (Newcombs) Black. Mr. and Mrs. Robertson have one son and a daughter living, Cora Edna and David Shaw. They buried Birdie Alice and Virgil Asher. Mr. Robertson is a member of the Masonic fraternity, the A. O. U. W., and he and wife are members of the Cumberland Presbyterian Church. Esther (Calhoun) Love, the grandmother of the subject of this sketch, was a cousin of John C. Calhoun, and the daughter of William Love, a gentleman of high standing in his community, who was county surveyor of Christian County, Ky., and who was murdered by the Harps, two outlaws who infested that country, and who subsequently paid the penalty of their crimes by death, one of whom was beheaded, and his head exposed on a pole for a number of days, the spot being known at the present day as "Harps Head Road," near Madisonville, Ky.

William J. Rodgers, Sr., farmer, was born in Knox County, Tenn., May 7, 1817, his parents being Thomas and Mary (Donaldson) Rodgers, the former born in Washington County, East Tenn., and the latter in the State of Pennsylvania, in 1770 and 1772, respectively. They were among the early settlers of East Tennessee, and after residing in Knox County for some time, moved to Roane County, where they spent the remainder of their days. They were well-to-do farmers, and were members of the Cumberland Presbyterian Church, the father being a Whig in his political views. He lived to be about eighty-two years of age and his wife to be eighty-six. William J.

Rodgers, one of their seven children, was reared on a farm, and received his education in the old log school-house of early days. After assisting his parents until about twenty-five years of age, he engaged in farming for himself, which occupation has been his chief calling since, and by good management and industry is now one of the wealthy farmers of the county. He resided in Tennessee until 1867, since which time he has been a resident of Texas County, Mo., and purchased on coming here 680 acres of land, 160 of which he still retains, having given the rest to his children. February 3, 1842, he was married to Julia Stubbs, a native of Tennessee, by whom he has twelve children: Thomas L., James M., Mary D., John, Samuel, Martha M., William J., George P., Jethro M., Archimedes, James M. and Margaret C. The mother of these children died on the 4th of September, 1870, and three years later Mr. Rodgers wedded Mrs. Ahalia (Johnson) Green, who was born in Mecklenburgh County, Va., in 1838, but was reared in North Carolina. They are members of the Methodist Episcopal Church, South, and Mr. Rodgers is a stanch Republican in politics. George P. Rodgers, his son, is also a farmer and stock raiser, and was born in Roane County, Tenn., December 3, 1855, and received good early educational advantages. December 7, 1875, he wedded Miss Nora Nichols, who was a daughter of Capt. John W. Nichols, and died July 26, 1878, without issue. January 8, 1880, Mr. Rodgers married his second wife, whose maiden name was Sarah E. Weller, who was born in Washington, Ohio, October 19, 1858, and by whom he became the father of four children: Lela M., Oscar and an infant. One child died in infancy. He owns 168 acres of land, with about 112 under cultivation, and takes considerable interest in raising blooded stock, being the owner of a fine Durham bull, a good jack and a splendid horse. The results of his efforts are already to be seen in the improvement of the stock of the neighborhood, and his fine farm testifies to his ability as a thorough-going farmer.

Peter Root, another successful tiller of the soil and prominent stock raiser of Burdine Township, was born in Middle Sweden, Skofde, November 11, 1850, and is the son of John and Joannah Root. The father was a blacksmith by occupation, and came to America in 1869. He settled at Moline, Ill., but subsequently returned to Sweden. Peter Root learned farming and railroading in the old country, and in 1871 crossed the ocean to America. He first located in Putnam County, N. Y., and worked in the Tilly Foster Iron Mines there for four years. In 1874 he came to Missouri, and worked at farming near Verona until 1878, when he started for Prescott, Ariz., and went from there to Albuquerque, N. Mex., where he spent eighteen months; thence to Silver Cliff, Colo., and finally to Cabool, Mo., where he has since remained. He was married at Verona, Mo., to Miss Anna Gustafson, a native of Sweden, who came to America in 1872. To this marriage were born four sons and one daughter: Albert, Carl, Edward, Ellen, Dora and John William. Mr. Root has 160 acres of nice land, and pays considerable attention to the raising of fine stock. He has served with credit as a member of the school board, and he and wife are worthy members of the Lutheran Church.

Columbus M. Ross, M. D., graduate of St. Louis Medical College, and physician and merchant at Houston, was born in Giles County, Tenn., February 8, 1833, and is the son of Elam L. and Dorcas (Vansandt) Ross, both natives of Tennessee. The parents left their native State in 1856, locating near Marshfield, Mo., and here the father followed agricultural pursuits the remainder of his life. He died in Marshfield in March, 1857, at the age of fifty-seven years. The mother is yet living, is seventy-four years of age, and is now a resident of Polk County, Mo. Both parents were members of the Methodist Episcopal Church, South. The paternal grandfather of our subject was a soldier in the Revolutionary War. He immigrated to Middle Tennessee about 1800, and there died at the extreme age of ninety-eight years. He and two sons were in the War of 1812. Columbus M. Ross was the eldest child born to his parents. He received his education at Pleasant Grove Male Academy, and began the study of medicine at Ashland, Tenn., receiving his diploma in 1866. In 1856 he came to Missouri, locating at Marshfield, and began the practice of his profession. At the breaking out of the late war he entered the Confederate army as assistant surgeon in the Seventh Brigade, Missouri State Guard, and was afterward surgeon. At the close of the war he went to Illinois, and remained in Montgomery County for three years; then in 1868 he came to Houston, where he was engaged in the successful practice of his profession until 1882, when he was elected county clerk. He held this position three years. Dr. Ross has been married three times, first in 1857 to Miss Adaline Matilda Cloud, who died at Springfield, Mo., in 1862, leaving two children, Beauregard and Adaline. In 1864 the Doctor took for his second wife Miss Susan A. McClary, who died in 1869, leaving two children: C. M., Jr., and Susan A. In 1870 Dr. Ross married Mrs. Mary A. McClellan. The Doctor is a member of the Methodist Episcopal Church, South; is a member of the I. O. O. F., and is one of the oldest Masons in Southern Missouri. He is a Democrat in his political views.

William Roy, farmer, of Texas County, Mo., is a native of Perthshire, Scotland, and was born on the 9th of July, 1837, being a son of William and Belle (McGregor) Roy, both of whom were born, reared and married in Perthshire, and there resided until 1850, when they immigrated to America, settling near Montreal, Canada. The father was an extensive railroad, bridge and ditch contractor, and although he began working as a day laborer, he became one of the prominent men of his county and held a number of offices of trust, being mayor of his district, an office which corresponds to our county judge. He and wife were members of the Presbyterian Church, and died in Canada. William Roy is the third of their eight children, and received a limited early education in his native land. At the age of fifteen years he became delivery boy in the wholesale grocery house of Kingan & Kinloch, of Montreal, and remained with them fifteen years, rising to the position of shipping clerk. In 1866 he went to New York City, where he became shipping clerk for Robert McDonald, remaining with him two years, and then came to Texas County, Mo., where he is now the owner of an excellent farm, consisting of 240 acres, and has given 160 acres to his sons. For the past thirteen years he has run a threshing machine, and although on coming to the county he had never driven a team, he has surmounted many difficulties, and is considered one of the successful farmers of the county. July 4, 1856, he wedded Miss Ellen Cameron, who was born in County Antrim, Ireland, and by her is the father of the following children: William M., John C., Robert J., George R., Ellen J., Agnes B. and Thomas A. Mr. and Mrs. Roy are members of the Methodist Episcopal Church, South.

Frank P. Rutherford, another prominent merchant of Houston, Texas Co., Mo., and the son of John and Mary (Taylor) Rutherford, was born in Anderson County, Tenn., May 16, 1853. The parents were natives of Anderson County, Tenn., the father born in 1815, and died in 1875 in Texas County, Mo. The mother was born in 1817, and died in Texas County, Mo., in 1887. They were married in Tennessee, where they lived until 1864, when they moved to Boyle County, Ky., and there resided three years. They then moved to La Fayette County, Mo., where they remained until coming to Texas County, Mo., in 1871. He was sheriff of Anderson County, Tenn., for four years, was a successful farmer, and was a Democrat in his political views. He and wife were members of the Methodist Episcopal Church. Besides his farming interest he was also engaged in merchandising at Chester at the breaking out of the war, but his business was broken up during this struggle. To his marriage were born seven children, four now living: Isaac, a carpenter at Mammoth Springs, Mo.; James, at Dayton, Wash. Ter.; Mary, wife of A. G. Bate, and Frank P. The last named, when a boy, learned the carpenter's trade, at which he worked until 1878, when he opened a cabinet-shop and furniture store, with a very small capital. He has been quite successful, although starting with limited means. September 29, 1879, he married Miss Alice Kelley, a native of Webster County, Mo., and the daughter of William C. Kelley. To this union were born two children, James and Ernest. Mr. Rutherford has a branch store at Cabool, furniture establishment, which is doing well at that place. He is Democratic in his political principles, and Mrs. Rutherford is a member of the Methodist Episcopal Church, South.

John Schissler, merchant, of the firm of J. Schissler & Co., and one of the most prominent and substantial business men of Texas County, Mo., was born in St. Clair County, Ill., January 15, 1847, being the son of John and Mary Anna (Roth) Schissler. The parents were natives of Bavaria, immigrating to the United States some years ago, locating in St. Clair County, Ill., where the father died in 1850. The mother received her final summons in the same county and State a few years later. Our subject, John Schissler, was then placed under the control of Adam Roth, the wholesale and retail grocer of St. Louis, and remained with him until twenty-one years of age, having all the advantages of a mercantile experience. He was also blessed with a liberal schooling, attending the public schools of St. Louis, and afterward graduated from Rohror's Commercial College. He was then engaged as book-keeper for his uncle, Adam Roth, and served in this capacity for three years. He was then connected with other business houses of the city, as salesman, until March, 1870, when he formed a partnership with August Masterbrook, and engaged in the retail grocery business in St. Louis. Five years later he embarked in the same business on his own responsibility, and followed this until 1878, when, in April of that year, he came to Houston, Mo., and opened the establishment of which he is now the head. At that time he was in rather stinted circumstances, but he went bravely to work, applied himself closely to business, and soon succeeded in building up one of the most profitable trades in the county. His store is, indeed, a model, the equal, in systematic arrangement, to any found in much larger towns. He is by far the heaviest dealer in this section, carrying a full line of goods, and reaching the $10,000 mark in valuation. Since locating here Mr. Schissler has conducted his business on strictly a cash basis. The County Wheel recognizes him as their merchant, it being the Wheel headquarters for supplies of Texas County. December 22, 1872, Mr. Schissler married Miss Catherine Doehler, a native of Indiana, born January 6, 1855, and the daughter of Peter Doehler. This union resulted in the birth of four children: Sophia M., Kate F., Annie F. and Alice A. Mr. Schissler is a member of the I. O. O. F., the A. O. U. W., and in politics is a stanch Republican.

George Shafer (deceased) was born in Berks County, Penn., November 28, 1816. His father, when a boy, was brought to America, and sold to pay his passage to this country. The man to whom he was sold, dressed him in a negro's clothes, worked him hard and abused him in many ways. When he had worked his time out he repaid all this kindness (?) by giving his master a good thrashing. George Shafer was reared on a farm, and educated in both the German and English languages, and was quite a good scholar. When young he and his parents moved to Mahoning County, Ohio, where he met and married Miss Christina Gilbert, who was born in Mahoning County, Ohio, and her parents were from Pennsylvania. The family farther back came from Germany. Grandfather Gilbert was a colonel in the Revolutionary War. Mrs. Shafer never attended school more than three months, and that in a German school. After marriage Mr. and Mrs. Shafer located in Mahoning County, Ohio, where Mr. Shafer carried on farming until he moved to Trumbull County, where for some years he speculated in oil lands and became quite wealthy. In 1869 he moved to Texas County, Mo., locating on the farm where Mrs. Shafer now resides, which consists of 960 acres. When they first settled in Mahoning County, Ohio, Mr. Shafer was in very poor circumstances financially. He purchased a rough piece of land in the woods, but he and his faithful companion worked almost day and night to pay for it. This they at last did, and he became quite wealthy before his death, which occurred April 12, 1887. He was a good man, and was beloved and respected by all who knew him. He was a Whig previous to the war, and afterward a Republican. His wife is still living, and is seventy-six years of age. Their family consisted of nine children: Catherine, Margaret, Mary, Sarah, Hosea, George, David Amanda and John. Only three are now living. David is the only one single and the only living son. He owns 629 acres of land, has a fine farm, and is a successful farmer and dealer in stock. He is a Republican in his political opinions, and is a member of the Methodist Church.

Joel Sherrill. Prominent among the early settlers of Missouri, and among those deserving special recognition for their long residence in Texas County, stands the name of the above mentioned gentleman, who is the son of John and Mary (Holbert) Sherrill. The father was born May 10, 1784, in South Carolina, and the mother was born in the same State April 10, 1791. They lived in their native State until 1819, then moved to St. Francois County, Mo., and from there, in 1831, to "The Lick," from which Licking took its name, purchasing land where the town is now situated, and here followed farming. During the latter part of the War of 1812 Mr. Sherrill volunteered, but served only a short time. He was a Democrat in his political views, and for six years served as justice of the peace. He died March 15, 1855. She died April 17, 1872, and was a member of the Baptist Church. In their family were four children, three of whom lived to be grown, and Joel Sherrill is the only one now living. He was born January 23, 1815; was reared on a farm, and received a limited education in the subscription schools. At the age of twenty-one he began for himself by farming, and October 2, 1836, he married Miss Jane Thornton, a native of Union County, Ill., born December 15, 1820. She came to what is now Dent County when about thirteen years of age. Her father, William Thornton, was a soldier in the War of 1812. In 1839 Mr. Sherrill moved to the place where he now lives, his nearest neighbor being six miles distant, and here he and his chosen companion began making their fortune. He now owns 1,000 acres of land. For two years he held the office of county judge, and has always affiliated with the Democratic party. To Mr. and Mrs. Sherrill were born seven children, of whom two lived to be grown, Mary E. and Joel S. Mr. Sherrill's chief business during life has been farming, although he has also been engaged in merchandising for a number of years. He has been a resident of this county for fifty-eight years, and is classed among its most respected citizens. He is a Royal Arch Mason, and he and wife are members of the Christian Church. The Sherrill family sprang from a young Englishman, who came to America in an early day, married, and settled in Virginia. Afterward the family went to South Carolina.

James B. Sherrill, one of the enterprising and successful citizens of Texas County, Mo., was born in that county December 27, 1853, and is the son of Nel and Margaret (Bradford) Sherrill, born in Tennessee and Texas County, Mo., respectively. When young, Nel Sherrill came with his parents to this county. He married Miss Elizabeth Campbell, who bore him one son. After her death he married Miss Bradford, and by her became the father of two sons. He was a farmer by occupation, and died in 1855. The mother afterward married Spencer Mitchell, who died at Little Rock, Ark., in the Confederate army. By this last marriage she became the mother of three children, one son and two daughters. Later the mother married Dr. Echols McKinney, by whom she had one son. She is still living, and is about fifty-three years old. James B. Sherrill was reared to farm life, and owing to the war received a rather limited education. After his mother was left a widow he assisted in supporting her, and at the age of nineteen he commenced working on the farm by the month, and became an independent farmer. February 25, 1874, he married Miss Margaret Campbell, who bore him three children, one son and two daughters. In 1879 he lost his wife, and two years later he married Miss Belle Wilson, a native of Dent County, born September 24, 1854, and to this union were born three children, one son and two daughters. Mr. Sherrill is the owner of 100 acres of land, well improved, and has lived in Sherrill Township all his life. For two years he was sheriff of that township. He is a Democrat in politics, a member of the Masonic lodge, and he and wife are members of the Methodist Episcopal Church, South.

Wiley B. Simmons, merchant at Summerville, Mo., was born in Claiborne County, Tenn., November 13, 1830, being a son of Enoch C. and Sarah (Lewis) Simmons, who were also natives of that State, and were married in Claiborne County. The father was reared on a farm, received a good education, and became a minister of the Baptist Church, preaching for about thirty-five years. At an early day he immigrated to Missouri, settling in Greene County, where he remained several years, afterward going to Arkansas, and from there to Dent County, Mo., dying in the latter place in 1860. His wife's death occurred in 1876, at the age of seventy-six years. Five of their ten children are now living: William D., Wiley B., Pulaski, Charles and Lettie. Wiley B. Simmons was reared on farms in Greene and Dent Counties, receiving a common-school education. He remained with his parents until he attained his majority, and in 1850 married Miss Minerva Nash, a native of Tennessee, by whom he has six children: John F., Julia Mary J., Sarah M., Charles L., Lucinda and Phoebe. After Mrs. Simmons' death, which occurred in 1881, Mr. Simmons married Mrs. Carrie Cox, a daughter of Christopher and Electa McNich. They were born, reared and married in Livingston County, N. Y., Mrs. Simmons being born in the same county. After her marriage to Mr. Cox they immigrated to Oregon County, Mo., in 1866, but were residing in Licking, Texas County, at the time of Mr. Cox's death. The following are their three children: James S., Esther E. and J. Leslie. Her union to Mr. Simmons was consummated May 1, 1884, and she has for a number of years been an earnest worker in and member of the Christian Church. August 9, 1862, Mr. Simmons enlisted in Company D, Thirty-second Missouri Infantry, enlisting at the end of four month in the Eleventh Missouri Cavalry, Company A, and after serving twenty months was discharged at Little Rock, Ark. Until 1886 he was engaged in farming, but at that date embarked in the mercantile business at Summerville, which has proved very profitable, the firm being now known as Simmons & Son. He is a member of the G. A. R.

Hon. James Riley Simmons, who figures prominently in the farming and stock raising interests of Cass Township, was born in Marshall County, Tenn., January 10, 1848, being the son of Lewis and Malinda (Gant) Simmons, both natives of North Carolina, and grandson of Lewis Simmons, Sr., who was also a native of North Carolina, and who made a home for himself and family in Tennessee at a very early date. The Simmons trace their ancestry back to a settlement made in North Carolina by a native of Ireland previous to the Revolutionary War. They were people of medium stature, of strong physique, and were rather tenacious of their religious belief, although their descendant, Lewis Simmons, Jr., was liberal in that regard and tending toward a belief in Universalism. The Gants were of Irish extraction, and made settlements in North Carolina after Revolutionary War times. They followed in general the characteristics of the Simmons. On both sides they were agricultural people, and never owned slaves. Hon. James Riley Simmons was one of three sons and two daughters born to his parents. He was reared in Texas County, where his father had located in 1855, from Marshall County, Tenn., and where his death had occurred from small-pox in 1864, after an active, useful life. The mother is still living, and makes her home with James R. The latter, as soon as grown, engaged in farming and stock raising, and has placed it on a good footing here. He pays attention to the raising and breeding of Short-horn and Durham cattle, Poland-China and Berkshire hogs, Cotswold sheep, etc. He owns 600 acres of land, 350 under cultivation. He was married in Texas County to Miss Mary E. Rust, a native of Warren County, Tenn., and the daughter of Robert and Margaret (Eddy) Rust, natives of Tennessee, who made a home in Texas County about 1854. Mr. Rust lost his life in the Confederate service, in 1863, under Gen. Price. To Mr. and Mrs. Simmons were born five sons and three daughters: Irene, Lewis, Gouley, Lee, Oscar, John R., Jr., Perley, and buried Annie, the second daughter. Mr. Simmons has given his children good educational advantages, which have not been neglected. Mrs. Simmons is a devoted member of the Christian Church. Mr. Simmons is a member of the Masonic Blue Lodge, is Past Master of both Texas and Barnes' lodges and is an Odd Fellow. He has always taken an active part in the politics of the Democratic party, and has ever advocated the principles of the same. In 1887 the people of Texas County signified their appreciation of Mr. Simmons' labors by giving him a unanimous election as their representative to the Thirty-fourth General Assembly, in which he has served on committees of Agriculture, Claims and Labor. He has always given an important support to all measures tending to the general advancement of his county and State, He has, for the past eleven years, taken an important part in the detection and bringing to justice of criminals, who have sought a haven of safety within the limits of Texas County, and has extended his work in this direction to many points far beyond the limits of this County.

Andrew J. Snelson, sheriff of Texas County, Mo., is a native of Crawford County, Mo., and was born on the 10th of June, 1849, being a son of John C. and Ann (Craig) Snelson, natives, respectively, of Ohio and Alabama. The father became a resident of Crawford County, Mo., when about fourteen years of age, but received very poor early educational advantages. He worked at blacksmithing and farming for a number of years, and then opened a general mercantile establishment, which he managed with success until the breaking out of the late war, when he gave up this work to enlist in the Confederate army, and after two months' service on detached duty, died of exposure, when in his fifty-third year. His father, Levi F. Snelson, was of Scotch descent, born in Ohio, and was a general mechanic by trade. The mother's ancestors were originally from Ireland, but at an early period became residents of Alabama. To John C. and Ann (Craig) Snelson twelve children were born, ten being yet living: Joseph N., John C., Missouri C., Levi F., Andrew J., Ann A., Samuel H., Alice E., Eldora P. and Margaret C. Andrew J. Snelson was reared on a farm in Crawford County, Mo., and gained a good education by his own exertions, although his brothers, sisters and widowed mother were mainly dependent on him for a living. He remained with and cared for them until twenty-three years of age, then was married to Miss Martha Ann Stoy, a native of Pulaski County, and seven children have blessed their union: Charley O., Effie O., William C., Dersey A., Walter M., Archie J. and Thomas J. G. Mr. Snelson resided in Crawford County, Mo., until 1881, engaged in farming, then removed to Texas County, and was connected with the firm of Farris & Co., as a partner, for two years, and was then associated with J. W. Miers and A. L. Cochrane until 1888, at which time he was elected sheriff of Texas County on the Democratic ticket. He and wife are members of the Cumberland Presbyterian Church, and he is a Mason.

Henry A. Steffens. Prominent among the enterprising and substantial citizens of Texas County stands the name of the above mentioned gentleman, who is a native of Phelps County, Mo. He was born July 4, 1865, and is the son of John H. and D. Josephine (Sutton) Steffens. The father was born in Hamburg, Germany, March 30, 1835, and died in Texas County, Mo., April 29, 1879. The mother was born in Texas County, Mo., March 15, 1846, and is now living in Houston, Mo. She is the daughter of Valentine Sutton, one of the first settlers of Texas County, Mo. John H. Steffens was a boy nine years of age when he came from Germany with his brother, and located first in New York City, and then joined the Regular Army, and served fifteen years. He then came to Missouri, locating in Texas County, where he received his final summons. He served during the late war in the First Missouri Light Artillery, and received the rank of first lieutenant. He was severely wounded at Pea Ridge by a bursting shell. While in the Regular Army he served as a Government scout on the plains, and was twice wounded by Indians. At one time he went with Jasper Walker to Nicaragua and other places. After the war he engaged in merchandising at Houston in connection with the hotel business, but shortly before his death he had retired from the mercantile business. He served Texas County two terms as county and circuit clerk and recorder, and was one of the prominent men of the county. He was a very successful business man, and attended strictly to his own affairs. He was a Democrat in politics, a Mason and Odd Fellow, and at different times represented his lodge at the Grand Lodge of Missouri. To his marriage was born one child, Henry A., the subject of this sketch. The latter received a liberal education in Houston, and in the academy at Rolla. He remained with his mother until twenty-one years of age. In 1888 he moved to his present location, where he is extensively engaged in farming and stock raising, etc. February 13, 1887, he married Miss Mollie Belew, daughter of E. A. Belew, of Texas County, Mo. She was born in Dent County, Mo., December 19, 1867, and by her marriage became the mother of one child, Herbert Clyde. Mr. Steffens is a member of the I. O. O. F., is a Democrat in politics, and Mrs. Steffens is a member of the Baptist Church.

William M. Stoy is the only surviving member of a family of four children born to the marriage of John W. Stoy and Elizabeth Price, and was born in St. Louis County, Mo., May 11, 1828. The father was born in Kentucky in May, 1801, and when four years old was taken to St. Louis, when that now popular city was only a small village. He received a good education, and growing to manhood among the French people, learned to speak that language fluently. After reaching manhood he engaged in farming, which occupation he continued the remainder of his days, and died in St. Louis County in May, 1882, in his eightieth year. His wife was a descendant of the old Price family of Kentucky, and became a resident of St. Louis County, Mo., when small, and died in 1832. Mr. Stoy afterward married Harriet Clifton, a Kentuckian, by whom he had six children: Julia A., Francis M., Martha E., Josiah, John and James. Mrs. Stoy died during the late war. Dr. Samuel Stoy, the grandfather, was a German, and a native of Philadelphia, and at an early day immigrated to Kentucky, and to Missouri in 1806, having followed his profession throughout life. His wife, Elizabeth (Kountz) Stoy, was also a native of Pennsylvania, and of German parentage. Grandfather Price was a Kentuckian, and a saddler by trade, and a participant in the Revolutionary War, and also immigrated to Missouri at an early day. Grandmother Price was a descendant of the Marshall family of Kentucky, Thomas Humphrey and Leroy Marshall being her brothers. William M. Stoy, our subject, learned the wagonmaker's trade in St. Louis, and received a common-school education. He remained in his native county until his marriage, then went to Pulaski County, but after the war closed returned to St. Louis County, there meeting his family. He then came to Texas County, entered land and remained six years, after which he returned to St. Louis, where he spent eight years working at his trade. Since that time he has resided on his present farm. January 31, 1850, he wedded Miss Eliza Neely, a daughter of David and Mary Neely, of Kentucky, who were born in 1792. Her father's parents were natives of Ireland, who immigrated to Kentucky in an early day. David Neely was a soldier in the War of 1812, was captured by the Indians, and confined in prison at Fort Wayne, subsisting eight days on raw corn. He was forced to run the gauntlet. His death occurred in Gasconade County during the late war, aged seventy-one years. His wife died in Franklin County, Mo., in 1875. Her parents, named Ball, were among the first settlers of Kentucky. Mrs. Stoy was born in St. Louis County, Mo. Five of the nine children born to her union with Mr. Stoy are living: Mary E., John E., Dorothea A., Francis M. and Charles V. Elizabeth M., William M., Walter M. and Sarah J. are deceased. The family attend the Missionary Baptist Church, and Mr. Stoy is a member of the Masonic fraternity, and a Democrat in politics. In 1862 he enlisted in Company G, Tenth Missouri Volunteer Infantry, and after serving one week was detached to work at his trade, and put in charge of the work by order of the general, an acquaintance of his. He participated in the battles of Prairie Grove and Mansfield.

Thomas G. Sturgeon. Closely associated with the farming and stock dealing interests of Texas County, Mo., stands the name of the above mentioned gentleman, who was born in Hart County, Ky., in 1854, and is the son of Isham and Delilah (Denison) Sturgeon, both natives of the same county as our subject. After marriage the parents lived in their native county until about 1851, and then came to Missouri, whence, after living in Phelps County for about three years, they returned to Kentucky. In 1856 they again returned to Missouri, locating in Texas County, and for a livelihood the father followed farming. He was a Democrat politically. During the war he moved to Arkansas, and while back looking after his farm he was killed, in 1863, by Monk's band. After some time his son, and a brother of our subject, sixteen years old, was killed. The mother spent her last days with her son, Thomas G. Sturgeon, who was one of eight children, four sons and four daughters, three of whom are now living. He was reared on the farm, and at the age of sixteen began working for himself. He had received a limited education, never attending school more than a month altogether, and as a consequence has never learned to read nor write. Since 1875 he has been dealing in stock, though he has followed farming in connection. November 26, 1882, he married Miss Mary L. Crow, a native of Texas County, Mo., born November 12, 1865, and the daughter of W. G. J. Crow. This union resulted in the birth of three children: Wilbird C. (deceased), James E. and Thomas W. Mr. Sturgeon is the owner of 150 acres of land, with about 105 under cultivation. He is one of the most extensive stock shippers in the county, and is accounted a good judge of the same. He is a Democrat in politics, and Mrs. Sturgeon is a member of the Methodist Episcopal Church.

Calvin Buchanan Taylor, M. D., a prominent practicing physician of Texas County, Mo., was born in St. Francois County, Mo., February 27, 1859, and is the son of William H. and Mary (Towery) Taylor, both natives of North Carolina, where they were united in marriage. About 1841 they moved to St. Francois County, Mo., and the following year to Texas County, where the mother died a few years later. Afterward the father married again, and died in Texas County, at the age of sixty-six. He was a farmer and wagon-maker by occupation. Both parents were members of the Baptist Church. Their family consisted of eight children, four sons and four daughters. The youngest child received a good practical education in the common schools and in the schools at Licking. He then worked on the farm and taught school until twenty-one years of age, when he began the study of medicine, under Dr. George Orr, of Licking. He took the first course of medical lectures at the College of Physicians and Surgeons at Keokuk, Iowa, and graduated from the Missouri Medical College, in St. Louis, Mo., in 1885. He then located in Licking, where he has practiced ever since. December 31, 1885, he married Mrs. Mary D. Ray, *nee* Fisher, who bore him two children, Grover (deceased) and Morgan. Dr. Taylor is a member of the Rolla District Medical Association and Texas County Medical Society. He is a Mason, being S. W., and he and wife are members of the Christian Church. He is a Democrat in politics. For three years he has run a drug store in

Licking. In June, 1885, he was appointed postmaster at Licking, and has given good satisfaction. He has been practicing for five years, and has met with success. Dr. Taylor is one of the few who have attained to the degree of his profession without aid from any one, working his own way arduously while obtaining an education.

Judge William Franklin Trail. One of the oldest and most honored citizens of Texas County, and president of the Old Settlers' Association, is Mr. Trail, who was born near Murfreesboro, Tenn., January 19, 1827, being the fourth of eight children born to the marriage of Young Trail and Catherine Rhodes, who were born in South Carolina and Georgia; Young Trail died in Hickman County, Ky., in 1851, at the age of fifty-one years, and Catherine Trail in Texas County, Mo., in 1861, aged sixty-one years. They were married in Rutherford County, Tenn., and there resided until 1840, when they immigrated to Kentucky. They were members of the Primitive Baptist Church, and the father was a school-teacher by profession and a Democrat in politics. Their son, William Franklin, was educated in Tennessee, under his father's supervision, and at the age of twenty-two years was married to Mary McMorris, and moved to Missouri, locating in Texas County, where he has since made his home. His wife was born in Graves County, Ky., and died in Kansas, having borne three children, Richard Y., a farmer of Howell County, Mo., being the only one living. March 31, 1861, Mr. Trail married Louisa Smothermon, who was born in Rutherford County, Tenn., in 1828, and four of their five children are living: Frances C., wife of J. H. Purcell, of Texas County; George W., in Colorado; Darriska R., wife of John S. Gregory, of Texas County, and Stonewall J. Christina died when two years of age. Mr. Trail came to this county with very limited means, but is now considered one of the thrifty farmers of the county. In 1865 he began merchandising at Licking, Mo., but afterward located at Raymondville, which place he had planned, and was appointed its postmaster, a position he fills at the present time. He has served a number of years as presiding judge of the county, and has also been justice of the peace and notary public, and was appointed by Gov. Hardin to select produce for the State of Missouri for the World's Fair at Vienna. He has always been a Democrat, and is a member of the Masonic fraternity. In September, 1862, he enlisted in Company K, Ninth Confederate Cavalry, and was a captain in the service for twelve months.

Chapman Walker Wade, dealer in flour and feed, lumber, fence posts and piling, was born in Bath County, Ky., February 27, 1830, and is the son of Greenberry B. and Mary (Kelso) Wade, and grandson of James Wade, who served with distinction on the staff of Gen. Anthony Wayne, as a spy and scout, in his battles with the Indians. He was a man of hardy constitution, and afterward settled on a farm in Bath County, Ky., where he died at a good old age. His son, Greenberry B., was a physician of good standing, and came to Missouri in 1839, made a settlement in Franklin County, and practiced medicine there for many years. He was a man of more than ordinary ability, and was an official of that county for many years. He was for several years presiding judge of the county court of Franklin, sheriff of that county for four years, assessor four years, and held many other honored positions. He died there at the age of seventy-eight. The boyhood days of Chapman W. Wade were spent in Franklin County, where he obtained a fair education. When in his twentieth year, or in 1850, he joined a party and went overland to California, spending four months and ten days in making the trip. He spent thirteen years in California engaged in mining and the lumber business, meeting with good success. In 1863 he returned to Franklin County, Mo., and here embarked in merchandising and farming, which he continued for several years. In 1882 he went to Springfield, Mo., spent a year there, and in 1883 he moved to Cabool, where he engaged in the flour and feed business, wholesale and retail, and has added to it the lumber and other business interests. He has built and improved largely upon city property of Cabool, and has given a cordial support to many other interests besides, with which he is individually identified. He has served as president of Cabool City Council two terms, and is a prominent citizen. He was married in Franklin County, Mo., to Miss Fannie Omohundro, a native of Virginia, whom he buried in Franklin County, in full communion with the faith of the Methodist Episcopal Church, South, leaving a daughter, Fannie W., who is now the wife of I. W. Rennick, of Franklin County, and farmer and merchant of Japan, Mo. Mr. Wade took for his second wife Miss Helen M. Cook, a lady of estimable attainments, a leader in Sabbath-school work in Cabool, and a devout member of the Methodist Episcopal Church, South. Their domestic circle has been blessed by the birth of a son and daughter, Ben C. and Julia B., both of whom are deceased.

Charles C. Ware, farmer, was born in Worcester County, Md., July 12, 1813, his parents being Hugh and Atlanta (Taylor) Ware. The father was of Scotch-Irish descent, and was born across the ocean, his early days having been spent in following the sea. He was a captain for many years, and was the owner of two ships, but died in the prime of life, in 1820, at the age of forty-five years, his wife's death occurring in 1828, at the age of forty-six. Their family consisted of nine children, the only living son, Charles C., receiving his education previous to his fourteenth year. He entered a wholesale hardware store in Philadelphia, Pa., where he remained until 1834, then came to St. Louis, and after clerking for a short time, opened a hardware store. He was unfortunate, however, in the choice of a partner, and soon closed out the business, and in 1838 came to Texas County, and opened a general mercantile store at Ellsworth. About two years later he sold out to an individual, who took the benefit of the bankrupt law, and cheated him out of all he had. Mr. Ware then engaged in hauling saw-logs, but soon became the owner of forty acres of timber land on which he settled, and engaged in clearing his land, and getting it under cultivation. He has been quite successful, notwithstanding several unfortunate business ventures, and is now the owner of about 400 acres of land, with about 100 acres under cultivation. October 15, 1840, he was married to Mrs. Elizabeth Haines, *nee* Carter, by whom he has six children: William H., Mary A., Ann E., Rhoda J., Charles H. and Martha M. Mrs. Ware died on the 23d of May, 1852, and February 1, 1855,

Mr. Ware wedded Miss Sarah Deweese, who was born in Massac County, Ill., March 7, 1837. The following are their children: Sarah F., John W., Solomon T., Minnie A., James W., Nancy C., Eunice L. J., William R., Isaac C., Frances C. and Benjamin F. Mr. Ware is a Democrat, and he and wife are members of the Methodist Episcopal Church, South.

David H. Watson, farmer and stock raiser, of Burdine Township, Section 32, was born in Fulton County, Ill., April 25, 1855, being the son of Washington and Maria (Clark) Watson, natives of Indiana and Ohio, respectively, and grandson of James Watson, who was a soldier in the War of 1812, and a commissioned officer. After the war he settled in Indiana, where he passed the remainder of his days. Washington Watson removed with his family to Nodaway County, Mo., in 1855, and there he died in 1860. His son, David H. Watson, attained his growth in Missouri and Louisiana. He followed farming there and in Iowa until 1885, when he came to Cabool, Mo., and here engaged in the hotel business. At the end of one year he abandoned this, and turned his attention to farming. He has a fine farm, situated three and a half miles northeast of Cabool, on the Houston road, and it is well watered by good natural springs from the solid rock. This farm is well adapted to stock farming and raising fruit. Mr. Watson was married in Nodaway County, Mo., to Miss Susan Roberts, a native of that county, and the daughter of Elijah Roberts, who was born in Indiana. To Mr. and Mrs. Watson has been born one child, Nathan Leslie. Mr. Watson has always affiliated with the Democratic party, and has rendered it important aid at this place on many occasions. He is a member of the A. O. U. W., and has held many official positions in that order. He is a member of the Wheel, and a prominent citizen.

Edward H. Wheeler, a prominent farmer of Texas County, Mo., was born in Monroe County, Ga., May 3, 1843, being a son of Robert M. and Henrietta (Hanson) Wheeler, who were also born in that county. They died in Humphreys County, Tenn., in 1884, and Monroe County, Ga., in 1866, respectively, the latter's birth occurring in 1805. They were members of the Methodist Episcopal Church, South, and the father resided in his native State until 1876, when he moved to Tennessee, and there spent the remainder of his days, having been a very successful farmer and stock dealer. His father, William Wheeler, was of English descent, born in Virginia, but after moving to and residing in East Tennessee for some time moved to Georgia. The children of Robert M. Wheeler are as follows: Garland F., John W., William Daniel, Edward H., Susan (deceased), Ardica A. and Nancy A. Edward H. Wheeler was educated in his native State, and March 18, 1861, enlisted in Company K, First Georgia Volunteers, Confederate States Army, and the following March joined Company K, Fifty-third Georgia Infantry, for the remainder of the war, participating in the battles of Laurel Hill, Greenbriar River, and was then with Stonewall Jackson (1862), then with Longstreet, and was in all the battles in which his army participated, the principal ones being Malvern Hill, Winchester, Second Bull Run, Harper's Ferry and Antietam, and served as a scout. Shortly before the close of the war he was captured and taken to Gen.

Butler's headquarters, thence to Hampton Roads, being a prisoner about forty days. After the cessation of hostilities he went to Washington, D. C., thence to Baltimore, then to Louisville, Ky., and afterward located in Clark County, Ind., where he resided five years. He was married there September 4, 1867, to Mary A. Watson, and soon after moved to Texas County, Mo., where he has since been one of the prominent citizens. He has always been a Democrat in politics, and in 1878 was elected presiding judge of the county, and served in this capacity for four years. He and wife are the parents of the following children: George E., Mabel (deceased), Robert T., Jesse A., Louisa, Lily F., Cora A., John M., Virdie, Grover C., and Charles (deceased). Mrs. Wheeler is a member of the Baptist Church, and was born in Wilkes County, N. C., September 10, 1849, being a daughter of Lewis and Clarissa Watson.

Charles W. White, A. M., president and proprietor of Houston Institute, was born in Randolph County, N. C., December 15, 1856, and is the son of Woodard R. and Mary A. (Wall) White, natives of Randolph County, N. C. Woodard R. White died in his native county in 1868, at the age of forty-three years. He received a good common-school education, and although starting with limited means, became a successful farmer; was also engaged in stock dealing, principally in horses, and prospered in all his undertakings. He was captain of a company of Confederate infantry of Gen. A. P. Hill's division; was in many battles during his service; was taken prisoner at Hill's surrender, and retained as such at Hart's Island until July, 1865. The White family were from Scotland, and settled either in Virginia or North Carolina. They took an important part during the Revolutionary War. The Wall family were originally from England. Mrs. Mary A. White was born in 1833, is still living, and is a member of the Methodist Episcopal Church, South, of which her husband was also a member. He was a Democrat in politics, and belonged to the Masonic fraternity. To their union were born seven children, six now living: Robert T., Thomas Logan, William F. M., Jennie, Susan E. and Charles W. The latter was reared on the farm, and graduated in the year 1877, with the degree of A. B., from Trinity College, where he received the degree of A. M. in 1880. He then taught at Trap Hill Institute as principal for five years, or until 1883, when he came to Missouri, and located at Houston. He there opened the Academy, which, by energy and perseverance, he has built to its now excellent standing. December 26, 1881, he married Miss Betty Dean, daughter of Henry and Nancy Dean, of Phelps County, Mo., and to this union have been born two children, H. Lee and Don. W. Prof. White is a member of the I. O. O. F., is Secretary, and has represented his lodge at the Grand Lodge. He is also D. D. G. M. He was elected school commissioner of Texas County in April, 1887, and re-elected in 1889; is a Democrat in his political views, and he and wife are members of the Methodist Episcopal Church, South.

James H. Wilson, one of the early settlers in Missouri, was born on the 1st of January, 1812, and is a son of Eli B. Wilson, a sketch of whom is given elsewhere. He was born in the "Buckeye State," but was reared in Kentucky, and in 1832 came to Missouri, where he was married to Lucinda Coppedge, who died in Crawford County in 1858, leaving eight children. After her death Mr. Wilson married Mrs. Nancy J. Yowell, *nee* Bradford, by whom he is the father of six children. He is an old Jacksonian Democrat, and is now residing in Phelps County, and is a member of the Primitive Baptist Church, both wives being members of the same. His fifth child, Taylor S., was born in Crawford County (now Phelps) December 24, 1849, and received the education and rearing of the average farmer's boy. He assisted his father until twenty years of age, when he began for himself, working by the month as a farm hand for nearly eight years. He now owns a good farm, with about seventy acres under cultivation. August 20, 1876, he was married to Miss Sallie E., a daughter of Col. James H. McBride. She was born in Springfield, Mo., September 15, 1856, and is the mother of the following children: James E., Albert C., David N., Dora A., Mildred J. and Lewis H. Both Mr. and Mrs. Wilson belong to the Christian Church.

Eli W. Wilson is considered one of the prosperous farmers and stock raisers of Texas County, Mo., and was born in Estill County, Ky., July 21, 1828, being a son of Eli B. and Nancy (Webber) Wilson, who were born in Virginia, and when young removed with their parents to Kentucky, and after becoming grown were married in Estill County, removing in 1832 to Missouri, and locating in La Fayette County, and about five years later in Crawford County, where the father died at about the age of fifty-five years. Subsequently the mother and younger children moved to Dent County, where the former's death occurred during the war. Mr. Wilson was a successful farmer, and during the War of 1812 belonged to that military organization known as Minute Men. He and wife were members of the Primitive Baptist Church, and he was a Whig politically. He was twice married, his first union being to a Miss Peak, who bore him four children. His second union resulted in the birth of eight children, the youngest, Eli W., being reared on a farm. His educational advantages were very poor, and after his father's death he cared for his mother as long as she lived. December 22, 1853, he married Ruth A. Early, a native of Virginia, by whom he is the father of nine children: Nancy B., Ruth A., Mary F., Eli B., Emily E., Alfred L., James R., Samuel E. and Agnes A. The mother of these children died January 9, 1870, and April 16, 1871, Mr. Wilson wedded Mrs. Louisa J. King (daughter of Gen. James H. McBride), who was the mother of two sons, James S., and William L., by her first husband. Her marriage with Mr. Wilson has resulted in the birth of six children: Minnie V., Leslie E., Lulu A., Nellie F., Elmer W. and Richard B. Since 1867 Mr. Wilson has resided in Texas County, and has held several official positions, such as sheriff, collector and assessor. He is a Democrat and Mason, and is the owner of 562 acres of land, with about 280 under cultivation.

Maj. George D. Woodward, of the firm of Woodward & Bartholomew, planing-mill and lumber manufacturers and dealers in all kinds of building material, at Cabool, is a gentleman of life-long experience in the lumber milling business. He was born in Pennsylvania, at Cherry Ridge, Wayne County, April 28, 1841, and comes of a long line of English ancestors in America, of Quaker stock. Three brothers of the name made a settlement in Pennsylvania in very early times as followers of William Penn. Maj. George D. Woodward attained his growth in Pennsylvania, and upon arriving at manhood he had completed the trade of carpenter and joiner. In 1858 he came West, and for two years was engaged in contracting and building in Chicago, Ill., leaving it to go into the war. Upon the first call for troops Mr. Woodward responded, and was the first soldier of Illinois to enroll himself upon that list of brave men who did noble service in defense of the Union, and whose acts of glory shed such a grand luster upon the history of the then young State. He rendered active and honorable service for four years and eight months, in Company H, Tenth Illinois Volunteer Infantry, serving in the ranks three months and for the balance in command, rising in regular gradations to the position of field officer, being retired at the end of the war as a veteran of his company and brevetted major, and serving in 127 battles. After the war he returned to the vocation of his choice, and for several years was engaged in milling and in the manufacture of lumber. He then left Illinois, and in 1884 went to Arkansas, where for a time he was occupied in Hot Spring County, at Donaldson, in milling. He then left this business as a traveling man and knight of the gripsack, in the interest of the lumber business, and came to this portion of Missouri in 1886 as superintendent of the interest of the Southern Missouri Land Company. He severed his connection with this company in 1888, and came to Cabool to place his present plant here, in which he takes an especial pride, and, to say the least, he is a master of his interests. The present plant has a capacity of 100,000 feet per day, and has the facilities of turning out all kinds of fine work done in this line of business. He has buried his wife, and has a son, Robert Atwater, a bright lad of eleven years, the relict of his marital union with Miss Fannie C. Atwater, whom he buried at Willow Springs, Mo. He is a Master Mason. For eight years he served on the board of aldermen of Moline, Ill., and presided over that body about four years of that time.

John D. Young, prosecuting attorney of Texas County, was born near Houston, Texas Co., Mo., January 7, 1854, his parents being William M. and Sarah J. (Fourt) Young, both natives of Missouri, he of Boone County and she of either Pulaski or Crawford County. The father died January 4, 1884, at the age of fifty-three years, but the mother is still living, and is residing on the old homestead. He was a farmer by occupation, and also was engaged in the milling business. During the late war he served six months in the State Militia, but previous to this, in 1848, he went to California, and worked in the mines until 1851, when he returned to Texas County, Mo. There were born to this marriage nine children, six now living: John D., Margaret C., wife of Jonathan Jones, a farmer of Texas County; Lynch J., Sarah, wife of John Hambleton, farmer of Texas County; Cordelia, Cora A., also married, and Charles R., now attending school at Mountain Grove. John D. Young received his education in the home schools and at Salem Academy, where he taught school four years. In 1879 he was elected collector of Texas County, and served two years. In the fall of 1881 he attended law school at Columbia, and graduated from the same in April, 1884. One year later he commenced the practice of law, and in November, 1888, he was elected prosecuting attorney of Texas County. July 28, 1887, he married Miss Cordelia A. Lynch, who was born in 1867, and who is the daughter of John T. Lynch. She is a member of the Christian Church, and he is a Republican in politics.

WRIGHT COUNTY.

James B. Adams, farmer and fruit grower of Wood Township, Wright Co., Mo., was born in Franklin County of the same State, February 25, 1831, and is a son of Burwell B. and Harriet (Allen) Adams, who were born in Charlotte County, Va., and Missouri, respectively. The father grew to manhood in his native State, and in 1818 came to Missouri, locating in St. Louis County, where he was married, but afterward moved to Franklin County, where he resided until 1844, when he was washed out by the freshet of that year, and moved to Montgomery County. Here he spent the remainder of his days, dying in 1877, at the age of eighty-three years. He was a soldier in the War of 1812. His wife died in 1856, having been a daughter of John Allen, who was born in Germany, and was a pioneer settler of America. James B. Adams is the fifth in a family of eight children, six of whom grew to maturity, and five of whom are still living, and was reared in Montgomery County, receiving a good education in the schools of Danville. After attaining a suitable age, he taught school in that county, and then went to Pike County, where he clerked in a dry goods store until about the opening of the war. He was married in that county to Miss Jane Settles, a native of Illinois, by whom he had one child, John Quincy. Ten months after their marriage the wife died, and after remaining a widower three years he married Russia Z. D. Zumwalt, who was born in St. Charles County, Mo., in 1849, to which union seven children were born, four now living: Burwell B., Minnie S., William T. and Mary L. About the opening of the war they moved to Montgomery County, where Mr. Adams enlisted in Company D, Missouri State Militia, United States Army, and served about a year and a half. He then returned home, and taught school and farmed until 1870, at which time he became a resident of Wright County, and although the war had left him without means, he set to work to retrieve his fallen fortunes, and homesteaded 100 acres of land, which he has since increased to 360 acres. He has taught school also during this time, and with the exception of about three terms has been engaged in teaching for the past twenty years. He belongs to the Masonic fraternity, and is a Republican in politics.

John B. Agee, liveryman at Mountain Grove, Mo., was born in Scott County, Va., in 1837. He is the son of Isaac and Hannah (Bounds) Agee, and grandson of William Agee, who was a native of

Virginia, and a tiller of the soil by occupation. He was one of the early settlers of Virginia, and died in Scott County of that State. While boating on the river he had the sight of one of his eyes destroyed. Isaac Agee was also a native of Virginia, and also followed agricultural pursuits. He moved to Tennessee when the subject of this sketch was a child, and followed farming in that State for several years. He passed his last days in that State. Hannah Agee was the mother of eight children, and also died in Tennessee. John B. Agee, his father and grandfather were all Union men, while all the rest of the connection were Southern sympathizers, and most of them were killed in the Confederate army. John B. Agee grew to manhood in Tennessee, and there married Miss Sarah Long, who bore him three children: William, James E., and Docia, wife of Harvey Young. Mrs. Agee died in April, 1874, and Mr. Agee afterward married Miss Elizabeth Hart, daughter of Judge Hart, of Norwood. These children were born to this union: Fred, Marion, Laura, Luie, Ada (deceased), John and Ben. Mr. Agee came to Missouri in 1860, and worked on the 'Frisco Railroad one year, but his principal occupation has been farming. He is the owner of eighty acres of land. In 1887 he moved to Mountain Grove, and has now the only livery in the place. Aside from this he owns some valuable town property. He is a Republican in politics; is a member of the Masonic fraternity, Tyler of Mountain Grove Lodge, and a member of the Methodist Episcopal Church.

Hon. Barney Amick, member of the Legislature from Wright County, Mo., was born in Randolph County, N. C., in 1836, being the son of Lorenzo D. and Cynthia (Burrow) Amick, and grandson of Peter Amick, who was a native of Holland, and immigrated to America, where he died, in Randolph County, N. C. The maternal grandfather of our subject, Barney Burrow, was a native of England; came to America when a young man, and located in Guilford County, N. C., where he was living at the breaking out of the Revolution. He was a farmer, and died at the age of about fifty-five years. The Burrows were of the Presbyterian denomination, and were very tenacious of their religious faith. Dobson Burrow, a brother of Barney Burrow, was a Revolutionary soldier, and fought on the Colonial side. Lorenzo D. Amick was also a native of Randolph County, N. C., born October 12, 1813, and was by occupation a farmer. He immigrated to Missouri in 1842, locating in what is now Webster County, and in 1848 moved to Morgan County, where he remained for ten years. He then returned to Webster County, Mo., in 1857, and located twelve miles west of where his son, Hon. Barney Amick, now resides, where he spent his declining years. He died in 1863. Mrs. Cynthia (Burrow) Amick was born in Guilford County, N. C., November 13, 1812, and died in 1886. They were the parents of eight children, of whom Barney Amick is the eldest, and only six of whom are now living. He received such an education as the common day-schools of that time afforded, but by observation and study he has fitted himself for any position, and is a well-informed man on any subject. At the age of fourteen he entered mercantile life as a clerk in a store at Versailles, Morgan Co., Mo., and remained there for five years. In 1857 he went to Webster County, Mo., and at Waldo entered business for himself by running a general mercantile store for three years. About this time the Civil War broke out, and Mr. Amick joined Company L, First Missouri Cavalry, and served three years. He was at the battles of Prairie Grove, Little Rock, and during Banks' expedition up Red River he was under fire forty days. Immediately after the war he was elected county and circuit clerk, and filled the position for eight years. In 1874 he was elected circuit clerk, and served four years in that capacity. He retired to his farm in 1878, and has since been engaged in agricultural pursuits. In 1886 he was elected a member of the Legislature, and is still the incumbent. In 1860 Mr. Amick was united in marriage to Miss Angeline Freeman, who bore him four children: John, Theodosia (deceased), Cynthia, and Cora, who died at the age of sixteen years. Mrs. Amick was born in 1837, and died in March, 1870. Mr. Amick, for two years before the war, and before his marriage, traveled as a salesman for J. C. McCoy, and was over Illinois, Arkansas and Missouri. He chose for his second wife Miss Margaret F. Freeman, and was married to her in May, 1871. Five children were born to their union: Charles, who died at the age of fourteen months; Edgar, Roscoe, Nena, and Samuel, who died in infancy. Both wives were the daughters of L. T. and Sarah L. Freeman, who were natives of Roane County, Tenn., and pioneers of Wright County, Mo., where they moved in 1843. Mr. Amick is a member of the Masonic fraternity, is a member of the G. A. R., and is a member of the Baptist Church.

James Archer, proprietor of Mountain Grove Roller Mills, was born in Leeds, Yorkshire, England, August 14, 1835, and there received his education. He followed the manufacturing of woolen goods (which his ancestors had followed for many generations before him) until 1859, when he came to America. His brother, Joseph Archer, fought through the Crimean War for England, and after peace was declared he was sent to Canada, but deserted and came to the United States. James Archer, after coming to the United States, located in Providence, R. I., first, and worked at his trade for some time, but afterward went to Philadelphia, Penn., where he worked for seven years. He was married in Philadelphia to the widow of Capt. David Potts, an Englishman, who was killed in the second battle of Bull Run, in 1862. He was commissioned first lieutenant, and acted as captain for five months. Mrs. Archer's maiden name was Elizabeth Clayton, and she was born in Manchester, England. To Mr. and Mrs. Archer were born five living children: Mary E., Fred W., Lizzie E., Ralph and Alice. Clara E. died at the age of two years. Mrs. Archer had one child by her first marriage, Eliza J., now the wife of William Crider. In 1868 James Archer went to Illinois, and remained at Shelbyville for about two years, engaged in the woolen mills. He then went to work for himself. He purchased a roll carding machine, brought it to Rolla, Mo., and before he got his carder in operation he was prevailed upon to take charge of and erect the pioneer woolen mill, west of the Mississippi River, at St. James. Mr. William James owned the Meramec Iron Works, and had the mills built to improve the town of St. James. Mr. Archer was the pioneer woolen man west of the Mississippi. He operated the mills one year, and then left work there and took charge of a wool carding machine at Hartville, which he operated for ten years. He then came to Mountain Grove, built a mill at the old town (stone process), and ran it for seven years. The railroad came through, and he then put in full roller process, and in December, 1886, commenced working, with a capacity of sixty barrels per day. He still has his carding machine running in connection with his mill proper. He ships flour South principally, and does a large shipping business, having shipped flour as far as Atlanta, Ga. Mr. Archer has taken a prominent part in building up Mountain Grove, and is one of the prominent citizens of Wright County. His mill cost $11,000. Mr. Archer was justice of the peace all the time he was at Hartville, and has also filled the same position since coming to Mountain Grove. He is a member of the board of aldermen. He is a member of both the Masonic and Odd Fellows lodges; is an Episcopalian, but affiliates with the Methodist Episcopal Church, and is an honest, upright citizen. In 1875 Mr. Archer made a trip to England to see his parents, William and Ellen (Robinson) Archer, the father being also a woolen manufacturer all his life. He was born June 10, 1806, in Leeds, England, and died suddenly shortly after his son's visit. The mother died in December of the same year. They were the parents of eleven children, six living still. The paternal grandfather, Joseph Archer, was also born in Leeds, England, and was also a manufacturer of woolen goods. The maternal grandfather, James Robinson, was a carriage manufacturer.

Jehu Barnes, a successful and energetic farmer of Wood Township, Wright Co., Mo., was born in Burke County, N. C., May 18, 1817, and is a son of Zachariah and Rosa (Anshin) Barnes, who spent their lives in their native State of North Carolina. They died when Jehu was quite young, but he was reared to manhood in North Carolina, and came to Missouri in 1838, locating in St. Francois County, where he spent some time in working by the month. He there married Elizabeth B. Parkes, who was born in 1826, also in North Carolina, and by her became the father of twelve children, nine of whom are living: William M., Ann (wife of William Conley), James T., Jehu F., John, Elizabeth J. (deceased), Wesley, Lillie (wife of Smith Abshere), Alice, Mary E. and Benjamin. Jehu Barnes went to Texas in 1848, where he spent one year, then returned home, and went to California to dig gold, coming home the following year. In 1866 he came to Wright County, and located on his present farm, which consists of 200 acres, after having given considerable to his children. He and wife are among the old and highly honored citizens of the county, and since the forming of the Republican party he has been identified with its interests. His first presidential vote was cast for Henry Clay. He is a member of the Dunkard Church. During his early settlement in Missouri game was very abundant, and many deer and other wild animals fell victims to his skill as a marksman.

Dr. D. L. Benson, of Mountain Grove, Wright Co., Mo., was born in Perry County, Ill., in 1836, and is the son of Samuel and Mary (Baker) Benson, and grandson of Daniel Benson, who was a native of Ireland, and who immigrated to America, locating in Tennessee, where he died. Samuel Benson was a native of Bedford County,

Tenn., born in 1806. When about eighteen years of age he immigrated to Boone County, Mo., and remained there for about two years, when he went to St. Louis and worked at his trade, that of a stonemason. While in St. Louis he married Miss Baker, and soon afterward moved to Perry County, Ill., where he followed agricultural pursuits the rest of his life. He died in March, 1888. Mary (Baker) Benson was born in Illinois in 1810, and died in 1886. They were the parents of thirteen children, three now living. Dr. D. L. Benson was the third child in order of birth. He grew to maturity on a farm in Illinois, and received his education in the common schools of his native county. Later he read medicine under a preceptor, but before practicing he married Miss Esther Staton, who was also born in Perry County, Ill., in 1842, and reared within half a mile of her husband. Dr. Benson practiced medicine in Perry County, Ill., and when forty years of age moved to Mountain Grove, Wright County, and his was the fifth family in the town. Here he continued the practice of his profession, and is next to the oldest practitioner in the place. He is strictly temperate in his habits, and has for many years been an elder in the Christian Church. Dr. Benson is an inveterate hunter, and every fall abandons his business and takes his annual hunt. During pioneer times he killed seventeen deer at one lick, from May until the 1st of August, and he has killed deer on what is now the public square of the town. He was surveyor of Perry County, Ill., for fourteen years, and is one of the sucessful practitioners of the town in which he now lives.

Judge George W. Calhoun, of Wright County, Mo., was born on the 24th of July, 1824, and is the eldest of ten children, four of whom are living. born to the marriage of James Calhoun and Barbara Pence. The father was born in the " Palmetto State" in 1803, and was reared on a farm in Alabama, coming to Missouri in 1844, and locating on Wolf Creek, and there died on the 10th of June, 1846. He was a second cousin of John C. Calhoun, of South Carolina. His wife was born in Madison County, Ala., about 1807, and died on the 5th of October, 1881. The paternal grandfather, William Calhoun, was born, reared and married in Ireland, and there his first wife died. He thereupon immigrated to America, locating in South Carolina, where he erected a large mill, and in time acquired considerable wealth. He married his second wife in South Carolina, and by her became the father of two children. The maternal grandfather of Judge Calhoun was a German, who emigrated to America at an early day, and took an active part in assisting the colonists to free themselves from the British yoke. He died in Tennessee about 1835. He was the eldest of seven brothers, the youngest of whom weighed 250 pounds, and all were noted for their large statures and great strength. Judge George W. Calhoun grew to manhood in Lawrence County, Tenn., and was there married to Rebecca Sanders, who was born in Tennessee in 1820, her father having been a prosperous farmer and blacksmith of Lawrenceburg. They had eleven children: Henry, who died at the age of twenty-six years; James F., Louisa J., wife of Rev. Jackson Barnett; Elizabeth, wife of Rev. Thomas Moody; William, Mary A., wife of R. Johnson; Barbara, wife of Rev. Joseph Young; John;

Martha L., wife of Gen. J. Strunks; Joseph, one of the popular local educators of Wright County, and Brantley S. Judge Calhoun located on a farm on Wolf Creek in 1844, and was there engaged in farming for forty-five years. In 1880 he was elected on the Republican ticket as judge of Wright County, being re-elected in 1882 for two more years. He owns a valuable farm of 160 acres in Douglas County and two lots in Norwood. In 1864 he enlisted in Company G of the Sixteenth Missouri Cavalry, having previously belonged to both the Home and State Militia, and served until the close of the war. For the past thirty-five years he has been a member of the Free Will Baptist Church, and throughout his career has always supported the cause of temperance.

James A. Claxton, farmer and stock raiser of Gasconade Township, Wright Co., Mo., was born in Bedford County, Tenn., in 1826; son of James and Temperance (Ratcliff) Claxton, and a grandson on the mother's side of Joshua Ratcliff, who was a soldier in the Revolutionary war, where he was wounded, and when he died, at the age of ninety, the scar was to be seen upon his breast. The paternal grandfather was a native of North Carolina, and one of the first settlers of Tennessee. He was of Dutch descent, and lived to be eighty years of age. James Claxton, father of our subject, was born on the road from North Carolina to Tennessee in 1801, and grew to manhood in the last named State, where he was married, and where he followed farming until the fall of 1853. He then moved to Missouri, located in Greene County, and in 1858 came to Wright County, Mo., where he died on the 6th of October, 1871; he was the owner of 600 acres of land, and was in quite comfortable circumstances. He was allowed a pension for services rendered under Jackson in the Black Hawk War, but did not draw it. Temperance (Ratcliff) Claxton was a native of North Carolina, and died in Missouri November 23, 1877. They were the parents of eleven children, James A. Claxton being the fourth child in order of birth. He was reared on a farm in Tennessee, and married Miss Eliza Jane Harrison, daughter of Edward Cannon and Eliza Jane (McClane) Harrison, who were married in Bedford County, Tenn. The former, a resident of Northern Missouri, was born in North Carolina in 1799; his wife in South Carolina in 1800. Mrs. Claxton bore her husband eleven children, nine now living: James Cannon, born January 20, 1849; William Calvin, June 16, 1853; Newton Cyrus, February 15, 1855; Dudley C., May 12, 1857; Margaret A., February 26, 1859; Henry C., April 21, 1861; Hepsey B., August 12, 1864; John R., February 27, 1870, and Edward D., December 28, 1871. Those deceased are: Manday M., born September 21, 1851, died December 24, 1863, and Jasper, born January 16, 1863, died March 27, 1863. James A. Claxton came to Missouri in the fall of 1852, and remained in Pulaski County one year, in Greene County five years, and then moved east of his present farm, where he remained for some time before he moved on the farm where he now resides. He has been on this farm for twenty-one years, and has 698 acres of good land. During the Civil War he was in the State Militia. He is a Democrat in his political views, and a good citizen. All his children are married with the exception of two.

Samuel Coday. Prominent among the successful and enterprising farmers and stock raisers of Gasconade Township stands the name of Mr. Coday, who was born in Kentucky in 1818, and who is one of the old and much esteemed citizens of the county. He is the son of John and Betsey (Summers) Coday. John Coday was born in Virginia, and was one of the pioneers of Kentucky. He moved from that State to Indiana, and came to Missouri about 1835, locating on the farm where his son Samuel is now residing. There he died at an advanced age. Mrs. Betsey (Summers) Coday is also deceased. They were the parents of eight children, five now living. The maternal grandfather was a miller by occupation, and was waylaid and shot. The maternal grandmother died in Wright County at a very great age. Samuel Coday grew to manhood in Wright County, and married Miss Mary J. Binkley, who bore him nine children: Samantha, wife of Samuel Adams, Henry, Lihew, Isaac, Emily E., James, Nancy, Parthina, and Martha, wife of F. Shaver. Mr. Coday can relate many interesting anecdotes relative to pioneer times, and has helped kill many bear. He and a party of two others entered a cave in Ozark Mountains, where they shot and wounded a bear. One of their dogs was killed and another was badly used up by the infuriated animal, which proceeded to the mouth of the cave, sat down and kept the hunters there all night. Panthers, deer and other wild animals were plentiful. Mr. Coday has about 300 acres of good land, and is in very comfortable circumstances. One of his sons is living on the farm. Mr. Coday is a member of the Agricultural Wheel.

Henry Coday, druggist at Mansfield, Mo., and a native of Wright County, was born June 2, 1848, his parents being Samuel and Mary J. (Binkley) Coday. [See sketch of Samuel Coday.] He was reared on the farm on which his father is at present residing, and attended school in Hartville for some time after he was grown. From 1873 to 1875 he was in St. Louis and Lebanon, Mo., but since the latter date has resided almost constantly in Wright County. Previous to that time, however, he traveled in Missouri, Arkansas, Texas, Illinois and Kansas, and was in business in Hartville until the fall of 1881, since which time he has been engaged in selling drugs in Mansfield, and has built up a large and lucrative trade. His stock is valued at from $1,200 to $1,500, and he has one of the handsomest residences in Mansfield, all of which he has earned by his own industry and good management. In 1883 he was married to Miss Lizzie Chapman, who was born in Crawford County, Mo., in 1859, and by her he is the father of two children, Winfield Scott and Blanche. Mr. Coday is a Democrat in his political views.

James H. B. Cope, a farmer of Elk Creek Township, Wright Co., Mo., was born in Middle Tennessee in 1831, being the son of Stephen and Comfort (Bolin) Cope. The paternal grandfather was born in one of the Carolinas, was a farmer and a member of the Baptist Church. He was a pioneer settler of Warren County, Tenn., was the father of four children, and died in Tennessee at the age of ninety-eight years. Stephen Cope was born in Warren County, Tenn., in 1803, and was a farmer by occupation. He was always a Democrat in his political views, and was constable in Warren County for six years. He was also justice of the peace for twelve years, and died in 1887. His wife, Comfort Cope, was also a native of Warren County, Tenn., and is still living. They were the parents of sixteen children, James H. B. Cope being the seventh in order of birth. He grew to manhood in Warren and Grundy Counties, Tenn., where he received a fair education in the common schools. At the age of twenty-six he married Miss Minerva J. Roberts, a native of Tennessee, born in 1835 and died in 1863. They became the parents of four children: William, who died at the age of two years; Sarah A., died at the age of twenty-three years, was married and left one child; James T., and Elizabeth, who died at the age of one year. In 1865 Mr. Cope married Mrs. (Nichols) Young, and the fruits of this union were seven children: Fannie E., Alonzo, James Newton, Cinda, Flora, John and Harvey. Mrs. Cope was the mother of two children by her former marriage: A. L. and Sarah J. Mr. Cope immigrated to Missouri in 1857, locating in Wright County, and has made his home here ever since, with the exception of a short time during the war, when he refugeed to Phelps County. He never took up arms against the Union, but his sympathies were with the South. He is a Democrat in politics, and a member of the Wheel. The maternal grandfather, Lewis Bolin, lived in Warren County, Tenn. He was a hero of the War of 1812, and the first man to enter the British fort at the battle of New Orleans. He had fourteen holes shot through his coat as he went in. He witnessed the death of Packenham and the general withdrawal of the British from American soil. He afterward served all through the Texas war, and when it closed he wrote to his family and said: "Come to Texas!" for he had enough land for all his children. He was never heard from afterward. He was a great traveler, and had been all over the Union.

J. A. Cover, dealer in saddles, harness, etc., at Mountain Grove, Wright County, Mo., was born in Union County, Ill., in 1862, the son of Alson and Melissa (Sams) Cover. Alson Cover was probably a native of Pennsylvania, and by trade a plasterer, but he also followed farming and merchandising. He died in Johnsboro, Ill., at the age of forty-nine years, when the subject of this sketch was seven years of age. Melissa (Sams) Cover died when her son, J. A. Cover, was fourteen years of age. She was of English extraction and the Covers were of German origin. J. A. Cover was one of eight children born to his parents. After the death of his mother he went to Dent County, Mo., and then lived with his sister, Mrs. Pendergrass, for two years, meanwhile attending school. He then went to Illinois, and in one and a half years returned to Missouri, where he served an apprenticeship to the saddler's trade at Salem, Dent County, Mo., for three years. He then came to Mountain Grove in 1883, built his present house and engaged in his present business. He is a young man of good business qualifications, and is respected by all. His average sales equal about $3,000 per year, and aside from this he is partner in the only furniture and undertaker's establishment in the town. This is run by his brother, S. H. Cover. J. A. Cover was married in 1885 to Miss Ada A. Hayes, a native of Ohio, born in 1865. She was taken to Missouri at the age of twelve years, and supplemented her common-school education with a course at a graded school in Dent County, Mo. She has been a teacher in the public schools of Wright and Texas Counties, and also worked in the post-office at Mountain Grove for many years. She and her mother carried on the post-office at that place for sixteen years. She is a member of the Old School Presbyterian Church. Mr. Cover is a Democrat in his political views.

S. H. Cover, proprietor of furniture and undertaker establishment at Mountain Grove, Mo., was born in Illinois January 20, 1865. He attained his growth in his native State and in Missouri, finishing an education received in the common schools by a course in the graded schools under Prof. William Lynch, and afterward worked at various pursuits until 1888, when he came to Mountain Grove and engaged in his present business. He carries a stock valued at $2,000, and is a wide-awake, thorough-going business man. In his political views he affiliates with the Democratic party.

Argus Cox, attorney at law, and prosecuting attorney of Wright County, Mo., was born in Van Buren County, Iowa, in 1856, and is the son of Randolph and Sarah (McIntosh) Cox. The father was born in Indiana, and is a farmer by occupation. He was reared in Illinois, being taken there when a child, but afterward moved into Iowa, where he married Miss Sarah McIntosh, and became the father of nine children. He moved to Wright County, Mo., in 1884, and is now located at Mountain Grove. His wife is also living. Argus Cox was the fourth child in the order of birth. He attained his growth in Van Buren County, Iowa, receiving a good literary education, and was a graduate from the law department of the State University in 1882. He then entered the law office of Sloanwork & Brown, Keosauqua, Iowa, where he remained for some time. Previous to his graduating in law he had taught school, being principal of the graded school at Milton, and he now returned to that profession. He first began the practice of law at Greenfield, Adair Co., Iowa, but went from there to Jasper County, Mo., remaining there for some time, and then moved to Mountain Grove, Wright County, Mo., in the spring of 1884, where he engaged in the practice of law. In 1886 he was elected prosecuting attorney of Wright County, and is one of the promising young men of the county. He is a Republican in politics, is a member of the I. O. O. F., and is a member of the Methodist Episcopal Church. He choose for his companion in life Miss Emma E. Starr, who was born in Wisconsin in 1862. They have one child, Roy.

E. H. Davis, a prominent farmer and stockman of Wright County, Mo., is a Tennesseean, born in 1850, and is a son of Jesse P. and Lucinda H. (Pibas) Davis, the former being born in Bedford County, Tenn., in 1818. He grew to manhood and was married in that county, and in 1844 immigrated to Missouri, but shortly after returned to Tennessee, where he resided until 1853, at which time he came back to Missouri, and located on the farm where he now lives. During the Civil War he was a member of the Forty-fourth Missouri Infantry, United States Army, and did honorable and active service. Miss Pibas was his second wife, and by him became the mother of nine children: K. M., E. H., J. B., T. J., R. I., J. L., and triplets, all of whom lived to be fourteen months old, and P. S. grew to manhood. E. H. Davis grew to manhood in Wright County, and attended the common schools. At the age of eighteen years he was married to Miss Sarah M. Randolph, who was born in Tennessee in 1847, and the following are the names of the children born to their union: V. B., N. I., J. T., M. E., W. A., J. R., and J. G., who died at the age of seven months. Immediately after his marriage Mr. Davis settled down to farming and trading in stock, at which he has been quite successful, and is now the owner of 200 acres of valuable land in Wright County. His wife is a daughter of G. R. Randolph, of Tennessee, who became a resident of Laclede County, Mo., in 1859, and he is one of the progressive and stirring men of the county, and makes every effort to keep up with the times. He inherits his stability and perseverance from his Dutch ancestors, and is a leading man in the business circles of the county. He votes the Democratic ticket, and is a member of the A. F. & A. M. and the Agricultural Wheel, and he and wife are members of the Christian Church. His grandfather was probably a native of North Carolina, and one of the family characteristics is their small stature.

Rev. W. S. Dennis was born in Roane County, Tenn., in 1831, and is a son of Joseph and Mary (Brown) Dennis, who were born in Tennessee in 1802 and 1806, and died in Wright County, Mo., in 1880 and 1878, respectively. They became residents of Missouri in 1859, and were the parents of fourteen children, eleven of whom are living at the present time. The paternal grandparents, Joseph and Mrs. (Beason) Dennis, were born in Tennessee, and became the parents of nine children. The grandfather died at the age of eighty years. Edward Brown, the maternal grandfather, was born in Tennessee, and lived in McMinn County, where he was accidentally killed. He was a hatter by trade. His wife was Miss Dyer, and lived to the extreme old age of one hundred and one years. Gideon Dennis, an uncle of Rev. W. S. Dennis, was a Baptist minister, and a strong Union man during the late war. While out hunting he was caught by the rebels and taken to Libby Prison, where he died of starvation. Our subject grew to manhood and was married in Tennessee, the latter event taking place October 9, 1851, to Miss Mary Burke, who was born October 11, 1835. The following are their children: Martha L., wife of M. M. Cooley; William Henry, Joseph, Theodocia, John A., Milton E. and Roetta. Those deceased are: Phoebe, aged twenty-six years, wife of M. G. Hensley; Elizabeth, aged twenty years; Sarah E., aged twenty years, blind from the time she was three years old; Jason E., died in childhood; Cynthia C., at the age of two years, and two infants. The mother of these children died September 14, 1883, and Mr. Dennis afterward married, December 25, 1884, Miss Nancy Irwin, who was born in East Tennessee in 1859. They have three children: Allie May, Ezra S., Della A., and one that died in infancy. Since 1856 Mr. Dennis has resided in Missouri, having been a resident of Camden County until 1867. Since January of that year he has lived in Wright County. He was ordained a minister of the Baptist Church October 9, 1867, and has been a local preacher ever since that time. He owns an excellent farm of 309 acres, and is in a prosperous condition financially. He is a Master Mason, a Republican in politics, and is a member of the G. A. R., having served in the Union army in the Light Artillery during the late war, and received his discharge November 20, 1865.

G. M. Dennis, farmer and stock raiser of Wolf Creek, Wright Co., Mo., was born in Roane County, Tenn., in 1838, and is a son of Joseph and Mary (Brown) Dennis. The father was born in Grainger County, Tenn., in 1799, and was a farmer by occupation. He came to Missouri in the fall of 1868, and located in Wright County, where he died in 1882. His wife was born in the same county as himself in 1803, and also died in Wright County, Mo., in 1878. The paternal grandparents, Joseph and Betsey (Beesley) Dennis, were born in North Carolina, and died in Tennessee. Grandfather Brown was also born in North Carolina, was a hatter by trade, and was killed by accident. G. M. Dennis is one of six surviving sons in a family of twelve children, and was born, reared and married in Tennessee. At the breaking out of the war he joined Company A, Fifth Tennessee, Federal troops, Army of the Cumberland, and served three years and two months. He was quite severely wounded at one time, for which he receives a pension of $2 per month. Five of his brothers were in the Federal service, and all are still living. G. M. Dennis was married in Tennessee to Sarah Crockett, a native of that State, born October 27, 1844, and by her has a family of eight children: William Henry, is a school-teacher, and is attending Mountain Grove Academy; James L., Joseph L., Sarah F., Albert M. and Bertie M. Tennessee L. and John A. are deceased. Mr. Dennis has a valuable farm of 200 acres, and is one of the industrious and enterprising farmers of the county. He is a Republican, a member of the G. A. R., and belongs to the Missionary Baptist Church. Mrs. Dennis is a daughter of John and Nancy (Patty) Crockett, the father being a native of Tennessee. Her paternal grandmother was a Rooker, whose father was stolen from England and brought to America. He was the only child of a man worth millions of dollars, but on his death no trace of his money was found.

George M. Douglas, proprietor of a blacksmith and wagon repair shop at Mountain Grove, Wright County, Mo., was born in Gasconade County, of the same State, July 23, 1847, the son of W. R. and Elizabeth (Watton) Douglas. W. R. Douglas was born in Missouri in 1818, probably in St. Louis County, and was a successful tiller of the soil. He immigrated to Gasconade County, Mo., and from there to Texas County, where he died in 1882. He was a volunteer to the Mormon War. His wife, Elizabeth (Watton) Douglas, was the mother of four children, and died when the subject of this sketch was quite small. He grew to manhood in Gasconade County, Mo., and at the age of eighteen moved with his father to Texas County, where he lived until 1876. He was married in Texas County to Miss Sarah C. Shorns, who was born in Texas County, Mo., in 1855, and who, by her marriage, became the mother of these children: Elizabeth L., James A., W. E., Benjamin B., Hattie E. and Charley E. One child they lost in infancy. Mrs. Douglas died in 1884, and Mr. Douglas took for his second wife Miss Maggie A. Ferguson, who was born in Missouri in 1858. To this union were born two children, one now living, Lyle

E. The other child died in infancy. Mr. Douglas learned the blacksmith's trade in Texas County, and followed this business in that county for about two years. In 1876 he came to Wright County, where he engaged in the blacksmith and wagon repairing business. This he has followed ever since, with the exception of one year, when he bought and ran a planer. He owns his shop and residence in Mountain Grove, and is a first-class citizen. He does about $1,000 worth of business per year. He is a Republican in politics, and is a member of the Baptist Church.

F. W. Duggan, attorney at law at Mountain Grove, Wright Co., Mo., and a son of J. F. M. and Sarah (Camp) Duggan, was born in McMinn County, E. Tenn., October 31, 1857. The father was born in East Tennessee, and was a Methodist Episcopal circuit rider for about thirty-two years. He was a leading preacher in the Methodist Church, and followed his ministerial duties all his life. The mother, Mrs. Sarah (Camp) Duggan, was a native of Virginia. They were the parents of five children, three now living. Mrs. Duggan died in 1875, and J. F. M. Duggan was again married, this wife bearing him one child. The paternal grandfather of the subject of this sketch, John Duggan, was probably a native of Virginia, and afterward located in Blount County, Tenn. He was a soldier in the War of 1812, and died in Tennessee. The great-grandfather Duggan was a native of Ireland, and immigrated to America. The maternal grandfather, W. B. Camp, was a cousin of Gen. Scott, and was a native of Virginia. He was in the War of 1812, and every subsequent war in which the United States has been engaged. At the age of seventy-four years he entered the Federal army, and died of small-pox at Nashville, Tenn., while in the service of the United States army. The maternal grandmother is still alive, and resides in Monroe County, Tenn. She still enjoys good health. The maternal great-grandfather and his brother immigrated from Europe at the time of the Revolutionary War, and disputed on the political issue of the day, the great-grandfather joining the American side and his brother the English side. The brother changed his name to Campbell, so that the Duggan family might never know what became of him, so great was the disgrace in joining the American cause, he thought. The maternal grandmother, spoken of above, and whose name was Elizabeth (Anthony) Camp, was in all probability a native of Virginia, and was related to Pocahontas. She was a pioneer of Tennessee. Her husband, W. B. Camp, was a strong Abolitionist, and got into difficulty with his father-in-law, because the latter wanted to present his daughter, Mrs. Camp, with a slave. Mr. Camp took his wife with him, went to Tennessee, and never let her parents know aught of his whereabouts. F. W. Duggan grew to manhood in his native State, and received a good collegiate education in McMinn County, Tenn. He read law for some time under a preceptor, and in 1885 moved to Missouri, and located in Douglas County, where he followed the profession of teaching for one year. He then came to Mountain Grove, Mo., and was admitted to the Wright County bar before Judge Wallace. He has a good practice at this place, and aside from this he is a partner in the city drug store of Duggan & Rall, this being one of the oldest drug houses in the place, though in new hands now. Mr. Duggan was married in Tennessee to Miss Mintie A. Cantrell, who was born in McMinn County, Tenn., in 1858. and who bore him four children: Chrisie, Myrtle, Harrison DeWitt and Frankie. The Cantrells were among the pioneers of Tennessee, and among the wealthiest families. Mrs. Duggan is a member of the Baptist Church. Mr. Duggan is a member of the I. O. O. F., and politically is a Republican.

Thomas Duncan, blacksmith, of Hartville, Mo., was born in East Tennessee October 20, 1839, being the son of Robert and Pollie (Duncan) Duncan, and was reared under the reign of slavery, but was a single man when the emancipation proclamation was issued. He then came to Missouri, and he and Anderson Hogue and Hugh White were the first colored men who located in Wright County. Thomas Duncan learned the trade of blacksmith in Tennessee, and in 1872 he located in Hartville, and purchased an outfit, and has been engaged in the business there ever since. Although several blacksmiths have come and gone, he does as much as $1,000 worth of business here in one year. He owns his residence in Hartville, also his shop, and aside from this is the owner of 120 acres of land. He was married to Miss Ellen Vernon, daughter of Lill Vernon, who is the son of Col. Vernon, of Laclede County, Mo., she having been the daughter of a slave in that family. By her marriage with Mr. Duncan she became the mother of five living children: Mary, Clarence, Flora, Toby and Clara. Mr. Duncan is a Republican in his political views, and is a much esteemed citizen. He learned to read and write during the war. His nephew, Prof. Solomon Gilliam, was born in Marion County, Tenn., September 17, 1858, his parents being Solomon, Sr., and Margaret (Duncan) Gilliam. Solomon Gilliam was also a native of Tennessee, and died there before the emancipation. He was a slave in the family of Dr. Gilliam, of Jasper, Tenn. Margaret Duncan became the mother of four children, of whom Prof. Solomon Gilliam is the youngest and the only one now living. Margaret Gilliam died in Tennessee October 3. 1864, and the subject of this sketch was left to the care of grandparents and uncles, and remained with them in Tennessee until January, 1880, when he joined his uncle, Thomas Duncan. He farmed one season here, and then concluded to supplement his common-school education received in Tennessee with a course at college, and with that intention in view went to Lincoln Institute, Jefferson City, Mo., and took the degree of B. S. D. from that institution in 1888. He has taught school for five years, and at intervals during those years he has attended school. He is a man of large vocal capacity, and is one of the best educated men of his race in South Central Missouri. He is a Republican politically.

W. C. Ellis, of the drug firm of Ellis & Lee, at Mountain Grove, Wright Co., Mo., was born in that county and State in 1857, and is the son of John and Arabella (Lee) Ellis. John Ellis was born in Tennessee, and came to Missouri when a young man. He first located in Wright County, and then moved to Arkansas, about 1861. He died in the Confederate army. Mrs. Arabella (Lee) Ellis is still living, and is a resident of Wright County. She is a sister of J. A. Lee, a member of the firm of Ellis & Lee. She became the mother of ten children. The paternal grandfather was a native of Tennessee, and immigrated to Wright County, Mo., where he passed the remainder of his days. The maternal grandfather was also a native of Tennessee, but moved to Missouri. W. C. Ellis grew to manhood in his native county, and was educated at Mountain Grove Academy. In 1876 he began as clerk in a dry goods store, and there remained until August, 1881, when he helped organize the firm of Ellis & Lee. He was married January 15, 1882, to Miss Lizzie Stephens, who was born in Texas County, Mo., in 1857. She was a student at Mountain Grove Academy for about three years, and later became a teacher in the public schools of Texas and Wright Counties. She acquired a good education and is a lady of much personal culture. The result of this union was the birth of five children: Fridda, Tommie, Lyle W. and two infants. Mr. Ellis is a member of the I. O. O. F., is a Democrat in politics, and is a prominent, enterprising citizen. Mrs. Ellis died September 17, 1888.

Paul Ellis, dealer in oak railroad ties, fence-posts and hard-wood lumber, and also general merchant at Cedar Gap, Wright Co., Mo., was born in Waldo, Webster County, Mo., September 28, 1858, and was there reared to manhood. He received his education in Mountain Dale Seminary, and began earning his own living, by teaching a district school, at the age of seventeen years. He became one of the popular educators of Webster and Wright Counties, but at the end of six years gave up this calling to become a mercantile clerk. He first engaged in mercantile pursuits on his own account at Duncan, but three months afterward came to Cedar Gap, where he engaged in his present business four years later. In 1888 he checked by the Greene County Bank $23,000, shipping the same year 517 car loads of lumber, and in February, 1889, shipped 147 car loads. Mr. Ellis has been remarkably successful, as he began business with nothing, and is now considered one of the prosperous young business men of the county. When twenty-four years old he was married to Miss Mollie Pyatt, a native of Wright County, Mo., born in 1862, by whom he became the father of three children: Jesse, living, and Victoria and Victor, deceased. Mr. Ellis is a Republican, a Mason, and a son of J. W. Ellis, who was born in North Carolina, and there married Rachel Mingus. He was a carpenter by trade, and in 1852 came to Missouri, enlisting from this State in the Confederate army, and was killed, while on his way home, by a band of robbers. His wife, who was born in North Carolina, is still living, and resides in Duncan. Her mother is also living. Mrs. Paul Ellis is a daughter of Judge Joseph and Jane (Allen) Pyatt, who were also natives of North Carolina, and were there reared and married. After coming to Missouri Mr. Pyatt was elected judge of the Wright County Court, and was a farmer and school-teacher by occupation. He was a Federal soldier in the late war.

Andrew J. Farmer, postmaster of Hartville, Wright Co., Mo., is a native of Anderson County, Tenn., born October 3, 1863, his parents being Henry and Erie (Davidson) Farmer. Henry Farmer was born in Tennessee July 17, 1818, and was a merchant by occupation. He was married in his native State, and became the father of five living children: James H., Arthur F., Alexander B., Robert G. and Andrew J. One child, Moses, died when quite young. Erie (Davidson) Farmer was born in Tennessee September 12, 1831, and came to Wright County, Mo., in 1874. Here they still remain, and are at present residents of Hartville. They own a house and lot, and are much respected citizens. Their son, Andrew J., was reared in Wright County, and there also received his education. December 26, 1881, he became deputy postmaster at Hartville, and served four years, when under Grover Cleveland's administration he became postmaster. His brother, Robert Farmer, has acted as his deputy for more than two years. He was born September 18, 1860. Andrew Farmer is one of the industrious and sober young men of whom Wright County may justly be proud, and that he has made an efficient and trustworthy postmaster is recognized by all. He is a Democrat in his political views, and is a promising young man.

James Forrest, proprietor of the Forrest Hotel at Hartville, Mo., and a genial, pleasant gentleman, was born in Greene County, Ark., February 3, 1835, being the son of John and Catherine (Sanders) Forrest, both natives of Tennessee. The father was born in 1811, and was one of the pioneers of Wright County, Mo. He was married in Greene County, Ark., and lived there for about thirteen years, when he came to Wright County, October 15, 1847. He was a farmer by occupation, and died in the year 1861. To his marriage were born eleven children, four now living, James being the eldest. Catherine Forrest was born in 1813 and died in 1882. The paternal grandfather, James Forrest, moved from North Carolina to Tennessee, and was a farmer by occupation. He died in Tennessee in 1861. The maternal grandfather and grandmother came to Missouri from Tennessee, and died in Wright County, the latter at the age of over one hundred years. James Forrest (subject) was educated in the common schools and at Mountain Grove. He spent the years 1859 and 1860 in Texas, after which he returned to Missouri, and in 1863 went to Illinois, where he spent over a year. He returned to Wright County, Mo., in 1864, and on September 29 of that year he was united in marriage to Miss Martha Ritchey, who was born in Indiana in 1840, and who bore him six children: Mary, wife of Edward Templeton; John W., Norah, Manda and Thula. William B. died when an infant. Previous to his marriage Mr. Forrest received the appointment of deputy county circuit clerk, and held this position until January, 1867. In the fall of 1866 he was elected judge of the probate court and *ex-officio* presiding judge of county court, holding the position four years, when he was appointed and served nine months more. In 1874 he was elected clerk of the county court, and was re-elected in 1878. After this he was again appointed judge of probate court and served his time out. He then retired, after sixteen years and five months of public service. After serving out his long period of clerkship he retired to his farm, and devoted five years to agricultural pursuits. He has 300 acres of land, and besides this he has town property. He has for the last three years been keeping hotel in connection with his farming interest. In his political views Mr. Forrest has always been an uncompromising Democrat; has stumped the county for the Democracy, and, notwithstanding the vast

Republican majority, has held his share of public trusts. He is a member of the Methodist Episcopal Church, and a prominent citizen.

F. B. Fuson, M. D., of Mansfield, Mo., was born in Wayne County, Tenn., in 1859, and is a son of John and Sophronia (Gallegly) Fuson, both of whom were born in Tennessee, the former's birth occurring in 1823 and the latter's in 1833. A short time previous to the breaking out of the Rebellion they moved to Illinois, and after serving for about three months in the Federal army, he engaged in farming, and in 1870 came to Wright County, but is now a resident of Webster County, and is engaged in the hardware business. F. B. Fuson is the third of their five children, and was educated in Missouri, and when starting out in life for himself commenced as a drug clerk, afterward embarking in the business on his own responsibility in Hartville, where he remained several years. He graduated from the Missouri Medical College at St. Louis in 1886, as an M. D., and soon after located in Mansfield, where he immediately entered upon the practice of his profession, and is considered one of the rising young physicians of the county. He is progressive and enterprising, and is taking steps to have a medical society organized in the county. He is a Master Mason, and a member of the A. F. & A. M. He was married to Miss Stella Johnson, of Kansas City, Mo., and by her is the father of one child, Gertrude. The name Fuson is of Welsh origin, but the paternal grandfather was born in Virginia, and was an early immigrant to Tennessee. The Galleglys are of Scotch-Irish lineage.

Hon. Dixon F. Gourley, member of the Legislature from Wright County, and minister of the Methodist Episcopal Church, South, was born in East Tennessee in 1849, and is the son of S. H. and Deliza (Carroll) Gourley. The paternal grandfather was a tiller of the soil, and lived in Tennessee He entered the Confederate army at the age of sixty-three, and died in Tennessee after peace was declared. The Gourley family were square-built, long-lived people. The maternal grandmother, who was a native of North Carolina, died at the age of eighty-nine years. S. H. Gourley, who was born in Tennessee about 1828, was married in that State, and there carried on mercantile pursuits until about 1856, when he came to Missouri and located in Phelps County. He is now residing in Laclede County. His wife died in 1882, and was the mother of eleven children, eight of whom are now living. S. H. Gourley enlisted for the Mexican War, but peace was declared before he entered the service. Hon. Dixon F. Gourley grew to years of maturity on a farm in Phelps County, Mo., and received his education in Springdale Academy of that county. He was married in Maries County to Miss Hester A. Matlock, a native of Crawford County, Mo., and this union resulted in the birth of these children: Mary E., Adam, Etta, Dixon E., Rebecca O., Elbert W. and Nancy R. Those deceased were George, an infant, and Emil, who also died in infancy. Mr. Gourley came to Wright County in 1884, and has been an active preacher in the Methodist Episcopal Church for eighteen years in Phelps, Maries, Stoddard, Laclede and Wright Counties. He was elected to represent Wright County in the Legislature in November, 1888, on the Union Labor Ticket. Mr. Gourley owns 430 acres of land, with fifty-five acres in Laclede County.

Dr. Samuel F. Grubb, now a farmer of Hart Township, Wright Co., Mo., was born in Wythe County, Va., in 1826, the son of Henry and Mary (Woolford) Grubb, and grandson of John Grubb, who was also a native of Wythe County, Va., and born back in the eighteenth century. The paternal great-grandfather came from Switzerland, and settled near Wytheville, Va. Henry Grubb was born in Wythe County, Va., in 1799, was reared on a farm owned by his father, and he there followed agricultural pursuits all his life. He was captain of the State Militia in Virginia, and died in 1873. Mary (Woolford) Grubb died in 1882, at the age of seventy-nine or eighty years. She was the mother of thirteen children, of whom Dr. Samuel F. Grubb is the fifth. He attained his growth in his native county, and studied and practiced dentistry under Dr. John Welsh, an expert in his profession. Dr. Grubb became a partner with him, and soon became one of the most popular dentists in the country. He practiced in Wythe and Grayson Counties for more than thirty years. He moved to Wright County, Mo., in 1887, and purchased 300 acres of land, on which he is now residing. He has had a few difficult cases since coming to Missouri, but has not attended to the dental business entirely. He expects, as soon as he can, to go to work here again. He was married in North Carolina to Miss Margaret Huddle, who was born in Wythe County, Va. They ran away, were married in North Carolina, and to their union were born two children, Nancy and Mary E. Dr. Grubb is a Republican in politics, and is an excellent citizen. His set of dental instruments are as good as can be found in the United States, and cost him $450 in gold. The handles of all his instruments are made of cameo, ivory and pearl, with gold bands.

R. H. Hanson, M. D. (homœopathist), of Hartville, Mo., was born in New York in 1843, and is the son of Cyrus and Lucinda (Hill) Hanson, and the maternal grandson of Richard and Betsey (Hill) Hill, who reared a family of twelve children. Cyrus Hanson was a native of New Hampshire, a farmer, and immigrated to New York, where he died. His wife, Mrs. Lucinda (Hill) Hanson, was born in Vermont, and became the mother of eight children, six now living. She is still living, and is residing in Minnesota. Of this family R. H. Hanson is the eldest. He remained and assisted his father on the farm until over twenty years of age, and his education was received principally by self study at home. He commenced studying for the ministry early in life, and also studied medicine. He first practiced medicine in Southwest and Central Missouri, and commenced his ministerial work at Ash Grove Circuit, where he remained for twelve years, and during that time he was also engaged in the practice of medicine. To this he has devoted his time entirely for the last three years. He was married in Missouri to Miss Zellah F. Hott, who was born in Missouri, and who by her union became the mother of three children: Viola M., Perry L., and Inez T., who died at the age of fifteen months. Mr. Hanson is a Republican in his political views, and is a licensed pharmacist. He was ordained deacon by Bishop Merrill in 1875, an elder in St. Louis, Mo., by Bishop Simpson, and has married forty-three couples in Hartville. Mrs. Hanson was born in Polk County, Mo., in 1853, and her father was a native of Springfield, Ill. He came to

Missouri in 1826, and died December 31, 1887, and his wife the day previous, of the same year. The mother was born on Christmas eve, married on Christmas eve, and died very near that time. Her maiden name was Joannah Douglass; she was of Scotch descent; her grandfather, William Douglass, was born in Virginia, and his father was a native of Scotland, and was of the Lord Douglass family. Her grandmother Douglass was a Kelso, and was a native of France. The father of Mrs. Hanson was a surveyor and engineer; was all through the Mexican War, and applied for a pension, which he never received until the time of his death. He belonged to the Advance Guards, and was an interpreter, speaking Spanish. During the Civil War he was a member of the secret service. He attended the same Sunday-school with Abraham Lincoln, and knew Mrs. Lincoln before her marriage. His grandfather on his mother's side was a Kelby, and was one of the first three white men that settled the site of Springfield, Ill.

Judge Isaac L. Hart, of the general mercantile firm of I. L. Hart & Co., of Norwood, Mo., was born in Tennessee in 1828, his parents being Leonard and Catherine (Emmett) Hart. The father was born, reared and married in Tennessee, and about 1852 immigrated to Missouri, but afterward moved from Wright County, where he had first settled, to Phelps County, where he spent the remainder of his days. Isaac L. Hart is the eldest of their nine children, and since attaining manhood has been a resident of Missouri. He was engaged in farming until 1878, and was then elected associate judge of the Wright County Court, in which capacity he served two years, then engaging in the hardware business, as a member of the firm of I. L. Hart & Co., at Mansfield. Ten months later, owing to the death of one partner, John Gorman, he sold to Calvin Spence, and returned to the farm, where he remained until his removal to Hartville in 1885. After working in Mr. Prophet's store some time he entered the firm of Mabon & Hart, buying out Mr. Mabon one year later, and moving to Norwood. The present firm are now doing a thriving business, their stock being valued at about $8,000. In 1863 Judge Hart was married in Wright County to Miss Tryphenah Pool, which union has resulted in the birth of four children: Sarah, Elizabeth, Laura and Frances (wife of S. E. Pope). The paternal grandfather, Leonard Hart, Sr., was a Pennsylvania Dutchman, and could neither read nor write the English language. He was an early immigrant to Tennessee. The maternal grandfather, George W. Emmett, was also a native of Pennsylvania, and both were soldiers in the Revolutionary War. The latter received a wound in the head by a sword, and was left for dead on the battle-field, but recovered from his wound. Judge Hart is a member of the A. F. & A. M.

Rufus L. Henderson, postmaster, grocer and druggist of Norwood, Mo., has been a resident of Wright County since 1883, and was born in Laclede County April 14, 1852. His father, Joseph Henderson, was born in Pennsylvania February 15, 1801, but was reared to manhood in Kentucky, and was there married to Miss Mary C. Williamson. About 1848 they removed to Missouri, locating in Laclede County, where the father worked as a farmer and mechanic until his death, June 3, 1874. His wife was born in Kentucky April 8, 1808. His father was born in Scotland, and was brought to America by his father, and located in Pennsylvania. He afterward moved to Caldwell County, Ky., being one of the pioneers of the State. Rufus L. Henderson is the youngest of ten children, and grew to manhood in Laclede County, Mo., receiving a common-school education. On the 1st of November, 1874, he was married to Miss Sarah I. McFarland, who was also born in Laclede County, but was a descendant of one of the old pioneer families of Kentucky. Her birth occurred on the 1st of November, 1857, and her union with Mr. Henderson resulted in the birth of six children: Freddie, Irvie, Burtie, Bessie, Jewel and Nellie. Previous to his arrival in Norwood, April 8, 1883, he was engaged in farming and blacksmithing, but has since been occupied in his present business. He also owns a one-half interest in a tract of 320 acres. He is a Democrat, and in 1885 was appointed postmaster of Norwood. He is a member of the A. F. & A. M., and he and wife belong to the Cumberland Presbyterian Church.

Thomas F. Henslee, retail liquor dealer, of Hartville, Mo., was born in North Carolina May 15, 1846, and is a son of Thomas and Betsey (Melton) Henslee, who were born, reared and married in North Carolina, the latter event taking place in 1838. To them were born three children, Thomas F. being the only one who grew to manhood. The mother died in 1848, and Mr. Henslee afterward married Mary Melton, by whom he became the father of one child, and is now living in Webster County, Mo. Thomas F. Henslee was reared and educated in Webster County, and was married in 1869 to Miss Eliza J. Dameron, who was born in North Carolina in April, 1845, and by her has one child, Anna B., the wife of W. H. Gorman. Mr. Henslee has farmed nearly all his life, and owns a valuable farm of 172 acres, but since engaging in the liquor business, in 1883, has rented his farm. He owns a good residence in Hartville, and is well fixed financially. During the late war he served in the Home Guards as forage master. He is a Democrat politically, and is Past Master in the Masonic fraternity.

M. G. Hensley, grocer, of Mansfield, Mo., was born in East Tennessee in 1852, and is a son of William and Elizabeth Hensley, who were born in Tennessee, the former's birth occurring in 1829. They were married in their native State, and in the fall of 1868 immigrated to Missouri, locating in Wright County, and now residing two miles north of Mansfield. The paternal grandfather, Benjamin Hensley, was of English descent, and lived and died in Tennessee. He was a soldier in the Mexican War, and for his services in that struggle received a pension. M. G. Hensley was seventeen years old when he came to Wright County, Mo., and his early days were spent in assisting his father on the home farm. He was first married to Miss Sarah White, who died in 1882, and he then married Mary E. Gorman, widow of John Gorman, and daughter of Mr. Rudd. Three children were born to her marriage with Mr. Gorman, and one child was born to her last marriage, Frank, who died at the age of two years. Mr. Hensley was in the mail service for three years, and entered the drug business in Mansfield in 1883, with a stock valued at $7,000. Two years later he closed out his establishment and began selling groceries, this stock amounting to $800. Mrs. Hensley owns the Hensley Hotel in Mansfield, which they successfully managed for about five years, but they now have it rented. Mr. Hensley is a Republican.

J. A. Hight, of Mansfield, Mo., is a son of John H. and Jane (Baker) Hight, and was born in Middle Tennessee in 1830. The father was also supposed to have been born in Tennessee in 1809, and there grew to maturity and married. He was a carpenter by trade, but also farmed, and after moving to Missouri, in 1839, followed both these occupations in what is now Wright County. He was killed in Arkansas, through mistake, by the Federal forces during the late war. His wife was born in Kentucky in 1810, and is now living in New Mexico. Five of their thirteen children grew to maturity, only two of whom are now living, J. A. and his sister. The Hights are of Irish descent, and the maternal grandfather and the grandmother immigrated to Tennessee from Kentucky, thence to Missouri, and died in the latter State. J. A. Hight received only the advantages of the subscription schools in his youth, and was engaged in assisting his father in tilling the farm. At the age of twenty years he was married to Miss Mary Ann Rippee, who was born in Indiana in February, 1831, and five children have blessed their union: Thomas Jefferson, John Wesley, Hiram Jackson, William H., and Mary J., wife of William B. King. Mr. Hight farmed in Wright County until the breaking out of the Civil War, and in 1862 joined the Eighth Missouri State Militia, entering as a corporal; through exposure his eyes became somewhat diseased. Since August, 1883, he has received a pension of $30 per month, and received back pay to the amount of $2,433.39. He is a member of the G. A. R. He owns four lots in the town of Mansfield.

Anderson Hogue, a prominent farmer, and the owner of 500 acres of land in Wright County, Mo., was born in Marion County, Tenn., in 1805, and was sold to a man by the name of Anderson Hogue, by his former master, who was also his father. From Anderson Hogue he takes his name. He was married in Tennessee to Miss Hannah Burnett, also a slave, and her master was also her father. She became the mother of six children: Nancy, wife of Thomas Haney; Fanny, who was married twice, and who is now deceased; Mary A. Tennessee, wife of James Payne; Henry A., Nelson and George. The mother of these children died in Tennessee, in the time of slavery. Three years after her death Mr. Hogue married Miss Theresa Hogue, one of the slaves of his last master, and to this union have been born twelve children: Sarah, (deceased), Robert, Lizzie, wife of William Trout; Adalaide, wife of Peter Hooper; Laura B., also married; Lonnie, Augusta M., wife of Newton Trout; Florence, wife of George Layer; William, Eddins R., Maude and Ida. Mr. Hogue was married before the war, and lived twenty-one miles below Chattanooga, on the State road. He saw Sherman on his march to the sea. Five years after peace was declared he and his family came north, settling in Wright County, and being the first colored family in the same. Mr. Hogue is a Republican in politics, and Mrs. Hogue is a member of the Cumberland Presbyterian Church.

D. W. Hoover, liveryman, of Mansfield, Mo., was born in Webster

County of that State in 1855. His father, Jesse Hoover, was born in North Carolina, and there married Amanda Cross, and came to Missouri in 1854, locating in Webster County. He was a farmer, and his union with Miss Cross resulted in the birth of eleven children, all of whom are living at the present time. The grandparents on both sides were from North Carolina, and were prosperous tillers of the soil. D. W. Hoover was reared in Webster County, and was educated in the common schools. At the age of eighteen years he was married to Miss Martha Winningham, a native of Tennessee, and by her has three children: Amanda, Samuel and Walter. Mrs. Hoover died in 1880, and Mr. Hoover took for his second wife Miss Mollie Jenkins, of Missouri, born in 1860. They have four children: Stella, Ada, Sophia and Gus. Mr. Hoover farmed in Webster County until 1881, when he sold out, and opened a livery stable at Seymour, which he managed for a number of years. On coming to Mansfield he bought out the livery firm of Spence & Rippee, and has been sole proprietor ever since. His stock is valued at about $3,200, and he does a large annual business. Mr. Hoover is a Republican in his political views.

W. H. Hopper, of the Hopper Furniture Co., of Mansfield, Mo., was born in Indiana on the 9th of February, 1827, and since ten years of age has been a resident of Missouri. He is the second of eleven children born to the marriage of Raleigh Hopper and Rebecca Malonee, and in early life received only the advantages of the subscription schools. He remained at home with his family until July 4, 1852, when he was married to Miss Ella J. Wilson, and began making a home for himself. His wife was born in Indiana in 1829, and became the mother of eight children, six of whom are living: Rachel, wife of W. F. Hulla; Margaret, wife of John Riley; Polly Ann, the deceased wife of Sampson Rippee; Rebecca A., wife of Jacob Gass; Rhoda, wife of Henry Tarbutton; Simpson, Catherine, and John, who died at the age of twenty-two years. Mr. Hopper lived in Douglas County until February 24, 1871, when he came to Wright County, and here has since been engaged in farming. In 1861 he served in the Home Guards, and the following year served in the Enrolled Missouri Militia. Being disbanded in the spring of 1863, in August of the same year he joined the Sixth Provisional Regiment, but was mustered out March 5, 1864, and entered the Forty-sixth Missouri Volunteer Infantry, serving until the close of the war as second lieutenant. He now belongs to the G. A. R., and in his political views is a Republican. The family worship in the Cumberland Presbyterian Church. His father, Raleigh Hopper, was born in Virginia in 1785, but grew to manhood in Kentucky, and there married his first wife, Polly Neill, who died after having borne a family of seven children. Mr. Hopper then married Miss Malonee, who was born in 1804. They moved to Missouri in 1837, and after residing in Pulaski, Wright and Ozark Counties located in Douglas County, where the father died October 17, 1844. At that time he was a member of the Missouri Legislature from Ozark County. The mother still lives, and resides in Douglas County. The paternal grandfather, Blackgrove Hopper, was a native of Virginia, and died in Kentucky, having followed the occupation of farming throughout life.

Benjamin F. Hudson, collector of Wright County, Mo., was born in Shelby County, Ill., in November, 1847. He is a son of Franklin and Margaret (Perryman) Hudson, and the maternal grandson of Allen Perryman, who was a native of Tennessee, but who immigrated to Illinois, and afterward to Missouri, where he died in Wright County, at the age of eighty-six years. Franklin Hudson was born and reared in South Carolina, and when a young man immigrated to Illinois, where he married Miss Perryman, who is yet living, and who resides in Wright County. Franklin Hudson was one of the popular educators of South Carolina before he left that State, and followed that avocation after coming to Illinois for about fourteen years. He then turned his attention to farming, which he carried on until his death, which occurred in the last named State. Benjamin F. Hudson was the second of seven children, six now living. He attained his growth in Shelby County, Ill., and received a good practical education in the common schools. In 1866 he immigrated to Missouri, and after one year in Pulaski County located in Wright County, and there he has since resided. He followed school-teaching for eight years, and, like his father, was a very popular educator. At the end of the above-mentioned time, or in 1880, he was elected county assessor, and was re-elected two years later, serving altogether four years. In 1884 he was elected county collector, and received the unanimous nomination of his party. He was re-elected collector in 1886, and because of having filled the period denominated by law, retired, and was no longer a candidate. In March, 1869, he was married to Miss Matilda Williams, a native of Missouri, and the daughter of Benjamin and Mary Williams, natives of Indiana, who came to Missouri at an early date, and located in Wright County. Mr. Williams was a Federal soldier, and died at Marshfield, while in service during the Civil War. Mrs. Williams is still alive. Benjamin F. Hudson is the father of five children living: Benjamin, Elizabeth, Minnie, Mary and John. One child, unnamed, died in infancy. Mr. Hudson is a member of the Masonic fraternity, a member of the Missionary Baptist Church, and is a Republican in his political principles.

H. E. Inman is a prosperous jeweler of Mountain Grove, Wright Co., Mo., and was born in Chemung County, N. Y., in 1862. His parents, Charles D. and Abigail M. (Robins) Inman, were also born in the Eastern States, the father having also been born in Chemung County, N. Y. From early boyhood he followed the occupation of farming, and after his removal to Missouri, in 1879, he continued to till the soil. He now resides in Wright County, Mo., and owns 280 acres of land. His union with Miss Robins resulted in the birth of nine children, H. E. Inman having been next to the youngest in order of his birth. He was educated in his native State, and came to Missouri with his parents, and in 1882 launched in business for himself at Mountain Grove, where his efforts have been attended with good results, his income amounting to about $1,000 for the year ending in 1888. He owns a good residence and two lots in the town, and owing to his energy and good management, bids fair to become one of the wealthy citizens of the county. He was married May 27, 1886, to Miss Mary E. Braselton, who was also born in 1862, and by her is the father of one child, Charley E. Mrs. Inman is finely educated, and was a successful teacher of music for some time. They are members of the Methodist Episcopal Church, and in his political views Mr. Inman is a stanch Republican. His paternal grandfather, Stephen Inman, was a successful farmer of Chemung County, N. Y.

William Johnston, another enterprising and successful farmer and stock raiser of Wright County, Mo., was born in Center County, Penn., December 11, 1832, and is the son of William and Elizabeth (Rider) Johnston. William Johnston, Sr., was born in Center County, Penn., in 1808, grew to manhood in that county, and was there married. His parents died when he was but a lad, and he was bound out. By personal application he became master of the German language, and also obtained a good English education by private study, from moments snatched from an unrelenting master. He was married April 25, 1830, to Miss Elizabeth Rider, a native of Center County, Penn., born February 19, 1809, and to them were born eight children, six of whom were natives of Center County. William Johnston, Sr., and family immigrated then to the western part of the State, Clarion County, Penn., in 1844. Here he carried on a rented farm and worked in an ore bank for five years. By that time he had accumulated sufficient money to purchase a farm, and went to farming until 1873. During this time there were two more sons added to the family. In 1873 oil was discovered on his land, and he sold twenty-nine acres for $3,000. He leased eighteen acres on a royalty, and the balance of the farm he and his sons undertook to manage. Previous to this William Johnston, Jr., had immigrated to Missouri, and located in that State in 1873. When oil was discovered on his father's farm in Pennsylvania he returned to assist in managing the oil business. They put down thirteen oil wells on the part of the farm they retained, the shallowest being 1,050 feet deep. The oil paid greatly at first, but soon fell from $4 per barrel to 60 cents. They finally quit the operation, and in about 1878 sold out. William Johnston, Jr., realized about $4,000 out of his portion of the business. He then came West, and again settled down to farming. He is now the owner of 493 acres of land in Wright County, Mo. On February 18, 1862, Mr. Johnston joined the Federal Army, Company F, Second Pennsylvania Cavalry, and was in the army ten months. August 27, 1862, he was wounded in the second battle of Bull Run. His horse was shot through by a piece of shell, and the fragment of shell struck his leg after passing through his horse and disabled him. He received his discharge for disability December 5, 1862, and now draws $8 per month pension. He was married in 1857 to Miss Mary Adams, a native of County Antrim, Ireland, born April 3, 1837, and to them have been born two living children: William, and Sadie Agnes, wife of John H. Simmons. They had three older children, who are deceased: Alexander Adams, who died at the age of three years and six months; Elizabeth, who died at the age of three months and eleven days, and Ira Lincoln, who died at the age of sixteen months. Mrs. Mary Johnston was but three months old when she came with her parents to America. They first landed in New York, but soon went from there to Carbon County, Penn., thence to Center County of that State, and in 1871 the father moved to

Wright County, Mo., where two of his sons and two daughters had preceded him. He was born in Ireland February 12, 1812, and came to America in 1836. He moved to Wright County, Mo., where he died June 18, 1883; was a prominent member of the Presbyterian Church. Isabella (McAlister) Adams was also born in Antrim County, Ireland, in 1813. She is still alive, and resides in Wright County. The family are of Scotch extraction. The paternal grandfather Adams was of English and the paternal grandmother, whose maiden name was Knox, was of Scotch descent. The paternal grandfather of William Johnston, David Johnston, lived in Pennsylvania; was a native of one of the Eastern States, and was a Revolutionary soldier. He was a farmer by occupation. The maternal grandmother was also a native of Pennsylvania. Mr. Johnston is a member of the Methodist Episcopal Church, and a Republican in his politics.

Rev. Peter Lair, minister of the Cumberland Presbyterian Church, Brush Creek Township, Wright Co., Mo., was born in Georgia in 1830, and his mother's name was Letty May. She married a man by the name of Nero, who was the father of our subject, Peter Lair. Mr. Lair was sold out of the Weaver family, to whom his mother, by transfer, belonged, and was bought by a family by the name of Lair, hence his name. He lived with them until the time of the emancipation, and was set free in Dallas County, Tex. He then went to work and earned $2 plowing. He has preached since he was eighteen years of age; has taught school and preached at Springfield. He drove a six-mule team through to Springfield for a man, in order to get his wife through to that city. In 1866 he purchased three acres of land on St. Louis Street, in Springfield, and lived there for seventeen years. He came to Missouri in 1880, and has 160 acres of land. He sold out of three acres, $2,545 worth of property, and owns about $1,000 worth of property there yet. Since the war he has preached nearly every week. He has preached in the Kansas City Cumberland Presbyterian Church, and was absent just lately on a tour through a number of the States, but was in Topeka, Kas., for seven weeks. He was married to Miss Fanny Carson, who was a native of Butler County, Ky. Her mother belonged to a family by the name of Carson, and her father to a family by the name of Porter. She was with her husband in Dallas County, Tex., when first set free. She earned her first money by spinning and knitting. They have never had any children of their own, but have several adopted children; one, George Lair, is the nephew of Mr. Lair.

Dr. Thomas Lane, Jr., of Mountain Grove, Mo., son of G. C. and Cynthia (Harris) Lane, was born on the 10th of August, 1858. He attended school in Mountain Grove Academy and at Blackburn University, Carlinville, Macoupin Co., Ill., for some time, and afterward studied medicine under Dr. I. R. Lane, an old and successful practitioner of Springfield, Mo. He entered the Missouri Medical College at St. Louis, Mo., in 1884, from which institution he graduated in 1886. He then located in Mountain Grove, Mo., where he commenced the practice of his profession, and has met with unusual success in town and vicinity. He was married on the 29th of September, 1884, to Miss Emma Dora McCurston, who bore him two children: Otto Ray and Gertrude May. Mrs. Lane is the daughter of George W. McCurston, of Mountain Grove, Mo. Dr. Lane, pleasant and agreeable in his manners, is one of the rising young men of Mountain Grove, and the prospect of the future is bright before him.

J. A. Lee, of the drug firm of Ellis & Lee, at Mountain Grove, Wright Co., Mo., was born in Perry County, Mo., March 9, 1847, being the son of John B. and Elizabeth (Simmons) Lee, and the grandson on his mother's side of John Simmons, who was a native of Louisiana, but who settled in Tennessee, and afterward came to Missouri, where he died in Wright County. He was a captain in the War of 1812 under Jackson. John B. Lee was born in North Carolina, and immigrated to Middle Tennessee, where he was married. He afterward came to Missouri (about 1845 or 1846), lived in Perry County for a time, and then came to Wright County, where he died when forty-five years of age. His wife, Elizabeth (Simmons) Lee, was born in Tennessee in 1817, and grew to womanhood in that State. By her marriage to Mr. Lee she became the mother of ten children (four boys), two living, J. A. and J. C. Mrs. Lee is still living, and resides in Mountain Grove. The family is of Irish origin. J. A. Lee was reared in his native county, and during the war went, in 1860, to Arkansas. After peace was declared he returned to Missouri, and followed agricultural pursuits and traded in stock until 1881, when he and W. C. Ellis built a room and put in a stock of drugs. Their average sales equal $8,000 per year, and they keep one or two clerks. Mr. Lee has continued to deal in stock in connection with his drug business, and aside from this is the owner of 140 acres of land. He is a Cleveland Democrat; a member of the I. O. O. F., and is treasurer of the Widow' and Orphans' Fund in the I. O. O. F. Mr. Lee was married in 1870 to Miss N. M. Finley, of Moniteau County, Mo., born in 1844. Seven living children were the result of this union: James F., John R., Annie B., Emaline, Robert, Mary E. and Essie.

Prof. William H. Lynch, principal of Mountain Grove Academy, Mountain Grove, Wright Co., Mo., was born in Texas County, Mo., in 1839. He is the son of David and Pollie Ann (Fourt) Lynch. David Lynch was a good old native of Kentucky, born in 1803, and immigrated to Missouri in pioneer days. He located in what is now Texas County many years before that county was formed, and followed milling on Piney River, which business he operated until the time of his death. In his early years he taught school, and in his later years was a patron of education. He was a member of the county court in Texas County, and the first circuit court ever held in the county was held at his house. Mrs. David Lynch was a native of Missouri, and became the mother of seven children, Prof. William H. Lynch being second in order of birth. Mrs. David Lynch died at the age of thirty-eight, and when the subject of this sketch was a child. The paternal grandfather was also a native of Kentucky, and immigrated to Missouri. When Prof. William Lynch was seventeen years of age he was sent by his father to Boone County, Mo., where he attended the public schools, and afterward Lathrop Academy. He then returned to his home, and taught school in his native county for some time. He was then appointed county clerk of Texas County, and served in that capacity until August 10, 1862, when he resigned the clerkship and joined the Federal army, Thirty-second Missouri Volunteers. He entered as a private, but his energy and education soon gained recognition, and at St. Louis, Mo., he was promoted to the rank of sergeant. At Arkansas Post he was promoted to first sergeant, then commissary-sergeant, then in Georgia, he was promoted to lieutenant, and afterward was promoted to regimental quartermaster. In 1865 he was promoted to the rank of captain, and was discharged with that title. Years of rough experience, in which he had distinguished himself, had taught him the value of education, and so eager was he to further pursue his collegiate course that he returned at once to the State University at Columbia, and there attended school another year. He then returned to his favorite pursuit, teaching. He officiated as principal at Steelville Academy four years; St. James Seminary, Phelps County, one and a half years; Salem, Dent County, twelve years; West Plains, Howell County, three years, and in 1887 he was elected principal of Mountain Grove Academy, at a salary of $175 per month, which position he is still occupying. Prof. Lynch's life as an educator has been one continual round of success, until he now stands in the front rank of a few leading educators of Missouri. C. I. Filley, of St. Louis, Mo., visited Mountain Grove, and pronounced Prof. Lynch second to no educator in the State. Hon. R. P. Bland also stated in public here that he had known Prof. Lynch for many years, and that "he is the best organizer of schools in the State." The author of this sketch, as a Normalite, can bear witness that Prof. Lynch's methods of teaching are in harmony with the methods adopted in the leading teachers' training schools of the country. In twenty-five years of work as an educator Prof. Lynch has lost only one and a half days' time. Commissioner of Education at Washington says that "this is the most faithful time on record." Prof. Lynch was married, in 1871, to Miss Mary Cook, a native of Tennessee, born in 1848, and the result of this happy union was the birth of two children, one only, Florence, now living. Prof. Lynch is a member of the Presbyterian Church, affiliates with the Republican party, is a Master Mason and a Royal Arch Mason.

J. M. McKee, justice of the peace of Pleasant Valley Township, Wright Co., Mo., was born in Frederick County, Va., in 1830, and is a son of Joel and Rebecca (Kline) McKee, who were born in Virginia, in 1800, and died in 1835 and 1880, respectively. The paternal grandparents were Virginians, and there spent their lives, but the maternal grandparents were of Irish descent. J. M. McKee grew to manhood in Virginia, and was educated in the common schools of that State, and after reaching a suitable age began traveling through his native State and Tennessee, in the employ of T. J. Doyle & Co., of Fredericksburg, Va., selling farming implements. At the age of thirty years he was married, in Scott County, Va., to Miss Elizabeth Grubb, who was born in Sullivan County, Tenn., in 1837. She is a daughter of Curtis A. Grubb, who was one of the early emigrants from Virginia to Tennessee. His wife, whose maiden name was Mary Ann Curtis, was born in Virginia, and is still living, and makes her home with her only surviving child, Mrs. McKee. Mr. McKee left Virginia in 1863, and moved to Kentucky, where he remained until 1869, having entered the Federal service, but at the end of eighteen months was mustered out of service at Lexington, Ky. In 1869 he went to Kansas, but two years later located in Missouri, residing in Douglas County until about four years since, when he retired from active life, and came to Mansfield. He owns a good residence and two town lots in Mansfield, and for some time has held the offices of notary public and justice of the peace. He is a member of the Missionary Baptist Church, the G. A. R., and in his political views is a Republican.

James J. McMullin. Among the prosperous agriculturists of Wright County, Mo., may be mentioned Mr. McMullin, who was born in Roane County, Tenn., in 1827, and was there reared and educated. He learned to read and write unaided, and the rest of his education was received in the old subscription schools. When about twenty years of age he was married, and soon afterward went to Iowa, and at the end of four years went to Lee County, Iowa, and from there moved to Scott County, Mo., and in 1857 took up his abode in Wright County, where he has since made his home. He was in the Federal service, in the Sixteenth Missouri Cavalry, during the late war, and was out three years, being mustered out of service at Springfield. He owns a good farm of 280 acres, and is considered one of the successful agriculturists and stock men of the county. He is a member of the A. F. & A. M., is a Democrat in politics, and he and family are members of the Cumberland Presbyterian Church. He was married to Miss Eliza J. Breazeale, who was born in Roane County, Tenn., July 4, 1830, and thirteen children, nine of whom are living, were born to their union: Samuel, Mary, Maude, Joseph, Frances, Laura, James, Jesse and Pearl. Three children died in infancy, and Martha at the age of fourteen years. Mr. McMullin's parents, James and Rebecca (Mattock) McMullin, were married in Tennessee, whither the father had moved from his native State, North Carolina, when a young man. He had been previously married in Pennsylvania to a Miss McDonald, who died in Roane County, Tenn., leaving four children. His union with Miss Mattock was blessed by the birth of nine children. After his death, which occurred in Tennessee, his widow married John Turner, and moved to Missouri, and died in Scott County, having borne Mr. Turner one child. James McMullin was a soldier in the War of 1812.

Thomas Jefferson Mansfield, of the Wright County Mercantile Co., at Mansfield, Mo., was born in Madison County, Mo., in 1858. His father, Robert Mansfield, was born in Tennessee in 1808, and there grew to manhood and was married. He moved to Wright County, Mo., in 1848, thence to Madison County, of the same State, but returned to Wright County in 1868, and about a year before his death moved to Laclede County, where he died in 1887. He was a farmer throughout life, and by his wife, Nancy Spears, had a family of twelve children, seven of whom are living at the present time. Thomas J. Mansfield, whose name heads this sketch, is the seventh of their children, and was reared to manhood in his native State, receiving his education in a common school in Illinois. Having learned the printer's trade, he returned to Wright County, Mo., where he was engaged in this work until about eight years since, when he entered the mercantile business at Hartville, and has been a member of the present firm for over a year. Their stock is valued at $10,000, and their annual sales amount to about $30,000. He was married in Hartville to Miss Susie Lee Perry, who was born in Missouri in 1861, and is a daughter of Rev. John W. Perry, of the Methodist Episcopal Church, South. They have one child, Marion Pearl. Mr. Mansfield is a Democrat, a member of the Methodist Episcopal Church, South, and belongs to the I. O. O. F., Fourth Degree, 992, Mountain Grove Lodge. His paternal grandfather, an Englishman, came to America prior to the Revolutionary War, and assisted the colonists in their struggle against the mother country. He was in the battle of Yorktown.

T. H. Marshall, agent and operator for the Gulf Railroad at Norwood, Mo., was born in Knox County, Mo., October 25, 1849, and is a son of William P. and Sarah A. (Herrington) Marshall. The father was born in Maryland in 1813, and after attaining manhood went to Ralls County, Mo., where he was married, his wife being a native of that county. He began merchandising in Kirksville, afterward farmed on Salt River, in that county, and after residing in Lewis County for some time, moved to St. Clair, where he died in 1872. His union with Miss Herrington resulted in the birth of eight children, T. H. Marshall being their third child. The latter was reared to manhood near Monticello, Mo., and received his education in the schools of that place. After acquiring an excellent knowledge of telegraphy he came to Norwood, where he has held his present position for over six years. He was married in this place to Miss Julia E. Wood, a native of Nashville, Ill., born January 13, 1867, and by her is the father of one child, Ollie. Mrs. Marshall is a daughter of B. F. and L. L. Wood, and a granddaughter of Maj. Wood, who was a soldier in the Mexican War, a pioneer of the State of Illinois, and was at one time a presidential elector for the same. Mr. Marshall is a Democrat in politics, is a man of excellent business qualifications, and thoroughly understands the business in which he is engaged.

H. C. Miller was born in Wilmington. Del., May 10, 1855, the son of E. F. and T. E. (Richmond) Miller. E. F. Miller was born in Saxony, Germany, in 1814, and was a machinist by occupation. He came to America when about the age of thirty years, and located in Philadelphia, but afterward moved to Wilmington, Del. After remaining there a short time he moved to Marshall, Tex., and then back to St. Louis, Mo., where he followed manufacturing for some time, but moved from there to St. Paul, Minn., and then to Rolla, Mo., where he first followed mercantile pursuits, and afterward the livery business. He is now living in Rolla. Mrs. T. E. (Richmond) Miller was born in Baltimore, Md., in 1832, and by her marriage to E. F. Miller became the mother of nine children, six now living, of whom our subject was the second in order of birth. He grew to manhood and was educated in St. Louis and Rolla, Mo. He then clerked from the time he was fourteen years of age until he was twenty-nine, when he engaged in business at Mountain Grove, when there were only twenty people in the place. He started with a capital of $300, and carried on merchandising two or three years, when he gradually became interested in the lumber business. He became a partner in the Lake Lily Mills, and helped remodel it. He is now a partner with his brother in the store here, and owns 3,000 acres of land in Cleveland County, Ark. He owns a saw-mill plant on his land, which annually cuts 7,000,000 feet, and they ship 800 car loads of lumber and timber per year. His whole investment there is about $25,000. In 1881 Mr Miller was married, his wife's birth occurring in Illinois in September, 1861. This union resulted in the birth of two children, Mabel and Minnie. Mr. Miller is a member of the A. F. & A. M., and is a Past Master; is a Republican in politics, and he virtually built the Methodist Episcopal Church building. He is one of the essentially progressive men of South Central Missouri, and has done more than any other one man to build up Mountain Grove. He is a young man of push and energy, and is truly a self-made man. E. J. Miller, who is twenty-eight years of age, is now running the store at Mountain Grove, and has absolute control of the same.

Col. William C. Mings, of Montgomery Township, Wright County, Mo., was born in Madison County, Ky., on the Kentucky River, December 17, 1831, son of George Wolfscale and Pollie (Kanatzar) Mings. The paternal grandfather was born in Charleston, S. C., April 10, 1754, and was one of the pioneers of Kentucky. He was married in North Carolina, and died in Illinois April 14, 1849. He was a Revolutionary soldier; was at the battle of Brandywine, and received a pension from the Government for services rendered. The great-grandfather was born in Scotland, but immigrated to America, and was with the colonial soldiers at Braddock's defeat. He had three sons: Joseph, Alexander and James. George W. Mings was born in Wayne County, Ky., July 16, 1806, grew to manhood in Kentucky and Tennessee, was married in Madison County, Ky., and was by trade a hatter, although he followed agricultural pursuits principally. He immigrated to Illinois, then back to Kentucky, then to Missouri, afterward to Arkansas, but finally settled in Missouri in 1861. He died at the residence of his son December 26, 1886. He volunteered to go to the Mexican War, but his company was not called. His wife, Pollie (Kanatzar) Mings, was born in Kentucky in May, 1810, and is still alive, and resides with her son. They were the parents of eleven children, four now living. Col. William C. Mings went to Arkansas with his father in 1849, and there attained his majority. He cast his first presidential vote for Gen. Winfield Scott, and was married December 21, 1854, to Miss Nancy A. Neel, who was born in Tennessee March 7, 1832. Her people came from North Carolina to Tennessee, and her grandfather was a native of Ireland. Col. W. C. Mings came to Missouri August 10, 1861, joined the Rangers, and afterward the Tenth Missouri Cavalry. He was a non-commissioned officer, and rendered effective and valuable service. He was at one time a candidate for Congress in this district, and previous to the War held several prominent offices in the State of Arkansas. He has held the office of commissioner, assessor, justice of the peace, and has been postmaster at Mingsville, which was named after him. He served two terms of four years each as county surveyor and eight years as notary public. He has 235 acres of land, and his farm is well stocked. He has five children living: Margaret E., George W., Joseph W., William R., John W., and James, who died at the age of four years. During the war Mr. Mings was elected colonel of a regiment then being organized, but refused to serve.

Prof. Thomas J. Montgomerie. Prominent among the enterprising men and successful educators of South Central Missouri stands the name of Prof. Thomas Montgomerie, principal of Hartville Public Schools. He was born in Wright County, Mo., August 19, 1841, and is the son of Jefferson and Nancy E. (Anderson) Montgomerie. The father was born in North Carolina June 9, 1800, but grew to maturity in Tennessee. At the age of twenty-five he came to Missouri, and in 1828 was married to Miss Nancy Anderson. He was an early pioneer of what is now Wright County, and Montgomerie Township bears his name. He died in Wright County. His wife was also a native of North Carolina, and her people moved to Tennessee when she was a child, and from that State to Missouri, when she was fifteen years of age. By her marriage to Mr. Montgomerie she became the mother of nine children. The paternal grandfather of our subject, John Montgomerie, was a native of Ireland, and after immigrating to America located in North Carolina. The paternal grandmother was a Moore, and died in Tennessee at the age of one hundred and four years. Prof. Thomas Montgomerie was the sixth child in order of birth born to his parents. He grew to manhood in Wright County, and supplemented his common-school education with a course in Mountain Grove Academy, under Prof. Phillips. Consistent with his tastes, he entered the profession of teaching at Springdale Academy, Mo., Rolla High-school, Richland Institute, Pulaski County, and Lebanon Public Schools, these being some of the places in which he has officiated as an educator. After coming to Wright County, although he is a Democrat in his political views, and the county vastly Republican, so strong a hold had he gained upon the affections of the citizens of Wright County that he was elected circuit clerk in 1878, and county clerk at the expiration of this term (1882). He leaves behind him the neatest county record in sixty-nine counties of the Mississippi Valley, besides records in several Western States, and in Chicago and other cities, which are acknowledged by all to be the neatest records ever seen. He was married in 1866 to Miss Elizabeth Bradford, and afterward, in 1878, to Mrs. Mott. Prof. Montgomerie has attained a high reputation in Southern Missouri as an educator, is a proficient mathematician, and a man of culture and high literary attainments. He is now engaged in writing a work, entitled "Logic of Mathematics," which will soon be given to the public.

William L. Murrell, a prominent citizen of Hartville, Mo., was born in Greene County, Mo., in 1844, the son of William and Frances C. (Cobb) Murrell. The paternal grandparents were natives of Tennessee, and the maternal of Germany. William Murrell was born in Tennessee, and there grew to manhood. He was married in that State, was a farmer by occupation, but moved to Greene County, Mo., where he was among the pioneers of that county, locating there about 1830. He organized a company for the Mexican War, was made captain of the same, and served all through the war. He then returned to Greene County, Mo., where he died in 1848. The mother died in Webster County, Mo., at the age of sixty-two years. They were the parents of nine children, of whom William L. is the youngest. He was taken to Wright County by his mother when about nine years of age, here attaining his growth, and was here educated. When the Civil War broke out he was eighteen years of age, and he joined the Eighth Missouri Cavalry, Federal Army, being in service for three years. He was at the battles of Prairie Grove, Pea Ridge, Little Rock and Pumpkin Bend, on White River. He was mustered out at Little Rock, Ark., and then returned to Wright County, Mo., where he followed farming for several years, and still owns a farm. In 1876 he was elected sheriff of Wright County, and served two years. In 1862 he was elected collector of Wright County, served two years, and then retired from public life. After that time he was engaged on his farm until two years ago, since which time he has lived in Hartville, in order to educate his children. He was married in 1866 to Miss Sarah A. Boiles, a native of Tennessee, born in 1843, and to this union were born six children: Darthulia E., James M., William D., Noah A. and George C. One died in infancy. Mr. Murrell is a member of the Masonic fraternity and G. A. R., a member of the Methodist Episcopal Church, and is a Republican in politics.

Hon. Thomas H. Musick, attorney at law and proprietor of the *Southwest Republican*, a journal published weekly at Hartville, Mo., was born in Pike County, Mo., May 27, 1834. He attained his growth in his native county, and supplemented his common-school education with a course at Ashley Seminary. He afterward followed the profession of teaching in Pike County for ten years. About this time the Civil War broke out, and he joined the Ninth Missouri Cavalry, and served until the close of the war. Having read law while teaching, he was admitted to the bar at Danville, Mo., and located at Mexico, Mo., and there practiced law until 1880, when he went to Douglas County, of the same State, and there remained one year. He then moved to Wright County, Mo., entered upon the practice of his profession, and was thus engaged until 1885, when he purchased the *Wright County Republican*, which he changed to *Southwest Republican*, and which he still runs in connection with his law practice. Mr. Musick was elected prosecuting attorney of Wright County, Mo., in 1882, re-elected in 1884, and served until 1887. He was a Republican candidate for Congress, Eleventh Congressional District, in 1888, and reduced the Democratic majority from 3,598 to about 400. Mr. Musick was married January 20, 1863, to Miss Lois E. Pickett, who was born in Pike County, Mo., in 1846, and who became the mother of three children, two now living: Ida, now married to J. C. F. Clark, and Shelley. Cyril died at the age of three months. Mrs. Musick died in 1870, and two years later Mr. Musick married Miss Kate Taylor, and by this union became the father of two living children: Ruth V. and Lois E. Mr. Musick is the son of Rev. Lafreniere C. and Jane D. (Hayden) Musick. The law firm of which Mr. Musick is now a member is Musick & McKenney. Mr. McKenney is a man of long years of experience in the practice of law, and has practiced in some of the highest courts of the country. Mr. Musick has been a consistent member of the Baptist Church for thirty-six years; has always been strictly abstemious, and an advocate of temperance and other reformatory measures. He is in favor of the equal rights of all before the law, and, as might be expected, is in favor of a strict enforcement of the law. Politically he was a Whig prior to 1860; since then he has been a steadfast, active and aggressive Republican. During his term as prosecuting attorney he was vigorous in his prosecution of criminals, but withal he was so just and kind in the discharge of his official duties that, contrary to the general experience of vigorous prosecutors, he made but few enemies by enforcing the law. Mr. Musick is a fluent and effective speaker, and pays more attention to bringing out the strong points than to mere oratory; yet, when he wishes, he can be very ornate in his language. He is a man of very cool, even temper, never permitting himself to be drawn into a quarrel, nor does he ever become perceptibly excited. But, notwithstanding this, his experience has proved that having a cool, even temper, and avoiding quarrels, will not always shield a man from the rough corners in life, for while he resided in Douglas County there was a most dastardly attempt made to take his life. He was sitting one evening, a little after dark, in his house in Ava, the county seat of Douglas County, with a babe on each knee, one of them being three years old and the other eleven months, when the would-be assassin, in a stealthy, cowardly manner, slipped up and fired at him through the window. The ball struck him in the breast, and followed a rib round for about four inches, then glanced off and went through his right arm above the elbow, fracturing the bone down to the elbow. It also passed through the wrist of the youngest child, shattering it in a fearful manner. The child, had it lived, would have been a cripple, but it died about six months after. Mr. Musick's wounds were so severe that he was not really in a proper condition to attend to business for six months after receiving them, yet, such was his energy that he went into court in about four weeks after he was shot and tried a murder case with success. The only cause known for the dastardly act is the fact that Mr. Musick had been employed to prosecute the claim of an old blind man, on a plain promissory note, against his sons, who had scheduled against it, and it is supposed that he was shot to prevent his doing so. While Mr. Musick enjoys a large, laborious and lucrative practice, he finds time to devote himself assiduously to literary and scientific pursuits, for which he has a strong liking. He controls the county paper in such a manner that it has a circulation of something over 1,000 in this sparsely populated country. In addition to this he has written a monogram of fifty-six pages on the "Conservation of Forces," a deep and intricate subject, yet treated by him in such a way that any scientist can read it with pleasure and profit. He is now engaged in re-writing, revising and enlarging it, and it is thought by scientific men that when the revised edition appears it will attract an enlarged attention. William H. H. Musick, a younger brother, born on the 26th of June, 1840, edits the *Southwest Republican*, making it not only a good newspaper but an able and fearless investigator of all current public questions, as well as a journal of high literary merits, considering its rural location. He is a gentleman of indomitable energy and industry, correct habits and stern integrity.

Dr. Lewis E. Musick, physician and surgeon at Mountain Grove, Mo., and brother to Thomas H. and William H. H. Musick, was born in Montgomery County, Mo., January 27, 1836. The genealogy of the Musick family is traced back several generations to its origin in George Musick, who was picked up when a child as the only survivor of a shipwreck on the coast of Wales, and was called Musick because of his musical talents. Growing to manhood in that country, he had five sons: Alexis, George, David, Abram and Ephraim, all of whom immigrated to America, and settled in Spottsylvania County, Va., early in the eighteenth century. Thomas R. Musick, son of Ephraim, who married a Roy, was born in Spottsylvania County, Va., in 1757. He united with the Baptist Church, and entered the ministry at seventeen years of age. Soon after he immigrated to North Carolina, where he enlisted in the army, served through the Revolutionary War, was twice a prisoner to the British, and was at the surrender of Cornwallis. After the war he removed to Kentucky, where he married Mary Nevel. About 1801 he came to Missouri, and preached the first Protestant sermon west of the Mississippi. He was for many years pastor of Fee Fee Baptist Church, in St. Louis County, and was buried there in 1843. Capt. Lewis Musick, son of Thomas R., and grandfather to the subject of this sketch, was born in Kentucky about 1783. He married Mary Fitzwater, whose maternal grandfather was a Bean. Lewis Musick was a captain in the military service, fighting the Indians in Missouri from 1811 to 1815. He died in California in 1849. Rev. Lafreniere C. Musick, the father of Dr. L. E. Musick, was born in St. Louis County in 1815, and is now living in Audrain County, Mo. Dr. Musick's mother, Jane D. Hayden, daughter of Elisha, Jr., and Mary W. Hayden, was born in Todd County, Ky., in 1815. Elisha, Jr., was the son of Elisha Hayden, Sr., who married Jane Donaldson, the daughter of Samuel Donaldson. Her mother was a Bailey. Mary W. Hayden was a daughter of Joshua and Susannah Harrison, and was born in South Carolina. Joshua was born in Virginia, and his mother was Mary Elza. Elisha Hayden, Sr., was born in Virginia, and was the son of William Hayden, who married Mary Ann Waller. Elisha, Sr., was a Revolutionary soldier. The Haydens originally spelled the name Headen, and the family was of Irish extraction. Jane Donaldson's maternal grandmother was a Clayton. Susannah Harrison was a sister to Elisha Hayden, Sr. The Harrisons were related to Gov. Ben. Harrison of Virginia, and the Donaldsons, a branch of the family of that name distinguished in the history of Tennessee. Dr. Lewis E. Musick is a man of more than average natural endowments, and laid the foundation of a good English education in the common schools. He took sides with the Union during the Civil War, entered the service in 1861, and served until May 15, 1865, when failing health forced him to abandon his post of duty. He served as sergeant, lieutenant and captain. Dr. Musick was married in 1864 to Miss Margaret H. Lewis, a native of Missouri, born in 1850, and to them was born one child, Ada, wife of E. L. Shinkle, of Pittsburg, Kas. Mrs. Musick is the youngest child of the second husband of Rebecca H. Lewis, whose first husband was her full cousin, and was named Walpole. The Walpoles are of English extraction, and related to the family of Sir Robert Walpole. Dr. Lewis E. Musick graduated from and took his degree in the American Medical College, St. Louis, Mo. He came to Mountain Grove in 1881, and here found an extensive business awaiting him. Dr. and Mrs. Musick are well preserved people for their years He attributes this remarkable preservation of youthful vigor to a strict observance of nature's laws and superior hygienic treatment. He is a member of the G. A. R., and is a Republican in his politics.

Mrs. Mary Newton, widow of Andrew Newton, was born in Kentucky in 1827, the daughter of William and Huldah (Young) Rippey, natives of Virginia. They were married in Kentucky, and afterward moved to Indiana, when the subject of this sketch was a child. The father was a farmer by occupation, and died in Indiana, where the mother also passed the remainder of her days. The paternal grandfather died in Wright County, Mo., and the maternal grandfather died in Kentucky. Mrs. Newton was left an orphan at an early age, and was reared by an aunt, who took her to Missouri, and settled in Wright County. Here she grew to womanhood, and was married to Mr. Newton in 1843. To them were born fifteen children, ten now living: James, William, Sarah, wife of Thomas Montgomery; John, Frances E., wife of William W. Edington; George W., Mary, wife of Rufus Scott; Julia A., wife of C. J. Crain; Jesse A. and Barney. Those deceased are: Rettie, who died at the age of eleven years and five months; Huldah, who died at the age of nineteen months; Clementine, Susan, who died at the age of four months, and an infant son. Andrew Newton was born in Kentucky in 1819, and died February 27, 1881, at the age of sixty-two years. He was reared in Indiana, and came to Missouri in 1839, where he homesteaded 400 acres, which is still in the hands of the family. George, Jesse and Barney are at home.

Jeremiah Newton, assessor of Wright County, Mo., was born in Lawrence County, Ind., in 1837, being the son of Alexander and Sarah A. (Henderson) Newton. Alexander Newton was born (probably) in Virginia in 1812, and reared principally in Kentucky. He moved to Indiana before he was grown, and in 1839 moved to Missouri, settling in this county, and there died in 1878. He was a farmer by occupation. Sarah A. (Henderson) Newton was born in Indiana in 1815, and died in Missouri in 1888. They were the parents of twelve children, ten of whom grew to maturity. The paternal grandfather was born in Virginia, was a farmer, and had a brother who fought in the War of 1812, and was never afterward heard of. Jeremiah Newton was next to the eldest child in order of birth. He was but a child when his parents moved to Missouri, and although he never attended school, he has a good knowledge of books by his own personal application. He was reared on his present farm, and in 1865 he was united in marriage to Miss Harriet J. Wynn, a native of West Tennessee, born in 1844. Eight children were the result of this union, only two now living. The children are named as follows: Rufus L., who died at the age of one year; Robert A., who died at the age of five years; John A., died at the age of four; Adella, when three years of age, and

Ida, died when an infant; Franklin is living; Docia E. and Julian. The mother of these children died in 1880. In 1876 Mr. Newton was elected to the office of county assessor, and was re-elected in 1878. After being out of office for four years he was elected, in 1884, and again in 1886, to the assessor's office, which he has filled in a capable and efficient manner. He has about 180 acres of good land, and is a successful farmer. Of the six brothers of the Newton family all are members of the Masonic fraternity. Mr. Newton is an excellent citizen, and has the respect of all who know him. During the fifteen years spent with his wife not one word of disagreement has passed between them.

Mrs. Mary J. Nichols, widow of Lazarus Nichols, was born in the "Blue Grass State," and is the daughter of Pleasant and Elizabeth (Cowden) McClure, also natives of Kentucky. They came to Missouri when our subject was about grown, settling in Webster County, near Waldo Post-office, and there passed their last days. The mother died in 1866 or 1867, and the father in 1886. Mrs. Mary J. Nichols was married to Mr. Lazarus Nichols about the close of the war, and to this union were born seven children: Laura, wife of Alexander Barnett; George, Narcissus, wife of J. G. Piatt; J. C., Lola, wife of A. N. Allen; Hattie and Charley. The youngest son accidentally received a gunshot wound, which terminated fatally for him eight days after the accident occurred. After marriage Mr. and Mrs. Nichols moved on the farm where Mrs. Nichols is now living, and there the family was reared. Mr. Nichols was a native of Kentucky, and was an early settler of Missouri. He was a man of industry, who accumulated much wealth in Wright County, and left to his family 800 acres of good land. He died in this county in 1877, and his son George is living on the farm and taking care of his mother, and looking after the interest of the farm. He was born in 1866, and received his education in the district schools and at Hartville, Marshfield and Seymour. J. C. Nichols attended the Christian Brothers College in St. Louis, and also attended the school at Marionville. The mother and all her daughters are members of the Baptist Church.

William C. Odell, a successful farmer and stock raiser of Union Township, Wright Co., Mo., was born in Pulaski County of that State in 1837, and is the son of Samuel and Mary L. (Devashier) Odell, and grandson of Enoch Odell, who was born in Virginia, and who was an old soldier in Jackson's war. He married and lived in Tennessee, and was the father of three sons and five daughters. He moved to Missouri, where he died. The paternal great-grandfather was a native of Virginia. The Odells were of Irish descent, and the Devashiers were of German, Grandfather Devashier coming from Germany. Samuel Odell was born in White County, Tenn., October 30, 1800, and attained his growth in his native State. He was married in White County, Tenn., to Miss Cynthia Walker, who bore him seven children. They afterward moved to Illinois, but six years later moved to Missouri, locating in Pulaski County, and lived on the Osage Fork of the Gasconade until 1881, when he received his final summons. He was one of the pioneer men of this section of the country. His second wife, Mrs. Mary L. (Devashier) Odell, was born in Maury County,

Tenn., in 1815, and died in December, 1888; she became the mother of nine children by her marriage, eight of whom grew to manhood. Abraham, one of the sons, was a Federal soldier, and was killed in the battle of Pleasant Hill, La. William Odell was married in 1858 to Miss Mary Randolph, who bore him eight children: James S., Enoch B., Mary A., wife of Thomas Colton; A. F., a young man, who has not attained his majority, but who weighs 203 pounds, and has traveled all over the United States; Isaac, Jacob, Billy and Cynthia. Mr. Odell was a member of Company B, Forty-sixth Missouri Infantry, and received his discharge at Springfield, Mo. He is a successful, enterprising farmer, and is the owner of 200 acres of land. He is a member of the Missionary Baptist Church, is a member of the Masonic fraternity, and is a Democrat in his political views.

W. W. Oliver, of Wright County, Mo., was born in Guilford County, N. C., November 7, 1833, the son of Allen and Mariah (Williams) Oliver, both natives of Rockingham County, N. C., and born in 1812 and 1814, respectively. The father died in his native county January 1, 1875, and the mother in North Carolina in 1858. W. W. Oliver was married in Guilford County, N. C., in 1852, to Miss Unica Calhoun, who bore him four children: Mariah, wife of Floyd M. Todd, and the mother of six children; James A., a native of Guilford County, N. C.; William H., born in Putnam County, Ind., and R. P., who was also born in Putnam County, Ind. Each of Mr. Oliver's children are well provided for, and are on farms of their own. Mr. Oliver moved to Indiana in 1856, and after remaining there for about ten years, where he rented land and followed agricultural pursuits for a livelihood, moved to Wright County, Mo. He here purchased a farm, and went to work with a determination to succeed, which by his industry and enterprise he eventually did. He now has about 500 acres, and has provided well for his children. Mr. Oliver started life without a cent, and is a fair example of what can be accomplished by push and energy. He is the model farmer of the county, and for neatness and economy has no superior anywhere. While in Indiana, and during the war, Mr. Oliver was a member of the State Militia. He is a charter member of the Masonic fraternity, a Master Mason, a member of the Missionary Baptist Church, and is a Republican politically.

Col. R. Boone Palmer. Prominent among the enterprising and successful citizens of Wright County, Mo., and among those deserving special recognition for their long residence in the county, stands the name of the above-mentioned gentleman, who was born in Pickens District, S. C., in 1816. He is the son of John and Nancy (Boone) Palmer, and the grandson, on his mother's side, of Ratcliff Boone, a relative of Daniel Boone. The paternal grandfather was a native of Virginia, and one of the pioneers of South Carolina. John Palmer, so far as known, was a native of South Carolina, and in that State was married to Miss Nancy Boone, who was also a native of South Carolina. After marriage he moved to Georgia, where he farmed until his death. They were the parents of eight children, six now living, of whom Col. Palmer is next to the eldest in order of birth. He moved with his parents to Georgia, there grew to manhood, and there, at the age of nineteen, was united in marriage to Miss Sarah Nix, who bore these children: William, Benjamin and Joseph; three died, two in infancy. One, Lucinda, was married to Noah Claxton, and before her death bore him two children. Col. Palmer moved to Missouri in October, 1840. He intended going to Texas, but finally located in what is now Wright County, where he purchased land, and was one of the pioneers of the place. Early in 1840 he was elected associate judge of the county court, and finally elected president. During one of his terms of office county warrants were raised in value from 50 to 95 cents on the dollar. He served as county judge for a period of four or five years. In the spring of 1849 he left Hartville and went overland to California, there following mining, and made $3,000 cash. He also followed ranching in that State, and in 1853 he returned by Panama and New Orleans to his family in Wright County, Mo., where he farmed until the opening of the war. He was then appointed colonel of the Seventy-third Enrolled Missouri Militia, to guard home property. In 1862 he was elected to the Legislature, and was re-elected in 1864 for two years more. He remained with that body until the close of the war. After that event he made a race for State senator, but was counted out. In 1870 he ran for the State Senate on the issue of enfranchisement, and was elected, serving four years. He was a member of the committee on education, and visited Kirksville Normal, and School of Mines and Metallurgy at Rolla. He is the author of the original bill in Missouri for the regulation of carrying concealed or exposed weapons. In 1879 Col. Palmer was elected as an Independent Democrat to the State Legislature, and served two years. He is official reporter for Wright County to the Agricultural Department of the United States. He is independent in his political views as well as in his religion, and is one of the leading men of the county. He has sold $5,000 worth of land, and has much on hand still. He is a member of the Wright County bar, being the oldest member, with one exception, in the county. In June, 1888, he traveled all through Illinois, Kentucky, Ohio and Indiana, and visited Lexington and the monument and homestead of Henry Clay, and although his early education was rather deficient, he has, by experience gained in traveling, and by his close application to study between business hours, become a well-informed man on any subject. He is now seventy-two years of age, is hale and hearty, and occasionally goes on hunting expeditions with his pack of hounds.

Judge T. H. Patterson, of Mansfield, Wright County, Mo., was born in Indiana, on the 9th of April, 1826, and was there reared to manhood and educated in the common schools, becoming, in after years, a popular local educator of Clark County. On the 17th of March, 1859, he was married to Miss Elizabeth Hunter, who was born in Pennsylvania, in 1831, but was reared in Indiana. She was also a successful teacher in the public schools of that State, and has taught one term of school since coming to Missouri. Of a number of children born to them, only one is known to be living at the present time, Hannah Florence. Thomas A. left home, and has not been heard from for five years. Those deceased are George W., aged three years; Margaret, an infant; Robert R., aged fourteen years; John, aged ten years, and Mary E., who was a public school-teacher of Wright and Webster Counties, and while visiting friends in another portion of the State took sick, and died quite suddenly. Her birth occurred in September, 1863, and her death July 24, 1888. The mother of these children died December 13, 1878. During the late war Judge Patterson served in Company C, Forty-fourth Indiana Infantry, and after the cessation of hostilities came to Missouri and located in Newton County, where he lived three years, and was engaged in pedagoguing. In 1871 he came to where Mansfield now is, where he followed the same occupation, and was also engaged in tilling the soil. He has held the office of justice of the peace for a number of years, and has also served one term of four years as presiding judge of the Wright County Court. He was a high license man for several years. He is a Republican in politics, a member of the Christian Church, and owns a good farm of 160 acres. His father, Robert Patterson, was a native of County Down, Ireland, and was born about 1789. After leaving there he lived in Scotland some time, and in 1811 came to America, and joined the United States troops in the War of 1812. He located in Maryland, and was there married to Miss Hannah Hill, and soon afterward moved to Kentucky, thence to Indiana, dying in the latter State, on Christmas Day, 1852. His wife was born in Maryland in 1797, and died in Clark County, Ind., in 1884. They were the parents of three sons and four daughters. Two of the daughters and one son are now living.

John T. Pope, attorney at law and prosecuting attorney-elect of Wright County, Mo., was born in Davidson County, N. C., January 25, 1849, son of Thomas and Mary A. (Hale) Pope. The father was also born in North Carolina, in November, 1819, and was a tiller of the soil. To his marriage were born seven children, four now living. Mr. Pope is still living, and is a resident of North Carolina. His wife, Mrs. Mary A. (Hale) Pope, died in 1862, at the age of thirty-seven years. The Pope family are of Pennsylvania Dutch descent, and the grandfather, Isaac Pope, was born in Maryland, and immigrated to North Carolina at an early date. He was one of the early settlers of that State, and was a farmer by occupation. The maternal grandfather, John Hale, was of Scotch descent. Edward Hale, uncle of subject, published the Fayetteville *Observer*, at Fayetteville, N. C., and his son is Hale, the publisher at New York City. John T. Pope left North Carolina at the age of nineteen years, and came direct to Wright County, Mo., where he located and received a good common-school education in Davidson and Bethany Academy, North Carolina. He taught school, read law at the same time, and when his term of school was over, he commenced the practice of law. He served as superintendent of public schools from 1870 to 1872, and then county attorney for four years. He was elected prosecuting attorney of the county, and re-elected in 1878. He has dealt extensively in real estate in Wright County, and now owns more than 1,000 acres with good titles. He was married, in Wright County, to Miss Mattie A. Bryant, a native of Phelps County, Mo., who bore him six children: Charles E., Guy C., Otto D., Thomas A., Alith, and Ruth, who died at the age of four months. Mr. Pope is a Republican politically, and one of the representative men of the county.

S. E. Pope, attorney at law at Hartville, is a native of Davidson County, N. C., born October 17, 1861, and entered Trinity College in 1878, joining the Sophomore class, but left two years later on account of failing health. He came to Missouri, and afterward went to Tom Green County, Tex. In 1884 he returned to Missouri, locating at Hartville, in Wright County, and there he has remained ever since. He was admitted to the bar, and became a practicing attorney at the September term of the circuit court in the year 1888. He was married August 2, 1888, to Miss Fannie Hart, and has one child, Emma Leigh. Attorney Ed. Pope, as he is familiarly called by the people at Hartville, is one of the self-made and rising men of whom Wright County can justly be proud. On being admitted to the bar he became a member of the firm in which he had studied, the firm becoming known as Mansfield & Pope, and he is also a member of the real estate firm of Pope & Stewart. This last named firm have the only complete set of abstract books in Wright County. Mr. Pope is an attorney of unusual ability, and does a large business in the county. He is the son of Thomas and Mary A. (Hale) Pope. The maternal grandfather, John L. Hale, was a native of North Carolina, and the maternal grandmother's maiden name was Hunt.

Hon. Joseph P. Raney, at present a retired merchant of Mountain Grove, Mo., was born in Pulaski County, Ky., in 1833, the son of William and Lucy (Graves) Raney, and is the grandson, on his mother's side, of Robert Graves, who was a native of North Carolina. The paternal grandfather was a native of Ireland, and after immigrating to the United States settled in North Carolina. The maternal grandmother, who was a Leighton, was of Carolina stock. William Raney was a native of Era, Ky., and was a farmer by occupation. He was married in his native State, and came to Macon County, Mo., in 1839, where he followed agricultural pursuits until 1854, when he received his final summons. Mrs. Lucy (Graves) Raney was born in 1803, and died in Shelby County, Mo., in 1874. William Graves, an uncle of Hon. Joseph P. Raney, has been a minister in the Baptist Church for over sixty years, and is now in his eighty-sixth year. He rides on horseback, and is still active in his ministerial duties. Hon. Joseph P. Raney grew to maturity in Macon County, Mo., and his early school advantages were limited. This he improved materially by his own individual efforts, and is considered a well-informed man on every subject. He was married in 1867 to Miss M. E. Grass. She was born in Indiana, and died in 1861. One child, who is now deceased, was born to this union. In 1862 Mr. Raney enlisted in the Union Army, Company M, First Arkansas Cavalry Volunteers, at Springfield, and was in service from July 22, 1862, to February 27, 1865. He participated in the battles of Prairie Grove, Fayetteville, and was in several severe skirmishes. He entered the service as a private, but was immediately promoted to the rank of orderly-sergeant, and later to first lieutenant, at Berryville, Ark., in March, 1864. He was mustered out as lieutenant February 27, 1865, because of disability, and now, for diseases contracted in the army, he receives a pension of $7 per month. After the war Mr. Raney located in Barry County, Mo., and was the first sheriff of that county after the war, being elected in 1865. He served one term, and then entered the saw-mill business, which he continued until September, 1867. He then left Barry County and moved to Wright County, Mo., locating one and a half miles east of Hartville, and was there engaged in tilling the soil. Later he engaged in merchandising with William Young, of that place, but abandoned that in the fall of 1870, and was elected to the Missouri Legislature. He served out that period, and later was elected to the position of treasurer, which he filled for two years. In 1882 he was re-elected to the Legislature, served that period, and then moved to Mountain Grove. He engaged in merchandising here in 1882, and entered the firm of J. P. Raney & Co. In 1884 the firm title changed to Robertson, Raney & Co. John Cundeer became a member of the firm in 1885. Mr. Raney retired, sold to Dr. J. R. Carson, and remained out of business until November, 1885, when he engaged in business at Hartville, but later moved his stock to Mountain Grove, and became associated with J. Raine & Co. He sold out in 1888, and is now retired. He was married to M. M. V. Quigg (Weaver), and six children were the result of this union, five now living: William, Lucy M., Dorcas P., James and Joseph H. The one deceased was named Guy, who died when young. Mr. Raney's second wife died in October, 1884, and he was married in May, 1888, to Miss Nancy W. Thomas, who was born in Shelby County, Mo. Mr. Raney is a member of the A. F. & A. M., and also the G. A. R. He is a member of the Baptist Church.

J. W. Rippee, druggist at Cedar Gap, Wright County, Mo., was born in Webster County, Mo., in 1850, the son of John and Catherine (Newton) Rippee, and grandson of William Rippee, who died when John Rippee was small, and hence no account of him. John Rippee was born in Kentucky in 1822, and grew to manhood in Indiana. He came to Missouri in 1837, locating in what is now Webster County, but then Pulaski, and is one of the pioneer men of the place. He is still alive; was married in Pulaski County, and is still a resident of Webster. His wife, Catherine Newton, was born in Indiana in 1833, and by her marriage became the mother of ten children, eight now living, and J. W. Rippee being the eldest in order of birth. He was reared in Webster County on a farm, and remained on the same until June 19, 1888, when he was united in marriage to Miss Melissa Potter, of Douglas County, Mo., born in 1869, and the daughter of William Potter, one of the early settlers. Mrs. Rippee received a common-school education, and is a refined and much esteemed lady. Mr. Rippee embarked in the drug business in May, 1887, and owns a half interest in the establishment. He also owns forty acres of land in Barry County, Mo. In politics, he is a Republican.

Mrs. Nancy Robinett, widow of James H. Robinett, was born in Tennessee in 1841, the daughter of Johanan and Sarah (McRoberts) Smith. The father was born in Tennessee in 1812, and came to Missouri in 1853. He has followed agricultural pursuits all his life, and is yet living. He is residing with his daughter. The mother was born in Tennessee in 1812, and is also alive, and resides with her daughter. They were the parents of five children, two now living, Mrs. Nancy Robinett and Francis Smith. The paternal grandfather, Johanan Smith, was a native of North Carolina, was a farmer by occupation, and died in Tennessee in 1857, at the age of eighty-three. He was of Irish descent. James H. Robinett was born in North Carolina in 1827, went to Tennessee with his parents when a boy, and when still quite young moved with them to Missouri. They settled in Wright County in 1838, and there his father, Jesse Robinett, entered land. The mother was Mrs. Frances (Jones) Robinett. Jesse Robinett was one of the pioneers of the county, and accumulated a great many acres of land during his life. He was for years one of the leading men of the county, and was judge of the county court. He was also appointed sheriff of the county, which position he held during the war. He was in the Federal army, and was a member of the Eighth Missouri State Militia. He died in Wright County, Mo., in 1881. He was the father of twelve children, all now living: James H., John, Charlie, Jesse A., Winfield, Lincoln, Frances, Nancy, Wilson, Avi, Cleo and Rebecca. There are now 1,300 acres of land in the Robinett estate. Mrs. Robinett is a member of the Methodist Episcopal Church, and is of Irish extraction. The Robinetts are of French. The voters of the family are Republicans in politics. Winfield Robinett attended school at Drury College, Springfield, Mo., and Jesse Allen, Charles and John also attended the same institution. James is a graduate of Eastman's Business College. Winfield was born February 11, 1868, and took a three years' course in school. He traveled through Kansas, Nebraska, Illinois, North Dakota and the Dominion of Canada, and was absent a year and a half.

J. H. Robinett, of the general mercantile firm of I. L. Hart & Co., of Norwood, Mo., was born on the 3d of August, 1861, and is a son of Judge J. H. Robinett, a short history of whom is given in the sketch of Nancy Robinett. Our subject received a high-school education, and completed his business course in the Eastman National Business College at Poughkeepsie, N. Y., and has a life membership in the same. He returned to Wright County, Mo., in 1882, and farmed one year, after which he engaged in the mercantile business with C. Lehman & Co., at Norwood. After being associated with that firm for about one and a half years, he withdrew, and went to Mountain Grove, where he was occupied in business for two years. His eyes had been troubling him for some time, and one year was then spent in having them treated. He was married to Miss Sarah N. Lee, who was born in Wright County in 1855, and their union has resulted in the birth of four children: Mabel, Oliver L., Annie and Nena. Mr. Robinett is one of the rising young men of Wright County, and is a shrewd and successful business man. He is a Republican in politics, and belongs to the A. F. & A. M. fraternity.

G. J. Roote is an extensive manufacturer and dealer in railroad lumber at Mansfield, and was born in Waukesha County, Wis., in 1845, being a son of Eleazer and Laura (Jenkins) Roote. The father was born in Columbia County, N. Y., March 6, 1802, and graduated from Williams College, Massachusetts, in 1821, being admitted to the bar of the supreme court of New York three years later. He was then engaged in practicing law until 1830, but was then compelled to go to a warmer climate on account of his health. From that time until 1845 he made his home in Virginia, then moved to Waukesha County, Wis., where he became the chief promoter and founder of Carroll College. In 1847 he was elected a member of the Second Constitutional Convention from his county, and was substantially the author of the present educational article in the constitution for the State of Wisconsin, as well as that providing for and founding a State University. In 1848 he was elected superintendent of public instruction, being re-elected to the office in 1852 and 1854, but at the latter date ill-health again forced him to return South, and, having taken orders in the Prostestant Episcopal Church, he was for three years rector of Trinity Church, St. Augustine, Fla. He was first married to Miss Hannah Dayton, of Hudson, N. Y., and secondly to Miss Laura Jenkins, who was born in New York City in 1815. She became the mother of four children, and died in 1876. Mr. Roote died July 25, 1887, at St. Augustine, Fla. His father was a native of Connecticut, and was a physician by profession. He was a descendant of Thomas Roote who emigrated from England at an early day and settled in North ampton, Mass. The maternal great-grandfather of our subject, Thomas Jenkins, was born at Nantucket, Mass., and amassed a great deal of wealth. He was a large ship owner, and was one of the chief founders of Hudson, N. Y. His son, Gilbert, was also a ship owner, and for over thirty years was a collector of the port at Hudson, N. Y. The latter's daughter, Laura, was the mother of the gentleman whose name heads this sketch, G. J. Roote. The latter was educated in Ripon College, Wis., but in 1863 left his studies to enter the Federal army, and was a faithful soldier until 1866. His literary and other mental endowments were soon recognized, and he became a clerk in the adjutant-general's office, under Maj.-Gen. Thomas. His ability as a clerk was very remarkable, and during all his wearisome routine of duty not one of his records was returned for correction. At the close of the war he wrote the history of the Fourteenth Army Corps. For several years after the war he was in the employ of different publishing companies, and then engaged in the real estate business in Jefferson County, Mo., but after some time went to Alabama, where he and a brother established the Tuscumbia *Chronicle*, a weekly journal, but sold out in 1874, returned to Missouri, and located in Wright County in 1884, where he engaged in prospecting and mining. In 1885 Mr. Roote became editor of the *Wright County Republican*, but the following year embarked in his present work, and does an annual business of $30,000. He is an uncompromising Union man, a strong Republican, and was the prime mover in establishing the G. A. R. post at Mansfield, and has been its Commander since its organization. He was married in 1872 to Mrs. Elizabeth Fotheringham, *nee* Bryan, who was born in Ste. Genevieve County, Mo., in 1844. Mr. Roote was the Republican candidate for the Legislature from Wright County in the late election.

Andrew Ross, judge of probate court of Wright County, Mo., was born in Polk County, Mo., April 27, 1841, the son of Henry and Mary

E. (Tarbutton) Ross, and grandson of Samuel Ross, who was a native of Kentucky, was a farmer by occupation, and received his final summons in his native State. The maternal grandfather was also a native of Kentucky, also a farmer by occupation, and died in Wright County, Mo. Henry Ross was born in Kentucky February 21, 1816, and left his native State at the age of sixteen, and in 1856 moved to Wright County, Mo., settling in the western part of the county. He remained there until 1868, when he moved to Polk County, Mo., and there he still resides. During the Civil War he was on the Federal side, in the Eighth Missouri State Militia, but only served one year. He was also in the Indian War. His wife, Mary E. (Tarbutton) Ross, was a native of Kentucky, born in 1824, and remained in her native State until sixteen years of age, when she came to Polk County, Mo. Here she married Mr. Ross, and to them were born nine children, eight of whom grew to maturity. Mrs. Ross died April 4, 1860. Judge Ross attained his growth in Wright County, Mo., on a farm, and secured a rather limited education in the common schools. This he greatly improved by individual study, and is considered a well-informed man on any subject. He was married to Miss Marjery Newton, daughter of William and Nancy Newton, and the result of this happy union was the birth of eight children, six now living: John H., Nancy E., Arthur A., Flora A., Mary A. and Naomi J. Those deceased are Jesse A., at the age of two years, and William N., at the age of three months. Judge Ross was in the Federal army, first in Phelps' regiment and afterward in Company L, First Missouri Cavalry Volunteers. He enlisted in August, 1862, and was discharged June 17, 1865. October 10, 1867, he lost his hand and half way to his elbow, just after the war, in a cane-mill. In 1868 he was elected assessor of Wright County, and re-elected in 1870. He was elected justice of the peace several times, and in 1884 was elected probate judge, and is the present incumbent. He owns 178 acres of land four miles north of Cedar Gap, and is a successful farmer and a prominent citizen. Judge Ross is a member of the Baptist Church, was ordained a minister in the same about six years ago, and has acted as a local preacher ever since. He has had charge of Pleasant View and Mansfield Churches. He is a Republican in politics; is a member and Chaplain of the G. A. R. at Mansfield.

A. J. Rudd, postmaster at Mountain Grove, Wright Co., Mo., was born in Greene County of the same State in 1864, and is the son of P. W. and Delilah (Messimar) Rudd, and grandson of William A. Rudd, who was a native of Scotland. He immigrated to America and located in North Carolina. The maternal grandfather, Peter Messimar, was a native of Germany, and immigrated to America at an early date. He located in Tennessee, but afterward moved to Georgia, where he now resides, and, although ninety-seven years of age, enjoys excellent health. P. W. Rudd was born in Cassville, N. C., but immigrated to Georgia, where he married Miss Messimar. He was a farmer by occupation, also a dealer in real estate and a merchant. He came to Missouri in 1859, and located in Greene County in 1866, but left that county and went to Washington County, Ark. After remaining in that State for a year he returned to Missouri, locating at Hartville, Wright County, and there followed the law and real estate business. He came to Mountain Grove in 1884; was appointed postmaster August 30, 1885, and served until his death, which occurred January 21, 1888. To Mr. and Mrs. Rudd were born nine children, seven of whom are now living, A. J. Rudd being the eldest son. He was married February 24, 1884, to Miss Jennie L. Rippee, who was born in 1868. She is now the mother of two children, Audrey L. and Ada. Mrs. Rudd is still in school, though married and a mother. She attended school at Richmond, Mo., before marriage, and was a teacher in Tennessee at the time of marriage. She is of a decidedly literary taste, and contemplates completing a classical course and still further pursue the business of teaching. Mr. Rudd, besides being postmaster, is a full partner with F. M. Garner in the hardware firm of Rudd & Garner. He is a member of the I. O. O. F. lodge, and is a decided Democrat in his political principles. Mrs. Rudd is a member of the Methodist Episcopal Church, South.

Rev. John A. Russell, minister of the Cumberland Presbyterian Church, of Brush Creek Township, Wright Co., Mo., was born in Alabama in 1851, the son of Samuel C. and Sarah G. (Crawford) Russell, and the grandson on his mother's side of Joseph Crawford, who was a minister in the Cumberland Presbyterian Church, Coffee County, Middle Tennessee. He was man of much ability, had a good English education, and became preceptor to many young men who entered the ministry. He died at the advanced age of over ninety years. The maternal great-grandfather was of Scotch-Irish descent, and was born in the Emerald Isle. He came to America about the first of the present century, and was the father of ten children, seven sons and three daughters. Of the seven sons, four are ministers, and one a physician. Samuel C. Russell was also a native of Alabama, and was married in Tennessee to Sarah G. Crawford, who bore him five children, of whom Rev. John A. Russell is the eldest. The parents moved to Tennessee in about 1852, and from there to Missouri in 1857 or 1858, locating in Wright County, two miles south of Hartville. Here the father died May 17, 1864. He was all through the Mexican War. His wife followed him to the grave June 18, 1864. The Russells are of Irish descent. Rev. John A. Russell was reared on a farm, and educated in Wright County and in Arkansas. He commenced studying for the ministry in 1878, and joined the church October 12 of that year. He was licensed to preach March 30, 1879, on the first essay he wrote, and was ordained in October, 1880, at Mount Moriah Church, Wright County, Springfield Presbytery. He preached for seven years at Norwood, and from 1883 to 1888 at Phillipsburg Church. He is the owner of 250 acres of land, but expects to devote his whole time to the ministry. He was married in November, 1875, to Miss Tennessee McClannahan, who was born in Tennessee May 25, 1854, and who is the daughter of Philip McClannahan. Her father came to Missouri about 1872, and died about 1874, at the age of sixty years. He was a successful tiller of the soil. To Mr. and Mrs. Russell were born six children: Floyd, Elmer E., Holan, Cora I., Vance E. and DeWitt T. Mr. Russell followed the teacher's profession for about ten years, and was school commissioner of Wright County for four years. He is a member of the Wheel, a member of the Masonic fraternity, and is a Democrat in his political views.

Samuel O. Shields, collector-elect of Wright County, Mo., was born in Pulaski County, Mo., in 1849, the son of Arnett and Nancy (Richardson) Shields. Arnett Shields was born in Roane County, Tenn., February 14, 1816, was a farmer by occupation, and came to Missouri in May, 1837, locating in what is now Wright County, and died there February 3, 1888. He was one of the associate judges of Wright County Court during the war. He enlisted for the Mexican War, but his company was not called out. During the Civil War he was a member of the Twenty-fourth Missouri Regiment Volunteers, but was discharged on account of being too old. He was married twice, in Missouri, his second wife being Miss Nancy Richardson, who bore him eight children, who grew to maturity. There were three children by the first wife, one of whom is now alive. Samuel O. Shields grew to manhood in Wright County, and has acquired a limited education by personal application. He was married at the age of twenty-one years to Miss Sarah J. Smith, who bore him four children, three now living: John, Arnett and Charles. The one deceased was named David. Mr. Shields has been engaged in farming, and for the past six or eight years has been occupied in trading in stock, shipping and driving cattle. He is the owner of 460 acres of land. He is a Democrat in politics, and was elected collector on the Labor ticket. His paternal grandfather was a native of Tennessee, and came to Missouri in 1837, where he died in Webster County, at the age of sixty-five years. He was a soldier in the War of 1812. The paternal great-grandfather was a native of Ireland, who immigrated to America, and located in Tennessee. The Richardsons were originally from Tennessee. Mr. Shields is one of the enterprising, progressive men of the county, and is respected, and esteemed by all who know him.

James A. Simpson, mayor of Mountain Grove, Wright County, Mo., and proprietor of Mountain Grove Marble Works, was born in Cannon County, Tenn., September 7, 1846, being the son of John A. and Margaret (Cherry) Simpson, and grandson of Valentine Simpson, who was a native of North Carolina, and was a farmer by occupation. He moved from his native State to Tennessee, and there resided until an old man, when he immigrated to Oregon County, Mo., and here received his final summons. He was born in 1790, and died in 1865. He was said to have been a soldier in the Black Hawk War. The paternal great-grandfather, Peter Simpson, was a native of North Carolina, and immigrated to Tennessee, where he died. The name Simpson is purely English. The maternal grandfather was born in North Carolina, and also immigrated to Tennessee, where he died. The maternal grandmother, Sarah Cherry, was a descendant of English ancestors. John A. Simpson, father of subject, was born in Tennessee February 27, 1821, and there grew to manhood and was married. He immigrated to Missouri in 1851, and located in Lawrence County, removing in 1861 to Randolph County, Ark., where he died in 1865. He was in the Confederate service during the late war, and participated in a number of battles. Margaret (Cherry) Simpson is still living, and resides in Lawrence County, Mo. She is the mother of eight children, of whom

James A. Simpson is the eldest. He was reared to man's estate in Lawrence County, Mo., received a common-school education, and came to Wright County, Mo., in 1873, where he was married to Miss Helen R. Ellis, a native of Wright County, Mo., born in 1852. Seven children were the fruits of this union: Loren E., Margaret E., Verona J., Annie V., John W., Francis Edward and James Arthur. Mr. Simpson followed farming until 1883, and then engaged in the marble business, which he has since continued, and does all his own work. He is also the owner of three houses and lots. He was elected justice of the peace of Mountain Grove Township in 1886, elected mayor in 1887, and filled the office of city treasurer for one year, previous to being elected to the position of mayor. He is a Democrat in politics, and is a member of the Methodist Episcopal Church, being a trustee of the same. Mr. Simpson comes of long-lived ancestors on both the paternal and maternal sides, having seen all his grandparents except the grandmother on his father's side, and in infancy was held in the arms of his great-grandparents on his father's side.

Mrs. Margaret Smith, widow of Henry Smith, of Pleasant Valley Township, Wright Co., Mo., was born in Roane County, E. Tenn., in 1826. She is a daughter of Daniel and Jane (Mattox) White, the father having lived all his life in Tennessee, where he was engaged in farming. After his death his widow with her six children came to Missouri. Margaret Smith grew to womanhood in Tennessee, and was married there, in October, 1851, to Henry Smith, who was a native of the "Old North State," born in 1824. He was taken by his people to Tennessee when a boy, and there grew to manhood. While a young man he served in the Mexican War, and after his return he and Mrs. Smith were married, came to Missouri in 1852, and located in Webster County, but at the end of two years came to Wright County, and located on their present farm. Mr. Smith entered the Union army, Company B, First Missouri Cavalry, and served about three years. His health at this time became very much impaired, but he has never applied for a pension. After his return home he was engaged in farming until his death, in 1880. He left a valuable 500-acre upland and bottom farm, which is still in possession of the family, with the exception of twenty-seven acres, which were sold for $50 per acre. Mrs. Smith became the mother of six children, five of whom are living: Eliza, wife of John A. Hensley; Houston, Huldah E., wife of Gid. M. Hensley; William J. and Samuel Lafayette. Her oldest child, Alexander, was born in 1852, and died in 1881, leaving a wife and three children. The family attend the Presbyterian Church. Mr. Smith was a Republican in politics.

J. C. Spence, a prominent merchant of Mansfield, Mo., was born in Roane County, E. Tenn., in 1830, and was the sixth child born to the marriage of Robert and Margaret (Alexander) Spence, who were early immigrants to Tennessee, where they were married and reared their family of eight children. In 1853 they immigrated to Wright County, Mo., where they were engaged in farming and spent the remainder of their days. The father's ancestors, paternal and maternal, who were of Scotch and Irish descent, immigrated to America prior to the Revolutionary War, and served in that conflict, the latter being in the battle of King's Mountain, where he had his "bee gum" hat pierced by seven bullets. The hat was kept in the family as a relic for many years. J. C. Spence, whose name heads this sketch, was the first of his father's children to leave the paternal roof to seek his fortune. While they were still residents of Tennessee he came to Missouri (in 1852), having been previously married to Miss Sarah E. Osborn, a native of Tennessee. She only lived two years after her marriage, their only child dying the same week that his mother did. Soon after this sad event Mr. Spence went to California, and remained on the Pacific slope for eleven years, and finally, after mining without success for several years, turned his attention to stock dealing, in which business he was quite successful. In 1868 he returned to Wright County, and engaged in merchandising, farming and stock trading, but after a time gave up the two latter employments, and since 1882 has been a resident of Mansfield, and has given his attention to merchandising. The first year of his residence in the town he built a barn and was occupied in the livery business, but soon sold out, and has since given his attention to his store. On invoicing his stock of goods January 1, 1889, it amounted to about $10,000. He has good town property, and is considered one of the wealthy citizens of the county. He is a member of the Cumberland Presbyterian Church, and is a Democrat in his political views.

Edward H. Stewart, attorney at law and member of the real estate firm of Pope & Stewart, of Hartville, Mo., was born in Buffalo, Dallas Co., Mo., in 1865, and was reared and educated in that State. He received more than average educational advantages from his earliest childhood, and being of a literary turn of mind, coupled with a studious temperament during his college course at Marionville Collegiate Institute, graduated with honors from that institution in 1884, having laid the foundation of a good English education. After leaving school he went to Texas County, Mo., where he engaged in the profession of teaching. He afterward became editor of the *Record*, a journal published at Cabool. Hard study at college caused Mr. Stewart's eyes to become affected, and he went to Wichita, Kas., where he joined a corps of civil engineers then in the employ of the Missouri Pacific Railroad Company, and helped locate 4,000 miles of railroad, in Kansas and Colorado. He afterward left the employ of the company, and engaged at a better salary with the Denver & Rio Grande Railway Company. He worked through Colorado, New Mexico and Utah Territories. Having regained his health, Mr. Stewart returned to Missouri in October, 1887. Having previously studied law, he was admitted to the bar at Hartville, Mo., in September, 1888. Since that time he and Attorney S. E. Pope have organized the real estate firm of Pope & Stewart. They are doing an extensive land, insurance and loan business. Mr. Stewart is a genuine Democrat by conviction, his ancestors having been Republicans. During the campaign of 1888 he stumped Wright County in favor of Grover Cleveland's administration. His efforts on the stump signalized his ability, and have been the cause of his being offered various honorable and remunerative positions outside of Wright County. Mr. Stewart is the son of A. J. and Anna (Gay) Stewart, and the grandson on his mother's side of William Gay, who was a native of Kentucky, and who was a colonel in the Creek and Seminole War. He became a pioneer of California, and lived near Oroville, where he amassed considerable property, and where he spent his declining years. He died in 1875. The maternal great-grandfather was a native of England, and the maternal great-great-grandfather was a native of Germany. Mrs. Anna (Gay) Stewart was born in Indian Territory in 1835, and is now living in a comfortable home in Barry County, Mo.

S. T. Talcott, editor of the *Mountain Prospect*, a weekly journal at Mountain Grove, Wright Co., Mo., is a native of Vernon, Tolland Co., Conn., where he was born in 1829, being a son of Samuel S. and Harriet S. (Smith) Talcott. Talcott is an English name, and the ancestors of the present family came from England to America at an early date. The paternal grandfather was a farmer and mechanic, and died in Connecticut, his native State. The maternal grandfather was a Revolutionary soldier, and was full of humor. At one time, while in the army, and when the soldiers were rationed on horse flesh and told that it was beef, he secured a horse's tail, fastened it to a pole, and started through the camp, crying "Beef! beef!" He came very near getting court-martialed for this bit of humor. Samuel S. Talcott was born in Vernon, Conn., in 1793, grew to manhood and died in that town in his ninetieth year. He was a farmer and manufacturer by occupation. He was first selectman and justice of the peace for several years, and also represented the county in the Legislature one year. His wife, Harriet (Smith) Talcott, was also a native of Connecticut, born in 1800. They were the parents of six children, three now living, and S. T. Talcott being the fifth in order of birth. He attained his growth and was educated in Connecticut, having in addition to his common-school education attended the graded schools for some time. He assisted his father on the farm, and worked in the paper mill belonging to his father until twenty-two years of age, when he married Miss Louisa Woodford, daughter of Romantia Woodford, a farmer in the town of Avon, Conn. One child was the result of this union, Arthur C., who died at the age of nine years. Mrs. Talcott died in 1859, and Mr. Talcott, in 1861, married Miss Sabra C. Bushnell, who was born in Norwich, Conn., and was educated at Norwich Free Academy. One child, Minnie L., was born to this union; she died at the age of two years. Mrs. Talcott was for several years a teacher in Mountain Grove Academy, and is a regular correspondent for the *Missouri and Kansas Farmer*. She now supervises the printing department of the office of the *Mountain Prospect*. She was very popular as a teacher at Mountain Grove. After marriage Mr. Talcott followed paper manufacturing for a number of years, when his health failed, and he traveled for some time. During the late war he enlisted in the Federal army under Hancock, Twenty-seventh Connecticut Volunteers, and was out nine months. He was at the battles of Fredericksburg and Chancellorsville, and was for a time in Libby Prison. After the war he returned to Connecticut, and was for a time engaged as a traveling salesman. He left Connecticut in 1869, and came to Texas County, Mo., where he took up a homestead. In 1874 he went to Colorado on horseback; was in Kansas, Colorado, Wyoming Territory, Iowa, and back through Missouri to his home in 1875. He remained on his homestead until his health broke down, when he changed business, and manufactured shingles, also superintended the building of a steam saw and grist-mill in the wilderness of Texas County. In 1877 he came to Mountain Grove, and has been here since. In 1882 he became editor of his present paper, and the same year was made mayor of the town. The year previous he was appointed justice of the peace. Mr. Talcott is a genial gentleman, of much push and enterprise, and in connection with his paper he does a large real estate business. The *Mountain Prospect* is devoted to the interests of South Central Missouri, and has a circulation of 600. Mrs. Talcott is a lady of much culture, and is thoroughly conversant with all topics concerning South Central Missouri.

James A. Tate, treasurer of Wright County, and one of its leading citizens, was born in that county September 25, 1859, being the son of John L. and Turzy J. (Quick) Tate, natives of Tennessee, and grandson of James Tate, who was born in Virginia, going from there to North Carolina, from there to Tennessee, and finally to Newton County, Mo., where he received his final summons. He was a fifer in the Revolution on the side of the Colonists, and in a fight at Norfolk, Va., had the fife shot out of his mouth, and was himself disabled. There is in the family a box which family tradition says was handed down from the ancestors in Scotland. The paternal great-grandfather was born in Ireland, but was of Scotch descent. John L. Tate was born in North Carolina, and moved with his parents to Tennessee when a child, and afterward in 1839, or when he was nine years of age, moved to Missouri, and was one of the pioneer settlers of Wright County. He was married in that State, was a farmer by occupation, was elected county surveyor, afterward sheriff, and died in Wright County November 20, 1880. The mother is still living, and resides in Hartville. They were the parents of five children, two now living: James A. and Thula (Murrell). James A. received a good, liberal education in the common schools of Wright County, and followed agricultural pursuits until November, 1884, when he was elected county treasurer of Wright County. He was re-elected in 1886, and, now that he has served as long as the law permits, has retired from public office for the present. He has also been one of the popular educators of the county. He is a member of the A. F. & A. M.; is a Republican in politics, and is one of the native young men of whom Wright County may justly be proud. He has gained the confidence and esteem of the people of the community, and has made a worthy officer. He lost in a fire at Hartville over $1,500 worth of drugs.

John Turner, farmer and stockman of Wright County, Mo., was born in Roane County, Tenn., in 1820, and was there reared to manhood and married. He immigrated to Missouri in 1849, and in October, 1860, took up his abode on his present farm in Wright County. He first married Rebecca McMullin, and by her had the following children: Sarah (Mrs. Hanks), Elizabeth A. (Mrs. Odell), Margaret (Mrs. Bell), Nancy (Mrs. Moore), Mary (Mrs. Ridgway), Frances

(Mrs. Bumont), Laura (Mrs. Henson) and John J. Those deceased are Jason, who died during the Civil War, and James, at the age of fifteen years. Mr. Turner took for his second wife, Miss Elizabeth White, and their children are as follows: Jesse, who married Sarah J. Hensley, and is the father of one child, Lillie; Triphena, wife of Will Hight; Joseph C., who married Ary L. Crippen, and has one child, John Andrew; John, and Fisher C., who was killed by accident when four years of age. John married Tennessee Evans, but since her death has lived with his father. Mr. Turner was in the Federal service during the late war, serving in a Missouri Company. He owns a good farm of 286 acres, and is well fixed financially. He is a Republican, a member of the G. A. R., and belongs to the Baptist Church. His parents, John and Sarah (TaLee) Turner, were married in New Orleans, whither the father had come from his native land of Ireland after he had attained manhood. He soon after moved to Tennessee, where he lived until his family grew to maturity, and in 1849 located in Scott County, Mo., where he died in 1889. He was a soldier in the War of 1812, and he and his sons, John, whose name heads this sketch, and Sterling, were in the Florida War. The father and Sterling held commissions as lieutenant. The latter was a captain in the late war on the Confederate side, and was killed at the battle of Vicksburg. Joseph, another son, held the rank of major under Gen. Sherman, in the United States army, and was at the siege of Vicksburg, where his brother was killed, and after the surrender found his brother dead. Besides this brother he had another brother, two nephews, and a brother-in-law in the surrender. John Turner, the father, and his wife were the parents of eight sons and three daughters, and after the mother's death he married a Mrs. McMullin, whose maiden name was Matlock. To them were born two children. The paternal grandfather immigrated with his large family from Ireland to America, and located in North Carolina, where he died at a very old age.

Judge Marion Ward, associate judge of the Southern District, Wright County Court, of Missouri, was born in Jefferson County, Tenn., in 1843, and is the son of James and Nancy (McKinney) Ward. James Ward was born in Virginia, and moved from that State to Tennessee, where he passed his last days. His father, John Ward, was one of the early settlers of Tennessee, from Virginia, and was of Irish descent, his father having been born in Ireland. Nancy (McKinney) Ward was born in Tennessee, and by her marriage to Mr. Ward became the mother of eight children, three now living. She died in Jefferson County, Tenn. Judge Marion Ward, the youngest of the above-mentioned family, received a common-school education, which he increased materially by individual study in later years. He moved to Missouri in 1860, locating in Wright County, and although only seventeen years of age, began working for himself, first by farming. When the war broke out he abandoned that business and joined the Federal army, Company H, Eighth Missouri Cavalry, and was with this company one year. He was wounded at the battle of Lone Jack, being shot five times, and was disabled from duty from 1863. He ran a confectionery house in Rolla until August, 1864, when he joined the Sixteenth Missouri Cavalry, and served until the close of the war. He was mustered out at Springfield, Mo., in June, 1865, and still has both of his discharges. He received his pension about 1879—$6 per month. Mr. Ward settled in Wright County after the war, and made his home in Gasconade Township, where he has remained ever since. He was elected judge of the county court in 1886, and after serving two years was re-elected in 1888. He was married to Miss Margaret L. Newton in September, 1864. She was born March 27, 1843, and by her marriage became the mother of eleven children, all now living: Ira E., Sarah (wife of E. C. F. Hickman), Jasper N., Robert N., Nancy M., John M., Bedie I., Ora V., Addie, Ollie and Otis E. Mrs. Ward is the daughter of Nevels Newton, one of the earliest settlers of Wright County, Mo., and a native of Indiana. Judge Ward is the owner of over 244 acres of land, and lives six miles due west of Hartville. He is a Republican in his political views, and a member of the Methodist Episcopal Church.

W. H. Wells, proprietor of Lake Lily Roller Mills, of Mountain Grove, Mo., is a native of Indiana, born in 1855. He grew to manhood in his native State, receiving a good common-school education, which he improved materially by attending college in Sullivan County, Ind. He was married at the early age of nineteen to Miss Rose Wesner, his junior by two years, and the result of this early and happy union was four children, only one now living, Edith. Of the three deceased but one lived to be three years of age. After his marriage Mr. Wells followed agricultural pursuits in Indiana for two years, and then, becoming convinced that some other pursuit in life would be more congenial to his tastes, and perhaps more remunerative in the outcome, he purchased a share in the Augusta Mills, at Augusta, Ind. He remained a partner in the mills for three and a half years, when he sold out his milling interest there and made a trip to Texas. He, however, remained in the Lone Star State but a short time, when he returned to Illinois, locating at Butler, Montgomery Co., and consistent with his taste, leased a mill, which he ran for nine months. He next went to Stanton, Ill., where he worked in a mill for five months. Previous to his milling at Stanton he was engaged for a short time in running an engine for the Litchfield Car Machine Co., at Litchfield, Ill. In 1882 Mr. Wells moved to Missouri, and settled at Hartville, Wright County, where he ran a water mill on the Gasconade River for one year. In 1883 he came to Mountain Grove, and was a partner with James Archer in a mill on the site of the old town of Mountain Grove. When the railroad came through Wright County this partnership was dissolved, and Mr. Wells purchased an interest in the mills, and finally became sole proprietor. In 1886 he changed the old stone process of the mill for a full roller process, with a capacity of ninety barrels per day. The total cost of machinery and property was $12,000. Mr. Wells now does an extensive merchant and exchange milling business, and ships flour as far as Memphis, Tenn. It is claimed by him that the superior quality of the flour ground by Lake Lily Mills is due not only to the excellent care and facilities for grinding, but to the superior quality of the native wheat as well; is the best he has ever ground in any country. Mr. Wells is abstemious; is a Democrat in politics, and is a member of the Christian Church. He is the son of

Andrew J. and Mary J. (Perkins) Wells, and the grandson of Frank Wells, who was born in Kentucky, and removed to Indiana, where he died. He was a farmer by occupation, and a soldier in the Revolutionary War. The parents of the subject of this sketch were both natives of Indiana, but the father's people were from Kentucky. The mother died in 1868. They were the parents of eight children, two now living. Andrew Wells followed various pursuits, viz.: merchandising, milling, farming, and owned considerable real estate. He went to Texas, and now lives in Palestine of that State, engaged in merchandising.

Moses White is one of the prosperous farmers and stockmen of Wright County, Mo., and deserves much credit for the success which has attended his efforts, as he started in life a poor boy. He was born in Roane County, Tenn., in 1829, and was the first of the family to leave home and fight the battle of life for himself. In 1848 he came to Wright County, Mo., having walked the most of the way, and on his arrival here had just $1. He worked by the month as a farm hand for three years, then returned to Tennessee, and brought his mother, brothers and sisters back to Missouri with him. He then entered a good piece of land, but sold his claim soon after, and bought 160 acres at the head-waters of the Gasconade River. This land he also sold, and bought his present property, which proved a good investment, and on which he located in the fall of 1858. On the 8th of March, 1855, he wedded Miss Amanda Freeman, who was born in Roane County, Tenn., in 1846, and five of their ten children are living at the present time: Robert Jason, Samuel, Louella (wife of Ralph Simmons), Minnie and Eva. Those deceased are Joseph, Alonzo, Emma, Sadie (wife of M. G. Henslee) and Martha (wife of C. C. Hensley). When the Civil War broke out Mr. White joined the Home Guards, then the Enrolled Militia, serving six months in each. He was taken prisoner by Marmaduke's men, but was afterward exchanged. Since the war he has been successfully engaged in farming. His farm consists of 230 acres, and is well adapted to raising the cereals or stock. He is a Republican, a member of the A. F. & A. M., and he and family worship in the Baptist Church. His father, Daniel White, was a native of North Carolina, and went to Tennessee with his parents when a boy, where he was reared, educated and married, the latter event being to Miss Jane Mattox. He was a farmer by occupation, and died in Tennessee. His wife died in Missouri in 1863. Five of their eight children are now alive. The paternal grandfather was probably born in North Carolina, and was married in Tennessee to a Miss Hawkins. She came with her children to Missouri, and died in Wright County at the age of seventy-two years.

J. W. Williams, lumber merchant at Mountain Grove, Mo., was born in Indiana, Spencer County, in 1850, the son of William and E. M. (Whitton) Williams. William Williams was born in England, and immigrated to America at an early date. He was married in Indiana, and lived in Spencer County of that State for many years, engaged in agricultural pursuits. He was born in 1828, and died in 1863. Mrs. Williams was born in 1822, in Kentucky, is still living, and is a resident of Mountain Grove, Mo. J. W. Williams was the eldest of three children. He was but fourteen years of age when his father died, and he began traveling around. He traveled over thirteen States and three Territories. He first worked on a steamboat between Pittsburg and New Orleans for over six years, and then became freight clerk on a boat, where he remained for some time. He then came to Missouri, and became a carpenter, a joiner, and a millwright. He followed the saw-mill business for four years in Douglas and Howell Counties, afterward sold out, and erected a planing-mill in Mountain Grove in June, 1877. He ran a large lumber yard, $5,000 of lumber invested. Mr. Williams has just returned from a trip through Arkansas, Georgia, Texas, Indian Territory and New Mexico. He has now determined to remain in Mountain Grove, and is the owner of considerable town property. He has been the owner of as much as 1,700 acres of land, and is the owner of eighty acres now. He was married in June, 1871, to Miss E. H. Huffman, who has borne him two children, Fred and Addie. Mrs. Williams is the daughter of James and Melvina (Lundy) Huffman, the father being a native of Virginia, and of German extraction. Mr. Williams affiliates with the Republican party in his politics. He is a member of the Methodist Episcopal Church, and also a member of the A. F. & A. M.

Dr. I. S. Wilson, secretary and general manager of Spring River Lumber Company, Cedar Gap, Wright Co., Mo., was born in Belmont County, Ohio, in 1845, and attained his growth on the farm. He took his first course of medical lectures in Cincinnati, Ohio, and graduated in New York City, when about twenty-one years of age, under the great Dr. Flint. After graduating he enlisted in the Federal service, as surgeon in Brown's staff, in March, 1865. He remained in the employ of the Government until 1871, when he returned to Ohio. He resided for a year and a half in Illinois, Henderson County, and came to Missouri in 1873. He located in Webster County when the Gulf Railroad came through, in 1882; later he moved to Cedar Gap; was made postmaster, and still holds that position. He was elected surveyor of Webster County two terms, and when he had served his term nearly out, resigned. He stumped the county for the Greenback nominee for representative. He practiced medicine at Waldo for about nine years, and then, in 1882, embarked in the lumber business at Cedar Gap, Mo., gradually withdrawing from active practice. May 7, 1886, he took a partner in the lumber business, G. W. Freeman, and this firm is worth $50,000. Dr. Wilson was married in Waldo to Miss Naomi Dixon, of Webster County, born in 1862 (now deceased), and one child (also dead) was the result of this union. His parents, Avery and Sarah (Hayes) Wilson, were both natives of Belmont County, Ohio, and both born in the year 1818. Avery Wilson was a farmer by occupation. He is now deceased. The paternal grandfather, Caleb Wilson, was a native of Ohio, and the paternal grandmother, whose maiden name was Mills, was a native of North Carolina. She was a Quaker, and was a member of Millwood Church in Ohio. The great-grandfather Wilson was also a native of Ohio. Dr. Wilson is the owner of a farm and some town property in Webster County. He was called to the chair of mathematics in Mountain Dale Seminary for one scholastic year.

P. R. Worsham, a retired farmer, residing at Mountain Grove, Mo., was born in East Tennessee May 18, 1827, his parents being Joseph and Melvina (Lewis) Worsham. They were born, reared and married in Virginia, after which they immigrated to Tennessee, locating in the eastern portion of the State, where the father died. He was the father of five children, four of whom lived to maturity, and after his death his widow, in company with her son, P. R. Worsham, came to Missouri, and died at her son's home, in Texas County, in 1880, aged seventy-seven years. P. R. Worsham grew to manhood in Tennessee, and was there married to Miss Nancy Scott, who was born in East Tennessee in 1825, and is a daughter of William and Susan (Parker) Scott. Their union was blessed in the birth of eleven children, the following of whom are living: Sarah J., wife of John W. Wallace; Mary E., wife of G. W. Hunter; Henderson, Susan, wife of James Cardwell; Catherine, wife of F. Cardwell; Cordelia, wife of Grant Seburn; Alice, wife of James Mabon, the present treasurer of Wright County. The children deceased are Eliza (Mrs. Mitchell), who died at the age of eighteen years; William, at the age of eleven months; David, at the age of two months, and Oliver, aged fourteen months. Mr. and Mrs. Worsham have also reared a grandson, Columbus Mitchell, who is now a student in Mountain Grove Academy. Mrs. Worsham's father was of Scotch-Irish descent, a farmer by occupation, and in 1841 immigrated from his native State of Tennessee to Missouri, and died in St. Louis County. Mr. Worsham came to Missouri in 1853, locating first in Wright County, afterward in Texas County, making the latter his home until 1886, when he concluded to retire from active business life, and moved to Mountain Grove, but still retains his farm, which consists of 340 acres. He also has thirty-seven acres one mile west of Mountain Grove, but lives in town. He is a Republican in politics, a member of the Methodist Episcopal Church and the Masonic fraternity. For twenty years he was postmaster of Pleasant Ridge, and holds his commission as justice of the peace.

Brown Wyatt, stock trader, of Mountain Grove, Wright Co., was born in St. Clair County, of that State, December 9, 1843, the son of John J. and Christiana (Duckworth) Wyatt, and grandson of John Wyatt, a native of Kentucky, and a farmer by occupation. The great-grandfather was also named John Wyatt. The Duckworth family are of Irish descent. John J. Wyatt was born March 20, 1811, in Kentucky, and died in Wild Cherry, Ark., in November, 1880. He was a merchant by occupation, but was also a minister in the Christian Church. By his own individual efforts he obtained a good education, and became a very prominent minister in the Christian Church in Missouri and Arkansas. He would never accept any money for his services in the church. His wife, Christiana Wyatt, was born in Illinois in January, 1822, and was the mother of eight children, of whom our subject is second in order of birth. He attained his growth in Arkansas, and has acquired by application a fine business education. He was married at the age of twenty-three to Miss Paulina Haughn, a daughter of Peter Haughn, who was born in Germany, and who was a soldier in the War of 1812. By this union Mr. Wyatt became the father of eight children: Henry Clay, Maggie, Jemima C., John, Dollie, Ada, Oliver and May Leora. These children are now in school. Mr. Wyatt is the owner of 160 acres of land and a residence in town. He ships stock, and has been following shipping to St. Louis for more than twenty years. He is a Republican in politics, and was in the Union army during the war, in Company G, Phelps' regiment, one of six companies organized in Fulton County, Ark.

Pleasant Wynne, who is closely associated with the farming and stock raising interests of Montgomery Township, Wright Co., Mo., is a native of Marion County, Tenn., born in 1829. He is the son of John and Margaret Wynne. John Wynne was born in Virginia in October, 1800, and was a pioneer of Tennessee. He was a great hunter, and spent many enjoyable hours with his gun. He died in 1865. By his marriage he became the father of nine children, three now living, and P. Wynne being the eldest alive, and the fifth child. He was reared in Tennessee, and was there married to Miss Anna Bullard, who bore him nine children: George Washington, William, Mary, Margaret, Pleasant, Jane, Alabama, Angenetta and Tennessee, The mother of these children died in 1883, when about fifty-three years of age. Pleasant Wynne was united in marriage to Mrs. Long, whose maiden name was Bohannon, and two children were the result of this union: Thomas J. and James Monroe. Mr. Wynne settled on his present farm in 1870. He bought 403 acres of land, and after doing well by his children he has about 300 acres yet. During the war Mr. Wynne was in the commissary department.

Mrs. Julia Wynne, widow of Julian F. Wynne, was born in Gibson County, W. Tenn., in 1854, and is the daughter of William and Julia (Gilbert) Caple. William Caple was born in Middle Tennessee in 1817, was a farmer and stock-trader by occupation, and was also engaged in merchandising. He died in Tennessee in 1862. The mother, Julia Caple, was born in North Carolina. They were the parents of ten children. Mrs. Julia Wynne, the subject of this sketch, was married to Julian Wynne in Arkansas, and bore him seven children: Barbara, Harriet, Ida, Vernie (deceased), Mary (wife of J. P. Box, who died in May, 1887, leaving two children, Blanche and Claude), William, who died at the age of four years, and Thomas, who died when six weeks old. Mrs. Wynne came to her present farm in 1878. This farm consists of 160 acres of land, with 120 acres under cultivation. Julian Wynne was born in Dyer County, W. Tenn., in 1840, and always followed agricultural pursuits. He died in 1881. He was the son of William and Barbara Wynne, natives of East Tennessee, who immigrated to Missouri, and both died in Wright County. Julian Wynne was in the Confederate army during the late war, and served with honor and credit for four years. Mrs. Wynne is a member of the Presbyterian Church, as was also her husband.

Archabal Young, an enterprising farmer of Gasconade Township, Wright Co., Mo., was born in Perry County, Ky., in 1822, and is a son of Samuel and Mary (Newton) Young. The paternal grandparents, so far as known, were born in Ireland, and the grandmother died in Kentucky. Samuel Young was born in North Carolina May 5, 1774, grew to manhood in that State, and there married. He farmed for many years in Virginia, Kentucky, Indiana and Missouri, moving into the last named State in the fall of 1841, and there died in 1850. His wife, Mrs. Mary (Newton) Young, was born in North Carolina November 10, 1777, and was the mother of ten children, all of whom lived to be grown. She died in Indiana when her son Archabal was six years of age. He remained in Indiana until nineteen years of age, when he moved to Wright County, Mo., and was one of the pioneer hunters of that State. He made hunting a business, and he now says that if all the deer he has killed were alive and turned into one herd, it would astonish people. The woods at that time abounded in many wild animals, and were a hunter's paradise. Mr. Young went to work, and now has an excellent farm. He has been married three times: first, to Miss Frances Rippee, and after her death to Mrs. Cynthia Blankenship, who bore him two children, Cynthia and Angeline. After her death Mr. Young married Miss Elizabeth H. McCain. To the first marriage were born six children. During the Civil War Mr. Young was a member of Company E, Eighth Missouri Cavalry. He is a Democrat in politics, is a member of the Wheel, and has been a member of the Cumberland Presbyterian Church for forty-five years.

Mrs. A. M. Young, widow of William Young, of Hartville, Mo., was born in Crawford County, Mo., in 1840, and is the daughter of John M. and Elizabeth (Bridges) Gorman. John M. Gorman was born in North Carolina in 1814, and grew to manhood in Crawford County, Mo. He first worked as a collier in that county, saved his money, and afterward engaged in merchandising in a log cabin three miles south of where Hartville now stands. He afterward located in Hartville, and was the first dry goods merchant in the town. There had been, previous to his location in the county seat, one man who had followed the grocery business on a small scale. Consequently Mr. Gorman may be called the pioneer merchant of Wright County. He followed this business in Hartville, and in connection ran a couple of extensive stock farms, until his death in 1854. When the report of his death was spread abroad many of the old people said, " The father of Hartville is dead." He was married in 1834, in Phelps County, to Miss Lizzie Bridges, a native of Tennessee, born in 1820, and the result of this happy union was the birth of eight children, four of whom grew to maturity. Of these Mrs. A. M. Young is the eldest. When her mother, who died in 1851, was about to close her eyes upon the scenes of this world, she turned to our subject, who was then but eleven years of age, and gave her the two younger children. After her death Mr. Gorman married Mrs. Cynthia Tunnel, and the usual result of step-mother curriculum was entailed upon the children. In this case Mrs. Young remembered the dying request of her mother, and in a truly womanly way looked after the interests of her two younger brothers. At the age of fifteen she was married to William Young, and the result of this pleasant union was five children, four of whom are now living: Frank, F. M. (deceased), Mattie, wife, of T. J. Kelly; Harvey and Oscar. William Young, the father of these children, was born in Indiana in 1833, the son of W. F. and Mary (Young) Young, cousins. While he was still a boy his parents immigrated to Missouri, locating in the woods on a fork of the Gasconade, and here William grew to manhood among the wild scenes of frontier life. After reaching years of discretion he became a merchant, and followed this business in Hartville for about five years after the Civil War. Just about the time that he was doing a most extensive business, failing health interfered, and he gradually became an invalid. After ten years of sickness he died of consumption, in 1883. During her husband's illness Mrs. Young, with the business trait that always distinguished her, took charge of her husband's affairs, and in 1871 commenced keeping hotel in her present building in Hartville, and in connection with this carried on her domestic affairs. For two years she kept hotel in Mansfield, Wright Co., Mo., but afterward returned to her home in Hartville, where the "Young House" is noted for its good board, general comfort and genial atmosphere. "Aunt Rilda," as Mrs. Young is familiarly called by her friends, is a pleasant faced, ruddy cheeked, stout woman, whose never-failing good humor makes her a favorite wherever she is known. Her paternal grandparents were natives of Ireland, who immigrated to America, settling in Tennessee first, and then became early settlers of Missouri. They settled in what was afterward formed into Phelps County, and there the Gorman family lived long, and were very much respected. A number of large apple trees now mark the site of the Gorman's old homestead. The seeds from which the apple trees were grown were brought by Grandmother Gorman from Tennessee, in the toe of a stocking. William Young's father, W. F. Young, was among the earliest settlers of the Wood's Fork of the Gasconade. In his house the first circuit court of Wright County was held, and also the first church services. W. F. Young was born in North Carolina; his father was also born in that State, but his great-grandfather was a native of Ireland, and immigrated to America in 1790 or 1792, where he became one of the pioneers of North Carolina. Frank Young, the eldest child of our subject, was born in Hartville, Mo., in 1856, and at the age of sixteen he became a page in the Missouri House of Representatives, where he remained two years. On his return home he attended school, and afterward engaged in the profession of teaching for four years, during which time he was also connected with a retail furniture establishment. In 1883 he was appointed treasurer of Wright County by Gov. Crittenden, and served two years. He took charge of the "Young House," a hotel in Marshfield, during 1884 and 1885, after which he went on the road as traveling salesman for Joseph Baum & Co., a boot and shoe house, at St. Louis. His health failed at this time, and he went to California, where he remained a season, and then returned to Hartville, where he has since been engaged in taking care of the Young estate, and also has charge of the livery business. He was elected chairman of the Democratic Central Committee September 20, 1888, and is one of the enthusiastic Democrats of the section; his influence, combined with the efforts of other young men of the county, defeated the most important part of the Republican ticket in Wright County for 1888. A bright future is in store for this young man, and he will no doubt be heard from in the highest circles of

Wright County politics in the near future. He is a member of the Masonic fraternity.

E. B. Young, furniture merchant and dealer in undertakers' goods at Mansfield, Mo., was born in Wright County, Mo., in 1854, and is a son of Fielding M. and Margaret E. (Montgomery) Young, who were born in Indiana and one of the Eastern States, respectively. The father grew to manhood and followed farming and merchandising in Wright County, and there died about 1858. His wife died in 1870, aged forty years, having borne a family of six children. [For paternal genealogy, see sketch of Mrs. A. M. Young, and for the maternal genealogy, see sketch of Prof. T. J. Montgomerie.] E. B. Young grew to manhood in Phelps County, and was educated at Richland, Mo., in the graded schools. He has been dependent on his own resources since the death of his mother, when he was sixteen years of age, and, with the aid of a patrimony which he received, he has been successful in his business ventures. For a number of years he worked at various occupations in Texas, Arkansas, Louisiana and Missouri, and followed saw-milling for two years in Texas. In 1881 he came to Missouri, and went into business in Hartville, the firm being known as E. B. Young & Co., and then came to Mansfield, and entered business in November, 1882, and here has since remained. He has recently taken William Hopper as a partner, and the firm is now styled the Hopper Furniture Co., their stock being valued at $1,500. Mr. Young owns a good lot and residence, and a half interest in the store. In April, 1886, he married Miss Ada Gorman, a daughter of M. D. Gorman, of Hartville, Mo., by whom he has one child, Virdie Mabel.

ADDENDA.

The following items are deserving of mention, and only appear at this place on account of the impossibility of obtaining information in time to secure proper insertion.

Pulaski County.—The first Agricultural Wheel in Pulaski County, Mo., was organized at Hopewell, in Piney Township, March 15, 1888, by J. H. Hanley, State Deputy, the names of nineteen constituent members comprising the organization. Since then forty-nine have been initiated into the lodge at this place. The growth of the order has been steady. April 17, 1888, a sufficient number of Wheels had been instituted to form a County Wheel, the organization of which was effected at Dundas on that date. There are now about forty-five Wheels in the county, with a membership of some 1,200. Four regular sessions of the County Wheel have been held, and a county trade committee appointed, the latter having located a central trade store at Richland, and a sub-central store at Waynesville, each now enjoying a large and satisfactory patronage. The Wheel at Hopewell is still working harmoniously, under the leadership of Rev. A. Hendrix, president.

The population of Pulaski County was, in 1840, 6,529; in 1850, 3,998; in 1860, 3,835; in 1870, 4,714, and in 1880, 7,250. The falling off of 1850 and 1860 was due to the smaller size of the county.

The election returns for President have been as follows: In 1836, Harrison and White (Whig), 49, Van Buren (Dem.), 230; in 1840, Harrison (Whig), 196, Van Buren (Dem.), 720; in 1844, Clay (Whig), 86, Polk (Dem.), 325; in 1848, Taylor (Whig), 124, Cass (Dem.), 241; in 1852, Scott (Whig), 39, Pierce (Dem.), 169; in 1856, Fillmore (American), 68, Buchanan (Dem.), 268; in 1860, Douglas, (Dem.), 107, Bell (Union), 62; Breckinridge (Dem.), 281, Lincoln, (Rep.), 7; in 1864, Lincoln (Rep.), 105, McClellan (Dem.), 28; in 1868, Grant (Rep.), 176, Seymour (Dem.), 199; in 1872, Greeley (Lib. Rep. and Dem.), 534, Grant (Rep.), 324; in 1876, Tilden (Dem.), 748, Hayes (Rep.), 408, Cooper (Greenbacker), 1; in 1880, Hancock Dem.), 772, Garfield (Rep.), 462, Weaver (Greenbacker), 19; in 1884, Cleveland (Dem.), 948, Blaine and Butler (Fusion), 615; in 1888, Cleveland (Dem.), 1,048, Harrison (Rep.), 662, Fiske (Prohibition) 0, Streeter (Labor), 59.

Wright County.—Mountain Grove, as a school point, dates its work back to 1856. The first school building was erected by the citizens by private subscription, among those who contributed being Thomas

Lane, Sr., Preston Day, Manning Harris, Richard Boatman, M. D., and Thomas White, M. D. This house, which still stands at the site of the old town, was presented to Prof. Simeon Phillips, and the parties who built the structure afterward supported the school by paying regular tuition for their children, besides making various donations. Prof. Phillips taught till about the opening of the war, after which no session was held until after peace was concluded. The names of some of the teachers who have officiated here since the war, are Profs. Bundy, Perkins and George Escott. At this period the old Mountain Grove District was formed, and a public school building erected. Since that time the school has been conducted as a district school, and has received an extended patronage from a broad area in South Central Missouri.

The present building of the new organization was constructed in 1886. The present spacious brick edifice was completed that year, and the first term of school was held in 1886 and 1887. Prof. Lynch was employed as principal. Five hundred dollars tuition was paid into the district treasury, by students out of the district and above school age, during that scholastic year. There are now ten counties of Missouri and five States represented in the school. Mountain Grove is essentially a school town, and its citizens have made many sacrifices for the cause of education.

Mountain Grove charge of the Methodist Episcopal Church was organized in 1883, by Rev. R. H. Hanson, with the following original members: L. F. Inman, Cornelia Inman, Peter Hoog, N. M. Hoog, Fannie Rainey, William Roper, Mary Roper, M. M. Cook, J. L. Hughes, J. F. Hughes, H. E. Inman, William Longacre, Wilmot Longacre, J. H. Simpson, H. R. Simpson, M. J. Brown, S. Brown, James Cockrum, Lizzie Cockrum, Mark Robertson, Ebenezer Hunt, R. Cox, S. A. Cox, E. Cox, Carrie Cox, Alice Cox, James Beaumont and Martha Beaumont. The first class leader was L. F. Inman, and the second, Ferguson Braselton; the present one is H. E. Inman. The ministers in succession have been Revs. R. H. Hanson, Allen, Wesley Nall, Groves, Parsons Mosher, Miller, and the present incumbent, Rev. Darby. The present church building is one of the neatest and best furnished in South Central Missouri. Its erection was commenced in 1885, when the membership numbered but fourteen. Except $140, the amount of $1,400 was raised from outside sources, largely through the influence of H. C. Miller, whose services as a member of the building committee proved of substantial benefit.

The Mountain Grove Christian Church was organized in 1877, under W. D. Campbell, a local preacher, with G. W. Workman and wife, Thomas Johnston and wife, D. L. Benson and wife, Mrs. P. Wyatt and G. S. Escott and wife among the original members. Dr. Benson was ordained elder, and also acted as church clerk. The growth of this body was unnoticed until 1883, when Rev. J. N. Murphy came, and preaching was resumed. A reorganization was effected, and D. L. Benson, H. J. Smith, William Dyer and I. N. Moore were chosen elders; John Odell and J. W. Doughty, deacons, and James Sales, church clerk. The membership at this time was forty-two. Following Rev. Mr. Murphy, C. C. Coffer, J. W. Frost, H.

Drennan, F. M. Houton and H. Drennan (present incumbent) have been the pastors in charge. Until the completion of the new church building services were held in the school-house of the old village. The new edifice was begun in 1883, and completed in 1885, at a cost of about $4,000. It is entirely paid for. The church roll includes the names of about seventy-five members.

Dent County.—The population of Dent County in 1860 was 5,654; in 1870, 6,357, and in 1880, 10,646.

The election returns of Dent (for President), beginning with 1852, are as follows: Scott (Whig), 74; Pierce (Dem.), 96. In 1856, Fillmore (American), 77; Buchanan (Dem.), 396. In 1860, Douglas (Dem.), 207; Bell (Union), 243; Breckenridge (Dem.), 338; Lincoln (Rep.), 7. In 1864, Lincoln (Rep.), 107; McClellan (Dem.), 1. In 1868, Grant (Rep.), 214; Seymour (Dem.), 161. In 1872, Greeley (liberal Rep. and Dem.), 515; Grant (Rep.), 394. In 1876, Tilden (Dem.), 826; Hayes (Rep.), 446. In 1880, Hancock (Dem.), 1,073; Garfield (Rep.), 707; Weaver (Greenbacker), 35. In 1884, Cleveland (Dem.), 1,171; Blaine and Butler (Fusion), 798. In 1888, Cleveland (Dem), 1,172; Harrison (Rep.), 957; Fiske (Prohib.), 16; Streeter (Labor), 55.

INDEX

Abbott, Lucly-808
Abbott, F.W.-688
Abbott, F.A.-688
Abel, John David-973
Abel, Margaret-973
Able, Etta-927
Able, Matilda-927
Abshere, Smith-1162
Adams, Mary-1181
Adams, Samuel-1165
Adams, Burwell-1159
Adams, James B.-1159
    John Quincy
    Burwell B.
    Minnie S.
    Wm. T.
    Mary L.
Adams, Catherine-1005
Adams, Elizabeth-1004
Adams, (Grandfather)-1004
Adams, Celia-993
Adams, Wm.-961
Adams, Francis M.-922
    Elzerene
    Emily D.
    Wm. A.
    Alta J.
    Frances R.
    Mary O.
    Philip A.
Adams, Eliza-961
Adams, Philip-922
    Francis M.
    Martin V.
    Jasper N.
    Julia D.
Adams, Elcanah-766
Adams, J. Spencer-766
Adams, W. Spencer-766
    Rufus
    Thomas Luther

    Nancy Jane
    Margarie Catherine
    Mollie L.
    Stacy
Adkins, H.-712
Adkins, Drury-689
Adkins, Abner-689
    Bailey
    Malinda
    Abner
    Wm.
Adkins, Bailey-689
Adkinson, Rebecca-1040
Agee, Isaac-1159
Agee, Anna-909
Agee, Sherman-917
Agee, John B.-1159
Agee, Wm.-1159
Aldredge, Harriet A.-835
Aldridge, Richard-822
Aldridge, Micajah-822
    Martha A.
    Candice S.
    Allie B.
    Sterling Roy
    Williamson
Alexander, Tobitha M.-836
Alexander, H.H.-836
Alexander, Margaret-964
Alexander, Margaret-1204
Alford, Wm.-931
Alford, M.-931
Alford, John-923
    Malinda
    Robert
    Orlando D.
    Thomas
    Margaret
    Rebecca
    Mary

Alford, John M.-1923
    Robert
    Wm.
    Pleasant
    Jeremiah
    Sarah
    Mathew
    Charles
    Thomas
    Owen
    Susan
    Mary
    John
Alford, Sarah-925
Alford, J.M.-925
Allaman, W.T.-1098
Allcorn, John-940
Allen, A.N.-1193
Allen, Jane-1172
Allen, Harriet-1159
Allen, John-1159
Allen, Dr.-830
Allen, John-790
Allen, Martha-790
Allen, John D.-966
Alley, Clara J.-944
Alley, Wiley-944
Alsup, W.L.-858
Amick, Barney-1160
    John
    Theodosia
    Cynthia
    Cora
    Charles
    Edgar
    Roscoe
    Neva
    Samuel
Amick, Lorenzo-Cynthia-842
Amick, Elizabeth C.-842
Amick, Lorenzo D.-1160
Amos, Rebecca M.-922
Anderson, Nancy E.-1188
Anderson, Martha C.-1125
Anderson, Edward-823
    V.W.
    Adaline
    Margaret J.
    Thomas
Anderson, Thomas-823
    Francis M.
    Henry R.
    Margaret J.
    I.N.
    Thomas J.
    Allen A.
    John L.
    Eula B.
    Minnie E.
    V. Ernest
Anderson, Tennie-815
Anderson, Jacob-744
Anderson, Rebecca J.-744
Anderson, Jesse C.-689
    James W.
    Dawson B.
    Jesse N.
Anderson, Jesse N.-689
    Ida
    Frances
Andrew, Mark-924
    Martha
    Virginia
    Emily
    Lucy
    Harriet
    Joseph
    Susan
    Mark
    John P.
Andrews, Susannah-1031
Andrews, Emily-936
Andrews, John P.-924
    Henrietta V.
    Zula R.
    Alice
    Rolla
    Bessie
Andrews, Sallie-706
Angel, John M.-1089
    James W.
    Isabella A.
    Susan B.
    Hershel A.

        John C.
        Willis
        Sarah Rebecca
        Horace
Angel, Martin-1089
Angell, J.M.-1089
Angell, G.W.-1090
Anshim, Rosa-1162
Ansley, Doreas-1135
Anthony, Elizabeth-1170
Anthony, Benjamin-1118
Anthony, John M.-981
Anthony, Permelia F.-981
Apperson, John-1067
Apperson, Elizabeth-1067
Appleton, John, Jr.-889
Appleton, John, Sr.-889
Appleton, R.H.C.-889
        Myrtle Evee
Appleton, Alsie-809
Appling, James-753
Appling, James M.-690
Appling, James M.-690
        Aurelius M.
        James W.
        John W.
        Columbus C.
        Miles L.
        Edward H.
        Sarah A.
        Ella M.
Appling, Joel-690
Appling, James W.-690
        Ella B.
        Jennie M.
        Alma M.
Archer, Wm.-1162
Archer, Joseph, Sr.-1162
Archer, James-1161
        Mary E.
        Fred W.
        Lizzie E.
        Ralph
        Alice
        Clara E.
Archibald, O.W.-864
Armitage, Hester-1005
Armstrong, Dialtha-1013

Armstrong, J.W.-899
Armstrong, James-890
        Mason
        Roland
        James
Armstrong, Mason-890
Armstrong, James M.-890
Armstrong John W.-890
        James W.
        Joseph S.
        Mary Ellis
        Benjamin
        John R.
        Charles H.
        Elizabeth D.
Armstrong, Susan-815
Armstrong, John W.-696
Arnhold, George-319
        August
        Wm.
        Ameil
        Henry
        Louisa
        Sophia
        Clara
Arnhold, Henry-891
        Christopher
        John
        Sophia
        Dora
        George
Arnholdt, Christopher-920
Arnholdt, Louisa-920
Arnot, W.L.-1026
Arnot, Halbert-1026
Arthur, Alice-1104
Arthur, Mattie L.-1103
Arthur, John-1027
        Mattie
        Samuel
        Alice
        Anna Mary
        Kate
        Julia
Arthur, Barnabas-1027
Arthur, John-974
        Samuel F.
        Mary

　　　　　　Mattie
　　　　　　Alice
　　　　　　Katie
　　　　　　John
　　　　　　James
　　　　　　Lewis
　　　　　　Ellen
　　　　　　Lizzie
　　　　　　May
　　　　　　Julia
Arthur, Samuel F.-974
Arthur, Lizzie-1083
Arthur, Bluford-Julia-1083
Asbridge, Joseph-1028
Asbridge, Samuel-1028
　　　　　　Sidney L.
　　　　　　Rachel Melvina
Ashbrook, Rosanna-1072
Asher, Narcissa-1142
Asher, Wm. R.-1142
Asher, Wm. Sr.-1142
Ashlock, John M.-1029
Ashlock, Wm.-1029
Ashlock, John M.-1029
Ashwell, Nancy E.-914
Askin, John Sr.-1030
Asking, John Jr.-1030
　　　　　　Wm. A.
　　　　　　Robert M.
Asking, Robert Mortimer-1030
　　　　　　Wm. Clarence
　　　　　　John Herbert
　　　　　　Arthur W.
　　　　　　Adney E.
　　　　　　Myrvin L.
　　　　　　Matie A.
　　　　　　Elia
Atchley, James-691
　　　　　　John B.
　　　　　　Benjamin
　　　　　　Freeman
Atchley, John-Lizzie-691
　　　　　　Noah D.
　　　　　　Morgan L.
　　　　　　Seth
　　　　　　Miles
　　　　　　Sarah
　　　　　　Elizabeth
　　　　　　Elder
　　　　　　Delilah
　　　　　　James
Atchley, Martin-692
　　　　　　Seth
　　　　　　Mahala
Atchly, Morgan L.-924
　　　　　　John A.
　　　　　　Jessie E.
　　　　　　Inez
　　　　　　Virgil M.
　　　　　　Maude
Atkins, Scott-824
Atkins, Morrie-824
Atkins, Samuel-824
Atkinson, John-826
Atkinson, Edith-826
Atteberry, F.S.-990
Atwater, Frannie C.-1158
Auckman, Andrew-1017
Auckman, Elizabeth-1017
Aurebach, Louis-1026
Austin, J.L.-931
Austin, G.B.-946
Avery, Mary-1015
Avery, John-Elizabeth-1000
Avery, Juliana-1000
Avery, James M.-1033
Avery, Roy-96
Avery, Foster-891
　　　　　　Jeremiah M.
　　　　　　Ephraim F.
　　　　　　Sarah
　　　　　　Eda A.
Avery, B.F.-891
　　　　　　Emma
　　　　　　Edna C.
　　　　　　Roy
　　　　　　Charles E.
****
**
Bacon, Elizabeth-1006
Bagerly, Mrs. Mildred E.-899
Bagley, Hiram-915
Bailey, Ogden-761
Bailey, Andrew R.-767
　　　　　　Preston T.
　　　　　　Mattie
　　　　　　Carrie L.

          Lester M.
          Jennie E.
Bailey, David-767
Bailey, Miss-1191
Bain, Asa H.-1031
          James F.
          Mary S.
          H. Asbury
          Susannah C
Bain, Wm.-1031
Bain, Frederick-1031
Baker, Mary-819
Baker, Mary Ann-876
Baker, Mary-931
Baker, J.A.-925
          James S.
          Mary A.
          Hannah E.
          Lucy
          Maude
          Susie
Baker, Abraham-925
Baker, John-975
          Sarah A.
          Mary H.
          James M.
          John W.
Baker, James-975
Baker, Matthew S.-975
          John N.
          Matthew S.
          Delila A.
          Elizabeth
          Hettie M.
          Nancy R.
          Oliver T.
          Thomas H.
          Malinda J.
          James H.
Baker, Mary-1162
Baker, Jane-1178
Ball, Miss-1151
Ballard, Mary-704
Ballard, Bland N. Sr.-767
Ballard, Bland N. Jr.-767
          Maggie
          Olive
          Charles
          Cora
          Sallie
          Lucy
          Samuel
          Neely
          Winnie
Ballard, B.N.-816
Ballard, Eliza-816
Ballenger, Benjamin-721
Ballew, Nancy-954
Ballou, Nathaniel-891
Bamber, W.F.-1016
Banch, Frank-Mary-1090
Banch, John-1090
          John H.
          Wm. Frederick
Bannen, John-990
Barber, T.Y.-1123
Barber, Miss D.L.-1123
Barker, Frances-938
Barksdale, Wm.-1031
Barksdale, Stephen I.-1031
          Wm.
          Henry
          Waller
Barksdale, Stephen I.K.-Sarah-1040
Barksdale, Mary V.-1040
Barksdale, Nancy-1053
Barlow, Jacob-768
Barlow, Wellington-768
          Pennis
          Joseph W.
          Sarah
          R. Lincoln
          Catherine
          Sherman
Barnard, Mrs. Susan-980
Barnard, Miss R.M.-780
Barnett, Rhoda-801
Barnett, Nancy J.-814
Barnett, Jackson-1163
Barnett, Alexander-1193
Barnes, Elizabeth-690
Barnes, Floyd E.-824
          Cora
          Minnie
          Warren
Barnes, E.W.-824

Barnes, S.K.-851
Barnes, W.S.-1010
Barnes, Nancy M.-1033
Barnes, Thomas-Elizabeth-1068
Barnes, Rachel M.-1068
Barnes, Rachel Minerva-1069
Barnes, John-1090
Barnes, John E.-1090
Barnes, Jehu-1103
Barnes, Sarah Ann-1103
Barnes, Emma H.-1100
Barnes, Mildred-1128
Barnes, Jehu-1162
    Wm. M.
    Ann
    James T.
    Jehu F.
    John
    Elizabeth J.
    Wesley
    Lillie
    Alice
    Mary E.
    Benjamin
Barnes, Zachariah-1162
Barnhart, T.-846
Barns, Rose-1019
Barr, Ellen J.-731
Barr, S.B.F.C.-731
Barr, Ann-840
Barrett, Mary-1013
Barricklow, Farrington-1091
Barricklow, Van Dyke-1091
Barricklow, Daniel-1091
Barricklow, Henry-1091
Barricklow, Perry-1091
Barrow, Mary-1137
Bartholomew, Robert-1092
Bartholomew, Wm. O.-1092
Bartlett, Nancy-971
Bartlett, Solomom-768
    Crocia Ann
    George W.
Bartlett, John M.-768
    Solomom
    Nancy
    Louisa

    John G.
    Reuben H.
    Hiram F.
    Sarah
Bartlett, Solomon-789
Basham, Edmond-788
    Elizabeth
    John
    Nancy
    Perry
    V.A.
    Amanda
    S.F.
    Florence
    Martelia
    James
Basham, Miss V.A.-788
Bass, John-825
    Sarah C.
    Jasper A.J.
    Jesse W.
    John W.
    Margaret F.
    Benton
Bass, Andrew-825
Bass, John T.-925
    Wellington
    Walter
    Ottie
Bass, Dolphin-925
    John T.
    Harriet
    Lucy
    Solomon
    Henry
    Nancy
    Wm.
    Louis
Bass, Robert-1032
Bass, John T.-1032
    Lee
    Jackson
    Benjamin
    Sarah
    Minnie
Bate, A.G.-1145
Bates, Larkin Ruffus-76

       Thomas
       Effie
       Alfred
       Viola
       Mattie
       Charles
Bates, Larkin-769
Bates, Albert-770
       James L.
       Mary J.
       Avirella
       Wm. A.
Bates, Wm. Addison-770
       Cora Lee
       Bertie G.
       Fred R.
       Walter A.
       Stella
       Claude M.
Bates, W.A.-787
Bates, Rebecca-788
Bates, James P.-1092
       Mary F.
Bates, P. Quinton-1092
Bates, James P.-1108
Battons, Mary-938
Baumgartner, Anton-Mary-976
Baumgartner, Peter-975
Bean, Mr.-1191
Beard, Lucinda-908
Beard, James W.-1093
Beard, Bird-1093
Beardon, Elizabeth-1093
Beasly, Louisa-930
Beason, Miss.-1168
Beck, Mr.-748
       Robert Elmer
       Wm. S.
       Edina
Beck, Isaac F.-932
Beck, Josie M.-932
Beck, John C.-926
       Rodolphus
       John M.
       Joseph R.
       Jasper N.
       Sarah E.
Beck, John M.-926

Beck, Leonard-1047
Beck, John-1112
Beckhorn, Eliza-916
Beckner, Danile-692
       Levi L.
       Daniel
       Aaron
       Eli Harrison
       May Ann
       Nioma
       Dilieah
Beckner, Levi L.-692
       Amanda
       John K.
       Abram L.
       Isabelle
       Adeline
       Isaac N.
       Louisa
       Mary Ann
Beckner, Daniel-693
       Siegel
       Jesse
       Chloe
       E.C.
       Dan
       Levi
Beeler, Daniel-1093
Beeler, Jacob-1093
Beeler, Jesse Franklin-1093
       Cynthia Jane
       Mary Orlena
       Matilda Caroline
       Martha Elizabeth
       Melissa Ann
       Margaret Ellen
       James K.P.
Beesley, Betsey-1169
Beers, Frank-1007
Beeson, Naomi-918
Beavers, Reeves-1094
Behrens, Christian H.-926
Behrens, Henry-926
       Christian H.
       Henry J.
       Wm. J.
       August C.
       Hannah
       Charles C.

           Martha
           Frederic E.
Belew, E.A.-1150
Belew, Mollie-1150
Bell, Lucinda-993
Bell, Daniel-994
Bell, Agnes-1090
Bell, Henry H.-1094
      Maggie L.
      Cora
      Edwin E.
      Henry J.
      Samuel G.
Bell, Samuel-1094
Bell, Agnes C.-1100
Bellerby, Kate-1039
Bellerby, Harry-Anna-1039
Bench, Riley-703
Bennett, Lydia E.-715
Bennett, J.M.-969
Bennett, Marion Francis-929
         Wm. S.
         George W.
         Edith
         John Q.
         Lizzie
         Ann
         Phillip
         Maude
         James L.
         Arthur
Bennett, Phillip-928
         Wm. M.
         Marion F.
         Lafayette
         Pauline J.
         Phillip A.
         Emerson
         Margaret A.
Bennett, John C.-928
         Emma
         Ella
         Sheridan
         Sherman
         Emmett
         John
         Odessa
         Ressa

Bennett, Nathaniel L.-927
         Moses W.
         Mary F.
         Lucinda J.
         Albert D.
         Ben D.
         Jack T.
         Edmond
         George M.
Bennett, Moses G.-927
         Nathaniel L.
         Harriet
         James C.
         Martha
         John M.
         Mary
         Lockey A.
         Margaret D.
         Jackson
Bennett, N.L.-944
Bennett, Rutha-925
Bennett, N.C.-944
Bennett, Martha-947
Benson, Alva-694
Benson, Amanda J.-841
Benson, Thomas-841
Benson, Lizzie-1030
Benson, Henry-Mary-1030
Benson, Samuel-1162
Benson, Daniel-1162
Benson, D.L.-1162
Benthall, Rosanah J.-964
Benton, Wm.-935
Benton, John Thomas-1032
        James E.
        Julia Ellen
        Birdie
Benton, Henry W.-1032
        Rhoda Ann
        James S.
        Catherine E.
        John T.
        Henry E.
        Julia Ann
        Elijah P.
Beet, Sarah Mountjoy-981
Betts, Wm.-951
Bevel, Elizabeth-1098

Bickford, L.F.-715
Biehler, Daniel-698
Bierman, John W.-Rosena-1121
Bierman, Jennie-1121
Bilderback, Daniel-693
    Margaret
    Susan
    Hester
    Daniel
    Henry C.
    Elizabeth
Bilderback, Thomas-693
    Henry L.
    Sarah J.
    Stephen W.
    Thomas J.
    Margaret E.
    Mary E.
Billings, Catherine-987
Billings, Margaret-47
Bills, Ailee-858
Bilyeu, Peter-811
Bilyeu, Nancy-811
Binkard, Susan-952
Binkley, N.F.-935
Binkley, Mary-986
Binkley, Mary J.-1165
Binns, Joseph-861
Birlew, Eliza-1038
Bishop, Christina-902
Bishop, Edmund Ward-976
    Jennie
    Julia
    Edmund W. Jr.
    Flora
Bishop, Morris-976
Black, Sarah-1123
Black, Miss. C. Shaw-1142
Black, John T.-1142
Blackwell, Diana-811
Blackwell, Z.-1000
Blackwell, Hardy-1033
    Arley Fulton
Blackwell, Franklin C.-1033
    Emmett H.
Blackwell, Wm.-1033
Blackwell, James H.-1033

    Eliza J.
    Frances
    James T.
    Rachel
    Franklin C.
    John P.
    Nancy
    Hardy
Blackwell, Mary Ann-1085
Blackwell, Wm.-1085
Bland, Richard P.-694
    Fannie
    Theodric R.
    Ewing C.
    George V.
    Margaret
Bland, Stouten E.-894
    Richard P.
    Charles C.
    Elizabeth
Bland, Joannah-704
Bland, S. Edward-977
    Richard P.
    Elizabeth
    Ella
    Charles C.
Bland, Charles C.-977
    Thomas C.
    Richard E.
    Harry O.
    Charles P.
    Ione
    Joseph
    George R.
Blankenship, Elizabeth-938
Blankenship, Mrs. Cynthia-1214
Blankenship, Spencer-1095
Blankenship, John R.-1095
Blanton, Val-1033
Blassingame, Mary-1129
Blay, Alex.-945
Bledsoe, Louisa-913
Bledsoe, Ambrose-914
Bledsoe, Mary E.-951
Bliss, Jerusha-1124
Blommfield, G.G.-721
Blunt, James-826

Blunt, Adam M.-825
    James L.
    Alfred M.
    Lavina
    Daniel L.
    George
    Huldah J.
    Sarah E.
    John C.
    Mary F.
    Martha E.
    Joseph A.
Blunt, Alfred M.-826
    Sarah E.
    Mary E.
    Celia
    James
    Thomas
Blythe, Mary-875
Bodenhamer, David-825
Bodenhamer, Jacob-827
    C.W.
    W.F.
Bodenhamer, P.G.-827
Bodenhamer, Joseph D.-827
    Ella Maude
Bodenhamer, Wm. Frederick-827
Bohannan, Catherine-702
Bohannon, John-730
Bohannon, Malinda-730
Bohannon, Miss-1213
Boiles, Sarah A.-1189
Boisselier, Emil G.-978
    Thomas H.
    Wilhemina
    Emil G.
    Charles W.
    Harry H.
    Katie G.
Bolin, Lewis-1166
Bolin, Comfort-1165
Bolles, R.C.-736
Bollinger, Fannie M.-764
Bollinger, Frederick-Margaret-764
Bollinger, Jacob M.-892
    George F.
    Nancy A.
    Hiram M.
    Lee
    Rosa Mary
    Wright M.
Bollinger, Wright M.-892
    Jacob M.
    Joseph C.
    Salina D.
    Sarah F.
    Jerusha B.
Bollinger, Jacob-892
Bond, Martha-769
Bondurant, Joseph A.-1011
Bondurant, Alice J.-1012
Bonner, Wm.-Anna-1029
Bonner, Jane-1029
Boone, Nancy-1194
Boone, Ratcliff-1194
Booth, Thomas-949
Booth, Jennie H.-772
Booton, Laban-695
Booton, Theodore A.-695
    Margaret
    Elizabeth
    Clark
    Ann
    Nancy
    Ellen
    Charles
Bostic, Mary-789
Bostic, B.B.-789
Bostic, Mrs. Emeline-819
Boswell, Fannie-838
Boswell, Letha-828
Botsford, Merab-976
Bottom, Nancy-947
Bottom, A.-949
Bouldin, Sarah S.-841
Bounde, Hannah-1159
Bourman, James-727
Bowen, Maria-1071
Bower, Emanuel-930
    Hannah
    Susan
    Mary
    Wm.
    Jennie

          Vernon
Bower, Michael-Susan-930
          Michael
          Margaret
          Emanuel
          Luvina
          Wm.
Bower, Ellen-949
Bower, E.-949
Bowers, Valentine-893
          Maggie
          Willie
          Mattie
          Mary
          Gracie
Bowers, Valentine, Sr.-893
Bowers, Abraham N.-893
          Daniel
          Valentine
          Reece
          James
          John
          Jacob
          Isaac
          Polly
          Barbara
          Archey
          Lyda
          Abigail
Bowles, Edward B.-1054
Bowman, John-724
Bowman, Mary C.-727
Bowman, James R.-979
Bowman, James-980
Bowman, John R.-1017
Bowman, Sarah-1017
Bowman, Benjamin-1034
Bowman, Sparling-1034
Bowman, Robert Jackson-1034
          James L.
          Benjamin
          Joseph
          Matthew
          John
          Wm.
          Juda
          Mary
Bowman, Thomas Jefferson-1034

          Benjamin F.
          Thomas J.
Bowman, Isaac-1034
Box, J.P.-1213
          Blanche
          Claude
Boyd, James W.-714
Boyd, Sarah-918
Bradfield, Elizabeth-1041
Bradford, Neely-768
Bradford, Elizabeth-768
Bradford, Adam-770
Bradford, Isaac Neely-770
Bradford, Wm. L.-770
Bradford, Adam-772
Bradford, James A.-771
          Ada L.
          Sally M.
          Marion E.
          Lucy E.
          Clara E.
          Mary L.
Bradford, I.N.-786
Bradford, Nancy J.-822
Bradford, Charles A.-875
Bradford, Martha Frances-1081
Bradford, John D.-1061
Bradford, Thomas N.-1097
Bradford, James-1097
Bradford, James-1096
          America
          Columbus
          Josiah G.
          Hugh
          Florence A.
          Arthur
          Huber
Bradford, Sarah-1133
Bradford, Mary A.-1141
Bradford, James-1141
Bradford, Margaret-1147
Bradford, Nancy-1157
Bradford, Elizabeth-1188
Bradley, Mary-733
Bradshaw, Francis-695
          Belle
          Edith
          James T.

                    Lydia
                    Edward
                    Andrew
                    Mamie
                    Maude
Bradshaw, J.T.-695
          Margaret
          Eugenia
Bradshaw, Laura-960
Bradshaw, J.A.-781
Bradshaw, Wm. A.-904
Brand, Calvin-1033
Brannock, Samuel-827
          Wm. W.
          Hulia A.
          Alexander N.
          Mary A.
Brannock, A.N.-827
Brannock, Wm.-827
Branson, David-980
Braselton, Mary E.-1180
Bray, Wm.-931
     Wm.
     Noah
     Reuben
Bray, Noah-930
     Elizabeth J.
     Mary N.
     Frances A.
     Wm. R.
     Joah J.
     General F.
     Naomi
     Margaret
Breakfield, Mr.-698
Breazeale, Eliza J.-1185
Breshears, Mary B.-925
Bressie, Mary A.-1076
Bressie, David-Lucinda-1076
Brewington, Sallie-815
Brickey, Miss E.J.-1057
Brickey, Cornelius-Keziah-1057
Bridges, Joseph-949
Bridges, Martha A.-949
Bridges, Elizabeth-1214
Briggs, Elizabeth-806
Brigman, Edmund-Nancy-1027

Brigman, Lucy J.-1027
Briner, Laura J.-783
Bringleson, Bringle-717
Britton, Sarah-972
Bronaugh, Sarah J.-742
Brookhaw, Moses-897
Brooke, Cyrus C.-705
Brooke, Florence-705
Brooke, Christopher W.-828
       McNey
       Robert H.
       Stella
       Nellie
       Edna
       Shirley
Brooke, Robert H.-828
Brooke, Henrietta-1029
Brookshire, Susanna-786
Brookshire, Rachel-1110
Brotherton, Marshall-732
Brotherton, James-732
Brotherton, Mary-732
Brown, George A.-696
       Arminta F.
       Neil S.
       Allen D.
       James J.
       Henry L.
       Martha E.
       George L.
       Millie N.
Brown, Henry L.-696
       Gracie S.
       Oscar L.
Brown, J.H.-727
Brown, Elizabeth-783
Brown, George A.-828
Brown, Dickson-828
       George A.
       Eliza Jane
       L.K
       Naomi R.
       J.W.
       E.M.
       Mary A.
       Dixon L.
       Julia Ann

Brown, Pascal-834
Brown, George A.-860
Brown, Mereilla-864
Brown, Eliza-894
Brown, Nancy-902
Brown, Jonas-902
Brown, Thomas M.-931
Brown, John M.-931
Brown, Caroline-953
Brown, Sarah-956
Brown, Jennie Ann-976
Brown, Elizabeth-984
Brown, Elizabeth-1005
Brown, Mehitabel-1042
Brown, Mary-1075
Brown, Sarah-1101
Brown, Alfred N.-1090
    Frank Earl
    Charles Joseph
Brown, John A.-939
Brown, Charles-1099
Brown, Wm. J.-1099
    George W.
    Lily Bell
    F.R.
    Thomas Jerry
    Mary Caroline
    Jimmie
    Cora Bell
Brown, John W.-1098
    Wm. Isaac
    John Wesley
    Thomas Benton
    James Harvey
    Albert L.
    Christopher C.
    Martha Delilah
    Mary Melvina
Brown, George W.-1098
    Thomas J.
    Albert M.
    Charles N.
    Josiah
    James W.
    John H.
Brown, George Wesley-1098

Brown, Wm. R.-1098
    Mary C.
    Eliza A.
    Francis
    George W.
    Wm. J.
Brown, Martin Collins-1097
    Jesse M.
    Emily
    Wiley Luther
    Julia
    Agnes
    George B.
    James M.
    Maggie T.
Brown, Jesse-1097
Brown, Cordelia-1097
Brown, J.M.-1116
Brown, W.I.-1118
Brown, Rachel-1118
Brown, Mary-1132
Brown, Edward-1168
Brown, Mary-1168
Brown, Solomon-1035
Brown, Millard F.-1034
Brownfield, A.B.-768
Brownfield, Sarah A.-918
Brownfield, Samuel-918
    Wm.
    Ellen
    Sarah
Brownlee, Artie M.-767
Brownlee, Thomas-Martha-767
Brownlow, J.P.-932
    Arabella F.
    Sallie P.
    John E.
    Joseph F.
    Cecil A.
    Cora Katie
Brownlow, James-932
Bruhlman, Jacob-1045
Brundridge, Cornelius-933
    Susan
    Sarah
    Martha J.

        G.F.
        Annie
        Ella
        John W.
        Bell
Brundridge, David-933
        Cornelius
        Wm. A.
        Sophronia
        John
        Nancy
        Abraham
        Delila
        James D.
Brunner, Levi-929
        Wm. H.
        Jacob
        John T.
        Sarah E.
        Emanuel
Brunner, Peter-Sally-929
Brush, B.L.-961
Bruton, Terrell-698
Bruton, D.P.-830
Bruton, Martha M.-830
Bruton, Enoch-832
Bruton, Anice Elizabeth-832
Bruton, David-832
Bruton, Ida-832
Bryan, Alexander-772
        Samuel
Bryan, Moses A.-772
Bryan, Alexander-Mary-781
Bryan, Ida-832
Bryan, Elizabeth-1200
Bryant, Rhoda-997
Bryant, Mattie A.-1196
Buchanan, Patsy-1091
Buchanan, James-1091
Buckner, Wm. H.-934
        Joseph A.
        Sarah E.
        David W.
        James D.
        Eliza J.
        John H.
        Margaret A.
        Levi A.
        Lavine
        Charles
        Ira P.
Buckner, Thomas-934
        Wm. H.
        John W.
        Elizabeth
        Nancy E.
Budreau, Fred J.-704
Bugg, Mary Jane-1063
Bullard, Anna-1213
Bumgarner, Henry-849
Bumpus, Penelope-884
Bunch, John-909
Bundy, Clara-1115
Burbanks, Mary-820
Burbanks, Moores-Nancy-820
Burchfield, Mary A.-847
Burgdorf, Hannah-926
Burhans, Mary E.-793
Burhans, James-894
        James W.
        Joseph W.
        Lavinia C.
        Mary E.
        Stephen S.
        Frank D.
        Nancy E.
        Adora
Burhans, Joseph W.-893
        Lizzie
        Mary E.
        Daniel
        Emma
        George
        Lottie
        Pliny J.
        Eva
Burke, Mary-1168
Burkitt, Mary E.-1048
Burkitt, Thomas W.-Catherine-10
Burkitt, Martha L.-1074
Burkitt, Wheeler-Catherine-1006
Burkitt, Sarah-1006
Burks, J.W.-859
Burks, Martha-859

Burks, Didama-1020
Burne, Ann-876
Burne, Elizabeth-924
Burnett, Hannah-1178
Burnes, Martha J.-1105
Burns, Edward S.-980
    Quintus D.
    Daniel D.
    Wm. C.
    Mary F.
    Nettie E.
    Eva M.
    Edward F.
    Elizabeth
Burns, Daniel D.-980
    Melvin H.
    Grover C.
    Elzie
Burns, John S.-697
    Foster
    James
    Wm.
    Denean
    Archibald
    Wilburn
    Eva
    Florence
Burns, Foster-697
    John S.
    Joseph
    James
Burns, John-697
Burrow, Barney-1160
Burrow, Cynthia-1160
Burton, Charles E.-950
Burwell, John-981
    Mary
    John B.
    Stephen B.
    Nathan L.
Burwell, Nathan L.-981
Bushnell, Sabre C.-1206
Butts, John-888
Butts, Andrew Johnson-935
    Mallie
    Willie

Butts, John W.-935
    A.J.
    Nettie
    Hassie
    Walter
Butts, H. G.-935
    **
Cabble, Margaret-1139
Caffey, Jesse W.-910
Cain, Wm.-696
Cain, George C.-772
    Mary
    George W.
    Frances
    Jesse
    Linda
    Thomas
    Louisiana
Cain, Jonathan-772
Cain, Malinda-775
Cain, Wm.-829
Caldwell, Samuel H.-829
    W.S.
    Frederick J.
    Ollie J.
Caldwell, Andrew-830
Caldwell, Sidney C.-830
Caldwell, Samuel-829
Caldwell, Sarah-877
Caldwell, Margaret-877
Caldwell, Robert-877
Calhoun, Louisa-959
Calhoun, Esther-1142
Calhoun, George W.-1163
    Henry
    James F.
    Louisa J.
    Elizabeth
    Wm.
    Mary A.
    Barbara
    John
    Martha L.
    Joseph
    Brantley S.

Calhoun, Wm.-1163
Calhoun, John C.-1163
Calhoun, James-1163
Calhoun, Unica-1194
Callahan, James-1036
Callahan, Margaret-774
Callahan, Sarah-774
Callahan, Robert-1036
Callahan, W.C.-1036
Callahan, James-1036
Callahan, Thomas-1038
Callahan, John Larkin-1036
    John Robert
    Larkin A.
    Sarah
    Thomas A.
    Eliza J.
Callaway, Parham-830
Callaway, James P.-830
    Roxie R.
    Atlee B.
    Parham P.
    Lawrence A.
Callaway, Mary C.-888
Cameron, John G.-1100
    Rosabella
    Ewan J.
    Eva E.
Cameron, John-1100
    Rose Ella
    Aggie
    John
    David M.
    Wm. W.
    Jennie B.
    James R.
Cameron, Malcolm-1100
Cameron, Christina-1086
Cameron, Ellen-1145
Camp, W.B.-1170
Camp, Sarah-1170
Campbell, Robert-980
Campbell, Elizabeth-980
Campbell, J.H.-714
Campbell, George W.-858
Campbell, Ann Eliza-858
Campbell, Isabella-1009

Campbell, Isabel-998
Campbell, Joseph-982
    Mary
    Joseph
    Kate
    Eugene
    Bessie
    John
Campbell, Alexander-1020
Campbell, Lewis-1043
Campbell, Susan-1109
Campbell, Margaret-1148
Campbell, Elizabeth-1147
Camper, Mary-872
Cannady, S.C.-1116
Cannefax, Joseph-774
    George R.
    Robert
    I. Binda
Cannefax, Redford-Louisa-774
Cannefax, John-774
Cannefax, Wm.-774
Cannafax, George R.-773
    Mattie
    Hattie
    Caroline
    Naomi
    Ruthie
    Loren
    Clyde
    Walter
Cannefax, Charley-774
Canoy, Margaret-1131
Cansler, Martha-1023
Cantrell, Mintie A.-1171
Cantrell, Alexander M.-830
    Alexander Hall
    Edward
    Hezikiah
    Charles
    John D.
    Elva
    Mary
    Dora
    A. Logan
    Martha
    Clementina

Cantrell, Gabriel-830
Cantrell, Felix C.-831
   Joseph Sherman
   Ulysses S. Grant
   Wm. Gabriel
   David Sheridan
   Martha Arabelle
   Abraham
Cantrell, Joseph P-831
   John G.
   Wm.
   Nancy
   Malissa
   Ada
   Joseph
   Emma
   Messie
   Mattie
Cantrell, Caroline-831
Caple, Julia-1213
Caple, Wm.-1213
Cardell, Lucinda-923
Cardwell, Edmund P.-832
   America F.
   Thomas G.
   Jesse May
   Caledonia W.
Cardwell, Thomas P.-832
Cardwell, Alexander G.-832
   Wm. Thomas
   Perry W.
   Linda B.
   Samuel Tilden
Cardwell, John-832
Cardwell, Thomas G.-832
   Albert L.
   Susan D.
   Robert E.
   Wm. E.
   Jesse N.
   Thomas A.
   Mattie R.
   Eugenia B.
Cardwell, F.-1212
Cardwell, James-1212
Cargill, Mary-882
Carleton, Franklin S.-922
   Merinda I.
   John
   Sarah A.
Carley, Mary B.-790
Carley, Herbert-790
Carlton, Milton-922
   Eveline E.
   Wm. R.
Carmack, Wm.-Elizabeth-772
Carmack, Sallie-770
Carmack, Mary-772
Carnahan, Maria-951
Carpenter, Lucretia-775
Carpenter, John D.-983
   Gertrude
   Grace
Carpenter, Benedict K.-983
   Wm. E.
   John D.
   Carrie
   Charles H.
Carrick, Wm.-853
Carrick, Martha Ellen-853
Carrigan, Mary A.-688
Carroll, George-Cordelia A.-889
Carroll, Rosa A.-889
Carroll, Deliza-1174
Carson, Fanny-1182
Cartall, Charles-983
Cartall, George-Johannah-983
Carter, C. C.-925
Carter, Reuben I.-934
Carter, Elizabeth-934
Carter, Sarah-1112
Carter, Diana-1132
Carter, Elizabeth-1154
Carthy, Jube-1034
Case, M.H.-968
Casey, Samuel-698
   Mary J.
   Shadrock V.
   Amanda H.
   Anna B.
   Thomas B.
   Lucretia E.
   Samuel H.
Casey, Shadrock V.-698

       Wm. S.
       Mary E.
       Eliza L.
       Thomas H.
       Anna P.
       Shadrock Allen
Cass, Theresa-833
Cass, Dudley-833
Cass, Lewis S.-833
       Mary
       Burdella
       Dudley
       Emma
       Fannie
       Lydia
Cassilly, Alice-1138
Casteel, Charity A.-705
Castleman, Sarah-693
Cates, Thomas-833
Cates, Daniel E.-833
       Zarilda F.
       Giles G.
Cates, John S.-833
       Mary E.
       John R.
       Martha J.
       Daniel E.
       Joseph H.
       Finetti F.
       Locadia R.
       Justinna E.
       Caldonia C.
       James P.
       Giles P.
Cavaness, Edward-1101
Cavaness, Wm. F.-1101
       Thomas M.
       Martha M.
       Mary E.
       Alfred O.
       Lorenzo
       Alexander W.
       Wm. E.
       Andrew D.
Cayoe, Lucretia B.-698
Chaffin, Robert-843
Chaffin, Jefferson P.-865

Chalfant, Job V.-704
Chalfant, L.P.-894
       Joab V.
       James L.
       Henry W.
       Wm. D.
       Edward C.
       Francis A.
       George R.
Chalfant, David H.-894
       L.P.
       Martha
Chalfant, David-894
Chalfant, H.W.-896
       Ida M.
       Sarah M.
       Fred O.
       Florence
Chambers, Charlotte-820
Chambers, Alexander-820
Chambers, James L.-1033
Chandler, Richard-Elizabeth-1023
Chandler, Lizzie M.-1023
Chapman, Rhoda J.-965
Chapman, Lizzie-1165
Cherry, Sallie A.-906
Cherry, Sarah-1203
Cherry, Margaret-1203
Childers, Matilda-1068
Childress, George L.-834
       Mary B.
       Frances E.
       Lillie E.
       Robert B.
       Creed A.
       Linna M.
Childress, R.L.-834
Chilton, Wm.-Louisa-1085
Chilton, Anna-1085
Chitty, Anderson H.-835
       Willie D.
       Gaylord Wallace
Chitty, Dixon-835
Christeson, R.L.-770
Christeson, Elijah Jordan-774
       James
       Thomas J.

```
                Cyrus E.                            Eddie
                Elizabeth                           Drura
                George E.                           Fannie
                John                                Belle
                Cynthia J.                          Inauda
                Sarah A.                            Carrie
                Frank                               Arthur
                Wm. H.                    Claiborn, Danile-Anna-776
                Martha                    Claiborn, Onsley-776
Christeson, Elisha-774                              John L.
            Elijah J.                               Wm. F.
            Permelia                                Susan J.
            Malinda                                 N.T.
            Walker W.                               Elvira E.
            Eljelima                                Daniel A.
Christeson, Robert-774                Clark, May-965
Christeson, Elisha-776                Clark, Spencer-752
Christeson, Robert L. Sr.-776         Clark, Margaret-752
Christeson, Robert L. Jr.-776         Clark, Benjamin-777
            Lida                      Clark, John J.-777
Christeson, Commodore P.-775          Clark, Zachariah-777
            Elijah C.                 Clark, Levi-Nancy-784
            Lillie P.                 Clark, Nancy C.-784
            Wm. C.                    Clark, J.J.-791
            Commodore F.              Clark, Rebecca J.-799
            Mary E.                   Clark, George-954
Christeson, Elijah-775                Clark, Julia W.-954
            Commodore P.              Clark, Mary A.-1019
            Lafayette                 Clark, Maria-1155
            James Pleasant            Clark, J.C.F.-1189
Christman, Eliza-1037                 Claxton, James A.-1164
Christman, James-1016                           James Cannon
Christman, Malinda-1016                         Wm. Calvin
Chumbley, Lewis-1037                            Newton Cyrus
Chumbley, Sarah A.-1037                         Dudley C.
Churchill, Effie T.-992                         Margaret A.
Churchill, C.B.-896                             Henry C.
            Effie                               Hepsey B.
            Armstead S.                         John R.
            Lena B.                             Edward D.
            Harry                               Manday M.
            John                                Jasper
Churchill, A.S.-896                   Claxton, James-1164
Cissel, Eliza-829                     Claxton, Noah-1196
Claiborn, Daniel A.-776               Clayton, Spencer-752
            Onsley                    Clayton, Matilda-752
            H.A.                      Clayton, John W.-859
```

Clayton, Alice-859
Clayton, Foster-1118
Clayton, Nancy Henry-1118
Clayton, Elizabeth-1161
Clayton, Miss-1191
Clendenin, Ephraim R.-699
        Emma G.
        Colburn C.
        Charles M.
        Adelle
        Sidney
        Penelope
        Clara
Clendenin, C.C.-699
        Etta
Clifton, Harriet-1151
Cline, Sarah V.-1111
Clinkinbard, Mary-736
Clinkinbard, James M.-736
Clomen, Martha Ann-872
Cloud, Timothy-944
Cloud, Adaline Matilda-1144
Clough, Jeremiah-700
      Celestia
      Jane
      Edwin R.
      Walter W.
      Charles
Clough, E.R.-700
Clute, Jane-989
Coalter, Elizabeth-712
Cobb, Deborah-903
Cobb, Frances C.-1188
Cockerell, Kitte-747
Cockerill, Catherine-1118
Cockerill, Amanda-785
Cockerill, Anderson-785
Cochrane, L.A.-1101
      Victor Hugo
      Leroy
Cochrane, John, Jr.-1101
Cochrane, John, Sr.-1101
Cochrane, A.L.-1150
Coday, Samuel-1165
      Samantha
      Henry
      Likew
      Isaac
      Emily E.
      James
      Nancy
      Parthine
      Martha
Coday, John-1165
Coday, Henry-1165
      Winfield S.
      Blanche
Cofer, Monroe-929
Coffin, Judith-710
Coffman, Abner L.-701
      Rachel E.
      Fernando /
      Ella
      Houston
      James C.
Coffman, James C.-701
      Rudolph
      Ulue
      Eugene
      Ernest
      Effie
      Ella
      James
      John
      Mary
Coffman, A.B.-701
Coffman, John-701
Coffman, Charles-702
      Lawrence E.
Coffman, Jennie-776
Coffman, John-Mary-776
Colby, Wm. A.-839
Coldiron, Wm.-975
Coldiron, Sarah J.-975
Cole, Hattie-848
Cole, Olive H.-892
Cole, Martha A.-959
Cole, Elizabeth-1039
Cole, Nancy-1096
Coleman, Jackson-1056
Colley, Sarah C.-974
Colley, Cyrus-775
Colley, G.W.-770
Colley, Daniel-779

                Clara
                Daniel Burkley
Colley, James M.-779
Colley, Cyrus-778
Colley, George W.-778
                Frank L.
                James W.
                Charles M.
                Ida V.
                Alfie
Colley, D.B.-787
Collier, Charlotte-833
Collier, D.T.-1103
Collier, David T.-1101
                Bryon
                Ida
                Mamie
                Claud
                Effie
                Everett
                Lillian
                Burt
Collier, Jesse-1101
Collins, America C.-1131
Colton, Thomas-1194
Combs, Maggie-785
Combs, A.J.-Mary E-785
Compton, Rachel-887
Comstock, Elbert C.-Kittie-1037
Comstock, Asa-1037
Condit, Lottie P.-864
Condit, Phillip-864
Condray, Thomas H.-1037
Condray, Wm. H.-1037
Conley, Phebe-1008
Conley, Aggie-1013
Conn, Eleanor M.-921
Conn, Josiah-921
Connell, Tennessee-1049
Connell, James C.-Emily-1049
Connelly, Wm. Burrell-1102
                Elvira
                Sarah Ann
                James Franklin
                Wm. Lincoln
                Cora Blanche
                Jehu

                        Lillie Jane
                        Estella Mabel
                        Mary Elizabeth
            Connelly, Wm.-1102
                        Sarah
                        Livinia
                        Wm.
                        Burrell
            Conner, Solomon-897
            Conner, Maria E.-897
            Conner, Armstrong-701
            Connor, Mary E.-701
            Conway, Pauline-699
            Conway, Clement C.-699
            Cook, Joel B.-702
                        Edward P.
                        John T.
                        Caroline
                        Mary
                        James
                        Sarah
                        George
                        Nathaiel G.
                        Welton
                        Wm. J.
                        Lydia A.
                        Martha
            Cook, John-702
            Cook, Lorenz D.-702
            Cook, Edward P.-702
                        Margaret
                        Wm.
                        Joel B.
                        John E.
                        Mary
                        Laura
                        Angeline
                        Lucy
            Cook, Mary E.-752
            Cook, Wm. J.-780
            Cook, J.B.-780
            Cook, J.L.-926
            Cook, Laderina-952
            Cook, Helen M.-1154
            Cook, Mary-1184
            Cooksey, Wm.-933
            Cooksey, John-933

Cooley, J.S.-1087
Cooley, M.M.-1168
Cooper, Sarah J.-871
Cooper, Humphrey-871
Cooper, Elvira J.-718
Cope, James H.B.-1165
    Wm.
    Sara A.
    Elizabeth
    Fannie E.
    Alenzo
    James Newton
    Cinda
    Flora
    John
    Harvey
Cope, Stephen-1165
Copeland, John-1039
Copening, Ellen-275
Copening, Jacob-875
Coppedge, Lindsey L.-991
Coppedge, Martha E.-991
Coppedge, L.L.-Amanda-988
Coppedge, Sallie J.-985
Coppedge, Henson-1018
Coppedge, Margaret-1018
Coppedge, Levisia-1051
Coppedge, Lucinda-1157
Corser, Wm.-703
Corser, C.H.-703
    Fred
    Augustus
    Nettie Louisa
Coshow, A.J.-748
Cossey, Sarah L.-694
Cotton, John H.-703
    Martha J.
    Addison R.
    Thomas B.
    Artelia E.
    Sarah A.
    Nannie E.
    Elvira
    John M.
Cotton, Samuel-703
    Jacob
    Elizabeth
    John H.

Couch, Sarah-701
Collie, Barbara-1130
Cover, J.A.-1166
Cover, Alson-1166
Cover, S.H.-1167
Cowan, Robert B. Jr.-985
Cowan, David E.-984
Cowan, Robert B.-985
    Elizabeth C.
    David E.
    Robert B.
    Wm. H.
    John W.
    Travis J.
    Francis M.
Cowan, Wm. B.-984
Cowan, Wm.-984
Cowden, Elizabeth-966
Cowden, Mary J.-938
Cowden, Sarah A.-962
Cowden, W.O.P.-962
Cowden, Elizabeth-1193
Cowen, Wm.-1061
Cowen, Robert B.-1061
Cowen, Wm. B.-1061
Cowen, Elizabeth C.-1061
Cowgill, B.E.-704
Cowgill, Elisha Y.-704
    B.H.
    Emma
    Anna
    George I.
Cox, Sarah-966
Cox, Mary-977
Cox, John-937
Cox, Nancy-937
Cox, Margaret-961
Cox, Nancy-1099
Cox, Nicholas-1038
Cox, Christopher C.-1038
Cox, Mr.-1148
    James S.
    Ester E.
    J. Leslie
Cox, Argus-1167
    Roy
Cox, Randolph-1167
Coy, Lewis-912

Craddock, Elizabeth J.-748
Craddock, Asa L.-Nancy-748
    Asa
    James
    Elizabeth
    Nancy
    Eliza
    Lucinda
    John
    Matilda
    Clayborne
    Mary
    Stark
Craddock, Miss-749
Craddock, Anna-754
Craddock, Edmond-Elizabeth-785
Craddock, Lucinda Jane-802
Craddock, John-1065
Craddock, Elizabeth-1055
Craft, Abraham-780
Craft, Wm.-780
Craft, Hiram D.-780
    Edwin
    Wm.
    Charley
    Albert
    Emery
    Neva
    Thomas
    Minnie
Craig, James E.-1031
Craig, Mary M.-1031
Craig, Rose-1100
Craig, W.H.-1052
Craig, T.C.-1114
Craig, Ann-1149
Craiger, James P.-1058
Craiger, Emma-1058
Crain, Frances M.-915
Crain, James A.-915
Crain, C.J.-1192
Craven, Frank-1028
Craven, Alfred-1028
Craven, John W.-1103
Craven, Louie J.-1101
Craven, Benjamin Franklin-1103
    John Arthur

Craven, James A.-1103
    Rosa D.
    Joel W.
    Elbert E.
    Wesley H.
    James M.
    Nunice
    Helen
    Alfred F.
Craven, Alfred Randolph-1104
    Mildred B.
    Mattie E.
    Ashbury F.
Crawford, Mary-818
Crawford, Samuel C., Jr.-836
    Martha Elizabeth
    Samuel L.
Crawford, Samuel C., Sr.-835
Crawford, Mary-935
Crawford, Joseph-1202
Crawford, Sarah G.-1202
Crider, Wm.-1161
Crippen, Avy H.-1208
Crites, Mrs. Sarah-1026
Crockett, John-1169
Crockett, Sarah-1169
Cronin, Wm. W.-1104
    Annie
    Jeremiah
Cronin, D.W.-1104
Cronin, Daniel-1104
Crook, John-890
Crook, Mary-890
Crosner, Henry-1056
Crosner, Julia-1056
Cross, Melissa-710
Cross, Amanda A.-853
Cross, Pearl-1038
Cross, Harry, Jr.-1038
Cross, Harry-Susannah-1038
Cross, W.Y.-1113
Cross, Amanda-1179
Crouch, Joel C.-Ellen V.-807
Crouch, Elizabeth R.-807
Crow, David T.M.-1105
    James F.
    Jennie

      Lucy
      Jacob D.
Crow, Dickerson-1105
Crow, Elizabeth-1141
Crow, W.G.J.-1152
Crow, Mary L.-1152
Crump, Wm. W.-836
      Mary A.
      Ella M.
      Georgie L.
      Inez R.
Crump, Adam-836
      John P.
      Wm. N.
      Nancy C.
      Mary E.
Crump, George W.-875
Culton, Elizabeth-790
Cummings, Frank-1099
Cummins, John-1039
Cummins, Samuel-1039
Cundiff, Mary J.-964
Cunningham, Nancy-713
Curry, Mary L.-695
Curtice, Charles L.-935
      Alice
      Willie
      Mamie
      Walter
      Cecil
      Neva
Curtis, Mary Ann-1184
      ****
      **
Dalton, Thomas-705
Dalton, Simon-705
      James B.
      Lethe
      Ruth
      Elizabeth
Dameron, Joe Stella-828
Dameron, John S.-836
Dameron, Winifred A.-863
Dameron, Eliza J.-1177
Daniel, Nannie-750
Daniel, M.E.-750
Daniels, Elizabeth-777
Darby, Elizabeth-930

Darby, Jedediah-936
Darby, Daniel-930
      Nzra
      Ruami
      Ephraim
      Wm. H.
      George W.
      Isabelle
Darby, Wm. H.-936
Darman, Sarah E.-964
Darnell, Samuel-897
      John
      Anna
      Richard
      Caroline
      Lewis
      S.E.
Darnell, Samuel, Sr.-897
Darnell, S.E.-897
      Ardella
      Emma
      James
      Cora
      Everett
Daugherty, Saciah-Sally-1032
Daugherty, Mary E.-1032
Daugherty, John M.-1040
      Jefferson B.
      Etta
      Ellen
Daugherty, Surkiah-1040
Daugherty, Jefferson-1052
Davey, Paul M.-1000
Davidson, George-707
Davidson, J.H.-934
Davidson, Erie-1172
Davis, Perneoia-705
Davis, James B.-705
Davis, James Monroe-705
Davis, James Franklin-705
      James Harvey
      Thomas Ernest
      Ellen
Davis, Nathan L.-717
Davis, Nancy-716
Davis, James-734
Davis, George W.-Elizabeth W.-734

Davis, Sarah-734
Davis, Sarah-764
Davis, Isaac N.-778
Davis, I.H.-779
Davis, Daniel E.-781
Davis, Charles H.-781
Davis, Wm. G.-836
    Charles B.
    Amanda J.
    James Edmond
Davis, Charles-836
Davis, Wm. A.-860
Davis, Sarah C.-887
Davis, S.J.-897
    Cornelia
    Sarah
    Belle
    Mattie
    Tea
Davis, Severe-897
Davis, Lucy-899
Davis, Lucy-901
Davis, Joseph-937
    Olive Lula
    Cora Nancy
    Oscar Lee
    Riuah Rewena
Davis, Ezekial-Rachel-937
Davis, Woodford-944
Davis, Minerva A.-944
Davis, Samuel-986
Davis, Lemuel C.-986
Davis, Noah C.-986
Davis, Alson W.-Hannah-985
Davis, George W.-985
Davis, Jesse P.-1167
    K.M.
    E.H.
    J.B.
    T.J.
    R.I.
    J.L.
    P.S.
Davis, E.H.-1167
    V.B.
    N.I.
    J.T.
    M.E.

    W.A.
    J.R.
    J.G.
Davidson, Bracket-838
Davidson, John H.-**837**
    Margaret R.
    Joel Thomas
    George W.
    Lewis H.
    Sarah J.
    Oliver C.
    Charles A.
    Catherine
Davison, George-939
    Joshua S.
    Mary J.
Dawson, Zena-913
Dawson, Eli-1114
Day, George A.-851
Day, John-947
    Edward
    Allen
    Hiley
Dayton, Hannah-1199
Deal, Lydia-1045
Dean, Susan-789
Dean, Jesse-808
Dean, Susanna-808
Dean, Stephen D.-987
    Daisy M.
    Edna Jane
    Mary Etta
    Harry
    Clifford
Dean. Charles M.-987
    Albert
    Bettie
    Ella
    Lewis
    Josie D.
    Wesley
    Grace
Dean, Moses-986
Dean, Henry-986
    Charles M.
    Mary M.
    Stephen D.
    Bettie

Dean, Henry-Nancy-1156
Dean, Betty-1156
Deardeuff, Lydia-800
Debery, Thomas-898
    Henry
    Alexander
    John
    George
    Mary
    Albert
    Isaac
    Thomas C.
Debery, Henry-898
    Ella
    Effie
    Charles
    Vallie
    Emma
    Lilburn
    Virgil
    Atha
    Montez
Debruin, John-798
Decker, Henry-781
    Landrick
    Wm. Thomas
    Polly J.
    Marion
    Richard
    Katie
    Jemima
    Jackson
    Ambrose
Decker, Landick-Patsy-782
Decker, Martha-782
Decker, Henry-Patsy-782
Decker, David-781
    Henry
    Caroline
    Mahala
    Tabitha
    Basheba
    Welcome
    Marion
    Martha
    Merritt
    Sarah

    Anderson
    Nancy
Deeman, Fannie-794
Deer, Mary Ann-786
Delaplain, George-937
    Elvira
    Orpha
    Eva
    Adam
    Charles
Delaplain, John-937
Demuth, Joseph-705
Demuth, John-705
Demuth, S.C.-705
    John V.
    Frederick
    Mary
Demuth, A.-1008
Denison, James H.-1106
    Maletena F.
    Mary E.
    McCuin Z.
    Ceba C.
Denison, Zachariah T.-110
    Henry C.
    Francis L.
    Samantha L.
    Delilah A.
    Lucy C.
    Frances L.
    Amanda E.
    Maggie T.
Denison, Zachariah-1105
Denison, Delilah-1152
Dennis, Gideon-1168
Dennis, Joseph-1168
Dennis, W.S.-1168
    Martha L.
    Wm. Henry
    Joseph
    Theodocia
    John A.
    Milton E.
    Rosetta
    Phoebe
    Elizabeth
    Sarah E.

           Jason E.
           Cynthia C.
           Allie May
           Ezra S.
           Della A.
Dennis, Joseph-1168
Dennis, G.M.-1169
           Wm. Henty
           James L.
           Joseph L.
           Sarah F.
           Albert M.
           Bertie M.
Dent, Miss-734
Denny, Elizabeth-833
Denney, Benjamin-838
Denney, John-838
           Crafford
           Thomas L.
           Mary T.
           Ellet G.
           Wm. T.
           Louisa H.
           Riley
           Sophronia
Denny, Minerva-880
Denny, Charles-880
Denny, E.G.-881
Denny, Elizabeth-931
Derrick, James-945
           Joshua
           Cynthia J.
Detherage, James, Sr.-706
Detherage, James, Jr.-706
           Martin
           Winnie
           Thomas
           Betsey
           Sarah
           Mary J.
           James
           Marian
           Jesse
Dethurum, G.-968
Devashier, (Grandfather)-1193
Devashier, Mary L.-1193
Devazier, Mary S.-741

Devilbliss, Frank C.-704
Devlin, Maria-746
Devlin, Charles D.-746
DeVore, Effie-733
Deweese, Sarah-1155
Dial, Jennie-751
Dial, Jeremiah-751
Dickard, Wm.-860
Diffenderfer, Michael-706
           Davis R.
           Mary
           Frank R.
Diffenderfer, D.R.-706
           Wm.
           Mary
           David
           Henry
           Jane
           John
           Grace
Diffenderfer, David-707
Dill, Martha E.-1041
Dill, Alfred-1077
Dill, Jane-1077
Dillard, R.D.-752
Dillion, Silas-938
           Mary Frances
           Jeremiah
           Anna E.
           Wm.
           Robert
           Jennie E.
           Crawford
           Dona Belle
           Jacob
           John L.
           Mella S.
           Rebecca J.
Dillion, Wm.-938
           Louis
           Jacob
           Lydia
           Silas
           Jesse
           Reed
           Tyra

        Becky
        Polly
        Moses
Dillion, Jesse-938
Dillon, Ann-1138
Dilworth, Jane Douthart-1041
        Mary
        Rebecca R.
        Julia Ann
        Emma
        Abbie
        Billie Green
Dilworth, Billy Green-1041
Dinwiddie, Mrs.-1032
Dixon, Naomi-1211
Dixon, James-775
Dixon, J.B.-829
Dixon, Hiram-892
        Wm. M.
        Sarah J.
        George W.
        John T.
        Margaret
Dixon, Margaret R.-892
Dixon, Margaret-1065
Doak, Martha A.-1057
Dobson, Spencer-964
Dobson, Julia A.-964
Dodd, Amanda-991
Dodge, Fanny-1057
Dodge, Jared-Sally-1057
Dodson, F.A.-784
Dodson, Joe Ann-798
Dodson, Benjamin D.-Joe Ann-798
Dodson, Lucy E.-890
Dodson, Wm. M.-899
        Lucy E.
        Penelope
Dodson, James-899
        Wm. M.
        James N.B.
        Lucy
        Zilpha
        Benjamin D.
Dodson, James N.B.-900
        Lola M.
        Joan Z.

Dodson, Benjamin D.-900
Dodson, Lucy-901
Dodson, James-901
Dodson, Lucy-917
Dodson, Penelope-995
Doehler, Peter-1146
Doehler, Catherine-1146
Doffeller, Theresa-762
Donahoe, Daniel-988
        Katie Marie
        Mary Anna
        Wm. Patrick
        Daniel Francis
        Sarah Blanche
        Cornelius M.
Donahoe, Wm.-988
Donaldson, Mary-1142
Donaldson, Jane-1191
Donaldson, Damuel-1191
Donnan, Alexander-1154
Dooley, Jennie-1010
Dooley, Thomas-1010
Dornan, Nathaniel-953
Doss, C.H.-817
Douglas, George W.-1169
        Elizabeth L.
        James A.
        W.E.
        Benjamin B.
        Hattie E.
        Charley E.
        Lyle
Douglas, W.R.-1169
Douglas, Joannah-1176
Douglas, Wm.-1176
Douthit, Emaline-845
Dover, J.-710
Dowel, Elizabeth-797
Downey, Mary M.-763
Downey, Abram-Patsy-763
Drake, Agnes-774
Drake, Jacob-938
Drake, Jacob, Sr.-928
Drake, Jacob-953
Draper, C.C.-732
Drennon, Mary Catherine-109
Drum, J.-950

Drum, Mary-950
Drumheller, Nicholas L.-945
Drumheller, Sarah M.-945
Dickworth, Christina-1212
Dickworth, Henry-1080
Dudley, Nancy-796
Dudley, Nancy-1012
Duggan, F.W.-1170
    Chrisie
    Myrtle
    Harrison DeWitt
    Frankie
Duggan, J.F.M.-1170
Duggan, John-1170
Dugger, Mary C.-968
Dugger, Samuel B.-838
    Jarrot P.
    Helen M.
    Mary C.
    Samuel O.
    Albert Arthur
Dugger, Jefferson L.-838
Duke, James R.-1106
    Arthur Wm.
    James R.
    Jennie J.
    Charles H.
    Bessie
Duke, Richard-1106
    James R.
    Wm. R.
Dumont, Margaret-1042
Dunbar, Sarah-731
Duncan, R.B.-770
Duncan, Martha-770
Duncan, Sophronia Isabel-997
Duncan, Thomas-1171
    Mary
    Clarence
    Flora
    Toby
    Clara
Duncan, Robert-1171
Duncan, Pollie-1171
Duncan, Margaret-1171
Dunham, Margaret-707

Dunham, Richard H.-995
Dunham, Rebecca J.-995
Dunham, James-1026
Dunham, Isaac-1049
Dunlap, Thomas-Nancy-1016
Dunlap, Belle-1016
Dunavant, C.A.-1072
Dupugh, J.-723
Durbie, John A.-750
Duval, Lizzie L.-747
Dye, Evelina-1099
Dye, Elbridge L.-1041
    Leslie E.
    Frank W.
    Mary A.
    Isaac R.
Dye, Alexander E.-1041
Dye, Vincent-1041
Dye, Isaac-1042
Dyer, Mary-1094
Dyer, Elizabeth-1021
Dyer, Miss.-1168
Dyker, Harriet A.-991
Dykes, Michael-850
Dwyer, John F.-834
Dwyer, J.B.-834
Dwyer, D.H.-834
****
  **

Eade, Mrs. Melvina-
    Lena Belle
Earley, Elizabeth-767
Earley, Rutha-1157
Earnest, Amos-900
    Addie
    Isaac
    Jerusha J.
    B.W.
    John M.
Earnest, Benjamin W.-900
    Lizzie
    Samuel
    Kelley
    Wm.
    Mollie
    James

Earney, Martin-1045
Earney, Missouri Jane-1045
Earp, John C.-901
    Josiah
    John C.
    Wm. L.
    Mary A.
    Narcissus
Earp, Grandfather-901
Earp, James C.-901
    Olive M.
    Annie S.
    Thompson J.
    Carrie M.
    John M.
    Frannie J.
    Virgil
Earp, John C.-909
Eason, E.E.-955
Eaton, Miss.-961
Eddy, Margaret-1149
Edgar, H.R.-1008
Edington, Wm.-1192
Edington, James-843
Edington, Sarah-843
Edmisson, Richard C.-707
Edmisson, John-707
Edmisson, John S.-939
    George T.
    Louisa R.
    Richard C.
    Nancy M.
    Robert N.
Edmisson, George T.-940
    Lizzie
    Felix C.
    George I.
    Robert E.
    Albert E.
Edmisson, Emanuel-939
    Martha
    Ellen
    Nancy
    Curtiss C.
    S.R.
Edmisson, Curtis C.-940
    John R.

    Nancy Celine
    Lillie Melvina
    Curtis O.
    Wm. R.
    James F.
    Ella R.
    Ida M.
    Cora L.
Edmondson, W.G.-1036
Edmondson, George T.-969
Edmondson, B.-953
Edwards, Ella-702
Edwards, Joseph-702
Edwards, George-708
    Sandy
    Orange
Edwards, Darius-708
    Josiah
    Cinderella
    George W.
    Alexander
    Darius
    John B.
    Mary
    Mandania
    Wm. H.H.
    Amos
    Martha
    Nancy J.
Edwards, Amos-708
    Rosa M.
    Cora B.
    Charley D.
    Lula G.
    Lillie
    Nettie
    Ally D.
    Floyd
Edwards, Lydia-764
Edwards, W.D.-826
Edwards, Fannie L.-903
Edwards, Augustus M.J.-955
Edwards, P.H.-1125
Elayer, Joseph-1042
    Minor
    Milo
    Marquis

Elayer, Minor-1042
    Harvey
    Edward W.
    Ruth
    Jessie
Elayer, Joseph, Sr.-1042
Elder, Miles-691
Elliott, Daniel G.-1107
    Sanders S.
    Mary Lucy
    Wm. T.
Elliott, Thomas-1107
    Simon
    Nathan
    Thomas
    Daniel G.
Elliott, Cynthia A.-1076
Elliott, Isaminda-1137
Ellis, Mahala F.-1101
Ellis, Helen R.-1204
Ellis, Elizabeth-896
Ellis, Mary-893
Ellis, Mes. Mary J.-1004
Ellis, Martha J.-1023
Ellis, W.C.-1171
    Fridda
    Tommie
    Lyle W.
Ellis, John-1171
Ellis, Paul-1172
    Jesse
    Victoria
    Victor
Elmore, Ebenezer-889
Elmore, Levina-889
Elmore, Jesse-1112
Elmore, Eliza Matilda-1112
Elza, Mary-1191
Emmett, Catherine-1176
Emory, Lucinda-849
Erton, Nancy-817
Esther, Elizabeth-730
Esther, John-735
Esther, Lou-735
Esterly, Mary-706
Estes, John G.-901
    Mary G.
    Susan
    Zilpha
    Penelope
    Andrew
    Elizabeth
    Lucy
Estes, Andrew-901
    Elizabeth
    Nancy P.
    Martha E.
    Jenora
    John W.
    Lucy A.
    Ethel
    Eltha
    Andrew A.
Estes, Andrew, Sr.-901
Estes, John G.-917
Estes, Lucy-917
Eubanks, Elizabeth-924
Evans, Tennessee-1205
Evans, Caroline-711
Evans, Freeman-825
Evans, Freeman-840
    Harvey K.
    Maggie
    Maude E.
    Bessie
Evans, James-840
Evans, Phoebe-936
Evans, John F.-989
    Wm. T.
    John W.
    Catherine
    George A.
    Caledonia
    Missouri A.
    Melvina
    Jennie
    Martha L.
Evans, Wm. T.-938
    Nancy A.
    Mary E.
    Sarah E.
    John A.
    Lucy E.
    Martha J.
    Wm. E.

Ezard, Thomas E.-909
Ezel, Elizabeth-845
****
**
Fairless, Charleton-861
Farmer, John-902
      Joshua
      Joseph M.
Farmer, Joshua-902
      Mary Frances
      Joseph Wm.
      James Edward
      Wm. E.
Farmer, Joseph-902
Farmer, Indiana A.-903
Farmer, Henry-1172
      James H.
      Arthur F.
      Alexander B.
      Robert G.
      Andrew J.
      Moses
Farmer, Andrew J.-1172
Farnham, Sarah E.-992
Farnsworth, L.-840
      Anna Laura
      Arthur Roscoe
      Lottie May
      Oscar
      Wm.
      Edgar
      Elmer
Farnsworth, John-940
Farrar, Reuben H.-782
Farrar, James M.-782
Farrar, Richard-782
Farrar, Reuben-Virginia-791
Farrar, Zippora-791
Farris, J.W.-696
Farris, J.W.-709
Farris, Hiram K.-Abigail-709
Farris, John R.-1108
      Rosa
      Albert
      Della
      Lee
      Walter R.

      Ferdinando
      Maggie
      Johnnie
Farris, James-1108
Farris, Drucilla-1137
Faulkner, James-797
Faulkner, Martha-797
Feaster, E.S.-903
      Mary
      George
      W.A.
      Elizabeth
      T.J.
      Emma
Feaster, T.J.-903
Fengler, Albert T.-1108
Fengler, Ernest-Emelia-1108
      Richard
      Emil
      George
      Albert
      Trangott
Ferguson, Alice-798
Ferguson, Maggie A.-1169
Ferrill, E.P.-1013
Fielder, Martha-932
Fifield, Marietta-882
Finley, Miss. N.M.-1183
Fisher, Mrs. Sarah-920
Fisher, Mary D.-1152
Fitzgerald, Eglentine-755
Fitzgerald, Joseph-755
Fitzwater, Mary-1191
Fizer, Mary J.-1088
Flannagan, Thomas-942
Fleck, Lavina-729
Fleming, Annie-796
Fleshman, A.A.-714
Flett, A.A.-992
Flint, Frederick C.-989
      Asa
      Wilbur
      Leonard
Flint, Wilbur-990
      Carrie
Flint, Edward-989
Florance, Thomas S.-841

```
                Inez                          Thula
                Ollie G.                      Wm. B.
                Walter J.             Forrest, James, Sr.-1173
                Robert                Forsythe, Richard-1136
Florance, Tolliver-841                Fort, Wm.-920
Florance, James-841                         Nellie
Floyd, Calvin-1043                          Edward L.
        Alphia                              Lillie
Floyd, Nimrod-1043                          Albert
Foard, Richard T.-1109                Fort, Wm., Sr.-Nancy-990
        Novella J.                          Henry
        Mary J.                             Mary
        Bulah F.                            Nancy
        Wm. B.                              Sarah
Foard, Wm. F.-1109                          Wm.
Folger, Charles, Jr.-710                    Libbie
        Nelson                              James
        Everett                             Charles
        Ginevra                             Rhoda
        Rosella                             Henrietta
        Samuel                        Fort, Thomas-990
        Winslow                             Wm.
        Clarkson                            Charles
Foote, James K.-783                         Thomas, Jr.
        Nora A.                       Fort, Nancy-1008
        Mabel M.                      Fort, Sarah-Wm.-1008
        Edson E.                      Fortner, E.D.-969
        Artiemecie                    Fortson, Elizabeth-841
Foote, Wm.-783                        Foster, Rebecca-743
        James K.                      Foster, Enoch-Rebecca-743
        Mary E.                       Foster, Mary P.-781
        Nancy A.                      Foster, George-827
        Cammaliza                     Foster, Susan-827
        Malinda F.                    Foster, John B.-967
        Wm. F.                        Foster, Jesse-867
        Minnie A.                     Foster, Annie-867
        Evaline M.                    Foster, J.D.-887
        Asher L.                      Foster, Mary-902
Ford, Joan A.                         Foster, Williamson-902
Fore, Lucretia-1004                         James
Forrest, John-1173                          Thomas
Forrest, James-1173                         Leonard
        Mary                                Mary
        John W.                       Foster, Nancy E.-911
        Norah                         Foster, Elizabeth M.-919
        Manda                         Foster, Susan-942
```

Fourt, L.A.-1116
Fourt, Polly Ann Margaret-1127
Fourt, Sarah J.-1158
Fourt, Pollie Ann-1183
Fowler, Julia A.-970
Fowler, John F.-929
Fowler, Ruth A.-1111
Fox, Enoch-1044
Fox, Wm.-1044
Fox, John B.-1043
Fox, James C.-1109
    Nancy C.
    Wm. B.
    Susan E.
    James M.
    Mary M.
    Thomas O.
Fox, Wm.-1109
Foy, Bridget-807
Foy, Bridget-917
Fraker, Christian-941
    Michael
    Margaret
    George W.
    Mary
    Robert
    Sarah
    Elizabeth
    Benjamin
    Catherine
    Martha J.
    Nancy E.
Fraker, Michael, Jr.-941
Fraker, Michael, Sr.-941
Fraker, Benjamin S.-941
Francisco, J.G.-903
    Sophia L.
    Anna J.
    Molly E.
    J.W.
Francisco, J.W.-903
    George T.
    Woodie E.
    Anna J.
    John S.
    Mary E.
    Murray C.

Francisco, John-904
Frank, Thomas-1033
Frank, Mary B.-1047
Frank, Philip-Mary-1047
Franklin, Dr.-710
Franklin, G.B.-923
Franklin, John, Jr.-942
    Andrew J.
    Wm. T.
    Albert J.
    George R.
    Joseph H.
    Almus M.
    Mary
Franklin, John, Sr.-942
    Nancy
    John
Frazer, Caroline-740
Frazier, Elizabeth-914
Freeland, M.D.-1133
Freeland, Anna-1133
Freeman, Amanda-1210
Freeman, James M.-991
    Mary E.
    Loring L.
Freeman, Britton-991
    James M.
    George W.
    Clemantine
    Wm.
    John
    Ellen
    Edward
    Dodson
    Marion
Freeman, James-991
    Thomas
Freeman, John-841
    Lorenzo D.
    Mary M.
    John T.
    Robert J.
    Laura M.
Freeman, Littleton-866
Freeman, B.D.-841
Freeman, Susan-866
Freeman, Littleton-884

Freeman, Laura B.-884
Freeman, Tircy-883
Freeman, Amanda J.-887
Freeman, Belle-907
Freeman, L.T.-Sarah L.-1161
Freeman, Margaret F.-1161
Freeman, Angeline-1161
French, Lucinda-760
French, Charles-775
French, John B.-892
Freudenstein, Ditmer-Mary-979
Freudenstein, Elizabeth-979
Freeze, Martin-708
Freeze, Sarah L.-708
Friar, Sarah A.-729
Frieze, John-906
    Louis
    George
    Ina B.
    Arty
Frish, Purlina-920
Frost, Simeon-991
    Hamilton J.
    James M.
    Cyrus H.
    Edmund F.
    Christopher E.
    George H.
    Martha J.
    Mary
Frost, John S...-992
    Esther Jane
    Henry Cleino
Frost, George W.-992
Frost, Cyrus H.-991
    Sarah J.
Fry, S.H.-1089
Fry, Catherine-930
Fry, Daniel-930
Fry, Catherine-1112
Fudge, Christina-814
Fulbright, Levi C.-710
    Susan J.
    John L.
    Matilda Ruth
    Wm. H.
    Anna E.
    Robert B.
    Roxanna
    Mary L.E.
    Caroline
    Ephraim R.
    Josiah
    Daniel
    Samuel
    Ellen
Fulbright, Wm.-710
    Levi C.
    Henry
    David N.
    E.R.
Fulbright, Ephraim R.-711
    Guy
    Floy
    Montia
    John W.
Fulbright, John, Jr.-711
Fulbright, John, Sr.-711
    Wm.
    David
    Martin
    Daniel
    John
    Elizabeth
    Catherine
    Susanah
    Christener
    Sarah
Fulbright, James H.-711
    Lucy J.
    Elizabeth K.
    John H.
    Emma L.
    Jemimah P.
    Jesse M.
    James H.
Fulbright, Daniel-713
    John
    Wm.
    Nahala
    Martin V.
    James H.
    Merritt C.
    Daniel L.

        Leonidas
        Jesse W.
        Samuel H.
Fulbright, Martin V.-713
        James D.
        Mary F.
        Louisa
        Mastin V.
        Joseph
Fulbright, Samuel R.-759
Fulbright, Daniel-997
Fuson, James W.-842
        Opal W.
Fuson, John-842
        W.T.
        J.A.
        R.B.
        Mary J.
        John M.
        James W.
        Emma C.
        Fanny
Fuson, Jonathan-842
Fuson, J.W.-867
Fuson, F.B.-1174
        Gertrude
Fuson, John-1174
Fusselman, Henry-1113
Fusselman, Sarah-1113
Fyan, Robert W.-1054
        ****
        **
Gaddis, Mary-695
Gaddy, Pleasant M.-993
        Louisa
        Sarah
        George W.
        Samuel
        Hila
        Harmon
        John
Gaddy, Jeremiah-993
Gaddy, Harmon A.-993
        F.M.
        Eliza
        Jeremiah
        Harmon A.

        Emily
        Louisa
        Harriet J.
        Rutha M.
        Martin F.
Galbraith, James-881
Galbreath, Malinda-943
Gallahorn, Rachel-1005
Gallegly, Sophronia-1174
Gallegly, Morris-842
Gallagly, Sophronia-842
Galloway, Ann-817
Gammelgaard, Mette-Marie-870
Gammon, George P.-926
Gammon, Emeline-926
Gammon, D.M.-943
        Charles C.
        Leonard T.
        Wm.
        Eva
        Margaret
        Stella
Gammon, George-943
Gammon, Mary A.-956
Gammons, Beverly-934
Ganes, Faney-832
Gann, Francis M.-943
        James W.
        Rebecca Ann
        John W.
        Martha J.
        Starling C.
        George R.
        Marion
        Joseph
        Franklin N.
        Lucy E.
        Thomas J.
Gann, Cornelius-943
        Sarah E.
        Martha J.
        Delilah
        Francis M.
        Thomas
        Nancy
        James M.
        John
        Henry D.

Gant, Malinda-1148
Garland, G.P.-876
Garner, Maggie E.-1033
Garner, Wm.-843
Garner, John-843
Garner, Valentine-843
    Nancy
    John
    Wm.
    Martha
    Dialtha
    Frances
    Mary
    Anna
    James
    George
    Julia
    Jane
    Susan
    Amanda
    Sarah
Garner, Louis-917
Garner, Lucretia-917
Garret, Elizabeth-947
Garrison, Lucy M.-810
Garrison, James B.-961
Garvey, Elizabeth-982
Garvey, James-982
Gass, James Anderson-822
Gass, Frannie E.
Gass, Jacob-1179
Gaston, Mary J.-789
Gatewood, Miss.-818
Gay, Sarah A.-989
Gay, Anna-1205
Gay, Wm.-1205
Garhart, James-1039
Gearhart, Ruth-836
Gearing, H.C.-894
Geer, Ann E.-1095
Geers, John-1110
    Nicholas G.
    Oklahoma
    Joan
    Wm. L.
    Mary C.
    Charles F.

    John E.
    Lucy D.
Geers, Wm. L.-1110
Geeslin, Jane-708
Geiger, W.F.-810
Gentry, Joiner-843
    Wille Sherman
    Amos B.
    Charles O.
    Mary J.
    Robert C.
    Martha Ann
Gentry, Bartlett-843
George, Ada-727
George, Nathaniel L.-865
George, H., Sr.-904
George, H.-904
    Josiah M.
    Elizabeth J.
    Samuel H.
    Milton L.
    Frederick A.
George, Ira H.-922
George, Melvina C.-922
Gerhardt, August-905
    Johanna E.
    Frederick J.
    Katherine E.
    Harmon W.
    Adolph N.
    Ulyssimus S.A.
    Laura
    Pinky A.
Gibbons, Mary-1085
Gibson, John J.A.-692
Gibson, John-Mary-713
    Eliza
    Jane
    Lydia
    Thomas M.
    Wm.
    Mary
    John
    Robert
    Julia A.
Gibson, Thomas M.-713
    Elizabeth

                    Mary J.
                    Sarah Y.
                    Rosaline
                    James G.
Gibson, Lucinda-751
Gibson, Samuel-816
Gibson, Lottie-816
Gibson, Mary-901
Gibson, Wm. F.-1110
       George W.
       Mary C.
       Amanda
       Sarah
       James W.
       Daniel R.
       David A.
       Thomas
       Martha A.
       Elizabeth
       John
       Robert L.
       Andrew J.
       Lucy
Gibson, Thomas H.-1110
       Huldah
       Jeanette
       Lloyd
       Dora
       Byron
       John T.
       Pearl
Gibson, Thomas N., Sr.-1111
Giddens, John K.-784
       Lidia May
       Hattie P.
       Susie A.
Giddens, Wm. G.-784
       Nancy E.
       John K.
       Mary C.
       Delilah A.
       George W.
       James F.
       Margaret
       Amanda
       Eliza A.
       R.T.

Giddens, Samuel F.-783
        John B.
        Samuel B.
        A.R.
        W.V.
        Wm. G.
Giddens, Roger-783
Giddeons, Mary E.-1093
Gift, Mary-990
Gilbert, Julia-1213
Gilbert, Grandfather-1146
Gilbert, Christina-1146
Giles, Samuel-818
Giles, Annie-818
Gill, John-1000/
Gilleland, Mr.-831
           Parthena
           Robert
Gillett, Harvey-916
Gillespie, Wm.-778
Gillespie, Rachel-779
Gillespie, Wm.-Mary-795
Gillespie, Elizabeth-795
Gillespie, Oliver-Caroline-810
Gillespie, Mary-810
Gilliam, Solomon, Sr.-1171
Glasby, Nancy-1074
Glass, Nancy-948
Glasscock, Jane-800
Glover, John-803
Glynn, Wm.-737
Glynn, Michael-737
       Mary
       Wm.
       Thomas
       John
Glynn, Mary-737
Goade, Amanda J.-1069
Godbey, Josiah-1044
        Wm. C.
        John E.
        Martha J.
        Sarah H.
        Milton
        Samuel M.
        Josiah
        Maggie

Thomas	Goodwin, Matilda A.-827
Sena	Goodwin, Thomas-844
Godbey, Milton-1044	Natilda
Annie	Thomas
Jervase	Hays
Frank	Rosa K.
Milton E.	Emaline
Pearl	Hattie
Elizabeth	Goodwin, Elijah-845
Godfrey, Hugh-784	Goodwin, Adam-844
Richard	Gordon, Malinda-971
Alexis	Gordon, Maggie L.-700
James	Gordon, Noah-971
Joseph	Gordon, John-810
Thomas	Gordon, Mary-810
Frank	Gorman, Miss. A.M.-1214
Caleb	Gorman, John M.-1214
George	Gorman, M.D.-1216
Isaac	Gorman, Ada-1216
Godfrey, Thomas-785	Gorman, John M.-862
Godwin, Mary E.-1021	Gorman, W.H.-1177
Goff, Margaret-1017	Gorman, John-1177
Goheen, Joseph S.-944	Goss, Sarah-852
JO-Nettie	Goss, Jacob-887
Charles	Goss, Frona-887
Harry	Goss, Joseph-1049
Goldsberry, George-Salisba-780	Goss, Elizabeth-1049
Goldsberry, Jesse-780	Gouge, Sarah-1129
Goloday, Miss.-788	Goureley, Dixon-1174
Gooch, Cicily-852	Mary E.
Good, Jacob, Jr.-844	Adam
Thomas A.	Etta
Joel B.	Dixon E.
John W.	Rebecca O.
Rutha A.	Elbert W.
Jacob W.	Nancy R.
Albert B.	Gourley, S.H.-1174
Mary C.	Gower, Elizabeth-862
Good, Jacob, Sr.-844	Grabiel, Susannah-794
Good, Mary E.-1101	Graham, Aquilla-845
Goodall, R.P.-714	Graham, Joel-845
R.P., Jr.	Graham, D.L.-845
Goodall, Richard R.-714	Grangoard, Hans C.-802
R.P.	Grangoard, Esther-802
Helen	Grass, Miss. M.E.-1197
Goodell, Wm. S.-1113	Graves, Lydia-729
Gooderich, R.-716	Graves, A.T.-830

Graves, Joshua H.-846
    Myrtle
    Clara
Graves, Ira-846
Graves, A.J.-945
Graves, Lucy-1197
Graves, Robert-1197
Graves, Wm.-1197
Gray, Blineld-1082
Gray, Joseph-791
Gray, Mary Ann-791
Gregory, Mary-1000
Gregory, Jane-1023
Gregory, John S.-1153
Green, John-690
Green, Jeanette-689
Green, Samuel-846
    John D.
    James
    Sarah
    Malinda
    Velneyrettie
    Delssia
    Martha J.
    Ortelia
    Wm.
    S.P.
Green, James-846
Green, John D.-846
Green, Catherine-859
Green, Mary-1050
Greener, Nicholas-Ellen-1121
Greener, Jennie-1121
Greenleaf, Thomas R.-715
Greenleaf, George H.-715
    Mary
    Anna
    Georgia
Greer, C.H.-847
    John W.
    Wm. M.
    Robert H.
    Ida L.
Greer, W.W.-847
Grier, Newton F.-847
    Tasso
    Samuel
    Dorsey
    Ollie
Grier, Samuel-847
Grier, N.F.-877
Grier, Dollie H.-877
Griesel, Hannah-897
Griesel, George-897
    Anna
    Adam
    Wm.
    George
    Louisa
    Matilda
    Sophia
    Antulp
    Della
Grielsel, Adam-905
    Jacob
    George
Griffith, Nancy-874
Griffith, Margaret Ann-1081
Griffith, Thomas-Sarah-1081
Grigsby, P.D.-843
Grimes, Wm.-842
Grimes, Mary E.-842
Grisham, Austin-1136
Groesbeck, A.D.-760
Groesbeck, Louisa-761
Groom, Enoch-785
Groom, James F.-785
Groom, I.D.-785
Groom, T.P.-910
Grooms, Sultana-853
Gross, John-768
Gross, Dorcas-768
Groves, Delilah-908
Grubb, Irwin-690
Grubb, John-1175
Grubb, Samuel F.-1175
    Nancy
    Mary E.
Grubb, Henry-1175
Grubb, Curtis A.-1184
Grubb, Elizabeth
Gumpertz, Simon-Sibiela-848
    David
    Gus
Gumpertz, Gus-848
    Simon

Gunter, Alvira P.-721
Gunter, James-721
    Thomas
    Louisa
    Alvira
Gustafson, Anna-1143
Gustin, G.B.-701
Gustin, Jonathan F.-715
    S.P.
    Esther A.
    M.W.
Gustin, M.W.-715
    Jesse D.
    Sempronius B.
    Myrtie C.
    Bertha F.
Gutherbridge, John M.-931
Gutherie, John-716
    Absalom
    Isaiah
    Louisa
Guthoerl, Jacob-1045
Guthoerl, Peter-1045
    Lydia C.
    Laura
    Ingersoll
    Firnim
    Wm. A.
  ****
   **
Haden, Joseph-Mary-798
Haden, Mary K.-798
Haffy, Adaline-705
Hagenbush, John-1094
Haggard, America E.-1106
Haggard, Coffee Carroll-849
    Wm.
    Carroll
    Amanda
Haggard, Samuel-849
Hagler, John-Rachel-1029
Hagler, Elizabeth-1029
Hahn, Adam-871
Hahn, Jane-871
Hailey, Peter F.-848
    Wm.
    Mary T.

    Martha J.
    A. Lincoln
    Joyce
Hailey, Tavner-848
Halbert, Mary Ann-1085
Halbert, James-1086
Halbert, Elizabeth-1095
Halbert, Joel S.-1111
    Eureka P.
    Eli C.
    Estella P.
    Ephraim G.
    Frances A.
    Mary E.
    Eva M.
    Bertha C.
    Bessie M.
    Carrie
Halbert, Eli G.-1111
Halbert, Mary L.-1133
Halbert, E.-1135
Halbert, Annie-1135
Halburt, Emma-1142
Halbert, Mary-1033
Hale, Edward-1196
Hale, John-1196
Hales, Mary A.-1196
Hales, Nancy-736
Hale, W.G.-786
Hale, Samuel R.-786
Hale, I.H.-818
Hale, Thomas-865
Hale, Wm.-950
Hale, Wm. R.-994
    Minnie L.
    Ida M.
    Nicholas L.
    John A.
    Lindsey L.
    Wm. R.
    M.C.
Hale, Elizabeth-994
Hale, Zachariah-994
Hale, M.C.-994
    Samuel G.
    Wm. R.
    Alexander B.

        John A.
        Caroline
        Lucy
Haley, George-774
        Josephine
        Azaline
        Ruth
        Bettie
Haley, Josephine-774
Haley, Wm. S.-874
Hall, Mrs.-1109
Hall, Salina-892
Hall, James-906
        Wm. Edgar
        James Harvey
Hall, James Harvey-906
        Thomas E.
Halloman, Hannah-924
Halla, Susan-843
Hambleton, John-1158
Hamilton, David-692
Hamlin, Clarissa-738
Hamlin, J.R.-849
Hamlin, Oscar T.-849
Hampton, Noah H.-825
Hampton, Emma-825
Hampton, N.H.-851
Hand, Spencer-861
Haney, Thomas-1178
Haneycutt, Edmond-786
Haneycutt, Mary E.-786
Hanigan, Bridget-1119
Hanrahan, Thomas M.-994
        Jeremiah
        Mary
Hanrahan, Thomas-994
        Jeremiah
        James
        Thomas
        Bridget
Hansford, Mary-1020
Hanson, Henrietta-1155
Hanson, R.H.-1175
        Viola M.
        Perry L.
        Inez T.
Hanson, Cyrus-1175

Hanson, C.-697
Hanson, Christian-717
        Emma
        Clare
        Sarah
        Jennie
Hanson, Han Christian-717
Hardin, Angeline-1099
Hardin, Miss.-1115
Hardin, Robert W.-1115
Hardin, R.W.-1116
Hardin, Nancy-1116
Hardison, J.L.-969
Hardison, Delilah-838
Hardison, Thomas-933
Hardison, Margaret-939
Hardy, R.O.-765
Harges, Abram-850
        John
        Wm.
        Canzada
        Thomas Jefferson
        Julia Ann
        Catherine
        Mary Mahuldia
        Abram, Jr.
Harges, Abner-850
Harkey, Wm.-1085
Harmon, Wm. H.-854
Harmon, Laura E.-854
Harmon, Henry-1112
        George W.
        Anderson
        Martha E.
        Ada
        Robert L.
        Mary E.
        Cordelia
Harmon, Philip-1112
Harmon, Gideon-1097
Harmon, James-969
Harmon, Mary B.-969
Harmon, T.R.-Catherine-811
Harmon, Nancy M.-811
Harper, Frances-963
Harrell, Dyca-749
Harrell, Miss.-749

Harrington, Green-1094
Harris, Cynthia-1182
Harris, Mary M.-971
Harris, Micajah-Barsheba-971
Harris, Phoebe-744
Harris, John D.-744
Harrison, Benjamin-1060
Harrison, James P.-1061
Harrison, Permelia M.-1060
Harrison, James-1080
Harrison, Abner-James-1053
Harrison, Levicia A.-1053
Harrison, George-1074
Harrison, Eliza Jane-1164
Harrison, Edward Cannon-1164
Harrison, Joshua-Susannah-1191
Harrison, Lou-715
Harrison, John B.-715
Harrison, Albert-766
Harrison, John P.-977
Harrison, James B.-995
    Benjamin H.
    Georgia
    Lucile
    James
Harrison, Benjamin B.-995
    Lyourgus L.
    James B.
Harrison, John P.-996
Harrison, Thomas C.-996
    Lizzie L.
    Daisy
    Edward
Harrison, Edward M.-996
Harrison, T.C.-1021
Harron, Elizabeth-835
Hart, Mr.-1160
Hart, Elizabeth-1160
Hart, Isaac L.-1176
    Sarah
    Elizabeth
    Laura
    Frances
Hart, Leonard-1176
Hart, Leonard, Sr.-1176
Hart, Fannie-1197
Hart, Mary B.-719

Hart, Mary-902
Hartley, Jesse-825
Hartley, Angeline-825
Hartley, Jesse-850
Hartley, R.B.-850
Hartley, John H.-850
Hassell, C.B.-872
Hatfield, James-966
Hathaway, Daniel-885
Haughn, Paulina-1212
Haughn, Peter-1212
Hawkins, Mary M.-757
Hawkins, Isabel-958
Hawkins, James Harvey-980
    Wm. Jefferson
    Joseph Marion
    Jacob Monroe
Hawkins, Perry D.-997
Hawkins, Robert P.-997
    Perry David
    John P.
    Rhoda J.
    Ivy Wilbert
Hawkins, Solomon-997
    Wm. J.
    James P.
    Robert P.
    Alfred
    Perry Eaton
    Malissa Susanna
    Mary M.
    Eliza Louisa
    John B.
    Amanda M.
    Permelia Elizabeth
Hawkins, Mary E.-1013
Hayden, Elisha Jr.-Mary W.-1191
Hayden, Elisha, Sr.-1191
Hayden, Wm.-1191
Hayden, Jane D.-1189
Hayes, Sarah-1211
Hayes, Martha-1036
Hayes, Reuben-765
Hayes, Harriet-764
Hayes, T.J.-950
Haymes, Wm. Z.-851
    Sarah T.

          Estella
          Virginia T.
          Mary R.
          Adelaide
          Martha E.
          Walter O.
          Jacob E.
          Maggie J.
          Wm. S.
Haymes, Wm.-851
Haymes, Rebecca J.-923
Haymes, Wm.-Rebecca-923
Haynes, Asa-695
Haynes, Miss.-695
Hazel, Alfred M.-883
Hazel, Mary Jane-883
Head, George A.-1046
Head, George W.-1046
Head, Wm.-1046
Headlee, Elisha-998
Headlee, Samuel H.-998
Headrick, Silas-1048
        Frederick
        May
        James
        Jeremiah
        Riley
        Annie
        Myrtle
Headrick, Christopher C.-1047
        James
        Franklin
        Silas
Headrick, Frank-1047
Headrick, Francis-1047
        Margaret
Headrick, David-1047
Heard, Wm. J.-717
        Mary Ellen
        Martha J.
        Elizabeth
        Ciles H.
        Wm. W.
        Frances O.
        Charles G.
        John H.
        Sarah A.

        Margaret C.
        Susan
Hedrick, Peter-1049
Hedrick, Alfred-1049
Hedrick, Cicero P.-1049
Hedrick, Adam-1049
Heffner, Elizabeth-874
Hemphill, Alfred-Maria-744
Hemphill, Nancy J.-744
Henderson, Catherine-1108
Henderson, Rufus L.-1176
        Freddie
        Irvie
        Burtie
        Bessie
        Jewell
        Nellie
Henderson, Joseph-1176
Henderson, Sarah A.-1192
Henderson, Priscilla-721
Hendricks, James-Sarah-742
Hendricks, Mary E.-742
Hendricks, Berry-913
Hendrickson, J.L.-970
Hendrickson, Mary-970
Hendrix, Henry L.-786
Hendrix, Jesse-786
Hendrix, Alexander-786
Henshaw, Levi-774
Henslee, M.G.-1210
Henslee, Thomas F.-1177
        Anna B.
Henslee, Thomas-1177
Henslee, Elizabeth-704
Hensley, C.C.-1210
Hensley, John A.-1204
Hensley, Gid M.-1204
Hensley, Sarah J.-1208
Hensley, M.G.-1168
Hensley, Benjamin-1177
Hensley, M.G.-1177
        Frank
Hensley, Wm.-Elizabeth-117
Hensley, Jane-1005
Henson, Mary-715
Henson, George-772
Henson, Marcissa-772

Henson, Benjamin-928
Henson, Elizabeth-928
Henson, B.W.A.-944
    Wm. T.
    Benjamin F.
    Augusta
    Charles F.
    Cora D.
    Mamie E.
    Thomas E.
    John I.
Henson, Benjamin-944
    Elizabeth
    Wm. T.
    Catherine
    B.W.A.
Henson, Wm. T.-945
Herald, W.R.-727
Herbert, Horatio S.-999
    Hattie
    Bessie
Herbert, James-999
Herd, George W.-945
    Rosa J.
    Eliza C.
    James T.
    Phoebe V.
    Sarah C.
    Lougenia M.
    Parthena
    Alma
    Mary R.
Herd, John-945
    James C.
    George W.
Herndon, R.F.-763
Herrick, Henry J.-1112
    Henry L.
Herrick, Lot-1112
    Catherine
    Electa J.
    Henry J.
    George W.
Herrington, Sarah A.-1186
Hess, Moses-692
Hess, Elias-692
Heymann, Arnistine-1114

Hibdon, Mary E.-920
Hice, Emeline-792
Hickey, George W.-991
Hicks, Mary-1097
Hicks, W.S.-787
    James W.
Hicks, James-787
Hicks, George W.-849
Hicks, Wm.-907
Hickman, E.C.F.-1209
Hickman, Timothy-1050
Hickman, James-1050
    Silas P.
Hickman, Wm.-1050
Hickman, Mastin-713
Hickman, Mary L.-713
Hickman, Thomas L.-718
    Charlotta
    Sarah J.
    Lavinia
    Charles
    James H.
    Mastin
    Frederick
    Ahaz
    Catherine
Hickman, Mastin-718
    Sarah J.
    Mary L.
    Joe Ann
    Emett F.
    James M.
    Joseph P.
    George W.
    Henry C.
    John F.
    Martha D.
    Thomas A.
    Nathaniel
    Charlotta C.
Hickman, John B.-719
    Joseph W.
    Hugh E.
    Georgia
    Kinsey R.
Hickman, Joseph-719
    Sarah A.

          Margaret A.
          Wm.
          John B.
Higginbotham, Joseph-1067
Higginbotham, Thomas-1067
Higgins, Desdemona-1110
Highfill, Messer-851
        Willie E.
Highfill, J.E.-851
Highman, Sarah A.-911
Hight, Will-1208
Hight, J.A.-1178
Hight, John H.-1178
Highley, Elizabeth-1084
Hightower, Thomas Russell-852
        Matilda A.
        John R.
        Albert
        Cleveland
        Irvin Earl
Hightower, Dovorex-852
        Joshua
        Eppa
        Abner
        Thomas Russell
Highshoe, David-924
Highshoe, Fintha-924
Hill, Bettey-1175
Hill, Richard-1175
Hill, Lucinda-1175
Hill, Hannah-1196/
Hill, V.B.-792
Hill, George H.-940
Hill, Thomas-940
Hill, Ada-998
Hill, V.B.-996
Hillhouse, Nancy E.-711
Hime, Elizabeth-833
Hines, Wm.-1113
Hines, Virgil M.-1113
        Leslie
Hines, Vincent K.-1113
        James H.
        John W.
        W.M.
        V.M.

        Frank B.
        V.G.
        Mary
        Jane
        Julia
        Ida
Hines, Eliza A.-908
Hobbs, Margaret E.-779
Hobbs, Joseph-779
        LeRoy J.
        Wm. W.
        Josie J.
Hibbs, Wm. Wilson-787
        Lena
        Roy
Hobbs, Vincent-787
Hobbs, Joseph J.-787
Hobbs, Elizabeth-804
Hobson, Arthur-1051
        Charles Wm.
        Joab
        Aaron S.
Hobson, Charles Wm.-1051
Hodges, B.M.-1064
Hodges, Hiram-1052
        Samuel
        Benjamin M.
        Hiram L.
        Elizabeth
        Ellen R.
        James J.
        Sarah J.
        Helen M.
        George W.
Hodges, Samuel-1052
Hodges, Richard-Sarah F.-1052
Hodges, Joseph-1028
Hoeck, Robert F.-1114
        Bertha
Hoeck, Gustav-1114
Hogan, Andrew-869
Hogan, Amanda-869
Hogg, Susanna-949
Hogle, Hannah S.-846
Hogue, Theresa-1178
Hogue, Anderson-1178

          Nancy
          Fanny
          Mary A.
          Henry A.
          Nelson
          George
          Sarah
          Robert
          Lizzie
          Adalaide
          Laura B.
          Lonnie
          Augusta M.
          Florence
          Wm.
          Eddins R.
          Maude
          Ida
Hohman, Peter-806
Hohman, Margaretta-906
Holbert, Mary-1147
Hollingsworth, Rutha-710
Hollis, Frank-858
Hollis, Eliza-945
Holloman, Mary-1013
Holloman, Edmund B.-1013
Holly, Nancy-942
Holman, Wm.-1053
Holman, Wm. T.-1053
Holman, Wm.-Nancy-1075
Holman, Mary-1075
Holman, John-719
Holman, George Y.-719
Holman, George T.-719
          James L.
          Mary L.
          John L.L.
          Andrew J.
          Wm.
          George T.W.
          Joseph B.
Holman, George T.W.-720
          Florence I.
          Ida M.
          Jessie M.
          Amanda F.
          Mary E.

Holman, Mary L.-733
Holt, Benjamin Osborn-1122
Holt, Mary Eliza-934
Holt, Josiah-Millie-934
Honsinger, Mary J.-703
Honsinger, Susan Q.-724
Honsonger, Thomas-724
Hooker, Mary-1140
Hooker, Eugene-763
Hooker, F.-906
          John A.
          Lena M.
Hooker, John A.-906
          Fernando
          Helena A.
Hooker, Tennie E.-999
Hooper, Peter-1178
Hooper, Nancy-689
Hooper, Woodley-721
Hooper, Benjamin-721
          Sarah J.
          Benjamin C.
          Mary P.
          Fannie
Hooper, Benjamin C.-721
          Carl V.
          Henry
Hoover, D.W.-1178
          Amanda
          Samuel
          Walter
          Stella
          Ada
          Sophia
          Gus
Hoover, Jesse-1179
Hoover, George-Sarah-852
Hoover, Jennie-851
Hoover, George-852
          Louis F.
          Jane
          Christina
          Mary
          Samuel C.
          George W.
          Maud Elizabeth
          Johnny

                Margaret
                Alice
                Robert Franklin
                Sarah F.
Hoover, Felix-852
Hoover, Silas A.-853
                Ida S.
                Daniel A.
                Amanda E.
                Mary E.
                Wm. S.
Hoover, Jesse-853
Hopkins, Ephraim-907
                John
                Rebecca
                Christopher C.
                Margaret
                James
                Alpha
                Charles
                George W.
                Sarah Ann
Hopkins, John-907
                Elisha C.
                Ephraim
                James F.
                Elizabeth
Hopper, W.H.-1179
                Rachel
                Margaret
                Polly Ann
                Rebecca A.
                Rhoda
                Simpson
                Catherine
                John
Hopper, Raleigh-1179
Hopper, Blackgrave-1179
Hoskinson, Isaac, Sr.-722
                Gamaliel
                Isaac Jr.
Hoskinson, Isaac, Jr.-721
                Myrtle
Hott, Zella-1175
Hough, Payton-722
                Josephus
                John
                Ashford
                David
Hough, Wm.-722
Hough, Josephus-722
                Eliza J.
                Martha A.
                Margerie
                Alvira
                Samuel B.
                Catherine
                Cary Frank
                Lou
                Susie
                Wm. H.
                Melvinia
                Elizabeth
House, Peter-999
House, Menzo-999
House, Coonrod P.-999
House, Abraham P.-999
Housman, Mary E.-1122
Howard, Ersly J.-1083
Howard, John-701
Howard, Miss. M.A.-701
Howard, Mollie-769
Howard, Matilda-769
Howard, Silas-769
Howard, Silas-778
Howard, Elizabeth-778
Howard, Wm.-779
Howard, Wm.-907
                Charlotte
                Elvira
                Elizabeth
                G.S.
Howard, G.S.-907
                Wm. J.
                Mary F.
                Virginia A.
                Effie C.
                Edna E.
                Ernest B.
                Fred
Howard, Mary-975
Howell, Christopher-1086
Howell, Caroline-1086
Howell, Joseph M.-1087
Howell, Wm. C.-744
Howland, Ira-761

Hubbard, Spencer M.-1114
    Eunice
    James H.
    Tom
Hubbard, John H.-1114
    James M.
    John H.
    Martha Ann
    S.M.
    Charles B.
    Frank P.
    Robert P.
Hubbard, Frank Payne-1118
    Gracie May
    Henry H.
Hubbard, Mattie S.-754
Hubbard, John H.-853
    Nellie S.
    Della Lee
    Ella O.
    John A.
Hubbard, Wm.-853
Hubbard, Bird-853
Huckins, F.S.-Emily J.-786
Huckins, Prudence-786
Huddle, Margaret-1175
Hudgens, James-775
Hudgens, Matilda-817
Hudson, Benjamin-1180
    Benjamin
    Elizabeth
    Minnie
    Mary
    John
Hudson, Franklin-1180
Hudspeth, Mary C.-1041
Huffman, Miss. E.H.-1211
Huffman, James-1211
Huffman, M.J.-777
    Jane E.
    Mary
    Caroline
    Robert
    Susan
    Missouri
    Martha
    John
    Jacob
    Jesse

Huffman, Jane E.-777
Huffsmith, M.-1010
Hufft, Nancy-692
Hughes, James-765
Hughes, Polly-773
Hughes, Wm.-788
Hughes, Eliza-788
Hulla, W.F.-1179
Hulse, John E.-723
    Edmund
    John
    Albert
    Wm.
    Adelaide
Hulse, Edmund-723
    Mary
    Jennie
    Edith
    Edmund
    John
    Margaret
Humphries, Mary-1117
Hunt, J.M.-857
Hunt, Warrenton-945
    Wm. T.
    James R.
    Ella
    Adolphus F.
    Marcus F.
    Jasper I.
    Varda V.
Hunt, Peter-945
Hunter, G.W.-1212
Hunter, Elizabeth-1195
Hunter, B.F.-774
Hunter, Mary-776
Hunter, Josephine A.-1019
Hutcheson, Wm. T.-1001
    Lulu D.
    Wm. R.
    M. Grace
    J. Emmett
Hutcheson, Robert E.-1001
    James M.
    Eliza J.
    Mary E.
    Sarah A.
    Robertus A.
    Theodore F.

Hutcheson, M.C.-1001
Hutcheson, John Gregory-1000
    Marion C.
    Mary
    Sarah E.
    Imogene
Hutcheson, James-1000
    James M.
    Wm.
    Martha
    Mary E.
    John G.
Hutchings, Charles-1088
Hutchings, Mary-1087
Hutson, Susanna-1005
Hude, Jane-719
Hude, John-Malinda-852
Hude, Martha-852
Hude, Perrir T.-867
Hyer, John-1054
    Elizabeth
    Martha L.
    Mary Ella
Hyer, John-1103
Hyer, Louis Frederick-1054
Hyer, Samuel-1054
Hyer, John-1048
Hyer, Martha-715
Hyer, John-974
Hyer, Elizabeth-974
Hyer, Samuel-Elizabeth-1028
Hyer, Elizabeth-1028
    ****
      **

Imboden, John-788
Imboden, George-788
    James W.
    John H.
    T.V.
    George W.
    J.S.
    B.F.
    C.A.
    Eliza A.
    Albertson
Imboden, John H.-788
    Minnie
    Mabel

Ingera, Miss.-801
Ingram, Miss.-1006
Inman, Ezekiel-Lillie-1077
Inman, Susan W.-1077
Inman, W.C.-1087
Inman, Stephen-1181
Inman, H.E.-1180
    Charles E.
Inman, Charles D.-1180
Irwin, Nancy-1168
Isbel, Margaret-1105
Isbel, Mary Ann-784
Isbel, James-Nancy-784
Ivey, Josiah-763
    ****
      **

Jack, James-Susannah-1055
Jack, Emeline-1055
Jackson, Nancy A.-738
Jackson, Elizabeth-773
Jackson, John-773
Jackson, W.R.-842
Jackson, Elizabeth-850
Jackson, Oscar-703
Jadwin, Valentine-1055
Jadwin, Joseph H.-1055
Jadwin, Wm.C.-1116
    W.C.
    Martha
    Laura
    Sarah
    Joseph E.
    Matilda
Jadwin, Alexander-1115
    Manson M.
    Mary Angeline
    Wm. C.
    Mattie A.
    Laura E.
    Sarah E.
    Joseph E.
    Matilda P.
Jadwin, Joseph-1115
    Martin C.
    Alexander
Jamason, Evaline-859
James, George-Dicey-724
    Wm.

```
            George R.                              Mary A.
James, George R.-724                               Frank Lee
       Mary Ellen                                  Martha E.
       George F.                 Jenkins, Mollie-1179
       Emily J.                  Jenkins, Laura-1199
       Quillana E.               Jenkins, Thomas-1200
       Wm. M.                    Jenkins, Laura-1200
       Laura D.                  Jennings, John-857
       Lur J.                    Jennings, Hiram-857
       Rosa B.                          Ellis
       Effie May                        Laura B.
       Edgar M.                         John E.
       Thomas                    Jinkins, Sarah-716
       Isom                      Johns, John Thomas-1056
       Charley W.                Johns, Elisha-1055
James, Catherine-727             Johns, John Thomas-1055
James, Wm. T.-727                Johns, Elijah-1055
James, Mary J.-1083              Johnson, Sarah C.-1106
James, Stephen C.-Keziah-1083    Johnson, Little B.-727
James, Wm. H.-854                        Lewis C.
       John T.                           Rachel
       W.C.                              Elizabeth
       Jefferson B.                      Elisha A.
       Virginia Lee                      James L.
       Edward                            Silas
       Mary                      Johnson, Edmund-727
James, John-854                  Johnson, Travis-727
James, Wm.-1008                          Malissa E.
Jameson, Robert W.-854                   Eliza A.
         Thomas T.                       Parley R.
         Sarah M.                        Mary C.
         Martha E.                       Charles L.
         Nancy F.                Johnson, Frank-1106
         Abigail J.              Johnson, Mary A.-1101
         Robert W.               Johnson, Stebbine-728
Jameson, Samuel-854                      Rhoda W.
Jamison, Miss. S.-718                    M.W.
Jamison, George W.-718           Johnson, M.W.-728
Jamison, Homer-1031                      Joseph M.
Jamison, Clara Alice-1031                Thaddeus S.
Janes, Miss. T.B.-1097                   Frank J.
Jarrell, Jarrett-724                     Fannie J.
Jarrell, W.G.-724                        Maggie R.
Jarrell, B.C.-724                        Charles D.
         Salinda I.                      Mary B.
         Wm. A.                          Louisa W.
```

           Emma C.
           Marshall W, Jr.
Johnson, Charles L.-742
Johnson, Mary-734
Johnson, Mary C.-732
Johnson, David-788
Johnson, James L.-788
           Oscar
           Effie
           Ernest
           Josephine
           Vera
Johnson, John-788
Johnson, Mary E.-841
Johnson, Frank L.-1116
           Decatur
           Columbus F.
           Sarah E.
           Mary
           Paulina J.
           Hettie A.
           Julia
           Nancy
           Elvira E.
           Wm. T.
           Lewis L.
           Charles M.
           Clinton A.
           Jeremiah
           Foster L.
           Amanda
           Malinda
           Margaret
Johnson, Margaret-898
Johnson, Wm.-1116
Johnson, Emma-898
Johnson, Elvira-920
Johnson, Adaline-938
Johnson, Nancy-938
Johnson, John J.-946
Johnson, C.F.-946
           Alfred L.
           Wm. O.
           Walter T.
           Minnie D.
           Charles F.
           Margaret
           Fannie J.

Johnson, P.-1006
Johnson, Henrietta-1103
Johnson, Cynthia-1061
Johnson, Bolly-1058
Johnson, Abner-1058
Johnson, Sarah-1116
Johnson, W.-1116
Johnson, Margaret-1116
Johnson, Ahalis-1143
Johnson, R.-1163
Johnson, Stella-1174
Johnston, Wm., Sr.-1181
Johnston, Wm.-1181
           Wm.
           Sadie Agnes
           Alexander Adams
           Elizabeth
           Ira Lincoln
Johnston, David-1182
Joiner, Elizabeth-956
Jones, Nancy Evaline-1033
Jones, James-1033
Jones, Mary-706
Jones, Henry-727
Jones, T.H.-753
Jones, Sarah-772
Jones, Mahala-788
Jones, Virginia-782
Jones, Alfred-823
Jones, Martha E.-819
Jones, Deborah-816
Jones, Nancy-816
Jones, Rebecca E.-851
Jones, Wm. E.-857
           Jacob
           Sarah
           Charles
           Mollie L.
           Robert A.
           Anna
Jones, Aquilla-857
Jones, Eli W.-858
           Edwind W.
           Medretta
           Mary Frances
           James F.
           Martha F.
           Joseph Lee

                Ida A.   Green S.
                Charley   Nancy
                Robert E.   Jones, Missouri Isabella-976
                Nella F.   Jones, Thomas A., Sr.-1002
                Lemuel A.   Jones, John G.-1002
        Jones, James-858   Jones, Thomas M.-1002
                Lemuel   Jones, Thomas A.-1002
                Susan C.   Jones, Wm. B.-1020
                Edwin C.   Jones, Nancy A.-1020
                Garsham B.   Jones, John A.-1062
                Polly Ann   Jones, Jonathan D.-1057
                Solomon B.   Jones, J.W.-1057
                Sarah M.   Jones, A.J.-1056
                James N.   Jones, Wm.-1056
                Elizabeth P.   Jones, James M.-Nancy-1056
                Eli W.   Jones, Mary-1056
                Keziah M.   Jones, James-1094
        Jones, J.B.-859   Jones, Jonathan-1117
        Jones, Isaac C.-858   Jones, James W.-1117
                Wm. Campbell   Jonathan
                V. May   John
                Charles L.   Jones, Michael C.-1117
                Bingham H.   Eliza
                Sadie   Jones, Felix W.-1117
                June C.   Michael C.
        Jones, Hettie-1098   Olive
        Jones, Thomas-1099   Chylon
        Jones, Eliza-903   Iradel
        Jones, J.-927   Marcellus
        Jones, M.D.L.-931   Jones, Onor-1117
        Jones, L.F.-945   Jones, Sarah-1078
        Jones, Solomon B.-945   Jones, Jonathan-1158
        Jones, John Washington-947   Jones, Frances-1199
                Moses B.   Jordan, John-760
                James F.   Jordan, Josephine-759
                Nathaniel L.   Joslin, Ezra-729
                Sarah A.   Joslin, Luke, Sr.-729
                Jackson B.   Orrilla
                Solomon L.   Fannie S.
                Christopher Alonzo   Luke
        Jones, Bills-947   Joslin, Luke-729
                Mary   Wilbert C.
                Sarah   Carrie E.
                Solomon B.   Luke
                John Washington   David D.
                Lemuel T.   Herbert W.
                Robert L.   Charles E.
                James E.   Mary E.
                                                Hattie E.

Joyner, Wm.-929
Judge, Catherine-982
Judson, Lucius-1064
Julian, Lydia-865
Justice, Rebecca-808
  ****
   **

Kaffinberger, L.J.-700
Kanada, Charles-Lucy-800
Kanada, Sallie-800
Kanatzar, Pollie-1187
Kapp, Jacob-704
Keatley, Thomas-1001
Keatley, Virginia-1001
Keen, Sarah-1099
Keen, Matthias-1118
Keen, Enoch-1118
 Allie Jane
 Thomas P.
 Mary
 George W.
 Sarah
 Lewis Wesley
 John P.
 Wm. M.
 James E.
Keen, Hattie B.-978
Keith, Anderson-789
 Wm. T.
 Albert N.
 Arthur L.
 Mary C.
Keith, John-789
 Anderson
 Elizabeth
 Paradine
 Polly A.
 James
 Henry
 Martha
 George
 Jonathan
 Sallie
 Francis
 Melvin
 Wm. R.
 Cordelia
 Simon P.
 Mary

Kellar, Mary-756
Keller, Joseph-859
 James F.
 W.R.
 John L.
 Mary J.
 Sarah C.
 Sophia E.
 Charles Winfield
Keller, F.A.-859
Keller, Mahala-1043
Kelly, T.J.-1214
Kelly, Sarah S.-717
Kelly, Julia-798
Kelly, Peter-Bridget-797
Kelly, Elizabeth-854
Kelly, Sarah-901
Kelly, Wm. C.-1002
 Alice
 Jefferson D.
 Christopher L.
 Lulu
 John
 James B.
Kelly, Hardy-1003
Kelly, Samuel-Nancy-1044
Kelly, Sena-1044
Kelley, Wm. C.-1145
Kelley, Diana-1122
Kelley, Alice-1145
Kelso, Wm. C.-790
 Martha
 Stotira
 Mary
 Joseph
 Wm. C.
 Alexander
 Lottie
Kelso, Joseph-790
 Hugh
 Ewing
 Martha
 Wm.
 Polly
 Jane
 Elizabeth
 Sallie
 John A.
 Speece

Walker
Kelso, Hugh, Sr.-790
Kelso, Hugh-790
Kelso, James-790
Kelso, Mary-1153
Kelso, Miss.-1176
Kenamore, George R.-1058
    Rufus Clare
    Charley
Kenamore, Grant Allen-1058
    Wm. R.
    George R.
Kenamore, Wm.-1058
Kendall, Nathaniel-1092
Kendall, Norma-1092
Kendall, Mary-1105
Kendrick, B.F.-908
    Wm.
    Eliza A.
    George
    Laura J.
    Mary
    John
    Lizzie
    Benjamin
    Dora
Kendrick, John-908
Kenneday, Sarah-1093
Keplinger, Elizabeth-871
Kerr, James H.-874
Kerr, Catherine-874
Kessler, Rudolph, Sr.-1059
    Rudolph
    Emily D.
    Charles
    Joannah
    Lena
    John
Kessler, Rudolph-1059
    Rudolph
    John
    Lizzie
    Rosa
Kessler, Jacob-1059
Kibler, Lucinda-723
Kibler, James R.-723
Kidd, Leroy A-Ann Eliza-821

Kidd, Emma C.-821
Kidwell, Sarah A.D.-1005
Kidwell, Wm.-1005
Kilburn, Nancy-696
Kilburn, Allen-829
Kilburn, Nancy-829
Kilburn, Allen-860
    Wm. P.
    James J.
    Joel N.
    Nancy Lee
    Mary
    Jane
    Eliza
Kilburn, Daniel-860
    Allen
    Martha
Kilburn, Joseph-863
Kilburn, Allen-888
Kilburn, Mary J.-888
Kilgore, Elizabeth P.-1126
Killion, I.C.-964
Kimberly, Sarah-1070
Kimbrough, Frank P.-839
Kinchloe, Mollie-749
Kindig, Eliza J.-1066
King, Thomas-705
King, Mary R.-721
King, Nancy-1032
King, C.L.-782
King, Joseph-Rhoda-1033
King, Mary A.-849
King, Frederick-860
King, Mary-865
King, Pleasant-908
    Ray
    Ilma
    Edith
    Edgar
    Nilla
King, Hugh L.-909
    Pleasant
    Laura
    Oliver L.
    Louella
    Sophronia
King, John S.-908

King, Florence M.-909
King, Frank M.-910
King, Nancy-954
King, Caroline-1108
King, Mr.-1157
    James S.
    Wm. L.
King, Wm. B.-1178
King, Mr.-1121
Kinney, Noel A.-1009
Kinney, Elizabeth-1050
Kinser, Elizabeth-885
Kirk, Nancy-830
Kirkman, Mary-1109
Kirkpatrick, Miss.-788
Kirkpatrick, Elizabeth-1026
Kirwan, Hugh-1119
    Timothy
    Ann
    Cecelia
    Della
    John
Kirwan, John S.-1119
    Ellen Cecelia
Kitchen, Wm. A.-1004
    Sarah E.
    George D.
    Wm. J.
    James E.
    Margaret E.
    Richard M.
    Cynthia A.
    Charles L.
Kitchen, George P.-1004
    Elias D.
    Conrad
    Margaret J.
    Mary N.
    Andrew J.
    Sarah E.
    George N.
Kitchen, Anthony-Margaret-1004
Kitchen, Nancy-1018
Kleener, Miss.-793
Kline, Rebecca-1184
Klymer, Rhoda Elizabeth-1099
Knerr, John-Julia-822

Knerr, Lizzie-822
Knight, Frank P.-751
Knox, Margaret-943
Kofahl, Hans Christopher-1121
Kofahl, Christopher-1121
    John C.
    Henry
    Wm.
    Magdalene C.
    Ellen
    Louis C.
    Robert E.L.
    James C.
    Benjamin F.
Kouns, D.H.-896
Kountz, Elizabeth-1151
Krame, Catherine-1045
Kunze, Emma-762
Kyle, John W.-1122
    Lilie May
    Mary J.
    James W.
    Charles A.
    John H.
    Elizabeth M.
    Caroline L.
    Ethel C.
    Cecily
    Florence
Kyle, Samuel-1122
Kyrkendall, Jane-711
Kyrkendall, Mary-711
    ****
    **
Lacy, Hannah-834
Lair, Peter-1182
    George
Lamb, John B.-1004
    America L.
    Lemuel W.
    Amanda C.
    Louisa E.
    John E.
    Nora E.
    Wm. Thomas
Lamb, John-1005
Lamb, Thomas-1005

        John B.
        Nancy J.
        Wm. Riley
Lambeth, Lucinda-720
Lambeth, Joseph-729
Lambeth, Josiah B.-729
        Joseph
        Wm.
        Madison
        Susan
        Nina
        Orlena
        Irving
Lambeth, Wm. F.-729
        John
        James
        Joseph
        Wm.
        Andrew
        Dee
        Roenia
Lamon, Polly-840
Lane, James M.-783
Lane, Thursia E.-784
Lane, Abigail-793
Lane, C.C.-1182
Lane, Thomas, Jr.-1182
        Otto Ray
        Gertrude May
Langston,,Mary E.-882
Langston, J.W.-882
Lanning, Mary A.-989
Lanning, Wm.-989
Larkin, Isaiah-1059
        Maley
        George
        Wm.
        Rosa
        Isaiah
        Dolly A.
        Effie
        Dovie
        Magnolia
        Albert
Larkin, George W.-1059
Larrimore, Sarah P.-1064
Larimore, James-1064

Lassiter, Matthew-727
Lassiter, Lucy A.-727
Latimer, Augustus-858
Latimer, Samuel T.-947
        Nancy A.
        Ida J.
        Wesley B.
        Cora B.
        Samuel A.
        Mary M.M.
        Sarah E.
        Nathan W.
Latimer, Samuel-947
        Samuel J.
        G.W.
        Margaret Ann
        Adaline
        Martha Ann
        Nancy G.
        Wm. H.
        Jacob L.
        Lydia M.
Latimer, Jacob-947
Latimer, Charles Harry-1123
        Elizabeth P.
        Joseph W.
Latimer, Elizabeth P.-1133
Laughlin, John J.-Catherine-791
Laughlin, Matilda-791
Lawny, Winnie-763
Lawson, Mahala-835
Lavender, Jane-1126
Layer, George-1178
Layton, Clara E.-886
Lea, Eppey H.-861
        H.H.
        Martha
        Elizabeth
        Nancy
        Gideon B.R.
        Frances
        Wm.
Lea, Herndon H.-861
Lea, John C.-1114
Leake, Cynthia-1002
Leake, Wm., Sr.-1002
Lease, Mary L.-692

Leavitt, Guilford A.-1124
    Albert W.
    Serene F.
    Amelia
    James B.
Leavitt, James-1124
Leckie, Dr.-955
Ledbetter, Matilda-960
Ledgerwood, Nancy-989
Lee, R.B.-965
Lee, Zerilda-901
Lee, Arabella-1171
Lee, J.A.-1171
Lee, John B.-1183
    J.A.
    J.C.
Lee, J.A.-1183
    James F.
    John R.
    Annie B.
    Emaline
    Essie
    Robert
    Mary E.
Lee, Sarah N.-1199
Leeds, James B.-Eva-1052
Leeds, Rhoda Ann-1052
Leek, Hanna-992
Legan, T.F.-944
Legg, Mary-1080
Leidheiser, John A.-905
    John A.
    Conrad
    Martha E.
    Catherine
Leidheiser, Catherine-897
Leighton, Mr.-1197
Leighty, Jennie-921
Leighty, Peter-Ellen-921
Lemmens, Robert-1094
Lenox, Hamilton-Maria-771
Lenox, Bettie C.-771
Lenox, David-974
Lenox, Francis M.-Elizabeth-974
Lenox, Josie M.-974
Lenox, W.W.-985
Lenox, Susannah B.-984

Lenox, David-984
Lenox, Charles-1005
Lenox, David-1005
Lenox, D.F.-1005
    Bessie
    Hamilton
    Catherine
    Kenard
    Isaac
    Madge
Lenox, John, Jr.-1005
    Mary J.
    Henry E.
    Samuel H.
    Willie Ann
    Francis E.
    Sarah L.
    Harriet E.
Lenox, John, Sr.-1005
    Thomas
    John
    Taylor
    Hamilton
    Elizabeth
    Susannah
    Margaret A.
Lenox, Miss.-1018
Lenox, J.M.-1037
Lenox, Hamilton-1060
Lenox, Wilson M.-1060
Lenox, Susannah B.-1061
Lenox, Margaret A.-1061
Leonard, J.C.-750
Leonard, Robert A.-1063
Leonard, Joseph-1063
Leonard, Robert-1061
Leonard, Abner H.-1061
    John W.
    Wm. R.
    James F.
    Eliza Ellen
Leonard, Wm.-1062
Leonard, Joseph S.-1062
Lermond, Elizabeth-816
Le Sueur, Martel-1006
Le Sueur, Wm. M.-1006
Le Sueur,-1007

                Ellen V.
                Ida C.
                Exeony E.
                Thomas G.
Le Sueur, Grandason B.-1006
                Wm. M.
                Rebecca E.
                Elizabeth
                James C.
                Martel P.
                Catherine O.
                Martha A.
                Stephen W.
                George G.
Letchworth, W.P.-843
Letchworth, Welcome-862
                Isabella Catherine
                Thompson
                John M.
Letchworth, Aaron-Elizabeth-862
Lewis, Melvina-1212
Lewis, Elizabeth-733
Lewis, Elizabeth-806
Lewis, John-806
                Elizabeth
                Hiram
                Mary I.
                Rebecca T.
                Emma A.
                Louisa V.
                Tabitha
                Samuel W.
                Sarah C.
Lewis, Julia-904
Lewis, Josiah-1063
Lewis, John-1063
Lewis, Mary M.-1133
Lewis, Sarah-1148
Lewis, Margaret H.-1191
Lewis, Rebecca H.-1192
Light, Dollie-705
Light, Noah D.-704
Light, Nettie-944
Lightner, C.C.-948
                Georgia C.
                Jessie L.
                Rosa Cornelia

Lightner, Christopher-948
Lightner, J.M.-948
                George W.
                C.C.
Lillian, Eleanor-724
Lindsey, Lycurgus-968
                Cynthia A.
                Mary E.
                Josephine
                Matilda
                Emma
                Laura
                Eugene
Lindsey, Amos-970
Lindsey, Emma-970
Lindsey, Josephine-968
Lindsey, Vivia-965
Lindsey, Virginia T.-925
Lindsey, Ezekiel-949
                Larissa
                Vivia
                Alice
                Luella
                Nellie
                Melvin
                Lester
Lindsey, Sterling-949
                Ezekiel
                Hannah B.
                Sterling W.
                Wm. C.
                Eliza
                Drucilla
                Mary
                Elizabeth
                John J.
                Emily J.
                Daniel A.
Lindsey, S.W.-950
                Carroll J.
                Bertha
                Daniel J.
                Blanche
                Ella
                Bernice Y.
                Minnie
                Roscoe

　　　　　　Anthony
　　　　　　Grant
　　　　　　Emmet
　　　　　　Jeannette
Lindsey, Cynthia A.-960
Linsey, Eliza R.-1070
Lingo, Tyre M.-1124
　　　　　　Liza J.
　　　　　　James R.
　　　　　　Miram
　　　　　　Charles F.
　　　　　　Mary E.
　　　　　　Laura
　　　　　　Benagah A.
　　　　　　Wm. E.
　　　　　　George M.
　　　　　　Alice
　　　　　　Berry A.
　　　　　　Lewis E.
Lingo, James-1125
Lingsweiler, John-730
Lingsweiler, John G.-791
Lingsweiler, Edward-790
Lingsweiler, John I.-790
Lingsweiler, John N.-Christiana-730
　　　　　　John G.
　　　　　　Julia
　　　　　　Louise
　　　　　　Edward
　　　　　　Mary
　　　　　　Wm. H.
　　　　　　Christiana
　　　　　　Carrie L.
　　　　　　Frank I.
Lingsweiler, J.G.-730
　　　　　　Charlie E.
　　　　　　Mabel I.
　　　　　　Arthur F.
　　　　　　Myrtle V.
Linn, George-843
Lipscomb, Miss.-758
Lipscomb, Wade-819
　　　　　　Sarah
　　　　　　Susannah
　　　　　　Amanda
　　　　　　Julia
　　　　　　John F.
　　　　　　Harriet

Lipscomb, Harriet-818
Little, L.D.-966
Livesay, Sarah A.-1002
Livesay, John W.-1007
　　　　　　James D.
　　　　　　Lewis A.
　　　　　　John S.
　　　　　　Mary J.
　　　　　　Amanda M.
Livesay, John Simpson-1007
Lloyd, Ella-981
Lloyd, Wm.-981
Lockwood, Isaac-731
　　　　　　Mary J.
　　　　　　Francis M.
　　　　　　George H.
　　　　　　Thomas F.
　　　　　　Wm. A.
　　　　　　Isaac O.
　　　　　　Ira E.
Lockwood, Thomas F.-731
　　　　　　Eda Ethel
Lofton, Thomas-875
Lofton, Cornelius-881
Lofton, John-934
Lofton, Serena-934
Logan, Anthony-Margaret-79
Logan, Margaret J.-791
Logan, Jane-897
Logan, Nancy-897
London, Emily Frances-1058
Long, Mary A.-1098
Long, J.M.-777
Long, Joseph Martin-791
　　　　　　Luther
　　　　　　Sarah Ann
　　　　　　Henry Martin
　　　　　　Lydia Adelia
Long, George W.-791
　　　　　　Wm. P.
　　　　　　Francis M.
　　　　　　Joseph M.
Long, Martin-791
Long, Thomas S.-794
Long, Lucinda-793
Long, Mary A.-794
Long, Matthew-863
　　　　　　Wm. L.

        Jacob T.
        Margaret E.
        Ellen
Long, Wm. L.-864
        Elizabeth C.
        Matthew P.
Long, Wm.-Rebecca M.-863
Long, A.S.-990
Long, A.S.-1008
Long, Joseph-1008
Long, Sarah-1160
Lorance, A.-701
Lowrance, A.A.-741
Lortz, Anna M.-805
Loudermilk, Irene-875
Lovan, Wm. M.-951
        James R.
        Marshall G.
        Mary E.
        Henry G.
        Gertrude
Lovan, M.G.-951
        Alfonso B.
        Leonidas
        Ida
        Marshall E.
        Edmund A.
Lovan, Mary E.-958
Love, Charlotte B.-796
Love, Thomas B.-862
Love, Martha-862
Love, Eliza E.-1007
Love, Robert A.-Amanda-1007
        Eliza E.
        Lea M.
        George L.
        Eddie A.
        Thomas E.
        Nellie C.
        Charles F.
        Triza Carrie
        James W.
Love, Isaac-1008
Love, R.A.-1013
Love, Nancy Jane-1013
Love, Pleasant M.-1013
Love, Mary Ann-1035
Love, Wm. O.-1035

Love, Andrew H.-1068
Love, John-1064
Love, Wm. Robert-1064
        Elizabeth
        Dallason
        Andrew H.
        Mary
        Wm. B.
        Horace J.
Love, Robert K.-Margaret C.-1064
        Wm. R.
        John A.
        Dallison S.
        Elizabeth J.
        Sarah A.
Love, Wm. R.-1052
Love, Wm.-1142
Love, Esther-1142
Lovell, T.C.-951
Lowrance, S.S.-894
Lusllin, Alexander S.-694
Lumbeck, I.J.K.-990
Lundy, Melvina-1211
Lutes, Jane M.-722
Lyles, Alfred Newton-1126
Lyles, Stephen D.-1126
        Mary
        Josephine
Lyles, Robert-1126
Lyles, Wm. Lavender-1125
        Pleasant L.
        Edgar K.
        Cecil F.
Lyles, Ephraim-1126
Lymon, Ruth-714
Lynch, R.B.-1115
Lynch, John T.-1127
        Cordelia Ann
        Minnie E.
        Thomas H.
        Mary F.
Lynch, Henry, Sr.-1127
Lynch, D.-1127
Lynch, Henry-1127
Lynch, David-1127
        Wm. H.
        John T.
        Ransom B.

        David A.
        Hayden W.
Lynch, Dabney B.-1127
        John H.
        Susan C.
        James S.
        Ervin T.
        Martin W.
Lynch, John T.-1159
Lynch, Cordelia-1159
Lynch, Wm. H.-1183
        Florence
Lynch, David-1183
Lyon, Dr.-907
  ****
   **
McAlister, Isabella-1182
Mc Berry, James-849
McBride, John-883
Mcbride, Hannah-883
McBride, James H.-1128
McBride, James H.-1157
McBride, Louisa J.-1157
McBride, Naomi-828
McCain, Elizabeth H.-1214
McCain, Hugh-717
McCaskill, James-1129
        Cecil
        Myrtle
McCaskill, Wm.-1129
        Eliza
        James—
        George
        John
        Elizabeth
        Wm.
        Zimri
        Levi
        Alice
        Donna
McCaupin, Mary-1063
McChane, F.M.-720
McClane, Eliza Jane-1164
McClannahan, Tennessee-1202
McClannahan, Philip-1202
McClary, Susan A.-1144
McClellan, Mrs. Mary A.-1144
McClendon, Elvira-1102

McCloskey, Catherine-744
McCloud, Phoebe-713
McClure, Pleasant-1193
McClure, Mary J.-1193
McClurg, Joseph W.-728
McClurg, Mary E.-728
McClurg, Joseph, Jr.-732
        James B.
        J.W.
McClurg, Joseph, Sr.-732
        Joseph
        Alexander
        Wm.
McClurg, J.W.-732
        Mary E.
        Fannie
        Joseph E.
        Sarah
        James A.
        Marshall J.
McCluster, Michael-1036
McCoin, Hugh-722
McComb, James, Sr.-733
        Wm.
        Lewis
        Mary
        Amy
        James
        David
McComb, Wm.-733
McComb, James, Jr.-733
        Charles A.
        James A.
        Virgil J.
        George E.
        Wm. E.
        Ernest H.
        Floyd J.
McCombs, Dr.-720
McCommon, Wm. M.-975
McCoren, Susan-1080
McCoren, Isaac-Rebecca-108
McCormmach, Russel-864
        Alfred J.
        Leroy
        Wm. T.
        Huldah J.
        John C.

          Joseph F.
          James Russell
          Harriet M.
          Sarah Ann
          Martha L.
          Mary M.
          Ollie L.
McCormmach, Johnson-864
McCowan, R.A.-970
McCoy, Daniel W.-952
    Maud
    Myrtle
McCoy, Andrew-952
McCoy, J.C.-1161
McCracken, Emily J.-878
McCrae, Frank-1009
McCrae, Charles M.-1009
    Charles Edward
    Rowe Francis
McCrary, Rachel-811
McCreary, Isabel-932
McCulloch, Martha W.-886
McCurston, George W.-1183
McCurston, Emma Dora-1182

McDonald, Lizzie-990
McDonald, F.E.-991
McDonald, Martha-1007
McDonald, Nancy-1055
McDonald, James-1065
MacDonald, Betsey-1065
McDonald, Robert-1144
McDonald, Miss.-1185
McDonnell, Sarah-1040
McDougal, Dell-991
McDowell, Alexander-920
McEffee, Catherine E.-820
McElhattan, Jane-923
McFadin, Herbert-858
McFall, Anderson-733
    Julia F.
    John L.
    Sidney C.
    Myrtle Etolia
McFall, Lindsey 733
    Sarah E.
    Wm.
    James

          Emmerson
          Susan E.
          Anderson
McFarland, Lottie-815
McFarland, Malinda Jane-823
McFarland, J.H.-1028
McFarland, Sarah I.-1177
McGee, Solomon M.-952
    Gilson F.
    Solomon A.
    Wm. K.
    Martin L.
    Dialtha C.
    Charles E.
    Amanda F.
    Sarah Louisa
    Rosie E.
    Jacob
    John T.
McGee, Wm.-952
    John O.
    Louisa T.
    Solomon M.
    Jane
    Wm. H.
    Delila B.
    Mary Ann
    Margaret
    James W.
McGee, John-1065
McGee, James D.-1064
McGee, Thomas-1075
McGee, Isabelle-1075
McGinnis, Hugh-Mary-1035
McGinnis, Maggie Ann-1035
McGinnis, Mary-966
MacGlashlan, Alexander-1065
MacGlashlan, Thomas-1065
    Thomas Angus Ewan
McGregor, Joe-792
    Ralph
McGregor, Allan L.-792
    Allan
    Joe
    James
    Pryor
McGregor, James-792
McGregor, Belle-1144

McIntire, J.W.-917
McIntosh, Sarah-1167
McKee, J.M.-1184
McKee, Joel-1184
McKenna, John-1121
McKenzie, George-1121
McKenzie, John-1010
McKinney, Nancy-1208
McKinney, Serena-1127
McKinney, David-1129
  Margaret
  Alonzo
  Missouri
  Ellen
  Ida
  Monroe
  Mary
  Jacob L.
  Martha J.
  Pinkney
  James Wm.
  J.D.
  Sarah
  Nancy
  Andrew J.
  C.G.
  Robert B.
  Chelly
McKinney, James-1129
McKinney, Echols-1147
McKorkle, Robert-980
McKorkle, Rachel-980
McLachlan, Margaret-1078
McLellan, Margaret-816
McMahan, Abraham-842
  Elijah
McMahan, Tempa-843
McMahan, John F.-865
  James T.
  Mason Y.
  John F.
  Samuel R.
  Robert C.
  Charles W.
  Mattie E.
McMahan, John-865
McMahan, James-865
  John F.
  Abram
  Joseph
  Elijah
  Wm. T.
  Elizabeth
  Dubson
  Temperance
  Robert
  Huldah
  James
  Samuel
McMahan, Wm.T.-866
  James
  Wm.T. Jr.
  Arabella
  Lillie
  Clella J.
  Rosa
  Mattie E.
  Tempa S.
  Hulda F.
  Samuel D.
McMahan, Robert-867
  Hulda Temperance
  John R.
  Bertha May
  Thomas W.
  Effie Myrtle
McMahan, James-868
  Rosa Lee
McMenus, W.S.-752
McMenus, Joseph-752
McMillan, Ellen-935
McMorris, Mary-1153
McMullen, Elizabeth-991
McMullin, Rebecca-1027
McMullin, James J.-1185
  Samuel
  Mary
  Maude
  Joseph
  Frances
  Laura
  James
  Jesse
  Pearl
McMullin, James-1185
McMurtrey, Wm.-1041

McMurtrey, J.N.-1066
    Jessie
    Walter
    Tessie
    Clifford
    Deane
    Percy
McMurtrey, Alexander-1066
McMurtrey, Alexander, Sr.-1066
McNeal, Elizabeth-816
McNeff, George T.-783
McNeil, Annie-1138
McNich, Christopher-Electa-1148
McNich, Carrie-1147
McPherson, Mary-690
McPherson, T.-690
McPherson, Hardin-881
    Alice Mattie
McQueen, Elizabeth-1026
McRoberts, Sarah-1198
McSpadden, Moses M.-1067
    Elizabeth
    Aloey Jane
    Emeline
    Joseph M.
McSpadden, John-1067
    John
    Randolph W.
    Moses M.
McSpadden, Moses H.-1068
McSpadden, Moses-1067
McSpadden, Lizzie-1058
McSwain, Sarah A.-892
McVey, Nancy-940
    ****
      **

Mabon, James-1212
Mackey, W.P.-843
Maddux, Nathaniel-Rebbeca-969
Maddux, Avaline-969
Maddux, Nathaniel-698
Maddux, Nancy-698
Maddux, J.K.P.-953
    Tamza C.
    Mary E.
    Rebecca
    John
    Burton
    Clarence
    Ernie
Maddux, Alfred B.-953
Maddux, Rebecca-957
Madison, Polly-970
Magill, John H.-868
    Della
    Ralph
    Logan
Magill, John-869
Mahaney, Lucinda-823
Malcolm, D.W.-1008
Malon, Margaret-842
Malonee, Rebecca-1179
Manchester, Levi W.-1018
Manes, Sallie E.-716
Manes, Samuel J.-792
    J.T.
    J.O.
    W.J.
    S.J.
    A.E.
    M.J.
    Ida M.
    Bertha E.
    S.J.
Manes, Jacob-792
Manes, Seth-793
Maness, Lucy-1135
Maness, Elijah-1135
Mann, George-874
Mann, Hannah R.-874
Manry, Edward-830
Manry, Harriet-830
Mansfield, Thomas Jefferson-118
    Marion Pearl
Mansfield, Robert-1185
Manuel, Mary-703
Margedant, Otto P.-1010
    Sarah J.
    Henrietta
    Agnes
    Lillian
    Edwin L.
    Albert
    Walter
    Oscar
    Florence

Margedant, Mattias-1010
Marks, George S.-793
    Alice J.
    Fannie B.
    Wm. S.
    Thomas Grant
    Addie May
    Charles E.
    Orpha B.
    Eva M.
Marks, Jacob, Jr.-793
    Phoebe A.
    Andrew N.
    Daniel H.
    Louisa J.
    Peter A.
    Margaret E.
    George B.
    Isaiah W.
    Lydia H.
    John L.
    Jacob S.
    Susannah
Marks, Jacob, Sr.-793
    John
    Jacob
    Luke
    Katie
    Polly
    Hannah
Marks, Peter-793
Marks, John-793
Marlin, Thomas-869
    James
    Spencer
    Archibald
    Malinda
    Wm.
    Mary
Marlin, Archibald-869
    Madison
    Wallace
    Helen
    Delmar
    Mary
Marlow, Mary-787
Marre, Ann-926
Martin, Lewis-1042

Martin, George-1068
Martin, Wm. C.-1068
    Eliza Jane
    Wm. T.
    John Westley
    Francis
    Marion
    George Washington
Martin, W.T.-1069
    Charles E.
    Ernest E.
    Minnie M.
    Pearl
    Mattie
    Lee
Martin, Wm. C.-1069
    Eliza J.
    Wm. Thomas
    John W.
    Francis M.
    George W.
Martin, Martha E.-1110
Martin, J.F.-715
Martin, Mary B.-1077
Martin, Sarah J.-802
Martin, Elisha-Emily-805
Martin, Sarah J.-804
Martin, Emeline-869
Martin, Wm. A.-869
    Laura M.
    Charles F.
    Mary S.
    James P.
    Matilda C.
Martin, James D.-869
Martin, Fannie-903
Martin, Samuel T.-903
    G. Thomas
    Samuel D.
    Charles
    Frank
    Fannie
    Bettie
    Mary
    Kate
    Helen
    Anna
    Hester

Martin, Rebecca-945
Martin, Louisa-952
Martin, Jane-1008
Martin, Adam-1012
Martin, Madison-1012
Martin, Charles N.-1011
Martin, David-1012
Martinson, Marian-717
Marsh, George-1097
Marsh, Sophronia-925
Marshall, Mr.-1151
    Thomas Humphrey
    Leroy
Marshall, T.H.-1186
    Ollie
Marshall, Wm. P.-1186
Marshall, George-997
    Lizzie
    Carrie
Marshall, Lizzie-997
Mashburn, Charity-908
Mason, Peter T.-1130
    Wm. D.
    Herbert C.
    James R.
    Frank
    Edwin
    Elizabeth L.
    Roy M.
    Grace
Mason, Dexter-1130
Mason, Temperance-865
Masterbrook, August-1145
Matkin, Malinda-1105
Matlock, Hester A.-1174
Matlock, Elizabeth-987
Matlock, John-987
Mattock, Rebecca-1185
Mattox, Jane-1204
Matthews, Ama C.-1092
Matthews, Ransom D.-1092
Matthews, Martha-769
Matthews, Wm.-769
Matthews, Alice Ann-769
Matthews, Sarah-1004
Maupin, Sallie B.-1015
Mautz, Frank-1137
Maxey, Sarah M.-703

May, Letty-1182
May, Emily J.-738
May, Robert-Ellen-738
Mayfield, Elizabeth-720
Mayfield, W.R.-720
Mayfield, James-734
    James
    Wm. R.
    Anna
Mayfield, Wm. R.-734
    Sarah E.
    Irvin W.
    W. Melvin
    Andrew O.
    L.S.
    Lulu Bell
Mayfield, W.M.-735
    Orin
Mayfield, James-738
Mayfield, Lucy E.-738
Mayfield, John E.
    Lucy E.
    Sarah N.
    James H.
    Wm. R.
Mays, Charles T.H.-795
Mays, Beverly-795
Mays, Wm.-795
Mays, James M.-795
Meade, Mary-914
Medley, Miss.-920
Meents, Feeke-735
Meents, Tantken-735
Ments, John-735
    Margaret
    Remmer
Mehaffey, A.D.-948
Mehaffey, Mary E.-948
Mellen, Jerusha B.-728
Melton, Betsey-1177
Melton, Mary-1177
Melton, J.D.-884
Mendenhall, Jacob-966
Meriner, H.E.-700
Meriweather, Robert-1012
    Carl
    Roy B.
Merrell, Dan-1131

          Missouri C.
          Margaret B.
          Hattie E.
          Amanda M.
Merrell, Alfred-1131
          John
          Dan
Merrell, John-1131
          Eleanor
          Mary
          Alfred
          Louisa F.
          John
          Philip
          Margaret M.
          George M.
Merritt, John-1102
Messersmith, Cena-809
Messimar, Peter-1201
Messimar, Delilah-1201
Mickler, G.W.-783
Miers, J.W.-1150
Mikkelsen, Christian-870
          Christian P.
          Hans
          Jacob P.
          Charles
          Louisa
          Christians
          Anna
Mikkelson, Hans-Christine-870
Milburn, Lucie A.-880
Milburn, Alexander-880
Millard, A.M.-999
Miller, Mary Elizabeth-1059
Miller, H.C.-1186
          Mabel
          Minnie
Miller, E.F.-1186
Miller, Sarah Ann-692
Miller, John-Elizabeth-692
Miller, J.J.-750
Miller, Joseph-766
Miller, Franklin-766
Miller, C.-795
          Flossa
          Gertrude May

Miller, John-796
Miller, Joseph-796
Miller, Richard-796
Miller, Jasper-826
Miller, Mary-830
Miller, John-871
Miller, John F.-871
          Frank
          Dean
          John
          Marion
          Harvey
          Melvin
          Bessie
Miller, D.R.-898
Miller, W.J.-901
Miller, George W.-909
Miller, Samuel D.-909
          Sarah
          Mary
          Anna E.
          George W.
          John R.
          Wm. J.
          Theresa C.
Miller, Elizabeth-919
Miller, John-Nancy-1009
Miller, Amanda-1009
Miller, Wm.-1018
Miller, Lois-1018
Miller, Levi-1013
          Margaret E.
          Martha F.
          Cynthia
          Augusta I.
          Josie A.
          Alfred L.
          Nancy J.
Miller, George-1013
Miller, Lea H.-1012
          Letitia
          T.W.
          Lea E.
Miller, John C.-1012
          Lea H.
          Chesteen
          Wm. W.

       George R.
Mills, Miss.-1211
Millsap, Joseph-Mary-1039
Millsap, Angeline-1039
Millsap, James-Elizabeth-1067
Millsap, Juliann-1067
Miln, James-699
Miner, Laban E.-1070
Miner, Jordan-1069
Miner, Cretis-795
Minium, John-Harriet-996
Minium, Linda-996
Mings, Wm. C.-1187
      Margaret E.
      George W.
      Joseph W.
      Wm. R.
      John W.
      James
Mings, George Wolfscale-1187
Mings, Elizabeth-980
Mires, George W.-Elizabeth Ann-1128
Mires, Cordelia Ann-1128
Mires, J.W.-1131
      Benjamin
      Edison
      Walter
Mires, George W.-1132
Mires, Peter-1132
Mires, Charles-1132
Misenbelder, Elizabeth-929
Mitchell, John-1054
Mitchell, Elizabeth-1054
Mitchell, Spencer-1072
Mitchell, Martha E.-1072
Mitchell, Martha E.-1073
Mitchell, Louisa C.-1114
Mitchell, Spencer-Susan-1114
Mitchell, J.J.-1118
Mitchell, Levi-1013
      Margaret E.
      Martha F.
      Cynthia
      Augusta I.
      Josie A.
      Alfred L.
      Nancy J.

Mitchell, Frances M.-1127
Mitchell, P.D.-1127
Mitchell, Sherrill Lewis-1133
      Nellie
      Ernest
Mitchell, Spencer-1133
Mitchell, Sherrill S., Sr.-1133
Mitchell, Philander Davis-1133
      Travis B.
      Spencer E.
      Frances M.
      Mary E.
      Philander H.
Mitchell, Martha-1136
Mitchell, Spencer-1147
Mitchell, Virginia E.-695
Mitchell, Martha-753
Mitchell, Samuel-770
Mitchell, Cytha Lorena-770
Mitchell, Samuel-778
Mitchell, Elwiza H.-778
Mitchell, James M.-787
Mitchell, Cora E.-787
Mitchell, John-850
Mitchell, Louisa-850
Mitchell, Greenstreet-949
Mitchell, Wm.-1013
      Polly
      James
      Mahala
      Andrew
      Peter
      Wm.
      Levi
      Julius
      Sallie
      Abigail
      James
      Jesse
Mitchler, Samuel-865
Mizer, Michael-736
      George W.
      Wm. H.
      Wesley W.
      Albert B.
      Lucinda
      Nancy
      Elijah H.

           Minerva
           Angeline
Mizer, Wm. H.-736
       Elder J.
       Noah E.
       Wm. L.
       Myrtle
       Virgil
       Luna
       Edna
       Alice
       Atna
Moffatt, Catherine-1051
Moffat, Flora-714
Molkey, Miss.-936
Moltke, Baron Von-936
Monday, Wm.-748
        Mary
        Robert
Monday, Priscilla-843
Monroe, Thomas-732
Montague, Jane-790
Montgomerie, Thomas J.-1188
Montgomerie, Jefferson-1188
Montgomery, Margaret E.-1216
Montgomery, Frances-1041
Montgomery, Thomas-1192
Montgomery, Elizabeth-849
Montgomery, John J.-954
            John Wm.
            Gilford W.
            Allie Virginia
Montgomery, Wm.-954
            John J.
            Margaret
            Charity
            Thomas J.B.
            Nancy E.
Montgomery, T.J.B.-954
            Evy M.
            Wm. C.
            Cora E.
            Irena F.
            Thomas B.
            Daisy D.
            Bunnie
Montgomery, Jane-987

Montgomery, Thomas-Mary-987
Moody, Thomas-1163
Moore, Thomas Lorenzo-1134
Moore, Mr.-1188
Moore, Nancy F.-693
Moore, James T.-722
Moore, Asa-736
Moore, L.A.-736
       Emanuel
       Albert
       Thomas E.
Moore, Wm.-Elizabeth Ann-787
Moore, Margare J.-787
Moore, Elizabeth-823
Moore, Dorcas-826
Moore, Wm.-865
Moore, Friley Washington-871
       Wm. J.
Moore, Mathias-871
Moore, Wm. B.-871
Moore, Jonathan-872
Moore, Joseph T.-872
Moore, Elizabeth-891
Moore, Maria M.-996
Moran, Elizabeth-1070
Moran, Derby-1134
       Moses W.
       John H.
       Thomas M.
Moran, John H.-1134
       Hampton
       Vesta
Moreland, Sarah-892
Morgan, Malitia-786
Morgan, John-797
        Rebecca
        George
        Loura R.
        Lottie W.
        John B.
        Mattie
Morgan, Reuben-797
Morgan, Rosina-824
Morland, Lydia-943
Morphis, Leonard H.-862
Morrel, Mary-710
Morris, Mary-755

Morris, Mary E.-822
Morris, James Thomas-873
      James C.
      Clarence R.
Morris, Robert-873
Morris, Caroline-989
Morris, Miss. A.-995
Morrison, Wm.-1070
Morrison, Samuel-1070
      Wm. S.
      Grace L.
      Clarence M.
      Guy W.
      Carl T.
Morrison, Joseph F.-797
Morrison, John O.-797
Morrison, Easter-945
Morrisey, Bridget-1134
Morrow, Phena-782
Morrow, David,-955
Morrow, W.L.-955
      Wm. L.
      Robert
      George
      Julia
      Harriet
      Tabitha
Morrow, Robert-955
      Thomas B.
      Robert A.
      Monroe I.
      Mary –
      Josephine
Morrow, T.B.-956
      Lizzie
      Etta
      Queeny
Morse, Wm.-Lucy A.-1002
Morse, Lucy B.-1002
Morton, J.M.-877
Morton, George-870
Morton, Sarah L.-870
Morton, Martha Jane-873
Mosby, Anna B.-792
Moser, Daniel-1071
Moser, Sarah A.-1071
Moser, John-1071
Moser, Eli-1071

Moser, Franklin M.-1071
Moser, Allen-Susannah-737
Moser, John J.,Jr.-738
      Lucy A.
      Charley W.
      George A.
      Harrison
      Ida L.
Moser, John-737
      Henry
      James
      Margaret
      John
Mosher, Eli-1034
Moss, Elizabeth-785
Mott, Mrs.-1188
Moulder, David-910
      Ellen
      Jessie L.
      Cora M.
      Thomas V.
      Charles
      George C.
      John D.
      Elect E.
      Emma M.
      Sallie
Moulder, Valentine-910
      David
      Mary E.
      Bertha R.
Moulder, Jessie-913
Moulder, Thomas H.B.-911
      Frederick J.
      Hattie L.
      Juliett
      Sidney
      Anna E.
      George A.
      Bettie
      John P.
Mounce, John-838
Mounce, Mary-838
Mouser, J.B.-780
Mowery, Sophia-722
Mowser, Margaret-702
Mulholland, Mary-931
Mulkey, Alice-970

Munday, Mary-886
Munger, Margaret L.-765
Murphy, Wm. H.-799
    Arthur P.
    Kate C.
    Mary
    Wm. H. Jr.
Murphy, Isaac-799
Murphy, Isiah T.-799
    Thomas A.
    Wm. H.
    Perron F.
    Frank W.
    Robert C.
    Lilburn
    Anvil M.
    Mary
    Emma
Murphy, Frances M.-912
Murphy, A.M.-997
Murray, Mary-Ann-988
Murray, Patrick-Mary-988
Murrell, Mary Ann-1135
Murrell, Wm.-1188
Murrell, Wm. L.-1188
    Darthulia E.
    James
    Wm.
    Noah
    George
Murrill, Elias-1135
Murrill, E.P.-1135
    Constantine
    George Riley
    Mary Ann
    Daisy May
    Ross Perkins
Murry, Mary-737
Musgrave, Sarah N.-787
Musgrave, George-798
Musgrave, Bennerr H.-798
Musgrave, W.S.-798
Musgraves, Andrew-784
Musick, Lewis E.-1191
    Ada
Musick, Lewis-1191
Musick, George-1191
    Alexis
    George
    David
    Abraham
    Ephraim
Musick, Thomas R.-1191
Musick, Thomas H.-1189
    Ida
    Shelley
    Ruth V.
    Lois E.
Musick, Wm. H.H.-1190
Musick, Lafreniere C.-1189
    ****
    **
Nall, Margaret-694
Nall, John-1135
Nall, John, Sr.-1135
Nall, Wesley-1135
    Samuel
    G.C.
    Sarah
    A.B.
    Naomi Jane
    John F.
Nalle, Margaret-977
Nanny, Rebecca-922
Napier, Patrick-1118
Nash, Elizabeth-778
Nash, Minerva-1148
Nasry, Jane-1032
Neal, A.H.-731
Neal, Rebecca E.-906
Neel, Nancy A.-1187
Neely, Frances-772
Neely, David-Mary-1151
Neely, Eliza-1151
Neese, Eleanor-878
Neice, Nancy-980
Neil, Margaret Ann-765
Neill, Polly-1179
Nelson, Wm.-Mahala-699
Nelson, Mary Ann-699
Nelson, John A.-738
    Fannie E.
    Absalom
Nelson, Elijah-738
Nelson, A.-738
    Homer A.

                Arthur T.   Ida
                Harry A.   Franklin
                Alfred J.   Docia E.
                Laura A.   Jilian
Nelson, America-1080   Newton, Marjery-1201
Nelson, John-768   Newton, Wm.-Nancy-1201
Nelson, Joe-1080   Nichol, Wm.-Scott-1136
Nelson, John W.-774   Nichol, David-1136
Nelson, Sarah-798   Nicholas, Walker-1137
Nelson, John-874   Nicholas, Thomas E.-1137
Nelson, John W.-874   Mary
                Myrtle   Orlena
                Mary E.   Daisy
                Maggie M.   Nichols, Nancy-966
                Elsie E.   Nichols, Lucinda-740
                Wm. Roy   Nichols, Sarah-881
Nelson, Grandfather-912   Nichols, Frances E.-879
Nelson, Owen A.-911   Nichols, John W.-1143
                Hugh R.   Nichols, Nora-1143
                Wm. G.   Nichols, Miss.-1166
                George E.   Nichols, Lazarus-1193
Nelson, Alexander C.-911   Laura
                Owen A.   George
                John W.   Narcissus
                George W.   J.C.
                Grant   Lola
Nero, Mr.-1182   Hattie
Nesbit, Mary J.-747   Charley
Nestor, Bridget-1138   Nichols, J.C.-1193
Nevel, Mary-1191   Nicholson, Catherine-908
Nestor, John-1138   Nicholson, Anna Margareta-802
Newcombs, M. Jane-1142   Nicholson, Sampson-876
Newcomer, W.H.-884   Nicholson, Emily-876
Newhouse, Sarah-746   Nicholson, Isaac-913
Newhouse, Martha-747   Nicholson, Elizabeth-913
Newport, Calvin-973   Nicholson, Lora-959
Newport, Rebecca-1004   Nicks, John, Sr.-739
Newport, Richard-1004   Nicks, John, Jr.-739
Newport, J.D.-927   Betsey A.
Newton, Margaret L.-1208   Alfred H.
Newton, Mary-1214   Mary
Newton, Louisa-835   Nicks, A.H.-739
Newton, Alexander-1192   Wm. M.
Newton, Jeremiah-1192   Mary B.
                Rufus L.   Brown S.
                Robert A.   Robert A.
                John A.   Niven, Mary-991
                Adella   Nix, Sarah-1195

Nool, Nancy-748
Norris, B.F.-922
Norris, Sarah Ann-1034
Norman, Moses-740
    Jasper N.
    Newton
    Caledonia
    Sarah J.
    Taylor
    Caroline
    Mattie
Norman, Jasper N.-740
    Ida
    Nellie
    Gracie
    Archie
    Harrison
Norman, T.J.-962
North, Elizabeth-1115
Norton, Wm.-969
Norton, Nellie-851
Nyberg, Wm.-723
    ****
     **

Oaks, John W.-734
Oaks, Mary C.-734
O'Bannon, John-929
O'Bannon, Mary-929
O'Bannon, John-951
O'Bannon, George W.-956
    Floyd
    Claude
    Daisy
    Myrtle
    Ralph
    Arthur
O'Bannon, John-956
    Phoebe
    George W.
    John
    Mary
    James P.
O'Bannon, John-957
    Wm.
    Effie
    Minnie
    Roscoe

O'Bannon, J.P.-958
    Howard
    Lillie
    Roswell C.
    Gertrude
Oberbeck, Wm.-740
    Carr
    Caroline
    Lottie
    Henry
    August
    Herman H.
    Frederick
    Minnie
Oberbeck, H.H.-740
    Minnie
    Annie
    Henry
    August
    Mary
    Lena
    Ida
O'Brien, Elizabeth-1014
Odel, Wm. C.-1193
    James S.
    Enoch B.
    Mary A.
    A.F.
    Isaac
    Jacob
    Billy
    Cynthia
O'Dell, I.M.-741
    Grace
O'Dell, Samuel-741
    Elizabeth
    Enoch
    Jonathan
    Jeremiah
    John
    James
    Eliza
    W.C.
    A.F.
    S.N.
    B.A.
    I.M.

```
                S.S.
                Maggie
                Jennie
                Kate
Odell, Katie W.-839
Odell, Samuel-1193
Odell, Enoch-1193
Odenweller, Mr.-906
Officer, Nancy H.-862
Officer, Jefferson-862
O'Halloran, James J.-913
                Bessie
O'Halloran, Thomas-912
                Wm.D.
                Thomas W.
                Edwin C.
                James
                Mary E.
                Fannie B.
                John M.
                Katie F.
O'Halloran, Mr.-912
                Thomas
                Maurice
                James
                Eliza
O'Hearn, Michael-1138
O'Hearn, John-1137
Olinger, Martha-946
Oliver, W.H.-867
Oliver, Giles-711
                Henry
                Mary M.
                Fannie
                Wm.
Oliver, Fannie-711
Oliver, W.W.-1194
                Mariah
                James A.
                Wm. H.
                R.P.
Oliver, Allen-1194
Onehundro, Fannie-1154
O'Neal, Martha-761
O'Niel, Catherine-1104
Orchard, John-1072
            Alexander H.
            George W.
            James M.
```

```
Orchard, James Madison-1072
            John M.
            Albert E.
            Charles H.
            Mary L.
            Julia R.
            Wm. D.
            Ruah
Orchard, Charles-H.-1073
Orchard, J.M.-1073
Organ, John E.-1073
            Minnie
            James B.
            Perry
            Daisy E.
Organ, James-1073
Orr, George M.-1126
Osborn, Stephen-913
            Ambrose
            Nelson
            Franklin
            Malinda
            Wm.
Osborn, James-914
Osborn, Wm.-913
            Isaac
            Franklin
            Wm.
            Lucy A.
            Malinda
            Mary J.
            Matilda
Osborn, Sarah E.-1205
Ostrander, Emma R.-731
Oszmus, Andrew-Jane-893
Oszmus, Mattie-893
Ousley, John-810
Overbey, James B.-Jane-809
Overbey, Zula-809
Overby, James-800
            Alfred W.
            Mary J.
            Lucy B.
            James R.
            Marcus L.
            Zulia F.
            Wm. T.
            Tura A.
            John L.
```

   Frankly E.
   Dora M.
   Elmar A.
   Docia B.
Overby, Cain-800
Overturf, Orpha-937
Owen, W.H.-741
  Wm. H.
  James W.
Owen, Sigel-863
Owens, Philip-744
Owens, Wm.-784
Owens, J.B.-857
Owens, Samantha-825
Owens, Sarah-937
Owsley, Florence-1114
Owsley, John H.-1114
   ****
   **
Paine, John J.-742
  Robert A.
  John T.
  Sarah N.
  Clara Bell
  Mary
  Lucia
  George
  Martha
Paine, A.-742
  George A.
  Marvin M.
  John J.
Paine, Clara-749
Paine, Martha-950
Palmer, Arthur L.-763
Palmer, John-1194
Palmer, R. Boone-1194
  Wm.
  Benjamin
  Joseph
  Lucinda
Pare, Anna-707
Parker, Lucy-969
Parker, Susan-1212
Parker, David A.-Sarah-1070
Parker, Margaret E.-1069
Parker, Wm. F.-761

Parker, Elizabeth-835
Parker, Laura-1130
Parker, Robert T.-1014
Parker, Robert-1014
Parker, Luman F.,Jr.-1015
  Luman F.
  Jackuelin 0.
  Grace M.
Parker, Luman F.,Sr.-1015
Parkes, Elizabeth D.-1162
Parks, Elizabeth Dodson-1103
Parr, Samuel-727
Parry, Amanda L.-1073
Patrick, Sarah-897
Patterson, James T.-750
Patterson, Robert-894
Patterson, Eliza-894
Patterson, Isabel-937
Patterson, A.J.-958
  Nellie
  Thomas
Patterson, Thomas-958
  Francis M.
  Campbell
  Lucretia
  A.J.
Patterson, Robert-1196
Patterson, T.H.-1195
  Hannah Florence
  Thomas A.
  George W.
  Margaret
  Robert R.
  John
  Mary E.
Patton, C.F.-990
Patty, Nancy-1169
Paul, John-Mary-780
Paulding, John W.-1138
  George
  John H.
  Hiram
  Walter
  Joseph
Paul, Mary Margaret-780
Paulding, John-1138
Paulding, George-1138

        John M.
        Wm. W.
        Alfred D.
        Adaline
        Isabella
        James P.
        Benjamin
        George
        Mary
        Henry
        Lizzie
        Agnes
        Ellen
        Joseph
Payne, Wm.-914
Payne, Wm.J.-914
        Wm. H.
Payne, Jane-1178
Payton, Laura L.-758
Payton, Henry-Elizabeth-758
Peak, Miss.-1157
Pease, John R.-914
        John R.
        Edwin E.
        Helen
        Francis
        Hiram L.
Pease, Hiram L.-914
Peck, Thomas-1034
Peck, Jane-1034
Peden, Nancy Jane-1034
Peden, Benjamin-Mary-1034
Pemberton, Wm.,Jr.-801
        Thomas
        Nancy J.
        Preston
        Sarah M.
        Wm. R.
Pemberton, Wm., Sr.-801
        Wm.
        Alexander
        Nancy
        Melvina
        Winnie
        Lewis
        Ruthie
Pemberton, Thomas-801
Pemberton, Richard-1074

Pemberton, Jesse B.-1074
        Levi T.
        Eliza J.
        J. Brown
        John W.
        Martha A.
Pemberton, Levi T.-1075
Pence, Barbara-1163
Pendelton, J.T.-959
        Luther E.
        Bertram E.
        Clara G.
Pendleton, George L.-959
        Tabitha P.
        John T.
        George T.
        Russell G.
        Mary S.
        Armedia
        Susan
        Sarah A.
Pepper, Polly-889
Perkins, Mary J.-1210
Perkins, Lotta-806
Perkins, John-1135
Perkins, Jane A.-1135
Perry, John A.-994
Perry, Jackson-1012
Perry, Anastasia-1012
Perry, John W.-1186
Perry, Susie Lee-1186
Perryman, Margaret-1180
Peter, Elizabeth-1139
Peter, Henry T.-1139
Peter, Charles E.-1139
Peterson, Loss-801
        Ingera
        Peter
        Anna Margareta
Peterson, Peter-801
        Loss
        Paer G.
Peterson, Anna M.-870
Pettigrew, Edward-Nancy-1065
Pettigrew, Sarah-1065
Pettigrew, Ebenezer-1075
Pettigrew, John T.-1075
        John Y.

                  Albert B.
                  Ida L.
Pettigrew, George Franklin-1139
                  Albert
                  Marshall E.
                  George R.
                  Mabel A.
Pettigrew, Edwin-1139
Pewett, H.-1029
Phillips, Gideon-743
Phillips, Matilda V.-969
Phillips, Hiram-970
Phillips, Rebecca-907
Phillips, Joshua-743
Phillips, Dain-743
Phillips, Richard-743
Phillips, Reuben-743
                  Joseph S.
                  Washington
                  Simeon W.
                  Reuben M.
                  A.J.
                  Rufus
                  Eliza A.
                  Lestina A.
                  Mary S.
                  Caroline E.
Phillips, Rufus-743
                  Heseltine A.
                  Reuben T.
                  Andrew D.
                  Rufus S.
                  Maggie E.
                  Isaac N.
                  Parker Duff
                  Celestine
                  John G.
                  Lucy Armintia
                  Wm. E.
                  Charles J.
Phillips, Robert-Nancy-744
Phillips, Wm.-744
                  Nancy
                  James Monroe
Phillips, Jesse-Polly-766
Phillips, Martha A.-766
Phillips, Martha-832
Philpot, Wm.-968

Piatt, J.G.-1193
Pibas, Lucinda H.-1167
Pickard, Mary A.-1084
Pierce, J.R.-892
Piercy, Lucy W.-754
Piercy, Baswell-754
                  Jack
                  Frank
                  Martha
                  Lucy
Piercy, C.M.-910
Pike, Gabriel M.-1140
                  Alva E.
                  Benjamin M.
                  Nancy T.E.
                  Robert
Pike, Benjamin-1140
Pinkney, Eliza J.-1043
Pinkney, C.P.-1043
Pinnick, Adaline-783
Pipkin, Lewis-853
Pipkin, Sarah F.-853
Pippin, George W.-802
                  Alvah
                  Thomas C.
                  Olive G.
Pippin, Hill-802
Pippin, Wm.-802
                  Virginia
                  George W.
                  Wm. J.
                  Thomas J.
                  Amiah
                  Alice
                  Charley
                  Joseph
                  Bland
                  Lizzie
                  Robert
Pitchford, Malinda Jane-8
Pitts, Nancy R.-892
Plain, Mary A.-812
Plain, John-812
                  Mary A.
                  Malinda
                  Isabel
                  Nancy
                  Ella

      Alice
      Laura May
Plank, Jasper-1087
Plank, Henry-862
      Della
      Sarah
      Laura
      Amanda
Plank, George-1033
Plank, Elizabeth-1005
Plank, Benedict-1005
Plank, Nancy-1049
Plank, Benedict-1049
Pleasatn, Lucy-822
Pleasant, Elizabeth-847
Plinkett, Mary-737
Plyburn, Mary-938
Poindexter, F.A.-889
Poindexter, Volumia I.-889
Pool, Robert-831
Pool, Trephena,-831
Pool, Joseph-977
Pool, Tryphenah-1176
Poole, J.W.P.-996
      Joseph W.
Pooler, Nancy-736
Pope, W.S.-746
Pope, S.E.-1176
Pope, Isaac-1196
Pope, Thomas-1196
Pope, S.E.-1197
      Emma Leigh
Pope, John T.-1196
      Charles E.
      Guy C.
      Otto D.
      Thomas A.
      Alith
      Ruth
Popejoy, Sarah T.-766
Popejoy, Alexander-766
Popejoy, John-953
Porch, Israel-1117
Porch, Mary-1117
Porter, Mr.-1082
Porter, Flora N.-739
Porter, Mary-906

Porter, Wm. P.-960
      Nettie F.
      Wm. W.
      Robert H.
      Lula B.
      Maude
      Ellis B.
      Mabel
      Mollie
Porter, Wm. C.-960
      Martha
      Mary
      Henry
      Sarah
      Wm. P.
Porter, Margaret S.-1046
Potter, Thomas W.-1046
Potter, Ruthie E.-826
Potter, Wm.-826
Potter, Wm.-1198
Potter, Melissa-1198
Potts, David-1161
      Eliza J.
Pounds, Sarah-1028
Powell, Elias-837
Powell, Nancy Caroline-837
Powell, Jerome H.-953
Powell, Eliza J.-1026
Powell, Rebecca-1066
Powell, Benjamin F.-1076
Powell, Joseph E.-1076
Powell, George W.-1076
Powell, German H.-1076
Powell, Henry E.-1076
Power, James-718
Poynter, T.J.-955
Pratt, Wm.-1102
Price, Fanny-792
Price, Hiram-802
      John
      Mary Ann
Price, John-802
Price, Wm.-1029
Price, Grandfather-1151
Price, Elizabeth-1151
Prillaman, Gabriel-1006
Proctor, Rhoda-864

Proctor, Nancy-956
Province, Evaline-1033
Pruett, Jesse-717
Pryer, John L.-874
    Nancy Olive
    Mary E.
    Amanda
    Dona Jane
    Araminta S.
    Lydia J.
Pryor, Wm.-974
Puett, Mary-836
Puett, Wm. M.-875
    John J.
    Virgie Irene
Puett, Joseph N.-975
    Mary
    Wm. M.
    Caroline S.
    Joseph N.
Pulland, Elizabeth Ann-1106
Pulliam, Nathan-817
Pulliam, Mary A.-817
Pullam, Delilah-1098
Pumphrey, Wm. G.-887
Pumphrey, Mary E.-887
Purcell, J.M.-1153
Purdin, Mary A.-1111
Purnell, Biddie-703
Puryear, Robert M.-875
Puryear, Samuel Y.-875
Putman, Alex-1049
Putman, George-1098
Pyatt, Joseph-1172
Pyatt, Mollie-1172
    ****
     **

Quick, Turzy J.-1207
Quinlan, Ellen-994
Quinn, Edward-744
Quinn, John M.-744
    Frank
    John
    James
    Mary E.
    Anna Teresa
    ****
     **

Rabenau, Henry-976
    Henry A.
    Wm. J.
    Caroline Louisa
    Charles J.
    Louis G.
Radcliff, Sarah A.-1110
Ragland, John-745
    Silas
    Wm. C.
    James H.
    John M.
Ragland, John M.-745
    Arthur H.
    Simeon W.
    Gertrude M.
    J.M. Hubert
    Clarence E.
    Nora E.
Ragland, John-758
Ragsdale, Susan V.-837
Rainey, D.-792
Ramsay, A.A.-952
Ramsay, Alice J.-952
Ramadall, Elizabeth-894
Ramsey, James-1015
    Noah
    Mary
    Monroe
    Ada
    Robert L.
    Margaret
    James
    Cora
    Charley
Ramsey, Robert L.-1015
    James
    Lewis N.
    Robert S.
    Dinah
Randales, Franklin-973
Randales, Alice-973
Randall, Jabes D.-1141
    James L.
    Esther A.
    Oscar A.
    Leslie C.
    Iva F.

Randall, Orman-1141
Randle, James L.-939
Randles, Rhoda-941
Randles, Robert O.-941
Randles, Robert-944
Randles, Altha-947
Randolph, G.R.-1168
Randolph, Sarah M.-1168
Randolph, Mary-1194
Raney, Joseph P.-1197
    Wm.
    Lucy M.
    Dorcas P.
    James
    Joseph H.
    Guy
Raney, Wm.-1197
Rapp, Martha-777
Ratcliff, Joshua-1164
Ratcliff, Temperance-1164
Ratcliff, Susannah-970
Ratleff, Wm.-Rachel-1044
Ratleff, Julia A.-1044
Rauch, Alexander J.-1016
Rauch, John-1016
Rauch, John Wm.-1017
Ray, Sarah Jane-1041
Ray, James H.-1041
Ray, James H.-1076
Ray, Robert-1076
Ray, John Reynolds-1076
    Lolo
    Bennie
Ray, David-1141
Ray, Wm.-1141
    Lizzie F.
    Sanford D.
    Theale V.
    Alra
Ray, Abigail-774
Ray, Wm.-920
Ray, Rebecca-993
Ray, Abner-993
Ray, James-1026
Rayl, J.A.-795
Rayl, Anastasia-1022
Rayle, J.A.-778

Razor, Elizabeth-1052
Razor, Peter-1052
Ready, Mary-784
Rease, Rebecca-854
Record, Mary-901
Reddick, Eliza-1086
Reddick, Ransom-1077
    James W.
Reddick, Daniel-1077
Reddick, James W.-1041
Redmond, John J.-876
    John N.
    Emily
    Sarah
Redmond, Matthew-876
Reed, Margaret-876
Reents, Reka-735
Reeves, J.O.R.-791
Regan, Robert B.-740
Renner, Mary Angeline-876
Renner, John-876
Rennick, I.W.-1154
Rennington, Phoebe-926
Reno, Ellen-718
Repsher, Elizabeth-1090
Reynolds, Alice-737
Reynolds, Bridget-745
Reynolds, R.D.-961
    Sarah A.
    Margaret J.
    George W.
    M.L.
Reynolds, Mark, Jr.-961
    John J.
    James K.
    Mark B.
    Sarah
    Nancy L.
    Margaret J.
Reynolds, M.L.-960
    Eliza J.
    Wm. D.
    Mark W.
    Eugene H.
    Lillie May
Reynolds, Mark, Sr.-960
    Elizabeth

                    John
                    Dianna
                    Nancy
                    Charlotte
                    Ailie
                    Wm.
                    Cyrus
                    Robert D.
                    Mark, Jr.
Reynolds, J., Jr.-965
Reynolds, Nancy-965
Rheinerson, Susan E.-1014
Rhodes, Catherine-1153
Rhodes, Nicholas-876
          Robert E.
          John F.
          Sarah H.
          Wm. T.
Rhodes, John-876
Rhodes, Robert E.-877
Rice, James L.-697
Rice, J.L.-829
Rice, John-869
Rice, Polly-869
Rice, Catherine-905
Rice, Polly A.-947
Rice, Wesley S.-963
       Luvernia F.
       Rosa B.
       Roadman B.
       Rosa T.
       Christian B.
       Virginia A.
       Wesley W.
       Levi H.
       Oliver O.
       Estella M.
Rice, James S.-963
      Harper H.
      Calvin H.
      Wesley S.
      Mahala L.
      Roadman H.
Richards, Anna-739
Richardson, Nancy-1203
Richardson, G.B.-837
Richter, Fredericks-1010

Rickman, Mr.-742
Ricjmond, Miss. T.E.-1186
Richs, Magdalens-1121
Ridenough, Elizabeth-994
Rider, Mary J.-1129
Rider, Elizabeth-1181
Riddle, Mr.-772
        Elias
Riddle, Isaac-777
Riddle, Matilda L.-777
Riegel, Eliza M.-839
Riggs, Wm. S.-678
       Mary
       Robert
       Wm. S.
       John A.
Riggs, A.J.-978
Riley, Margaret-879
Riley, John-1179
Richey, Wm.-746
Richey, James-746
        Newton
        Martha
        Nancy
        Wm.
        May
        Eura
        James
Richey, Wm.-746
        Eliza
        Robert
        Alexander
        Sarah
        Ralph
        Ada
        Samuel
        Mary
Rillmon, John H.-991
Rimmer, J.L.-694
Rimmer, John-694
Rimmer, Sarah J.-694
Rippee, Frances-1214
Rippee, Eliza-1112
Rippee, Mary Ann-1178
Rippee, Sampson-1179
Rippee, J.W.-1196
Rippee, John-1198

Rippee, Wm.-1198
Rippee, Jennie L.-1202
Rippey, Wm.-706
Rippey, Huldah-1192
Ritchey, Martha-1173
Riven, J.M.-834
Roach, L.I.-915
    Rebecca J.
    Susan E.
    James L.
    Sidney C.
    Martha A.
    Wm. N.
Roam, Isaac-804
Roam, Henry-803
Roberson, Margaret-1101
Roberson, Joshua-1101
Roberts, Susan E.-1050
Roberts, Hugh-Sarah-1051
Roberts, C.M.-1103
Roberts, James-1116
Roberts, Mary-1116
Roberts, Elijah-1155
Roberts, Susan-1155
Roberts, Minerva J.-1166
Roberts, Allen C.-Amanda-699
Roberts, Mary E.-699
Roberts, Z.B.-845
Roberts, Miss. E.J.-845
Roberts, Elizabeth-881
Roberts, John J.-881
Roberts, Zeruviah A.-903
Roberts, Uranah-907
Robertson, Peter-1078
Robertson, Duncan-1078
Robertson, David Asher-1142
    Cora Edna
    David Shaw
    Birdie Alice
    Virgil Asher
Robertson, Stephen-1142
Robertson, Wm.-1142
Robertson, Joshua-734
Robertson, David-776
Robertson, James R.-878
    M.N.
    A.J.
    John S.
    James M.
    Elizabeth Ann
Robertson, Daniel Wesley-878
    Ida Ellen
    Wm. Martin
    John Wesley
    Charles Calvin
    James Garland
    Daniel Alphonso
    Joseph Henry
    Ann Nettie
    Robert Josiah
    Eva Blanch
    Christopher Wallace
Robertson, S.C.-934
Robertson, S.B.-945
Robertson, E.T.-967
Robertson, James A.-964
Robertson, W.G.-964
    Ida B.
    Laura A.
    Eva W.
    Lula E.
    Harry W.
    Minnie
    Gracie
Robertson, Sarah J.-994
Robbins, Martha-933
Robbins, Delilah-939
Robbins, Wm.-Catherine-953
Robbins, Margaret E.-953
Robbins, Louisa E.-958
Robinett, Jesse-1199
    James H.
    John
    Charlie
    Jesse A.
    Winfield
    Lincoln
    Frances
    Nancy
    Wilson
    Avi I.
    Cleo
    Rebecca
Robinett, J.H.,Jr.-1199
    Mabel
    Oliver L.

                Annie
                Nena
Robinett, James H.-1198
Robins, Abigail M.-1180
Robinson, Basil-1140
Robinson, Rebecca-1139
Robinson, James-1162
Robinson, Ellen-1162
Robinson, T.E.-700
Robinson, John-770
Robinson, Lottie-809
Robinson, Rebecca-891
Robinson, Mary-1029
Robinson, John-1029
Rocter, Mary-706
Rodenbo, Sarah Ann-983
Rodgers, Sarah H.-1128
Rodgers, Nathaniel K.-Elizabeth-1128
Rodgers, George P.-1143
                Lela M.
                Oscar
Rodgers, Wm. J.-1142
                Thomas L.
                James M.
                Mary D.
                John
                Samuel
                Martha M.
                Wm. J.
                George P.
                Jethro M.
                Archimedes
                Margaret C.
Rodgers, Thomas-1142
Roe, Samuel-901
Roe, Molly-901
Roe, Jeduthan-976
Rogers, Edward-1010
Rogers, George-784
Roll, S.B.-952
Rollins, H.E.-778
Rollins, Wm-789
Rollins, Ransom-797
Rollins, James M.-802
Rollins, Docia-802
Rollins, James M.-804
Rollins, Harrison-804

Roney, Marilla-908
Roney, Thomas G.-Elizabeth-908
Roney, Samuel-1033
Root, John-Joannah-1143
Root, Peter-1143
                Albert
                Carl
                Edward
                Ellen
                Dora
                John Wm.
Root, Martin-Lucy L.-771
Root, Martha W.-771
Roote, Eleazer-1199
Roote, G.J.-1199
Rose, Tilda-811
Ross, Elizabeth-1067
Ross, Elam L.-1144
Ross, Columbus-1143
                Beauregard
                Adaline
                C.M.,Jr.
                Susan A.
Ross, Samuel-1201
Ross, Andrew-1200
                John H.
                Nancy E.
                Arthur A.
                Flora A.
                Mary A.
                Naomi J.
Ross, Henry-1200
Ross, Margaret D.-1003
Roster, John-994
Roster, Henry-1017
Roster, Charles-1017
Roth, Mary Ann-1145
Roth, Adam-1145
Rouff, Becky-701
Roundtree, Louisa A.-967
Roundtree, Joseph-966
Roundtree, Amanda L.-966
Roupp, Frank-718
Routh, F.M.-A.J.-939
                James P.
Routh, Thomas-969
Roy, Wm.,Jr.-1144

          Wm. M.
          John C.
          Robert J.
          George R.
          Ellen J.
          Agnes B.
          Thomas A.
Roy, Wm., Sr.-1144
Rubey, Urbin E.-747
       Thomas T.
       Charles W.
       Sarah J.
       Nancy C.
       Wm. L.
       Alice E.
Rubey, Charles W.-747
       Thomas L.
Rudd, Mr.-1177
Rudd, Mary E.-1177
Rudd, Wm. A.-1201
Rudd, P.W.-1201
Rudd, A.J.-1201
       Audrey L.
       Ada
Rudd, Mary E.-827
Ruffin, Emeline E.-844
Rupard, James-742
Rupard, Peter-748
Rupard, Erasmus-748
       Benjamin F.
       Parlee
       Lewis R.
       Elizabeth
       Wm.
       John D.
       Erasmus
       Peter
       Nancy
Rupard, Lewis R.-748
       Erasmus
       Nancy Ann
       Wm.
       John
       James
       Joseph
       Mary
       Matilda
       Lucinda

       Grant
Rupard, Wm.-749
       Pearl
       Beulah
Rupard, Erasmus-749
       Ella
       May
       Elijah
Rupard, Joseph-749
       Bettie
       Nancy A.
       Robert
       Ethel
       Joseph
Rupard, James-749
       Elsie
       Edward
       Wallace
Rush, John H.-879
Rush, James Lawrence-879
Rush, D.M.-949
Rush, David M.-965
       Dolores
       Lascelles
       Loise
       Norma L.
Rush, Daniel W.-965
       David M.
       Mary E.
       Rhoda A.
       Wm. R.
       John J.
       Maletha
Rush, John-965
Rusk, Lodema-761
Russell, John A.-1201
       Floyd
       Elmer E.
       Holan
       Cora I.
       Vance E.
       DeWitt T.
Russell, Samuel C.-1202
Russell, Jeremiah-749
       George W.
       W.R.
       Francis M.
       Theresa

                    Mary
Russell, Francis M.-749
          Mary Ella
          Florence Leona
          Ida Lee
          Emma Josephine
          Jeremiah Edwin
          Clara
Russell, Elizabeth-768
Russell, Isiah-895
Russell, Maria-895
Russell, Mary A.-912
Russell, Andrew A.-917
Russell, Mary J.-917
Rust, Miss. E.A.-1099
Rust, J.R.-1100
Rust, Robert-1149
Rust, Mary E.-1149
Ruth, Wm.-Eliza-1054
Ruth, Mary Ann-1054
Rutherford, Frank P.-1145
            James
            Ernest
Rutherford, John-1145
            Isaac
            James
            Mary
            Frank P.
Rutherford, F.P.-1003
Rutland, Margaret Missouri-1133
Rutt, Lucy-772
Ryan, Charles-1113
        ****
         **
Sailing, B.P.-769
Sally, George-1018
Sally, John A.-1018
Sally, James B.-1017
Sally, Lucinda F.-1026
Salsman, W.E.-837
Sample, Sarah E.-938
Sample, John-Elizabeth-938
Sams, Melissa-1166
Sandes, Mary-941
Sandes, Benjamin-941
Sandes, Christian-Mary-941
Sanders, Lucy-1107
Sanders, Rebecca-1163

Sanders, Catherine-1173
Sanderson, Alice-705
Sanderson, Alice-705
Sankey, Ira D.-1080
Sankey, Ezekiel, Sr.-1078
Sankey, Ezekiel-1078
Sankey, Eben Blanchley-1078
        Bessie P.
        Paul H.
        Ruth V.
        Eben Wallace
Sartin, Elizabeth-857
Saunders, John-934
Sawyer, Caleb-785
Sawyer, Susan-785
Sawyer, Henry-950
Schelling, Anna-1022
Schissler, John-1145
          Sophia M.
          Kate F.
          Annie F.
          Alice A.
Schissler, John, Sr.-1145
Schmalhorst, Henry Christopher-750
Schmalhorst, Anna Maria-750
Schmalhorst, Wm. H.-750
            Nancy N.
            Mary E.
            Cordelia I.
            Frances
            Margaret
            Samuel H.
            Levi
            Victoria
            Moses D.
            Wm. L.
            David E.
Schofield, James-965
Schofield, E.L.-965
          James C.
Schoolfield, Ellen-693
Schortt, Dora-891
Schlicht, John A.-805
          Charles
          Theresa
Schlicht, Paul-805
          John A.
          Frank

Scofield, Amanda J.-912
Scoggins, Mariah-1095
Scott, Wm.-1212
Scott, Nancy-1212
Scott, Jesse-751
Scott, Joab-751
Scott, Jordan-751
Scott, Solomon-865
    Larken R.
    Mary L.
    Stephen R.A.
Scott, Wm. C.-1004
Scott, Larah Louisa-1004
Scott, Lucinda-1098
Scott, Rufus-1192
Scruggs, John-760
Scruggs, Sarah-760
Searcy, Mary J.-890
Searing, Sarah-742
Seaton, Mary-715
Seburn, Grant-1212
Seely, Cornelia-965
Selby, Sallie-911
Selby, Thomas-Hulda-906
Selby, Legrand-906
Selby, Edna-906
Self, Wm. J.-965
    James H.
    Francis M.
    Wm. R.
    Mary E.
    Mark L.
    Nancy J.
    Albert J.
    Minnie P.
    Lulu E.
    Edward W.
Self, Peter-965
    Polly
    Wm. J.
    Charlotte
    Eliza
    Ruth
Self, Charles-961
Self, Peter-961
Self, Fountain-1136
Self, Nancy-1136

Sellard, Jane-977
Sellard, James-Judith-977
Sellers, Elizabeth-1094
Sellers, Martha-720
Settles, Jane-1159
Shackford, Helen A.-688
Shackford, Prof.-688
Shackelford, Mattie A.-878
Shafer, George-1146
    Catherine
    Maragaret
    Mary
    Sarah
    Hosea
    George
    David
    Amanda
    John
Shaha, Samantha-898
Shaha, Jackson-Elizabeth-898
Sharp, Victoria-756
Sharp, Mary-898
Sharp, Anna E.-905
Sharp, Jacob-905
Sharrartz, Margaret-1093
Sharrartz, Conrad-1093
Shaut, Elizabeth-999
Shaut, Jacob-999
Shaver, F.-1165
Shaw, Sarah-966
Shaw, Thomas-1018
Shaw, Hiram-1018
    Louis E.
    Hiram M.
    George T.
Shaw, Hiram-1018
    Lois J.
    Kate E.
    Josephine A.
    Olive Helen
    Hiram Miller
    Oliver Clark
Shea, Wm.-1030
Shea, Sarah S.-1030
Sheapley, Mr.-1082
Sheline-Sarah-938
Shemberger, Lydia A.-968

Shelton, Charlotta-944
Shelton, Stephen-1003
Shelton, Elizabeth-1003
Shelton, May-1032
Shero, Christina-790
Sherrill, Joel-1104
Sherrill, Mary E.-1104
Sherrill, Minerva-818
Sherrill, Samuel-818
    Catherine
Sherrill, Frances-1111
Sherrill, James-1147
Sherrill, Nel-1147
Sherrill, John-1147
Sherrill, Joel-1147
    Mary E.
    Joel S.
Shields, Arnett-1203
Shields, Samuel O.-1203
    John
    Arnett
    Charles
    David
Shields, Benjamin-843
Shinkle, Mr.-1191
Shinman, Adam-Henrietta-1019
Shinman, F.W.-1019
    F.W., Jr.
    Etta
    Albert
    Lena
    Walter
    Louis
Shipman, Martin D.-736
Shirley, Sarah J.-1082
Shirley, Jacob-Lucinda-1082
Shrock, Rebecca-1111
Shockley, Owen-806
    Sarah
    Oliver W.
    Mahala
    Andrew J.
    Samuel J.
    James M.H.
    Matilda
    Malinda
    Nellie

Shockley, Oliver W.-806
    Robert F.
    Cora
    Elizabeth
    Isaac
    Emmett
    Charlotte
    John O.
    Oliver
    Ollie
Shoemaker, Catherine-695
Shook, John-843
Shook, Mary L.-882
Shook, Wm.B.-882
Shoop, Mary E.-919
Shorns, Sarah C.-1169
Short, Reuben-1020
Short, John-1020
Short, Wesley-1020
Short, Evan L.-1020
Short, John L.-1020
    Rosa E.
    Nancy A.
Short, Thankful-1063
Shubert, George-807
Shubert, Charles-807
    Leslie
Shubert, Garret B.-807
Shubert, G.B.-916
    Charles
    Henry
    Eliza
    Edward F.
    Mary F.
    George
Shubert, George-916
    Garrett B.
    Henry
    Georgiana
Shults, Jacob-1060
Shults, Joseph Y.-1080
    Reuben O.
    Haden L.
    Emma E.
    Henry J.
    Joseph M.
    Elisha M.

          Lewis A.
          Mary L.
          Walter C.
          Effie M.
          Spurgeon R.
Shully, Leah-790
Sieg, Mary-1114
Sigler, Margaret-1025
Silvey, George W.-880
          Charles
          Smiley
          Letitia Ann
          Catherine
          Jackson
          Zerilda
          Susan
          James
          Thomas
          Elizabeth
Simmons, Ralph-1210
Simmons, Levi-Eliza-923
Simmons, Emily A.-923
Simmons, Wiley B.-1148
          John F.
          Julia Mary J.
          Sarah M.
          Charles L.
          Lucinda
          Phoebe
Simmons, James Riley-1148
          Irene
          Perley
          Lewis
          Annie
          Lee
          Gouley
          Oscar
          John R., Jr.
Simmons, Enoch C.-1148
          Wm. D.
          Wiley B.
          Pulaski
          Charles
          Lettie
Simmons, Lewis-1148
Simmons, Lewis, Sr.-1148
Simmons, John H.-1181
Simmons, John-1183

Simmons, Elizabeth-1183
Simms, J.W.-1073
Simpson, Valentine-1203
Simpson, Peter-1203
Simpson, James A.-1203
          Loren E.
          Margaret E.
          Verona J.
          Annie V.
          John W.
          Francis Edward
          James Arthur
Simpson, John A.-1203
Simpson, Emily-1082
Simpson, Joseph-1082
Simpson, Susan-700
Simpson, Alex-718
Simpson, George-764
Simpson, Wm. F.-917
          Wm. Andrew
Simpson, Wm. C.-917
          Sophia Ann
          Nancy E.
          John D.
          Wm. F.
Simpson, Julia-955
Simpson, James-Mary E.-1011
Simpson, Valeria-1011
Simpson, Robertha P.-1045
Sisk, Telitia J.-1093
Skaggs, Abraham-770
Skaggs, Nancy-801
Skaggs, Wm. A.-807
          Mastin
          Jesse
          Jacob
Skaggs, Jacob-808
Skaggs, Mastin-808
Skeaters, Wm.-1080
Skeeters, Samuel-1087
Skeeters, John L.-1080
          Wm. I.
          Elizabeth
          Samuel W.
          Martha C.
          Vickie
          Dora
Skelton, Elvira C.-705

Skinner, Elizabeth-898
Skyles, Wm.-1034
Skyles, Millie-1034
Slavens, L.J.-967
    Joseph Roundtree
    Mary Louisa
    Inez Lucy
Slavens, James H.-966
    Z.L.
    Nancy A.
    Lucius B.
    Luther J.
    Joseph W.R.
    Thomas F.
    Louisa Almarinda
Slavens, Z.L.-966
    Alice
    H.T.
    M.I.
    Robert
Slavens, Stewart-967
Small, Rebecca-975
Smalley, Lot-1126
Smelser, Margaret-767
Smiley, Wm.-1046
Smiley, Zanetta M.-1046
Smith, Sarah J.-1203
Smith, Henry-1204
    Eliza
    Houston
    Huldah E.
    Wm. J.
    Samuel
    Lafayette
    Alexander
Smith, Harriet S.-1206
Smith, Parthena-1082
Smith, Erasmus B.-1081
Smith, Wm. F.-1081
Smith, Benjamin-1081
Smith, Wm. S.-1081
Smith, Fannie A.-691
Smith, Joseph F.-691
Smith, John H.-696
Smith,,John W.-751
    Margaret Ann
    John Wesley

Smith, John Wesley-751
    Sarah Jane
    Nancy E.
    Rebecca F.
    John W.
    Margaret Ann
    Finis E.
    Martin S.
    Marcus B.
    Albert R.
Smith, Albert R.-752
    Albert R.,Jr.
Smith, Francis-753
    Samuel
    Joseph F.
Smith, Joseph F.-753
    Fannie
    Isabel
    Charles A.
    Jennie
Smith, C.A.-753
    Charles T.
    Homer F.
    Virgil A.
    Pauline
    Arthur Paul
Smith, Wm. H.-754
    George
    Wm. B.
    Mary
Smith, George-754
    James H.
    Ellen
    Wm.
    George
Smith, George-755
    Wm. H.
    Robert
    Martenia
Smith, Wm. B.-755
    James
    Lulu
    Joseph
    George
    Edwin
    Willie
    Mollie

        Robert
        Imogene
        Hugh
        Merton
        Egletine
        Ethel
Smith, Sarah-756
Smith, Nancy J.-803
Smith, Malinda J.-803
Smith, Daniel-803
Smith, Martha E.-789
Smith, Thomas L.-789
Smith, Nancy-850
Smith, James-850
Smith, Sarah E.-848
Smith, Wm.-848
Smith, Martha-844
Smith, Amos-Jane-844
Smith, Nancy-830
Smith, John-829
Smith, Ellen-825
Smith, Josiah-Minerva-814
Smith, Susan-814
Smith, Sarah-813
Smith, Moses-813
Smith, James R.-809
        Minnie M.
        Rosa N.
        Edna E.
        James T.
        Ida J.
Smith, Thomas M.-809
Smith, Daniel-808
Smith, Albert-808
Smith, Wm.-881
Smith, Nathan T.-881
        Mary
        Lucy
        Jessie Lorena
        John W.
        Bessie Adella
        Oscar Lee
Smith, Wm. L.-881
Smith, C.C.-881
Smith, Sarah A.-896
Smith, Nancy-987
Smith, Sarah-1014

Smith, Thomas-1021
Smith, Samuel-1021
Smith, James L.-1021
        Wm. H.
        Edmund W.
        Joseph S.
        Charles B.
        Wesley M.
        Allen
        Frank
Smith, Joseph A.-1021
        Ella
        Tenna
        Carrie
        Joseph H.
        James M.
        Annie
        Kate
Smith, Elizabeth-1047
Smith, Lucinda-1075
Smith, Jojanan-1198
        Nancy
        Francis
Smith, Nancy-1198
Smithpeter, W.-968
        Charles W.
        Herbert V.
Smithpeter, Alfred-968
        Angeline
        Albert
        Wilburn
        Ellen
        Marirtta
        Florence
Smothermon, Louisa-1153
Snapp, Elizabeth-948
Snelson, Missouri-1108
Snelson, John-1108
Snelson, John C.-1140
Snelson, Anna A.-1140
Snelson, Levi F.-1149
Snelson, John C.-1149
        Joseph N.
        John C.
        Missouri C.
        Levi F.
        Andrew J.

               Anna A.
               Samuel H.
               Alice E.
               Eldora P.
               Margaret C.
Snelson, Andrew J.-1149
               Charley O.
               Effie O.
               Wm. C.
               Dersey A.
               Walter M.
               Archie J.
               Thomas J.G.
Snow, Laura Ann-710
Snow, James-734
Snyder, Simon-794
Snyder, Anna-793
Snyder, John-794
Soest, Ernest, Jr.-1022
               Adelia
               Walter
               Herbert
Soest, Ernest Von-Emily-1022
Soest, Ernest Von, Sr.-1022
Solomon, Pleasant-810
Solmon, Edwin W.-879
               Milburn Tutt
Solmon, Ezekiel-880
Solmon, Wm. W.-880
Southard, W.A.-931
Southard, Martha A.-953
Sparkman, Ruth-993
Sparks, Reuben-1082
Sparks, Wm.-1082
Spear, Thomas-829
Spearman, Edmund-909
Spears, Nancy-1185
Spence, Martha-745
Spence, Robert-1204
Spencer, Miss.-719
Spencer, Esther-993
Spense, Martha-888
Sphar, Martin M.-731
Spohn, Elias-756
Spohn, W.-756
               Clara
               Myrtie

               Chase
               Justin
               Ernest
Spradling, George-826
Sprague, Ary B.-1042
Spriggs, Enoch-1039
Spring, James P.-1003
Sprout, John-798
Sprout, Joannah-900
Staff, A.L.-819
Stafford, James M.-969
               Amanda M.
               Lucy E.
               Newton C.
               Laura E.
               Martha A.
               John P.
               Mary Ellen
               Harriet T.
               Margaret S.
               Nathaniel B.
               Wm. A.
               Sarah E.
               Lydia L.
               Felix C.
               Heitte B.
               Floyd
Stafford, Bird-969
               James M.
               L.L.
Stafford, Amanda-940
Stafford, Esther-1141
Stagg, Anna G.-868
Stagner, Mary Ann-1062
Stagner, John-Anna-1062
Stamper, Nathaniel-768
Stamper, Nancy-768
Stanley, Polly Ann-969
Stanley, Horance-967
               Minerva
               I.V.
               Irene Z.
Stanley, Irene Z.-967
Stanley, Josiah-918
               Albert Sherman
Stanley, Richard H.-918
               Nancy A.

        Josiah
        Lydia
        Richard
        Henry
        Melissa
Starr, Emma E.-1167
Staton, Esther-1163
Stearnes, Martha J.-753
Steele, Rachel-998
Steele, Samuel-998
Steen, G.W.-749
Steffen, Catherine-1090
Steffen, Joh Peter-1090
Steffens, Henry A.-1150
Steffens, John H.-1150
Steinberger, Minnie-741
Stephens, Lizzie-1172
Stepp, Samuel-1082
Stepp, Wm. T.-1082
Stevens, Aggie-799
Stevens, Allen-Perlina-799
Stevens, Monroe-901
Stevens, Aultana J.-909
Stevenson, G.W.-809
        Emily
        Mary
        George
Stevenson, Zadock-809
Steward, Barbara C.-811
Steward, Katie-832
Stewart, Edward H.-1205
Stewart, A.J.-1205
Stewart, P.M.-694
Stewart, Wm.-778
Stewart, Charles-810
Stewart, Wm.P.-810
Stewart, John W.-810
Stewart, J.L.-1022
Stewart, J.M.-1023
Stiles, Louis-891
Stimson, Wm.,Jr.-1023
Stimson, Wm.,Sr.-1023
Stobaugh, Elizabeth J.-1059
Stogdill, J.R.-1118
Stokley, John-959
Stone, T.M.-862
Stone, B.W.-1020

Stone, Ann M.-1113
Stonecypher, Elizabeth-1013
Stotts, Morgan-1097
Stover, Lucy-1089
Stow, John L.-727
Stoy, Martha Ann-1150
Stoy, John W.-1151
    Julia A.
    Francis M.
    Martha E.
    Josiah
    John
    James
    Wm. M.
Stoy, Samuel-1151
Stoy, Wm. M.-1151
    Mary E.
    John E.
    Dorthea A.
    Francis M.
    Charles V.
    Elizabeth M.
    Wm. M.
    Walter M.
    Sarah J.
Strain, Thomas J.-Lydia-803
Strain, Rhoda-803
Stratton, W.A.-825
Stratton, Daniel-932
Strickland, Unity-701
Strong, Mary J.-820
Stroud, Lola M.-900
Stroup, Mary G.-699
Stull, Sarah-1088
Strunks, J.-1164
Stubbs, Andrew J.-Malinda-1078
Stubbs, Nancy-1078
Stubbs, Julia-1143
Sturgeon, John N.-1083
Sturgeon, W. Andrew-1083
Sturgeon, Isham-1152
Sturgeon, Thomas G.-1152
    Wilbird C.
    James E.
    Thomas W.
Sullins, Sarah-1136
Sullivan, Ellen-1138

Suminett, Margaret-1071
Summer, Jesse-Ditha-1129
Summer, Alice-1129
Summers, Betsey-1165
Sutherland, Mina O.-1092
Sutlif, Lola-1112
Sutton, Valentine-1107
Sutton, Nannie A.-1107
Sutton, A.G.-707
Sutton, Sarah E.-733
Sutton, Jesse-Nancy J.-734
Sutton, Wm.-811
Sutton, Alexander P.-811
Sutton, Valentine-1150
Sutton, D. Josephine-1150
Swain, Emma-815
Swain, George T.-Metilsa-815
Swiney, Edward-1084
    Elizabeth
    Ellen
    Julia A.
    John M.
    James H.
    Isaiah N.
    Edward L.
    Thomas D.
Swiney, John-1084
Swenson, Margaret A.-946
Swords, Mary A.-719
    ****
    ** -
Tabor, James-Delila-975
Tacher, Susanna-857
Talcott, Samuel-1206
Talcott, S.T.-1206
    Arthur C.
    Minnie L.
TaLee, Sarah-1208
Talliaferro, James-717
Tarbutton, Henry-1179
Tarbutton, Mary E.-1201
Tate, James A.-1207
Tate, John L.-1207
    James A.
    Thula
Tate, J.A.-843
Tate, James-1108

Tate, Ruth E.-1131
Tatum, Eaton-961
Taylor, Wm.-861
Taylor, Mary-1145
Taylor, Wm. H.-1152
Taylor, Calvin Buchanan-1152
    Grover
    Morgan
Taylor, Atlanta-1154
Taylor, Kate-1189
Teel, Sarah-847
Teeple, Jacob,Jr.-811
    Charles Elbert
    John Elmer
    James A.
    Hannah Lavonia
    Robert Lee
    Minnie F.
    Lillie May
Teeple, Jacob,Sr.-811
    Peter
    G.W.
    John R.
    Isaac
    Margaret
    Diannah
    Nancy
    Hannah
    Jacob Jr.
Telcher, Frederica-1016
Telford, Hugh A.-1132
Telford, Elizabeth A.-1132
Templeton, Edward-1173
TenEyek, John W.-1024
TenEyek, Wm.,Jr.-1023
TenEyek, Coorod-1024
TenEyek, Wm.,Sr.-1024
Tennison, Mary A.-718
Tennison, Joseph A.-718
    Newman
    Sarah H.
    Mary A.
    Thomas J.
    Elizabeth L.
    Frances M.
    Wm. M.
Tetley, Fred-978

Tew, Drusilla-888
Thackery, H.-878
Thomas, Jane-1087
Thomas, Nancy-755
Thomas, James-755
    Sarah
    Mary
    James
    Esther
    John
    Eglentine
    Joseph
    Edward
    Margaret
    Rachel
Thomas, J.M.-834
Thomas, Miss. E.V.-840
Thomas, Esther L.-854
Thomas, Joseph-851
Thomas, Wm. W.-882
    Edgar
Thomas, Edgar M.-882
Thomas, Ageline-907
Thomas, Nancy W.-1198
Thompson, Thomas-691
Thompson, Susan-1084
Thompson, Morgan-Nancy-1084
Thompson, Joyse-848
Thompson, Catherine-869
Thompson, Andrew-883
Thompson, Moses-883
Thompson, Mary-883—
Thompson, George W,-882
    George W.
    Francis Marion
    Wm. Jackson
    Eva Ellar
Thompson, Mollie E.-888
Thompson, John A.-888
Thompson, Virginia W.-924
Thompson, J.W.W.-934
Thompson, Virginia-936
Thompson, J.W.W.-945
Thompson, John*Sarah-1024
Thompson, Jane-1024
Thompson, Platt-1024
    Lewis Henry
    George F.

Thompson, Lewis Henry-1024
Thompson, Elizabeth-1034
Thompson, Robert-Prudence-1034
Thompson, Jane-1125
Thons, Sarah G.-1099
Thons, R.G.-1099
Thornton, John-766
Thornton, Wm.-766
Thornton, Martha-873
Thornton, Martha J.-1111
Thornton, Wm.-1147
Thornton, Jane-1047
Thorp, Jane-1043
Thrailkill, W.-736
Thrailkill, Elizabeth-769
Thrapp, Fannie-722
Thurber, D.B.-1084
Thurber, N.A.-1084
Thurman, Samuel B.-819
Thurston, J.S.-969
    Wm. Lycurgus
    Shepard Oscar
    Thomas Fulton
Thurston, Wm. S.,Jr.-969
    J.S.
    Maggie A.
    Sally
    Robert
    John C.
    Nancy A.
Thurston, Wm. S.,Sr.-969
Tibbs, Hannah-897
Tibmar, Ann E.-905
Tice, L.-770
Tiller, Elizabeth-697
Tiller, James-697
Tilley, Mahala-1102
Tilley, Missanaiah Sophia-771
Tilley, Wilson-771
Tilley, Elizabeth-776
Tilley, Charlotte-776
Tilley, Margaret E.-787
Tilley, Wilson-Elizabeth-797
Tilley, Mary A.-797
Tilley, Nancy J.-802
Tinsley, Nancy E.-936
Tinsley, Thaddeus S.,Sr.-970
    John H.

        Lydia
        Alice
        Lee
        Vanus E.
        T.S.
        May
        Zela
        Clay
        Idylle
Tinsley, John-970
        Wm.
        Phillip
        Emily
        Ruth
        Amos
        Milton
        Elizabeth
        Thaddeus S.
        Martha
        Lucretia
        Lucinda
Tippett, Elizabeth-771
Tippin, G.T.-962
Titterington, Adam L.-756
        James
        John Q.
        Daniel
        Alfred
        Elizabeth
        Caroline
Titterington, John Q.-756
        Jesse M.
        Mary
        James H.
        Sarah A.
        Robert D.
Titterington, Richard M.-813
Titterington, Adam-813
Titterington, Alfred W.-813
Toby, Lucy-968
Todd, Floyd M.-1194
Tompkins, John-965
Tory, George-852
Toughstone, James M.-881
Towery, Mary-1152
Towns, Wm.-743
Townsend, Mary-781
Trail, Wm. Franklin-1153
        Richard Y.
        Frances C.
        George W.
        Darriska R.
        Stonewall J.
        Christina
Trail, Young-1153
Tramble, Martha Jane-1020
Traw, David-814
Traw, Simeon-813
        John
        Josiah
        James P.
Traw, Josiah-899
Tredway, Margarie-766
Tredway, Joel-766
Trimble, Eva A.-867
Trimble, A.D.-M.E.-868
Trimble, Samuel C.-884
        Anna Lee
        Fannie May
        Samuel E.
Trimble, John C.-884
Triplett, Wm. H.-883
        James A.
        Wm. T.
        Martha J.
        Della
        Mary L.
        Grant
        Charles F.
        Reuben W.
        Elsa Ann
Triplett, James M.-883
Trout, Newton-1178
Trout, Wm.-1178
Truedell, Mary-1140
Tuck, Jane W.-1109
Tuck, Nancy-1109
Tuck, Grandfather-1109
Tucker, R.H.-752
Tucker, Frank-784
Tune, Wm.-1080
Tunnel, Mrs. Cunthia-1214
Tunnell, Wm-884
        F.M.
        Joseph L.
        Nancy J.

          Sarah C.
          George W.
          Wm. J.
Tunnell, Burgess-884
Turley, Louisa J.-885
Turley, Zadock-Margaret-1060
Turley, Ruthie-1060
Turner, Joseph C.-1208
          John Andrew
Turner, Jesse-1208
          Lillie
Turner, John-1207
          Sarah
          Elizabeth A.
          Margaret
          Nancy
          Mary
          Frances
          Laura
          John J.
          Jesse
          Triphena
          Joseph C.
          John Fisher C.
Turner, Elizabeth-701
Turner, Hilary M.-757
          Wm.
          Alice
          John
          May
          Edward
          Blanche
          Virgil
          Zoe
          Robert
Turner, Martin-Elizabeth-758
Turner, Thomas-757
          Hillory M.
          Wm.
          Meriwether
          John C.
          Robert D.
          Mildred S.
          Andrew J.
          Thomas B.
Turner, Andrew J.-758
          Ella

          Thomas A.
          Robert B.
          Bettie F.
          Maude A.
          Henry P.
          Elmo M.
          Edna E.
          Myrtle O.
Turner, Thomas B.-759
          Claude J.
          Walter L.
          Jeane L.
          Ora T.
Turner, Thomas-704
Turner, Cordelia L.-790
Turner, Mary L.-870
Turner, Mary-881
Turner, Margaret L.-1104
Turner, Thomas K.-1007
Turner, Paulina J.-1006
Turner, A.M.-1108
Turpin, Christian-770
Turpin, Joseph H.-814
          Thomas H.
          Amanda J.
          John E.
          James R.
Turpin, Josiah-1096
Turpin, Thomas-814
          Joseph H.
          Eliza A.
          Martha
          Mary
          Thomas
          John
Turpin, Anna-1097
Turpin, Anna-1096
Turpin, Jilua A.-1130
Tutley, Frederick-694
Tutt, Ann G.-880
Tuttle, David-836
Tuttle, Dr.-863
Tuttle, Mary-863
Tyler, Laura-885
Tyler, Wm.-886
       ****
       **

Ulmon, Luticia-904
Umphries, T.P.-714
Underwood, Rebecca-773
Underwood, Samuel-Martha-773
Ussery, Miss. J.H.-933
****
**
Van Campen, Jennie-883
Vance, Frances Mary-771
Vance, Andrew-772
Vance, Samuel-772
Vanderford, Eli-970
Vanderford, Susanna-962
Vanderford, R.M.-962
Vanderford, A.R.-970
  Monroe
  John C.
  Jasper N.
  Marion F.
  James B.
  Julia A.
  Nancy P.
  Almira
Vanderford, Jasper N.-971
  Wm. M.
  Laura B.
  Ida M.
  Joseph A.
  Charles N.
  Annie
  Dora E.
  Minnie J.
  Pearl
Van Horn, Jane-971
Van Hooser, Mary-1115
Vansandt, Dorcas-1144
Varner, Mary-705
Vaughan, Jeremiah-938
Vaughan, Margaret-1094
Vaughn, Elizabeth J.-938
Vaughn, Nancy-1027
Vernon, Elizabeth A.-949
Vernon, Miles-949
Vernon, Ellen-1171
Vernon, Lill-1171
Vetter, Clarl-Frederica-1025
Vetter, Wm.-1025

Viemonn, L.D.-990
Vincent, J.W.-918
  Mabel
Vincent, Joshua S.-918
  Joshua W.
  Henry M.
Vining, Emma-1014
Vogel, Frederick-919
Vogel, John-919
  Bertha
  Ida
  Wm.
  Henry
  Charles
  Peter
  George
****
**
Wade, Wm.-1130
Wade, Nancy-1130
Wade, James-1153
Wade, Chapman Walker-1153
  Fannie W.
  Ben C.
  Julia B.
Wade, Greenberry B.-1153
Wade, Celia-749
Wade, John-801
Wade, Lucinda-801
Wade, Lucy A.-854
Wafford, Smith-1087
Wafford, Martha E.-1087
Wagner, Minnie-984
Wagner, Wm.-984
Wait, Russell-752
Wait, Fidelia-752
Wale, Martin-815
Wale, H.O.-815
Wale, C.D.-815
Waler, Sarah-1031
Walker, Mary-1126
Walker, Cynthia-1193
Walker, Cynthia-741
Walker, George-743
Walker, H.L.-844
Walker, Robert-852
Walker, Martha-852

Walker, Lucy-88
Wall, E.H.-1114
Wall, Mary A.-1156
Wallace, John W.-1212
Wallace, Elizabeth-1076
Wallace, Martha-721
Wallace, Seth-760
Wallace, Zebina-760
    Wm.
    Christopher
    Dewitt C.
    Jonathan C.
    Washington I.
    Joseph W.
Wallace, W.I.-760
    Clara
Wallace, Mary-835
Wallace, Wm.-835
Wallace, Jacob-905
    Eliza
    Ellen
    George W.
    James
    Wm.
    Mary Sally
    John Wesley
Wallace, Eliza J.-904
Waller, Mary Ann-1191
Waller, R.B.-823
Wallis, C.S.-841
Walls, Elizabeth-1063
Walpole, Mr.-1192
Walsh, Sarah-988
Walters, Joseph-822
Walters, Ida-822
Walton, Samuel W.-885
    Daisy D.
    Charles B.
    Hattie T.
    Wm. P.
    Mollie E.
    Jesse S.
    James E.
    Freeman
Walton, Wm.P.-885
Wammack, Martha Ann-849
Ward, Marion-1208
    Ira E.
    Sarah
    Jasper N.
    Robert N.
    Nancy M.
    John M.
    Bedie I.
    Ora V.
    Addie
    Ollie
    Otis E.
Ward, James-1208
Ward, Martha J.-1101
Ward, Sarah-718
Ward, Hannah-742
Ward, Elizabeth-804
Ware, Charles C.-1154
    Wm. H.
    Mary Ann
    Ann E.
    Rhoda J.
    Charles H.
    Martha M.
    Sarah T.
    Frances C.
    John W.
    Solomon T.
    Minnie A.
    James W.
    Nancy C.
    Eunice L.J.
    Wm. R.
    Isaac C.
Ware, Hugh-1154
Warner, Mary A. L.-1091
Warner, Joseph B.-761
    Wm. J.
    Mary D.
    Octavo
    Sarah
    James
    George S.
    Francis
    Antoinette
Warner, George S.-761
    Frances Lodema
Warren, Charley-815
Warren, Henry E.-815
Warren, Chloe-1023

Wate, Jacob-894
Wate, Lizzie-894
Waters, W.R.-904
Watkins, James D.-1051
Watkins, Cynthia A.-1051
Watkins, J.W.-851
Watkins, Pleasant-860
Watkins, Millie-860
Watkins, Nancy-860
Watkins, Millie-888
Watros, Frances Amelia-1031
Watson, John Emery-1185
    John Thomas
    James A.
    Mary A.
    Lorenzo Dow
    G.T. Beauregard
    Rhoda R.
    Price Albert
    Orin P.
    Samuel J.
    Tilden
Watson, Wm. G.-1085
Watson, Leonard B.-1085
Watson, John T.-1069
Watson, John Thomas-1068
Watson, David H.-1155
    Nathan Leslie
Watson, James-1155
Watson, Washington-1155
Watson, Clarissa-1156
Watson, Lewis-1156
Watson, Mary A.-1156
Watson, Cornelius-920
    Harriet E.
    Andrew J.
    Henry F.
    Eliza
Watson, A.J.-920
    Sarah A.
    Dolly E.
    Rosa B.
    Maude D.
Watts, Wm., Sr.-816
Watts, John-816
Watts, Samuel-816
Watts, Wm.-816

Watts, John J.-816
Watts, James-857
Watts, Artelia-857
Way, Hattie L.-703
Waymon, Mary-1092
Weakley, Wm.-Eliza-1129
Weakley, Drpha-1129
Weast, Sarah-990
Weatherby, Hobart-981
Weaver, John C.-1058
Weaver, Rosa-1059
Weaver, Mary E.-1054
Weaver, M.M.V.-1198
Weaver, Eliza-772
Webber, Nancy-1157
Webber, Wm.E.-819
Weber, A.J.-1026
Weber, John-1025
    John O.
    Elizabeth
    Wm. E.
    James H.
    Annie J.
    Mary E.
    Archibald N.
    Andrew J.
    Margaret E.
    Americus C.
    Joseph
    Sarah E.
    George E.
    Mattie A.
    Laura
    Minnie L.
    Charles A.
    Albert F.
    Nellie I.
Weber, John M.-1026
Webster, D.P.-817
    Ethel
    Zoe
Webster, George-817
Webster, John T.-817
    Nathan W.
    Norman
    George W.
    Moody J.

           D.P.
           J.G.
Weeks, Hiram-Mary-1000
Weeks, Harriet Helen-1000
Weigle, Mary-763
Weirauch, Mollie-741
Weissgerber, Adam-Catherine-761
Weissgerber, Conrad-761
           George
           Lena
           Otto
           Theresa
Welborn, Sarah I.-1096
Welch, Mary-1036
Welch, John-Elizabeth-1036
       Mary
Welch, Joseph-1037
Welch, Elizabeth-1037
Welch, John-1086
Welch, John Calvin-1086
       James C.
       Thomas F.
       Wm. G.
       Joseph M.
       Iona
       Bertha
       Walter H.
Welch, Thomas-1086
       Melissa
       Joseph M.
       John C.
       Thomas J.
       Eliza
       Jane
       Phoebe E.
       Current R.
       General A.
       James G.
       Josephine
       Albert D.
Welch, Michael-1138
Welch, James-Maria-784
Welch, Susan-784
Welch, Thomas P.-947
Welch, Rebecca P.-947
Welch, John-1013
Weller, Mary-1137

Weller, Sarah E.-1143
Wells, W.H.-1209
       Edith
Wells, Andrew J.-1210
Wells, Emily-1081
Wells, I.M.-734
Wells, P.P.-886
       Rachel F.
       W.C.
       J.F.
       Rosa E.
       Maggie M.
Wells, W.W.-887
Wells, Oliver-886
       Mary Edith
       Daniel Lee
       Cora Jane
       Thomas
Wells, James-886
Wells, James, Sr.-886
Wells, John-961
Wesner, Rose-1209
West, Z.L.-971
      Wm.M.
      Mary E.
      Courtney
      Zachariah
      Sarah M.
      Wesley
West, Wm.-Elizabeth-971
Weston, Harriet-999
Wharton, Wm. L.-692
Wharton, Emsley-873
Wharton, Mary L.-873
Whatcher, Josephine-796
Wheeler, Edward H.-1155
         George E.
         Mabel
         Robert T.
         Jesse A.
         Louisa
         Lily F.
         Cora A.
         John M.
         Virdie
         Grover C.
         Charles
Wheeler, Robert M.-1155

          Garland F.
          John W.
          Wm. Daniel
          Edward H.
          Susan
          Arcadia A.
          Nancy A.
Wheeler, Wm.-1155
Wheeler, John W.-818
          Minerva
          Ollie
          Wm.
          Luna
          Mary
Wheeler, Wm. E.-818
          John W.
          Nathan
          George W.
          Ray
          Ellen
          Mollie
          Fannie
          Cora
Wheeler, John-818
          Charlotte M.
          Frances A.
          Wm. E.
          Lydia B.
          Luther H.
Wheeling, Lucinda E.-1068
Whipple, Silence-773
White, Moses-1210
          Robert Jason
          Samuel
          Louella
          Minnie
          Eva
          Joseph
          Alonzo
          Emma
          Sadie
          Martha
White, Mary Emily-1109
White, J.C.-1109
White, Allie-1118
White, Thomas G.-1124
White, Julia W.-1124

White, Charles W.-1156
          H. Lee
          Don W.
White, Sarah-1177
White, Woodard R.-1156
          Robert T.
          Thomas Logan
          Wm. F.M.
          Jennie
          Susan E.
          Charles W.
White, Elizabeth-1208
White, Margaret-1204
White, Daniel-1204
White, Wm.-714
White, Sarah-767
White, Sallie-800
White, R. Jason-887
          Charles H.
          Verba
White, Moses-887
White, John-920
          Ellsworth Oron
White, Thomas-920
          John
          Riley H.
          Caroline
          Luroney Carlisle
          Robert
          James T.
White, Moses-920
White, Martha J.
White, Daniel-Elizabeth-935
White, Nathan-937
White, Rosetta-937
White, P.T.-953
White, J.H.-964
White, -1007
          Henry B.
          James W.
White, Harriet-1024
Whitehurst, J.W.-834
Whitelaw, James T.-1028
Whittenburg, J.D.-860
Whittenburg, Jonathan D.-887
          Thomas
          Martha

            Margaret
            Dickey
Whittenburg, James-Sarah C.-887
Whittenburg, Christopher H.-923
Whittle, Catherine-789
Whybark, Samuel P.-750
Whybark, Isabella-750
Wickersham, Isaac-762
            Sarah
            Richard
            James
            John
Wickersham, James H.-763
Wickersham, R.J.-762
            Nannie
            Ella
            Lou
            Mattie
            Bettie L.
            Sallie
            Mary
            Abra
            Vice
Wideck, Eve-844
Wiggs, Nancy-762
Wilburn, Elizabeth-846
Wild, Mary-723
Wilder, Margaret-723
Wilder, Hiram-723
Wilder, Ella E.-724
Wiley, James-1094
Wilhoit, Alexander-752
Wilks, Elizabeth-757
Wilks, Mary E.-712
Wilks, P.S.-842
Willams, Maria-1042
Williams, J.W.-1210
            Fred
            Addie
Williams, Wm. E.-1210
Williams, W.P.-Eliza-1042
Williams, Wm.-1087
Williams, Wm. W.-1087
Williams, David-Sarah-1087
Williams, Mary E.-1110
Williams, Benjamin-Mary-1180
Williams, Matilda-1180

Williams, Mariah-1194
Williams, Mattie-733
Williams, Emily-780
Williams, Alfred H.-783
Williams, Price-784
Williams, Sarah E.-803
Williams, Edward D.-819
            Samuel C.
            Martha E.
            Albert W.
            Henrietta B.
            Marie S.
            Edward G.
            James M.
Williams, Samuel-819
Williams, Edward G.-819
Williams, John-Fannie-826
Williams, Nancy G.-826
Williams, Joseph-862
Williams, Lydia C.-862
Williams, J.H.-876
Williams, David A.-888
            Gertrude
            Hallie E.
Williams, Richard M.-888
            J.T.
            George W.
            Richard C.
            David A.
            Annie
            Willie
            Charles
            Charles T.
            James R.
            Zanada F.
            Marion E.
Williams, Susan-918
Williams, Harrison-987
Williamson, Mary C.-1176
Williamson, Susan-933
Williamson, John H.-939
Willoughby, Sarah-967
Willoughby, Rev.-1100
Wilson, Caleb-1211
Wilson, Avery-1211
Wilson, I.S.-1211
Wilson, Dora-1097

Wilson, Wm. H.-1121
Wilson, Belle-1148
Wilson, Taylor S.-1157
    James E.
    Albert C.
    David N.
    Dora A.
    Mildred J.
    Lewis H.
Wilson, Eli B.-1156
Wilson, Annie M.-696
Wilson, James H.-1156
Wilson, Eli W.-1157
    Nancy B.
    Ruth A.
    Mary F.
    Eli B.
    Emily E.
    Alfred L.
    James R.
    Samuel E.
    Agnes A.
    Minnie V.
    Leslie E.
    Lulu A.
    Nellie F.
    Elmer W.
    Richard B.
Wilson, Ella-1179
Wilson, Margaret-697
Wilson, Anderson-697
Wilson, Frank C.-972
    Minnie A.
    Annie B.
Wilson, James, Jr.-972
    Wm. L.
    Frank C.
    Mary J.
    Martha M.
    Allen H.
    Charles H.
Wilson, James, Sr.-972
    Sampson
Wilson, Sanford-747
Wilson, Samuel-813
Wilson, Clara-813
Wilson, J.H.-822
Wilson, Mary-846
Wilson, Wm.-850
Wilson, Malcolm-888
    John A.
    Wm. H.
Wilson, Mary-900
Wilson, Jane-904
Wilson, Peter-951
Wilson, Frank C.-952
Wilson, F.M.-964
Wilson, Sarah A.-994
Winfrey, Josiah L.-921
    Mary E.
    Valonia J.
    Rebecca M.
    Eliza E.
    Melissa S.
    Sarah A.
    Josiah L.
    Zilpha J.
Winfrey, James M.-921
    Thomas
    Wm. C.
Winfrey, James M., Jr.-921
    Josiah L.
    Benjamin E.
    Sarah E.
    Eleathea
    Zilpha
    James M.
    Thomas L.
    Pennington
    John C.
    Marshall C.
    Francis T.
Winfrey, John-756
Winfrey, James-Winnie-801
Winfrey, Dica-801
Wingo, John, Sr.-1088
Wingo, John W.-1087
Wingo, Edmund T.-1087
    Jacob W.
Wingo, George S.-969
Wingo, Eliza-969
Wingo, I.J.-953
Winkler, Catherine-845
Winningham, J.S.-1130

Winningham, Isabella-1130
Winningham, Martha-1179
Winters, Edwin-747
Wisdom, Pollard-908
Wisdom, Lucy-908
Wisdom, Parson C.-926
Wisdom, Sarah E.-926
Wisdom, Colum-961
    Elizabeth
Wisdom, Darcus-961
Wise, Louis-692
Wise, Eliza B.-818
Wiseman, Wilson-704
Withaup, F.L.-E.E.-1073
Withaup, Alice M.-1073
Wollard, Elizabeth-707
Wollard, Nathaniel-973
    Louisa P.
    Nathaniel J.
    Silas B.
    James M.
Wollard, Elizabeth-939
Wollard, Nathaniel-972
    Mary L.M.
    James F.
    John S.
    Moses W.
    Sarah E.M.
    Robert P.
    Estella D.
    Quincy Lee
    Martha
    Permelia E.
    Omega F.
Wollard, Nathaniel-939
Wollard, Fanny-944
Womack, Wm.-Abigail-1074
Womack, Mary-1074
Wommack, Almarinda-850
Wood, Charles-998
Wood, S.W.-1102
Wood, Frances J.-1089
Wood, John C.-1089
Wood, Julia E.-1186
Wood, Major-1186
Wood, B.F.-L.L.-1186
Wood, Susanna-706

Wood, Henry-706
Wood, George,Sr.-763
Wood, George,Jr.-763
    Martha E.
    Carter
    Thomas
    Jane
    David W.
    Eli
    Charley
    Alice
    Mary
    Frank
    Winnie
    Abram
Wood, James-764
Wood, Isom-764
    Albert L.
    Henry
    Richard
    Margaret
    Julia A.
Wood, Sarah-903
Woodard, Sophia-754
Woodford, Romantia-1206
Woodford, Louisa-1206
Woods, Green-Elizabeth-1038
Woods, Josephine-1038
Woods, Zilla-1053
Woods, Mary-991
Woodward, Julia E.-1079
Woodward, George D.-1157
    Robert Atwater
Woolard, Sarah-927
Woolford, Mary-1175
Woolsey, Nancy-713
Woolsey, Wm.-817
Woolsey, Mary Jane-817
Workman, Green-Martha-741
Workman, Lizzie-741
Workman, Mary A.-812
Worsham, Joseph-1212
Worsham, P.R.-1212
    Sarah
    Mary E.
    Henderson
    Susan

    Catherine
    Cordelia
    Alice
    Eliza
    Wm.
    David
    Oliver
Worthington, Abi-786
Wray, Paternella-878
Wright, Lucretia-723
Wright, Benjamin-Elizabeth-723
    Eliza J.
    Benjamin
    Wm. C.
    Lucretia
Wright, Mary S.-740
Wright, L.W.H.-747
Wright, C.F.-753
Wright, Henry B.-764
Wright, Christopher-765
Wright, H.T.-764
    Harriet B.
    Grace E.
    George R.
    James H.
    Henry F.
    Louisa T.
Wright, Wm. J.-819
Wright, M.W.-819
Wright, David T.-820
Wright, Wm. T.-820
Wright, Frank-881
Wright, John-881
Wright, Rachel-929
Wright, Alice-960
Wrinkle, John R.-724
Wrinkle, Jacob-821
Wrinkle, George-821
Wrinkle, Jacob N.-821
Wrinkle, John-Sophia A.-821
Wrinkle, H.H.-821
Wyatt, John, Sr.-1212
Wyatt, John-1212
Wyatt, Brown-1212
    Henry Clay
    Maggie
    Jemima C.

    John
    Dollie
    Ada
    Oliver
    Mary Leora
Wyatt, John J.-1212
Wylie, Elizabeth-1015
Wynn, Harriet J.-1192
Wynn, Matthew-1013
Wynne, John-Margaret-1213
Wynne, Pleasant-1213
    George Washington
    Wm.
    Mary
    Margaret
    Pleasant
    Jane
    Albama
    Angenetta
    Tennessee
    Thomas J.
    James Monroe
Wynne, Julian F.-1213
    Barbara
    Harriet
    Ida
    Vernie
    Mary
    Wm.
    Thomas
Wyshon, W.M.-977
  ****
   **

Yaden, Ann-910
Yarbrough, E.J.-962
Yeagor, Livona C.-979
Yeagor, James-Sarah-979
Yeager, Pelina-949
Yeager, Euina J.-930
Yeager, Elijah-Hannah-930
York, Caroline-772
York, Curtis-797
Young, Nancy S.-714
Young, Jeremiah-765
    Campbell W.
    Mary C.
    Maggie

           Robert M.
Young, Ronert N.-765
           Charles J.
           Timothy N.
Young, Mary-1080
Young, James-866
Young, Margaret E.-866
Young, Agnes-1034
Young, Mary E.-997
Young, Green D.-Mary-1075
Young, Ruthie S.-1075
Young, John D.-1128
Young, Wm. M.-1158
           John D.
           Margaret C.
           Lynch J.
           Sarah
           Cordelia
           Cora A.
           Charles R.—
Young, John D.-1158
Young, Harvey-1160
Young, Joseph-1163
Young, Mr.-1166
           A.L.
           Sarah J.
Young, Mary-1192
Young, Wm.-1192
Young, Samuel-1213
Young, Archibald-1213
           Cynthia
           Angeline
Young, Wm.-1214
           Frank
           F.M.
           Mattie
           Harvey
           Oscar
Young, W.F.-1214
Young, Mary-1214
Young, Fielding M.-1216
Young, E.B.-1216
           Virdie Mabel
Yowell, Easton-822
Yowell, Wm. J.-822
Yowell, Lindsey L.-994
           Napoleon B.
           Amanda J.
           Lindsey L.
           Charles E.
Yowell, Susan A.-994
Yowell, Wm.-1026
    ****
    **
Zeigler, Rebecca-851
Zimmers, Hester-874
Zink, Mary A.-857
Zumwalt, Russia Z.D.-1159
Zumwalt, H.G.-748

www.ingramcontent.com/pod-product-compliance
Lightning Source LLC
Chambersburg PA
CBHW020630300426
44112CB00007B/70